# Handbook of Research Design
# in Mathematics and Science Education

# Handbook of Research Design in Mathematics and Science Education

Edited by

**Anthony E. Kelly**
*Rutgers University*

**Richard A. Lesh**
*Purdue University*

**LEA**
2000

LAWRENCE ERLBAUM ASSOCIATES, PUBLISHERS
Mahwah, New Jersey                              London

The final camera copy for this work was prepared by the author, and therefore the publisher takes no responsibility for consistency or correctness of typographical style. However, this arrangement helps to make publication of this kind of scholarship possible.

Copyright © 2000 by Lawrence Erlbaum Associates, Inc.
    All rights reserved. No part of this book may be reproduced in any form, by photostat, microfilm, retrieval system, or any other means, without prior written permission of the publisher.

Lawrence Erlbaum Associates, Inc., Publishers
10 Industrial Avenue
Mahwah, NJ  07430

Cover design by Kathryn Houghtaling Lacey

**Library of Congress Cataloging-in-Publication Data**

Handbook of research design in mathematics and science education /
edited by Anthony E. Kelly and Richard A. Lesh.
p.  cm.
    Includes bibliographical references and index.
ISBN 0-8058-3281-5  (cloth : alk. paper)
1. Mathematics—Study and teaching—Research.   2. Science—Study and
    teaching—Research.     I. Kelly, Anthony E.    II. Lesh, Richard A.

QA11.H256   1999
507.1 —dc21
                                                                    99-28610
                                                                    CIP

Books published by Lawrence Erlbaum Associates are printed on acid-free paper, and their bindings are chosen for strength and durability.

Printed in the United States of America
10  9  8  7  6  5  4  3  2

# Contents

# Preface

This book is based on results from a National Science Foundation-supported project aimed at clarifying the nature of principles that govern the effective use of emerging new research designs in mathematics and science education. The project involved a series of mini-conferences in which leading researchers in mathematics and science education developed detailed specifications for the book, as well as planning and revising chapters to be included. Chapters also were field tested and revised during a series of doctoral research seminars that were sponsored by the National Center for Improving Student Learning & Achievement in Mathematics & Science at the University of Wisconsin. In these seminars, computer-based videoconferencing and World Wide Web-(WWW)-based discussion groups were used to create interactions in which authors of potential chapters served as guest discussion leaders responding to questions and comments from doctoral students and faculty members representing more than a dozen leading research universities throughout the United States and abroad. Early sites for these seminars included Cornell University, Rutgers University, the State University of New York-Buffalo, Syracuse University, the University of Massachusetts, the University of Wisconsin, the University of Georgia, and Purdue University. Also, during later stages of the project, the seminar was extended to include sites in Australia, Canada, England, Israel, Mexico, and Taiwan. Finally, additional revision cycles of chapters were based on feedback obtained during presentations at professional conferences associated with the National Council of Teachers of Mathematics, the National Association for Research on Science Teaching, the American Association for the Advancement of Science, the American Educational Research Association, and the National and International Groups for the Psychology of Mathematics Education.

Additional resource materials related to the book can be found at the WWW site for Purdue's School Mathematics & Science Center: www.soe.purdue.edu/~lesh/ This Internet site includes directions for: (a) enrolling in seminars, (b) participating in ongoing discussion groups, and (c) submitting or downloading resources, which range from videotapes and transcripts, to assessment instruments or theory based software, to publications or data samples related to the research designs being discussed.

The editorial board for this book included representatives from both the National Science Foundation and the Department of Education, as well as representatives from a variety of relevant research journals in mathematics and science education. That is, these representatives included: Bob Davis from *The Journal of Mathematical Behavior*, Lyn English from *Mathematical Thinking & Learning*, representative from the National Association for Research in Science Teaching, and from the *Journal for Research in Science Teaching*, Carole Lacampagne from the Department of Education, Frank Lester from the *Journal for Research in Mathematics Education*, Mary Budd Rowe from the National Research Council, and Nora Sabelli from the National Science Foundation. Audrey Pendergast served as the technical editor.

During the course of the project, the mathematics and science education communities were stunned at the deaths of a series of its leading researchers. These giants included not only Bob Davis and Mary Budd Rowe, from our editorial board, but also Merlyn Behr, Alba Thompson, and Jack Easley—each of whom strongly influenced our deliberations and results. Words cannot express our shared sense of sorrow from the loss of these friends and colleagues. We humbly dedicate this book to their memory.

—*Anthony Kelly*
—*Richard Lesh*

# THE NEED TO ADDRESS
# PRIORITY PROBLEMS

In Part I, chapter 1 by Lesh, Lovitts, and Kelly describes some of the most important assumptions and purposes of this book. Many of these purposes are related to the fact that, during the past decade, rapid increases have occurred in the sophistication of research in mathematics and science education; and, these rapid increases have ushered in a series of paradigm shifts for thinking about: (a) the nature of teaching, learning, and problem solving, (b) the nature of students' developing constructs in elementary mathematics and science, (c) what it means to develop deeper or higher order understandings of the preceding constructs, (d) interactions among the development of individual students, groups of students, teachers, programs, curriculum materials, or relevant learning communities, and (e) interactions among (many levels and types of) researchers and (many levels and types of) practitioners—who may range from teachers, to curriculum developers, to policymakers. In general, regardless of whether researchers are focusing on the developing capabilities of students, teachers, programs, or relevant learning communities, it has become necessary to move beyond machine metaphors and factory-based models to account for patterns and regularities in behavior.

In educational psychology, there has been a tendency to try to explain the mind using analogies, models, and metaphors that are based on familiar powerful technologies. Thus, there has been a gradual transition:

- From analogies based on hardware—where whole systems are considered to be no more than the sum of their parts, and where the interactions that are emphasized involve no more than simple one-way cause-and-effect relationships.
- To analogies based on software—where silicone-based electronic circuits involve layers of recursive interactions that often lead to emergent phenomena at higher levels that cannot be derived from characteristics of phenomena at lower levels.
- To analogies based on wetware—where neurochemical interactions may involve "logics" that are fuzzy, partly redundant, partly inconsistent, and unstable.

In fact, as an age of biotechnologies gradually supersedes an age of electronic technologies, the systems that are priorities to investigate are no longer inert; they are living entities characterized by complex, dynamic, continually adapting and self-regulating systems.

Furthermore, they are not simply given in nature. Their existence is partly the result of human constructions.

More information about the nature of relevant paradigm shifts is given in the second chapter in this section, where Kelly and Lesh describe trends and shifts in research methods. According to chapter 1, one problem that resulted from these paradigm shifts is that, when researchers adopt new ways of thinking about mathematical thinking (or teaching, learning, and problem solving), this often creates the need for new research methodologies that are based on new assumptions, and that focus on new problems and opportunities. But, in mathematics and science education, the development of new research methodologies has not kept pace with the development of new problems and perspective; and, the development of widely recognized quality standards has not kept pace with the development of new methologies. Consequently, a crisis has arisen in the funding and publication of research. There is a widely held perception that naive or inappropriate standards frequently cause excellent studies to be rejected for funding or publication; or, conversely, potentially significant studies may be marred by methodological flaws. For example, in chapter 2 on research agendas, Lesh and Lovitts describe how, at National Science Foundation's Program for Research on Teaching and Learning, the most innovative and potentially powerful projects tended to be precisely those that are most negatively affected by poorly developed standards for assessing quality. This is because a hallmark of these studies is that they are aimed at making a difference in both theory and practice. That is, the research focuses on problems or issues that are priorities to address; and, the results also lead to significant developments (e.g., revisions, refinements, extensions) in what is known—or how we think about problems and opportunities. Therefore, because these investigations involve novel ways of thinking about problems and opportunities, they often stretch the limits of research tools and methodologies. Yet, research proposals allow only a small amount of space to explain new problems, perspectives, and procedures. Therefore, principal investigators may face the following dilemma: (a) Use simpler-to-explain or more traditional methodologies, and risk compromising the potential power of the proposed research, or (b) use more complex or less traditional methodologies, and risk rejection because insufficient opportunities are available to explain these novel approaches.

The project that led to this book was founded on the belief that the time has come to clarify the nature of certain research methodologies that have proven to be especially powerful for research in mathematics and science education; and, the time also has come to establish standards that can be used to optimize (or assess) the quality of these research designs. Of course, if obsolete or otherwise inappropriate standards are adopted, then the results could hinder rather than help. But, as long as decisions must be made about funding, publications, and presentations, it not possible to avoid issues of quality assessments. Decisions will be made. Therefore, our goal is to try to optimize the chances that productive decisions are made.

The fourth chapter in this section focuses on the impact of standards-based reform on methods of research in schools. In it, Romberg and Collins advocate a view of learning that borrows heavily from Greeno's notion (discussed in their chapter) that expertise involves a growing competence in "finding one's way" around a domain and using resources in that domain appropriately and productively. This topographical-environmental metaphor is proposed as a replacement for what these authors characterize as the current (and outmoded) metaphor for schooling, in which learning is seen as a mechanistic process of mastering atomistic pieces of knowledge and skill, and in which "student processing" takes place in a factory-like atmosphere.

One important point that Romberg and Collins emphasize is that the preceding metaphors, like others that might be adopted, often have profound effects on what questions are asked, on what problems are seen as worthy of study, and on what methods of research are judged to be appropriate. For example, Romberg and Collins are strong advocates of field-based methods of research. Therefore, the questions they raise reappear in later sections of this book that focus on links between research design, curriculum design, program design, and assessment design.

In the final chapter in this section, Confrey focuses on another major theme that strongly influenced discussions that led to this book. That is, the design of research often involves decisions similar to those that occur when businesses make choices about trade-offs involving quality and costs, safety and speed, diversity and simplicity, and so on. For example, in research involving curriculum reform, discussions about standards generally focus on issues about content quality, whereas discussions about systemic reform traditionally emphasize issues of equity. Yet, when Confrey describes ways of improving research and systemic reform towards equity and quality, she makes a strong case for not conflating equity with quality and, in particular, for not placing them in opposition. Confrey argues that equity and quality must coarise for either to be addressed effectively; and, she argues that both must be addressed within the context of systemic reform that goes beyond piecemeal approaches to educational change.

Confrey's chapter also highlights another theme that reverberates across many of the later sections of this book: Should educational research strive to produce universally applicable findings about educational change and improvement, or should it be construed as being similar to applied engineering in the classroom? Confrey appears to favor the latter view in which educational research produces new educational "products," curricular revisions, and rich repositories of "best practices." In this view, educational research does not stop with identifying problems and analyzing them; it must go further to craft solutions that make sense to local practitioners and that respond to the complexity of the local situation. Consequently, Confrey, just like Romberg and Collins, challenges readers to reject simple input–output views of schooling in which progress is made by "inputting" the insights of research into the system. Rather, she argues that school systems act more like organic, complex, self-adapting entities that act independently of the research community, but that also may react and change in response to communications from the research community.

Before reading the chapters in this section, readers may find it useful to formulate responses to the following questions:

1. In the context of research that you yourself might plan to conduct, what meanings do you associate with the following terms: replicability, reliability, validity, generalizability?

2. Among the constructs that you describe in Question 1, how relevant and significant do you consider each to be for assessing (or optimizing) the quality of your own research?

3. The results of research have limited value unless they are meaningful and useful to others (such as teachers, curriculum developers, assessment specialists, administrators, policymakers). Who are the

decision makers that should find your research useful? In addition to meaningfulness and usefulness, what other factors do you believe that these decision makers might consider to be important to assess (or optimize) the quality of your research?

4. Write a one-page list of guidelines that you would like reviewers to emphasize if a proposal for your research project appeared in a collection of other proposals that were competing with yours for funding or publication. In particular, what guidelines might emphasize the need to forge better working relationships between research and practice?

5. In mathematics and science education, the results of research often involve software development, curriculum development, teacher development, or program development in addition to the development of knowledge. In your own research, what relationships exist among these various types of activities?

6. Throughout this book, many authors challenge readers to reenvision the role of the educational researcher from an objective observer to a systematic observer who is also a caring advocate and reformer. How does the reader respond to this characterization of the researcher? In your own research, how does the choice of research methods differ depending on the "hat" worn by the researcher? Is one orientation more scientific than the other? Why or why not?

# 1 Purposes and Assumptions of This Book

**Richard Lesh**
*Purdue University*

**Barbara Lovitts**
*AIR*

**Anthony Kelly**
*Rutgers, the State University of New Jersey*

## SOME OF THE BOOK'S PURPOSES

A primary goal of this book is to describe several of the most important types of research designs that:

- Have been pioneered recently by mathematics and science educators.
- Have distinctive characteristics when they are used in projects that focus on mathematics or science education.
- Have proven to be especially productive for investigating the kinds of complex, interacting, and adapting systems that underlie the development of mathematics or science students and teachers. or for the development, dissemination, and implementation of innovative programs of mathematics or science instruction.

We also chose to emphasize research designs that are intended to radically increase the relevance of research to practice, often by involving practitioners in the identification and formulation of the problems to be addressed or in other key roles in the research processes. Examples of such research designs include:

- *Teaching experiments*, such as those that involve technology-intensive learning environments.

- *Clinical interviews*, such as those that focus on students' early conceptions of foundation-level constructs in mathematics or the sciences.

- *Analyses of videotapes*, such as those that involve real-life problem solving or classroom-based teaching and learning.

- *Action research studies*, such as those where researchers help to improve the system being studied or where teachers and other practitioners collect, analyze, or interpret information that is most relevant to perceived decision making priorities.

- *Ethnographic observations*, such as those in which attention is focused on abilities that might not be apparent to those who were unable to view the world through sophisticated mathematical or scientific lenses.

- *Software development studies* (or curricula development studies, more generally), where learning environments are developed to embody or instantiate conjectures about ideal principles in order to facilitate achievement in specific topic areas.

- *Computer-modeling studies*, such as those that are intended to describe, explain, or predict students' complex problem solving abilities.

Another goal of this book is to begin discussions about the nature of appropriate and productive criteria for assessing (and increasing) the quality of research proposals, projects, or publications that are based on the preceding kinds of research designs; and, a final objective is to describe the preceding guidelines in forms that will be useful to graduate students and others who are novices to the fields of mathematics or science education research.

# SOME OPERATING ASSUMPTIONS THAT INFLUENCED DISCUSSIONS LEADING TO THIS BOOK.[1]

## Observation 1

Authors in this book emphasize the term *research design* rather than *research methodology*. One reason for this choice is because, in general, the authors considered the process of research to be more like constructing a complex design than merely executing a correct procedure. For example, planning research often involves trade-offs similar to those that occur when an automobile is designed to meet conflicting goals (such as optimizing speed, safety, and economy). Therefore, various solutions frequently are possible involving different constellations of interacting factors. Another related reason for emphasizing *research design* is that, in graduate school experience in the social sciences, the term *research methodology* has tended to be associated with statistics-oriented courses in which the emphasis is on how to carry out computational procedures for analyzing data. Issues are seldom emphasized that involve alternative ways to formulate problems, gather relevant information, interpret patterns

---

[1] Although the projects that contributed to this book received funding from the National Science Foundation and the U.S. Department of Education and although the book's authors and editorial board included representatives from a number of relevant professional or governmental organizations, this volume should not be construed as expressing the views of any of these organizations or agencies. We have no authority to speak for others. Furthermore, action-oriented organizations and agencies change their priorities and policies continually in attempts to keep pace with current perceptions about what kinds of problems or opportunities are priorities for action and what kinds of theoretical perspectives seem to provide strategic leverage points for addressing these problems or opportunities. Therefore, anything that this book could say about research priorities or review procedures should be expected to change from one agency to another and from one time to another. Nonetheless, there exist some important principles and themes that are likely to endure, even as new priorities evolve to respond to changing conditions and new funding programs arise to replace current ones. Therefore, the authors who contributed to this book were challenged to emphasize principles and to review criteria that should remain fairly stable, even in the face of the preceding kinds of changes in perspectives and policies.

or regularities, or analyze underlying assumptions. In contrast to perspectives that focus on the data analysis stages of research, the research designs that are emphasized in this book seldom lend themselves to the selection and execution of standard data analysis techniques. In fact, combinations of qualitative and quantitative approaches tend to be needed (F. L. Schmidt, 1996; Stake, 1988).

## Observation 2

Doing research is not merely a process of using "accepted" techniques in ways that are "correct." Above all, the design of research involves developing a chain of reasoning that is coherent, shareable, and auditable, and that should be persuasive to a well-intentioned skeptic about issues that are priorities. In particular, the chain of reasoning should include clear statements about what assumptions are being made, how decisions are being made to determine which kind of information is relevant and less relevant, and what kinds of results are intended to be produced for what purposes. Then, the criteria that are most appropriate for assessing the quality of these research designs depend on the nature of the products that are being produced. For example:

- If the goal of a research project is to test a hypothesis (stated in the form of "if-then" rules), then advancing the state of knowledge may depend on determining whether (or to what extent) the rule produces accurate results under a variety of circumstances.
- If the goal is to produce a *description* of a complex system (such as those that underlie the development of students' or teachers' knowledge, or the development, dissemination, or implementation of sophisticated programs of instruction), then truth and falsity may not be at issue as much as fidelity, internal consistency, and other characteristics that are similar to those that apply to quality assessments for photographs, portraits, or verbal descriptions.
- If the goal is to demonstrate *possibilities*, perhaps by creating or refining new types of technology-intensive learning environments, then the advancement of knowledge may emphasize constructing, elaborating, refining, or extending such systems and the criteria for

success may emphasize factors such as shareability, power, and usefulness.

## Observation 3

Just as doing research entails more than gathering and analyzing data, reporting research involves more than conforming to styles that are correct. Research deals with the development of knowledge. In particular, the goal of research in mathematics and science education is to develop a body of shared knowledge consisting of rules, models, conceptual systems, conjectures, or ways of thinking that are powerful, meaningful, and useful for a variety of purposes and in a variety of situations. Each of the preceding characteristics implies different criteria for assessing the results produced by research investigations. For example, to be meaningful and useful, gains in knowledge often need to be accompanied by (or embedded in) exemplary software, informative assessment instruments, or illustrative instructional activities, programs, or prototypes to be used in schools. Also, the development of new ways of thinking frequently involves the development of new language, new models, and new metaphors as well as the formulation of abstract rules or principles.

## Observation 4

Research in mathematics and science education often bears the following similarity to research in more mature sciences such as biology, astronomy, geology, or physics. When entities such as subatomic particles are described using such fanciful terms as *color, charm, wisdom, truth*, and *beauty*, it is clear that the practitioners of the relevant sciences are quite comfortable with the notion that reality is a construct. When they recognize that researchers are integral parts of the systems they are hoping to understand and explain, they demonstrate their cognizance of the fact that observations that are made often induce changes in the systems being observed. Therefore, in such cases, there is no such thing as an immaculate perception. Similarly, in mathematics and science education, when attention is focused on the development of students, teachers, programs, or schools, it is clear that each of these "individuals" (or entities) involves complex systems that are interacting, self-regulating, and continually adapting. When they are acted on, they tend to act back by molding, shaping, and reacting to the information that they encounter. Consequently, when they learn and develop, the process tends to involve far more than merely "delivering" information to passive subjects; it involves complex interactions, sophisticated adaptation cycles, and feedback loops that lead frequently to breakdowns in traditional distinctions between researchers and teachers, assessment experts and curricula developers, observers and observed. For this reason, in the presence of such complexity, interactivity, and adaptivity, it often becomes necessary to reexamine traditional conceptions of constructs such as reliability or reproducibility, which past generations of researchers generally thought of in ways that presupposed the existence of researchers who strive for detached objectivity.

## Observation 5

Unlike researchers in the natural sciences (such as physics, astronomy, and chemistry), researchers in mathematics and science education generally deal with systems that do not develop naturally. For example, classrooms, schools, programs, and conceptual systems are not given in nature; they are created by humans. Furthermore, the models that are used to construct, describe, explain, manipulate, and predict the behaviors of these systems are also very much products of human construction. Finally, as we emphasized in Observation Four, the systems that are created are seldom inert; they tend to involve living, self-regulating, and self-organizing entities that modify themselves and adapt in the presence of information that is generated about them. Therefore, second-order effects occur frequently, especially when researchers go beyond generating information that is *reactive* (in the sense that it answers questions that are posed by teachers, policymakers, or other educational decision makers) to generating information that is *proactive* (in the sense that it is designed to help decision makers ask better questions, perceive new possibilities, and look at problems from more productive points of view). Hence, because mathematics and science educators tend to investigate living systems that are complex, interacting, and continually adapting, constructs and principles that explain the behaviors of these systems often appear to be less like "laws of nature" and more like "laws of the land" that govern a country's legal system. Issues of truth or falsity may be less pertinent than issues of consistency, meaningfulness, and the desirability of ensuing outcomes.

## Observation 6

Scholars in history and philosophy of science (including N. Campbell, 1920/1957; Harre, 1961; Hesse, 1967; Nagel, 1961; Suppe, 1977) suggest that scientists frequently think in terms of theoretical *explanatory models*, such as molecules, waves, fields, and black holes, which provide different ways of expressing hypotheses from empirical laws. These models are not simply condensed summaries of empirical observations. Rather, they are organizing inventions that contribute new mechanisms and concepts that are part of the scientist's view of the world, not "given" in the data. We agree with Clement's chapter in this book (Chapter 20), which explains that "one of the most important current needs in basic research on student learning processes is the need for insightful explanatory models of these processes"; and, we also agree that such basic research is often most fruitfully undertaken via clinical interviews, or teaching experiments, or other approaches to research that are emphasized in this book.

Clement describes a distinction between what he calls an "empirical law hypothesis" summarizing an observed regularity versus an "explanatory model hypothesis." In a frequently recalled example, Campbell (1920/1957) pointed out that being able to make predictions from the empirical gas law stating that pressure times volume is proportional to temperature is not at all equivalent to understanding the explanation for gas behavior in terms of a visualizable physical explanatory model of elastic billiard ball–like molecules in motion. The model describes a hidden process or mechanism that explains how the gas works, and it answers "why" questions about where observable changes in temperature and pressure come from. The empirical law PV = KT on its own does none of these things. In fact, the role of the model is to make such formulae comprehensible. Causal relationships are often central in models of this type; and, the model adds significant explanatory power to one's knowledge, as well as adding heuristic power that stimulates the future growth of the theory in which they are embedded.

A phenomenon that is similar to the one described in the preceding paragraph often occurs for middle school children who have difficulty using proportional reasoning (A is to B as C is to X) to calculate indirect measurements using the standard method suggested by the similar triangles shown in FIG. 1.1. Such children often find it useful to be able to explain the relevant quantitative relationships using "tessellated triangles" similar to those shown in FIG. 1.2. That is, if base of the "big triangle" equals 10 "little triangles," then the height of the "big triangle" also equals 10 "little triangles." Yet, to calculate the correct answer, these tessellations contribute nothing that was not given in the written equations.

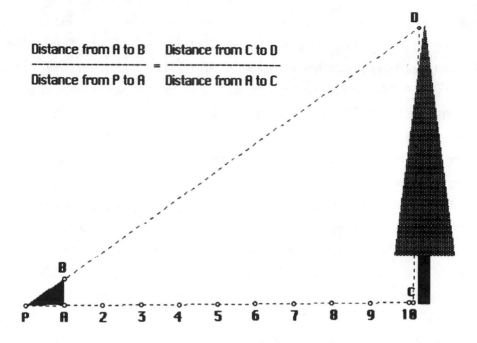

FIG. 1.1. Indirect measurement using similar triangles.

In research, just as in the proportional reasoning situation illustrated in FIG. 1.2, explanatory models are often iconic and analogical in nature, and are built up from more primitive and familiar notions. In this view, the visualizable model is a major locus of meaning for a scientific theory; and, it connects the observational side of science to the theoretical side. (Summaries of these views are given in Harre, 1967, and Hesse, 1967.) An implication of these considerations is that a central goal of science is to develop explanatory models that give satisfying explanations for patterns in observations.

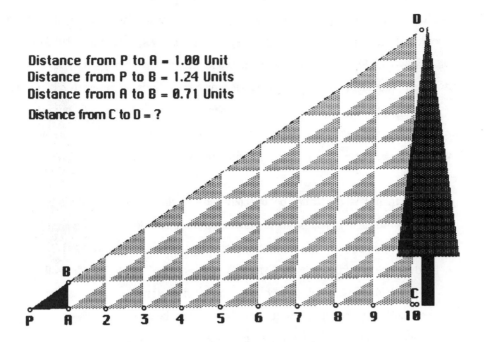

Distance from P to A = 1.00 Unit
Distance from P to B = 1.24 Units
Distance from A to B = 0.71 Units
Distance from C to D = ?

FIG. 1.2. Using tessellations to explain proportional relationships.

## WHAT PROBLEMS LED TO THE PERCEIVED NEED FOR THIS BOOK?

Several decades ago, mathematics and science educators were inclined to borrow both their theories and their research methodologies from other areas of research, such as developmental psychology, sociology, or agriculture (psychometrics). Therefore, during this period that was dominated by theory borrowing, discussions about research designs were not markedly different in mathematics and science education than in other content areas. Generally, the dominant research methodologies emanated from machine-based metaphors for thinking about the nature of teaching and learning; and, they also tended to assume that outcomes were based on simple linear combinations of uni-directional, cause-and-effect mechanisms that could be described using rules based on elementary algebra and statistics. Nonetheless, over the course of the past 30 years, theory *building* has replaced theory *borrowing* in mathematics and science education; and, as a result, mathematics education and science education have evolved into distinct disciplines with their own problems, theoretical frameworks, and rapidly expanding bodies of literature (Bybee & McInerney, 1995; Grouws & Cooney, 1988; Hiebert & Behr, 1988; Sowder, 1989; Wagner & Kieran, 1989).

Unfortunately, the development of widely recognized standards for research has not kept pace with the development of new problems, perspectives, and research procedures in mathematics and science education. Consequently, two kinds of undesirable results are likely to occur when proposals are reviewed for funding or when manuscripts are reviewed for publication:

- High-quality studies may be rejected because they involve unfamiliar research designs, because inadequate space is available for explanation, or because inappropriate or obsolete standards of assessment are used.

- Low-quality studies may be accepted because they employ traditional research designs, even though their research designs (as well as the standards that are used to assess them) may be based on naive or inappropriate ways of thinking about the nature of teaching, learning, and problem solving (or about the nature of program development, dissemination, and implementation).

For the aforementioned kinds of reasons, one of the main purposes of this book resulted from the authors' collective beliefs that the fields of mathematics and science education have arrived at a critical stage when future progress is likely to be compromised unless it is made easier for researchers to use innovative research designs in ways that increase their acceptability, sharability, usefulness, and cumulativeness. For example:

- At the time this book was being written, all three of the authors of this chapter were serving as program officers for the National Science Foundation's (NSF) Program for Research on Teaching and Learning. When they reviewed feedback during the assessment of preliminary proposals, or when they recorded the deliberations of peer review panels or mail reviewers, they became concerned about the following dilemma. Assessment issues often arose precisely because the most innovative and potentially powerful proposals stretched the limits of established theories and traditional methodologies. Yet, the NSF's 15-page limit on proposals allowed little opportunity for innovative proposals to include clear and detailed explanations of the three components that were needed in outstanding projects: (a) insightful interpretations of priority problems, (b) groundbreaking interpretations of useful, new, theoretical perspectives, and (c) cogent descriptions of innovative new research methodologies. As a result, because easy-to-cite references existed only for traditional research designs, researchers could face an undesirable choice: (a) propose novel research designs and risk rejection because of limited opportunities to explain the rationale and procedures, or (b) propose more traditional methodologies and risk compromising the applicability of their research results to emerging problems and perspectives.

- At approximately the same time that we embarked on this project, two international meetings took place at which a primary goal was to discuss quality standards for research in mathematics education. One was held at Gilleleje, Denmark, in 1992; it focused on "criteria for scientific quality and relevance in research on the didactics of mathematics" (Bishop, 1992; Brousseau, 1986; Kilpatrick, 1993a; Sierpinska, 1993). The other was held at the University of Maryland in 1994; it focused on the question: What is mathematics education research and what are its results? (Balacheff et al., 1993; Ellerton & M. A. Clements, 1996). As a direct consequence of these gatherings, a third related series of meetings was held as part of the 1996 International Congress of Mathematics Education in Seville, Spain (M. A. Clements & Ellerton, 1996). Each of these three meetings was born of the concern that, at international conferences involving mathematics and science education research, it is common to encounter sessions where flagrant violations seemed to occur related to traditional criteria such as validity, objectivity, rigor, precision, predictability, and reproducibility (Kilpatrick, 1993b; Mason, 1994; Shumway, 1980; Skovsmose, 1994). For example, studies purporting to be teaching experiments often consist of little more than anecdotes from a course taught by the researcher; or, videotape "analyses" often are based on out-of-context snippets that are used as a justification for telling a story for which the only justification that is offered is "trust me" (although many other interpretations seem equally plausible). Yet, in spite of the preceding concerns, participants expressed equally strong reservations about the fact that criteria based on statistical methods in behavioral psychology may be inappropriate for assessing the quality of, say, qualitative methods in cognitive psychology.

## NEW PARADIGMS CREATE THE NEED TO REVISE QUALITY ASSURANCE STANDARDS

Because the kinds of research designs that are emphasized in this book are based on newly evolving assumptions about the nature of students' knowledge, problem solving, learning, and teaching, they frequently involve lines of reasoning that are fundamentally different from those that applied to industrial-era factory metaphors for teaching and learning. Therefore, new standards of quality may be needed to assess the significance, credibility, and range of usefulness of the results that are produced by such studies. In general, basic issues, such as those related to validity, reliability, and generalizability, continue to be relevant and appropriate; but, usually, significant changes are needed in the ways that these criteria are defined operationally. For instance:

- In the past, one form of *validity* tended to be assessed based on correlations with results from standardized tests, which were in turn presumed to be measuring something important. But, in the case of nationally significant standardized tests, most have proven to be poorly aligned with national standards, grounded in obsolete forms of behavioral psychology, and not reflective of modern views about what it means to understand important constructs underlying the K–12 mathematics curriculum (Webb & Romberg, 1992). Moreover, mathematical thinking does not reside in the problems; it resides in the responses that students generate to problems. Consequently, mathematics educators have needed to become more sophisticated in the design of thought-revealing tasks in which the results that students produce include descriptions, explanations, constructions, and justifications that directly reveal significant aspects about students' ways of thinking (see chap. 21, this volume).

- In the past, research *credibility* often was interpreted in a way that appeared to demand almost omniscient objectivity on the part of the researcher. Yet, throughout the natural and social sciences, there is a growing recognition that, between the beholder and the beheld stretches a gulf of elaborate systems of theories and assumptions that are needed to distinguish signal from noise and to shape the interpretations of the phenomena under investigation. Therefore, given the current perspectives on knowledge that emphasize its cultural and social bases, the role of the researcher is less like that of a detached and disinterested judge, and more like that of an excellent defense lawyer who knows an area of study well, who cares deeply about it, but who nonetheless has the responsibility to present a case fairly, using evidence and lines of argument that are auditable and credible to a skeptic.

- In the past, *reliability* often was interpreted in a way that seemed to demand a naive type of reproducibility of results. That is, if one researcher repeated what another had done, then identical results were expected. For example, "standardized test questions" were designed with the intention that $N$ different students would be assumed to interpret the task in the same way, and repeated measurements of the construct were assumed to vary around students' "true" scores. But, for a researcher investigating the ways that students interpret a given situation, the expectation is that $N$ different students may interpret the situation in $N$ different ways. Also, if the goal of a complex task is for a student to develop an interpretation that is useful for making sense of the situation, then completion of the task generally involves significant forms of learning. Therefore, the student would not be expected to perform in the same way if the task were repeated or if a similar task were presented. Consequently, reliability cannot be interpreted to mean that behavior should be invariant across a series of related tasks. Nor does it mean that experts always should be expected to agree about the quality of a piece of work. Is a Jeep Cherokee better than a Ford Taurus? Such questions beg other questions: Better for what purpose? Better under what circumstances? Clearly, different evaluations will be made by experts who have different situations and purposes in mind; and, assessments of curriculum innovations require similar clarity about context and purpose. Furthermore, because the "subjects" being investigated are complex systems whose behaviors are extremely sensitive to small changes in conditions or purposes, what is expected from research is not some simplistic notion of reproducibility. Instead, what is needed are descriptions, explanations, and models that are meaningful, shareable, and useful to others in situations beyond those in which they were developed.

These observations are not intended to suggest that constructs such as validity, objectivity, and reliability are irrelevant to modern research in mathematics education. In fact, we consider the underlying constructs and concerns to be highly relevant. But, new problems and new theoretical perspectives require us to reexamine how we interpret these constructs. As researchers adopt new theoretical perspectives, even issues such as "burden of proof" frequently change due to the fact that what is taken as being "obvious" from one perspective may be regarded as "requiring proof" in other perspectives. For example, from the viewpoint of traditional psychometric theories, if a researcher wanted to partition a general mathematics aptitude test into components focusing on, say, algebraic and geometric thinking, the burden of proof would lie on the side of those who claim that aptitude in these areas involves something more than general intelligence. But, according to theoretical perspectives that are more relevant to current mathematics instruction, where geometric knowledge and abilities tend to be treated as being quite different from algebraic knowledge and abilities, and where (for example) a transfer of learning is seldom expected to occur automatically from one domain to another, the burden of proof would reside with those who would lump together achievement in such different conceptual domains and refer to the result as general mathematical aptitude (F. L. Schmidt, 1996; A. Strauss & Corbin, 1990).

An important purpose of this book is to reexamine the assumptions and goals underlying some of the most important and innovative new research designs that are being used extensively in mathematics and science education, and to describe them in ways that facilitate future progress in the field. We regard this as a work in progress where criteria for assessing quality will continually need to evolve along with the problems and perspectives they are intended to inform.

## THE DECADE OF THE "STANDARDS"

In mathematics and science education, this past decade has been characterized as the decade of the "standards." The development of standards has been a focus of activity at many different levels: local, district, state, and national; and, at each level, professional and governmental organizations have developed standards for assessing the quality of entities ranging from programs, to textbooks, to teaching, to tests (e.g., American Association for the Advancement of Science, 1993; Mathematical Sciences Education Board, 1990; National Board for Professional Teaching Standards, 1994, 1997; National Center of Education and the Economy and the University of Pittsburgh, 1997; National Council of Teachers of Mathematics, 1989, 1991b; National Research Council, 1996; U.S. Department of Education, 1991a).

Many different participants have joined in the preceding process: from teachers to researchers and administrators, and from representatives of business and industry to politicians, parents, and other concerned citizens. The standards that have been produced by these efforts have been used to provide powerful new tools to influence badly needed curricula reforms in mathematics and science education. However, in cases where these standards have been formulated inappropriately or assessed unwisely, they have led to serious debilitating effects on both what is taught and how it is taught (Ellerton & M. A. Clements, 1994). Therefore, it is critical that these standards be formulated wisely and assessed appropriately.

At their best, the newly developed standards often reflect deep and fundamental shifts in paradigms for thinking about what it means to understand the most important and powerful elementary constructs in mathematics and the sciences along with equally deep paradigm shifts in thinking about the nature of teaching, learning, and problem solving in mathematics, the sciences, or everyday situations. In general, emerging new perspectives have tended to move away from industrial-era, factory-based, assembly line metaphors for describing the development of knowledge (or the development of students, teachers, or programs). Instead, they are characterized by assumptions and interpretations that are consistent with more modern, postindustrial understandings about the development of complex, continually adapting, self-regulating systems (Kauffman, 1995; Shulman, 1986a).

Ironically, although many members of the mathematics and science education research communities have been leading contributors to the development of new standards to reflect new ways of thinking about problem solving, teaching, and learning, these communities of researchers as a whole have tended to overlook the need for similar standards for their own research practices. This is not altogether surprising because leading practitioners at all levels tend to be so busy with day-to-day problems that they seldom have adequate time for metalevel considerations. As the folk saying states: "When you are up to your neck in alligators, it's difficult to find time to think about draining the swamp." Yet, at a time when the mathematics and science education research communities increasingly are accused of failing to produce useful information to address the priority problems that their practitioners confront, researchers cannot afford to neglect discussions about the standards and principles that should apply to their own professional behaviors.

In past attempts to find measurable ways to think about constructs such as shareability, usefulness, and power, the results often have been counterproductive (M. A. Clements & Ellerton, 1996). This is because the criteria were defined operationally in ways that were inconsistent with basic assumptions about the systems being investigated; or, they were inadequate or inappropriate to deal with emerging problems, perspectives, or priorities in the development of knowledge. It was not because discussions about standards of quality were inherently irrelevant or inappropriate (Gamoran, in press; Newmann & Associates, 1996).

In some respects, the general objective of this book can be thought of as an attempt to take initial steps toward developing standards for research, similar to the standards that have been developed for curricula and assessment, or for teaching and teachers' education. However, we view the present effort as a beginning, more than as an end, of a process that must continue. New standards and new paradigms for thinking about teaching and learning have led to new research issues, which often cannot be addressed effectively with the experimental designs that were established to answer different kinds of questions or that are based on now-obsolete ways of thinking about the nature of mathematics, problem solving, teaching, and learning. Therefore, as new problems and perspectives continue to be generated, and as new research designs are created to address them, it will be equally important to continue to devise and revise appropriate criteria for assessing and increasing the quality of the efforts that are undertaken.

## ACKNOWLEDGMENTS

The project that led to this book was funded primarily by a cooperative agreement between Rutgers University and the National Science Foundation's Program for Research on Teaching and Learning (RTL). However, the Department of Education's National Center for Improvement of Student Learning & Achievement in Mathematics and Science Education also supported a series of seminars and follow-up activities that led to the gradual refinement and elaboration of many of the chapters.

# 2 Trends and Shifts in Research Methods

**Anthony E. Kelly**

*Rutgers, the State University of New Jersey*

**Richard Lesh**

*Purdue University*

All scientists choose, adapt, and create tools appropriate to their reading of problems and opportunities in their fields. In turn, new or adapted tools can change the questions asked and the answers given, leading to new research cycles. The dialectic between the evolution of tools and the refinement of problems characterizes growth in a field.

We are now at a point where the growing maturity of mathematics and science education research has shifted attention from strict adherence to traditional experimental methods as the best path to scientific insight to renewed interest in the development of alternative methods for research. In the past few number of decades, educational researchers have moved into school systems, classrooms, and workplaces and have found a complex and multifaceted world that they feel is not well described by traditional research techniques. In the past, educational phenomena derived their status by surviving a variety of statistical tests. Today, nascent educational phenomena are accorded primacy, and the onus is on research methods to describe them in rich and systematic ways.

What characterizes the sentiment of this book is the recognition that the legitimacy of educational research questions should not be predetermined by or constrained to the potentialities and capabilities of a particular research methodology. Rather, the needs of learning and teaching, and the descriptive, analytic, and communication needs of the

35

community of researchers should help bring forth and test a diversity of research methods. These methods may include those borrowed from other traditions (e.g., anthropology) as well as those emerging from within the practices of mathematics and science education research (e.g., teaching experiments, design experiments, action research). Educational research not only wishes to answer questions such as, "Which instructional approach leads to the greatest growth in learning under controlled conditions?" Research also involves model development and model validation—developing productive ways of thinking about problems and opportunities.

More ambitious curricula and more pluralistic pedagogies directed toward understanding, sense making, and broadly applicable intellectual skill, employing new tools and embodying new content, engaging new connections with the world outside the school and university, new connections among different levels of education—all these conspire to complexify the endeavor to achieve reliable knowledge and to limit the effectiveness of simple measures and strategies. These changes in education also interact complexly in a political environment that is tuned for rapid, egalitarian improvement of practice where the meaning of "improvement" is not only unclear, but is in serious contention. Further, innovation is highly decentralized horizontally across sites and, especially, disjointed vertically across levels. Indeed, perhaps the most important factor, not yet built into plans and expectations of most researchers, is the fundamental fact that virtually every idea appearing in later mathematics has conceptual and developmental roots in the earlier years—which means that our understandings of idea growth at the later levels necessarily must take into account the structure of such ideas and the ways those ideas grew from earlier experience, especially but not exclusively, educational experience. The existing political and economic factors and institutional arrangements pull researchers toward simple, local comparisons of isolated innovations in the face of all the contextual change and complexity just identified.

## SHIFTS

Behind this shift in methods, there are also shifts in some basic assumptions about the role of research in mathematics and science education. Table 2.1 summarizes a number of these shifts.

TABLE 2.1

Some Shifts in Emphasis in Educational Research in Mathematics and Science with Sample Chapters

| Less Emphasis On | More Emphasis On |
|---|---|
| researcher remoteness or stances of "objectivity" | researcher engagement, participant-observer roles: Chapters by Ball; Cline & Mandinach; Cobb; Confrey & Lachance; Doerr & Tinto; Feldman & Minstrell; Lesh & Kelly; Moschkovich & Brenner; Simon, Steffe & Thompson; Tobin |
| researcher as expert; the judge of the effectiveness of knowledge transmission using prescripted measures | researcher as coconstructor of knowledge; a learner-listener who values the perspective of the research subject, who practices self-reflexivity: Chapters by Ball; Cline & Mandinach; Cobb; Confrey & Lachance; Doerr & Tinto; Feldman & Minstrell; Lesh & Kelly; Moschkovich & Brenner; Simon, Steffe & Thompson; Tobin |
| viewing the learner as a lone, passive learner in a classroom seen as a closed unit | viewing the learner both as an individual and social learner within a classroom conceived of as a complex, self-organizing, self-regulating system that is one level in a larger human-constructed system: Chapters by Cline & Mandinach; Cobb; Lesh & Kelly; Steffe & Thompson |
| simple cause-and-effect or correlational models | complexity theory; systems thinking; organic and evolutionary models of learning and system change: Chapters by Cline & Mandinach; Lesh & Kelly |
| looking to statistical tests to determine if factors "exist" | F values and Pearson coefficients replaced by thick, ethnographic descriptions; recognition of the theory-ladenness of observation and method: Chapters by Cline & Mandinach; Cobb; Doerr & Tinto; Feldman & Minstrell; Moschkovich & Brenner; Simon, Steffe & Thompson; Tobin |
| the general applicability of method | the implications of subjects' constructions of content and subject matter for determining meaning: Chapters by Lesh & Clarke; Stroup & Wilensky |
| one-time measures of achievement (often summative or pre-post) | iterative cycles of observations of complex behaviors involving feedback; design experiments; engineering approaches: Chapters by Battista & Clements; Cobb; Lesh & Kelly; Steffe & Thompson |
| multiple-choice or other standardized measures of learning | multisensory/multimedia data sources; simulations; performance assessments: Chapters by Clements & Battista; Cooper; Hall; Mestre; Roschelle; Steffe & Thompson |
| average scores on standardized tests as learning outcomes | Sophistication of content models; the process of models; conceptual development: Chapters by Mestre; Steffe & Thompson; Lesh, Hoover, Hole, Kelly, & Post |

(continued)

| singular dependence on numbers; apparent precision of numbers | awareness of the assumptions of measurement; understanding the limitations of measures; extracting maximum information from measures, and involving interactive, multi-dimensional, dynamic, and graphic displays:  Chapters by Lesh, Hoover, Hole, Kelly, & Post; Liebovitch, Todorov, Wood, & Ellenbogen; Stroup & Wilensky; Mestre; Tatsuoka & Boodoo |
|---|---|
| accepting curricula as given | the historicity of curricula – Dennis; scientific and systematic reassessment of curricula – Battista & Clements; reconceptualization of curricula given technology – Roschelle & Jackiw; reconcepualization of curricula given research – Confrey & Lachance |

Over time, field-based educational researchers have come to recognize the sociocultural, historical, systemic, political, cognitive, affective, and physiological aspects of teaching and learning, which motivates them to expand their researchers' armamentarium. Accordingly, the reader will not find in these chapters a silver bullet research methodology. Rather, the authors invite the reader to struggle with them as they propose methods that they feel capture better the saliences in their growing understanding of learning and teaching, while producing an internally consistent, systematic, scientific account of it. Furthermore, the research products are increasingly the result of design studies that involve contributions from teachers, curriculum designers, and students.

# RESEARCHERS AS INTERESTED LEARNERS: BACKGROUND FACTORS

Researchers are learners, and their methods reflect their experiences and personalities. The proclivities of the researchers' represented in this book are supported by a number of background factors, many of which apply to all of the authors:

- Pride in their identities as teachers, teacher educators, curriculum developers, software developers, and program developer. In other words, educational researchers are beginning to draw upon more than their narrow training in research methods as a basis for designing and executing studies.

- Direct experiences with the realities of school and workplaces as entities within larger systems.

- A commitment to equity and fairness.

- The growing legitimization of field-based and qualitative methods, particularly ethnographic techniques and participant-observer studies.

- The legitimization of the study of cognition, as exemplified by the emergence and strength of cognitive science. Many early educational researchers began their training during the dominance of behaviorism; from that perspective, learners were organisms to which treatments were applied and whose environments were engineered. With the ascendancy of cognitive psychology, such narrow conceptions of learning have been abandoned.

- The transformative nature of technology, both as a tool in learning and in scientific advances. A number of research projects exemplify this insight, particularly the work in calculus (SIMCALC: http://tango.mth.umassd.edu/simcalc/) and scientific visualization (CoVis: http://www.covis.nwu.edu/). Researchers are using technology to question not only what content is taught, but also to whom it is taught and at what age.

- A commitment to the position (expressed variably) that all learners (researchers included) are active constructors of knowledge. There is a growing rejection of the researcher as the expert—the judge of the effectiveness of knowledge transmission. This view is being replaced by one of self-reflexivity in which the researcher is seen as a learner-listener who respects and models the worlds of others and views him- or herself as a learner (e.g., see chaps. 5, 9, 13, 18 this volume).

# RESEARCHERS AS INTERESTED LEARNERS: FOREGROUND FACTORS

In addition to the background factors described in the preceding section, the researchers in this book also share many proactive factors, which evidence themselves in the research methods they advocate. These factors include:

I.    A commitment to subject matter. For example, Steffe and Thompson (chap. 11, this volume) are less concerned with how students learn "formal mathematics," but more with how students construct their own understanding of mathematics. Their goal is to *replace* traditional mathematics curricula with curricula informed by insights from the mathematics of students.

Ia.   In their chapter, Confrey and Lachance (chap. 10, this volume) explore the teaching of multiplication not as repeated addition, but as involving the operation of splitting. They attempt to meld the functions of research as the disciplined observation of mathematical teaching practice, with research as a transformative process.

Ib.   In the analysis by Ball (of her own and Lampert's, Heaton's, and Simon's experiences; chap. 14, this volume), she notes that she and other teacher-researchers have experienced the need to understand mathematics itself more deeply in order to teach it in line with reform efforts, which, in turn, broadens the number and quality of the research questions that can be asked and addressed.

Ic.   Mestre (chap. 7, this volume), whose field is physics education, points out that the design of effective assessment task assumes a substantial grounding in subject matter. Moreover, the design of assessment devices (quantitative and qualitative) can effectively limit what a researcher can learn about students' understanding of subject matter knowledge by constraining or overdirecting students' responses to tasks. Mestre argues that the interplay between framing research questions, building and refining assessment tools, the character of evidence, and theory building and refinement is delicate and nonlinear and involved intimately with considerations of subject matter knowledge.

II. A desire to go beyond the identification and documentation of educational phenomena to their reform and improvement (e.g., Confrey, chap. 5, this volume).

III. An openness to employing techniques that provide more bandwidth in the recording, analysis, and dissemination of findings (e.g., chaps. 22, 23, and 24, this volume). In this case we find that researchers are using videotape archives, computer-generated trace files, and Internet-based records to create and support their claims.

IV. A desire to create not only research archives, but also revisable and augmentable, persuasive resources that form the basis for effective action by practitioners (e.g., videotapes of best practice, see Confrey, chap. 5, this volume).

V. An undertaking to increase the sophistication of the various measures used to judge the efficacy of a study. The simplistic uses of number and its apparent precision are disfavored increasingly, as is the thoughtless use of statistics (e.g., Liebovitch, Todorov, Wood & Ellenbogen, chap. 32, this volume). In particular, many authors recognize the immense loss of information that occurs when numbers are used to represent rich phenomena (e.g., Stroup & Wilensky, chap. 31, this volume). In fact, there is a growing effort to develop techniques to extract maximum information from educational measures (e.g., chaps 29 and 31, this volume). There is less singular reliance on "objective" data collection measures (characteristically, multiple-choice paper-and-pencil tests taken by students in isolation from one another) toward the use of multimedia and multisensory data collection approaches (e.g., see chaps 22, 23, and 27, this volume) and toward new approaches to task design such as model-eliciting problems (e.g., Lesh, Hoover, Hole, Kelly & Post, chap. 21, this volume). Greater attention is paid to the models that learners construct, to using the processes of model development as outcomes, and to creating representations of conceptual development compared to descriptions of behavior (e.g. chaps 7, 11, and 21, this volume). In addition, single measures of achievement are being replaced by attention to iterative cycles of observation of complex behaviors involving feedback (e.g., chaps. 9, 11, 12, 14, 17, and 23, this volume), a commitment to self-reflexivity in all aspects of the research endeavor (e.g., chaps. 9 and 11, this volume), and as exemplified by the entire book, an openness to learn from other traditions of research not only their techniques and methods, but also their approaches to the construction of researchable questions.

# RECOGNIZING THE SYSTEMS NATURE AND COMPLEXITY OF EDUCATION

Simple, cause-and-effect models are being replaced by models that take a more systemic, organic, or evolutionary approach to changes in learning and teaching (e.g., chaps. 8, 9, 11, 12, 15, and 17, this volume). The emerging view considers the learner as both an individual and a social learner in a learning environment conceived of as a complex, multilevel, human construction that is self-organizing and self-regulating and that is a part of, and responds to, the needs of larger systems (e.g., chaps. 8, 9, 11, 12, 13, and 30, this volume). There is also a movement away from attempts to draw cause-and-effect implications from data toward greater attention being paid to thick descriptions, narratives, and ethnographic methods, generally. It should be noted that this trend is not without its detractors (see chaps. 19 and 20, this volume).

# PROMOTING IMMEDIACY

A number of the authors have seen a need for more immediacy, both in terms of their interaction with their "subjects" and in the connection between research and effective action in practice. There is a shift from a stance of remoteness and researcher "objectivity" to a stance of engagement and immersion. For many of the book's authors, the delay between the findings of "basic research" in psychology (often conducted in laboratory settings) and their effective application in the classroom became too long or was unsatisfactory otherwise. Both factors have led to the development of research-teacher and teacher-researcher models. Examples of efforts to bridge the research-practice divide include varieties of action research (see Feldman &

Minstrell, chap. 16, this volume); varieties of teaching experiments (e.g., Steffe & Thompson, chap. 11, this volume), and transformative teaching experiments (Confrey & LaChance, chap. 10, this volume). This trend can be seen too in chapters 11–15, 17, and 18, this volume.

## CHALLENGING THE CURRICULUM AS GIVEN

Many of the book's authors question the curricula as given. Dennis (chap. 28, this volume), for example, points out the historicity of some aspects of mathematics curricula. Roschelle and Jackiw (chap. 27, this volume) call for a reconceptualization of curricula, given advances in technology. Confrey and Lachance (chap. 10, this volume) and Steffe and Thompson (chap. 11, this volume) call for a reconceptualization of curricula, given the findings from research into learning. Finally, Battista and Clements (chap. 25, this volume) call for a scientifically informed systematic reexamination of curricula.

## CAVEATS

As we have emphasized in other chapters in this book, it is not the goal of this book to establish a new set of standard techniques. The research designs that are described herein refer to works in progress. Many cautions may be applied to these efforts, some of which are noted here. As Stroup and Wilensky (chap. 31, this volume) point out, "radical individualism"—that is, the tendency to oversell data on individual cases, regardless of how rich the descriptions might be—must be avoided. Both Stroup and Wilensky and Tatsuoka and Boodoo (chap. 29, this volume) are working on statistical solutions to this problem. Lesh, Hoover, et al. (chap. 21, this volume) are addressing the problem by making a mathematical model and its development the focus of attention rather than individual differences, per se. A related concern is avoiding "radical localization," that is, overimmersion in one school or district in which the (re)engineering of its solutions is not mined for lessons that have broader application.

There is also the need to avoid relativism, to avoid sophomoric arguments claiming that, because there are many perspectives, there can be no agreement on robust phenomena. Chapter 19, by Goldin (see also Clement, chap. 20, this volume), explores some of this territory, particularly the political risks of downplaying concerns of replication and generalization, and defaulting to "storytelling." As Goldin points out, educational researchers must remain aware of the risk of losing political battles through the lack of "hard data." More generally, it is important not to lose sight of content concerns in mathematics and science and the real needs of students and teachers by engaging in esoteric, epistemological, sociological, and anthropological debates.

The final caution is to realize the increased demands on what is a very small community in educational research (see Confrey, chap. 5, this volume). To function as a competent educational researcher, it is now necessary to have increased sophistication in content knowledge in mathematics or science, in new technologies, and in psychology, sociology, ethnography, and methodology. Those who are training the next generation of researchers must pay close attention to this "capacity problem."

# 3 Research Agendas: Identifying Priority Problems and Developing Useful Theoretical Perspectives

**Richard Lesh**
*Purdue University*

**Barbara Lovitts**
*AIR*

Although a goal of this book is to discuss some of the most important criteria for assessing and optimizing the quality of research designs that appear to be especially promising for research on mathematics and science education, we make no attempt to establish an agenda for such research. In particular, this book is not about what kind of problems should be the most important to address, nor is it about what kind of theoretical perspectives should be favored. Yet, when panels of reviewers assess the quality of research proposals or publications, they consider more than the quality of the research design. For example, in mathematics and science education, high-quality research projects generally are intended to make a difference to both theory and practice. They tackle important problems or issues, and they lead to extensions, modifications, or revisions of a significant base of knowledge. Therefore, to assess proposals or publications for a particular organization or agency, reviewers take into account answers to the following types of questions:

- What kinds of decision makers and decision making issues does the organization or agency believe should be given priority? For example, should the policy-level decisions of administrators and politicians be given priority over the classroom decision-making issues that confront teachers and students? Should projects be supported in which *mathematics* or *science* could be replaced by such terms as *literature* or *social studies* or *art*? That is, should investigations be supported that deal with general education issues, or general management issues, or general policy issues, or general issues involving the dissemination of knowledge and the implementation of new scholarship in which the quality of the subject matter is not considered?

- What levels and types of subjects does the organization or agency want to generate more knowledge about? For example, should new information or new ways of thinking about the development of students and teachers be given priority over information about the development of schools or school systems, or the development, dissemination, and implementation of programs or curricular materials? What balance should an organization attempt to achieve among these factors?

- What "grain size" (level of detail) does the organization or agency consider to be most productive for describing the preceding subjects? What dimensions does it believe should be emphasized? For example, is information about the general behavior of groups viewed as being more significant than information about the detailed behaviors of individuals? Does a social perspective appear to be more useful than a cognitive perspective? Does a developmental perspective seem more likely to be useful than "status studies" at isolated intervals?

- What problems or issues does the organization or agency consider to be the most important to address about the preceding subjects? For example, should attention be focused on issues involving equity, content quality, standards, assessment, or school-to-work transitions? Should problems be emphasized that focus on policy issues or school-level decision making, even if these issues have little to do with the quality of mathematics and science instruction? To what extent should research be proactive (by attempting to investigate tomorrow's issues, perhaps related to innovative uses of technologies) rather than reactive (by restricting attention to solutions to problems that are priorities today)? Should the problems of inner-city minority students be given priority over those of other populations of students? Should the problems of nonindustrial societies be favored over those associated with technology-based, job opportunities?

- What kinds of conceptual frameworks or theoretical perspectives does the organization or agency consider to be most useful? For example, does the agency consider studies based on constructivist philosophies to be more promising and, therefore, more worthy of support than studies based on other perspectives?

- In what form does the organization or agency believe that relevant information should be delivered in order to be useful? For example, should the deliverables emphasize the development of *knowledge* (e.g., shareable and reusable information that is relevant to the priority, decision-making issues in mathematics or science education), the development of *materials* (e.g., textbooks, software, or videotapes), the development of *programs* (e.g., workshops or sequences of experiences that can be replicated and disseminated), or the development of *teachers* (e.g., enabling them to become certified as having achieved certain specified goals)?

Generating answers to the preceding types of questions is one of the most important challenges faced in formulating a *research agenda* for a particular organization or agency. But, in general, this book is not intended to address such questions. For our purposes, answers to such questions become relevant only if they have bearing on principles that researchers should consider in order to conduct (for example) high-quality clinical interviews, teaching experiments, or videotape analyses. Therefore, instead of attempting to provide answers about priority problems and perspectives, the authors in this book were asked to assume that most of these agenda-setting issues will be resolved by the funding agencies or professional organizations that will review proposals or publications. Our goal is to address a much more restricted set of issues that arise after decisions have been made about which problems and perspectives should be treated as priorities. That is, we focus on the internal logic of the processes of gathering, analyzing, and interpreting information, namely:

perspectives should be treated as priorities. That is, we focus on the internal logic of the processes of gathering, analyzing, and interpreting information, namely:

- Are the processes of data collection, analysis, and interpretation consistent with relevant assumptions about the nature of the subjects being investigated? For example, in research on teaching and learning, the subjects being investigated may range from students, to groups, to ideas, to software, to teachers, to schools, to programs, and to other kinds of complex systems that tend to react and modify themselves as a result of being observed. Therefore, in such instances, it often is inappropriate for researchers to rely on data collection methods that presuppose measurements that are completely unobtrusive.

- Are the processes for analyzing data consistent with assumptions about relevant characteristics and behaviors of the systems being investigated? For example, when complex, adapting, self-regulating systems are investigated, relevant characteristics and patterns of behavior often interact in complex ways that involve recursion and chaos. Consequently, in such instances, it may be inappropriate for researchers to rely on data analysis techniques that are based on simple linear models in which relevant characteristics and behaviors are treated as if they were independent or dependent variables within simple cause-and-effect interactions.

- Are the criteria for assessing the usefulness of constructs consistent with assumptions about the nature of relevant decision making issues and the relevant decision makers that these constructs are intended to inform? For example, in the assessment of students' achievement, information and ways of thinking that are useful for critical decision making by college admissions officers may be relatively insignificant in the context of less momentous iterative decision making by classroom teachers. Therefore, to design relevant research, decisions must be made that involve trade-offs among factors such as accuracy, precision, timeliness, and consistency. This is because research design strategies that have a positive effect on one of these factors often have negative effects on others.

## WHAT FACTORS INFLUENCED OUR CHOICE OF THE RESEARCH PROCEDURES EMPHASIZED?

Although the editors of this book considered it neither feasible nor desirable to restrict attention to any single theoretical perspective or any one set of problems, the research procedures that we chose to emphasize include clinical interviews, teaching experiments, videotape analyses, ethnographic observations, and other qualitative methods that often incorporate action research in which the roles of practitioners and researchers become blurred. Not only are these research procedures that have taken on distinctive characteristics when they have been used in mathematics and science education, but they also are research procedures that have been used extensively around the world for addressing many types of problems from many different perspectives. Yet, most of these perspectives emphasize constructivist ways of viewing students, teachers, classrooms, schools, and school districts; also, most of the research procedures that we emphasize were designed specifically to decrease the gap between researchers and practitioners, perhaps by including teachers and other practitioners in the research process or perhaps by stressing field-based, rather than laboratory-based, investigations.

In general, we have emphasized qualitative research procedures more than quantitative procedures mainly because a wealth of resources exists already in which quantitative methodologies are highlighted. Further, we have underlined psychological issues more than other perspectives because, during the past few decades, some of the most productive branches of mathematics and science education research have focused their investigations on how the ways of thinking of students, teachers, or others who are involved in mathematics and science education develop. Therefore, these are the areas where the development of new research designs has flourished.

Beyond the aforementioned prejudices, our discussions about research designs take place in the context of specific problems and perspectives. Consequently, to help coordinate the discussions in various chapters of the book, it was useful to choose a few themes (problems and perspectives) that might help to ground the discussions in specifics. Yet, at the same time, these themes needed to be chosen in such a way that they did not narrow the relevance of the book needlessly to include only those who share these prejudices. The research agenda that we chose in order to provide unifying themes is the one that was adopted by the organization that funded most of our efforts: the United States' National Science Foundation Program for Research on Teaching and Learning (RTL).

The research agenda for the RTL Program is given in the Appendix to this chapter. It was ideal for our purposes because it was formulated explicitly to enable most mathematics and science education researchers to fit within its framework. Yet, the themes that it emphasized enabled the program as a whole to describe the results of funded research projects in a form that is meaningful to politicians, bureaucrats, business leaders, and others who must support such efforts ultimately. Also, the subjects to be investigated can range from students, to teachers, to classrooms, to schools, and to programs; and, the general issues that it addresses can range from equity, to content quality, to preparation for success beyond school, and to technology in education. Therefore, the framework imposed few constraints on our discussions of research designs; nevertheless, it helped the authors to coordinate their efforts.

## WHY DO PROFESSIONAL ORGANIZATIONS AND FUNDING AGENCIES CHANGE THEIR RESEARCH PRIORITIES FREQUENTLY?

Another reason to avoid restricting attention to a narrow research agenda is that a variety of reasonable responses can be given to the kinds of agenda-setting questions that are described in the previous section. There is no single set of "right answers." Also, no professional organization or funding agency has more than a small amount of resources that it can use to help improve educational practice. Therefore, each tends to focus on a niche that will provide maximum leverage in the problem areas that it considers to be the most strategic for achieving the sorts of significant impacts that it seeks. As a result, different organizations and agencies tend to answer the preceding questions in different ways, and, in order to respond to the changing realities of both theory and practice, they review and revise continually their official opinions about priority problems and strategic directions for research and practice.

# IN WHAT WAYS DO CHANGES IN RESEARCH AGENDAS IMPACT CHOICES OF RESEARCH DESIGNS?

When a research agenda is specified, there are various ways that choices about problems and theoretical perspectives influence the kinds of research designs that are emphasized. Possibilities may range from proof-of-concept studies (such as those involving the use of innovative software or curricular materials), to case studies (such as those concerned with the dissemination or implementation of complex programs, or professional development), to surveys (such as those aimed at information for policy makers), to action research studies or teaching experiments (such as those featuring the classroom practices of effective teachers), to ethnographic observations (such as those whose purposes are to identify the kinds of mathematical or scientific understandings that are needed for success in various contemporary professions), and to detailed clinical interviews or videotape analyses (such as those seeking to clarify the categories of mathematical understandings and abilities that contribute to success in targeted types of real-life, problem solving situations).

To decide which of the preceding kinds of investigations may be most appropriate, another important factor to consider is the maturity of the relevant theoretical models. Sometimes, what is needed most is model construction, or model elaboration, or model extension; but, at other times, model testing and verification, or model revision and refinement are called for. Sometimes, hypothesis-testing studies are required; at other times, exploratory hypothesis-generating studies aimed at finding productive ways to think about the relevant situation are needed in order to advance the state of knowledge. Sometimes, premature attempts at quantification may be foolish, but, at later stages of development, the lack of measurable and clearly defined constructs may hinder progress.

Whereas the products that some studies yield may consist of rules or generalizations for which it is appropriate to ask whether the construct is true or false, other types of investigations may lead to products consisting of descriptions or explanations of complex systems, so that the kinds of criteria that are appropriate for judging quality are similar to those that apply to portraits of people, or to blueprints for houses. One does not ask whether portraits or blueprints are true or false; instead, we ask whether they are meaningful and useful, revealing and illuminating, internally consistent, sufficiently detailed, fuzzy and flawed. Therefore, among the research designs described in this book, many of the most important issues that we need to address are those that are related to criteria for judging and optimizing the quality of the results that are produced by the various kinds of investigations.

## NEW WAYS OF THINKING ABOUT COMMUNICATION BETWEEN RESEARCHERS AND PRACTITIONERS

Another factor that influenced strongly the research procedures stressed in this book was the sensed need to increase the timeliness and usefulness of the results that are produced by mathematics and science education researchers. On the one hand, from the perspective of practitioners who are critical of the mathematics and science education research communities, a perceived shortcoming is that researchers often seem to be driven by their whims and curiosities rather than by an attempt to investigate real problems. Therefore, the advances in knowledge that such researchers make often seem to practitioners to be irrelevant to the decision-making issues that they consider to be priorities. On the other hand, some of these dissatisfactions are the result of inappropriate traditional ways of thinking about productive links between theory and practice.

To develop more productive links between theory and practice, it is naive to think in terms of a one-way process in which practitioners present problems and researchers provide answers that are distributed through external agents. Traditionally, in education, ideas about *information dissemination* have been based on models and metaphors borrowed from agriculture, where new ideas were distributed in much the same way as fertilizer. But, today, in mathematics and science education, this way of thinking has proved to be inadequate. For example:

- It is misleading to imagine that mathematics and science educators can be sorted into nonoverlapping categories such as "researchers" and "practitioners." There are many other types of people besides teachers and researchers who are involved in the mathematics and science education enterprise. For example, other significant participants include curricula developers, teacher-educators, and school district curricula supervisors. Furthermore, many leading researchers are among the nation's most influential teachers, teacher-educators, curricula developers, or curricula reformers. Similarly, many outstanding practitioners are deeply involved in projects whose main goals are to generate new ways of thinking about the development of students or teachers or new ways of thinking about program development, implementation, and dissemination. Therefore, the kinds of research designs that are emphasized in this book include teaching experiments, action research, and other approaches to the development of knowledge in which the distinctions between researchers and practitioners are blurred.

- In mathematics and science education, the flow of information between researchers and practitioners is not the kind of one-way process that is suggested by such terms as *information dissemination*. Instead, to be effective, the flow of information usually must be cyclic, iterative, and interactive. One reason this is true is because researchers are not necessarily skilled at communicating their results in forms that are useful to teachers, and teachers are not necessarily skilled at describing their problems in forms that are researchable. As folk wisdom suggests, a fish is not necessarily the animal most likely to discover water. Quick fixes often focus on symptoms rather than causes; thus, a clear recognition of a pain is not the same thing as a clear conception of a solvable problem. Furthermore, research is similar to other forms of learning in the sense that an important goal of research is to look beyond the immediate and the obvious and to focus on what *could be* in addition to what *is*. Consequently, some of the most important contributions that researchers make to practice often involve finding new ways to think about problems and potential solutions, rather than merely providing answers to specific questions. Similarly, some of the most important contributions that practitioners make to research cannot be delayed until the final stages of projects when results are translated into a form that is intended to be meaningful and useful. Therefore, the kinds of research designs that are stressed herein often involve teachers, as well as other types of practitioners, at early stages of the projects, and the knowledge that is developed often is embedded in curricular materials, educational programs, or models for teaching and learning.

- Traditional views of program implementation tend to be based on machine metaphors in which schools are treated as if they are factories that can be broken into components and assembled one piece at a time. But "delivery-and-reception" models have proved to be far too simplistic to describe the development of complex systems, regardless of whether the "individuals" involved are students, teachers, groups, classrooms, schools, or school systems. As the chapter of this book on operational definitions (Lesh & Clarke, chap. 6, this volume) explains, all of these individuals involve systems that are more like complex and continually adapting biological systems than they are like simple machines. In each case, the system as a whole is more than the sum of its parts; the parts interact in complex and recursive ways, and, when actions are applied to these systems, the systems react. Therefore, when the goal is for a particular system to evolve in desirable directions, it is not enough for "good ideas" to be delivered and "bolted down" like isolated components in a machine. Instead, new ways of thinking need to be developed through extensions of, and adaptations to existing sound systems. As a result, the research designs that are highlighted in this volume frequently go beyond investigating isolated individuals and focus also on interactions among and between the development of students, teachers, curricular materials, and programs of instruction.

- Because of the complexity of the problems and the systems that need to be understood in mathematics and science education, single, isolated, research studies seldom produce results that are useful immediately for solving real-life problems. In most of the cases that occur in mathematics and science education, both the problems and the solutions are far too complex to lend themselves to simplistic, one-study-to-one-solution approaches to progress. Instead, a series of investigations conducted over a considerable tends to be needed. For real progress to be made, knowledge must accumulate. Therefore, rather than judging the usefulness of research projects based on the notion of a one-to-one correspondence between problems and projects or solutions, a more productive approach is to expect each study to contribute to the development of a community of knowledge, materials, and programs that should be expected to produce significant results over a reasonable period of time. In research, as in curricula reform, piecemeal approaches to progress are seldom effective to induce changes in knowledge and abilities, systemic and systematic research programs are needed.

## FOR PROGRESS TO BE MADE, KNOWLEDGE MUST ACCUMULATE

Another force on many of the research procedures described in this book was the desire to find appropriate balances and interdependencies among projects that focus on the development of knowledge versus those that focus on the development of curricular materials, students, teachers, groups, classrooms, programs, or other relevant complex systems.

To achieve appropriate balances among these kinds of projects, one question that we considered was: How much progress have mathematics and science education projects made since the time of the "new math" projects of the 1960s? Our conclusion was that, regardless of whether the projects being considered focused on materials development, students' development, teachers' development, or program development, the following generalizations tended to be true: In projects where progress has been made, it is because more is known at the end of the project; in projects where little significant progress has been apparent, it is because these projects have failed to build on one another's work in systematic ways. Consider the following examples:

- *Projects that focus on the development of curricular materials.* Have curriculum development projects built on their successes and failures in systematic ways? Have assessments of projects gone beyond simplistic claims that "It works!" to address such questions as: who, what, when, where, and why? With whom does it work and in what ways? What components work best for which purposes, and what components are missing or relatively ineffective? When and where does it work and under what conditions? Why do the preceding components work and how could improvements be made? In cases where these kinds of questions have been addressed in nonsimplistic ways, and in cases where the results were expressed in a form that was meaningful and useful to others, such materials development projects have contributed not only to the development of new curricular materials but also to what is known about teaching and learning. Unfortunately, relatively few curriculum development projects have treated "knowing more" as a major goal of their efforts. Consequently, progress has tended to be serendipitous.

- *Projects that focus on the development of teachers.* Are preservice or inservice projects for the development of teachers today improvements over their counterparts from 30 years ago? In cases where the answer is "yes," projects have tended to be based on research that focused on the development of students' knowledge, teachers' knowledge, and classroom practices. Examples of such projects include many whose directors are authors represented in this book or other well-know researchers (Ball, 1991; T. Carpenter & Fennema, 1992; T. Carpenter, Fennema, & Lamon, 1988; Cobb & Bauersfeld, 1995; Confrey, 1986, 1990; R. B. Davis, Maher, & Noddings, 1990; Hestenes, 1994; Lampert, 1985, 1988; Post, Behr, Lesh, & Harel, 1988; M. Simon & Schifter, 1991; A. Thompson, 1984, 1989; Warren, Rosebery, & Conant, 1994). Conversely, in the area of teachers' education where little progress has been made, the same mistakes tend to occur repeatedly in one project after another. For example, the results of development projects for teachers often are assessed using such naive indexes as minimizing dollars-per-contact-hour or maximizing the number of teachers "touched." Yet, it is well known that brief and superficial experiences are seldom effective in promoting sustainable changes in classroom practices. Similarly, models for teachers' inservice education continue to rely on brief summer workshops followed by a small number of brief, school-based observations, demonstrations, or discussion. Further, models for disseminating (or scaling up) these programs tend to rely on a cascading, "chain-letter" mechanism in which mentors pass on good practices to colleagues who, in turn, pass them on to others. However, it is well known that far more sophisticated forms of support are needed in order for the half-life of an intended change in practice to survive more than a single link in this cascading chain.

- *Projects that focus on the development, dissemination, and implementation of innovative programs of instruction.* Again, are today's projects an improvement over their counterparts from 30 years ago? The answer to this question is more definitely "no" than the answers to the questions about changes in projects for the development of curricular materials and teachers. Although simpleminded, "delivery-and-reception" metaphors are recognized widely now as being inappropriate for describing the development of students, teachers, or other complex systems, these same machine-based metaphors continue to be applied to the development of programs of instruction. The goals of such programs continue to be reduced to naive checklists. Tests that are aligned poorly with the goals of instruction continue to be used. Accountability practices typically have largely negative influences on what is taught and how it is taught and activities that are means to other ends tend to be treated as if they were ends in themselves. For example, teachers' workshops tend to be held, or new computer laboratories are created, as if they were ends in themselves apart from any goals related to students' achievement. In an attempt to avoid having curricula reforms appear to be top-down impositions, blue ribbon panels of teachers often rewrite local versions of national standards for curricula and instruction, and/or they attempt to write new materials for assessment or instruction. Yet, asking a small committee of expert teachers to create local standards seldom makes these standards any more local than those that were defined by national committees. Furthermore, curricular goals that are defined only by "school people" usually do not enlist support from knowledgeable parents or leaders in the community. Also, because teachers usually are given insufficient time to perform the preceding tasks, which they often are expected to carry out in addition to their other duties, the materials they produce seldom pass through the kind of quality assurance procedures that are needed in order to ensure that adequate attention has been given to such issues as equity, reliability, or validity. Furthermore, teachers who are involved in such efforts usually must take time away from precisely what they do best, which is interacting with students.

Among the difficulties mentioned in the preceding examples, nearly all of them resulted in pressing needs to develop new information and new ways of thinking about teaching, learning, and problem solving or the development, dissemination, and implementation of instructional programs and materials. Yet, many people involved in the reform of curricula claim that: "We know enough! All we need to do is to do it!"

We agree that curricula reform does not need to be delayed until many years and millions of dollars have been spent on more research. But, at organizations such as the United States' National Science Foundation (NSF), there never has been a danger that this possibility would occur. For example, traditionally, the NSF has spent orders of magnitude less money on educational projects that were aimed at the development of knowledge than those that focused on the development of curricular materials, instructional programs, teachers, and school systems. In fact, in recent years, the NSF has dedicated less than 1.6% of its education budget to projects whose main deliverables involved basic research on teaching and learning. Furthermore, whereas RTL-funded projects typically involved significant components related to the development of instructional materials, programs, or teachers, it has been rare for projects funded in these areas to involve significant components aimed at knowing more about problem solving, teaching, and learning.

The preceding observations are important because they suggested to the editors of this book that if research in mathematics and science education is going to get enough support to be effective, the kinds of research designs that need to be emphasized are those that: (a) can be conducted within the context of other types of projects, (b) are likely to lead to results for projects whose main goals stress the development of materials, software, teachers, programs, or effective school systems, and (c) go beyond studies aimed at yielding information about the development of individual students and teachers to focus also on information about the development of classrooms, schools, curricular materials, and other kinds of complex systems that need to be understood better in order to make significant and sustainable improvements in mathematics and science education.

The examples described throughout this section suggest that there should be an enormous return from giving greater attention to the development of knowledge projects whose objectives are the development of materials, programs, and teachers. For example, new math projects of the 1960s experienced many difficulties because little was known about the nature of students' ways of thinking about the fundamental principles of mathematics and science. But, today, a great deal has been learned about how students and teachers develop their mathematical and scientific knowledge. This fundamental research on teaching and learning has been one of the main factors leading to the successful development of standards to assess the achievements of mathematics and science instruction. Conversely, in areas where the research base on teaching and learning is least solid and extensive, standards-based efforts to improve curricular have been proportionally weak. For instance, the development of standards for curricula and evaluation has been far more effective in mathematics than in the sciences; it has been far more effective for elementary school and middle school courses than for high school or college courses; it has been far more effective for the education of students than for the education of teachers; and it has been far more effective in physics than in most of the other sciences. Moreover, the impact of standards-based curricula reform has tended to be directly proportional to how much is known about students' relevant ways of thinking and about how to mold and shape students' knowledge through the use of appropriate, small-group interactions, manipulatable materials, and other devices designed to increase representational fluency.

For certain topic areas in mathematics and science, a great deal is known about how students develop their ways of thinking about important constructs. But what does it mean for teachers to have deeper or higher order understandings? Do teachers need to develop understandings beyond those that are appropriate for their students? Surely, most people would agree that, for complex topics such as linear equations, teachers need to know more than their students. But how much more do they need to know? Also, do they need to know what they know differently? For example, beyond knowing what their students should know, teachers probably should know something about how relevant ideas develop: (a) psychologically (in the minds of students), (b) historically (among earlier generations of mathematicians), and (c) instructionally (in high-quality, curricular materials). They also should know something about the ways in which these ideas are used in real-life, problem solving situations. But what other understandings and abilities are required? Clearly, more research is needed.

## SUMMARY

This chapter describes some of the most important criteria that were used to choose the research designs featured in this book. It is important to consider these criteria not only because they influence strongly the choices that researchers make when they design specific research projects, but also because they influence the extent to which the results of research produces are likely to be viewed as useful by practitioners.

As noted earlier, one reason for giving special attention to the research agenda for the NSF's RTL Program is because it helped to coordinate the discussions in various chapters of this book. Another reason for considering this program is because even though other countries, organizations, and agencies emphasize different problems, perspectives, and approaches, the kinds of issues that influenced the mission of the RTL Program were similar to those that influence the research agendas of nearly every organization or agency that supports research in mathematics and science education. Therefore, discussions of the issues that influenced the RTL research agenda may be useful for interpreting the research agenda of other organizations or agencies active in similar areas.

# Appendix I

## The National Science Foundation's
## Program for Research on Teaching & Learning

(Since superceded by other research programs at NSF)

Research that makes a difference
*. . . in theory and practice.*

## GENERAL PROGRAM GOALS

The National Science Foundation's Program for Research on Teaching and Learning (RTL) is distinctive within the Directorate for Education and Human Resources (EHR) because funded projects focus on delivering knowledge and theory-based prototypes rather than materials, programs, or enhanced human resources. Also, unlike research and development programs in other federal agencies whose goals are to deal with issues that are of general educational, social, and economic significance, and where issues in mathematics and science education are simply treated as special cases, the RTL Program emphasizes issues in which: (a) the quality of mathematics, science, and technology education is a central concern, and (b) distinctive characteristics of mathematics, science, and technology education are highlighted in learning, problem solving, or instruction.

In addition to traditional types of research that emphasize data gathering, data analysis, data interpretation, and hypothesis testing, RTL projects frequently involve activities such as:

- Anticipating problems and needs-for-knowledge before they become impediments to progress.
- Translating future-oriented problems into researchable issues.
- Translating the implications of research and theory development into forms that are useful to practitioners and policy makers.
- Facilitating the development of research communities to focus on neglected priorities or strategic opportunities.

The goal of the preceding activities is to develop a body of knowledge that is theoretically sound, experience tested, and meaningfully instantiated in order to address emerging and anticipated problems in science, mathematics, and technology education. RTL-funded projects are not simply curiosity driven; they aim at strategic opportunities or significant leverage points for improving educational practice; they are proactive rather than reactive in terms of the problems they emphasize; and, projects that are treated as priorities usually involve much more than simply taking the next step in a productive program of research. Research on teaching and learning is research that makes a difference . . . in theory and in practice.

## RELATIONSHIPS TO OTHER EHR PROGRAMS

Because only limited funds are available, the RTL Program must focus its resources on projects that emphasize issues and problems that are anticipated to be critical to the success of current and future EHR initiatives. Therefore, to ensure maximum relevance to such initiatives, negotiations for RTL funding typically involve input from, and joint funding with, programs such as:

- State, urban, and rural systemic initiatives.
- Instructional materials development .
- Course and curriculum development.
- Teacher enhancement.
- Teacher preparation.
- Applications of advanced technologies.
- Networking infrastructure for education.
- Advanced technological education.
- Informal science education.

## A MATRIX OF CURRENT FUNDING PRIORITIES

The matrix that follows identifies areas that are current funding priorities in the RTL Program. The columns are content-specific versions of four general themes: (a) school-to-work transitions in a technology-based society, (b) equity, (c) educational quality, and (d) technology. The rows, as well as their ordering from learners and teachers to learning environments, focus on trends related to the "unit of analysis" that is emphasized in RTL-funded projects. That is, the RTL Program 's traditional strength has been research on the nature of individual student's knowledge, learning, and problem solving; but, recently, the emphasis has expanded to include research on the nature of teacher knowledge, attitudes, and beliefs about mathematics, science, technology, teaching, learning, and problem solving; and, currently, there is growing recognition that attention must go beyond individual students and teachers to include systemic factors involving groups, learning environments, programs, and implementations.

| | Preparation for Success in Postindustrial Societies | Equal Access to Powerful Ideas | Standards & Assessments for Documenting Progress | Influences of Technologies on Teaching & Learning |
|---|---|---|---|---|
| Learners | | | | |
| Teachers | | | | |
| Learning Environments | | | | |

## THEORETICAL PERSPECTIVES AND RESEARCH METHODOLOGIES

RTL-funded research has involved a wide range of theoretical perspectives and research methodologies, borrowing from and building on fields as diverse as cognitive science, sociology, anthropology, economics, and engineering; also, in many areas, mathematical sciences education research has evolved beyond theory borrowing to theory building. For example, the application of cognitive science to mathematics or the sciences is not just a general psychology applied to mathematics and science; rather, it has features that reflect the distinctive characteristics of knowledge, learning, problem solving, and instruction in these domains. Similar trends are apparent in areas evolving out of sociology, anthropology, and other disciplines.

Cognitive psychology has replaced behavioral psychology as the dominant source of theoretical models in mathematical sciences education research. Consequently, students' knowledge (and learning and problem solving) is likened, not to a machine, but to evolving, self-regulating, and adapting organisms. Similar "constructivist" paradigm shifts also have occurred in theories related to the development of teachers, programs, and learning environments.

To accompany the preceding paradigm shifts, the development of appropriate research methodologies is, in itself, a significant product of RTL-funded research. Examples include: teaching experiments in technology-intensive learning environments, computer modeling of complex problem solving behaviors, sophisticated videotape analysis techniques for real-life problem solving situations, and ethnographic observations in which attention is focused on abilities that go far beyond "shopkeeper arithmetic" from the industrial age. Therefore, competitive proposals must take special care to keep abreast of rapid advances in research methodologies and relevant theoretical models, as well as rapid transitions from hypothesis generation to hypothesis testing.

# MORE ABOUT THE CELLS IN THE MATRIX OF FUNDING PRIORITIES

For each column of the RTL Program's Matrix of Funding Priorities, this section identifies examples of the kind of issues that are of concern to RTL for learners, teachers, and learning environments.

## Preparation for Success in a Postindustrial Society

To live and work in a technology-based society, preparation for success includes much more than simply: *geometry* from the time of Euclid, *algebra* from the time of Descartes, *shopkeeper arithmetic* from the industrial age, elementary *logical reasoning* from the time of Aristotle, and a few science topics from the time of Newton. The world outside of schools is changing rapidly. The essential characteristic of an information age is that the constructs (conceptual systems, models, structural metaphors) that humans develop to make sense of their experiences also mold and shape the world in which these experiences occur. For example, many of the most important mathematical or scientific "objects" that impact everyday lives are systems—complex, dynamic, interacting systems—which range in size from large-scale communication and economic systems, to small-scale systems for scheduling, organizing, and accounting in everyday activities; and, many of the most important characteristics of these systems require students to go beyond surface-level data that can be counted or measured directly, and to focus on powerful patterns and regularities beneath the surface of things. Consequently, a primary goal of mathematics and science education is to help students develop powerful constructs (or conceptual technologies) that can provide them with the power to understand, use, create, manipulate, and control these systems for a variety of purposes, and to generate descriptions, explanations, and predictions for purposes that range from simple understanding (to avoid difficulties) to optimization or stabilization.

*Issues Related to Learners.* What kinds of problems and problem solving situations are priorities to address in a world increasingly dominated by complex, dynamic, interacting systems? What knowledge, abilities, and skills provide the most useful foundations for life-long learning, problem solving, and adaptability, especially when new types of teams, tools, and resources are used to address new kinds of problems within systems that did not exist in the past?

*Issues Related to Teachers.* What knowledge and abilities must teachers develop when it is no longer possible to be an "expert" in every area of student inquiry and when teachers' roles must shift from delivering facts and demonstrating skills toward being professional knowledge guides, information specialists, and facilitators of inquiry? How can teachers maintain a familiarity with the tools, resources, and problems that are priorities for success in the rapidly changing world outside of schools?

*Issues Related to Programs and Learning Environments.* What kinds of programs and learning environments are needed when lifelong learning must replace one-time instruction and certification? When instruction increasingly occurs in response to the needs, experiences, and purposes of individual learners? When the ability to create, seek out, and use information is as important as remembering and repeating facts and rules? When learning can take place anytime, anywhere, with anyone—rather than in rigidly structured spaces and time slots?

## Equal Access to Powerful Ideas

In a world characterized by increasingly complex, dynamic, and interacting systems (including systems of ideas), people who have not had the opportunity to develop the most powerful elementary but deep constructs in mathematics and the sciences are at a major disadvantage, especially in jobs beyond the entry level. In general, the educational system we have inherited was not designed to prepare students for adaptive functioning in technically complex environments where continuous learning is necessary. For example, its goals seldom emphasize the ability to explain structurally complex systems, the ability to construct convincing arguments, the ability to use sophisticated tools and resources, or the ability to analyze problems in a way so that they can be addressed by teams with diverse specialties. Therefore, by the time most students complete their K–12 mathematics and science education, they are seldom proficient at describing, explaining, creating, or manipulating elementary systems in which the "objects" go beyond simple counts, measures, and shapes to include entities such as ratios, rates, proportions, coordinates, rules, transformations, propositions, continuously changing quantities, accumulating quantities, or patterns or characteristics of sets of data (rather than isolated pieces of data).

*Issues Related to Learners.* Among the conceptual technologies that have the potential to provide the greatest power in the future lives of most students, which are elementary in spite of their depth, and to what extent are they accessible to all students? How is the development of low-level facts and skills related to the development of deeper or higher-order understandings and abilities? How can the development of deeper and higher-order understandings be stimulated, facilitated, and focused? How can students increase the power and generalizability of the constructs they develop?

*Issues Related to Teachers.* How can teachers shift attention beyond superficial "coverage" of a large number of small ideas (facts and skills) to focus on depth and power for a small number of big ideas (models, conceptual technologies, reasoning paradigms, and unifying themes and principles)? What understandings do mathematics and science teachers need about the ways the most important "big ideas" develop—in time (historically), in polished modern reinterpretations (mathematically, scientifically), in available curriculum materials (educationally), in class (pedagogically), and in the consciousness of students (psychologically)?

*Issues Related to Programs and Learning Environments.* What kind of programs and learning environments are needed to provide democratic access to powerful ideas and to capitalize on the experiences, goals, and learning styles of more than a narrow range of students? What kind of learning environments are needed to encourage students to develop, test, extend, or refine their own increasingly powerful constructs? What alternatives exist to the current layer-cake curriculum that acts structurally as a filter and delays access to the big ideas of mathematics so that only few students manage to engage those ideas? How can we build curricula that offer more longitudinal coherence and greater gestation time for major strands of mathematical and scientific  ideas, such as the mathematics of change or the mathematics of uncertainty and their relationship to scientific processes? Such curricula should offer meaningful access to these ideas for all students.

## Standards and Assessments to Document Progress

In a world where new ideas, tools, and resources are being used in new kinds of problem solving situations, past conceptions of mathematical and scientific ability are often far too narrow, low-level, and restricted to provide unbiased guidelines for recognizing and rewarding the abilities and achievements of students, teachers, or programs of instruction. Above all, research on assessment should help clarity the nature of instructional goals. Yet, most existing high-impact standardized tests are poorly aligned with national standards for instruction and assessment and the operational definitions of competence that they presuppose tend to be based on obsolete "industrial age" analogies to the assembly and functioning of simple machines. The negative influence of these assessments on the education system have been widely documented.

Issues about assessment are not restricted to the improvement of testing. Regardless of whether the instruments focus on learners, teachers, programs, or learning environments, educationally responsible assessments should gather information from a representative and balanced variety of sources. The descriptions that are generated should go beyond naive "good/bad" labels to include information about issues such as: Good for what purposes? Good in what ways? Good under what conditions?

Assessment instruments should contribute to both learning and to assessment; they also should have positive instructional value in the sense that they do not take students away from learning, or teachers away from teaching. That is, high-quality assessments should enable students, teachers, and programs to *make progress* while simultaneously *documenting* the nature of the progress that is being made. For example: (a) feedback  should enable individuals to develop in ways that are continuously better, without reducing goals to overly-simplistic definitions of best, and (b) documentation often can be gathered in ways that produce continuous traces of progress, without relying on naive subtracted differences between pretests and posttests (which often embody simplistic and distorted conceptions of actual instructional goals).

*Issues Related to Learners.* In mathematics and the sciences, as well in other areas in which advanced technologies are use extensively, many different kinds of personalities, knowledge, and abilities can lead to success, many different types of success are possible, and most people have irregular profiles of expertise—strengths in some areas, weaknesses in others. Therefore, new forms of assessment are needed that go beyond comparing individuals along one-dimensional good/bad scales to assessments that focus on instruction-relevant strengths and weaknesses.

*Issues Related To Teachers.* One of the primary purposes of assessment is to provide useful information to improve the quality of informed decision making by teachers, students, parents, and others whose goals are to optimize achievement. What information and feedback do teachers need to support wise instructional decision making? What knowledge and abilities should teachers develop in order to recognize and reward a broader range of mathematical and scientific abilities in their students? How can they stimulate and facilitate the development of problem solving personalities that involve productive beliefs, styles, attitudes, and values, as well as specific mathematical or scientific knowledge and abilities?

*Issues Related to Programs and Learning Environments.* In the same way that assessments of students should be integrated seamlessly into learning, problem solving, and instruction, assessments of programs should be integrated seamlessly into implementation, dissemination, and program refinement. It is misleading to label programs "successes" or "failures" as though everything the successful ones did was effective, everything the un-successful ones did was not effective. All programs have profiles of strengths and weaknesses. Most "work" for some types of results but "don't work" for others. Most are effective for some students (or teachers, or situations) but not for others. In general, most work some of the time in some circumstances, but none work all of the time in all circumstances. In fact, characteristics that lead to success in one situation often turn out to be counterproductive in other situations. Therefore, the goals of program assessments should be to facilitate and stimulate continuous development. No fixed and final state can ever be reached as though continuous growth is no longer necessary.

## Influences of Technologies on Teaching and Learning

Some educationally relevant technologies relate directly to teaching and learning whereas others are part of the infrastructure that support the management of instruction and communication among teachers, administrators, parents, policymakers, and others. Each type of technology brings a host of research questions regarding its implementation, use, and impact. For example: How may the effects of new tools and environments differ across different populations or across time? How can we best redefine the curriculum to exploit the power of new technologies to democratize access to powerful ideas and ways of thinking? How are emerging technologies changing nature of mathematics and the sciences as well as their uses in society?

*Issues Related to Learners.* Advances in technology have produced dramatic changes in how students are able to learn, what they should learn, what kind of problem solving situations they should be able to address, and what stages of problem solving tend to be emphasized. However, new technological tools, representations, and learning environments not only change the means and goals of learning, they also change the learners themselves. Generalizations that might have been valid for students-without-tools often simply do not apply to students-with-tools. Therefore, careful research is needed to document technology-related changes in thinking, visualization, communication, and problem solving. Research also is needed about how communication technologies may change the ways learners interact productively with one another, with teachers, and with information and data.

*Issues Related to Teachers.* Powerful conceptual technologies are not simply new ways to address old ideas. New types of knowledge and abilities become important, and new levels and types of understanding become important for old ideas and abilities. Furthermore, just as learners are changed by technology, so too are teachers. Indeed, the profession itself is changing. Research on teacher enhancement and preparation must take into account the new technological tools and contexts for the practice of teaching. Especially important is research that deepens understanding about how teachers can exploit opportunities to promote active learning and assessment, and how technology itself can serve the process of this integration into everyday practice.

*Issues Related to Programs and Learning Environments.* Although new technologies have produced radical changes in the worlds of work and entertainment, they have not yet made comparable impact in education. One reason for this lack of impact is that intended technological innovations have tended to be superimposed on an existing sets of practices that were taken as given. Yet, it is clear that realizing the full potential of new technologies must be systemic. It will require deep changes in curriculum, pedagogy, assessment, teacher preparation and credentialing, and even the relationships among school, work, and home. Consequently, RTL-funded research should anticipate possible new circumstances resulting from rapidly changing technologies and it must recognize that the real impact of research is usually several years away. Therefore, such RTL research will take place in the context of the development or deployment of new technologies; and, a question that all proposed projects must confront is: "How might new technologies change what is important to teach and learn as well as how this knowledge and information is taught and learned? How might emerging technologies undermine the importance of anticipated results?"

## FIVE QUESTIONS FOR PEER ASSESSMENTS OF RTL PROJECT PROPOSALS

1.  How significant is the project from the point of view of practice?
    *   Is the issue a priority in mathematics, science, & technology education?
    *   Is the issue a priority for NSF curriculum reform initiatives?
    *   Will the results address an important neglected issue?
    *   Are the results likely to make a significant difference?
    *   Will the results provide key leverage points for change?
    *   Will the results fill a void, or capitalize on a unique opportunity?
2.  Is the issue a *priority for RTL* to address?

Does the project fit the RTL Program's distinctive niche compared with other programs inside NSF? compared with other programs outside NSF?

3.  Is the project highly significant from the point of view of *theory development*?

- Will the results significantly advance what is known?

- Are the results likely to make a significant difference?

- Will the results provide key leverage points for change, fill a void, or capitalize on a unique opportunity?

4. Is the *methodology* clear, appropriate, and sound?

- Is it clear what the project is going to do?

- What theoretical framework will be used to select, filter, weight, organize, and analyze data?

- What patterns and regularities will be investigated?

- Will the results and conclusions be credible to a skeptic?

5. Is this the right person and place to conduct this particular project?

- What is the *track record* or the PI, staff, and organization?

- past influences on nationally significant efforts.

- contribution of "big ideas" to other projects.

- contribution of (former or current) staff to other projects or efforts.

# 4 The Impact of Standards-based Reform on Methods of Research in Schools

**Thomas A. Romberg**

*Sears Roebuck, Bascom Professor of Education*
*Director of NCISLMS, University of Wisconsin–Madison*

**Angelo Collins**
*Vanderbilt University*

In 1990, President George Bush and the nation's governors adopted a set of ambitious education goals for the schools of America to be reached by the year 2000. Then, in 1991, the administration adopted a strategy, labeled *America 2000*, designed to reach those goals (U.S. Department of Education, 1991a). Two of the national goals refer explicitly to mathematics and science: "All students will leave grades 4, 8, and 12 having demonstrated competency in challenging subject matter including...mathematics, science..."; and "U.S. students will be first in the world in mathematics and science achievement." In addition, three other goals refer implicitly to the need for reform in school mathematics and science: the increase in the high school graduation rate, adult literacy (including quantitative and scientific literacy), and professional development of the nation's teaching force (pp. 9–15).

As a nation, if we are to reach these goals, we need to set high expectations of achievement in school mathematics and science for all students, and we need to provide every student the means and the opportunity to achieve those expectations. The focus of the strategy to implement the changes needed in schooling practices to meet these goals has been labeled *standards-based reform* because national standards for the content, teaching, and assessment of school mathematics and science have been produced. These standards, developed for mathematics by the National Council of Teachers of Mathematics (1989, 1991b, 1995) and for science by the National Research Council (1996), are to be used to judge the adequacy of what content is taught, how the content is taught, and how student performance is judged in both school mathematics and science.[1]

The purposes of this chapter are to:

- Present the shifts in perspectives about schooling embodied in this reform movement.
- Describe the impact of these shifts on the types of questions that need to be answered.
- Define the ways in which scholarly evidence needs to be developed.

Issues of concern include:

- The need for reform in the content, teaching, and learning of school mathematics and science.
- The explicit and implicit questions about the impact of the reforms on the teaching and learning of mathematics and science in American schools.
- The degree to which the questions being raised about changes in schooling practices demand particular scholarly methods of collecting reliable and consistent evidence so that school mathematics and science in the United States have the potential to be "world class."

Although all of the knowledge about the teaching and learning of mathematics and science is tentative, scholarly evidence gathered in classrooms represents the best data available about the reform efforts and must be derived from diverse sources. Thus, the reform movement demands research in mathematics and science education and demands that reliable evidence must come from field studies of students and teachers interacting in classrooms about

---

[1] Also noteworthy are the efforts of Project 2061 of the American Association for the Advancement of Science (Rutherford & Ahlgren, 1990).

important problems leading to the goal of the reform movement—students' understanding of mathematics and science.

# THE NEED FOR REFORM

## The Legacy of Machine-Age Thinking

During the past century, public schools in this country have evolved toward a coherent system designed to transmit a large quantity of information to students through an organized schedule of courses. This system grew out of the machine-age thinking of the industrial revolution. The intellectual content of this age rested on reductionism, analysis, and cause-and-effect explanations (Ackoff, 1972). The machine age was preoccupied with taking things apart. The argument was that if something needed to be explained or a problem solved, it was broken into its components by analysis, and the components studied to determine cause-and-effect relationships. In this sense, the world was regarded as a machine operating in accordance with unchanging laws. It is this machine-age world view that is being challenged by the reform movement in school mathematics and science in the United States.

For schools, machine-age thinking led to information being segmented into subjects, courses, topics, and lessons, eventually getting down to its smallest parts—behavioral objectives. Then, the objectives were related through hierarchies and mechanized through textbooks, worksheets, and tests. Thus, over the last century, the consequences of machine-age thinking have influenced curricula, teachers, instruction, technology, assessment, and classroom environments to such an extent that their features are considered by many as sacrosanct traditions (e.g., the "layer-cake" curriculum; the teacher as teller; five-step instruction in 45-minute class periods; standardized tests; isolated, "egg-crate" classrooms with chalkboards and rows of desks). Traditions in the social sciences, as Popper (1965) once noted, are like laws in the natural sciences: They are to be adhered to until challenged and replaced. Therefore, if we want educational institutions to change, we also must challenge directly the mechanistic traditions underlying current educational institutions, build examples where the conditions for learning with understanding exist, and demonstrate their impact on students' learning. Only then will the implied changes in educational practices occur.

## Why Mathematics and Science Education "Failed"

Several reasons have been given for the claim that the current system is failing to provide all students the opportunity to become mathematically and scientifically literate. Three related reasons are equity, employment, and democratic citizenship. For mathematics, the basis of this claim rests on the fact that nearly half of American students never study any mathematics beyond arithmetic, and the majority of those who do are White males (Mathematical Sciences Education Board [MSEB], 1989). Similarly, for science, at present only 16% of all employed scientists and engineers are women, fewer than 3% are Black, and fewer than 3% are Hispanic (Matyas & Malcom, 1991).

Mathematics and science courses, more than most other curricular offerings in schools, have become a filter in our society that restricts access to knowledge. Too often, women and minority students are encouraged to stop taking mathematics and science or denied any opportunity to study more mathematics and science. This denial has major consequences for employment and citizenship. The MSEB (1989) argued that:

> Of 4 million that begin [school], only 500,000 are still studying mathematics 12 years later. Most students receive little of lasting value from the final mathematics course they study—typically high school geometry or algebra II. Many of those who drop out harbor life-long feelings of guilt or distaste for school mathematics. Some of those who become disenchanted with mathematics become teachers; others help decide educational and research policy for the nation. Very few adults in the United States have had the benefit of successful completion of a mathematics curriculum. (p. 5)

The arguments in A *Nation at Risk* (National Commission on Excellence in Education, 1983) and *Educating Americans for the Twenty-First Century* (National Science Board Commission on Precollege Education in Mathematics, Science, and Technology, 1983) focus on the fact that schools are failing to educate students to be productive employees in today's workplace. Schools, as presently constituted, were the products of an industrial era that has ended. School mathematics and science curricula still reflect the industrial needs of the 1920s, not the workplace or the societal needs of the 1990s. The MSEB (1989, 1990) reinforced the National Council of Teachers of Mathematics, National Research Council, and American

Association for the Advancement of Science positions that to be economically competitive and to practice responsible citizenship in the 21$^{st}$ century, all students will need to know more and a somewhat different mathematics and science than is covered currently in the programs of most American schools.

Furthermore, a recently completed curricula analysis for the Third International Mathematics and Science Study found:

> U.S. mathematics and science curricula reflect juxtaposed goals competing for the same limited resources of time and attention. Our official mathematics and science curriculum statements have no central focus or strategic ideas or approaches to what should be learned in mathematics and the sciences. (U.S. National Research Center for the Third International Mathematics and Science Study, 1996, p. 2)

Such lack of focus in both school mathematics and science has influenced the textbooks, instruction, and, consequently, the achievement of students.

## New Directions

It should not be surprising that there has been a clamor for change. However, documenting the inadequacy of current programs does not identify potentially powerful new practices. One way of approaching the changes needed is to alter our metaphor of schooling. The MSEB (1990) illustrated the kind of modification that is needed: "To the Romans, a curriculum was a rutted course that guided the path of two-wheeled chariots" (p. 4). This metaphor about a path to be followed is an appropriate description of the curricula for most school subjects. The MSEB went on to describe current mathematics curricula in terms of this metaphor:

> Today's mathematics curriculum—a course of study—follows a deeply rutted path directed more by events of the past than the changing needs of the present. Vast number of learning objectives, each associated with pedagogical strategies, serve as mile posts along the trail mapped by texts from kindergarten to twelfth grade. (p. 4)

Furthermore, again quoting MSEB about this path, "Problems are solved not by observing and responding to the natural landscape through which the mathematics curriculum passes, but by mastering time tested routines, conveniently placed along the path" (p. 4). It is this mechanistic metaphor about what should be taught that is being challenged. Scheffler's (1975) denunciation of this metaphor points the direction for rethinking the structure of a curriculum:

> It is no wonder that this [mechanical] conception isolates mathematics from other subjects, since what is here described is not so much a form of thinking as a substitute for thinking. The process of calculation or computation only involves the deployment of a set routine with no room for ingenuity or flair, no place for guess work or surprise, no chance for discovery, no need for the human being, in fact. (p. 184)

One interpretation of the reform vision of school mathematics presented by the National Council of Teachers of Mathematics in its *Curriculum and Evaluation Standards for School Mathematics* (1989) is that the image of the curriculum, as a tedious, uninteresting path to follow with lots of hurdles to clear, must be changed toward one emphasizing engagement and exploration of problem situations where thinking is valued.

For science education, Hurd (1995) addressed issues similar to those in mathematics education. He grounded the need for revising goals and forms for science education by noting the shifting view of the world:

> We are living in a critical period in our history, characterized by radical changes in how we live, learn and work. We are shifting from an industrial age to a knowledge-intensive society. The traditional purposes for science education and the supporting curriculums are viewed as inadequate … massive changes have taken place in America altering the character of society including our demography, lifestyles, values, family structures, social institutions, economy, patterns of American life, and the nature and ethos of science. (p. 6)

Hurd explained that current science curricula are rooted in a 200-year-old tradition that places science in a vocational context. In this context, students are to "think like scientists" and "do science" (p. 3). Hurd went on to say that:

> If students are to "be like scientists" they must first learn the language of scientists?… This means learning technical terms, symbols and mathematics expressions characteristic of each discipline studied. As the sciences have progressed over the years, so has the volume of technical

terms students must learn?... By performing experiments, it was expected that students would gain experience in "doing" science and an appreciation of the objectivity of science?... The requirement that all students get the same answer from an experiment supposedly confirmed the objectivity of a finding. The student's position in these experiments was that of a detached onlooker or spectator. (pp. 3–4)

Hurd described a broad shift in science education curricula:

> As science teaching now stands, all goals, objectives and concepts are *internal* to specific disciplines. The quest in the reform movement is for goals and curriculums in a social context. Briefly, this is a movement from the *esoteric* to the *exoteric* in science teaching. (p. 4, emphasis in the original)

Hurd described some of the characteristics of this shift in science education such as an increased focus on interdisciplinary science research fields that deal with complex systems, the inclusion of science and technology as an integrated system, an increased emphasis on looking toward the future and learning how to be lifelong learners, and increased emphasis on both quantitative and qualitative thinking skills. He predicted that "The trend is toward unity of the sciences and unification of the sciences with society" (p. 8).

A way to start creating new metaphors and practices for mathematics and science education is to consider mathematics and science knowledge, as any field of knowledge, organized into several related domains (or "conceptual fields;" Vergnaud, 1982). This domain view differs from the mechanical view in at least two important ways. First, the emphasis is not with the parts of which things are made but with the whole of which they are part (how concepts and skills in a domain are related) and, in turn, how those parts are related to other parts, other domains, and ideas in other disciplines. Second, this conception does not rest on a deterministic base of fundamental parts from which everything else is created. Instead, it rests on the signs, symbols, terms, and rules for use—the language that humans invent to communicate with each other. From this perspective, Greeno (1991) proposed a different metaphor:

> Students develop understanding when a domain is thought of as an environment, with resources at various places in the domain. In this metaphor, knowing is knowing your way around in the environment and knowing how to use its resources. This includes knowing what resources are available in the environment as well as being able to find and use those resources for understanding and reasoning. Knowing includes interactions with the environment in its own terms—exploring the territory, appreciating its scenery, and understanding how its various components interact. Knowing the domain also includes knowing what resources are in the environment that can be used to support your individual and social activities and the ability to recognize, find, and use those resources productively. Learning the domain, in this view, is analogous to learning to live in an environment: learning your way around, learning what resources are available, and learning how to use those resources in conducting your activities productively and enjoyably. (p. 175)

To engineer curricula based on this domain knowledge view, what is needed is a collection of problem situations that engage students so that they explore each domain in a structured manner. To accomplish this, two distinct dimensions need to be considered. The first is that the domain needs to be well mapped. This is not an easy task, as Webb and Romberg (1992) argued:

> knowledge of a domain is viewed as forming a network of multiple possible paths and not partitioned into discrete segments?... Over time, the maturation of a student's functioning within a conceptual field should be observed by noting the formation of new linkages, the variation in the situations the person is able to work with, the degree of abstraction that is applied, and the level of reasoning applied. (p. 47)

This dimension demands that the key features and resources of the domain that are important for students to find, discover, use, or even invent for themselves are identified.

The second dimension is that activities need to be identified that encourage students to explore the domain, and then the activities need to be organized in a structured manner that allows for such exploration. Doing both is not easy. For example, although there is no doubt that many interesting activities exist or can be created, "Do they lead anywhere?" is a serious question. Keitel (1987) argued that an activity approach in mathematics may lead to "no mathematics at all," and Romberg (1992b) stated that:

> Too often a problem is judged to be relevant through the eyes of adults, not children. Also, this perception is undoubtedly a Western, middle-class, static vision. Concrete situations, by themselves, do not guarantee that students will see relevance to their worlds, they may not be relevant for all students nor prepare them to deal with a changing, dynamic world. (p. 778)

In summary, there is a need to change the curriculum metaphor from following a path, to exploring an environment. As the new metaphor acquires detail and exemplars, it needs to describe how students engage in exploration as well as current understandings of the nature of science and mathematics as it relates to society. The new metaphor needs to be powerful in promoting the design of activities that require students to explore valued knowledge, and it should include multiple ways for students to demonstrate understanding.

## Implications of These Shifts for Schooling

The standards-based reform efforts imply that all students need to learn more, and often different, mathematics and science and that instruction must be revised significantly. The key notions embedded in this statement are the following:

- Teaching mathematics and science to "all students" emphasizes the fact that all need to be mathematically and scientifically literate if they are to be productive citizens in the 21$^{st}$ century. In particular, this emphasis on all students includes the traditionally underrepresented groups in mathematics and science—women, persons of color, and persons with disabilities.

- "Learn more" has two implications. First, in all mathematics and science courses, students need to learn more than how to manipulate symbols or to memorize terms. This implies that emphasis in every course should shift from coverage of a lot of procedures and facts toward a more indepth examination of selected important topics (the motto is "less is more"). Second, all students should expect to study mathematics and science every year that they are in school.

- "Often different mathematics and science" refers to the fact that, for mathematics, the mathematics that all students need to learn includes concepts from algebra, geometry, trigonometry, statistics, probability, discrete mathematics, and even calculus; for science, all students need to develop a rich and useful understanding of the major ideas through a process of inquiry and, in so doing, come to understand and master the process of inquiry.

- "To learn" means more than to be shown or to memorize and repeat. Learning involves asking, investigating, formulating, representing, reasoning, and using strategies to solve problems, and then reflecting on the mathematics and science being used.

- "Revised" instruction implies that classrooms need to become discourse communities in which conjectures are made, arguments presented, strategies discussed, and conversations the norm.

It is in classrooms that exhibit these features that research on the effects of reform needs to be conducted.

## RESEARCH QUESTIONS

Propelled by the need to educate all of America's students to levels of achievement in mathematics and science not thought possible over a decade ago, the challenge of the reform movement is to create classrooms where all students have the opportunity to understand mathematical and scientific ideas. This assertion is based on the belief that there is a direct and powerful relationship between student understanding and student achievement. In fact, the way to achieve the high expectations that we have for all students rests on their understanding of important mathematical and scientific ideas taught in school classrooms by professional teachers. This challenge needs to be addressed directly by researchers so that real change in the teaching and learning of mathematics and science occurs in the next decade. A sustained research program, conducted collaboratively with school personnel in school classrooms, needs to be carried out.

There is a pressing need to investigate how classrooms that promote understanding in mathematics and science can be created. Although much extant work can help to address this need, there are important gaps in our knowledge. To guide specific research studies, we suggest that attention be focused on the following eight general questions:

1. How is learning for understanding in both school mathematics and school science best characterized?

2. What are the important ideas in both school mathematics and school science that we expect students to understand?

3. What are the critical instructional features in classrooms that promote understanding for all students?

4. What is the appropriate role for teachers in such classrooms? (How can they be helped to assume their appropriate role effectively? How can changes in teachers' beliefs and practices be made self-sustaining?)

5. What is the impact on students' achievement of their understanding of the important ideas in mathematics and science? (That is, what information can be collected to demonstrate that students have grown in their understanding of the important ideas in both disciplines and to show their high levels of achievement?)

6. What organizational capacity—in the school and larger community—is required to support and sustain the development of classrooms that promote understanding?

7. How can we ensure the equitable distribution of opportunities to learn mathematics and science with understanding?

8. What strategies are effective in providing both information and support to policymakers, school administrators, and teachers so that they utilize the findings to create and support classrooms that promote understanding in mathematics and science?

## RESEARCH METHODS

As Lesh and Kelly (chap. 9, this volume) and Mestre (chap. 7, this volume) have argued, an investigator must match the methodology to the research questions. The specific research questions based on the eight general questions raised previously demand particular scholarly methods of collecting evidence and drawing inferences from that evidence. Because an object of the reform movement is classrooms that promote understanding, field studies of students and teachers interacting in classrooms about important problems leading to students' understanding of mathematics and science are warranted.

Although such field studies usually will involve experimentation, in that the impact of new content, strategies, instructional procedures, and so forth are being investigated, this does not mean that the classical experimental methods are appropriate (e.g., those summarized for education by D. T. Campbell & Stanley, 1963). Experimentation in reform classrooms occurs in a complex social environment that must be examined in a manner that attempts to capture the complexity of the interaction. Thus, general field methods discussed in detail in other chapters of this book should be considered when plans are made to investigate any specific research question related to the reform agenda. Such methods include teaching experiments (see chaps. 2, 11, and 12, this volume), case studies (see Cline & Mandinach, chap. 8, this volume), action research (see Feldman & Minstrell, chap. 16, this volume), developmental studies (see Battista & Clements, chap. 25, this volume), and ethnographic observational studies (see Moschkovich & Brenner, chap. 17, this volume).

Furthermore, in conducting field studies, multiple sources of evidence usually need to be gathered so that a well-grounded story can be told about the classroom situation being investigated. Studying students' understanding often will include creating construct-eliciting activities (see Hole, Hoover, Kelly, Lesh, & Post, chap. 21, this volume) or clinical interviews (see Clement, chap. 20, this volume). Studying classroom interactions may involve using video equipment for data collection and analyses (see chaps. 23 and 24, this volume).

## SUMMARY

If the education goals for the schools of America (U.S. Department of Education, 1991b) are ever to be met, considerable research needs to be carried out. The reform expectations involve creating classrooms that promote student understanding of mathematics and science. To bring about such reform, numerous investigations derived from a set of questions need to be carried out. What has been argued in this chapter is that to conduct such studies involves following field methods of inquiry utilizing multiple sources of evidence.

# 5    Improving Research and Systemic Reform Toward Equity and Quality

**Jere Confrey**
*University of Texas at Austin*

The reform of mathematics and science education in the United States has become a national priority, but teaching improved content in these subjects successfully to the majority of students is in jeopardy. As federal, state, and local agencies commit to improving the performance of our students in mathematics and science, they must come to terms with the extent of the problems first. The situation resembles this one. Imagine cranking the handle of a well and finding a very leaky bucket. Along comes an official who asks, "Who is responsible for this intolerably leaky bucket?" The subsequent questions are: Will the responsibility for the condition of the bucket be placed with those who left it too long without attention and care? Those who actively poked holes in it? Those who used it and ignored the leak? Or those who lifted the bucket up and let the state of disorder and neglect become evident to the public? A short-sighted Congress demanding immediate accountability is unlikely to be particularly circumspect, and any agency or political group advocating educational reform aggressively is in the precarious position of being left "holding the bucket," as it were. Added to this is a skeptical scientific community whose funding cuts in research leave some inclined to jettison the unruly and expensive efforts entailed in reforming science and mathematics education. Sadly, too, public debate and controversy are increasing as reformers make it clear that their goal is to educate all children better, not solely the narrower, albeit important, objective of preparing an elite few to become mathematicians or scientists.

In this chapter, I make the fundamental claim that in this unstable but vigorous climate of reform, the reorganization of science and mathematics education needs to be guided by a wisely chosen, strategic, and secure research base. Whereas, to this point, research has contributed toward a vision of what reform should look like in the classroom, in terms of curricula, pedagogy, and assessment, what is needed urgently now is a complementary body of research that can support explanations and predictions about the *process* of reform. This call for research leaves investigators with an important choice to make in the relatively young and overtaxed field of research in science, mathematics, and technology education; namely: Should we continue to engage in the types of studies that have created the climate and demand for reform, or should we turn to implementation issues and take on the challenges that the trajectory of reform is creating? Or is there another choice?

I claim that there is another choice and that it lies in the acknowledgment that research never anticipated all of the leaks in the bucket, nor did it bring strongly enough into relief the fact that the bucket is only a small part of a large system. It is undeniable that researchers identified critical issues. We identified the importance of the active involvement of students in constructing their knowledge (Confrey, 1994b; R. Glaser & Silver, 1994; Steffe, 1995; Tobin, 1993), documented the negative impact of unaligned assessment systems (with problem solving or conceptual thinking; Lesh & Lamon, 1992), harnessed the power of new forms of semiotics using new technologies, and described the character and intensity of successful professional development (Schifter, 1996a, 1996b; Schifter & Fosnot, 1993). Despite the importance of these results, changing any one of them alone was proving insufficient to fix the problems of mathematics and science. Carrying the analogy one step further, the preferred solution may lie not only in replacing or repairing the bucket, but also in selecting different water sources, redesigning the crank, moving the well, or building a reservoir and pumping station.

The fact is that the results of research must be implemented in the educational system. If the system is not prepared to change, then identifying the problems will not lead in any direct fashion to solutions. For instance, consider these examples: Learning to listen equitably to all students will not eliminate policies that systematically lead to the disappearance of some underrepresented groups in the upper division, thus denying them equal opportunity; designing new assessment systems will not tell schools how to respond to parental outcry about new forms of report cards; and introducing new semiotics will not prepare textbook publishers to produce electronic or multimedia materials automatically. All of these changes require one to look more broadly, beyond the restricted focus of a research study. All of them require us to move beyond the level of the classroom, a move that occurs only rarely in educational research. Briefly, the problems in mathematics, science, and technology education are systemic and, thus, require a systemwide intervention strategy.

## THREE PREMISES

### Premise 1: A Need for Systemic Reform

Therefore, I begin with the premise that some type of *systemic reform*[1] is needed. Let us define this term at the outset. Systemic reform is a phrase that melds the concepts of systems and change and, accordingly, refers to processes of continuous examination, feedback, and improvement in organizational systems that are working toward providing high-quality science, mathematics, and technology education to all children. Such systems include an array of interested parties (teachers, students, parents, administrators, professors, business people, taxpayers, volunteers, service providers, etc.) at multiple organizational levels who converge to work toward the goal of high academic performance by all students in science and mathematics. Reform efforts must acknowledge that instructional systems generate feedback, impetus, resistance, and controversy—issues of specific interest in systemic research, but ignored in much existing research. The complexity and natural diversity of such systems must be addressed realistically if decision making is to support positive and enduring change.

---

[1] I have comments in this chapter that are reflections of my experiences with the systemic reform programs of the National Science Foundation's Directorate of Education and Human Resources. Over the last few years, I have served on numerous panels, technical assistance teams, and discussion groups in these programmatic efforts. All comments in this chapter are my own responsibility, but many benefited from numerous discussions with members of these communities.

When undertaking research in systemic reform, we must keep in mind that the number of people involved in education is second in number to the health professions, and that researchers are a tiny but critical fraction of the educational field. In education, we are working with what Heinz von Foerester (1982) called a "principally undecidable system," too complex in its feedback cycles to be modeled causally, but nonetheless improvable by an iterative design process. This suggests that instead of viewing research as establishing universal principles for learning or teaching, it could be conceived of more productively as meeting design challenges. If this were the case, then the bulk of educational research must change to be more like engineering research, with targeted goals, explicit deliverables, prototyping, iterative design, and direct and widespread field testing in existing programs of reform.

Because systemic reform is being carried out widely already, we are dangerously behind on guiding, assessing, and modeling this process carefully and systematically. Even if we import a semiengineering approach, we also must attend directly to the fact that most of our colleagues in science and mathematics are trained to evaluate research according to scientific and mathematical standards, not the standards of social science. Thus, when the Mathematical Sciences Education Board of the National Academy of Sciences worked to produce a document linking research to reform, its members (I was one of them) struggled mightily over the question of what counts as evidence. This is not to deny that we need to insist on clear standards of evidence in social science and to recognize the need to include both qualitative and quantitative measures, but we also need to realize that one primary goal of social science research is to guide informed decision making. Unlike the claims of many in science, evidence does not provide us universal solutions, but it does permit us to find better ways to envision our work, lead the development of improved products, describe the conditions under which effective solutions have thrived and so on. Social science is unapologetically value-laden (see Confrey & Lachance, chap. 10, this volume); consequently, research results should be debated and interpreted. This is not a failure of the system but a strength. We can document, make careful argument, link theory with practice, evaluate, and, importantly to note, guide the careful design of programs and products.

Research is critical to achieving an informed vision of how to proceed. To do this, researchers must acknowledge more widely the role of research in our current understanding of the directions for reform and strengthen intentionally its connections to the overall system in which education is practiced. With regard to the role of research, I point out briefly that much of the basis of the standards for mathematics (National Council of Teachers of Mathematics, 1989), and for science (National Research Council, 1996) came out of the research base on children's learning. It was early research on the inadequacy of standardized tests and, subsequently, on children's conceptions that fostered the constructivist approach, group learning, and the role of reflection and communication. That this is poorly acknowledged by the authors has been useful in making the standards populist documents, politically strategic but unfortunate and inaccurate in relation to research. Although many of us in research recognize that it could and should be more influential in its impact on practice, I submit that its fundamental contributions to the teaching, learning, curricular, and pedagogical parts of the new approaches to science and mathematics education need to be acknowledged more extensively too.

To increase its influence, research can respond to the issues that are evolving from systemic reform and continuing to generate new and inventive ideas. Education is inherently a practice, and, as such, research must be linked closely to this practice, but that term should be defined broadly. For instance, research on the application of new technologies to education may not find its link in typical school practices but may relate first to the practices of scientists and mathematicians, financiers and architects, computer scientists and engineers working in the field, solving complex problems (Hall & R. Stevens, 1995, 1996; M. Resnick & Ocko, 1991; Wilensky, 1995). However, informed by the actual activities and tools of these professionals, researchers must create quickly the bridges into classroom activities and tie to children's ways of thinking and acting as well as to school-level accessibility to technological tools.

Thus, I suggest that research directions could be changed to guide and support reform more effectively by identifying fruitful and strategic topics for investigation, the results of which will advise existing systemic reform and direct future efforts, and by finding ways to make the research itself more systemic. When considering topics, we should conduct research on systemic reform too (Chubin, in press; O'Day & M. Smith, 1993; Porter, Archbald, & Tyree, 1991). Most of the remainder of this chapter is devoted to discussing some suggested research targets. However, I also claim that it is essential for research to be viewed as a part of systemic reform, not separate from it. Accordingly, we need, as a community, to define what it would mean to make research itself function more systemically. By conceptualizing research more systemically and by linking it more closely to systemic projects, the research is likely to lead to increasingly diverse, challenging, and rigorous theories, methods, and questions.

## Premise 2: Equity and Quality as Complementary Goals

Before discussing equity and quality, I suggest two basic principles that must underlie even more fully all calls for research and that should guide the selection of priorities. The first concerns the relationship between equity and quality. Most people advocate for both of them as overarching principles, but of crucial importance is clarification of the relationship between them (Confrey, 1995a).

Too many people in mathematics and science education see equity and quality as competing, and not complementary, goals. Too many of the underemployed or underfunded scientists and mathematicians in this country view themselves as victims of social engineering programs designed to force equity on them at the cost of quality. Instead, it would be helpful if they understood that one cause of their state of underemployment, is the failure to educate a broader base of the citizenry who understand the importance of their work and see its pursuit as in their own interests. Likewise, the reform of mathematics and science education is facing the immediate challenge of the pursuit of equity and quality being viewed by some very influential people as divergent paths. To obtain equity, they fear the loss of a quality education for their children and, therefore, are understandably unwilling to pay the price. To others, the system has underserved them repeatedly, and they believe that neither equity nor quality are likely to be provided them or their children. Without addressing these beliefs, the satisfactory reform of mathematics and science education will remain in serious jeopardy.

In biological terms, it is as if we believed that evolutionary success and biodiversity were incompatible and that we adhered to a naive belief that survival and dominance of the fittest were the ultimate criteria for achievement. To counter such views, we must educate the public to comprehend that the number of survivors is only one measure of evolutionary success and that being adaptive to a changing environment is a far superior, evolutionary trait. Symbiosis, commensalism, and mutualism are all forms of cross-species cooperation on which survival depends, and they are obligatory for all parties, not only for survival but also for enhancing the quality of that survival. To obtain a competitive advantage, one must know what one is competing against, and, in the current educational conflicts, one wonders if the correct threat is being identified and answered. For instance, in our culture when dropping tracking leads to community crisis and dispute, although the lack of decent technologies in virtually any school is seldom acknowledged, one must ask if, perhaps, the wrong source of competition has been identified.

Reform efforts must be dedicated to demonstrating that both equity and quality are the rights of all of the citizens in our country and that they can be achieved only in tandem. For reform to be successful, all of its participants must seek aggressively to uncover, clarify, and challenge the view that to achieve or protect quality, the price must be equity. Reform must differentiate between *expertise* in mathematics and science and *elitism*, and make expertise an accessible goal for all citizens. Primarily through their efforts in research and systemic reform, researchers and practitioners must lead the country in a courageous stance on these issues, largely by insisting that funding decisions and the continued support of systemic reform value equity, demand quality, and, therefore, are based on merit and not entitlement.

Specific research goals should include investing in inquiries that will clarify the relationship between equity and quality, both philosophically and empirically, and developing more sensitive measures of outcome and participation to ensure that equity considerations are not reduced to the mere counting of participants' ethnicity, gender, age, or class (Darling-Hammond, 1992; Tate, 1995a, 1995b).

## Premise 3: A Situation of Urgency and Strategy

In addition to my commitments to systemic reform, equity, and quality, I add a third premise: that we are working in a situation of urgency. This urgency is created by the basic rate of change being experienced in the world today. We are racing toward a global community where, for example, a five-person, senior, editorial staff for a new journal, the *International Journal of Computers for Mathematics Learning*, sits on three continents and communicates daily about acceptances and schedules; a precarious environment struggles to sustain the demands heaped on it; and an intertwined international economy operates in which the United States must participate both competitively and collaboratively. Add to this the increasing economic disparity in this country between its most and least wealthy, and one sees an educational system under significant pressure to maintain its democratic ideals.

As a result, the investment in research must be strategic. To be strategic, research should be viewed as an interactive design process, during which conditions and constraints are identified, aggressive field testing is done, and close attention is paid to market conditions. The outcomes of research should be identified explicitly, and the pathways to widespread dissemination should be built into the system. Means of identifying mutual problems and defining them as strategically accomplishable tasks need to be institutionalized.

## SPECIFIC TARGETS FOR RESEARCH ON SYSTEMIC REFORM

After reviewing a number of systemic programs, one becomes aware of certain issues that haunt the reform process repeatedly. I identify in the following list specific targets for new research and development. In order to decide how to address these targets, it can be helpful to consider them in light of what the National Science Foundation's (NSF) Division on Education and Systemic Reform calls the "drivers" of systemic reform (NSF, 1996). The term *driver* is used to suggest that how this component is carried out determines whether the overall program has impetus; like a mechanical driver, it is the interlinking of the "gears" that gives the systemic program its force. The six drivers are:

- Standards-based content, curricula, pedagogy, assessment, and professional development.
- Policies to support and enforce standards-based instruction.
- A convergence of resources to support the first driver.
- Broad-based partnerships that include public awareness, community involvement, and private enterprises.
- High-quality and multiple-outcome measures.
- Data analysis to examine the equity of the outcomes.

If we wish to achieve our equity goals, we must report the disaggregated outcomes of achievement gains obtained by both traditional and novel assessments, beginning in kindergarten. One logical way to eliminate a gap in performance between such groups as Whites, Asians, and students of high socioeconomic status in relation to African Americans, Hispanics, and students of low socioeconomic status is by halting our contributions to that gap in the early grades.

The drivers can assist us in proposing research approaches to the targets and the new territories identified in the next sections. As one proposes a research approach to a problem, one should consider how each of the six drivers relates to it and broaden one's approach to view them as covarying factors.

## Target 1: Vignettes on Learning Core Ideas

The heart of schooling lies in the interactions among teaching, learning, curricula, pedagogy, and assessment, and the bulk of the research needed lies in attaining improvements in everyday classroom activity (Ball, 1993a; Piliero, 1994). Systemic reform has made the linking of these components of education a possible target of reform such that if interventions fail to improve their interactions, we will have accomplished little of direct benefit to children. Research has made the most progress in the area of learning, where numerous typical conceptions and conceptual challenges have been identified (Confrey, 1990). In some areas, much investigation has been done—physics, certain biological processes, early number, ratio and proportion, basic probability, geometry, and functions—whereas in others virtually none has been done—trigonometry, algebraic structures, engineering education, chemistry, and agriscience.

By now, we should have examples of students working on interesting tasks, at grade level, so that teachers can access them systematically, watch videotaped interactions with children of diverse backgrounds, and reconsider the content in light of the result. Subsequently, teachers will be able to instruct with better depth of content and more sensitivity to their students. These examples should deal with core ideas, and they should be curricularly specific while avoiding being curricularly diosyncratic dependent. A strategic target would be the creation of a centralized repository of examples of students' approaches edited carefully, replete with students' work, and make it accessible to practicing teacher-educators and schools. The examples should illustrate not only students' typical approaches, but also the fertile possibilities that they raise, the challenges that children are deemed capable of meeting, and sociocultural views of what mathematics and science are, acknowledging diverse processes and perspectives. This repository should be expanded by adding additional samples and soliciting research on topics that have been neglected. Research on the impact on professional development of making such resources systematic and available, teachers' knowledge of content, and effective and inclusive pedagogy should follow. The use of new technologies, multimedia and the Internet, for example, should be exploited in this process.

We still need to focus on issues of learning, but place that focus in an interactional framework among learners and teachers. To do this, we must conduct more transformative teaching experiments (see Confrey and Lachance, chap. 10, this volume). These should be longitudinal experiments where we subject our approaches to the everyday constraints of classroom teaching and are explicit and bold about how instruction can be reformed dramatically so that students' learning will improve. Research on efficacy and on motivating achievement demonstrates how essential it is to believe that children can learn (Anderman & Maehr, 1994). After recognizing the importance of this critical element of the equity agenda, teachers also need to master how to make good use of the learning opportunities created by children when they are engaged in interesting tasks. Classroom observations show that teachers frequently miss or obliterate these opportunities repeatedly because they concentrate on narrow conceptualizations of the tasks and their outcomes, seeking premature closure with the goals that they initially set. Consequently, children's "wonderful ideas" (Duckworth, 1987) get overridden or ignored. This is the result of such problems as insufficient or, too often in the case of secondary and postsecondary teachers, inflexible knowledge of the subject matter, failure to engage students in motivating tasks, lack of belief in students' capacity, an overburdened curriculum, and/or an accountability in assessment systems that reward superficial behaviors.

To meet this goal, we need to create a number of longitudinal test-beds or field-sites for reform. The engagement with the staffs at the sites should be as a partnership where the joint modification and revisioning of approaches is studied and documented simultaneously with the creation of the extended vignettes.

## Target 2: Reforming the "Gatekeeper" Courses

Research on learning, teaching, and pedagogy should concentrate on whether the investments made in reforming the "gatekeeper" courses such as algebra and calculus (entry-level courses that students must pass in order to be able to progress onward) are achieving their desired outcomes in terms of equity and quality. Documentation of the extent of the reform needs to accompany careful descriptions of the changes in what happens in classes and to assess their impact. Increasingly, we need to be certain that the algebra we substitute is an intellectually powerful one, not merely the manipulation of symbols, but the application of quantitative reasoning and modeling to interesting and important phenomena. Of fundamental concern is to ensure that all schools and students have access to the most recent advances from research on learning about functions and relations, efficient algebraic manipulations, the revitalized role of geometry, and the use of appropriate technologies.

## Target 3: Reform at Secondary and Postsecondary Levels

Reform in algebra at the middle or early high school levels will necessitate a much stronger intervention into reform at the upper levels. There is some evidence that this will not follow automatically from reform in the elementary and middle grades. That reform in high school is stalling is due largely to the tendency of high school teachers and parents to look to the universities and colleges for guidance. How can we advocate for dramatic restructuring at the kindergarten through Grade 8 levels without assuring ourselves that high school and university expectations and experiences will be realigned suitably? Across the country, only the Montana State Systemic program (SIMMS) has begun by reforming secondary mathematics courses; then has attempted to work back down the system to align mathematics instruction from kindergarten through Grade 8. Another approach to secondary reform that shows potential promise is the idea of vertical teaming, both among elementary, middle, and secondary schools and between high schools and community colleges, colleges, and/or universities (UCAN Rural Systemic Initiative).

Effectiveness of vertical teaming between high school and university faculties can be restricted because of students' mobility. However, in many regions, such mobility is limited, and large numbers of students advance to local community colleges, colleges, or state universities. This is particularly the case as the cost of higher education increases. Exploring these kinds of local collaborations can suggest ways to escalate reform in the upper grades.

## Target 4: New Curricula and Implementation Strategies

A constructivist approach assumes that children are being given interesting and challenging curricular tasks to work with. We need to know to what extent this is happening and to foster its growth (Ferrini-Mundy & M. A. Clements, 1994; Raizen & Britton, 1996–1997; Silver & Cai, 1996). Two research areas can assist here: funding attempts to build on, modify, strengthen, and evaluate the curricular innovations of the last 6 years and studying the strengthen, and evaluate the curricular innovations of the last 6 years and studying the implementation models that work. The NSF's work to develop alternative curricula has led to stronger curricula (although most of them were dated technologically by the time they were published because of rapid changes).

Also, a number of schools are trying implementation strategies such as replacement units, cluster approaches, or schoolwide reform. Replacement units, where a teacher commits to a 2 to 6 week experiment using a particular part of a novel curriculum, are an interesting strategy because they focus multiple teachers' attention on the same event; they are a manageable amount of change for most teachers, even reluctant ones; and they can lead stepwise toward deep and lasting reform.

We need to identify and study these implementation strategies systemically. How do they interface with state mandates? Do they reach the unwilling or uneasy teachers? Are there hooks to accountability? How are publishers responding? Is the penetration as deep in different settings (rural, suburban, and urban), regions, and grade levels? What are the professional development implications of these approaches? Is curricularly dependent professional development a useful model? What are the trade-offs between depth of implementation and the pressure to increase the scale of activity?

## Target 5: School Restructuring

Having recently completed 8 weeks of work introducing algebra through ratio and proportion, the use of motion detectors, and multirepresentational software to all of the students in seventh grade, I can attest to the fact that the limited length of the class period was the greatest deterrent to reform. Teachers' doubts that students could tackle challenging problems in the class time allotted were reaffirmed as 42-minute periods made high-quality intellectual pursuit a race against the clock. When we began this endeavor, we were told that it would take 3 years to restructure class times in order to arrange for back-to-back mathematics, science, or technology periods. This kind of temporal inflexibility is a major impediment to reform. In restructuring, we also need to investigate such factors as the feasibility of hiring mathematics and science specialists in the upper elementary grades. With changes in the use of Chapter I funds, there are pivotal opportunities to reorganize the deployment of school personnel to assure that all children receive high-quality mathematics and science instruction.

## Target 6: Assessment Pools

We need to implement a strategic plan for assessment so that researchers can contribute to systemic reform from this area too. At least two states (Arizona and California) have experienced serious setbacks as political change in the state derailed statewide assessment programs that were designed to be more aligned with reform. Furthermore, at the assessment meeting of the NSF Urban Systemic Initiatives in 1996, there was a clear call for a pool of assessment items that are semi-open-ended. The practitioners indicated that they needed an easy way to acquire such items and tailor them to their local contexts, while still asserting stamps of validity and approval for them. This is an attainable target for researchers who could provide such approval, and it suggests a collaborative effort of researchers, practitioners, technical assistance teams, private corporations, and professional organizations. In its design, we need to consider how to expand such a system after its initial development. Assessment instruments that include the expertise and active participation of local teachers are sure means of strengthening reform. In addition, local school districts not only must be held strictly accountable for the educational systems over which they exercise control, but also they must accept national guidance.

## Target 7: Effective Models for Teachers' Professional Growth.

To my mind, developing effective approaches to teachers' professional growth is the thorniest and most troublesome challenge in reforming education because classroom teachers are the key to good instruction. There is evidence that we continue in a downward spiral here, with teachers less well prepared to teach in a world in which more and more mathematical, technical, and scientific knowledge is demanded (U.S. Department of Education, 1996). Two-hour or one-day workshops on trendy topics still dominate professional programs, and when given opportunities to engage in intellectually challenging professional development, too many teachers shy away. Furthermore, much of what is provided in teachers' preparation programs or inservice training is weak, poorly informed by research or content expertise, and only minimally connected to classroom practices. Even when teachers are given strong in-service activities, frequently they are under no obligation to implement the methods in their classes, and school pressures make it difficult for even the staunchest reformers to persist.

Moreover, site-based management teams who often are charged with identifying and planning professional development directions typically fail to be well enough informed on the opportunities and possibilities in science and mathematics education. We desperately need research to identify professional development models that work well. Nationally, we have moved from approach to approach in an attempt to identify the ones that are successful: teacher-leaders, teachers' collaboratives, action research, site-based management teams, and community- or school-based interventions (National Institute for Science Education, 1996). Systemic reform has added cluster approaches, networking, vertical alignment, and regional centers to the mix. To date, there is no clear evidence of which of these approaches are the most effective.

Research on teachers' education has seldom taken a systemic approach. However, it has demonstrated convincingly that teachers find case studies of other teachers undergoing professional changes leading toward reform influential sources for their own learning. Many are motivated deeply by discovering the consistency and persuasiveness of students' methods of learning. When this leads them to need to reconceptualize their own understandings, many admit to feelings of uneasiness, defensiveness, and reluctance to acknowledge and address their inadequate knowledge of the subject matter. This leaves professional development in systemic reform in a quandary. In a system in which participation in specific kinds of inservice training usually is not mandated and in which its professionals are reluctant or scared to address their inadequacies, how does one move a reform agenda forward?

Some answers to this quandary suggest that enabling teachers to change can be accomplished most readily in ecologically embedded settings of real classroom practices, real students, and real curricula—elements that they define as central to their profession. Multiyear summer programs of 2 weeks' or more duration, with follow-up classroom observations, seem reasonably effective. When teams of teachers from the same school participate in such activities, change can accelerate.

Early results from systemic reform suggest that teachers' professional relationships to the educational system need to be reconceptualized. Top-down mandates, poorly informed by the constraints of everyday teaching, inadequately planned, and likely to last no longer than the school year, are met with teachers' understandable skepticism and make them conservative about changing their instructional methods. Thus, effective reform leaders must partner with teachers to define the necessity to change and provide them support, incentives, and rewards to do so, while simultaneously enforcing policies to remediate, remove, or penalize those teachers whose instructional practices are detrimental to children's intellectual development.

Besides giving teachers adequate education and materials, achieving improvements in their professional development means changing the accountability in the system. Systemic reform permits accountability to be focused clearly toward the realization of measurably improved and equitable outcomes for all students. Accountability, then, must be a reciprocal process of convincing all of the interest groups that students are well served and that people are held responsible for negative results over which they can be fairly expected to exert some control. Recertification for teachers, steps for professional development credit, changes in their employment contracts to 11 months with obligatory summer coursework, and the addition of elementary-level specialists are all means to strengthen teachers' professional development; their effectiveness as strong methods of enforcing improvements must be investigated. The enforcement of anticipated progress must be balanced by providing incentive programs and rewards and recognition for leadership. Furthermore, teachers need assurances that their school principals know how to provide instructional guidance that will respect and facilitate the work of teacher-leaders and experts. If the principals fail to do so, reciprocal accountability means that the teachers need some recourse to ensure that their efforts are not impeded at this level.

In terms of new research, there is an acute need to increase capacity for middle-range professionals by creating viably institutionalized positions linking universities and schools and by guaranteeing continued professional growth and collegial interactions for these talented and dedicated individuals. To stabilize and strengthen reform, research on effective ways of educating and nurturing these professionals and providing them stable employment must occur (Lein, J. Johnson, & Ragland, 1996).

## NEW TERRITORIES FOR RESEARCH ON SYSTEMIC REFORM

Just as there are specific targets to suggest for research on systemic reform, there are also new territories for it that are not common yet need to be researched and developed proactively. I would offer five suggestions.

## New Territory 1: Technology Education, Statistical Data Management, and Agriscience

Emerging as important areas in which research can inform us of future directions are technology education and engineering preparation at the middle school level, the management of statistical data, and aspects of agriscience and environmental science. Simultaneously, we need to take a critical and invigorated look at the role of vocational technology courses. As it stands now, in secondary schools, college-bound students are not educated to use their hands, whereas non-college-bound students are not expected to use their intellectual capacity to the fullest. Clearly, both attitudes are problematic, and these traditions ignore the fact that some of the most important, future, scientific and mathematical work will be in new mathematical and scientific fields. The interface between the environment and agricultural practices will be developing. We are seeing employment opportunities with new technologies go unfilled; we will see a similar need developing in applied biology and biotechnology. Mathematicians and statisticians are working feverishly to manage huge, online, real-time data sets. Furthermore, the new technologies are merging scientific, artistic, and visual fields at a rapid pace. If we do not begin to develop curricula in these areas now, we will experience an underprepared workforce. By combining these new field opportunities with a revitalized and systemic approach to career exploration and apprenticeship, we can meet the dual goals of equity and quality.

## New Territory 2: Interdisciplinary Inquiry

We are drifting toward increasing interdisciplinary inquiry, and we need to know more about if and how it can be done. Project-based approaches are clearly highly motivating to students and can build conceptual understanding and receptivity to technology if coherence and progressiveness are carefully monitored. However, their success depends on determining what conditions ensure that students are gaining appropriate skills and increased expertise as they proceed through the activities. Careful sequencing of the projects proved key to satisfactory results in my own research (Confrey, 1995a; Lachance, 1996). My research group has had considerable success in implementing a physics-trigonometry course using motion detectors, Interactive Physics©, and Function Probe© in four 9-week units, but it took years to get the curriculum to work, even partnering with highly talented and determined teachers (Doerr,

1994; Noble, Flerlage, & Confrey, 1993). Project-based instruction still requires careful developmental sequencing, practice of skills, mastery of terminology, and control over one's tools. Interdisciplinary inquiry is probably the ultimate direction for curricula, but we must begin to study its development and use now in order to be ready for it (Tinker, 1996a).

## New Territory 3: Discourse Analysis and Networking

The analysis of discourse that takes the place during classes continues to offer rich opportunities for understanding quality and equity. New classroom-based methodologies are evolving in which interactions in the classroom are evaluated in terms of both content and process. One promising area is to examine how discourse promotes the development of forms of reasoning and argument (Hicks, 1995; Lehrer, Horvath, & Schauble, 1994). In the 3-year teaching experiment that I conducted with third- to fifth-graders, we saw significant gains in their sophistication of argument and spontaneous roots of proof. Verbal exchange is an important part of securing the foundations of inquiry-based approaches and being sure that they lead to high-quality learning. Discourse analysis is also an excellent way to see how participation patterns and language use can lead to unequal opportunity. Additionally, bilingual instructional settings can help to build a better understanding of the different roles played in conceptual development by different semiotic systems.

## New Territory 4: New Technologies

In each of the topics for research proposed earlier, the role of new technologies is an important aspect of the investigation (C. Fisher, Dwyer, & Yocam, 1996; Keitel & Ruthven, 1993). A central research question is: Which technologies used under what conditions lead to smarter users and which lead to only an appearance of expert behavior?

Vygotskian perspectives have established convincingly that the mind and the concept of knowledge are defined in relation to a culture's access to and use of tools, but it is still not clear what technologies and approaches are appropriate for the development of the mind. We must avoid seeing education reduced to technical fluency and schools regulated to teaching outdated and irrelevant skills. We need some skeptical and inventive studies on the uses of new technologies, while continuing our efforts to seek educational applications of advanced technologies and to increase their accessibility and compatibility. More of these studies must take place on site. In mathematics, a researchable question is: What does it mean to be "rigorous" in a symbol-manipulating environment? In science, we can ask: "What is an appropriate balance between technical facility with complex routines and the planning and interpretation of experiments?

The role of the new technologies as means of communication and of providing equitable access to resources must be researched too. Ideally, the Internet should be accessible easily, but, in reality, gaining access to equipment, getting online, knowing how to move in the system, and representing oneself in it are far from being available equally. Nonetheless, we must continue to develop educational applications of these new technologies and must see them applied to reform. In this arena, practical outcomes, advice to schools on installing networking, and the dissemination of funding opportunities can be centrally facilitated. An interesting potential area for new technologies is to inquire how they can be used in professional development. Multimedia courseware with hooks to the Internet are being developed aggressively by publishers who are investing considerable funds in such endeavors. We could be forging relationships with them to engage in related professional development in exchange for agreements to make these materials accessible for professional growth and researching the potential of such approaches to stimulate change in schools.

## New Territory 5: Methodologies

These research challenges are unlikely to be met by using traditional methodologies. They leave one asking the question: How can I produce results if I have to take into account so many different factors? The answer to this question will evolve as the studies evolve, but it will require that we untangle, describe, debate, and refine our approaches to be certain that the methodologies coevolve with our understanding of systemic reform.

# MAKING RESEARCH SYSTEMIC

We must begin by admitting that we lack the human resources capacity to make research systemic. If research is not serving our needs as fully as we might wish, it is in part because there are too few of us and we lack diversity. This is a critical problem that can be addressed only with significant changes in how researchers are educated and who is recruited into research in mathematics and science education.

One approach is to connect research to systemic reform through institutional changes. A critically important opportunity to do this is through the technical assistance initiatives associated with systemic reform projects. In helping to identify possible technical assistants for systemic reform, my research group was challenged by the need to locate individuals who were well informed in research and in the resources available, had the practical experience to enter school settings knowledgeably and comfortably, and possessed the necessary cultural and social sensitivities and expertise. Furthermore, effective technical assistance requires credibility, endurance, and trust at the sites where it is given, which means long-term relationships between providers and recipients.

A second intervention is to make use of the rich recruiting grounds provided by current systemic initiatives to find future researchers. However, to do this, one must recruit these potential researchers as students entering graduate institutions that have strong commitments to equity and quality and be sure that their studies do not deter them from, or cause them to develop a disrespect for, school-based practices. If programs to educate such individuals were tied to strategic intervention activities that allowed for reflective study, one would see programs that would serve multiple purposes.

Finally, we must beware of disincentives for the current research community whose commitments to research have helped us to see how to proceed. As universities face budget cuts, grantees face increased pressures to teach more courses, advise more graduate students, and document their worth to their institution to the tiniest detail. Doing research in a more systemic way must not put even more demands on the research community. At present, it is not unusual to expect researchers to identify the problems, propose the possible solutions, carry out the research, disseminate the findings, design the products needed, then seek new funding—and the half-life of a researcher is disturbingly short. Instead, we must organize to allow for high-quality and productive research teams who have stable and long-term funding and to work toward and support profound and lasting reform.

## CONCLUSION

Decoupling educational research and reform has perhaps never been so consequential. If systemic reform accelerates away from a research base, it may collapse from the failure to progress strategically, efficiently, and securely. Such a trajectory is equally dangerous for the research enterprise. Unless researchers contact successfully all of the practices of education in all of their complexity, the research enterprise will be left behind by a systemic reform movement that regards it as increasingly irrelevant and sterile. Both researchers and reformers have much to gain by opening dialogue and creating and supporting active collaborations. Returning to where I began this chapter, the responsibility to fix the leaky bucket and its associated system, and to be sure that all of the users receive high-quality nourishment, rests with all of us—practitioners, community members, and researchers alike. The educational system is no more than the sum of the intelligence and expertise of the people who make it up, and its care and upkeep can be improved and maintained if, and only if, we work strategically, urgently, and collaboratively toward these goals.

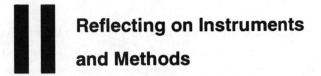

# II Reflecting on Instruments and Methods

Part II, about reflecting on instruments and methods, presents chapters that turn attention toward some of the most important "tools of the trade" as objects of study in themselves. Lesh and Clarke begin by asking readers to reconsider how to operationally define the constructs we wish to investigate. They argue that, regardless of whether the "individuals" we want to investigate are students, groups, teachers, classrooms, programs, or schools, their "ways of thinking" tend to involve systems that are complex, dynamic, self-regulating, and continually adapting—and that generally cannot be reduced to simple checklists of condition-action rules. Also, it may not be possible to isolate many of their most important constructs we want to investigate because their entire nature may change if they are separated from complex holistic systems in which they are embedded. Or, they may not be observable directly, but may be knowable only by their effects. Or, when they are observed, changes may be induced in the "subjects" being investigated. So, the researcher becomes an integral part of the system being observed.

One reason why the preceding factors occur so frequently in mathematics and science education is because of the complex systemic nature of many of the most important "subjects" that need to be understood; and, it also is because many of these systems are products of human construction. But, whatever the reasons may be, because the preceding kinds of phenomena occur so frequently in mathematics and science education research, it has become commonplace to hear researchers talking about rejecting traditions of "doing science" in the physical sciences (where, they would have us believe, researchers treat "reality" as though it were objective). But, when such educators speak about rejecting notions of objective reality, these statements generally are based on antiquated notions about the nature of modern research in the physical sciences—where the notion that reality is a construct is very familiar. For example, Lesh and Clarke discuss the fact that, in the physical sciences, a variety of levels and types of operational definitions commonly are employed to deal with constructs such as neutrinos, charm, and strange quarks whose existence is related to systems whose behaviors are characterized by mathematical discontinuities, chaos, and complexity. In particular, their behaviors tend to be extremely sensitive to initial conditions; when they are acted on, they act back; and, second- and third-order effects often are more significant than first-order effects. Yet, these characteristics do not make it impossible for researchers to formulate operational definitions that are meaningful and useful to others, nor do they make it impossible to develop useful measures for many of the underlying constructs. Consequently, there are strong reasons to believe that similar approaches may be productive in mathematics and science education.

Chapter 7 by Mestre revisits many of the themes introduced by Lesh and Clarke. But, Mestre describes these themes in a retrospective analysis of his own work where he shows how the capabilities of measuring instruments often significantly narrow or broaden the nature of the data that can be collected. Mestre especially emphasizes the interplay between theory and experimentation that is orchestrated (and constrained) by the capacities of the instruments that are used for measurement or assessment. In this way, he sidesteps debates about the relative merits of qualitative versus quantitative methods by demonstrating how the character of data that can be collected under either approach influences the nature of the theory that can be developed.

Just as Mestre's chapter provides clear insights into the analytical and theoretical values that can accrue from paying special attention to the design of outcome measures in research, chapter 8 by Cline and Mandinach shows how inadequacies of research methodologies may mask significant characteristics of the phenomena being investigated. They argue that it is unwise to preadopt a research methodology and then blindly "apply" this methodology to a phenomenon. Rather, they recommend that researcher should begin by trying to ascertain the character of the phenomenon. Then, research methods should be chosen, constructed, or adapted that are based on assumptions consistent with this character. For example, for the educational issues investigated in the studies described by Cline and Mandinach, they abandoned a quasi-experimental design and they instead adapted a research design rooted in case study methodology. Given that they were investigating the use of a new technology in education, the reader may be intrigued by their assertion that the question, "Does it work?" is "not an appropriate question." The reader also may wish to reflect on the authors' characterization of the roles of research subjects, as well as the roles of the researchers themselves.

Taken as a whole, Part II shows how the results that investigations produce often are strongly influenced by choices about methodologies, measurement instruments, and ways of thinking about the possibility of observing isolated phenomenon in carefully controlled laboratory-like environments.

Before reading the chapters in Part II, readers may find it useful to formulate responses to the following questions:

1. The underlying themes that are emphasized in Part II reemerge in many other parts of the book where the subjects being investigated may go

beyond children and teachers to also involve the development of groups, software, curriculum materials, programs, classrooms, schools, or school systems and surrounding communities—as well as interactions among the preceding kinds of entities. In the context of research that you yourself might plan to conduct, who (or what) are the subjects that you want to investigate? If your investigations involve several distinct types of subjects, what kind of interactions do you believe will be most important to investigate?

2. Part II focuses on the assessment of students and teachers. But, the discussions raise important issues about outcome measures for other types of developing subjects. For example, in research projects designed to investigate the development of programs, simple pretest–posttest designs often are used to describe changes that occur. Yet, simply describing a series of states often fails to yield good information about the nature of processes and mechanisms that lead to change. For a study that you yourself might want to conduct, describe how much you are interested in dynamic transitions, processes, or mechanisms—rather than simply describing static states.

3. In later parts of this book, research designs that are emphasized range from teaching experiments, to clinical interviews, to studies using videotapes as data, to case studies, to participant-observer studies, to action research studies, to ethnographic observational studies, to longitudinal development studies of individuals, groups, classrooms, or other subjects suggested in Question 1. One factor that distinguishes one approach from another is the extent and type of interactions that the researcher(s) have with the other participants in the study. What kind of interactions will be involved among researchers and participants in the research that you yourself plan to conduct?

4.  The main products that a research project is designed to produce may consist of hypotheses that are to be tested. But, other products include: (a) models or prototypes that need to be developed, (b) existence proofs that need to be demonstrated, (c) possibilities that need to be created or explored, and (d) other types of "deliverables" that may or may not involve measurement or quantification. For a research project that you yourself might plan to conduct, what is the nature of the products that you plan to produce? Will these products be refined or elaborated through several iterations? Or, if it is possible that several different levels or types of results could occur, what kind of issues should be considered to judge the relative strengths and weaknesses of these alternatives?

# 6 Formulating Operational Definitions of Desired Outcomes of Instruction in Mathematics and Science Education

**Richard Lesh**
*Purdue University*

**David Clarke**
*University of Melbourne*

The central question this chapter is intended to answer is: "What other options are available, beyond traditional standardized tests, or curriculum standards consisting of naïve checklists of low-level facts and skills, to operationally define educational goals in ways that provide direction for both instruction and accountability?" Suggestions for alternatives will be drawn from both the physical and social sciences, as well as from common experiences in business, engineering, and other areas where science is applied.

## LIMITATIONS OF STANDARDIZED TESTS TO OPERATIONALLY DEFINE GOALS OF INSTRUCTION

Productive assessment involves clarifying goals; and, the goal of this chapter is to describe several ways that mathematics and science educators can approach the task of developing measurable ways to specify the nature of their most important goals for instruction. To highlight some important issues that arise in such efforts, it is useful to begin by sorting out distinctions among a variety of assessment-related terms that educators often treat as if their meanings were identical—even though they are interpreted in ways that are quite distinct from one another in many other professions (ranging from business to engineering) or sciences (ranging from physical sciences to life sciences). By sorting out such distinctions, we believe that several significant needs, opportunities, and errors become apparent that should be taken into account when developing new perspectives about "operational definitions" of educational goals.

TABLE 6.1

| Terms Commonly Emphasized in Traditional Testing | Terms Commonly Emphasized in Performance Assessment |
|---|---|
| *Testing*<br><br>creating an ordeal (barrier, or filter) for accepting or rejecting (but not helping) | *Examining*<br><br>inspecting closely and generating high-fidelity descriptions |
| *Measuring*<br><br>partitioning (fragmenting) into indistinguishable pieces | *Documenting*<br><br>gathering tangible evidence which is credible to decision-makers |
| *Evaluating*<br><br>assigning a value without specifying conditions or purposes | *Assessing*<br><br>taking stock, orienting with respect to known landmarks and goals |

As Table 6.1 suggests, it is possible to inspect students' work closely without putting them through an ordeal; and, it also is possible to put students through an ordeal without closely inspecting their work. Similarly, it is possible to measure students without documenting their progress in forms that are useful to most decision makers; or, it is possible to document progress along a variety of dimensions without specifying a common unit of measure—and without collapsing all comparisons into a single linearly ordered dimension. Finally, it is possible to make value judgements (about a position or path) without getting oriented; and, it is possible to get oriented without making value judgements. For example, when travelers see an arrow on a map that says "you are here," they may be able to *assess* whether progress has been made toward some goal. Yet, judgements about whether a given location is good or bad may depend on a variety of factors. For example, if the travelers are hiking through the Grand Canyon, and if they are making judgements about how close they are to some specific goal, then these decisions may depend on factors related to time or effort rather than a geometer's notion of the straight-line distance between two points. Under some circumstances, time may be more important than effort; or, under other circumstances, the opposite may be the case.

Similar points are apparent when a person uses a consumer guidebook to compare automobiles, restaurants, or vacation plans. It is neither necessary nor desirable for the guidebook to reduce comparisons to a single dimension, nor is it necessary to compare items using a single standard unit of measure. Is a Jeep Cherokee better than a Ford Taurus? Judgements about "better" and "worse" beg the question "Better for what?" — Clearly, answers to this question vary from person to person, and can only be anticipated to a limited extent by testing companies or guidebook publishers. Similarly, in mathematics and science education, it usually is inappropriate to pretend that students can be put in order from "worst" to "best" without recognizing the facts such as: (a) all students develop complex profiles of strengths and weaknesses[1]; (b) different jobs often demand quite different profiles of understandings and abilities; (c) a person who has excellent credentials for one job may be ill suited for another; (d) progress can be made along a variety of paths; and (e) the significance of achievements often depend on the conditions under which they occur.

The first table in this section suggests that the kind of operational definitions that will be emphasized in this chapter should be less concerned with making value judgements in the context of artificial ordeals. Rather, they should focus on finding ways to produce auditable trails of documentation that yield assessments of productivity which are based on representative samples of closely inspected student work. Table 6.2 also emphasizes the fact that productive operational definitions should lead to useful information for decision makers.

---

[1] An algebraist is not necessarily a good topologist. A topologist is not necessarily a good tax consultant. A tax consultant is not necessarily a good programmer. A person who is good at following rules is not necessarily a person who is good at creating new sets of rules (when new programming languages need to be created). A person who is good at working along to produce answers to other peoples' well framed questions is not necessarily a person who is good a designing solutions to problems in which teams of specialists must work together. and there is no single "correct" ways to balance conflicting factors such as cost. quality, speed. and simplicity.

TABLE 6.2

Distinctions Between Traditional Testing and Representative Samples of Assessed Work

| *Traditional Tests* | *Representative Work Samples* |
|---|---|
| Generally focus on: | Generally focus on: |
| (a)  A small number of high-stakes but low-interest situations. | (a)  A larger number of low-stakes but high-interest |
| (b)  Short-answer questions that emphasize a large number of low-level facts & skills. | (b)  Project-sized activities emphasizing smaller numbers of deeper & higher order understandings and abilities. |
| *Summative Information* | *Formative Information* |
| Focuses on decision-making issues of administrators & policy makers. | Focuses on decision-making issues of students and teachers. |
| *Pretest–Post Designs* | *Dynamic Feedback* |
| Are intended to prove that "it" works; but, they often promote conditions which minimize the chances of success by measuring progress in terms of deficiencies with respect to simplistic "check list" of benchmarks (facts, skills, behaviors). | Focuses on monitoring and documenting progress while also encouraging development in directions that are increasingly "better". . . without using simplistic (mechanistic) definitions of "best" to determine next steps. |

The following kinds of questions shouldn't be overlooked when judgements are made about the relative strengths and weaknesses of alternative forms of assessment (and operational definitions of goals). Who are the most important decision makers whose needs should be addressed? What are the priority-type decisions they must make? What kind of information is needed to make wise decisions? Is rapid feedback more important than accuracy? Is it sufficient to reduce all information to a single-number score? Or, is it important to see details about profiles of strengths and weaknesses. Is it sufficient to receive information about groups? Or, is it important to get details about individuals? Is it sufficient to get information only infrequently, and to generate reports only after long delays? Or, is it important to get rapid feedback so strategic improvements can be made?

Instruments that address some of the preceding needs do not address others. So, a "one size fits all" strategy is not likely to be appropriate for all decision makers. Also, it is not necessary in an age when most modern decision makers have computers sitting on their desks. Even decision makers who don't have access to computers are familiar with modern newspapers in which nearly every section from business to sports includes a complex display of computer-generated information that is graphic, multidimensional, and (perhaps) interactive. Consequently, in such a society, technology makes it possible to gather information from multiple sources, to display the results for multiple purposes, and to produce reports that are simple without being simplistic. In particular, there is no need to simplify information only by relying on one-number characterizations of students, teachers, programs, or schools.

Another distinction that is relevant to our discussions is highlighted in the cartoonist Gary Larson's book "Night of the Crash Test Dummies" (1988). That is, in many everyday situations when we test something, we don't care whether the thing being tested is being injured or destroyed in the process. But, in education, in general, we *do* care. This is why, educators usually should obey a basic principle that was emphasized long ago in the preamble to the Hippocratic Oath in medicine. That is: *First, don't do harm!*

The preceding point is especially important in mathematics and science education because the need for severe artificial constraints on time and resources usually causes traditional standardized tests to restrict their attention to extremely brief and superficial work samples, as well as to equally simplistic scoring procedures. Consequently: (a) these tests tend to focus on shallow, narrow, and biased subsets of the understandings and abilities that are needed for success in more representative samples of work (Resnick & Resnick, 1993); (b) the understandings and abilities that they assess tend to be poorly aligned with the deeper and higher order knowledge emphasized in high quality curriculum standards (Romberg, et al., 1991); and (c) they seldom give adequate attention to the most important achievements of outstanding students, teachers, and programs. In other words, standardized tests tend to emphasize what is *not* important, while neglecting what is important. Therefore, when scores on such tests are used to predict performance in more realistic problem solving situations, they generally account for far less than 20% of the variance (Willingham, et al., 1983; Gardner, 1993a; Goleman, 1997). Yet, such tests continue to be used as de facto "operational definitions" to specify goals of instruction. Why?

Even testing companies don't use standardized tests to make high stakes decisions about employees' promotions and salary increases, or about the productivity of various components of their businesses. This is because many other cost-effective ways usually exist to produce auditable trails of documentation that provide information about achievement and productivity. Yet, in education, in spite of obvious alternatives to testing that are familiar in other areas of life, it is common to assume that expensive testing programs offer the only possible way to hold students, teachers, and schools accountable for high achievement.

At the same time that standardized tests are touted as the best way to emphasize accountability, and to encourage students, teachers, and schools to take responsibility for their own achievements, they actually provide ideal ways to *avoid* responsibility. This is because they rarely provide feedback that is in time or on target to do anything about the results. For example, unlike professional people in real life job situations, students are encouraged to imagine that high scores on a college entrance examination will relieve them of the responsibility to produce other forms of credible evidence showing productivity in challenging situations over long periods of time. Or, schools imagine that, by claiming to teach to tests, they can avoid responsibilities to provide better courses, better counseling, and better support to actually help students to get admitted (and to be successful) in excellent colleges and professions.[2]

---

[2] It is misleading to speak of treating students fairly on a test (or in a textbook or teaching program) if the test as a whole reflects obsolete, superficial, and instructionally-unproductive biases about the nature of mathematics, problem solving, teaching, and learning. Yet, if a narrow conception of mathematical ability is correlated with a more representative interpretation, then testing specialists often treat modest (.38) correlations as if they are sufficient (i.e., sufficient for selecting small-but-adequate numbers of students for access to scarce-but-adequate resources). Yet, today, even beyond concerns about fairness and equity, national assessment priorities have changed. At a national level, our foremost problem is not to *screen* talent; it is to *identify* and *nurture* capable students. The pool of students receiving adequate preparation in mathematics is no longer adequate; and, far too many capable students are being "shut out" or "turned off" by textbooks, teaching, and tests which give excessive attention to views of mathematics and problem solving that are fundamentally inconsistent with national curriculum and assessment standards for school mathematics and science.

The most serious shortcomings of standardized tests tend to occur when they go beyond being used as *indicators* of achievement to being used as if they *defined* what we mean by achievement. One argument in favor of teaching-to-tests is based on the fact that international assessments of students' mathematical abilities continually show that students in the United States rank far below their counterparts in other countries with prosperous economies. Yet, there is no country that has a stronger tradition of teaching to tests than the United States; and, the United States spends orders of magnitude more money on standardized testing than any other country. This is why there is no other country that has anything like the testing industry that exists in the United States. Consequently, while the United States is preoccupied with trying to catch up in low level "basics" emphasized on tests, many competing countries are shifting toward "thinking about complexity" and toward preparation for success in a technology-based society. Implications of these trends are clear. If the USA catches up, it will once again be left behind!

It is well known that pressures to teach to tests often exert strong forces on schools to "dumb down" their curriculum offerings in order to emphasize the simplistic conceptions of expertise that standardized tests embody. For example, consider the Educational Testing Service's to Scholastic Aptitude Test (SAT) that is used to select students for admission to many colleges.[3]  It has been a long-standing ETS policy that the SAT should include no

---

[3] Both of the authors of this chapter have served as deans as well as faculty members working with admissions officers at a variety of highly selective universities in the United States and Australia. Consequently, we've learned that, contrary to popular beliefs of those not directly involved in the decision making process, scores on standardized tests tend to be given far less attention in admissions decisions than factors such as: rank in class, teachers recommendations, recommendations from credible alumni, consistent records of good grades in challenging courses in schools whose programs are known to be strong, and other evidence of productivity and diversity. For example, at Purdue University, the admissions office clearly states that scores on standardized tests are considered only after at least six of the preceding kinds of factors have been assessed—and, even then, test scores are used mainly to grant admissions to students who are able to provide little other evidence of their capabilities. Unfortunately, many other colleges who follow similar policies are less forthright in acknowledging that their decisions are based on professional judgements rather than on rigid decision formulas. That is, to avoid the responsibility

(continued)

content that goes beyond ninth grade mathematics. Furthermore, SAT only claims to be measuring general aptitude rather than achievement. That is, it claims to be measuring "intelligence" that is presumed to be uninfluenced by particular instruction. Therefore, teaching to this test implies encouraging students to focus on mathematics that never goes beyond the ninth grade level; and, it also implies neglecting deeper and higher order thinking that is tied to the use of powerful and highly content-specific tools such as those needed for success in a technology-based society.

The preceding facts are among the most obvious reasons why there is only an unimpressive .38 correlation between SAT scores and success in introductory college courses—even when the only college courses that are considered are those in which students' grades are based on nothing more than performance on easy-to-score tests (Willingham et. Al., 1990). In other words, standardized tests don't even do an especially impressive job of predicting performance on freshman tests; and, correlations fall toward zero if success in post-graduation work experiences is considered—or if judgements about success are based on work samples that require more complex forms of thinking than those emphasized on standardized tests (Goleman, 1997; Shavelson & Baxter, 1992).

Later in this chapter, other explanations will be given about why teaching to tests, over a long period of time, tends to be a losing strategy. For now, a brief explanation is that: (a) students soon forget disorganized lists of facts and skills; (b) when facts and skills are "mastered" one-at-a-time and in isolation, students may never learn when to chose which one to use in particular situations; and (c) when instruction emphasizes only facts and skills, or content-independent problems solving processes, other exceedingly important goals of instruction are ignored.

---

of informing students that they didn't get admitted because they had poor records of performance in weak programs, it is easier and less risky to simply lead people to believe that they were rejected because of low test scores.

# RELATIONSHIPS BETWEEN MEASUREMENT INSTRUMENTS AND OPERATIONAL DEFINITIONS OF UNDERLYING CONSTRUCTS

Why is it so common, in education, to assume that *indicators* of achievement must be used to *define* goals of instruction? Thermometers measure temperature; but, this doesn't lead us to believe that simply causing the mercury to rise will do anything significant to change the weather.

Relationships between measurement, meaning, and dictionary-style definitions can be complex. Yet, these complexities need not lead to confusion about differences between measurement instruments and the constructs they are intended to measure. For example, consider the case of clocks and wrist watches. They are used to measure time; yet, even today, many basic issues remain unresolved about the measurement and meaning of time. In fact, during the past decade, many of the world's leading scientists have written books that attempt to explain various ways of thinking about the nature of time (Aveni, 1989; Coveney & Highfield, 1990; Davies, 1995; S. J. Gould, 1988; Hawking, 1988; Sachs, 1987; Shlain, 1991; Thorne, 1994). Yet, even though many deep issues remain unresolved about the nature of time, most ordinary people believe that they understand the concept of time sufficiently well simply because, for most practical purposes, they know how to measure time and they know how to deal with its effects.

Why do confusions persist in education about relationships between our ability to *measure* a construct and our ability to *define* it? Some reasons are because, in education: (a) it is common to treat means-to-ends as if they were ends-in-themselves; (b) it is common to treat effects as if they were causes; and (c) it is common to treat the consequences of new knowledge as if these consequences were the most essential parts of the underlying knowledge itself. In particular, high scores on tests often are treated as if they went beyond being *indicators* of achievement toward actually *being* the goals of instruction. If similar lines of reasoning were used in fields such as medicine, we would treat symptoms as if they were the underlying diseases.

The preceding fact is especially important in mathematics and science education because many of the most important constructs that students should learn are not reducible to facts and skills (*behavioral objectives* of instruction) nor to global processes (*process objectives* of instruction). Instead, they represent a third type of instructional goal that modern cognitive psychologists might refer to as *cognitive objectives* of instruction. They are models, metaphors, or other complex conceptual systems that are used to describe, to explain, or to construct complex systems in real or imagined worlds. For example, in science education, children develop their own ways of thinking about electricity, heat, light, magnets, and many other phenomena that they encounter in everyday situations; and, changing students' ways of thinking usually must involve more than simply forcing them to learn a few new facts or skills. Unless previously developed ways of thinking are challenged and tested, they tend to persist. For instance, if a child explains electricity as if it were like water running through tubes, then new facts and rules that are memorized are incorporated into these existing ways of thinking—rather than leading to new models, metaphors, and conceptual systems.

To illustrate the way that holistic conceptual systems resist change, there is perhaps no better example to consider than the way many educators think about assessment. In past stages of history, educators have tended to think about the mind (and about the nature of mathematical knowledge) as if it were similar to the most sophisticated technology of the preceding age. For example, as civilizations evolved from the industrial revolution through the electronics revolution to the current age of biotechnologies, educators have shifted from machine metaphors (based on hardware) to computer metaphors (based on software) to organic metaphors (based on wetware of the type that characterizes the processes of the human brain). Yet, in the area of assessment, simple input–output models continue to dominate that are based on machine metaphors. Consequently, to improve the assessment practices of schools and other educational agencies, it is not enough to introduce better test items. An entire paradigm shift will be needed which fundamentally rethinks issues ranging from data collection, data interpretation, data analysis, and the nature of reports (Lesh & Lamon, 1992).

Similar observations have been made about other components of curriculum reform, such as those that focus on teacher development, curriculum development, or program development. For example, to explain why piecemeal approaches to curriculum innovation are seldom effective, a report from the National Council of Teachers of Mathematics makes the following observation.

> In spite of the best intentions of developers and implementors, it was unreasonable to expect that new products or programs would be used as intended in most schools and classrooms. The reason for this is that public schools as they now operate are integrated social systems. Tinkering with parts, such as changing textbooks or the number of required courses, fails to change other components of the system. The traditions of the system force new products to be used in old ways. Current educational

> practice is based on a coherent set of ideas about goals, knowledge, work, and technology that came from a set of "scientific management" principles growing out of the industrial revolution of the past century. These ideas about schooling need to be challenged and replaced with an equally coherent set of practices in light of the economic and social revolution in which we are now engaged. Current school mathematics operates within a coherent system; reform will happen only if an equally coherent system replaces it. (National Council of Teachers of Mathematics, 1989)

According to ways of thinking borrowed from the industrial revolution, teachers have been led to believe that the construction of mathematical knowledge in a child's mind is similar to the process of assembling a machine, or programming a computer. That is, complex systems are thought of as being nothing more than the sums or their parts; each part is expected to be taught and tested one-at-a-time, in isolation, and out of context; and, the parts are assumed to be defined operationally using naive checklists of condition-action rules.

In contrast to the preceding perspective, scientists today are investigating complexity theory where the processes governing the development of complex, dynamic, self-organizing, and continually adapting systems are quite different than those that apply to simple machines. Parts interact. Logic is fuzzy. Whole systems are more than the sums of their parts; and, when the relevant systems are acted on, they act back.

Piaget was one of the earliest and most prominent researchers to reveal the nature of some of the most important conceptual systems that students must develop to make judgements about quantities ranging from simple counts, to lengths, to areas, to speeds, to forces, to probabilities (Piaget & Beth, 1966; Piaget & Inhelder, 1958). Similarly, during the past 30 years, some of the greatest achievements of mathematics and science education research have been to generate detailed information about what it means to develop deeper or higher order understandings of the conceptual systems that underlie students' developing knowledge about constructs ranging from fractions (Behr, Harel, Lesh, & Post, 1991) to forces (Hestenes, M. Wells, & Swackhamer, 1992) to functions (Kaput & Nemirovsky, 1995), to frequencies (Gal & Garfield, 1997).

The preceding increases in knowledge have been primary factors leading to the successful development of curricula standards produced recently by organizations such as the National Council of Teachers of Mathematics (1989), the American Association for the Advancement of Science (1993), and the National Research Council-National Academy of Sciences (National Research Council, 1996). Yet, in spite of enormous progress clarifying the nature of students' developing mathematical and scientific knowledge, many leaders in research have been reluctant to specify ways to measure what they mean by "understanding" for relevant conceptual systems. Why? One reason is because of fears that educators will confuse measurement instruments with the constructs they are intended to assess; but, another reason is because, when mathematics and science educators describe what kinds of understandings and abilities should be stressed in instruction, these curriculum standards for *instruction* do not necessarily provide straightforward performance standards for *students* (Romberg, et al., 1991). For example, saying that mathematics instruction should stress connections among ideas does not make clear how "connectedness" can be assessed in a student's thinking. Or, saying that flexibility of thought should be encouraged in instruction does not make it clear how flexibility could be assessed in ways that are useful, reliable, and unbiased. Similarly, specifying what we mean by terms like *understanding* tends to become especially problematic when modifiers are added such as: *concrete* understanding, *abstract* understanding, *symbolic* understanding, *intuitive* understanding, *situated* understanding, *higher order* understanding, *instrumental* understanding, *relational* understanding, *deeper* understanding, or *shared* understanding. In fact, even in the case of familiar terms such as *teaching*, *learning*, and *problem solving*, definitional difficulties often arise when modifiers like *good* are added. What do we mean when we speak of good teaching, good problem solving, good assessment tasks, or good instructional activities?

So far in this chapter, we've seen that the relationships often are not straightforward between measurement instruments and operational definitions of underlying constructs, or between curriculum standards for *instruction* and performance standards for *students*. The next section will describe some alternative types of operational definitions that are familiar in fields outside education, and that may provide useful ways to deal with the preceding kinds of complexities.

## ALTERNATIVE TYPES OF OPERATIONAL DEFINITIONS FOR SPECIFYING GOALS OF INSTRUCTION

In sciences ranging from physics to astronomy to biology to geology to anthropology, many levels and types of operational definitions are commonly employed to deal with constructs such as neutrinos, strange quarks, and other subatomic particles that have characteristics with whimsical names like *charm* or *flavor*. Furthermore, many of these constructs have characteristics similar to those that are of greatest interest in mathematics and science education. For example, the existence of a given entity may be inseparable from the complex holistic systems in which it is embedded. Or, the entity may not be observable directly, but rather may be knowable only by its effects.

Consider the case of the neutrino where huge vats of heavy water are surrounded by photo-multipliers in order to create situations in which the effects of neutrinos are likely to be observable and measurable. Yet, even under these conditions, neutrinos cannot be observed directly. They can be known only through their effects; and, between the beholder and the beheld, elaborate systems of theory and assumptions are needed to distinguish signal from noise, and to shape interpretations of the phenomena under investigation. Also, small changes in initial conditions often lead to large effects that are essentially unpredictable; and, observations that are made induce significant changes in the systems being observed. Consequently, both researchers and their instruments are integral parts of the systems that scientists are hoping to understand and explain.

Educators are not alone in their need to deal with constructs and phenomena that have the preceding characteristics. Furthermore, in sciences where fanciful terms such as *charm* and *flavor* are used to refer to characteristics of inanimate objects, it is clear that educators calling themselves constructivists are not alone in their recognition that reality is a construct. Throughout the physical sciences, life sciences, and social sciences, many of the most important "entities" that we need to understand and explain are products of human construction.

When devices such as cloud chambers and cyclotrons are needed to record and measure illusive constructs, it is clear that being able to measure a construct does not guarantee that a corresponding dictionary-style definition will be apparent. Conversely, even when scientists can give a dictionary-style definition of a construct (such as a black hole in astronomy), this doesn't guarantee that procedures will be clear for observing or measuring the construct.

In general, in the physical sciences, to develop useful operational definitions of complex phenomena (photons, neutrinos, etc.), a minimum requirement is that explicit procedures must be described specifying: (a) how to create a situation in which the relevant construct will occur; (b) how to detect its effects and sort out relevant from irrelevant information; and (c) how to make comparisons among various observed occurrences. Therefore, such operational definitions involve three parts that are similar, in some respects, to the following three parts of traditional types of behavioral objectives in mathematics and science education.

## Behavioral Objectives Involve Three Parts

Given {specified conditions} the student will exhibit {specified behaviors} with identifiable quality {perhaps specified as percents correct on relevant samples of tasks, or perhaps specified in terms of a correspondence with certain criteria for excellence}.

In mathematics and science education, the main problem with behavioral objectives is that not all forms of learning consist of rules (facts, skills, procedures); and, if attempts are made to reduce more complex conceptual systems to checklists of rules, the following sorts of difficulties arise. Even though students (teachers, programs, or schools) who develop a given conceptual system (C) may be expected to exhibit certain behaviors (B1, B2, B3, . . . Bn) on tasks (T1, T2, T3, . . . Tn), it usually is possible for these problem solvers to exhibit behaviors B1, B2, B3, . . . Bn *without* developing the underlying conceptual system C. This is because the relationship between C and its various manifestations B1, B2, . . . Bn tends to be associative rather than causal, and symptomatic rather than definitive.

In general, the development of complex conceptual systems is similar to the development of complex and dynamic systems that occur in other types of situations (such as sports, arts, or business). For example, coordinated and smoothly functioning systems usually involve more than the simple sums of their parts. In fact, characteristics of the parts tend to be inherited from characteristics of the system as a whole at least as much as the converse is the case. For instance, it may be true that a great artist  (or a great athlete) should be able to perform well on certain basic drills and exercises (calisthenics); nonetheless, a program of instruction (or assessment) that focuses on nothing more than these checklists of basic skills is unlikely to provide adequate approaches to excellence. For example, if we taught (and tested) cooks in this way, we'd never allow them to try cooking a meal until they memorized the names and skills associated with every tool at stores like Crate & Barrel and Williams Sonoma. Or, if we taught (and tested) carpenters in this way, we'd never allow them to try building a house until they memorized the names and skills associated with every tool at stores like Ace Hardware and Sears. Yet, whereas such an approach clearly is foolish in fields like cooking, carpentry, art, or sports, it is employed routinely in mathematics and science education. If fact, when students' performance deteriorates after schools focus instruction on a checklists of low level skills, a common reaction is for schools to focus on an even more detailed checklist. In fields such as cooking, carpentry, or sports, such an approach would be recognized as being the disease for which it purports to be the cure! But, in education, such approaches persist.

The next section of this chapter will describe some additional relevant shortcomings associated with the use of behavioral objectives in mathematics and science education. But, in this section, the goal is to describe alternatives to behavioral objectives as means of defining observable and assessable goals of instruction. In past publications, we have referred to some of the most productive of these new types of operational definitions as "cognitive objectives" of instruction (Lesh & Lamon, 1994). This name seems appropriate because they focus on students' *interpretations* of situations rather than focusing on their *actions* in these situations.

Whereas behavioral objectives collapse three different kinds of statements into a single condition-action rule, cognitive objectives function similarly to the ways cyclotrons, cloud chambers, and vats of heavy water are used in physics. That is, they are defined operationally by specifying: (a) *situations* that optimize the chances that the targeted construct will occur in an observable form; (b) *observation tools* that enable observers to sort out signal from noise in the results that occur; and (c) *quality assessment criteria* that allow meaningful comparisons to be made among alternative possibilities. For example:

> *Situations*: At the end of this chapter, Appendix A gives an example of a thought-revealing activity in which three-person teams of middle school students confront the need to develop weighted sums, weighted averages, or some other construct to aggregate information of qualitatively different types (such as times, distances, rankings, or qualitative information that must be quantified). Other examples are given in Chapters 21 and 23 of this volume. For instance, the tasks called "The Sears Catalogue Problem" (Chapter 21, this volume) and "The Summer Jobs Problem" (Chapter 23, this volume) both require students to deal with situations in which they must quantify relationships among quantities, then aggregate these relationships into a single measure.

For the purposes of this chapter, the main point that we want to emphasize about the preceding types of activities is that they have characteristics similar to those that apply to cloud chambers or other devices that are used to observe or measure subatomic particles. For example, the relevant construct is *elicited by* the task description or the device, but it does not *reside in* the task description or the device. In particular, for the kind of thought-revealing activities that we emphasize, the mathematical constructs do not reside in the problem statements, and hence they are not task variables; instead, they reside in the responses that students generate, and hence might be called response variables.

*Observation Tools*: In mathematics education, the kind of thought-revealing activities that we describe in Chapters 21 and 23 of this volume are examples of tasks that require students to reveal their ways of thinking. This is because the products that students develop include more than calculated results consisting of a single number answer; they also involve descriptions, constructions, explanations, or justifications that may be embedded in spreadsheets, graphs, equations, and other representational systems. Consequently, as students goal mathematize (quantify, coordinatize) the problem solving situations, the explicit mathematical interpretations that are generated reveal significant information about what kind of mathematical relationships, patterns, and regularities the student is taking into account. Furthermore, because the descriptions, constructions, explanations, and justifications that students produce are not merely parts of the processes of producing answers to questions, but are essential parts of the products themselves, it sometimes is possible for these products to reveal significant information about the processes that produced them. Also, because these products often need to be shareable, modifiable, transportable, and reusable, students often must go beyond thinking with a given construct to also think about it; and, they also must think about them in a way that generalizes beyond the specific situation that is given. Thus, it often is straightforward to deal with deeper and higher order understandings and abilities. Nonetheless, even if the products that students produce explicitly reveal significant aspects about the ways of thinking that they are using to make sense of the situation, various levels and types of products nearly always are possible, and it is not necessarily a straightforward task to analyze and interpret their results. For example:

- It nearly always is possible for students' responses to make use of a variety of representational systems (involving written symbols, spoken language, graphs or graphics, diagrams, and concrete models).
- It nearly always is possible for several, equally acceptable responses to be based on different decisions about trade-offs involving factors like accuracy, precision, simplicity, or timeliness.

To deal with the preceding kinds of complexities, teachers participating in the authors' past research projects have found it useful to develop "Ways of Thinking Sheets" that sometimes resemble large posters displaying snippets from the products that students produce for a given problem (Katims, Lesh, Hole, & Hoover, 1994a). For example, for the "Softball Problem" that is given in Appendix B, some relevant snippets might show several ways in which average-ability, middle school students often develop creative ways to: (a) quantify qualitative information (such as the weights or values that they assign to various categories of information given in the problem); (b) combine information involving diverse, qualitatively different, types of information (entailing ranks, distances, times, or value points); (c) make their assumptions explicit, and allow modifications to be made to deal with alternative assumptions; and (d) use a range of graphs, equations, or other representations. Other "Ways of Thinking Sheets" are described in Chapter 21 of this book.

> *Quality Assessment Criteria*: For the thought-revealing activities that we describe in Chapter 21 of this book, the constructions, descriptions or explanations that students produce provide conceptual tools that are requested by a specified client and for a specified purpose. Furthermore, the client and purpose are specified in such a way that this information provides straightforward criteria for making judgments about the strengths and weaknesses of alternative approaches. Nonetheless, to assess final results that are produced by different teams of students, teachers (and students) generally find it useful to use guidelines for assessing the usefulness of results. An example set of guidelines that can be used for the "Softball Problem" is given in Appendix B at the end of this chapter.

Note:   It has become common, in projects emphasizing performance assessment, to use the term *scoring rubric* to refer to guidelines for assessing the quality of students' work. But, we prefer to avoid this term because many scoring rubrics that have been developed operate on principles that are aligned more closely with checklists of behavioral objectives than with the kind of cognitive objectives that we wish to emphasize. Instead, we emphasize procedures similar to those used in Olympic competitions (basketball, gymnastics, and equestrian events), performing arts or crafts (dancing, playing musical instruments, and building houses), or businesses (assessing productivity for individuals, groups, and sites). In such contexts, the goal of assessment often involves complex systems; and, to assess these systems, the procedures that are used often involve three parts similar to those being described here. That is they involve creating: (a) situations in which these systems will be elicited and observable; (b) tools to help recognize important characteristics of the relevant systems that occur; and (c) tools to assess the relative strengths and weaknesses of the learner's systems that are elicited. Frequently, in these situations, the act of assessing complex performances is itself a complex performance. But, this need not be the case. For example, in complex businesses, or in sports or arts where complex performances are emphasized, final tests of success often are measured by scoring points, by making money, or by winning against an opponent. Yet, in the preceding situations, performers seldom do well if they are too preoccupied with only scoring points, making money, or winning. Because it is clear that the goal is to develop complex systems, there is no confusion between the goal and the criteria for assessing the goal. So, participants are not likely to imagine that complex performances can be reduced to a checklist of simple behaviors.

Taken together, the preceding kind of situations-plus-observation-tools-plus-quality-assessment-criteria often provide useful operational definitions of complex systems. This is because they include explicit procedures for describing: (a) how to create situations in which the relevant constructs will be likely to occur; (b) how to recognize and describe the relevant constructs when they occur; and (c) how to make comparisons among the alternatives that occur. In particular, in the case of conceptual systems that students develop during the solution of individual problem solving sessions: (i) model-eliciting activities put students in situations where they confront the need to produce a given type of construct, and where the products that they generate require them to reveal explicitly important characteristics of their underlying ways of thinking; (ii) ways of thinking sheets focus on ways of recognizing and describing the nature of the constructs that students produce; and (iii) guidelines for assessing the quality of students' work provide criteria that can be used to compare the usefulness of alternative ways of thinking.

## COMPLEX SYSTEMS HAVE DYNAMIC MULTIDIMENSIONAL PROFILES OF COMPETENCE

To identify other issues that are important to consider when operational definitions are formulated, it is useful to recognize that, in mathematics and science education, three-part operational definitions are especially useful because many of the "entities" to be observed and assessed involve complex, interacting, self-organizing, and continually adapting systems that cannot be reduced characterizations based on a checklist of condition–action rules. These complex systems include cognitive structures (which underlie a given student's understanding of a particular idea), conceptual systems (which underlie a student's understandings of relationships among ideas in a given topic area), biological systems (involving children's development), and social systems (within classrooms and schools).

Regardless of whether the individuals we want to assess are students, groups, teachers, classes, programs, or schools, the following two characteristics usually apply to the individual we want to investigate.

1.  In general, there is no single "best" type of individual; every individual has a complex profile of strengths and weaknesses; and, individuals who are effective in some ways and under some conditions are not necessarily effective in others.

2.  Individuals at every level of expertise must continue to adapt and develop; there exists no fixed and final state of excellence; in fact, conceptions of excellence tend to be among the most important characteristics that evolve during the development of individuals.

These two characteristics have important implications for the types of operational definitions that need to be emphasized in mathematics and science education. For example:

*For Programs*: When evaluating large and complex program innovations, it is misleading to label them "successes" or "failures" (as though everything that successful programs did was effective and everything that unsuccessful programs did was not effective). All programs have profiles of strengths and weaknesses. Most of them work some of the time, for some students, in some ways, and in some circumstances, but none of them work all of the time, for all students, for all purposes, and in all circumstances. Furthermore, success depends generally on how much and how well the program is implemented. If only half of a program is implemented, or if it is implemented in only a half-hearted way, then complete success is not expected. Also, as soon as a program begins to achieve success, fundamental changes tend to be induced into the situation where they are expected to function, and new rounds of adaptation tend to be needed. Therefore, when programs are observed and assessed, the kinds of descriptions that are needed should be multidimensional, conditional, and continually evolving.

*For Teachers*: As teachers develop, they frequently notice new things about their students, about their instructional materials, and about the ideas and abilities that they are trying to help their students learn. Consequently, these new observations often create new needs and opportunities that, in turn, demand additional development. Current capabilities be characterized by a single point on a "good–bad" scale; profiles of strengths and weaknesses always can be identified; and, the conditions in which these profiles have been achieved must be taken into account. For instance, no teacher is equally effective for all grade levels (kindergarten through calculus), for all types of students (handicapped through gifted), and for all types of settings (inner-city to rural). No teacher can be expected to be "good" constantly in "bad" situations; not everything that experts do is effective, nor is everything that novices do ineffective. Characteristics that lead to success in one situation (or for one person) often turn out to be counterproductive in other situations (or for another person). Finally, even though gains in students' achievement should be one factor considered when documenting the accomplishments of teachers (or programs), it is foolish to assume that the best teachers always produce the largest student learning gains in students. What if a great teacher chooses to deal with only difficult students or difficult circumstances? Clearly, expertise in teaching is plural, multidimensional, nonuniform, conditional, and continually evolving.

*For Students*: Chapter 23 of this book (Lesh & Lehrer) gives examples to show how students' responses to model-eliciting activities involve the development of complex descriptions or explanations. Furthermore, it also shows how these interpretations tend to develop through a series of modeling cycles in which the results of each cycle enable students to take into account new and different kinds of information, which, in turn, creates the need for additional refinements or embellishments in the underlying interpretation. In such problem solving situations, the development of students' ways of thinking tends to involve sorting out unstable conceptual systems at least as much as it involves assembling stable systems; and, as more sophisticated interpretations evolve, students often go beyond thinking *with* a given construct to thinking *about* the construct (e.g., by identifying assumptions that have been made and by identifying alternatives that might be appropriate under a variety of conditions).

Also, development tends to occur along a variety of relatively independent dimensions such as concrete–abstract, intuitive–formal, or situated–decontextualized. So, again, improvements tend to be multidimensional and unbounded, and, in general, the evolution of these systems obeys rules similar to those that apply to other complex, self-regulating, and continually adapting systems.

Three final characteristics should be mentioned that pertain to operational definitions involving the development of students, teachers, and programs. First, the development of these problem solvers tends to be highly interdependent. Even though, for some purposes, it may be possible to deal with the development of students, teachers, and programs as if they were isolated and independently functioning entities, in reality, they tend to be interdependent and indissociable. Second, when something (or someone) acts on any one of these complex systems, they tend to act back. Therefore, development is not solely the result of the passive acceptance of information. Third, researchers (as well as the instruments that they use) usually are integral parts of the systems that they are hoping to understand and explain. Therefore, observations often induce significant changes in the systems being observed, and small influences often lead to large effects that are essentially unpredictable. In other words, investigations involving the interdependent development of students, teachers, and programs involve many of the same characteristics that occur when complex and continually adapting systems are investigated in fields like physics, geology, astronomy, and biology. These characteristics include the following:

*Selectivity*: Observation involves an act of selection to distinguish signal from noise, to distinguish significant patterns from meaningless perturbations, and to select a productive level of detail to guide analysis. Therefore, different observers may emphasize or omit data (actions or contextual details) that are viewed as significant by participants, by other observers, or from other perspectives.

*Indeterminacy*: Observations often have a powerful influence on the phenomena being observed, and the only way to observe certain "objects" may be to induce changes in them and to observe their interactions with other phenomena.

*Subjectivity*: Observers cannot claim to represent the meaning that the activity has for the observed participant(s), only the meaning that the researcher-observer has developed.

*Reductionism*: The systems being investigated are not completely decomposable; that is, the systems as a whole are more than the simple sums of their parts, and characteristics of the parts are influenced by characteristics of the system as a whole.

*Decontextualization*: When a given system is isolated from other relevant systems and from the contexts that led to its development, some of its characteristics may be changed in significant ways.

*Reification*: Observations often accord a reality to the "observables" that conceals the inferential chain by which the researchers build representations of the relevant constructs.

*Dissociation*: Research observations occur within a larger social event (the research enterprise as a whole), which has its own participants (observer and observed), context (immediate social setting and surrounding research setting), purpose (observed task and overarching research aims), actions (including those of the researcher), and consequences.

# MULTITIERED TEACHING EXPERIMENTS PROVIDE MULTIDIMENSIONAL INTERACTING TRACES OF DEVELOPMENT

In Chapter 9 of this book, Lesh & Kelly describe techniques that were designed especially to investigate the multidimensional development of complex, interacting, self-regulating, and continually adapting systems (such as those associated with the models and conceptual systems that are used by students, groups, teachers, classes, schools, or school systems to structure their experiences). Consequently, multitiered teaching experiments were designed to investigate situations in which the challenges described in the previous section occur with regularity. Also, because multitiered teaching experiments focus on cognitive objectives of instruction, they provide alternatives to pretest–posttest designs for assessment, where the goals of instruction tend to be restricted to checklists of behavioral objectives. For this reason, it is possible for multitiered teaching experiments to go beyond being research designs for *observing* development; they also can be used as assessment designs for *documenting* development, and, at the same time, they can be used as instructional designs for *stimulating* and *facilitating* development. Within such a framework, optimization and documentation are not incompatible processes. In fact, the reflexivity of assessment and instruction is an analogue of the self-adaptive behaviors displayed by many living things that are capable of optimizing their performance in response to changing circumstances.

A typical multitiered teaching experiment involves three parallel and superimposed studies into the interacting development of students, teachers, and programs. The student-level study might be a 15-week investigation about the nature of students' developing ways of thinking about specially selected sequences of thought-revealing activities (Chapter 21, this volume). The teacher-level study might use the preceding tasks for students as the basis for teacher-level activities in which it is possible to investigate the development of teachers' integrated, mathematical, psychological, and pedagogical ways of thinking about students' evolving learning and problem solving abilities. Finally, the program-level study might use the tasks for students and teachers as contexts for investigating the development of relevant ways of thinking for administrators, parents, and policy makers concerning both the nature of their goals of instruction, and concerning the nature of high-quality teaching and learning environments.

Whereas thought-revealing activities for students are designed especially to reveal important characteristics of students' ways of thinking, multitiered teaching experiments also need to employ teacher-level activities in which teachers continually reveal, test, and refine or revise their ways of thinking. Examples of such teacher-level activities include generating: (a) observation sheets that colleagues could use to make significant observations about students as they are working in groups; (b) "ways of thinking sheets" that colleagues could use to give feedback to students about the strengths or weaknesses of their work; and (c) quality assessment procedures that colleagues could use to lead discussions with students aimed at assessing the quality of the products that students produce.

For the purposes of this chapter, three of the most important characteristics of multitiered teaching experiments are that:

1. They use formative feedback and consensus-building to provide conditions that make it possible for students, teachers, and/or programs to develop in directions that are continually "better" without basing the next steps on preconceived notions of "best."

2. They emphasize the use of self-documenting activities that encourage students, teachers, and/or programs to learn while simultaneously producing trails of documentation that reveal important characteristics about the nature of what is being learned.

3. The preceding trends allow inferences to be made about future developments that are likely to occur.

In other words, multitiered teaching experiments generate information that includes more than unorganized collections of isolated data points. The results also include traces of interactions, and these trajectories often lead to multidimensional descriptions of developing expertise.

One of the most important assumptions underlying the teacher level of multitiered teaching experiments is that, to improve teachers' teaching practices, it is not enough to ensure familiarity with a checklist of behavioral objectives; teachers also need to develop productive ways thinking about their teaching experiences. In particular, teachers need to develop productive ways of thinking about their students' learning and problem solving experiences.

## IN MULTITIERED TEACHING EXPERIMENTS, THE NATURE OF DEVELOPING ENTITIES EMERGES RETROSPECTIVELY

Cognitively guided instruction is a name that's been given to an approach to teacher development that focuses on helping teachers become "reflective practitioners" by becoming familiar with new insights about the nature of students' developing mathematical knowledge (T. Carpenter & Fennema, 1992). To implement cognitively guided instruction, one difficulty that arises is that, for nearly any given topic area in the K–12 mathematics or science curricula, too little is known about the nature of students' developing knowledge, and too little is known about the types of understanding that represent expert teacher-level knowledge. For example, for topics dealing with fractions or ratios, teachers surely need to develop deeper and higher order understandings than those needed by their students. But, what is the nature of such deeper and higher order understandings? It's clear that, in addition to understanding how relevant ideas develop psychologically (in the minds of students), teachers also benefit from knowing how the ideas developed historically (why did our ancestors need this idea?), logically (what alternative ways can the truth of the idea be established?), and instructionally (what alternative approaches to the topic are offered by textbooks or other curricular materials?). But, what other understandings might be needed? For most topic areas, researchers do not know the answers to this question yet. This is why multitiered teaching experiments emphasize the use of formative feedback and consensus-building, which do not require researchers to formulate a dictionary-style definition of an expert teacher before it is possible to help teachers develop in directions that are increasingly more effective. Also, rather than *telling teachers* about their students' ways of thinking, thought-revealing activities are used so that teachers can *make firsthand observations* about their students' ways of thinking.[4]

The preceding capabilities have important implications for those who are trying to formulate productive operational definitions for their instructional goals. To see why (and how) this is true, consider an educator who says, "I don't know how to define what I mean by a great teacher, but I know some important kinds of situations to look at, and I can point to

---

[4]Teachers' observations can lead to rich portrayals (or models) of their students provided that teachers have an adequate vocabulary of constructs with which to build their evolving ways of thinking. Given this, teachers construct a bottom-up model of the student that documents and celebrates each capability (and is informed by each difficulty) rather than documenting the gap between the student's current state of knowing and an idealized goal of a state of expertise. Emphasis on this gap commits the teacher to the documentation of deficiency rather than of accomplishment. Sweller (1992) has contrasted means–ends analysis with bottom-up approaches to problem solving in favor of the latter. Sweller's argument is that schema development or conceptual connectedness is facilitated by a bottom-up approach. Teachers' cumulative construction of their pupils' capability represents an analogous form of learning.

good teaching when I see it." What such educators are saying is that they know how to create situations to elicit and assess critical aspects of teaching, but they do not know yet how to deal with the third component that is needed to generate a three-part operational definition. That is, they do not know how to formulate an adequate multidimensional description of teachers' developing knowledge and abilities. But, within the kind of dynamic feedback systems that are emphasized in our multitiered approaches to research, assessment, and instruction, the nature of developing systems emerges at the end of the experience rather than being presupposed at the beginning.

When researchers or teachers know how to elicit and assess a construct (or system), these capabilities often make it possible to create a series of construct-refinement activities that will generate progressively clearer and more useful descriptions of developments that occur. For example, in studies of developing expertise of teachers (Lesh & Kelly, 1998), it is not necessary for a given description of expertise to be locked in at the beginning of a study (and used as the basis for a pretest–posttest design). Instead, increasingly sophisticated descriptions can be refined and documented gradually over the course of the study; and, at the end of the study, the validity of the description can be based on the trajectory of development that is revealed. In fact, as teachers, programs, and schools develop, their notions of excellence in teaching are primary factors that change. Therefore, if their progress continues to be measured using conceptions of excellence that existed at the beginning of a study, this practice tends to have significant negative influences on development.

## WHAT ARE "WAYS OF THINKING" FOR PROGRAMS, SCHOOLS, OR SCHOOL SYSTEMS?

Regardless of whether researchers investigate the development of individual students, groups, teachers, programs, schools, or school systems, a fundamental assumption underlying this chapter is that it is seldom sufficient to describe increasing expertise using only a checklist of behavioral objectives. For any of the preceding kinds of problem solvers, complex systems are involved, and excellent performance on complex tasks generally involves the development of powerful models (or *ways of thinking*) that provide meaningful ways to structure these experiences. But, what does it mean to speak about the ways of thinking of a program, a school, or a school system? By ways of thinking, we mean a system's interpretation (descriptions, explanations) of experiences. How can the nature of these ways of thinking be observed? How can their efficacy be assessed? Our answer to these questions is that procedures should be investigated that have been effective in other sciences where the systems being investigated also are complex, dynamic, and continually adapting.

Chapter 3 of this book, which is about identifying priority problems for research (Lesh & Lovitts), describes several ways that, during the past decade, researchers in mathematics and science education have fundamentally revised their ways of thinking about: (a) the nature of mathematics or science, (b) the nature of real-life decision-making situations in which these ideas are useful, and (c) the nature of productive teaching and learning. In general, when attention focuses on students or teachers, emerging new perspectives have shifted away from machine metaphors for describing development; instead, they emphasize perspectives that are more systemic, more organic, and better aligned with constructivist philosophies about the nature of learning and development. Yet, when attention shifts beyond students and teachers to focus on programs, schools, or school systems, development continues to be described using factory-based metaphors borrowed from an industrial age.

When old-fashioned factory models are used to conceptualize the development of complex systems, both teaching and learning tend to be treated as if they were similar to the process of assembling an automobile or another inert machine. Rather than molding and shaping the activities of living systems, these systemic wholes are treated as if they were nothing more than the sum of their parts. Furthermore, it is assumed that, when someone (or something) acts on these systems, they do not act back. In particular, observers (and tests) are considered to be completely objective and detached from the systems being observed.

When machine metaphors are used to think about curricular improvements in schools, the overall process might be called a conformance model for trying to improve instruction. Such an approach begins by defining fixed conceptions of desired outcomes. Then, participants are coerced to teach to tests that tend to be treated as de facto operational definitions of these standards. But, for reasons we've described earlier in this chapter, negative characteristics of this approach arise because the scope, length, and depth of tests generally force them to restrict attention to simplistic notions of expertise and to low-level tasks that are aligned poorly with intended instructional goals.

An alternative to conformance models for curriculum change might be called planned experimentation. It is an approach that is used commonly in modern businesses; and, it tends to be especially useful in situations where: (a) rapid adaptation is needed, (b) a "one size fits all" policy is hopelessly out of date, and (c) huge centralized, top-down, management styles are far too slow and insensitive to local needs. It also is an approach that is especially relevant to the development of nearly any community of complex adapting systems, including those that are similar to biological organisms rather than to inert machines.

As Darwin's theory of evolution suggests, diversity and variation are necessary ingredients for evolution to occur. They are not incompatible processes. In fact, if there is no diversity or no selection, then the relevant systems are not likely to evolve. Other necessary processes include selection, cross-fertilization, and preservation across time.

In the context of schools and programs of instruction, what the preceding principles imply is that the goal of assessment should be to improve performance, not merely to audit it. In particular, assessment should anticipate action (Clarke, 1996). It should be longitudinal and recursive; optimization and documentation should not be treated as if they were incompatible processes, and diversity should be encouraged as long as it is coupled with effective selection procedures to promote development.

When a planned experiment is used to improve instruction in schools, an important assumption is that, as the system develops, participants' conceptions of goals become much more clear, powerful, and sophisticated. Therefore, descriptions of expertise should not be locked in at the beginning of projects. Instead, these descriptions should be tested, revised, and refined gradually over the course of the project; and, the conceptions of excellence that evolve can be based on trails of documentation that accumulate. How can systems get better without beginning with a fixed and final definition of best? Regardless whether we are investigating complex systems that develop in education, the arts, crafts, sports, or professions like business or engineering, what we need are the abilities to elicit, observe, and assess the relevant constructs - not necessarily the ability to produce dictionary-style definitions, and certainly not the willingness to reduce goals to checklists of simple rules.

Contexts that elicit complex performances don't necessarily require the relevant participants to reveal observable ways of thinking; and, they also don't necessarily provide useful tools for comparing or assessing the quality of competing systems. Nonetheless, it often is not difficult to identify situations that require the relevant systems to be elicited and revealed, and it often is not difficult to identify ways to compare and assess the results that are produced. For example, we may not know how to define what makes Granny a great cook; however, it still may be easy to identify situations that will elicit and reveal her capabilities, and it also may be easy to compare and assess alternative results that are produced.

In general, to formulate useful operational definitions of complex, dynamic, and continually adapting systems, it is not always necessary to begin by producing a precise dictionary-style descriptions accompanied by ways to measure distances from this ideal. Sometimes, it is sufficient to specify: (a) how to elicit the system; (b) how to observe its characteristics; and (c) how to compare the alternatives that occur. Then, when these capabilities exist, it often is possible to create a series of interactions that involve iterative, formative, feedback loops that produce a trail of documentation that reveals the nature of the evolving system.

If we apply this approach to the development of programs, schools, or school systems, the first tools that are needed are contexts that can be used to get programs (or schools, or school systems) to reveal their relevant ways of thinking. Possibilities include: (a) curricular goals that are formulated; (b) alternative assessment instruments that are developed; (c) progress reports that are created to describe achievements; (d) dissemination and implementation plans that are adopted to facilitate improvement; and (e) teacher development activities that are offered to promote change. Then, in addition to identifying the kinds of contexts that are required for eliciting and revealing relevant ways of thinking, criteria also are needed that can be used to compare or assess the products that are generated.

Fortunately, finding ways to compare or assess the effectiveness of products that are generated by schools tends to be no more mysterious than finding ways to compare and assess the results of Granny's cooking. But, in the case of schools, judgments about quality nearly always should involve students' achievement. Therefore, when carrying out such processes, some important principles to keep in mind include the following:

1.  Achievement usually needs to be assessed using something more than brief tests that reduce expertise to simplistic lists of condition–action rules.

2.  Students' relevant products or performances usually should include more than those that can be interpreted and assessed easily by a machine.

3.  Emphasis needs to shift beyond superficial coverage of a large number of small tasks to the comprehensive treatment of a small number of big ideas.

4.  Quality ratings should not ignore the conditions under which complex performances occur, and complex profiles should not be collapsed into simplistic scores on a scale that recognizes only a single dimension along which progress can be made.

## COMPLEX SYSTEMS: TO KNOW THEM IS TO CHANGE THEM

To end this chapter about ways of formulating productive operational definitions of complex constructs in mathematics and science education, it is appropriate that we find ourselves returning to issues about students' ways of thinking, and about relationships between behavioral objectives and deeper cognitive objectives of instruction. It also is appropriate that we reconsider one of the most prevalent and damaging myths related to educational assessment: the assumption that assessment does not (and should not) induce changes in the entities being assessed.

For those familiar with Heisenberg's indeterminacy principle in physics, it is a familiar notion that to measure a construct is to change it. Therefore, it should come as no surprise that similar principles also may apply to the kinds of complex, dynamic, and continually adapting systems that occur in mathematics and science education. To know them is to interact with them; and, to interact with them often involves changing them in fundamental ways. For example, in the case of studies assessing the effectiveness of teaching (or programs, or curricular materials), standardized tests often go beyond being used as neutral indicators of learning outcomes. If they are used to clarify instructional goals, they often become powerful components of the initiatives themselves (Clarke & Stephens, 1996). Consequently, far from being passive assessments of non-adapting systems, they may have powerful positive or negative effects, depending on whether they support or subvert objectives of the relevant systems.

In mathematics and science education, there is another fundamental way that assessments often change the nature of the systems being observed. That is, even at the level of students' thinking about individual problem solving situations, it tends to be undesirable (and virtually impossible) to devise assessment tasks in which no learning is likely to occur. For example, for the kind of thought-revealing activities that we have advocated in this chapter, the interpretations that students are challenged to produce inherently involve significant forms of learning. This is because the new models and ways of thinking that develop often require previously existing conceptual systems to be integrated, differentiated, extended, or refined in significant ways. Furthermore, if the graphs, charts, diagrams, spreadsheets, and other symbolic descriptions that students generate are shareable, reusable, easily modifiable, and transportable beyond one particular situation, then they often represent significant forms of generalization and higher order thinking.

The preceding kind of thought-revealing activities emphasize that, above all, thinking mathematically involves interpreting situations by quantifying them, coordinatizing them, and mathematizing them in other ways. It is at best a half-truth to claim that elementary mathematics is about numbers and computation; it is also about quantities and quantitative relationships. Consequently, by treating mathematics as being (only) about numbers and operations with numbers, traditional textbooks and tests have tended to trivialize the interpretation stages of problem solving. For example, the results that students are requested to produce seldom include descriptions, explanations, or justifications in which they must reveal and test explicitly how they interpret problem solving situations; and, even in cases where a mathematical interpretation needs to be generated, the kinds of quantification that are involved rarely go beyond simple counts and measures. Yet, the kinds of situations that children should be able to use numbers to describe include those involving ranks and positions (coordinates), signed quantities (such as those involving negatives and positives), quantities assigned to qualitative information (such as those involving weights or values), multivalued quantities (such as those involving magnitude and direction), relationships among quantities (ratios), actions or transformations (such as those involving stretching, shrinking, or exchanging operations), changing quantities (rates involving "per" quantities), intensive quantities (such as those involving "-ness" quantities like denseness, and speediness), or accumulating quantities.

## SUMMARY AND CONCLUSIONS

An abiding goal of education is the specification of the desired outcomes of instruction in observable and assessable forms. As our conception of valued outcomes becomes more sophisticated, as we move from behavioral objectives to cognitive objectives, as we come to acknowledge the complexity of the settings in which we work, and as we come to recognize the symbiotic character of the constructs that we seek to assess within their encompassing systems, so our assessment (and research) must develop in subtlety and complexity.

In this chapter, analogies with detection systems from physical science have been used to point to similarities in the challenges posed by the study of constructs only observable indirectly, whether in educational systems or in physical systems. These similarities are important. They allow us to benefit from conceptual advances made in other disciplines and to validate the rigor of our own methods through their correspondence with the endorsed practices of other communities.

The identification of the three-fold character of model-eliciting activities provides a generalizable structure for the practical manifestation of valued educational constructs. This structure focuses attention (as classroom practitioners or as educational researchers, for instance) on activities that create situations conducive to the constructs to be studied, requires products or observation tools through which the construct is made manifest, and produces these products in a form amenable to assessment against specified criteria for quality. In their combination, these three elements—situations, products, and quality assessment criteria—constitute the operationalization of the construct in question.

This chapter has identified cognitive objectives as appropriate goals for contemporary instruction. Ways of thinking represent an elaboration of this conception of cognitive objectives in a form applicable to individuals and to educational systems. Multitiered teaching experiments represent one approach to the study of such systems; they are discussed in greater detail in other chapters.

Starting from an acknowledgment of the inevitable perturbation of the observed system in the act of assessment, perhaps the most contentious of the suggestions put forward in this chapter is advocacy of the use of assessment to change the observed system purposefully toward the desired outcomes. In this, the authors anticipate the development of assessment systems that both reveal valued constructs and deliberately prompt adaptations within the systems studied in directions advantageous to the system or to the individual whose performances are assessed.

# APPENDIX A: Quality Assurance Guide

This Quality Assurance Guide is designed to help teachers (and students) evaluate the products that are developed in response to model-eliciting activities with the following characteristics: the goal is to develop a conceptual tool. (b) the client who needs the tool is clearly identified. (c) the client's purposes are known, and (d) the tool must be sharable with other people and must be useful in situations where the data are different than those specified in the problem.

| Performance Level | How useful is the product? | What might the client say? | What questions should be asked? |
| --- | --- | --- | --- |
| Requires Redirection | The product is on the wrong track. Working longer or harder won't work. The students may require some additional feedback from the teacher. | *"Start over. This won't work. Think about it differently. Use different ideas or procedures."* | To assess students' work, put yourself in the role of the client. To do this, it's necessary to be clear about answers to the following questions. 1. Who is the client? 2. What conceptual tool does the client need? 3. What does the client need to be able to do with the tool? |
| Requires Major Extensions or Refinements | The product is a good start toward meeting the client's needs, but a lot more work is needed to respond to all of the issues. | *"You're on the right track, but this still needs a lot more work before it'll be in a form that's useful."* | Then, the quality of students' work can be determined by focusing on the question—*How useful is the tool for the purposes of the client?* To assess usefulness, and to identify strengths and weaknesses of different results that students produce, it would be helpful to consider the following questions. |
| Requires Only Minor Editing | The product is nearly ready to be used. It still needs a few small modifications, additions, or refinements. | *"Hmmm, this is close to what I need. You just need to add or change a few small things."* | 1. What information, relationships, and patterns does the tool take into account? 2. Were appropriate ideas and procedures chosen for dealing with this information? 3. Were any technical errors made in using the preceding ideas and procedures? |
| Useful for this Specific Data Given | No changes will be needed to meets the immediate needs of the client. | *"Ahhh, this will work well as it is. I won't even need to do any editing."* | But, the central question is—*Does the product meet the client's needs?* |
| Sharable or Reusable | The tool not only works for the immediate situation, but it also would be easy for others to modify and use it in similar situations. | *"Excellent, this tool will be easy for me to modify or use in other similar situations—when the data are slightly different."* | The product should make it clear that: (1) The students went beyond producing a tool that *they* themselves could use to also produce a tool that *others* could use—by including needed explanations, and by making it as simple, clear, and well organized as possible.; (2) the students went beyond thinking *with* the tool to also think *about* it—by identifying underlying assumptions (so that others know when the tool might need to be modified for use in similar situations); (3) the students went beyond *blind* thinking to also think *about* their thinking—by recognizing strength and weaknesses of their approach compared with other possible alternatives. |

This guide is the fourth of four tools that are useful for making sense of students' work related to model-eliciting activities. The first tool is an "Observation Sheet" that can be used to observe the processes that students' thinking goes through to develop final responses. The second tool is a "Ways of Thinking Sheet" that can be used to sort out strengths and weaknesses of the alternative results that students produce. The third tool is a "Self Reflection Sheet" that helps students reflect about roles they may have played during problem solution, feelings, and attitudes that may have influence performance.

# APPENDIX B

## The Softball Problem

To begin the Softball Problem, teachers often read the newspaper article and discuss the warm-up questions on the day before they want students to begin work on the main activity. This helps students become familiar with the situation before they are expected to begin work, and it also eliminates a lot of "wheel spinning" during the actual problem solving session.

### The 'Crack' of the Bat Rings Throughout Central Indiana Town and Across Fields During Summer Evenings

Summer is underway which means only one thing to the people in town of Gasburg: softball season has arrived. For many children in this Central Indiana town, softball is an annual tradition where players learn about competition, friendship and establish many fond memories.

But some parents are trying to make changes to the Gasburg Town Summer League, which has basically remained unchanged since the league was founded in 1946. The main change which parents want is equal competition between the teams. And they want it now.

This season—like seasons past—one team will most likely run away with the league title. Each year, one coach seems to get the best players in the town to be on the same team, which demolishes the competition. "Last year the Rib Shack won all of their games. Their closest win was a 10-3 win," said Kelsey Emonds. Emonds, a four-year veteran outfielder in the league, will compete in her final season before moving on to play softball in high school next year. "It's kind of sad. One part of me wants to play at this park forever and another part of me wants to move on to high school softball this season because I am tired of the unfair teams."

During her four years in the league, Emonds was on a team that breezed through the competition and then re-assigned the next year to a team that "was the joke of the league," said Emonds.

"I remember for the first three years, I was on a team with the neighborhood girls and we all played softball competitively," said Emonds. "Then I was placed on this new team which had players that couldn't play very well. It was a really bad year."

The team only won one game all season long in the 25-game season. "I just hope we have a better year. It's my last year and I want to go out with a better record and have a chance at winning a championship."

Mike Browning, league president, has expressed a concern about how teams are chosen and is trying to establish a new method of dividing interested players into fair teams.

"Attendance has dropped a lot," said Browning. "It's really not asking much to want to see a game in which the two teams are actually competing against one another."

Some changes might be coming in the way teams are assigned. Every spring, the league holds tryouts and practice games before the season starts. At the tryouts, players are tested in three different events: batting, throwing, and base running.

Currently, each player will get 10 at-bats at the tryouts. Players will be timed running from first base to second base three times and will have five chances to throw from centerfield after catching a ball.

If Browning and other parents have their way, the current system of having coaches pick the players would be abolished and the league would assign the players every year.

"The softball league hasn't changed much in over 50 years," said Browning. "If we don't make changes now, people will be so turned off to softball that we won't exist in another 10 years."

## Warm-up Questions

Answer the following questions after reviewing the article and the data.

1. Why are people, e.g. parents, coaches and players, upset with the current system?
2. Who is Mike Browning?
3. Who is Kelsey Emonds?
4. What team dominated the league last year?
5. Has this been the case in other instances in the past?
6. Who threw the farthest of all the participants?

7. Who ran the fastest of all the participants?

8. Did the same person throw the farthest and run the fastest also?

9. Who had the highest batting average?

TABLE B1

| Person | Throw in ft. | | Batting | | | | Run in seconds |
|---|---|---|---|---|---|---|---|
| Tisha | 81 | 65 | double | Single | single | pop-fly | 7.2 |
| | 79 | 61 | single | pop fly | pop fly | single | 6.9 |
| | 69 | | pop-fly | sac fly | | | 6.9 |
| Kim | 67 | 61 | Pop-fly | Pop-fly | Sac-fly | Home | 5.1 |
| | 66 | 59 | Sac-fly | Sac-fly | Triple | run | 5.3 |
| | 66 | | Triple | Ground out | | Double | 5.1 |
| Sally | 83 | 75 | Home run | Ground out | Pop-fly | Sac-fly | 5.9 |
| | 80 | 82 | Single | Double | Ground-out | Double | 6. |
| | 80 | | Sac-fly | Pop-fly | | | 6.2 |
| Barb | 97 | 89 | Triple | Ground-out | Pop-fly | Sac-fly | 6.4 |
| | 98 | 90 | Ground-out | Ground-out | Single | Sac-fly | 6.3 |
| | 91 | | Single | Pop-fly | | | 6.3 |
| Melissa | 98 | 88 | Pop-fly | Home run | Single | Double | 6.3 |
| | 90 | 86 | Double | Ground-out | Sac-fly | Ground- | 6.5 |
| | 84 | | Sac-fly | Pop-fly | | out | 6.7 |
| Charlene | 86 | 77 | Single | Strike out | Pop-fly | Ground- | 6.5 |
| | 83 | 80 | Double | Ground out | Pop-fly | out | 7.1 |
| | 65 | | Strike-out | Sac-fly | | Sac-fly | 6.5 |
| Cynthia | 72 | 72 | Strike out | Pop-fly | Strike-out | Double | 6.9 |
| | 72 | 69 | Ground-out | Strike-out | Double | Strike- | 6.1 |
| | 71 | | Strike-out | Pop-fly | | out | 6.4 |
| Rebecca | 49 | 56 | Strike-out | Strike-out | Single | Strike- | 5.5 |
| | 52 | 54 | Strike-out | Pop-fly | Double | out | 5.7 |
| | 56 | | Ground-out | Double | | Single | 5.6 |
| Beth | 61 | 54 | Single | Sac-fly | Ground-out | Pop-fly | 5.9 |
| | 61 | 59 | Double | Triple | Single | Home- | 6.0 |
| | 57 | | Strike-out | Ground-out | | run | 5.9 |
| Mary Pat | 53 | 50 | Strike-out | Strike-out | Pop-fly | Triple | 6.5 |
| | 57 | 37 | Sac-fly | double | Single | Single | 6.2 |
| | 52 | | Sac-fly | sac-fly | | | 6.4 |
| Kathy | 98 | 90 | Strike-out | Pop-fly | Double | Strike- | 5.6 |
| | 97 | 92 | Single | Pop-fly | Pop-fly | out | 5.9 |
| | 99 | | single | Sac-fly | | Sac-fly | 5.4 |
| Esther | 90 | 87 | Strike-out | Strike-out | Single | Sac-fly | 6.1 |
| | 90 | 85 | Strike-out | Double | Single | Double | 6.4 |
| | 86 | | Sac-fly | Sac-fly | | | 6.2 |
| Kelly | 80 | 80 | Home-run | Strike-out | Home-run | Pop-fly | 5.2 |
| | 79 | 82 | Strike-out | Double | Strike-out | Pop-fly | 5.1 |
| | 77 | | Strike-out | Triple | | | 4.9 |

## Key For Hitting Evaluation

1.  A strike-out occurs when a person gets three strikes before she hits the ball or gets four balls (a walk).
2.  A pop-fly occurs when a person hits the ball in the air and another individual catches the ball before it hits the ground. An out is achieved.
3.  A ground-out occurs when a person hits the ball and a fielder catches it and throws it to first before the batter arrives. An out is achieved.
4.  A Sac-fly occurs when a person hits the ball in the air and a person catches it. Unlike a pop-fly a base-runner advances to the next base.
5.  A single occurs when a person hits the ball and she gets to first base before the ball arrives.
6.  A double occurs when a person hits the ball and she gets to second base before the ball arrives.
7.  A triple occurs when a person hits the ball and she gets to third base before the ball arrives.
8.  A home-run occurs when a person hits the ball over the fence or when a person hits the ball and arrives home before the ball arrives.

## Coaches' Comments

Tisha: She has great fielding skills. Also she is very easy to work with. Her father was a professional baseball player.

Kim: Very fast athlete. She can get around the bases quickly and to balls quickly. She has gotten along well with teammates in the past.

Sally: No comments available.

Barb: She has a very strong arm and she is capable of playing several positions in a game.

Melissa: Fields exceptionally well. Her batting was improved near the end of the year.

Charlene: She's very mature for her age. When her coordination catches up with her age, she could be quite good.

Cynthia: Does many things well.

Rebecca: She knows more about the game than anyone else that I've coached. Her father played college baseball.

Beth: She's a very good offensive weapon and she plays well in the outfield.

Mary Pat: She does many things well, but she doesn't stand out in one area.

Kathy: She has a great throwing arm. This was the first year she ever played and she has the potential to become a great athlete.

Esther: No comments available.

Kelly: She helps the younger athletes. However, she has been known to miss games.

# 7 Progress in Research: The Interplay Among Theory, Research Questions, and Measurement Techniques

**Jose P. Mestre**

*University of Massachusetts–Amherst*

One often thinks of research as a cumulative endeavor by which "bricks" of empirical evidence are laid one on top of the other to form a "building" of knowledge. Long before the building is complete, we often construct theories to predict the building's looks and functionality, and further research provides additional bricks of knowledge that can be used to confirm, or refine, our theories. Although this architectural analogy may bear a close similarity to how research and theory progress in the natural sciences, I would argue that the analogy is more an idealization than a reality when dealing with educational research. In many cases, the construction or refinement of a theory is hampered by the very technique used to answer research questions. That is, the techniques and measures used to answer research questions, especially in the early stages of developing a theory, drive both the kinds of research questions one can ask and the refinement of the theory itself.

In this chapter, I provide a personal perspective on the interplay among theory, research questions, and measurement techniques for answering research questions. I draw upon my own field of expertise—physics education research—and upon my own research to provide concrete examples of how the measures we use in research often drive the development of theories. I argue that once a technique has been chosen to address research questions, the *type* of information that we hope to extract from the study is limited to a great extent. It is often the case that what we are interested in finding out from an investigation cannot be extracted from the data obtained from a single measuring technique. How, then, does one decide on the appropriate mix of techniques in order to make steady progress in building and refining our theories? There is no simple answer to this question; at least, there are no clear-cut criteria for

151

devising techniques for attacking particular research questions or for building or refining theories. What this chapter attempts to do is to provide researchers with perspectives to help them frame an answer.

## MATCHING THE METHODOLOGY TO THE RESEARCH QUESTIONS

Having a set of well-defined research questions precedes the selection of measuring techniques for investigating them. Once the research questions have been identified, one can begin to consider multiple measuring techniques that will generate multiple perspectives on the research questions. Perhaps what is most difficult about designing a research study is playing devil's advocate and second-guessing nagging questions that might remain after the methodology and techniques have been selected and the data have been collected. Is it likely that the methodologies and techniques chosen might yield data that are open to several interpretations? If so, can one devise complementary methodologies and techniques that help one to distinguish among them?

### Example 1: Just How "Novice" Are Novices and How "Expert" Are Experts?

#### *Background*

The first example that I use comes from studies on the nature of expertise in physics initiated over a decade ago. Our research group was engaged in a series of studies investigating whether it was possible to induce expertlike behavior in physics novices following a treatment in which the novices were asked to solve problems using a specific regimen. Undergraduate students who had completed successfully a calculus-based, introductory mechanics course with a grade of B or better (i.e., "good" novices) were asked to solve a number of physics problems over a period of several weeks using a computer-based, menu-driven tool that constrained them to follow a hierarchical problem analysis before solving the problems. The analysis began by asking the students to identify the major principle(s) that could be applied to solve the problem under consideration. Once the major principle was selected, the analysis proceeded to narrow the application of the principle to the specific context of the problem and included the identification of procedures for applying the principle and the resulting equations. The computer-based tool was designed to be consonant with the best knowledge at that time of how experts analyzed and solved physics problems. The study compared this hierarchical treatment's ability to induce expertlike behavior with the ability of other treatments in which the subjects used other more novicelike approaches to solve the same problems.

I do not go into great detail on the general thrust of the studies.[1] Rather, I draw on one small but crucial question on which our investigations hinged, namely: How does one measure expertlike behavior among novices? That is, in order to be able to answer our most fundamental research question: Did good novices exhibit expertlike, problem solving behavior following the hierarchical treatment?, we needed to have ways of measuring expertlike, problem solving behavior. This led to spin-off studies that attempted to evaluate techniques for measuring the degrees to which novices behaved like experts.

At the time, the seminal works of several researchers had shed light on the general, problem solving, behavior patterns exhibited by experts and novices in physics. For example, it was known that experts tended to solve problems strategically, proceeding from principles, concepts, and procedures toward equations, whereas novices tended to solve problems tactically, manipulating equations forward and backward in an attempt to "reduce the distance" between the "knowns" in the problem and the "unknown" that the problem asked for (Larkin, 1981, 1983; Larkin, J. McDermott, D. P. Simon, & H. A. Simon, 1980; D. P. Simon & H. A. Simon, 1978). When asked to articulate the approach they would use to solve a problem, experts usually started by describing the principles, concepts, and procedures they would apply, whereas novices tended to identify the equations they would use to get an answer. Finally, when asked to categorize problems according to similarity of solution, experts tended to group together problems that were solved using the same principle(s), whereas novices tended to group together problems that shared the same surface characteristics (e.g., problems involving inclined planes were grouped together regardless of whether or not they could be solved by applying the same principle) (Chi, Feltovich, & R. Glaser, 1981).

---

[1] For those interested in going beyond what is covered in this article, the results of these studies have been published in the following sources: Dufresne, Gerace, Hardiman, and Mestre (1992); Mestre, Dufresne, Gerace, Hardiman, and Touger (1992, 1993).

We thought a problem categorization task offered promise for measuring gradations in level of expertise, but previous categorization techniques did not have the sensitivity to measure the gradations that we desired. The technique that had been used by Chi et al. (1981) was a card-sorting task: A physics problem was written on an index card, and the subject was handed a stack of cards and asked to group them into piles, with the problems in the same pile being those that would be solved using a similar approach. The data were analyzed with cluster analysis techniques, which highlight the salient categorization differences among groups of subjects (e.g., experts and novices) but do not provide detailed information about progression along the expertise dimension. For example, although two novices could show the same tendencies to categorize according to the surface characteristics of problems, the piles of problems they formed were likely to differ enough to prohibit making any precise statement about which of the two novices was further along the expertise dimension. Hence, the "theory" at the time from card-sorting categorization studies could provide broad generalizations about the problem attributes that experts and novices cued on when solving problems, but it could not provide fine gradations about the degree of deep-structure versus surface-feature cuing as a function of degree of expertise.

## Designing the Techniques

*The Three-Problem Categorization Task.* The treatment that we were evaluating lasted five hours. In this short time, we did not expect that any possible shift toward expertlike behavior among novices would be very large. If it were, the findings would imply that we should be able to turn out experts in short order, something that is clearly not possible. Hence, we needed a measurement technique that would be sensitive to small pre- to posttreatment differences in expertlike behavior, and the card-sorting task did not offer this level of sensitivity. To get around this problem, we devised our own categorization methodology, which yielded only quantitative data (Hardiman, Dufresne, & Mestre, 1989). This methodology, which I call the *three-problem categorization task,* consisted of a paper-and-pencil assessment containing many items, each item consisting of three problems, a "model problem" and two "comparison problems." The subject was asked to read all three problems and to decide which of the two comparison problems would be solved most like the model problem, without solving any of the problems. The following is an example of such an item:

*Model Problem*: A 2.5 kg ball of radius 4 cm is traveling at 7 m/s on a rough horizontal surface but not spinning. Some distance later, the ball is rolling without slipping at 5 m/s. How much work was done by friction?

*Comparison Problem 1*: A 3 kg soccer ball of radius 15 cm is initially sliding at 10 m/s without spinning. The ball travels on a rough horizontal surface and eventually rolls without slipping. Find the ball's final velocity.

*Comparison Problem 2*: A small rock of mass 10 g falling vertically hits a very thick layer of snow and penetrates 2 m before coming to rest. If the rock's speed was 25 m/s just prior to hitting the snow, find the average force exerted on the rock by the snow.

Four different types of comparison problems were constructed to share certain attributes with the model problem. An "S" comparison problem was one that shared the same surface characteristics as the model problem; the first comparison problem just described is of the "S" type. A "D" comparison problem shared the same deep structure with the model problem (e.g., the same principle(s) and procedure would be used to solve it and the model problem); the second comparison problem in the previous example is a "D" type. An "SD" comparison problem matched the model problem on both surface characteristics and deep structure. Finally, an "N" comparison problem shared neither surface characteristics nor deep structure with the model problem. Four pairings of comparison problems were used in the items: S-D, S-SD, N-D, and N-SD, so that only one of the comparison problems in each item matched the model problem on deep structure; and consequently, it and the model problem would be solved using a similar approach.

Previous research suggested that a "true" novice would categorize on the basis of surface characteristics and that a "true" expert would categorize on the basis of deep structure. Table 7.1 gives the predicted, as well as actual, performance patterns of experts and novices, where correct performance on an item here means selecting the comparison problem that matched the deep structure of the model problem.

Unlike the card-sorting task, this technique provided additional details to help refine the "experts sort according to deep structure and novices sort according to surface features" theory. In addition, the technique yielded data that were easy to analyze and that resulted in a "score" that presumably was based on a subject's ability to select problems that are solved by applying the same principle(s). Hence, at first glance, it appeared that it might be possible from this technique to begin to refine the theory with statements about the interaction (i.e., competing influence) of surface features and deep structure in problem categorization between novices and experts.

TABLE 7.1

Predicted and Observed Percentage of Correct Responses for Experts and Novices in Three-Problem Categorization Task

| Item Type | Experts (N = 10) | | Novices (N = 45) | |
|---|---|---|---|---|
| | Predicted | Observed | Predicted | Observed |
| S-D* | 100 | 66 | 0 | 26 |
| S-SD[†] | 100 | 71 | 50 | 54 |
| N-D[†] | 100 | 84 | 50 | 67 |
| N-SD[§] | 100 | 91 | 100 | 87 |
| Total | 100 | 78 | 50 | 59 |

\* S-D = surface features, deep structure
† S-SD = surface features, both surface features and deep structure
‡ N-D = no match, deep structure
§ N-SD = no match, both surface features and deep structure

On closer scrutiny, however, this score provided limited information about the subject's reasoning. It became evident that we could not presume that, just because a subject matched the deep-structure comparison problem to the model problem, the subject was cuing on deep structure. Despite the fact that the performance pattern was aligned with the predicted performance pattern, without knowing the reasoning that the subjects used to make their decisions, we could not use this technique to assign a level of expertlike behavior to a subject's score. Further, inferring the subjects' reasons for their categorization decisions from this technique could be misleading. For example, a misidentified principle might have led to an incorrect response, even though the novice might be cuing on deep structure, or, perhaps, a subject could have arrived at a correct response without cuing on deep structure.

Although the methodology did not meet our needs, it did reveal some interesting findings. The deviation of the experts' performance from their predicted performance was large enough to be surprising. At 78%, the overall ability of the experts to select the comparison problem that matched the model problem in deep structure was far from the 100% predicted from the theory. Therefore, the findings suggested that surface characteristics could distract experts from cuing on deep structure, something that was not known prior to this experiment (for a discussion of the ramifications of this finding, see Hardiman et al., 1989). In short, this technique demonstrated that the current theory was too simplistic and that there was "fine structure" to the theory. However, without further details about the reasoning used to make categorization decisions, we could not describe this fine structure in any detail, so we were not able to advance the theory to any great extent with this technique. In terms of the architectural analogy presented earlier, although this technique provided another brick of empirical evidence, when this brick was laid upon the existing building of knowledge, it did not reveal a great deal more of the building's looks or functionality.

*The Two-Problem Categorization Task.* Clearly, there was a need for another methodology that would allow better triangulation on the type of reasoning that the subjects used to make categorization decisions. We believed that if we had the subjects' reasoning available, we would be able to judge the degree to which they were cuing on principles to make categorization decisions and, thereby, reveal the "fine structure" in the general theory.

The new technique that we devised differed from the former in two respects. First, the items in the new categorization task had only two problems: a model problem and a comparison problem. The comparison problem could match the model problem on surface characteristics (S), on deep structure (D), on both surface characteristics and deep structure (SD), or on neither (N). The second difference was that, now, the subjects were asked to state not only whether or not the two problems would be solved using a similar approach, but also the reasons underlying their decisions. With the subjects' reasons available, we would have an independent way of determining the degree to which they cued on surface characteristics versus deep structure. Thus, this technique was able to produce both quantitative and qualitative data.

The data now revealed that the experts performed more in accord with projections. Overall, the experts' performance was correct 95% of the time (i.e., they stated that the two problems would be solved similarly in the D and SD items and that they would not be solved similarly on the S and N items). Their reasoning was based on physics principles 93% of the time, with the principles being identified correctly 98% of the time. On the other hand, the novices' performance was correct 62% of the time. Further, the percentage of items on which novices used reasoning based on physics principles was 28%. Despite this seemingly low frequency of principle-based reasoning, the qualitative data revealed that 25% of the novices used principle-based reasoning over 70% of the time, whereas 39% of the novices used principle-based reasoning only 6% of the time. The remaining subjects used a mixture of principle-based, surface-feature-based, and equation-based reasoning. In keeping with what one might expect, the type of reasoning used by the novices correlated well with problem solving performance. On an independent assessment of problem solving, the 25% of the novices who categorized problems based on principles scored highest (57% score), whereas the 39% of the novices who did not categorize problems based on principles scored considerably lower (14%); the remaining subjects who used a mixture of reasoning scored 32% on the problem solving assessment (for details, see Hardiman et al., 1989).

As it turned out, it was the "state-your-reasons" qualitative data from the two-problem categorization task that were the most useful for measuring the gradations along the expertise dimension that we sought for the novice group. Although performance based on the quantitative matching data tracked with the degree of principle-based reasoning (overall performance for the principle-based, mixed, and surface-feature reasoners was 69%, 63%, and 56%, respectively), the overall categorization performance of the three groups did not differ enough to give us the sensitivity we needed. On the other hand, regardless of whether the actual reasoning employed was correct, we were able to use the subjects' predisposition to use principle-based reasoning in making categorization decisions as a sensitive measure of "expertlike behavior."

## How "the sum of the parts was greater than the whole" in refining the theory

Looking at the two experiments together provides an additional perspective on the theory, which one experiment by itself could not do. To illustrate this point, consider the fact that in the two-problem task, the performance of the experts was much closer to that predicted by the theory than in the three-problem task. Was this because, in the two-problem task, the experts had to provide an explanation, and the explanation forced them to evaluate the deep structure of the problems, whereas in the three-problem task, they may have become lazy and made an educated guess more often? We explained this somewhat surprising result (see Hardiman et al, 1989) in terms of a model of the threshold type (E. E. Smith, Shoben, & Rips, 1974).

For example, if in the three-problem task, the initial perception of similarity of one of the comparison problems to the model problem was high, a threshold model would predict that the subject would be predisposed to make a response on the basis of this overall impression of similarity without conducting a thorough analysis. There is evidence for this in the experts' relatively high rate of choosing the surface feature alternative in the S-D and N-SD items where surface features were in competition with alternatives that had no obvious superficial similarity to the model problem. If neither comparison problem succeeded in crossing the threshold of similarity (e.g., the N-D items), then the subjects were forced to consider other criteria on which to base their categorization decision (e.g., deep structure). The two-problem task suggests that when asked to provide their reasoning, experts tend not to be tempted to rely on the impression of similarity; asking for their reasoning appears to bypass the temptation to rely on surface similarity, as the threshold model would suggest. Additional research is required to verify this theoretical conjecture.

## Example 2: Probing Conceptual Understanding in Physics With a New Technique

Example 1, discussed in the previous section, illustrates how measurement techniques can place severe limits on the research questions that we can answer as well as on the theories that we can build. Example 2 illustrates how possessing a somewhat refined theory allows one to be critical of the measurement techniques, which in turn leads to advances in measurement techniques that allow one to answer more refined questions and to refine the theory further.

### Background

A prerequisite for skilled performance is a rich and well-structured knowledge base in the domain. However, a rich knowledge base is insufficient for skilled performance without the knowledge being highly proceduralized and tied to conditions of applicability (R. Glaser, 1994). The skilled performer not only knows the subject matter well, but also has the knowledge linked to contexts in which it applies and to procedures that can be used to apply it. Beginners in a domain lack a rich knowledge base and the extensive interconnection between the knowledge they possess, the contexts in which it applies, and the procedures for applying it.

Lacking the well-structured, proceduralized, and contextualized knowledge base of the expert, the novice relies on "pieces" of knowledge that often lack coherence and are tied loosely, if at all, to procedures and to contexts of applicability. The *knowledge-in-pieces framework* of diSessa (1988) and the *facets framework* described by Minstrell (1992) provide useful ways of thinking about novices' performance. Minstrell argued that when confronted by a problem to solve or a situation to explain, novices draw on specific pieces of knowledge that are triggered by the salient characteristics of the context involved. What may appear to be inconsistent reasoning on the part of novices when viewed from the expert's perspective is usually quite consistent when viewed from the facets that students bring to bear on the context.

About 7 years ago, I became interested in investigating the types of problem contexts that are linked to the conceptual and procedural knowledge of novice physics students. Put a different way, to what extent are novices' concepts and procedures tied to the conditions under which they apply? Although the current theoretical perspectives of experts' and novices' reasoning provided valuable generalizations about their knowledge structures and performance, they did not provide any detailed information about the degree to which novices' concepts and procedures were linked to problem contexts and to conditions of applicability. Further, the techniques that had been used to investigate novices' and experts' reasoning, whether they produced qualitative or quantitative data, typically focused on tasks related to problem solving. For example, problem categorization tasks provided subjects with problems (i.e., contexts) and explored what concepts, if any, the features of the problems triggered. Think-aloud protocols of subjects solving problems also have provided useful insights into the type of knowledge that novices bring to bear in solving problems.

I was interested in a technique that afforded novices a more open-ended task in which to display the types of contexts that they linked to concepts and procedures. *Problem posing* met this condition. In contrast to the techniques that employed problem solving tasks in which the subject is provided with a problem that not only has been formulated in advance by an expert, but also is well defined and solvable, problem posing requires that the subject perform the job of the expert in constructing a suitable problem, a job that entails combining a viable story line with appropriate surface features in ways that embody specific concepts. Hence, to do well at posing problems, the subject must be well versed in how concepts apply across a wide range of problem contexts, whereas it is possible for the solver to avoid the meaning of concepts altogether by solving problems by means–ends analysis.

Having decided on using problem posing, it then seemed evident that merely asking novices to construct problems was too open-ended a task to yield any useful information. The challenge was to come up with techniques that employed problem posing and that contained enough structure to allow an exploration of the links that novices make between concepts, procedures, and contexts of applicability.

## Designing the Techniques

*Posing Problems From Problem Situations.* The first technique that I explored focused on giving novices a problem situation, which consisted of a story line describing the interplay of various physical objects and asking them to use the situation to pose "textbooklike" problems that could be solved by applying specified principles of physics. Two different problem situations were paired with two different physics principles (Newton's second law and work–energy theorem), for a total of four situation–principle pairings. Table 7.2 summarizes the two problem situations and two principles used to construct the four pairings as well as the general instructions given to the subjects.

### TABLE 7.2

Problem situations, specified principles, and instructions to subjects.

Problem Situations:
1.  A block of mass $M$ on a frictionless horizontal surface is connected to a second block of mass $m$ by a light string over a light, frictionless pulley. The system is released from rest with no slack in the string.

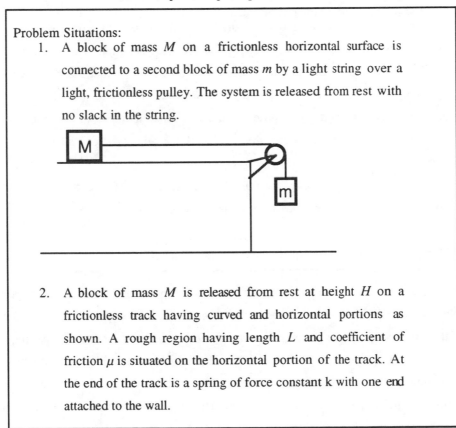

2.  A block of mass $M$ is released from rest at height $H$ on a frictionless track having curved and horizontal portions as shown. A rough region having length $L$ and coefficient of friction $\mu$ is situated on the horizontal portion of the track. At the end of the track is a spring of force constant k with one end attached to the wall.

(continued)

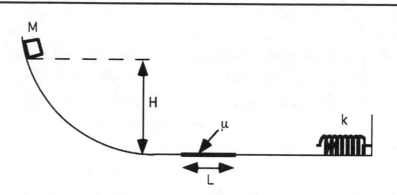

Specified Principles:

1.  Newton's second law: $\vec{F}_{net} = M\vec{a}$

2.  Work–energy theorem or conservation of mechanical energy

General instructions given to subjects:

This experiment takes about 1 hour. You will be asked to *pose* (i.e. make up) physics problems. You will be given several problem *situations*, and a list of *physics principles*. Use the situation to make up a problem that can be solved by applying the concept(s) selected. You will not be asked to solve the problems. The problems you pose should be similar to those that appear in physics textbooks. After you are done, we will ask you questions about what you did.

You will pose problems for four different situations. For each situation, you will be given 10 minutes to pose as many textbooklike problems as you can.

Please ask the proctor to explain anything that is not clear.

In order to investigate the subjects' ability to apply principles flexibly across problem contexts, the two problem situations and two principles were chosen such that when paired, two of the situation–principle pairings were *harmonious*, whereas the other two pairings were *disharmonious*. A harmonious pairing was one where, in traditional physics instruction, the problem situation is used very commonly in problems embodying that principle, whereas a disharmonious pairing was one where the problem situation is used rarely in problems solvable by that principle. For example, in Table 7.2, Situation 1 paired with Newton's second law is a harmonious pairing because, traditionally, this situation is used to ask for either the tension in the string or the acceleration of the blocks, both being questions that would require the application of Newton's second law. Situation 2 paired with the Work–energy theorem is the other harmonious pairing because, typically, this situation is used in problems requiring the application of the Conservation of mechanical energy or the work–energy theorem (e.g., in problems asking for the speed of the block immediately following the rough region or for the maximum compression of the spring). The remaining two pairings were disharmonious; for example, Situation 2 is not well-suited for the construction of a textbooklike problem that would require the application of Newton's second law. In order not to create the wrong impression, it is possible, albeit more challenging, to construct textbooklike problems from the two disharmonious pairings (e.g., asking for the acceleration of the block in the rough region for Situation 2 paired with Newton's second law or asking for the speed of the two blocks after the smaller block has fallen a certain distance in Situation 1 paired with the work–energy theorem).

Four college novices who had earned a B or better in a calculus-based mechanics course were given 10 minutes to pose as many problems as they could think of for each of the four situation–principle pairings. Following each 10-minute posing session, I conducted an interactive individual interview with the subjects during which I asked them to look over the problems they had posed and to explain how each one could be solved with the designated principle. (Details of the study can be found in Mestre, 1994a.)

The data collected provided a wealth of information. Here, I focus on only two complementary pieces of information that could be extracted from the data: whether the problems posed were solvable by the specified principle, and whether the subject provided a correct and coherent explanation of how the problem posed could be solved by the specified principle. These two pieces of information provided insights into the degree to which the subjects were able to link concepts and procedures to the conditions of applicability.

Although 83% of the problems posed by the four subjects were solvable, only 53% were solvable by the specified principle. In accord with expectations, twice as many of the problems posed in the harmonious pairings were solvable by the specified principle compared to the disharmonious pairings. Out of all of the problems that could be solved by the specified principle, only in 63% of them were the subjects capable of providing an adequate explanation of how the principle could be applied to solve the problem. These quantitative data are in agreement with the generalization that the novices' knowledge is linked poorly to conditions of applicability.

The qualitative data from the interviews could be interpreted readily in terms of the knowledge-in-pieces framework or the facets framework and provided detailed information about the types of associations that novices make between concepts and problem contexts. Often, the facets applied by the subjects conflicted, causing irreconcilable confusion in many cases. For example, one subject posed the following two solvable problems for Situation 1 paired with Newton's second law: "Give an expression relating the ratio of mass 1 to mass 2 to the acceleration of the system," and "When the masses are equal, what is the acceleration of the system?" In reasoning about the first problem, the subject relied on two pieces of information: one correct, the other incorrect. The incorrect piece consisted of assuming that the gravitational force exerted by the earth on $m$, namely $mg$, is transferred in total to the string, making the tension in the string also mg. (This assumption would imply that the net force on mass m is 0; hence, it should not accelerate.) He then applied his second correct piece of information. He used Newton's second law (Newton's second law states that the net force on a body is equal to its mass times its acceleration) to find the acceleration of the mass, $M$, on top of the table. Because he had assumed that the tension in the string was mg, this tension is also equal to the net force pulling on mass $M$; so, according to Newton's second law, its acceleration would be $a = mg/M$. This result caused irreconcilable confusion for the subject in discussing the second problem. His equation meant that when the masses are equal, the acceleration of the system is g, which implied that both blocks would have the same acceleration as that of an isolated mass dropped in the earth's gravitational field. The subject was unable to isolate and evaluate the two pieces of knowledge that he had applied. He became quite distraught about the conflict between his mathematical result and his intuitions, stating emphatically at one point during the interview: "Math doesn't lie!"

This technique was quite useful for providing detailed information about the degree to which the novices' conceptual knowledge is linked to conditions of applicability, and, in that sense, it expanded our theoretical perspectives of the novices' performance and of the transition from novice to expert. The data revealed that, although novices could pose solvable problems, they were not facile at posing solvable problems that were solvable by the specified principles. The data also shed light on the degree to which novices could apply concepts across novel contexts; in the disharmonious pairings, novices found it quite difficult to generate problems solvable by the specified principles if the context was not one typically associated with the principle. What this technique could not do is to indicate what contexts are triggered by the mentioning of specific concepts because the contexts from which the subjects were asked to generate problems were provided. The second posing technique provided information on this issue.

*Posing Problems From Concept Scenarios.* The previous technique provided a context (the problem situation) within which to generate a problem that could be solved with a specified principle. Therefore, both the context and the principle were available for the subject to consider together while generating the problem. The second technique I examined provided the subject with concept scenarios—namely, descriptions of the principles and concepts that apply to a problem and the temporal order in which they apply—and asked the subject to pose textbooklike problems that matched the concept scenarios. In this case, the subject had to generate a context (i.e., objects, story line, and physical setup) and then use the context to generate a problem that matched the scenario. Table 7.3 shows the three concept scenarios used as well as the general instructions given to the subjects.

Four college novices participated in this study, which was administered using the same procedure as the previous problem-posing study.

Overall, the task proved quite challenging, with a percentage of solvable problems of 53%; 47% of the problems posed matched the scenarios, with about twice as many matchings for Scenario 2 than for Scenarios 1 and 3. Out of all of the problems that matched the scenarios, only in 71% of the cases were the subjects able to provide a correct explanation of how the problem posed matched the scenarios.

The data revealed that the contexts that were triggered by the concepts contained in the scenarios were quite limited. It was common to find that the subjects had one archetypical context that was associated with a concept (e.g., bodies falling in the earth's gravitational field with the conservation of mechanical energy), which proved rather restrictive in generating problems to match the scenarios. Even if the subjects devised a context that was quite useful for generating problems that embodied the concepts in a scenario, this did not mean that they could generate problems that actually matched the scenarios. Consistent with the knowledge-in-pieces framework, the novices found it difficult to match the scenarios holistically; that is, in Scenarios 2 and 3, which contained more than one concept, the problems posed often matched only parts of the Scenario.

TABLE 7.3

Concept Scenarios and Instructions to Subjects

---

*Concept Scenario 1*: Newton's second law (i.e., $F_{net} = Ma$) is applied to determine the acceleration of an object.

*Concept Scenario 2*: Mechanical energy is conserved, potential energy diminishes, and kinetic energy increases.

*Concept Scenario 3*: Mechanical energy is conserved, followed by conservation of momentum, followed by conservation of mechanical energy, with potential energy increasing and kinetic energy decreasing.

*General Instructions Given to Subjects*:

This experiment takes about 1 hour. You will be asked to *pose* (i.e. make up) physics problems. You will be provided with *concept scenarios* (i.e., a sequence of concepts that apply to a problem, and the order in which they apply) and asked to pose textbooklike problems that match the concept scenarios. You will not be asked to solve the problems you pose. The problems you pose should be similar to those that appear in physics textbooks. After you are done, you will be asked questions about what you did.

You will pose problems for 3 different scenarios. For each scenario, you will be given 15 minutes to pose "textbooklike" problems.

Please ask the proctor to explain anything that is not clear.

---

The interview data revealed that, except for Scenario 2 where the subjects generally were able to articulate coherent explanations of how the problems they had posed matched the scenario, the explanations supplied displayed a superficial understanding of the conditions under which the concepts could be applied to solve problems. The subjects' explanations of how the problems they posed matched Scenarios 1 and 3 often relied on discussing the equations that would be used to solve the problems posed.

## General Comments on the Posing Techniques

I found problem posing to be a very useful tool for probing conceptual knowledge as well as the ability to apply concepts in problem solving contexts. The data generated from the two methodologies helped me to gain insights into the degree of fragmentation or coherence of conceptual knowledge, the degree to which the subjects were making appropriate links between the concepts and the contexts in which they can be applied, and the degree to which the subjects understood the conditions under which the concepts and the principles can be applied. The interview portion of the methodologies was crucial in attempting to interpret the subjects' reasoning, especially because the subjects often were able to pose problems that could be solved by the specified principles or that matched the concept scenarios, yet they furnished an inadequate explanation of how the principles provided applied to the problems posed. The interactivity of the interviews was also a very positive feature of the technique because it gave the interviewer the flexibility to ask questions that probed the depth of the novice's knowledge. Although these methodologies are extremely time consuming to administer and the data are difficult to analyze, they can provide detailed information of a subject's conceptual knowledge and its links both to contexts in which it can be applied and to conditions of applicability; they also could be used to devise a scale to estimate where an individual is along the expertise dimension.

The posing techniques also provided a link between theory and practice. In traditional physics instruction, we train students to solve many problems, believing that in solving problems correctly, the student also understands the underlying concepts. The posing data (and other researchers' data reviewed in Mestre, 1994a) revealed that this is not the case. Instructors often delude themselves that problem solving proficiency implies conceptual understanding. When one probes more deeply, however, it becomes clear that good novices (who even might become expert physicists eventually) have a tenuous fragmented understanding of concepts and principles and the conditions under which they apply.

## CONCLUDING REMARKS

I have argued that the view that progress in educational research and theory building is incremental and linear is more of an idealization than a reality. The examples discussed herein suggest a delicate interplay among theory, research questions, and measurement techniques. Measurement techniques can limit the kinds of answers that we can obtain from our research questions and, in turn, limit the refinement of a theory. On the other hand, a more refined theory can help us to devise new measurement techniques, which in turn allow us to answer more refined questions, which in turn can lead to further refinement of the theory.

At a more practical level, the aforementioned examples also speak to the issues of triangulation, of qualitative versus quantitative data, and of resources available to conduct our investigations. Different techniques generate different types of information, and it is often the case that a single technique will not provide the breadth of information necessary to answer unequivocally the research questions under investigation. Therefore, it is important to devise complementary techniques that help to triangulate on answers to the research questions. There also appears to be some debate in the mathematics and science education research communities about whether techniques that result in qualitative data are "better" than techniques that result in quantitative data (or vice versa). The issue of what type of data is better depends largely on the research question(s) under investigation and the resources available. Some research questions are perfectly answerable by techniques that yield quantitative data, whereas others require the probing of information that can be acquired only through techniques that yield qualitative data. The examples I provided illustrate how qualitative and quantitative data often can be collected by a single technique, with the two types of data complementing each other. Also, quantitative data are easier to analyze than qualitative data, which typically means that many more subjects can be included in experiments generating quantitative data. Hence, the time, costs, and personnel required to conduct a research investigation can constrain the research questions themselves, or the methodologies that can be used, or both.

## ACKNOWLEDGMENTS

I would like to thank Robert Dufresne and Anthony Kelly for providing valuable feedback on the manuscript of this chapter.

# 8 The Corruption of a Research Design: A Case Study of a Curriculum Innovation Project

**Hugh F. Cline**
*Columbia University*

**Ellen B. Mandinach**
*Educational Testing Services*

This chapter describes the corruption of a research design. It explains why and how a computer-based curriculum innovation project was transformed from a quasi-experimental design to a comparative case study. The project, the Systems Thinking and Curriculum Innovation Network (STACI[N]), is a multiyear curriculum development, implementation, and research effort conducted by the authors, who are research staff members at Educational Testing Service (ETS). The project examines the impact of technology on teaching and learning activities (Mandinach & Cline, 1994a). More specifically, the STACI[N] Project implements systems thinking and systems modeling in precollege curricula and examines their impact on:

- Student learning processes and outcomes.
- Classroom dynamics and teachers' behavior.
- The organizational structure and functioning of schools.

The first section of this chapter tells the story of how the STACI[N] Project evolved over 8 years, drawing specifically on anecdotes and data that illustrate how the comparative case study methodology was developed, expanded, and adapted both to facilitate an educational innovation and to document its ontogenesis. The second part of the chapter focuses on methodological issues, including the need for longitudinal design, multiple methods, multiple levels of analysis, and systems analysis.

# THE STORY OF THE SYSTEMS THINKING PROJECT

## Objectives

The STACI[N] Project began in 1986. It was funded by the Office of Educational Research and Improvement (OERI) of the U.S. Department of Education and a collaboration between ETS and the Educational Technology Center (ETC), located at the Harvard University Graduate School of Education. The original purpose of the STACI[N] Project was to examine the impact of technology on students' acquisition and transfer of higher order thinking skills, using system dynamics as the instructional vehicle. As defined by Hulse (1995):

> System dynamics is the study of how the behavior of systems arises from the mutual interactions of their component parts and processes. The need to understand such behavior is ubiquitous—a common intellectual thread unifying the study of the sciences, technology, economics, business, social systems, etc. (p. 2)

At the time, system dynamics seemed to be a promising choice because it had the potential to stimulate the acquisition of important cognitive skills, was generic in nature, and had not been used extensively at the precollege level yet.

The field of system dynamics was created by Jay Forrester (1968), with the Sloan School of Management at the Massachusetts Institute of Technology (MIT). Drawing on their experiences in creating computer models of assembly line manufacturing, Forrester, his colleagues, and students developed a simulation and modeling language, DYNAMO, for mainframe computers that allowed them to create models of many economic and social systems. The titles of Forrester's books, starting with *Industrial Dynamics* (1961), continuing with *Principles of Systems* (1968), *Urban Dynamics* (1969), and eventually *World Dynamics* (1971), document the expanding complexity and scope of the simulations produced by the MIT group.

In 1985, Barry Richmond, a student of Forrester's, developed a Macintosh microcomputer version of DYNAMO called STELLA (Systems Thinking Experiential Learning Laboratory with Animation). Richmond established his own company, High Performance Systems (HPS), in New Hampshire, to market STELLA (Richmond, 1985) and produce new software to facilitate modeling and simulation. With the implementation of system dynamics principles on microcomputers, the capability of developing models and using simulations for instruction became available to any teacher and school able to afford the relatively inexpensive Macintosh computer. A computer-based, curriculum innovation project using systems thinking suddenly became an affordable possibility.

The systems thinking approach, as operationalized in the STACI$^N$ Project, consisted of three interdependent components:

- The theoretical perspective of system dynamics.
- The graphical user interface computer (GUI), at that time the Macintosh.
- The simulation and modeling software package STELLA.

The systems thinking approach was viewed as an instructional tool that could be integrated into curricula to facilitate students' acquisition of declarative and procedural knowledge.

## Project Inception

The systems thinking project began with the establishment of a mutually beneficial collaboration among three parties: ETS, ETC, and Brattleboro Union High School (BUHS) in Vermont. ETC was seeking a meaningful role for ETS as a part of their collaboration. ETS had conducted an extensive survey of educational software in pursuit of a program that would engender higher order thinking skills across the curricula. In the summer of 1986, we at ETS were introduced to STELLA and systems thinking. We recognized its potential for instructional enhancement immediately. Concurrently, we learned that BUHS was planning to use STELLA in its science department. BUHS had applied for and received a U.S. Department of Education Secretary's Discretionary Grant to support its implementation of systems thinking. Four enthusiastic teachers were ready to implement systems thinking by the beginning of the 1986-1987 academic year.

The four teachers at BUHS who had applied for the grant were thrilled to receive $20,000. Initially, it seemed like a great deal of money. However, it soon became clear that they had underestimated substantially the time, money, and resources that would be needed to develop and introduce systems thinking in their classes. At that time, faculty, students, and parents had received only limited exposure to systems thinking, which was initiated by an interested parent who had studied under Forrester. The teachers needed substantial and sustained support for learning systems thinking and the use of STELLA. Very few materials for systems-based curricula at the precollege level existed. The teachers would have to develop any materials that they needed, and they would have to consult with experts to help in that development process. Also, the school had only three Macintosh computers on which to run STELLA. More computers would be needed if the teachers were to begin using systems thinking on a broad scale. All these activities would require a good deal of time and money. Time was required to come up to speed with systems thinking and STELLA, to begin to develop curricular materials, and then to implement them in their classes. Money was required to support the requisite resources and to pay for the staff time. Although the teachers did not recognize it then, BUHS faced a virtually impossible task.

ETS was seeking a platform that would enable it to conduct research on the impact of technology. BUHS provided such a platform. With financial support from OERI through ETC, ETS could provide BUHS with the resources to use technology in their classrooms. The External Research Division at Apple Computer, Inc. donated 15 Macintosh computers to BUHS. With the funds from ETC, the teachers were paid stipends and provided with opportunities to learn systems and STELLA. A system dynamics expert from MIT paid frequent visits to BUHS to work directly with the students and teachers on modeling techniques. Support for systems thinking was given to the project by the BUHS principal, superintendent, and school board. ETS also was authorized to conduct a research study examining the impact of systems thinking on the students, teachers, and the school. Seemingly, everything that was needed to facilitate the implementation of and research on systems-based curricula was in place. Thus, the original STACI Project was launched. Little did we know that it would be a long time before we could do any research on its impact.

## A Rocky Beginning

ETS worked exclusively with BUHS for 2 years, with the assistance of the system dynamist from MIT and the staff of HPS. We were implementing what we thought was an almost perfect quasi-experiment. Systems thinking would be introduced into the science courses taught by the four project teachers; other science department members would serve as the controls. Although students were assigned randomly to systems or traditional courses, there was no reason to suspect any bias. As envisioned, we would be able to compare students who had taken systems-based courses with their counterparts who had received traditional instruction. Furthermore, over successive years, we hoped that we would be able to obtain data about the transfer of systems thinking skills as students progressed through the science curricula.

By Halloween of 1986, we realized that it would be impossible to integrate enough systems thinking materials into BUHS's science courses to enable us to detect any impact on students' learning by the end of that first academic year. While juggling their normally heavy load of academic and administrative responsibilities, the teachers were trying furiously to develop new materials. They had neither the time nor the energy to achieve their new pedagogical objectives. The materials that did get produced were completed with substantial assistance from the MIT and HPS consultants, and they were plagued with many pedagogical problems. The consultants had little experience with precollege instructional materials, and the teachers had not developed yet a feel for what systems topics might be readily applicable to high school curricula. The teachers selected topics that, when translated into systems models, were far too complicated for their students. Furthermore, the teachers held such high expectations for their students' achievement that the tests they devised were too difficult. There was a huge chasm between expectations and outcomes, causing the students and their teachers to become frustrated. This frustration sabotaged the effective use of systems thinking for both the students and the teachers. The teachers had failed to make the educational objectives of systems thinking clear to their students. Consequently, many students perceived it to be irrelevant, abstract, or too difficult.

As we tracked the progress or lack thereof at BUHS, a number of issues became apparent. First, it made no sense at all to conduct research on the impact of systems thinking until there was a critical mass of instructional materials being used in the classrooms, and this was not going to happen quickly. Second, the quasi-experimental design was not appropriate. What was needed was a more flexible research design, closer to what Newman (1990) later termed the formative experiment. Third, the teachers needed more time, support, training, and colleagues with whom they could collaborate. Fourth, a few teachers in rural Vermont could not promote a substantial growth in materials for systems thinking curricula. Fifth, the research project needed to be preceded by a concerted effort to develop and implement the appropriate curricula. Then, and only then, could the research occur.

Sixth, the role of the teachers needed to change from those who impart knowledge to their students to facilitators, mentors, and coaches. Finally, we, the researchers, realized that our roles had changed rapidly from objective observers to involved participants. Despite the minimal implementation, we recognized the potential that systems thinking had for the improvement of teaching and learning activities. In the process of helping with the project's implementation, we had become participants and colleagues. The questions that confronted us were how we could help the teachers at BUHS best, implement systems thinking more effectively, and study its impact on students' acquisition of knowledge, classroom dynamics, and organizational change.

## Project Expansion

Encouraged by what we had learned from the project thus far, we began to explore the feasibility of expanding it. The issues mentioned previously intrigued us, and we wanted to pursue them. ETC's funding was ending, and we needed to seek additional sources of support. Concurrently, we needed to conceptualize a project that would build on what we had learned during the two years at BUHS and to move forward. With additional assistance from the External Research Division at Apple and ETS, we created a consortium of schools whose teachers formed collaborative content teams to develop, share, and implement systems-based, instructional materials. We needed a critical mass to build on the BUHS experience and to work with those teachers to produce materials in a number of content areas.

Recognizing the potentials of the instructional perspective, Apple wanted to provide additional support, but requested that the schools be located in the Silicon Valley. We sought schools that varied along a number of dimensions: the academic aspirations of the students, administrative commitment, and the ethnic and socioeconomic characteristics of the community served. We wanted to explore those characteristics of students, schools, and communities that might either facilitate or impede the implementation of such technology-based innovations in the curricula.

In spite of uncertain funding at that time, four high schools and two middle schools in the San Francisco Bay Area agreed to work with us. In each school, a minimum of five teachers volunteered to participate. Thus, the STACI$^N$ Project was launched as an extension of STACI. The superscript N denotes the fact that the teachers formed a network of collaborators. Apple again provided hardware to the schools, but, this time it donated much more equipment. Each school received 20 Macintosh microcomputers, 15 for a school laboratory and 5 for the personal use of the teachers. HPS also agreed to continue to serve as instructors in systems thinking, modeling, and STELLA for the teachers as well as to be available as on-call expert consultants for the entire project. The teachers' workshops became more formalized, structured, and extensive. HPS learned from STACI$^N$ how to work effectively with precollege teachers, and the STACI$^N$ participants received regular and ongoing instruction, consultation, and guidance about modeling and the integration of systems thinking into their courses.

Perhaps most important, the teachers had a number of colleagues with whom they could collaborate. Originally, we thought that the teachers would align themselves by their content areas with, for example, the biology teachers working together. This happened sometimes, although not as frequently as expected. Some teachers preferred to form school teams or cross-disciplinary groups. Whatever the structure, the project had teachers from seven schools (and, ultimately, an eighth school, a high school in Tucson, Arizona) coming together at least twice a year to implement the systems thinking approach in their classes. Furthermore, all the schools were connected by a project-sponsored electronic mail network that allowed the teachers to communicate, share curricular materials, and discuss progress and problems.

## Lessons Learned

Six additional years of funding from various U.S. Department of Education awards and contributions from ETS sustained the project's work. During that time, the project involved almost 100 teachers into whose classes the systems thinking approach was integrated. The approach worked for most teachers, but failed to match pedagogical objectives for others. In the successful applications, teachers were able to implement systems thinking in such a way that its use enhanced teaching and learning activities in their classrooms. Systems thinking stimulated students' acquisition of declarative and procedural knowledge as well as increased their level of motivation and cognitive engagement. The approach provided teachers with fresh ways of presenting topics that had been difficult to structure formerly. Regardless of their level of expertise and experience, the approach also stimulated the teachers' professional development. Many of the teachers reported that the use of the systems approach had sparked a new level of enthusiasm for their careers. It gave them novel ways of presenting materials as well as access to a powerful technology.

In contrast, approximately one third of the teachers found the use of systems thinking too difficult, labor intensive, intrusive, or contrary to curriculum mandates, accountability factors, or pedagogical styles. Therefore, they resigned from the project. The reasons for some of these failures are informative. To implement the systems thinking approach effectively as it was defined originally, teachers needed to be facile not only with a GUI computer and the STELLA software, but also with the theory of system dynamics. Overcoming computer phobia was a hurdle for some teachers. Mastering the software was an issue for others.

The most difficult tasks for the unsuccessful teachers were to recognize how the systems thinking approach could be applied to their subject area and then to design curricular modules and systems models based on that understanding. Although many of the teachers acknowledged the potential applicability, they had difficulty translating it into workable curricular materials. Some of them wanted to be handed packaged curricular materials rather than to develop them on their own. The process of becoming a proficient systems thinking teacher, particularly for some of the early participants, required more time and effort than they were willing or able to devote.

This particular problem began to diminish when curricular materials became more readily available and the teachers had colleagues with whom they could collaborate. In addition to increases in the critical mass of materials and colleagues, there had been substantial enhancements to STELLA, making it more user friendly. Furthermore, STELLA was not the only systems-based software available. Other modeling tools had come on the market. Also, some teachers started using the series of simulations produced by Maxis that included SimCity (Maxis, 1989) and SimEarth (Maxis, 1990). These software packages are based on the principles of system dynamics too, albeit in a more "edutainment-like" format. Moreover, teachers can obtain systems thinking training courses from HPS and other organizations now. There are increasingly more and better resources at teachers' disposal to enable them to adopt systems thinking.

Some teachers saw an immediate fit for systems thinking in their curricula. For others, the fit was not readily apparent. In some instances, the course content was structured so tightly that no more material could be squeezed into the curriculum. These teachers perceived the use of systems thinking as forcing the removal of some previously mandated material. In other words, if systems thinking were introduced, other content would have to be sacrificed. In contrast, those teachers who used systems thinking effectively, saw it as an enhancement to the existing curricula, not as an additional component. They used the approach to teach topics that heretofore had been difficult or could benefit from a new instructional perspective. They did not have to sacrifice existing course content in favor of systems thinking.

However, the pressure to cover the curriculum in light of accountability to prescribed goals is a very real phenomenon, particularly at the high school level and for advanced placement courses. Schools use standardized test scores for a variety of reasons. However, teachers frequently think that their performance evaluations are based on the test scores of the students in their classes. We found that a number of the STACI[N] Project teachers who were teaching high-stakes courses in highly competitive schools were among those who embraced systems thinking most enthusiastically. They saw it as a way to increase their students' learning. As an aside, several teachers advised that some of the most able students preferred traditional instructional methods. The better students knew how to succeed under the previous conditions, and they opined that the systems thinking approach required too much work, effort, and thought.

However, many of the teachers who worked at the other end of the ability spectrum also embraced systems thinking, but for very different reasons. Traditional instructional methods had been unsuccessful with their students. These teachers reported that the systems thinking approach engaged students in content areas that were nearly inaccessible using traditional methods. In fact, many of the at-risk students were unable to read textbooks, but they could learn from the GUI computer and the systems-based, curricular modules.

It also became apparent that certain pedagogical styles either impeded or facilitated the use of a constructivist approach such as systems thinking. Generally, teachers who were able to create a constructivist learning environment were effective in implementing the systems thinking approach. One of the more major changes in pedagogical style observed among teachers involved in the project was a shift from teacher-directed to learner-directed environments, in which students became active participants in the educational process. One measure of effective teachers is the ability to relinquish control of the classroom, shifting from being a transmitter of knowledge to becoming a facilitator of learning. Such teachers encourage intellectual exploration on the part of their students, focusing on the acquisition of procedural knowledge and problem solving skills, and their application to real-world situations.

Teachers who had difficulty adapting to the constructivist approach were unwilling to allow students to assume responsibility for their learning. These teachers preferred to maintain a didactic classroom environment in which students adhere to the more traditional, passive role. We refer to this as the funnel method of instruction in which teachers serve as the transmitters of information and students as the passive receptors of it. The teachers' role is to fill their students' heads with facts and figures, and the students' role is to allow their heads to be filled passively. One can imagine a funnel attached to a student's head into which the teacher pours the facts. Many students are frustrated by this method of instruction. The reaction to it of our students in the school in Tucson was to develop the motto, "No More Funnels!"

We believe that the systems thinking approach will decrease the funnel method by engaging students to pursue learning in an active, "hands-on" manner. Students become more engaged and, therefore, more likely to learn more effectively. Many teachers also benefit from the constructivist approach because it infuses excitement into teaching and learning activities. Despite being labor intensive and more work than traditional methods, most of our teachers advise that the systems thinking approach has brought renewed enthusiasm to their classrooms and has stimulated professional development.

It is clear from the preceding description of the STACI$^N$ Project that the application of a quasi-experimental research design to it was neither sufficiently sensitive nor powerful enough to be fruitful. The overriding evaluation question in many educational innovation projects is, "Does it work?" It is clear from the example of the STACI$^N$ Project that this question needs to be refined further and broken into a large number of more explicit questions. For example, what kinds of students have what kind of learning experiences with what types of materials and instructional approaches? Then, each of these questions needs to be subdivided into even more specific questions.

It would be highly desirable if, in the next section of this chapter, we could propose a specific research design for most or, at least, many of these questions. However, in our view, it would be premature to suggest such designs. We feel strongly that it is necessary to apply multiple perspectives to a project of this sort. Therefore, rather than finishing the chapter with a description of alternative or more effective research designs, we present a series of observations and inferences relevant to the conduct of such projects.

## Methodological Implications

During the eight years of the STACI$^N$ Project, the methods used to implement and evaluate systems thinking underwent substantial revision and adaptation. In many respects, we innovated as we implemented, so to speak. Methods were adopted to meet the immediate needs. Some things, like indepth interviews with teachers and students and classroom observations, produced useful information. Other efforts, such as a cognitive analysis of teachers' think-aloud protocols of model-building exercises, did not prove useful. What emerged gradually was a variety of perspectives and procedures that probably are described best as a comparative case study.

From the experiences recounted earlier, it is possible to infer a number of important methodological implications relevant to the design and execution of a comparative case study that examines the impact of a mathematics and science educational reform project. We find it convenient to classify these inferences in four interrelated categories: (a) longitudinal design, (b) multiple methods, (c) hierarchical analyses, and (d) system dynamics.

In the remainder of this chapter, we discuss these methodological perspectives. However, first, an initial comment: Perhaps the most important lesson we have learned from the STACI$^N$ Project is that it is absolutely necessary for researchers to remain flexible in applying their methodological knowledge in a field setting. The common, dominant leitmotif that pervades our discussion here is the obligation to adapt continuously to the needs of the participants in a project. Perhaps those of us who are engaged in educational research projects can learn from the world of business where, today, there is a growing awareness of the imperative to stay attuned to the needs of one's customers.

In educational research we must develop sensitivity to the needs of the participants in our projects, be they students, teachers, administrators, parents, or policymakers at any level. Particularly in the case of educational reform efforts, we may have to change our conceptions about our research activities and think of the participants more as collaborators and colleagues. This transition occurred in our perspectives, particularly of the teachers and administrators in the STACI$^N$ Project. As the previous description made abundantly clear, flexibility in meeting the requirements of our colleagues was the hallmark of our efforts.

The STACI$^N$ Project did not resemble at all the accounts of research methods found in most social and behavioral science methodology textbooks. It was necessary to make continuous adjustments in all aspects of its implementation and assessment phases. We did have initial hypotheses concerning learning and transfer, but they were set aside quickly as we struggled with all sorts of problems associated with the delivery and installation of hardware and software. In fact, very few of our initial expectations were realized, and we were revising our strategies, priorities, roles, and schedules continuously in order to accommodate a plethora of unexpected problems and contingencies. Furthermore, during the course of the project, it became necessary to provide a variety of services and assistance to the schools and the teachers.

At different times, we served as hardware installers, technicians, software instructors, troubleshooters, guidance counselors, travel agents, caterers, and even lay psychotherapists. If a researcher makes a commitment to teachers and schools to implement and evaluate computer-based innovations in their curricula, it is not realistic to expect to perform only those activities customarily associated with research, such as subject assignment, data collection, analysis, and scholarly reporting.

Had we been unwilling or unable to take on all the roles just enumerated, the STACI$^N$ Project would have faltered in the early months, and one would have been tempted to conclude that another effort at educational reform fell short of its desired objective. Technology-based innovations such as the STACI$^N$ Project require the acquisition and installation of hardware and software on the one hand and the continuous support of teachers on the other. Flexibility in applying traditional social and behavioral science research methods has to be complemented with common sense and an orientation to be of service to the students, teachers, and schools participating in the project.

## Longitudinal Design

In the application of both methodological expertise and flexibility, it is likely that the researcher will have to sacrifice the quasi-experimental methodological design that has become the idol of so many social and behavioral scientists. Since the publication of the now classic article by D. T. Campbell and Stanley (1963), many researchers have striven to attain or approximate this design. It is an adaptation of the classic laboratory experiment in which all the extraneous conditions that might influence the outcome are supposedly eliminated or controlled by randomization and appropriate data analyses. Indeed, there are many occasions in which this design is appropriate and viable. However, most of the instances involving computer-based innovations in the curricula that take place in real time in classrooms are not amenable to the quasi-experimental design. Two fundamental aspects of the quasi-experimental design were problematical in the STACI$^N$ Project: Before and after measurements and the use of experimental and control groups.

Inherent to the concept of the experiment is the requirement that measurements be taken before and after the application of a stimulus or treatment. To have these measurements correspond to before and after states, there must be some specific point or points in when the stimulus or treatment is applied. However, as the earlier description of the STACI$^N$ Project shows clearly, the implementation of systems thinking by the participating teachers was a gradual process that took many years. In each succeeding year of the project, the students enrolled in classes using systems thinking were exposed to more curricular modules that had this dynamic, problem solving perspective embedded. Furthermore, the nature, extent, and effectiveness of those modules expanded each year as the teachers became more knowledgeable and adept in using the systems thinking approach. Therefore, in the STACI$^N$ Project, it was impossible to identify before and after conditions. Rather, there was one continuous process of change.

Corresponding to the teachers' gradual professional development in using systems thinking was the incremental intellectual growth of the students as they applied their modeling and simulation skills in different courses. For these reasons, comparing measurements gathered in the beginning with those collected at the end of any particular school year made no sense. In 1 year, the differences that were detectable were likely to be minimal. The noticeable changes began to appear after several years, particularly when students employed systems thinking in a sequence of science and mathematics courses.

The second feature of the quasi-experimental design that was problematical in the STACI$^N$ Project was the use of experimental and control groups. A canon of all research experimentation is the application of the stimulus or treatment to the experimental group and the withholding of it from the control group. The essence of a quasi-experiment is the random assignment of subjects to these groups. Randomization is assumed to control for all other possible extraneous factors that might be considered to have a causal relationship with the treatment. However, it is essential to the integrity of the design to avoid contamination by preventing any of the treatment occurring inadvertently with the subjects in the control group.

In a laboratory setting, such contamination is avoided more readily. When the research is being conducted in a school setting over several years, it is impossible to block such contamination. For example, in several schools in the STACI$^N$ Project, teachers who were not members of the project became interested in systems thinking and started using some of the curricular materials in their classes, which we had intended using as control groups. It would have been imprudent to ask those teachers to stop using our materials, and it is quite likely that they would have refused. Administrators in those schools would have been perplexed by such a request, for we had spent considerable time and effort convincing them and their school board members that systems thinking would help their students to learn and their teachers to become more effective. Why, then, would we want to prevent other students and teachers from benefiting from the project as well? In fact, one of the long-range objectives of the STACI[N] Project is to promote widely the use of the systems thinking approach. It would have been both impossible and contradictory to our goals to obstruct its spread to the control classes in a futile attempt to protect experimental integrity.

Furthermore, during the course of a school year, students would change classes, shifting from what we called experimental groups to control groups and contaminating the design further. In some of the schools, there were huge changes in the composition of the classes during the course of one school year. Several teachers reported that as many as 50% of the students enrolled in a course in the fall would be gone by the spring. A recent statewide study in California documented similar mobility patterns (Lash & Kirkpatrick, 1994). To make matters even more complicated, from one year to the next, students were exposed to an increasingly complex pattern of treatments and nontreatments. Over a 4-year high school or a 7-year middle and high school progression, the mix of experimental and control exposures eventually became unwieldy.

In the previously cited Campbell and Stanley monograph, 16 different designs are discussed, corresponding to various patterns in which subjects are assigned randomly to experimental or control groups and measures of the impact of the treatment are repeated. When the researcher is able to control the introduction of the treatment and their subjects are assigned randomly to experimental and control groups, the quasi-experiment can be assumed to take on most of the characteristics of the true experimental design. However, in the STACI[N] Project, the stimulus was by no means a single event and the students moved freely into and out of the so-called experimental and control classes.

It is virtually impossible to indicate precisely when the treatment was administered and, therefore, when comparisons between measures would be meaningful. For this reason, the quasi- experimental design as planned for the STACI[N] Project originally had to be abandoned, and the research design employed was closer to a continuous time series, as also described by D. T. Campbell and Stanley (1963). Today, we would refer to this as an ongoing longitudinal design. In this research design, multiple data sets documenting the nature of the innovation and its impact on a variety of dimensions are collected, analyzed, and reported in a continuing cycle. In a very real sense, research focusing on the impact of a computer-based innovation to a curriculum should be designed and executed as an ongoing activity. Data collection and analyses should be carried out continuously and indefinitely. Only in this way is it possible to provide timely and regular feedback to refine the treatment further and to enhance teaching and learning.

## Multiple Methods

In the early stages of the project, it became clear that incorporating systems thinking would generate multiple impacts, among them how knowledge of a subject is acquired; the development of higher order, problem solving skills; improvement in the students' capabilities for working in groups; changes in the dynamics of the classroom; and professional development opportunities for the teachers involved in the project. All these were legitimate and positive expectations resulting from the introduction of systems thinking. Obviously, different methods would need to be employed to document and describe the nature and extent of these various consequences.

As mentioned previously, no existing assessment instrument was appropriate. During the course of the project, we developed several versions of a paper-and-pencil test that gauged the extent to which the students were mastering the concepts, vocabulary, and problem solving skills of systems thinking. The students' performance on regular tests, quizzes, examinations, and the like were recorded, and the teachers were asked to indicate whether or not they perceived improvements in their students' achievement. Both observations of classrooms and in-depth interviews with teachers were employed at various points. In many classes, students wrote essays on assigned topics, and the teachers and we analyzed their contents documenting the occurrence of systems thinking themes. Also, think-aloud protocols were collected from students while they solved problems.

All these data collection methods provided a rich and diverse set of evidence, documenting changes and advances made in teaching and learning activities. It was clear that the only hope for an adequate description of the many facets of change and innovation that accompanied the introduction of systems thinking was to rely on virtually all the data collection techniques that are available to the social and behavioral sciences. To do less would have resulted in incomplete documentation of the project. Unfortunately, there is no simple way to integrate all these analyses into an overall metaevaluative summary.

## Hierarchical Analyses

As mentioned in the previous discussion, the impact of the systems thinking approach occurred at three different levels: (a) students' learning, (b) classroom dynamics, and (c) the school as a social organization.

Clearly, a systems thinking model of computer-based revisions to curricula would lead us to anticipate changes at these three levels. Thus far in the STACI[N] Project, we have been able to document and describe changes at each of these levels. The more systematic analyses of the data examining relationships across the different levels remain to be completed. For example, it will be interesting to examine the relationship between a student's declarative and procedural knowledge in varying contexts of learner-centered classrooms. The challenge now is to devise methodologies that allow such hierarchical or contextual analyses.

At the first level, the project focused on gathering data that described how students learn and what they do with the knowledge that they have acquired. The focus here was on how learning that reflected systems thinking occurred. We were interested in both declarative knowledge and problem solving skills. The systems thinking pencil-and-paper test, students' essays, course examinations and grades, and think-aloud protocol analyses were all used. Because the teachers collaborated with us in the collection and analyses of data, different techniques were used in different schools at different times. Therefore, there is no analysis that summarizes all the results across all the schools. However, we can report uniform patterns of improved learning in all instances (Mandinach & Cline, 1996).

At the second level, classroom dynamics, we collected data documenting the changing patterns of interactions among students and teachers. The methods of data collection at the classroom dynamics level were structured observations of classes and indepth interviews with teachers. In several instances, teachers observed and recorded activities in each other's classrooms. Because students typically worked in pairs using their systems thinking materials, the teachers lectured to the entire class far less frequently and spent more time working with the dyads providing advice, encouragement, and technical expertise. One of the teachers described this experience as similar to a butterfly pollinating the students' minds by flying around the room and touching down here and there to provide assistance. Many computer-based, educational innovations have noted a shift in classroom dynamics from the traditional lecture style to a more student-centered, student-directed learning environment (Mandinach & Cline, 1994b).

Of the three levels of analyses in the STACI$^N$ Project, the one of the school as a social organization is the least well developed. The objects of inquiry here are the sociological changes that occur in a school, focusing on its structure and function. The data that do exist for this level so far were collected during interviews with teachers, administrators, and school board members. The analyses will include changing patterns of role performance, interpersonal communication, personal influence, power and authority, and job satisfaction. Future publications will communicate the results of these analyses and explore their policy implications for supporting reform in mathematics and science education.

## System Dynamics

By now, it must be clear that the longitudinal, multimethod, hierarchical perspective that emerged over the eight years of the STACI$^N$ Project was system dynamics. Gradually, we learned to apply to the STACI$^N$ Project the same perspective that we were helping the teachers to use in their classrooms. However, this transition caused a strain in our relationships with our funding agencies and sources of support. Many people, including staff in the organizations that supplied the resources for the project, OERI, ETC, ETS, and Apple Computer, as well as the students, teachers, administrators, and school board members, wanted an answer to the question, "Does it work?" Of course, it is an understandable and legitimate question. They all wished to know whether the substantial investment that they are making in the promotion of systems thinking is having the desired, and at least implied if not promised, positive impact. However, as noted previously, the history of the STACI$^N$ Project makes it obvious that this is not an appropriate question.

In fact, in any educational reform project, it is now clear to us that to ask a single question about impact or outcome is naive. Furthermore, to search for the ideal experimental or quasi-experimental design for evaluation research is fruitless. Reform endeavors take place in real-world contexts that are composed of many, interrelated, dynamic factors. Any attempt at educational reform will have multiple components and multiple impacts, and they will interact across levels of organization and over time. Many questions must be asked repeatedly, and the answer to any one of them is almost always related to many others. We need to ask what the factors are that facilitate or impede effective teaching and learning. The answers to some of these specific questions have been set forth by us elsewhere (Mandinach & Cline, 1994a, 1994b).

In recent years, an appreciation of the need for a systems thinking approach has grown in the educational reform and research communities. A joint undertaking of OERI and the National Science Foundation (NSF) is attempting to promote systemic reform. Each state has been invited to create a comprehensive plan to effect systemic reform of public education from kindergarten through Grade 12. As of this writing, close to 40 states have had their plans approved, and federally funded systemic reforms are underway. Unfortunately, the power of systems thinking is not realized fully in these efforts. NSF offers the following definition:

> "Systemic reform" is a process of educational reform based on the premise that achieving excellence and equity requires alignment of critical activities and components. It is as much a change in infrastructure as in outcomes. Central elements include—high standards for learning expected from all students; alignment among all the parts of the system—policies, practices, and accountability mechanisms; a change in governance that includes greater school site flexibility; greater involvement of the public and community; a closer link between formal and informal learning experiences; enhanced attention to professional development; and increased articulation between the precollege and postsecondary education institutions. (Suter, 1996, p. 5)

Notice that there is no mention of systems analysis in this definition. Simulation and modeling as aids in the analysis of reform efforts are ignored. Although the components of the definition are commendable and there is a call for alignment of the elements of systemic reform, no attention is devoted to the issues of interaction and feedback—the core of systems analysis. Consequently, the discipline, rigor, and precision in planning and assessment that derive from the systems thinking approach are not realized in a project that is devoted to systemic reform. In a recent work, we presented our first draft of a systems thinking model of a computer-based, educational, curricular reform project (Mandinach & Cline, 1994a). FIG. 8.1 is a revised draft of that model.

It contains a proposed set of variables describing the components of changes fostered by computer-based revisions to curricula at the student learning, classroom dynamics, and organizational change levels. This diagram is useful as an early approximation of the many factors involved in an educational reform venture such as the STACI[N] Project. However, it should be pointed out that FIG. 8.1 is not a STELLA model of the STACI$^N$ Project. Rather, it is a preliminary step to a model. In the vernacular of STELLA, it is a map, which will be elaborated on and converted to an operating model subsequently.

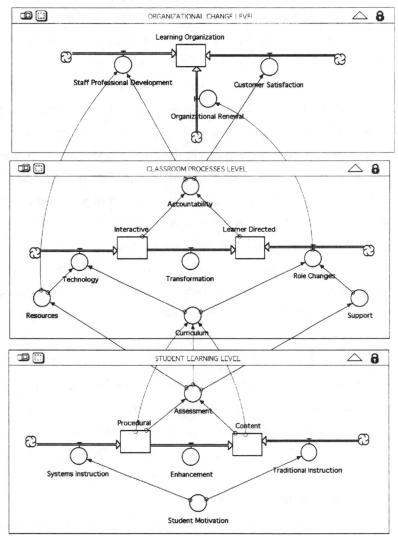

FIG. 8.1. A systems thinking model of a computer-based educational, curriculum reform project.

This chapter is not the appropriate place to present a detailed description of our map. The interested reader is referred to our original presentation (Mandinach & Cline, 1994). Here, we provide a brief overview to give a sense of the power of the systems thinking approach in analyzing dynamic phenomena. The STELLA language employs four elements for defining models: stocks, flows, converters, and connectors. Stocks are repositories where accumulations occur and are represented in the map as rectangles. Flows are the regulators of the accumulations and are depicted as pipes with valves attached. Converters and connectors provide the linkages among the stocks and flows and are portrayed as circles and arrows. An analogy to grammar is that stocks are the nouns, flows are the verbs, and converters and connectors are the modifiers or adjectives and adverbs of the STELLA language.

The first level of the map—student learning—depicts two stocks: procedural and content knowledge. The second level of the map—classroom dynamics—also has two stocks: interactive and learner-directed environments. The third level—organizational change—contains only one stock: the learning organization. As depicted in the map, all the stocks are regulated by various flows, converters, and connectors. Notice that there are numerous instances of connectors across the three levels, denoting contextual relationships. For example, the two stocks at the student learning level—procedural and content learning—are connected to the converter, curriculum, at the classroom dynamics level. Also, the flow—staff professional development—at the organizational change level is connected to both the resources and the accountability converters and the interactive and learner-directed environments stocks at the classroom dynamics level.

It should be pointed out that, as in all simulation activities in the STACI$^{N}$ Project, the objective is to facilitate the analysis of the problem, not to create the correct model. This point stresses that our interest in systems thinking is not to get the right model for the purpose of prediction. Rather, it is the heuristic value of creating the model that excites us. Students and teachers alike all report gaining a deeper understanding of the phenomena they are studying through the use of systems thinking. Therefore, we never attempt to find the correct answer. It probably is not attainable, and there would be no way of ever testing its accuracy. Rather, it is the search for a reasonable model that approximates the data available that is an incredibly rich and stimulating experience for all learners.

## SUMMARY

In this chapter, we have guided the reader through a description of our activities over an eight-year period in which we carried out innovations to curricula using computer-based curriculum technology. During that time, we took on many roles in addition to that of researcher to facilitate reform. The efficacy of the innovation depended heavily on the teachers' capability to integrate use of the theoretical perspective of systems thinking, the hardware, and the software in their classrooms. Therefore, we had to spend enormous amounts of time and resources on implementation issues. Most of what we did in the early period pertained to administrative and technical issues, rather than research activities. Also, because it took much longer than we or the teachers anticipated to make systems thinking operational, there never was a time when we could say that the experimental stimulus or the treatment had been administered.

Consequently, our plans for a quasi-experimental design had to be replaced with a more comprehensive case study perspective. We adopted a variety of methods on a continuing or longitudinal basis to examine a host of outcomes from the curricular innovation at three different levels: student learning, classroom dynamics, and organizational change. In all these administrative, technical, and research aspects it was necessary to be adaptive, flexible, and patient. These are skills that are rarely, if ever, discussed in methodology textbooks. In the case of the STACI[N] Project, they were developed in the field and just-in-time. In many respects, our experiences mirror closely those reported by Newman (1990) in his attempts to use electronic networks connecting schools for teaching and research activities with elementary school students in learning geography. We strongly suspect that such experiences will become commonplace as more endeavors are initiated to use technology to support reforms in mathematics and science education.   Editors' note: Since this chapter was first written, significant reformulations have occurred in NSF's systemic reform programs.

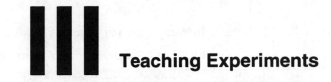

# III Teaching Experiments

Each of the five chapters in Part III takes a different approach to a single basic type of research design, called a teaching experiment, that often distinguishes itself by its conscious breaking down of the researcher-teacher divide. The role of the research is recast, sometimes as a teacher, always as a co-learner. Similarly, the roles of students and teachers often are recast as cocollaborators in the search for critical issues, promising perspectives, relevant data, or useful interpretations. In all cases, the characterization of research is transformed beyond that of a remote viewing of classroom life in which the researcher acts by judging the classroom life against a prefabricated ideal. In fact, to emphasize this point, it perhaps would have been appropriate to retitle Part III as teaching and learning experiments.

It is fitting that teaching experiments were chosen as the first type of research design that we deal with in depth in this book. There is perhaps no other type of research that more clearly illustrates distinctive characteristics of research in mathematics and science education. Yet, the five chapters in this part of the book make clear the diversity of the approaches that referred to as "teaching experiments." In fact, beyond the five chapters in Part III, at least half a dozen more chapters in later sections also deal with related methodologies involving action research (e.g., chaps. 15 and 16), classroom-based research (e.g., chap. 14), ethnographic observations (e.g., chap. 17), clinical interviews (e.g., chaps. 19 and 20), videotape analyses (e.g., chaps. 22 and 23), and investigations in which studies of student development interact with parallel investigations focusing on teacher development, software development, or the development of other relevant entities (e.g., chaps. 26 and 27).

In general, teaching experiments focus on development that occurs within conceptually rich environments that are explicitly designed to optimize the chances that relevant developments will occur in forms that can be observed. The time periods that are involved may range from a few hours, to a week, to a semester or an academic year. Furthermore, the environment being observed may range from small laboratory-like interview rooms, to full classrooms, to even larger learning environments.

Some of the teaching experiments that are described in Part III focus on the development of *students* (Steffe & Thompson, chap. 11); some focus on the development of *ideas* in groups, teams, or individuals (Lesh & Kelly, chap. 9); and, others focus on the development of *teachers* (Simon, chap. 13), *classroom instructional environments* (Cobb, chap. 12), or *instructional activities* such as those involving software (Confrey & Lachance, chap. 10). Furthermore, most of these research designs inherently involve interactions among the preceding kinds of developing entities. Nonetheless, regardless of which subject is chosen for emphasis, regardless of what kind of interactions are salient, and regardless of what "grain size" the analysis adopts, each chapter in this part of the book is concerned with ways to investigate the development of complex, self-organizing, interacting, and adapting *systems* whose evolution is often extremely sensitive to small changes in conditions. Therefore, many of the issues that were raised in Part II re-emerge in forms that focus on issues about replication and the generalizability of results.

Regardless of whether attention is focused on the developing ways of thinking of students, teachers, programs, or schools, one difficulty that generally arises is that the relevant underlying systems cannot be observed directly, but can be known only by their effects. To observe them, researchers must interact with them; and, when researchers act on these systems, the systems typically act back by molding, shaping, or reacting to the information that they encounter. Consequently, when the relevant problem solvers or decision makers solve problems (or learn, or develop), development involves far more than simply "delivering" information to passive subjects. It involves complex interactions, sophisticated adaptation cycles, and feedback loops that frequently lead to breakdowns in traditional distinctions between researchers, teachers, and learners; and, similar breakdowns occur between assessment experts and curriculum developers, or observers and observed. Therefore, researchers often must become integral parts of the systems they investigated.

Before reading the chapters in Part III, readers may find it useful to formulate responses to the following questions for a teaching experiment that they might want to conduct:

1. When different problem solvers are expected to interpret a single problem solving situation in fundamentally different ways, what does it mean to speak about "standardized" questions? When different learners are expected to interpret a given learning experience in fundamentally different ways, what does it mean to speak about "the same treatment" being given to two different participants? When researchers are integral parts of the systems being investigated, what does it mean to say that other researchers should see the "same" things" in the "same" situations? What do your answers to the preceding questions suggest about the "replicating" research results?

194

2. If your study involves interactions among several distinct types of problem solvers or decision makers, how will you go beyond describing isolated individuals to also describe relevant interactions? How will you go beyond describing isolated states to also describe transitions from one state to another?

3. What kind of generalizations do you hope to be able to make about the subjects who are involved in your own research? (Notice that generalizations about *students* tend to have a different character than generalizations about students' *ideas*. For example, generalizations about *students* tend to involve statements such as: "This child is a preoperational thinker." "This child is impulsive." "This child is a type B thinker." Whereas, generalizations about students' *ideas* tend to involve statements such as: "The development of this idea involves increasing representational fluency." "Higher order understandings of this conceptual system involves going beyond thinking *with* the conceptual system to also thinking about it in a variety of problem solving situations.")

4. Mathematics and science education research often focuses on the evolving conceptual systems used by learners or problem solvers. But, for many of these conceptual systems, significant developments are not likely to occur unless artificially rich environments are created that stimulate, focus, and facilitate development. In research that you might want to conduct, how important do you think it is for these learning environments to be similar to those that might readily occur in typical classrooms? To what extent is it important to focus on atypical learning environments (such as those that are technology rich) that might not be achievable in regular classrooms?

5. Regardless of whether attention is focused on students, groups, teachers, or other learners or problem solvers, most modern theories of

teaching and learning believe that the way learning and problem solving experiences are interpreted is influenced by *both* (internal) conceptual systems and (external) structured environments. Nonetheless, some teaching experiments are intended to result in statements about "natural" development (or development that is likely to occur in ordinary circumstances). Or, other teaching experiments focus on "induced" development (or development that appears to be almost completely determined by special and unusual circumstances). For a teaching experiment that you yourself might want to conduct, how important will it be for you to disentangle the relative contributions of internal and external factors? What seem to be promising techniques to accomplish this goal?

# 9 Multitiered Teaching Experiments

**Richard Lesh**
*Purdue University*

**Anthony Kelly**
*Rutgers, the State University of New Jersey*

In this chapter, special attention is given to three-tiered teaching experiments in which a 15-week teaching experiment for students is used as the context for a 15-week teaching experiment for teachers, which in turn is used as the context for a 15-week teaching experiment for researchers. As Table 9.1 suggests, Tier 1 of such projects may be aimed at investigating the nature of students' developing knowledge and abilities; Tier 2 may focus on teachers' developing assumptions about the nature of students' mathematical knowledge and abilities; and, Tier 3 may concentrate on researchers' developing conceptions about the nature of students' and teachers' developing knowledge and abilities.

For the kind of three-tiered teaching experiment outlined in Table 9.1, each tier can be thought of as a longitudinal development study in a conceptually enriched environment (Lesh, 1983). That is, a goal is to go beyond studies of typical development in natural environments to focus on induced development within carefully controlled environments. For example, at the student-level tier, three-tiered teaching experiments have proved to be especially useful for studying the nature of students' developing knowledge about fractions, quotients, ratios, rates, and proportions (or other ideas in algebra, geometry, or calculus), which seldom evolve beyond primitive levels in natural environments that are not enriched artificially.

TABLE 9.1

A Three-Tiered Teaching Experiment

| Tier 3: The Researcher Level | Researchers develop models to make sense of teachers' and students' modeling activities. They reveal their interpretations as they create learning situations for teachers and students and as they describe, explain, and predict teachers' and students' behaviors. |
|---|---|
| Tier 2: The Teacher Level | As teachers develop shared tools (such as observation forms or guidelines for assessing students' responses) and as they describe, explain, and predict students' behaviors, they construct and refine models to make sense of students' modeling activities. |
| Tier 1: The Student Level | Three-person teams of students may work on a series of model-eliciting activities,[a] in which the goals include constructing and refining models (descriptions, explanations, justifications) that reveal partly how they are interpreting the situation. |

In the United States, the term *teaching experiment* became popular following the publication of a series of books entitled *Soviet Studies in School Mathematics* (Kilpatrick & Wirszup, 1975). One reason this term struck a responsive chord among mathematics and science educators was because of a long-standing tradition in which significant research tended to be embedded within an integrated approach to research and development (with interactions between teaching and learning). For example, in some studies, learning environments were developed using software and/or concrete manipulatives; yet, at the same time, investigations were conducted to examine the development of students' knowledge within these environments. Therefore, the research tended to involve feedback loops in which information about the development of students influenced the development of software, and information about the development of software influenced the development of students. Nonetheless, even though most teaching experiments tend to involve some form of teaching, it is not necessarily for them to involve teachers, nor is it necessary for the organism that is learning or solving problems to be an individual . For example:

- *Studies in which no teacher is involved.* Some teaching experiments are intended to explore the nature of "good" software or productive activities

---

[a] Details about such problems are given in the chapter 21, this volume.

with concrete manipulatives. If the goal is to investigate development under optimum conditions, then researchers or other experts may serve as teachers (of individuals or small groups of students), regardless of whether these conditions are realistic in a normal classroom. Therefore, the interactions that are emphasized may be between a student and a researcher (or a student and a computer program), and a classroom teacher may not be involved in any way (see chap. 11, this volume).[1]

- *Studies in which an individual learner (or problem-solver) is not the focus.* Some studies may focus on a group (or a team, or a community) of students, rather than on a single isolated student (see the chapter by Cobb in this volume). Furthermore, depending on the extent to which the researcher is interested in student-student interactions or student-problem interactions (rather than student-teacher interactions), the presence of an authority figure (or a teacher) may not be of interest in the study. [2]

---

[1] In model-eliciting activities that the authors tend to emphasize in their teaching experiments, they have found that three-person teams of average-ability students are able to develop descriptions or explanations that embody important mathematical ways of thinking. That is, students frequently invent (or at least modify or refine significantly) major mathematical ideas, and meaningful learning is often a by-product of problem solving. Consequently, intrusions from an authority figure (a teacher or researcher) generally may not be needed.

[2] In model-eliciting activities where several modeling cycles are required in order for students to produce ways of thinking that are useful, one of the goals of the research is usually to observe and document these cycles as directly as possible. Consequently, because ways of thinking tend to be externalized in a group, the authors tend to focus on problem solving situations in which the problem solving entity is a three-person team of students, rather than individual students working in isolation. Then, they compare team problem solving with individual problem solving in much the same way that other researchers have compared problem solving by experts versus novices or gifted students versus average-ability students.

In general, for the type of teaching experiment that is emphasized in this chapter, the goal is not to produce generalizations about: (a) students (e.g., she is a concrete operational child; he is impulsive, or creative, or left-brained, or suffers from dyslexia); (b) teachers (e.g., his beliefs are consistent with a constructivist philosophy of learning); or (c) groups (e.g., they have not adopted a taken-as-shared notion of what it means to justify a claim). Instead, the primary goal is to focus on the nature of developing *ideas* (or "smart tools," models, or metaphors in which these ideas are embedded), regardless of whether the relevant development occurs in individuals or in groups.

## A PRIMARY DILEMMA UNDERLYING TEACHING EXPERIMENT METHODOLOGIES

Because a goal of most teaching experiments is to go beyond descriptions of successive *states* of knowledge to hypothesize the processes and *mechanisms* that promote development from one state to another, it is important to create research environments that induce changes in the subjects whose knowledge or abilities are being investigated while minimizing uninteresting influences that are imposed by authority figures (e.g., teachers or researchers).[3]

---

[3] In a chapter entitled "Conceptual Analyses of Problem Solving Performance," Lesh (1983) described briefly similarities and differences among task analyses, idea analyses, and analyses of students' cognitive characteristics. For example: (a) in task analyses, the results of the research are statements about tasks; (b) in idea analyses, the results are statements about the nature and development of ideas (in the minds of students); and (c) in analyses of students' cognitive characteristics, the results are statements about the nature and development of students themselves.

To recognize the implications of the preceding distinctions among the analyses of students, tasks, and ideas (or tools or conceptual technologies), it is useful to keep in mind the following analogy. In his book, *The Selfish Gene* (1976), Richard Dawkins explained Darwin's theory of evolution using "a gene's-eye-view of development" in which animals and other human-size organisms are interpreted as "survival machines" that genes develop in order to optimize their own chances of survival. Then, later in this book, in a chapter entitled "Memes: The New Replicators," Dawkins described why the law that all life evolves through the differential survival of replicating entities applies equally well to both genes and "memes" (a term coined by Dawkins to refer to ideas) and

(continued)

Regardless of whether a researcher's primary aim is to observe, or to document change, or to measure, when teaching experiment methodologies are used, the following fundamental dilemma tends to arise. If the research is designed to find ways to think about the nature of students' mathematical knowledge (or abilities), then how can the researchers also be inducing changes in that knowledge?    If the researcher is inducing changes in subjects (e.g., through teaching or through carefully structured sequences of problem solving experiences), then how can the researcher also be studying the nature of the change that occurs? How can researchers avoid simply observing what they themselves created? How can they measure change (or document change or observe change) at the same time that they are changing the measures (or the documentation systems or the observation schemes)?

Answers to these questions hinge on the fact that, in well-designed teaching experiments, it is possible to create conditions that optimize the chances that development will occur without dictating the directions that this development must take. For instance, this can be accomplished by: (a) creating environments where investigators (students, teachers, and researchers) confront the need to develop new conceptions (or interpretations) of their experiences; (b) structuring these interactions so that the preceding constructs must be tested, assessed, extended, refined, rejected, or revised for a specific purpose (e.g., to increase their

---

why the "survival of the stable" is a more general way to think about Darwin's law of the "survival of the fittest."

Similar themes have been developed in more recent publications by Dawkins (1976, 1986, 1995), Gould (1981), and others who are investigating complexity theory and the development of complex, self-organizing systems (Barlow, 1991, 1994; Kauffman, 1995).   For the purposes of this chapter about research design in mathematics and science education, the heart of the preceding analogy is that it explains why it makes sense sometimes to go beyond (or beneath) our prejudice of focusing on (only) people-size organisms.   In particular, focusing on the development of ideas (regardless of whether these ideas develop in the minds of individual students or groups of students) often is productive for many of the same reasons why Dawkins, Gould, and Kauffman have found that, in order to understand the development of humans, it sometimes makes sense to focus on the development of other kinds of interacting complex systems.

usefulness, stability, and power in the execution of a concrete task); (c) providing tools that facilitate (but do not needlessly constrain) the construction of relevant models; and (d) using formative feedback and consensus building to ensure that these constructs develop in directions that are continually "better" without merely testing preconceived hypotheses about a predetermined definition of "best." In other words, the environment should "press for adaptation" (Noddings, 1990) by facilitating the construction and testing of basic constructs, so that some will be ruled in and others ruled out.

Using techniques that are described in chapter 21 of this book, about model-eliciting activities, it also is possible to structure tasks in such a way that each of the relevant investigators (students, teachers, and researchers) simultaneously learns and documents what he or she is learning. To accomplish these goals, it is important to provide rich opportunities for the investigators (students, teachers, and researchers) to represent and reflect upon their knowledge. This can be done by focusing on problem solving or decision making activities in which the results that the investigators develop inherently involve descriptions, explanations, or justified predictions that reveal explicitly how they are interpreting the problem solving situation (Kaput, 1985, 1987). In this way, as constructs develop, a continuous trail of documentation is produced that automatically provides traces of development. Thus, investigators at all levels can view them in retrospect to clarify the nature of the learning that occurred. In other words, by providing rich opportunities for investigators to express, test, and refine their evolving constructs, it is possible to simultaneously stimulate, facilitate, and investigate the development of key constructs, understandings, and abilities. Also, because significant changes often occur during relatively brief periods of closely monitored time, many changes and inducements for change can be documented explicitly so that it is possible to go beyond descriptions of successive states of knowledge to focus also on the mechanisms that promote development from one state to another.

## DIFFICULTIES THAT LED TO THE DEVELOPMENT OF MULTITIERED TEACHING EXPERIMENTS

The following difficulties are among the most significant that led to the development of the kind of multitiered teaching experiments that is described in this chapter.

First, for many concepts that we want to investigate, most students' relevant knowledge seldom develops beyond primitive levels as long as their mathematical experiences are

First, for many concepts that we want to investigate, most students' relevant knowledge seldom develops beyond primitive levels as long as their mathematical experiences are restricted to those that occur naturally in everyday settings. Therefore, to investigate the development of these concepts, artificially rich mathematical environments need to be created, and observations need to be made during time spans when significant developments are able to occur.

Second, in the preceding investigations, after conducting interviews designed to identify the nature of a given student's knowledge, the authors often conducted instructional activities designed to change the student's understandings and abilities. During the course of these instructional activities, the authors often found the conclusions that they had formed that were based on initial interviews needed to be revised significantly. Often, one of the best ways to find out about a student's state of knowledge is to try to teach him or her something (or to induce changes in that state of knowledge). Consequently, for yet another reason, a goal for relevant research is to preserve traces that document the nature of the developments that occur.

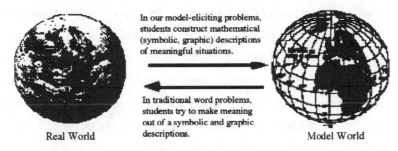

Real World                    Model World

In our model-eliciting problems, students construct mathematical (symbolic, graphic) descriptions of meaningful situations.

In traditional word problems, students try to make meaning out of a symbolic and graphic descriptions.

FIG. 9.1. The difference between model-eliciting problems and traditional word problems.

Third, as FIG. 9.1 suggests, for many of the problem solving situations that the authors want to emphasize, the processes that are involved are almost exactly the opposite of those that are involved in traditional word problems where the most important stages of problem solving seldom involve mathematization (i.e., quantification or other types of mathematical interpretation), and the results that students produce seldom involve descriptions, constructions, explanations, or justifications in which they must reveal explicitly how they interpret the problem solving situation. Consequently, if nontraditional problems are emphasized, the following dilemmas tend to arise, which require researchers to think in new ways about issues such as the possibility of standardized questions:

symbolic, or spoken description nearly always is appropriate (with trade-offs involving accuracy, timeliness, complexity, simplicity, precision, etc.). Therefore, because $N$ different students may interpret a single situation in $N$ different ways, traditional conceptions of standardized questions need to be revised considerably. Also, to identify the nature of the mathematics that a student uses to make sense of a given problem, it is not enough to look only at the problem and at whether or not an acceptable response is given. The mathematics that needs to be identified is in the student's solution; it is not in the author's problem.

- If the solution of a problem inherently requires students to develop a construct (or an interpretation), then construct development is bound to occur. Furthermore, if the construct involves a mathematically significant system, then significant learning inherently occurs. In other words, in the context of such problems, the process of trying to gather information about students' knowledge inherently causes the state of that knowledge to change. Therefore, if students' knowledge involves continually adapting systems, and not only static structures, then relevant research must go beyond static glimpses of development and must preserve traces that document the nature of the developments that occur.

## THE NEED FOR SHARED RESEARCH DESIGNS

The kind of multitiered teaching experiment that is described here was designed to be useful in action research projects in which teachers act as investigators (as well as participants) and/or researchers act as teachers or learners (as well as investigators). Furthermore, it is intended to be useful as a shared research design for large research and development projects in which it is important to coordinate the activities of multiple researchers with multiple purposes at multiple sites. For example, it has been used extensively in *The Rational Number Project* (Behr et al., 1991), *The Project On Using Mathematics in Everyday Situations* (Lesh, 1985b), *The Project on Models & Modeling in Mathematics & Science Education* (National Center for Improving Student Learning and Achievement in Mathematics and Science, 1998), and *SimCalc* (Kaput & Roschelle, 1993).

In these projects, one goal was for the overall research designs to be sufficiently structured to give shape to the information that was being drawn from different levels and types of isolated studies. Yet, it was also important for the overall research designs to be sufficiently open to provide access for participants whose perspectives and interests often varied because of different assumptions and perspectives related to the following kinds of factors.

## What Factors Are the Center of Attention?

For the type of teaching experiment that is emphasized in this chapter, the subjects may range from individual students, to groups of students, to teachers, to classroom discourse, communities involving both teachers and students, or schools and surrounding communities Also the entities whose development is being investigated may be the smart tools (models, metaphors, or representational systems) that students develop for dealing with a given class of problems. Therefore, some teaching experiments result in generalizations about the nature of students' conceptual and procedural tools, whereas others result in generalizations about the nature of students, teachers, groups, software, or other entities. Some of the most common sources of design flaws  in teacher experiments tend to result from a lack of clarity and consistency about what entities the research is intended to yield generalizations. For example, studies that are intended to yield generalizations on the nature of productive learning environments (software, concrete manipulatives, or realistic problem solving activities) generally need to be governed by a logic that is quite different from that in studies intended to yield generalizations on the nature of students' (or teachers') knowledge or tools.

## What Theoretical Windows Are Emphasized?

Regardless of whether the researcher focuses on *ideas* developing in students, *students* developing in groups, *groups* developing in classrooms, or *classrooms* in schools, each level of analysis tends to highlight or clarify some aspects of the situation while, at the same time, de-emphasizing or distorting others. Choices about the subjects and the level of detail of the analysis are similar to choices about how far up or down to turn a microscope or telescope in a laboratory for a biology or astronomy task. Furthermore, when a research project chooses to adopt a given theoretical perspective, the choice is also somewhat like choosing a window through which to view the subjects.

Depending on the choices that are made about theoretical windows and level of detail, a given investigation is likely to collect different information, and different patterns or regularities are likely to be emphasized. For example, in a multitiered teaching experiment, a teacher's-eye view of a situation may produce results that are quite different than those generated from a student's-eye-view or a researcher's-eye view. Or, when a teaching experiment includes a series of interviews, the nature of these interviews often differs significantly depending on whether the researcher interprets the interviews to involve mainly student–teacher interactions (see FIG. 9.2a), where the problem may be seen as being a relatively insignificant device to facilitate this interaction, or student–problem interactions (see FIG. 9.2b), where the teacher may be seen as being mainly a device to facilitate this interaction.

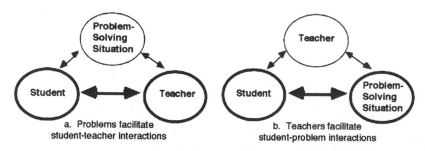

FIG. 9.2. Different viewpoints and philosophies produce different interpretations.

Perhaps social constructivists might emphasize interviews of the type the depicted in FIG. 9.2a, whereas cognitive constructivists might emphasize interviews of the type shown in FIG. 9.2b. But, such labels tend to be far too crude to predict accurately the assumptions or procedures of individual researchers. For example, in their research, the authors of this chapter generally take an integrated approach to both the cognitive and social aspects of learning. Yet, in the components of their projects where interviewing or teaching are involved, situations that are characterized mainly by FIG. 9.2a tend to be far less productive than those characterized mainly by FIG. 9.2b.[4] On the other hand, in chapter 13 of this book, by Steffe and Thompson, the interviews that they describe clearly emphasize interactions of the FIG. 9.2a type; however, both Steffe and Thompson usually considered to be leading spokesmen for the cognitive constructivist perspective.

The points here are not to label people or to make a simplistic association of specific interviewing techniques with crude labels for theoretical perspectives. In fact, in this chapter, the authors do not even want to argue that one approach or perspective is more productive than another. Instead, the point is that one of the main operating principles underlying multitiered teaching experiments is to juxtapose systematically several alternative perspectives and to seek corroboration through triangulation.

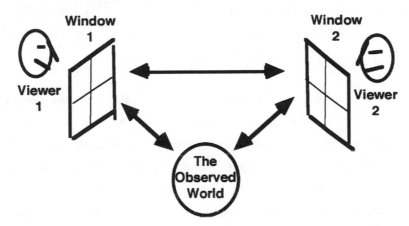

FIG. 9.3. The corroboration-through-triangulation principle.

For the kind of multitiered teaching experiment discussed herein, a corroboration-through-triangulation principle (see FIG. 9.3) may involve three distinct types of mismatches:

---

[4] Details of why this is the case are described in chapter 21.

- Between-observer mismatches; for example, comparing the interpretations of students, teachers, and researchers.

- Within-observer/between-window mismatches; for example, when teachers put on their "social-cognitive-mathematical-pedagogical glasses" when viewing a learning or problem solving activity.

- Within-observer/between-role mismatches; for example, when teachers are cast in a variety of roles that range from interviewers, to observers, to subjects, or to participants.

For instance, a given person's interpretation of a situation may vary from time to time depending on factors such as whether their perspective is articulated during the course of an ongoing activity, or whether it is based on a more detached, after-the-fact view of a videotape of the completed session. Therefore, one way to encourage the development of each interpretation is to juxtapose these two perspectives and to press for their integration or another form of adaptation.

## What Practical Problems Are Treated as Priorities?

What is observed in a research setting also depends on the perceived purpose of the information that is to be collected or generated. For instance, for the type of teaching experiment that is the topic of this chapter, these purposes include issues that involve:

- *Content quality*: For example, what does it mean to have a deeper or higher order understanding of a given concept? What does it mean for a curriculum and an instruction to focus on detailed treatments of a small number of big ideas, rather than on superficial coverage of a large number of small ideas?

- *Technology*: For example, what kinds of activities are most productive to facilitate specific types of knowledge or understanding? In what ways can specific types of tools be used to help provide early democratic access to powerful ideas?

- *School-to-career transitions*: For example, what kinds of knowledge and abilities are needed for success in a technology-based society (where people often work in teams of specialists, using powerful tools and diverse resources)?

- *Equity*: For example, what kinds of problem solving situations are especially effective and should be used to recognize and reward students with a broader range of abilities than the narrow, shallow, and obsolete conceptions of ability that are stressed usually in traditional textbooks, tests, and teaching?

- *Teacher development*: For example, how can information about the nature of students' knowledge be used to influence how teachers teach?
- *Instructional design*: for example, what are the strengths and weaknesses associated different types of activities using computer-based graphics?

Regardless of whether a given researcher focuses on the development of students, teachers, groups, software, or other entities that interact during teaching and learning, a basic assumption that underlies the kind of teaching experiment that is described in this chapter is that none of these adapting, and self-regulating systems develops in isolation from one another. Consequently, the kinds of research designs that have proved to be most productive for investigating the nature of these entities tend to focus on both *development* (not just on isolated static glimpses of development) and *interactions* (not just on isolated entities). In general, only incomplete pictures of development arise from isolated studies that focus exclusively on one or two of the preceding entities, or from studies that focus exclusively on isolated states of development rather than on the mechanisms that drive development from one state to another. Therefore, to conduct the kind of complex, multidimensional, and longitudinal studies that are needed, the notion of a partly shared research design has evolved to help coordinate the work of multiple researchers at multiple sites. The multitiered teaching experiments described in this chapter are examples of these *partly shared research designs*.

# THE CONSISTENCY PRINCIPLE FOR RESEARCH DESIGNS AT ALL THREE LEVELS OF THREE-TIERED TEACHING EXPERIMENTS

Another basic assumption underlying the design of multitiered teaching experiments is that, in spite of obvious differences among the three levels of investigators (students, teachers, and researchers), all of them are engaged in making sense of their experiences by developing smart tools (constructs, models, conceptual systems, belief systems, and representational systems) that are used to generate descriptions, explanations, constructions, and justifications using a variety of representation systems (e.g., systems of written symbols, systems of graphic images, or systems involving concrete manipulatives, experience-based metaphors, or spoken language). Two corollaries of this assumption are that similar cognitive characteristics should be expected from the investigators at each tier, and that at each tier, similar mechanisms also should be expected to contribute to the construction, integration, differentiation, reorganization, and refinement of each of the relevant conceptual systems.

To see how these preceding two corollaries influence the design of multitiered teaching experiments, this section focuses on relevant results from several recent studies in which the student-level teaching experiments consisted mainly of 60-minute sessions in which three-person teams of students worked on a series of model-eliciting problems with the following characteristics:

- Interpretation of the problem solving situation is an important part of the task, and, during a single, problem solving session (which lasts approximately 40–60 minutes), students are able to produce responses that are appropriate in terms of factors such as accuracy, precision, reliability, timeliness, or costliness.

- Several alternative levels and types of responses are possible, and the students themselves are able to make judgments about the strengths and weaknesses of alternative descriptions, explanations, constructions, or justifications.

- The responses that students construct tend to require 3–10 modeling cycles where each cycle involves a progressively more refined and elaborated interpretation of the givens, goals, and solution paths.

## Cognitive Characteristics of Investigators (Students, Teachers, and Researchers)

When student-level teaching experiments are centered around sequences of the preceding kinds of model-eliciting activities, the results showed consistently that the students' initial interpretations tend to be strikingly barren and distorted compared with the conceptions that developed later (chap. 23, this volume). For example, early interpretations frequently are based on only a small subset of the information that is relevant; yet, at the same time, inappropriate prejudices are often "read into" the situation that were not given objectively.

Based on this observation, the consistency principle for research design suggests that, when teacher-level and researcher-level teaching experiments are used to accompany such modeling cycles also, and that for the researchers and teachers, just as for the children, first-cycle interpretations should be expected to be rather barren and distorted compared to those that should evolve after several cycles.

In a multitiered teaching experiment, it is seldom enough for researchers to view videotapes only once or twice before extracting quotations that they believe are indicative of the students' ways of thinking. As its name implies, teaching experiments usually need to involve a series of experiments during which the constructs that are being developed should be tested repeatedly while they are being gradually modified, extended, and refined. As FIG. 9.4 suggests, at each tier of a multitiered teaching experiment, a series of modeling cycles usually is needed, and, during each cycle, the relevant investigators should be challenged to: (a) reveal their current interpretations by making them explicit, (b) test and assess their current interpretations, (c) reflect upon their current interpretations, and (d) gradually refine, reorganize, extend, or reject their current interpretations. In particular, researchers are not exempt from these rules.

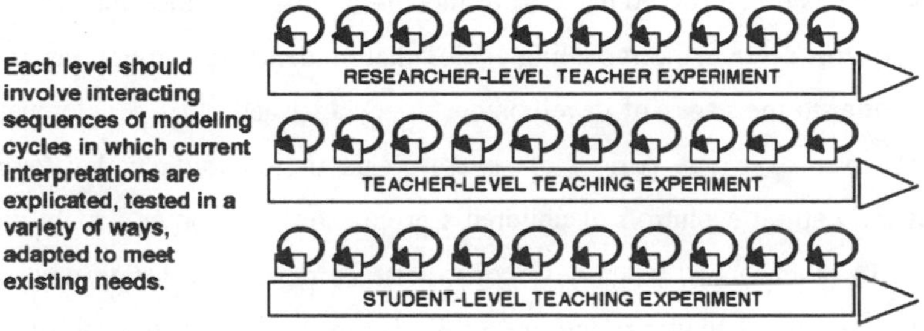

**Each level should involve interacting sequences of modeling cycles in which current interpretations are explicated, tested in a variety of ways, adapted to meet existing needs.**

RESEARCHER-LEVEL TEACHER EXPERIMENT

TEACHER-LEVEL TEACHING EXPERIMENT

STUDENT-LEVEL TEACHING EXPERIMENT

FIG. 9.4. The iterative model-refinement principle.

For researchers as well as for teachers and students, data interpretation should not be left until the end of the project when all of the data collection has been completed. The iterative model-refinement principle says that if no researcher-level model testing takes place throughout the study, then no modeling cycles are likely to occur, and little model development is likely to take place.[5]

---

[5] For additional details about videotape analyses, see chapter 23 of this book.

throughout the study, then no modeling cycles are likely to occur, and little model development is likely to take place.[5]

## General Mechanisms That Promote Construct Development

Observations in the previous section raise another key question that a coherent research design should address, namely: How is it that investigators (students, teachers, and researchers) are able to develop beyond the inherent inadequacies of their initial interpretations of their experiences? Or to express it differently: When early interpretations of the givens and goals are barren and distorted, what processes can students, teachers, and researchers use to guide themselves through a series of models that are progressively better without having a predetermined conception of best?

Results from student-level teaching experiments suggest that the driving forces underlying the development of conceptual systems are similar to those that apply to other types of adapting and self-organizing systems (Kauffman, 1993, 1995). For example, in student-level teaching experiments that involved the kind of model-eliciting activities that were described at the beginning of this section, the modeling cycles that students go through are inclined to be remarkably similar to the stages of development that Piaget and other developmental psychologists had observed over time periods of several years in longitudinal development studies investigating the natural evolution of children's proportional reasoning capabilities (Lesh & Kaput, 1988). In other words, when new constructs are developed during the solution of a single 60-minute model-eliciting activity, this is merely another way of saying that significant local conceptual developments tend to occur, and the mechanisms that contribute to development tend to be strikingly similar to those that have been identified by Piaget (Piaget & Inhelder, 1974) and by current researchers investigating complexity, chaos, and adapting self-organizing systems (Kauffman, 1993, 1995).

Implications from modern theories of dynamic systems are similar in many ways to those that have been used in the past to explain the development of complex systems. For example:

---

[5] For additional details about videotape analyses, see chapter 23 of this book.

- In mathematics education, Lesh and Kaput (1988) have related how mechanisms similar to Piaget's contribute to the modeling cycles that lead to the solution of individual, model-eliciting activities.

Therefore, the consistency principle for research design implies that, for development to occur at any of the levels of a multitiered teaching experiment, researchers should anticipate that mechanisms must be created to provide for mutation, selection, propagation, and preservation of the relevant systems whose development is to be encouraged (see FIG. 9.5). Examples are given shortly. First, it is useful to describe a few more similarities and differences between the models and modeling activities of students, teachers, and researchers.

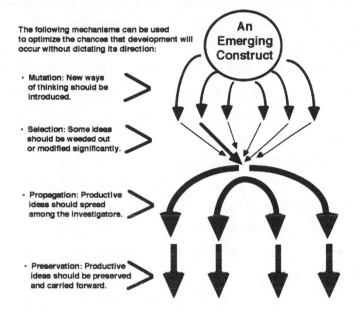

FIG. 9.5. Mechanisms that are driving forces for construct development.

## SIMILARITIES AND DIFFERENCES BETWEEN STUDENTS, TEACHERS, AND RESEARCHERS

The language of models and modeling has proved to be a powerful unifying theme for describing similarities among the construct development activities of students, teachers, and researchers; and, it also has proved to be useful for helping researchers and curricula designers

# SIMILARITIES AND DIFFERENCES BETWEEN STUDENTS, TEACHERS, AND RESEARCHERS

The language of models and modeling has proved to be a powerful unifying theme for describing similarities among the construct development activities of students, teachers, and researchers; and, it also has proved to be useful for helping researchers and curricula designers to establish relationships connecting their work in mathematics, science, and everyday problem solving situations.

To make use of modeling theory in the context of three-tiered teaching experiments, it is important to emphasize that students, teachers, and researchers are all decision makers (i.e., problem-solvers) who often make decisions at times when: (a) an overwhelming amount of relevant information is available, yet, the information needs to be filtered, weighted, simplified, organized, and interpreted before it is useful; (b) some important information may be missing, or it may need to be sought out, yet, a decision needs to be made within specified time limits, budgets, constraints, and margins for error, or (c) some of the most important aspects of the situation often involve patterns or regularities beneath the surface of things, or they may involve second-order constructs (such as an index of inflation) which cannot be counted or measured directly but that involve patterns, trends, relationships, or organizational systems that can be described in a variety of ways and at a variety of levels of sophistication or precision (to fit different assumptions, conditions, and purposes).

When humans confront problem solving situations where both too much and not enough information may be available, they simplify and make sense of their experiences using models (or descriptive systems embedded in appropriate external representations). For example:

- Because models embody explanations of how the facts are related to one another, as well as descriptions and explanations of patterns and regularities beneath the surface of things, they can be used to base decisions on a minimum set of cues, to fill holes, or go beyond the information given (Bruner, 1973).

- Because models give holistic interpretations of entire situations, including hypotheses about objects or events that are not given obviously (or that need to be generated or sought out), they can be used to select, filter, analyze, and interpret the information that is most relevant, while ignoring or de-emphasizing the information that is less relevant (Shulman, 1985).

According to these perspectives, expertise (for students, teachers, or researchers) is not considered to be reducible to a simplistic list of condition-action rules. This is because mathematics entails seeing at least as much as it entails doing. Or, to state the matter somewhat differently, one could say that doing mathematics involves (more than anything else) interpreting situations mathematically; that is, it involves mathematizing. When this mathematization takes place, it is done using constructs (e.g., conceptual models, structural metaphors, and other types of descriptive, explanatory systems for making sense of patterns and regularities in real or possible worlds). These constructs must be developed by the students themselves; they cannot be delivered to them through their teachers' presentations.

Similarly, the ability of teachers to create (or interpret, explain, predict, and control) productive teaching and learning situations quickly and accurately depends heavily on the models that they develop to make sense of relevant experiences. For example, research has shown that: (a) some of the most effective ways to change what teachers do is to change how they think about decision making situations (Romberg, Fennema, & T. Carpenter, 1993); (b) some of the most effective ways to change how teachers interpret their teaching experiences is to change how they think about the nature of their students' mathematical knowledge (T. Carpenter, Fennema, & Romberg, 1993); and (c) some of the most straightforward ways to help teachers become familiar with students' ways of thinking are by using model-eliciting activities in which the teachers produce descriptions, explanations, and justifications that reveal explicitly how they are interpreting learning and problem solving  situations (Lesh, Hoover, & Kelly, 1993). Nonetheless, in spite of the preceding similarities between students' mathematical models and the conceptual systems (or models) that are needed by teachers in their decision making activities, some striking dissimilarities exist too. For instance, the conceptual systems that underlie children's mathematical reasoning are often easy to name (e.g., ratios and proportions) and easy to describe using concise notation systems (e.g., $A/B = C/D$), but when attention shifts from children's knowledge to teachers' knowledge these illusions of simplicity disappear.

Clearly, teachers' mathematical understandings should involve deeper and higher order understandings of elementary mathematical topics; and, equally clearly, these understandings should be quite different from the superficial treatments of advanced topics that tend to characterize the mathematics courses in most teacher education programs.  But what does it mean to have a deeper or higher order understanding of a given, elementary-but-deep, mathematical construct?

One can speak about the development of a given mathematical idea in terms that are: (a) *logical*, based on formal definitions, explanations, or derivations; (b) *historical*, concerning the problems, issues, and perspectives that created the need for the idea; (c) *pedagogical*, relating to how the idea is introduced in available curricular resources (e.g., textbooks, software, videos) or how to make abstract ideas more concrete, or formal ideas more intuitive; or (d) *psychological*, including knowledge about common error patterns, naive conceptualizations, typical stages through which development generally occurs, and dimensions along which development generally occurs. Therefore, a profound understanding of an elementary mathematical idea surely involves the integration of these mathematical-logical-historical-pedagogical-psychological components of development. But what is the nature of this integrated understanding? How does it develop? How can its development be encouraged and assessed? These are precisely the sorts of questions that teacher-level teaching experiments, of the type described in the next section, are designed to address.

# AN EXAMPLE: SPECIFIC WAYS TO STIMULATE AND FACILITATE CONSTRUCT DEVELOPMENT AT THE TEACHER LEVEL OF A THREE-TIERED TEACHING EXPERIMENT

To investigate teachers' (typically undifferentiated) mathematical-psychological-pedagogical understandings about the nature of mathematics (or about the ways in which mathematics is useful in real-life situations), one type of three-tiered teaching experiment that has proved to be especially effective is one in which the student level consists of students working in three-person teams on a series of model-eliciting activities designed to reveal useful information about the nature of these students' mathematical understandings. When students are working on sequences of such tasks, these settings provide an ideal context for teacher-level teaching experiments focusing on the following kinds of real-life, decision making activities for teachers that involve: (a) writing performance assessment activities that are similar to examples that are given of model-eliciting activities and that yield information about students that informs instruction;[6] (b) assessing the strengths and weaknesses of such activities;[7] (c) assessing the strengths and weaknesses of the results that students produce in response to the preceding problems;[8] (d) developing observation forms to help teachers make insightful observations while students are working on the problems, and (e) developing a classification scheme that teachers can use, during students' presentations of their results, to recognize the alternative ways of thinking that students can be expected to use. In other words, real-life

---

[6] Because of the current popularity of performance assessment, teachers who participated in the authors' projects tended to think of model-eliciting activities within this frame of reference. However, even though well-designed model-eliciting activities are quite useful for assessment purposes, they are equally productive from the point of view of instruction. Furthermore, a survey of existing performance assessment materials has shown that few satisfy the kinds of design principles that are described in the chapter of this book about principles for writing effective model-eliciting activities.

[7] Usefulness can be assessed in a variety of ways. Perhaps the goal is to identify a wider range of abilities than those typically recognized and rewarded in traditional textbooks, teaching, and tests, and, consequently, to identify a wider range of students who are mathematically able. Perhaps the goal is to identify students' conceptual strengths and weaknesses, so that instruction can capitalize on the strengths and address or avoid the weaknesses. Perhaps the goal is for teachers to tailor their observations of students' work to produce examples illustrating what it means to develop deeper or higher order understandings of a given concept (e.g., involving ratios, fractions, and proportions). Or perhaps the goal is to predict how students will perform on interviews, tests, competitions, or challenges. In any case, the purpose of the activities must be identified clearly, or it will be impossible to assess their quality.

[8] Again, because of the current popularity of performance assessment, teachers who participated in the authors' projects tended to think of these quality assessment schemes as scoring rubrics, even though typical kinds of scoring rubrics tend to be completely incompatible with the theory underlying model-eliciting activities.

problem solving activities for students provide the basis for some of the most useful kinds of real-life decision making activities for teachers.

As an example of a three-tiered teaching experiment in which the aforementioned kinds of teacher-level tasks were used, it is helpful to focus on the series of studies that led to the design principles that are described in chapter 21 of this book. Throughout these studies, the goals for the teachers were to work with the research staff to develop a collection of performance assessment activities for their own students and to design principles to help other teachers develop such problems, together with the appropriate observation forms, response assessment forms, and other materials to accompany the collection of example problems.

To accomplish these goals, a series of diverse groups of expert teachers worked together in weekly seminars over 15-week periods. Each seminar lasted approximately 2 hours. In each session, participating teachers engaged in the following kinds of activities in which they continually articulated, examined, compared, tested, refined, and reached consensus about their shared conceptions of about excellent problem solving activities for their students:

- *Critiquing example problems*: Teachers discussed the strengths and weaknesses of example problems that had been published by relevant professional or governmental organizations.

- *Role-playing*: Teachers participated, as if they were students, in the solution of example problems whose quality was being assessed. Then they reported and discussed their reflections on things that were significant about the session from a student's point of view.

- *Trying out problems*: Teachers field-tested problems in their own classrooms and reported their observations and interesting examples of students' work.

- *Observing videotapes*: Teachers observed videotapes of three-person teams of students as they were working on example problems whose quality was being assessed. Then they reported and discussed their observations of things that were significant about the session from a teacher's point of view.

- *Writing problems*: Each week, each teacher wrote one problem (or modified a problem that had been written earlier). Then they identified and discussed trial rules for writing excellent problems that satisfied the required characteristics.

- *Assessing students' written work*: Teachers field-tested problems that they or their colleagues had written. Then they assessed the strengths and weaknesses of the students' responses.

Throughout these sessions, the main criteria that were used to judge the quality of the activities that teachers wrote were based on empirical results with students. That is, tasks were judged to be excellent mainly because the results that students produced provided useful diagnostic information about their conceptual strengths and weaknesses. So, when teachers wrote activities for their students, their goal was to develop problems with the characteristic that when they (the teachers) roamed around their classrooms observing students who were working on these problems and when they examined the results that their students produced, the results would yield information similar to the kind that might have been generated if the teachers had had enough time to interview most of the students individually.

Similarly, as teachers were trying to create activities to investigate the nature of students' mathematical knowledge, researchers were trying to create activities to investigate the nature of teachers' knowledge. To accomplish this goal, the key to success was based on the fact that, when teachers explained why they thought specific tasks were good (or why they thought specific pieces of their students' work were good), they automatically revealed a great deal of their own assumptions about the nature of mathematics, problem solving, learning, and teaching.

As the teachers' authoring capabilities improved, the records from their seminars and written work produced a continuous trail of documentation that could be examined by both them and the research staff to reflect on the nature of the teachers' developing knowledge and abilities. The mechanisms that served as drivers for this development were particular instances of those that were described earlier in this chapter: mutation, selection, propagation, and preservation.

## Mutation

The goal here is to "perturb" the constructs (models) that teachers have developed about what mathematics is, how students think mathematically, and how to encourage growth in mathematics through instructional interventions. New modes of thinking were stimulated in the following kinds of ways by: (a) identifying examples of students' work where surprising insights often were apparent about their conceptual strengths and weaknesses; (b) using discussion sessions in which teachers generated specific problems and rules of thumb for writing such problems; (c) discussing perceived strengths and weaknesses of example problems that were chosen by the researchers or the teachers; or (d) using brief brainstorming sessions in which the goal was to generate interesting, "wild, new ideas" to consider during the following week's authoring activities.

## Selection

As a result of the mutation activities, a number of new ideas tended to be produced about good problems, how to write them, and the nature of students' developing knowledge and abilities. However, the new ideas were not necessarily good ideas. Therefore, in order to help teachers select the better from the poorer ideas, the following three types of selection activities were used: (a) *trial by consistency*, in which individual teachers were encouraged to make judgments about whether or not a suggestion makes sense or is consistent with their own current conceptions and experiences; that is, the teacher, as the constructor of knowledge, is the ultimate arbiter; (b) *trial by ordeal*, in which a teacher's ideas and examples were field-tested promptly with students and were found either to be useful or not, based on the results that students produced; (c) *trial by jury*, in which teachers were encouraged to compare ideas with their peers and to discuss the likely strengths and weaknesses of alternative suggestions. This introduces the notion of community apprenticeship into the model. These discussions were not intended to be punitive. Instead, they were designed to help teachers develop defensible models of mathematics, problem solving, teaching, and learning and organize the various suggestions into a coherent conceptual system so that suggestions were not adopted merely because they were novel. The goal was not to develop individual constructs for thinking about the nature of excellent activities; it was to develop shared constructs.

## Propagation

The goal here was for good ideas, which had survived the preceding tests, to spread throughout the population of teachers. This was accomplished not only through the seminars and discussions, but also by using electronic mail and easily shared, computer-based files. In this way, it was easy for teachers to share useful tools and resources, effective authoring procedures, and productive conceptual schemes.

## Preservation

Again, the accumulation of knowledge was encouraged by using videotapes and computer-based files to preserve written records of ideas that proved to be effective and by putting these ideas in a form that was easy for teachers to edit and use in future situations. Therefore, the "survival of the fittest" meant that successful ideas and strategies continued to be used and that they continued to be refined or improved by other teachers. Thus, the body of shared information that developed was grounded in the personal experience of individual teachers.

As a consequence of these teacher-level teaching experiments, the teachers developed, tested, and refined six principles for creating (or choosing) excellent tasks that they referred to as performance assessment activities. The results of these activities are described in chapter 21 of this book.

# AN EXAMPLE: SPECIFIC WAYS TO STIMULATE AND FACILITATE CONSTRUCT DEVELOPMENT AT THE RESEARCHER LEVEL OF A THREE-TIERED TEACHING EXPERIMENT

The consistency principle of research design suggests that, in general, similar research design principles that apply to student-level and teacher-level teaching experiments also apply in straightforward ways to research-level teaching experiments. In particular, it is important to generate environments in which researchers need to create explicit descriptions, explanations, and predictions about teachers' and students' behaviors. Then, mechanisms need to be preplanned to ensure that these constructs will be tested, refined, revised, rejected, or extended in ways that increase their usefulness, stability, fidelity, and power and that a trail of documentation will be created that will reveal the nature of the evolution that takes place.

For the series of three-tiered teaching experiments described in the previous section, students developed constructs to describe mathematical problem solving situations; teachers developed constructs to describe activities involving students; and researchers developed constructs to describe activities involving teachers (and students). One of the ways in which researchers got feedback about their evolving conceptions of teachers' expertise was to select and organize illuminating snippets from the transcripts that were made during teachers' discussion groups that were held each week. Then, participating teachers selected, rejected, revised, and edited these snippets in ways that they believed to be appropriate. Consequently, these teachers were true coresearchers in the researcher-level teaching experiments which, from the researchers' point of view, were aimed at clarifying the general nature of the teachers' evolving conceptions or at the development of expertise in teaching.

It should be noted that the procedure described in the foregoing paragraph is in stark contrast to research studies in which researchers collect a mountain of records and videotapes, and then go off by themselves in a single attempt to make sense of their data, with no feedback from the participants and often no refinement cycles of any kind.

One is led to wonder what researchers would think if participating teachers were given records and videotapes of the researchers' activities during the project and if the teachers published papers about the nature of researchers that used unedited fragments of things that researchers had been quoted as saying at some point in the study. Surely, researchers would consider these spontaneous sound bites to be poor indicators of their real thinking on the relevant topics. Surely, researchers would want to edit the quotations and make them more thoughtful. The consistency principle of research design suggests that teachers might feel similarly about the ways that researchers might use quotations from their activities and discussions. For example, in one of the three-tiered teaching experiments of the type described in the previous section, the following conclusions were stated:

- *There is no single "best" type of teacher.* "It doesn't matter whether we're talking about basketball players or business executives, 'stars' often have personalities and capabilities as different as Michael Jordan, Magic Johnson, and Larry Bird . . . . Some of the characteristics that contribute to success for one person lead to failures for another . . . . People who are really good are very flexible. They can change personalities when they move from one situation to another."

- *Expert teachers have complex profiles of strengths and weaknesses*, and they learn to optimize their strengths and minimize their weaknesses. "Not everything an 'expert' does is good, and not everything that a 'novice' does is bad . . . . Just because a teacher is an expert at dealing with 30 students in a whole class, this doesn't necessarily mean they're experts at one-to-one tutoring with an individual student."

- *The results of teaching are multidimensional and conditional.* "Tutors who are effective in some ways aren't necessarily effective in others!. . . . How effective you are depends on students and the situation . . . . A tutor who is good at dealing with geometry for inner-city, eighth-grader girls isn't necessarily good at all at dealing with algebra for rural, sixth-grader boys . . . . The things that 'turn on' one student sometimes 'turn off' others; or, they get better here, at the same time they get worse there."

- *There is no fixed and final state of expert knowledge.* Teachers at every level of expertise must continue to adapt and develop. "As soon as you get better at teaching [e.g., by getting more sophisticated about what it means to understand a given idea], you change the students you're dealing with . . . and you change the whole classroom situation, so you have to get better all over again. If a teacher ever quits trying to improve, they often get stale and aren't very good at all."

- *It is possible to help both students and teachers to develop in directions that are continually better,* without basing learning activities on a pre-conceived (rule-based) conception of "best." "In the Olympics, in gymnastics and diving competitions, or in music recitals, or in other types of competitions, I don't need to know how to define what makes someone a 'star' in order to point to performances that are good and not so good...or in order to help kids who aren't so good get better. I just need to be able to keep giving them tasks where targeted kinds of performances will be needed and where students themselves can judge which ways they need to improve . . . . Good activities are usually too complex to have only a few ways to perform them correctly; and, performances that are really great are usually the ones that 'show off' the performer's individual characteristics and styles . . . . Coaching is a lot like whittling wood. What you produce is shaped by the personality of the material, but, basically, to carve a horse, you start with a promising piece of wood and chip away everything that doesn't look like a horse. They sort out or refine what they do by borrowing from similar situations."

- Successful people (students, teachers, and researchers) must go beyond thinking with a given model to thinking about how they think about their experiences. "Good players aren't necessarily good coaches and vice versa, but people who are good learn to be one of their own coaches. They're always going beyond the limits of their own current abilities or ways of thinking about what they're doing."

In considering these points, it is important to emphasize that, rather than using the teachers' unrehearsed, unpolished, impromptu comments as data that were interpreted exclusively by the researchers, a large share of the responsibility for their selection, interpretation, elaboration, and refinement devolved on the teachers themselves as they gradually refined their notions about what it means to be a consistently effective tutor. This does not imply that the researchers did not play an important role in the production of the aformentioned conclusions. In fact, the researchers were very active in filtering, selecting, organizing, and assessing the potential importance of the information that was available. However, as this process took place, the teachers were not cast in the demeaning role of "subjects" (vs. "royalty") in the construct development enterprise.

During the multiweek studies, the snippets that were collected were revised and edited several times by the participating teachers, and efforts were made to convert their quotations from unpolished statements made by individuals into well-edited statements that reflected a consensus opinion that had been reached by the group. Also, because of the peer editing and consensus building that took place, the constructs and conceptual systems that the teachers used to make sense of their experiences were much more multidimensional, varied, and continually evolving than most expert–novice descriptions tend to suggest. Furthermore, the portrait of expertise that emerged was quite different from those that have emerged from more traditional types of researcher-dominated research designs.

Even though, from the researchers' point of view, the central goal of many of the studies mentioned earlier was to investigate the nature of expert teachers' knowledge, their aim was not to label one type of teacher an expert or to characterize novices in terms of deficiencies compared with a predetermined ideal defined at the beginning of the project. Instead, the "real-life" teachers' activities that were used provided contexts in which the teachers themselves could decide in which directions they needed to develop in order to improve, and simultaneously, they could learn and document what they were learning. By using activities and seminars in which participating teachers continually articulated, examined, compared, and tested their conceptions about excellent problems (or observation forms, or assessment forms, or tutoring procedures), the teachers themselves were treated as true collaborators in the development of a more refined and sophisticated understanding of the nature of their integrated, mathematical-psychological-pedagogical knowledge.

By the end of the 10- to 16-week teaching experiments, expert teachers produced a trail of documentation that revealed the nature of their evolving conceptions about: (a) the nature of modern elementary mathematics; (b) the nature of "real-life" learning and problem solving situations in an age of information; and (c) the nature of the understandings and abilities that are needed for success in the preceding kinds of situations. Therefore, these experiments also can be described as "evolving expert studies" in which the participating teachers functioned as both research subjects and research collaborators.

To accomplish such goals, the techniques are straightforward: Bring together a diverse group of teachers who qualify as experts according to some reasonable criteria; then, engage them in a series of activities in which they must continually articulate, examine, compare, test, refine, and reach consensus about such things as the nature of excellent problem solving activities for their students. In the end, what gets produced is a consensus that is validated by a trail of documentation showing how it was tested, refined, and elaborated.

Evolving expert studies are based on the recognition that teachers have a great deal to contribute to the development of instructional goals and activities. Yet, no one possesses all of the knowledge that is relevant from fields as different as mathematics, psychology, education, and the history of mathematics. Furthermore, because formative feedback and consensus building are used to optimize the chances of improvement, teachers are able to develop in directions that they themselves are able to judge to be continually better (without basing their judgments on preconceived notions of best).

In this kind of research design, the main way that researchers are different from teachers is that the researchers need to play some metacognitive roles that the teachers do not need to play. For example, the researchers need to ensure that sessions are planned that are aimed at the mechanisms of mutation, selection, propagation, and preservation. Also, some additional clerical services need to be performed to ensure that records are maintained in a form that is accessible and useful.

The evolving expert studies described in this section lasted approximately 10–16 weeks, and the teachers met at least once a week in seminars or laboratory sessions that usually lasted at least 2 hours. The teachers' activities included: (a) participating as if they were students in trial excellent activities; (b) observing students' responses to trial activities in their classrooms or on videotapes; (c) assessing students' responses to trial activities; or (d) assessing the strengths and weaknesses of trial activities. In other words, each study involved two interacting levels of activities (for middle school students and for their teachers), and both levels emphasized the development of models and constructs by the relevant investigators. That is, real-life, problem solving activities for students provided ideal contexts for equally real-life, decision making activities for teachers. In addition, at the same time that the teachers were developing more sophisticated conceptions about the nature of mathematics, learning, and problem solving, they also were able to serve as collaborators in the development of more refined and sophisticated conceptions about the nature of excellent, real-life activities for their students.

## SUMMARY, AND A COMPARISON OF MULTITIERED TEACHING STUDIES TO OTHER RESEARCH DESIGN OPTIONS

The kinds of multitiered teaching experiments that have been described in this chapter were designed explicitly to be useful for investigating the nature of students' or teachers' developing knowledge, especially in areas where the relevant ideas seldom develop naturally. However, according to the theoretical perspective that underlies this chapter, the distinctive characteristic about students' knowledge is that it is a complex dynamics and self-organizing system that is adapting continually to its environment. Consequently, the research design principles that have been discussed also sometimes apply in straightforward ways to other kinds of complex and adapting systems, which include students, groups of students, teachers, classroom learning communities, and programs of instruction. For each of these types of developing systems, relevant research may include teaching experiments with the following characteristics:

- Development, in the sense that they involve interacting longitudinal development studies in structurally rich, learning environments.
- Teaching, in the sense that, at each level, experiences are created to ensure that development will occur without predetermining its specific nature or direction.

- Experiments, in the sense that, at each level, they involve repeated construct development cycles in which the relevant investigators (students, teachers, and researchers) repeatedly reveal, test, refine, and extend their knowledge.

To conduct teaching experiments to investigate the development of any of the aforementioned types of complex systems, some of the most important research design issues that arise pertain to the fact that, when the environment is structurally (conceptually) enriched, the constructs that evolve will be partly the result of how the relevant investigators interpret and structure their experiences and partly the result of structure that was built into the learning experiences (by teachers, administrators, or researchers). This is why, at the student level of the teaching experiments described in this chapter, it was equally important to (1) describe how students' interpretations developed along a variety of dimensions and (2) how effective teachers structured productive learning environments (e.g., by choosing to emphasize particular types of problems, feedbacks, and activities).

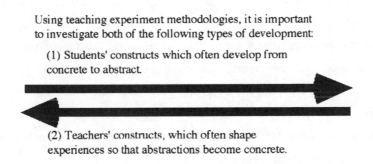

FIG. 9.6.  Students' and teachers' constructs can evolve in opposite developmental directions.

As FIG. 9.6 suggests, to investigate how students' constructs gradually evolve (for example) from concrete experiences to abstract principles, or from crude intuitions to refined formalizations, or from situated prototypes to decontextualized models, it also is useful to investigate how effective teachers reverse these developmental directions by making abstract ideas concrete, by making formal ideas more intuitive, or by situating decontextualized information meaningfully. Information about the nature of students' developing knowledge comes from interactions involving both of these kinds of development.

## Teaching Experiments Offer Alternatives to Expert–Novice Designs

In many ways, the goals of teaching experiments often are similar to those in traditional types of expert–novice studies; that is, the objectives may be to investigate the nature of teachers' knowledge for both experts and novices (or the ways in which expertise develops in other domains of problem solving or decision making). But, in any of these cases, when teaching experiments are used as evolving expert studies, an important feature is that they be designed to avoid the following kind of circularity in reasoning, which often occurs in traditional kinds of expert–novice studies. Expressed in another way, the traits or abilities that are used (implicitly or explicitly) to select experts often turn out to be precisely the same ones that, later, it is discovered the experts possess.

Evolving expert studies are based on the recognition that: (a) there is no single best type of teacher, student, or program; (b) every teacher, student, or program has a complex profile of strengths and weaknesses; (c) teachers, students, or programs that are effective in some ways are not necessarily effective in others; (d) teachers who are effective under some conditions are not necessarily effective in others; and (e) there is no fixed and final state of excellence—that is, teachers, students, and programs at every level of expertise must continue to adapt and develop or be adapted and developed. Instead, expertise is plural, multidimensional, nonuniform, conditional, and continually evolving. Yet, it is possible to create experiences in which a combination of formative feedback and consensus building is sufficient to help teachers, students, or programs develop in directions that are continually better even without beginning with a preconceived definition of best.

## Teaching Experiments Offer Alternatives to Pretest–Posttest Designs

In much the same way that multitiered teaching experiments can be used to investigate the development of groups of students (teams, or classroom communities), they also can be used to investigate the evolution of other types of complex and continually adapting systems, such as programs of instruction.

A traditional way to investigate the progress of innovative instructional programs is to use a pretest–posttest design and perhaps to compare the gains made by a control group and a treatment group. However, pretest–posttest designs tend to raise the following research design difficulties: (a) it is often not possible, especially at the start of a project, to specify the project's desired outcomes in a fixed and final form; (b) it is often not possible, especially at the start of a project, to develop tests that do an accurate job of defining operationally the desired outcomes of the project; (c) the tests themselves often influence (sometimes adversely) both what is accomplished and how it is accomplished; (d) it is often impossible to establish the actual comparability of the treatment group and the control group, taking into account all of the conditions that should be expected to influence development and all of the dimensions along which progress is likely to be made.

Pretest–posttest designs also tend to presuppose that the best way to get complex systems to evolve is to get them to conform toward a single one-dimensional conception of excellence. But, in such fields as modern business, where complex and continually adapting systems are precisely the entities that need to be developed, conformance models of progress are often discarded in favor of continuous progress models that rely on exactly the same kinds of mechanisms that underlie the types of multitiered teaching experiments that were described in this section; that is, the mechanisms they emphasize are designed to ensure planned diversity, fast feedback, and rapid and continuous adaptation.

When such continuous progress models are used for program assessment and accountability, the evidence that progress has been made comes in the form of a documentation trail. It does not come only in the form of a subtracted difference between pretest and posttest scores. Optimization and documentation are not incompatible processes. Instead, (a) assessment is continuous and is used to optimize (not compromise) the chances of success; (b) assessment is based on the assumption that different systems may need to make progress in different ways, in response to different conditions, constraints, and opportunities; and (c) assessment is based on the assumption that there exists no fixed and final state of development where no further adaptation is needed.

## Teaching Experiments Offer Alternatives to Simple Sequences of Tests, Clinical Interviews, or Neutral Observations

Again, optimization and documentation need not be treated as if they were incompatible processes. But, when teaching experiment methodologies are used, it is important that activities and interactions be more than a simple string of tests, clinical interviews, or observations. Instead, at each level of a multitiered teaching experiment, the purpose of the sessions is to force each of the relevant investigators to reveal, test, refine, and extend their relevant constructs continually; and, from each session to the next, construct-development cycles should be occurring continually. Therefore, considerable amounts of planning and information analysis usually must be done from one session to the next. It is not enough for all planning to be done at the beginning of a 15-week study, and all of the data analysis to be done at the end of it.

## Multitiered Teaching Experiments Offer the Possibility of Shared Research Designs to Coordinate the Activities of Multiple Researchers at Multiple Sites

When multitiered teaching experiments are well designed, they often enable researchers to work together at multiple sites, even in cases when: (a) one researcher may be interested primarily in the developing knowledge of students, (b) another may focus on the developing knowledge of teachers, (c) yet another may be concerned mainly with how to enlist the understanding and support of administrators, parents, or community leaders, and (d) still another may emphasize the development of software or other instructional materials. Furthermore, teachers who are participating in the project may be interested mostly in the development of assessment materials, observation forms, or other materials that promote learning and assessment; whereas, the researchers may be most interested in the formation and functioning of classroom discourse communities.

None of these perspectives can be neglected. Piecemeal approaches to curriculum development are seldom effective. For progress to be made, new curricular materials must be accompanied by equally ambitious efforts aimed at teachers' development, assessment, and ways to enlist the support of administrators, parents, and community leaders. Similarly, piecemeal approaches to the development of knowledge are likely to be too restricted to be useful for supporting these other efforts. Therefore, it is important for researchers to devise ways to integrate the work of projects where (for example) the teacher development interest of one researcher can fit with the curriculum development interest of another. It was precisely for this purpose that the authors and their colleagues have developed the kind of multitiered teaching experiment described in this chapter.

# 10 Transformative Teaching Experiments Through Conjecture-Driven Research Design

**Jere Confrey**

*University of Texas at Austin*

**Andrea Lachance**

*Cornell University*

Educational research must serve a variety of purposes. One of these purposes is to invent, develop, and test novel ways of teaching mathematics. Until quite recently, research frequently was confined to out-of-school laboratory settings (Kilpatrick, 1992). This allowed theories to be tested in a fairly controlled environment. However, results and findings from these types of studies have been criticized for being of limited applicability to classroom instruction (Romberg & T. P. Carpenter, 1986). The basis for this criticism was that the instructional methods used in these experiments were not subjected to the constraints of schooling, and, thus, teachers were skeptical that they would prove sustainable in everyday situations.

Such critiques led to a period in which we witnessed an increase in research on existing exemplary classroom practices and an argument that new practices need to evolve from the "best practices" that exist in schools currently. However, some researchers worry that the development of best practices for wide-scale implementation would require a significant period of study and theory building. This might result in a reform movement that is too constrained, too incremental, or too delayed to meet the needs of the country's children. Therefore, there is a need for classroom research that is more speculative and in which some of the constraints of typical classrooms are relaxed while others remain in force.

In this chapter, we describe a research design model that utilizes both theory and common, core, classroom conditions in order to create and investigate new instructional strategies. The strategies developed through this design are meant to change and even to reform current

231

teaching practices drastically. We call this design *transformative and conjecture-driven teaching experiments* and we argue that such a design holds much promise for instituting significant positive changes by establishing a better connection between research and practice.

# DEVELOPING THE CONJECTURE

## Ideological Stance

We want to make clear that we situate this design in the realm of social science. More and more, social scientists are recognizing how our values and beliefs frame our choice of research problems, our selection of methods, and our interpretation of data (Guba & Lincoln, 1989; J. K. Smith, 1989). Take, for example, the traditional emphasis on computational skills in mathematics assessments. Such an emphasis grew out of our society's value of computational skills (National Council of Teachers of Mathematics, 1989). These skills allowed students to secure jobs and to become informed citizens in an industrial society. However, with advances in technology, such computational skills are no longer as important. Instead, students need to develop critical-thinking skills to interpret data appropriately and to use technology to solve more complex problems. Thus, changes in our society have led to a change in what we value in mathematical skills. With this change in values has come a change in the mathematics education community's research agenda.

In any aspect of social science, there are many examples like the one aforementioned where it is clear that what is valued by society and/or various research communities guides the specifics of a research agenda. Furthermore, because our particular field of social science is education, not only will interpretations derive from this work, but also the research itself inevitably will constitute an intervention. We believe that because education consists of ongoing practices, intervening through research makes "replication," as a simplistic concept, unattainable. However, we claim that the ways in which research acts as an intervention will inform discussions on how the research is carried into practice.

Thus, we are obligated to acknowledge the influence of our values on our interpretations, while ensuring that our interventions are educationally sound and reflect our values. In recognition of this, we make our values explicit before discussing the specifics of our research design model. We unapologetically acknowledge that our experiences, beliefs, and values influenced the shape and structure of our research model.

Our transformative and conjecture-driven teaching experiment is motivated by our commitment to equity, and we consider this the basis of our ideological stance.[1] In our work, we seek continually to advance the kind of research that entails active attempts to ensure equal opportunities for all students to participate in and succeed at mathematics. There are several reasons for this stance. The first one stems from current problems with the lack of equity in mathematics education.

Among students in levels as low as middle school, researchers have found significant gaps in achievement in mathematics between different groups of students (girls vs. boys, African American vs. White, lower socioeconomic groups vs. middle and higher socioeconomic groups, etc.), (Secada, 1992). These achievement gaps translate into participation gaps in high school and college where researchers have documented a decline in the numbers of ethnic and racial minorities participating in higher level mathematics courses and an underrepresentation of women in quantitative fields. Nonparticipation and a high rate of failure in mathematics by underrepresented groups mean limited access to certain, higher paying prestigious careers and jobs and a lack of influence on the course of technological development (Secada, 1992). Even among the entire population, we see inordinate levels of failure in mathematics. As it exists, we are supporting an elaborate mathematics education system that succeeds for only a tiny percentage of the population.

Because we see these inequities as stemming from how mathematics education is structured, we see unfairness and unnecessary failure arising from a myriad of common instructional methods. Typically, mathematics is taught with an undue and a premature emphasis on the abstract and formal, which, we argue, prevents many students from accessing mathematical concepts. In many schools across the nation, students are assigned to mathematics courses by the use of "ability grouping" schemes that are often arbitrary and lack flexibility and bidirectionality (Oakes, 1990). This lack of equal access to opportunities to learn, to resources, and to sound instruction leads to the systematic disenfranchisement of certain groups (Oakes, 1990; Secada, 1992; Tate, 1994).

Finally, we affirm that our stance, formed by our belief that mathematics is a human construction, would benefit from the inclusion of contributions from more diverse constituencies. We hold this commitment in spite of a well-documented history of

---

[1] Because ideological stance, unlike political correctness, is not merely an attitude that one assumes or discards, we are not prepared to consider whether other ideological stances fit with this methodology, but we would not rule out such considerations by others.

mathematics that suppresses and excludes broad participation and point instead to other fields in which struggles to overcome bias have succeeded in enriching the quality of the scholarship (e.g., the disciplines in the humanities that are influenced by women's, Afrocentric, Latino, and Asian studies).

In mathematics education, we propose to incorporate diversity by close listening. Years of experience of working with children and listening to their ideas and innovations carefully demonstrate that they frequently produce insights and innovations that have escaped the experts. The variety of questions, representations, and solutions that students have constructed has both intrigued and astounded us. However, recognizing the novelty and power of students' ideas takes practice, an expectation of diversity in approach, and a willingness to envision things from their point of view (Confrey, 1991, 1993, 1994).

Consequently, into our ideological stance, we place the belief that a novice can often envision possibilities, arrangements, and logical relations that experts have been trained to overlook. Successful close listening requires the expert to revise his or her perspective in light of a student voice as well as to acknowledge the source of these revisions in the teaching and learning acts. This can be particularly difficult given the dominant culture's portrayal of mathematical constructions as pure, highly symbolic, and existing outside human experience. This makes one unlikely to hear students' constructions and, therefore, limits and narrows them. Furthermore, classroom climates that emphasize only the quick and ready display of mathematical competence lead to the suppression and destruction of "voice"; students learn to stifle and deny their insights, creating oppressive circumstances. The researcher must be able and willing to allow these novel constructions to emerge and support them, despite the limitations potentially set by the content under examination, the classroom environment, and mathematical tradition (Confrey, 1991, 1994). We describe the examination and revision of expert perspective in light of student voice as a *voice-perspective heuristic* and use it to guide our interventions and interpretations.

Our claim is that one's ideological stance informs and saturates one's research design model. Having defined our ideological stance, we now describe the components of our design model.

## The Conjecture

A crucial part of this type of teaching experiment is the conjecture. But what is a conjecture? According to the dictionary, one definition of a conjecture is an inference based on inconclusive or incomplete evidence. In the context of mathematics education, this inference may pertain to how mathematics for educational purposes should be organized or conceptualized or taught. Thus, the conjecture is a means to reconceptualize the ways in which to approach both the content and the pedagogy of a set of mathematical topics. Most often, it comes from a dissatisfaction in the researchers' minds with the outcomes of typical practices. It transforms how one views teaching and learning activities. Over the course of the teaching experiment, a strong conjecture should shift one's perspective and bring new events, previously insignificant or perplexing, into relief. At points in its evolution, the conjecture should feel like a grand scheme beginning to emerge from many, previously disparate pieces, making them more cohesive.

Unlike a formal hypothesis in an experimental design approach, a conjecture is *not* an assertion waiting to be proved or disproved. Research guided by a hypothesis merely attempts to discover if a given intervention worked or not or if a given theory was supported or not. But research guided by a conjecture seeks to revise and elaborate the conjecture while the research is in progress. Thus, whereas a hypothesis remains static throughout an experiment, a conjecture evolves constantly as the research progresses. This is similar to Lakatos' (1976) recognition that theory is established "through the incessant improvement of guesses by speculation and criticism" (p. 5).

The conjectures that we envision as essential in this type of research have two significant dimensions. First, the conjecture must have a mathematical content dimension. This means, for example, that a conjecture would not concern itself with the impact of conflict management skills on group problem solving. Instead, the conjecture would have to include a mathematical component such as how a full understanding of radical mathematics is critical to low-socioeconomic-class students gaining full citizenship in a technological society (Frankenstein, 1995) or how the mathematics of change can lead to the introduction of calculus-related concepts as early as elementary school (Nemirovsky, Tierney, & Wright, 1995; Roschelle & Kaput, 1996b; P. W. Thompson, 1994a). Although the content of the conjecture does not have to come out of traditional school mathematics curricula, the researcher should be able to define and describe clearly the mathematical content of the conjecture. In brief, the content dimension answers the question: What should be taught?

Second, there must be a pedagogical dimension linked to the content dimension that answers the question: How should this content be taught? This aspect of the conjecture guides the researcher on how the classroom needs to be organized for instruction and on what kinds of tasks, activities, and resources need to be provided for the content.

For example, in the Algebra Project (Silva, Moses, Rivers, & P. Johnson, 1990), Moses recognized the role that algebra serves as a critical gateway to success and participation in higher level mathematics for inner-city students. He conjectured that what is needed to help students move successfully from elementary school arithmetic thinking to high school algebraic thinking is a transitional curriculum. At the same time, Moses claimed that students must develop these transitional skills through familiar physical experiences and must be supported in their learning by an organized network of community members. Consequently, the content of Moses' conjecture is the need for a curriculum that will teach transitional skills that allow students to access to abstract algebraic notation. The pedagogical dimension of the conjecture becomes the teaching of these skills through engaging and experiential tasks with explicit and intensive community involvement and advocacy. This conjecture crystalizes the notion that as the level of symbolic abstraction is raised, students need to work with experientially familiar frames of reference that help them to learn algebraic notation.

## The Theoretical Framework

A conjecture is necessarily situated in a theory or it cannot be interpreted. Theory, such as intellectual development theory, social organizational theory, or cognitive theory, relates the conjecture to other aspects of education or mathematics. Whatever the particular theoretical aspect of the conjecture is, it serves to structure the activities and methodologies in the teaching experiment. In relation to the conjecture, the theory helps to weave together the content and pedagogical dimensions.

A critical element of the theoretical framework is a careful review and analysis of the existing literature. Seldom, if ever, does a robust conjecture fall full-blown from the sky. Usually it comes from a thoughtful and critical review of the literature to discern an anomaly that has been overlooked, unsolved, or addressed inadequately by one's colleagues. As a result, a theoretical discussion should funnel one from a broad set of theoretical claims to the specifics of the content to be imparted and how the conjecture is situated in that literature. A full discussion of theory is beyond the scope of this chapter, but, in the next section, we present a brief discussion of the theories that guided the "splitting" conjecture. Its role in guiding the research, in defining what counts as evidence, and in creating the observational categories is well documented in other literature (Steffe & Gale, 1995).

## An Example: The "Splitting" Conjecture and Related Theory

To illustrate better what we mean by a conjecture, we describe an example from our work involving teaching experiments. In this case, the content of the conjecture was a topic known as *splitting*. The notion of splitting (Confrey, 1988, 1989, 1994; Confrey & E. Smith, 1995) grew out of Confrey's research into students' conceptions of exponential functions. From this work, Confrey and her research team began to see that mathematics curricula tend to rely too heavily and almost exclusively on counting and, consequently, on the model of multiplication as repeated addition. According to Confrey (1994), the problem with conceptualizing multiplication exclusively as repeated addition is that such a conception cannot accommodate many of the students' intuitive and primitive actions that *are not* repeated addition but that often *are* multiplicative in nature. Some of these actions include sharing, folding, dividing symmetrically, and magnifying.

These types of action, Confrey (1994) claimed, are the basis for a "primitive, cognitive scheme" that she called splitting: "In its most primitive form, splitting can be defined as an action of creating simultaneously multiple versions of an original, an action often represented by a tree diagram" (p. 292). In this sense, students are splitting when they divide a piece of paper into four equivalent sections or break a candy bar in half and in half again to share it among four people. They are splitting also when they are organizing a set of objects into an array because it requires the production of groups of equal size. When students do this, they are not relying on counting to verify that they split the areas or sets correctly. Rather, they are relying on the geometric equivalence of the resulting parts or a one-to-one (or a one-to-many) correspondence of the parts. Thus, the splitting construct can live independently of counting and repeated addition.

The construct of splitting provides a foundation and a context for the concept of ratio (Confrey & E. Smith, 1995). One of the attributes of ratio that emerges from the splitting conjecture is that it is connected inherently to the operations of multiplication and division. Through splitting actions, multiplication, division, and ratio form a trio of mathematical ideas that mutually support and define each other. Confrey (1988, 1989, 1994) argued that in order to support the intuitive splitting actions of children, students should be introduced to the constructs of multiplication, division, and ratio as a trio of ideas while they are in the primary grades. As a result, the content component of the splitting conjecture proposes the transformation of traditional school mathematics curricula so that, in addition to exposing students to additive structures, it also will support their understandings of multiplicative structures.

The literature on multiplication and division and on ratio and proportion was critical to the evolution of this claim. The Rational Number Project (Lesh et al., 1989) had identified already myriad of rational number constructs that begged to be simplified and unified. The work of Fischbien, Deri, Nello, and Marino (1985) on primitive notions had an asymmetry; division had two roots (partitive and quotative) but multiplication had only one—repeated addition. Alleviating this asymmetry was a powerful impetus in the proposal of the conjecture. The careful work of Steffe and colleagues (Steffe, 1994) on number made counting the centerpiece and eventual underlying structure of multiplication, and yet counting failed to capture the geometric intuition of arrays, symmetry, and similarity, which also are multiplicative in nature. And, finally, the conceptual change literature (Strike & Posner, 1982) prompted a historical investigation that revealed that the Greek concept of ratio was lost in the modern arithmetization of number. Each of these literature reviews pushed Confrey to articulate a new conjecture.

For the authors of this chapter, the pedagogy of the conjecture was embedded deeply in our theoretical framework, which we would describe as situated in a constructivist paradigm informed increasingly by a sociocultural perspective and a sensitivity to students' voices (Confrey, 1994, 1995, 1995). In mathematics education, constructivist theory makes the claim that all mathematical ideas are grounded in human schemes of action. Mathematics is viewed as a result of personal constructions made through one's actions and reflections on those actions. In a teaching situation, mathematical constructions are influenced by the conditions that spur children to action as well as the experiences and insights that children bring to those actions (Confrey, 1994, 1995, 1995; von Glasersfeld, 1984).

At the same time, all actions and reflections are assumed to be saturated by one's cultural settings and interactions. Typically, actions do not take place in a vacuum, but involve social interactions with other people. Usually, the norms of the environment in which these interactions take place are dictated by the dominant culture. Thus, students' mathematical constructions are influenced by the social and cultural norms that regulate their activity. In this perspective, language serves as a means of both acculturation, personal expression, and exchange (Confrey, 1994, 1995, 1995; Vygotsky, 1986).

Our ideological stance influenced the conjecture in both of its dimensions of content and pedagogy. Ratio and proportion are critical topics for success in advanced courses, and, as a result, increasing the success of a diverse group of students' with them is a worthy target for reform. That increased success would come with the support and articulation of student voice was a central component of the research. In this manner, we see how theory and ideology interact with the construction and articulation of the conjecture.

In addition, theory and ideology affect all of the components of instruction designed to operationalize the conjecture in actuality. In our case, this interaction resulted in the intervention's attention to the following areas:

- In order to construct knowledge, students need opportunities to explore activities that are rich in possibilities for multiple solutions and various tool use.

- Students need tools, materials, and other people with which and with whom they can build the constructions associated with these activities.

- As new starts and alternative approaches surface, structures to support and develop them must be present.

- The listener or researcher must be compelled to examine simultaneously and dialectically both his or her own understanding of the ideas under construction (and their places in sociocultural history) and understandings of the students.

## DEVELOPING THE TEACHING EXPERIMENT[2]

Having defined and described what we mean by conjecture, we outline now what a transformative and conjecture-driven teaching experiment is. We see the teaching experiment as a planned intervention that takes place over a significant period of time in a classroom where a continuing course of instruction is taught. The experiment will involve a dialectical relationship between the conjecture and the components of instruction, which are: (a) the curriculum; (b) the method of instruction; (c) the role of the teacher; and (d) the methods of assessment.

---

[2] We have chosen to retain the label *teaching experiment* despite the connotations of the term *experiment*. This is because the term has established itself with a varied set of meanings in mathematics education, as demonstrated by its different uses in chapters in this book (e.g., Steffe & Thompson, chap. 11, this volume).

The research questions and the methods of data collection and analysis must be informed by both parts of the dialectic, and it is in this redefined relationship that we see the basis for the redefinition of the research-practice relationship. We offer a general description of each of the components of instruction and illustrate how we developed those components in our work.

It should be noted that this form of complex research requires a team of researchers working on the project. This is not merely a response to the need for multiple data collectors, rather because of the need to discuss and refine our interpretations and plans continuously. Identifying the appropriate roles of the team's members and their foci of attention are important parts of the project. We found it useful to have individuals who would concentrate on the design and analysis of separate segments of the curriculum, whereas the project director was continuously responsible to guide the overall directions and work for the elaboration of the conjecture. Within a university where graduate students are in different stages of their studies, this design works very well.

## Refining the Conjecture and Developing Research Questions

As stated previously, the conjecture is the driving force in this research design model. It will determine exactly what questions the transformative teaching experiment will explore. Because so much of the research design is dependent on the conjecture, it might be wise to do some preliminary smaller investigations into the power of the conjecture before beginning a large-scale teaching experiment based on it. These smaller investigations might involve working with a small group of students for a short time to explore a single aspect of the conjecture. This will lead to a better understanding and definition of it. Ultimately, such a process will frame the questions for a full-scale, conjecture-driven teaching experiment.

In the case of the splitting conjecture, several smaller studies had contributed to the evolving construct of splitting. One study focused on college students' conceptions of exponential functions (Confrey, 1991), which led to the understanding of how students reason with multiplicative units. Another study looked at first-grade students' understanding of similarity (Confrey, 1992) and found that similarity is a strong intuitive notion for young children. The results of these early investigations of splitting confirmed, among other things, that students do have a variety of conceptions of multiplication that go beyond repeated addition. Furthermore, as mentioned earlier, an examination of history revealed that the Greek conception of ratio was very different from the construct held today. The Greeks' idea of ratio was grounded in action just as students' early experiences with splitting are believed to be

(Confrey & E. Smith, 1989). Through these various activities, the construct of splitting was refined and strengthened. Eventually, this process led to these questions:

- How would mathematics education be different if the intuitive notions of splitting were supported?
- What would curricular activities that support splitting look like?
- What mathematical strengths and weaknesses would students develop if their sense of splitting were developed?

These questions led to a more extensive teaching experiment using the splitting conjecture.

Because components of this teaching experiment are discussed throughout the rest of this chapter, a brief overview of the experiment is provided now. Over a 3-year period (1992–1995), Confrey conducted a transformative and conjecture-driven teaching experiment with a heterogeneously grouped class of elementary school students ($N = 20$) in a public school of a small city. Confrey taught most of the sessions. A research team consisting of two to four graduate students (depending on the year) assisted Confrey.

During the course of the experiment, the elementary school students passed through Grades 3, 4, and 5. In the third grade, the students were introduced to multiplication, division, and ratio as a trio of mathematical ideas. When this same group of students was in the fourth grade, their instruction focused on strengthening the construct of ratio and introducing fractions as a subset of ratio (Confrey & Scarano, 1995). While studying ratios and fractions, the students worked in such contexts as scaling recipes, using shadows to estimate height, and building an access ramp with an appropriate slope for handicapped persons. As fifth-graders, after having developed a rich network of mathematical ideas, the students were introduced to decimal numbers. Further details of this teaching experiment can be found in Confrey (1995, 1996), Lachance (1996), Preyer (1996), and Scarano and Confrey (1996).

In instruction, we identified four design and implementation components that need to be conceived and carried out progressively during the teaching experiment. These are: (a) curriculum; (b) classroom interactions; (c) teaching; and (d) assessment.

## Four Design Components of Instruction

*Curriculum.* The conjecture will determine what content areas will be covered by the curriculum used in the classroom intervention. However, because the teaching experiments take place in classrooms where a course of instruction proceeds continuously, the researcher must take into account what students and teachers are expected to cover at that grade level. Most schools must answer to a system of accountability—such as end-of-year school district examinations or national standardized tests—to ensure that the designated material has been covered.

There are many ways to handle this. The researcher can plan to conduct the teaching experiment during a period of review so that the teacher and students will have ample time to cover the prescribed material. Or the researcher could propose to cover the content dictated by the school district's mandate within the confines of the teaching experiment. Or the researcher could get a waiver for the teacher and students involved in the teaching experiment so that they will not be held accountable for the material that could not be covered because of the time used by the teaching experiment.

Whatever the researcher decides to do, it needs to be done in consultation with the teacher and the other relevant parties (parents, administrator, and others). The setting of this type of research in working classrooms brings with it an ethical responsibility to ensure the progress of all of the students. This means that one must accept the commitment to the students, the parents, and the staff members to act only on behalf of the children's academic and emotional well-being. Should this commitment require one to compromise the quality of the research, the commitment must prevail. Typically, what happens if an accommodation has to be made is a modification of the curriculum that is a compromise between what the researcher might wish to do and the practical demands of the setting.

An example of a compromise occurred in the splitting research when we needed to teach the addition of fractions. Our dilemma was that in the two-dimensional plane, ratios, as vectors, can be added with vector addition. However, conventional mathematics frowns on notating this as:

$$\frac{a}{b} + \frac{c}{d} = \frac{a+c}{b+d}$$

although combining ratios is a somewhat commonly encountered operation. Because we were concerned that our students not be penalized on the end-of-the-year achievement tests for using this type of operation in an inappropriate context, we gave them a project involving the addition of measurements followed with an assessment asking them to evaluate the responses of two students. In the assessment activity, the response of one student was

$$\frac{2}{5} + \frac{2}{5} = \frac{4}{10}$$

whereas the other was

$$\frac{2}{5} + \frac{2}{5} = \frac{4}{5}$$

In our classroom discussion, we made it clear that only the second of these responses would be scored as correct on typical achievement tests, even though the first notation made sense in certain contexts.

The major influence on the content of the teaching experiment's curriculum is the conjecture and determining how it could influence the choice, sequence, and duration of what is presented as well as the types of activities used. In discussing the curriculum component of a the teaching experiment, it is essential to point out that one cannot design a complete curriculum in advance. If it is truly a conjecture-driven intervention, rather than a program implementation, one enters it knowing that future decisions in the experiment will be made based on what happens during the earlier parts of the intervention. We have called this type of curriculum development "responsive and emergent" (Lachance, 1996).

Although the researcher certainly will have specific content areas and topics that he or she intends the conjecture-driven intervention to cover, curricular activities should be structured so that they are flexible and open-ended. This enables the researcher to observe and monitor students' interactions with the curriculum and its activities. As a result of these observations, the researcher can adapt curricular activities according to the responses and innovations contributed by the students. Hence, the development of this type of curricular intervention can be seen as responsive.

Responding to students' needs and inputs also makes the curriculum development process in this type of research design emergent. As the students work through the curriculum and offer different and often innovative insights into the mathematics, the researcher's own insights into the content will evolve. This is expected to be particularly striking because the researcher is looking at the students' work through the lens of the conjecture.

If the conjecture is not robust, there will be insufficient information to start and then guide the new design. On the other hand, if the curricular intervention is not aggressive enough, the guardians of the traditional approach may resist and drown out the new intervention eventually. Moreover, if the curriculum and the conjecture are both robust enough, the changes in the curriculum should be more substantial than those in the conjecture. As we discuss further in the section on the preliminary data analyses, although changes in the conjecture are expected, these changes can be described as "evolutionary refinements" and "elaborations." The conjecture's changes are in contrast to the curricular changes that are responsive and emergent. Relatively, the rate of modification of the conjecture should be slower than that of the curriculum. An analogy might help. Imagine looking at a complex and changing scene through a lens. As the scene changes dramatically, small adjustments with the lens must be made in order to bring all of the aspects of the scene into focus. In relation to the changes in the scene, the focus adjustment is incremental. Because the conjecture functions as a lens to the complex scene, we expect small shifts in its position, but a deeper elaboration of it when viewing the sometimes major "scene" changes of the curriculum.

In the splitting conjecture experiment, both the splitting content and the constructivist theory influenced the types of curricular activities used. In terms of content, it was the intention of our curricular intervention to cover many of the topics mandated by the traditional elementary school mathematics curricular for Grades 3 through 5, such as multiplication, division, fractions, decimals, and geometry. In addition, we sought to expand the content of the traditional curricular by deepening the treatment of the traditional topics and introducing new arrangements such as making ratio and proportion by two-dimensional graphing superordinate to fractions and including an early introduction to algebra.

To accomplish all of this, we developed a model for approaching these topics through the splitting conjecture. This model (see FIG. 10.1) has at its center the trio of mathematical constructs of splitting: multiplication, division, and ratio. It is through this trio that other topics such as fractions, decimals, geometry, two-dimensional graphing, and, eventually, percents can be developed and explored.

With our intervention's use of a wide range of concrete and contextual experiences, we hoped to encourage students to develop a firm grounding in the central trio of constructs. From this foundation, richer understandings of all related subsidiary constructs could be developed and the conjecture could be elaborated. Because this model views the subsidiary constructs as being connected to and through the central trio of concepts, the relationships between and among all of the concepts can be explored, seen, and understood more readily by students.

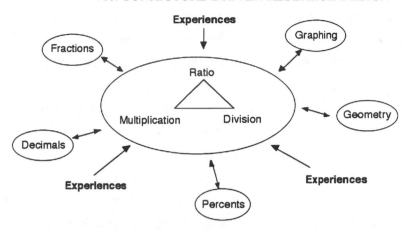

FIG. 10.1. A model for approaching selected topics through a trio of splitting constructs.

Consistent with our theory, the curriculum was organized around modeling activities where students were engaged in tool-based investigations. Although the activities in the splitting experiment were called for at different points throughout the intervention, they did have a number of common characteristics. They were designed to be fun and compelling, with the intent of creating the need for students to construct various understandings. Consistent with our equity stance, the activities included experiments, demonstrations, puzzles, and design projects, one of whose purposes was to make it easy for all of the students to begin them. Because many of the problems had multiple facets with varying levels of challenge, all of the children in the class learned that they could participate in these projects successfully and advance to the next activity. Similarly, these tasks typically allowed for differing degrees of completion, permitting interested students to pursue them further. Finally, with a strong use of context, commonplace tools, and varied student experiences the problems were widely attractive and generally offered multiple possibilities for their representation (i.e., tables, graphs, pictures, etc.). All of this was essential to create sufficient space for interesting and novel approaches to emerge.

For instance, in Grade 4, using their understanding of ratio, the students had to design a wheelchair ramp that would fit a specific entryway and have an appropriate slope and supports. Eventually, actual ramps were constructed with each group's chosen slope. To test their designs, the students traveled up and down the ramps in a wheelchair.

The conjecture provides the impetus to develop careful intra-activity sequencing as well as interactivity sequencing to allow the systematic, albeit emergent, conceptual development of mathematical ideas. For instance, the curriculum activity of the handicapped ramp problem *emerged* as we *elaborated* the conjecture. We knew that we wanted to use the two-dimensional plane to compare ratios and to progress into operations with them. We entered the teaching experiment with a conjecture that splitting had strong geometric connections, and we sought to bring them out in our curricular examples. Constructing a ramp met our needs on a variety of levels. The students could engage in tool-based activities, they could work in a context with which they are familiar (especially in schools as mainstreaming is implemented), and they would make the concept of slope an effective bridge from ratio and proportion to algebra and geometry.

As we approached the time to undertake the ramp problem, we realized that the students needed more experience in working with large whole numbers and a fixed ratio relation. This led us to insert an activity that involved finding the heights of trees from the lengths of their shadows. Again, one can see how curricular changes are more likely to be revised in response to classroom observations, whereas the implied changes to the conjecture are more delicate and refined.

*Classroom Interactions.* Because this type of research necessitates a teaching experiment, the researcher will need to decide how the instruction will be structured. Will the students work individually, in small groups or as an entire class? Should there be problem solving activities or a lecture format? Or will there be a combination of these instructional approaches? Both the content and the pedagogical dimensions of the conjecture, informed by the theoretical framework, will influence the methods of instruction chosen. In addition, the types of curricular activities that the researcher hopes to employ will dictate in some respects the forms of classroom interactions used in the intervention. Decisions on the forms of these interactions are essential in planning the methods of data collection.

Because of the emphasis on the use of tools and model-building tasks, much of the activity in the splitting experiment took place in small heterogeneous groups of students. The groups remained intact during particular activities, with changes in participants occurring as new activities were introduced. Before, during, and after small-group work, sessions were devoted to whole-class discussion. Sometimes, these whole-class discussions were used to "create the need" for the activity or to share and discuss progress during group work on the activity.

However, because of the conjecture's focus on the students' voices, the whole-class discussions also allowed for the development and emergence of students' voices in relation to the teacher's and the researcher's perspectives. In these exchanges, it was the interactions among the students and between the teacher and the students that determined what would be discussed and pursued, and ultimately, what meanings would be negotiated.

*The Role of the Teacher.* In a transformative and conjecture-driven teaching experiment, two questions related to the role of the teacher must be answered. The first is: Who will act as the teacher during the intervention? In some situations, it may make sense for the current classroom teacher to be the main teacher in the intervention. This would allow the researchers to spend more time observing the interactions taking place in the classroom and the effects of the intervention. However, in order for the classroom teacher to be the teacher during the experiment, she or he would have to agree to be a full member of the research team. This means that the classroom teacher would have to be very familiar with the conjecture. It also implies that the teacher would have to be able to participate in the intervention's development and to assist in analyzing the data from the experiment during both the preliminary and final analyses. Obviously, this would entail a substantial commitment of time and energy by the teacher. Because of these requirements, it may be better to have a member of the research team act as the classroom teacher during the intervention. Clearly, the particular characteristics of the classroom setting and the people involved in the research will influence how the teacher for the teaching experiment will be chosen.

No matter who acts as the teacher during the experiment, a second question needs to be answered: What role will the teacher play during the intervention? Will the teacher act as the expert, dispensing knowledge as necessary? Will the teacher act as the facilitator, assisting students as they act on their own or in small groups? Or will the role of the teacher change according to the curricular activities? The answers to these questions must be informed by the conjecture itself and by the types of curricular activities that the intervention will use.

In the splitting experiment, the leader of the research team acted as the classroom teacher. The novelty of the splitting conjecture and its lack of extensive articulation at that time made it both too difficult to communicate to a classroom teacher as well as too onerous, risky, and threatening to the fidelity of the study to have it taught by someone insufficiently versed in it.

As the teacher, Confrey took on a variety of roles. At points, she was an expert resource person, a listener, a facilitator, a discussion leader, a coach, and an evaluator. As both a teacher and a researcher and given the focus of the splitting conjecture, she had to approach the task of teaching with a profound respect for and curiosity in the possible alternative approaches used by the students. She also had to draw upon a broad knowledge of the content, which sometimes meant that she needed to confer with mathematical experts on such topics as vector spaces, linear algebra, and projections. This was true despite the fact that the intervention was at the elementary grade level. Furthermore, because one of the tasks of the research was to discern the students' novel approaches to the conjecture and to assess their fruitfulness, listening was one of the teacher's major responsibilities.

*Assessment.* As with the other components of the teaching experiment, the assessment activities used to evaluate the students' learning and progress must be informed by and consistent with the content, pedagogy, and theoretical framework of the conjecture along with the other components of the intervention. The results of assessments not only will provide outcome data related to the impact of the intervention, but also will allow for an ongoing formative evaluation of the intervention process. This formative assessment will guide the evolution of the conjecture and the related curricular materials continuously. Thus, it will be important for the researcher to vary the types of assessment practices used and to employ both informal and formal evaluations.

In the splitting experiment, multiple assessment practices were employed. For example, group projects always ended with a performance assessment. Often, a small panel of guest evaluators were invited to the classroom so that students could present and defend their solutions to problems. As the intervention continued and group work progressed, the students themselves often became the best source of questions about and criticisms of other students' solutions.

Homework was assigned four nights a week and was collected and corrected. This gave the research team an opportunity to perform frequent checks of the students' understanding. Short, in-class assignments, which the students might work on individually or in groups, also were used to gauge the group's general understanding of the topic.

Other assessments were used to evaluate the overall impact of the intervention. The researchers created longer, end-of-unit assessments that consisted of open-ended tasks or nonroutine problems suggested by other research. The regular classroom teacher also administered tests on skill development and gave the researchers access to their results. Finally, standardized achievement tests, mandated by the school district, were taken by the students. The district made these results available to the researchers in order to ascertain how the intervention might have influenced students' performance.

## Putting It All Together: The Research Design Model

We can now present a model for the transformative and conjecture-driven teaching experiment (see FIG. 10.2). The teaching experiment is embedded in social science and education, an ideological stance on equity, diversity, and the importance of student voice and a theoretical framework. The conjecture and the instructional components are drawn as separate entities in a dialectical relationship. Together, they are labeled the teaching experiment. The two dimensions of the conjecture and the four components of instruction are listed.

The conjecture, the instruction, and their relationship change over time, which is signaled by their dialectical relationship and by the two feedback loops. The feedback loop to instruction is labeled *emergent* and *responsive*; the feedback loop to the conjecture is labeled *evolving* and *elaborating*.

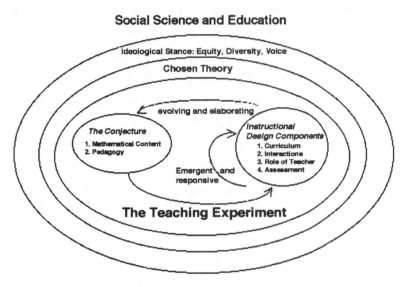

FIG. 10.2. A model for the transformative and conjecture-driven teaching experiment.

# DATA COLLECTION AND ANALYSES

## Data Collection

In a transformative and conjecture-driven teaching experiment, multiple methods of collecting data should be used. First of all, there should be some way to capture the day-to-day interactions in the classroom. One of the most straightforward methods of doing this is videotaping classes. A combination of videotaping and careful notes of classroom observations is often ideal.

In addition, some data should be collected on individuals. Certainly, some of the assessment activities provide data on what students have learned. However, more indepth understanding of students' learning and development can be obtained through task or open-ended interviews. Again, the content and the theoretical framework of the conjecture will help to determine both the number and the form of the interviews.

Following a group is also a valuable source of information in classes where children are taught by the group instructional method. In small groups, the articulation of students' voices is rich and revealing of their conceptions. The decision to follow one group instead of multiple groups is a difficult one. The trade-off is to witness the conceptual development of one group more fully as opposed to broadening one's sampling of students' methods by viewing multiple groups.

Finally, and importantly to note, data need to be collected about the researchers' thinking about and actions during the intervention. Because so much of this type of teaching experiment depends on what emerges from the classroom interactions, such data are vital to refining and understanding the conjecture and its impact. Ideally, video and/or audio records of the researchers' meetings should be made. Furthermore, the researchers should keep field notes or journals to record their thoughts and reflections about the intervention as it continues. It even may be helpful or necessary for a member of the research team, or perhaps someone outside the research team, to interview the different researchers about the research process.

In the splitting experiment, videotaping was the primary form of data collection (see Roschelle, chap. 24, this volume). Both the whole-class and small-group interactions were taped. Generally, two cameras were used. During whole-class activities, one camera recorded the presenter at the front of the room, who could be the teacher or one of the students, along with the board or large paper display. The second camera recorded the students and tended to focus on the student who was speaking.

During small-group work, a study group was chosen and one camera followed it throughout a series of activities in a given unit. The second camera moved among the remaining groups to record the diversity of methods that emerged from the students' work. Using this method, we were able to gather data that allowed us to follow the conceptual development of one group, while collecting a sample of data from the other groups.

One technique used to achieve better insight into what the students were thinking and doing was to have small groups give a progress report to the entire class. Sometimes, these progress reports took the form of the groups recounting their work from the previous day. At other times, the groups discussed their current plan of action. On occasions, the groups shared their concerns about the obstacles they faced in accomplishing a task. These reports were a source of significant data.

Besides the videotapes, other sources of information included the students' written homework, and other written assessment activities, and the verbal responses gathered from them during intermittent interviews. As mentioned previously, homework was given, collected, and corrected each week in order to maintain a continuous record of students' conceptual development. Also, low-stakes assessments involving short (less than 15 minutes), open-ended items were used to gauge the depth and breadth of the students' understanding.

Generally, we interviewed students when we were unsure of their perspectives on and depth of understanding of a certain topic. Some of these interviews took place as a student worked on the short, low-stakes assessment items described previously. Additionally, at the end of the decimal unit, the members of the study group were interviewed to ascertain how they had made sense of the entire decimal unit.

The records of our own meetings and thinking tended to be kept by a member of the research team. For the most part, these records were summaries of the contents of a given discussion as opposed to verbatim transcripts. Usually, such meetings were not video- or audiotaped because they took place mainly in the classroom or in the car on the drive back from school directly after the class session. Given these circumstances, keeping minutes of these conversations seemed to be a more effective method of recording their content. Some members of the research team also kept field journals to track their thinking during the intervention.

## Preliminary Data Analysis and Curricular Revision

In a transformative and conjecture-driven teaching experiment, we see two types of data analysis. The first type is the ongoing and preliminary analysis, which takes place during the intervention. This is necessitated by this design's anticipation of emerging issues. Thus, at frequent intervals (perhaps after each class), the research team needs to meet and discuss the implications of the students' activities for future plans. Although this extensive reflection on practices and careful modification of plans could not occur to the same extent with a regular teaching load, it is essential for the success of the teaching experiments. It is through this preliminary analysis that both the conjecture and the curricular activities are reflected upon, developed, and revised.

In the splitting experiment, there were several objects of preliminary analysis. Generally, almost no stable analysis could take place in the first few days of a new activity. Typically, these were chaotic and noisy times. The intent of the projects would be clarified, and the research team would feel overwhelmed by the level and variety of activity. Seldom did things go as planned. During this time, it was difficult to conduct any kind of systematic examination of the data, although the research team met nearly every day, if only to recount the day's tumultuous events.

However, by the end of two or three days, coherence would emerge. Students would have transformed the activity into their own, would have asked questions to clarify the task, and would have made a reasonable schedule and timeline for completing it. Simultaneously, the research team became more confident of their observations and ability to respond to the emerging needs of the students.

At points in every activity, the teacher-researcher would hold whole-class discussions with a specific goal in mind. The topics of such discussions could be a review of a specific homework problem that might inform a current activity or the teaching of a particular skill that students saw necessary for the larger, problem solving activity. These discussions were important territory for an initial analysis of the data. The students' proposals, how they represented the problem (tables, graphs, pictures, etc.), and their mode of language were examined carefully.

For instance, as reported elsewhere (Confrey, 1995), in one group discussion, the students were asked to find different amounts of lemon juice and water that would taste the same as a recipe for lemonade that consisted of 9 parts lemon juice to 12 parts of water. They did this by searching for the smallest whole number ratio (3:4) that fit perfectly into the given ratio (9:12). When asked what this could be called, they replied "the littlest recipe" or "the base combination." The first of these two terms ("the littlest recipe") was used extensively throughout the teaching experiment by the students to describe a ratio in its "lowest terms."

Not only was this a finding that would endure in its viability to the students, but also its theoretical value was significant. We called it a ratio unit to signal its importance, and it became an important part of the conjecture. In the past, other researchers concentrated on students "building up" the littlest recipe to make larger batches (Streefland, 1991). This examination of ratio focuses mostly on the additive component of ratio building. What we had found was that students were willing and able to "scale down" a large recipe to its smallest, whole number equivalent. This process focuses more on the multiplicative, scaling down aspect of ratio, rather than on the more additive process of building up.

As important as the expression of these perspectives of the students was, it also was essential to consider the times when we revised and or modified our curricular interventions in order to reflect the students' proposals during these periods of preliminary data analysis. An example from the activities used to teach decimals illustrates this point.

The first activity used in our decimal unit, the Weights Problem, was intended to be a transitional problem that reviewed ratio concepts and, at the same time, laid a foundation for decimal notation. In the first part of the Weights Problem, students were given four shapes (sticks, rectangles, circles, and blobs) made of similar materials (light wood or plastic) and were asked to ascertain the relationships in weight between the shapes. They were given the materials to construct a pan balance to uncover these relationships. By design, the weights of the shapes had a multiplicative relationship with each other (e.g., the weight of two circles equaled the weight of one stick; the weight of four sticks was equivalent to the weight of one blob; the weight of three blobs equaled the weight of four rectangles). The students were told that these shapes made up the weight system of a fictional country. When they had determined all of the relationships in this weight system, they had to create a tourist guide that explained the weight system to visitors.

Originally, we envisioned a transition to decimals by introducing a weight system that involved an increasing set of 10-to-1 relations. However, two considerations encouraged us to revise this plan. First, to understand their weight systems fully, it was clear that the students needed and desired an opportunity to use them. Second, we wanted this particular activity to lead them to reexamine the relationships among the weights in a specific system and to begin to think about how to create a notation and a set of operations in that system. We had seen previously the necessity of thinking hard about how to build a numeration system when we developed the operation of the multiplication of rational numbers. However, with the introduction of decimals, we encountered ordering, place value, ratio relations, addition, and subtraction, all combining to produce decimal notation and a new kind of number. Such a conceptualization was in marked contrast with other researchers who deal solely with issues of ordering in decimals and concern themselves only with the contrasts between decimal and whole number ordering (L. B. Resnick et al., 1989).

Our conjecture about the importance of ratio was giving us a different perspective on decimals. This led us to create the following tasks. Once the students became familiar with the weight system and made their tourist guides, they were given a bag containing different kinds of candy bars. They were asked to weigh each type of candy in the weight system and come up with a type of notation for recording the weight of each of the candies—what we called a receipt for the candy weights. Then they were asked to total up the values on the receipt and to weigh all of the candies together. This led them into a feedback system in which they expected the two results to confirm each other. It was a powerful way to strengthen their awareness of a numeration system. Developing this task is a clear example of how analyzing preliminary data can lead to changes in both the curriculum and the conjecture. The curricular changes were substantial; on the other hand, the core of the conjecture was elaborated rather than altered.

## Final Data Analysis

The second type of analysis occurs after the classroom activity has finished. The research team then plunges into the pile of data it has collected to begin the more indepth analysis of what occurred during the intervention. The methods of analysis used will depend on the methods used to collect the data, the results of the preliminary data analysis, and, of course, the conjecture itself. If more quantitative testing methods are used, some kinds of statistical analysis may be appropriate. To analyze the qualitative data, processes will be needed to organize it and then analyze its content for emergent patterns and themes. There are many ways in which to structure such a process. One could use matrix organization systems recommended by Miles and Huberman (1984) or a grounded theory approach described by A. Strauss and Corbin (1990). Patton (1990) discussed, among other analytic techniques, the process of coding and creating a category system for analyzing qualitative data.

Whatever analytic methods are used, this final stage is the slowest and most time-consuming. It is in this stage that the research team returns to the data to attempt to construct a coherent story of the development of the students' ideas and their connection to the conjecture. Once this story has been constructed, decisions about how it will be publicized and told need to be made. These decisions are discussed later.

In the splitting experiment, we used a variety of techniques to conduct the final analysis of the data. One of the unique aspects of the splitting experiment was that it was designed to accommodate multiple graduate students' theses projects. Several of the graduate students on the research team chose an aspect of the splitting experiment as the topic of their thesis. For instance, one graduate student examined the decimal unit for her master's thesis (Lachance, 1996), whereas another graduate student investigated students' use and development of tools (Preyer, 1996) throughout the last year of the intervention. In these cases, the graduate students tended to take the lead in the final analysis of the data. However, their results and tentative conclusions were always subjected to review, discussion, and refinement by the larger research group.

Each type of data collection required a different set of analytic techniques. For example, sometimes, written assessments were looked at in purely quantitative terms. How many items did the students complete correctly? How did the class fare overall? How did different groups of students (e.g., girls vs. boys) perform in comparison to each other? However, these assessments were also subject to content analysis. What types of methods did the students use to solve problems? How do we categorize those methods? What types of evidence of the students' thinking are present in these solutions?

One of the most time-consuming aspects of our final analysis was sifting through the videotapes. Generally, one or two of us viewed them and tried to code various sections. Like the experiment itself, our coding system changed as it developed. We kept notes describing the various groupings and categories of videotaped interactions. These categories grew and changed as we incorporated more data. In the end, we came up with a system of categories for describing the data. Because such research allows for these categories to emerge, they are important products of the work too.

For instance, in making sense of the decimal unit, four major categories described much of the videotaped data:

- *Precursors*: episodes in which students seemed to be developing precursors for decimal notation.

- *Concrete referents*: episodes where students used concrete referents as a means of understanding decimal notation.

- *Ratio reasoning*: episodes in which students appeared to use ratios as a means of making sense of decimals.

- *Mathematical connections*: episodes where students, attempting to make sense of a new idea, were relating various mathematical constructions to each other.

The development of these categories was also dependent on review and revision by the larger research team (see Lachance (1996) for a description of how these categories were linked to her analysis of the relation between decimals and ratio reasoning).

By the end of the study, a much more elaborated articulation of the conjecture was proposed. The elaborated conjecture can be communicated by means of examples from the research, but it should be analyzed for the robustness of its structure and connections as well. A model of the elaborated splitting conjecture is reproduced in FIG. 10.3. the reader may refer to Confrey (1996) for a fuller explanation of its contents.

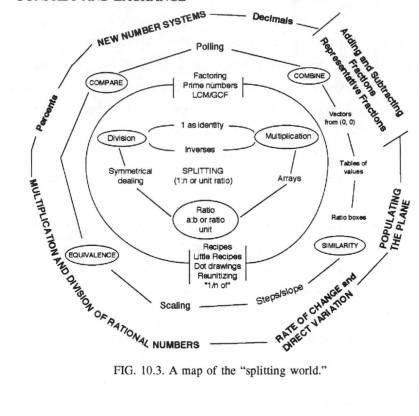

FIG. 10.3. A map of the "splitting world."

# PRODUCTS OF TRANSFORMATIVE AND CONJECTURE-DRIVEN TEACHING EXPERIMENTS

An outline of the potential products of the transformative and conjecture-driven teaching experiment should be included in the research design's overall plan. Such products should be consistent with the rest of the design of the research and, thus, must take a variety of forms. Some researchers argue that the obligation of research is only to contribute to the knowledge base of the community of researchers, leaving others to interpret and translate the findings for practitioners. Consistent with our reform model, we take issue with such a narrow definition of the products of research. Producing multiple products of varied shape and structure will ensure that the conversation about the conjecture will be carried on by a diversity of audiences who will contribute to its further elaboration. It also ensures that the dialectical relation between conjecture and instruction carried out in the experiment is reproduced between the practitioner and the researcher as research results are prepared.

Potential products from this research include:

- Research papers on topics related to the conjecture such as its relationship to particular conceptual development, its forms of representations, the types of classroom interactions it promotes, and the associated outcomes of student assessments.

- Curricular materials, including software and multimedia products, that are informed by the research's findings.

- Professional development materials, such as videotapes of students' and teachers' work.

- Implementation studies looking at how the results are put into effect in various settings.

- Policy briefs for school personnel. These might be most in the school and school district where the research took place.

## EVALUATING THE QUALITY OF A TRANSFORMATIVE AND CONJECTURE-DRIVEN TEACHING EXPERIMENT

This approach to research design combines multiple elements: evolving conjectures, shifts in curricula, external instructors, and new forms of assessment. Finally elements are not found in "conventional" educational studies. Therefore, a legitimate question is: Is this merely an exercise in design, notoriously serendipitous, or are there well-defined criteria for judging the adequacy and quality of such studies? Although we acknowledge that design is indeed a significant element in this work, we argue that what makes this type of work a worthwhile and significant research model is that the design element is regulated by an explicitly stated and well-developed conjecture. The burden is on the researcher to demonstrate that the conjecture guides the design of the classroom practice and the analysis of the data.

It follows that a concern with this type of guided research is *how* it is guided. Is the conjecture's development truly guided by the data or does the researcher seem to pursue an independent agenda? Because of this concern, research of this type must be subjected to a careful demonstration of its quality. However, because of the novelty and the emergent nature of this research, we cannot adopt quality standards from traditional research models and leave it at that. Such standards as internal validity, external validity, reliability, and objectivity do not seem to fit. Instead, we must identify standards that conform to the components of our model and gauge their successful application. Thus, such standards will address issues related to ideological stance, theoretical framework, and the dialectical interaction between the conjecture and the intervention. Because the research must demonstrate its own consistency, we see one goal as ensuring the quality of the internal processes of the research. At the same time, because we acknowledge that educational research entails an intervention and aims at reform, we also must ensure quality through an assessment of the potential impacts on practice. An outline of this quality assurance plan is offered in FIG. 10.4.

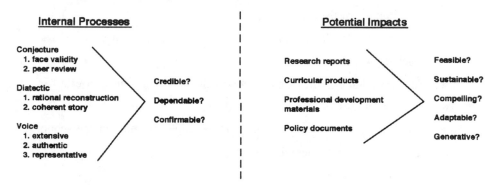

FIG. 10.4. Evaluating the transformative and conjecture-driven teaching experiment.

## Ensuring the Quality of the Internal Processes

Clearly, one cannot evaluate whether all of the aspects of the research process are of high quality. However, there are some aspects that deserve special attention because of the key roles they play in both our interpretation of events and the shape and structure of the intervention itself. Perhaps the most important question about this research concerns the explanatory power of the conjecture (Robinson, 1993). Recall that one of the catalysts for creating a conjecture was a dissatisfaction with the ways in which traditional practices treat a given set of mathematical topics and the belief that such treatment prevents many students from accessing mathematical understandings. So, one of the main questions of this type of research has to be: Can the conjecture point to a better way to reconceptualize this set of topics that will allow *all students* to construct an understanding of these concepts? This question leads to the identification of three targets for evaluating the quality of the research.

First, the quality of the conjecture can be looked at as an issue of face validity in relation to peer review. At the end of the study, an audience of researchers or practitioners can evaluate the face validity of the elaborated conjecture. This will be done by an analysis of its content and its path of evolution, which will require the judgment of an expert knowledgeable in the content, and by its relationship to the literature. The researcher must provide the audiences interested in these issues with enough background information about the conjecture, its content, pedagogy, and theoretical framework to make such an assessment in light of the research's findings.

Second, the quality of the process can be judged in relation to the coherence of the story recounting the dialectical relationship between the events in the classroom and the conjecture. How closely are the two forces in the dialectic interwoven? Does it result in a coherent story? We see this "story" as similar to Lakatos' (1976) description of his own work as a "rational reconstruction." In order to do this, the researcher will need to provide the readers with evidence of the research process, in terms of both preliminary and final data analysis.

Third, the fidelity of the study to its ideological stance can be judged. An outside audience should be able to determine whether the data allowed for the emergence of the students' voices. By this, we mean that an audience must be able to determine if the student expressions are extensive and authentic enough to convince a reader of the depth of the students' commitment to and ownership of the ideas. To do this, the researcher would need to provide ample data in the form of quotations from the students and examples of their work in discussions of the research. Along with these data, sufficient citations about the characteristics and contexts of the student-speakers, along with comments about how representative of the various student groups a given set of interactions is, must be included. Although we recognize that some students may be more articulate than others, in order to fulfill the diversity requirement, the research is obligated to demonstrate that the educational benefits have been experienced widely. In addition to the students' voices, the results of various assessment activities may support these claims. Fidelity to the ideological stance also can be gauged by whether there are concrete indicators of increased successful access to learning for all students. In terms of increased equality of outcomes, in the splitting work, we examined how the gap between better and less well prepared students changed over the course of the intervention. At the end of the 3-year splitting experiment, we found that not only did 17 of 20 students score in the 19th percentile on standardized achievement tests, but also that in contrast with comparison schools, the margin in achievement levels between better and less well prepared students had decreased significantly. In large part, this was due to the vastly improved performance of the less-well-prepared group (Scarano & Confrey, 1996).

The claims for the quality of the conjecture, of the rational reconstruction, and of the fidelity to the ideological stance are based on interpreted data. However, how does an audience know whether these data are trustworthy? Some audiences may feel that such interpreted data have been "corrupted" by the researchers' interpretations. They may ask: "How do we know that the researcher just saw what she wanted to see or only paid attention to the data that supported her conjecture?" Such concerns speak to the issue of trustworthiness; in other words, how does an audience know that it can trust the methods and interpretation of the researcher?

To address these concerns, we turn for a moment to the field of program evaluation. Guba and Lincoln (1989) promoted a design that they called "responsive constructivist evaluation," which bears similarity to some aspects of the transformative and conjecture-driven teaching experiment. Most significantly, their evaluation model seeks to respond to the claims, concerns, and issues raised by interested parties in a given setting. As such, the design is viewed as emergent because the focus of the evaluation emerges and evolves from inputs by and negotiations among those concerned with its results. This is very similar to how we see the conjecture evolving through the interaction of students' voices and researchers' perspectives.

As a part of their proposed model for evaluation, Guba and Lincoln (1989) offered a set of criteria by which we can judge the "trustworthiness" of a given inquirer's methods and data. Because their evaluation design stresses the importance of evolving and emerging constructions and our research design has a similar focus, we have adapted several of Guba and Lincoln's notions to speak to the issue of the trustworthiness of interpreted data in conjecture-driven research. Specifically, we believe that the audiences who question the quality of interpreted data needed to be assured that these data are credible, dependable, and confirmable (Guba & Lincoln, 1989).

In terms of the credibility, a judgment of quality needs to be based on how well the constructed perspectives of the respondents (in this case, the students) matched the versions of these constructions presented by the researcher. In other words, how well did the researchers reconstruct what the students were experiencing? In several branches of social science (anthropology, sociology, etc.), specific ways of ensuring that such reconstructions are credible have been developed. Examples of them that might be used most easily in conjecture-driven research are prolonged engagement with the context of the research, persistent observation of the interactions and the setting, analysis of cases that are not in keeping with the conjecture, and checking with students to be sure that we understand what they are trying to communicate to us. By using such methods, the researcher may help to ensure that he or she is representing the constructions of the students in a credible manner.

The concept of dependability speaks to the stability of the data. For some audiences, assuring the stability of the data could be a major problem for a conjecture-driven teaching experiment where "methodological changes and shifts in constructions are expected products of an emergent design dedicated to increasingly sophisticated constructions" (Guba & Lincoln, 1989, p. 242). However, as Guba and Lincoln saw it (and we concur):

> Far from being threats to dependability, such changes and shifts are hallmarks of a maturing—and successful—inquiry. But such changes and shifts need to be both tracked and traceable (publicly inspectable) so that outside reviewers . . . can explore the process, judge the decisions that were made, and understand what salient factors in the context led the [researcher] to the decisions and interpretations made" (p. 242).

Thus, to ensure dependability, researchers involved in conjecture-driven teaching experiments must keep careful track of their methodological and analytical decisions. Such evidence of the research process will allow outside parties to follow and assess the reasoning behind the methodological path taken through the data.

Finally, the construct of confirmability involves ensuring that the findings of the research are grounded in the data rather than in the whims of the research team. If the findings are confirmable, an external observer should be able to reconstruct them by way of the data. To allow this to happen, Guba and Lincoln (1989) suggested that the researcher provide an audit trail. With an audit trail, the researcher keeps evidence of the processes by which the methodological decisions were made and the data were analyzed. Then, an external auditor should be able to reconstruct the process and confirm the findings. Such an audit also can be used to ensure the dependability of the data.

Obviously, an audit is not possible in many settings because it is time consuming and requires the services of a committed individual from outside the research group. If an auditor is paid, this would entail considerable expense as well. However, in discussing research findings and presenting reports on their results, some information about what decisions were made and how and why they were made would allow audiences to have some ability to assess the dependability and confirmability of the findings.

In summary, because the quality of this research is so dependent on how well the researchers reflect upon the data and challenge themselves with respect to their evolving understandings, the question of "How do we know we can trust the researchers?" is paramount. Assuring the credibility, dependability, and confirmability of the research certainly will answer this question adequately for some audiences. However, we recognize that other audiences will remain skeptical about the quality of this type of research. With these audiences, the researcher will have to continue to struggle with how to present compelling and convincing arguments that confirm the findings of the research.

## Assessing the Potential Impact

The second part of our quality criterion is linked to our motivations for doing this type of research. One objective of this research model is to connect research and practice better so that changes in classrooms will be initiated more quickly and effectively. Thus, the second part of the quality criterion concerns how well the findings of the study are connected to achievable change. This is perhaps the most difficult criterion to meet because, in the past, bridging the gap between research results and practice has not been efficient or easy. However, because this type of research is coupled with a reform agenda, we believe that an assessment of quality must be made on its potential ability to act as a catalyst for change.

The research team needs to devise ways of making this information useful to the audiences of policymakers, teachers, parents, administrators, students, and others who initiate changes in the system. The targets for assessing the potential impacts of the research project are its products and dissemination practices discussed in the section Products of Transformative and Conjecture-Driven Teaching Experiments.

We maintain that one should expect more positive evaluations of the potential impacts on practice of a conjecture-driven teaching experiment because, unlike research designs that are isolated from classrooms, this research takes place inside them. However, such research takes place in one classroom only and, as we specified at the beginning, certain classroom constraints could be altered or relaxed. Thus, there is still a need to evaluate the potential impacts of this type of research.

Criteria for assessing these impacts include:

- *Feasibility*: Any type of research findings can be implemented if there are ample resources, both financial and human. However, schools' resources are limited, particularly at those less advantaged schools that have larger populations of at-risk students. In the quest for equity, it must be feasible for the products of research to be implemented and useful in all classrooms.

- *Sustainability*: High-quality products will have to endure and sustain their impacts over a substantial period of time. Although only time will allow one to assess the sustainability of the impact fully, it can be explored in advance by comparing the products to similar ones.

- *Compelling Nature*: The research findings must convince practitioners of the urgency with which the proposed changes should take place. The findings and products must compel them to change. Many innovations are viewed as interesting to practitioners, but only a few create an imperative that practitioners are unlikely to ignore.

- *Adaptability*: With sensitivity to the unique and diverse contexts of schools, these products must be adaptable to a particular context. In a diverse and multicultural society with a variety of configurations of schooling, a product of research must demonstrate flexibility.

- *Generativity*: Just as it did for the research, the conjecture should provide practitioners with a powerful means of reconceptualizing a variety of classroom events, relationships, and practices. Products of research that become models for innovations will prove fruitful beyond their initial conceptualizations.

Because research has been relatively isolated from practice in the past, these criteria appear too demanding of any one team of researchers. However, as research becomes more integrated with classroom practices, we are confident that we will gain skill in assessing these criteria prior to actual implementation studies. At this point, though, implementation studies or field tests may be required in order to learn more about them.

There is no question that in our splitting work we have struggled with integrating research and practice. Finding creative ways to translate our research into practice while combating the educational system's resistance to profound change continues to be a challenge. However, we have been most successful with preparing presentations for practitioners that illustrate what students can do if given the proper activities and environment. We often bring to these sessions videotapes of students working on various projects or presenting their solutions to problems in order to demonstrate how capable and creative students are.

Although this may seem somewhat trivial compared to what we have found about the splitting conjecture, we feel it is an important effort to make. For example, whenever we talk about introducing decimals by means of the Weights Problem, we get questions that reveal the low expectations others have of students. Recall that the Weights Problem involved weights (circles, rectangles, blobs, and sticks) that have various multiplicative relationships to each other. For example, there might be a 4-to-1 relationship between the weight of circles and the weight of blobs, and perhaps a 2-to-3 relationship between the weight of rectangles and the weight of circles. Students' work with a variety of ratios was meant to build a foundation from which they would see our decimal system as a particular set of 10-to-1 ratio relationships.

Inevitably, when we explain this problem to various groups, we are asked such questions as: "Why did you start with all those odd ratio relationships? Why didn't you make the weights all into 10-to-1 relationships? Didn't the kids get confused?" The assumption underlying these questions is that students can learn by simple straightforward methods only. Sophistication and complexity are not only unnecessary, but also may be dangerous or confusing to students, according to this line of reasoning. Having encountered these challenges frequently, we see the need to demonstrate what students are able, willing, and eager to do when given sophisticated sets of problems and how powerful their constructions are when given the chance to develop. Although they fall short of some of the changes that our findings could promote, we do believe that our presentations to teachers and peers are helping to lay the foundation for what we hope will be more transformative changes in the future.

# CONCLUSION

We believe that the strengths of this type of research are its unique characteristics. By listening to children and allowing theoretical understandings to evolve from what we hear, we can pave the way more effectively for increasingly equitable mathematics education practices. After all, we know that traditional models of instruction do not work for many groups of students. What better way to uncover what does work for them than to let their voices guide our emerging conjectures and theories?

The impacts that such a process can have are multiple:

- Such research is a means of articulating clearly and specifically how we want to reconceptualize mathematics curricula so that they are accessible to all students.
- By combining some of the limitations of classroom practices with the theoretical underpinnings of educational research, this model helps to build a stronger bridge between research and practice. Such a bridge can lead to a more efficient and effective reform movement.

- By making others aware of what it is possible to accomplish with children, this research model can inform decision making about what can and should be going on in mathematics education.

We believe it is vital that mathematics education research be committed to equity. By framing our research with this commitment, we are aiming for a high water mark. Intellectually interesting findings are no longer enough. Today, the worth of our work must be judged on the extent to which it improves access to learning for all of our children.

# 11 Teaching Experiment Methodology: Underlying Principles and Essential Elements

**Leslie P. Steffe**
*University of Georgia*

**Patrick W. Thompson**
*Vanderbilt University*

With Contributions by
**Ernst von Glasersfeld**

> The constructivist is fully aware of the fact that an organism's conceptual constructions are not fancy-free. On the contrary, the process of constructing is constantly curbed and held in check by the constraints it runs into. (von Glasersfeld, 1990, p. 33)

A primary purpose for using teaching experiment methodology is for researchers to experience, firsthand, students'[1] mathematical learning and reasoning. Without the experiences afforded by teaching, there would be no basis for coming to understand the powerful

---

[1] We use the term *student* generically to emphasize that our remarks apply to, for example, investigating children's understanding of number or college mathematics majors' understandings of the fundamental theorem of calculus.

mathematical concepts and operations students construct or even for suspecting that these concepts and operations may be distinctly different from those of researchers.

The constraints that researchers experience in teaching constitute a basis for understanding students' mathematical constructions. As we, the authors, use it, *constraint* has a dual meaning. Researchers' imputations to students of mathematical understandings and operations are constrained to language and actions they are able to bring forth in students. They also are constrained by students' mistakes, especially those mistakes that are essential, that is, mistakes that persist despite researchers' best efforts to eliminate them. Sources of essential mistakes reside in students' current mathematical knowledge. To experience constraints in these two senses is our primary reason for doing teaching experiments. The first type of constraint serves in building up a "mathematics of students" and the second type serves in circumscribing such a mathematics within conceptual boundaries.

In our teaching experiments, we have found it necessary to attribute mathematical realities to students that are independent of our own mathematical realities. By "independent of our own" we mean that we attribute mathematical concepts and operations to students that they have constructed as a result of their interactions in their physical and sociocultural milieu.[2] In this attribution, we remain aware that we may not, and probably cannot, account for students' mathematics using our own mathematical concepts and operations. Although our attribution of mathematical realities to students is a conceptual construct, it is grounded in the mathematical realities of students as we experience them. We use the phrase "students' mathematics" to refer to whatever might constitute students' mathematical realities; we use the phrase "mathematics of students" to refer to our interpretations of students' mathematics.[3]

---

[2] Although we stress construction as a result of interaction, we do not assume that information is transferred directly from an environment to the individual in an interaction. Whatever constitutes information for the individual is constructed by the individual using his or her own conceptual constructs.

[3] We formulated this sentence to highlight the fact that there is no one "mathematics of students." In principle, there could be variations in what researchers emphasize in teaching experiments as they study students' mathematics. We believe that these variations, rather than being a weakness of

*(continued)*

The distinction we make between students' mathematics and mathematics of students was captured by Ackermann (1995) in speaking of human relations:

> In human relations, it is vital to attribute autonomy to others and to things—to celebrate their existence independently from our current interaction with them. This is true even if an attribution (of existence) is a mental construct. We can literally rob others of their identity if we deny them an existence beyond our current interests. (p. 343)

Students' mathematics is something we attribute to students independently of our interactions with them. In doing so, we reason as follows: If we acknowledge that students are autonomous organisms not unlike ourselves, and if we claim that our consensual mathematical reality is the only one, then certain difficulties arise. If our, the researchers', consensual mathematical reality is the only one, then the mathematical reality of any student would be solely in our imagination. But a student, being not unlike ourselves, can insist that his or her mathematical reality is the sole mathematical reality and that the mathematical reality of everyone else is in his or her imagination, including our, the researchers', consensual reality. Being autonomous also, we would not want to accept that our consensual mathematical reality is merely a concoction of the student's imagination. So, we have to accept the student's mathematical reality as being distinct from ours. We call those mathematical realities "students' mathematics," whatever they might be. Students' mathematics is indicated by what they say and do as they engage in mathematical activity, and a basic goal of the researchers in a teaching experiment is to construct models of students' mathematics. "Mathematics of students" refers to these models, and it includes the modifications students make in their ways of operating (Steffe, 1988).

We regard the mathematics of students as a legitimate mathematics to the extent we can find rational grounds for what students say and do. Looking behind what students say and do in

---

teaching experiments, are one of their greatest strengths because different possibilities for students' mathematics education emerge.

an attempt to understand their mathematical realities is an essential part of a teaching experiment. The process involved in looking behind what students say and do was called conceptual analysis by von Glasersfeld (1995), and it is here one becomes explicitly aware of one's own engagement in a kind of mathematical research. For us, this awareness is essential because teaching experiment methodology is based on the necessity of providing an ontogenetic justification of mathematics, that is, a justification based on the history of its generation by individuals. This kind of justification is different from the impersonal, universal, and ahistorical justification often provided for mathematics, but we believe it is an appropriate way to regard mathematics, especially in the case of specifying a school mathematics. In fact, we contend an ontogenetic justification of mathematics is generally no less rational than its alternatives. But it is different to regard mathematics as a product of the functioning of human intelligence (Piaget, 1980) than to regard it as a product of impersonal, universal, and ahistorical reason. Our view of mathematics as a product of functioning human intelligence defines mathematics as a living subject rather than as a subject of being; this is the core belief from which our research methodology flows.

By regarding mathematics as a living subject, we are faced with a different mathematics than appears in contemporary school mathematics. Our practical stance is that the better we understand it, the better positioned we are to affect students productively. Indeed, it is our intention that the mathematics of students replace contemporary school mathematics (Steffe & Wiegel, 1992). This is the main thrust of our work, and we want it to be understood in this way. We strive to specify the mathematical concepts and operations of students and to make them the conceptual foundations of school mathematics.

## HISTORICAL PERSPECTIVES

### Reasons for the Emergence of Teaching Experiments

Teaching experiments were not always an accepted way of doing research in mathematics education. It was not until approximately 1970 that teaching experiments in mathematics education emerged in the United States. They emerged for two reasons. First, models out of which one might make a mathematics of students were developed outside of mathematics education and for purposes other than educating students (e.g., Brownell, 1928; McLellan & Dewey, 1895; Piaget & Szeminska, 1952). After intensive efforts to use these models to study the mathematical development of students, it became clear that new models were needed that had their roots in mathematics education. Some researchers came to understand that mathematics educators could not simply borrow models from the fields of genetic epistemology, philosophy, or psychology and use them with the expectation that they could be used to explain students' mathematical learning and development in the context of teaching. Models were needed that included an account of the progress students make as a result of interactive mathematical communication. Although it was not the intention of researchers to explain students' mathematics using known mathematical systems, it was felt researchers needed to learn how to use their own mathematical knowledge in actual interactions with students. The models of students' mathematics available at the time were not sensitive either to the issues involved in sustaining students' mathematical activity over extended periods of time or to the issues involved in how teachers might participate in students' modifications of that activity.

Second, a large chasm existed between the practice of research and the practice of teaching. Essentially, the experimental methodology used prior to the emergence of teaching experiments had its roots in the "agriculture paradigm." In this paradigm, the researcher selects one or more samples from a target population and subjects it or them to various treatments. The effect of one treatment is compared to the effects of others, with the intention of specifying differences between or among them. This seemed to be a reasonable way to proceed in research, and it was the one advocated by D. T. Campbell and Stanley (1963): "By experiment we refer to that portion of research in which variables are manipulated and their effects upon other variables are observed" (p. 1).

Researchers' attempts to formulate possible factors that could be varied systematically in such a way that a corresponding variation in other variables might be observed seemed logical enough. But the research essentially failed. In hindsight, classical experimental design in the spirit of D. T. Campbell and Stanley (1963) suppressed conceptual analysis in the conduct of research. One reason for this suppression was the assumption that an experimental manipulation would causally affect other variables—such as measures of students' mathematical achievement—quite apart from the individuals involved in the treatment. The subjects in experiments were recipients of treatments and usually were not the focus of conceptual analysis. The subjects were subjected to treatments; they did not participate in the coconstruction of the treatments in the context of teaching episodes. How students made meanings or the meanings they made was not of primary interest.

Classical experimental design inhibited efforts to investigate students' sense-making constructs. It also inhibited efforts to engage in the kind of research we believe is essential in establishing mathematics education as an academic field. Researchers found it all too easy to appear "scientific" by using advanced statistical methods and by writing in the passive voice—the latter giving an objective, "hard science" appearance to claims. Too often, conceptual analyses of mathematical understanding and mathematical performance were absent.

A strong reliance on psychometrics was another significant difficulty researchers came to have with classical methods. Psychometrics was founded upon the idea that a student's actual score on an item is composed of a "true" score and some amount due to error. For this to make sense, one needed to assume a cause–effect relationship between the item presented and a student's resulting performance. This led to all sorts of pseudoscientific constructs, such as test items having "dimensions" that would account for different students' behaviors (P. W. Thompson, 1982, p. 156).

Psychometrics lent support to classical experimental design—that to experiment means to manipulate variables. In classical experimental research, tasks, items, dimensions, and so forth were objects to be manipulated. It was through such manipulation that researchers controlled students' environments and, hence, uncovered the reality of their knowledge. From a constructivist perspective, however, there is no such thing as a "constant" stimulus; students construct for themselves the tasks in which they actually engage, and it is the constructive process and the constructed task that are interesting scientifically (Powers, 1973, 1978).

## Reasons for the Acceptance of Teaching Experiments

There seem to be several reasons teaching experiments were accepted almost at face value by mathematics educators without being developed and analyzed more extensively. First, the methodology seemed intuitively correct. The word *teaching* in the title appealed to the common sense of mathematics educators and resonated with their professional identification as mathematics teachers.

Second, versions of the methodology were being used already by researchers in the Academy of Pedagogical Sciences in the then Union of Soviet Socialist Republics. Reports of this research became available in the United States through the efforts of Izaack Wirszup at the University of Chicago (Wirszup & Kilpatrick, 1975–1978) and provided academic respectability for what was then a major departure in the practice of research in mathematics education. The Soviet versions of the teaching experiment were examined by a small group of researchers in the United States in their formulation of a new methodology for mathematics education research.[4]

Finally, the field of mathematics education was entering a postmodern period (von Glasersfeld, 1987a). Major shifts in the way in which mathematical knowing was understood were under way, and they became expressed in the paradigm wars of the next decade (e.g., Brophy, 1986; Confrey, 1986; Kilpatrick, 1987; Sinclair, 1987; Vergnaud, 1987; Wheeler, 1987). Mathematics education researchers began to change their concept of normal science, and the teaching experiment filled a void in the methodologies available for investigating mathematical learning and development.[5] In fact, over the past 20 years, growing numbers of researchers have sought to understand students' mathematical experience. They have tried to account for students' mathematical activity in the context of teaching as manifestations of their current imagery, reasoning, and understandings. They also have tried to build accounts of how students learn specific mathematical concepts. Rather than become interested in these issues in a pure form, researchers explicitly acknowledged that mathematical activity in school occurs as a result of students' participation in teaching. Experimental methodologies used in the 1970s were inadequate for addressing these issues. In particular, the foundational assumptions of psychometrics conflicted profoundly with assumptions that gave meaning to the idea of understanding another's mathematical experiences without assuming a God's-eye view of those experiences (P. W. Thompson, 1982).

So, new research methodologies emerged to support avenues of inquiry that current methodologies could not sustain, and the teaching experiment marked a revolution in the

---

[4] For example, a symposium entitled "The Soviet Teaching Experiment: Its Role and Usage in American Research" was presented at the 1978 annual meeting of the National Council of Teachers of Mathematics in San Diego, California.

[5] See Zweng, Green, Kilpatrick, Pollack, and Suydam (1983) for an interesting discussion of alternative methodologies.

practice of mathematics education research (Cobb & Steffe, 1983; Hunting, 1983; P. W. Thompson, 1979, 1982). The methodology of the teaching experiment will unavoidably continue to evolve among the researchers who use it. It certainly did not emerge as a standardized methodology nor has it been standardized since. Rather, the teaching experiment is a conceptual tool that researchers use in the organization of their activities. It is primarily an exploratory tool, derived from Piaget's clinical interview and aimed at exploring students' mathematics. Because it involves experimentation with the ways and means of influencing students' mathematical knowledge, the teaching experiment is more than a clinical interview. Whereas the clinical interview is aimed at understanding students' current knowledge, the teaching experiment is directed toward understanding the progress students make over extended periods. It is a dynamic way of operating, serving a functional role in the lives of researchers as they strive to organize their activity to achieve their purposes and goals. In this, it is a living methodology designed initially for the exploration and explanation of students' mathematical activity. Our comments concerning the teaching experiment should be interpreted in this context because they are not meant to be prescriptive.

# THE ELEMENTS OF TEACHING EXPERIMENT METHODOLOGY

A teaching experiment involves a sequence of teaching episodes (Steffe, 1983). A teaching episode includes a teaching agent, one or more students, a witness of the teaching episodes, and a method of recording what transpires during the episode. These records, if available, can be used in preparing subsequent episodes as well as in conducting a retrospective conceptual analysis of the teaching experiment. These elements are germane to all teaching experiments.

## Exploratory Teaching

There is a case where it may be appropriate to emphasize the experiential aspects involved in teaching and not to concentrate on hypothesis testing or retrospective analyses. For example, one of the first teaching experiments conducted in the United States was done for a reason that does not appear in the report of the experiment (Steffe, Hirstein, & Spikes, 1976). After working for a period of approximately eight years trying to apply Piaget's cognitive-development models to mathematics education, a point had been reached where children's construction of number, as explained by Piaget and Szeminska (1952), was not useful in furthering the researchers' goals. New models for children's construction of number were needed that were more sensitive to their mathematical concepts and operations (cf. Steffe, Cobb & von Glaserfeld, 1988). So, the researchers in the Steffe et al. (1976) study returned to their professional commitment as mathematics teachers in order to learn students' mathematics firsthand. Based on their past experience as mathematics teachers, they understood that teaching students for short periods of time could not serve as a basis for a solid understanding of their thinking and how it might be influenced. They taught two classes of first-grade students for one school year, an experience that contributed some of the basic ideas about teaching experiment methodology.

Any researcher who hasn't conducted a teaching experiment independently, but who wishes to do so, should engage in exploratory teaching first. It is important that one become thoroughly acquainted, at an experiential level, with students' ways and means of operating in whatever domain of mathematical concepts and operations are of interest. In understanding this, one must adopt a certain attitude if substantial progress is to be made toward learning a mathematics of students. The teacher-researcher must attempt to put aside his or her own concepts and operations and not insist that the students learn what he or she knows. Otherwise, the researcher might become caught in what Stolzenberg (1984) called a "trap"—focusing on the mathematics the researcher takes as given instead of focusing on exploring students' ways and means of operating. The researcher's mathematical concepts and operations can be orienting, but they should not be regarded, initially at least, as constituting what the students should learn.

## Meanings of Experiment in a Teaching Experiment

*Testing Research Hypotheses.* Other than the goal of becoming thoroughly familiar with children's mathematics in an experiential sense, our purpose for engaging in exploratory teaching was to begin making essential distinctions in students' ways and means of operating. For example, when teaching the two classes of first-graders, we observed children who could count, but who needed objects in their visual field in order to carry out the activity. We also observed other children who could count as these children did, but who also willfully created substitute countable items such as tapping their finger on a table when the items to be counted were hidden from view. Children of the second type were obliged to always count from "one" in order to give meaning to a number word. There was another group of children who could count as children of the first two types did, but they also could start from any number word and count further when the items they intended to count were not in their visual field.

These distinctions proved to be essential in two senses. First, we did not teach these children to count in the ways they did. Rather, their ways of counting arose from within them and we as their teachers had nothing to do with it.[6] Second, the ways in which the children counted were resistant to our efforts to teach them to count in ways that, to us, were more advanced. We tried to teach the children in the first group to count as the children in the second group did, and the children in the second group to count as the children in the third group did, but we were essentially unsuccessful. We also tried, again with little success, to teach the children in the third group to count forward or backward interchangeably in what, to us, were missing addend situations.

So, we had found a problem that seemed to have educational significance. Consequently, a 2-year teaching experiment was mounted to explore if progress could be made in solving this problem. By using individual interviews (Ginsburg, 1981), six children were selected, three who gave every indication of counting as the children in the first group did and three who gave every indication of counting as the children in the second group did (Steffe et al., 1988). The experiment was to explore the consequences of being in one of the two groups. Would the three children in each group remain fundamentally alike over the duration of the teaching experiment and distinctly different from the three children in the other group? Or, would all of the children tend toward homogeneity in their mathematical understandings and interactions?

We use *experiment* in "teaching experiment" in a scientific sense. The hypotheses in the teaching experiment mentioned previously were that the differences between children of different groups would become quite large over the 2-year period and that the children within a

---

[6]This assertion may seem to contradict the idea of a mind-dependent reality. However, the comment is made to acknowledge our awareness that these students had a history of interactions of which we were not a part. It also acknowledges that in our interactions, the students contributed their ways of counting to the situations without being told by us how to count or even to count.

group would remain essentially alike. That the hypotheses were confirmed is important, but only incidental to our purposes here. What is important is that teaching experiments are done to test hypotheses as well as to generate them. One does not embark on the intensive work of a teaching experiment without having major research hypotheses to test.

The research hypotheses one formulates prior to a teaching experiment guide the initial selection of the students and the researchers' overall general intentions. However, the researchers do their best to "forget" these hypotheses during the course of the teaching episodes, in favor of adapting to the constraints they experience in interacting with the students. The researchers' intention is to remain aware of the students' contributions to the trajectory of teaching interactions and for the students to test the research hypotheses seriously. Researchers have students "test the research hypotheses seriously" by teaching them with the goal of promoting the greatest progress possible in all participating students. The researchers return to the research hypotheses retrospectively after completing the teaching episodes. This method—setting research hypotheses aside and focusing on what actually happens—is basic in the ontogenetic justification of mathematics.

*Generating and Testing Hypotheses.* In addition to formulating and testing major research hypotheses, another modus operandi in a teaching experiment is for the researchers to generate and test hypotheses during the teaching episodes. Often, these hypotheses are conceived "on the fly," a phrase Ackermann (1995) used to describe how hypotheses are formulated in clinical interviews. Frequently, they are formulated between teaching episodes as well. The teacher-researcher, through reviewing the records of one or more earlier teaching episodes, may formulate one or more hypotheses to be tested in the next episode.

In a teaching episode, the students' language and actions are a source of perturbation for the teacher-researcher. It is the job of the teacher-researcher to continually postulate possible meanings that lie behind students' language and actions. It is in this way that students guide the teacher-researcher. The teacher-researcher may have a set of hypotheses to test before a teaching episode and a sequence of situations planned to test the hypotheses. But, because of students' unanticipated ways and means of operating as well as their unexpected mistakes, the teacher-researcher may be forced to abandon these hypotheses while interacting with the students and to create new hypotheses and situations on-the-spot. The teacher-researcher also might interpret the anticipated language and actions of the students in ways that were unexpected prior to teaching. Impromptu interpretations occur to the teacher-researcher as an insight that would be unlikely to happen in the absence of experiencing the students in the context of teaching interactions. Here, again, the teacher-researcher is obliged to formulate new hypotheses and to formulate situations of learning to test them.

Through generating and testing hypotheses, boundaries of the students' ways and means of operating can be formulated—where the students make what to us are essential mistakes. These essential mistakes are of the same nature as those Piaget found in his studies of children, and we use them for essentially the same purpose he did. They arise from students' failures to make adaptations when interacting in a medium. Operations and meanings we impute to students within the boundaries of their essential mistakes constitute what we call living models of the students' mathematics. The boundaries of a living model are usually fuzzy, and what might be placed just inside or just outside them is always a source of tension and often leads to creative efforts on the part of the researchers. Essential mistakes provide stability in a dynamic living model of students' mathematics. We understand better what students can do if we understand what they cannot do. We understand what students can understand better if we understand what they cannot understand. It also helps to understand what a child can do if we understand what other students, whose knowledge is judged to be at a higher or lower level, can do. In this, we are in accordance with Ackermann (1995) that: "The focus of the clinician [teacher] is to understand the originality of [the child's] reasoning, to describe its coherence, and to probe its robustness or fragility in a variety of contexts" (p. 346).

When a student makes what appears to be an essential mistake, our purpose is not "to judge or evaluate the child's performance in relation to performances of other children who might come up with the right answer" (Ackermann, 1995, p. 346). In this, we interpret Ackermann as speaking about the attitude of the teacher-researcher toward the child. Rather than believing that a student is absolutely wrong or that the student's knowledge is immature or irrational, the teacher-researcher must attempt to understand what the student can do; that is, the teacher-researcher must construct a frame of reference in which what the student can do seems rational. This is a basic challenge facing the researcher.[7]

## Meanings of Teaching in a Teaching Experiment

Teaching actions occur in a teaching experiment in the context of interacting with students. However, interaction is not taken as a given—learning how to interact with students is a central issue in any teaching experiment. The nuances of how to act and how to ask questions after being surprised are among, in our experience, the most central issues in conducting a teaching experiment. The researchers may have research hypotheses to test at the beginning of a teaching experiment, but even researchers experienced in teaching may not know well enough what progress students will make or know well enough their mathematical thinking and power of abstraction to formulate learning environments prior to teaching. Wholly unexpected possibilities may open up to the teacher-researcher in the course of the teaching experiment.

If the researchers knew ahead of time how to interact with the teaching experiments' students and what the outcomes of those interactions might be, there would be little reason for conducting a teaching experiment. So, frequently, the researchers are obliged to engage in responsive and intuitive interactions with the students when they are, in fact, puzzled about where the interactions are headed. As the teaching experiment progresses, the researchers become more experienced with the students and often change from interacting in a responsive and intuitive way to interacting analytically.

*Responsive and Intuitive Interaction.* In responsive and intuitive interactions, the teacher-researcher is usually not explicitly aware of how or why he or she acts as he or she does and the action appears without forethought. He or she acts without planning the action in advance

---

[7]Establishing a mathematics of students is essential in support of the current reform efforts in mathematics education. It is insufficient to focus on reforming mathematics teaching and learning without also reforming the mathematical aspects of those activities (Steffe & Wiegel, 1992).

of the action. In this role, we see ourselves as agents of action (or interaction). As agents of action, we strive to harmonize ourselves with the students with whom we are working to the extent that we "lose" ourselves in our interactions. We make no intentional distinctions between our knowledge and the students' knowledge, and, for us, experientially, everything is the students' knowledge as we strive to feel at one with them. In essence, we become the students and attempt to think as they do (P. W. Thompson, 1982, 1991; van Manen, 1991). Researchers do not adopt this stance at the beginning of a teaching experiment only. Rather, they maintain it throughout the experiment.

By interacting with students in a responsive and an intuitive way, the goal of the researchers is to explore the students' reasoning. For example, when working with two third-grade children named Jason and Patricia,[8] Jason drew a stick spanning the computer screen, as shown in FIG. 11.1. The teacher asked the two children if they could cut the stick into two equal pieces. This question was asked with no apparent expectation of what the children might do:

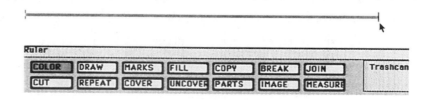

FIG. 11.1. The child was using TIMA.[9]

# PROTOCOL I

---

[8] Jason and Patricia were two children in the teaching experiment entitled "Construction of the Rational Numbers of Arithmetic," National Science Foundation Project No. RED-8954678.

[9] Sticks a computer microworld that we designed especially for the teaching experiment. In this microworld, the child could use the button labeled *CUT* to cut the stick.

Jason: (Using the CUT command, he makes a cut in the stick, then leans back to inspect his choice visually.)

Teacher: How do you know these two sticks are equal? How do you know they are the same size?

The two pieces were obviously of different lengths, and the two children made a visual comparison between the two pieces. But, Jason went further and suggested: "Copy the biggest one and then copy them again," and then said "No," shaking his head. After that, the two children sat in silent concentration.

The teacher-researcher tried to imagine finding a way of cutting the stick into two equal pieces as if he were one of the children. Based on his interpretation that the children could find no action in their computer microworld that would yield two equal pieces of the stick,[10] he suggested to Patricia that she draw a shorter stick that would be "easier to divide." In this suggestion, the tone of the researcher's voice indicated to the students that even he could not find where to cut this rather long stick. The teacher-researcher had no foreknowledge of where his suggestion might lead the students. That they led to productive interactions and spontaneous contributions by Patricia and Jason as exhibited in Protocol II:

## PROTOCOL II

Teacher: (After Patricia had drawn a stick about 1 decimeter in length.) Now, I want you to break that stick up into two equal pieces of the same size.

Patricia: (She places her right index finger on the right endpoint of the stick, then places her middle finger to the immediate left of her index finger. She continues in this way, walking her fingers along the stick in

---

[10]The children were not familiar yet with "PARTS," which could be used to partition a stick into equal-sized pieces.

synchrony with uttering.)   One, two, three, four, five. (She stops when she is about one half of the way across the stick.)

Jason: (He places his right index finger where Patricia left off; he uses his right thumb rather than his middle finger to begin walking along the stick. He changes to his left index finger rather than his right thumb after placing his thumb down once. He continues in this way until he reaches the left endpoint of the stick, uttering) Six, seven, eight, nine, ten. (Then) they're five and five. (He smiles with satisfaction.)

P: (She smiles also.)

The actions that the children took after the researcher's directive in Protocol II were contributed by the students and were not suggested by the teacher-researcher. Patricia introduced independently the action of walking her fingers along the stick until she arrived at a place that she regarded as one half of the way across the stick. Jason picked up counting where Patricia left off, which indicates that he shared her goal to find a way to establish equal pieces of the stick. Patricia's counting activity was meaningful to him, and he could be said to engage in cooperative mathematical activity with Patricia.

In a teaching episode, as in a clinical interview, the students' reasoning is the focus of attention (Ackermann, 1995). When the students' reasoning proves to be rich and full of implications for further interaction by the teacher-researcher, he or she often turns to analytical rather than to responsive and intuitive action. Researchers' abilities to engage in analytical action frequently follows an insight into the mental operations that make students' language and actions possible. The teacher-researcher formulates an image of the students' mental operations and an itinerary of what they might learn and how they might learn it.[11] Initially, this itinerary is articulated loosely or not at all. Nevertheless, the teacher-researcher has a sense of direction and a sense of possibilities for where he or she might try to take the students. The teacher-researcher now has initial goals along with a sense of possibilities for how the goals

---

[11]Learning may be *provoked* by instruction, providing an impetus for students' attention and reflection, but it is not *caused* by instruction. See Piaget's (1964) quotation, in the section on Learning and Development in a Teaching Experiment, and ensuing discussion.

might be achieved in future teaching episodes. As the teacher-researcher engages the children in further teaching episodes, this goal structure becomes extended and articulated. The most important feature of the extension and articulation is that the teacher-researcher modifies the goal structure constantly while developing it to fit the students' mathematical activity. Extending and modifying the goal structure lasts until the students' schemes seem to be well established and the students seem to have reached a plateau. At this point, where the teacher-researchers might try to take the students and how they might take them again become major issues.

*Analytical Interaction.* The teacher-researcher sometimes will have a precise hypothesis about students' schemes or operations. These are testable through an analytic interaction—an interaction with students inititated for the purpose of comparing their actions in specific contexts with actions consonant with the hypothesis. For example, because of the independence of Patricia's and Jason's contributions in Protocol II, a witness of the teaching episode inferred that the numerical operations of both children were activated and that they used these numerical operations in their attempts to partition the stick into equal pieces of indefinite size. This inference proved to be crucial in this particular teaching experiment because it served as a foundation for generating and testing a hypothesis of how these two children constructed fraction schemes.

Based on our interpretation that Jason and Patricia partitioned the stick mentally in Protocol II into an indefinite numerosity of sticks of equal but indefinite size before counting, the hypothesis was formulated that these children could establish an equipartitioning scheme. We generated the situation of learning of Protocol III in a test of our hypothesis in a teaching episode just three days after the one of Protocol II. The two children drew a stick of approximately 1 decimeter in length and the teacher-researcher asked the children to find the share for one of four people.

## PROTOCOL III

Teacher: Let's say that the three of us are together and then there is Dr. Olive over there. Dr. Olive wants a piece of this candy (the stick), but we want to have fair shares. We want him to have a share just like our shares, and we want all of our shares to be fair. I wonder if you could cut a piece of candy off from here (the stick) for Dr. Olive?

Jason: (Using the MARKS command, he makes three marks on the stick, estimating the place for the marks visually.)

Patricia: How do you know they are even? There is a big piece right there.

Jason: I don't know. (He clears all the marks and then makes a mark indicating one share. Before he can continue making marks, the teacher-researcher intervenes.)

Teacher: Can you break that somehow? (The teacher-researcher asks this question to explore the nature of Jason's partitioning operations.)

Jason: (Using the BREAK command, he breaks the stick at the mark; then he makes three copies of the piece and aligns them end-to-end under the remaining piece of the stick starting from the left endpoint of the remaining piece as in FIG. 11.2.)

FIG. 11.2. Jason testing if one piece cut from a stick is one of four equal pieces.

Teacher: Why don't you make another copy? (This suggestion was made to explore if Jason regarded the piece as belonging to the three copies as well as to the original stick.)

Jason: (He makes another copy and aligns it with the three others. He now has the four copies aligned directly beneath the original stick, which itself is cut once. The four pieces together are slightly longer than the original stick, as illustrated in FIG. 11.3.)

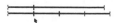

FIG. 11.3. Jason's completed test.

We regard the scheme that Jason established in Protocol III as an equipartitioning scheme because he copied the part he broke off from the stick three times in a test to find if three copies would reconstitute the remaining part. After the suggestion to make another copy, Jason joined the four copied parts to ascertain if they were the same length as the original stick. This indicated that he was trying to find if the piece that he broke off from the stick was a fair share. This way of working was a modification of his numerical operations displayed in Protocol II.[12] It was presaged by his comment: "Copy the biggest one and copy them again," following Protocol I.

To claim that a modification constitutes an accommodation, it is necessary to observe the modification in subsequent interactions. Toward this end, after Jason had compared the copies with the original in Protocol III, we observed Patricia draw a stick a bit longer than the piece that Jason had cut off, and she, too, made copies and compared them with the original stick. This was not merely an imitation. After finding that her copies made a stick that was too long, Jason drew a shorter stick, and, after copying and joining, he found that the four pieces together were too short. The two children proceeded in this way until they finally drew an appropriate stick. These sustained attempts were executed independently of the teacher's directives, and they confirm the internal necessity that the children must have felt that the four pieces together must be exactly the same length as the original stick. The two children had constructed an equipartitioning scheme out of the raw material of the numerical operations manifest in Protocol II. In the teaching experiment, this was a critical event and we could see possibilities for the children in their construction of fraction schemes that were unavailable to us before. We now had a definite direction to pursue, even though we fully expected to generate and test many more hypotheses.

Any knowledge claim that we make concerning students' mathematical knowledge is based on what students contribute independently to the situations that they establish. This is indispensable, but unless we had presented Jason and Patricia with the situation of Protocol

---

[12]We focus on learning as accommodation in the context of scheme theory. In this, what students learn is defined in terms of changes in their schemes rather than in terms of the mathematical knowledge of the researchers.

III, we would not have experienced their equipartitioning scheme. This observation is crucial because adults' concepts and operations modify their interaction in the same way that students' concepts and operations modify their interaction. Not only are situations of learning a function of what we impute to students, but also their zones of potential construction are essentially a function of our interpretations. We are in accordance with Maturana (1978) that "We literally create the world in which we live by living it. If a distinction is not performed, the entity that this distinction would specify would not exist" (p. 61).

*The Role of a Witness of the Teaching Episodes.* Communication with students can be established more easily if the teacher-researcher has a history of interactions with students similar to the students involved in the teaching experiment. This is, in part, why we recommended strongly that the teacher-researcher engage in exploratory teaching before attempting to conduct a teaching experiment. Recognizing mathematical language and current students' actions in an interaction that one has experienced before is a source of confidence for the teacher-researcher that communication is indeed being established. However, the teacher-researcher should expect to encounter students operating in unanticipated and apparently novel ways as well as their making unexpected mistakes and becoming unable to operate. In these cases, it is often helpful to be able to appeal to an observer of the teaching episode for an alternative interpretation of events.

Being immersed in interaction, the teacher-researcher may not be able to step out of it, reflect on it, and take action on that basis. This is very difficult because the teacher-researcher would have to "be" in two places in a very short time frame—in the interaction and outside it. It is quite impossible to achieve this if there are no conceptual elements available to the teacher-researcher that can be used in interpretating the current situation. In this case, the teacher-researcher would be caught up in trying to respond to what the student just said or did and would not reflect on the student's contribution. In this case, the observer may help the teacher-researcher both to understand the student and to posit further action.

There are also occasions when the observer might make an interpretation of a student's actions that is different from that of the teacher-researcher for any one of several reasons. The observer also might catch important elements of a student's actions that apparently are missed by the teacher-researcher. In these cases, the observer may ask the teacher-researcher if he or she would like another opinion. The teacher should have the right of refusal if he or she is confident of having a clear understanding of what the student is doing or has plans for action.

The experiences of being a teacher in a teaching episode and being an observer of a teaching episode are quite distinct. We have mentioned already the difficulties of a teacher becoming an observer of his or her own circumstances of observation, and this is why there should be a witness of every teaching episode. It is helpful for the witness and the teacher to interchange roles in an attempt to improve their communication. It also is helpful for both of them to be involved in planning the next teaching episode.

*Teaching as a Method of Scientific Investigation.* As indicated earlier, a primary goal of the teacher in a teaching experiment is to establish living models of students' mathematics, as exemplified in the protocols. The goal of establishing living models is sensible only when the idea of teaching is predicated on an understanding of human beings as self-organizing and self-regulating. If students were not self-regulating and self-organizing, a researcher would find that they would make no independent contributions in the way Jason contributed to what transpired in Protocol III. That is, without being told to make three copies of the stick and compare the copies with the part remaining and without having observed such activity, Jason engaged in these operations purposefully. We did not observe Jason's operations in any social interaction in which he engaged. Rather, they were initially observed in his interactions in the microworld.

Moreover, if students were not self-regulating or self-organizing, they would not modify their numerical schemes independently, as Jason and Patricia did in the establishment of an equipartitioning scheme. Clearly, in the absence of independent contributions from the students, there would be no scientific reason for conducting a teaching experiment. The researchers would not be constrained to the students' ways and means of operating, and there would be no basis for attributing to students a mathematical reality independent of the researchers'. On the other hand, the experience that students are self-organizing systems in the sense explained by Maturana (1978) suggests that they do have their own mathematical reality.

It is easy to undervalue teaching as a method of scientific investigation where the emphasis is on the researchers' learning the students' mathematical thinking and modifications of that thinking. In their attempts to learn students' mathematics, the researchers create situations and ways of interacting with students that encourage the students to modify their current thinking. It is with respect to these situations and interactions that the students emerge as self-regulating and self-organizing.

Stressing self-regulation and self-organization does not mean that the students are not teachable or that we do not attempt to induce learning in them. Quite to the contrary, we consider students to be teachable if, first, we can engage them in situations in which they use their mathematical schemes independently and, second, if we can observe independent modifications in their use of these schemes. We contrast this idea of students being teachable with Maturana's (1978) idea of an instructable system:

> The general idea of an instructable system is this: If the state a system adopts as a result of an interaction were specified by the properties of the entity with which it interacts, then the interaction would be an instructive interaction. Systems that undergo instructive interactions cannot be analyzed by a scientific procedure. In fact, all instructable systems would adopt the same state under the same perturbations and would necessarily be indistinguishable to a standard observer. (p. 34)

If students were instructable in Maturana's (1978) sense, they would be uninteresting scientifically because it would be possible to explain their mathematical knowledge by appealing to the teacher-researcher's mathematical knowledge. The teaching experiment's coherence resides in what the teacher-researcher can say about bringing forth, sustaining, and modifying students' mathematical schemes.

Toward this end, we establish schemes of action and operation that fit within our constraints and attempt to induce changes in these schemes. This production of schemes is compatible with El'konin's (1967) assessment of Vygotsky's research that the essential function of a teaching experiment was the production of models: "Unfortunately, it is still rare to meet with the interpretation of Vygotsky's research as modeling, rather than empirically studying, developmental processes" (p. 36).

So, we can begin to appreciate how important the independent contributions of our students are to us as we work with them in teaching experiments. Just as important are those boundaries that we establish on students' ways and means of operating by using their essential mistakes. These essential mistakes serve as constraints for the researchers and are a basic source of their problems. In fact, it is our goal to eliminate the constraints that we experience when teaching students, and the only way that can happen is if we succeed in helping students to eliminate the constraints that they might experience by modifying their schemes. The only way that we can learn to solve our problems is for the students to learn to solve the problems that we present to them. This is a most sobering realization because we have found that it can take students long periods of time to construct the knowledge necessary to overcome their essential mistakes.[13]

## Learning and Development in a Teaching Experiment

A virtue of a teaching experiment is that it allows the study of constructive processes, which is in part understood as the accommodations that students make in their functioning schemes. Because of the researcher's continued interaction with students, he or she is likely to observe at least the results of those critical moments when major restructuring is indicated by changes in a student's language and actions. Documenting such major restructuring of mathematical schemes is compatible with a vital part of Vygotsky's (1978) emphasis on studying the influence of learning on development. Further, our emphasis on modeling such mathematical development is compatible an essential part of Vygotsky's experimental-genetic method, which El'konin (1967) described as allowing "a dissection in abstract form of the very essence of the genetic process of concept formation" (p. 36).

A way to think about development in the context of teaching is that the essential mistakes of students most often disappear through the processes involved in development. These processes are set in motion in particular interactions, but continue beyond any specific interaction. Learning, on the other hand, occurs in particular interactions in which students modify their current schemes using available operations in new way. A study of both development and learning is involved in teaching experiments. Neither is *caused* by teaching actions and, in this sense, both are spontaneous.

Our focus on mathematical development in the context of teaching does not exclude us from taking advantage of the products of spontaneous development. In Piaget's (1964) view,

---

[13]The "mistakes" of Patricia and Jason in Protocol II were not essential mistakes because the children modified their ways and means of operating only three days later.

spontaneous development was regarded as the results of children's interactions in their physical and sociocultural milieu. To make these results accessible to us in teaching experiments, we focus on what students contribute independently to our interactions with them. In this way, we are able to bring the history of students' spontaneous development into their mathematical education and to formulate and test hypotheses concerning the contributions of this history to their mathematical education. In particular, our goal is to bring forth the schemes that students have constructed through spontaneous development and to use them in the formulation of the major research hypotheses of the teaching experiment.

Because we focus on the schemes that students construct through spontaneous development, we are able to take advantage of the products of spontaneous development in our study of learning. In particular, we are able to regard learning as spontaneous in the frame of reference of the students. However, Piaget (1964) regarded learning as provoked as opposed to spontaneous:

> In general, learning is provoked by situations—provoked by a psychological experimenter; or by a teacher with respect to some didactic point; or by an external situation. It is provoked in general, as opposed to spontaneous. In addition, it is a limited process—limited to a single problem, or to a single structure. (p. 8)

Learning is not spontaneous in the sense that the provocations that occasion it might be intentional on the part of the teacher-researcher. In the child's frame of reference, though, the processes involved in learning are essentially outside of his or her awareness. This is indicated by the observation that what students learn often is not what was intended by the teacher-researcher. It also is indicated when a child learns when the teacher-researcher has no such intention. Even in those cases where students learn what a teacher-researcher intends, the event that constitutes learning arises not because of the teacher's actions. Teaching actions only occasion students' learning (Kieren, 1994). Learning arises as an independent contribution of the interacting students. In the case of Jason learning the equipartitioning scheme in Protocol III, asking him to cut one of four equal pieces from a stick, would have been totally ineffective if he were yet to construct iterable units. Moreover, although Jason's actions followed from the teacher's query, we could not say that the query caused his actions. There was a break between Jason's actions and the teacher's query in that his (Jason's) actions were contributed by him, not by the teacher-researcher. To an observer, the conjunction of Jason's actions and the teacher's query may appear related, but the actions are distinct from the query. Other queries might occur that would seem fully as causal.

We do not use *spontaneous* in the context of learning to indicate the absence of elements with which the students interact. Rather, we use the term to refer to the noncausality of teaching actions, to the self-regulation of the students when interacting, to a lack of awareness of the learning process, and to its unpredictability. Because of these factors, we regard learning as a spontaneous process in the students' frame of reference.

If learning is placed in the context of accommodation of the products of spontaneous development, it need not be regarded as limited to a single problem or as a limited process. In fact, in a teaching experiment, it is never the intention of the teacher-researcher that the students learn to solve a single problem, even though situations are presented to them that might be a problem for them. Rather, the interest is in understanding the students' assimilating schemes and how these schemes might change as a result of their mathematical activity. Neither Jason nor Patricia was limited to the situation in which they established their equipartitioning schemes. Rather, their schemes applied to any situation in which a whole was shared into a specific number of parts.

We can now make our reasons for engaging in exploratory teaching more clear. Through exploratory teaching, our goal is to bring forth the schemes that students have constructed through spontaneous development. It is essential for researchers to have constructed a topography of students' spontaneous schemes prior to engaging in the individual interviews at the beginning of a teaching experiment for the purpose of selecting student-participants. Our recommendation that the spirit of exploratory teaching be continued throughout a teaching experiment is based in part on the reality that schemes different from those that were identified before the experiment began may emerge during it.

## Learning as Accommodation

In Piaget's (1964) position that learning is subordinate to spontaneous development, *learning* referred to the results of specialized interactions. In teaching experiment methodology, *learning* also refers to the results of specialized interactions. But, here, learning is regarded as being based on spontaneous development rather than being subordinate to it. What is of interest to us is how students might modify their spontaneous schemes in the context of specialized mathematical interactions.

Because it is a goal of the teacher-researcher to bring forth students' spontaneous schemes, an important function of the teacher-researcher in a teaching experiment is to foster students' successful assimilation. In this, we emphasize students' mathematical play as a particular form of cognitive play (Steffe & Wiegel, 1994). In mathematical play, the teacher-researcher tries to engender generalizing assimilation.

An assimilation is generalizing if the scheme involved is used in situations that contain sensory material or conceptual items that are novel for the scheme (from the point of view of an observer), but the scheme does not recognize it (until possibly later, as a consequence of the unrecognized difference), and if there is an adjustment in the scheme without the activity of the scheme being implemented (cf. Steffe & Wiegel, 1994). Another case would be where giving meaning to utterances entails a coordination of the schemes involved in interpretation again without the activity of the schemes being implemented. Stressing generalizing assimilation is compatible with Ackermann's (1995) rule that, in a clinical interview, constraints of the situations used in a test of the limits of the child's thinking should be varied. But, it is only compatible because, rather than testing the limits of the child's thinking initially, we encourage students to use their schemes in situations that not only include novel elements from the researchers' point of view, but also are so similar to situations constituted by students' current schemes that they may not identify the novelty (P. W. Thompson, 1994a). In doing this, limitations in students' thinking may occur unexpectedly.

The situations used to encourage generalizing assimilation should be interesting and challenging for students and excite their mathematical imagination, but they should not be so far beyond their current schemes that they require students to make major accommodations in the scheme. The teacher-researcher intentionally varies the context, the material, and the scope of the situations, but not the conceptual operations involved.[14]

---

[14] Varying the context and material of the situations is similar to Dienes' (1960) perceptual variability principle. But it is similar only because the teacher also can vary certain mathematical parameters of a situation without varying the mathematical operation. For example, the teacher may

*(continued)*

Mathematical play, as a form of cognitive play, is a necessary prelude for students' engagement in independent mathematical activity. Independent mathematical activity is goal-directed,[15] and it can evolve out of mathematical play with the subtle guidance of the teacher-researcher. Independent mathematical activity can be either an individual or a social activity. As social activity, from the researchers' perspective, students' independent mathematical activity comprises a self-regulating and possibly self-sustaining social system in the sense that Maturana (1978) spoke of a consensual domain of interactions.[16]

Learning how to bring forth and sustain students' independent mathematical activity is a part of learning how to interact with students in a teaching experiment. A goal in this is for students to make their mathematical knowledge explicit and to find limits in their ways and means of operating. Another goal is for students to come to understand mathematics as something that belongs to them. In other words, two of the goals of the teaching experiment are to establish the zones of actual construction of the participating students and to specify the independent mathematical activity of the students in these zones.

*Functional Accommodations.* By an accommodation of a scheme, we mean any modification of the scheme that is permanent.[17] An accommodation is functional if it occurs in the context of the scheme being used (Steffe, 1991). To encourage accommodation, the

---

use number words in the teens for students who can count only to 10 with the goal of encouraging them to learn the number words past *ten* without changing anything else about counting.

[15] We speak of shared goals in the case of cooperative mathematical activity.

[16] A consensual domain is established when the individuals of a group adjust and adapt their actions and reactions to achieve the degree of compatibility necessary for cooperation. This involves the use of language and the adjustments and mutual adaptations of individual meanings to allow effective interaction and cooperation.

[17] By *permanent,* we mean that the modification reemerges independently in situations where the scheme is used.

teacher-researcher chooses learning situations within the assimilatory power of the students that contain elements that might engender perturbation in the use of the schemes. The elements might block use of the schemes, they might lead to inadequacies in the schemes' activity, or they might lead to ambiguities in the results of the schemes. The accommodations that we have in mind differ from generalizing assimilation (which also can be regarded in the context of accommodation) in that they consist of a novel composition of the operations available or changes in the activity of the scheme. They go beyond use of the scheme in a situation in which it has not been used previously, which is an essential characteristic of generalizing assimilation.

When fostering accommodation, the teacher-researcher's intention is for the students to use their schemes in novel ways. In fact, the teacher-researcher must decide when he or she can pose situations of learning[18] that take them appropriately beyond their current independent mathematical activity. The teacher-researcher is engaged in hypothesis generation and testing now, where hypotheses are formulated about what the students might learn mathematically beyond their current ways and means of operating.

A major part of the teaching experiment, then, is for the teacher-researcher to generate situations of learning systematically and to test conjectures and local hypotheses about the mathematical learning of the students. In these activities, conjectures and local hypotheses of the teacher-researcher are documented along with how they were tested. Protocol III is an example of a test of the hypothesis that Jason and Patricia had constructed partitioning operations. It is important to note that a test of this hypothesis did not require a simple reproduction of the observation that the children used their counting schemes in partitioning in Protocol II. Rather, it entailed a test of the generative power of the children in learning situations quite distinct from the original situation of observation. This is a major modus operandi in a teaching experiment. We are not as concerned with replicating an observation to

---

[18] The way in which we generate these situations is similar to Dienes' (1960) mathematical variability principle. It differs in that we base our decisions on the students' mathematical schemes as well as on our own mathematical knowledge.

establish the viability of the interpretation involved in the observation as we are with establishing what else the student can do that follows on from the interpretation.

*Developmental Accommodations.* Sometimes, the teacher-researcher chooses situations within the students' assimilatory power that, from the point of view of the teacher-researcher, contain elements that are outside of the students' schemes. The students would notice these elements only if their schemes did not work or if their attention were drawn to them. In either case, from the researcher's perspective, these elements would block a resolution of the situation unless a major reorganization of the students' schemes occurred. For example, a child may compare the boys and the girls when asked if there are more children or more boys in the classroom because of a lack of hierarchical classification operations. If this were the case, class inclusion would be irrelevant to the child's scheme of classification, and the child would not establish relations between the boys and the children, or the girls and the children. From the child's perspective, comparing the boys and the girls directly solves the situation, and it may not be possible for the teacher-researcher to engender an awareness of the inclusion relation in the child.

These kinds of situations constitute currently unsolvable problems for students from the researchers' perspective, and we use them to check students' current developmental levels. We also use them in an attempt to induce an awareness in the student of the possibility of a result different from the one that they may have established. In doing so, the teacher-researcher might ask a question or make a comment that is intended to induce an element of doubt in the students: for example, the teacher-researcher might make countersuggestions such as "Another child we saw yesterday thought that. . . . Do you think this makes sense" (Ackermann, 1995, p. 347). The teacher-researcher also might ask the students to explain what situation they solved. Then, the teacher-researcher can repose the situation in an attempt to make a contrast between it and the students' situations. In making the contrast, it is the teacher's goal that the students reorganize their thinking in a way that will lead to a solution of the situation.

Still another technique that we use is to ask students to anticipate the outcome of their operations. This technique is similar to Ackermann's (1995) idea of inviting the child to make guesses (anticipations) and expressing these guesses in various ways. Using this approach, we often encourage the students to take action as Ackermann (1995) did: "Let's try and see what happens!" (p. 347). In any event, the teacher-researcher must be prepared to abandon a situation when it becomes apparent that the students cannot find an action that would lead to the reorganization envisioned.

## Retrospective Analysis and Model Building

*Retrospective Analysis.* Retrospective analysis of the public records made of the interactive mathematical communication in a teaching experiment is a critical part of the methodology. It is even more labor-intensive than the activity of teaching. In fact, most researchers who propose teaching experiments fail to plan adequately for retrospective analyses of the teaching episodes. Through teaching and witnessing, researchers have mental records of the interactions with students, and it becomes clear to the researchers who engage in videotape analyses that much of what was learned when working with the students was learned spontaneously and outside their awareness. Careful analysis of the videotapes offers the researchers the opportunity to activate the records of their past experiences with the students and to bring them into conscious awareness.

When the researchers recognize an interaction as having been experienced before, past interpretations of the students' activity that were made on the fly may reoccur to the teacher-researcher. However, through watching the videotapes, the teacher-researcher has the advantage of making an historical analysis of the students' mathematics retrospectively and prospectively, and both of these perspectives provide insight into the students' actions and interactions that were not available to the teacher-researcher when the interactions took place. It is especially important that the teacher-researcher be able to take a prospective view of the interacting child and interpret the significance of what the students may or may not have been doing from that perspective. In this way, the researcher can set the child in a historical context and modify or stabilize the original interpretations, as the case may be.

There are also those inevitable cases where the researchers do not recognize an interaction as having been experienced before. In these cases, the teacher-researcher can make novel interpretations in terms of his or her evolving concept of the students' mathematics. In any event, what the researchers are trying to do is to construct elements of the models of the constructing students over the course of the teaching experiment. It is a distinct advantage to understand these constructing minds as being occasioned by the teacher-researcher's own ways and means of operating because that understanding holds the potential of bridging the gap between research and practice that plagued us earlier on.

*Model Building.* Through retrospective analyses, we attempt to bring to the fore the activity of model building that was present throughout the teaching episodes. In the modeling process, we use concepts in the core of our research program like assimilation, accommodation, cognitive and mathematical play, communication, development, interaction, mental operation, self-regulation, scheme, zone of potential construction, and others. These concepts emerge in the form of specific and concrete explanations of students' mathematical activity. In this regard, the modeling process in which we engage is compatible with how Maturana (1978) regarded scientific explanation:  "As scientists, we want to provide explanations for the phenomena we observe. That is, we want to propose conceptual or concrete systems that can be deemed intentionally isomorphic to the systems that generate the observed phenomena" (p. 29).

Our modeling process is only compatible because we have no access to students' mathematical realities outside of our own ways and means of operating when bringing the students' mathematics forth. So, we cannot get outside our observations to check if our conceptual constructs are isomorphic to the students' mathematics. But we can and do establish viable ways and means of thinking that fit within the experiential constraints that we established when interacting with the students in teaching episodes.

These ways of thinking allow us to "get inside the heads" of students and specify explanatory concepts and operations. So, through the use of the core concepts of our research program, we make concrete claims about the mental functioning of students, and these claims draw their operational character from the framework itself. The unavoidable circularity in model building between the framework and the models is what drives and sustains our research programs in that the core concepts are subject to modification in their use, and new concepts arise out of model building that modify our core concepts substantially.

Model building involves the creativity of the researchers, and the processes involved are themselves open for investigation. One important aspect is trying to think as students think (Thompson, 1982):

> [A researcher] constructs a model just as [he or she would construct] any
> other conceptual system—by reflectively abstracting and relating operations
> which serve to connect experientially derived states. Here I am applying
> Piaget's notion of reflective abstraction to the researcher. As he or she

watches a student ease through some problems and stumble over others, or successively ease and blunder through parts of a problem, the researcher asks himself, "What can this person be thinking so that his actions make sense from his perspective? . . . " This is the ground floor of modeling a student's understanding. The researcher puts himself into the position of the student and attempts to examine the operations that he (the researcher) would need and the constraints he would have to operate under in order to (logically) behave as the student did. (p. 161)

One does this for each student in an investigation, and, as soon as one begins to see a pattern in one's mode of explanation, the job must be expanded to abstracting reflectively the operations that one applies in constructing explanations. When the researcher becomes reflectively aware of these operations, and can relate one with another, he or she has an explanatory framework. This explanatory framework usually opens new possibilities for the researcher who turns to using it for new purposes.

Because the models that we formulate are grounded in our interactions with students, we fully expect that the models will be useful to us as we engage in further interactive mathematical communication with other students. The models are also useful instruments of communication with others interested in the mathematical education of students. However, unless the models reemerge in interactions with students, they would not be useful to anyone, including the model builders.

## ARE TEACHING EXPERIMENTS SCIENTIFIC?

As we have indicated, teaching experiments are concerned with conceptual structures and models of the kinds of change that are considered learning or development. This focus entails two specific conditions. First, it is important to emphasize that no single observation can be taken as an indication of learning or development. Change is the transition from one point to another and therefore requires at least two observations made at different times.[19] Second, when we speak of learning or development, we have in mind not any change, but change in the students' current mathematical schemes that occur in interactive mathematical communication. Such change might be anticipated by the researchers, but, often, it can be known only in retrospect because the researchers might experience a different change than the one anticipated, or even no observable change. In any case, it is the researchers who learn as well as, perhaps, the students. This point is fundamental in a teaching experiment; it is the researchers who are striving to learn what change they can bring forth in their students and how to explain such change.

Regardless of whether students change as anticipated or change in ways that are known only in retrospect, the researchers do become aware of a directionality of change. This awareness has a consequence that would be considered unusual in other kinds of research. It is quite often the case that an observation can be reinterpreted from the vantage point of a later one as a preliminary step of a change that was not discernible at the time. Such reinterpretation of past findings might be deemed improper in other branches of science, but in an investigation of mental operations that relies more on the microanalysis of videotapes than on the brief live observation of the students' activity, it is no less legitimate than, for example, the reevaluation of microbiological evidence on the basis of enlargements of a microscopic image.

Teaching experiments serve the construction of models of conceptual change. In this regard, they follow what two founders of the discipline of cybernetics have described as accepted scientific procedure:

---

[19] We do not specify any minimal duration between the two times. The two times may be distinct moments within a single experiential episode or distinct moments across two different experiential episodes. What happens in between the two moments of time is critical and constitutes the study of the interactions involved. Rather than merely document the observations at the two times, what is of interest is to specify a trajectory of changes from one time to another.

An intuitive flair for what will turn out to be the important general question gives the basis for selecting some of the significant among the indefinite number of trivial experiments which could be carried out at that stage. Quite vague and tacit generalizations thus influence the selection of data at the start. The data then lead to more precise generalizations, which in turn suggest further experiments and progress is made by successive excursions from data to abstractions and vice versa. (Rosenblueth & Wiener, 1945, p. 317)

In the teaching experiment, hypothesis formulation, experimental testing, and reconstruction of the hypothesis form a recursive cycle. The researcher may begin with a hypothesis, a preliminary model, constructed on the basis of his or her theoretical assumptions and prior experience. Whatever the students say or do in the context of interacting with the researchers in a medium is potential data for inferences about the students' conceptual operations and serves as confirming or disconfirming the hypothesis. Initially, these inferences are necessarily vague and often spring from as yet tacit assumptions. As a rule, they suggest further experimentation that may help to make the assumptions more explicit and the inferences more precise. As the cycle continues, a firmer model of the students' mental activity begins to take shape and the cycle proceeds.

There are two basic goals that seemingly stand in opposition as the cycle of model building proceeds. First, we want to find if the model remains viable in the face of the experiments conducted by the researchers. That is, the researchers strive to generate observations that would force them to modify their models of the students' mathematics. If no such observations are forthcoming, then the researchers can regard their model as being at least temporarily viable. On the other hand, given that the researchers strive to work at the boundaries of the students' knowledge for the purpose of testing hypotheses, they always stand ready to modify their model to account for perhaps unexpected observations. Here, it is important to note that we have found that students' mathematical schemes change slowly over time and that students work at the same learning level for extended periods (cf. Steffe et al., 1988).

Even if other researchers find the inferences made about students' mathematics compatible with their observations, this would not mean that the researchers have found an objective insight into the workings of the students' minds. This other mind remains as fundamentally inaccessible to observation as the clockwork of the watch that Einstein chose as a metaphor for the universe:

> Physical concepts are free creations of the human mind, and are not, however it may seem, uniquely determined by the external world. In our endeavor to understand reality we are somewhat like a man trying to understand the mechanism of a closed watch. He sees the face and the moving hands, even hears its ticking, but he has no way of opening the case. If he is ingenious he may form some picture of a mechanism which could be responsible for all the things he observes, but he may never be quite sure his picture is the only one which could explain his observations. He will never be able to compare his picture with the real mechanism and he cannot even imagine the possibility or the meaning of such a comparison. (Einstein & Infeld, 1938/1967, p. 31)

If it was scientific in that case to invent a mechanism and to test it against the observable features of a watch, it is no less so for an educational researcher to posit conceptual structures and mental operations and to investigate their fit with whatever seems relevant in the students' observable behavior. In doing this, the researcher engages in the process of experiential abstraction in a retrospective analysis of videotaped teaching episodes. The researcher may have engaged in a conceptual analysis already in establishing the conceptual constructs used in the experiential abstraction. But this does not mean that the products of such a conceptual analysis would constitute the mathematics of students without the constructs emerging in their mathematical language and actions. It is essential to note that the construction of the mathematics of students is based on a conceptual analysis of the mathematical language and actions of students as well as on theoretical constructs perhaps established in an earlier conceptual analysis not involving students. There is a dialectical relationship between the two kinds of analyses. Theoretical constructs are used in analyzing students' language and actions and thus modify the teacher-researcher's ways of interacting with students. Conversely, the theoretical constructs are modified in their use. In fact, a need may be established for constructing novel theoretical constructs. The idea of establishing a fit, then, is not merely one of confirming a previously conceived conceptual construct. Rather, establishing a fit may involve major accommodations by the teacher-researcher.

What Einstein and Infeld (1938/1967) called a "picture of a mechanism" (which could be held responsible for what one observes) is precisely what cyberneticians now call a "model"; the construction of models that can be seen in some way as analogous to a student's thought processes is the main scientific purpose of teaching experiments. From the researcher's standpoint, the conceptual structures and their change in the heads of students are very much like the workings inside a closed watch. We believe that the understanding and solving of problems that involve abstract entities such as numbers and their relations is dependent on mental operations, and there is no way to observe mental operations directly. At best, they can be inferred from a variety of observable manisfestations. From the side of the researchers, a teaching experiment includes the generation and testing of hypotheses to see whether or not the experiential world that the students' language and actions comprise allows the current interpretation that the developing model proposes. It is a question of fit rather than of match. Thus, a model is viable as long as it remains adequate to explain students' independent contributions. But no amount of fit can turn a model into a description of what may be going on. It remains an interpretation that seems viable from a particular perspective.

There is a difference between this point of view and Einstein's. In spite of the fact that he saw clearly that the scientist could no more compare his theoretical models with the real universe than the man in his metaphor could compare his invented mechanism with the closed watch, Einstein had the metaphysical belief that "God was not playing dice." In other words, he believed that, in principle, an intrinsic order could be found in reality independent of the investigator. As constructivists, we are more modest. We believe that a model's viability pertains to a domain of our experience and we make no ontological claims about the nature of students' mathematics.[20]

---

[20]This is not to say that we do not seek order and regularity in students' mathematical activity. Quite to the contrary. By making the comment, we intend to highlight that what we experience as students' mathematics is unavoidably dependent on our actions as researchers. This is the main reason we believe that the researchers in a teaching experiment must be experientially involved themselves in the students' mathematical activity.

# FINAL COMMENTS

A claim that one has constructed a model of students' mathematics is a strong claim. One could question the replicability of a teaching experiment on which a model was based and the generalizability of the model itself. These are important issues. However, we do not recommend that teaching experiments be replicated in the sense that Piaget's work was replicated (Lovell, 1972). The Piagetian replication studies were useful in the sense that they encouraged the researchers doing the replications to learn the theory. Moreover, Piaget's research became widely known through the work of his replicators, but it became known in a rather distorted way. Few replication studies extended his theory because the replicators did not seem to understand that Piaget was concerned with conceptual development and not with performance. The concept of replication seemed predicated on the concept of theory testing rather than on theory building—using aspects of a theory to build models that supersede current ones.

## On Replication

At the very minimum, researchers in a teaching experiment who make a claim about what students know are obliged to make records of the living models of students' mathematics that illustrate aspects of the claim available to an interested public. Second, researchers can build an important aspect of replication into a teaching experiment. One example is to select at least three students whose language and actions indicate similar spontaneous schemes. In this way, one can attempt to replicate case studies of individual students in the same teaching experiment. Replicate case studies contribute significantly to building models of students' mathematics (Steffe, 1991).

Third, when the researcher's goals change sufficiently to warrant conducting another teaching experiment, the current model can be used as input—as conceptual material to be reorganized. However, the primary emphasis should be on constructing superseding models.

One model is said to supersede another if it is a reorganization of the preceding model, if it solves all of the problems that the preceding model solved, but solves them better, and if it solves problems that the superseding model did not solve. It is in the sense of constructing superseding models that we advocate that researchers replicate their own teaching experiment or a teaching experiment of other researchers. In our opinion, this way of thinking about replication will serve in the scientific progress of mathematics education and will provide stability in what we regard as the mathematics of students.

## On Generalizability

The intent to build models that supersede current ones encourages communication among researchers. It is a way of making public the community's more or less private results as well as of checking those results. The intent to build superseding models also serves generalizability—the aim of building models that apply in principle to settings beyond the ones that gave rise to the models originally.

Asking a question about the generalizability of any model of students' mathematics is similar to asking about the generalizability of number and quantity. The issue is not that number and quantity are ideas that are generalizable. Rather, the pertinent issue is that they are concepts that prove useful in settings other than those in which they are built. It does not make sense to demand of teaching experiments that they "generalize" in the way in which one might hope that claims thought to be true about a random sample would be true as well about the population from which the sample was drawn.

The issues involved in generalizability are quite different for us. By being explanatory, the researcher's conceptual schemes are dynamic concepts in his or her life that can be used and even modified in further interactions with students. Any conceptual scheme that is constructed through experiential abstraction has this quality. If it does not, it has no place as a part of the mathematics of students. So, at the bottom line, if we find our way of thinking about students' mathematics useful in interpreting the mathematical activity of students other than those in the original teaching experiment, this provides critical confirmation of our way of thinking. It is not a matter of generalizing the results in a hypothetical way, but of the results being useful in organizing and guiding our experience of students doing mathematics.

Further, if we can reorganize our previous ways of thinking in a new teaching experiment, that is, if we can learn, aspects of the old model become involved in new relations in the new model and, thus, become generalized conceptually. When it is possible to communicate with other researchers doing teaching experiments independently of us, this also serves as a vital confirmation of our way of thinking and perhaps as a site for each of us to construct a superseding model. The element of generalization that is involved is strengthened if that other researcher launched his or her teaching experiment for the purpose of constructing a superseding model of our current model of students' mathematics.

There are cases when sampling procedures can be useful. For example, after the hard work that has gone into constructing a model of students' mathematics, the researchers may become interested in interviewing a group of students of the same age as those in the teaching experiment that gave rise to the model. The goal of the researchers would be to find disconfirmations of aspects of the model with an eye toward building a superseding model in a future teaching experiment. Questions such as finding the ratios of students entering their first grade in school with certain spontaneous schemes are of educational interest. These questions can be answered by an expert clinician using clinical interviews and appropriate sampling procedures, but we do not regard such queries as being related to questions of the generalizability of a model of students' mathematics.

## On Self-Reflexivity

At every point when interacting with students in a teaching experiment, the students' and teacher's actions are codependent. The realization that the researchers are participants in the students' constructions and the students are active participants in the researcher's constructions is precisely what recommends the teaching experiment methodology. Rather than being regarded as a weakness of the methodology, it is one of its greatest strengths because it provides researchers the possibility of influencing the education community's images of mathematics teaching, learning, and curricula. In fact, the teaching experiment was designed for the purpose of eliminating the separation between the practice of research and the practice of teaching.

But the principle of self-reflexivity (Steier, 1995)—applying the principles of the methodology first and foremost to oneself—is even more deeply embedded in the methodology than portrayed previously. For example, the researchers must look within themselves to make explicit what is analogous to the practice of establishing students' spontaneous schemes. Neither the researchers nor the students start as blank slates in a teaching experiment, and the knowledge of the researchers become the most critical issue. Although we have appealed to researchers to set aside their own mathematical knowledge that they would not attribute to students for the purpose of learning from them, this does not mean that the researchers who are more or less successful in doing this will be devoid of knowledge. On the contrary, it is the researchers who attribute mathematical meaning to students' language and actions using their own instruments of assimilation.

This idea may seem to contradict almost everything that we have said. But although students' language and actions constrain the researchers' constructions, it is the researchers who bring this language and action forth in the students. Of course, what is brought forth is always a function of the researcher's current knowledge and this is why we find von Foerster's (1984) aesthetical and ethical imperatives so important in doing a teaching experiment: If you desire to see, learn how to act, and act always so as to increase the number of choices.

In previous sections, we spoke of researchers being involved in teaching experiments. One can "be involved" in teaching experiments in many ways, some direct and some indirect. But the essential involvements in a teaching experiment are as a witness and as a teacher-researcher in teaching episodes. We want to make our position completely clear in this regard. It is essential that at least some of the people doing the theorizing are active integrally both as witnesses and as teacher-researchers in any experiment's teaching. Those remaining are, at a minimum, active integrally in the retrospective analysis conducted at the end of the teaching episodes. A teaching experiment run by an "executive researcher"—someone who supervises but is essentially uninvolved in teaching or witnessing—is fundamentally flawed on methodological grounds. Such teaching experiments are unacceptable.

# ACKNOWLEDGMENTS

This chapter was written as part of the activities of the National Science Foundation Project No. RED-8954678. We would like to thank Richard Lesh, Jim Kaput, Anthony Kelly, John Olive, and Heide Wiegel for their comments on earlier drafts of the chapter. However, all of the opinions expressed are solely those of the authors.

# 12 Conducting Teaching Experiments in Collaboration With Teachers

**Paul Cobb**
*Vanderbilt University*

The past decade has witnessed a number of profound shifts in the ways in which the problems and issues of mathematics education have been framed and addressed. The first of these shifts concerns the characterization of individual students' mathematical activity. The central metaphor of students as processors of information has been displaced by that of students acting purposefully in an evolving mathematical reality of their own making (Sfard, 1994). As a consequence, analyses of students' mathematical reasoning have moved away from specifying cognitive behaviors and toward inferring the quality of their mathematical experience. A second shift concerns the increased acknowledgment of the social and cultural aspects of mathematical activity (Nunes, 1992; Voigt, 1994). As recently as 1988, Eisenhart could write with considerable justification that mathematics educators "are accustomed to assuming that the development of cognitive skill is central to human development, [and] that these skills appear in a regular sequence regardless of context or content" (p. 101). The growing trend to go beyond a purely cognitive focus is indicated by an increasing number of analyses that question an exclusive preoccupation with the individual learner (Cobb & Bauersfeld, 1995; Greeno, 1991; Lave, 1988; Saxe, 1991; Whitson, in press). In this emerging view, individual students' activity is seen to be located both within the classroom microculture and within broader systems of activity that constitute the sociopolitical setting of reform in mathematics education.

A third shift in suppositions and assumptions concerns the relation between theory and practice. In traditional approaches that embody the positivist epistemology of practice, theory is seen to stand apart from and above the practice of learning and teaching mathematics

(Schön, 1983). Then teachers are positioned as consumers of research findings that are generated outside the context of the classroom. In contrast to this subordination of practice to theory, an alternative view is emerging that emphasizes the reflexive relationship between the two (Gravemeijer, 1995). From this latter perspective, theory is seen to emerge from practice and to feed back to guide it. This view, it should be noted, provides a rationale for transformational research that has as its goal the development and investigation of theoretically grounded innovations in instructional settings. Taken together, these shifts in the ways in which problems of teaching and learning mathematics are cast have precipitated the development of a range of new methodologies, many of which are discussed in this volume. The focus in this chapter is on a particular type of classroom teaching experiment that is conducted in collaboration with a practicing teacher who is a member of the research and development team. Experiments of this type can vary in duration from a few weeks to an entire school year and typically have as one of their goals the development of instructional activities for students. The concerns and issues discussed by the research team while the experiment is in progress are frequently highly pragmatic in that the teacher and the researchers are responsible together for the quality of the students' mathematics education. As a consequence, initial conjectures typically emerge while addressing specific practical issues. These conjectures later orient a retrospective analysis of data sources that can include videorecordings of classroom sessions, videorecorded interviews conducted with the students, copies of the students' written work, daily field notes, records of project meetings and debriefing sessions, and the teacher's daily journal.

In the following sections of the chapter, I first discuss the theoretical orientation that underpins this methodology and outline the types of problems that might be addressed in the course of a classroom teaching experiment. Then, I place the methodology in the context of developmental research and consider three central aspects of the approach: instructional design and planning, the ongoing analysis of classroom events, and the retrospective analysis of all the data sources generated in the course of a teaching experiment. Against this background, attention is given to specific methodological issues, among them generalizability, trustworthiness, and commensurability. Finally, I focus on the process of establishing collaborative relationships with teachers and conclude by discussing problems for which other methodologies might be more appropriate.

# THEORETICAL ORIENTATION

As M. Simon (1995) observed, several different forms of constructivism have been proposed in recent years. A key issue that differentiates these positions is the relationship between individual psychological processes and classroom social processes. At one extreme, researchers who take a strong psychological perspective acknowledge the influence of social interaction, but treat it as a source of perturbations for otherwise autonomous conceptual development. Such approaches recognize that the *process* of students' mathematical development has a social aspect in that interpersonal interactions serve as a catalyst for learning. However, the *products* of development—students' increasingly sophisticated mathematical ways of knowing—are treated exclusively as individual psychological accomplishments. At the other extreme, sociocultural approaches in the Vygotskian tradition tend to elevate social processes above psychological processes. For example, it is argued in some formulations that the qualities of students' mathematical thinking are *generated by* or *derived from* the organizational features of the social activities in which they participated (van Oers, 1996). Such approaches account for development primarily in social terms and leave little room for psychological analyses of individual students' constructive activities.

The theoretical stance that underpins the type of classroom teaching experiment I discuss should be distinguished from both strong psychological and strong social versions of constructivism. This alternative stance has been called the emergent perspective (Cobb, 1995). One of its central assumptions is that learning can be characterized as both a process of active individual construction and a process of mathematical enculturation (cf. Dorfler, 1995). On the one hand, the emergent perspective goes beyond exclusively psychological approaches by viewing students' mathematical activity as being necessarily socially situated. Therefore, the products of students' mathematical development—increasingly sophisticated ways of reasoning—are seen to be related to their participation in particular communities of practice such as those constituted by the teacher and the students in the classroom. On the other hand, the emergent perspective questions the subordination of psychological processes to social processes and attributes a central role to analyses of individual students' mathematical activity. The basic relationship posited between students' constructive activities and the social processes in which they participate in the classroom is one of reflexivity in which neither is given preeminence over the other. In this view, students are considered to contribute to the evolving classroom mathematical practices as they reorganize their individual mathematical activities. Conversely, the ways in which they make these reorganizations are constrained by their participation in the evolving classroom practices. A basic assumption of the emergent perspective is, therefore, that neither individual students' activities nor classroom mathematical practices can be accounted for adequately except in relation to the other.

It should be noted that this view of mathematical learning as a participatory activity has immediate pragmatic implications for the conduct of teaching experiments. For example, if one wants to investigate students' development of what the National Council of Teachers of Mathematics (1991b) called a mathematical disposition, then it is crucial that they participate in classroom mathematical practices in which they are expected to judge what counts as acceptable mathematical explanations and as different, efficient, and sophisticated mathematical solutions (Lampert, 1990; Yackel & Cobb, 1996). Similarly, if one wants to investigate how students might come to use conventional and nonstandard notations in powerful ways, then it is important to document the ways in which they participate in practices that involve the development of ways of recording mathematical activity for communicative purposes (Bednarz, Dufour-Janvier, Porrier, & Bacon, 1993; van Oers, 1995).

Theoretically, the emergent perspective emphasizes the importance of analyzing students' mathematical activity as it is situated in the social context of the classroom. Therefore, accounts of their mathematical development might involve the coordination of psychological analyses of their individual activities with social analyses of the norms and practices established by the classroom community. The particular psychological perspective that I and my colleagues adopt is broadly compatible with that outlined by other contributors to this volume (cf. Steffe & Thompson, chap. 11, this volume). The social perspective draws on symbolic interactionism and ethnomethodology as they have been adapted to the problems and issues of mathematics education (Bauersfeld, Krummheuer, & Voigt, 1988). Discussion of this perspective can be found in Bauersfeld (1988) and Voigt (1994).

In a subsequent section of this chapter, I clarify the relationship between these two perspectives while outlining an interpretive framework for analyzing individual and collective mathematical activity in the classroom. For the present, my concern is to emphasize the more general point that classroom teaching experiment methodology requires a way of relating individual students' mathematical activity to the local social world of the classroom in which they participate. In my view, teaching experiments that fail to acknowledge this theoretical issue are suspect. Almost by default, analyses are produced in which mathematical development seems either to occur in a social vacuum or to be attributed directly to social processes. The emergent perspective I have outlined constitutes one way of relating social and psychological analyses.[1] As becomes clear, this perspective itself emerged while conducting a series of teaching experiments in the classroom. Its focus on mathematical activity in a social context provides a strong rationale for developing classrooms as action research sites.

## Problems and Issues

Classroom teaching experiments have a relatively long history in mathematics education, particularly in the former Soviet Union (Davydov, 1988). However, the particular type of classroom teaching experiment with which I am concerned evolved most directly from the constructivist teaching experiment (Cobb & Steffe, 1983; Steffe, 1983; see also Steffe & Thompson, chap. 11, this volume). In the constructivist teaching experiment, the researcher acts as teacher and usually interacts with students either one-on-one or in small groups. As Steffe and Thompson explain in chapter 11 in this book, the researcher's primary goal "is to establish a *living model* of children's mathematical activity and transformations of this activity as a result of mathematical interactions in learning environments." The decision that I and my colleagues[2] made to extend this approach to the classroom was precipitated by investigations that documented the undesirable mathematical beliefs and conceptions that students typically develop in the context of traditional instruction (e.g., Carraher & Schliemann, 1985; Schoenfeld, 1983). The initial issue the classroom teaching experiment was designed to address was that of investigating students' mathematical learning in alternative classroom contexts developed in collaboration with teachers. The methodology therefore provides a way of exploring the prospects and possibilities for reform at the

---

[1] The emergent goals model developed by Saxe (1991) represents an alternative, though broadly compatible, approach that deals with both individual and collective processes.

[2] The type of teaching experiment described in this chapter was developed initially in collaboration with Erna Yackel and Terry Wood. More recent modifications have been made in collaboration with Erna Yackel and Koeno Gravemeijer. Where appropriate, I use the first-person plural throughout the chapter to indicate these collaborations.

classroom level. This focus on students' mathematical development immediately leads to a number of related issues. The first of these concerns the social context of development. The classroom microculture in which students participate influences profoundly the goals they attempt to achieve, their understanding of what counts as an acceptable mathematical explanation, and, indeed, their general beliefs about what it means to know and do mathematics in school. Consequently, it is essential to document the microculture established by the classroom community even if the primary concern is to formulate psychological models of the processes by which students transform their mathematical activity. However, beyond this minimalist approach, aspects of the classroom microculture (and students' participation in it) can become legitimate objects of inquiry. For example, analyses might be conducted that focus on the teacher's and students' negotiation of general classroom social norms, standards of mathematical argumentation, or particular classroom mathematical practices. Further, teaching experiments can be conducted to investigate the extent to which students' participation in particular social arrangements such as small-group, collaborative activity or whole-class discussions supports their mathematical development.

A second cluster of related issues that are appropriate for investigation centers on the activity of the teacher. It is generally acknowledged that the classroom is the primary learning environment for teachers as well as for students and researchers (Ball, 1993b; Cobb, T. Wood, & Yackel, 1990; Knapp & Peterson, 1995; M. Simon & Schifter, 1991; A. Thompson, 1992). In particular, it appears that teachers reorganize their beliefs and instructional practices as they attempt to make sense of classroom events and incidents. Hence, teachers' learning, as it occurs in a social context, can become a direct focus of investigation in a teaching experiment.[3]

---

[3] In chapter 9 in this book, Lesh and Kelly describe a three-tiered teaching experiment in which the tiers or levels focus on the students, the teachers, and the researchers respectively. The classroom teaching experiment methodology outlined in this chapter can be used to investigate students' and teachers' learning as it occurs in a social context. Such investigations are located at the lower two tiers of Lesh and Kelly's model. However, the teaching experiment methodology is not well suited to the problem of analyzing systematically the researchers' learning as it occurs in a social context. An adequate treatment of this issue would require a second group of researchers who study

(continued)

Additionally, it should be noted that teachers who participate in teaching experiments typically become extremely effective in supporting their students' mathematical development. This, therefore, constitutes an opportunity to delineate aspects of effective reform teaching as they are manifested in the teachers' interactions with their students. Analyses of this type can make an important contribution in that reform teaching often is  characterized with reference to traditional instruction, and the emphasis is on what teachers should not do. In my view, there is a pressing need to clarify further how teachers support their students' mathematical development *proactively* as they act and interact in the social context of the classroom.

A third set of issues that might be addressed by conducting a classroom teaching experiment centers on the development of instructional sequences and the local, domain-specific instructional theories that underpin them (Gravemeijer, 1995). In the course of a classroom teaching experiment, the research team develops sequences of instructional activities that embody conjectures about students' constructive activities. An analysis of students' learning in a social context requires that the instructional activities be documented as they are realized in interaction. This analysis can be used to guide both the revision of the instructional activities and the elaboration of their rationale in terms of students' potential construction in the social situation of the classroom. I discuss the process of instructional development in more detail in the next section of this chapter. For the present, it suffices to note that if this cyclic process of design and analysis is repeated a number of times, the rationale can be refined until it acquires eventually the status of a local instructional theory that underpins an instructional sequence (Gravemeijer, 1995). Streefland's (1991) analysis of a

---

the first group working with students and teachers. (An example of an outside analysis of this type in which I and my colleagues became subjects was reported by Dillon, 1993.)  Nonetheless, the research team conducting a classroom teaching experiment does compile a record of its own learning in the spirit of Lesh and Kelly. Typically, this documentation includes audiorecordings of project meetings as well as paper documentation. Further, the researchers attempt to remain aware that their activity is, like that of the teachers, socially situated and that the products of the research are grounded in their classroom-based practice. I attempt to indicate this sense of situation throughout the chapter.

series of teaching experiments that focused on students' understanding of fractions is paradigmatic in this regard.

A final set of issues for which the teaching experiment methodology is appropriate is located at a metalevel and concerns the development of theoretical constructs that might be used to make sense of what is going on in the classroom. When discussing the theoretical orientation, I noted that the emergent perspective itself emanated from a series of teaching experiments. The viewpoint that I and my colleagues held at the outset was primarily psychological in that we intended to focus on the conceptual reorganizations that individual students made while interacting with their peers and the teacher. However, it soon became apparent that a psychological perspective, by itself, was inadequate to account for students' mathematical activity in the classroom. Thus, it was while trying to make sense of what was happening in classrooms that we revised a number of our basic assumptions and formulated the goal of developing a complementary social perspective. The delineation of this global objective was, however, merely a first step. It is one thing to make general pronouncements about the coordination of psychological and social perspectives and another to conduct empirical analyses of classroom events based on this intention. A fundamental issue that we have addressed while conducting teaching experiments is that of developing theoretical constructs that are tailored to our needs as mathematics educators interested in reform at the classroom level. One of the strengths of the classroom teaching experiment methodology is that it makes it possible to address both pragmatic and highly theoretical issues simultaneously. It is in this sense that the methodology enacts the reflexivity between theory and practice.

## TEACHING EXPERIMENTS IN THE CONTEXT OF DEVELOPMENTAL RESEARCH

In broad outline, the process of conducting a classroom teaching experiment can be characterized by the developmental research cycle as described by Gravemeijer (1995). As can be seen from FIG. 12.1, this cycle consists of two general, closely related aspects.[4] The first focus is concerned with instructional development and planning and is guided by an evolving instructional theory. The second aspect involves the ongoing analysis of classroom activities and events, and is guided by an emerging interpretive framework. This cycle proves to be analogous in many ways to the mathematics teaching cycle developed by M. Simon (1995) and shown in simplified form in FIG. 12.2. In the following paragraphs, I draw heavily on M. Simon's analysis as I consider the two aspects of the developmental research cycle.

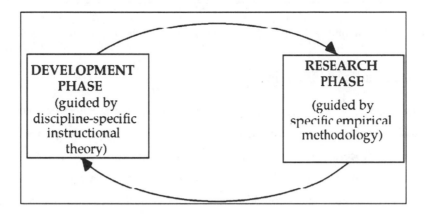

FIG. 12.1. Aspects of the developmental research cycle.

---

[4] As becomes apparent, this cycle occurs at two distinct levels (Gravemeijer, 1995). The most basic is the microlevel, where the anticipatory thought experiment and the teaching experiment concern the planning and trying out of instructional activities on a day-to-day basis. At this level, the analysis of what happens in the classroom informs the planning of the next instructional activity to be enacted in the same classroom. At a second broader level, the developmental research cycle centers on an entire instructional sequence. The thought experiment at this level concerns the local instructional theory that underlies the sequence, and the teaching experiment involves the realization of the whole set of instructional activities in the classroom, even as they are being revised continually . This broader cycle builds on the learning process of the research team inherent in the daily microcycles and is complemented by a retrospective analysis of the entire data set generated in the course of the teaching experiment.

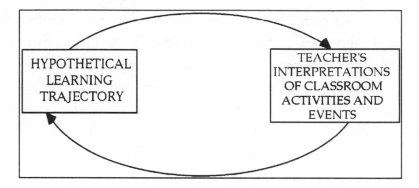

FIG. 12.2. A simplified version of M. Simon's (1995) mathematics teaching cycle.

## Instructional Design and Planning

A classroom teaching experiment typically begins with the clarification of mathematical learning goals and with a thought experiment in which the research team envisions how the teaching–learning process might be realized in the classroom (Gravemeijer, 1995). In M. Simon's (1995) terms, this first step involves the formulation of a hypothetical learning trajectory that is made up of three components: learning goals for students, planned learning or instructional activities, and a conjectured learning process in which the teacher anticipates how students' thinking and understanding might evolve when the learning activities are enacted in the classroom. This approach acknowledges the importance of listening to students and attempting to assess their current understandings, but also stresses the importance of anticipating the possible process of their learning as it might occur when planned but revisable instructional activities are enacted in an assumed classroom microculture. In this approach:

> The development of a hypothetical learning process and the development of the learning [or instructional] activities have a symbiotic relationship; the generation of ideas for learning activities is dependent on the teacher's hypotheses about the development of students' thinking and learning; further, the generation of hypotheses of student conceptual development depends on the nature of anticipated activities. (M. Simon, 1995, p. 136)

This formulation implies that even if social processes in the classroom remain implicit, purely psychological analyses that characterize learning independent of situation are inadequate when designing and planning for instruction. What is required is an *instructional theory*, however tentative and provisional, that gives rise to conjectures about possible means of supporting students' reorganization of their mathematical activity. A theory of this type embodies positive heuristics for the process of supporting students' development that have emerged in the course of prior teaching experiments conducted by both a particular research group and the research community more generally (Gravemeijer, 1995).[5] In my view, anticipatory heuristics of this type are particularly critical when the instructional activities involve technology-intensive learning environments such as microworlds in that it is frequently difficult to make substantial modifications once the teaching experiment is in progress.

The particular instructional theory that I and my colleagues have drawn on in recent classroom teaching experiments is that of *realistic mathematics education* (RME), developed at the Freudenthal Institute (Gravemeijer, 1995; Streefland, 1991; Treffers, 1987). In the following pages, I outline the tenets of this evolving theory to illustrate the importance of going beyond a purely psychological analysis when planning teaching experiments and designing instructional activities. As background, it should be noted that RME is broadly compatible with the emergent perspective in that both are based on similar characterizations of mathematics and mathematical learning (Cobb, Gravemeigher, Yackel, McClain, & Whitenack, in press). In particular, both contend that mathematics is a creative human activity and that mathematical learning occurs as students develop effective ways to solve problems and cope with situations. Further, both propose that mathematical development involves the bringing forth of a mathematical reality (Freudenthal, 1991). In social terms, this can be viewed as a process of enculturation into a historically evolving, interpretive stance (cf. Greeno, 1991; Saxe & Bermudez, 1996). In psychological terms, it involves the internalization and interiorization of mathematical activity by a process of reflective

---

[5] Gravemeijer (1995) argued that the development of an instructional theory of this type involves a third cyclic process that is more distanced from classroom practice than either the daily microcycles or the cycles that center on entire instructional sequences. At this macrolevel, an instructional theory is generated by generalizing from local instructional theories that underpin specific instructional sequences. In this case, the empirical grounding of the evolving instructional theory is mediated by the developmental research cycles at the lower levels.

abstraction so that the results of activity can be anticipated and activity itself becomes an entity that can be manipulated conceptually (Sfard, 1991; P. W. Thompson, 1994b; von Glasersfeld, 1991a).

One of the central tenets of RME is that the starting points of instructional sequences should be experientially real to students in the sense that they can engage immediately in personally meaningful mathematical activity (Streefland, 1991). In this regard, P. W. Thompson (1992) noted from the emergent perspective that:

> If students do not become engaged imaginistically in the ways that relate mathematical reasoning to principled experience, then we have little reason to believe that they will come to see their worlds outside of school as in any way mathematical. (p. 10)

As a point of clarification, it should be stressed that the term *experientially real* means only that the starting points should be experienced as real by the students, not that they have to involve realistic situations. Thus, arithmetic tasks presented by using conventional notation might be experientially real for students for whom the whole numbers are mathematical objects. In general, conjectures about the possible nature of students' experiential realities are derived from psychological analyses. It also can be noted that even when everyday scenarios are used as starting points, they necessarily differ from the situations as students might experience them out of school (Lave, 1993; Walkerdine, 1988). To account for students' learning, therefore, it is essential to delineate the scenario as it is constituted interactively in the classroom with the teacher's guidance.

A second tenet of RME is that in addition to taking account of students' current mathematical ways of knowing, the starting points should be justifiable in terms of the potential endpoints of the learning sequence. This implies that students' initially informal mathematical activity should constitute a basis from which they can abstract and construct increasingly sophisticated mathematical conceptions as they participate in classroom mathematical practices. At the same time, the situations that serve as starting points should continue to function as paradigm cases that involve rich imagery and thus anchor students' increasingly abstract mathematical activity. This latter requirement is consistent with analyses that emphasize the important role that analogies (Clement & D. E. Brown, 1989), metaphors (Pimm, 1987; Presmeg, 1992; Sfard, 1994), prototypes (Dorfler, 1995), intuitions (Fischbein, 1987), and generic organizers (Tall, 1989) play in mathematical activity.

In dealing with the starting points and potential endpoints, the first two tenets of RME hint at the tension that is endemic to mathematics teaching. Thus, Ball (1993b) observed that recent American proposals for educational reform "are replete with notions of 'understanding' and 'community'—about building bridges between the experiences of the child and the knowledge of the expert" (p. 374). She then inquired:

> *How* do I [as a mathematics teacher] create experiences for my students that connect with what they now know and care about but that also transcend the present? *How* do I value their interests and also connect them to ideas and traditions growing out of centuries of mathematical exploration and invention? (p. 375.)

RME's attempt to cope with this tension is embodied in a third tenet wherein it is argued that instructional sequences should contain activities in which students create and elaborate symbolic models of their informal mathematical activity. This modeling activity might entail making drawings, diagrams, or tables, or it could entail developing informal notations or using conventional mathematical notations. This third tenet is based on the psychological conjecture that, with the teacher's guidance, students' *models of* their informal mathematical activity can evolve into *models for* increasingly abstract mathematical reasoning (Gravemeijer, 1995). Dorfler (1989) made a similar proposal when he discussed the role of symbolic *protocols of action* in enabling reflection on and analysis of mathematical activity. Similarly, Kaput (in press) suggested that such records and notations might support the taking of activities or processes as entities that can be compared and can come to possess general properties. To the extent that this occurs, students' models would provide eventually what Kaput (1991) termed semantic guidance rather than syntactic guidance. In social terms, this third tenet implies a shift in classroom mathematical practices such that ways of symbolizing developed to initially express informal mathematical activity take on a life of their own and are used subsequently to support more formal mathematical activity in a range of situations.

A discussion of RME as it relates to the design of instructional sequences involving technology-intensive learning environments was provided by Bowers (1995). It is apparent that the interpretation of RME I have given implies conjectures about both individual and collective development. For example, the speculation that students' models of their informal mathematical activity might take on a life of their own and become models for increasingly abstract mathematical reasoning implies conjectures about the ways in which they might reorganize their mathematical activity. Further, this conjecture about individual development is made against the background of conjectures about the nature of the mathematical practices in which students might participate in the classroom, and about the ways in which those practices might evolve as students reorganize their activity. In general, conjectures of this type provide an initial orientation when planning a teaching experiment and designing instructional activities. However, the activities are modified continually in the course of the teaching experiment, and it is to this issue that I turn next.

## Experimenting in the Classroom

As a pragmatic matter, it is critical in our experience that the researchers be present in the classroom every day while the teaching experiment is in progress. We also have found that short, daily, debriefing sessions conducted with the collaborating teacher immediately after each classroom session are invaluable. In addition, longer weekly meetings of all members of the research team, including the teacher, have proved essential. A primary focus in both of these meetings and the short debriefing sessions is to develop, consensual or "taken-as-shared" interpretations of what might be going on in the classroom. These ongoing analyses of individual children's activity and of classroom social processes inform new thought experiments in the course of which conjectures about possible learning trajectories are revised frequently. As a consequence, there is often an almost daily modification of local learning goals, instructional activities, and social goals for the classroom participation structure. Therefore, we have found it counterproductive to plan the details of specific instructional activities more than a day or two in advance.

This emphasis on an ongoing process of experimentation is compatible with M. Simon's (1995) observation that "the only thing that is predictable in teaching is that classroom activities will not go as predicted" (p. 133). He also noted that ideas and conjectures are modified as one attempts to make sense of the social constitution of classroom activities. In this view, the emerging interpretive framework that guides the researchers' sense-making activities is of central importance and influences profoundly what can be learned in the course of a teaching experiment. Therefore, it is important that the research team articulate a provisional framework before the teaching experiment commences by clarifying theoretical constructs that might be used to make sense of what is happening in the classroom. The framework that my colleagues and I use currently is shown in Table 12.1. As was the case when discussing RME, my intent in outlining the framework is to provide an illustrative example.

TABLE 12.1

An Interpretive Framework for Analyzing Individual and Collective Activity at the Classroom Level

| Social Perspective | Psychological Perspective |
|---|---|
| Classroom social norms | Beliefs about our own role, others' roles, and the general nature of mathematical activity |
| Sociomathematical norms | Specifically mathematical beliefs and values |
| Classroom mathematical practices | Mathematical conceptions and activity |

The framework can be viewed as a response to the issue of attempting to understand mathematical learning as it occurs in the social context of the classroom. I want to avoid the claim that the framework might capture somehow the structure of individual and collective activity independently of history, situation, and purpose. The most that is claimed is that it has proved useful when attempting to support change at the classroom level.[6] With regard to the specifics of the framework, the column headings "Social Perspective" and "Psychological Perspective" refer to the two, reflexively related perspectives, that together, comprise the emergent viewpoint. Recall that these are an interactionist perspective on communal classroom processes and a psychological constructivist perspective on individual students' (or the teacher's) activity as they participate in and contribute to the development of these collective processes. In the following paragraphs, I discuss classroom social norms first, then sociomathematical norms, and finally classroom mathematical practices.

*Classroom Social Norms.* As has been noted, the theoretical stance that underpinned the first classroom teaching experiment my colleagues and I conducted was primarily psychological. However, an unanticipated issue arose in the first few days of the school year. The second-grade teacher with whom we cooperated engaged her students in both collaborative, small-group work and whole-class discussions of their mathematical interpretations and solutions. It soon became apparent that the teacher's expectation that the children would

---

[6] An elaboration of the framework that takes account of school-level and societal-level processes was discussed by Cobb and Yackel (1995).

explain publicly how they had interpreted and solved instructional activities ran counter to their prior experiences of class discussions in school. The students had been in traditional classrooms during their first-grade year and seemed to take it for granted that they were to infer the response the teacher had in mind rather than to articulate their own understandings. The teacher coped with this conflict between her own and the students' expectations by initiating a process that we came to term subsequently the renegotiation of classroom social norms. Examples of norms for whole-class discussions that became explicit topics of conversation include explaining and justifying solutions, attempting to make sense of explanations given by others, indicating agreement and disagreement, and questioning alternatives in situations where a conflict in interpretations or solutions has become apparent. In general, social norms can be seen to delineate the classroom participation structure (Erickson, 1986; Lampert, 1990).

A detailed account of the renegotiation process was given elsewhere (Cobb, Yackel, & Wood, 1989). For current purposes, it suffices to note that a social norm is not a psychological construct that can be attributed to a particular individual, but is instead a joint social construction. This can be contrasted with accounts framed in individualistic terms in which the teacher is said to establish or specify social norms for students. To be sure, the teacher is an institutionalized authority in the classroom (Bishop, 1985). However, from the emergent perspective, the most the teacher can do is express that authority in action by initiating and guiding the renegotiation process. The students also have to play their part in contributing to the establishment of social norms. A central premise of the interpretive framework is that in making these contributions, students reorganize their individual beliefs about their own role, others' roles, and the general nature of mathematical activity (Cobb et al., 1989). As a consequence, these beliefs are taken to be the psychological correlates of the classroom social norms (see Table 12.1).

*Sociomathematical Norms.* The analysis of general classroom social norms constituted our initial attempt to develop a social perspective on classroom activities and events. One aspect of the analysis that proved disquieting was that it was not specific to mathematics, but applied to almost any subject matter area. For example, one would hope that students would challenge each other's thinking and justify their own interpretations in science and literature lessons as well as in mathematics lessons. As a consequence, the focus of subsequent analyses shifted to the normative aspects of whole-class discussions that are specific to students' mathematical activity (Lampert, 1990; Voigt, 1995; Yackel & Cobb, 1996). Examples of such sociomathematical norms include what counts as a different mathematical solution, a sophisticated mathematical solution, an efficient mathematical solution, and an acceptable mathematical explanation and justification.

The relevance of the first of these norms—that concerning mathematical difference—became apparent when attention was given to the process by which the collaborating teachers guided the development of an inquiry approach to mathematics in their classrooms. As a part of this process, the teachers asked the students regularly if anyone had solved a task a different way and then questioned contributions that they did not consider to be mathematically different. The analysis indicated that the students did not know what would constitute a mathematical difference until the teacher and other students accepted some of their contributions but not others. Consequently, in responding to the teacher's requests for a different solution, the students were both learning what counts as a mathematical difference and helping to establish what counts as a mathematical difference in their classroom. In the course of these interactions, the sociomathematical norm of mathematical difference emerged through a process of (often implicit) negotiation. The analysis of this norm has proven to be paradigmatic in that a similar process of development appears to hold for other sociomathematical norms such as those dealing with sophisticated and efficient solutions and with acceptable explanations and justifications (Yackel & Cobb, 1996).

It also is worth noting that the process of negotiating sociomathematical norms can give rise to learning opportunities for teachers as well as for students. For example, the teachers with whom we worked were attempting to develop an inquiry form of practice for the first time and had not, in their prior years of teaching, asked students to explain their thinking. Consequently, the experiential basis from which they attempted to anticipate students' contributions to classroom discussions was extremely limited. Further, they had not decided necessarily in advance what would constitute a mathematical difference or an acceptable justification. Instead, they seemed to explicate and elaborate their own understanding of these and other normative aspects of mathematical activity as they interacted with their students.

The analysis of sociomathematical norms has proved to be significant pragmatically when conducting teaching experiments in that it clarifies the process by which the collaborating teachers fostered the development of intellectual autonomy in their classrooms. In particular, these teachers attempted to guide the development of a community of validators in the classrooms by encouraging the devolution of responsibility (cf. Brousseau, 1984). However, students could assume these responsibilities only to the extent that they developed personal ways of judging that enabled them to know both when it was appropriate to make a mathematical contribution and what constituted an acceptable contribution. This required, among other things, that the students could judge what counted as a different mathematical solution, an insightful mathematical solution, an efficient mathematical solution, and an acceptable mathematical explanation and justification. These are precisely the types of judgments that they and the teacher negotiated when establishing sociomathematical norms. This suggests that students constructed specifically mathematical beliefs and values that enabled them to act as increasingly autonomous members of classroom mathematical communities as they participated in the negotiation of sociomathematical norms (Yackel & Cobb, 1996). These beliefs and values, it should be noted, are psychological constructs and constitute a mathematical disposition (National Council of Teachers of Mathematics, 1991b). As shown in Table 12.1, they are taken to be the psychological correlates of the sociomathematical norms.

*Classroom Mathematical Practices.* The third aspect of the interpretive framework—concerning classroom mathematical practices—was motivated by the realization that one can talk of the mathematical development of a classroom community as well as of individual children. For example, in the second-grade classrooms in which my colleagues and I have worked, various solution methods that involve counting by ones are established mathematical practices at the beginning of the school year. Some of the students also are able to develop solutions that involve the conceptual creation of units of 10 and 1. However, when they do so, they are obliged to explain and justify their interpretations of number words and numerals. Later in the school year, solutions based on such interpretations are taken as self-evident by the classroom community. The activity of interpreting number words and numerals in this way has become an established mathematical practice that no longer stands in need of justification. From the students' point of view, numbers simply are composed of 10s and 1s—it is a mathematical truth.

This illustration from the second-grade classrooms describes a global shift in classroom mathematical practices that occurred over a period of several weeks. An example of a detailed analysis of evolving classroom practices can be found in Cobb et al. (in press). In general, an analysis of this type documents instructional sequences as they are realized in interaction in the classroom, and therefore, draws together the two general aspects of developmental research: instructional development and classroom-based research (see FIG. 12.1). This type of analysis also bears directly on the issue of accounting for mathematical learning as it occurs in the social context of the classroom. Viewed against the background of classroom social and sociomathematical norms, the mathematical practices established by the classroom community can be seen to constitute the immediate local situations of the students' mathematical development. Consequently, in identifying sequences of such practices, the analysis documents the evolving social situations in which students participate and learn. Individual students' mathematical conceptions and activities are taken as the psychological correlates of these practices, and the relation between them is considered to be reflexive (see Table 12.1).

*Summary.* The framework that I have outlined illustrates one way of organizing and structuring analyses of classroom activities and events. The primary function of such a framework is to provide a way of coping with the messiness and complexity of classroom life. By definition, a framework influences to a considerable extent the issues that are seen as significant and problematic when a teaching experiment is in progress. In our case, for example, it is not surprising that sociomathematical norms became an explicit focus of attention in the daily debriefing sessions and weekly meetings held during a recently completed teaching experiment. In a nontrivial sense, the interpretive framework is an integral aspect of the reality with which the research team is experimenting. As a consequence, the importance of attempting to articulate provisional theoretical constructs that might inform the interpretation of classroom events cannot be overemphasized.

## Retrospective Analysis

Thus far, the discussion has focused on both the planning of a teaching experiment and the ongoing experimentation in the classroom that is central to the methodology.[7] A third aspect of the methodology concerns the retrospective analysis of the entire data set collected during the experiment. One of the primary aims of this analysis is to place classroom events

---

[7] It is this process of ongoing experimentation inherent in the daily microcycles that differentiates the classroom teaching experiment from traditional, formative-evolution designs in which the research team starts with ready-made innovations, implements them in the classroom, and assesses their effectiveness.

in a broader theoretical context, thereby framing them as paradigmatic cases of more encompassing phenomena. In this regard, the retrospective analysis can be contrasted with the analysis conducted while the experiment is in progress in that, typically, the latter is concerned with issues that relate directly to the goal of supporting the mathematical development of the participating students. For example, in the course of the teaching experiment reported by M. Simon (1995), the ongoing analysis appears to have focused on the immediate goal of helping students develop an understanding of the multiplicative relationship involved in evaluating the area of a rectangle. However, in the retrospective analysis, classroom events were considered to be paradigmatic of instructional processes guided by a constructivist view of learning. The goal of this analysis, therefore, was to develop a model of teaching that is compatible with constructivism. Similarly, in a first-grade teaching experiment that I and my colleagues conducted recently, the immediate goal was to support the students' development of increasingly sophisticated arithmetical conceptions. To this end, we modified and refined tentative instructional sequences compatible with RME while the experiment was in progress. As a result, the sequences that were enacted in the classroom involved conjectures about the role that modeling and symbolizing might play in the children's mathematical development. One of the retrospective analyses that has been completed thus far focuses on this issue and treats classroom events as paradigmatic situations in which to develop a theoretical account of modeling, symbolizing, and using cultural tools (Cobb et al., in press).

It is apparent from the prior discussion of experimenting in the classroom that the day-to-day concern of supporting the participating students' mathematical development has a theoretical aspect. However, this concern is located in the immediate context of pedagogical judgment. In conducting a retrospective analysis, the research team steps back and reflects on its activity of experimenting in the classroom. Therefore, interpretations of particular events can be located both retrospectively and prospectively in the unfolding stream of classroom activity (cf. Steffe & Thompson, chap. 13, this volume). As a consequence, theoretical analyses grow out of and yet remain grounded in the practice of doing classroom-based developmental research. Further, in the longer term, the research agenda evolves as theoretical analyses completed in one experiment feed forward to inform future experiments (cf. Yackel, 1995).

# GENERALIZABILITY, TRUSTWORTHINESS, AND COMMENSURABILITY

In discussing specific methodological issues, I find it useful to distinguish between two types of products developed in the course of teaching experiments: theoretical analyses and instructional innovations. I consider each in turn.

## Theoretical Analyses

A theoretical analysis is the result of a complex, purposeful, problem solving process. Therefore, one would not expect that different researchers would develop similar theoretical constructs when analyzing a data set created in the course of a teaching experiment.[8] This implies that the notion of replicability is not relevant in this context. Following Atkinson, Delamont, and Hammersley (1988), I suggest, instead, that the relevant criteria are those of the generalizability and the trustworthiness of the analysis.

The issue of generalizability was touched on when discussing retrospective analyses. There, the importance of viewing classroom events as paradigmatic of broader phenomena was emphasized. It is this treatment of classroom activities and events as exemplars or prototypes that gives rise to generalizability. Of course, this is not generalization in the traditional sense that the characteristics of particular cases are either ignored or treated as interchangeable members of the set to which assertions are claimed to apply. Instead, the theoretical analysis developed when coming to understand one case is deemed to be relevant when interpreting other cases. Thus, what is generalized is a way of interpreting and acting that preserves the specific characteristics of individual cases. For example, I and my colleagues conjecture that much of what we learned when analyzing first-graders' modeling can inform analyses of other students' mathematical learning in a wide range of classroom situations, including those that involve the intensive use of technology. It is this quest for generalizability that distinguishes

---

[8] Instances in which a group of researchers develops a range of differing analyses of a single data set can be of interest in their own right (cf. Cobb & Bauersfeld, 1995).

analyses whose primary goal is to assess a particular instructional innovation from those whose goal is the development of theory that can feed forward to guide future research and the development of activities.

Whereas generalizability is associated closely with the notion of paradigm, trustworthiness is concerned with the reasonableness and justifiability of inferences and assertions. This notion of trustworthiness acknowledges that a range of plausible analyses might be made of a given data set for a variety of different purposes. The issue at hand is, therefore, that of the credibility of an analysis. The most important consideration in this regard is the extent to which the analysis of the longitudinal data set is both systematic and thorough. This is an extremely pressing issue given that large sets of videorecordings and transcripts are generated in the course of a teaching experiment. What is required is a systematic analytical approach in which provisional claims and conjectures are open to continual refutation. Cobb and Whitenack (1996) illustrated one such approach that draws heavily on B. G. Glaser and A. L. Strauss's (1967) constant comparative method. Irrespective of the specific approach adopted, it is important to document all phases of the analysis process, including the refining and refuting of initial conjectures. Then, final claims and assertions can be justified by backtracking through the various levels of the analysis, if necessary to the videorecordings and transcripts. This documentation of the research team's learning process provides an empirical grounding for the analysis (Gravemeijer, 1995). Further, it provides a means of differentiating systematic analyses in which sample episodes are used to illustrate general assertions from questionable analyses in which a few, possibly atypical, episodes are used to support unsubstantiated claims. Additional criteria that enhance the trustworthiness of an analysis include both the extent to which it has been critiqued by other researchers and the extent to which it derives from a prolonged engagement with students and teachers (S. J. Taylor & Bogdan, 1984). Typically, this latter criterion is satisfied in the case of classroom teaching experiments and constitutes a strength of the methodology.

## Instructional Innovations

A central assumption of developmental research is that instructional innovations developed in the course of a classroom teaching experiment can lead to productive patterns of learning when they are enacted in other classrooms. However, as we know only too well, the history of research in education in general, and in mathematics education in particular, is replete with more than its share of disparate and often irreconcilable findings. From the emergent perspective, a primary source of difficulty is that the independent variables of traditional experimental research are relatively superficial and have little to do with either context or meaning. We have seen that in the emergent view, students are considered to perceive, act, and learn as they participate in the self-organization of a system that is larger than themselves—the community of practice established in the classroom. In such an approach, learning is characterized as "an aspect of self-organization, not just of the human organism as a biological system, but of ecosocial systems in which the organism functions as a human being" (Lemke, in press). It is this participation in an evolving community of practice that is not addressed by traditional experimental research.

In my view, the primary concern is not so much that past findings have been disparate as that they have been irreconcilable. Hence, it has not been possible to account for the differences in findings when different groups of students receive supposedly the same instructional treatment. In contrast to traditional experimental research, the challenge from the emergent perspective is not that of replicating instructional innovations by ensuring that they are enacted in precisely the same way in different classrooms. The conception of teachers as professionals who adjust their plans continually on the basis of ongoing assessments of individual and collective activity in the classroom would suggest that complete replicability is neither desirable nor, perhaps, possible (cf. Ball, 1993b; M. Simon, 1995). Instead, the challenge, as it is construed from the emergent perspective, is to develop ways of analyzing innovations that make their realization in different classrooms commensurable. The interpretive framework that I have outlined evolved in the context of developmental research and, therefore, constitutes one possible way to organize such analyses. The central point is not, however, that others should use this particular framework. Instead, it is to emphasize the potential contributions of interpretive frameworks that are concerned with context and meaning. Frameworks of this type can support greater precision in developmental research by making it possible to compare, contrast, and relate different enactments of innovations. In the case of the framework outlined in this chapter, for example, an analysis of the mathematical practices established as an instructional sequence is enacted in a particular classroom documents that sequence as it is realized in interaction. Viewed against the background of classroom social and sociomathematical norms, the instructional sequence as enacted by a particular classroom community also can be seen to constitute the evolving social situation in which the students' mathematical development occurred. Consequently, an analysis of two different enactments of the same instructional sequence conducted in terms of constructs such as classroom social norms, sociomathematical norms, and classroom mathematical practices involves a comparison of the evolving social worlds in which the two groups of students participated. Such an analysis, therefore, makes different enactments of the same innovation commensurable. In addition, it emphasizes context and meaning by bringing to the fore the practices in which the students participated as they reorganized their mathematical activity. We contend that an approach of this type, in which commensurability is based on context and meaning, can facilitate disciplined systematic inquiry into reform and change that embraces the messiness and complexity of the classroom.

# COLLABORATING WITH TEACHERS

The type of classroom teaching experiment in which researchers collaborate with one or more teachers can be contrasted with that in which a researcher also acts as the teacher. The close relationship between these two approaches is indicated by the frequent references I have made to an experiment reported by M. Simon (1995), in which he acted as the teacher. The decision of whether or not to act as the teacher involves a trade-off. On the one hand, in experiments conducted in collaboration with a teacher, the researcher typically learns something about the process by which teachers reorganize their instructional practices even if this is not an explicit focus of investigation. Such insights are of immediate pragmatic relevance in that they can inform ongoing teacher development efforts. On the other hand, researchers who collaborate with teachers probably have less flexibility in pursuing particular visions of reform than do researchers who act as teachers. In the latter case, the researcher can follow up immediately on his or her own conjectures and intuitions in the classroom. In contrast, the role of a researcher who collaborates with a teacher is that of a leader in a local pedagogical community comprising the research and development team. One of his or her primary responsibilities is to guide the development of this community as it seeks to arrive at taken-as-shared decisions and judgments. Thus, whereas a researcher who serves as the teacher can act solely on the basis of his or her own judgments, a researcher who collaborates with a teacher can be effective only by acting as a member of a local community. In the former case, the researcher acts with fewer constraints, but, in the latter case, the context of the teaching experiment is closer to that in which reform must take place eventually. Consequently, researchers who collaborate with teachers accept what can be called realistic constraints as they explore what might be possible in students' mathematics education.

With regard to the process of conducting a teaching experiment in collaboration with a teacher, the overriding concern should be that of establishing an effective basis for communication so that the teacher and the researchers constitute a pedagogical community united by a common purpose. The possibility of developing such a basis for communication should be considered very seriously when deciding whether or not to collaborate with particular teachers. In our experience, we have found it critical to identify initial common ground from which an adequate basis might evolve. These taken-as-shared assumptions and beliefs could concern what the teacher and the researchers value mathematically, or they could involve general views about what constitutes students' intellectual and social welfare in school. As a next step, usually, an extensive series of interactions is necessary before the teaching experiment begins so that the teacher and the researchers can understand each other's viewpoints. These interactions, which should be negotiated mutually, could include mathematical problem solving, videorecorded interviews conducted by the teacher with his or her students, or pilot work conducted in the teacher's classroom in order to provide a context in which to discuss interpretations of particular events. The overall goal is that the teacher and the researchers will develop a taken-as-shared understanding of the rationale for and intent of the agreed-upon innovation before the teaching experiment begins.

Once the experiment is in progress, daily debriefing sessions and weekly meetings provide occasions in which to develop taken-as-shared interpretations of what is happening in the classroom. In our experience, the discussions in these meetings can be far-ranging and might focus on the quality of an individual student's mathematical activity, the nature of classroom norms and mathematical practices, or the planning of instructional activities. As a general rule, we have found it helpful to draw on our understanding of learning as it occurs in a social context to guide our interactions with collaborating teachers (Yackel, 1995). In doing so, our primary concern has been to support the teachers' development while simultaneously learning from them rather than to ensure that they act in accord with our personal interpretations and judgments. This attempt to be consistent when conducting teaching experiments stems from the concern that collaborating teachers might assume that their role is merely to translate researchers' decisions and judgments into practice. However, it is possible to explore the prospects for reform in collaboration with teachers only if they develop personally justifiable forms of practice as they participate in a teaching experiment. Therefore, the highest priority should be given to establishing with the collaborating teachers relationships that are based on mutual respect and trust.

# CONCLUSION

In this chapter, I have discussed the strengths of the methodology of the classroom teaching experiment. The most important of these derives from the researchers' participation in a collaborative team that is responsible for the quality of students' mathematical activity on a daily basis. This prolonged engagement with teachers and students provides an experiential grounding for theoretical developments that can inform practice. Throughout the discussion, I have emphasized that the teaching experiment methodology has emerged from attempts to address a range of problems and issues, including those of reform at the classroom level. In these concluding remarks, I consider situations in which other methodologies might be more appropriate.

When conducting a classroom teaching experiment, a recurring challenge is that of documenting in detail the quality of individual students' mathematical reasoning. A number of techniques can be used to alleviate this difficulty. They include the regular use of classroom tasks and activities designed specifically to solicit informative records of students' mathematical interpretations. In addition, interviews can be conducted with selected students immediately after classroom sessions, and interventions can be made on camera to ask clarifying questions or to pose impromptu tasks. However, even when these techniques are used, researchers conducting a classroom teaching experiment cannot maintain a continuous focus on the mathematical activity of all of the participating students. In my view, the constructivist teaching experiment developed by Steffe and his colleagues is a more appropriate methodology when the primary concern is to analyze the psychological processes by which individual students reorganize their activity (cf. Steffe & Thompson, chap. 13, this volume). I would observe only that this methodology does not provide a window into students' mathematical cognitions independent of situation and purpose. Instead, it provides a means of investigating the conceptual developments that students make while interacting with the researcher. From the emergent perspective, it is important to document the social situation of students' development even in the case of a series of one-on-one teaching sessions. Accordingly, the examination of these sessions should involve the coordination of a psychological analysis of the students' activity with a social analysis of the relationship established jointly by the researcher and the student.

A second set of issues for which the classroom teaching experiment is not well suited concerns the broader sociopolitical context of reform. In the type of teaching experiment that I have described, explanations of teachers' and students' activities typically are formulated in terms of processes located at the classroom level and focus on individual interpretations and face-to-face interactions and discourse. These explanations do not make reference to students' and teachers' participation in practices located outside the classroom at the school and community levels. A variety of other methodologies, including ethnographies, may be more appropriate for investigations that focus on cultural diversity and the restructuring of the school as it relates to reform in mathematics education (cf. Doerr & Tinto, chap. 15, this volume; Moschkovich & Brenner, chap. 17, this volume).

As is the case with any methodology, the classroom teaching experiment allows researchers to address some issues better than others. Its primary contribution is in allowing researchers to investigate the implications of reform as they play out in interactions between teachers and students in classrooms. Throughout this chapter, I have drawn on my own and my colleagues' experience of collaborating with teachers to clarify what is involved in conducting classroom teaching experiments that can inform ongoing reform efforts. In the last analysis, the relevance of the methodology will rest on the extent to which it continues to provide such guidance.

## ACKNOWLEDGMENTS

The author is grateful to Anthony Kelly and Martin Simon for helpful comments on a previous draft of this chapter. The analysis reported in this chapter was supported by the National Science Foundation under grant RED-981498 and by the Office of Educational Research and Improvement under grant number R305A0007. The opinions expressed do not necessarily reflect the views of either the Foundation or OERI.

# 13

# Research on the Development of Mathematics Teachers: The Teacher Development Experiment

**Martin A. Simon**
*Pennsylvania State University*

The publication of Curriculum and Evaluation Standards for School Mathematics by the National Council Teachers of Mathematics in 1989 marked the beginning of a large-scale endeavor to reform mathematics education. The success of this effort hinges on the effectiveness of attempts to provide education and support for teachers to prepare them to carry out this reform in their classrooms. Because the perspectives on mathematics, learning, and teaching that characterize this reform are radically different from those that underlie traditional school mathematics (Cobb, Wood, Yackel, & McNeal, 1992), the challenge to create appropriate educational opportunities for practicing and prospective teachers, themselves products of traditional school mathematics, is great.

A knowledge base is needed that will guide the creation of novel and effective teacher education[1] programs. It must include identification of key aspects of teacher knowledge and

---

[1] I use *teacher education* to refer to all intentional educational opportunities for both prospective and practicing teachers. *Teacher development* refers to changes in knowledge, beliefs, dispositions, and skills that support teachers' increased ability to implement successfully the principles of the current mathematics education reform. Thus, the goal of teacher education is teacher development.

skills (the goals of teacher education), useful frameworks to describe how such knowledge and skills develop, and useful models of interventions that can promote such development.[2] [3]

In order to generate the requisite knowledge base, new research methodologies are needed. The need is based on the following dilemma. Descriptive research on teaching and teacher development generates accounts of what is in place at present. However, the current reform in mathematics education requires not only the reinvention of mathematics teaching, but also the reinvention of teacher education. Therefore, research must contribute to understanding a process that is largely unrealized at this time. We seem to have a "catch 22:" we are unable to foster adequate teacher development because we do not understand the developmental processes sufficiently, and we are unable to understand the developmental processes because we do not have situations to observe where teachers are developing this expertise.

A methodology is emerging that shows promise of addressing this dilemma. I refer to this methodology, which is the subject of this chapter, as a *teacher development experiment*[4] (TDE). This methodology for studying the development of teachers builds on the central principle of the constructivist teaching experiment (Cobb & Steffe, 1983; see also Steffe & Thompson, chap. 11, this volume), that is, that a team of knowledgeable and skillful researchers can study development by fostering development as part of a continuous cycle of analysis and intervention. This feature of the TDE and of the teaching experiment methodologies provides a framework for researchers to work at the edge of their evolving knowledge. The TDE methodology also integrates a case study approach into its adaptation of

---

[2] These three categories for a useful knowledge base are interrelated and interdependent.

[3] Currently, small- and large-scale efforts to help teachers understand the principles of the mathematics reform and to modify their teaching practice have been limited by a lack of knowledge of how teachers develop from traditional perspectives to those consistent with the current reform.

[4] The term *teacher development experiment* is an attempt to distinguish it from the teaching experiment while recognizing the teaching experiment as a central building block of the methodology.

the teaching experiment in order to collect and coordinate individual and group data on teacher[5] development.

## THE PSYCHOLOGICAL AND SOCIAL THEORETICAL UNDERPINNINGS OF THE TDE

The TDE builds directly on the "emergent perspective" articulated by Cobb and his colleagues (Cobb, chap. 12, this volume; Cobb & Bauersfeld, 1995; Cobb & Yackel, 1996). (The reader is encouraged to read Cobb's contribution in this volume before continuing with this chapter.) From the emergent perspective, learning can be seen as both a psychological process of the individual and a social process of the group:

> The basic relation posited between students' constructive activities and the social processes in which they participate in the classroom is one of reflexivity in which neither is given preeminence over the other. In this view, students are considered to contribute to the evolving classroom mathematical practices as they reorganize their individual mathematical activities. Conversely, the ways in which they make these reorganizations are constrained by their participation in the evolving classroom practices.
> (Cobb, chap. 12, this volume)

Thus, the emergent perspective eschews debate over whether learning is primarily psychological or social. Rather, it asserts the usefulness of coordinating the analyses that result from taking each perspective (psychological and social) as primary. "Therefore, accounts of [students'] mathematical development might involve the coordination of psychological analyses of their individual activities with social analyses of the norms and practices established by the classroom community" (Cobb, chap. 12, this volume.)

---

[5] *Teacher* is used to designate both prospective and practicing teachers unless otherwise specified.

Whereas Cobb and his colleagues have focused mainly on classroom communities consisting of students and a teacher, the TDE is concerned with an additional community of practice—a group of teachers with a teacher-educator. However, prior to describing the methodology in more detail, I wish to focus on a third community of practice—the community of mathematics education researchers.

By applying the emergent perspective to the development of knowledge in the research community, we create a context for research on the development of mathematics teachers and define the potential contributions of the TDE.[6] We can consider the enterprise of mathematics education research as the individual learning of researchers (and research teams) occurring within the social context of the research community. As such, the learning of individual researchers and research teams is guided and constrained by the knowledge, tools, norms, and practices of the mathematics education research community. Conversely, the learning that occurs in individual projects contributes to the taken-as-shared[7] knowledge of the research community, to the tools and methodologies that it has available, and to its norms and practices. Applying these notions specifically to the TDE, we can examine the nature of the knowledge that could be expected to derive from the application of this methodology. I would suggest that the TDE can allow researchers to generate increasingly powerful schemes for thinking about the development of teachers in the context of teacher education opportunities. The TDE takes as its object of study a teaching–learning complex that encompasses three levels of participants: the researcher/teacher-educator, the teacher, and the teacher's students, and two levels of curricula: the teacher education curricula and the mathematics students' curricula.[8] By focusing on different aspects of this complex (indivisible) whole, one generates

---

[6] Steffe and Thompson (chap. 11, this volume) apply their radical constructivist lens to the researcher's learning. This is parallel to my application of the emergent perspective to examining the activity of researchers.

[7] Researchers judge knowledge to be "taken as-shared" when participants use it without need for justification, taking for granted a shared meaning (Streeck, 1979).

[8] The levels of participation are similar to those described in Lesh and Kelly's chapter on multitiered teaching experiments, chapter 9, this volume.

schemes about development (potentially at three levels), schemes about teaching (at two levels), and schemes about curricula (at two levels). This perspective includes, but is not limited to, what Cobb identifies as the two products of the whole-class teaching experiment (see chap. 12, this volume): "theoretical analyses and instructional innovations."

## SITTING ON THE SHOULDERS OF GIANTS

The TDE methodology is an adaptation and extension of groundbreaking research approaches: the development of the constructivist teaching experiment and, later, the whole-class teaching experiment. In this section, I discuss the contributions of these methodologies to the TDE.

### Contributions of the Constructivist Teaching Experiment

The constructivist teaching experiment methodology originated among researchers attempting to understand children's concept development in particular areas of mathematics (Behr, Wachsmuth, Post, & Lesh, 1984; Cobb & Steffe, 1983; Lesh, 1985a; Steffe, 1983, 1991). The original work was done with individual children and pairs of children. (As background for this section, the reader is encouraged to read Steffe and Thompson, chap. 11, this volume.) Following, I highlight those aspects of this teaching experiment methodology that play a significant role in the TDE.

*The Researcher-Teacher.* The advent of the constructivist teaching experiment provided an alternative to existing research paradigms in which researchers are observers or quantifiers of either "natural" or "experimental" situations. The merged role of researcher and teacher provides an opportunity for the researcher to develop knowledge through multiple iterations of a reflection-interaction cycle (see Fig. 13.1).

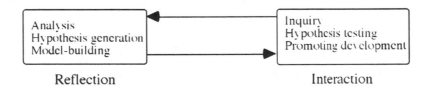

FIG. 13.1. Researcher's reflection-interaction cycle.

In chapter 11 in this book, Steffe and Thompson point out that "Students' actions and constructions are influenced by a teacher's actions and constructions, and vice versa. But neither is totally dependent on or independent of the other." Therefore, we can postulate a reflection-interaction cycle for the student similar to the researcher's cycle pictured in FIG. 13.1[9]. However, in most cases, the student's cycle is less conscious.

As a part of the reflection-interaction cycle, the researcher-teacher applies knowledge shared by the research community and personal knowledge, including current hypotheses, to the interactions with the students. The researcher's intuition and action patterns, which are not parts of his or her explicit knowledge, also contribute to the interaction. The researcher's interpretation of the interactions supports some aspects of his or her knowledge and challenges other aspects, resulting in the modification of that knowledge. Thus, this cycle, central to the teaching experiment, allows researchers to work at the growing edge of their knowledge of how students learn.

*The Observer.* The observer(s) is an important contributor to the teaching experiment. This role complements the role of the researcher-teacher and amplifies the overall analytical power of the research team.[10] In particular, the observer[11] (a) represents a perspective from outside the teacher–student interaction, (b) calls attention to aspects of the data set that might be overlooked by the researcher-teacher, (c) introduces alternative explanations that broaden the analysis of the data, (d) challenges the researcher-teacher's interpretations and

---

[9] Gravemeijer's (1994) developmental research cycle of development and research seems to be congruent with my characterization of a reflection-interaction cycle. The difference in language is attributable to Gravemeijer's focus on research into the design of curricula in contrast to my focus here on research into the development of students and teachers. The similarities between these two endeavors are probably greater than the differences.

[10] The roles of the observer and the researcher-teacher are important; however, these roles do not have to be occupied by the same person throughout the study. In some studies, a pair of researchers may decide to exchange these roles.

[11] Items a, b, and c are described in Steffe and Thompson, chap. 11, this volume.

formulations, and (e) (by the nature of the collaboration) requires the researcher-teacher to articulate and communicate his or her ideas (and vice versa).

*Ongoing and Retrospective Analyses.* The teaching experiment involves two important levels of data analysis: the ongoing analysis, which occurs during and between sessions with students, and the retrospective analysis, which focuses on a sequence of sessions (see Steffe and Thompson, chap. 11, this volume). These two levels of analysis serve the research in particular ways.

The ongoing analysis is the basis for spontaneous and planned interventions with the students, interactions that gather additional information, test hypotheses, and promote further development.[12] A key aspect of the ongoing analysis is the generation and modification of the researcher's models of the students' knowledge, actions, and dispositions. The teaching experiment has been used mainly to generate models of students' mathematics (cf. Steffe & Thompson, chap. 11, this volume; Steffe & Tzur, 1994). It is on the basis of the researcher's current models of students' thinking that subsequent interventions are generated.

The retrospective analysis involves a reexamination of a larger corpus of data, either the entire teaching experiment to date or a subset of those data that are considered to be a useful unit of analysis. This analysis involves a careful structured review of all of the relevant records of the teaching experiment. The purpose of this analysis is to continue to develop explanatory models of the students' mathematical development.

*Model Building.* The goal of the teaching experiment is the development of explanatory models of students' mathematical development:

> A constructivist research program in mathematics education has, as its central problem, the explanation of the process of construction of mathematical objects as it actually occurs in children. . . . The teaching

---

[12]I use *intervention* to indicate a teacher's behavior designed to further students' learning. *Interaction* refers to communication and coordinated action among teacher and students.

experiment is a technique which is used to construct explanations of children's constructions. (Steffe, 1983, pp. 469–470)

These explanatory models begin to be developed during the ongoing analysis. However, it is during the retrospective analysis that the models are articulated more fully.

*Hypothesis Generation and Testing*. The teaching experiment entails ongoing cycles of generating and testing hypotheses. The researchers' current hypotheses guide their interactions with the students. These interactions provide data that support or engender modification of these hypotheses and also foster the generation of new hypotheses. The initial hypotheses of the research team guide the development of the initial research plan.

*Recording*. Recording of sessions with students is usually accomplished by videotaping. These recordings and their transcriptions are essential for the retrospective analysis. Frequently, the tapes are watched between sessions to support the ongoing analyses as well. Audiotapes of or notes from the ongoing analysis meetings between the researcher-teacher and the observers provide an additional source of data for the retrospective analysis.

*Summarizing the Contribution of the Constructivist Teaching Experiment to the TDE*. Each of the aspects of the teaching experiment mentioned in this section are fundamental to the TDE. The observer's role, the reflection-interaction cycle, the ongoing and retrospective analyses, the emphasis on model-building and hypothesis generation and testing, and the role of recording are all applied directly to the TDE. The researcher-teacher role is expanded because of the researchers' focus on and engagement in teacher development. (This role is described in the subsequent section, The Teacher Development Experiment Methodology.)

## Contributions of the Whole-Class Teaching Experiment

The work of Cobb, Yackel, and Wood (Cobb, chap. 12, this volume; Cobb, Yackel, & Wood, 1993) has created a methodology for studying mathematics learning in classrooms based on the teaching experiment. This section discusses several features of the whole-class teaching experiment methodology that are incorporated in the TDE.

*Emergent Perspective*. This social and psychological perspective on learning, discussed earlier in the chapter, provides the theoretical underpinning for every aspect of the TDE methodology. Cobb (chap 12, this volume) points out that the emergent perspective itself developed in the context of whole-class teaching experiments. Thus, theoretical constructs are generated and modified in the context of such studies.

*Conceptual Framework.* Cobb and his colleagues have developed an interpretive framework for analyzing individual and collective activity at the classroom level. The framework emphasizes the complementarity of a focus on classroom norms and practices with a focus on individuals' beliefs about the respective roles of the participants (teacher and students) and conceptions of the content domain (mathematics). Such inquiry involves attention to individual, small-group, and large-group engagement in the content and to classroom community members' explicit conversations about the functioning of the learning community.[13]

*Framing Paradigm Cases.* Cobb (chap. 12, this volume) suggests a useful way to think about the products of a whole class teaching experiment:

> One of the primary aims of this analysis is to place classroom events in a broader theoretical context, thereby framing them as paradigm cases of more encompassing phenomena. In this regard, the retrospective analysis can be contrasted with the analysis conducted while the experiment is in progress in that, typically, the latter is concerned with issues that relate directly to the goal of supporting the mathematical development of the participating students.

The notion of framing paradigmattic cases is a useful construct for many types of qualitative research. It suggests that researchers examine the particular situation that they have documented in order to identify "paradigmatic situations in which to develop a theoretical account" that can address issues relevant to the mathematics education research and/or teaching communities.

This focus on framing paradigmattic cases addresses the issue of generalizability, one of the three criteria described by Cobb in chapter 12 in this book: "[T]he theoretical analysis

---

[13] In this paragraph, I have broadened the language beyond what Cobb uses to focus on mathematics classrooms because the TDE methodology looks at development more broadly, not only the learning of mathematics.

developed when coming to understand that one case is deemed to be relevant when interpreting other cases. Thus, what is generalized is a way of interpreting and acting that preserves the specific characteristics of individual cases."

Thus, generalizability, according to Cobb, does not mean that the context is irrelevant, but, rather, that the paradigm case is considered in light of the context in which it developed.

*Trustworthiness and Commensurability.* In addition to generalizability, Cobb describes in his chapter herein two other criteria of research quality that can be applied to the TDE: trustworthiness and commensurability. Trustworthiness is dependent on analyses that are "both systematic and thorough." Commensurability suggests that a goal of the research is to develop theoretical constructs that allow researchers to make sense of the variation in outcomes of particular interventions in different contexts.

*Summarizing the Contribution of the Whole-Class Teaching Experiment to the TDE.* As mentioned earlier in this chapter, the emergent perspective that undergirds the whole-class teaching experiment serves the same function in the TDE methodology. Cobb's notion of framing paradigmattic cases and holding the research to standards of trustworthiness and commensurability are appropriated and built on. Furthermore, the TDE's conceptual framework makes use of constructs developed by Cobb and his colleagues and is described in ways that highlight the parallels and contrasts between these related methodologies (see the next section).

## THE TEACHER DEVELOPMENT EXPERIMENT METHODOLOGY

### Overview

The TDE methodology is an adaptation and extension of the constructivist teaching experiment and whole-class teaching experiment methodologies, building particularly on those aspects highlighted in the previous section. However, the TDE is concerned with the development of teachers, which encompasses more than mathematical development, the focus of its predecessors. Guided by an emergent perspective, the TDE uses the developmental stance of the teaching experiment to study the different aspects of mathematics teacher development at the various sites where it occurs. This is pursued by coordinating whole-class teaching experiments (in the context of teacher education) with adaptations of individual case studies.

## Developmental Stance

The TDE takes a parallel stance to that of the teaching experiment: the researcher promotes the development of teachers as a means of studying their development. Because the development of mathematics teachers involves pedagogical development, as well as mathematical development, and because that development happens not only in mathematics classes for teachers, but also in mathematics education courses, teachers' own classrooms, and professional collaborations, TDE researchers participate in teacher development at these diverse sites. Thus, the TDE coordinates analyses of group and individual development through whole-class teaching experiments in mathematics classes for teachers and mathematics education classes (such classes as students' mathematical thinking, big ideas in mathematics curricula, and mathematics classroom teaching) and the clinical supervision of teachers in their own classrooms as a part of case studies of individual teachers.

*TDE Teaching Experiments.* One major component of the TDE is whole-class teaching experiments in mathematics courses for teachers and mathematics education classes. The researcher-teacher (teacher-educator in this case) promotes development through the course activities. All of the classes are videotaped. The researcher-teacher meets with the observers between class sessions to analyze the previous session, generate and modify models of the teachers' development (ongoing analysis), and plan the instructional interventions for the next class.

Whereas, generally, teaching experiments have focused on mathematical development, the TDE classroom teaching experiments are used to generate models for the teachers' pedagogical development as well as their mathematical development. This distinction is meant to communicate the breadth of the TDE focus, nonetheless recognizing that we can view mathematical and pedagogical development as interrelated. Teachers' pedagogical development (with respect to mathematics) may be influenced by their mathematical development, and, conversely, their mathematical development may be enhanced as a result of their pedagogical inquiry. Thus, TDE teaching experiments make use of the structure of their predecessors while broadening and changing their areas of concentration. Even in the mathematics courses for teachers, the concentration is broader than in Cobb's whole-class teaching experiments because of the researchers' interest in how the teachers' concepts of teaching and learning mathematics evolve in the context of the mathematics courses.

The TDE retrospective analysis involves not only attempts to analyze data gathered over time, but also attempts to relate development from one course to the next, including both mathematics courses and mathematics education courses. The models of teachers' development generated in the retrospective analysis have the quality of Cobb's paradigm cases as defined in his chapter in this book; that is, they articulate ways of viewing teacher development that may be useful in considering other teacher development situations.

## Analyzing Teaching Experiment Data: An Example

The Construction of Elementary Mathematics Project included a teaching experiment in a mathematics course for prospective elementary teachers that focused on understanding multiplicative structures (Simon & Blume, 1994a, 1994b). In the ongoing analysis of data from this teaching experiment, mathematical justification emerged as a key issue. The researchers analyzed "situations for justification" (Cobb, et al., 1992) to generate models of the students' conceptions of justification and to determine ways to promote the development of these conceptions in subsequent class sessions. The ongoing analysis over the entire semester indicated that significant change had taken place in the nature of the students' engagement in situations for justification. Whereas many of the students' early attempts to justify a mathematical idea (e.g., the multiplication of length times width to evaluate the area of a rectangle) involved invoking authorities (texts, past teachers) and proof by example, later discussions of justification involved deductive proofs and the students taking on the role of arbiters of validity. (The detailed analysis of justification in this teaching experiment is documented in Simon & Blume, 1996.)

The prominence of justification in the ongoing analysis led to a retrospective analysis centered on two broad questions:

- How were classroom norms with respect to justification and validation negotiated in this classroom community?
- What issues affected the development of these norms?

These relatively unfocused questions represented our attempt to explore what the data could teach us about validation and justification in the context of this mathematics class for prospective teachers (Simon & Blume, 1996).

In the retrospective analysis, situations for justification were extracted from the class transcripts. Then, referring to the classroom videotapes as needed, we conducted a line-by-line analysis of these transcript episodes in order to account for all of the students' actions (including language) related to justification. This process included interpreting justifications offered, responses to justifications, the extent to which students were persuaded by particular arguments, and the apparent norms and practices that existed in relation to justification. Informed by previous work in the field (e.g., Balacheff, 1987; Bell, 1979; Hanna, 1990; van Dormolen, 1977), our analysis generated three products: an extension of existing taxonomies of students' mathematical justifications, a description of the important factors that contribute to students' engagement in mathematical justification, and an explication of the norms and practices that were developed with respect to justification.

Other examples of the results of analyzing these teaching experiment data include two papers on prospective teachers' mathematical knowledge (Simon & Blume, 1994a, 1994b) and a paper (McNeal & Simon, 1999) on the development of mathematical and social norms. (McNeal & M. Simon, 1994, contains a short segment of that analysis.)

In general, issues that emerged as significant in the ongoing analysis became the foci of retrospective analyses. In the latter, relevant data were identified, and detailed analysis and model building ensued.

## Case Studies of Individual Teachers

The TDE provides a dual perspective on teacher development by coordinating analyses of individual and group development. As discussed in the preceding paragraphs, the latter is accomplished through whole-class teaching experiments. The former is accomplished through an adaptation of the individual case study. I want to emphasize, however, that both the teaching experiment component and the case study component involve the coordination of social and psychological analyses. (The two-by-two matrix in Table 13.1, addresses this point.) The whole-class teaching experiment entails looking at individuals' conceptions as well as at the development of social practices. Likewise, the case study requires making sense of the social context within which individual development occurs, including courses for teachers and the classroom community of the mathematics class taught by the teacher.

TABLE 13.1

Purposes and Perspectives of the Teacher Development Experiment

| | | Perspectives Used | |
|---|---|---|---|
| | | *Social Perspective* | *Psychological Perspective* |
| Purposes of the Research | Analysis of collective development | Whole-class teaching experiment | |
| | Analysis of individual development | Case studies of individual teachers | |

The case studies of individual teachers that are included in the TDE make use of traditional case study methodology (Stake, 1978), but with a particular modification based on the TDE developmental stance (discussed earlier). Extending the notion of fostering development as a context for studying development, TDE researchers take on the role of clinical supervisor in order to foster and study teachers' development in their own classrooms. M. Simon and Schifter (1991) found that the role of "classroom consultant" (clinical supervisor of teachers in their own classrooms) was a key component in supporting the development of mathematics teachers. The researcher uses the supervisor role to promote further development, engaging in a cycle of reflection and interaction analogous to the cycle that characterizes the teaching experiment.

The researcher's role as a clinical supervisor (based on Simon, 1989) involves regular observations of the teacher during the teacher's mathematics class and regular meetings with the teacher following these classes. Conversations may focus on the lesson; what came before it or what will follow it; the teacher's thinking prior to, during, and after the lesson (including the teacher's evaluation of the lesson); the mathematics involved; and the activity of individual students. The researcher also serves as a resource for the teacher by providing references for textual and instructional materials, ideas for lessons, and insights into aspects of the teaching–learning process. Further, the researcher acts as a support person for the teacher and as a confidant for the teacher's emotional experiences that accompany engagement in radical professional change. Each aspect of the researcher's classroom supervision role contributes to the research team's ability to understand the social, affective, and cognitive components of the teacher's development.

The teacher sets the agenda for the interactions with the researcher, choosing how to make use of the researcher's support at any given time.[14] Nonetheless, the researcher has her or his own evolving hypotheses of what might contribute to the teacher's development. These hypotheses guide the researcher's responses to the teacher's agenda.

Data for the case studies include periodic videotaped observations of the teacher teaching mathematics. These observations are the topic of interviews with the teacher before and after each observation. The interviews explore the teacher's conceptions, motivations, and thinking with respect to the instructional decisions made before and during the lesson. Further understanding of the teacher's perspectives comes from inviting his or her interpretations of classroom interactions and individual students' behaviors.

The TDE teaching experiments also provide data for the case studies of individual teachers. Analyses of the teacher's participation in the teaching experiment classes are an essential part of understanding the individual's development. (During class sessions, we organize the videotaping of small groups to assure that the case study teachers appear regularly on the tapes.) A more elaborated discussion of the TDE case study methodology can be found in (Simon & Tzur, 1999).

## Interpretive Framework

The TDE interpretive framework builds on the emergent perspective and the framework developed by Cobb as described in chapter 12 herein. However, because the TDE studies pedagogical as well as mathematical development and because that development occurs at multiple sites, the framework requires extension beyond the framework described by Cobb for studying elementary classrooms. Using a tabular structure similar to Cobb's, this framework is outlined in Table 13.2.

---

[14]This relationship between researcher and teacher is different from that articulated by Cobb in chapter 12 herein. In Cobb's teaching experiments, the teacher is a member of the research team. As such, the researchers share pedagogical responsibility with the teacher, although I assume that the teacher maintains the ultimate authority for decisions affecting students.

TABLE 13.2

Interpretive Framework

| From a Social Perspective | | From a Psychological Perspective | |
|---|---|---|---|
| *Norms and Practices* | *Affective* | *Cognitive* | *Affective* |
| Social norms | Effectiveness power, cooperative–competitive | Beliefs about one's own and others' role | Effectiveness power, inclusion |
| Mathematical and pedagogical practices | Emotional content arising from practices | Concepts, skills, individual practice, personal development | Emotional content arising from learning confidence |

*Social Norms.* In the TDE framework, social norms include norms that are established in mathematics courses for teachers, in mathematics education courses for teachers, and in teachers' own classrooms. Whereas Cobb and Yackel distinguished between social norms and sociomathematical norms in a mathematics classroom (Cobb, in this volume; Yackel & Cobb, 1996), this distinction does not fit classes where the content is mathematics pedagogy, a major part of the TDE. Thus, in order to make the framework applicable to all of the courses of the TDE, Cobb and Yackel's two categories are subsumed under "social norms."

The dotted line between "social norms" and "mathematical and pedagogical practices" signals that there is an overlap between these two categories. That is, norms related to teachers' roles, developed in mathematics classes, may have essentially the same content as pedagogical practices that are established in the context of mathematics education classes for teachers. For example, in a mathematics class for teachers, a norm for the teacher's role in facilitating communication in large-group discussions may be established. Such a norm also may be constituted in the context of the teacher's own mathematics classroom. These would be considered examples of social norms. However, in a course on classroom mathematics teaching, the same type of "practice" might become a taken-as-shared part of a mathematics teacher's responsibility; this facilitation function would be a component of what this pedagogical classroom community assumes about teaching. In this latter case, this aspect of the role of the teacher would be categorized appropriately as "mathematical and pedagogical practices."

*Mathematical and Pedagogical Practices.* This category designates the development of shared knowledge and practices in accordance with group goals. In the mathematics classroom, the focus is on mathematical knowledge and practices that become part of the taken-as-shared functioning of the group. When mathematical knowledge and practices become taken-as-shared, they no longer require explanation or justification. Similarly, in a mathematics education class, pedagogical knowledge and practices become taken-as-shared. For example, in a pedagogical learning community, probing students' thinking about computation or inquiring into how students might come to abstract a particular mathematical operation might become accepted practices that require no justification.

*Affect.* In the interpretive framework that I present for the TDE, I include a focus on the affect involved in development. Learners' affect was not an explicit emphasis of mathematics teaching experiments until Tzur's recent work (1995). In the TDE, which involves teachers changing their basic orientations toward mathematics, learning, and teaching, attention to the participants' affect is essential because some of the developmental obstacles that must be overcome by teachers are affective in nature. Table 13.2 denotes a consideration of both group and individual affect.

The organization of Table 13.2 suggests that the development of social norms entails a group affect (e.g., a sense of power or powerlessness). Correspondingly, the development of individual beliefs about one's role and the role of the other community members entails individual affect (e.g., a sense of personal effectiveness in that community). The development of shared knowledge and practice and the development of individual abilities also entails affective response.

*Cognitive Component.* By "cognitive," I designate a category parallel to Cobb's "psychological" while attempting to distinguish between the cognitive and the affective components of individual psychological development. The cognitive component covers the development of the individual's abilities, knowledge, and beliefs, both mathematical and pedagogical. The cognitive components of beliefs about one's own and others' role correlate with the development of group social norms. The development of concepts, skills, and so on, correlates with the collective development of mathematical and pedagogical practices.

## Coordinating the Analyses of the Teaching Experiments and the Case Studies of Individual Teachers

Though both of the components of the TDE (teaching experiments and case studies) contribute to the researchers' understanding of teacher development, the methodology affords the coordination of the analyses of the two components. The attempt to make sense of the results of the study of the group with the results of studies of individuals has the potential to deepen, sharpen, and modify the analyses generated by the study. The researchers' understanding of the development of the group is amplified by detailed analysis of the development of individuals in that group. Likewise, the individuals' development is understood in the context of the group in which much of the teacher development activities took place.

## Additional Issues of Data Collection and Analysis

Who teaches in the teaching experiments? In discussing classroom research, A. Brown (1992) pointed out:

> Central to the enterprise is that the classroom must function smoothly as a learning environment before we can study anything other than the myriad possible ways that things can go wrong. Classroom life is synergistic: Aspects of it that are often treated independently, such as teacher training, curriculum selection, testing, and so forth actually form part of a systematic whole. (pp. 142–143)

Because the classroom teacher has a major influence on many of these aspects of the functioning of the classroom, "Who teaches in the teaching experiments?" is a key question for a research team planning a TDE. The decision involves choosing between two categories of potential teachers, researchers versus practitioners recruited specifically for this position. Although our work (cf. Simon, 1995) has been done with the principal investigator in the role of researcher–teacher-educator, this is not the only reasonable decision.

In particular, it is important to explore who has the greatest experience in carrying out the type of teaching needed for the research project. Because so much of the teaching occurs spontaneously, in response to students, the researcher–teacher-educator must be able to engage in teaching that is consistent with the framework of the project (see Simon, 1997, for a discussion of models of teaching as elements of research frameworks) and that represents the current level of knowledge of the research team. The teaching experiment is designed to build on the cutting edge of relevant knowledge and practice. It is the quality of the interventions that determines the potential for what can be learned from those interventions. The researcher who serves as teacher-educator is the instrument through which the research team enacts these interventions. The following are to be avoided in selecting a teacher-educator for the TDE classes:

- A teacher-educator who is just beginning to develop the kind of teaching practice needed. This is particularly relevant in the current climate of changing pedagogical paradigms (Cobb, et al., 1992; Simon, 1995). Fundamental change in teaching practice is an uncertain journey that takes place over an extended period of time.[15] A teaching experiment demands appropriate practice from the outset, a practice consistent with the basic pedagogical paradigm of the project. The teacher-educator's practice must allow the research team to function at the growing edge of its knowledge in exploring teacher development.

- A teacher-educator who is not likely to understand deeply the analyses and hypotheses of the research team. Without profound understanding, the teacher-educator cannot be an optimum research instrument in the interactive sessions. I suggest that someone who is not well prepared to be one of the major contributors to the analyses and hypothesis generation is unlikely to understand consistently at sufficient depth. As von Glasersfeld (1989) remind us, "The human knower can only know what the human knower has constructed" (p. 123).

In lieu of a teacher-educator with the particular experience necessary, Steffe and Thompson (chap. 11, this volume) "strongly recommend":

---

[15] Studying the development of novice teacher-educators may be a valuable endeavor, but different from the TDE, which tries to study teacher development in a context that includes a teacher educator with appropriate knowledge, skills, and experience.

Any researcher who has not conducted a teaching experiment independently, but who wishes to do so, first engage in exploratory teaching in order to become thoroughly acquainted with students' ways and means of operating with respect to whatever particular domain of mathematical concepts and operations are of interest.

*Handling Teacher Self-Report Data*. The TDE generates a considerable amount of teacher self-report data. Criteria to determine in which cases self-report data can be accepted at face value are important. As noted earlier, the TDE incorporates Cobb's (chap. 12, this volume) notions of generalizability, trustworthiness, and commensurability. Related to trustworthiness, we have identified two criteria for teacher self-report data: *genuineness* and *legitimacy*. By genuineness, I mean that the communication represents the teacher's experiential reality. By legitimacy, I mean that the teacher is the appropriate person to assess the situation. Let us consider the ramifications of each of them. In the context of a TDE, teacher-participants are likely to develop conceptions of the idealized participant, as a student and as a classroom teacher. As a result, self-report data may be affected by teachers' natural (and often unconscious) attempts to show themselves as competent according to these conceptions. For example, in the context of a TDE in which a focus on students' mathematics is developing, the researchers would have to question the genuineness of the comment, "I really see how important it is to understand students' mathematics." The statement may indicate what the teacher perceives as valued in the program rather than the teacher's deep personal commitment.

Because the researchers have no way of knowing directly whether a communication is genuine, we have developed the following criteria for genuineness:

- If the communication by the teacher-participant could be motivated by a desire to appear competent (consistent with the "party line"), these data may not be used as primary data. They may be used only as secondary data to corroborate inferences made by the researchers based on observations of that participant in action.

- If the communication by the teacher-participant varies from what would be expected if she or he were attempting to demonstrate competence (e.g., expressions of lack of understanding, resistance to instructional interventions), these data may be considered genuine and used as primary data sources assuming that they are unchallenged for other reasons (e.g., legitimacy).

Evaluation of genuineness, therefore, involves viewing teacher self-report data in the context of emerging norms and practices as identified by the researchers. When the self-report data are consistent with the norms of what it means to be an effective group member or teacher, the genuineness of the data is questioned. This does not imply that the teacher's self-report is not accurate, only that the researcher cannot be confident of its accuracy; data that reflect the teacher's involvement in teaching and/or learning situations from which inferences can be made are needed.

Turning to the question of whether self-report data are legitimate, we distinguish between issues for which the teachers' perceptions are needed and those for which the researchers' evaluations are more appropriate. An example of the former might be an expression of a teacher's own experience (as long as it meets the criterion of genuineness); for example, "I feel really conflicted between trying to cover the textbook and spending the time that I feel the students need for understanding." An example of the latter is, "Now, I really understand proportions." To determine whether the teacher does understand proportions, it is more appropriate that the researchers evaluate that understanding. One could argue that it may be relevant to note that the teacher believes that he or she understands the mathematics involved and chose to comment on it. However, the teacher's statement would not be seen as evidence of understanding (not legitimate) and might be questioned also on the basis of genuineness.

*Studying Teacher Thinking in Context.* Interviews are used regularly to collect data on teachers' current conceptions. These interviews are structured so that teachers are challenged to make sense of particular learning–teaching interactions and to address specific pedagogical problems. In so doing, teachers are not making general claims about their beliefs, claims whose genuineness might be questioned and whose utility and meaning to the teachers the researchers would have difficulty understanding. When the interviews precede or follow a teacher's lesson with a class, the interviewer can focus the discussion on specifics of the lesson or the lesson plan. In cases where there is no specific lesson on which to focus (e.g., interviews to collect preprogram baseline data from prospective teachers), videotapes, pedagogical scenarios, and role-plays can be used.

*Prestudy Assessment.* Prior to the TDE, it is essential to collect data on the participants in the case studies. It also may be useful to collect some data on all of the other participants. These data aid the research team's subsequent attempts to make sense of the participants' actions and development. This prestudy data collection consists of mathematical, pedagogical, and relevant affective issues. Examples of types of prestudy instruments follow:

- Mathematical problems given as written assessments and in individual or pair interviews: Interviews may be used to clarify issues raised by the participant's responses to the written tasks. Here, the goal is to assess understanding of mathematical concepts, problem solving, affect related to the tasks, and conceptions of mathematics.

- Pedagogical interviews: These interviews revolve around pedagogical problems, which may be posed verbally, through role-playing, or by using videotape. The use of pedagogical problems creates a context for observing the participants in "action" (simulated or imagined), rather than inviting them to tell the researchers what they know and believe.

- Observations of teaching: These are important for collecting data on practicing teachers and, sometimes, may be possible for prospective teachers. Postlesson, or pre- and postlesson, interviews are helpful in order to gain a sense of the teacher's thinking about the plan for, conduct of, and reflection on the lesson.

Issues of genuineness and legitimacy are relevant to prestudy data collection as well. Of course, no project norms have been established yet. However, the question of what the participant thinks that the "experts" (the researchers) want to hear is still a concern.

*Videorecording in Classrooms.* According to the emergent perspective, the classroom culture is constituted interactively by the teacher and the students. Thus, in keeping with this perspective, it is important to record classroom activity in ways that include the teacher and the students. Two videocameras, providing different views, seem to be a minimum. Finding a way to assure high-quality sound recording is essential and entails experimentation with the particular physical setting.

## Limitations of the TDE

As in all qualitative research, the quality of TDE research depends directly on the knowledge, skills, and interactive abilities of the researchers involved, because the researcher, are the "instrument." However, the TDE has an additional layer: teaching. Beyond the usual competencies in observation, questioning, data management, and data analysis, the TDE is dependent on the researchers' ability to promote development. (This is also true of individual and whole-class teaching experiments.) Consequently, preparation for conducting TDE research combines two difficult processes: learning to conduct research and learning to teach (in ways that are appropriate for the TDE).

Because of the extensive nature of the TDE, the research is labor intensive and, therefore, costly. Management of the great quantity of data generated can seem overwhelming. An appropriate time frame for studying teacher development is probably several years, and funding sources may balk at financing a long intervention followed by an appropriately long period for retrospective analysis of the data.

The comprehensive nature of the TDE, in which the context and the nature of the interactions are crucial to understanding the outcomes, causes researchers who use the methodology to confront an issue common to a number of qualitative research methodologies: namely, the lack of appropriate vehicles for sharing results. Usually, the average length of an article in a research journal is inadequate for this purpose. The research community likely will look to advances in technology for solutions to this problem. Solutions might involve readers' access to videotaped segments and complex data sets (transcripts, individual's work, etc.).

One of the limitations on current TDE research is the lack of domain-specific knowledge with respect to the pedagogical development of mathematics teachers. Whereas researchers aiming to study students' development of particular mathematical knowledge are likely to have access to empirical and theoretical work that identifies key concepts, the TDE researchers have little to guide their investigation of the pedagogical development of teachers. Much work is needed to describe the nature of teaching (the goal of teacher development) and its component competencies (Simon, 1997).

The TDE is understood correctly as a research methodology that involves promoting the development of teachers. This is in contrast to teacher development projects that incorporate a research component. In a TDE, optimum conditions are created for generating empirically based knowledge. In a teacher development project, many of the conditions are determined by the need to serve a particular population of teachers, research considerations being secondary. Thus, the TDE methodology may not be appropriate for research in the context of a teacher development project or may need considerable modification in order to be useful. Also, considerable modification would be needed if the TDE methodology were to be used in situations where teachers are required to participate or in settings where researchers are interested in studying systemic change.

My final point in this section concerns researchers' relationships to classroom teachers. In the educational community, there is a strong sentiment that teachers should be equal partners with researchers and collaborate on the preparation of research reports. The TDE methodology that I have described stands in contrast to this perspective. Though leaving to other venues the discussion of teachers as researchers and teachers as partners with researchers, I assert the importance of having a context for studying the development of teachers in which an observer (the researcher) can analyze the process of development from a perspective not available to the developing teacher.[16] Nonetheless, two issues that are raised by considering teachers as research partners can guide the TDE approach. First, it is important that a climate of mutual respect and support exist. Both the researcher and the teacher are learning in the context of the TDE; the teacher is learning about teaching, and the researcher is learning about the teacher's development. Each is key to the other's learning. Asymmetry in expertise does not have to be accompanied by a powerlessness of one of the parties. Second, the teachers can and should have a voice, in the context of their professional life, to communicate their developmental experience and their views of practice. This is a different role from that of the TDE researcher.

## CONCLUSIONS

The TDE represents an application and adaptation of the whole-class teaching experiment and the case study. The methodology is new and evolving and is intended to generate a motion picture of development as opposed to snapshots provided by earlier methodologies. The TDE takes a stance in relation to the development of mathematics teachers that involves researchers in promoting teacher development in order to increase understanding of teacher development. It involves using the full extent of what is understood already about fostering teacher

---

[16]This issue is further developed in M. Simon and Tzur (1999).

development as the starting point. Each subsequent intervention is guided additionally by what the researchers have learned in their previous interactions with the teachers. Thus, the TDE is a tight spiral of hypothesis testing and hypothesis modification and generation.

The comprehensive nature of the TDE study derives from its inclusion of three pairs of conditions:

- study of groups of teachers and of individual teachers;
- study of how teachers develop during coursework and in their own classrooms; and,
- study of teachers' mathematical development and their pedagogical development.

The teaching experiment and the TDE have contributed to blurring the boundaries between research and teaching. These methodologies change the nature of research by engaging the researcher in the practice of teaching in order to learn about the development of the student population (in the TDE, the teachers are the students). However, this blurring of the boundaries also potentially affects what constitutes teaching. The role of researcher–teacher (or researcher–teacher–educator) can be the basis of a new model of teaching. Teaching as a process of inquiry in which the teacher is engaged in an ongoing cycle of interaction and reflection has great potential. Simon (1995) described an emerging model of teaching based on an analysis of the teacher-researcher's role in a teaching experiment with prospective teachers. This rapprochement of teaching and research is consistent with Cobb's view of the changing relationship between theory and practice, which he recounts in chapter 12 of this book. He writes, "Theory is seen to emerge from practice and to feed back to guide it."

# IV Classroom-Based Research

For the kind of teaching experiments that were emphasized in Part III, teachers often functioned as coresearchers (e.g., chap. 9), or researchers functioned as coteachers (e.g., chaps. 10 and 11). Also, in some cases, the researcher's goals went beyond investigating the nature of students' developing knowledge to also investigate the nature of effective teachers (e.g., chaps. 12 and 13), curriculum materials (e.g., chaps. 9 and 10), software (e.g., chap. 10 and 11), or classroom learning environments (e.g., chaps. 12 and 13). Consequently, in many of the preceding cases, the researchers are not simply disinterested observers; instead, they often are significantly involved in projects aimed at improving instruction. Also, they may be more interested in "what's possible" (in ideal situations) than in "what's typical" (in ordinary classrooms); and, in most cases, the site for research moves out of the laboratory and into real classrooms, or other naturalistic environments for teaching, learning, or problem solving.

In Part IV, each of the chapters describes research paradigms in which researchers move even further away from laboratory settings, and even further away from the role of a "disinterested observer." For example, in Ball's research, she is first and foremost a teacher whose concerns about the good of her students often outweigh concerns about maintaining laboratory-like purity concerning the possibility of describing interactions that occur. Similarly, Doerr and Tinto and Feldman and Minstrel focus on action research paradigms in which the roles of teachers and researchers become blurred, with both becoming agents for change in the status quo. But, whereas Doerr and Tinto emphasize the role of researcher as teacher, Feldman and Minstrel focus on the teacher as researcher.

All of the preceding chapters raise interesting issues about themes that traditional researchers might have referred to as dealing with (a) the "replicability" of results or (b) the "objectivity" of the researcher. But, when the subjects being investigated are understood to be complex, dynamic, self regulating, and continually adapting systems, and when a basic assumption is made that a single situation will be interpreted differently by different subjects, then replication cannot refer to simplistic notions about doing the same things again under the same conditions.

When researchers attempt to develop theoretical models and perspectives that will yield powerful insights for others, this does not necessarily imply that two observers should be expected too see the same things in a single situation. In mathematics and science education, the systems being observed tend to be far too complex and interacting for such simplistic notions to apply. Furthermore, what counts as facts and data is far from being objectively given—partly because too many layers of theory are needed to sort out signal from noise.

Ball deals with the preceding themes when she emphasizes ways that researchers may benefit from the viewpoint of "insiders"—perhaps by adopting the role of teachers. Similarly, Moschkovich and Brenner deal with these issues when they describe a "naturalistic" paradigm in which learning inside the classroom can be studied as a part of a larger account of children's learning outside the classroom. Finally Tobin provides an introduction to what he calls "the interpretive method" in science education research.

A recurring theme throughout this book is that the goal of research is not always to test the truth or falsity of hypotheses, or condition-action rules. For example, for several of the chapters in Part IV, the main goal is to develop descriptions of existing situations, or conjectures about possible situations. Or, in other sections of this book, other types of research results are discussed such as those that involve existence proofs, model development, or the design of software or ideal learning environments. In these latter types of investigations, the point is not to test whether a given design or model is true or false. Instead, the pertinent questions to ask involve the extent to which a model or design is sufficiently meaningful and detailed to be useful and powerful for specific "customers" to achieve specific goals. For example, in Part III, Confrey and Lachance conjecture that it should be productive for the curriculum to give more attention to "splitting" interpretations of multiplication, in addition to the "repeated addition" interpretations that are emphasized in most traditional textbooks. In many ways, judging the productivity of such a conjecture is similar judging the usefulness of an architect's plans for building a complex house. Trade-offs may involve factors such as costs and benefits, size and efficiency, precision and accuracy, or complexity and detail. It is not necessarily the case that one house, or one house plan, is better or worse than another; and, to some extend, usefulness depends on the needs and perspectives of the customer. Nonetheless, rules exist for creating or improving houses and house plans. Similarly, if the goal of research is to produce a description of complex, adapting, and interacting systems, then judgments about usefulness and sharability may emphasize factors such as fidelity, internal consistency, or explanatory/predictive power—rather than truth or falsity.

Before reading the chapters in Part IV, readers may find it useful to formulate responses to the following questions for a research that you yourself might want to conduct:

1. Quality assessment standards that apply to existence proofs (or to model development, or to design development) tend to be somewhat different than those that apply to hypothesis testing. What kind of

product do you plan to produce in the research project that you are planning? Do you anticipate that the refinement and elaboration of your results may go through several iterations? If so, what characteristics do you think may distinguish early iterations from later iterations?

2. To what extent will you be a participant–observer in your investigations? What other participants' perspectives should be represented in your final results? To what extent, or in what ways, do you think that the notions of objectivity and replicability should apply to your investigations?

3. Authors in this book generally subscribe to the philosophical notion that reality is a construct; and, they also recognize that, in mathematics and science education, many of the most important systems that we need to investigate are products of human construction. That is, the systems being investigated do not occur naturally in the world. To what extent will you or others be involved in creating the situation that you plan to investigate in your own research?

4. When investigating the behaviors of complex systems, the most important characteristics of these systems tend to focus on underlying patterns and regularities that cannot be simply perceived. What steps may be needed to help you go beyond surface-level characteristics to focus on relationships and interactions that may not be apparent based on superficial inspection of relevant phenomena?

# 14 Working on the Inside: Using One's Own Practice as a Site for Studying Teaching and Learning

**Deborah Loewenberg Ball**
*University of Michigan*

This chapter examines benefits and pitfalls inherent in studying teaching and learning *from the inside*, where the teacher is also the principal investigator of the research. Such "first-person" writing about teaching is situated in the much wider domain of "inquiry in teaching" and includes such genres as action research, teacher narratives, teacher research, as well as multiple forms of research on teaching.[1] Although first-person approaches to inquiry vary, they overlap and share many similar aims, methods, questions, standards, and perspectives. They focus on issues of practice. They seek to probe beneath the surface of the obvious and taken for granted. Grounded in practice, with tools that can transcend the boundaries of practice, these approaches to inquiry aim to produce knowledge that can contribute to the improvement of teaching and learning.

Of course, most research on teaching shares these aims. What most clearly distinguishes first-person inquiry from other approaches to the study of teaching and learning is that it deliberately uses the position of the teacher to ground questions, structure analysis, and represent interpretation. In contrast, other research on teaching deliberately divides the work of

---

[1] For examples of each of these, see: reflection in and on teaching (e.g., Schön, 1983, 1991), action research (Rosenthal, 1994), teacher narratives (Kohl, 1967, 1984; Paley, 1979, 1981, 1995; Schifter & Fosnot, 1993, 1996a, 1996b); teacher research (Cochran-Smith & Lytle, 1993), researcher-teacher (Ball, 1993a, 1993b, 1995, in press; Chazan, 1992, 1996; Heaton, 1994; Lampert, 1986, 1990, 1992, in press; Osborne, 1993; Wilson, 1990, in press).

practice from the undertaking of inquiry. Researchers bring questions into a classroom, sit on its periphery, or move into its flow. They watch and talk with teachers. They sit near and listen to students. Equipped with theories, questions, and yellow-lined pads, they seek as outsiders to understand, analyze, and explain what goes on there. As participant–observers, they inherit an inherently ambiguous role of outsider trying to understand inside. On one hand, their outside perspectives as psychologists, anthropologists, or simply adult nonmembers of the context, offer them perspective that insiders lack. As outsiders, they can see and hear things that insiders take for granted. On the other hand, as outsiders they cannot completely understand local meanings, language, norms, and practices. They miss nuances, make faulty connections, and inappropriately infer motives. They ask questions of their own making, questions insiders might not think to pose. But also they miss questions that lie at the heart of the puzzles of practice.

Whereas conventional research on teaching looks *in at* teaching and learning, the work in this chapter seeks instead to examine teaching *from the inside*, from what Lampert (1998) called "the perspective of practice." Those who do this kind of work blend the construction of practice with its analysis. They do so in ways that offer special possibilities of insight and understanding, viewed through the firsthand experience of the teacher. Looking from inside, they probe aspects of the enterprises of teaching and learning often invisible to outsiders. For example: What are the special anxieties and issues entailed in changing one's practice? What is it like to try to excite and engage first-graders in studying abstractions of number theory? What content and pedagogical dilemmas arise in teaching a heterogeneous high school algebra class (Chazan, 1992, 1996)? What struggles inhere in trying to unlearn pedagogical habits and to learn to teach differently (Heaton, 1994)? What is it like to be a White woman teacher working with children of color, leaning into and across divides of social class, race, gender (Paley, 1979, 1981, 1995)? What are some of the challenges of trying to teach a mathematics methods course in ways that depart sharply from the usual "cover the curriculum" approach, focusing deeply instead on the mathematics itself, and on children's thinking (Ball, 1990; Suzuka, 1996)?

Different as they may be from other forms of research on teaching, "inside" approaches to inquiry in teaching nevertheless differ from one another significantly in both purpose and method. For example, "reflection" in and on teaching has as its primary goal to heighten deliberation in and about practice, to consider alternative interpretations, to seek information for next steps as a teacher of the class or child at hand. It is a form of inquiry most closely tied to the ongoing work of teaching. It pays least attention to the production of insights, ideas, or theories to be shared broadly with others. It also need have no special design or conjecture. "Action research," although tied closely to one's own ongoing work as a teacher, is typically more planful. With a focal question in mind, the teacher investigates an issue, designs and tries a new method or new materials, and seeks to examine it or them systematically. Some forms of inquiry make communication with others central—teacher narratives, for example. Teachers writing about their teaching concentrate on representing the experience—problems, puzzles, excitements—of practice to themselves, to close colleagues, and sometimes to a wider audience.[2]

Within this arena, practitioners examine their practice thoughtfully with the goal of learning about teaching and learning and ultimately, improving it. Some write about teaching after the fact, offering narrative, analysis, or commentary. Others set out with a project to write about their teaching. Moreover, across all of these approaches to inquiry in teaching, communication with others about teaching is usually an aim, thereby working to change the traditional isolation of practice. The agendas may vary, from representing teachers' experiences to asserting the primacy of teachers' perspectives to contributing to scholarship and theory.

To probe what is entailed in "working on the inside," I have organized this chapter in three sections. I begin with a first-person account of my own trajectory: initially, using inquiry as a means of practice and later using practice as a medium for research. I turn next to examining three cases of researcher-teachers' work. All three focus on mathematics teaching and learning, but differ in question, in design, and in what is afforded by the first-person perspective. I first describe and analyze each case, then appraise comparatively the nature of these inquiries and their yield. In the third section, I consider three special challenges of

---

[2] I draw here on Lampert's (1992) notion of the "continuum of justification" in doing mathematics. She argued that, in proving a mathematical claim, one faces the challenges of (a) convincing oneself that something that one thinks *might* be the case, *is*; (b) convincing others with whom one is closely connected—colleagues with similar commitments and orientations; and (c) convincing others working in other paradigms who may not share the same assumptions. In constructing knowledge in and for teaching, a similar continuum may be conceived (see Lampert, 1998)—talking with oneself about one's work, sharing with colleagues who belong to the same community, and communicating with broader audiences concerned with teaching and learning.

first-person research. The chapter concludes with issues crucial to the ongoing development of this approach to the study of teaching and learning.

## LOOKING AT FIRST-PERSON RESEARCH FROM A FIRST-PERSON PERSPECTIVE: A NARRATIVE

When I began teaching in 1975, I was given an extraordinary but significantly formative teaching assignment for a first-year teacher: four sections of elementary school science (two third-grade classes, one fourth-grade, and one fifth-grade) and one section of language arts in a departmentalized elementary school. Equipped with three grade levels worth of *Science Curriculum Improvement Study* (SCIS) materials, I set out, bravely, to begin teaching (Karplus, 1974). I could not have been less prepared for this assignment. In college, I had majored in French and minored in English, and I had not studied any science other than the two basic courses required for my teaching certificate. Hence, by necessity, my teaching was an investigation into science and how to engage children in learning science. Not unimportant, the materials that I was using to construct my teaching used an investigative design for children's learning. They set out lessons that set the children to exploring, experimenting, and discussing what they saw. The teacher was to guide these discussions gently.

The simultaneous reality of my own pedagogical experiments and my early efforts to engage children in scientific investigation intertwined for me the learning of my students and my own learning as a teacher. I had no real alternative than to design my lessons, drawing heavily from the curriculum materials, and to work with my students on those lessons. Afterwards, it was useful to stand back to see what I and they had done, where we had veered off unproductively, where I had made a fortuitous move, where we needed to head. The iterative process of design, experimentation, and analysis was etched into my work during these first two years, mostly as a matter of survival. Quite likely, the guidance I received from the curriculum materials, with their heavy emphasis on guiding my students to explore, conjecture, design, experiment, and analyze, oriented me strongly in this way. My pedagogical inquiries ran in parallel with the children's scientific ones.

In the ensuing years, I continued to work in this way. I examined my students' learning and work, and generated alternative ideas about ways to help them learn. I designed different strategies and curriculum units, tried them with the children, and watched closely what happened. I revised and revamped what I did. Although I would not have known the term, I was developing what we now call a "reflective stance" as a teacher, and I was designing little "action research" projects, although there were no formal structures to my approach. I would not have been able to imagine teaching in any other way. My students came from over 30 countries, spoke languages I had never heard of, and I had five different teaching assignments in the first 6 years of my career: multigrade science (1975–1976), second–third grade combination (1976–1977), second grade (1977–1978), first–, second–, third–grade team room with another teacher (1978–1980), and fifth grade (1980–1981). There was a great deal I had to learn, and no opportunity to learn what I needed other than to try to develop ways to learn in and from my own teaching.

I hit a critical point in my work after 6 years of teaching. I was teaching fifth grade, and mathematics suddenly emerged as a problem for me. Despite my good intentions and careful, step-by-step, conceptual explanations, long-division and complex work with fractions loomed as an impenetrable curricular wall for many of my students. Alex, one of my students, would go home on Friday able to solve a long division problem and, on Monday, no longer seem to remember how to begin. Neither he or his classmates could explain what we were doing despite my efforts to model and explain the procedures I so desperately sought to teach them. When I graded papers, students got many answers wrong. Merely reexplaining and then asking them to correct their papers—a common pedagogical strategy—seemed futile. All the imagination and cleverness in the world was not helping my students grasp the material. Studying their errors did not help. I was at a loss. For the first time, neither my own resources nor those of my colleagues were adequate to help me figure out what to try. It was 1980—the year that the National Council of Teachers of Mathematics (NCTM) published *An Agenda for Action*, the forerunner of the coming wave of mathematics reform. But there was little available to help me examine what was happening in my room, or to help me improve my teaching.

My long-term investigation into the improvement of mathematics education had its root that year, as I struggled, less successfully than in my previous work, to increase my effectiveness with those students. My intense interest in mathematics teaching and learning, my own and my students', began to grow, and expanded into increasingly formal inquiry. As my questions multiplied, my strategies of investigation expanded. I engaged other teachers in my inquiry and began to pay attention to both my own and others' learning. I realized that I needed to learn more mathematics myself, for unlike the other areas in which I was developing my teaching, I was inadequately educated in mathematics. At that point I had taken no mathematics since my first year of college, when I passed out of the required course for elementary teachers and took an independent study with a professor in the mathematics department. I remembered little from that study and realized that, in order to develop my capacities to help my students, I would need to know more mathematics myself. I did not know what I was seeking, only that I needed to have the kind of fluency with mathematics that I had with language. That fluency had been a crucial resource in the development of my teaching of reading and writing.

Perry Lanier, a professor at Michigan State University where I was enrolled in a master's degree program, introduced me to the Comprehensive School Mathematics Program (CSMP) curriculum (Central Midwest Regional Educational Laboratory, 1982). It was a stroke of good luck. Profiting from his wise experience and from conversations with him, I began experimenting with CSMP in my classroom, and the next year, teaching first grade, I used the materials as the primary mathematics curriculum. The materials were structured in a completely unfamiliar way, and the central mathematical ideas were big ones, as in SCIS: structure of number, functions and their composition, classification. A few powerful representational tools, all pictorial, were used and encouraged. Intertwined on a ground of curriculum, there was a lot for me to learn, both mathematics and about pedagogy.

Following the CSMP curriculum produced a classroom full of 6-year-olds talking about mathematical ideas. I was astonished at the serious intellectual work in which the children could engage. Although I did not yet appreciate sufficiently what of their work was significant mathematically, I began to see connections between the way I had learned to teach science several years earlier and what teaching mathematics might be like. My own and my students' mathematical learning began to grow, and it developed into increasingly formal inquiry. If I was going to be able to hear my students' mathematical bundles of insights and confusions, stumbles and leaps, I had mathematics to learn. My journey took me into mathematical coursework. I also became involved in "staff development" in mathematics. So weak were the infrastructure and resources for teacher development that someone like me who was both learning and interested was quickly catapulted into leadership roles. For me, professional development and teacher learning soon became new arenas for puzzling, experimenting, and analyzing domains of intertwined practice and inquiry.

When I entered the world of formal educational research as a graduate student, I became increasingly interested in teacher learning. The years I had spent so far as a teacher, developing my own knowledge and skills, trying to improve my teaching, working with colleagues, had piqued my interest in what teaching entails and how teachers learn to change what they do, assume, know, or believe. My dissertation research grew from my wonderment at the lack of attention to teachers as learners in the literature I had been exploring. Although, in the mid-1980s, it was widely believed that students' prior experiences and ideas shaped what they learned from instruction, this perspective was not applied in the context of teacher learning. Teachers, it seemed, could be filled up with information and techniques, with little regard for what they currently believed or did or knew. I designed a study to explore what teacher education students brought with them to their formal preparation to teach mathematics. I studied both prospective elementary teachers and prospective secondary mathematics teachers and interviewed them about mathematics, mathematics teaching and learning, and students as learners of mathematics. What I learned was the vast extent to which these prospective teachers already had ideas about all of these issues. And what they believed was often at odds with what teacher educators wanted them to think or know. For example, many believed that mathematical ability is innate and that many people simply cannot be good at mathematics. Most thought of mathematics as a cut-and-dried area of truths to be memorized and procedures to be practiced, and they thought of good math teaching as that which makes its dry material "fun." I began to glimpse possible new explanations for the ineffectiveness of teacher education. If teacher educators designed their curriculum with little sense of what their students already knew or believed, then they were unlikely to meet their students' current thinking. It was easy to imagine that students could pass through their professional education with their entering ideas both unchallenged and unchanged.

When I was writing my dissertation, I realized that readers would need a sense of the kind of mathematics teaching that teacher educators were hoping to prepare beginners to do. Without that image, interpreting what prospective teachers knew made little sense. Knew in relation to what goal? Three years prior to the emergence of the NCTM *Standards*, I wondered how to provide such an image as a grounding for the reader. Instinctively, I reached into my own experience and wrote a description of a recent day in a third-grade class I was teaching, in which the children and I were exploring a contextualized, area-perimeter problem. Although I used my own teaching as the source for the detailed description, the reader could have had no clue about this in the way I wrote it. I began with an entirely detached explanation:

> To illustrate concretely what a mathematical pedagogy might look like, I
> use an example from a third grade classroom in which students are learning
> about perimeter and area and the relationship between these two measures.

On the day that I will describe, students were presenting their solutions to the following problem which the teacher had posed the day before:

> Suppose you had 64 meters of fence with which you were going to build a pen for your large dog, Bozo. What are some different pens you can make if you use all the fence? Which is the pen with the *most* play space for Bozo? Which pen allows him the *least* play space?

The students have worked on this problem in a variety of ways, using tools and strategies which they have acquired: graph paper for drawing alternative dogpens, rulers for drawing constructions of dogpens on plain paper, making tables of the possible combinations of dimensions that total 64 and calculations of area using $L \times W$ (length times width). Some students have worked together on the problem; others have worked alone.

The teacher opens discussion by asking who would like to present a solution to the problem of finding the most play space for Bozo. A girl comes up to the board and carefully draws a $18 \times 14$-inch rectangular pen on the board. Turning to face the class, she announces that this is the largest pen that can be built with 64 meters of fence. The teacher asks her to explain. (Ball, 1988, p. 3)

The description of the lesson continues for almost four pages, with detailed account of the discussion, the teacher's moves, and the children's work. The section ends with a commentary on the mathematics lesson, but nowhere do I reveal that I am using my own practice as a source for understanding the nature of teaching, that I am "the teacher."

In other research I was doing, my practice was a source for behind-the-scenes work that supported my formal inquiry. For example, in the development of instruments for our longitudinal study of teacher learning at the National Center for Research on Teacher Education, we devised a strategy in which we attempted to probe prospective and practicing teachers' understandings of mathematics and their ideas about teaching and learning, and about students by presenting them with carefully described classroom scenarios. The inspiration for many of these were from experiences I had had in my own teaching. Using situations that I knew arose in trying to teach mathematics—such as a student coming up with an unexpected mathematical idea, or trying to explain something that one has only learned as a rule oneself, or interpreting students' written work—it was possible to design good items to tap teachers' ideas, beliefs, and understandings, and how these interacted in the context of a specific pedagogical situation. The inquiry I had been doing in my own practice was a valuable source of raw material to be shaped into theoretically framed research questions.

In these first two border experiences, practice was guiding research rather than the other way around. Gradually, my continuing work as a teacher became a more explicit and formally designed part of my approach as a scholar. Interested in teacher learning, I was convinced that the ongoing study of teaching, both from the inside and from the sidelines, was essential. I needed to continue to probe the kinds of personal and intellectual resources that seemed to bear on teaching mathematics. Old questions, newly sharpened: What do teachers need to know of and about mathematics in order to teach for understanding? What kinds of understanding, orientation, and belief shape teachers' reasoning, decisions, and moves?

Making progress on such questions requires, in my mind, multiple strategies. One is highly empirical: Watch teachers at work, and analyze what they do; interview them about their reasons, and seek to learn what they know and believe about mathematics and how that interacts with other ideas to shape their moves and decisions. Another is conceptual–analytic: Start with mathematical goals and analyze logically the kinds of understandings that it would take to manage and navigate them in a classroom. A third is a combination of the other two, yet it is radically different, for it looks at practice from the inside: Design a mathematical terrain or course, try to work with a group of students in pursuit of its goals, and examine carefully what it takes to manage that undertaking. What mathematical issues arise? What do students say and do, and what does this require of the teacher? Analyses such as these can offer other illumination of what teachers need to know to teach mathematics.

My own experience as a researcher was convincing me that my history and insight as a teacher were useful resources. I set out to harness and discipline their potential. I sought to develop uses of the first and third approaches—some study of other teachers and some first-person research in which I am the teacher and the researcher. When I study other teachers' practice, I stand back and watch people both like and different from me navigate a curriculum in which I have had no hand. In other work, I examine from the inside what it takes for me to help my students accomplish certain kinds of mathematical goals. I have a firsthand role both in what is being attempted and how it evolves in practice.

# RESEARCH ON AND INTO PRACTICE FROM THE PERSPECTIVE OF THE RESEARCHER-TEACHER

We turn now to take a closer look at research on teaching and learning where the principal investigator of the research is also the teacher and where at least one central goal is to contribute to scholarly discourse communities and to the development of theory.[3] Important to note, first of all, is that, viewed this way, the work can be seen as a special case of the genre of qualitative case studies (Borko, C. Brown, Eisenhart, & Underhill, 1992; C. A. Brown & Cooney, 1982; Eisenhart et al., 1993; Erlwanger 1973; A. Thompson, 1984; T. Wood, Cobb, & Yackel, 1991). Like other case study research, this kind of work interweaves the empirical with the conceptual. It strives to illuminate a broader point, probe a theoretical issue, develop an argument or framework. It faces challenges in convincing others that something worthwhile can be learned from the close probing of a single instance. This raises the crucial question of what any "single instance" is an instance *of* (S. M. Wilson & Gudmunsdottir, 1987).

Take Erlwanger's (1973) analysis of Benny, a well-known study of student learning. The challenges Erlwanger faced in convincing his readers that a close look at Benny can contribute to a much larger set of theoretical and practical issues are similar to those faced by all case study researchers. What is it about the study of this one child that warrants it as part of a larger discourse on learning and teaching? Despite the fact that this is a study of an individual sixth-grade child, this seminal case is not seen merely as a study of a single child's experience in the fractions unit of his sixth-grade class. Rather, it represents an inquiry into, and analysis of, the underside of students' experiences of mathematics teaching and illuminates the gap between what school assessments may reveal and what students may think about the content.

---

[3] The reason to bound it in this way is that an increasing number of such studies are being attempted, in many cases by doctoral students for their dissertation research. It is a quietly growing field of research and, like the early years of ethnography in education, it is at risk as it grows. Explicitly considering what it might take to do such work well, and what the standards of such work would need to be, is crucial. As I have published several articles, all in refereed academic journals, and a number of book chapters, where my teaching is centrally the site for the research, I have been paying attention to precisely these issues. (I have published other pieces that also draw heavily on my teaching, but where my teaching is not the centerpiece of the analysis.)

Few readers would dismiss Erlwanger's piece as an isolated "nonrepresentative case." Nor would many readers worry that Erlwanger relied on so few instances about Benny to make his argument. Readers understand the article to be about problems of learning and assessment, at that time a serious challenge to the enthusiasm for individualized instruction—not a full and extended analysis of Benny. The claims are only in part about Benny.

Research in which researchers use their own practice as teachers as a site for scholarly work is relatively recent. Arising as it does simultaneously with critiques of the dominance of researchers' ideas in what is considered "knowledge of teaching" (Carter, 1990, 1993), such work can be seen as a means to legitimate perspectives of practice in the construction of knowledge about teaching. First-person research enters a teacher's voice and perspective into the discourse of scholarship. However, for the most part, the research on which I focus in this chapter is a form of qualitative case study whose agenda is less centered on the politics of teacher voice and more centered on an epistemology of practice that structures and examines the work from the inside. The researchers are usually university based educators, some with extensive experience as practicing teachers, some with less. What characterizes this kind of work so far?

In this section, I examine three examples of first-person research on teaching and then stand back to comment on the common features of the inquiries: one piece of work each by Magdalene Lampert, Ruth Heaton, and Martin Simon. My emphasis here is on these particular works, not on the researchers themselves or their overall programs of scholarship. Although, in all three pieces the researchers use their own teaching as a centerpiece of their inquiry, there are many differences among them as well.

## Lampert (1986): Inquiry Into Elementary Mathematics Teaching

I begin with Lampert's article, "Knowing, Doing, and Teaching Multiplication," an article she published in *Cognition and Instruction* in 1986. Significant is that this piece was Lampert's first published work using her own teaching as a site for research. Perhaps as significant is that it was also a first for the research community to whom she was writing. The publication of this article in *Cognition and Instruction* marked a watershed in research on teaching and learning, for it was the first piece written by a researcher-teacher to be published in a scholarly journal in the United States.

In this article, Lampert analyzed the teaching and learning of multidigit multiplication in fourth grade.[4] Her question centers on how the computational way of knowing and doing multiplication, which is favored by and more familiar to most teachers and parents, can be intertwined with a more conceptual perspective, commonly the domain of mathematicians. Lampert sought to explore instructional strategies that favor neither computational nor conceptual approaches, but rather foster connections between these two ways of knowing mathematics. She used her teaching of fourth grade, explaining at the outset that:

> The classroom research reported here is not oriented toward conclusions about how to teach the multiplication of large numbers. . . . It is intended to be conjectural—that is, to outline an approach to instruction that is "worth trying" (cf. Noddings, 1985)—and is grounded in actual classroom experimentation. (p. 306)

Lampert asked what it means to know multiplication and identified four different ways of knowing it. A first is computational: counting or memorizing or performing operations on numbers. A second is intuitive, as in milkmen counting their units of milk on racks (Scribner, 1984). A third is concrete, that is, manipulating objects to find answers with such tools as base-10 blocks for grouping and trading. Principled knowledge, a final way of knowing, is procedural knowledge that includes understanding of why the procedures are warranted.

Based on observations of student work and on theoretical knowledge about cognition, Lampert set out to explore the potential for certain forms of classroom instruction that would allow for the strengthening of connections among these different ways of knowing multiplication. She described three experimental lessons that she taught to her fourth-graders. Each lesson that she designed used a different kind of multiplication problem: The first used coin problems, such as "Using only two kinds of coins, make $1.00 with 19 coins." The second used stories and pictures to link the concreteness of the coin problems with the third

---

[4]Worth noting is that 1986 predated the NCTM *Standards* (1989, 1991b, 1995). Lampert's (1986) analysis in this article of her efforts to teach multiplication contributed to the development of images of the possible in school mathematics teaching. Such images were critical to the mathematics education community as the NCTM began its major undertaking of defining and developing articulated views of curriculum, assessment, and teaching.

set of problems that were symbolic in form but highly narrated with conceptual terms. With structured experiences in decomposition and recomposition strategies and orders of operations, the three experimental lessons represented Lampert's operating conjecture about how to link different ways of knowing multiplication for her students. Her teaching of these three kinds of problems was part of her experiment in pursuing the conjecture. Designing both the problems and the pedagogy, Lampert constructed a context in which to investigate how students might be helped to "know" multiplication in the different ways she had posited. In her observations of students, she found evidence that they were inventing procedures using mathematical principles and that they had come to see mathematics as more than a set of procedures for finding answers.

In the last section of the article, Lampert moved away from the specific context of multidigit multiplication to consider larger questions about the teaching and learning of mathematics in school. She used the outcomes of her experimental lessons to argue that fourth-graders can do mathematics and think mathematically, that they are capable of learning to represent their thinking, to listen to one another, and to invent useful and sensible, problem-solving strategies. She described the kind of teaching that she thought would allow children to develop mathematical skill and confidence:

> I would suggest that they need to be asked questions whose answers can be "figured out" not by relying on memorized rules for moving numbers around but by thinking about what numbers and symbols mean. They need to be treated like sense-makers rather than rememberers and forgetters. They need to see connections between what they are supposed to be learning in school and things they care about understanding outside of school, and these connections need to be related to the substance of what they are supposed to be learning. They need to learn to do computation competently and efficiently without losing sight of the meaning of what they are doing and its relation to solving real problems. The lessons I have taught and described here suggest that it is possible to do these things in a conventional school classroom. (p. 340)

Lampert's work also generates questions about the epistemology of mathematics and the ways in which this kind of teaching might alter or challenge students' and teachers' conceptions of mathematics as a discipline. She described her role as a teacher thus:

My role is to bring students' ideas about how to solve or analyze problems into the public forum of the classroom, to referee arguments about whether those ideas were reasonable, and to sanction students' intuitive use of mathematical principles as legitimate. I also taught new information in the form of symbolic structures and emphasized the connection between symbols and operations on quantities, but I made it a classroom requirement that students use their own ways of deciding whether something was mathematically reasonable in doing the work. (p. 339)

How are these processes of acquiring mathematical knowledge related to the nature of mathematical knowledge itself? How will these ways of teaching and learning mathematics in the classroom affect teachers' and students' abilities to understand higher mathematics? How might they limit their future appreciation of other meanings and uses of multiplication? Ultimately, Lampert asked how disciplinary dispositions are, and can be, acquired, and used her teaching as evidence of what is possible. Whether and how this would play out in other classrooms is not a question she sought to answer, but she concluded by saying that it would be useful to understand what the outcomes for students might be over the long run and what it might take to do this sort of teaching and learning in other classrooms.

What does working on Lampert's questions from the inside offer? Lampert examined whether more computational ways of knowing and doing multiplication might be integrated fruitfully in teaching fourth grade. Rather than choosing to emphasize concrete and conceptual modes over symbolic ones, she sought to develop an approach that intertwines and connects different elements of knowing and doing multiplication and to see how it works. Being the teacher as well as the researcher afforded Lampert a space in which to work that is not easily available otherwise.

The approach to teaching multiplication in which she was interested is rare in practice. Although Lampert may not be alone in imagining such instruction, instances of it in action do not abound. Lampert could not simply locate a classroom with this sort of mathematics teaching. As such, Lampert had to create an instance of such teaching in order to examine how it works. This experiment also allowed her to probe what students are capable of doing in alternative instructional settings.

As creator and critic, designer and analyst, Lampert had to keep her eye on what would count as legitimate claims from her work. One kind of claim can of course be local, about what she did with these students on this topic. What did she do? How did it play out for the class and for particular children? What did the students learn? Although these sorts of analyses matter, they are not what matters most, for they situate knowledge in particulars. Knowing about Ko's (one of her students) thinking is not immediately of use to others.

So what can others learn from Lampert's work about settings, students, and content different from hers? She proposed two implications of her work, one derived from the work her students did in the context of her approach and the second raised from the very structure of the design itself—her teaching. First, Lampert claimed that the work her students did "raises theoretical questions about the relationship of intuitive, concrete, and computational knowledge . . . and principled conceptual knowledge" (p. 337). Did the students know to use principles because they had had direct experience with the ideas in a concrete realm? Were they understanding what they were doing or were they simply applying a procedure from one context to another? Could the teacher be seen as reconnecting procedures to their conceptual underpinnings? These are all important questions about how to help students develop both conceptual and procedural understandings of mathematics. Lampert's examples offer insight into what the composition of these understandings can look like, and her analyses of the connections offer readers ways to look at other students.

Lampert took a second tack as well. She claimed that, in addition to the potential insights into the development of mathematical understanding of concepts and procedures, her work also raises questions about the nature of teaching and of the teacher's role in helping students to learn. She suggested that what she was doing as the teacher offers an example to be scrutinized about the ways in which teachers might bridge students' intuitive and procedural understandings with formal abstract principles. Lampert argued that, viewed this way, teaching mathematics "content" is not easily separated from developing a culture of mathematical sense making. Her examples illustrate this bond and offer readers an image of a different conception of the teacher's role in students' learning to know and do mathematics.

In Lampert's work, then, we see that in order to pursue the question she had about learning to know and do multiplication in ways that linked different ways of knowing mathematics, Lampert had to create the context for her research. In creating the context, she also produced an instance worth examining of what is entailed in such creation—hence, insights into the nature of instruction and of the teacher's role. As researcher of these questions, she used herself as teacher. And as teacher, she created new possibilities not only for practice, but for research.

We turn next to Heaton's work, which contrasts with Lampert's both in focus and design. Whereas Lampert studied student learning in the context of teaching, Heaton studied teacher learning in the context of teaching. Moreover, unlike Lampert, Heaton did not explicitly set out to design a context for her study. Instead, as a teacher, she found herself in a challenging situation ripe with possibilities for inquiry. An experienced and skilled teacher, Heaton found herself struggling to change her teaching from a traditional approach to one grounded in reform ideas about good teaching. What she found difficult, and why, as well as what helped her to learn, emerged as important questions worth examining in a disciplined way. These questions were of interest more broadly, for Heaton was not alone in the struggle to remake herself as a teacher of mathematics.

## Heaton (1994): Inquiry into Changing One's Practice

In her dissertation research, *Creating and Studying a Practice of Teaching Elementary Mathematics for Understanding*, Heaton (1940) framed her inquiry by asking, "What would it take to teach elementary mathematics in ways envisioned by the current reforms in mathematics education? What struggles would be experienced by teachers as they transform their teaching?" (p. ii). To explore these questions, Heaton studied her own mathematics teaching in a fourth-grade classroom. She described her own education beginning with elementary school, her experiences in school mathematics, her teacher education program, and her years of successful teaching in various settings. Without fanfare, she let the reader know that she was awarded "Teacher of the Year" in Vermont. In her doctoral work, Heaton was exposed to reform ideas about mathematics teaching and her world began to change. As part of a research project on which she worked, Heaton (1992) did fieldwork, following two teachers in California in their efforts to teach mathematics in the context of the massive wave of reform. She began to wonder if she, an experienced teacher, could do the kind of teaching reformers were promoting, and she arranged to teach mathematics for a year in a local fourth grade. Although it was developed before the NCTM *Standards*, the curriculum in use in that school reflected many aspects of the contemporary reform visions of mathematics teaching and learning. However, the task of changing her teaching turned out to be even more challenging than she had anticipated and, after the fact, she decided to make her efforts to change her teaching the focus of her research.

What does working on Heaton's questions "from the inside" offer? Heaton analyzed the challenges of learning to teach mathematics for understanding by documenting her own learning over the course of that year. The going was tough at times. Despite the fact that the curriculum was scripted, Heaton got stuck as she struggled to understand the design of a lesson. She lost her mathematical bearings in the middle of class discussions. Everything seemed to take longer than the teacher's guide indicated, and she felt herself falling behind. Her frustration and embarrassment well up repeatedly.

What can others learn from Heaton's struggles? In documenting and analyzing this year of teaching, Heaton sought to make claims regarding the challenges that might face any teacher attempting to take on the task of teaching this way:

> What is it that I—an experienced and successful elementary school teacher—have had to learn to make fundamental changes in my mathematics teaching? More broadly, I was asking: What do teachers need to know, care about and be disposed to do to teach mathematics for understanding?" (p. 90)

To manage the fact that she was studying her own learning, which meant that she—the very object and tool of her own inquiry—was changing even as she was conducting her research, Heaton invented a methodological strategy that afforded her separation from herself by using different voices to represent different points on her trajectory: Ruth 1, the self that was doing the teaching at the time; Ruth 2, the self that was reflecting on that teaching at the time; and Ruth 3, the self that made sense 3 years later of the teaching she did during that year.

Heaton came to a number of realizations about the challenge of what she set out to do. For example, she saw that she lacked understanding about the purposes and significance of specific content and about how mathematical ideas interconnect. She suspected that becoming more fluent in conceptual understandings of mathematical ideas will help her to be more able to listen to students' understandings and to guide fruitful conversations about them. Heaton learns that she could no longer use the textbook as a strict timetable for where this kind of teaching might take her and her class. She saw that this kind of teaching would require an ability to see multiple ways of representing a mathematical issue.

Some of Heaton's analysis focuses more on the pedagogical aspects of the work. She learned the importance of what she called "improvisation" in teaching, that is, "to be responsive to students' understanding and to the mathematics" (p. 222). She struggled with managing disagreements in the classroom, both the content and the standards of discourse. Heaton came to think that this kind of teaching would require "sharing the lead" with her students, a practice to which she was unaccustomed.

Ultimately, Heaton concluded that "continuous invention of a practice is inherent to the work of teaching mathematics for understanding" (p. 341). The metaphor of invention captures this kind of mathematics pedagogy for Heaton this kind of teaching is necessarily situation-specific, it is fundamentally responsive to the particular students in a given context, and because coming to know mathematics is intimately linked with the ways that knowledge is constructed. Heaton then proposed some ways in which prospective and experienced teachers might prepare for the endemic uncertainties of this kind of teaching. One is "educative curricula," materials that could enrich teachers' understandings of mathematical concepts and help them to anticipate student thinking based on these deep understandings of the mathematical terrain, its relevance, and its interconnectedness. Learning to teach this way will require a capacity for seeing, creating, and choosing among a wide repertoire of options at a given moment of practice. It will demand an ability to anticipate, hear, and interpret students' understandings. It will depend on a deep knowledge of mathematics, and a sense of its fundamental questions and ideas, how they interrelate and their purposes in the curriculum. Finally, it will acknowledge the tentative and uncertain nature that this kind of teaching entails.

In Heaton's work, we have an example of studying from the inside what it takes to change one's practice from good traditional teaching to teaching in the spirit of the reforms. The changes entailed are not minor. The reforms lead teachers to reconsider fundamental aspects of who they are, the role they play in their students' learning, the way they establish and maintain the classroom culture, the content they teach. These changes are at the core of teachers' identities and practice. Heaton's experience not only helps us analyze what it takes to manage the challenges of trying to change, but also offers us something Lampert's does not: what it is *like* to face these changes. What does it feel like? What arises? This understanding, not readily accessible from the outside, is important in seeking to understand the challenges of teacher learning and change.

We turn next to a third case of studying teaching from the inside: Simon, a teacher-educator, conducted his research in the context of his own teaching of mathematics methods. Like Lampert, Simon designed his context as a site for his inquiry. But like Heaton, Simon's focus was on teachers' learning.

## Simon (1995): Inquiry into Mathematics Teacher Education

For this last case, I examine M. Simon's "Reconstructing Mathematics Pedagogy From a Constructivist Perspective," published in the *Journal for Research in Mathematics Education* in 1995. Simon's point of departure is that although constructivist views have provided rich models of how students learn, they do not extend to how teachers should teach. He pointed to the lack of theoretical frameworks for a pedagogy of mathematics consistent with constructivist theory. Several reasons account for this, according to Simon. First, some assume "constructivist teaching" as a direct entailment of learning theory. This common view is often simplistic, envisioning a removed and inactive teacher whose role is principally one of noninterference in students' learning. Second, within research on learning, many projects focus on individual learners; fewer look at classrooms. A third source of this gap emerges from a disjuncture between research on teaching and research on learning. Because researchers who study teachers' thinking, beliefs, and practices rarely end up studying teachers who have "well-developed constructivist perspectives and [are] implementing reform ideas" (p. 118), more such research is done in traditional settings. Consequently, research on teaching has focused on relatively traditional practice, whereas research on learning has focused on constructivism. These reasons combine to create a gap between theories of learning and theories of instruction.

M. Simon identified some research that has focused on mathematics teaching grounded in a constructivist perspective, particularly on the deliberative and design aspects of practice—selecting tasks or problems, choosing representations, and facilitating the development of community (e.g., Ball, 1993a; Brousseau, 1981; Cobb, T. Wood, & Yackel, 1993; Lampert, 1990). Simon positioned his work to extend and elaborate this line of inquiry. Designing what he called a "teaching experiment," he set out to analyze situations in which a constructivist perspective on learning comes up against "realities of real students in real classrooms" (p. 121) in order to bridge what he saw as a critical disjuncture between the development of theories of learning and of teaching. What is the nature of the design work when constructivist theory underlies the pedagogy?

To pursue this question, Simon studied his own teaching of prospective elementary teachers within an experimental teacher preparation program consisting of a mathematics course, a course on mathematics teaching and learning, and two practica. The goals of the program he designed were to increase beginning teachers' knowledge of mathematics and to develop their understanding of mathematics teaching and learning consistent with current theory and reform documents such as the NCTM *Standards*. Through analysis of his own actions as a teacher in this context, Simon develops a model of teaching and teacher decision-making that is rooted in constructivism. Being the teacher gives him inside access to a case of a teacher working within twin commitments to content and to students' thinking.

In his analysis, Simon sought to make his own pedagogical decision making in posing problems explicit. He attended carefully to the hypotheses that he made about what the learners might learn and what he might do to foster this learning. These hypotheses are based on his knowledge of the mathematics content and his knowledge about how students learn mathematics. He found that his hypotheses were constantly changing, based on his work with his students, and this led him to develop new problems that would address his revised hypotheses about what students might learn. Simultaneously, his own understanding of mathematics content and his knowledge about how students learn mathematics were altered. For example, he wrote:

> As we proceeded to explore the multiplicative relationship involved in evaluating the area of a rectangle, I came to believe that the context in which we were working (area) was not well understood by many of the students. They seemed to think about area as generated by multiplying length times width. Although my primary focus was on multiplicative relationships, not on area, it seemed clear that an understanding of area was necessary in order for students to think about constituting the quantity (area) and evaluating that quantity. What action could I take as a teacher? (p. 127)

Through such deliberation and reflection on his students' understandings and misunderstandings, Simon revised his hypotheses about what they might learn and how to go about providing contexts that would foster such learning.

What does working on Simon's questions from the inside offer? Using his own teaching, Simon was able to probe practice that is grounded in constructivist theories of learning. He saw patterns emerging in his teaching role that constitute what he called the mathematical teaching cycle. This model includes what Simon called the "hypothetical learning trajectory," which is determined by the teacher's original learning goal, the learning activities, and the thinking and learning that the teacher predicts will occur. He called it "hypothetical" because it cannot be known in advance and students' learning often does not proceed exactly as predicted. In order to plan, the teacher must form viable hypotheses about how the learning trajectory might develop and design on the basis of those hypotheses. Surrounding this hypothetical learning trajectory is the mathematical teaching cycle, which draws on other areas of teacher knowledge: the teacher's theories of learning and teaching mathematics, the teacher's mathematical content knowledge, and the teacher's knowledge about materials, problems, and activities. Reflexively, what happens in the classroom is informed by these areas of teacher knowledge and, in turn, informs the teacher's knowledge. In Simon's model, the teacher's hypothetical learning trajectory is continually modified to take into account the teacher's expanding knowledge about his students.

Simon also noticed other aspects about his role as a teacher in this kind of mathematics teaching. One is the experimental nature of teaching, which is exemplified by the discrepancy he found in the amount of time that he had planned to dedicate to certain topics and the amount of time that these topics actually occupied. Precisely because the teacher bases his planning on hypotheses about what students know and how they will learn, the actual process may take longer or shorter amounts of time. Second, again because the teacher bases his planning on hypotheses about student understandings and because he revises his activities, goals, and hypotheses in response to what he perceives to be actual student understandings in various contexts, he cannot perfectly anticipate the hurdles that students may encounter as they work on the ideas. Third, in appraising his teaching episodes, Simon concluded that he was not able to provoke the disequilibrium that he believed would be useful in his students' learning. He came to believe that he could only attempt to promote disequilibrium, that this attempt is predicated on sometimes inadequate pictures of his students' understandings, and that learning does not proceed in a linear fashion.

Working from analyses of these particular cases, Simon developed the mathematical teaching cycle to describe a more general model of pedagogy based on constructivist views of learning. At the same time, he was cautious about how the data from this study will apply to other contexts. For example, teaching students in a teacher education program is distinct from teaching third-graders mathematics in some ways. Still, the mathematics teaching cycle suggests ways teachers might think about mathematics pedagogy, with particular emphasis on the ability to generate hypotheses about student understandings, to form hypothetical learning trajectories, and to consider the conceptual knowledge of the mathematics being taught. Further, the model strives to address the inherent tension in teaching this way: the tension between teacher planfulness on the one hand, and responsiveness to students on the other.

From the inside, Simon examined this tension of planfulness and response. Using this tension, he proposed a model of teaching centered in the teacher's role in guiding student learning in relation to considered mathematical goals. This role is framed by both attention to students and analysis of the mathematical terrain, composed in an iterative cycle of design and revision. With a close view of the nature of this effort in practice, including its uncertainties and challenges, its imperfections and struggles, he was able to specify a theoretically grounded, normative model of design and construction in teaching.

## What Is Distinctive About First-Person Research?

In some ways, these researcher-teacher, first-person projects might appear to be highly similar to other case study research. However, two features characterize important distinctions. First, design—not only of the methodology but also of the phenomenon and its context as well—plays a critical role. Instead of merely studying what they find, they begin with an issue and design a context in which to pursue it. The issue with which they begin is at once theoretical and practical, rooted in everyday challenges of practice but also situated in a larger scholarly discourse, and they create a way to examine and develop that issue further. What they ultimately focus on may emerge out of the situation and its unfolding, but they have an important hand in constructing fundamental features of the arena of study.

Lampert (1986) began by identifying a long-standing divide about the aims of school mathematics. On one side are the many school people who focus on computational skill; on the other are mathematicians for whom abstract mathematical principles and structures are central. She set out to examine how these different ideas about knowing mathematics might be designed to interplay in real classroom practice. Through her own efforts to teach multidigit multiplication to fourth-graders, Lampert explored what is possible in a regular classroom in which making principled knowledge of mathematics connected to procedures is a central aim. What does that look like? What is entailed?

Heaton (1994) started with the practical problem of experienced teachers who face the sea change of ideas about elementary mathematics teaching, and she raised central theoretical questions about making these kinds of fundamental changes in one's practice. Using her personal experience of change to study experienced teacher learning, she probed not only what happens, or what it takes to do this, but also what it is like. She developed a strategy for straddling the inside and the outside, moving across time and perspective to look with precision at the work involved in facing off with the demands and opportunities of change.

M. Simon (1995) began with a different concern, one more rooted in theory but with direct connections to practice. Arguing that constructivist theory (which has been so central to recent developments in mathematics education) is not a theory of pedagogy, he sought to develop a model of the design work entailed in using constructivist principles as the root of a pedagogy of mathematics. He used his own teaching to posit a provisional theoretical model that can capture elements of this design process in other mathematics teaching contexts.

Each of these researchers can be seen as conducting research in which the phenomenon they want to study must be *designed* in order to study it. Rather than studying what is, they work in a mode closer to what Ann Brown (1992), citing Allan Collins, referred to as "design experiments."[5] More like certain work in the "design sciences," such as aeronautics or artificial intelligence, this approach to research on teaching and learning involves both designing an educational innovation and simultaneously studying it. The design work does not proceed linearly; instead, the design is iteratively adjusted in the course of the research. The adjustments are themselves objects of study, and contribute to theory building.

Unlike Brown, however, Lampert, Heaton, and Simon are themselves firsthand tools of the research on teaching. Lampert (1985) described this as using the self as a tool in teaching and in research on teaching, and later she (Lampert, 1995) cited Garrison's (1995) observation that "the teacher is the most fundamental technology in educational practice." The designs of these three first-person researchers require their skilled hand and eye in construction; in different ways, their questions require them to be inside the interplay of design and construction.

In Lampert's case, her design is a kind of teaching and learning, and she studied its features in practice. She produced an image of a kind of teaching and learning and probed its elements, seeking also to describe it in ways that make the pursuit of its principles viable in real classrooms. As such, creating it in a regular, fourth-grade classroom is an essential part of the approach. Like Brown, Lampert wanted to build description and theory in the "blooming, buzzing confusion" of real classrooms (A. L. Brown, 1992, p. 141). Simon took this one step further: His project was to create a theory of design. So his teaching efforts, including the creation in process, were the objects of inquiry. Being the designer of the teaching gave him intimate access to the processes and considerations of design. For both Lampert and Simon, to have another teacher do the teaching would be to introduce issues of teacher learning that would interfere with their aims in these particular projects. Lampert wanted to shape the

---

[5]It might be helpful here, too, to examine the similarities and differences between *design experiments* and *teaching experiments*, because the latter term is used so much more in the mathematics education community and literature.

teaching in particular ways and to adjust her designs to keep her eye on a kind of learning. Simon wanted to study the complex intricacies of design. In both cases, being both designer and builder was essential to their goals. Heaton, in intriguing contrast to the other two, also used only herself but made teacher learning a major focus of the analysis by examining closely what she confronted and had to learn in trying to create the kind of teaching she envisioned.

First-person research offers the researcher a role in creating the phenomenon to be investigated coupled with the capacity to examine it from the inside, to learn that which is less visible. As architect, builder, and critic, the researcher-teacher moves fluidly and without interference across roles and functions of the work. These features make possible many inquiries that would be difficult to pursue from the outside. Still, first-person research is threaded with challenges. We turn next to an examination of three special issues, one related to questions, one related to stance, and a third related to claims.

# SPECIAL VALUES AND PITFALLS OF THE FIRST-PERSON PERSPECTIVE

Considering these three cases of first-person research offers a preliminary glimpse of what such inquiries make possible. Researchers may design experimentally contexts, curricula, modes of teaching, experiences, or situations that they want to be able to probe. Rather than having to find an instance of the phenomenon in which they are interested, they can create it and then study it. Moreover, in some cases, the challenge is the creation, and having a firsthand role in the construction offers the opportunity to study what it takes to enact a certain kind of teaching, classroom, or curriculum. Another possibility of first-person research is to access, uncover, and probe elements of the situation or experience invisible to the outsider. What is it like to do this sort of teaching? What tensions arise? What are the feelings entailed? What are the incentives? What is the underlying reasoning?

## Research Questions: Connecting Problem and Perspective

Studying teaching and learning from the inside is not equally fruitful, or even generative, for all questions. It is useful to ask, for a given question, whether and how the first-person perspective can play a role.

For example, consider Heaton's central focus on the effort to change her mathematics teaching. What was it like to try to make the kinds of changes she was trying to make? What did she struggle with? How did she feel about it along the way, and what experiences stood out as critical? Certainly, it is possible to imagine a researcher following another teacher around, seeking to understand the experience of a teacher engaged in significant changes in her practice. Such a researcher would interview the teacher about what she was doing and why, how it was different from what she usually did. The researcher might try to probe what the teacher knew and believed, and what she was learning, and might seek to describe and analyze her practice. She might talk with the teacher and try to understand the challenges of the work. This would be useful. But the researcher would also be limited. Aspects of the teacher's experience, of the struggle, would not be readily evident or easy to probe. What Heaton was able to probe about the work of changing one's teaching was different from this. Heaton sought to explore, and later represent, the journey of a serious effort to change one's teaching, using her own firsthand experience as a window onto the process. It was the experienced teacher's embarrassments, chagrins, and sources of exhilaration that she wanted to capture and analyze. From the vantage point of her own experience, she recorded what she did and felt, and she created analyzable data from that experience. The data she was able to capture and later analyze were different from those that would have been collected by another researcher. That she was able to do it was not simply that she was "there," however; I return to this later.

By way of contrast, imagine wanting to study how different children experience the curriculum and pedagogy of a mathematics class and what they are learning. Investigating this likely would require watching, listening, and talking to various children. It would mean probing their reactions and making it safe for them to be as candid as possible about other students, about the class, about the teacher. It would mean examining both generously and skeptically what they seem to be learning.

What might be the contribution of the first-person perspective in this case? The teacher has an ongoing relationship with students that may permit her to know them more closely than would someone less involved with the class. The teacher has access to detail of the class that others would not: She may be able to sense tender issues, may know about particular pivotal episodes, and may understand the children's talk and manner in ways that others would not. She knows the history of shared examples, problems, and discussions that she can use to probe the children's ideas and experiences. At the same time, her relationship with the children is itself a central part of their experience of the class. What might they not want to say to her? What might it be risky to disclose? Moreover, the teacher's commitment to help children can impede the capacity to see and hear problems and difficulties. She may not be able to notice subtle ways in which her manner affects particular children and, hence, may not be able to probe their responses. She may want the children to understand and to learn so much that a necessary skepticism is difficult to maintain. Quite naturally, it may not be easy to see how particular activities or discourse modes might be experienced in ways quite different from what she had intended, and thus she would not be able to ask students about things they themselves do not raise.

Turn for a moment away from research on mathematics teaching, to explore a rich and well-developed example of first-person research in another area, elementary school writing: namely, the work of Timothy Lensmire (1991, 1994). Lensmire's study of the writing workshop in his fourth-grade classroom faced challenges of the first-person perspective. His management of the role of researcher-teacher illuminates the interplay of agendas present in this work and what it might mean to exploit the first-person perspective for ends aimed pointedly at both theory and practice. The writing workshop, as a pedagogical structure, is envisioned by its designers as a means to change traditional writing instruction in school, which rarely provides opportunities for students to develop voice and to play with language and text. According to Lensmire (1994), "with the support of the teacher and numerous opportunities to collaborate and share texts with peers, children [in writing workshop classrooms] are supposed to gradually become more and more able to realize their intentions in text" (p. 3). Working from a design already in part created, Lensmire sought to construct a substantial workshop in his classroom, and to study it. He intended to describe the workshop and to investigate his experiences as the teacher trying to create it. But, as he acknowledged wryly, the story he had to tell afterwards was different from the one he had expected to be telling. Children wrote unkind things about one another, and the freedom of expression afforded an open door for class and gender biases from the wide society. Absent an explicitly political agenda of social challenge, the writing workshop surfaced a host of problems that he had not anticipated. He was faced with being both designer and builder, not simply the observer and analyst of the construction—a fundamental change in his envisioned project, which he turned to insightful advantage.

Though teachers' questions "often emerge from discrepancies between what is intended and what occurs" (Cochran-Smith & Lytle, 1990, p. 5), many teachers would not have taken the simultaneously theoretical and practical tack on the problems that Lensmire accomplished. Instead, they would have worked primarily to alter the shape of the classroom culture and the children's participation with one another. This classroom might also have been studied from an outside researcher's perspective, that of a participant-observer, who might have probed the interaction of sociological, personal, and pedagogical dimensions of Lensmire's classroom. But Lensmire, as the researcher-teacher, turned neither to an adjustment of his classroom nor to a probing study of the social class and gender dynamics.  Instead, he adapted his study to what was happening in his class. He took his pedagogical puzzle and worked on it while he also probed the complex theoretical tangles it revealed within romantic ideals for the improvement of schools. He documented and analyzed his struggles to guide and direct the children's writing and interactions. How to manage the commitment to let children find their voices, to write about the topics they chose, in the ways they wanted, and also create a classroom dedicated to social and political commitments of equity and respect? As the teacher, Lensmire was ideally situated to probe this pedagogical tension. At the same time, he needed to understand different children's experiences in his class in order to grasp the complexity of the dilemma into which he had collided headlong. Recognizing the limits of his own position to probe in the ways he wanted, he engaged colleagues in interviewing children in the class. His colleagues helped to focus the questions students were asked, and they were able to delve in ways that he might not have been able to. In this manner, Lensmire was able to design a strategy that allowed him access to students' perspectives in ways that complemented his own perceptions and experiences, but without complicating the data collection with his complex role as both researcher and teacher.

In considering the appropriateness of the first-person perspective for a particular research agenda, three questions are crucial. First, does the phenomenon in which the researcher is interested exist? Does the researcher have a conjecture or image of a kind of teaching, an approach to curriculum, or a type of classroom that is not out there to be studied? And, if it is this need to create the phenomenon that underlies the impulse to engage in first-person research, does the researcher think he or she is particularly well equipped to be designer, developer, and enactor of the practice or would an experienced practitioner be a more reliable partner in this construction? Second, is what the researcher wants to know uniquely accessible from the inside or would an outsider be able to access this issue as well, or perhaps better? Third, is the question at hand one in which other scholars have an interest, or should have an interest, and if so, will probing the inside of a particular design offer perspectives crucial to a larger discourse?

## Scholarly Stance: Composing Distance and Insight

Studying teaching from the first-person perspective offers a special kind of personal inside view that is difficult to gain through even close participant observation. Because teaching and learning are deeply personal—that is, they are in fundamental ways relational and about persons—approaches to scholarship that use the personal as a resource offer the possibility of insights that are more difficult to gain from an outsider's perspective. Some aspects of experience are inarticulable; the chasm between what we know and what we can say is variable, but rarely closed. Limited in what can be asked or explained across any interpersonal divide, a challenge for the inside perspective is how the inarticulable can be represented, probed, and ultimately examined. Ironically, such scholarship depends also on a kind of distance between the researcher and the context and problems of study. How does the first-person researcher create the conversation with herself that makes it possible to excavate, name, and analyze aspects of experience unseen to the outsider?

Disciplined inquiry relies inherently on both faith and doubt: The researcher needs to listen and watch sympathetically, assuming that people in the setting make sense, but must also notice strange or discontinuous events or phenomena. If the researcher remains entirely inside the experience, the critical edge needed for analysis is difficult to establish; what remains may be more narrative than research.

Because research methodology is so often fraught with imperatives to separate the self from the inquiry, we need to develop disciplined methods that deliberately use the self as a tool to construct insights, perspectives, and knowledge that expand our capacity to know (Krieger, 1991). At the same time we need to guard against the tendency toward the personal on the basis of some kind of basic appeal or, worse, naive ideas about what constitutes knowledge. That it is asserted from the first-person perspective cannot make it automatically true.

What is entailed in managing the first-person perspective in the construction of this stance? One thing it implies is that researchers using this approach must be able to treat their experiments, settings, and work as matters for scrutiny. They must be able to view the teaching, the students, and the learning in the context of, but also apart from, their efforts and desires. For example, when examining videotape from his classroom, the researcher-teacher must cultivate a stance of inquiry and curiosity and must overcome a natural urge to defend against questions others raise. This is complicated, for it must be combined with an insider perspective. At the same time, to silence the interior voice, to deny the personal is to undo the very project of first-person research, shutting out part of what is experienced on the inside. In part, this kind of research requires both an unusual concentration on, and use of, self, combined with an almost unnatural suspension of the personal.

How can the researcher work to gain alternative perspectives and interpretations of his own and others' actions and thoughts in the session, while also seeking to use the intimate and the personal as resources? Heaton (1994) managed this problem by inventing a methodological device of distancing herself by using Ruth 1, Ruth 2, and Ruth 3, to separate her data and vantage point across the work. Ruth 1 is what she named the teacher teaching and struggling online to reconstruct her teaching. Ruth 2 is the teacher who was making sense of that teaching and learning and who offers perspectives gained through the reflective writing, recorded conversations, and journal exchanges of the teacher during that same school year, but with a temporal distance from particular events. These entries capture the interpretive work of the teacher involved in the challenges of inventing and relearning how she teaches mathematics. Ruth 3 is the perspective of the teacher, 3 years later, who knows the experiences intimately but who has increased conceptual distance on them. Heaton explained her struggles as a researcher, trying to sort out her "multiple selves":

> What makes the work of this study somewhat more complicated is that not
> only do the multiple selves at any given point in time matter, a particular
> self changes over time. Since the point is . . . to understand my learning,
> the changes in self are important to analyze and represent. (p. 64)

Using these temporally distinct selves helped Heaton to focus on the changes in herself, crucial because hers was a study of her own learning as a teacher. The device of multiple Ruths allowed her access to the different perspectives and experiences that she had recorded across time and also afforded her a stance in analyzing the data. This problem of using the self while also standing back from it is an endemic challenge of this kind of work. Getting clear about ways to do it is highly related to the claims one wants to be able to make.

## Claims: Navigating the General and Particular

Close study of a single teacher, in a particular setting, with specific content and students, no matter how carefully done or how captivating, always raises questions about the domain of the results. What are the claims of the work about? This problem is still greater in first-person research because the fusion of researcher and teacher can make location of the claims still more complex. At times, moving beyond the particulars can be difficult because of the tight interconnection of voice, experience, and analysis. At other times, the researcher's interest in theory can excessively inflate the level of claims. That the author is both subject and narrator, both actor and critic raises special questions about the nature of claims born of first-person research. Answers to these questions are crucial for the disciplined development of the insider perspective in inquiry.

About the three cases in this chapter, we ask: Are Lampert's claims about Lampert and what she did? Is Heaton merely retelling the troubles she encountered? Is Simon showing what he did in his teacher education classes? Or are their claims about teaching, or learning, more generally? How do the claims of these three authors relate to the questions, stance, and design of their research? After reading Lampert, Heaton, or Simon, what are we to think about? What new insights have we gleaned? What do we understand differently, and are there special issues in separating from the interplay of the person of the researcher and the claims of the research?

Let us consider Lampert first. Surely we are not primarily to understand how she, as an individual teacher, taught multiplication. Neither was she merely trying to show us the problems she personally encountered with this group of students in East Lansing, Michigan, over 10 years ago. If not that, then what? Near the end of her article, Lampert wrote:

> The experimental lessons described in this article stand as evidence that fourth-graders can do mathematics and think mathematically. - - - The lessons I have taught and described here suggest that it is possible to do these things in a conventional school classroom. (p. 340)

One claim of Lampert's work is that the sort of work that her students were doing in learning about multiplication is work that one can expect other fourth-graders to do. How is this general claim related to the analyses in the article? At first glance, Lampert's students do not seem atypical. She described her 28 students as ranging widely in computational skill, hence, like many other fourth-grade classes. She placed a heavy emphasis on the teaching that shaped their opportunities to learn mathematics, implying that it is the opportunity to use information, organize it strategically, generate and test conjectures, and experiment with solutions and solution methods that matters. The particularity is here, in Lampert's approach. As readers, we know little about how bound up with her and her personal style and understanding the pedagogical design may be. She strove to de-center the description from herself, asking instead, "What sort of help do children need from *adults* in order to do these things and to be confident in their ability to do them" (p. 341)? Lampert described her approach to teaching, focusing in particular on the structure of asking students to explain how they "figured out" their answers (asked even when the answer is not conventionally correct).

She explained that she had two reasons for doing this: first, to give herself a glimpse of how students are thinking and what they are using to reason mathematically, and, second, to cultivate the intellectual habit of moving the locus of authority from the teacher and the answer key to the students as knowers and to standards of mathematical evidence.

Lampert used her classroom as a setting for creating particularly designed opportunities for learning mathematics. As such, her claims are about what is possible for students to do and to think about, not what is or must be. That she was the teacher of the class means that she was able to work from inside the design. The architecture of the class—its pedagogy and curriculum—is hers in concert with her students. In seeking to explore and later to show readers what is possible, she used herself as designer and builder. This affords her the opportunity to make claims about what is possible. She was, in A. L. Brown's (1992) terms, clearly working as "a design scientist. . . . [attempting] to engineer [an] innovative educational environment" (p. 141) and, at the same time, studying what happens in such an environment—what students do, what struggles she faced as a teacher, how the mathematics develops. Lampert acknowledged that if the objective was to examine closely both instructional strategies and learning, then other programs of research might need to be designed that were more rigorous. Her claims are not about what to do, but about the nature of curricular aims in mathematics education and what it might be possible to aim for pedagogically. In her design to "[reconnect] principled conceptual knowledge with procedural knowledge" (p. 338) on the argument that these connections have been severed in most school instruction, Lampert claimed that this can be done in a regular school.

Simon's teaching experiment in preservice mathematics teacher education yields a different kind of result or claim. He used his analysis of three teaching episodes from his own mathematics methods teaching to develop a provisional general theory of pedagogy based on constructivist principles of learning. He saw this as crucial because:

> Although constructivism provides a useful framework for thinking about mathematics learning in classrooms and therefore can contribute in important ways to the effort to reform classroom mathematics teaching, it does not tell us how to teach mathematics, that is, it does not stipulate a particular model. (p. 114)

The mathematics teaching cycle that M. Simon developed is "a schematic model of the cyclical interrelationships of aspects of teacher knowledge, thinking, decision making, and activity that seems to be demonstrated by the data" (p. 135).

How did Simon leverage this from the insider work he had done on teaching? At the beginning of the section of his article in which he developed this theoretical perspective, he explains:

> In this section, I use the first person singular to refer to my actions and
> thinking as the teacher. I use the third person, often referring to "the teacher"
> to designate ideas I am lifting from the particular context in which I was the
> teacher. (p. 132)

Simon's model is a descriptive one, showing the teaching cycle rooted in the construction of a hypothetical learning trajectory, which includes the teacher's learning goal, plan for learning activities, and a hypothesis about the learning process. He examines the components of the teaching cycle, showing domains of knowledge and processes of knowing in practice that interact in the course of teaching to modify the trajectory of instruction. This section is an abstracted model of the process of planning, doing, listening, adjusting that Simon argued is at the heart of teaching—not just his teaching, but teaching more generally. In the next section of his article, Simon returned closer to the data from his teaching to articulate some elements of teaching that "embodies the reform principles." Here, he described some aspects of what he was doing in the episodes offered earlier in his article, drawing more directly on his firsthand experience. He described the experimental nature of this kind of teaching, hence, elaborating the "hypothetical" and "experimental" nature of the work. Speaking from the inside again, he layered practice against his provisional model.

Interesting to note is that Simon strove to move beyond the particulars of his own context in more than ways related to who he is individually. His aim was broader than Lampert's. His model of mathematics teaching is provisionally applicable to any teaching, not solely the teaching of preservice teachers in a mathematics methods course. In his conclusion, he reminded his readers that: "The data from this study must be seen in its particular context. The teaching practice was embedded in a teacher education program; the mathematics students were prospective elementary [teachers]" (p. 142).

Like Lampert, he also notes the important relationship between his first-person research and other lines of inquiry: Mathematics teaching with other populations involves a set of different constraints. Research in other contexts will inform us about the degree of context dependence of the ideas generated" (p. 142).

M. Simon's article is followed by a response written by two other researchers, Leslie Steffe and Beatriz D'Ambrosio (1995), who engaged the model as an abstraction about mathematics teaching. Like Simon, they referred to examples from his teaching to argue their points, but the argument is not about Simon's teaching itself but about the model and its role in research and its relationship to constructivist theory. As such, their response reflects their reading of his claims as theoretical, abstracted from the particulars of his own situation, yet developed and supplied by it.

What about Heaton's study of learning to teach mathematics for understanding? What are the claims of this study about? Arguing that her experiences in trying to change her mathematics teaching are not unique to her, Heaton explained that she, nonetheless, intended her work to be "both an autobiographical account of learning to teach and a piece of scholarship" (p. 29):

> What I have written is not just a story of my experience. It is also a close
> and careful study of my learning experiences over two points in time based
> on an analysis of a variety of source of documentation of my teaching. (p.
> 29)

Heaton sought to surface issues about learning to teach mathematics for understanding that she wanted her readers to understand as endemic to the challenges of trying to change one's teaching in these directions. However, of the three researchers examined in this chapter, Heaton used her self the most centrally. Perhaps because her work is as autobiographical as it is, she endeavored to establish carefully who she is in relation to the central questions of the study. She sought to do this both so that her readers can make sense of her experiences, but, more important, so that she could be seen as similar to many other capable, experienced teachers. She argued that:

> This study yields theory and questions about teaching generated in a rigorous
> way by an insider. As in medical research, when charting new territory, the
> value of the work does not come only from the questions answered but from
> new questions that get asked because of it. (p. 91)

Heaton's original question was, "What does it take for an experienced and successful elementary teacher to make changes in teaching mathematics" (p. 339). A central claim she made is that "learning to teach mathematics for understanding entails, simultaneously, learning to continuously invent a practice of teaching mathematics for understanding while you do it" (p. 339). With an analysis of the reforms and the sorts of guidance they do and do not provide for teaching, Heaton argued that the reform visions are underdetermined and, hence, require teachers to invent versions of teaching that fits with these aims. This claim is meant to apply to all who begin trying to teach this way. What she was claiming, drawing from both her careful analyses of her own experiences and her examination of the reform sources, is that there is no single practice of teaching for understanding. Hence, she claimed, interpreting and constructing it are parts of the process of learning to do it. Heaton continued with an analysis of her expectations in setting out to remodel her teaching and argued that learning to change one's teaching is not helpfully construed as complete abandonment of past practices. Instead, it requires "a skillful merger of old and new practices" (p. 358). A third area of claims for her study entailed subject matter understanding needed to teach in this way. She claimed that teachers have to be able to construct new understandings of mathematics as they explore the ideas with their students. Again, she drew from her experiences with the curriculum and with students' responses and work to make a broader claim about the nature of the subject matter understandings necessary in this kind of teaching.

Lampert set out to design a kind of teaching so as to be able to make claims about what is possible. Simon also very consciously designed a way of working with students, carefully documenting the decisions he made as he worked, and then he used his teaching as a platform to construct a provisional model of teacher decision making and teaching in this kind of teaching for understanding. Heaton did something distinct from these two. Heaton used herself and her experience to examine what happens to an experienced teacher who tries to change her teaching. She did not design the processes by which she would learn, other than setting out to do it. She put herself in a position to try to learn to teach, making herself quite vulnerable, for it was her experience that would form the material for analyzing the process of making such change. She, and what happened to and with her, was the central material of the study. Her claims are about herself as a case of an experienced, good teacher; her intellectual project was to convince her readers that her experience was logically rooted in things endemic to learning this kind of teaching and how to do it. That is, she aimed to make claims that would help us to consider closely the demands of learning to change one's teaching to this kind of teaching in general, not only her own experience.

Across these three cases, all three researchers were self-conscious and careful about the relationship among questions, stance, and design. Lampert, wondering about a particular way to manage the multiple ways of knowing central to mathematics, designed an approach to teaching on the basis of a conjecture about teaching and learning. Focused on learning, she traced her students' work and thinking across a series of lessons and examines how their mathematical understanding evolves. She had her eye on her students, and she used her researcher-teacher perspective to scrutinize what they do. Seeing what they do convinced her, and she, in turns, sought to convince her readers that what they did demonstrates what is possible to do more generally in the teaching of mathematics in school. She offered a way of thinking both about the nature of mathematical knowing and of the teacher's role that underlie her efforts, and, by implication, others' efforts. Simon, like Lampert, had to design a situation for his work. In so doing, he was able, like Heaton, to examine what goes on for the teacher in trying to work in that context. He examined the process of pedagogy and curriculum in action, using his own efforts as a source of insight. He probed the interplay of attention to the curriculum and to the students, elaborating what this attention is like and what it means to navigate the two in constructing a class. Unlike the others, Simon's yield is a model, a schematic for conceptualizing the relationships of teacher knowledge, student thinking, and teacher learning in the course of teaching. Heaton, unlike the other two researchers, did not design her situation. Using her own naturally arising experience also makes her challenge to move beyond her case more difficult. Although, as she acknowledged, she represents many other good, experienced teachers faced with changing how they have apparently successfully taught mathematics, her story is more autobiographical, and it takes more attention to locate the claims beyond her story. She did so by reminding the reader who she is and what her experience offers in considering the learning of other practicing teachers. And she did so by pushing herself to consider what the features of her struggles were and what sorts of support might help: curriculum materials, opportunities to learn with and from them, opportunities to learn mathematics.

## FIRST-PERSON RESEARCH: FACING THE RESPONSIBILITY FOR DEVELOPING A GENRE

In writing about recent trends in anthropology to acknowledge and use the self in writing, Ruth Behar (1996) posed a crucial question for our interest in first-person research on practice. Acknowledging the inevitable interpermeation of the self and what is being studied, she asked:

> How do you write subjectivity into ethnography in such a way that you can
> continue to call what you are doing ethnography? Should we be worried that
> a smoke alarm will blare in our ears when the ethnography grows too hot
> and "too personal"? (p. 7)

On one hand, Behar argued firmly for the need to find a place for the self in the scholar's voice and position. At the same time, she cautioned against the unexamined move to include the "personal." She explained that writing the conventional, "author-evacuated texts"[6] produces scholarship that is at worst boring and unenlightening. Using oneself explicitly in one's work ("author-saturated texts") has the potential to be humiliating, embarrassing, and useless unless one can connect the particulars of one's perspective and experience to the subject under study, to the "enormous sea of . . . issues" related to theory and experience. Otherwise, it runs the risk of realizing its critics' claims that such work is little more than a "nouveau solipsism" (Patai, 1994).

Behar (1996) wrote eloquently an impassioned story of her own evolution as an anthropologist gradually rejecting the traditional and almost unnatural isolation of self from a form of work that so centrally uses the self. Her story is itself an exemplar of inquiry that uses and moves beyond the first-person perspective, for her story can be read as a case of inquiry into the very terrain of her own scholarly work. As an anthropologist involved in changing her practice, she—like Lampert, Heaton, and Simon—was at once creating a new practice of anthropology and investigating the issues entailed in both doing and creating this new practice:

> When I began, nine years ago, to make emotions part of my ethnography, I had no idea where this work would take me or whether it would be accepted within anthropology and the academy. I began with a sense of urgency, a desire to embed the diary of my life within the accounts of the lives of others that I was being required to produce as an anthropologist. As a student I was taught to maintain the same strict boundary Malinowski had kept between his ethnography and his autobiography. But I'd reached a point where these forms of knowing were no longer so easily separated. (p. 19)

She wrote about her experiences as she changed her work: struggles with the tenure process, reactions of other scholars, and questions from her Aunt Rebecca about what anthropology "is." But Behar (1996) did not write only about her own change; she wrote also

---

[6]Behar cited Geertz's *Works and Lives* (1988) for this characterization of conventional social science texts.

about changes in the fields around her: the rise of "first-person narratives written by those who previously had been more likely to be the ethnographized rather than the ethnographer," which challenged anthropology's traditional views of "truth"; new debates about what it means to be an "insider" to a culture; and the rise of "native anthropology." As in other fields where shifts in epistemology and politics are altering practice, research on teaching is opening previously closed approaches to the construction of knowledge.[7] Behar issued a caution to which all who are involved in such projects would be wise to attend:

> As is the case with any intellectual trend, some experiments work out better than others. It is far from easy to locate oneself in one's own text. Writing vulnerably takes as much skill, nuance, and willingness to follow through on the ramifications of a complicated idea as writing invulnerably and distantly. I would say it takes still greater skill. (p. 13)

If first-person research on teaching and learning is to take a legitimate and developed place in the lexicon of scholarly work on teaching and learning, the challenges examined in this chapter will require ongoing attention. For what sorts of questions is first-person research appropriate, or even ideal? For what sorts of questions is it inappropriate? How can distance and insight be composed in the creation of this genre of research such that the inside view is coupled with analysis, that belief and conviction born of intimate involvement are threaded with skepticism and critical perspective? And how can shared notions evolve about what count as reasonable claims, and what it means to warrant them with evidence?

In addition to the thoughtful development of this approach to the study of teaching and learning is the need to consider the learning of new researchers. How might doctoral students learn to design and write first-person dissertations? What are the kinds of experiences and opportunities, distinct from other aspects of research preparation in which they already participate, that graduate students may need in order to develop the capacity to do such work? When might it be unwise to choose such an approach?

Three possible avenues seem fruitful to pursue as this genre of scholarship develops. One is to consider more explicitly the relation of different forms of "teacher research" and research

---

[7] Susan Krieger (1991) offered a view of her own and others' shifts within sociology away from traditional approaches to knowing to include the knower much more prominently within the processes and products of the work.

on teaching (which I mentioned briefly at the beginning of this chapter), to articulate more broadly the relations of question, purpose, stance, audience, and knowledge claims across these different forms of inquiry in, on, and from the perspective of practice.

A second avenue is to consider more explicitly what might constitute "methods" of first-person research. In what ways do the structures and concepts of other, more established approaches to inquiry provide the ingredient skills, methods, and ideas for this, a variant on other forms of qualitative research? What special methods might be invented or needed to face some of the special problems of focus, analysis, interpretation, and writing?

A third promising avenue is to look to the development of method and scholarship in other fields as sources of insight into the relationship of the self to the objects of inquiry: anthropology and sociology, history and literary criticism, psychology and philosophy. How have scholarly approaches and texts evolved as issues of voice, perspective, and representation have emerged? The study of other practices could broaden ideas about the role of the practitioner in developing knowledge about practice: other professional practices, some of the performing arts, writing. How do practitioners have a voice in the study of these practices? Are there ideas about knowing and knowledge in these other realms that might inform or inspire the development of insider approaches to the study of teaching?

Knowing that there are important things to know about the work of teaching that may best be investigated from the inside brings these questions to the fore. An interest in neither being seduced into a simple-minded enthusiasm for first-person approaches to inquiry, nor an unthoughtful dismissal of them as solipsistic, makes the challenge of developing this kind of work worthy of attention.

## ACKNOWLEDGMENTS

This work profited from the helpful comments of Magdalene Lampert, Elaine Howes, Jennifer Lewis, and Kara Suzuka. I am also grateful to Jennifer Lewis and Mark Hoover for their helpful assistance with the chapter.

# 15  Paradigms for Teacher-Centered, Classroom-Based Research

**Helen M. Doerr**
**Patricia P. Tinto**
*Syracuse University*

The terms *action research*, *teacher research*, and *collaborative action research* have been used as umbrella terms to cover a wide range of classroom-based research activities. The images for teacher research include a reflective process aimed at the professional development of the individual; an approximation of university research that is carried out by teachers; a new methodology with its own epistemology, standards, and questions; or a cyclic process of problem identification, action, and reflection aimed at changes in practice. Just as the history of action research has its roots in an agenda for social change through practitioner research, a common thread among these images is the study and creation of practice-centered change. In this chapter, we elaborate some guidelines for, and methodological variations of, action research approaches to the study and creation of change in mathematics education. We focus on the interplay between the evolving research on, and changes in, mathematics practice, which occurred in the schools and the classrooms of experienced high school mathematics teachers. This is not to suggest that the only model of classroom-based research is action research (see, e.g. chaps. 9, 11, and 13, this volume), but merely to state that teacher research of necessity occurs in classrooms in schools.

We begin with a discussion of two issues that have become particularly salient for us as researchers: the role and relationship of the teacher and the researcher, and the nature of the knowledge that is generated by practitioner research and how it is made public. Through these two issues, we identify two of the dilemmas or tensions posed by the action research paradigm. Then, we describe some guiding principles for the design of action research projects and the specific methodological approaches taken in three particular studies. We report briefly on the results of these studies in order to illuminate some of the significant characteristics of this methodology. Finally, we conclude with some remarks intended to offer a critical perspective on any action research project.

## THE ROLES OF TEACHERS AND RESEARCHERS

Traditional books on the methodologies of qualitative research acknowledge the crucial role played by the relationship between the researcher and the subjects of the research. Researchers are admonished to establish rapport with field informants while simultaneously being cautioned against the bias that can result from the failure to maintain an "objective" or neutral stance. More recently, both feminists and postmodern qualitative researchers have criticized the very notion of an "objective standpoint," arguing that it leads to an object treatment of human subjects while at the same time hiding the human side of the researcher (Fine, 1994; Reason, 1994). This has led some researchers to engage in more collaborative relationships between researcher and teacher. In the work of Ulichny and Schoener (1996), their teacher-researcher team conceptualizes their research stance along two dimensions, one of relationship and one of action. They saw the relationship between the researcher and the teacher as situated along a continuum from relative strangers to mutual friends.

In terms of action, Ulichny and Schoener (1996) viewed the researcher as positioned along a continuum from distant observer to full participant in the work under study. The teacher, on the other hand, though a full participant in the classroom work being studied, may be only a very distant observer of the research project, the data analysis and interpretation, and the communication of the results. Although there is much literature on collaborative research, much of it is reported only in the voice of the researcher and only on the results of the research from that perspective. In their study, Ulichny and Schoener provided two distinct interpretations of the teaching and learning questions that were central to the research and a view of the dynamic evolution of the relationship between researcher and teacher. When the teacher shares the role of researcher, classroom-based research moves from the teacher being the passive object of study to an active state in which the teacher is a participant in the research process. This participation leads to a greater role for the teacher in defining researchable questions, gathering and interpreting data, and communicating results. It also leads to changes in the relationship between the researcher and the teacher. This relationship needs to promote the development of knowledge through shared dialogue, and this knowledge then lives in the joint world of theory and practice. Glesne and Peshkin (1992) suggested that an increased emphasis on issues of power and control in the research process has led to the emergence of alternative modes of qualitative research, such as action research.

Some investigators have advocated a model that replaces the university researcher with the teacher, as an investigator of his or her practice. This shift potentially enables the teacher's voice to be heard fully and gives recognition to the creation of new professional knowledge by practitioners (Tripp, 1990). At the same time, it alters the research project and process fundamentally by posing different questions and by redefining what data are collected and how they are analyzed and reported (Glesne & Peshkin, 1992). Furthermore, as teachers become the "subjects" of their own research, the research process necessarily becomes one that is self-reflective. The cycle of problem identification, action, and reflection encourages changes in teachers' beliefs and in their classrooms (Calhoun, 1993; Oja & Smulyan, 1989).

Action research and teacher research shift the knowledge base for teaching from one that is built primarily on university-based research and then applied in classroom practice to one that recognizes teachers as generators of knowledge from practice. An essential characteristic of this shift in the knowledge base is not merely the location of the site (i.e., the classroom as a target of a technical rationalist approach to research grounded in the university), but rather the centrality of the involvement of the teacher as a poser of researchable questions, collector of data, and generator of knowledge. This then leads to one of the fundamental dilemmas posed by action research, which is how to account for the stance and perspectives of the teacher-researcher who is researching her or his own practice.

## KNOWLEDGE ABOUT TEACHING AND LEARNING

The primary purpose of much traditional academic research is to generate theories and test hypotheses, thereby creating new knowledge. Action research, on the other hand, often has as its goal the transformation of practice (cf. Goswami & Stillman, 1987; Noffke & Stevenson,

1995; G. Wells, 1994). Other goals of action research include closing the gap between research and practice, providing opportunities for teachers' development, enhancing the professional status of teachers, and investigating the solution of practical problems in schools (hence, the word *action* research). In their work, A. Feldman and Atkin (1995) made a distinction between contributing to the knowledge base of the academy and developing greater wisdom about educational practice. This claim is built on an epistemological framework that draws on an understanding of the nature of professional knowledge in fields other than education. By analogy, Feldman and Atkin argued that, "much of the wisdom associated with the intelligent use of practical information lies in a particularized understanding of the circumstances in a specific classroom (and, indeed, of the particular teacher)" (p. 131). These case-based, person-specific understandings of particular events, people, and conditions are built and developed by educational practitioners through the action research process.

Cochran-Smith and Lytle (1993) were both cautionary and critical of the notion that the structure of knowledge as practical wisdom is only experiential and pragmatic and argued that such a view may well lead to the devaluation and marginalization of such knowledge. They asserted that teachers do bring a theoretical framework to their research questions, analyses, and interpretations. These frameworks encompass knowledge of content, pedagogy, curricula, characteristics of learners, and educational contexts, purposes, and values. According to Cochran-Smith and Lytle, "if we regard teachers' theories as sets of interrelated conceptual frameworks grounded in practice, teacher researchers are both users and generators of theory" (p. 17). They went on to argue that those teachers who are researchers in their own classrooms can and do construct knowledge about teaching, learning and schooling.

One of the current challenges of action research, according to Noffke (1994), is to clarify if and how action research can contribute to the traditional knowledge base of educational research or if it is, "a new form of research whose methods, methodology, and epistemology are now being clarified" (p. 16). Elliott (1991) argued that in action research, theory is derived from practice and is constituted by a set of abstractions and generalizations about it. This contrasts sharply with a technical rationalist view that sees practice as the application of theories and principles that are understood prior to engagement in practice. According to Schön (1995), the epistemological foundation of action research is precisely a rejection of a technical rationalist approach to knowledge and a valuing of "knowing-in-action." This knowing-in-action is tacit and implicit in the actions of competent professionals as they make judgments and perform tasks in an everyday setting. Schön suggested that there is an "epistemology of practice that takes fuller account of the competence practitioners sometimes display in situations of uncertainty, complexity, uniqueness, and conflict" (p. 29). However, knowledgeable practitioners are often at a loss to produce adequate descriptions of what it is that they know. By reflecting-in-action, the practitioner restructures her or his understanding of the problem situation and of the strategies of action that she or he has been using. According to Schön (1983, 1987, 1995), reflecting on reflection-in-action makes explicit the action strategies, assumptions, and problem settings that were implicit in reflection-in-action. This, in turn, can lead to the critique and testing of strategies ("Why didn't that work?" or "What should I try next time?"), assumptions, and problem settings implicit across a range of situations. Drawing on Dewey's notion of inquiry, Schön argued that action research becomes generative when it moves beyond the solution to a particular problem to the generation of new problems. This then leads to the generation of new knowledge and multiple cycles of inquiry, which we illustrate in FIG. 15.1.

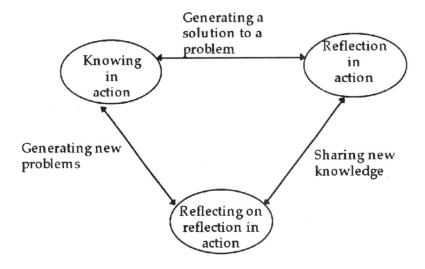

FIG. 15.1. Cycles of inquiry through teacher research.

The steps of reflecting on reflection-in-action and the generation of new problems are what distinguish the knowledge gained from action research and the knowledge held by an individual who is a "good reflective practitioner." The sharing of knowledge, the generation of new problems, and the active application of knowledge in practice lead to the close intertwining of theory and practice.

Increasingly, this teacher-generated knowledge is finding new forums for presentation and publication (Burnaford, Fischer, & Hobson, 1996; Cochran-Smith & Lytle, 1993; Goswami & Stillman, 1987; McNiff, 1993; Raymond, Rafferty, & Dutt, 1996; G. Wells, 1994; Zack, Mousley, & Breen, 1997). According to Schön (1995), action research suggests that teaching is a new form of scholarship and, as such, must lead to new categories of scholarly activities and the "building up [of] communities of inquiry capable of criticizing such research and fostering its development" (p. 34). A fundamental dilemma posed by any action research project, then, is to understand how to move beyond the particular story told by a skilled reflective practitioner in order to understand, critique, and foster the development of the new knowledge that is embedded in the practice of teaching and learning and to nurture the expression of that knowledge in new forms and by new voices.

## GUIDING PRINCIPLES

The centrality of the relationship between the researcher and her or his practice and of the nature of the knowledge that is generated form the basis of the two most significant characteristics of action research:

- Its primary purpose is to simultaneously study and generate knowledge about the very practice that it seeks to change.
- The study is carried out by the practitioners (in varying degrees of close collaboration with university researchers) rather than by an outside group of researchers.

Because of these defining characteristics, action research does not fit neatly within those research frameworks that tend to be hypotheses-testing or hypotheses-generating studies. Above all, the goal of action research is to be action generating. As such, projects designed with this methodological approach are much more likely to guide practitioners toward practical next steps that can be taken to resolve a specific local problem and are somewhat less likely to provide findings that will guide a major rethinking of policy, curricula, instruction, or theories of learning. The knowledge gained by action research tends to be local, often at the level of a particular element of instructional practice in a particular classroom or at the level of an issue that affects several groups of participants (such as teachers, parents, and administrators) in a school building.

With these two central characteristics in mind, we offer the following five guiding principles that are intended to uncover some of the assumptions underlying action research, to assist in the design of an action research project, and to provide a perspective from which to take a critical view of the results of action research:

*Systematic Cycles of Inquiry.* Because action research studies simultaneously both teaching practice and the changes taking place in that practice, the research process itself should be characterized by the intertwining of research questions that are refined and reformulated as changes take place and data are collected and analyzed. New questions emerge, new actions are taken, and new data are collected. The systematic definition of emerging queries and the systematic collection of supporting data throughout these cycles of action likely will lead to results that tend to be perceived as supporting or challenging the changes in practice and as evolving continually into better understandings of practice.

*Grounded in Evidence Gathered by Practitioners.* In action research, data gathering and analysis should be seen as ongoing and mutually informing the research questions. These cycles of inquiry should inform and modify the participants' roles in the study and should support the changes that occur in the context of the study. Although the final product of a qualitative study may be documentation or the generation of a framework to elicit understanding, the product of an action research project should include the change of practice based on the evidence gathered by the practitioners. As noted previously, action research tends to be defined somewhat locally. However, within the limits of this local definition, be it within a single classroom for a short period of time or across several classrooms within a school, the design of the project should support thorough collection and analysis of the data by practitioners.

*Generative of New Questions.* The action researcher is in interaction with and transforming the problematic situation. In the spirit of what John Dewey called inquiry, action research proceeds from a problematic situation to the resolution of the problem to the generation of a new problem. This new problem comes in combination with changes in the context that result from interactions with the original problematic situation. Hence, the test of a cycle of action research is not only a critique of the interactions and that transformation of the problematic situation, but also a critique of the value of the new problems that are generated.

*Generative of Shared Knowledge.* Often, the stories of teacher-researchers are told as the particular knowledge gained by teachers in their own classroom setting. Indeed, at the extreme, one could claim that teacher research is merely reflective practice. Though we recognize that reflective practice is certainly a highly desirable attribute of a practitioner in education, we would argue that merely reflecting on one's own practice and acting on those reflections are not sufficient to contribute to the educational community's knowledge about teaching and learning and will not lead to powerful ideas for growth and change. An essential element of effective action research is that the findings of that research become generative of new shared knowledge for the larger educational community. However, we are not suggesting, as is seen later, that the forums for sharing teachers' knowledge should be limited to the traditional currency of the academic research community. Rather, new forums and new forms for shared knowledge will emerge as teacher-researchers gain new professional voices for speaking about what they have learned about their practice. The audience for action research products should include both theoreticians and practitioners because the results of the research should stay within the overall paradigm of a close intertwining of theory and practice.

*Diversity and Multiplicity of Participants.* Action research is characterized by the involvement of the participants as researchers. Classroom teachers move from hosting university researchers in their classrooms to becoming members of the research team or the researcher. In addition, the action-oriented researcher seeks to study a system and to introduce changes into that system simultaneously. Whereas the observer who documents change ordinarily guards and values the distance that she or he keeps from being involved in the setting, the researcher in an action research project participates directly in the project both as a participant and as a researcher. To balance this lack of distance by an individual researcher, action research projects should employ several participants with a variety of viewpoints about the project as members of the research team. Such diversity and multiplicity across both participants and settings serve to strengthen the validity of the research findings.

These guidelines are intended to suggest the potential strengths of action research approaches as well as to indicate cautionary notes for those who design and participate in such projects. In the next section, we describe three of the various methodological approaches that we have used as practitioners who study the very systems we wish to change. The second author of this chapter is a university researcher and participated in varying roles in each of these studies. In addition, this chapter was read and critiqued by Barbara A. Shelly, one of the teacher-researchers in the first study and a codirector of the second study.

# METHODOLOGICAL VARIATIONS WITHIN ACTION RESEARCH

The methodology of action research always is situated in a particular context or setting and is directed toward actions to be taken by teachers and other members of the community of practice, often in a collaborative role with university researchers. As noted earlier, we describe three methodological variations of action research, followed by details of the actual studies. Each variation is recounted in terms of:

- The purpose of the study.
- The role of each of the players in it.
- The data collection and analysis processes.
- The presentation of the findings.

## Variation 1

In the first approach, two teachers and a university researcher (the second author) defined their collaborative inquiry as the examination of two classes whose teachers were beginning the process of changing their instructional routines. The purpose of the research was twofold: to document the effects of these instructional changes from the perspectives of the students, and to continue to shift the normative teaching practice from a traditional, passive, lecture mode to one that involved the students actively. Thus, the focus of the research was on changing the culture of two classes. Because the research was guided by the purposeful decision to veer away from what had been well-established practice, both the school's administrators and the students' parents were informed about the intent of the research. The students were asked to sign consent forms, so that they, too, were aware that their teachers were making and studying changes that would take place in their classes.

Whereas the university faculty member had a background in qualitative research, the teachers' roles as researchers were evolutionary. At the beginning of the study, the roles were defined more traditionally. The university researcher's initial role was primarily that of an outsider observing and documenting both the teachers' and the students' actions and voices in the secondary mathematics class. However, as data about the students were collected and as the teachers and the university researcher discussed the data and formed conclusions that shaped the actions in the next day's class, the process of the study left the more traditional, observational, research paradigm and became aligned more closely as an evolving, collaborative relationship for the researcher and the teachers. The university researcher progressed from observer to participant by designing instructional materials, whereas the two teachers shifted from solely classroom practitioners to observers and researchers of classroom life. The teachers became full partners in establishing research priorities and in collecting and analyzing data. The university researcher began to play a role in designing the strategies that would bring the desired changes into the classroom.

The study evolved into one that documented classroom reform as experienced by the students and provided data to guide the teachers initiating and revising the reform efforts (Tinto, 1993a; Tinto, Shelly, & Zarach, 1994a, 1994b). Data collection techniques focused on capturing the students' voices. As the students realized that their perspective was playing a part in the shaping of the class, they, too, began to see themselves as participants in the research. The outcomes of the 2-year research study were presented at conferences related to practice for teachers and at research conferences and provided evidence for the creation of a large-scale teacher development project (Tinto, Shelly, & Zarach, 1992, 1993; Tinto, Zarach, & Shelly, 1993). In this manner, the study reached the joint goals of speaking both to theory and to practice.

## Variation 2

In the second action research variation, the research study was initiated as a part of a continuing staff development effort. It was designed as a model of collective inquiry, where each project teacher would be involved in her or his own small-scale study. The intent of the project was to use these small-scale research projects as vehicles for moving teachers beyond reflective practice to initiating and sustaining changes in how they teach. The project's codirectors (who included the two teacher-researchers from the first study and the second author) acted as coaches to respond to questions about conducting research, but they did not participate actively in the resulting studies. The function of the university researcher was defined as that of mentor, assisting the teachers with the development of questions or facilitating dialogue among them that would help them to identify a research focus. Greater details on how teachers go about designing an action research project can be found in Altrichter, Posch, and Somekh (1993), Elliott (1991), Hubbard and Power (1993), and Mohr and MacLean (1987).

Each teacher defined an area of inquiry and carried out her or his own study individually. The teachers' questions were targeted at examining aspects of specific instructional strategies. The project emphasized the systematic gathering of data and learning how to "look" at a class from the perspective of a researcher as well as a teacher. A summer institute for the participating teachers included classes on qualitative research methods, and time was given during the academic year to helping shape the questions being asked by the teachers. For the participating teachers, it was very important that the "doing" of the research study was seen as manageable, so that the dual role of teacher and researcher was necessary only for a very specific part of each teacher's day. On the whole, data collection methods were those that were seen by the teacher-researchers as being integrated closely with classroom instruction and assessment (Tinto, 1996a, 1996b). These methods involved collecting students' writing or recording students' talk. In these small-scale studies, the teachers did not take on the role of advocate completely. In fact, many of the teachers were somewhat skeptical of the instructional strategies that they were implementing. The classroom context was one of experimentation, with the teacher-researcher developing her or his understanding through participation in the research process.

The power of the research process to change practice was seen in the collective reporting of research efforts by the participating teachers (Tinto & Shelly, 1996). Although the focus of each research study was necessarily narrow, the overall significance was heightened by the number and the diversity of the research sites. As a consequence, the project moved from being a story of good practice in one classroom to becoming a model for breaking traditional teaching routines in many classrooms. The results of these studies were presented by the teacher-researchers at local, regional, and national forums for mathematics teachers (Tinto, Shelly, Zarach, & Graver, 1995).

## Variation 3

The purpose of the research in the third variation was to respond to a perceived need of a local school community to improve the quality of the mathematics education of students. Much of this concern was focused on perceptions about students' failure rates—which students were failing, whose students were failing, and why they were failing. In this case, the goal of hearing the many perspectives present in the situation was a major force in defining the data collection methods. Students, parents (among them the second author), and teachers were involved from the beginning as central players in the study. Interviews were deemed essential in order to gather each person's words (and this included administrators' voices as well) in order to help build a collective view of the problem. To establish mutual trust and, ultimately, common ownership of the findings, it was critical that the researchers not be outsiders to the community. To address concerns about potential biases in data collection and analysis, the researchers needed to represent each segment of the community and to work together in defining the focus of the study, developing interview questions, and analyzing the data. The relationship between the participant-researchers and the community members at large was seen as a significant issue in the research process. The results of the data collection and analyses were presented to the community as a collective understanding of the various perspectives on the problem. This joint ownership of the process and its outcomes helped to ensure acceptance of the findings by the larger community.

In the next section of this chapter, we describe more fully each of the action research studies whose methodologies were discussed earlier. These three studies are used to explore and illuminate:

- The relationship between the university-based researchers and the teachers.
- The nature of the research questions posed.
- The changes that took place at the level of the individual teacher and in a departmental setting.
- The articulation of the results of the research.
- The emerging voices of the teachers.

These three studies show a range of relationships between teacher and researcher, from collaborating with a university researcher in designing the focus of the research to participating in a network of teacher-researchers reciprocally defining the questions, gathering the data, and interpreting the results. Through their engagement in this research, teachers made changes in their own classroom practices and in those of their school. At the same time, they participated in local and national forums for communicating the results of their work. The first action research study focuses on the professional development and their emerging roles as teacher-researchers of two experienced secondary mathematics teachers, whereas the second study shows how this development led to the creation of a larger network of teacher-researchers. The third study focuses on school-level changes that were motivated through questions brought about by the changes in practice of these teacher-researchers.

## TEACHERS AS COLLABORATIVE RESEARCHERS FOR CHANGES IN CLASSROOM ENVIRONMENTS

During a local conference on using technology in the classroom, two secondary mathematics teachers, one from a suburban district, the other from an urban district, and a mathematics educator (the second author) began to talk about teaching practices in the classroom. Though both teachers were perceived by parents, students, colleagues, and administrators as exemplary teachers, both were dissatisfied with their current classroom culture. Both teachers were teaching computer classes also and had observed the startling contrast in students' engagement between their computer classes and their mathematics classes. The teachers noted that their computer classes were more in keeping with the standards of the National Council of Teachers of Mathematics (NCTM, 1989) than their mathematics classes were. Unlike their mathematics classes, the computer classes were characterized by the active involvement of the students in the learning process. Problem solving was the focus of the activity, and the teacher played the role of facilitator, rather than authority.

Both teachers wanted to employ more active learning strategies in their mathematics classes and to implement technology. They expected such changes to impact the culture of their classes. Realizing that they had no obvious external support for making such changes, they decided to join with the university researcher and to document their efforts. They wanted to be able to answer the question, "How will we know if we have made a positive difference in the learning environment for students?"

A collaborative teacher-researcher team was formed. The teachers brought to this team expertise in technology and an interest in group work and writing in the classroom. The mathematics educator became a mentor in the research process. She listened to the teachers' reflections about classroom practice and helped them to formulate questions for their students in order to gather the data that would inform their inquiry. Over the course of 2 years, the teachers implemented a number of changes designed to involve their students actively in learning mathematics. These changes included using cooperative group strategies, problem solving with technology, teaching the "big ideas," and encouraging the students' written expression of mathematical reasoning. The teachers hypothesized that the students who were involved in these activities would learn to think mathematically. Together, the team formalized specific questions such as:

- What types of cooperative group experiences are useful in teaching specific mathematics content?

- How does the use of technology facilitate students' conjecturing?

- Do these changes in instructional strategies support more active class involvement for students?

To document their efforts at changing the learning environment of their classrooms, the team identified the kinds of data that they would collect. Seeing change as a year-long process, the team decided to capture data by collecting students' journals and learning logs, audiotaping students' talk during group work, and videotaping both whole-class and small-group work. Initially, the teachers focused on ways to document change. They needed to describe what went on in their classrooms. Students responded to journal questions such as, "For me, a typical math class is. . . . " and, "Math is like. . . . ." As the teachers heard the voices of the students and saw how the students responded to the innovations, they moved from merely trying to document changes to trying to understand more fully the reasons for those changes.

The team reexamined the students' journals and learning logs to identify the sources of authority in the classroom. As the teachers read the journals and analyzed the students' responses, they found that in the beginning of the year, students wrote about mathematics class in terms of the teacher. Several months later, the students were describing the classroom routine in terms of their own actions. Early in the year, the students had articulated a transmission model of teaching and learning. This led the two teachers to rethink the group structures that were used in class. They moved from group models where students were assigned special roles to a model that promoted conjecturing on the part of each student. Data were gathered in the form of students' written reactions to photographs taken during group work. Responses to the "What's going on here?" query gave the teachers evidence that the students were beginning to see themselves as engaged in the process of doing mathematics. Listening to the audiotapes of group discussions and reading the transcripts helped the teachers to understand the dynamics of small-group interactions. Thus, the teachers felt increasing confidence about their strategies for moving the students toward a model of more active participation in their classes.

Though both the teachers and the university researcher benefited professionally from the action research and their interactions on the research team, the impact of their work had potential beyond their own professional development. One of the results of their study showed that effective, small-group interactions were characterized by conversations in which students' talk included explanatory remarks, students shared the role of expert, social talk was brief and noninterruptive, and students gave and received genuine mathematical responses for help and feedback (Tinto, Shelly & Zarach, 1994a, 1994b). The teachers and the mathematics educator were invited to join a national panel of researchers at the National Science Foundation Catalyst Conference in 1991, which provided further validation for the teachers of their roles as researchers and collaborators. At the conference, the audience of university-based researchers noted that the perspective of the teacher in the classroom is central to developing an understanding of the teaching and learning process in mathematics classes. It became apparent that this perspective becomes available only when the teachers are active in the research process—when, in fact, they are researchers. The teachers reported that they gained an understanding of the potential of educational research. Rather than seeing such research as distant and distinct from the classroom, through their ownership of the research questions and the data, they came to value classroom-based research. This led to the development of the collective action research project, described next.

# COLLECTIVE ACTION RESEARCH FOR CHANGE IN TEACHERS' PRACTICES

In the summers of 1993 and 1994, 42 secondary mathematics teachers from 15 school districts began a multiyear project to build a local network of secondary mathematics educators rethinking their practice. The teachers came from rural, urban, and suburban middle schools and high schools. Part of the selection criteria included support from school building and school district administrators and evidence that the teachers had a history of commitment to professional development activities. Preference was given to pairs of teachers from the same school. When small rural schools were involved, teams could be teachers from neighboring towns.

These teachers were asked to rethink their practice but were not told what to change. Instead, they were asked to look at the teaching routines that they had developed over the years, select a part that they were not satisfied with, and begin to change that piece (Tinto, 1993b; Tinto, Shelly, & Zarach, 1993a, 1993b, 1994a). They were challenged to collect evidence so that they would know if their innovations were effective. During 4-week summer workshops, the teachers engaged in exploring mathematics, learning about computer and graphing calculator technologies, and adapting new strategies to involve students in mathematical thinking. The learning opportunities for the teachers were created as models for best practice and were discussed as part of the workshop.

The summer workshops also involved the teachers in discussions of their teaching routines and of how to go about documenting what takes place in their classrooms. The teachers commented that although they continually gathered informal data that played a role in their thinking about the students and about themselves as teachers, they did not gather these data in any systematic fashion. The teachers realized that many of the questions they had about their practice could not be answered by the conventional data (tests, quizzes, and homework scores) that they had collected. This led to a cycle of refining their questions about the process of teaching and defining the kinds of data needed to answer these questions. The university researchers responded to this need by introducing the ideas and processes of using qualitative data as a basis for decision making. One teacher spoke for many when he said: "I found that the research, in the collection of some kind of data which may verify that we are doing something in the right direction, is an important step."

Following the emphasis on writing suggested in the NCTM standards (1989), the teachers focused on adding new types of questions to their traditional assessment instruments. Developing questions that were open-ended and nonleading became a part of their new routine for many of the project's teachers. The systematic collection and analysis of these data were the next steps. When students responded to the teachers' beginning-of-the-year query, "When I enter math class, I . . . ," the teachers gained two important perspectives on it. First, they acquired insights into each individual student's perspective on the mathematics class, and, second, they formed a collective vision of what was defining the culture of the class from the students' viewpoint. Both perspectives then became data for the teacher-researcher in making changes in her or his classroom. In beginning-of-the-year journal entries, students spoke often about the teacher, describing very conventional roles for both the teacher and the student. The similarity of students' perspectives on the teaching routines across all teachers and schools was a powerful motivational force for teachers to begin to rethink their teaching practice. For these teachers, this type of data supported their emerging beliefs that their efforts to change the role of the teacher in the classroom were warranted.

Other teachers focused their research questions on students' discourse during group work. Many teachers, who had monitored and filtered all of the conversation in their mathematics classes, were concerned that students would solely engage in social talk. These teachers organized group work and audiotaped their students' discussions. Some teachers took the time to listen to each group conversation carefully, whereas others had the tapes transcribed and read through the transcripts. After analyzing the students' talk from several of her classes, one teacher noted, "Why did I wait so long!" She was amazed at the level of mathematical talk taking place student-to-student. It was clear that this level of conversation had not occurred when she had directed and controlled all of the discussions.

Several teachers from different schools decided to break their routine by forming student homework groups. The rationale for forming homework groups was to bring students into class, involve them in discussion, and cut down on the time that most secondary mathematics teachers spend reviewing problems at the blackboard. These groups would consist of three to four students and would be formed for an entire grading period. Homework groups would meet at the beginning of each class period, and students were expected to use the time to discuss homework questions. If a group member had difficulty with a question, other members were expected to assist in an explanation until all of the members felt confident of their responses. The teacher would provide an answer key depending on the type of homework and the purpose of the homework. Again, teachers had many questions about this structure. Would students stop doing their homework and attempt to "piggyback" on the responses of other students? Would students engage in social talk only? Would students merely give others the answer? Would students who were handing in their homework consistently feel that the discussion groups were wasting their time? Teachers structured journal questions to hear the reflections of the students and they listened to audiotaped discussions. Each teacher analyzed the data that she or he had collected over several months. The outcome was powerful. Each teacher had come to similar conclusions about the positive impact of homework groups on their students' learning and on the class culture in general, and these teachers represented different courses and different schools. The replication of the study across different schools enhanced the power of the results for the teachers. When they presented the results to other teachers, these teachers looked at the studies as a whole, believing in the validity of the research and believing that they, too, could try this innovation in their classroom. Thus, the results became generative of new problems for action for these other teachers.

The teachers in the project were asked to present the results of their studies to each other and to their administrators. The presentation format selected by the teachers was a poster session on each research project. During the regular Saturday sessions, the teachers would display their posters during the coffee hour and time was given for them to talk with each other about the progress of their studies. At first, the idea of bringing to the public the results of their research was somewhat overwhelming. Once the poster session began, however, teachers soon realized that they gained from discussing their own study and they gained by listening to others. At the end of the academic year, teachers shared the results of their studies more formally with other teachers and administrators. The success of this miniconference prompted the teachers to present their posters at their own schools, both to fellow teachers and to parents.

The teachers stated that they felt more secure in talking with parents about the changes because they had the data to support the positive impact of their innovations. They could point to students' responses and students' dialogue to justify their changes in teaching strategies. Later, several teachers brought their posters to a research conference on mathematics education hosted by the local university. Thirty teachers took their research studies to a session at NCTM's annual conference in 1995. Subsequently, teachers reported that although they were somewhat negative at first about the amount of time that they perceived would be involved in the work of creating a research study, finding a focus, being diligent about collecting data, and analyzing it, not only did they gain from the final results of their study, but also they learned from doing it. Many noted that the process of doing the research became a part of the process of teaching. Moreover, they began to value the research conversations that they were having with each other. One of the most noticeable outcomes of the project, for the teachers, was the development of this network of professional voices.

Not every teacher continued to do research on a regular basis in her or his classes. However, most of them have redefined their routine assessment tasks to include the collection of qualitative data. Many have stated that the routine of the Friday quiz is a thing of the past. Learning logs, group-processing forms, and homework headings provide teachers with the data that they need for an ongoing assessment of their students and their classes. As one teacher commented:

> If I am going to try something new that I am not sure about, I'll purposely collect student data. It might be a journal question or I might take pictures and ask students what is going on here? But I know that if I really want to know whether this is a good idea or not, I'll need to do something more organized, more systematic.

Thus, the project's teachers developed a new sense of creating a knowledge base about teaching practices through a cycle of posing questions, defining and gathering data, analyzing and interpreting results, sharing insights and findings, and investigating new questions.

## COMMUNITY ACTION RESEARCH FOR CHANGES IN SCHOOL ENVIRONMENTS

As the teachers involved in the project described previously began to rethink their teaching practices, their classrooms began to look and sound different from conventional classrooms. This led to conflicts in one of the schools. Students and parents became aware of the differences in teaching practice between the project's teachers and other members of the department. One evening, parents arrived at a parent-teacher meeting angry about the prior year's low test scores and the perceived inequities in current teaching practices. Some of the parents blamed the curriculum; others blamed the teachers. The teachers talked about unmotivated students and the lack of administrative support for needed materials, whereas the project's teachers tried to address the need for group work and the use of technology. The situation was rife with anger and frustration. It had the potential for dividing the faculty and the students even further apart.

The project's teachers, having found new roles for themselves as teacher-researchers, negotiated with the parents to form a task force consisting of parents, teachers, and students to study the problem. The group met and decided to interview members of the school's community. With the assistance of a qualitative researcher from the Mathematics Teacher/Researchers Collaborating for Collaboration in the Classroom (MTRC3) project, the group developed open-ended interview questions to gather the perspectives of students, parents, teachers, and administrators about mathematics at the high school. The task force asked: "What is the students' experience in mathematics at City High?" "What do parents expect?" "What do teachers experience as mathematics teachers at City High?" "How does the administrative staff view the mathematics program and how do they react to the issue of low test scores?" To honor confidentiality and to increase participants' levels of comfort with the process, graduate students trained in qualitative research methods were asked to join the project and to conduct some of the interviews with teachers and administrators. The research project took a critical turn when task force members themselves engaged in the collection and interpretation of data. Students interviewed students and parents. Parents interviewed parents and some students. Teachers interviewed teachers.

This participation helped to ensure that different perspectives about the problem would be heard and valued and that, as members of the inquiry team, all of the constituents would take responsibility for the problem. Biklen (1991) observed that qualitative research holds this capacity to build community. In finding out how each of the groups interpreted the mathematics experience at City High, the groups began to understand the broader context of concerns and expectations in which their particular view was embedded. Three themes emerged from the interview data, and the task force began to organize its findings around these thematic issues:

- *What is mathematics?* Students and teachers agreed that mathematics is different from other school subjects in the ways in which it is taught and learned. Mathematics is perceived as distant from interpersonal relationships. Students saw it as disconnected from the real world. It was socially acceptable to dislike and be unsuccessful at mathematics, yet failure at it made many students feel that they were not smart.

- *What are the most common explanations that students, teachers, and parents use to account for problems with mathematics?* Teachers felt that mathematics classes were too large and blamed the lack of students' motivation and their prior elementary preparation for the high failure rates. Students also felt that the mathematics classes were too large and faulted teaching strategies for their failure. They expressed a need for better explanations by teachers, a better attitude by teachers toward students, and less disruption of the class by peers. Students believed that most of the problems came from students either having "math genes" or not having "math genes." Students also faulted "mixed-grade" classes for many of the problems that individual students faced. These mixed-grade classes had students from more than one grade level in the same class; indeed, some classes had students from all four grade levels in the same class. Parents expressed frustration with their inability to help with homework. Parents, too, attributed students' success or failure to "math genes." They felt that teachers held low expectations of success for many students and that teachers viewed students as either "getting" mathematics or not. Parents were concerned that problems in mathematics frequently led to problems in other courses as well.

- *How did parents, students, and teachers perceive the relationships between groups in ways that would account for the lack of communication they all felt?* Parents, students, and teachers all felt that there was too little time for teachers to get to know students in and out of class. Teachers noted that the physical separation of the school building kept students from lingering at class but promoted good departmental relations among teachers because teachers of like content had rooms close by. Students' impressions of the helpfulness of teachers varied, as did their impressions about the positive and negative effects of student–student relationships in the classroom. Although teachers said that they welcomed parental collaboration, they noted that issues such as working parents, family instability, and hostility toward schooling were reasons they had not been successful at achieving positive relationships with parents. Parents saw such collaboration as important because of their own perceived inadequacies with the subject.

The task force met with the parent–teacher organization and then made these recommendations in each of the three areas:

- *What is mathematics?* The task force felt that it was critical to begin to change beliefs about the use of mathematics, about who should be studying it, and about the expectations of who should be successful at it. The task force recommended that all of the groups (students, teachers, parents, and administrators) should continue to engage in dialogue about mathematics at City High. Algebra should be required for all students. The task force argued against the concept of "math genes" and urged that mathematics teachers, students, and parents each take responsibility to believe that all of the students in the class can succeed in mathematics. All of the groups were adamant that more tracking would not be a solution. All of the groups must work on diminishing the distinctions between mathematics and other subjects. Writing across the curricula was suggested as a strategy that would emphasize the connections of the other subjects with mathematics. Multicultural influences on mathematics should be stressed in various courses; instructional changes utilizing technology were needed.

- *What are some possible solutions in response to the most common problems with mathematics?* Teachers and students alike argued that class sizes must be reduced. Teachers wanted to have longer class periods as well. Students should form study groups for mathematics, and schools should offer parents classes on Saturdays to help them become more competent at helping their children. Clearly, administrative support was needed for these changes, including release time for teachers to plan changes in their classroom routines, a professional library, richer classroom materials, and inservice programs for teachers that focus on the pedagogy of mathematics. A mathematics clinic freeing teachers from study hall to staff the clinic and establishing a dialogue among teachers of mathematics from the 3rd to the 12th grade were seen as potential solutions.

- *How might relationships among teachers, parents, and students be improved?* Teachers and students both need to work on relationships in the classroom. Community-building activities should be added to classroom routines. The school could host an open house when parents could drop by any classroom at any time during the day.

By participating in this research process, teachers, students, and parents were able to understand better the different perspectives that they all held about mathematics at City High and were able to develop recommendations for change. The Task Force's Final Report (Biklen et al., 1992) noted that "our recommendations aim to change what currently seem to be normative values about mathematics at our school. We hear students focus on 'getting it.' We want to change this norm to 'thinking through mathematics'" (p. 25). Over time, the school moved to meet many of the recommendations. The site-based school improvement team used the recommendations as a starting point for many schoolwide discussions. The mathematics department also used the recommendations as a basis for discussion. At the suggestion of the mathematics department, laboratory periods were added to the first-year algebra courses so that more diversity in instructional strategies could be employed. The school began to investigate the use of 90-minute periods for all mathematics classes. The school and the school district moved to mandate algebra for all students. A parents' open house day was established each semester so that parents could drop in during the day and obtain a sense of what was happening in classes at City High. Faculty and graduate students from a nearby university were invited to give workshops and to model the use of hand-held technologies in mathematics classes. One teacher began to investigate the use of community building exercises in the context of her mathematics classes. Her success at changing the culture of her classroom to one in which students participate freely and help each other readily led other teachers to adopt this strategy. Ongoing, inservice workshops encouraged teachers to have students write in the content areas. These results created a climate for teachers to rethink their own practices systematically, through cycles of inquiry leading to further changes at both classroom and school wide levels.

## CONCLUSIONS

Because action research is grounded in practice, it is more a model of incremental change and growth in knowledge than a fundamental rethinking or restructuring of the entire educational enterprise. Nonetheless, action research can lead to more far-reaching changes in relationships and knowledge because it leads practitioners and researchers to mutually redefine their roles and to share their knowledge with the larger community of practitioners. In each of the three cases, we have addressed the critical issue of keeping the distance and preserving the distinction between researcher and participant. As the distances and the distinctions blurred, collaborative team inquiry nurtured and supported the willingness of teachers to take risks in their classes by trying out innovative strategies without the promise of success along the way. The speed with which these teachers changed their teaching practice depended on the cycle of collaborative data collection and analysis. Next steps were predicated on findings based on the teachers' own analysis of the evidence. The complexity of a classroom in flux mandates that the boundaries between research and practice become blurred.

As we looked into single classrooms, we found evidence that the lessons learned from the process of documenting change informed both research and practice. It brought to the forefront issues that needed further research, such as the interaction between group structures and mathematical content. It highlighted good practice such as ensuring that students have multiple opportunities to share their thinking. It opened up new forums for teachers to communicate their findings with other professionals and together to build on those results. In the second study we examined, teachers initiated their own small-scale studies. Here, the emphases were on defining the research questions that were significant to the individual teacher and on collecting and analyzing data. The juxtaposition of each teacher's beliefs about teaching and learning with the findings from her or his study often caused teachers to begin to rethink and change their teaching practices. As these specific changes were shared among the collective group of participating teachers, more fundamental beliefs about teaching and learning became open to question and discussion. In many cases, this led to broader changes in a teacher's overall practice.

Teachers are asked frequently to change how they teach, but they seldom have meaningful data that encourages them to do so. The teacher-researchers gained an insider view that was a catalyst for change. The lack of distance from the teacher-researcher to the phenomena being studied was related directly to the level of trust in the findings. The collective findings from multiple classrooms began to have meaning for other teachers. The biases of the insider as the researcher became diminished by the diversity of sites and the multiplicity of teacher-researchers across many settings. As more teacher research becomes reported in the voices of the teacher and less in the voices of the university researchers, we are beginning to forge more equitable, collaborative relationships that seek to respect practice-based, teacher-generated knowledge seen in newly emerging forms.

## ACKNOWLEDGMENTS

The research reported in this chapter was supported in part by a Small Grant for Exploratory Research (SGER) (RED-9255375) and in part by a Teacher Enhancement grant (ESI-9253298) from the National Science Foundation. The opinions expressed herein do not necessarily reflect those of the Foundation.

# Action Research as a Research Methodology for the Study of the Teaching and Learning of Science

**Allan Feldman**

*University of Massachusetts–Amherst*

**Jim Minstrell**

*Talaria, Inc.*

## WHAT IS ACTION RESEARCH?

Increasingly, action research has become a part of funded educational research and curricular development projects. There have been two main arguments for this. The first is that it reduces the time lag between the generation of new knowledge and its application in the classroom. If teachers are the researchers, the time lag may be reduced to zero. The second is that teachers represent a highly educated population who, with proper training, could act as classroom researchers. This offers at least two potential benefits. One is that it could reduce the cost of doing research or development. Teachers would be researchers doing inquiry as a part of their normal practice, with little additional compensation or release time. The other is that teachers spend large amounts of time in schools working with children and are experts at what they do. The inclusion of teachers as researchers in funded projects is a way of utilizing that expertise.

At the same time, there are significant concerns about the use of action research as a research methodology. First, how is the success of action research measured? If it is done by looking for a product such as an addition to the knowledge base on teaching or learning, then issues related to the validity and reliability of the research arise. Can teachers generate sufficient warrant to support propositional statements that arise from their research? Can they avoid or overcome the bias that is inherent in doing research on their own practice? Other products, such as changes in teachers or students, are possible, but difficult to measure. For example, it may be claimed that the teachers' practice has improved, that they have reached better understandings of their educational situations, or that they feel empowered through their involvement in action research. It also may be claimed that students find themselves in situations that are more supportive or challenging, or that they have learned more or differently as a result of their teachers' action research.

A second set of concerns relates to the ways in which the worlds of university-based research and teaching in kindergarten through Grade 12 intersect. Chief among these are questions that relate to the setting of a research agenda. Who sets the agenda? What tensions may arise between the goals of the principal investigators (PIs) of a funded project and the teachers' goals that relate to their own professional development or their "need to know" (A. Feldman, 1994a) that their work has had the desired effect on their students? There are issues that arise because of possible differences between the structure of funded projects and teachers' work and lives. These may be as mundane as the constraints imposed by school schedules, funding timetables, and the isolation of teachers. They also may arise from conflicting assumptions of what constitutes research or from the "contradictions of control" (McNeil, 1988) that can arise from the top-down, center-periphery management of action research configured as a grass-roots activity (A. Feldman, 1995b).

Finally, there is the issue of how teachers learn to do action research, and how others learn how to teach them how to do it and how to facilitate it. Must every project that attempts to use action research start from the beginning, or is there a way to build on the successes and failures of others?

In this chapter, we address these issues by examining action research from three perspectives. The first is an overview of what it means to engage in action research as a methodology for investigating teaching and learning in science education. In that section, we make explicit various conceptions of action research and provide readers with our definition of it. The second perspective is that of an individual (Minstrell) engaged in action research in his classroom to improve his teaching, his students' learning, and to advance knowledge of the teaching and learning of physics. The third perspective is that of a facilitator (Feldman) of action research done by others. By providing views from these three perspectives, we intend to address these concerns and issues and help readers develop their understanding of what action

research is and can be, so that it can be used as a methodology for the study of teaching and
learning in the sciences.

## Conceptions of Action Research

In writing this chapter, we are aware that *action research* is charged with meaning  In other
words, our readers bring with them their conceptions of it. Although some have abandoned the
label because of these connotations and, instead, call this methodology "teacher research" or
"practitioner inquiry," we have decided to continue to use it. Because of this, we find it
necessary to make explicit some of the conceptions that readers may have of action research.

For some, their conceptions depend on whether they put the accent on *action* or on
*research*. When the accent is on action, there is an assumption that when teachers do action
research in their classrooms, their primary purpose is to modify their practice in some way.
This may mean that the collection and analysis of data are used to guide the development of an
action plan. Others do action research by changing the system through action as a way to
determine what works and does not work in the classroom, and why. When research is
accented, action research is seen as a modification of traditional educational research that
incorporates teachers in a nontrivial way. The teachers may pursue their own research agendas,
aid in research initiated by university researchers, or be alpha- and beta-testers as in industrial
product-testing models.

There are other conceptions that readers may have of what action research is and is not,
and should be or should not be. To some, it is tied to a desire to do good in the world, through
direct social action (e.g., McTaggart, 1994). Others come to it from a critical theory
perspective that sees teachers' engagement in action research as an emancipatory process (Carr
& Kemmis, 1986). Still others assume that action research, as a form of research, is separate
from the political sphere and is concerned primarily with knowledge accumulation (e.g., Borg,
Gall, & Gall, 1993).

Action research has become linked to both pre- and inservice teacher education, too.
Increasingly, one finds a form of action research as a required component of preservice teacher
education programs (Noffke, 1996). It also is seen as a way to encourage the professional
development of teachers either by providing them with skills that will allow them to be
reflective and inquiring practitioners (e.g., Gore & Zeichner, 1991) or through the knowledge

that they will acquire from the completion of action research projects in their classrooms (e.g., Fals-Borda & Anisur, 1991).

Clearly, there are many ways in which readers conceive of action research. We have made some explicit here, not to suggest that certain of them are "misconceptions" and others "true," but rather as a reminder that action research, as a social and political endeavor with a history that stretches throughout this century, has multiple meanings and is understood in different ways by different people in different contexts. After saying that, we proceed to explain what we mean by action research.

## A Definition of Action Research

By action research, we mean teachers researching their own practice of teaching. It is an inquiry into *their* teaching in *their* classrooms. Because this research is focused on the work of teacher-researchers, it is developmental in nature and has two main purposes. The more immediate of the two is the improvement of their teaching practice in order to improve their students' learning. That is, when teachers engage in research on their teaching, they do so to get better at what they do. The second purpose is to seek an improved understanding of the educational situations in which they teach so that they then can become a part of the knowledge base of teaching and learning. From this operational definition of action research, it should be seen that it is a research *methodology*, a paradigm within which research is done, rather than a set of specific research *methods*. It is characterized by the focus of the research—the teaching done by the researcher—and the goals of that research—the improvement of teaching and learning and a better understanding of the researcher's educational situation.

## Doing and Facilitating Action Research

By defining action research in this way, we raise several questions that are embedded in the issues that we have raised already. First, action research appears to be a local and highly contextualized form of research. It is done by a teacher on his or her own practice in his or her own classroom. Does this result in research that is highly biased and from which it is difficult to generalize to other cases? Second, because it is highly contextualized, teachers choose problems to investigate that are of interest or concern to them. What if the teachers' agendas do not match those of the projects' PIs? Third, the goal of action research is greater understanding that can be linked to improved practice. This makes it an interpretive rather than an explanatory form of research (Bruner, 1996). Interpretive scholarship, which is ubiquitous in the humanities, has been accepted in the social sciences only recently and has made few inroads into the natural sciences. This then raises the question of whether this methodology would be accepted by the large number of scientists who are a part of the science education research community.

We explore these issues through reference to our own professional experiences with action research. Minstrell presents a case of a physics teacher engaged in action research. In it, he provides a narrative of his more than 20 years of doing research in his classroom on how his students learn physics and how that has affected his teaching and other professional practice. Feldman relates his work with various groups of teachers engaged in action research to these methodological issues and suggests possible remedies.

## The Products of Action Research

One of the most significant questions about action research concerns its products and how it can be determined whether they are of importance. There are several different types of products of action research: the generation of knowledge about teaching and learning, increased understanding of practice, and improvements in teaching and learning. These products differ significantly in how they are evaluated. Typically, teaching and learning are evaluated relative to specific benchmarks or standards. These benchmarks may be determined as a result of research, or they may relate to social and political norms. And, depending on what the benchmarks look like, an evaluation relative to them may be rather straightforward and traditional, such as a standardized examination or a Flanders-type checklist (Flanders, 1970), or quite complex if, for example, one is seeking evidence of deep conceptual understanding or constructivist teaching (see, e.g., several chapters in this volume, including the one by Tobin, chap. 18).

Changes are other possible outcomes for teachers who engage in the process. These changes include an increase in the teachers' knowledge and in their stances toward their work. From 1990 to 1993, Feldman studied teachers engaged in action research to understand the ways that knowledge and understanding are generated and shared in collaborative action research (A. Feldman, 1994b; 1996). During that time, he worked with a group of physics teachers in the San Francisco Bay Area who call themselves the Physics Teachers Action Research Group (PTARG). PTARG is a group of seven high school and community college physics teachers (Andria Erzberger, Sean Fottrell, Larry Hiebart, Tim Merrill, Annette Rappleyea, Lettie

Weinmann, and Tom Woosnam) who have undertaken a collaborative systematic inquiry into their own teaching for more than 6 years. The group began as an occasional meeting of physics teachers in the Bay Area to discuss the teaching of physics and to hear presentations from physicists on current research.

In his analysis of the group's meetings, Feldman was able to demonstrate that knowledge about physics, teaching, and learning, and what Shulman (1986b) called pedagogical content knowledge was generated and shared among the teachers (Feldman, 1995b). It also was apparent that the teachers began to see themselves as *researchers* as well as classroom teachers. They began to make presentations at meetings of the American Association of Physics Teachers (AAPT) and have published as a result of their action research (Erzberger et. al., 1996). Similar changes in stance occurred among teachers who did action research as a part of the California Scope, Sequence, and Coordination (SS&C) Project (A. Feldman, 1998). All of the teachers found that they were capable of improving or understanding better the implementation of new curricula in their schools. Several presented papers at national and state conferences for the first time, and one mentioned that being called an action research "fellow" had had a positive impact on his conception of himself as a professional. These changes in how they viewed their practice can be called *empowerment*, and it has been seen in other studies of teachers engaged in action research (Cochran-Smith & Lytle, 1993; Hollingsworth, 1994;).

Though improvements in teaching and learning are the ultimate goals of educational research, and growth in teachers' knowledge, as well as their empowerment, can be ways to achieve these goals, there is the assumption that funded research will result in a product that enhances the knowledge base for teaching and learning. For this to happen, knowledge must be generated. Whether the knowledge is in the form that Shulman (1986b) has called propositional, case, or strategic it must be warranted in some way (Phillips, 1987).

Knowledge is generated by doing research. If action research is to generate knowledge, it must be a legitimate form of research, and the results must be seen to be valid. Is action research, and is it a *valid* form of research? As Feldman has worked with teachers doing action research, whether the physics teachers in PTARG, the science teachers in California in the SS&C project, or the teachers enrolled in a graduate seminar on action research (A. Feldman, 1998; A. Feldman, et al., 1998), they have explored the question of the validity of action research. During his investigation of PTARG, it was Andria Erzberger who voiced most often the question, "Is this really research?"  At one point she asked, "How do I know if my students are learning any better? How do I know if I've changed? How do I know if the students have changed?" (A. Feldman, 1994a).

Feldman has attempted to answer Erzberger's questions about whether action research is research by referring to Lawrence Stenhouse's (1975) definition of research: systematic critical inquiry made public. Because this definition goes beyond the idealized notion of research as quantifiable hypothesis testing that produces generalizable propositional statements, it allows for human inquiry activities that are interpretive as well as explanatory to be labeled as research. Using this definition, the scholarly work of social scientists who use the ethnographic methods of anthropology or the clinical methods of psychology as well as that of historians, philosophers, and literary and art critics can be recognized as legitimate forms of research.

Returning to action research, if Stenhouse's definition is accepted, action research is a legitimate form of research if it is systematic and critical inquiry made public. In Feldman's work with teachers doing action research, they have tried to make it so by the teachers systematizing their inquiries and by subjecting them to critique from within and from outside (A. Feldman, 1996; 1998). However, several factors make this difficult for the teachers to do. First, because action research is inquiry into one's own practice, the distance between inquiring subject and object of study has been reduced to zero; they are the same person. Second, the action research is inherently non-reproducible. Teaching situations change continuously and no two classes are similar enough to control variables in experimental designs. It also must be noted that there are times when a teaching technique that would be considered the "experimental treatment" has enough inherent strengths that ethical issues are raised if it is withheld from a "control group" of students. And, third, the methods of the social sciences that can be used to mimic scientific experimental designs can lead to frustration and obfuscation because of temporal, spatial and social constraints on the teacher action researcher (A. Feldman & Atkin, 1995).

Although these factors suggest that action research cannot meet the demands of traditional research, this turns out not to be the case because the goals of action research are often interpretive rather than explanatory. Because most action research is concerned with seeking understanding or meaning, teachers do not need to demonstrate that what they have learned are viable explanations for all cases. Rather, they need to show that what they have learned is true in the particular case of their teaching in their classrooms. To do this, they can use a variety of techniques borrowed from the social sciences that improve on the verisimilitude of their research. These include triangulation, the consideration of alternative perspectives, testing through practice, practical compatibility, and ethical justifiability (A. Feldman, 1994a).

Triangulation consists of collecting data that represent several views of the same situation. For example, when action researchers try out a new teaching idea, they can write an account of what happened. The account is based on what the teacher remembered while in the role of teaching the class. This can be triangulated in a variety of ways. The teacher can audiotape or videotape the class. Other teachers may be asked to sit in on the class to record their observations. Students can be interviewed formally or informally after the class for their perspectives. The students could be asked to write their own reflective notes on the class. These methods have been used by all of the teachers whose action research Feldman has facilitated. Moreover, it is possible to get a variety of outcome measures, such as traditional and alternative forms of assessment.

Whereas triangulation is done to gather a variety of data from different views, the data can be interpreted from a variety of different perspectives, too. This is particularly useful in trying to understand students' responses to classroom situations. For example, a teacher may observe that students do not cooperate with one another when they are asked to work in groups. This may be interpreted as students competing rather than cooperating in response to their desires to be accepted to competitive colleges. But this also may be interpreted as a failure of the students to understand the purpose of, or instructions for, the activity, or the teacher's failure to communicate. New data can be collected, or existing data reinterpreted, to check these hypotheses.

Action researchers, like engineers and others in the applied sciences, can test their ideas by putting them into practice. The teachers develop new ideas about teaching, or reconfigure others, and try them out. Action researchers can evaluate the effectiveness of their new instructional methods or materials through outcome measures, or they can use ongoing formative assessments within the context of the teaching situation. Although this formative testing through practice cannot "prove" that a particular instructional method works, it can demonstrate that it did not work in its present form and requires modification. This is what the PTARG and CA SS&C teachers have done.

In addition to testing ideas about teaching to see whether they affect students' learning, action researchers can test whether their ideas are practical and compatible with their teaching situations. They get an immediate evaluation of the implementability of the suggested improvement. Some ideas can be rejected out of hand; for example, minuscule budgets may prevent the use of sophisticated technology in a particular classroom. Other ideas may need to be modified because of large class size, multiple presentations, or the socioeconomic status of the students.

Finally, because teachers can have profound effects on the lives of their students, the results of their action research must be justifiable ethically. Therefore, the self-evaluation of teaching practices through action research should pass tests of accessibility and equity, and should promote the health and well-being of the students and others in the schools (Altrichter, et al., 1993).

Teachers who engage in action research can take steps to ensure that their data are trustworthy through triangulation: They test their ideas through practice in their own classrooms, they check that their findings are practical and ethical, and they share what they have learned with other teachers, as ways of "publishing" what they have learned and of opening it to the scrutiny of their peers. In this manner their research is systematic and critical inquiry made public. In the next section of this chapter, we present an example of one teacher doing action research. In it, we look at how Jim Minstrell has done systematic critical inquiry in his classroom, and made it public.

## DOING ACTION RESEARCH: AN EXAMPLE OF ACTION RESEARCH IN ONE TEACHER'S CLASSROOM

Much of the experience of being an action researcher occurs alone in one's own classroom. Consistent with that tradition, this section is written in the first person. In it, one of us (Jim Minstrell) recounts how he arrived at, and developed gradually, the methods and learning perspectives that he has used during more than two decades as an action researcher attempting to understand his students' thinking and the effects and practice of his teaching in the context of classroom activities in science and mathematics. More recently, he has been working with networks of teachers who are engaging collectively and independently in their own action research to improve their students' learning.

## Why Classroom Research?

At some level, I have known that I was interested in questions of human learning since I was in the eighth grade. When studying science, we were "forced" to memorize steps of "the" scientific method. I remember voicing my disapproval during a class discussion that "nobody thinks like that."

During my first few years of teaching, I was told by my administrators and by my students that I was "one of the best teachers" they had had, and I wondered precisely what "learning" effects I had had on my students. The students did well on my tests as long as I kept the questions close to the procedures that I had "trained" them to do. But, when I slipped in questions that required a deep understanding of the concepts and reasoning I supposedly had been teaching, I was disappointed. I became more curious about the nature of learning in the classroom.

After only four years of teaching, I had the opportunity to participate in research at the national level with Project Physics (Rutherford, Holton, & Watson, 1970). Although the methods used by the researchers in that project were very sophisticated and served the needs of a large curriculum development project, they were not useful to my interest in improving my effectiveness as a teacher in my own classroom. Although the results seemed too far from my issues of learning in my classroom, the experience initiated my interest in research.

Six years into my teaching career, I began working part time at the University of Washington with Professor Arnold Arons, a colleague and mentor through whom (not from whom) I learned a lot about science and about the capabilities and difficulties of developing conceptual understanding. In working with our university students (mostly teachers and prospective teachers), Arons used to coach me to keep my hands in my pockets and make the students show me what they did, or what they would do, about the problem. Prior to that, my inclination was not unlike many, well-meaning teachers whose approach is: "Here, let me show you how to do it," from which the students learned little more than how "smart" I was.

Arons also coached me to listen to what the students were saying, reminding me that I had two ears but only one mouth and to use them in that proportion. In addition to my learning much about physics, I changed my perspective from a focus on me as a deliverer of knowledge to a focus on my students and what they were learning. My critical questions as a teacher became: "What is the understanding of my students?" and "What experiences can I put before the students to cause them to have to rethink their present understanding and reconstruct that understanding in order to make it more consistent with a broader set of phenomena?"

This has evolved into my line of classroom research and has affected my teaching greatly. When I finished my doctoral dissertation, I applied for a grant to buy part of my time so that I could stay in my high school classroom and conduct research on the teaching and learning of my students. That has become the natural, and practical, setting within which I conduct a line of research. At the same time, my primary responsibility has been to teach, or, more correctly, to be responsible for my students' learning. Now, in the classroom, I always wear both the hat of a researcher and the hat of a teacher. Each perspective helps me to direct, and to make sense of, the results of the other.

## My Classroom-Based Action Research

How better could I understand my students' thinking, their conceptual understanding, and their reasoning in the natural setting of the classroom? What effects, if any, did my teaching have on their learning? How could I effect better learning? Will my results be of use beyond my classroom?

In the early stages of my action research, my activities as a researcher were informal. They amounted mostly to anecdotes that, to me, represented evidence of either the learning I intended or the learning that did not occur. I looked for correlation between gross measures like grades in my class (e.g., high school physics) and possible predicting variables like grades in other courses (e.g., geometry) and more "standardized" measures (e.g., "the Classroom Test of Formal Operations"; Lawson, 1977).

Sometimes, I was testing an intervention as short as a particular lesson and, at other times, the effects of aspects of an entire year's program. At times, I could conduct a controlled experiment. At others, I was gathering data and attempting to interpret the results.

Gradually, there evolved a line of investigation in my classroom that focused on describing my students' initial and developing understanding and reasoning about the content of the courses I was teaching. Later, that line of investigation evolved into designing and testing instructional interventions adapted explicitly to address students' difficulties in understanding and reasoning.

*Data Gathering in My Classroom.* After I began to listen to my students more carefully and to solicit their ideas, I needed to gather data systematically. I enlisted the help of my students and their parents who, at the beginning of the school year, were asked to consider and sign consent forms for participation in my studies. I warned my students that I might be doing some atypical teaching and assessment during my research to understand and address their thinking. I bought a small, battery-run audiorecorder that I kept on my desk in the classroom. Later, I bought a videocamera and recorder that I set up when I anticipated discussions that might be informative to other teachers. While students interacted in small groups, I carried the audiorecorder with me and turned it on when I came to an interesting discussion or when students came to me with questions or ideas they had about the phenomena under investigation. During large-group discussions, when it appeared that an informative discussion was likely to develop, I started the recorder and let it run throughout the class period. After the discussion, if I felt there were not research quality data, I erased the tape and prepared it for another class.

On one such occasion, early in my experience as a classroom researcher, the audiorecorder was running when we were beginning the study of force and motion. I had asked the students about the forces on a book "at rest" on the front table. The students drew and wrote their answers on paper quietly. While I was walking around the room, I noticed that two answers, involving whether the table exerted a force, dominated. One suggested that the table exerted an upward force, and the other suggested no such upward force. When our discussion began, I drew those two diagrams on the board and took a poll. There was an observer in the class that day, so I asked him to record the number of students who raised their hands during these brief surveys. The answers were divided approximately evenly between those who thought that the table exerted an upward force and those who thought that it did not.

I asked for volunteers to support one or the other of these positions and discovered that the difference revolved around whether one believed that passive objects like tables could exert forces. I decided to test this by putting the book on the outstretched hand of a student. We took a poll on the students' beliefs about this situation. Nearly everyone thought that the hand exerted an upward force. I inquired about the difference between the two situations, and the students argued that the hand was alive and that the person made muscular adjustments to support the book, especially when I stacked several additional books on top of the first one. The observer recorded the number of students who raised their hands. The teacher side of me wanted the students to be able to see the similarities between the situations, but it was clear that the students were seeing the differences. Again thinking about how I would address their concern, I pulled a spring out of a drawer, hung it from hardware, and attached the book to the spring. The spring stretched until the book was supported. I asked again for diagrams and took another poll, recorded by the observer. Nearly all of the students believed that the spring must be exerting an upward force. I countered by asking whether the spring was alive or how this situation was like the book on the hand. The students did not believe that the spring was alive with muscular activity, but that it could stretch or deform and adjust in a way to support the book. And, how was this different from the table? They suggested that the table was rigid: It did not stretch or deform like the spring. "Ability to deform or adjust" now seemed to be the difference between these situations and my target situation of the book on the table. I put on my teacher hat, darkened the room, pulled out a light projector, and set it up so that the light reflected off the table top onto the far wall. Using this "light lever," I alternately put heavy objects on and off the table, and we noticed the movement of the light on the far wall. The students concluded that the table must be bending also. With my teacher hat still in place, I summarized by suggesting that force is a concept invented by humankind. As such, we are free to define force in any way we want, but the scientist notes the similarity of "at rest" in several situations. Then, wanting to be consistent, he thinks of one explanation that works for all of the situations: the explanation involving balanced forces. This means that the scientist's definition of force will include "passive" support by tables as well as "active" support by things like hands or springs.

The description of this action research became the material in my first published research article (Minstrell, 1982a). The situation has been analyzed since by other researchers and incorporated into curricular materials (Camp et.al., 1994). It is important to note that, in this discovery mode, the "hats" of researcher and teacher are being interchanged quickly in efforts both to understand the students' thinking and to affect their learning.

It was a memorable lesson for me and for my students. It made them think differently about whether actions are active or passive and about the idea of force. These lessons that students keep referring back to later in the year, or in subsequent years, I have come to call "benchmark lessons," a metaphor from the geographical survey reference benchmarks that one finds cemented into rocks (diSessa & Minstrell, 1998).

This interplay between conducting research focused on students' understanding, and making adjustments in instruction to address their understanding, is similar to the design process of engineering as well as the investigatory process of science. Prototype lessons are planned, tried, altered, and tried until the product is a lesson that works within the design constraints of addressing the students' concerns and the target learning of the curriculum. As a teacher-researcher, I was at the same time a scientist, trying to understand the students' thinking, and an engineer, trying to develop a product lesson that works within the constraints.

This interplay places demands on me to be creative in designing and redesigning relevant experiences that bring into question some of the initial ideas of the students. In that way, I test my models of their thinking. I also need to know the subject matter well so that I can appreciate the issues from the students' view and how those issues relate to the formal discipline. Then, I need to know the curriculum possibilities well so that I can choose or redesign activities.

*Description of My Students' Thinking.* With more experience as an action researcher, I became more systematic in my methods. To find out what students are thinking, I designed and set problematic situations before them at the beginning of most units of study. These tasks were typically in the form of preinstruction quizzes, but only the students' honest effort, not the "correctness" of the answer, counted for credit (Minstrell, 1982b). Students were asked for an answer and reasoning for how the answer made sense. From the sorts of tasks I set and from the answers and the rationale students gave, I inferred their conceptual understanding. In this research approach, I was using methods similar to the interviews conducted by cognitive scientists except that I was interviewing my whole class (Bruer, 1993). As a teacher, the activities I set out in class tended to be driven by the class as a whole, rather than by an individual learner. Still, the method allowed me to "know" the tentative thinking of most of the individuals in my class as well as the thinking of the class in general.

The aforementioned procedure allowed me to "discover" aspects of my students' thinking. For example, before I started a dynamics unit, I used the University of Massachusetts Mechanics Diagnostic (Clement, 1982b) to identify ideas my students seemed to have about the forces that objects exerted on each other during interaction. Even though most high school students were able to repeat the phrase "for every action, there is an equal and opposite reaction," they did not apply the idea to objects interacting. I found that most students initially attended to surface features and argued that the heavier, or the stronger, or the most active object, or the one that inflicted the greater change in the other object, exerted the greater force. Often, that was as far as I could go in terms of learning about students' thinking, creating the hypothesis, and then instructing with that thinking in mind.

However, as time and opportunity allowed, I also attempted to "verify" my hypotheses about students' thinking. I designed problematic situations that contained those features specifically, and, based on my assumptions about the students' thinking, I predicted the outcomes. If they responded according to my prediction, I had some degree of confirmation that my assumptions about their thinking were correct.

Notice that the procedure is consistent with science as a method. As a researcher, I was generating and testing hypotheses about students' thinking. As a teacher, I wanted to know generally what the thinking was so that I could choose or design more relevant activities, benchmark lessons that might have a better chance of changing students' conceptions, for example, by incorporating a broader set of phenomena, constructing new conceptions or new models that likely would be more consistent with formal scientific thinking.

The results of these more systematic approaches to identifying students' ideas have appeared in a working document accumulating facets of students' thinking (Minstrell, 1992). Are students' facets of thinking consistent from one situation to another? If one looks at the data from the perspective of principled formal physics, the answer is a clear no. However, if one looks at the surface features of problems, students' thinking is much more consistent (Minstrell & Stimpson, 1986). To the extent that we can triangulate students' understanding from test results, discussions, laboratory activities, and written work, we establish the reliability of our findings. The facets developed from classroom research provide a set of potential hypotheses of students' thinking in most topics of physics. As a classroom teacher, I use these facets to diagnose the ideas of students and to prescribe my instruction based on the diagnosis. The facets and facet-based instruction have been incorporated into a computerized diagnoser for physics instruction developed by me and my colleagues in the psychology department at the University of Washington (Hunt & Minstrell, 1994; Levidow, Hunt, & McKee, 1991).

*Testing the Effects of My Instructional Intervention.* Being a teacher and wanting to see that I have an effect on the learners in my class, I write or adapt an instructional activity that is designed to perturb the assumed thinking of the students. To test for effects, I needed to identify the students' initial thinking first. The facets are helpful in designing a preinstruction quiz or survey to do that. Then, I used an instructional intervention, designed specifically to address the students' thinking. This usually amounted to a series of lessons, including the benchmark lesson, that took a few days for the students to work through. Repeatedly, the issues, questions, and ideas that were voiced in the initial problematic situations were revisited. Finally, at a later time, I set another task before the students in order to assess their resulting thinking, looking for apparent change. Out of this process, I and my fellow teachers have developed a physics pedagogy program, an evolving set of activities that can be used by teachers to help them focus on their students' learning of critical ideas about the physical world. The classroom-measured effectiveness of these research-based products provides our source of validity for the research.

## Summary: Lessons From Doing Action Research

Most of my current research is directed at modeling students' thinking and testing the effectiveness of interventions to change that thinking. It is no accident that most of my current teaching involves guiding students' modeling of physical phenomena. The methods of the research are eclectic. Sometimes, they are chosen to be consistent with the rhythm of the classroom. Occasionally, they interrupt the flow. Although somewhat constrained by the context of the classroom, the research methods I choose are associated with the questions involved in the research and are not necessarily unique to the classroom.

Many of my findings can add to the general knowledge of learning and teaching and are not limited to my classroom only. My "rule of thumb" has been that if about 10% or more of my students exhibit a similar sort of thinking, then I need to acknowledge and describe the conceptions and reasoning they are using, and I need to design instruction to address that thinking. These findings have been generalizable beyond my classroom. Although one might think that there would be as many different ideas as there are students in the classroom, this is not the case. Usually, there are between two and eight approaches to thinking exhibited by the class when confronted with a particular situation. When we present similar sorts of situations, I see the same behavior replicated in the classrooms of other teachers. And, in most cases, the lessons that work to perturb the problematic thinking in one classroom also work in another. Thus, these findings are considered generalizable.

Teaching is a complex, problem-solving activity. There is no single way to do it. Some goals are predictable, and some emerge during classroom activities. Adopting the perspective of the researcher as well as the teacher in my classroom has given me professional vitality. Feeling free to do the research allows me to inquire into my own questions about teaching and learning. When I see learning, I can feel success as a teacher. When learning does not happen, I do not need to cover it up to preserve my self-esteem. Instead, I have another problematic situation to investigate as a researcher. Wearing both the hat of the teacher and the hat of the inquiring researcher allows me to produce more effective learning environments for my students and for the field of science education.

To be a teacher-researcher takes time. My personal development has taken years. I was fortunate to have survived competition for research funding that bought a portion of my time to enable me to think about issues of teaching and learning in my classroom. I also benefited from university colleagues who have challenged me to improve my research techniques. Finally, I have benefited from working with students, administrators, and especially teacher colleagues who have allowed me to investigate their classroom environments. They have been instrumental in testing the validity and reliability of apparent findings.

Conducting action research has allowed me to maintain a line of personal inquiry in the context of the classroom, where most formal learning takes place. I am able to test my own hypotheses about learning and about teaching for more effective learning. Now I am working with several teachers, and we question each other, redesigning and testing instructional activities. Many of them claim, as I do, that conducting action research in their classrooms has revitalized their professional lives. All of us agree that taking on an inquiry perspective about our classroom activities has yielded significant changes in our teaching and, more important, in the learning of our students.

My action research and my actions as a teacher have become one. I can no longer teach without conducting research in the same instructional setting.

## FACILITATING ACTION RESEARCH

In his narrative, Minstrell has described how action research can result in a teacher's professional development, increased learning by students, and additions to the knowledge base on teaching and learning science. However, Minstrell's experience with action research is unique. He has been able to develop his own research agenda and carry it out through years of inquiry in his classroom in collaboration with colleagues in colleges and universities throughout the world. When action research is selected as a research methodology to be used by teachers as a part of funded projects, problems can arise that were not inherent in Minstrell's situation. In this section of the chapter, we explore these methodological concerns in relation to Feldman's experience as a facilitator of teachers' action research.

## Setting the Agenda

The first of these methodological concerns is how the research agenda is set and who sets it. Tensions can arise between teachers and the project directors when the teachers are asked to do action research to meet the needs of a research agenda that they did not help to determine. These tensions arise because the teachers' reasons for engaging in the research do not match the goals of the funded project.

There are three ways that Feldman has seen this occur:

- Teachers' own research questions can push aside the agenda set by the projects' principal investigators.
- The project can call for teachers to do documentation or evaluation when they would prefer to focus on their professional development.
- The teachers' primary concern can be to satisfy their "need to know" that their teaching has the desired effect on their students' learning (A. Feldman, 1994a).

For example, in the original PTARG project, which was funded by the Spencer Foundation (A. Feldman, 1993), the teachers were aware of the goals of the project when they agreed to join it. However, as they engaged in collaborative action research, the problems and concerns that they had about their own practices, including their "need to know," pushed aside the PI's agenda.

During the academic year that PTARG was a part of the Spencer Foundation–funded research project, each of the teachers received a small honorarium for their participation ($500), a modest dinner was provided for each meeting, and several of the teachers were provided with travel funds to attend and make a presentation at a meeting of the American Association of Physics Teachers. In addition, the teachers and Feldman invested significant amounts of time in the project during that year. Was this a good use of the resources? If measured against the goals of the funded project, the answer would be no. It should be clear that although the PTARG teachers agreed to be a part of the project and were aware of its goals, they were reluctant to participate fully in it. Eventually they did, but the outcomes were significantly different from those that the PI had expected, and as soon as the funded year ended, the teachers abandoned that agenda for their own. This raises two issues: The first is whether we can expect teachers to engage enthusiastically in research that is not of primary concern to them. The PTARG teachers indicated to Feldman that they would and, in fact, did follow through with what they agreed to do. But this appeared to be more because of a feeling of professional obligation than of interest. This raises the question of why they joined the project in the first place if they had little interest in the stated goals. When asked, the PTARG teachers responded that it was a way for them to learn more about their own practice and to improve it by interacting with other physics teachers in ways that were not possible in their schools (A. Feldman, 1993).

Once in the projects, the teachers were aware of the commitment that they had made. In fact, the PTARG teachers told Feldman, in separate interviews, that they would have followed closer to the PI's agenda if they had been pressed to do so. This raised a second concern, one that has political and ethical dimensions: Given the hierarchical differences between university researchers and school teachers and the teachers' feelings of professional obligation once they agree to participate in a funded project, what can, or cannot, the directors of the projects do to keep the teachers focused on the project's agenda? And, possibly even more important, is it necessary to make sure in some way that the teachers truly buy into the goals of the project before they are accepted into it?

A similar conflict of goals occurred in the action research component of the California SS&C Project (A. Feldman, 1995b). Over the course of 2 years, 24 teachers engaged in action research on the implementation of SS&C in their high schools. In the original proposal for the California SS&C Project, the action research component was envisioned to be a way for teachers to assist in the overall evaluation of the project and to generate knowledge about how students learn when science is taught in a coordinated manner. Only three of the teachers' action research projects could be considered evaluative in any way, and none was designed to generate knowledge about students' learning. In addition, these three evaluation studies were not done to satisfy the needs of the PIs or the National Science Foundation (the agency that funded the SS&C project), but rather to satisfy the teachers' own "need to know" that the effort that they were putting into the reform of their teaching was having the desired effects on their students. All of the others were concerned either with curriculum design and instruction or with structural problems in the school, the school district, or the region in the implementation of SS&C. It is important to note, however, that the action research component did meet the PIs' goal to create a mechanism that would provide teachers with information about the implementation of SS&C in other schools (A. Feldman, Mason, & Goldberg, 1992, 1993).

## Structural Concerns

Feldman's work with the California SS&C Project led him to identify methodological concerns that arose from the structure of the overall project and of the action research component. These included:

- A constrictive timetable.
- Conflicting conceptions of what constitutes research.
- Contradictions of control.
- The physical isolation of the teachers.

The first three of these flaws relate to what A. Feldman (1995b) has called the *institutionalization* of action research. By this, he means that an organizational institution had been created and given legitimate status to promote a cause—the implementation of SS&C in California.

It is apparent that the institutionalized nature of this action research and the fact that these teachers are practicing professionals have impeded the research process. First, because the action research was embedded in the larger project, the timetable of the California SS&C Project determined the pace of the action research. From the analysis of the action research component, it appears as if one academic year is not enough time for teachers to complete an action research project that is expected to generate new knowledge or be useful for program evaluation purposes. In fact, it appears that the first year is a time for sorting through priorities, coming to an understanding of the research process, and redefining the goal of the research. A second year would have been needed to proceed with the project. This is even more apparent when compared with Minstrell's action research biography, which began with his involvement with Project Physics in the late 1960s, developed through the 1970s, and resulted in his first publication in 1982.

A second impediment was due to the institutionalized nature of the action research, too. No distinction was made between research for professional development or curriculum implementation and research for the purpose of program evaluation. To many of the teachers involved and to the directors of the California SS&C Project, action research was seen as a way for teachers to evaluate the program at their schools. The teachers who attempted to do this found that it was a task well beyond the resources available to them. Related to this was an unforeseen conception that many of the teachers held of research in educational settings. Although it may be expected for them to hold a conception of research similar to what is presented as "the" scientific method in introductory science textbooks, many thought of educational research as the collection of data about students to report to governmental agencies for accountability purposes.

Third, there were the contradictions of control (McNeil, 1988) inherent in this project, which was designed to be a site-based curriculum development effort, but was situated in a government initiative with its top-down, center-periphery, information transfer and control. Although this had little effect on the day-to-day activities of the teachers in the California SS&C Project, it had significant repercussions for the teacher leaders in the project (Kota & A. Feldman, 1993) and made the action research fellows unsure of what it was that they could focus on as problematic in their implementation of SS&C.

Finally, there was the geographic spread of the teachers involved. During the first year, most of the teachers were isolated physically from one another. They were spread throughout the entire 1,000-mile length of California, although most of them were concentrated in the San Francisco, Los Angeles, and San Diego areas. This isolation led to two significant problems: The first was that the action research fellows did not know that their lack of time and other resources were not unique to them. The second was that they were not able to get the frequent critical feedback that would have allowed them to move ahead with their inquiries. Again, a look back at Minstrell's experience reinforces this. During much of his development as an action researcher, he had a supportive collegial relationship with Arnold Arons at the University of Washington.

## Constraints of Schooling

In addition to the methodological concerns that arise from the structure of the funded project, there are those that are due to the constraints imposed by the structure of schools and of teachers' work. Chief among these are the lack of time to engage in any professional development activities other than those that are the normal part of teaching. In his work with PTARG and his teaching of a graduate seminar on action research, Feldman has developed a model of action research that is an enhancement of normal practice and relies on the use of sustained conversations in collaborative settings (A. Feldman, 1996, 1998; Hollingsworth, 1994).

In enhanced normal practice, teachers engage collaboratively in action research through three mechanisms: anecdote-telling, the trying out of ideas, and systematic inquiry. In this context, "collaborative" refers to a group of teachers—or other practitioners—who form a group within which they work together to engage in action research on their individual practices. When the teachers gather together, they share stories of practice. One teacher may tell an anecdote; the others listen. The listeners respond with their own anecdotes, with questions that ask for details, or with questions that take a critical turn and explore the nature of teaching and learning in schools in the context of the anecdote told. This is not a transmission model; rather, it is a conversational exchange in a particular situation that relies on the teachers' expertise and experiences—what Searle (1984) called the "Background," "the set of skills, habits, abilities, etc., against which intentional states function" (p. 68).

As might be expected, ideas about practice are exchanged and generated in the anecdote-telling process. The teachers go back to their classrooms and try out these ideas. They then return to the group with new anecdotes that describe how these ideas were enacted and how the students responded to them. Again, the other teachers in the collaborative group respond to the anecdotes with their stories and with new questions. In this way, through both the taking of actions and through conversation, there is an improvement of practice and a better understanding of the teachers' educational situations.

The third mechanism of enhanced normal practice, systematic inquiry, is similar to classroom action research (Altrichter, et al, 1993; Calhoun, 1994; Sagor, 1992). It relies heavily on the collection and analysis of data in the modes of operation of the university. In the model of enhanced normal practice, systematic inquiry begins as the result of the uncovering of dilemmas or dissonances in practice that can be resolved only through a more detailed, systematic look at the practice situation.

As can be seen, sustained conversations are a significant part of enhanced normal practice. These conversations aid in research because they promote the exchange of knowledge and the generation of understanding through dialectical, meaning-making processes. Again, it is important to note that this is not a transmission or conduit model in which words are the intermediaries between people that result in the transfer of thoughts, knowledge, or feelings (Reddy, 1979). Conversations play an important part in action research because they are critical inquiry processes. They are inquiry processes when the participants enter into conversations for the purposes of exchanging and generating knowledge and understanding, and when people enter into them to make defensible decisions about goals or actions. In this latter case, the participants are engaging in a form of practical reasoning, such as Aristotelian phronē sis (Irwin, 1985). Conversations are critical inquiry processes because of the ways in which understanding grows among the participants (Gadamer, 1992). In conversations, the participants move between the conversational situation, their immediate understanding, and a more global understanding of what is being said, listened to, reflected upon, and responded to. Thus, conversations are analogous to the manner in which text is interpreted critically (Gadamer, 1992). When we come to understand a text, it helps us to understand its meaning in new ways. In the same way, conversation is a critical process that leads to new understanding and the new understanding shapes the conversation. It follows then, using Stenhouse's (1975) definition of research as systematic critical inquiry made public, that conversations, which can be mechanisms for critical inquiry, serve as a research method when systematized through the anecdote-telling mechanism of enhanced normal practice (A. Feldman, 1996).

## The Teaching of Action Research

Finally, there are the issues of how teachers learn to do action research and how others learn how to teach them to do it and how to facilitate it. It appears that learning how to do action research, as with learning how to do any type of research, is accomplished best by doing it. Therefore, if teachers are expected to have some level of expertise in action research when they do it as a part of a funded project, they should have had some experience with it already. What this means is that if projects are to incorporate teachers as action researchers, they must recruit teachers who have had experience with action research or another significant research experience, or there should be the expectation that the teachers' initial use of action research will serve mainly to teach them how to do it.

The same would hold true for those who teach teachers to do action research and facilitate it. Therefore, it is important for projects to include people with expertise in the teaching and facilitating of action research unless time is allowed for project personnel to gain that experience.

## Summary: Lessons From Facilitating Action Research

When teachers engage in action research as a part of funded projects, methodological issues arise that relate to teachers' resources, goals, structures of the projects, and the constraints of schooling. Through our experience and inquiries into action research, we have developed the following set of suggestions for those who would like to include teachers' action research as a part of a funded project:

- Give it time. It appears that it may take up to 1 year for teachers to learn how to do action research. Then, a second year is needed for the teachers to look critically and systematically at their teaching.

- It is a group activity. Teachers get the most out of doing action research when it is done collaboratively with other teachers. It also appears, both from Feldman's experience with PTARG (A. Feldman, 1993) and his teaching of an action research seminar (A. Feldman, 1998), that groups of teachers that transcend school boundaries may be more effective than groups within schools. His data suggest that when teachers collaborate with teachers from other schools, they are both less constrained by the cultures and structures of their own schools and more likely to find other teachers who can become invested in the idea of being teacher-researchers.

- The research questions should be generated by the teachers involved, or in collaboration with the PIs. The ownership of the questions can result in more ownership of the research.

- The methods, both quantitative and qualitative, of the natural sciences and the social sciences may not be appropriate for developmental teacher research. The methods require resources that many teachers do not have, they may not satisfy the teachers' need to know, and they often do not match the rhythm of teaching (A. Feldman & Atkin, 1995). And, unless teachers are provided with time and other resources, the methods of action research need to be embedded in what teachers already do. In addition, ways should be found to allow teachers to maintain sustained conversations about their action research.

- In order for teachers to engage in research, or any noninstructional professional activities, ways need to be found to provide them with release time.

How can these lessons be applied to the use of action research in funded projects? The items in the list suggest that if action research is to be an integral part of funded research or development projects, it must be well structured and highly organized by the starting date of the action research component. Teachers need to be clear about what they are committing to, they must be provided with adequate resources including release time, and there must be ongoing support by trained facilitators. Teachers should be aware that not only are they committing to being a part of a project that provides them with colleagues and status, but also that they have a specific job to do. Although the specific job may evolve as the overall project progresses, they need to be clear about what the agenda of the project is and who has set it. It is important to realize that the project directors have a responsibility to have thought this out carefully before asking teachers to make their commitment and to have enlisted the aid of individuals who have expertise in action research.

It also is important for the project directors to recognize that teachers' professional lives differ significantly from those of university researchers. Teachers have very little unscheduled time during the school day, are responsible for large numbers of students, are often involved in extracurricular and other professional activities, and have personal lives, too. If the teachers are being asked to do more than what Feldman has described as enhanced normal practice, they must be provided with real release time; for secondary school teachers, this means a reduction in the number of classes taught each day. Obviously, that would result in action research not being as cost-effective as some assume.

The project directors also should be clear that there are multiple conceptions of action research and that the type that they promote as a part of their project should be consonant with the goals of the project. From Feldman's experience with the California SS&C Project and with PTARG, he has come to realize that a self-developmental form of action research can be at odds with the goals of a funded project.

Finally, it is important to build into the project methods for the maintenance of sustained conversations among the action researchers. This may mean having regular meetings about once every 3 or 4 weeks throughout the academic year and someone who can convene and facilitate those meetings. Without these gatherings and conversations, the action research may get put into that "next thing to do" pile and emerge only when the teachers feel the professional obligation to deliver what they had agreed to.

As we come to the end of this chapter, there remains one more lesson that we must articulate. It is clear from Minstrell's narrative that, under the right conditions, a teacher who has the proper resources can engage in classroom-based action research that meets all of the validity demands of university based research and adds significantly to the knowledge base on teaching and learning science. This suggests to us that, in addition to thinking about how teachers can be utilized as researchers in others' funded research and development projects, the possibility should be considered that they can be researchers in their own right. Clearly, they would need to learn how to be researchers and most likely go through some sort of apprentice experience—in effect, what Minstrell did when he completed his doctorate at the University of Washington. But, more important, ways would need to be found to support them in their roles as teachers and researchers through significant funding opportunities.

# CONCLUSION

The purpose of this chapter has been to help readers develop their understanding of what action research is and can be, and how it can be used for the professional development of teachers, the formative and summative evaluation of programs, and the generation of new knowledge about teaching and learning.

There are four main points that we want to reiterate and relate to the use of action research as a part of funded projects:

- Action research has a history. As with any human endeavor, that history can be told in many ways, and how one reads it affects the understanding of what action research is.

- Learning how to do action research is a part of the process of becoming an action researcher. In other words, it is a developmental process that occurs over time. We saw that in Minstrell's action research autobiography and in the projects that Feldman facilitated. Teachers begin with a curiosity about teaching and learning, which may be tied to a moral imperative that they feel to help students learn. This leads them to try out different ways to teach and then to their feeling a need to know that their new methods are having the desired effects. By grappling with ways to satisfy that need, teachers begin to realize that systematic inquiry can be used to understand the educational situations in which they practice and to help them change those situations so that learning can take place.

- Doing action research can result in teachers feeling a tension between teaching and researching. This tension arises from the uncertainty about their role in the classroom as well as questions about the validity and reliability of their research. Whereas Minstrell has been able to construct his practice so that he is a teacher, a researcher, and an action researcher, others have felt the dilemma that results from that tension (A. Feldman, 1994a; Wong, 1995).

- We have produced a list of suggestions and concerns about the use of action research. It should be clear that although this list may provide useful guidelines for engaging teachers in action research to improve their practice, they can be at odds with the use of action research for the furthering of the goals of funded research and development projects.

How, then, do these points relate to the use of action research as a part of funded research and development projects? The first suggests to us that it is important to make explicit what one means by the term whenever action research is considered as a method for these projects. The second raises the issue of time. Although becoming an action researcher can stretch over a teacher's career, funded projects have definite timetables by which they are constrained. The third point reminds us that the demands on teachers and their teaching goals may be in conflict with the agendas of the projects or the methods that help to ensure reliability and validity. And the list of lessons highlights the differences between action research for the professional development of individual teachers and action research that is institutionalized to meet the needs of a funded project. All of this suggests that if teachers' action research is to be used successfully in funded projects, the PIs of those projects need to give careful consideration to what the purposes of that action research are, how it fits into the overall goals of the project, and how teachers will be supported so that they can become action researchers.

## ACKNOWLEDGMENTS

Preparation of this chapter was supported partially by The James S. McDonnell Foundation and The Spencer Foundation. The ideas presented are those of the authors and do not represent necessarily the thoughts and opinions of the foundations.

# 17

## Integrating a Naturalistic Paradigm Into Research on Mathematics and Science Cognition and Learning

**Judit N. Moschkovich**
*University of California–Santa Cruz*

**Mary E. Brenner**
*University of California–Santa Barbara*

The fields of mathematics and science education no longer accept a model of the mathematics or science learner as an individual grappling with a body of predetermined concepts and facts. It is recognized that the learner is a member of multiple communities and that, within and through these communities, the content and meaning of mathematics or science are continually renegotiated as parts of the learning process. Thus in order to understand the individual's thinking fully, it is necessary to analyze the individual's home and community cultures (Abreu, 1995; Brenner, 1998a, 1998b) as well as the classroom cultures (Cobb & Bauersfeld, 1995) within which learning occurs. In fact, current models of mathematical problem solving include beliefs and practices that individuals develop through interaction with their physical and social environments as important aspects of cognition (Bishop, 1991; Schoenfeld, 1992). These new models of mathematics and science cognition call for new approaches to research. In this chapter, we discuss the approach we have used for two research projects that integrated a naturalistic paradigm into the study of mathematics cognition and learning.

We refer to this paradigm, derived from the social sciences that traditionally have studied communities, cultures, and social interactions, as the *naturalistic research paradigm* (Erlandson, Harris, Skipper, & Allen, 1993; Lincoln & Guba, 1985). Because we assume that the reader is more familiar with cognitive research approaches in mathematics and science education, such as cognitive science (Schoenfeld, 1987a) or constructivism (Steffe & Gale, 1995), we focus on the naturalistic research paradigm. We review the main principles for using a naturalistic paradigm, describe two studies that used a spiraling design for integrating this paradigm with other research methods, and outline some standards of quality for naturalistic research studies. We are not proposing that the naturalistic paradigm is more advantageous than any other paradigm. Our claims are that it can be integrated into studies of cognition, that naturalistic and cognitive (or experimental) methods can be combined in complementary ways, and that this integration and combination can move mathematics and science education research forward. We present two research projects as examples of how this integration is possible and what it can contribute.

In the two studies in which we have used the naturalistic paradigm to examine mathematics cognition and learning, the paradigm from sociology and anthropology was integrated with cognitive science methodology in a spiraling design that combined naturalistic and cognitive science methods for collecting and analyzing data. These studies are not presented as exemplary in any sense but, rather, to provide a focus for dialogues about methodology in mathematics and science education research.

In this chapter and through the descriptions of these two studies, we address several questions that focus on naturalistic inquiry and how to include it in research on mathematics and science education:

- What principles guide research studies using a naturalistic paradigm?
- How can a naturalistic paradigm be combined with other research approaches to explore questions about mathematics cognition and learning?
- How can researchers use ethnographic methods to investigate aspects of mathematics cognition and learning?
- What are the standards for quality in naturalistic research?

The naturalistic paradigm that undergirds our work is an emergent paradigm about the nature of the research enterprise (Lincoln & Guba, 1985; Erlandson et al., 1993).[1] This paradigm arose in contrast to positivistic traditions in which the scientific method was considered the route to discovering an objective reality. The naturalistic paradigm assumes that meaning is constructed by both participants and observers so that, in effect, there are multiple realities (Erlandson et al., 1993). Because these multiple versions of reality are shaped by both theoretical and value frameworks, it is not possible to achieve pure objectivity (Guba, 1990). The goal of the naturalistic research enterprise is, "to identify the variety of constructions that exist and bring them into as much consensus as possible" (Guba, 1990, p. 26). To fulfill this purpose, naturalistic research takes a holistic view in order to examine these various constructions in relation to each other as they interact in their own contexts. It should be noted that naturalistic research is not synonymous with qualitative research, although qualitative methods tend to be the preferred methods used in the naturalistic paradigm (Erlandson et al., 1993; Guba, 1993). A close examination of the assumptions underlying different qualitative traditions in educational research, such as those described by Jacob (1987), shows that the naturalistic paradigm is inherent to some qualitative traditions, but not all.

## PRINCIPLES OF NATURALISTIC RESEARCH STUDIES

So far, we have used the term *paradigm*, rather than *methodology*, to emphasize that we are not referring to a collection of methods but to an epistemological stance. Although the term methodology is misunderstood sometimes to refer only to "methods," theory and methods are intricately related, mutually constructive, and informing of each other. Methodology includes the underlying theoretical assumptions about cognition and learning: what cognition and learning are; when and where cognition and learning occur; and how to document, describe, and explain them. In the rest of this chapter, we use the terms *paradigm* and *methodology* interchangeably, assume that both of these terms refer to theory and methods together, and

---

[1]Although more recently it has been called the constructivist paradigm by some of its main proponents (e.g., Guba, 1990), we prefer to use the term *naturalistic* in order to distinguish it from *cognitive constructivism*, which term is used by many educational researchers (Steffe & Gale, 1995).

assume that integrating a naturalistic paradigm into research involves using both methods and theory.

A naturalistic paradigm is not defined by the methods used or the place where data are collected but, more important, by a theoretical stance and a set of research principles. The theoretical stance can be summarized as the assumption that meaning is socially constructed and negotiated in practice. The research principles include considering multiple viewpoints, studying cognition in context, and connecting theory generation and verification. This stance and these principles do not exist on their own; they are tied complexly to several disciplines and traditions and draw meaning from these disciplines. The naturalistic methods we mention are couched within the practices of an academic discipline also and take their meaning from these practices.[2]

The three basic research principles that we have followed when integrating a naturalistic paradigm into the study of mathematics cognition are given next. These principles derive in large part from ethnography, a methodology (not a collection of methods) connected closely to the theoretical principles of anthropology, such as the centrality of the concept of culture (Spindler & Spindler, 1987).

## Principle 1: It Is Essential to Consider Multiple Points of View of Events

A naturalistic research paradigm provides both theoretical and methodological leverage for capturing multiple points of view of an event. There are many advantages to this for researchers who accept constructive processes that begin from a learner's existing base of knowledge. In some cognitive research for educational purposes, there has been a traditional assumption that there is only one correct way to do mathematics or science and that there are optimal cognitive structures for learners' knowledge. Some examples of research epitomizing this assumption most strongly include work using the expert–novice paradigm (Larkin et al., 1980), the work on misconceptions (for reviews, see Confrey, 1990; Driver & Easley, 1983; L. McDermott, 1984), bugs (J. S. Brown & Burton, 1978; J. S. Brown & VanLehn, 1980; Burton, 1982), errors (Matz, 1982), and ideal task analysis (L. Resnick & Ford, 1981). This assumption results in portraits of a learner's knowledge that emphasize its relative accuracy or

---

[2]See Jacob (1987), for a detailed analysis of qualitative traditions and their relationships to academic disciplines.

completeness when it is compared with an ideal model held by an expert. But this often unexamined assumption can lead researchers to miss the unexpected structure of novices' knowledge, the alternative understandings held by learners (Confrey, 1990), or the potential for progress in students' initial conceptions (Moschkovich, 1992, 1999). A naturalistic paradigm provides a road map for understanding learners in their own terms and for highlighting the potential in what they know, rather than only comparing their knowledge to that of an expert.

From anthropology and sociology come notions of relativity that acknowledge and honor the knowledge of the people we study (Spindler & Spindler, 1987; Spradley, 1979). A relativistic stance in research means that we try to understand the knowledge of others in their own terms as much as possible prior to comparing it to other knowledge systems, including those of experts. Cognitive anthropology (Spradley, 1980; Werner & Schoepfle, 1987) and grounded theory (B. G. Glaser & A. L. Strauss, 1967) prescribe specific research techniques that enable the systematic elicitation of participants' knowledge, although each of these methodologies has its own set of assumptions about the nature of knowledge that may have different utility for any given research agenda in education.

Thus, relativism allows us to move from deficiency models of students to exploring their potential for progress, a move that is especially relevant to research with minority students. Closely aligned to notions of relativity is the recognition that culture plays a role in learning. The notion of culture is central in moving from deficiency models of students to exploring and defining culturally relevant pedagogy.[3] The continuing failure to meet the needs of diverse students adequately points to the need for an infusion of fresh ideas for working with learners from different cultural backgrounds.

In a naturalistic paradigm, the point of view of the researcher becomes explicit. Because many forms of naturalistic research utilize the individual researcher as a tool in the data collection process, recent standards for data collection (Emerson, Fretz, & Shaw, 1995; Lincoln & Guba, 1985) dictate that researchers set down their own reactions to the events being recorded and analyzed. Thus, the researcher becomes a variable to be described in the

---

[3] Here we are not referring to culture as a factor or a variable for understanding students' performance (such as socioeconomic status, ethnicity, or gender) but to the concept of culture: the assumption that everyone has a culture and that this culture plays a role in cognition and learning.

research report. Rather than aspiring to perfect objectivity, a naturalistic methodology prescribes a controlled and acknowledged subjectivity.

## Principle 2: It Is Useful to Connect Theory Verification and Theory Generation

In addition to verifying or extending existing theoretical frameworks, research in mathematics and science education needs to generate new theories grounded in data. Combining the verification and generation of theories is most likely to move the field forward for two reasons. Verifying existing theories builds on previous work and makes connections to theories outside mathematics and science cognition. Building on previous work prevents the reinvention of the wheel that may exist already. Connecting to other areas prevents theories of cognition in mathematics and science from becoming isolated from theories in other domains.

As we show in our descriptions of two projects, a naturalistic research paradigm can be used for generating and verifying both substantive and formal theory (LeCompte & Preissle, 1993). Substantive theory provides explanations for a circumscribed area of inquiry such as linear functions, proportions, or metacognition. In contrast, formal theory is an interlocking set of assumptions, concepts, and propositions that frame the research enterprise. This set of assumptions typically derives from specific disciplinary traditions such as sociolinguistics or structuralist sociology (Jacob, 1987; LeCompte & Preissle, 1993). Mathematics and science education can benefit from using not only the techniques of other social sciences but also the formal theories. In fact, to use the methods appropriately, it is necessary to acknowledge and understand the theories underlying these methods. In a later section, we discuss ethnography in more detail in order to illustrate the relationship between ethnographic methods and theory.

## Principle 3: It Is Important to Study Cognitive Activity in Context

Research on mathematics and science cognition needs to pay particular attention to context. We would like to make an explicit distinction between setting and context.[4] We use the term

---

[4]These definitions are parallel to, but different, from Lave's definitions of arena, setting, and context. In particular, Lave used the term *arena* to refer to what we call setting, and the term *setting* in a different sense than we intend, defining setting as the "repeatedly experienced, personally ordered and edited version" (Lave, 1988, p. 151) of an arena. We use context in the same sense that Lave did, to refer not to a single entity, such as a place, but to "an identifiable, durable framework for activity, with properties that transcend the experience of

*setting* to refer to the physical and social environment. We use the term *context* to refer to the relationship between a setting and how participants interpret the setting, including the meaning of practices. Thus, a description of a setting might include what objects, people, and activities are present. A description of a context would need to delve more deeply into the different meanings that a setting and the practices taking place in a setting have for different participants.

Studying cognitive activity in context means not only considering the place where the activity occurs, but also considering how context, the meaning that the place and the practices have for the participants, is socially constructed. It is not possible to neutralize the "distracting" effects of contextual variables as early "think-aloud" studies tried to do (Schoenfeld, 1985). Rather, cognition and its context constitute aspects of the same phenomenon. As Lave and Wenger (1991) pointed out, "learners inevitably participate in communities of practitioners and that the mastery of knowledge and skill requires newcomers to move toward full participation in the sociocultural practices of a community" (p. 29). This notion of situated learning means that it is not sufficient to describe the setting in which learning takes place (classrooms, stores, homes); rather, learning and cognition need to be described within the larger set of practices that happen to occur in particular physical and social settings.

One way to address the importance of context is to study cognition in the settings in which it naturally and regularly occurs without intervention.[5] Of course, naturalistic research methods were developed to study behavior within such "natural" settings and here they have much to offer educational research. However, because the mathematics content in which we are

---

individuals, exist prior to them, and are entirely beyond their control. On the other hand, context is experienced differently by different individuals" (Lave, 1988, p. 151).

[5] Although we could define a "natural" setting as one in which a cognitive phenomenon occurs regularly without intervention, in using a naturalistic paradigm, it is more important to consider and describe in detail the characteristics of the setting and how they might impact cognition and learning in that setting than to decide whether one setting is more or less "natural" than another.

most interested may not always be visible in these "natural" settings,[6] researchers may need to combine data from a "natural" setting and a more structured situation that includes an intervention, a quasi-experiment, or a design experiment (Brown, 1992). Nonetheless, to understand the process of learning from the naturalistic research stance, it is essential to include at least some data from a natural setting, such as a classroom or other complex setting, in the research design. The descriptions of the two studies that follow exemplify a design for doing this.

# A DESIGN FOR INTEGRATING A NATURALISTIC PARADIGM INTO THE STUDY OF COGNITION

This account of a spiraling design which we have followed integrates a naturalistic paradigm into the study of cognition. This spiraling design combines central aspects of a naturalistic paradigm, such as ecological validity and an ethnographic stance, with some of the advantages of using a more cognitive approach, such as a focus on cognition, content, and individual performance.

We propose that research studies examining cognition and learning can integrate a naturalistic paradigm by spiraling between the use of different naturalistic methods (e.g., natural observation and conversational interviews) and more cognitive-oriented methods (e.g., written tests, controlled experiments, quasi-experiments, and clinical interviews). These methods can be used in tandem with a cyclical reiterating movement through the different phases of project development (planning, data collection, analysis, and theory building). This spiraling design combines the linear structure of the traditional psychology experiment with the more circular research process usually described for qualitative research designs (Marshall & Rossman, 1995; Spradley, 1980).

As FIG. 17.1 illustrates, the typical phases of experimental research on cognition can be outlined as:

- Define a research question or a hypothesis.

---

[6] In fact, Newman, Griffin, & M. Cole (1989) emphasized that even during carefully structured classroom lessons, sometimes problems get solved and yet the researcher cannot detect who did the cognitive work or how the work was accomplished.

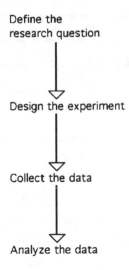

FIG. 17.1. The four phases of experimental research.

In contrast, in a naturalistic study, each of these phases is revisited several times and each phase informs other phases, as FIG. 17.2 demonstrates.

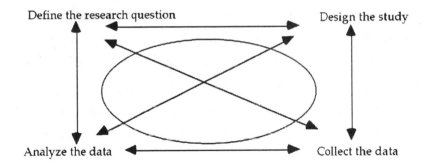

FIG. 17.2. The cycle of naturalistic research.

A project can shift between these two models as needed to achieve optimal understanding of the cognitive process in question. The spiral shown in FIG. 17.3 combines cycling between the phases of a naturalistic research study with the linear phases of an experimental cognitive study.

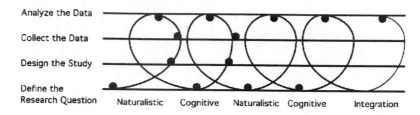

FIG. 17.3. An example of a spiral design for research. The black dots indicate steps that might be carried out at each phase of the project.

When using this spiraling design, our suggestion to integrate a naturalistic paradigm does not imply abandoning experiments. Rather, researchers can consider experiments (or quasi-experiments) as one possible aspect of the research cycle and can design them to be as "ecologically valid" as possible. Ecological validity has been addressed in psychological studies before (Bronfenbrenner, 1977; M. Cole, Hood, & R. P. McDermott, 1978). Bronfenbrenner suggested that for a study to be considered ecologically valid it should be designed to fulfill the three conditions:

> First, it must maintain the integrity of the real-life situations it is designed to investigate. Second, it must be faithful to the larger social and cultural contexts from which the subjects came. Third, the analysis must be consistent with the participants' definition of the situation. (p. 35)

Cole, et al. (1978) recommended, specifically, that "the analysis of any behavior should begin with a descriptive analysis of at least one real world scene" (p. 4). Then, this descriptive analysis can inform the design of an experiment (or quasi-experiment) that preserves some aspects of the real-world setting while modifying others. We have followed this recommendation in our own research by starting a study with observations in a setting where cognitive phenomena occur regularly without intervention. To explore further the cognitive phenomena observed in the natural setting originally, we designed interviews, quasi-experiments, tests, interventions, and so on, that were based on those observations.

## TWO STUDIES

In this section, we describe two studies that integrated a naturalistic paradigm into the study of mathematics cognition, focusing on how each study follows a spiraling design for the research cycle and exemplifies the principles proposed for using a naturalistic paradigm.

## Making Sense of Linear Functions

The purposes of this study (Moschkovich, 1992, 1996, 1998, 1999) were to explore secondary students' conceptions of linear functions and to examine how these conceptions change. The model used for the design of the study was an anthropological one, following studies conducted in workplaces that integrated different data collection and analysis methods (Brenner, 1985; Lave, 1988; Scribner, 1984). Whereas these studies with a similar spiraling strategy had focused on mathematics cognition at work, this study focused on cognition in school. The project included the collection of data from two settings: classroom observations and videotaped discussions between pairs of students conducted outside classroom time. The data were examined by analyzing the field observations, responses to written assessments, and the protocols of the videotapes.

To integrate an ecological perspective into the study, the research started with observations in a setting where students learned regularly about linear functions: two ninth-grade algebra classrooms.[7] Students were observed working in groups or with a teacher during two curricular units, one covering linear functions and the other quadratic functions. Each unit lasted approximately 8 weeks, and classroom observations were conducted for every lesson in each unit. The researcher also participated in several tutoring sessions after school where students discussed their homework assignments. Whole-class discussions and one student group were audiotaped during 10 lessons in one classroom. Students also were videotaped while they worked on the computer during one lesson. Ten pairs of students from the two classrooms observed volunteered to complete written assessments and to participate in discussion sessions. During the discussion sessions, pairs of students were videotaped while exploring linear functions with a peer, using graphing software and problems designed by the researcher.

---

[7] This setting can be considered "natural" in that the daily classroom practices were occurring regularly with little or no intervention from the researcher. The important questions are not whether classrooms, in general, are natural settings or how one classroom might be a more natural setting than another. For example, it is possible to use a naturalistic research paradigm to conduct research in a classroom with an instructional intervention, without needing to worry about whether this is a more or less natural setting. Instead, it is most important to consider and describe in detail the characteristics of the setting and how they might impact cognition and learning.

This study reflects a strategy that spirals between different methods in both the design and analysis phases of the study. The cycle of data collection began by observing students in a natural setting, the classroom, making conjectures based on these observations, and then addressing these conjectures directly in the design of the written assessments and the problems for the peer discussion sessions. Starting the research cycle with a natural setting was important for establishing the ecological validity of the student conceptions that were observed. Inherent to this spiraling strategy is triangulation through using different sources of data and methods of analysis. Conjectures based on field observations were corroborated through the analysis of written and videotaped data for individual students. For example, during the classroom observations the researcher noted that some students were using the *x-intercept* to generate equations of the form $y = mx + b$ and that some students were having difficulty describing lines on the computer screen. These two working hypotheses, which emerged from the analysis of the fieldwork, were verified and refined through the quantitative analysis of the written assessments and the protocol analysis of the videotapes. Thus, the central arguments were developed through the "constant comparative method" (B. G. Glaser & A. L. Strauss, 1967) across settings, data sources, and case studies of pairs of students.

A central objective of the study was to consider multiple points of view, especially the points of view of the students. The goal was to describe how the students approached the connection between lines and equations (Moschkovich, 1992). One technique for maintaining this focus on the students' perspectives was to take special notice of those of their actions or statements that seemed at odds with the researcher's understanding of lines and their equations. The researcher then constructed hypotheses about the students' points of view, based on these initial observations. These hypotheses were addressed more explicitly and in more detail in the written assessments and discussion problems. For example, several of the discussion problems targeted the students' use of the *x-intercept*. Throughout the analysis, an attempt was made to maintain at least two concurrent perspectives of the subject matter: the researcher's perspective, informed by training in mathematics and science, and the students' perspectives, as they were reflected in their conversations about lines and equations.

The study also aimed at verifying and generating theories. Two goals here were to corroborate previous laboratory case study data on student conceptions in this domain, such as their focus on the *x-intercept* for equations of the form $y = mx + b$ (Goldenberg, 1988; Schoenfeld, J. P. Smith, & Arcavi, 1993), and to extend these findings to a classroom setting. However, new themes, such as the students' use of descriptive terms and the negotiation of the meaning of these terms (Moschkovich, 1996), arose from the field observations and the analysis of the videotapes.

This study explored cognitive activity in both a naturally occurring setting, a classroom, and in a setting not occurring naturally but constructed specifically for the research study, the peer discussion sessions. The classroom observations served several methodological purposes. First, these observations informed the analysis of the videotaped peer discussions. Instead of conjecturing or wondering what the students' classroom experiences had been, the researcher had detailed data on their experiences with linear functions. Second, the students' classroom activities were used as a model for the design of the peer discussion sessions. Although the discussion sessions were more structured than the classroom group work and constituted a short instructional intervention, in order to maintain as much ecological validity as possible, the discussion sessions were devised to resemble classroom group work as much as possible. For example, the directions for the students were similar to those given to them in the classroom and the structure of the discussions was taken from a model for classroom science discussions (Hatano, 1988; Inagaki, 1981). However, because one of the goals was to document conversations between peers, the researcher intervened as little as possible during the discussion sessions, in contrast to the classroom setting where the teacher was a resource for students.

One reason for conducting the peer discussion sessions was that this setting provided "quieter" data than a classroom, both in terms of the noise level in a classroom and the factors that can be controlled there. Students chose their partner for the discussion sessions, instead of being assigned to a group randomly, as was the case in the classroom. Students worked with a peer of their choice (they were instructed to pick a peer of the same gender), the social situation that has been suggested as being optimal for collaboration (Azmitia & Perlmutter, 1989). Also, during the discussion sessions, the students worked on problems designed to address particular conceptions more specifically than their classroom activities did and they completed written assessments that addressed the conceptions targeted in the discussion problems.

Several results from this study have some ecological validity for students in reform-oriented mathematics classrooms, are grounded in data, and have both verified and generated theories. Students' use of the *x-intercept* was documented in the classroom work, in their answers to the written assessments, and in their discussions with a peer (Moschkovich, 1992, 1999). The protocol analysis of the videotapes was used to describe the nature and transformation of this conception and to develop a theoretical framework for the transformation of students' conceptions (Moschkovich, 1998, 1999). The analysis also described how students negotiated descriptions of lines, especially the meaning of the term *steeper* (Moschkovich, 1996).

## Hawaiian Children's Understanding of Money

Anthropologists have developed a theory of culture conflict that has been used to analyze and change classroom practices that have prevented the academic achievement of children from nonmainstream cultures. Most of the research has been done in the area of instructional methods (Au & Mason, 1981; C. Jordan, 1985) and literacy (Heath, 1983). The theory states that there are key differences between schools and homes that block children from participating in school activities effectively, whereas other differences do not seem to make a difference. In addition, comparisons of home and school can enable content from children's everyday life to be integrated successfully into classroom lessons for enhanced learning of the regular curriculum (Brenner, 1989, 1998a).

This study (Brenner, 1998a, 1998b) was conducted to determine if differences existed between the ways in which Native Hawaiian children learned about mathematics at home and the ways in which it was taught at school, and if such differences had any importance for their learning school curricula. Although culturally compatible instructional methods had been adopted by teachers, including cooperative peer work and altered discourse styles, Native Hawaiians continued to underachieve in mathematics in both research classrooms and in the entire school system (Hannahs, 1983; U.S. Congressional Senate Committee on Indian Affairs, 1994). The topic of money was chosen because children from ages 4 to 8 have a large interest in it and they learn about it both in and out of school. Not only is money a topic in its own right in early elementary mathematics curricula, it is used as a model for place value concepts and often in applications such as word problems.

A multifaceted research design was employed (Brenner, 1989, 1998b). Children were studied in three settings—stores, homes, and schools. Nonparticipant observation was used in stores on a regular basis for 6 months to determine what kind of shopping children do, what kinds of money they use, and how they interact with peers and shopkeepers while they are shopping. The researcher chose to begin the study with observations of children engaged in shopping because of the desire to overcome assumptions about children's use of money. As a newcomer to the Hawaiian Islands and as an adult who grew up in an era when penny candy really cost a penny, the researcher had reason to expect that her childhood shopping experiences would differ from those of Native Hawaiian children. In addition, the researcher wanted to observe the shopping routines used by children because prior studies had shown that the mathematical skills used in shopping are shaped strongly by other factors operating in particular settings such as who is present and what goals are being fulfilled (Lave, 1988; Saxe, 1991). Because the research focus was on the early elementary years, it was believed that the children would be unable to explain their shopping in an adequate level of detail. Nor were the questions that would elicit the best information from the children known beforehand. Werner and Schoepfle (1987) emphasized the importance in ethnography of negotiating culturally relevant questions: "Just because another group speaks some variety of English does not mean that we are capable of asking significant questions" (p. 321). The observations were begun before the first interviews and continued for another 2 to 3 months after the first round of interviews was completed. In this way the observations helped to shape the interview questions, and continuing observations cross-validated what the children said in interviews, an example of how the research spiral builds on different research approaches. In addition, it was important to spread the shopping observations over a period of time in order to capture variations in children's routines, which are influenced by the school year and summer vacation.

Children's money experiences at home were studied in two ways. A sample of six families was visited weekly for a year. The researcher functioned as a participant observer with the target child in each family, shopping and playing games that involved money with the child, whereas another interviewer interacted with the parents. The parents in these families were interviewed regularly. A larger sample of 100 families was surveyed to determine the money and shopping practices of children in kindergarten through Grade 3. Through this component of the study, it was possible to ascertain which kinds of money and shopping knowledge were transmitted and valued by parents and how shopping experiences fit into children's everyday lives. The survey also enabled an assessment to be made of whether observations in stores and observations in six homes were characteristic of a larger sample of Native Hawaiian children.

The school environment for money was studied by following a cohort of 24 children from the beginning of kindergarten through the end of second grade. The same children were interviewed about money three times over this period of time, they were observed regularly in their classrooms, and all school materials dealing with money (textbook lessons, worksheets, etc.) were catalogued, including tests that contained questions on money. By combining the data from these various sources, it was possible to trace the longitudinal development of knowledge about money for this sample of children in relation to both school instruction and their shopping practices outside school.

Cognitive models were developed from the data to show what children needed to know about money outside school in order to be competent shoppers, what they actually knew about money at ages 4 to 8, and what model of knowledge about money was taught by the school for this same age range. Key differences were described in what the children knew at each age and what the school expected them to know, thus confirming that there is a difference in the knowledge learned at home and at school by Native Hawaiian children in this aspect of mathematical information. The interviews with the children and the analysis of their school work showed that these differences were important because they caused a negative effect on some children's motivation and blocked comprehension of some aspects of their school curriculum. Not all children showed this pattern. About 25% of the children had no spending money and little shopping experience, as reported both by the children during interviews and by their parents on the survey. These children showed a growth of knowledge that conformed more closely to what was taught in school. Studies of children from other ethnic groups (Abreu 1995; Guberman, 1992; Nunes, Schliemann, & Carraher, 1993; Saxe, 1991), as well as informal observations in non-Hawaiian neighborhoods, revealed that the Native Hawaiian children's shopping patterns and knowledge of money were distinctive from those of many other groups of children.

Observing children in their natural settings of stores and homes turned out to be the key to understanding children's behavior during interviews and in school. For instance, the children in kindergarten appeared not to know anything about money because, on the school's test, they were unable to identify pennies, nickels, and dimes. However, a more open-ended interview and simulated shopping tasks revealed that the children knew the value of a quarter and a dollar and could use these denominations accurately for making purchases. A review of the data from the shopping observations confirmed that children seldom used anything but quarters or dollars for making purchases. Furthermore, although the school organized lessons about money around pennies, the children organized their knowledge of money with quarters as the central value.

This study demonstrates how naturalistic methods can be combined with the kinds of methods used more typically in cognitive studies (clinical interviews and task simulations) to explore the utility of a formal theory from anthropology (culture conflict theory) for studying how mathematics is learned as well as to develop a substantive theory about children's understanding of the domain of money. At the formal theory level, this study was one of the first to substantiate a difference between children's everyday mathematical knowledge and their school mathematical knowledge, including verification that the children recognized and were affected by this difference. At the level of substantive theory, the researcher was able to develop models of mathematical knowledge about money that were informative for teachers of Native Hawaiian children, but whose generalizability to other populations requires further research. Although only the research methods used to examine the differences between school knowledge and everyday knowledge about money for Native Hawaiian children have been described, in subsequent studies, some teachers and the researcher designed new mathematics activities that built more directly from children's everyday mathematical experiences (Brenner, 1998a). The effectiveness of these interventions provided further verification that conflicts between everyday practices and school practices were a source of difficulty for some children.

The inclusion of both observations and interviews was planned from the beginning of the study. The researcher did not believe that she could understand children's everyday knowledge of money without including multiple methodologies. In line with the basic assumptions of the naturalistic paradigm, it was assumed that children's knowledge of money was constructed from their experiences or lack of experiences with shopping and the use of money. Therefore, it was important to obtain information about these experiences, and, in this instance, the children were not able to tell us about them directly. The observations also permitted the elimination of some rival hypotheses about the nature of children's understanding of money. The initial evidence from classroom observations that kindergarten children did not know about pennies, nickels, and dimes had several possible explanations. It was reasonable to suggest either that children just beginning kindergarten did not have the underlying knowledge of numbers in order to be able to understand the quantities represented by the coins or that they had trouble understanding that five pennies were the same as a nickel in value because of undeveloped concepts about part–whole relations. Alternatively, it was possible to hypothesize that they had not done any shopping and, therefore, were simply unfamiliar with money in general. However, the initial observations showed that many young children do go shopping, but not with pennies, nickels, and dimes. In the observations, it was noticed that children used quarters and dollars almost exclusively. So the interviews with the kindergarten children were extended to include these denominations and they were asked about the relation between them. Other questions to test children's numerical skills were incorporated too, and, generally, it was found that they understood number concepts well enough to understand the values of pennies, nickels, and dimes. Without the observations, these kinds of questions would not have been included in a clinical interview with children beginning kindergarten.

The inclusion of multiple methods can entail significant additional expenditures of time and money on the part of researchers. However, this was not a significant issue in this study. The initial study was planned to cover a full year, so the use of multiple methods did not prolong its duration of the study because the researcher alternated between methods over the course of the year. Because the observations of children took place after school in either homes or public shopping areas, it was possible to interview them and to observe them in classrooms during the school day and to carry out other parts of the research in complementary times in the afternoons and evenings. In addition, colleagues collaborated in collecting data from the home study, enabling other important issues about the home experiences of young Native Hawaiian children to be addressed (Levin, Brenner, & McClellan, 1993).

## ETHNOGRAPHY AND ETHNOGRAPHIC METHODS

The naturalistic paradigm reflected in the two studies described previously relies largely on an ethnographic stance toward research. Using this ethnographic stance to study cognition means more than borrowing methods; it means integrating theories and methods. In this section, we use ethnography to illustrate the distinction between methods and methodology and to discuss important issues that need consideration when using ethnographic methods. A similar discussion could be held for grounded theory, case studies, discourse analysis, and other methodologies from anthropology, sociology, or linguistics.

A number of authors have differentiated using ethnographic methods from the goal of writing an ethnography. An ethnography involves much more than using ethnographic methods such as participant observation, taking field notes, or conducting interviews. A true ethnography is a long-term project, involves participant observation as well as other methods, and aims to describe the participants' perspectives (Emerson et al., 1995; Glesne & Peshkin, 1992; Shimahara, 1988; Spradley, 1979, 1980). Ethnography is a methodology that is intricately related to the theoretical principles of anthropology, such as the centrality of the concept of culture (Spindler & Spindler, 1987). In the words of these two educational anthropologists:

Many people, who are quite innocent of anthropology as a discipline and who have only vague notions of cultural process, claim to be doing ethnography. We have nothing against anyone doing qualitative, field site evaluation, participant or nonparticipant observation, descriptive journalism, or anything else if it is well done. It will produce some tangible result and may be useful, but it should not be called ethnography unless it is, and it is not ethnography unless it uses some model of cultural process in both the gathering and interpretation of data. (p. 151)

Although not every naturalistic study is an ethnography, ethnographic methods can be integrated into a research study that may not be a full ethnography. One of the central goals of using ethnographic methods is to identify the issues for the participants (Malinowski, 1922; Spradley, 1979). However, ethnographic methods also help the analyst to raise issues that the participants may not have been aware of themselves. For example, in uncovering the mathematics that is involved in candy selling in the streets, one main goal was to describe events from the point of view of the participants. However, another aim was to describe the mathematical principles underlying the selling activities, even if the participants themselves might not identify these mathematical principles (Nunes et al., 1993; Saxe, 1991).

In using ethnographic methods to study learning in classrooms, it is important to keep in mind that we are conducting observations not only across cultures, but also across ages and educational experiences. One criterion in anthropology for how well one understands the participants in a study is being able to act like them (Goodenough, 1956; Shimahara, 1988). When one is observing students who are younger and have less schooling, it is perhaps less important to be able to act like them and more important to remain aware of how one's experience can affect the research. Eckert (1989) provided a number of observations that are pertinent to mathematics and science education researchers, based on her ethnographic research in a high school:

Doing ethnography in one's own culture brings obvious problems and an American doing ethnography in an American high school certainly stretches the limits of the ethnographic method. My challenge in doing this work was not to pretend to be a complete outsider to the community, but to assess the real nature of my status. (p. 26)

There is no special way to deal with the potential interference of personal experience. My responsibility as an ethnographer was not to forget my own story, but to know it well and to refer to it constantly to make sure that it was not blinding me to what I saw or focusing my attention on only some of what I saw. Careful articulation of my previous beliefs about school and adolescence was interleaved with a constant questioning of every observation and every interpretation. (p. 27)

When using ethnographic methods, researchers need to be aware of the difference between conducting short-term (a few weeks) and long-term observations (a few months). In ethnographic work, it takes time to be admitted into a community:

In the end, the challenges and responsibilities of doing participant observation in an American high school are not very different than those facing an ethnographer working in any other culture or age group. I was an outsider trying to get to know and understand a community. I needed to gain the confidence and trust of the members of the community so that they would allow me access to their activities and knowledge, and I needed to become sufficiently part of the local woodwork to be able to observe activities without producing a distraction. (p. 25)

Another important distinction between using ethnographic methods and doing an ethnography is in the different ways to collect data when using ethnographic methods. There is a difference between what people say they do (self-reports), what people are observed doing (observation), or what the researcher concludes from participation in an activity (participant observation). There is also a difference between being a "participant-observer" and an "observing participant." A participant-observer observes and participates in activities without being identified as belonging to one of the social categories of the community being observed. On the other hand, an observing participant, such as a teacher-researcher, is a part of the classroom community. This distinction, however, is not a dichotomy. A researcher can engage in a spectrum of activities that ranges from the first, observing and participating while not belonging to the community, to the second, belonging to a community and observing one's own activity as well as those of others.

One important aspect of using ethnographic methods is knowing the purpose of different note-taking techniques (Emerson et al., 1995). A researcher can jot down observations online, write low-inference descriptions, or make analytical, methodological, or personal memos. Each type of note has different implications for analysis. In analytical memos, inferences are made beyond low-inference description. For instance, questions or curricular reflections are noted and hypotheses are made. In writing methodological memos the researcher might consider what to do next and how to do it. And, last, in writing personal memos the researcher records feelings, impressions, and reactions that may or may not become a part of the research analysis. However, these personal memos can become part of the audit trail that helps to establish the overall quality of a study as explained later.

We also would like to point to the connection between using ethnographic methods and collecting video data. Video data can be collected concurrently with ethnographic observations or without any ethnographic observations. Conducting observations while being present physically provides a researcher with multiple impressions that may not be reproduced by reading someone else's field notes or watching a tape of activities in a classroom the analyst has not visited. We are not suggesting that researchers only analyze tapes of activities in classrooms where they have conducted observations personally. Instead, we suggest that researchers consider and describe the methods used to collect and analyze their data, including whether observations and field notes were collected while videotapes were made and whether the videotaping or observations were conducted by the analyst or another researcher. In this way, we can specify and discuss the advantages and disadvantages of each situation.

The last aspect of ethnographic methods that we would like to address is transcription. Transcripts and tapes are not equivalent, nor are all transcripts alike (Kvale, 1996). The act of transcribing is an interpretive act. The choice of a system of transcription conventions reflects the analyst's theoretical stance, analytical focus, and relationship to the audience (Linde, 1993; Ochs, 1979). When transcribing tapes it is important to be explicit about how and why certain aspects of the data were not included in the transcripts and why others were. For example, gestures, expressions, and tone of voice usually help the analyst interpret utterances on a videotape in a way that needs to be communicated in a transcript.

# STANDARDS OF QUALITY FOR NATURALISTIC RESEARCH STUDIES

The methods and assumptions used in naturalistic research raise serious questions about the rigor and objectivity of data collected within this paradigm. For instance, the issue of subjectivity is often raised about naturalistic research. Because researchers working within a naturalistic paradigm assume that there are multiple constructions of reality, they also assume that any descriptions of these constructions will have subjective overtones. At the same time, naturalistic researchers are sensitive to issues of how the characteristics and beliefs of individual researchers can bias results. Another important concern is that of reactivity to the researcher. Because naturalistic researchers observe people as they are engaged in their everyday activities and even participate in these activities at times, there is a chance that their presence changes these activities. Naturalistic research designs can incorporate safeguards for these threats to the validity of research results. Another issue brought up frequently about naturalistic studies is the possibility of generalizing beyond the people studied because samples are often small or specific to particular settings. One of the basic assumptions of naturalistic research states that the highest priority is given to understanding and theorizing adequately about the particular research context in the form of substantive theory before the relevance of the findings is discussed for other groups or contexts (Erlandson et al., 1993). However, there are techniques that enable researchers to assess the transferability, if not the actual generalizability, of results. In this section, we discuss specific ways that naturalistic research addresses the issues of bias, reactivity, and generalizability.

Because naturalistic research methods derive from particular disciplinary traditions, the standards for judging the adequacy of research using these methods should derive from these traditions too. Although there is consensus that naturalistic research requires a redefinition of the traditional research concepts of validity, reliability, and generalizability, researchers have not reached consensus yet about the nature of this redefinition (for discussions of the issues involved, see Firestone, 1993; LeCompte & Preissle, 1993). We have chosen to follow the recommendations of Lincoln and Guba (1985) and Erlandson et al. (1993) by calling the qualities that establish the credibility of a study its *trustworthiness*. By using a different term such as trustworthiness, we stress that distinct sets of standards and strategies are appropriate for judging naturalistic research.

Despite clear differences in traditional and naturalistic approaches to defining the quality of a research project, at the heart of most research is the need to establish the systematicity, rigor and believability of its results. Lincoln and Guba (1985) identified four dimensions that frame the concern for quality in both traditions: (a) truth value, (b) applicability, (c) consistency, and (d) neutrality.

As Table 17.1 displays, we consider each of these in turn by comparing briefly the traditional and naturalistic definitions with examples of specific strategies that can be used within a naturalistic paradigm. The strategies included here are by no means exhaustive. Further strategies and variations have been described in LeCompte and Preissle (1993),

Erlandson et al. (1993), Lincoln and Guba (1985), Firestone (1993), Jick (1979), Lincoln (1990), and Marshall and Rossman (1995), among others.

TABLE 17.1

Standards for Naturalistic Research

| Dimension of Quality | Traditional term | Naturalistic term | Sample strategies |
|---|---|---|---|
| • Truth value | • Internal validity | • Credibility | • Prolonged engagement<br>• Persistent observation<br>• Triangulation<br>• Member checking |
| • Applicability | • External validity<br>• Generalizability | • Transferability<br>• Analytical generalizability | • Thick description<br>• Purposeful sampling<br><br>• Multisite designs<br>• Critical case selection |
| • Consistency | • Reliability | • Dependability | • Audit trail<br>• Multiple researchers<br>• Participant research assistants<br>• Recording devices |
| • Neutrality | • Objectivity | • Confirmability | • Audit trail<br>• Researcher's role defined |

*Note.* The sources of the terms and strategies are Erlandson, Harris, Skipper, and Allen (1993), Firestone (1993), LeCompte and Preissle (1993), and Lincoln and Guba (1985).

## Truth Value

The truth value of traditional research is addressed as internal validity, that is, the real relationship between accurately identified variables. In the trustworthiness approach, truth value is defined as credibility: In other words, how well do the results capture the constructs used by the participants in a context and the particular dynamics of that context. Several research strategies are used to assure that the basic database is adequate for capturing the major features of the phenomenon under study. Prolonged engagement (see Table 17.1) means that the researcher spends enough time in the context to eliminate or control distortions in the data that might occur because of unusual or atypical events, including the presence of the researcher herself. Prolonged engagement is the naturalistic researcher's strongest defense against reactivity. People have trouble maintaining atypical or ideal patterns of behavior over extended periods. In addition, everyday activities tend to be very robust. As Jean Lave put it (Lave & Kvale, 1995):

> There are common practices in American life that I dislike very much and if, just by being a participant-observer, I could change them, I would certainly do so. It turns out not to be easy to change social formations, or communities, or peoples' ways of life. In fact, it is very difficult. (p. 226)

In traditional ethnographic studies, a period of fieldwork usually lasts at least a year so as to allow the researcher adequate time to learn the culture and to see a full cycle of events. Frequently, the cycles of activity in contexts relevant to science and mathematics education will differ from this. For the study about linear functions (Moschkovich, 1992), one such cycle was the approximately 8 weeks taken to cover a curriculum unit. The researcher spent two of these cycles with each of her study classrooms in order to observe all of the instruction that had direct relevance to linear functions. For the money study (Brenner, 1989, 1998b), the observations in stores spanned 6 months and covered several distinct cycles that influenced children's spending—the school year/summer cycle and the monthly cycle in which there is more money to spend at the beginning of the month when paychecks and food stamps arrive.

Spending an extended period of time also gives the participants the opportunity to become accustomed to the researcher's presence. For example, at the beginning of data collection for the money study, the researcher was asked frequently by children who she was and why she was "hanging around." After a few weeks these questions seldom arose or the children told their friends, "She's somebody's mom" or, "She's looking at how kids spend money."

Another concern about credibility that arises in naturalistic research is deciding how much information is enough. The answer from the perspective of prolonged engagement is that enough time has been spent in a context when recurrent patterns become clear and fewer new types of data are being collected. Credibility is also enhanced by the use of persistent observation. This entails taking an analytical view of the data, looking for important patterns, and then seeking out further information that confirms or contradicts the emerging understanding of the researcher. The use of persistent observation ensures that the researcher achieves adequate depth in the most important aspect of the phenomenon under study.

In the linear functions study (Moschkovich, 1999), the researcher initially noticed and documented students' use of the *x-intercept* and their difficulties in describing graphs and in resolving disagreements during the classroom observations. A special effort was made to collect a substantial body of examples confirming or contradicting these initial themes, as well as other themes that emerged during the analysis of the videotapes. The discussion problems were designed to explore the initial themes further and the videotapes of the discussion sessions were analyzed by focusing on both initial and emergent themes.

In the case of the money study (Brenner, 1989, 1998b), the researcher noticed after a few weeks of observation that there were not many observations about the use of pennies. This became increasingly important as a research theme when she discovered during interviews that the kindergarten children had trouble identifying pennies and said consistently that they were "junk" and not money. To explore this theme, over a period of months the researcher included observations that focused on the coins and bills used by the children and the kind of change given to them by the storekeepers. These observations generated several hundred accurate records of the actual money used that confirmed that, indeed, the children seldom used pennies and never received them as change. The researcher also began to record the prices of the items that children bought most frequently and discovered that they were priced so that pennies were unnecessary. For instance, cheap candies were always two for 5¢ and storekeepers would not sell one piece for 3¢.

Triangulation, the use of multiple sources of data, is the best known of the techniques for establishing credibility. In the linear functions study (Moschkovich, 1992, 1996, 1998, 1999), written test results were used to corroborate some of the conclusions from the analysis of the peer discussions. In addition, the researcher compared students' discussions across her two research sites: the classroom and the peer discussions. Student conceptions documented in both settings, such as the use of the *x-intercept*, confirmed the robust nature of these conceptions. Student conceptions and descriptions were observed to be similar in both the classrooms and in the discussion sessions organized by the researcher. This confirmed the transferability of the analysis of the students' conceptions and their use of language; that is, it was not particular to one context only. The observation of these conceptions in the classroom established that they were not an artifact of the observer's influence as students carried out tasks designed by the researcher. During the money study (Brenner, 1998b), the researcher cross-checked the results from the interviews with the results from the tests that teachers gave as a regular part of their instruction. For instance, it was surprising that a comparison of interview data from the beginning and the end of the kindergarten year did not show much improvement in the children's knowledge of coins, even though they had covered a unit on money in class. The teacher's records showed that their test scores at the end of this unit were correspondingly low, confirming that this result was not an artifact of an interviewing technique or reflective of a bias brought to the interview session.

Another control for research bias is member checking, a technique in which the researcher's constructed understanding of the research results is presented to the informants for comment and revision. At its simplest, this can entail asking the informants to review interview transcripts for accuracy and completeness or to provide commentary on raw data such as a videotape. More complex variations consist of asking the informants to comment on drafts of final reports or subjecting tentative conclusions to the systematic scrutiny of the participants. This latter approach was taken by J. W. Wilson (1994) in her study of motivating and nonmotivating instructional activities. After three months of participant observation during which she lived the life of a sixth-grade student (at least during school hours!), Wilson interviewed every student in the class to confirm that the activities she had identified as salient by personal experience during her participant observation were seen as such by a majority of the students. During the money study, the initial draft of the school's model of knowledge about money was shown to the teachers for comment and confirmation. Although it was not included in the textbook materials explicitly, it seemed that the students were expected to know by the second grade that a dollar is made up of 100¢. The teachers agreed that, even though it was not in the textbook, this knowledge was a part of what the students should learn in school and they intended to include it in their lectures to the class.

## Applicability

Applicability is the dimension of quality that ascertains that the results of a study are relevant to a different or larger context. This may be the dimension of quality that differs most radically between the traditional and the naturalistic paradigms. In the traditional framework, this is called external validity or generalizability. The goal is to establish that the results obtained hold, regardless of the specific sample or context, most often with reference to a larger population. From the point of view of trustworthiness, this is referred to as transferability. Because understanding the context is one of the principles guiding naturalistic research, naturalistic researchers do not always try to establish how well their results will apply to other contexts. Some naturalistic researchers assert that it is not the researcher's task to suggest how the results may be relevant to others; rather, it is the reader's task to determine what is relevant from a study to a context of interest (Lincoln & Guba, 1985).

Two strategies are suggested for optimizing transferability, from the perspective of both the researcher and the reader, with particular reference to allowing the reader to make judgments about transferability. The first is the use of thick description in which the context and the dynamics within the context are detailed thoroughly. In our studies, this included collecting both specifications of the participants with the usual demographics (e.g., age, ethnicity, and socioeconomic status) and the more particularistic details of a unique physical location. For instance, in the full report of the linear functions study (Moschkovich, 1992), the curriculum units and the problems that the students worked on each day were included to, "illustrate that the exercises the students worked on were reasonably good tasks to try, and thus the student difficulties discussed later . . . were not the result of a poor curriculum" (p. 46). In the money study, the researcher (Brenner, 1989, 1998b) provided a description of the food trucks (manapua trucks), snack shops (crackseed stores), and neighborhood stores that constituted the main settings for the children's independent shopping because they are particular to Hawaii in some ways and perhaps relevant only to certain other kinds of urban neighborhoods.

The second strategy for supporting transferability is purposeful sampling in which sites and informants are included in a study in order to choose optimally informative sources of information rather than to represent a larger population randomly. Patton (1990) described 16 purposeful, sampling strategies that can be used to choose a sample that is most likely to elucidate the questions driving the research. The researcher is responsible for describing the procedures used to choose a sample and the rationale behind it. Some naturalistic researchers advocate sampling for maximum variability, whereas others explicitly choose limited variability in order to highlight other aspects of the context. Multisite designs, such as those described later are used by some researchers to control for irrelevant aspects of particular contexts. Other researchers are interested in what makes some events or sites unusual and will use critical case selection to assure that they capture the phenomenon of interest, particularly when it is somewhat rare.

In the linear functions study (Moschkovich, 1992), the two classrooms were chosen purposely to represent reform curriculum and exemplary teaching. The students' groups observed in the classroom were selected because they were composed of average-achieving students. Although the students who participated in the discussion sessions were volunteers, they turned out to be mostly average students, with only two low achievers, as determined by their course grades and evaluation by the teacher. After ascertaining the achievement levels of the volunteer students, the researcher deliberately approached two students identified as high achievers in order to round out the sample. In the money study (Brenner, 1989, 1998b), three distinct kinds of stores were included in the sample to ensure that the shopping routines identified were not results of the products sold (prepared food, toys, groceries) or idiosyncratic routines set up by a few storekeepers. In addition, businesses in lower socioeconomic neighborhoods were chosen because the research was part of a project intended to improve instructional methods for poorer Native Hawaiian children who are more at risk for school failure.

## Consistency

The third dimension from Lincoln and Guba's (1985) approach is that of consistency, which stipulates that under the same circumstances, the same results should be found. In traditional designs, this is called reliability; in the naturalistic paradigm, it is labeled dependability. Once again, these techniques can be seen as ways to minimize researcher bias and/or to assess the amount of researcher bias. The overall dependability of a researcher's project can be established by an audit trail in which the process of the research is documented in such a manner that it can be scrutinized by others outside of the project. In the linear functions study (Moschkovich, 1992), the researcher kept records according to university human subject standards. For the money study (Brenner, 1998b), the researcher was required to submit annual reports on the details of the research and to archive the originals of all data (field notes, interview tapes, tests forms) as forms of institutional as well as individual accountability. The use of multiple researchers also can provide corroboration when observations are compared in a process somewhat like measuring interrater reliability. In the linear functions study (Moschkovich, 1992), the researcher was supervised by senior investigators, shared data with other researchers, and conducted some of the analysis in the context of a research group. In the home study component of the money study (Levin, et al., 1993), the researcher was one member of a three-person team that shared the task of home visits for a year. In addition to pooling their field notes and interview transcripts, the researchers also read each other's materials as a cross-check for the themes that were thought to be occurring across households and to confirm that their methods were consistent over time.

The help of participant research assistants (i.e., "natives" of the location) can serve as a check on the subjective meanings of the events occurring at a site, thus addressing one of the basic principles of naturalistic research. In the money study (Brenner, 1989, 1998b; Levin, et al., 1993), one of the members of the home study team was Native Hawaiian and a mother. She was able to provide useful insights about patterns of behavior that were observed in some homes. Also, using recording devices (e.g., videocameras and audio taperecorders) can aid the researcher in achieving and proving the dependability of certain kinds of data, particularly in classrooms where recording may be relatively nondisruptive. However, an overreliance on recording devices can introduce or mask some threats to dependability because their use depends upon repeated judgments by the researcher of when and what to record.

## Neutrality

The last dimension addresses the neutrality of the research, namely, how the biases of the researcher are dealt with throughout the research process. In traditional approaches, this is called objectivity; in the naturalistic paradigm it is referred to as confirmability. One clear difference between traditional and naturalistic research is that naturalistic researchers do not seek to distance themselves from the research participants; rather they immerse themselves in the lives of the participants.

The audit trail is useful for establishing the confirmability of a research project because it allows both the data and assertions based on the data to be traced to their origin over the course of a project. Naturalistic researchers readily admit that it is impossible to eliminate completely the effects of the observers when using methods such as participant observation and intensive interviewing. Thus, it becomes important to describe the researcher's role in the research context. This entails describing personal attributes such as ethnicity or the ability to participate in the discourse of a site (this can mean speaking Spanish or talking about mathematics), how one obtained access to the site, and the reactions of the participants to the researcher. For example, in the money study (Brenner, 1998b), the researcher was construed to have quite different roles depending on the particular context. When the researcher was observing at food trucks at public parks, the children assumed that she was someone's mother because local adults regularly spent time at these places. In contrast, in the small neighborhood stores, it was not normal for people to spend time while not actively shopping and the researcher was asked on a number of occasions if she was the store detective.

Because the spiral design that we propose for research allows for emergent research questions, new strategies for trustworthiness may need to be incorporated as new questions emerge. For instance, it may be necessary to add new cases to a study, thus shifting the nature of the purposeful sampling, or new ways of triangulation may emerge over the course of a study. These new and developing strategies used in a spiraling design research project would need to be described and carried out in a principled way.

Any one research project is limited to including only some of these specific strategies for establishing trustworthiness. However, it is essential to consider how to incorporate some of these strategies into the initial design of the research, especially the documentation underlying the audit trail. We feel that the spiral design proposed offers increased opportunities for assessing the trustworthiness of results through its combination of multiple research methods. Further, triangulation of the results of data collected from multiple sources is a principled and integral aspect of the spiral research design.

## LEARNING TO USE A NATURALISTIC PARADIGM

The principles and standards for using a naturalistic paradigm discussed in this chapter were developed in several disciplines. Learning to use these principles involved participating in a community of researchers who were engaged in research practices reflecting these principles. The two authors of this chapter have different trajectories of participation. One was trained in anthropology and has conducted traditional fieldwork in other countries. The other was trained as a natural scientist originally and then as an educational researcher (in part by the second author). Nevertheless, both authors learned similar skills through their participation and collaboration with other researchers involved in the daily practice of conducting research. These skills involve not only explicit aspects of sound research practice but also implicit knowledge such as rules of thumb and how to decide what constitutes a good research problem or question.

Mathematics and science education are drawing on several academic disciplines to develop methodologies for research. Participating in interdisciplinary collaborative work and staying connected with the fields that generated these methods (sociology, anthropology, linguistics, etc.) either through reading texts, attending conferences, or talking with colleagues are crucial aspects of learning to include a naturalistic paradigm in cognitive research.

## ACKNOWLEDGMENTS

The participation of the first author in writing this chapter was supported in part by a National Academy of Education Spencer Postdoctoral Fellowship. The second author would like to acknowledge the Center for the Development of Early Education, Kamehameha Schools, Honolulu, Hawaii. The names of the authors appear in reverse alphabetical order. This chapter was written collaboratively. Each author contributed equally to all sections of the chapter except the section on the two particular studies which were written separately by each author.

# 18 Interpretive Research in Science Education

**Kenneth Tobin**

*University of Pennsylvania*

Interpretive research is an umbrella term used to describe studies that endeavor to understand a community in terms of the actions and interactions of the participants, from their own perspectives. Interpretive research seeks to answer broad questions and can address sociocultural factors not accessed easily using other methodologies. For example, the first interpretive study undertaken by our research group investigated the question of what is happening in high school science classrooms. Initially our explanations of what was happening were related to patterns that could be observed directly by members of our research team (Tobin & Gallagher, 1987). We identified numerous factors that shaped the science curricula being taught, such as students who monopolized interactions with the teacher, gender equity issues, and the nature of the assessment system (Tobin, Espinet, Byrd, & Adams, 1988). Gradually our foci shifted to patterns that related teachers' beliefs to the enacted science curricula (Tobin & Espinet, 1989). The study of teachers' beliefs then evolved to include the role of metaphor in constraining teachers' and students' actions (Briscoe, 1993; Tobin, Kahle, & Fraser, 1990; Tobin & LaMaster, 1995; Tobin & Tippins, 1996). As a landscape of understandings about teaching and learning emerged, we began to examine the manner in which specific subject matter was taught in a context of the social forces that distribute power and constrain the actions of participants in a community (Tobin, McRobbie, & D. Anderson, 1997). Throughout this succession of studies, I worked with my colleagues to explore the potential of interpretive research and to develop forms of practice in which the epistemology associated with the actions and interactions of the researcher was compatible with that applied to the interpretive frame used to construct and explain data.

What I find most appealing about interpretive research are its flexibility to explore the issues of greatest salience in a particular setting and the emergent nature of the design. Of most importance are the meanings that researchers assign to experiences in the field. The design of a study at any time depends on what is being learned, the questions that guide the design being: What is known now? and What do we want to learn next? Any visit to the field can take into account what has been learned in a study already. Therefore, the critical components of the design of an interpretive study are its emergent nature and, as the study progresses, the provision of sufficient time for interpretation.

The following sections present discussions of:

- The criteria that pertain to the quality of interpretive research.
- Authenticity criteria.
- An example of the procedures employed and the outcomes of an intensive interpretive study undertaken by McRobbie and me in an Australian high school (e.g., McRobbie & Tobin, 1995; Tobin & McRobbie, 1996a, 1996b).

## QUALITY CRITERIA FOR INTERPRETIVE RESEARCH

Because interpretive research acknowledges its subjectivity, it does not follow that everything is permissible and that there are no standards. On the contrary, as noted already, an interpretive researcher seeks to learn through systematic activity focused on efforts to understand the interactions between participants in social settings in terms of the perspectives of the participants. The "re" in research is important in that researchers not only seek to know but also are skeptical about what is learned; therefore, they look again in a search for evidence to counter the assertions of a study. That is, the knowledge gained from research is put to the test so that there is a close link between what is learned and the evidence used to support claims made from a study. The standards that apply to interpretive research and ensure that it is a credible and moral activity are described in this section.

## Getting Started

Although the tradition in research has been to concentrate on the identification of patterns or major trends, that is, the central tendencies, and to regard divergence from the central position as error, the underpinnings of interpretive research mandate that we learn not only from central tendencies but also from data sources at the periphery of a community. In interpretive research, efforts are made to get a clear picture of the central tendencies and to understand the phenomena that are discrepant from the patterns of central tendencies. This principle is enshrined in the design of interpretive research by selecting participants serially and contingently. Accordingly, binding decisions are not made beforehand about who will participate in a study or how many participants will be involved. Having started with one participant, extensive observations can reveal certain patterns that become foci of interest. When the substantive issues suggest that it is time to add another participant, then that participant should be selected to provide experiences that will advance our understandings of the issues on which the research is centered. One criterion that often is employed is to choose someone who is most different from the first participant selected and studied. In other words, a dialectical principle is applied in the selection of participants so that the diversity of a given community is reflected in the data sources scrutinized during a study.

In an interpretive study of the teaching and learning of college physics, we were interested in examining the nature of learning environments in the class. The context for the study was a course for science education majors who were seeking certification in a science area other than physics. Any community involves a relatively large number of participants who are concerned about what is happening in their area of interest. These participants tend to cluster into groups such as students, teachers, administrators, parents, and business representatives. It is important to identify those concerned who will be regarded as sources of data. Usually, it is not possible to include all of the stakeholder groups in a study, so it is necessary to pick the most salient ones to participate. Which groups to include and which to leave out can become clearer as a study progresses. I try to concentrate initially on only the essential primary data sources and include others as a study becomes more focused. In this example of the college physics class, those most affected by the outcome were the professor and the students. So only they were chosen at the outset. This decision was based on what we judged to be the best use of scarce human resources on the research team. We preferred to reserve our resources for intensive case studies of relatively few individuals rather than less intensive activities with a larger number of participants.

Selecting the students for the study necessitated careful consideration of a number of alternatives. First we identified a female undergraduate, Diedre, who was struggling with the scientific content covered in the class. She was very determined to succeed and had shown that she was willing to seek outside assistance and to make extra efforts. Her selection would enable us to see how she made sense of physics and would provide a window into the problems she encountered. Furthermore, we believed that her participation could help her to learn physics through her conversations with the researchers about the subject matter. The student who was most different from Diedre was Joel, an undergraduate student who had attained the highest scores on the initial assessment tasks. A third choice was selected as a potential participant. He was as different from Joel and Diedre as possible, a man who was not succeeding and who frequently made self-demeaning remarks.

The three participants were all approachable and occupied different places in the classroom community. Although we felt that three students would be an ample number, we selected a fourth who we thought was closer to the center of the group in that he was regarded as typical. We then commenced an intensive analysis of Diedre's participation in the study, including the others as secondary sources whenever we felt a need to test the diversity of the students' beliefs on issues that emerged from our interpretations. By adopting this approach, we were able to place Diedre in relation to the others on issues that she regarded as critical to her learning. After several weeks of intensive research, we handed our interpretive remarks to Diedre for her comments and began a case study of Joel. At this stage, the study took a sudden turn because of an incident involving Joel.

Because of his dissatisfaction with how the students were building a scientific discourse, the professor reorganized them into heterogeneous groups of four for discussion. During the first discussion, it was apparent that Joel did not appreciate being in a group with someone like Diedre, who was not learning at the same rate. Joel did not think that her explanations to Diedre were pertinent to her own goals as a learner, regarded additional discussions as counter to her best interests, and left the group to join others who she perceived were working at a more appropriate pace. Her actions stunned the professor and the other students in her group. Subsequent analysis of the incident revealed dramatic differences among the participants in their beliefs about learning and the importance of different roles and activities. Diedre, Joel, and the professor remained key data sources along with the other students in the group of four, both of whom were not identified in the original set of four participants.

Significant issues in any study are identifying appropriate hypotheses and ensuring that suitable data are obtained to test them in a credible manner. For this reason, it is important to stay on top of the analysis and interpretation of data. Unlike other forms of research in which analysis and interpretation follow data collection in a linear way, interpretive research requires that continuing interpretations permit successive assumptions on which the design of a study is built. Thus, the principles of an emergent design require ongoing analysis and interpretation, and successive assumptions permit the agendas of researchers to reflect what appear to be the most salient issues. However, it is important not only to recognize that an emergent design permits interpretive research to be responsive to what happens in the classroom but also to acknowledge that what is noticed in the events of the field will reflect the values and personal history of the researcher. Similarly, what is not noticed or what is regarded as unimportant also will reflect a value system of the observer. Accordingly, an account of the theoretical frame of the observer is of crucial importance in interpretive research. Of course it is difficult to know about this, and, as a study progresses, it is likely to change. Therefore, it is important that researchers record those beliefs that they think are of most significance to devising and carrying out a study. These beliefs, once recorded, can be referents for reflection and critical analysis by researchers, who ought to be aware of the ways in which their beliefs are affecting the formulation of a study. Discussion of them might lead to the identification of other beliefs, hitherto intuitive, that also are framing their perspectives.

## Data Sources

The data of a study emerge from analysis of their sources, which, in turn, are selected for their potential alignment with the goals of the research. Qualitative data sources can take many forms that include, but are not limited to:

- Transcripts of oral texts.
- Videotaped images of teaching and learning.
- Photographs of classroom events and phenomena.
- Sketches and diagrams from the field.
- Artifacts collected from the classroom or school.

- Field notes and analytical memoranda related to observations of teaching and learning or visits to the site of the study (i.e., the field).

An interpretive study would employ a variety of data sources in order to increase the credibility of what is learned, and it is expected that multiple data sources would support any assertion.

Multiple data sources need to be explored in order to establish the warrants for knowledge claims. If multiple data sources produce a pattern that makes sense, then there is greater confidence that the pattern is not dependent on a particular form of data, such as field notes or interviews. Also related to credibility is prolonged engagement in the field. Here, the interest is to ensure that patterns persist over time and are not idiosyncratic of events at a particular time. The framing of data over time needs to take place in a context of the changing perspectives of the researcher, which also ought to be documented over the same period. In addition, intensive investigation of the phenomena of the study ought to occur. The intention is that such intensive observations will facilitate the detailed description necessary to contextualize what is learned from an interpretive study.

## Creating Viable Assertions

Having accessed a variety of data sources, the next task of an interpretive researcher is to prepare them for analysis and interpretation. The first challenges are to create an archival system for each source (so that it can be accessed as necessary) and to enable analyses and interpretations to be linked to their original sources.

The preparation of research texts from data sources depends in large part on the nature of the source. Several examples are discussed so that some of the issues can be illustrated.

*Field Notes.* Generally, notes taken in the field are usually reworked as soon as possible after a researcher returns from the field. At this time, while the memories of events are fresh, details can be added to the written notes and interpretive accounts can be added as analytical memoranda. Usually I adopt the practice of adding questions to the field notes so that, when I get time I can have some of the participants review my notes, read the questions, and clarify items that might need their insights.

*Transcriptions.* A verbatim transcription is made of segments of interviews and sections deemed irrelevant are deleted. Transcriptions also are made of segments of videotapes. To the extent possible, notations are used to link the lines of transcribed text with the place on the tape whence it was transcribed. This can save time when it is necessary to refer to primary sources to obtain additional information.

*Artifacts From the Field.* Documents, photographs, and objects often are brought from field sites because of their potential relevance to a project. In each case, it is useful to link some text to these sources. In most instances, an analytical memorandum is written for each artifact, and documents and photographs can be transformed into a digitized form to permit storage, analysis, and inclusion in interpretive texts.

The first step I take in analyzing a field text is to read it and make notes on a paper copy or on a notepad in my computer. This preliminary analysis is tentative and allows me to obtain an overview of the potential of the data source and how it fits with earlier analyses I have undertaken in this and other studies. This initial reading allows me to prepare the field text in ways that will facilitate subsequent analyses. One task is to identify textual units that are relatively coherent in that they deal with only one issue. Occasionally textual units are less than one complete sentence; usually, they involve one or more sentences. Even if a textual unit is coherent and only represents a single event or a solitary idea, it frequently is possible to classify it according to multiple categories. For example, a textual unit might be an excellent example of both pedagogical content knowledge and gender equity. As I review each textual unit, I create category labels for it and record appropriate descriptors for each category.

When I have read the entire text, I use a word processor to prepare a research text that separates each textual unit from the next with a carriage return. During this process, I edit fully the text. To facilitate analysis with a computer program I save a text file, being sure to delete the soft returns at the end of each line inserted by the word-processing application when the text wraps around automatically at the end of each line in a textual unit. Before beginning subsequent analyses, I ensure that all of the editing is done in a word processor because computer applications for analyzing qualitative data usually do not have well-developed text editors.

The analysis of texts involves several iterations. Most computer applications permit the user to read each unit and assign one or more category labels to it. As I read through each textual unit, I use existing categories to classify the text or I create new categories. When all of the textual units have been classified, most qualitative research programs can provide a display of the text associated with each category. The subsequent stages in the analysis are to sort the textual units in each category into subcategories and to identify the linkages between categories. This process is interpretive and is an opportunity for different perspectives to clarify alternative groupings within and between categories. Emerging from these analyses are assertions that are claims about the relationships that underlie the decisions to group specific categories and textual units.

Once assertions have been created, they can provide direction for the design of a study. If a study is to be credible, it is imperative that efforts are made to obtain data that are pertinent to each of the emergent assertions. At this stage, researchers will ensure that each assertion is supported by a variety of data sources and that the amount of data in support of an assertion is substantially more than the amount of data that would refute it. Intensive efforts should be made to locate sources whose information might lead to an assertion being rejected or adapted. By grouping assertions, it is possible to create theoretical entities that are grounded in a study. If the analyses and interpretations have been undertaken with care, it should be possible to link all of the levels of assertions through trails of data to sources that constitute their base of support.

For every pattern that is discernible, there will be discrepant data. A feature of interpretive research is the manner in which discrepant data are investigated thoroughly, so that assertions can be suitably contextualized, elaborated, clarified, and, on some occasions, changed. Negative case analysis operationalizes the significance of maintaining and learning from diversity. A standard to which interpretive researchers might aspire is to understand thoroughly all of the cases that are at variance with a given assertion. An intensive analysis of discrepant cases has the potential to explicate the boundaries of a data set and thereby give added meaning to the assertions that define the central tendencies.

## Credibility

Verification of information by the participants in a study is a critical part of an interpretive study. Because one of the goals is to understand the actions of the participants from their own perspectives, researchers are endeavoring to construct texts that address two broad issues: What is happening here? and, What are the reasons for what is happening? In arriving at answers to these questions, there are many levels at which interpretation requires researchers to produce texts that purport to capture the perspectives of participants. Member checks place these interpretive documents in the hands of participants and ask them to indicate whether or not their perspectives are depicted accurately. Participants might be asked to mark up the text, suggest changes, make elaborations or clarifications, and provide examples to enrich the text. The purposes of member checks are to test the accuracy of researchers' interpretations, by indicating the extent to which participants agree with them. The procedure allows participants to critique the interpretations of the researchers and is an additional source of data for a study. Examples of member checks are the provision of field notes, research texts, and interpretive extracts to participants to review and to indicate specific areas of agreement and disagreement. In the case of young children, we have undertaken such checks orally, explaining to them what we think is happening and why we think it occurred. Their comments are analyzed as member checks. No doubt there will be occasions when researchers will argue that even though a participant claims the researcher has not understood something correctly, an interpretation is retained because of other evidence available to support the assertion. Although the member check is a critical part of interpretive research, the notion that different perspectives can add to the richness of a study permits a researcher to include the differing perspectives on interpretation as another layer of informative description that increases the potential to learn from the investigation. In one study in which a teacher-participant disagreed strongly with the interpretations of our research team, we developed a new research text that included his points of view with ours, evidence for readers that our interpretations and the belief set that supported them were disputed by the teacher (Tobin, et al., 1988).

Erickson (1986) described two challenges for interpretive researchers as making the familiar strange and the strange familiar. The insider's view is essential in an interpretive study and, for that reason, attention is paid to the voices of the participants and such mechanisms as member checks. Those with an insider's view face the challenge of making what is familiar to them seem strange. As necessary as the insiders' perspective might be, it also is essential that a study have an outsider's judgment of what is happening. The outsider's view concerns making the strange seem familiar. More often than not, researchers are from the outside and do not belong to the community that they are studying. Their perspectives are enriched by the theoretical frameworks used to make sense of what they are seeing and to frame what is relevant and noteworthy. An outsider is more likely to notice events that have salience but are accepted as normal practices by an insider and may go unnoticed. An interpretive study should incorporate both insiders' and outsiders' perspectives because they are potentially complementary.

One way to include outsiders' perspectives is to use a panel of peers to review interpretations and other aspects of a study in what are referred to as peer debriefing sessions. A critical aspect of peer debriefing is that those involved in it should have no direct interest in the study. Two types of peer groups can be selected: to reflect the research team and to reflect other interest groups. Peer debriefing requires researchers that assemble arguments to support assertions and constitutes a critical check on the viability of what has been learned from a study. When peer committees that reflect specific interest groups are selected, peer debriefing provides opportunities to obtain perspectives held to be viable by different communities. The value of debriefing by one's peers is that new issues and alternative interpretations emerge and require researchers to critique their potential viability. Provided that the researchers learn from them, these perspectives can improve a study.

## Preparation of Research Texts

The preparation of research texts is an important part of a study. Many issues have arisen, as we have learned from our practices over the decade, in which I have engaged in interpretive research with a number of my colleagues. The first problem I encountered involved my history of valuing assertions about central tendencies. Accordingly, I organized groups of researchers with an expectation that we would negotiate and arrive at consensus, and my initial studies regarded assertions as being akin to negotiated truths about the settings we studied. After some early problems with members of the research team who were concerned about their inability to convince others of their ways of seeing matters, and many studies in which teachers were affronted by what we wrote about them, I learned an important lesson about diversity.

In a group of researchers, it is not necessary for consensus to be reached on interpretations or on what is to be done next. A group can be a forum for discussing research texts of various types, learning from the perspectives of others, and presenting cogent points of view to peers. In research meetings, it is important to maintain a diversity of interpretations and to identify areas on which there is consensus. We found it necessary to structure research meetings so that all of the researchers could be heard and could participate in a shared discourse in which power was distributed equitably. One of the strengths of having a team of researchers was that the team could be informed from multiple perspectives. Each researcher was afforded an opportunity to prepare interpretive texts and to subject them to member checks, peer debriefing, and critical analyses by their colleagues engaged in the research. Rather than having one negotiated text, it was considered desirable to have multiple texts and to recognize that different researchers would have different goals and would want to represent those goals and their learning through their participation in research. The differing interpretations of members of a research team were regarded as a strength of a research design, and an essential part of any research text was the acknowledgment that other texts existed representing alternative accounts of what had happened and why it had happened.

The necessity of taking into account the voices of all of the participants in the research setting was a challenge, because an authentic representation of their perspectives might entail relating a story that is of little interest to a researcher. That is to say, the values of teachers that would be represented in their perspectives might differ significantly from those of researchers. In addition, the problems of intertextuality are continual (Lemke, 1995). Researchers pore over documents, such as transcripts from interviews, and identify parts that are relevant and parts that are less relevant to the stories that they want to tell about what they have learned in a study. Relevant textual units are retained and aggregated with others like them into categories that then are associated with one another. In this process, the context in which textual units were given meaning originally can be substantially different because a research text is a rhetorical event in which selected textual units are used as evidence for an assertion that is a part of an emerging thesis that constitutes a research text. A most important aspect of the member-checking process is that the participants have opportunities to review the final research texts as well as the interpretive texts reviewed throughout the study.

## The Moral Practice of Research

It is increasingly common for researchers to include teachers among the researchers rather than to design studies where teachers are not a part of the research team. However, whether or not there are teachers on the research team, it is essential that the plans for any study take account of the morality of the interactions between the researchers and the other participants. The researchers should disclose their goals fully and should refrain from developing research agendas that are not understood by all of the participants. Understanding fully what is happening from the perspectives of all of the participants can build from a respect for those perspectives to a realization that the participants interact as they do because they believe that their actions are viable. Valuing the importance of learning from the perspectives of the participants increases the likelihood that the participants' voices will be elicited and efforts will be made to ensure that the researchers' interpretations bear at least a family resemblance to the participants' descriptions of their own perspectives. Our approach to interpretive research has been guided by an ethical framework proposed initially by Sockett (1993), in which practical wisdom is employed by being fair, caring, honest, and courageous. It is never a matter of displaying one or several of these virtues separately, but of demonstrating practical wisdom that makes full allowance for the contexts in which interactions occur. The plan of a study needs to ensure the morality of all interactions. As a study is conducted, consideration should be given to the dynamic nature and context dependence of the interactions between the participants in a community.

## AUTHENTICITY CRITERIA FOR INTERPRETIVE RESEARCH

How much researchers learn from a study is an important authenticity criterion. The researchers' perspectives, used to organize experiences, describe what is happening, and support implications, should evolve in ways that relate to what they are learning from the diverse perspectives of the participants as they (the researchers) come to understand issues that eluded them previously. In this process, it is desirable to obtain interpretive accounts of the perspectives of each of the significant stakeholder groups involved in a study and to check with them that these accounts are similar to what they consider to be their perspectives. This system of member checking enables participants to provide additional data to clarify or elaborate the researcher's efforts to capture their perspectives. Having obtained authentic descriptions of the perspectives of others, it is necessary for researchers to demonstrate that they have learned from them by documenting carefully the issues thought to be salient throughout a study and to show a trajectory of learning over time.

A second measure of authenticity is whether the participants in a study understand and appreciate the constructions and value systems of others, whether they agree with them or not. This measure requires researchers to obtain diverse accounts of the perspectives of stakeholder groups. Once these accounts are available, they can be shared systematically among those concerned with the findings of the study so that the participants not only are aware of the perspectives of other interest groups but also have opportunities to understand and learn from them. Erickson (1986) suggested that actions be interpreted from the viewpoints of participants and that checks be undertaken to ascertain the extent to which the interpretations of researchers are accepted by participants as authentic descriptions of their perspectives. Member checks, whereby interpretive accounts are returned to stakeholders for comment, are a critical component in assuring that interpretive research provides opportunities for all of the participants to learn from others' perspectives.

Interpretive research is regarded as a catalyst for change. Accordingly, a third test of authenticity concerns the extent to which actions are initiated by participation in a study. The design of a study should anticipate opportunities for strategizing possible changes, examine the potential consequences of enacting particular changes, and plan to study the implementation of changes so that decisions can be made on whether to continue to implement, adapt, or discontinue new practices.

A final authenticity criterion relates to how much the participants in a study are empowered to act. This criterion bears upon the participatory nature of interpretive research and the desire that all stakeholders have significant roles and opportunities to contribute to the study in meaningful ways. The products of the research process, then, should be texts that have been shaped mutually through recursive processes involving negotiation between the researchers and all of the other interested parties. Throughout a study, documents can be released to selected individuals from the most important interest groups so that each is aware of the perspectives of the others and can contemplate changes that might be a consequence of the study. If effective communication is maintained between and within the stakeholder groups it is plausible that consensus can be reached on actions that are acceptable to all concerned.

# AN INTERPRETIVE STUDY OF THE TEACHING AND LEARNING OF CHEMISTRY

## Transferability

What we learn from interpretive research is grounded in the histories of the researchers. For example, what we learned in the following interpretive study of a veteran chemistry teacher and his class was constrained by the researchers' histories of being science teachers and science teacher-educators for more than 30 years and having engaged in research in science classrooms for more than 20 years. The extent to which what we learned from this study can be applied to contexts that readers might encounter is constrained by the perspective of the reader and by the potential applications that the reader might consider. In any set of publications, only a part of what has been learned can be reported, and the authors decide how to describe the context of what has been gleaned. In this sense, the authors delimit the extent to which knowledge from a study can be applied by a reader. Accordingly, transferability (Guba & Lincoln, 1989) is viewed as a transaction of a reader with a text, and the extent to which the reader sees the relevance of what has been learned to the problems that he or she has defined.

## Social Perspectives

The study incorporated two broad views of social phenomena: actor oriented and structure oriented (Galtung, 1980). Although both perspectives deal with human action and interaction, the actor-oriented position perceives action as related to the intentions and capabilities of the actors whereas the structure oriented position regards action as a function of the position of the actor in a social setting. Thus, the actor-oriented perspective considers actions in terms of the actors' goals, beliefs, behaviors, and constructions of context and the structural perspective examines factors such as diversity, growth, equality, and social justice. The actor-oriented and structural perspectives are conceptualized as existing in a recursive relationship to one another. Neither view is regarded as privileged and each contributes to the description of what is happening and why, the two fundamental foci of interpretive inquiry.

## The Setting and Structure

The setting for the study (McRobbie & Tobin, 1995; Tobin & McRobbie, 1996b) was an urban high school with an enrollment of about 1,000 students in Brisbane, Australia. The roles of the researchers were confined, as much as possible, to research. We negotiated entry into the school site to undertake a study that would provide a platform for changes to be considered by the schools' faculty at a later time. The participants in the study were Jacobs (a pseudonym), a 20-year veteran teacher, who also was the chairman of the Science Department, and his Grade 11 chemistry class consisting of nine boys and six girls. We listened with empathy to the stories of the teacher and his students and did not counsel or suggest alternatives. When asked, we assisted students with their learning. Throughout the study, we did not endeavor to change the teacher's or the students' actions. However, by providing the teacher and the students with field notes, interviewing them, and then giving them transcripts of the interviews, we acknowledge that a context was created in which the reflections of all of the participants were different than would have been the case had we not been there. This was a participant observation study where the presence of the researchers changed what happened although we had not intended that the teacher's and the students' actions would change to fit our goals. As changes occurred, we endeavored to describe and interpret them in a context that took account of our presence.

Two researchers visited the chemistry classroom every day of the week for 4 weeks to observe a unit that explored titrations and electrochemistry. Each lesson was videotaped to facilitate analyses of classroom transactions. Because we were in the field for a prolonged time, the tendency of the participants to exhibit contrived behaviors for the benefit of the researchers was minimized, and we were able to see whether given behaviors were typical or atypical. We maximized the probability that the emergent assertions were consistent with a variety of data through the use of the following sources:

- Field notes and analytical memoranda based on observations of teaching.
- Interviews with Jacobs.
- Interviews with six students, colleague teachers, and administrators.
- Videotaped lesson segments.

Jacobs was interviewed on five occasions, each of about 1 1/2 hours' duration, and six students were interviewed for approximately 1 hour each. The students selected for interview were those identified by the researchers and Jacobs as interesting, in the sense that they represented the diversity of the classroom. We felt that by interviewing these students and observing them intensively, we would come to understand the boundaries of this classroom as well as the central tendencies. The interviews and initial observations revealed that many of the students were immigrants and spoke a language other than English as their mother tongue. More than 20 languages were used by students in the school. English was spoken in the homes of 83% of the students; for 77% percent of them, English was their native tongue. About 10% of the students spoke and wrote English to a limited extent only or hardly at all. In the chemistry class, four of the students had come from Hong Kong or Taiwan. These students informed us that they had elected to study science and mathematics because they felt that their lack of proficiency in English would be less of a barrier to their success in these subjects.

Because of the relatively high number of students with limited proficiency in speaking English, we decided to look closely at their performance in chemistry. Initially, we expected to witness their success despite language limitations. This expectation fueled our observations, and it was the use of the hermeneutical dialectical circle that afforded us an opportunity to examine the handicap of limited proficiency in English and the relative importance of cultural capital in assisting students to overcome adverse learning conditions.

Chao (a pseudonym), who immigrated voluntarily to Australia from Hong Kong, was the highest-achieving LEP (limited English proficient) Chinese student in the class. She was selected as the first of two participants in the study because she was older than her peers and, in spite of her limitations with the English language, was easy to talk to and willing to speak with us about her experiences in Australia and Hong Kong. Fortunately for Chao, several of her peers at school were native speakers of Cantonese, and, when necessary, she was able to use Cantonese to clarify and elaborate her chemistry concepts. Chao was successful in Grade 11 but did not complete Grade 12 and returned to Hong Kong for personal reasons. The following year she came back to Australia to complete Grade 12 at a different school in which relatively large numbers of Cantonese speakers and adults were enrolled.

To obtain insights into the differences in the group of LEP Chinese students, we decided to include Poon (a pseudonym) in the study. Poon was chosen because he was quite different from Chao, sat next to and often worked with her, and was a native speaker of Cantonese. Unlike Chao, he was not achieving at a high level, appeared uncertain, and often did not participate in whole-class, verbal interactions because he lacked confidence in speaking English. Poon failed Grade 11, repeated all of the subjects the following year, and passed them all except chemistry. When Poon commenced Grade 12, there were only two Chinese students in Grades 11 and 12: Poon and a male student from Taiwan. As the only speaker of Cantonese, Poon felt isolated and lonely. He rarely spoke to other students, and, although he found them friendly, they often did not speak to him. Thus, his limited proficiency in English minimized his opportunities to learn from his peers.

Data on the teacher's and the students' perceptions of their learning environments were obtained from a 25-item questionnaire referred to as the Classroom Environment Survey

(CES; McRobbie & Tobin, 1997), which ascertained perceptions of the following five constructs:

- The involvement of students in discussions with each other.
- The autonomy of students in making decisions about their learning.
- The relevance of the chemistry subject matter to students' careers and daily lives.
- The commitment of students to learning.
- The inhibitors to learning.

For each dimension, there were parallel questions to measure what the respondents preferred and experienced. The teacher's form of the CES was worded differently from that of the students, asking for his perceptions of the extent of the students' actions. For example, question 1 on the students' form became "Students ask one another about their ideas" on the teacher's form.

The teacher and the students responded to the CES by indicating the extent to which an activity took place in the classroom on a 5-point scale, with intervals representing:

- Very often (assigned scale value of 5; the accompanying description meant that this represented more than once a lesson).
- Often (4; about once a lesson).
- Sometimes (3; weekly).
- Seldom (2; once a month).
- Almost never (1; less than once a month).

On completion of the CES, the teacher and the students were asked to describe aspects of their learning environment in general terms in order to obtain their broad impressions of the classroom. Then they were asked to recount their impressions of their learning environment in terms of involvement, commitment to learning, autonomy, relevance, and disruption. Finally, the respondents were presented with their completed survey forms and asked to explain their responses. This procedure resulted in thick descriptions for each individual at three levels:

- At a holistic level where the students were asked to describe the suitability of the classroom for learning.
- At a level corresponding to each of the five dimensions incorporated in the CES.
- At the specific level of each item in the CES.

These interviews provided ample accounts of the students' and the teacher's learning environments and their preferences. Questions also were posed about the roles of the teacher and students and the nature of the teaching–learning process, their views on the nature of science and scientific knowledge, and the constraining and facilitating aspects of the context.

Jacobs and the students, including Chao and Poon, also were requested to comment on the manner in which LEP Chinese students engaged in tasks, asked for and received help from the teacher and their peers, used resources to assist their learning of chemistry, and interacted with one another and with English-proficient students in the school. Both Chao and Poon were interviewed 2 years after the initial observations in order to check on their educational progress and to provide them with opportunities to review research texts that related to them. Although both of them were limited still in their use of English, they had improved their competence. As was the case during the classroom observations, in comparison to Poon, Chao was more competent and confident in her use of English.

Although we did not measure achievement in learning chemistry in this study, we analyzed performance data used by Jacobs and other teachers of Grade 11 chemistry in the school to assess such achievement. The assessments for the year were based on a summation of performance in four areas: chemistry content, simple application, complex application, and scientific process. We compared the performance in these four areas of 8 LEP Chinese students with 37 English-proficient students in the Grade 11 chemistry cohort.

Throughout the study, my colleague McRobbie and I met regularly to discuss and analyze data and to formulate assertions that provided focal points for subsequent field activities. These focal points reflected our initial interests (the nature of science reflected in the enacted curricula, the teaching and learning of challenging concepts, and teacher's and students' perceptions of the learning environment) and the role of language in the learning of science for students with limited proficiency in English. The latter focus evolved after our curiosity was sparked by the relatively high proportion of Chinese students in the school. Initially, we had assumed that the Chinese would be among the highest achievers in the class based on our stereotypical view that Asian students excel at science.

Any evidence that was counter to an assertion was explored in detail, and care was taken to build an understanding of the discrepancy. In this process, assertions were elaborated to take account of all of the data. Serious attempts were made to refute assertions. The best example of this involved our initial assertion about Chinese students. This early assumption about high accomplishment needed to allow for Poon's performance; as we focused on his relative lack of success in chemistry, our assertions changed. The focus then shifted to the role of English for those with limited proficiency in it in the context of a country where the instruction is entirely in English.

Data and interpretations were shared with the participants so that they could check intentionality and errors that might have been made either by the participants or the researchers. Extensive member checks allowed the participants to review data and interpretations, agree or disagree with the assertions of the research, and suggest corrections, elaborations, and summary statements. For example, Jacobs was provided with copies of all the field notes, in which we often wrote questions that he answered, written transcripts of four interviews with him, written interpretations of data, and research reports such as papers. Students also were provided with transcripts of their interviews, written interpretations, and copies of draft papers. Reactions from the participants were used as sources of data and provided bases for revising earlier drafts of this chapter.

Over a 2-year period, we continued our association with the participants in the study by asking them to read our interpretations and to suggest changes that would improve the authenticity of our accounts. In addition, in 1995, we shared our interpretations with other students and teachers like those who participated in the study. For example, the narratives of Jacobs, Chao and another student were printed and distributed to another Grade 11 chemistry class taught by Jacobs. Students in these classes were asked to read the narratives and to identify the parts with which they agreed and disagreed. They also were invited to write comments about the narratives.

Drafts of the papers written for the study were distributed to colleagues who had relevant expertise. For example, a paper on limited proficiency in English and the learning of science was distributed to 15 colleagues with backgrounds in science education, English as a second language, or language and literacy. All of them provided critical comments on the paper and 10 attended a peer debriefing session that critiqued our theoretical rationale, procedures, and interpretations. Criticisms raised in the peer debriefing session were used as a basis for numerous changes to that paper (Tobin & McRobbie, 1996a, 1996b).

We decided to use narrative accounts to convey the context of our study and the knowledge that was implicit in the stories of Jacobs, selected students, and the researchers. In this fashion, we felt that we could emphasize the voices of the teacher and the students in a credible manner and, in the latter parts of another paper emphasize our interpretations. The narrative for Jacobs was an aggregate of segments from interviews with him that were pertinent to the performance of LEP Chinese students and other issues deemed significant by either him or the researchers. Jacobs read and edited the narrative and advised us that it was an authentic report of his beliefs about teaching and learning chemistry. A student narrative was a composite of interviews with several, Australian-born students in the chemistry class. Chao's narrative also was a composite made from transcripts of interviews with her, selected to provide insights into the world of an LEP Chinese student studying chemistry in an Australian school where English is the language for teaching, most learning activities, and assessment. In addition, other narratives were prepared to provide readers with detailed descriptions of our research into teaching and learning. For example, a vignette describing a typical day in the chemistry classroom was based on the field notes of the two researchers for that lesson and on those before and after it, videotapes of the lessons (one that tracked the teacher and the other that concentrated on the learners), and interviews with the teacher and the students about that lesson.

## What Did We Learn?

Jacobs made sense of his teaching roles in terms of beliefs related to the transmission of knowledge, being an efficient teacher, maintaining the rigor of the curriculum, and preparing students to be successful on examinations. These beliefs were supported by the teacher and the students and provided a strong rationale for maintaining the types of classroom practices that educational reformers want to change. If teachers can be brought to a level of consciousness about such beliefs as these, there is a chance that their viability can be addressed directly and alternative referents can be generated to propel reform in the direction advocated in the myriad reports that presently exhort changes in educational policy and classroom practice (e.g., National Research Council, 1996).

Although the teacher and his students tended to see science as an evolving discipline that was uncertain and changed over time, the manner in which the curriculum was implemented was a direct contrast. In the enacted curriculum, science was represented as a catalogue of facts to be memorized and as algorithmic solutions to problems. The beliefs that had the greatest impact on shaping the curriculum were the teacher's assumptions of how students learn, his beliefs about the distribution of power between himself and his students, and the extent to which he accepted restraints as reasons for maintaining a traditional approach to teaching and learning chemistry.

Initially, Jacobs and the students had difficulty describing their beliefs. However, as the study progressed, they used language to recount their practices and to construct mental models that fitted with their practices and beliefs about learning. The teacher's and students' goals, their beliefs about the teacher's and the learners' roles, and their constructions of the context were coherent to such a degree that there was little impetus for change. An objectivist system of semantics was used by the teacher to justify an approach to teaching that was consistent with transmitting knowledge to student-receivers and maintaining a high level of control over their activities. Little autonomy was provided for the students to decide what or how they should learn and chemistry was perceived to have limited relevance.

To a significant measure, the students accepted their learning environment and justified what happened in terms that were consistent with objectivist semantics. Hence, as noted above, there was no motivation to make changes, and the principal concern was to cover the work program in the most efficient way possible. The teacher was in tune with the students' reasons for studying chemistry, and his teaching approaches reinforced their actions. Any endeavor to reform teaching and learning practices should take into account the implications of this congruence between teacher's and students' actions. When teachers and students construct their goals and the contexts in which progress toward those goals will occur, these constructions are not merely a process of mediation between one teacher and his class. The constructions of goals and contexts are saturated with the mediating effects of a cultural press that shapes a referential system that gives meaning to, and criteria for assessing the potential viability of, the actions of either a teacher or a student.

Jacobs' beliefs about the transmission of knowledge, teaching efficiently, and maintaining rigor comprised a coherent array of thoughts that influenced the manner in which he planned his lessons and taught them.

The transmission metaphor views the teacher as a principal source and the students as receivers of knowledge. These beliefs were supported by three dimensions: an objectivist view of knowledge (M. Johnson, 1987), a mental model for teaching and learning that is characterized by memorization, and the conviction that the teacher should have power over the students in most classroom situations. Jacobs also believed that he had the responsibility to ensure that students learn at a level that is consistent from one set of students to another and from one year to the next. As the guardian of the standards, he considered it his job to maintain the rigor of the chemistry course by covering the prescribed subject matter, nurturing high standards, preparing students for the next educational level, and recognizing that the specification of the curriculum was the prerogative of external agencies.

Because of his beliefs about transmission, efficiency, and rigor, Jacobs made few efforts to elicit reactions from his students and usually was unaware of how they were making sense of what they were to learn. Similarly, because of his beliefs about learning, he did not perceive a role for himself in mediating the construction of linkages in semantic webs of understanding. Even though Jacobs knew his electrochemistry thoroughly, his knowledge probably was based on his extensive teaching experience and did not seem to extend beyond what he needed to know in order to transmit certain facts and perform particular demonstrations. Jacobs did not believe in an interactive model of learning, and for that reason, did not encourage coparticipation. By maintaining a distance from his students and relying on the transmission of facts, he was not conscious of his failure to anticipate probable misconceptions so that he could address them during his activities. In addition, he did not encourage his students to interact to facilitate their learning because he believed that he needed to have control over the coverage of the subject matter to ensure efficient learning and to maintain high standards. Thus, there is an interaction between the subject matter that needs to be known and beliefs about teaching and learning. With few exceptions, Jacobs' pedagogical content knowledge seemed adequate for the restricted roles he played while teaching. However, from the perspective of the roles that he might have filled as a mediator of understanding, his pedagogical content knowledge can be seen as limited. He needed to know not only his facts about electrochemistry but also how to assist his students to demonstrate what they know and how to constrain their experiences such that they build particular canonical understandings.

Two forms of discourse were apparent in Jacobs' class: one associated with the students and the other with Jacobs' voice and canonical science. The extent to which the two forms of discourse overlapped was negligible, even though Jacobs made some efforts to paraphrase and elaborate on students' responses to his questions. Jacobs' concern was to progress through the subject matter, interacting with his students sufficiently so that at least the correct understandings could be provided and ensuring that he completed most of the work planned for the lesson. The main goals of the lesson were to present correct answers and to cover the content rather than to ensure that the students understood the subject matter. Comprehension of the subject matter was left to the students to accomplish, either as a result of their own thinking during the class or in external settings. Although there are many types of activities that enable students and the teacher to forge a new discourse, each of them would involve the students in being able to create written and oral texts around which interactions, negotiation, and consensus building would occur. It is assumed that all of the participants would, over time, build knowledge that was more scientific.

Despite the efforts to learn of a group of students with limited proficiency in English, their difficulties in speaking and writing English were factors that hampered their ability to learn chemistry with understanding. A shared belief that appeared to permeate the school, that all students should use English to learn chemistry and to demonstrate what they have learned, placed students with little knowledge of English in a position of potential failure. Chinese students tried to use English to make sense of what had happened in class and to demonstrate how much chemistry they had learned. At the same time, they spoke and wrote Cantonese and showed high levels of commitment to learn, make an effort, and remain engaged in productive tasks in and out of school. These practices were consistent with those expected by the teacher and with those that typically occur in schools in their native Hong Kong. The research supports the assertions that learning chemistry can be facilitated when LEP students are given opportunities to use their native language fully and when the microculture of the classroom fits the macroculture of their life outside the classroom.

## CONCLUSIONS

To what extent are the products of interpretive research generalizable? Because of the traditions of experimental and quasi experimental research, generalizability has been a concept that has been claimed by researchers when writing about their findings. The warrants for their claims have comprised statistical and logical analyses based on putative links between a sample and a defined population. The argument for generalizability is that the findings of a study, based on a sample, are applicable to the defined population as long as certain criteria are met. Of course, to a reader and a potential user of research, generalizability has little relevance. The credibility of the research is of most importance and so, too, is the persuasiveness of the argument used to sustain the conclusions. Notwithstanding the extent to which my argument is accepted, many will criticize what is learned from interpretive research on the basis of a small sample size. This inclination has been described by manuscript and proposal reviewers as "the small $N$ problem" or "the sample of one phenomenon." To make such statements is to misunderstand a basic goal of interpretive research.

The goals of interpretive research are to make sense of experience, build patterns of meaning and relationship that are linked to well-described situations, and communicate what has been learned in ways that are connected to context. By presenting what has been learned in a context of the evidence for and against the assertions, detailed descriptions of illustrative vignettes, and examples of explanatory data, a text prepared for dissemination can enable a reader to decide how credible and authentic the research is and whether or not anything in the account of it is potentially applicable to the contexts in which he or she practices education. The extent to which what is described in a report is transferable to other contexts or needs to be adapted is for the reader to determine, not the researcher. Thus in preparing research texts, it is important for researchers to provide sufficiently detailed descriptions of the context and the evidence to enable readers to assess the potential transferability and adaptability.

One of the constant problems faced by educational researchers is producing research that can be used by practitioners. Even though the *Journal of Research in Science Teaching* and other journals insisted in the 1970s and 1980s that all articles should include a section on implications for practice, it was generally the case that such journals were not read by teachers and research was not seen as an agent for change and reform as funding agencies and researchers had hoped. If the authenticity criteria described in this chapter are adopted, studies will be planned to make a difference, not only as a result of what is written as a product, but also as a result of the conduct of the research in schools and the moral concern that all of the participants in research should benefit from the activity, not solely the researchers. The belief that knowledge and context are linked inextricably leads to the moral position that research should be designed to be authentic and to produce improvements in the institutions that engage in the research.

A concern that I faced as a beginning researcher in the 1970s and early 1980s was a preoccupation with understanding central tendencies through the partitioning of variance components. Part of the concern was the linear causal modeling associated with many of the designs I used and a reductionist way of looking at life in complex entities such as classrooms and schools. In addition, an assumption that all of the persons associated with a factor in a design were the same and that any differences were due to random error was problematical for the people I knew. I was not even sure that such an assumption was particularly robust for the agricultural contexts from which many of our statistical approaches had been borrowed. As I explored alternative ways of doing research that would enable me to address meaningful educational problems in a powerful way, interpretive research appealed to me as being most appropriate (Erickson, 1986, 1998). It was legitimate to go to an educational setting and investigate intensively those problems that were of most interest to the participants throughout a study. The questions that could be addressed were significant and the focus was on making sense, not on defining operationally entities that could be controlled and manipulated. After 15 years of research in a paradigm based on quasi-experiments, I was searching for a new methodology and found an appealing alternative in a draft of Erickson's chapter on interpretive research (Erickson, 1986). For me, one of the appealing aspects of interpretive research is that it can be adapted to different, underlying, theoretical referents. Thus, as I have learned more about the social and cultural theories that pertain to the studies in which I engage, I have been able to apply them to the methods I employ in educational research. One referent that has made a considerable difference to how I think about educational research is what Guba and Lincoln (1989) referred to as the hermeneutical dialectical circle.

To my mind the hermeneutical dialectical circle is a way of thinking about the diversity in social settings. Generally, we look for organizations of phenomena in terms of patterns of regularity, and these patterns have been the main quest in educational research. In this chapter, I have referred to them as central tendencies, which often are described in interpretive research as assertions. However, an undue emphasis on central tendencies can favor retention of the existing situations. Use of the hermeneutical dialectical circle can guard against this inclination by going to the opposite extreme. In the selection of participants in a study, one can choose a first participant and then another who is most different from the first. When putting together a research team, one can include different participants so that diverse viewpoints can be represented in the theoretical perspectives that frame the planning and performance of a study. In the interpretation of given data, one can create an assertion and then search for evidence to support an opposite assertion. Thus, use of the hermeneutical dialectical circle is a factor that enhances the credibility of research and is a guard against the values of a group of interpretive researchers influencing what they choose to notice and to ignore. Finally, application of the hermeneutical dialectical circle ensures that the diversity in an interpretive study will be preserved. Whenever a central tendency is described, a researcher ought to begin to describe the various positions that define the periphery of perspectives that have been identified and preserved as a part of the overall description of the context to which all knowledge is linked.

Research involving human subjects necessarily entails moral actions. Too often in the past, studies have been designed by investigators operating on an assumption that knowledge and context can be separated meaningfully. In this chapter, I have assumed that knowledge and context cannot be separated. Accordingly, the morality of how the research is conducted needs to be considered at all times during a study. The considerations are context-dependent and do not reduce easily to a set of rules that typically govern the performance of research in universities and schools. On the basis of what I have described earlier in this chapter, it might be concluded that a researcher should demonstrate practical wisdom in terms of being honest, courageous, caring, and fair. However, such an exhortation ignores the complexity of most social systems and the paradox that to interact appropriately with one set of participants might be regarded as uncaring or unfair by other sets of participants. Participation in many communities carries with it an inherent ambiguity, especially for outsiders. Accordingly, I conclude this chapter with the suggestion that research be planned and performed with issues of ethical practice kept in the foreground and the subject of ongoing critical discussion throughout the progress of a study. If this becomes widespread practice in educational research, it is possible that those involved will be receptive to enacting changes on the basis of what they learn through their research activity. In such circumstances, the conduct of research will mean much more than the preparation and acceptance of researchers' accounts of their work.

# V Clinical Methods

Part III explained that one of reasons why teaching experiments have become popular in mathematics and science education is that one of the best ways to learn about the nature of a student's *state* of knowledge is to try to teach something new—by inducing changes in existing states of knowledge. Also, rather than being interested in *states* of knowledge, researchers may be more interested in dynamic *processes* or *mechanisms*. But, for either of the preceding reasons, many teaching experiments can be viewed as being extended clinical interviews; or, conversely, clinical interviews often can be viewed as being brief teaching experiments. Therefore, most of the issues that were discussed in Parts III and IV also are relevant in Part V.

To begin Part V, Goldin and Clement discuss the pragmatics and semantics of alternative questioning techniques used in clinical interviews. Then, Lesh and his colleagues explore the design and testing of tasks that are intended to reveal the thought processes of students and teachers. Next, Hall focuses on videotaping, and on issues that need to be considered when collecting and reporting videotaped research sessions; and, he describes a variety of ways that videotapes should not be confused with "raw data." For example, every time a camera or microphone focuses on one aspect of a situation rather than another, prejudices are introduced about what is important and what is not. Similarly, even after videotapes have been transcribed, Lesh and Lehrer describe why the interpretation of videotaped records should not be thought of as being a one-time event, and why it generally must involve many iterations and recursions for researchers to go beyond surface-level phenomena to recognize deeper patterns of behavior. Finally, Roschelle provides practical guidelines for selecting and using video technologies.

In both Parts III and IV, questions were raised about replication and objectivity. In Part V, these issues become particularized in discussions about "standardized" questions and "standardized" questioning techniques. To illustrate why these issues tend to become especially problematic in mathematics and science education, consider the fact that a large part of "thinking mathematically" or "thinking scientifically" focuses on developing mathematical or scientific interpretations of relevant learning or problem solving situations. Sometimes these interpretations involve quantification; sometimes they involve coordinatizing; and, sometimes they involve other types of mathematization or scientific modeling. But, in any case, in situations where the interpretation of the situation is not trivial: (a) A variety of levels and types of interpretations generally are possible; (b) a variety of different representations may be useful (each of which emphasizes and de-emphasizes somewhat different characteristics of the situations they are intended to describe); and (c) different analyses may involve different grain sizes, perspectives, or trade-offs involving factors such as simplicity and precision. The result of these facts is that, in general, if $N$ learners or problem solvers are asked to interpret a situation, then $N$ different interpretations should be expected to occur; and, this fact is especially true when clinical interviewers use different sequences of questions to probe the thinking of individual research subjects. Therefore, when such situations occur, questions arise about what it means to speak about standardized questions or about standardized sequences of questions; and, similar questions arise about the kinds of generalizations that can be made from results of specific interviews or videotaped episodes.

Before reading the chapters in Part V, readers may find it useful to formulate responses to the following questions for a research that you yourself might want to conduct:

- Are you planning for $N$ different subjects to participate in a single teaching, learning, or problem solving situation? If so, do you think that it will be important for you to deal with the fact that the different subjects may interpret the situation in significantly different ways?

- Are you planning to interview your research subjects? If so, what attempts do you think it will be important for you make to standardize the questions or sequences of questions?

- Are you planning for each research subject to deal with $N$ different problem solving or decision making situations? If so, do you think it will be important for you to be able to claim that these situations represent a sample from some larger class? What evidence will you need to produce to support this claim?

# 19

## A Scientific Perspective on Structured, Task-Based Interviews in Mathematics Education Research

**Gerald A. Goldin**

*Rutgers, the State University of New Jersey*

This chapter considers one methodological aspect of qualitative research—the use of structured, task-based interviews in observing and interpreting mathematical behavior. Several scientific issues and their implications are discussed briefly, including: (a) the reproducibility, comparability, and reliability of observations; (b) the generalizability of research findings; (c) the importance of mathematical content and structures; (d) the role of cognitive theory in designing and interpreting interviews; and, (e) the interplay among task and contextual variables. In evaluating task-based interview methods scientifically, I argue against some claims that have been advanced in the name of epistemological schools of thought ranging from radical positivism and behaviorism to radical constructivism, social constructivism, and postmodernism. Finally, some broadly applicable principles and techniques are proposed for improving the quality of task-based interview research.

The perspective offered here is that of a physical scientist as well as a mathematics educator who has been involved in empirical and theoretical research on mathematical problem solving for 25 years. I maintain that sound principles of scientific investigation, as developed and applied in modern science, should be applied to this endeavor too. This should never be done dogmatically or automatically. However, it should be done rigorously, paying careful attention to the reasoning behind the application of the methodological ideas of science. Although I have learned much from the research of others who hold different views, I remain entirely unconvinced by the arguments that are advanced occasionally, claiming that scientific methods of inquiry are inadequate for, or irrelevant to, the study of human psychosocial activities such as teaching and learning mathematics and mathematical problem solving.

Because one purpose of this book is to consider quality standards for qualitative research methods, it is essential to consider the fundamental scientific issues.

My experiences with task-based interview methodology originated and evolved through a series of studies of individual mathematical problem solving by elementary school, high school, and college students and adults, conducted in collaboration with my students (Bodner & Goldin, 1991a, 1991b; DeBellis & Goldin, 1991; Goldin, 1985; Goldin & Landis, 1985, 1986; Goldin & Luger, 1975; Goldin & Waters, 1982; Luger, 1980; Waters, 1980). Most recently, members of a group of investigators that I led at Rutgers University have been analyzing and interpreting the results of a series of five task-based interviews in elementary school mathematics. We created these interviews as part of a longitudinal study of individual children's mathematical development (Goldin, 1993a; Goldin, DeBellis, DeWindt-King, Passantino, & Zang, 1993). Between 1992 and 1994, structured interviews were conducted with an initial group of 22 third- and fourth-grade children, 19 of whom completed the full series. Partial results have been reported (DeBellis, 1996; DeBellis & Goldin, 1993, 1997; Goldin & Passantino, 1996; Zang, 1994, 1995). The development of interview scripts for this series was guided by the views described in this chapter; in turn, my views were influenced by insights gained during the study.

It is not my intention to describe the specifics of these studies here, but to focus on methodological suggestions and conclusions drawn in part from them. The chapter is organized as follows. The next section summarizes the meaning, importance, and limitations of task-based interview research in mathematics education. Here I try to explain the notion of structured interviews that are designed to investigate hypotheses using qualitative analyses of data, and offer some brief examples. The ideas presented carry forward and expand considerably on earlier deliberations about the measurement of mathematical problem solving outcomes (Cobb, 1986; Goldin, 1982, 1986; L. Hart, 1986; Lucas, et al., 1980) and the relation between cognitive theory and assessment (Goldin, 1992c). This is followed by a discussion of key scientific issues in connection with the methodology, and the case for explicit rejection of certain damaging conclusions derived from dismissive epistemological belief systems. The final section offers a preliminary set of broad, guiding principles and techniques for establishing and enhancing the quality of task-based interview research in the domain of mathematics.

# TASK-BASED INTERVIEWS

Structured, task-based interviews for the study of mathematical behavior involve minimally a subject (the problem solver) and an interviewer (the clinician), interacting in relation to one or more tasks (questions, problems, or activities) introduced to the subject by the clinician in a preplanned way. The latter component justifies the term *task-based*, so that the subjects' interactions are not merely with the interviewers, but with the task environments. Group interviews with two or more subjects fall also within the purview of this discussion, leading to the need to expand our interpretations of some of the ideas.

Normally, provision is made for observing and recording for later analysis what takes place during the interview, through audio- and/or videotaping, observers' notes, and the subject's work. Explicit provision is made too for contingencies that may occur as the interview proceeds, possibly by means of branching sequences of heuristic questions, hints, related problems in sequence, retrospective questions, or other interventions by the clinician. It is this explicit provision for contingencies, together with the attention to the sequence and structures of the tasks, that distinguishes the "structured" interviews discussed here from "unstructured" interviews, which may be limited to "free" problem solving (where no substantial assistance that would facilitate a solution is given by the clinician to the subject) or to the handling of contingencies on an improvisational basis. By analyzing verbal and nonverbal behavior or interactions, the researcher hopes to make inferences about the mathematical thinking, learning, and/or problem solving of the subjects. From these inferences, we hope to deepen our understanding of various aspects of mathematics education. We may aim to test one or more explicit hypotheses, using qualitative analyses of the data; we may seek merely to obtain descriptive reports about the subjects' learning and/or problem solving; or we may hope to achieve an intermediate goal, such as refining or elaborating a conjecture.

Of course, the design of structured task-based interviews needs to take into account their research purposes. These may include (for example) exploratory investigation; refinement of observation, description, inference, or analysis techniques; development of constructs and conjectures; investigation or testing of advance hypotheses; and/or inquiry into the applicability of a model of teaching, learning, or problem solving. In addition the design is affected by the complexity of the phenomena in the system being investigated.

Task-based interviews can serve as research instruments for making systematic observations in the psychology of learning mathematics and solving mathematical problems. They also can be adapted as assessment tools for describing the subject's knowledge and/or improving the practice of mathematics education (cf. R. B. Davis, 1984). The value of task-based interviews for either of these purposes lies in the fact that they provide a structured mathematical environment that, to some extent, can be controlled. Mathematical tasks can be adjusted in wording, content, setting, sequence, and structure, based on express criteria and the outcomes of prior research. Interview contingencies can be decided explicitly and modified when appropriate. In comparison with conventional, paper-and-pencil test-based methods, task-based interviews make it possible to focus research attention more directly on the subjects' processes of addressing mathematical tasks, rather than just on the patterns of correct and incorrect answers in the results they produce. Thus, there is the possibility of delving into a variety of important topics more deeply than is possible by other experimental means—topics such as complex cognitions associated with learning mathematics, mechanisms of mathematical exploration and problem solving, relationships between problem solving and learning, relationships between affect and cognition, and so forth. A few examples may illustrate some of these ideas and their evolution.

During the 1950s and 1960s, many researchers investigated the use of strategies by problem solvers. These studies were consistent with the prevailing behavioral focus in psychology, considering a "strategy" to be essentially a pattern in behavior. Strategy scores were defined, based on the kinds of discrete choices made by subjects during problem solving. For example, Bruner, Goodnow, and Austin (1956) distinguished various sorts of "focusing" and "scanning" strategies in conjunctive concept identification tasks, whereas Dienes and Jeeves (1965, 1970) found "operator," "pattern," and "memory" strategies in card tasks that had the underlying structure of a mathematical group. The nature of the interviews was to pose problems where the spectrum of choices available at each point (i.e., the set of possible "behaviors") was limited—for instance (depending on the task) to trying an exemplar, making a guess or conjecture, or choosing a card. The tasks and questions were highly structured in order to circumscribe the outcomes. Then, certain kinds of hypotheses could be investigated quantitatively: ways in which strategy scores might depend on task variables, subject variables, or training experiences; the consistency of strategies across isomorphic or homomorphic task structures, and the like (Dienes & Jeeves, 1970; Jeeves & Greer, 1983).

Newell and H. A. Simon (1972) pioneered the analysis of subjects' verbal problem solving protocols. They modeled the individual's problem solving process as a search through an internal problem space; basically, the purpose of the task-based interviews was to test and refine such a model. The tasks in their studies were selected (tacitly) so that they embodied fairly well defined external state-spaces: cryptarithmetic, symbolic logic, and chess problems, for example. They encouraged their subjects to "think out loud" during problem solving that was otherwise without overt interventions, or "free." Thus, the interview contingencies were almost unstructured, but important structures were imposed in the choices of structured tasks and the thinking-aloud procedure. The analysis of the protocols, through which the interviews were interpreted, was highly structured as well—being carried out in relation to then-current information-processing models for problem solving based on state-space tree search (cf. Wickelgren, 1974). In retrospect, it can be said that the advance commitment to this type of protocol analysis contributed to the insufficiently justified conclusion that the data supported the adequacy of the internal problem-space model.

Combining some features of earlier techniques, a task-based interview study was designed to test certain hypotheses about the effects of task variables on the strategies used in conjunctive concept identification tasks (Goldin & Waters, 1982; Waters, 1980). Here, subjects were asked to choose cards to test as exemplars or nonexemplars of a conjunctive concept; but, after each choice, they were asked, "Why did you make that choice?" The purpose was to be able to classify the kinds of reasons they offered as being of a focusing or scanning nature, thus introducing a quantifiable distinction between the (qualitatively defined) *intended* use of the strategies, and the *behavioral* strategy scores studied earlier. However, our analysis of the outcomes was confined to strategy scoring. Of course we recognized that the repeated asking of a specific question requiring self-monitoring would affect the subjects' problem solving processes importantly. In fact, it is a general feature of structured task-based interviews that the interventions are a part of the task environment. What is observed is always the subjects' behavior in the presence of the structured interventions. What may be inferred are aspects of the subjects' internal cognitions and/or affect in the presence of the interventions. Though results cannot be interpreted as corresponding to what would have occurred in an entirely free situation, this is not a "limitation." It is simply a fact about human interaction, about the phenomenon under study; mathematical problem solving during discourse with another person. There is nothing in this to discredit the methodology.

In subsequent work designed to explore a heuristic process called "Think of a Simpler Problem," we posed this question to mathematically talented children (after some preliminary activity): "What is the remainder when 2 to the 50th power is divided by 3?" (Goldin, 1985; Goldin & Landis, 1985, 1986). In the script for the structured, task-based interview, we developed the technique of providing hints or heuristic suggestions that might guide the children past obstacles. These interventions were preplanned. They were based on, and in accordance with, the particular structured, heuristic process whose development we wished to study. With specified exceptions, they were provided only at points in the interview when the child's free problem solving came to such a firm halt or impasse that further progress seemed unlikely. Thus, the interventions could be understood to bridge gaps in the child's own, partially developed, heuristic planning competencies. The richness of the subsequent problem solving behaviors indicated to us that these suggestions were meaningful to the subject. In this way, we were able to observe (often, very sophisticated) problem solving behavior, much further along a path toward solution than would have been possible otherwise. We inferred various aspects of the children's planning and executive control structures as they related to the "simpler problem" heuristic process. Results here were in the form of qualitative descriptions of (inferred) competencies and competency structures, rather than quantitative scores. The plan for intervention was overt, not tacit. Again, it is clear that intervening in the problem solving resulted in its following a very different path from that which it might have taken without any intervention.

Finally, I shall say a little about the most recent series of five task-based interviews (Goldin et al., 1993). These interviews were designed to explore individual children's mathematical development longitudinally, through case studies focusing on the growth of internal representational capabilities and their interplay with external representations constructed by the children. The clinicians were trained with interview scripts that describe branching sequences of possible questions and interventions, ranging from relatively "neutral" ones such as, "Why do you think so?" or, "Can you show me what you mean?" to more specific heuristic suggestions, questions, or even explanations. The scripts vary in size from 27 to 55 pages (with a lot of blank space) and are designed to be administered in a single class period of 45 minutes to 1 hour. Each task-based interview is organized so that, for each main question, the exploration proceeds in four stages:

- Posing the question (free problem solving), with sufficient time for the child to respond and only nondirective follow-up questions, such as, "Can you tell me more about that?"

- Minimal heuristic suggestions, if the response is not spontaneous, such as, "Can you show me using some of these materials?"

- The guided use of heuristic suggestions, again only when the requested description or anticipated behavior does not occur spontaneously, such as, "Do you see a pattern in the cards?"

- Exploratory, metacognitive questions, such as, "Do you think you could explain how you thought about the problem?"

After some preliminary questions, each interview includes by design a sequence of nonroutine mathematical tasks, that can evoke complex heuristic processes together with imagistic representation (especially visual and kinesthetic) and/or numerical representation, verbal discussion, and affective responses. The tasks involve sequences that can be interpreted as embodying whole number and/or geometrical patterns, and activities inviting the use of additive structures, multiplicative structures, and rational number structures. The goals of the clinician, before continuing to the next question, are to elicit, with specified exceptions, a complete, coherent verbal reason for each of the child's responses, and a coherent external representation constructed by the child. A complete, coherent reason means one based on a described or modeled pattern. However it is *not* required that this pattern be the "canonical" response or the "desired correct answer" in order that the response or external representation be considered complete and coherent.

During the interviews, the children and their work were videotaped; the tapes were transcribed, and the protocols and tapes are being analyzed in a variety of exploratory ways. These range from inferred focusing by the child on particular visual components during strategic thinking, to inferred interactions between affect and heuristics in the child, to the inferred use by the child of various fraction models. Representations, both external and internal, are a key construct in the analysis of outcomes, including their development over time in individual children as evidenced by comparisons between later and earlier interviews.

In contrast to the earlier studies described, the current investigations are wholly exploratory and descriptive. Their interim products are a set of complex, detailed, qualitative reports, without yet quantitative tests of hypotheses or generalizable conclusions. Indeed, although interviews of this design could be used to test hypotheses, they have the particular strength that they do not require advance commitment to a particular set of hypotheses. Nevertheless, despite the open-ended aspect of the study, we strive through careful task-based interview design to become as explicit as possible about the task environment in which we are conducting our explorations, including the interview contingencies. We also seek to describe carefully the reasoning or evidence behind the inferences about the children's internal representations that we make from observations of their problem solving behavior. The interview scripts are sufficiently detailed to enable other researchers to conduct "the same" or structurally similar interviews with other subjects, using "the same" or similar mathematical tasks. Though these characteristics are difficult to achieve (and I readily acknowledge limitations in the extent of our group's success), they are important ingredients of high-quality scientific investigation, even in the earliest exploratory stages of research.

As the practice of mathematics education has moved away from an earlier, nearly exclusive focus on rules, procedures, and algorithmic learning, it has come to emphasize more categorically conceptual understanding, complex problem solving, and children's internal constructions of mathematical meaning (R. B. Davis, et al., 1990; National Council of Teachers of Mathematics, 1989; Steffe, Nesher, Cobb, Goldin, & Greer, 1996). The task-based interview, of the type mentioned, becomes then an increasingly important tool in designing research. As an instrument for gathering qualitative data, it can help us infer and describe the deeper understandings in students that we seek to achieve through improved emphases in education. Research is thus joined more directly with educational practice, as the interview can aid us in understanding how to characterize and achieve higher order learning goals in a variety of domains of school mathematics.

As a qualitative assessment tool, the task-based interview also has great potential for evaluating whether we are succeeding (Lesh & Lamon, 1992). It offers the opportunity for research-based inferences about students' achievement of higher and deeper mathematical understandings, going beyond the more superficial measures in wide use now. Information may be gathered about students that bears directly on improved classroom goals in mathematics, addressing the questions most central to the educational reform process; for instance: What powerful problem solving processes are students learning that go beyond mathematical facts and algorithmic procedures? What kinds of cognitive representations are they developing? What beliefs about mathematics, or affective pathways in relation to mathematics, are children acquiring? What consequences are innovative teaching methods having for their mathematical development? In the context of new educational practices, it is increasingly important to be able to describe and assess the mathematical development of individual children over time; a longitudinal series of task-based interviews is one tool for achieving this objective.

The potential for extension from research to assessment is a strength of task-based interview methods, but poses its own challenges. Sometimes, the societal purposes of assessment are very different from those of research. For example, traditional assessment goals may include maximizing the spread in individual performance scores, a goal that can be in conflict with the research purpose of obtaining better understandings and descriptions of various structures of mathematical competencies in students. Contrasts between different uses of clinical interview methods were discussed recently by Hunting (1997). Being explicit about the goals for which task-based interviews are designed, so as to develop them accordingly, is one important ingredient in achieving a high level of quality.

Indeed, to serve the ends for which task-based interviews are suited, their construction must reach the point that permits researchers to generalize from their findings, and to build systematically on each other's work. This requires attention to the scientific issues raised in the discussion that follows.

Besides their intellectual necessity, there is an important practical reason for urgency in addressing these concerns. Reforms in school mathematics in the United States are open to opposition, including politically motivated opposition. Revising teacher-centered, direct instruction that values memorization, rules, mathematical algorithms, and standard problem types, to emphasize guided explorations by children, nonroutine problem solving, the discovery of patterns, and the ways of reasoning that lie behind mathematical procedures, involves risk. To survive anticipated challenges, the reform movement needs to define its goals and document its achievements in ways that withstand scientific scrutiny and criticism. This cannot be said too strongly! If the research base for promoting reform relies exclusively on qualitative research in the form of anecdotal accounts, interesting stories, and irreproducible results, while the research base for opposing reform is based on quantitative replicable evidence (such as easily obtained scores on traditional skills tests in mathematics), the results are foreseeable and potentially disastrous. The research community will, by default, provide powerful ammunition to reform's opponents. Already this "research gap" is, in my opinion, a serious one.

# SCIENTIFIC CONSIDERATIONS

Whether we regard task-based interviews as research instruments or assessment tools, their use to observe and draw valid inferences from mathematical behavior requires the consideration of important scientific issues. This section takes up some of them.

## Control and Design, Observation and Inference

In scientific research, one seeks to describe one's observational methods as completely as possible. This includes distinguishing carefully between what is controlled or partially controlled in the research design, and what is uncontrolled. It also means characterizing what is observed as precisely as possible, and distinguishing what is observed from what is inferred or deduced from the observations. These steps lay the foundation for drawing valid inferences based on overt reasoning about empirical observations.

In task-based interview research, we generally can control or partially control the tasks (addressing such variables as mathematical content and structure, complexity, and linguistic and semantic structure), the interview questions and any suggestions or hints offered (including various contingencies on which these may depend), the interview setting, the choice of subjects, the physical materials available to the subjects, the time allotted for problem solving, and related task and situational variables. In a high-quality study, these choices are not accidental. Rather, they are made carefully in the course of the interview design, in order to achieve the observation of certain sorts of mathematical behavior (often, behavior appropriate to an exploratory, problem solving context in mathematics).

The goal of careful description means arriving at the point that other researchers can conduct task-based interviews with the same or similar controls exercised, that is, with the same or similar tasks, questions, contingencies, and so forth. This is a key step toward replicability (see later discussion), and without it the goal of research generalizability is sacrificed from the outset.

It should be completely clear in this discussion that it is the *presented* task, not the *interpreted* task, that is subject to experimental control. Of course, the same or similar presented tasks will be interpreted similarly by some students, and very differently by others. I do not advocate making, "the assumption that there is nothing problematic about the interpretation of givens, goals, and legitimate solution steps, and the only difficulty consists of finding a way to get from here to there" (R. Lesh, personal communication, May 1997).

Whether or not the interpretations by individuals of givens, goals, solution steps, or other problem features vary greatly or are problematic is an *empirical* question subject to scientific investigation. But we can address it only if we are willing to treat the task that is presented as subject to control.

Quality research not only addresses the variables that are controlled, but also includes explicit consideration of known variables that are uncontrolled, seeking to understand and allow for their possible effects. For instance, in the task-based interview involving "2 to the 50th power" mentioned earlier, we had no way to control for the children's prior study or understanding of exponents in arithmetic. However, we had every reason to think that it would have important effects. Therefore, we sought to minimize the consequences of this variation by beginning the task-based interview with a short teaching sequence, with examples. Every child in the study interpreted the exponent correctly as repeated multiplication in arithmetic examples, before proceeding to the main interview question.

If the design of task-based interviews is haphazard—with variables that can be controlled remaining uncontrolled—the validity of the inferences drawn from the resulting observations becomes questionable. Proposed interpretations are open to objection because the results may be accidental, or spurious, one-time consequences of unobserved, uncontrolled particulars of the situation. This is the meaning of characterizing a research report as "anecdotal."

As noted, task-based interviews typically do not focus on easily defined outcomes such as patterns of correct and incorrect answers by subjects. Rather, investigators try to observe, record, and interpret complex behaviors and patterns in behavior, including subjects' spoken words, interjections, movements, writings, drawings, actions on and with external materials, gestures, facial expressions, and so forth. Decisions regarding what to observe are a part of the research design. Quality research distinguishes what is *observed* from what is *inferred*, and this is especially important when what is observed is already complex and qualitative. In chemistry, for many decades, atoms and molecules were not observed: They were inferred (as theoretical constructs) from quantitative, macroscopic, and most importantly, reproducible observations of patterns in chemical reactions. Some thought atoms could never be observed, as their (inferred) sizes were typically smaller than the (inferred) wavelength of visible light. In the psychology of mathematics education, we similarly cannot observe subjects' thinking, reasoning, cognitive processes, internal representations, meanings, knowledge structures, schemata, affective or emotional states, and the like. These are all model-dependent constructs by researchers, viewed as descriptive of important phenomena internal to individual subjects.

Through research one can hope (at best) to make inferences about them, using what *can* be observed to infer what cannot.

Thus it becomes imperative to examine in detail how we make such inferences. The goal must be to become as explicit as possible about the criteria for drawing particular sorts of inferences from particular sorts of observations. This includes careful statements of the theoretical assumptions behind the constructs themselves and the justifications for specific inferences made. The alternative to such explicitness is to rely entirely on the tacit assumptions and subjective judgments of the researchers or clinicians, or those who have studied with them.

Because, in mathematics education research, the researcher often interacts with the subjects, because the process of observation itself has effects on the persons being observed, and because the inferred constructs are of necessity quite complex, some advocate rejecting entirely the idea of an "objective reality," and, with it, the scientific methods that have succeeded so dramatically in the natural sciences. But the interactive, complex features of experimentation are familiar to physical and biological scientists. They are particularly evident in the study of quantum phenomena, and uncertainty, and in the domain of classical dynamical systems sensitively dependent on initial conditions. In no way do they invalidate the scientific methods of investigation that have led to understandings of these phenomena. Although quantum mechanics raises important philosophical issues about the meaning of the word *objective*, the alternative for most physicists who understand the subject is *not* that reality is "subjective" or a "social construct." It is that reality may be fundamentally probabilistic, indeterminate, stochastic, or unpredictable at the subatomic level. Whether these things are so (and present evidence seems to be in their favor) is again an *empirical* question.

The result of rejecting scientific methods of inquiry is to replace them with subjective, albeit possibly well informed, judgments. I would like to stress that to argue against reliance on subjective individual judgment in research is *not* to challenge the expertise of particular researchers in exercising those judgments. Rather, it is to advocate the goal of scientific generalizability of conclusions over the collection of anecdotal evidence.

## Reproducibility, Comparability, Reliability, and Generalizability

Task-based interviews, intended as they usually are to yield qualitative observations, do not lend themselves easily to quantitative generalization through research. Every interview is different, and not all variables can be controlled. At a minimum the subjects, the clinicians, and the specific context of task administration all differ from one interview to another. Nevertheless, generalization—including, in this case, generalization of the qualitative findings—is critical to applying and building on what we learn. In what sense, then, do such interviews constitute genuine scientific investigation? How can we achieve any reproducibility or replicability of research findings if we use this methodology? How can we compare the results of different studies, hope for reliability in our observational and inferencing methods, or validly assert the generalizability of findings from the studies we conduct?

Perhaps a good example is provided by Piaget's discovery and description of the nonconservation of number by young children, and his more detailed characterization of stages that children go through in acquiring number conservation (Piaget, 1965). Piaget gathered information principally through well-described, individual task-based interviews. His findings were confirmed by many researchers working independently in a variety of contexts and cultures. They certainly involved complex observations and inferences, and the need to make these reliably and compare them in different studies. Suppose that Piaget's findings had turned out to be irreproducible, occurring only sporadically, occasionally, or unpredictably, or occurring only with certain, not clearly specifiable, task materials and not with other materials, or occurring only for a few clinicians whom Piaget himself had trained and not for others. His conclusions would then have been far less influential on the research community—and quite rightly so.

A first step in achieving our scientific goals is to recognize the urgent necessity of keeping them, rather than abandoning them. In my view this is such an important need that it should be included from the outset in developing standards of quality for task-based interview research.

There is a troubling tendency in the mathematics education community to regard these goals not only as unimportant but also, in principle, unachievable; appropriate perhaps for the physical sciences, but not for the study of human beings as unique, cognizing individuals in a social and cultural context. Some researchers advocate replacing the goal of research objectivity or validity with that of "viability," meaning that the knowledge gained "fits into the world of the knower's experience" (von Glasersfeld, 1996, p. 310) or (from the social constructivist perspective) that it offers some degree of continuing acceptability or utility in discourse within the community of mathematics education researchers. The notion of viability is an interesting and useful one in describing the psychology of individuals' knowledge and belief structures, but it is a very different thing from scientific validity. Such a replacement should be regarded as scientifically unacceptable. It would eliminate the fundamental notion that scientific knowledge and preconceptions be empirically demonstrable or falsifiable through research.

Without establishing the comparability of research findings in different studies, we place ourselves in the prescientific stage of being unable even to identify similarities or differences among individuals or populations. Without achieving reproducibility or replicability, we have no scientific evidence on which general conclusions can be based. The observation that particular events seem to have occurred in particular interviews or a particular study tells us little about good educational practice for a population of students. It remains at best a suggestive story, one that may serve the preconceptions of those who like it, or disturb those who do not. Without attention to the reliability of observation and inference, we do not even know if the story itself is an artifact of the researcher's imagination or wishful thinking. Such stories are *viable* when they please those who tell and hear them, but viability alone characterizes superstitious belief systems such as astrological forecasting as well as scientific belief systems such as astronomical theory. It is no substitute for scientific evidence. To abandon scientific goals in task-based interview research is to leave the field of generalizable research in mathematics education, by default, to those who rely exclusively on quantitative, rather than qualitative, methods.

The second step, then, in achieving scientific goals must be to include progress toward them among the criteria for quality in research. We must consider the use of all available techniques for making such progress in evaluating research quality.

To move toward the generalizability of research findings, we must aim to describe methods and results in ways that gives sense to the term *replicability*, namely, they must permit the community of researchers to employ similar methods, compare results, and confirm or contradict each other. Not only should the variables subject to control be addressed explicitly, but also the kinds of observations to be made and the methods of inference to be used should be characterized in advance as much as possible. One important way to do this in task-based interview research is to create, wherever possible, interview scripts. The scripts prescribe the tasks, the questions posed, and the major interview contingencies. With such scripts, at least some of the clinician's decisions enter the domain of scientific discourse. The choices made in designing scripts can be discussed and criticized because they are explicit. The same, or nearly the same, tasks, questions, and contingencies can be employed by other researchers for presentation. The concrete materials made available to the subject can be controlled, described, and reproduced or modified,\ as desired. In addition, the population of subjects in a study can be characterized sufficiently well so that important similarities and differences with other subject populations can be identified. Some aspects of the interview context can be controlled, and these, too, become a part of the experimental protocol.

Inevitably, other quantitative and qualitative variables or features will differ from study to study. It is important to remember that, in general, scientific reproducibility does not mean that a study is performed a second time under identical conditions. It means that the described outcomes of the research—whether they be patterns in behavior, inferred stages of development, schemata, internal representations, particular cognitive obstacles occurring in specific mathematical domains, the variability of strategies, a range of children's affective responses, population differences, and so forth—are observed repeatedly in subjects under a variety of known conditions, and continue to be observed as the experimental methods are refined and improved so that the conditions are determined more clearly. This ensures that the conclusions claimed are not spurious, one-time events or merely artifacts of a researcher's subjective judgments, and that any trained researcher can replicate the study and observe them.

The goal of the comparability of research findings refers to the need for descriptions of conditions, observations, and inferences from the observations to be sufficiently precise that, when other observers under different conditions make observations and inferences, the findings of the studies can be compared with respect to some defined outcome variables. How do the conclusions of a study depend on the population of subjects? How do they depend on the task variables? How do they depend on contextual factors? All such questions presuppose the comparability of the controlled variables and the outcome measures.

The concept of reliability includes measuring the consistency with which a task-based interview is conducted, observations are taken, and inferences are made from the observations using defined criteria. It also includes measures of consistency among different observations intended to permit the same or similar inferences. For example, it is important to ask: Do different clinicians follow the interview script correctly, and do they do so repeatedly? Do various clinicians interpret contingencies the same way? Are observations made and recorded reliably? Is there consistency within and between researchers in the application of criteria for making inferences? Do different observers arrive at similar conclusions in interpreting subjects' behavior? Does the behavior of the subjects support the inference that they understand the mathematical tasks in a consistent way? Do independent observations in a single interview, or across several interviews, support the conclusions reached?

It may be extremely difficult or impossible, as a practical matter, to define or meet quantitative criteria for the reliability of most observations and inferences made from task-based interviews. Nevertheless, progress can be achieved for particular kinds of task variables, observational variables, or inference criteria that are deemed crucial to each study.

Ultimately, the generalizability of the findings of mathematics education research means our ability to predict validly, based on many research studies performed under controlled or partially controlled conditions, something about a population of students who are interacting with certain mathematical tasks in a defined context. It is essential to understand that a large accumulation of anecdotal evidence, in and of itself, does not provide grounds for generalization; indeed, anecdotal accounts abound in support of astrology, psychic phenomena, medical quackery, and other pseudoscientific beliefs. I argue that the generalizability of task-based interview research can follow only from close attention to scientific concerns such as those discussed here. Statistical methods and standardized experimental designs are tools for achieving generalizability, but they are not the only tools. Indeed, the pressures to conform to conventional, standardized experimental designs earlier skewed mathematics education research away from the study of complex mathematical learning and problem solving processes, whereas traditional psychometric models and methodologies have been misused and misinterpreted badly. I have also been one of those pointing out how meta-analysis is subject to abuse in the search for generalizability (Goldin, 1992a, 1993b). But we must not be led by examples of questionable research performed in the name of generalizability to sacrifice generalizability itself as a fundamental goal, any more than we should be led by abuses and misuses of statistics to abandon statistical methods.

## Mathematical Content and Structures

Among the most important of the variables subject to control in task-based interview design are the mathematical characteristics of the problems on which interviews are based. In discussing these characteristics, it is important to go beyond the superficial level to address both the deeper semantic structures and the deeper mathematical structures that may occur in various task-content domains.

The value of regarding abstract mathematical structures as variables external to the subjects is well established. This perspective permits researchers to design tasks that will facilitate particular interactions between mathematical structures and structures internal to the subjects. The analysis of such structures—the possible interactions among mathematics, cognition and learning, and affect—is an important theoretical ingredient of task-based interview research. Thus, in referring to mathematical structures in the tasks presented in our longitudinal series of five task-based interviews as "whole number and/or geometrical patterns," "additive structures," "multiplicative structures," and "rational number structures," it is not assumed that the subjects have developed just these structures already, or that they all will interpret the tasks according to such structures. Rather, the purpose is to infer interactions between the subjects' internal cognitive and affective structures and the external mathematical task structures. The characterization of the tasks as "having" such structures means that there is reason to believe that meaningful interactions in relation to these structures are possible or likely. Whether and how they occur is then subject to empirical investigation.

Related problems in task-based interviews can be selected to embody, for example, homomorphic or isomorphic mathematical structures, or a cross-section of diverse structures, or to embed different, specific problem state-space structures in different contexts, and so forth (Goldin, 1980; Greer & Harel, 1998; Jeeves and Greer, 1983).

## Cognitive Theory and Models

The role of theory in structuring task-based interview research is crucial, just as every scientific investigation is fundamentally theory based and theory guided. What we observe depends on the definitions that we adopt, and on what we decide should be looked for; this depends, in turn, on theory. The earliest task-based interviews that I was involved in designing were based on the analysis of task variables (Goldin & McClintock, 1980); whereas, more recent studies made use of a model for learning and problem solving competency based on the development of several kinds of internal, cognitive representational systems and their interplay with external representations (Goldin, 1987, 1992c).

It never should be regarded as sufficient to conduct an interview "without preconceptions," merely to observe what will happen. In my view, this means merely that the researchers' preconceptions will be tacit, rather than explicit. With no proposed theoretical model and guiding questions framed within the model, what can be learned from the interview is of severely limited scientific value. Thus, one attribute of quality task-based interview research is the careful description of the theoretical framework within which the research is conducted. What is assumed, and what is sought to be learned, about the subjects' competencies or competency structures, cognitions or cognitive structures, concepts or conceptual structures, attitudes, affective pathways or structures, belief systems, stages of development, systems of internal representation, problem solving strategies, and so forth, should be considered in detail in the design of the interview.

Obviously, the choice of tasks influences the outcomes in a task-based interview, and it is theory that guides us in how this may be expected to happen. What we set out to observe affects the structure of the contingencies in an interview; again, it is theory that guides us—in how to design the contingencies and in how to draw inferences from the observations. Ultimately, the best research questions help us to modify and improve our theories based on the outcomes of interview-based research.

## Social, Cultural, and Psychological Contexts

The question of describing the constraints, limitations, or influences resulting from the social and cultural contexts of task-based interviews, as well as their individual psychological contexts as experienced by the subjects, is a challenging one that should be considered expressly in task-based interview research. From what evidence might we infer interactions between the subjects' expectations, apprehensions and intentions, the task variables, and mathematical cognitions and affect? For instance, children drawn from their regular classes to participate in interviews may see the interview as fundamentally a school activity, and respond both mathematically and emotionally as if the expectation is for them to produce "school mathematics"—correct answers through previously learned algorithms—although that is not the interviewer's intent. Overt consideration and analysis of such issues, even when they are not the main focus of the research, can contribute substantially to the quality of the research study through improved interview design and more careful inferences drawn from the outcomes observed.

## Interplay Among Variables

The variables discussed here should not be considered to act independently. For example, task-based interviews present a mathematical environment in a social/cultural environment, and the subject's internal representation of social expectations and their possible consequences may influence his or her mathematical behavior in a way that depends on the mathematics, too. To illustrate this possibility, consider again an interview taking place in an elementary school, whose purpose the child may believe is to test his or her understanding of the mathematics taught in school. The child may respond very differently to the mathematical content of the interview tasks—both cognitively and affectively—according to whether or not the mathematical topics were discussed in class recently, discussed long before, or never encountered previously; or according to whether or not they were tested in class.

Such complex interactions mean that in the design of the interviews, there always will be trade-offs that sacrifice some potential observations for others. They also suggest the need for perpetual openness to the observation and interpretation of new or unanticipated events.

# DISMISSIVE CLAIMS BASED ON EPISTEMOLOGICAL BELIEF SYSTEMS

In this section, I argue that standards of quality in task-based interview research should include the clear rejection of certain unsound claims, sometimes made in the name of epistemological belief systems that have been fashionable—from logical positivism and behaviorism to radical constructivism, radical social constructivism, and postmodernism and related ideas. The characteristic these claims share that warrants their rejection is that each dismisses as inadmissible certain kinds of evidence or explanatory tools; not on scientific grounds, but on the basis of asserted a priori philosophical stances. This dismissal is a major obstacle to the progress of scientific research in mathematical learning and problem solving. It is an obstacle that extends back to the 1950s. It is time that we rejected such dismissive, nonscientific thinking once and for all.

It will, of course, be pointed out that the rejection of dismissive, a priori claims itself constitutes a "dismissal," as if that demonstrated a sort of inconsistency in the position advocated here. There is no inconsistency. I do not favor the prior rejection of such claims, as the claimants favor the prior rejection of one or another aspect of empirical scientific study. Rather, their rejection should be based on the identifiable damage to scientific research and educational practice that has resulted from the dismissive claims themselves.

For example, during the first half of this century, logical positivists argued in favor of operational definitions as the basis of scientific investigation. They took the position that statements about "in-principle-unobservable" events and other nonverifiable statements are inherently meaningless (Ayer, 1946). Accepting this analysis, some radical behaviorists ruled out of bounds all "mentalistic" explanations of behavior. Because stimulus situations and subjects' responses are observable and measurable directly; whereas cognitions, affect, internal representations, mental states, and the like are not, the latter were to be excluded in advance from the domain of legitimate research discussion.

The focus on stimulus-response psychology derived quite clearly from the radical behaviorist perspective (Skinner, 1953, 1974). It was likewise argued that the need to define "behavioral objectives" in education, notably mathematics education, followed from the necessary, "scientific," epistemological requirement that observable and measurable learning outcomes be specified in advance (Mager, 1962, Sund & Picard, 1972). This was required in order that educational objectives satisfy the verifiability criterion of meaningfulness. In mathematics, radical behaviorism dominated classroom practice for a considerable period of time. It tended to result in an exclusive emphasis on discrete, rule-based, easily testable skills, and the explicit de-emphasis of "understanding" as an educational goal. Behaviorism in task-based interview research led to an exclusive focus on subjects' stimulus situations and discrete behaviors, without the needed focus on what can be inferred from them about internal processes, and without the needed consideration of psychological, social, and cultural contexts. All such nonbehavioral constructs were dismissed a priori, without examination.

I use the past tense in the preceding two paragraphs because the ideas of the radical behaviorists are much less fashionable today than they were in the recent past. But it is hard to overestimate the influence that they had on research (from the 1940s at least through the 1960s), and on school practices in mathematics (from the late 1960s through the 1980s). Nevertheless the dismissal before consideration of constructs that cannot be observed directly is contrary to scientific methodology, where as already noted a great deal that cannot be observed directly is inferred.

In stark contrast to behaviorism, radical constructivism allows and encourages the construction of models for cognition or mental processes. In this view, all knowledge is constructed by necessity from the knower's world of experience, and the "real world" is regarded as existing but, in principle, unknowable (von Glasersfeld, 1991b). In the name of radical constructivism, some seek to exclude notions such as "reality," "truth," or "correctness" a priori from legitimate discourse. Mathematical structures and truths, as well as problem structures viewed as external to learners and problem solvers, are seen as invalid objects of discussion because they do not exist apart from individuals' constructed knowledge. Furthermore, as we have no direct access to each other's cognitions, there is no way of knowing that a concept or problem in mathematics is "the same" for different individuals. In short, though in the name of behaviorism some dismissed in advance any discussion of the internal, in the name of constructivism some dismiss today any discussion of the external

(Goldin & Kaput, 1996). Controlled experiments in mathematics education are rejected, because there is nothing apart from the knower that is subject to control.

In mathematics education, these dismissive claims have led to the widespread devaluation of generalizability as a research goal. We now have many case studies of constructivist classroom practices, but very few generalizable results. In task-based interview research, strict adherence to dismissive claims based on radical constructivism would eliminate the needed goal of generalizability entirely, and preclude the analysis of tasks as independent of the ways in which individual subjects interact with them.

Social constructivists (Ernest, 1991), and in the extreme case some advocates of postmodernist "scientific criticism," view mathematics and science fundamentally and exclusively as social and cultural systems. Social viability replaces validity as the basis for acceptance. Dismissive claims based on this view hold that the warrants or criteria for viability cannot refer to any superior status for the rational processes used in mathematics, or the experimental methods used in science. Viability reduces only to social or cultural consensus (the experience of shared discourse) and to relationships of power in the culture. All variables are deemed cultural a priori, and attempts to arrive at scientifically justified generalizations are seen merely as the implementation of social conventions having by necessity no greater claim than alternative social conventions (although at some point they may have greater political power, which itself becomes a basis for challenging them).

In mathematics education, dismissive claims based on radical social constructivism have contributed to a tendency to ignore the correctness or incorrectness of students' work, accepting instead all classroom reasoning as equally valid. This inclination is consistent with an extreme cultural relativism, a certain politicization of the educational process, and an overt devaluation of mathematical abstraction in favor of contextualized or situated learning. In the setting of task-based interview research, the dismissive claims would require us to focus in each interview essentially and exclusively on its social context, on shared social assumptions of clinician and subject, and (possibly) on tacit power relationships. The analysis of mathematical tasks or problems, subjects' cognitions, or other variables, independently of their sociocultural aspects, is ruled out a priori.

In my view, each of these radical epistemologies is unsound in fundamental ways, a discussion of which is beyond the scope of this chapter (cf. Goldin, 1990). But whether or not the epistemologies themselves are unsound or inconsistent, the dismissive claims based on them have been fundamentally damaging. Despite this, each has had some positive effects in its own way, and my criticisms are not based on opposition to things radical. Radical behaviorism successfully removed many of the outdated ideas associated with the psychology of mental states, reminding us that a scientific theory of psychology must rely ultimately on what can be observed. In arguing against it, I do *not* advocate the adoption of introspective methods or a return to explanations in terms of mental states. Radical constructivism, in turn, has been successful in helping to overcome the hegemony of behaviorism, reminding us to pay attention to knowledge as experienced by the knower, and not to impose the assumptions of the researcher. In arguing against it, I do *not* advocate behaviorism or psychometrics, nor do I adopt the view of knowledge as "transmitted" or deny the value and importance of knowledge constructed through discovery and learning by doing. Radical social constructivism has reminded us of the essential importance of social and cultural contexts in mathematics education research. In arguing against it, I do *not* advocate disregarding or ignoring these contexts. Unfortunately, in each case the useful effects were accomplished through the expedient of an advocacy movement that denied without scrutiny the admissibility of other key variables.

In the scientific development of task-based interview research, variables of all types should be addressed, at least in principle. This is required to maximize our understanding of mathematical learning and problem solving. External behavioral and representational modes must be considered explicitly, as well as representations internal to the subjects. Mathematical structures of tasks must be analyzed, as well as the subjects' interactions with the tasks. Social and cultural contexts need to be considered, as well as the psychology of individual students. Patterns of incorrect responses must be considered and understood, but part of that understanding needs to be in relation to the existence of correct responses. It should be a standard of quality task-based interview research to be inclusive of all of these, unless some are shown experimentally to be without importance or validity.

Therefore, I would characterize claims based on epistemological systems that throw out key variables a priori, without investigating them, as *dismissive claims*. It may seem overly bold to argue that standards of quality in task-based interview research should be established that reject such claims. I would point out that adherents of each radical epistemological school have not hesitated to argue that research based on other epistemologies should be rejected. In practice today, it would not (and should not) be acceptable to take a strictly behavioral approach in task-based interview research, namely, to argue that all internal constructs should be rejected in advance, and to rely on stimulus–response psychology or operant conditioning as the sole explanatory mechanisms for complex mathematical behavior. But if we are prepared to reject radical behaviorism as failing to meet scientific standards of quality research, we should be equally firm in rejecting the elimination of important constructs when this is advocated in the name of radical constructivism, radical social constructivism, or postmodernism.

One possible response to the scientific goals for task-based interview research described in the last section, a response encouraged by the failure of behaviorism (which claimed to be very scientific) and made sometimes in the name of radical constructivists and radical social constructivists, is to make the argument that the goals cannot be achieved. At most, it is argued, a story can be constructed about what occurred during an interview. Each problem solving episode is unique—an interaction between a unique clinician with personal and/or sociocultural preconceptions, and a unique subject—and each person has access only to his or her own world of experience. However, if we follow this path, we relinquish the possibility of distinguishing the spurious from the genuine. The latter is not merely in the eye of the beholder or in the eyes of a community of beholders. The central feature of scientific method, a point missed by those who insist on denying it validity on first principles, is that it enables research to filter out the biases, to arrive at conclusions that do not depend on, and even contradict, the preconceptions and perceptions of beholders—whether these preconceptions are individual or shared across a culture. If we want to find out what genuinely makes a difference in children's learning of mathematics, we need ways of observing, inferring, and assessing that can be done independently of particular individuals' subjective judgments, and that can stand up to scientific scrutiny.

The political difficulty in maintaining this position is that it opens the door again to those who want to rely on low-level skills tests, standardized tests, and psychometric methods with their own major oversimplifications and scientific flaws. The solution to this difficulty is to study the complexity, allowing for and making use of all of the diverse, interesting variables and constructs, and to strive for generalizability through scientific methods. The task-based interview is an essential tool for achieving this.

## PRINCIPLES AND TECHNIQUES FOR DESIGNING QUALITY INTERVIEWS

I would like to close this chapter by suggesting 10 broad methodological principles for designing and constructing task-based interviews. These principles are based on my own experience with creating interview scripts, in which they are implemented at least partially, and on the work of others. I believe that they provide a solid foundation for optimizing systematically the research information gathered in interviews, and that they further the scientific goals discussed here. Thus, they are offered as a step toward establishing quality standards suitable for acceptance by researchers in mathematics education.

- *Design task-based interviews to address advance research questions.* There is no one, "best," research methodology. Rather, a research design must be tailored to answering the questions asked (not the other way around). Ideally, one has formulated ahead of time clear, specific research goals and well-posed research questions, which the task-based interview or interviews are designed to help answer. The advance research questions should influence the development of instruments—the choice of tasks and materials, the contingencies in the interview, the decisions about what behaviors to observe, and the criteria for making inferences—and the other controllable variables, such as the subject population and the interview context. Design decisions should be guided by the criterion of making precisely described choices that aid in addressing the research questions.

- *Choose tasks that are accessible to the subjects.* Interview tasks should embody mathematical ideas and structures appropriate for the individuals being interviewed. This means that the subjects should be able to represent meaningfully at least some task configurations, conditions, and goals—internally and, where appropriate, externally. The issue of task accessibility should always be addressed consciously and openly by the researcher.

From the standpoint of accessibility, it can be helpful in a task-based interview to pose successive tasks of increasing complexity, culminating in one or more questions that challenge the most able of the subjects in the study population.

- *Choose tasks that embody rich representational structures.* Mathematical tasks with depth and response flexibility, that allow evidence of widely differing subject capabilities to emerge, are highly desirable. To achieve this, tasks should embody carefully selected mathematical (arithmetical, algebraic, geometrical, etc.) structures susceptible to abstract characterization, as well as meaningful semantic structures capable of being represented imagistically through visual, spatial, and kinesthetic internal representation. They should incorporate simultaneously rich formal, symbolic structures capable of notational representation in a variety of ways. There should be opportunities for subjects to connect these different representational modes. Provision for external representational constructions (see later discussion) should be sufficiently rich to allow observations from which complex internal representational steps appropriate to the tasks can be inferred.

The tasks should suggest or entail strategic thinking of some complexity, involving the planning and executive control level representation. Time for reflection, introspection, and retrospection, and explicit consideration of affective variables, should be incorporated according to the goals of the study.

As tasks are selected, opportunities to structure sets of interviews in conscious mathematical and cognitive relation to each other should be considered also.

- *Develop explicitly described interviews and establish criteria for major contingencies.* Every aspect of the design and implementation of the interview should be available to the research community in as detailed a form as possible, in order to permit discussion and to invite replication and extension of the studies. This enables independent judgments of the appropriateness of the choices made in the interview design. It also permits independent investigation of the same mathematical ideas and structures in other contexts with other populations.

Major contingencies should be addressed in the design of the interviews carefully and clearly. When the goal is to explore the subject's cognitions without imposing those of the researcher, the contingencies should but rarely distinguish "correct" from "incorrect" responses. Instead, structured questions should be devised to provide subjects with opportunities to self-correct, in any contingency. The establishment of well-defined criteria for various interpositions by the clinician is a major point in the design of task-based interviews where trade-offs necessarily occur. As questions are selected for incorporation in an interview script, some kinds of information will be gained whereas other kinds of (potential) information will be lost.

One way to recapture some information is to consider including in each interview a set of reflective questions posed retrospectively. These can be at the very end or after each task.

The essential feature, an important key to the replicability and generalizability of task-based-interview methodology, is that such choices be made overtly rather than tacitly. The impromptu judgment of the clinician may be exercised occasionally in a surprising situation; but in general, it is an inadequate basis for making choices.

- *Encourage free problem solving.* Subjects should engage in free problem solving during the interview to the maximum extent possible, in order to allow observation of their spontaneous behaviors and their reasons given for spontaneous choices before prompts or suggestions are offered. Hints, prompts, or new questions should be provided only after ample opportunity has been given for free problem solving, and each instance of assistance should be followed by further periods without directive intervention. This technique permits exploration of the subjects' freely chosen strategies, representations, and so forth, maximizing the information gained; whereas providing premature guidance results in the loss of information. However, this principle does mean some sacrifice of the speed with which the subjects understand the problem, or progress through it.

In implementing this principle, one should accept *for the time being* all productions generated during the interview, without imposing preconceived notions about appropriate ways to solve the problem. "Wrong" responses are treated similarly to "correct" ones for a period of time (with conscious exceptions decided in advance if certain understandings are essential for subsequent questions). However, the fact that some responses are incorrect should not be forgotten. The interview structure should provide opportunities for the subjects to correct themselves, through planned follow-up and retrospective questions or suggestions.

- *Maximize interaction with the external learning environment.* Various planned, external representational capabilities should be provided to the subjects during each interview, to permit their interaction with a richly diverse, observable learning or problem solving environment. This will permit the subjects to exercise a range of possibilities in representing their responses observably. Inferences about internal representations or mental processes can be drawn from the subjects' external manipulations and productions; thus, maximizing opportunities for interaction also maximizes the possibilities for making useful inferences.

- *Decide what will be recorded and record as much of it as possible.* The advance specification of research questions and the advance decisions regarding the criteria that will be used to make inferences from observations can assist in planning what kinds of observations should be recorded and how. The subjects may be asked to show the clinician what they mean at key points, using materials provided for the purpose to draw or model mathematical ideas. Videocameras may focus on the subjects' hands as well as their faces and bodies, and/or film the clinician with the subject to allow their interactions to be observed. Facial expressions may be recorded through close-up video. Observers may note particular aspects of behavior during the interview as the subject solves problems or responds to questions.

Clear distinctions should be made between observations and inferences, with the bases on which inferences are to be made described as fully and specifically as possible, and in advance to the maximum extent feasible. By planning and structuring beforehand what will be recorded and how inferences will be made, researchers can go far beyond posing tasks merely to observe and analyze what happens. At the same time, it is important to remain as alert as possible to novel or unanticipated occurrences during mathematical problem solving, whose detection and reporting are always vital.

- *Train the clinicians and pilot-test the interview.* With interviews scripted in advance, and contingencies decided carefully in advance, rehearsals with clinicians and pilot subjects are needed to ensure that each script will be followed, not only with fidelity but also with ease and comfort. After preliminary rehearsals, additional, systematic pilot administration of the interview can prevent unintended consequences of language use, discover possible points of mathematical misunderstanding or ambiguities, and elicit behaviors reflecting unanticipated contingencies. This information should be used to refine and adapt the original script before a full study is carried out with it.

- *Design to be alert to new or unforeseen possibilities.* One of the values of good research, whether using structured, task-based interviews or other methodologies, is that it makes possible new perspectives—provided we are open to them. Based on what we have learned, we strive to revise our ideas, sometimes in major ways, and to ask new or better questions. If we are listening and observing carefully, and do not impose our own processes in advance, our students often surprise us with their thinking. The best task-based interview designs, though incorporating categories of anticipated observations, also will allow for new or unforeseen possibilities outside the preset categories.

- *Compromise when appropriate.* Principles should not be implemented mechanistically in complex endeavors. In designing and carrying out task-based interviews, conflicts between principles will sometimes occur—for example, encouraging free problem solving for too long may mean that under the time constraints of the interview, information in relation to planned, subsequent, interview questions will be lost. One should be prepared to compromise these principles, but to do so consciously and explicitly, when that will optimize the achievement of specific research goals.

## CONCLUSION

I have reviewed a number of scientific issues in relation to structured, task-based interviews in mathematics education research. Their use in place of more traditional outcome measures, such as tests and questionnaires with scales that lend themselves easily to quantitative scoring, does not require the abandonment of scientific methods of inquiry. But designing interviews in accordance with scientific principles is a difficult undertaking. It is made more difficult by the tendency of some researchers to dismiss scientific methodology as irrelevant or inapplicable in this domain. I have tried here to respond to such arguments, based on my own experience and expertise. At the same time, I have proposed tentatively 10 practical, guiding principles for the design of high-quality interviews. If adopted in a considered way, such standards should strengthen substantially the scientific value of studies using structured, task-based interview methods.

# 20 Analysis of Clinical Interviews: Foundations and Model Viability

**John Clement**

*University of Massachusetts–Amherst*

The clinical interview is a technique pioneered by Piaget (1975) to study the form of knowledge structures and reasoning processes. Since the mid–1970s, it has evolved into a variety of methods, including open-ended interviews and think-aloud problem solving protocols. These techniques have played key roles in seminal studies in science and mathematics education as well as developmental psychology. Their strengths, in comparison to nonclinical, data-gathering techniques, include the ability to collect and analyze data on mental processes at the level of a subject's authentic ideas and meanings, and to expose hidden structures and processes in the subject's thinking that could not be detected by less open-ended techniques. These abilities are especially important because of Piaget's discovery that people have many interesting knowledge structures and reasoning processes that are not the same as academic ones—they have alternative conceptions and use nonformal reasoning and learning processes. Mapping this "hidden world" of indigenous thinking is crucial for the success of instructional design. Students cannot help but use their own prior conceptions and reasoning processes during instruction, and these have strong effects on the course of instruction. Because tests are almost always written from the point of view of the teacher and are designed to detect standard forms of academic knowledge, they can fail to detect key elements in students' thinking. Clinical interviews, on the other hand, can be designed to elicit and document naturalistic forms of thinking. In some exploratory varieties of clinical interviewing, the investigator can also react responsively to data as they are collected by asking new questions in order to clarify and extend the investigation. Even where the detection of academic knowledge is sought, clinical interviews can give more information on depth of conceptual understanding, because oral and graphical explanations can be collected, and clarifications can be sought where appropriate. However, the analysis of interviews can be difficult and time consuming, always involving a degree of interpretation on the part of the researcher. One purpose of this chapter is to discuss the scientific foundations that provide a basis for sound analysis.

Partly because of their open-endedness and qualitative and interpretive nature, some individuals have implied that clinical interview studies may be "unscientific" (Nisbett & T. Wilson, 1977); witness the recently advertised international handbook of *Educational Research, Methodology, and Measurement* (Keeves, 1988, 1997), in which research methodology is divided into two camps: humanistic (including interviewing for clinical research) and scientific analysis (including quantitative methods.) The present chapter argues that carefully done clinical interview studies are an essential and irreplaceable part of the scientific enterprise of investigating a student's mental processes and that, in the context of the history of science, such simplistic associations between the scientific and the quantitative are grossly misplaced.

There are also controversies at a more detailed level. A variety of protocol analysis methods are available; see, for example, Clement (1979, 1989b), Driver (1973), Easley (1974), Hayes and Flower (1978), and Newell and H. A. Simon (1972). In fact, there are some fairly diverse methods of clinical interviewing; these vary from the most *convergent* approach involving the detailed coding of individual clauses in transcripts by multiple independent coders to the most *generative* approach involving the open interpretation of large episodes by an individual analyst. This raises several questions: (a) One can ask whether the two approaches aforementioned are in opposition or are complementary (I claim the latter); (b) generative/interpretive analyses focus on constructing new observation concepts and theoretical models. Because they concentrate on discovering new constructs rather than attaining high reliability with established constructs, they have been criticized by some as being less scientific. So a second question is whether generative studies in particular can be placed on firmer methodological ground as scientific studies in a more explicit way than in the past. (c) In this regard, I want to examine first whether some new trends in the history and philosophy of science focusing on mental models and naturalistic studies of reasoning in scientists can be used as a foundation for analysis methodology.

Thus, I begin by stepping back to consider the bigger picture of the scientific research enterprise in general. I believe that there is some very good news here. Recent views of the nature of theory generation and evaluation in science lend substantial support to the scientific value of protocol analysis in general and of generative methods in particular. I develop this conclusion from the view that the core of what an investigator is doing in analyzing a clinical interview is constructing a model of hidden mental structures and processes that are grounded in detailed observations from protocols. Making sure that these models are viable is a central goal. Therefore, there are two main topics in this chapter:

- The foundations of techniques for constructing models—from history of science.
- A description of different types of clinical interview methods used for different purposes, concentrating on generative methods that foster the production of viable models of students' mental processes.

## FOUNDATIONS: FINDINGS FROM RECENT HISTORY OF SCIENCE STUDIES ON PROCESSES FOR CONSTRUCTING MODELS IN SCIENCE

The work of a group of scholars in the history and philosophy of science (N. Campbell, 1920/1957; Harre, 1961; Hesse, 1967; Nagel, 1961) provides the following view of the types of knowledge involved in science. The work suggested that scientists often think in terms of theoretical *explanatory models,* such as molecules, waves, fields, and black holes, that are a separate kind of hypothesis from empirical laws. Such models are not merely condensed summaries of empirical observations but, rather, are inventions that contribute new mechanisms and concepts that are part of the scientist's view of the world and that are not "given" in the data. I first wish to put forward the view that one of the most important needs in basic research on students' learning processes is the need for insightful explanatory models of these processes. To do this, I first need to examine the different types of knowledge used in science.

TABLE 20.1.

Four Levels of Knowledge Used in the Physical and Cognitive Sciences

| | | Physical Science: Study of Gases | Cognitive Science: Study of Disequilibrium | Cognitive Science: Diagnostic Algebra Research |
|---|---|---|---|---|
| **T H E O R I E S** | 4. Formal Principles and Theoretical Commitments | $P = \dfrac{\frac{1}{3} NMV^2}{L^2}$ (Refers to theory of molecules) | Psychological need for local coherence | Tendency to symbolize static rather than operational relations |
| | 3. Researcher's Explanatory Models | Colliding elastic particle model | Mental disequilibrium between conceptions and perceptions | Static versus operative conceptions of equations |
| **O B S E R V A T I O N S** | 2. Observed Behavior Patterns and Empirical Laws | PV = kT (refers to observations of measuring apparatus) | Subjects make predictions and express concern or surprise at opposite result | Reversal pattern in equations; references to relative sizes of quantities |
| | 1. Primary-Level Data | Measurement of a single pressure change in a heated gas | Individual subject expresses concern or surprise | Individual reversals |

## Four Levels of Knowledge in Science

As shown on the left-hand side of Table 20.1, the authors mentioned in the previous paragraph describe science as having at least four levels of knowledge. In particular, they saw a distinction between an empirical law hypothesis (at Level 2 in Table 20.1), summarizing an observed regularity, and what I call an explanatory model hypothesis (at Level 3). N. Campbell's (1920/1957) oft-cited example is that merely being able to make predictions from the empirical gas law stating that pressure times volume is proportional to temperature is not equivalent to understanding the explanation for the behavior of gas in terms of an imageable explanatory model of billiard ball-like molecules in motion. The model provides a description of a hidden process, or mechanism, that explains how the gas works and answers "why" questions about where observable changes in temperature and pressure come from. On its own, the empirical law PV = KT does none of these things. Causal relationships are often central in explanatory models. The model not only adds significant explanatory power to one's knowledge but also heuristic power, which stimulates the future growth of the theory.

These models do not consist merely of formulas and statements of abstract principles; rather, they consist of visualizable physical models, such as the elastic particle model for gases, which underlie the comprehension of formulas. Explanatory models are often iconic and analogical in nature, being built up from more primitive and familiar notions. In this view, the visualizable model is a major locus of meaning for a scientific theory. (Summaries of these views were given in Harre, 1967; Hesse, 1967; and a related hierarchy was proposed in Easley, 1978.) Thus, the two lower rows of Table 20.1 constitute the observational level of science and the two upper rows constitute the theoretical level. These distinctions can be applied to studies of cognitive processes as well. For example, the second column in Table 20.1 shows four types of knowledge for the psychological construct of disequilibrium following a prediction. Disequilibrium as an explanatory model of a mental process is distinguished from expressions of surprise as an observed behavior pattern. The upshot of these considerations is that a central goal of science is to develop explanatory models that give satisfying explanations for patterns in observations.

## The Need for Generative Case Studies

Unfortunately, in general within the learning sciences, there has been a significant shortage of explanatory models for higher order processes. For example, there has been a notable lack of research on theories of content-rich, higher level, cognitive processing in proportion to other areas of human thought. This is not surprising, because psychology favors studies that include controlled experiments comparing behavior patterns at Level 2 in Table 20.1 and because doing controlled experiments on higher order processes is extremely difficult. This is the case because, first, some of the processes are so poorly understood that what the most important variables are is not at all clear. Second, there are likely to be many difficult choices open to a human problem solver, and many possibilities for feedback loops, processes that compete or coordinate with each other, and recursion. For such cases, these non linear properties make the use of a controlled experiment designed to identify simple linear relationships between variables very difficult to apply at best. This perspective gives us a way to see why quite different methods might be required for some studies within the learning sciences (in Table 20.1), as well as why special methods might be required to generate new hypotheses at level three (explanatory models of mental processes) for complex, higher order thinking.

## An Example Illustrating the Role of Generative Case Studies

Here and throughout this chapter, I cite examples from one line of research that depended heavily on generative case studies. It concerned solutions to algebra word problems and the nature of students' difficulties with "reversal errors" (Clement, 1982a). The problem shown in Table 20.2 was given on a 45-minute written test to 150 freshmen engineering students.

TABLE 20.2.

An Example of the Reversal Error in an Algebra Word Problem

| Test Question (n = 150) | Correct Answer | % Correct | Typical Incorrect Answer |
|---|---|---|---|
| | $S = 6P$ | 63% | $6S = P$ |

Write an equation using the variables $S$ and $P$ to represent the following statement: "There are six times as many students as professor at this university." Use $S$ for the number of students and $P$ for the number of professors.

Fully 37% of the engineering majors, most of whom were taking calculus, solved this very basic algebra problem incorrectly. With a similar problem involving a fractional rather than an integral ratio, 73% failed to solve it. At first, it was thought that the errors on such simple problems must be due primarily to carelessness. However, there was a strong pattern in the errors. Sixty-eight percent of the errors were reversal errors: $6S = P$ (or an algebraically equivalent statement) instead of $S = 6P$. Placing this example in Table 20.1 at level 2 (behavior patterns), one might propose *empirical* hypotheses concerning correlations between the incidence of reversal errors and subject variables such as age and mathematical background. These could be tested purely at the observational level without the development of a theory.

On the other hand, at Level 3 (explanatory models), one might try to form *theoretical* hypotheses concerning the alternative reasoning patterns that cause these errors, and the reasoning pattern(s) responsible for correct answers. In order to do this, audiotaped and videotaped clinical interviews were conducted with 15 freshmen who were asked to think aloud as they worked. From the analysis of transcripts of the subjects making reversal errors, one model of the faulty reasoning that emerged was a "word-order-matching" approach in which the students assume that the order of the key words in the problem statement will map directly into the order of the symbols appearing in the equation. For example, subject $S1$ immediately wrote $6S = P$ and said, "Well, the problem states it right off: '6 times students';

so it will be six times $S$ is equal to professors." In this case, some of the protocol data were very suggestive of an explanation. There is no evidence here for any more complicated a strategy than that of mechanically matching the order of the symbols in the equation to the order of the words in the problem statement. This provides a possible explanation for the difficulty. This is a syntactic strategy in the sense that it is based on rules for arranging symbols in an expression that do not depend on the meaning of the expression. (Eventually, we found another source of the error, which is discussed later.)

Although the analysis process was unusually easy in this first example, it gives an illustration of constructing a model for a subject's reasoning process—a model that is grounded in the primary level observations in a transcript. The clinical interviews played an important role here because they furnished a unique and comparatively direct source of information on the source of the error. Also, the model of the faulty, word-order-matching process (at Level 3 in Table 20.1) goes well beyond the observed behavior pattern of the reversed equation (at Level 2 in Table 20.1) in providing a description of the mental process underlying the behavior.

Thus, by using generative case studies in these areas, one can propose initial explanatory models of cognitive processes that are grounded in naturalistic observations. Now that the nature of explanatory models has been introduced, the question of how such models are constructed in science in general can be examined.

## The Construction of Explanatory Models in Science: Abduction Versus Induction

If generative interviews are to generate grounded explanatory models, this raises the fundamental issue of how the explanatory models at Level 3 of Table 20.1 are formed in the mind of a scientific investigator. Much of the recent progress in history and philosophy of science can be seen as a struggle to move away from a simplistic view of how theories are formed in science as being either pure induction upward from observations or pure deduction downward from axioms, followed by testing. Instead, we see movement toward a view that includes both top-down and bottom-up processing in a cycle of educated conjecture, criticism, and revision, as shown in FIG. 20.1. Many modern scholars in the history of science and cognitive studies of science now view the process of how models are constructed in science as a cyclical process of hypothesis generation, rational and empirical testing, and modification or rejection. It is difficult to describe so complex a process in a single diagram, but the simplified model in FIG. 20.1, integrating the work of a number of scholars, aids in this analysis. A major change in the basis for such views is that the most recent work has been grounded in systematic studies of scientists rather than in abstract analyses of the nature of science. Theory formation and assessment cycles of this kind were discussed by Gruber (1974), Nersessian (1984, 1992), Tweney (1985),  Thagard (1992), Giere (1988), and Darden (1991) based on studies in the history of science, and by Dunbar (1994) and Clement (1989b) based on naturalistic and "think-aloud" studies of expert scientists. This work means that major elements shown in FIG. 20.1 now have empirical grounding in studies of  scientists.

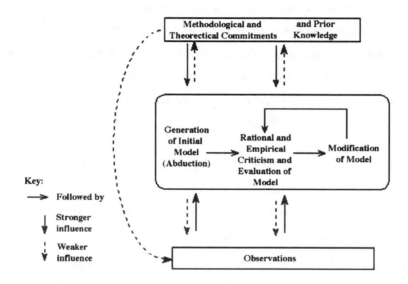

FIG. 20.1. Basic model construction cycle with top-down and bottom-up influences.

Essentially, the scientist aims to construct or piece together a theoretical model in the form of a conjectured story or a picture of a hidden structure or process that explains why the phenomenon occurred. Peirce (1958) and Hanson (1958) used the term *abduction* to describe the process of formulating a hypothesis that, if it were true, would account for the phenomenon in question. The initial hypothesis for a hidden mechanism is often more like an abduction than a recognized pattern or induction, and it can be a creative invention as long as it accounts for the observations collected so far.

However, it also should be a very educated invention, reflecting constraints in the scientist's prior knowledge about what might be the most plausible mechanisms involved. Thus, an initial hypothesis for an explanatory model often can be formed by an abductive process, possibly for just a single instance of the phenomenon. Then, the initial model is evaluated and revised in response to criticisms. This can involve evaluations by comparisons with new data, or it can involve evaluations via rational criteria such as simplicity and consistency. By such a process of successive refinements, we cannot arrive at absolute certainties, but a viable and successful explanatory model may be formed. As von Glasersfeld and Steffe (1991) put it: "The most one can hope for is that the model fits whatever observations one has made and, more important, that it remains viable in the face of new observations" (p. 98). And as Hanson (1958) and Kuhn (1962/1970) have emphasized, observations are theory-laden in that they can be shaped and influenced by the investigator's prior conceptions and theories. This is shown by the downward arrows leading to the observations in FIG. 20.1, which indicate that observation concepts and categories can change and develop along with the theoretical model. (See Lakatos, 1978, for a parallel view of mathematics.)

## Maintaining the Distinction Between Observation and Theory

In all of the aforementioned, however, there is an effort to maintain the distinction between observation and theory. Although these two processes interact, they still can be seen as separate, semiautonomous processes rather than a single process. When they conflict, it is seen as essential to assign greater, but not overwhelming, weight, in the long run, to documented, publicly agreed-upon observations over prior theoretical commitments and newly invented theories. It is also desirable, where possible, to describe explicitly relations of support between observations and theory. Although intermediate examples can be raised that suggest viewing the theory-observation distinction as more of a continuum, the effort can be made still to progress toward separating these two modes of thinking for doing science so that they constrain and stimulate each other. The important goal is to progress toward observation processes that may not be fully "objective" but that are still independent enough from one's theories to yield surprises and anomalies that can motivate revisions in, or even eventual rejections of, the theories.

## Using the Interpretive Analysis of Generative Clinical Interviews to Construct Models

The above perspectives from the history of science provide a methodological grounding for analyzing protocols in generative studies in education. In this method, analysts construct, criticize, and revise hypothesized models of mental structures and processes repeatedly while using them to explain as much of the data in a protocol or a set of protocols as possible. According to the framework developed here, this process is one of abduction, repeated criticism (from both rational and empirical sources), and responsive revision.

Returning to the algebra study example, we gradually became more and more dissatisfied with the word-order-matching hypothesis as the only source of the reversal error. Sections of transcript such as the following one from a parallel problem served to discount this hypothesis as the only explanation. The problem is to write an algebraic expression for the statement: "There are eight times as many people in China as there are in England."

The student wrote: $8C = 1E$.

Transcript line 9: Student: "for every eight Chinamen, but then again, saying for every eight Chinese, yeah, that's right, for every eight Chinese, there's one Englishman." [The interviewer asks the student to explain his equation.]

12  Student: "All right, it means that there is a larger number (points to $8C$) of Chinese for every Englishman" (points to $1E$).

13  Interviewer: "So you're pointing to the $8C$ and the $1E$?"

14  Student: "Yeah, and there is a larger number of Chinese than there are Englishmen; therefore, the number of Chinese to Englishmen should be larger—$8C = 1E$."

In line 12, subject $S2$ indicated clearly that he had comprehended the relative sizes of the two groups in the problem—that there are more people in China. This suggests that he had gone beyond a syntactic, word-order-matching approach and was using a semantic approach dependent on the meaning of the problem. At this point, the word-order-matching model was no longer a viable one for these parts of the protocol. The student's intuitions about how to symbolize this relationship were to place the multiplier (8) next to the letter associated with the larger group. This approach is a very literal attempt to compare the relative sizes of the two groups in a static manner, and we detected it in a significant number of students. Therefore we labeled this the *static comparison* approach.

This appears to be an incorrect, but meaningful, way for this group of students to symbolize the relative sizes of two groups—indicating the "base ratio" of eight people in China associated with each person in England. At first, we were blind to this thought pattern because we had come to take for granted the idea that the students were using word-order matching. But an intensive case study of a single student led to generating (abducting) the hypothesis that a meaningful but incorrect symbolization strategy different from word-order matching was being used in these cases. Once we had formulated this hypothesis for one student, *it sensitized us to new observations to look for,* such as the relative-size references. We ultimately found evidence for the static comparison approach in a majority of the subjects making reversal errors on such problems, although we had not "seen" the evidence in our initial look at the transcripts. This second source of the reversal error was harder to detect, requiring us to go through several of the cycles shown in FIG. 20.1. Thus, by criticizing and revising one's models of the student's thought process repeatedly, one can develop progressively more adequate models and observation concepts through a model construction process that is used by scientists in general.

# AN INITIAL DICHOTOMY OF CLINICAL INTERVIEW METHODS: GENERATIVE PURPOSES LEAD TO INTERPRETIVE ANALYSES WHEREAS CONVERGENT PURPOSES LEAD TO CODED ANALYSES

The previous examples prepare us to distinguish two major purposes of studies conducted in educational research: *generative* and *convergent*. I begin by painting these contrasting purposes as a dichotomy in order to introduce the issues, then broaden it later into a spectrum with intermediate points, in order to suggest some of the options available for different research purposes.

## Purposes of Clinical Interview Studies

- *Generative* purposes usually lead to an *interpretive* analysis. Such a study can deal with behaviors that are quite unfamiliar, for which there is very little in the way of existing theory. The purpose of a generative study is to generate new observation categories and new elements of a theoretical model in the form of descriptions of mental structures or processes that can explain the data. This method can deal with larger and richer sections of interview data involving more complex processing. It entails higher levels of inference on the part of the researcher.

- *Convergent* purposes usually lead to a *coded* analysis of interviews that attempts to provide reliable, comparable, empirical findings that can be used to determine frequencies, sample means, and sometimes, experimental comparisons for testing a hypothesis.

An interpretive analysis in a generative study tends to present a relatively large section of a transcript, followed by the author's inferences concerning the thought processes of the subject. In contrast to a coded analysis (see the next subsection), observation categories are not fixed ahead of time. Analysis can generate new observation categories and models of mental processes giving plausible explanations for the observed behavior. (For example, all of the models of reasoning modes that produce reversal errors were generated during intensive interpretive analysis of individual case studies done for generative purposes.)

There are a number of reasons for the importance of generative studies:

- They are a primary source of grounded theoretical models for learning processes.
- They are a primary source of key observation concepts.
- They are not restricted to collecting immediately codeable observations that fit into existing categories of description; they *allow investigators to develop new categories for description.*
- They provide a foundation for the design of convergent studies.

## Interpretive Versus Coded Analysis

This contrasts with a coded analysis in a convergent study that focuses on observations that are assigned to predefined categories by a coder, usually from relatively small segments of a transcript. A transcript is coded when the analyst formulates criteria for recognizing a phenomenon and then lists the places where that phenomenon occurs in the transcript. The conclusions may be at the level of observation patterns alone, or, they can be used as data to support or reject theoretical hypotheses that may have been generated by other means. Two examples of research questions in this type of study are:

- Among a set of previously characterized behaviors, which do these subjects exhibit?

- Among a set of previously characterized mental concepts or processes with previously hypothesized behavioral indicators, which do these subjects possess?

By using the words *coded* and *interpretive* I do not intend to deny that coding of a transcript in natural language that is ungrammatical and incomplete is also an act of interpretation. The intent is only to signify a greater degree of interpretation in the analysis of generative studies.

# THE VIABILITY OF THEORETICAL MODELS IN THE ANALYSIS OF CLINICAL INTERVIEWS

## Viability Versus Validity

Generally, in this chapter, the issue of the viability of a model speaks to our interest in attaining models that are useful to us, that have support in the data, that fit or interact productively with our larger theoretical framework, and that give us a sense of understanding by providing satisfying explanations about hidden processes underlying the phenomena in an area. The literature on validity is tangled with multiple meanings and interpretations for the term. Validity of what? Widely differing referents occur including the validity of an observation, of a theoretical model, or of the relation between an observation and a model. For the sake of avoiding confusion with these past uses, the best strategy, used in this chapter, is to put aside the term *validity* altogether in this context and to define a new methodological term—*viability* of a model—based on the relation between models and observation in science as described by modern historians of science.

Because the job of generating a framework at this level is such a basic one, it makes sense to use a broad definition of viability: the view that the viability of a model should be no less than an estimate of its usefulness or strength as a scientific theory compared to other theories. The bad news here is that strength is a complex thing to measure, and the criteria for it involve human estimates and judgments. The good news is that modern work in the history of science has shown that this is a problem common to all of the developing sciences and has made considerable progress on describing these criteria in more realistic terms. Criteria for evaluating scientific theories have been discussed by Kuhn (1977) and extended by Darden (1991) among others, and I use a condensed version of their standards in what follows.

## Determinants of Viability

The "explanatory power and usefulness" of a model corresponds roughly to what we mean by the viability of a model. Given a set of observations, the major factors that affect the viability of a theory or a model that explains them are its plausibility, empirical support, rational (nonempirical) support (such as its coherence with previously established models), and external viability  (or "tests over time"), such as its extendability to new contexts. These factors are discussed separately in the following and are summarized in Table 20.3.

TABLE 20.3.

Viability of a Model: Criteria for Evaluating Theories

*1. Plausibility*
> a. Explanatory adequacy
>
> b. Internal coherence

*2. Empirical Support*
> a. Triangulation and number of  supporting observations
>
> b. Strength of connection to each observation
>
> c. Lack of  anomalies

*3. Nonempirical Criteria*
> a. Clarity
>
> b. Simplicity
>
> c. Lack of "ad hocness"
>
> d. External coherence

*4. External Viability*
> a. Generalizability
>
> b. Predictiveness
>
> c. Extendability
>
> d. Fruitfulness

*Plausibility: Explanatory Adequacy and Internal Coherence.* The most basic requirement for a model of a person's cognitive structures and processes is that it gives a plausible explanation for the observed behavior. We cannot provide merely an informal mixed metaphor as the model. It must be a description of a thought process, that we can easily imagine taking place in the subjects, that explains their behavior and that is internally coherent. This last criterion refers to whether the model is internally consistent, both logically and pragmatically, in terms of the story it tells about a mental mechanism (e.g., it does not speak of conscious processing on unconscious material).

*Empirical Support.* Interviews are subject to what Hayes (1978) called the porpoise effect: We only see a part of the porpoise a part of the time, and we only derive partial and indirect information on intermittent parts of mental processes by viewing the data in interview transcripts or tapes. Mental processes are by nature hidden processes. Thus, our concluding hypotheses about models of processes in a report will be stronger or weaker depending partly on how much support they derive from empirical observations; and that depends on how prevalent and how pertinent the data are. The strength of empirical support depends primarily on the following three factors:

- *Explanatory adequacy and scope by means of triangulation and number of supporting observations.* The empirical support that a model has rises with the number of supporting observations that it has, in other words, the number of connections to data. When a model gives a plausible explanation for an observation, it, in turn, receives a degree of empirical support from the observation. When a model provides an explanation for more than one observation or aspect of a transcript and derives support from all of them, we say that we can triangulate from the observations to the model. In this way, model construction is responsive to the multiple constraints provided by the transcript. Inferring new models from evidence in protocols is an inherently difficult and creative construction process. When one can triangulate by explaining multiple observations with the same hypothesized model, shown schematically as hypothesis E in FIG. 20.2, that gives one a stronger degree of support for the model.

  For example, in the case of the static comparison approach as an origin of reversal errors discussed earlier, a central assumption of this model was that the students comprehended and heeded the relative sizes of the two groups (implying they thought that they were symbolizing that relationship). This assumption distinguishes the static comparison approach from a purely syntactic one of word-order matching. There are three different indicators of this in the excerpts from the previous transcript, in Lines 9, 12, and 14. Thus, we can triangulate from these statements to the hypothesized model that a correct, relative-size idea is a part of subject S2s comprehension of the problem.

(Note: Here, support usually means "corroborates" rather than "strongly implicates." On its own, each observation may not provide substantial evidence. Furthermore, a single observation can have explanations other than the one proposed for it, as symbolized by the pairs of lines reaching upward from each observation symbol in FIG. 20.2. But when one hypothesis fits more observations than any of the other hypotheses, this can support the hypothesis as the most plausible explanation. Thus the relation between observations and hypothesized models used here is not one of unique implication but, rather, of collective abduction and support.)

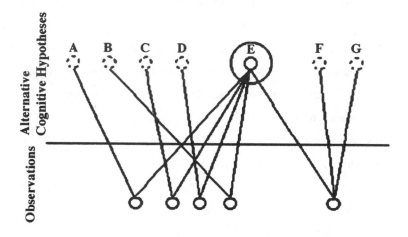

FIG. 20.2. Triangulation: Hypothesis E with multiple sources of support.

- *The strength of each connection of support between an observation and a hypothesis*—that is, the directness and quality of each supporting observation (e.g., if a subject solving a mathematics problem mentions the name of each step of a standard algorithm as it is used, that observation has a strong connection of support to the hypothesis that he or she is using an algorithm). FIG. 20.3 shows a simplified case where theoretical aspect $T1$ is supported by observations $O1-O3$ and $T2$ by $O3$, $O4$ and $O5$. The $T$s stand for theoretical models of a cognitive process (such as the static comparison approach). The $P$s stand for segments of transcript that constitute relatively raw data used in the analysis. (Even here, the transcribing of slurred words or incomplete phrases will involve some top-down interpretation, but, in general, the transcript level will involve the least amount of interpretive inference.) The $O$s stand for observation concepts (behavior patterns such as reversed equations and stated, relative-size comparisons) that have been identified as relevant. One particular observation (e.g., $O1$ in FIG. 20.3) may provide more direct evidence for (have fewer layers of interpretation leading to) a theoretical model (shown as a heavier line of connection to the theory) than another observation. (Some would call this the validity of using that observation to infer that hypothesis. Of the aspects of viability in FIG. 20.3 that have been discussed, this is the closest one to "content validity" in the testing literature.)

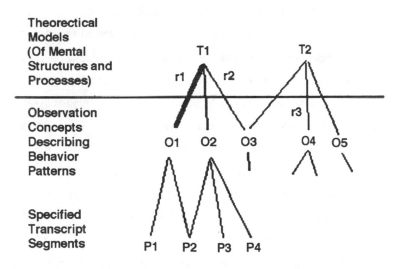

FIG. 20.3. Levels of analysis in a clinical interview.

- *Absence of conflicting evidence or anomalies that are inconsistent with the model.* In any study of rich behavior, there will be some observations that are not explained by the current theoretical model, and perhaps some that are in conflict with it; the latter are called anomalies with respect to that model. If there are too many anomalies, a model may lose its viability in comparison to another competing model.

The above three factors determine the empirical support for a hypothesized model and are one component of its viability, as shown in Table 20.3. Wide triangulation from multiple instances is desirable when available, but it is not the only criterion, especially in initial studies of an area where "existence proofs" (read "arguments from even a single observed instance for instituting a new category of behavior or category of mental processing") are needed.

*Nonempirical Criteria.* Other criteria given in Darden (1991) and Kuhn (1977) for evaluating scientific theories are nonempirical. I discussed two of these earlier in the subsection Plausibility: Explanatory Adequacy and Internal Coherence. Others are:

- *Clarity*: whether the model is clearly described and comprehensible, allowing it to be used as a tool for thinking.
- *Simplicity and lack of ad hocness*: whether the model introduces arbitrary elements in order to "kluge" (contrive) an explanation. Other factors being equal, a simpler model is preferred.
- *u*: whether the model is coherent with other accepted theories in one's larger theoretical framework, again both logically and pragmatically. For example, the theory that students can tend to use an overly static approach to algebraic symbolization becomes more plausible when one sees related behaviors in a very different domain such as Cartesian graphs. There, one can observe some students symbolizing the speed of a bike coasting over a hill with a speed versus time graph that shows the same hill-like shape!  This error has the same character of an overly literal correspondence between the symbol and the symbolized (Clement, 1989a).

*External Viability of a Model Across Contexts and Populations.* Further criteria from Kuhn (1977) and Darden (1991) concern the extent to which the model has explanatory power in the sense that it can be applied to contexts outside the realm of the original study. By other contexts, I mean a different task, setting, or population for the study. These criteria are:

- *Generalizability (of a model)*: Can the existing model be applied to other contexts in order to explain existing data? For example, the static comparison approach helps to explain why reversal errors are also observed in problems where students translate from pictures (rather than sentences) to an equation. (These errors could not be explained by the word-order-matching model.)

- *Predictiveness (predictive validity)*: Does the model lead to new predictions for other contexts that turn out to be correct? For example, Clement (1982a) discussed how the above model led to a prediction for fewer reversal errors in a computer programming context.

- *Extendability*: Can the model be modified or extended to account for even more widely varying contexts?

- *Fruitfulness*: Whether the model is ultimately fruitful as a heuristic for promoting the identification of further interesting observations and hypotheses.

The last three criteria are essentially tests of a model over time, indicating whether a model leads to further productivity in the field.

## A Constructivist Approach to Investigation

The preceding guidelines constitute a far more extensive set than usually are mentioned in clinical interview studies, including my own. I believe that we need to be more explicit about them in preparing and reviewing reports, especially larger reports that describe a program of research.

In this view, a model of mental processes is generated initially from a protocol by process of constrained inventive abduction and refined by means of an evaluation and improvement cycle. As argued in the first part of this chapter, the model need not necessarily predict observations deductively nor does it need to summarize a strong statistical pattern of observations; it need provide only a viable plausible explanation for a set of observations. It should have internal coherence, empirical support, and usually, external coherence with an existing framework. In such a system, one can argue for the viability of a theoretical model both from above and below in FIG. 20.1. In this constructivist approach, one can claim to have a powerfully viable model that is firmly grounded in an empirical foundation, without overreaching by claiming to have found certain truth.

## The Survival of the Most Viable Model

In the long run, the viability of the hypothesized model will be compared to the viability of competing hypotheses, and the one with the highest viability should survive. This will take some discussion in the scientific community because, according to the aforementioned criteria, the viability of a theory or model is a complex judgment call. As an estimate of how much confidence one places in a model currently, it is the weighted sum of a variety of factors listed in Table 20.3. Even the factor of empirical support is itself a weighted sum. This makes writing conclusions about models in a clinical, interview study more difficult because the author should indicate, at least approximately, his or her view of the relative strengths of each portion of the conclusion based on all of these factors. An author will not discuss every item in Table 20.3 always, but the relevant items should be considered in determining the judgments of how strongly to state each conclusion.

## RECOMMENDATIONS FOR FOSTERING MODEL VIABILITY

### Recommendations for Increasing Model Viability in Reports on Interpretive Analyses of Generative Studies

The new view of scientific theory evaluation above provides a firmer foundation for suggesting the following general recommendations concerning viability in reporting on analysis work. I begin with generative studies and base the recommendations on the goal of generating viable scientific models. Some of these recommendations (as well as those concerning reliability discussed later) overlap to a certain extent with those discussed by D. Campbell (1979), Chi (1995), Ginsburg (1983), Goetz and LeCompte (1984), Howe (1985), Howe and Eisenhart (1990), Lincoln and Guba (1985), Patton (1980), and M. L. Smith (1987). Initially, the most basic research questions in this approach are: What might be the important mental states or processes involved? What might be the observation patterns that provide evidence for these processes?

   *Plausibility and Explanatory Adequacy.* The first task is to achieve rudimentary explanatory adequacy—the investigator must construct a plausible model that explains the behavior in question and, at the same time, must refine and sometimes construct the descriptors for the behavior. This is done by means of the cyclical, interpretive analysis cycle of segmenting the protocol, making observations from each segment, formulating a hypothesized model of mental processes that can explain the observations (and suggest others to look for), returning to the data to refine and look for more confirming or disconfirming observations, criticizing and modifying or extending the model, and so on. (For an early description of a similar process called the constant comparison method, see B. G. Glaser & A. L. Strauss, 1967.)   Models will attain progressively more and more viability with each cycle as mental process concepts with supporting observation concepts are formed and stabilized.

*Empirical Support and Absence of Anomalies.* The analyst interested in developing a viable, robust model must be alert constantly for aspects of a protocol that conflict with the current model. They are what inspire improvements in the model. After the model is as well developed as possible for the current analysis, the "lack of multiple anomalies" criterion for the viability of a model should be examined in the report. It should state whether there are any data elements still in conflict with the model; if they are numerous or important, they will expose limitations in the model. Some of the most valuable observations are those that do not fit any current hypotheses. These can stimulate later construction and revision of a model. Analysts have an obligation to be open to such observations and to report them. Not everything in a generative study has to be explained; new empirical findings can be provocative and valuable in themselves.

*Attending to Nonempirical Factors in Evaluating the Viability of a Model.* Reviewing the list of criteria for evaluating a theory presented earlier, one can recommend that for both generative and convergent studies, authors should take pains to:

- Display the external coherence of the model—how it fits with other prior models in the investigator's paradigm. This should include a discussion of the background assumptions from the investigator's prior theoretical framework that are part of the argument leading to the conclusions.
- Criticize and revise models for internal consistency and coherence.
- Construct models that are as simple as possible and describe them with as much clarity and transparency as possible. One should be able to *think* and *reason productively* with the models.
- Compare modular parts of the favored model to other rival models.

- Construct models that are as detailed as possible, but not so detailed that they are hard to support from the available observations. This is the basic tension that determines the appropriate grain size of the model.
- Say how the model might be extendible, fruitful, or predictive in other areas to be examined.

*Methodological Heuristics and Trade-Offs.* Darden (1991) pointed out that the criteria for evaluating models are heuristics, not algorithms. She emphasized the fact that different criteria can pull the investigator in different directions; that is, there are some difficult trade-offs to be considered when attempting to improve a theory. For example, increasing detail so that the theory is closer to a deterministic computer simulation may increase predictiveness, but it may reduce plausibility, simplicity, and transparency. If the model becomes too complex for the investigator to think with, that must count as a negative factor for an *explanatory* model. This is a major reason that most scientists prefer to retain visualizable qualitative models even in fields where they have led to the formation of much more complex and detailed mathematical models or simulations. In summary, one cannot simply act to maximize each of the aforementioned characteristics because they sometimes lead to conflicting goals—compromises must be chosen that make the model as viable as possible relative to other models.

*Other Heuristics for Constructing Viable Models.* The criteria discussed earlier are derived from characteristics of scientific theories as described in recent portrayals of thinking in scientists and may have as much or more to do with evaluating models as with generating them. As such they do not provide very down to earth advice about the difficult initial task itself—the creative act of formulating new theories of cognitive processes. For this reason, I also make some less esoteric recommendations based on personal experience with constructing models of processes from protocol data:

- In an area about which very little is known, a case study can be very powerful. Choosing a transcript that is especially challenging to conventional wisdom or to one's existing theories can be very important because its anomalies will stimulate the growth of a new theory. Once initiated, the theory can be tested and refined by determining whether it can explain the behavior of many other subjects as well.

- When the investigator understands very little about such a case study tape, one may have to view the tape 10 or 20 or more times in order to generate an explanation. Often one needs to "live with" such a tape for a period of time in order to create a viable model.

- Successful scientists appear to engage in model construction cycles in which they alternate between a freely creative, divergent mode of work, and a highly critical, convergent mode (Clement, 1989b). It may be helpful for analysts to use these two modes to first generate possible models, then aggressively criticize and eliminate or revise them.

- Having more than one analyst can stimulate the creative mode via brainstorming and the critical mode via argument. Sometimes these modes can be consciously fostered (as in the "no criticisms" rule for brainstorming).

- A good heuristic is to try to **draw** what happened in the mind of the subject. Mental processes can involve many interconnections and relationships over time. Creative representations in the form of many varieties of diagrams can be very helpful devices for keeping track of such complexity, drawing inferences, seeing new connections, and criticizing and improving one's model. New computerized tools such as graphics packages, Semnet (K. Fisher, 1990) and Inspiration (Helfgott, & Hoof, 1994) can also be very helpful. The creation of new graphical systems for representing thinking processes can be an important part of a theoretical contribution (Clement, 1979; 1989b; Driver, 1973; Easley, 1974; Newell & H. A. Simon, 1972).

- Creative metaphors can serve as fertile starting points for a theoretical model without committing one to being "stuck" with the metaphor and precluding further development of the model beyond the metaphor. For example, thinking of conceptions competing or cooperating, or having momentum or autonomy may start as somewhat anthropomorphic metaphors, but may eventually lead to very useful theoretical perspectives.

## General Recommendations for Fostering Empirical Support as a Component of Viability in Both Generative and Some Convergent Studies

Some convergent studies may focus simply on establishing a pattern of observations in a sample without dealing with theoretical models of internal processes. However, in other convergent studies within an advanced area of work, the aforementioned criteria for the formation of models have been largely satisfied already before the study begins. In other words, viable models have been developed along with stable observation categories. The task remains to show clear connections of support between observations and models, and this is reflected in the following guidelines applying to such convergent studies as well as generative studies.

In a report, an analyst assesses aspects of the model and supporting observations and makes judgments of the model's viability. The strength of each conclusion should reflect this assessment. Investigators also should provide material that enables readers to make judgments of viability, so that readers can compare theories and data, and make global judgments of plausibility and viability. By displaying the patterns that one has identified, or at least sections of raw transcript, the writer allows readers to make their own judgments of the viability of the theoretical claims made.

Whenever possible, studies should display triangulated connections to an aspect of the model from the observations that support it. Readers will be able to make even better judgments about the viability of the model when this is done explicitly. Triangulation, in the broad sense, can occur not only across parts of a transcript but also across observation methods, tasks, and subjects.

As discussed earlier, in any study of relatively rich behavior, an analyst will construct models for different aspects of a protocol that have varying amounts of support in the data. There will be strong support for some models and only initial support for others. Conclusions about models should be stated with different levels of strength to reflect such variations. This suggests that there should be at least two sections in the discussion of the theoretical findings in a report. The first can be written conservatively, with only specific, well-supported conclusions about (models of) the subjects in the experiment. By making explicit the arguments and warrants for each conclusion whenever possible, the author should try to give readers enough information to allow them to make parallel judgments. The availability of transcripts, upon request, to interested readers is helpful in this regard. Then, a section that is described as more speculative can be written about the hypotheses that the investigator feels are reasonable, based on his or her entire past experience. In addition to contributing to existing theory, this can provoke new studies for evaluating these hypotheses.

## The Quality of Subjects' Reports

Investigators can try to improve the quality of the subjects' reports of their thinking. Ericsson and H. A. Simon (1984) discussed studies of the extent to which subjects' reports reflect an incomplete, biased, or inconsistent account of their thinking during problem solving. The quality of these reports affects the quality of the data in the study. They conclude that, under the right conditions, thinking aloud does not create major distortions in a subject's thought processes. They urge that subjects be encouraged to think aloud but not to reflect, at a psychological theory level, on their own thought processes. In this way one circumvents some of the classical objections to introspection raised by others (e.g. Nisbett & T. Wilson, 1977). Reporting is assumed to be restricted to processes that come into conscious attention. Therefore subjects will be able to report on some processes better than others, and their statements will always be incomplete. Ericsson and Simon argued that thinking that uses nonverbal representations, such as imagery, will be somewhat harder to report in detail because it must be translated into language, but the cognitive load required to give at least partial information on these aspects of thinking is not so heavy as to distort them appreciably.

In this chapter, I cannot do justice to the extensive work in this area, but the reader is referred to Ericsson and H. A. Simon (1984) for further discussion of the status of think-aloud protocols as data, the quality of subjects' reports, and associated issues of reliability and validity. Here, I comment only on one consideration involving the design of interview probes (questions that an interviewer uses to elicit a subject's thoughts within a problem solution). Some techniques for trying to increase the quality of the subject's reports are: training a subject to think aloud without theorizing about their thought processes, probing to encourage a sufficient amount of thinking aloud or output from a subject, and probing to request that the subject clarify a report. The controlled application of these three techniques can be important in determining the quality of the reports that subjects give. However, while using probes, the interviewers should try to minimize the interference or influence that they might have on the subjects' thinking. This sets up a major trade-off in the decision of how much probing to do during an interview. Put in the simplest terms, the need for completeness argues for doing more probing, whereas the need for minimizing interference argues for doing less. A compromise appropriate for some purposes is to do only nonintrusive probing early on (e.g., the interviewer can say: "Please think aloud"; or "Say that again, please?") and more intrusive probing only later in an interview. How one resolves this trade-off also depends on the purpose of the interviews. Researchers trying to describe stable knowledge states (e.g., persistent preconceptions) can allow more intrusive probing than describers of transient reasoning processes (e.g., nonroutine, problem solving processes) because there is a smaller interference effect. Also, training subjects to think aloud before starting an interview can sometimes reduce the amount of probing needed. Thus the quality of subjects' reports is another factor that an investigator can try to maximize in both generative and convergent approaches.

## BEYOND THE GENERATIVE VERSUS CONVERGENT DICHOTOMY: A SPECTRUM OF CLINICAL INTERVIEW METHODS

I began this chapter by describing a dichotomy between generative-interpretive research and convergent-coded research. It is time to expand this dichotomy into a spectrum by adding some intermediate methods. They illustrate the variety of techniques that are needed for a field as complex as educational research.

### Constructing New Observation Categories

First, however, I need to expand on the idea of what it means to define an observation construct or category. In even a 10-minute section of videotape, we are faced with a continuous stream of behavior that can be extremely rich. Assuming that we transcribe each statement, should we go beyond this to record each type of gesture, each voice intonation, each action with materials, and each line of a drawing? Or should we use larger meaningful units of activity such as "draws a bisected triangle"? A difficulty with a rich source of data source like a videotape is that there is too much data to analyze in a meaningful way! The investigator must decide what aspects of such a continuous stream of behavior are most relevant to the purpose and context of the study. This is the problem of identifying and describing observation concepts. The investigator must also determine what is relevant depending on the level of the research questions in which he or she is interested. Some of these choices will be obvious. But, for others, investigators must narrow their focus gradually to relevant observations and their descriptions and labels. Often this happens as they converge on an insightful theoretical model. For example, in the case of the static approach as a source of algebra reversal errors, it was not at all clear in the early case studies that students' references to the relative sizes of the two variables were an important observation category. Only as the theory of a static comparison approach was developed did that observation become important.

This illustrates that it is not only the case that theory emerges from observations. In generative studies, emergence sometimes occurs in the opposite direction or hand in hand, consistent with authors who refer to observations as more or less "theory laden."

## A Spectrum of Clinical Methods and Their Relation to Levels of Development in Observation Concepts

Table 20.4 shows a spectrum of methods from the generative to the convergent, with intermediate methods between them. There is an increasing level of observational reliability and quantifiability as one moves from Approach A to Approach D. Approaches A and B correspond to generative studies whereas C and D correspond to convergent studies. An exploratory study on a new subtopic may use Approach A alone. As theory and especially observation concepts become defined more explicitly, studies can be designed at the higher lettered approaches of Table 20.4.

Although this chapter concentrates on model viability, I touch briefly as well on the problem of the reliability of observations in the analysis of interviews. FIG. 20.3 can be used to contrast the concepts of reliability and viability as used here: Whereas viability refers essentially to the "strength" or believability of the theoretical models or findings about mental processes (Ts) at the top of the figure that explain behaviors, reliability refers to the "strength" or believability of the observation findings (Os) that summarize behaviors. Concerns about observational reliability stem most fundamentally from an interest in establishing agreement between scientists on believable findings at the level of observations (at Levels 1 and 2 in Table 20.1). This is a slightly broader and more fundamental use of the term *reliability* than is used in some circles because it is not limited to notions of consistency in the measurement of observables, although it includes that notion. Just as an important determinant of the viability of a model is the empirical support that a theoretical model receives from the multiple observations connected to it, an important component of the reliability of an observable behavior pattern is the combined strengths of the connections to sections of primary-level, protocol data represented as Ps in FIG. 20.3.

From one point of view, Table 20.4 describes a sequence of methods by which observation concepts can achieve high reliability gradually from top to bottom. The upper portion of the spectrum in Table 20.4 is associated with a concentration on the development of viable new models and observation concepts in areas where that is needed, whereas the bottom portion is associated with a concentration on pursuing greater reliability of observations. As concepts are criticized and refined and as observation concepts become more replicable, investigators may move downward on the spectrum in progressing from one form of analysis to the next.

Seeking improved reliability does not imply seeking a level where observations become "infallibly true readings of the book of nature." Rather, one seeks to establish a database of conclusions about summaries of behavior that are derived more directly from that behavior and that will attract as wide a span of agreement as possible. These observations can then be used as a relatively solid foundation for supporting more interpretive theoretical claims in a study.

Studies of each type listed in Table 20.4 are needed and each is important scientific work. A guiding principle is that work on an area of behavior should take place using the approach most appropriate to that area. In general, an area that is more complex, implicit, unexplored, or "hidden" in some other sense will require work using a lower lettered approach.

Higher level thinking of the kind usually studied in educational research is arguably the most complex process of all those studied by the sciences. Thus, in areas where processes are complex and relatively unexplored, it may take several investigators years to move through the lowest lettered approaches. The generative stage is crucial. As illustrated by Darwin and Faraday, the ability to experiment with interpretations of data and to reorganize and modify critical qualitative concepts is part of a criticism and improvement process that can play an essential role in scientific progress (Gruber, 1974; Tweney, 1985). This task will be facilitated by communication between groups. Therefore, it is important that there be channels for publishing the work that takes place in each of the approaches, including the lower lettered ones.

## Additional Guidelines for Fostering Model Viability in Each of the Four Types of Studies

In general, Approaches A and B in Table 20.4 correspond to generative studies whereas Approaches C and D correspond to convergent studies. Recommendations on maximizing viability from the previous sections of this chapter apply accordingly, with the additional considerations for each category itemized in Table 20.4:

TABLE 20.4.

Spectrum of Clinical Analysis Approaches From Generative to Convergent

A.  Exploratory Studies: Relatively large sections of transcript are explained by a global interpretation that may contain several elements. The analyst formulates an initial description of the subject's mental structures, goals, and processes that provides an explanation for the behavior exhibited in the transcript. This involves the construction of new descriptive concepts and relationships on a case-by-case basis. Examples of transcript sections are usually exhibited in reports along side the analysts' interpretations. In exploratory studies, sensitivity to subtle observations is important; for example, investigators may make use of facial expressions, gestures, and voice inflections. Although it may be impossible at this stage to code some of these observations reliably with multiple independent coders, analysts who become sensitive to them may generate key insightful hypotheses that would otherwise be difficult to attain. This generation technique does not prevent one from evaluating and increasing the support for these hypotheses later by other, more reliable means.

B.  Grounded Model Construction Studies: Analysts generate descriptions as in Approach A. In addition, some initial observation ($O$) concepts are identified that describe patterns of behavior. Investigators analyze smaller segments of transcripts and begin to separate theoretical ($T$) concepts (partial models or process characteristics) from observations. They also begin to connect theoretical models to specific observations that support them, triangulating where possible (as in FIG. 20.3). Interview procedures are standardized that are needed to provide a stable context for those observations that will be compared across different subjects and episodes.

(continued)

C. Explicit Analysis Studies: Investigators criticize and refine observation concepts and theoretical concepts (model elements) on the basis of more detailed analyses of cases; articulate more explicit definitions of observation concepts (definitions of observations should approach independent codeability); code for certain observations over a complete section of transcript according to a fixed definition or criterion; if the study has a theoretical component they will point to sets of observations in a transcript and explain them by means of a model; articulate more explicit descriptions of theoretical models; and describe explicit triangulated lines of support from observations to theoretical models.

D. Independent Coder Studies: Analysts refine concepts as in Approach C. In addition, coding of observation patterns (Os) is done by independent coders; interrater reliabilities are calculated. Note that it is much easier to define rules or guidelines for coding observable $O$s than for theoretical unobservable $T$s in FIG. 20.3. Coding that is restricted in this way still can provide a strong source of support for a constructed model $T$ when coded $O$s are judged by readers to provide evidence for $T$. In advanced fields explicit criteria may also be established for the subsequent inferring of $T$s from the presence of certain $O$s after $O$s have been coded.

*Note*. More generative and interpretive studies use Approaches A and B; whereas more convergent, confirmatory studies Approaches use C and D.

## RELIABILITY OF OBSERVATIONS: PROGRESSIVE LEVELS OF DEVELOPMENT

### Reliability Concerns Observations, not Theories

In the terms used here, concerns about reliability stem from an interest in establishing agreement between scientists on believable findings at the level of *observations*. In the broad sense, observational reliability refers to the "strength," or, believability of the observation findings that summarize behaviors. More reliable findings will be more convincing to other members of the scientific community. In contrast to this, *theories* are evaluated with respect to broader criteria (cf. the criteria for evaluating viability described earlier). Thus, we are concerned here primarily with the reliability of observations, not theories.

## Varying Needs for Reliability

I discuss the factors involved in fostering the reliability of observations according to the different approaches in Table 20.4. It makes sense that there will be emphasis on very different aspects of reliability at the two ends of the spectrum in Table 20.4. For example, there is no mention of measuring reliability across multiple coders in the lower lettered approaches; this is possible only after a criticism and improvement cycle has operated long enough to create relevant and stable observation concepts.

We also have the following very central trade-off. The more complex or implicit the mental process being investigated, the more difficult it will be to gather evidence on it. It will be harder to find relevant observables that can be coded and harder to connect them directly to the process in a concluding argument. Related to this is the idea that the longer a mental process takes to complete, the larger the sections of transcript that will refer to it. It will be easier, initially at least, to interpret such a section as a molar unit, rather than breaking it down first into coded fragments. I am not saying that it is impossible to eventually develop relevant and supporting codings that can contribute to evaluating certain models of complex processes, but I am saying that it becomes more difficult as the complexity increases. The more complex the process, the more difficult it will be to develop coding techniques for multiple coders to use to gather direct evidence for it at very high levels of reliability. It is possible that, for some topics, this level of reliability may be unattainable. Therefore investigators determine whether the purposes and topic of the research justify the expenditure of resources required to document high levels of reliability. Procedures for fostering reliability will vary across the approaches in Table 20.4, as is described next.

## Recommendations for Fostering Reliability

*Mechanical Recording of Data.* In all of the approaches in Table 20.4, audiotape, and, even better, videotape, are a great help because they retain a rich record of behavior that can be reexamined again and again. Of course, differences in what is "heard" and "seen" by investigators can still occur, but an automated record of this kind can raise the level of observer agreement significantly on simple behaviors like speech and actions. Portions of them can be included in reports as transcripts and shared with readers. Two-camera, picture-in-picture recording systems are useful for capturing subjects and a computer screen or written work at the same time.

*Procedural Replicability of Interviewing Procedures.* This refers to the extent to which the procedure of presenting questions and probes to the subjects is specified explicitly enough to be replicable across different subjects within the study or, possibly, by a different investigator with different subjects. Replicability of the interviewing procedures should be designed into all of the approaches in Table 20.4 as appropriate to the research objectives. It can help to increase the generality of observational findings across subjects in and outside of a study. Which procedures are standardized will depend on the issues that one wishes to reach conclusions about over groups of subjects. Readers are referred to chapter 19 in this volume for an extensive discussion of many key points in this area.

*Observational Reliability for Approaches A and B in Table 20.4.* The new studies of scientists described at the beginning of this chapter tell us that the model generation process also involves the construction of new observation concepts. This means that in generative clinical interview approaches, theory and observation concepts are developed together. Observation is highly constrained by the primary level data, but observation categories are still being formulated, and questions will remain about what part of the data will be the focus. These initial observations can still be extremely valuable as suggesters of initial hypotheses for models that can start and fuel a criticism and revision cycle. Because the observation concepts are continuing to change and improve, this lessens the focus on (and the possibility of) formal demonstrations of observational reliability at this stage. The primary focus will be on the ambitious tasks of forming viable models of what the subject is thinking and, at the same time, finding initial observation categories that are relevant to what the subject is thinking.

Nevertheless, one can estimate the relative believability and strength of one's different observations in a report and reflect them in the level of certainty expressed in one's descriptions. For example, one can report high estimated reliability for an observation referring to relative-size relations for a subject who gives a very clear and full report focusing on the relative sizes of two groups in an algebra solution, as opposed to a subject who gives a very short, muddled report. Readers can make their own judgments whether they would describe patterns in the data in the same way by comparing sections of transcript to the observation summaries of the investigator. Thus, displaying at least sample sections  of transcript to illustrate the bases for the investigator's observations can enhance readers' judgments of potential reliability.

In summary, even with generative approaches, there are opportunities to increase certain types of reliability in a useful way. I have identified four major factors to which generative studies can pay attention even though, typically, they do not attempt to replicate observations across samples in any formal way. They are:

- Increasing the quality of the subjects' reports (discussed earlier).
- Mechanical recording of a permanent data record.
- Replicability of interviewing procedures for presenting tasks and probes, where appropriate to research questions.
- Estimating the credibility or reliability of the observations that were made from a transcript and helping the reader do the same by sharing transcript sections.

Attention to these factors can help an investigator more firmly ground the findings of a study in a set of observations.

*Approach C: Explicit Analysis Studies.* In these studies, the separation of observations from theoretical mental processes makes possible some stronger considerations of the reliability of the observation concepts. Here, there is movement toward precise description of observation procedures in a way that could potentially be done by others as well as the analyst. The analyst attempts to arrive at clear criteria that can be used to assign events from transcript data to observation categories. In defining observation concepts, there is an attempt to find low-inference descriptors—those that require minimal interpretation—as a way of facilitating agreement between observers. However, seeking low-inference descriptors at the level of observations should not inhibit an analyst from also using high-inference descriptors at the level of theoretical models. When such descriptors explain multiple observations, they can be quite powerful.

As one's definitions of observation concepts approach a level where they can be used independently by others, but prior to any attempts at independent coding, the reader who is given sections of raw data and these observation criteria can use the criteria to make a more accurate assessment of whether he or she would be likely to code the data in the same way.

In addition, in Approaches A, B, and C, nonindependent multiple observers, if available, can consider data together and try to come to consensus on observations. Agreements and disagreements are reported. For the former, one can say that the possibility of agreement between observers has been shown.

*Approach D: Independent Coder Studies.* Here multiple observers are first trained to use explicit coding criteria, usually with practice items. Then they code the protocol data independently, tallying instances of each coding category. Interrater reliabilities can be calculated as the percentage of agreements out of the total number of judgments. Space does not permit a complete discussion of coding procedures here but an extensive discussion is given in Ericsson and H. A. Simon (1984).

Multiple observers need careful training and discussions to attain a common understanding of the criteria to be used for coding. Trained observers from the same research team are used in all branches of science; one is not required to replicate observational findings using laypersons recruited at random from the street. This acknowledges that observations can be somewhat theory laden. Successful agreement between independent coders requires subject verbalizations that are relatively clear and prolific, disciplined coders, and highly explicit and clear coding criteria (usually involving low-inference descriptors only).

Some studies may use several levels of coding such as primary-level transcript data, low-inference observations, patterns in those observations, and so forth. A less common and more ambitious goal is for the study to be replicated by a different research team on a new sample of subjects. Such external replicability requires, in addition to the other criteria in this chapter, high procedural replicability and the ability to select a similar sample. Such findings are only applicable to a context and sample with very similar attributes.

*The Choice of Method Depends on the Goal of the Research.* In summary, there is a spectrum of methods used in clinical interview studies that vary according to whether the purposes of the study are more generative or more convergent. On this dimension, the aim is to choose the level of analysis appropriate to the topic depending on the extent to which the observation categories either are established already or are being generated and refined. (*Note*: Some studies may use more than one method in Table 20.4. However, even in these cases, I find this breakdown useful in helping to separate and define the purposes of different activities in such a "compound" study.)

# TWO TYPES OF GENERALIZABILITY

## Theoretical Versus Observational Generalizability

The ability to replicate observations externally across samples also can be seen as a test of the generalizability of the observations across subjects within a population from which the sample has been drawn. For example, one hopes that the observations of reversal errors in freshmen engineering majors in our study would generalize with only minor differences to other samples in the population of freshmen engineers in general. We can contrast this observational generalizability to a second kind of generalizability—that of the theoretical model. Here, instead of being restricted to replicating the same set of conditions, the investigator can use the theoretical model to explain behavior under a new set of conditions. For example, in our study of reversal errors in algebra, we found that students would reverse the placement of coefficients in an equation that they wrote from problems where they translated from sentences to equations, as described earlier. We assumed that this was due to a rather mechanical, word-order-matching algorithm. However, we then discovered by generative protocol analysis that some students were doing meaning-based, nonalgorithmic thinking about images of quantities during solutions and still making the reversal error by placing the larger coefficient next to the letter symbolizing the larger quantity in the equation. From this model of the error source, we formed the prediction that the reversal error should appear in other contexts that could not involve word-order-matching, such as problems that started from pictures, data tables, or even graphs. This prediction turned out to be correct. Thus our generative study developed a model of a nonstandard, mathematical-reasoning process with predictive validity because it generalized to different contexts.

Also, by designing slightly more difficult problems, we were able to elicit considerable evidence for this difficulty in very different populations from the original (including a sample of university deans!). This illustrates the ability of a good theoretical model in science to apply adaptively to quite different circumstances from the original experiment, in contrast to the much more narrowly defined generalizability of a set of observations to other subjects in a particular population, using a particular procedure in a particular context. This reflects the fact that models are intended to be more general than observation patterns; that is, the generality or power of the model is strong enough to allow it to be applied to a different context or population where we do not expect particular observations to be replicated. Table 20.5 contrasts the features of generative and convergent studies that affect generalizability.

TABLE 20.5.

Characteristics of Generative Versus Convergent Studies

| Generative Studies | Convergent Studies |
|---|---|
| Generate new observation categories and new model elements that can explain relatively unexplored phenomena. | Use fixed observation categories and model elements and document where these are present in records of relatively familiar phenomena. |
| Interpretive analysis concentrates on model viability and relevance of focus for observations. | Coded analysis concentrates on the reliability of observations and, in advanced studies, the tightness of their connections to models. |
| Some attention to nonformal aspects of reliability. | Some attention to viability through explicit connections between observations and models. |
| Major strength is the external transfer of a new model. | Major strength is the external replicability of observations. |
| Theoretical generalizability of models across investigators and some populations and contexts. | Empirical generalizability of observations across samples and investigators, but generalizations are limited to a narrowly defined population and context. |
| Need procedural replicability conclusions that compare subjects. | Need procedural replicability for observational replicability as well as conclusions that compare subjects. |

Thus, there are two, different, major pathways for generalization to occur: *theoretical generalizability* of a model over contexts and populations, and *observational generalizability* of an established observation pattern over samples. However, the range of situations to which coded observations generalize is rather narrow, being limited to cases using the same interviewing procedure and sample characteristics. The predictive applicability of an observation pattern to a new sample is comparatively easy to determine. On the other hand, greater judgment is involved in deciding when and where to apply a theoretical model. The power or potential scope of its application is much wider, given that models are intended to apply to a wider range than the particular observations that they were created to explain. There are limits here, as well, to how different the situation or population can be for the model to apply. But the limits should be much less restrictive than for observation patterns.

In summary, there is a theoretical route for generalizability that operates through a theoretical model, which, if successful, can be applied more widely to other contexts and populations. This is the main route of generalizablity for generative studies. On the other hand, there is an observational route for generalizability to similar samples that extends from observation patterns in one study to similar observations in another study in which the experimental conditions are very similar. The latter type gives us a means for generalizing over samples in a restricted population; the former gives us a means for generalizing over contexts and populations.

## Objectivity

Note that the observation concepts for all of the approaches in Table 20.4 are theory laden to some extent. Consequently, we do not reach anything like "perfect objectivity" in Approach D. Agreement between independent observers in Approach D does not guarantee objectivity because those observers may share the same theories and special schemata that effect those observations. Again, the most important foundation for progress seems to be to work toward empirical constructs that may not be completely "objective," but that are still independent enough from one's theories to have the potential to yield surprises and anomalies that can motivate revisions in, or rejections of, the theories. There is a sense in which observations in the higher lettered approaches are "less likely to be unique" to an individual investigator. But what is of equal or greater value here is that one's own observations be independent to some extent from (and be capable of conflicting with) one's own theories. That is something that can happen with any of the four approaches in Table 20.4. This is equivalent to saying that if the analyst is doing his or her job, observations will not be completely theory determined and will be a semiautonomous process. This means that although researchers cannot help but be influenced by their theories when making observations from a tape or transcript, they do try to minimize this influence and attempt to be as open as possible to new or anomalous phenomena.

In summary, observations are not fixed properties of the world. They are fallible processes of the observer that can be affected by the observer's theories, but, in general, they are recognized as typically more trustworthy than theories, and procedures should be designed so that observations are independent enough to generate criticisms of those theories.

## WHY BOTH GENERATIVE AND CONVERGENT STUDIES ALONG ALL PARTS OF THE SPECTRUM ARE IMPORTANT

### Why Generative Studies Do Not Focus on Formal Measures of Reliability

Returning to the original dichotomy of generative versus convergent studies for the sake of simplicity, I can now discuss why generative studies do not focus on formal measures of reliability. In a previous section, I listed a number of recommendations for fostering the viability of models generated in generative studies. The main activity of these studies is to: (a) formulate well-grounded, viable models that are central and general enough to transfer to other situations and contexts (in other words, we wish to develop models of the most important structures and processes involved in learning); and (b) formulate relevant observation concepts that are important in the context of what the subject is doing. In generative studies these two activities will interact.

Studies of scientists' thinking tell us that hypothesized models of hidden processes are most often formed by an abductive generation, criticism, and revision process. In the early stages of this process, observation concepts will be generated and modified along with the new theoretical models. This means that in the early investigations in a subfield, seeking traditional measures of reliability and replicability of observations may be quite inappropriate because observation concepts will still be under formation and will not yet be stable. And a preoccupation with formal reliability may inhibit the process by which the concepts are revised and improved. It makes little sense to attempt independent coding with high interrater reliability while the relevant observation categories in an area are still being revised and defined. At this stage, the frequent modifications of the definitions of the categories would sabotage any attempts to measure coding reliability. That is possible only after a criticism and improvement cycle has operated long enough to create stable observation concepts.

Rather, in generative studies, model and observation concept formation can take place productively without yet insisting on formal measures of reliability such as agreement ratios between judges. The other, less formal types of reliability and viability discussed as appropriate for generative studies can still provide criteria for fostering productive, high-quality research at this level. Models produced by this process should still have the potential to generalize to other contexts and populations in a manner that goes beyond traditional concepts of the external replicability of observations, as summarized in Table 20.5.

## Higher Lettered Approaches Allow Enumerative Observations

In Approaches C and D in Table 20.4, once criteria for observation categories have been articulated, observations can be coded and frequency counts on observations can be used as collapsed data. In that case, the approach is *enumerative* in the sense that instances of something can be counted (e.g., there were 31 analogies produced by 10 expert subjects solving a certain problem; Clement, 1988). These data can be used either descriptively (e.g., to support the contention that experts generate analogies) or experimentally (e.g., to compare the number of analogies produced under two different conditions). Thus, observations also become more quantifiable in the convergent, higher lettered approaches.

It also is possible to imagine observation categories from Approach D evolving into measurable variables in more traditional, quantitative research using written instruments. These methods do not use clinical interviews and do not appear in the table but can be imagined to appear below the table. In this manner, clinical studies can play another role in developing important, new, observation variables that can then be used in more traditional, quantitative measurement studies.

## Study Sequences

One way to view Table 20.4 is as the downward path of possible development of work on a single topic over a period of time (usually years), as models become more fully developed and observation concepts become more explicit, replicable, and enumerative. However, that is only a part of the story; movement can occur in the other direction as well. FIG. 20.4 illustrates how work at a convergent level (or from a traditional, experimental measurement study) on one subtopic can raise questions that trigger work on new subtopics at a generative level. Therefore, the establishment of a reliable pattern of observation at Level D does not necessarily mean that a topic is closed to further investigation. Asking *why* the pattern occurs can reopen the investigation on a deeper plane that will benefit greatly from generative methods. Consequently, the overall picture is not always one of a uniform progression of a large field of study through the various approaches in Table 20.4. Rather, the progression can be cyclical, and different approaches will be appropriate for different subfields and subquestions at different times.

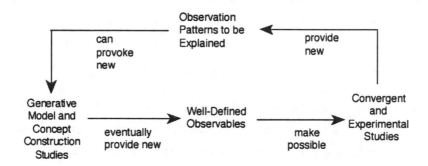

FIG. 20.4. How work at a convergent level can initiate work at a generative level.

## Maintaining a Balance Between Theoretical and Empirical Work

From this point of view, it does not make sense to push ahead for years with developing a very fine-grained model with, say, 10 times the number of elements as the number of sections referred to in a transcript, when one does not report on data that are fine-grained enough to support it. Such an exercise may be a worthwhile heuristic in the short run, but empirical analysis should keep pace with theoretical development in the long run. Conversely, it is undesirable to collect large amounts of unanalyzed data because model development should eventually steer the direction for collecting new data.

## Comparative Advantages of Generative Versus Convergent Methods

*Advantages of Generative Methods.* Following the contrasts in Table 20.5, generative methods are effective for formulating new observation concepts and explanatory models of cognitive processes that are grounded in protocol data. Generative methods can be used with interview data that are very rich in studies of complex mental processes (there has been a shortage of studies that map out such processes). Generative methods are appropriate to the embryonic state of this field. They can deal with behaviors that are unfamiliar and for which there is little in the way of established theory. The weakness of convergent methods is that if they are used too early in an investigation, the investigator can fail to identify key conceptions being used by the subject, key natural-reasoning methods, key processes, and hidden pitfalls in learning. Generative studies are more appropriate for constructing models of these hidden structures and processes.

A successful model can enable generalizations to different contexts and populations. I gave an example of this earlier in the section on generalizability in which reversal errors are predicted to occur in problems where students translate from *pictures* or data tables to an equation as well as from words to an equation. Thus models from generative studies may be shown to have predictive validity.

Although convergent studies place a higher priority on empirical replicability, a study that has achieved high replicability at the observational level is not guaranteed to have identified viable models at the theoretical level. This is reminiscent of the accuracy and reliability with which Ptolemy was able to predict the positions of the stars using a geocentric model with epicycles. Although he lacked a parsimonious model of the universe, he was able to make extremely replicable observations and accurate predictions. This did not prevent his core model of the universe from being rejected and replaced subsequently. Thus, the reliability or replicability of observations achieved by a convergent study does not on its own imply the presence of a viable and powerful model.

*Advantages of Convergent Methods.* On the other hand, the value of convergent studies leading to potentially replicable observations lies ultimately in the ability to tie one's conclusions to a relatively stable platform of fixed observation categories with a demonstrated level of agreement between observers and across samples. Observations of behaviors that are widespread and that are shared by other scientists in the field provide the strongest possible foundation for the arguments that will be made in the conclusion of such a study. Arguments to conclusions can be less implicit, complex, and interpretative than in generative studies. In addition, enumerative data from convergent studies allow one to count instances and, therefore, to compare frequencies between two types of conditions. This information can be used as a variable for descriptive, comparative, evaluative or experimental purposes.

Thus, Tables 20.4 and 20.5, along with FIG. 20.4, show how *both generative and convergent methods are essential to the scientific enterprises of educational research and the study of higher level thought processes.* Most generative studies have been done in the fields of education and developmental psychology; this illustrates a key role that these fields have played in cognitive science.

# CONCLUSION

Although some have argued that clinical methods are "less scientific" than more traditional methods in educational research, this chapter argues that clinical methods are an essential part of the scientific enterprise of investigating students' mental processes. In confronting the task of giving an explicit description of a methodology for clinical interviewing, it has been somewhat daunting for me to observe the wide disparities of views on this subject within the field. There are those who do clinical work that resist notions of standards of reliability or replicability in their findings. There are others who insist just as adamantly on formal coding procedures during analysis in order to ensure reliability. This chapter has proposed a rapprochement between these camps in saying that, depending on the goal of a particular clinical study, reliability will have a higher or lower priority relative to other considerations. It is my view that both generative and convergent clinical approaches are required for different purposes and that investigators need to be aware of the strengths of, and appropriate uses for, each of them, as indicated in Table 20.5.

In particular, there are generative studies using interpretive analysis techniques where the first priority is generating viable models and relevant observation concepts. Generative studies allow us to formulate new observation concepts and models of mental processes that are grounded in protocol data in order to explain important, but poorly understood, behaviors. On the other hand, convergent studies using coding techniques allow us to frame conclusions that are anchored in more verifiable observations. Hence, generative studies will be done more often at an early ("Darwinistic") stage in a research topic and convergent studies at a later stage (although this cycle can repeat itself at a deeper level on the same topic). The other approaches shown in Table 20.4 present intermediate options between these two extremes. These considerations should apply to the analysis of learning processes in studies such as tutoring interviews as well. They should also be extendible to the analysis of social phenomena in groups, but that extension is beyond the scope of this chapter.

Recent history of science studies and studies of cognition in scientists can provide foundational principles for designing methodologies in the learning sciences. What is new in modern history of science studies is that they are willing to describe and analyze theory (model) generation processes in addition to theory testing processes. This has given us an important new resource in formulating methodologies for generative clinical research. There is considerable evidence now that explanatory models in science are generated by an abductive generation, criticism, and revision process. In generative studies, model formation can take place productively through this process without formal measures of reliability, such as agreement ratios between judges. A higher priority goal for these studies is the viability of the proposed model—the strength or usefulness of the model as an explanatory mechanism—although some aspects of reliability are still very relevant. The history of science provides guidelines for defining forms of viability and reliability that are appropriate for generative, clinical interview studies and that can provide criteria for fostering productive, high-quality research. Models of student thinking produced in this way have the potential to generalize to other contexts and populations in a manner that goes beyond traditional concepts of the external replicability of observations. In this view, generative, convergent, and quantitative measurement methods are seen as linked complementary techniques for generating, supporting, and testing models of students' thinking, rather than as rival approaches. Thus, both generative and convergent clinical methods have roles to play as essential elements of a scientific approach to educational research.

## ACKNOWLEDGMENTS

The research reported in this study was supported by the National Science Foundation under Grant RED-9453084. Any opinions, findings, conclusions, or recommendations expressed in this chapter are those of the author and do not necessarily reflect the views of the National Science Foundation. I thank Ryan Tweney and Cliff Konold for their comments on this work.

# 21 Principles for Developing Thought-Revealing Activities for Students and Teachers

**Richard Lesh**
*Purdue University*

**Mark Hoover**
*University of Michigan*

**Bonnie Hole**
*Educational Testing Services*

**Anthony Kelly**
*Rutgers University*

**Thomas Post**
*University of Minnesota*

The central goal of this chapter is to describe six principles that have proven to be especially useful to help researchers (or teachers, curriculum designers, or assessment specialists) create thought revealing activities that we refer to as *model-eliciting activities*. The first section describes general characteristics and purposes of model-eliciting activities. The second section gives examples of several model-eliciting activities, and it also describes typical solutions that students generate to such problems. The third section states several disclaimers about model-eliciting activities, which tend to cause confusion if they are not addressed early. The fourth section describes difficulties that model-eliciting activities were designed to address in research; and, the fifth section describes principles for designing productive model-eliciting activities.

Finally, the last sections describe several common misconceptions or questions that often are raised about how model-eliciting activities can be used in teaching, research, or assessment.

# PURPOSES AND GENERAL CHARACTERISTICS OF MODEL-ELICITING ACTIVITIES

This chapter is especially concerned about thought revealing activities that focus on the development of constructs (models or conceptual systems that are embedded in a variety of representational systems) that provide the conceptual foundations for deeper and higher order understandings of many of the most powerful ideas in precollege mathematics and science curricula.[1] Therefore, the activities that are emphasized herein are not only thought revealing,

---

[1]It is especially appropriate to use the term *construct* in this chapter because, as constructivist philosophers surely would want us to emphasize, the term suggests that these conceptual systems simply be delivered to students solely through teachers' presentations. To a great extent, they must be developed by students themselves. On the other hand, the term *construct* is unnecessarily vague and misleading for at least three reasons:

First, the term *construction* often is interpreted as if it were synonymous with terms such as *assembly*; and, many conceptual entities that can be assembled are not *constructs* in the sense intended in this chapter. For instance, assembly may involve nothing more than systems of low-level facts and skills that have little to do with conceptual systems for making sense of experience. Thus, construction processed don't necessarily lead to constructs of the type that we want to emphasize in this chapter.

Second, among the processes that <u>do</u> contribute greatly to the development of the kind of constructs emphasized in this chapter, many do not fit the term *construction*. For example, development usually involves sorting out, differentiating, reorganizing, and refining unstable conceptual systems at least as much as it involves assembling or linking stable conceptual systems.

Third, in this chapter, we want to focus on the noun *construct* more than the verb *construct*, so it is helpful to use terminology that highlights this distinction and preference. Just as past curricula

(continued)

but also model-eliciting. That is, the descriptions, explanations, and constructions that students generate while working on them directly reveal how they are interpreting the mathematical situations that they encounter by disclosing how these situations are being mathematized (e.g., quantified, organized, coordinatized, dimensionalized) or interpreted.

The kind of thought revealing activities discussed in this chapter are useful for instruction and assessment as well as for research; and, they also are useful for investigating (or promoting) the development of teachers as well as students. How can they serve such diverse functions? First, to learn more about the nature of students' (or teachers') developing knowledge, it is productive to focus on tasks in which the products that are generated reveal significant information about the ways of thinking that produced them.[2] Second, if intermediate solution steps are externalized in forms that can be examined (by researchers, teachers, or students themselves), then the by-products of these learning or problem solving activities often generate trails of documentation that go beyond providing information about final results; they also reveal important information about the processes that contributed to these results.[3] Third, when a series of trial ways of thinking is externalized, tested, and

---

reform failures occurred when "discovery" was treated as if it were an end in itself, regardless of the quality of what was discovered, curricula reformers today often treat "construction" as an end itself, regardless of what gets constructed. In both cases, the means to an end is treated as the end in itself, whereas more important ends receive too little attention.

For the preceding reasons, and for the other reasons given in this chapter, the philosophical perspective adopted in this chapter might be called a "constructivist" theory, to distinguish it from "assemblyist" interpretations of constructivism and to shift the emphasis beyond construction as a process toward constructs as products of learning and problem solving. But, even if thes distinctions are stressed, it still is important to emphasize that many of the most important processes that contribute to the development of constructs do not fit well with common meanings of the term *construction*.

[2]For details, see chapter 6 in this book.

[3]For an example, see chapter 23 in this book.

refined or extended repeatedly, such thought revealing activities often go beyond providing documentation about completed learning or problem solving experiences; they also support the productivity of ongoing learning or problem solving experiences. Therefore, thought revealing activities of this type not only help to document development; they also promote development. Furthermore, because one of the most effective ways to help teachers improve their teaching practices is to help them become more familiar with their students' ways of thinking, thought revealing activities for students often provide ideal contexts for analogous types of thought revealing activities for teachers.

Of course, if our only goals were to investigate students' understandings of behavioral objectives of instruction, then model-eliciting activities would not be needed because proficiency with low level facts and skills tend to be directly observable using the kind of problems that are emphasized in traditional textbooks and tests. But, even when these latter types of traditional problems are modified by asking students to explain the reasoning they used to arrive at their solutions, this chapter explains why such problems are seldom effective for revealing students' understandings of the process objectives of instruction. Moreover, they tend to be completely inadequate for investigating the kinds of *cognitive objectives* of instruction that are the central concerns of this chapter.

For most problems or exercises that occur in mathematics textbooks and tests, the problem solver's goal is merely to produce a brief answer to a question that was formulated by others (within a situation that was described by others, getting from givens to goals that are specified by others, and using strings of facts and rules that are restricted artificially by others). But, for model-eliciting activities, the heart of the problem is for students themselves to develop an explicit mathematical interpretation of situations.   That is, students must mathematize situations.

Mathematizing involves making symbolic descriptions of meaningful situations, whereas the kinds of word problems that are in traditional textbooks and tests tend to emphasize almost exactly the opposite kind of processes. In other words, beyond difficulties associated with relevant computations, the problematic aspects of most textbook problems usually involve making meaning out of symbolic descriptions.

# WHO FORMULATED OUR CURRENT CONCEPTION OF MODEL-ELICITING ACTIVITIES?

Because the goal of this chapter is to describe six principles that have proved to be especially useful in creating thought revealing activities for research, assessment, and instruction, it is significant to emphasize that the principles described in this chapter were not invented by researchers sitting in laboratories. Instead, they were proposed, tested, and refined by hundreds of teachers, parents, and community leaders who worked with researchers in a series of 15-week, multitiered teaching experiments of the type recounted in the chapter on multitiered teaching experiments (Lesh & Kelly, chap. 9, this volume). The goal of these projects was to develop activities for instruction and assessment with the following general characteristics:

- Solutions to the problems should involve important mathematical ideas. In fact, attempts were made to emphasize 10 or so major ideas that the participating teachers considered to be the most important at any grade level or in any course. The goal was to focus on detailed treatments of a small number of major ideas rather than on superficial coverage of a large number of small and disconnected facts, rules, and skills. In short, the aim was to concentrate on deeper and higher order understandings of these major ideas.

- It should be apparent to parents, schoolboard members, and community leaders that the tasks emphasize the kinds of problem characteristics, understandings, and abilities that are needed for success in real life situations—not just in schools.

- The tasks should help teachers to recognize and reward students with a broader range of mathematical or scientific abilities than the narrow and often low-level skills typically emphasized in traditional textbooks, teaching, and tests.

- When teachers observe their students working on such tasks and when they examine the results that their students produce, they should be able to gather useful information about their students' conceptual strengths and weaknesses, so that teaching can be more effective.

Among the tasks that participants in the authors' studies ranked highest on the aforementioned criteria most were similar to case studies used in professional schools in fields ranging from business to engineering and medicine. These tasks were not merely surrogates for activities that are meaningful and important in real life situations. They directly involved samples of work taken from a representative collection of complex tasks that are intrinsically worthwhile, rather than only providing preparation for something else. Highly rated activities also tended to require no less than a full class period for students to complete, and realistic tools and resources generally were available (including calculators, computers, consultants, colleagues, and "how to" manuals). Also, teams of people with diverse expertise often worked together to generate appropriate responses. Consequently, planning, communication, monitoring, and assessing were important processes in addition to the computational and factual recall abilities traditionally considered to be the (sole) components of mathematical thinking.

## EXAMPLES OF MODEL-ELICITING ACTIVITIES

An example of a model-eliciting activity is given in Appendix A; it is called The Sears Catalogue Problem (Lesh & Zawojewski, 1987). As with other model-eliciting activities that the authors have emphasized, The Sears Catalogue Problem was designed to require at least one full class period for three-person teams of average-ability middle school students to complete. To set the stage for the problem, the data that students are given includes two newspapers (which include "back to school minicatalogues), one published recently and one published 10 years earlier.  The 10-year-old newspaper includes an editorial article that describes the typical allowance that students in a given community received at the time that the old newspaper was published. The goal of the problem is for students to write a new newspaper article describing to readers what a comparable allowance should be expected to be 10 years in the future. The new newspaper article should be persuasive to parents who might not believe that students' allowances should increase, like adults' salaries, to reflect increasing prices that are revealed in the newspapers and minicatalogues.

Other examples of model-eliciting activities are given in the chapter on operational definitions (Lesh & Clarke, chap. 6, this volume). Also, in chapter 23, this volume, the complete transcript is given of a solution that was generated by one group of average-ability seventh-graders who worked on a problem that we call "The Summer Jobs Problem" (Katims,

Lesh, Hole, & Hoover, 1994b). The goal of The Summer Jobs Problem might be described (by a scientist) as focusing on the formulation of an operational definition that describes the problem solvers' notion of how to measure the productivity of workers who are applying for a particular kind of summer job. Or, from the perspective of a business person, the students' goal might be described as producing a rule that is useful for making decisions about who to hire for a particular job. In either case, an important characteristic of such problems is that the descriptions, explanations, and justifications that are needed to respond to the problem are not only accompaniments to useful responses; they are the heart of useful responses. Also, because the problem is to be addressed by three-person teams of students, solution processes usually make heavy demands on metacognitive abilities involving planning, monitoring, and assessing as well as on communication capabilities and representational fluency for purposes such as: (a) justifying and explaining suggested actions and predicting their consequences; (b) monitoring and assessing progress; and (c) integrating and communicating results in a form that is useful to others. Therefore, solutions to the problem tend to emphasize a much broader notion of mathematical competencies than those stressed in traditional textbooks and tests.

Another important characteristic of model-eliciting activities is that students generate useful solutions (description, explanations, and constructions) by repeatedly revealing, testing, and refining or extending their ways of thinking. Consequently, they tend to go through sequences of interpretation-development cycles in which the givens, goals, and relevant solution processes are thought about in different ways. For example, a typical series of these cycles is described in the transcript that accompanies the chapter about iterative videotape analyses (Lesh & Lehrer, chap. 23, this volume), where a sequence of 14 distinct interpretation cycles can be identified. In general, the transition from initial to final interpretations often can be described in the following manner.

## CHARACTERISTICS OF STUDENTS' EARLY INTERPRETATIONS

As the transcript of The Summer Jobs Problem illustrates, students' early interpretations of model-eliciting activities frequently consist of a hodgepodge of several disorganized and inconsistent ways of thinking about givens, goals, and possible solution steps. For example, when three people are working in a group, they often fail to recognize that each individual is: (a) thinking about the situation in somewhat different ways; (b) focusing on different information and relationships; (c) aiming at somewhat different goals; and (d) envisioning different procedures for achieving these goals. In fact, even a single individual often fails to maintain a consistent interpretation and switches unconsciously from one way of thinking to another without noticing the change.

Because problems similar to The Summer Jobs Problem frequently involve both too much and not enough information, students' first representations and ways of thinking typically focus on only a subset of the information available; and, they often seem to be excessively preoccupied with finding ways to simplify or aggregate (sum, average) all of the information. For example, in their early interpretations of The Summer Jobs Problem, students often concentrate on earnings while ignoring work schedules; or, they become engrossed with fast sales periods while ignoring slow and steady periods; or, they center on only 1 month and ignore the other 2 months. Yet, at the same time that they are preoccupied with finding ways to simplify or reduce the information, they also may express concerns about not having additional information that they believe is relevant. For example, for The Summer Jobs Problem, such information may include facts about the needs, flexibility, or friendliness of potential employees, or their willingness to work. Although this information is not available, Maya, the client in the problem, would not be helped if students refused to respond to her request merely because some potentially relevant information was unavailable. Even at the early stages of thinking about the problem, students generally recognize the need to develop a simplified description (or model) that focuses on significant relationships, patterns, and trends and that simplifies the information in a useful form, while avoiding or taking into account difficulties related to surface-level details or gaps in the data.

## Characteristics of Intermediate Interpretations.

Later, more sophisticated ways of thinking tend to go beyond organizing and processing isolated pieces of data toward focusing on relationships, patterns, or trends in the data. For example, in The Summer Jobs Problem, students often place increasing emphasis on ratios or rates involving time and money (e.g., dollars per hour). Whereas, in their earliest interpretations, they may have failed to differentiate between (1) an average of several rates and (2) a single rate that is based on average earnings and times. In the first case, they may begin by calculating rates within each category (slow, steady, fast; June, July, August); then, (3) they find ways to aggregate these rates. In the second case, they begin by calculating sums or averages across categories (slow, steady, fast; June, July, August); then, they calculate rates based on these aggregates.

## Characteristics of Final Interpretations

Students' final responses often contain conditional statements, including various ways to take into account additional information that wasn't provided. For instance, final solutions of "The Summer Jobs Problem" may enable Maya to assign different "weights" to reflect her views about the relative importance of information from different months or different periods of work. They may enable her to adjust suggested weights to suit her preferences. They may use supplementary procedures, such as interviews, to take into account additional information; or, they may consider new hiring possibilities that were not suggested (such as hiring more or fewer full-time or part-time employees). Also, rather than applying a single rule uniformly across all of the employees, students may use a series of telescoping procedures. For example, as the transcript in Appendix to chapter 23 illustrates, one solution began by selecting employees for a "must hire" category; then, a different procedure was used to select employees among the remaining possibilities. Also, instead of relying on sums or averages to simplify the information, graphs like the ones shown in the Appendix may be used to focus on trends.

In general, for model-eliciting activities, solution process seldom conform to the following pattern. Initial interpretations organize and simplify the situation (so that additional information can be noticed or so that attention can be directed toward underlying patterns and regularities, which, in turn, may force changes in the interpretations that was used). That is, the new information that is noticed creates the need for more refined or more elaborate descriptions or interpretations. Then, in turn, the new interpretation that emerges often creates the need for another round of noticing additional information. Thus, interpretations can be unstable and evolving; and, the general cycle of development repeats until students judge the match between the model and the modeled to be sufficiently close and sufficiently powerful to produce the desired results without further adaptations.

## FOUR DISCLAIMERS

Before describing principles for designing effective model-eliciting activities, this section makes four brief disclaimers which tend to cause confusion if they are not addressed early.

### Disclaimer 1

Although emphasizing model-eliciting activities and problems that involve simulations of situations that might occur in students' everyday lives, the authors are not claiming that these are the only kind of thought revealing activities that can play useful roles in research, instruction, or assessment. Rather, they represent an especially informative and productive class of problems that emphasize productive perspectives about the nature of mathematics, the nature of real life situations in which mathematics is useful, and the nature of the abilities that contribute to success in situations encountered in everyday life.

Teachers who helped to develop our six principles discovered that, when they examined traditional textbooks and tests, nearly of the problems violated all of the principles described in this chapter. In fact, even in current curricular materials being developed under such banners as authentic assessment, performance assessment, or applications-oriented instruction, few problems could be found that satisfy the principles that they believed to be critical for the purposes emphasized in this chapter.

Although some people might be concerned that attention to pure mathematics might suffer if a small amount of attention is paid to problem solving situations that might occur in the present or future lives of students, the authors of this chapter believe that there is little danger that school mathematics will swing too far in the direction of emphasizing mathematics or science understandings and abilities that are genuinely useful outside school. Furthermore, most of the design principles that apply to model-eliciting activities apply equally well to other types of activities, such as skill-building activities or pure mathematics activities in which mathematical constructs are explored or compared, rather than being elicited or applied.

## Disclaimer 2

When the authors advocate problems that might reasonably occur in everyday lives outside of schools, they are not attempting to define real life formally or to argue that any particular view of reality is superior. Instead, the main point emphasized is that if a goal of research is to investigate the nature of students' developing knowledge, then it behooves researchers to be willing to enter the reality of students occasionally instead of always expecting them to come to the world of the researcher and educator. Nonetheless, throughout this chapter, it is stressed that naive notions about what is "real" for a given student often lead to actions that are antithetical to the design principles underlying model-eliciting activities. Certainly, most middle school childrens' realities are different from those that many adults attribute to them.

Another relevant observation about real life activities is that, in modern jobs beyond the entry level, and especially in jobs that make heavy use of sophisticated conceptual technologies, a surprising number of the mathematical activities address "what if" questions that stretch the boundaries of reality. For example, the conceptual systems that humans create to make sense of their experiences also mold and shape the world in which these experiences occur by creating new types of complex, dynamic, interacting systems ranging in size from large-scale communication and economic systems to small-scale systems for scheduling, organizing, and accounting in everyday activities. Thus, reality itself tends to be filled with human constructs, and the line between applied and pure mathematics activities blurs. Similarly, even in the case of pure mathematics activities of creating, exploring, or transforming patterns that do not resemble existing systems (e.g., communication systems, management systems, accounting systems, economic systems, organizational systems), the products that are produced often turn into applications when the world is transformed by their existence.

## Disclaimer 3

The authors are not identifying model-eliciting activities with current curricula reform movements focusing on performance assessment. Yet, experiencing the kinds of activities that are described in this chapter, it is true that many participants thought of performance assessment as a primary function that these model-eliciting activities would serve. That is, the activities were designed explicitly to be useful for instruction and assessment as well as for research, and they were explicitly designed so that students would be able to learn and document what they are learning at the same time. Nevertheless, there are several reasons to be cautious about associating model-eliciting activities with performance assessment. First, focusing on performance is often very different from focusing on powerful constructs. Beyond this, the term *assessment* often is treated as if it refers to nothing more than testing, which suggests a number of unfortunate connotations that the authors do not wish to associate with model-eliciting activities. For example, tests usually come at the end of instruction; whereas model-eliciting activities often are most useful at the start, where the emphasis is on identifying students' conceptual strengths and weaknesses and on optimizing progress rather than making value judgments about work that has been completed or skills that have been mastered already. The goal of testing tends to be to place a "good–bad" label on students or their work; however, the goal of model-eliciting activities is to reveal the nature of students' thinking. Tests are designed to measure what is, not to change it; on the other hand, during model-eliciting activities, students routinely develop constructs that are new to them, which is another way of saying that they are learning.

## Disclaimer 4

The authors are not identifying model-eliciting activities with traditional conceptions of applied problem solving. In mathematics and science education, problem solving often is defined as "activities in which students must get from givens to goals when the path is not immediately obvious." Similarly, productive heuristics traditionally are thought of as providing answers the question, "What can you do when you are stuck?" But, when attention focuses on model development in situations that can occur in everyday life, then the essence of many problem solving situations is finding ways to interpret them mathematically. In such situations, it is generally more important for students to find ways to adapt, modify, and refine ideas that they do have, rather than to try to find ways to be more effective when they are stuck (i.e., when they have no relevant ideas or when no substantive constructs appear relevant, as often happens in puzzles and games).

Table 21.1 describes a shift in emphasis from the traditional view of problem solving to an alternative that is based on model-eliciting activities. This perspective highlights a paradigm shift with potentially deep roots and extensive implications. For a brief account of other key elements of this paradigm shift, see chapter 2 in this volume (Kelly & Lesh).

TABLE 21.1.

The Differences Between Traditional Applied Problem Solving and Alternative,

Construct-Eliciting Activities

| *The Traditional View*<br>Applied problem solving is treated as a special case of traditional problem solving. | *An Alternative View*<br>Traditional problem solving is treated as a special case of construct-eliciting activities. |
|---|---|
| 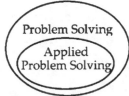 |  |
| If problem solving is thought of as "getting from givens" to goals then it makes sense to assume that:<br>- Both applied problem solving and construct-eliciting activities are special cases that involve confusing data and real-world knowledge in addition to the knowledge needed in more general situations.<br>- Heuristics and other mechanisms that apply to general problem solving should particularize to be productive in applied, problem solving situations.<br>Therefore, learning to solve real life problems should be expected to involve three steps:<br>- First, learn the prerequisite ideas and skills.<br>- Next, learn some general (content-independent) problem solving processes and heuristics.<br>- Finally (if time permits), learn to use the preceding ideas, skills, and heuristics in situations where additional, real life information is required. | If the essential characteristic of mathematical problem solving involves interpreting situations mathematically (modeling), and if nonroutine problems involve more than a single modeling cycle, and if multiple modeling cycles involve different ways of thinking about givens, goals, and/or solution paths, then it makes sense to assume that:<br>- Traditional problem solving is a special case where multiple modeling cycles are not needed.<br>- Solution processes involve much more than information processing using a single invariant model; they also involve model transformation because it is the model or interpretation itself that is being modified, extended or refined.<br>- Model construction and refinement are the same as construct development, so applied problem solving experiences are important *on the way* to learning the underlying constructs. |

# WHAT CREATED NEED FOR MODEL-ELICITING ACTIVITIES IN OUR OWN PAST RESEARCH PROJECTS?

What specific difficulties have model-eliciting activities been designed to address? When ideas for this chapter were discussed in the project on innovative research designs in mathematics and science education (chapters 1 & 2, this volume, give the background of this project), the topic of "problem characteristics" came up most directly in discussions about clinical interviews. For example, in some of the authors' research (Lesh et al., 1989), one of the original reasons why the notion of a model-eliciting activity was developed was to address important problems and opportunities that occurred during classroom-based clinical interviews.

One of the most important factors determining the success of most clinical interviews is the quality of the underlying tasks; and, this is especially true when mathematics and science education research shifts beyond surveying performance on a large number of small problems and moves toward probing students' thinking on a smaller number of larger problems. For example, in productive clinical interviews, it generally is desirable to reduce the number of interventions that researchers are required to make; and, in general, this is possible only when extremely well designed tasks are used.

When some of the authors conducted one-to-one interviews in their research, some of the most significant difficulties that arose occurred because such approaches tend to be costly and time consuming for both students and interviewers as well as for the people of many levels and types who analyze the data. Therefore, time constraints made it difficult to include enough sessions, enough subjects, and enough tasks to thoroughly investigate the many phenomena that it was desirable to emphasize. On the other hand, opportunities also arose when teachers and colleagues saw how much useful information often came out of these labor-intensive interviews. As a result, it was wondered if there might be some way to scale up the interviews so that they could be used with larger numbers of students — or by busy teachers who did not have long hours to spend interviewing individual students or watching videotapes.

The following three observations suggested productive strategies to respond to the challenges and opportunities described on the preceding page.

## Observation 1

One reason the authors believed that one-to-one interviews were needed was based on the assumption that sophisticated branching sequences of probing questions were required in order to follow the thinking of individual students and to document a variety of levels and types of responses. However, it was observed that the most expert interviewers varied a great deal in the frequency and duration of their interventions. For some interviewers, the ratio of "researcher talk" to "student talk" was nearly one-to-one, and the time lag between interventions was short. But, for other experts who were equally adept at producing convincing documentation about the nature of students' thinking, the interventions tended to be both brief and infrequent. Consequently, the model-eliciting activities described in this chapter were developed, in part, by studying the interviewing techniques of the "quieter" types of clinical interviewers. A goal was to design problems that keep students thinking productively but depend on only a minimum number of interventions and that encourage them to reveal explicitly a great deal of information about their evolving ways of thinking.

To accomplish this goal, it was important to design problems that would be: (a) self-adapting, in the sense that students would be able to interpret them meaningfully using different levels of mathematical knowledge and ability, as well as using a variety of different types of mathematical descriptions or explanations; (b) self-documenting, in the sense that the responses that students produce would reveal explicitly how they are thinking about the problem situation; and (c) self-monitoring, in the sense that students themselves would have a basis for monitoring their own thinking and would continue thinking in productive ways without continually needing to depend on adjustments by interviewers.

When tasks with these three characteristics are emphasized, it was found that interviewers usually do not need to make as many adjustments in the problem solving situation because students themselves are able to adapt the problem to fit their own ways of thinking. Ideally, after posing such self-adapting and self-documenting problems, interviewers can be free to roam about a classroom full of students, looking over shoulders, taking notes, and making only those few interventions that are absolutely necessary at appropriate times. In other words, in much the same way that an expert chess master may be able to carry on complex interactions with a roomful of individual chess players, we have found that model-eliciting problems often provide powerful yet practical ways for busy teachers or researchers to carry on simultaneous "interviews" with groups of students.

## Observation 2

Another reason one-to-one interviews tend to be expensive is that students' ways of thinking often seem to be observable only by examining the processes that they use to arrive at their responses; and, the only way to observe these processes seems to be through the use time-consuming analyses of videotapes and transcripts. Therefore, the model-eliciting activities described herein were developed, in part, by studying ways to pose problems so that the final products that students generate would reveal as much as possible about the ways of thinking that created them.

One way to achieve this objective is to state the purpose of the problem in such a way that the solution process becomes an essential part of the product itself. A potential route to do this is to establish problem goals (such as developing constructions, descriptions, explanations, or justifications) that require students to reveal explicitly how they interpreted the situation by imparting what types of mathematical quantities, relationships, operations, and patterns they took into account. For example, in the transcript that is given in the Appendix to the chapter on iterative videotape analyses (Lesh & Lehrer, chap. 23, this volume), the students solve the problem by constructing tables and graphs that serve as "smart tools" to enable them to describe the productivity of workers so that decisions can be made about who to rehire. Consequently, the goal of the problem is to develop a tool for decision-making, not only to make a decision. That is, these smart tools are not only parts of the process of producing responses to the problem, they are important parts of the responses themselves. Furthermore, the product that results can reveal a great deal of information about how students were thinking about the problem solving situation.

If model-eliciting activities are thought of as one-to-many interviews, then it is clear that some information may be lost that might have been available otherwise during one-to-one interviews followed by detailed videotape analyses. For instance, even for the best designed model-eliciting activities, students' final results seldom reveal information about rejected ideas that nonetheless influenced the final interpretation that was used and roles that various students played during the solution process. On the other hand, if researchers or teachers are freed from other time-consuming interactions, they often are able to record a great deal of this type of information while students are working. Furthermore, although some information inevitably will be lost when one-to-many interview techniques are used, other information is likely to become available that would not have been apparent using only one-to-one interviews. For example, when model-eliciting activities are used in classroom settings, many more students can be "interviewed," many more problems can be addressed, and the interviewer's time and expertise can be used efficiently when it is most productive, such as during data gathering and data analysis.

## Observation 3

When one-to-one clinical interviews are conducted, one goal may be to determine the state of knowledge of a given learner or problem solver, but another goal may be to investigate how this state of knowledge develops over time in response to various types of conceptual challenges. Also, the learner or problem solver who is of interest is not always an individual isolated student. For example, teams of students solve problems; and, they also develop shared knowledge. Of course, if the learner or problem solver is a group, then questions may arise about the state of knowledge of individual students in the group. But, for many research questions that are of interest, the goal is not to form conclusions about either individuals or groups. For instance: What does it mean for students to develop a particular type of deeper or higher order understanding of a given mathematical construct? What is the nature of a typical primitive understanding of the preceding construct? What mechanisms enable learners or problem solvers to develop such a construct from situated to decontextualized knowledge? What factors tend to create the need for learners or problem solvers to develop a particular construct?

None of the answers to these questions involves statements about particular learners or problem solvers, regardless of whether the "individual" is a single person or a group. Instead, they involve statements about the nature of productive learning environments, or about what it means to achieve certain levels or types of understanding for particular mathematical constructs, or about the nature of various dimensions of development for the constructs. Nevertheless, even for researchers or teachers who are interested in making statements about individual students, it still may be useful to investigate model-eliciting activities involving teams of students. One reason is because many of the mathematical understandings and abilities that are desirable for students to develop are meaningful only within social contexts.

For example, to the extent that mathematics is about communication, justification, or argumentation, the development of social norms tends to be highly relevant, and student-to-student or student-to-teacher interactions are as relevant as student-to-problem interactions. Furthermore, if Vygotskian perspectives on learning are adopted (Vygotsky, 1978), then one of the most important dimensions of conceptual development involves the gradual internalization of external processes and functions. In group problem solving sessions, it is natural for students to externalize ways of thinking that might remain internal otherwise. Also, the goals of learning or problem solving situations may involve developing shared knowledge, rather than only personal knowledge.

# PRINCIPLES FOR DESIGNING PRODUCTIVE MODEL-ELICITING ACTIVITIES

To judge the productivity of model-eliciting activities, the most important criterion to keep in mind is that, when students work on them, they should reveal explicitly the development of constructs (conceptual models) that are significant from a mathematical point of view and powerful from a practical point of view. If this single criterion is satisfied, then the activity generally will be useful for purposes such as providing information that (a) helps teachers to plan effective instruction; (b) helps researchers to investigate the nature of students' developing mathematical or scientific constructs; and (c) helps assessment specialists to recognize and reward a broad range of mathematical capabilities that contribute to success in a technology-based age of information. This section describes six principles for designing activities that meet this criterion. In other words, it describes six principles for creating productive model-eliciting activities.

## The Model Construction Principle

Above all, model-eliciting activities are intended to be thought revealing activities. The ways of thinking that need to be highlighted are the conceptual systems that students use to construct or interpret (describe, explain) structurally interesting systems. Therefore, to develop model-eliciting activities that are thought revealing, the first principle to emphasize is that it is desirable for the goal of the activity to include the development of an explicit construction, description, explanation, or justified prediction.

Whereas the problematic aspects of traditional textbook problems tend to involve trying to make meaning out of symbolically stated questions (in addition to computational difficulties associated with the correct execution of relevant skills), model-eliciting activities emphasize almost exactly the opposite kinds of processes. They involve trying to make symbolic descriptions of meaningful situations; that is, they involve mathematizing.

If the solution to a problem involves mathematizing (e.g., quantifying, coordinating, expressing something spatially), then one of the most important products that students create is a model in which a variety of concrete, graphic, symbolic, or language-based representational systems may be needed in order to describe the relationships, operations, and patterns that the underlying model is intended to illustrate. For this reason, to satisfy the model construction principle, a primary question that needs to be asked is:   Does the task put students in a situation where they recognize the need to develop a model for interpreting the givens, goals, and possible solution processes in a complex, problem solving situation? Or, does it ask them to produce only an answer to a question that was formulated by others?

What is a model? A model is a system that consists of (a) *elements*; (b) *relationships* among elements; (c) *operations* that describe how the elements interact; and (d) *patterns* or *rules*, such as symmetry, commutativity, or transitivity, that apply to the relationships and operations. However, not all systems function as models. To be a model, a system must be used to describe another system, or to think about it, or to make sense of it, or to explain it, or to make predictions about it. Also, to be a mathematically significant model, it must focus on the underlying structural characteristics of the system being described. Therefore, if an activity satisfies the model construction principle, the developers of the activity should be able to name the kind of system that the students are being challenged to construct, and the system should focus on a mathematically significant construct.

How can activities create the need for students to develop, revise, refine, and extend a mathematically significant model? To answer this question, task developers often find it useful to ask themselves: What kinds of situations require anyone—including myself and other adults—to create models? Answers to this question tend to be similar regardless of whether one is working in mathematics, the sciences, everyday life, business, engineering, or another profession in which mathematics is useful. To illustrate:

- Models are needed when it is necessary to make *predictions* based on underlying patterns or regularities, for example, to anticipate real events, to reconstruct past events, or to simulate inaccessible events.

- Models are needed when *constructions* or *explanations* are explicitly requested for the purpose such as describing hypothesized patterns and regularities or for describing decision-making situations in which too much or not enough information is available.

- Models are needed when it is necessary to *justify* or *explain* decisions, for example, by describing underlying assumptions, conditions, and alternatives.

- Models are needed to *analyze* or *assess* alternative conclusions, explanations, or interpretations generated by others, for example, by resolving interpretation mismatches between hypotheses and reality or between two competing interpretations, predictions, or explanations of a given situation.

In traditional mathematics textbooks, tests, and teaching, problems tend to be classified according to the kinds of numbers and number operations that they involve.—Do they involve whole numbers, fractions, decimals, ratios, or percents?  Do they involve addition, subtraction, multiplication, division, or exponentiation?—But, when only such questions are asked, unit labels tend to be treated as if they were mathematically uninteresting (e.g., 30 miles per hour $\times$ 20 minutes = [?]); and, even less attention tends to be given to the situations that these numbers are used to describe.  Such omissions are important because mathematics is about quantities and quantitative relationships at least as much as it is about numbers and number operations, and because the quantities that are involved include much more than simple counts and measures.  For example, they may include any of the following:

- Composite counts.
- Quantified qualitative information.
- Derived measures (e.g., based on a formula).
- Student-invented constructs (e.g., based on a formula).
- Very large (or small) quantities.
- Signed quantities (e.g., positive or negative).
- Directed quantities (e.g., simple or intuitive uses of vectors [arrows]).
- Ratios of quantities.

- Rates (i.e., per quantities or intensive quantities).
- Coordinates.
- Accumulating quantities (in which graphs or tables may be needed).
- Continuously changing quantities (in which graphs or tables may be needed).
- Transformations (e.g., actions on counts, measures, locations, or shapes).
- Rules (e.g., simple functions).
- Probabilities (measures associated with frequencies of events).
- Statistics (measures associated with sets of data).
- Sets (or elements of sets that are organized using lists, matrices, tree diagrams, etc.).
- Patterns (trends, sequences, series, etc.).
- Logical statements (e.g., simple directions, programming commands, calculator commands).

Model-eliciting activities emphasize the fact that mathematics is about seeing at least as much as it is about doing. Similarly, in science, it is obvious that some of the most important goals of instruction involve helping students to develop powerful models for making sense of their experiences involving light, gravity, electricity, magnetism, and other phenomena; and, it also is obvious that young students invent models of their own for making sense of these phenomena and that changing their ways of thinking must involve challenging and testing these models. But, because mathematics textbooks and tests usually have been preoccupied with computation situations in which interpretation is not problematic, students seldom develop more than extremely impoverished descriptive systems for making sense of situations involving the aforementioned kinds of quantities. In fact, it often is assumed that students do not (and cannot) develop metaphors, diagrams, language, and symbol systems for describing anything more than simple systems involving counts or measures.

Research on model-eliciting activities suggests a very different picture of what is possible (Lesh et al., 1993).—If you build it, they will come!—If students clearly recognize the need for a mathematical construct, then, in a remarkable number of instances, we've found that they will invent it. For example, when the authors first began to gather information about students' solutions to The Sears Catalogue Problem, which is given in Appendix A of this chapter, the main model (or reasoning pattern) that students were expected to construct was proportional reasoning of the form A/B = C/D; and, in fact, most of the students observed did end up thinking about the problem using a type of proportional reasoning. However, a high percentage of students went far beyond an interpretation of the problem based on simple ratios, proportions, or linear equations (Lesh & Akerstrom, 1982). For example, to find a useful way to think about the situation, students often invented surprisingly creative ways to deal with issues involving weighted averages, trends, interpolation, extrapolation, data sampling, margins of error, or other ideas that their teachers thought were "too sophisticated" for them to learn.  Furthermore, students who proved adept at such problems often were not the same ones who excelled at rule-following exercises or symbol-string manipulations (Lesh, 1983).

What created the need for students to develop descriptions and explanations in this situation? On the one hand, problems like The Sears Catalogue Problem contain an overwhelming amount of relevant information. So, students needed to think about issues such as: How many, and which, items should be considered? Which should be ignored? What should be done about unusual cases (such as the fact that the cost of pocket calculators decreased, whereas the cost of most other items increased)? How should the data be classified or organized? What kinds of patterns and relationships (e.g., additive, multiplicative, exponential) should be hypothesized? On the other hand, such problems often contain insufficient information because students frequently identified relevant issues for which no facts are available (e.g., how comparable are old and new radios?). Therefore, students must filter and weigh information.   Also, they must make assumptions to compensate for information that is missing. Consequently, issues related to sampling, variability, and averages tend to arise, as well as information about ratios and positive or negative changes in costs. Also, in order to aggregate information about many different types of items, several methods were possible. For example, some students compute changes in individual prices and then aggregate the changes for many items while others students aggregate prices and then calculate one single price increase.

After reviewing the answers that hundreds of teams produced in response to this problem, one conclusion that the authors reached is that many students who have been labeled *below average* in ability routinely develop more sophisticated mathematical constructs than anybody tried to teach them (Lesh et al., 1993). Also, the interpretation cycles that students go through during 60-minute problem solving sessions often correspond to compact versions of the developmental sequences that psychologists and educators have observed over periods of several years concerning the "natural" evolution of children's concepts of rational numbers and proportional reasoning (Lesh & Kaput, 1988). For example, Table 21.2 describes stages in the development of proportional reasoning and in modeling cycles during a multicycle, problem solving sequence such as that entailed in The Sears Catalogue Problem in Appendix A.

TABLE 21.2.

A Comparison of General Stages of Development and Local Modeling Cycles

| *Stages in Development for Proportional Reasoning* | *Modeling Cycles in Problem Solving Episodes* |
|---|---|
| Developmental psychologists (Piaget, 1950; Piaget & Inhelder, 1958, 1974) have observed the following stages in the evolution of children's general proportional reasoning capabilities:<br><br>*Reasoning based on only a salient subset of relevant information:* In their most primitive responses, students tend to ignore part of the relevant data, e.g., in balance beam tasks, students may notice the size of the weights on each arm but ignore the distance of the weights from the fulcrum.<br><br>*Reasoning based on only qualitative relationships:* Students may be able to solve problems that require qualitative reasoning only, but may fail on problems in which quantitative reasoning is needed also, e.g., For the two pairs of ratios below, it is easier to compare the first pair than to compare the second pair partly because: (a) if $A < B$ and $C > D$, then it is always true that $A/C < B/D$; but (b) if $A < B$ and $C < D$, then the relative sizes of the quantities must be taken into account in order to determine whether $A/B < C/D$ or $A/B > C/D$. | The multiple-cycle solution process described below is typical of those produced by middle school through adult students (as long as those students are eliminated for whom the problem posed is only an exercise in which an answer can be produced using a previously constructed, answer-giving routine).<br><br>The solution described below was constructed by three average-ability seventh-graders, working as a group for nearly 60 minutes on The Sears Catalogue Problem (see Appendix A).<br><br>*Conceptualization 1:* The students' first interpretation was based on additive preproportions involving only a biased subset of the given information; that is, without much reflection, the group began to calculate (by subtracting) "price differences" for pairs of (presumably comparable) old and new items. However, only a few items were considered, which were those that were noticed first (i.e., one or two items in the catalogue), and nothing was said to indicate how these subtracted differences would allow a new allowances to be determined. |

(continued)

10 cookies to 2 children <=> 8 cookies to 3 children

10 cookies to 3 children <=> 8 cookies to 2 children.

*Reasoning based on preproportional (additive) relationships:* Early attempts at quantifying often involve directly perceivable "additive" differences (i.e., A–B = C–D) rather than multiplicative relationships (which, in general, do not correspond to single, directly preceivable quantities, e.g.,

If a student is shown a $2 \times 3$ rectangle and is asked to "enlarge it," a correct response often is given by "doubling" to make a $4 \times 6$ rectangle. However, if the request then is made to "enlarge it again so that the base will be 9," the same students often draw a $7 \times 9$ rectangle, adding 3 to both sides of the $4 \times 6$ rectangle.

*Reasoning based on pattern recognition and replication:* Students' earliest uses of multiplicative "preproportional reasoning" often are based on a sort of "pattern recognition and replication" strategy, which some have called a "build up" strategy (e.g., K. Hart, 1984; Karplus & Peterson, 1970; Piaget & Inhelder, 1974). For example, if youngsters are given a table of values, they often solve the problem by noticing a pattern that they can apply to discover an unknown value, e.g.,

A candy store sells 2 pieces of candy for 8 cents. How much do 6 pieces of candy cost? Solution:

- 2 pieces for 8 cents

- 4 pieces for 16 cents

- 6 pieces for 24 cents.

Later, after calculating several price differences (in the apparent hope of discovering some sort of pattern), the tediousness of computation prompted the students to ask, Why are we doing this anyway? Then, without answering this question explicitly, the group began trying to determine a sensible collection of things that a given student might want to purchase.

In general, conceptualization 1 was characterized by repeatedly "losing the forest because of the trees"; that is, the overall goal was forgotten when the students got caught up in procedural details. On the other hand, as the group worked out computational details, students began to recognize difficulties that had been ignored at first (e.g., Which items should we consider? Why are we doing this anyway?).

*Conceptualization 2:* The students' second reconceptualization of the problem was based on an even more biased subset of the given information than their first conceptualization. The students guessed that, because 10 years had passed, perhaps the new allowance should be 10 times as large as before!

Although this "brainstorm" was quickly recognized as foolish, it served several positive functions: (a) It introduced a (primitive) multiplicative way to think about relationships between "old and new prices."; (b) It refocused attention on the overall goal of finding a way to determine current allowances.

Whereas the first conceptualization lost sight of the overall goal when attention was focused on details (individual subtractive differences), the second conceptualization ignored details when attention was focused on the relationship between old and new allowances and their respective buying power.

(continued)

According to Piaget (Piaget & Inhelder, 1958), the preceding type of reasoning does not represent "true proportional reasoning" necessarily because, to answer such problems correctly, students do not have to be aware of the reversibility of the relevant operations; that is, if a change is made in one of the four variables in a proportion, the student should be able to compensate by changing one of the remaining variables.

*Reasoning based on multiplicative proportional reasoning:* According to Piaget (Piaget & Inhelder, 1974), the essential characteristic of proportional reasoning is that it must involve a reversible relationship between two quantitative relationships. In other words:

- It must involve more than qualitative reasoning.

- It must involve more than a relationship between two concrete objects (or two, directly perceivable quantitative differences); it must involve a "second-order" relationship between two relationships.

- It must be reversible in the sense that it involves a recognition of structural similarity between two elementary mathematical systems (the simplest of which involves only two "objects" and a single "relationship" or "operation").

In general, according to Piaget and other developmental psychologists, an adolescent's proportional reasoning capabilities develop from global conceptualizations (often additive in nature), which focus one at a time on only the most salient (and often superficial) cues, to multiplicative conceptualizations, which deal with sets of information (or relationships) several at time within a well-organized "A is to B as C is to D" type of (proportional) systems.

*Conceptualization 3:* The third reconceptualization of the problem was based on a "pattern recognition and replication" type of preproportional reasoning. The students noticed a pattern of items whose price increases were (approximately) a simple integer ratio (i.e., approximately a factor of 2). So, they guessed that new allowances should be approximately "two times the old allowances."

This third reconceptualization showed real promise. However, the new clarity of thought that it introduced enabled the students to notice that (for example) some items decreased in price, even though most of the prices increased. So, the group recognized the need for a new way to think about the problem.

*Conceptualization 4:* The fourth reconceptualization was really a refinement of the third. It was based on a more sophisticated way of dealing with the difficulty that not all items increased by the same amount (and some decreased). That is, the students calculated what they referred to as "percent increases" (which were simple integer ratios). Then, these "percent increases" were averaged. This approach solved the problem that not all items increased by the same amount, but it did not resolve the difficulty of determining which items to include and which to exclude in the sample. Therefore, the students began to treat this sampling issue as the key point to address.

*Conceptualization 5:* Conceptualization 5 resolved the sampling issue explicitly! For the first time, the students wrote a (crude) mathematical proportion of the form "A is to B as C is to D." The values for A and B were based on the sums of prices for a number of "typical" items, and the students noticed that after a sufficient number of items had been included in the sum, the ratio was not affected much by the addition of more items.

Because of striking similarities between the two columns of the preceding chart, the authors sometimes refer to such problem solving episodes as local conceptual development

(LCD) sessions.[4] This LCD characteristic has important consequences for implementing other principles that have proved to be important for developing model-eliciting activities.

## The Reality Principle

In many respects, the reality principle could be called the meaningfulness principle. This is because, in order to produce the impressive kinds of results described in the preceding section, it is important for students to try to make sense of the situation based on extensions of their own personal knowledge and experiences.

One way for curricula developers to test whether the reality principle is satisfied is to ask, "Could this really happen in a real life situation?" Nonetheless, the key to satisfying the reality principle is not for the problem to be "real" in an absolute sense. The key to success is to recognize that students often have "school mathematics abilities" (and disabilities) that function almost completely independently from their "real life sense-making abilities" and to acknowledge that superficially real problems are often precisely the ones that do the most damage in terms of discouraging students from basing their responses on extensions of the real life knowledge and experiences. So, if questions about reality are asked, it is important to keep

---

[4]The idea of interpreting multiple-modeling-cycle, applied problem solving as "local conceptual development" has many practical and theoretical implications because: Mechanisms that developmental psychologists have shown contribute to general conceptual development can be used now to help clarify the kinds of problem solving processes (or heuristics, or strategies) that should facilitate students' abilities to use (and even create) substantive mathematical ideas in everyday situations; and mechanisms that appear important in "local conceptual development sessions" can be used to help explain general conceptual development in such areas as proportional reasoning. In other words, productive techniques that are well know among applied mathematicians may help developmental psychologists to create more prescriptive models to describe the mechanisms that are driving forces behind general conceptual development in mathematics and the sciences.

in mind that an adult's reality can be quite different from a child's reality, and that one child's reality is not necessarily the same as another's.

It is not the purpose of this section to define what is meant by real life problems. Neglected characteristics of such problems have been described in a number of publications (e.g., Lesh, 1981; Lesh & Akerstrom, 1982; Lesh & Lamon, 1992; Lesh & Zawojewski, 1987) where numerous examples are given. Instead, the goal here is to give examples to show how the reality principle can be used to develop effective model-eliciting activities where the effectiveness of an activity is measured by its success in eliciting informative and significant work from students.

In textbooks and tests, it is easy to find problems that refer to real objects and events. Boats go up and down streams; trains pass one another going in the same or opposite directions; swimming pools fill with water; ladders slide down walls; and students are asked questions about how long, how fast, when, or where. But, very few of these questions are likely to be posed in the everyday lives of students, their friends, or families. Furthermore, the answers that the authors consider "correct" often would not be sensible in real situations. For example, consider the multiple-choice exercise in Table 21.3, which was extracted directly from a famous test produced by a famous test maker. Clearly, answer choice b is the one that the authors considered correct; but, in a real situation, none of the answer choices is very reasonable. Choices c, d, and e imply that the whole board is shorter than the sum of its parts. Yet, choice b (the intended "correct" answer) is impossible too! This is because saw blades are not infinitely thin, so some material must be lost during sawing, and the amount of loss depends on such factors as the type of wood being cut (hardwood vs. soft pine), the type of cut (ripping vs. crosscutting), and the type and width of the saw blade. Answer a is the only feasible solution; however, it implies a huge loss in sawing (perhaps by a very wide and dull saw blade, followed by vigorous sanding). The result is that real woodworkers who encounter such problems could give the "correct" answer only by turning off their "real heads" and engaging their "school math" reasoning (where such foolishness often is rewarded!).

TABLE 21.3

A Multiple-Choice Question From a Major Test Maker and Some Teachers' First

Attempt to Improve the Question

| Multiple-Choice Question from a Major Test Maker | Teachers' First Attempts to Improve the Question |
|---|---|
| A board 7 feet 9 inches long is divided into three equal parts. What is the length of each part?<br>• 2 ft.  6 1/3 in.<br>• 2 ft.  7 in.<br>• 2 ft.  8 1/3 in.<br>• 2 ft.  8 in.<br>• 2 ft.  9 in. | A board 7 feet 9 inches long is divided into three equal parts. What is the length of each part?<br><br>Answer:_____<br>Explain your answer: |

In Table 21.3, the exercise on the right is an early attempt by a group of teachers to improve the multiple-choice question that's given on the left side. The first suggested improvement was based mainly on the current widespread aversion to multiple-choice (preanswered) items.  That is, the original, multiple-choice format was replaced by the more politically correct, "constructed-response" format. But, in terms of failing to elicit interesting work from students and of having negative effects on the students interviewed by the authors, the second version of the problem proved to be even worse than the first. To see why, imagine what would happen if we asked a professional woodworker the revised question. What kind of response would we expect? Is it possible that 7 feet 9 inches (a rip cut) might be an acceptable answer to the new question? Should the cuts preserve the thickness and width, but divide the length; should they preserve the width and length, but divide the thickness; or should they preserve the length and thickness, but divide the width? How quickly is the answer needed? Is overestimating preferable to underestimating? How important are accuracy, precision, and lack of waste? What assumptions should be made about the effects of sanding and finishing the parts? And so on. To answer such questions, a real woodworker would need to know the purpose of cutting the wood. If an explanation is needed, the woodworker would need to know who needs the explanation and why. Without being given such information, there is no basis for deciding (for example) whether a 30-second or a 30-minute explanation is appropriate. Therefore, the only way to respond to such questions in the absence of relevant information is for students to turn off their real life, sense-making abilities.

Appendix B at the end of this chapter gives two more examples to illustrate how several groups of expert teachers used the reality principle to select and improve performance assessment activities that have been published by the National Council of Teachers of Mathematics (NCTM) and other relevant professional or governmental organizations. The first example, called The Softball Problem, was found in a popular *NCTM Addenda Series: Grades 5–8, Developing Number Sense in the Middle Grades* (1991a). The second example, called Exploring the Size of a Million Dollars (see Table B1 in Appendix B), was found in the NCTM's *Curriculum and Evaluation Standards for School Mathematics* (NCTM, 1989). In both cases, the problems obviously refer to realistic events. But, in both cases, interviews with students revealed that the questions that were asked encouraged significant numbers of them to turn off their real life sense-making abilities and to give only the "school answers" that they thought were expected. The teachers' critiques illustrate why a "real" problem is not merely one that refers to a real situation. The question that is asked also needs to make sense in terms of students' real life knowledge and experiences.

To develop problems that encourage students to base their solutions on extensions of their personal knowledge, the topics that work best tend to be those that fit the current local interests and experiences of specifically targeted groups of students. But, in order to demonstrate their proficiency with a given mathematical or scientific construct, it often is not necessary for all of the students in a given classroom to work on exactly the same problem. Generally, clones, or structurally isomorphic problems, can be used so that students with different experiences and interests can demonstrate their competencies in different kinds of contexts.

To encourage students to make sense of problems using extensions of their real life knowledge and experiences, one device that the authors have found useful is to base problem solving situations on articles that describe real life situations in a mathematically rich newspaper (Katims et al., 1994). When such mathematically rich newspapers are used, researchers or teachers often pass them out the day before a given, problem solving episode is planned. Students also are given a set of preparatory questions that focus on reading the relevant newspaper article "with a mathematical eye." Then, following brief discussions of such preparatory questions, students usually spend less time floundering when they begin to work on the project. Also, for practical purposes, the newspaper articles help parents to recognize the significance of the work that students are doing.

## The Self-Assessment Principle

If problems are meaningful and if students recognize the need for a given construction, description, explanation, then an explosion of ideas is likely to occur in a group of students. But, for these conceptual systems to evolve, selection and refinement and elaboration also are needed. So, the self-assessment principle asks: Does the problem statement strongly suggest appropriate criteria for assessing the usefulness of alternative solutions? Is the purpose clear (what, when, why, where, and for whom)? Are students able to judge for themselves when their responses need to be improved, or when they need to be refined or extended for a given purpose? Will students know when they have finished? Or will they continually need to ask their teachers, "Is this good enough?"

Good business managers know that getting good work from employees depends, to a large extent, on stating assignments in such a way that workers know what is to be produced, when it is to be produced, why it is to be produced, and for whom it is to be produced. Otherwise, employees may have no way of knowing when the results are good enough, and no way of making judgments about such issues as whether speed is more important than precision, details, and accuracy. If workers cannot judge the quality of their work, then the quality of their work usually suffers. Therefore, it should be no surprise that a similar principle also applies to school work also. In fact, this principle is especially important in the case of model-eliciting activities because acceptable solutions generally require several modeling cycles and because students work in teams where disparate ways of thinking generally must be sorted out, refined, or integrated. At the outset of such problem solving episodes, teams of students usually start with different ideas from team members. Therefore, to make progress, groups need to: (a) detect deficiencies in their current ways of thinking; (b) compare alternative ideas and select those that are most and least useful; (c) integrate strengths and minimize weaknesses from alternative ways of thinking; (d) extend or refine the interpretations that are most promising; and (e) assess the adaptations that are made.

If students are unable to detect deficiencies in their primitive ways of thinking, then they are not likely to make significant efforts to develop beyond their primitive interpretations. If interpretation-reality mismatches are not detected, then students are not likely to proceed from their $(n-1)^{st}$ to their $n^{th}$ interpretation. In addition, if there are no criteria available for assessing mismatches among alternative interpretations, then these potential conflicts are not likely to lead to productive adaptations. Therefore, effective, model-eliciting activities should be stated in such a way that students themselves can assess their progress and the usefulness of the preliminary results that they produce. During each modeling cycle, students must be able to judge whether current solutions need to be revised, in which directions they should move, or which of several alternative solutions is most useful for a given purpose. In particular, the problem statement should make clear the criteria for answering the question, "Are we done yet?"

In the PACKETS Project (Katims et al., 1994), from which several examples cited in this chapter were taken, one device that is used to encourage students' self-assessment is to employ the notion of a client—a person or group of people in everyday roles who request that students construct a product for a specific purpose. As a result of specifying such a client and purpose, the evaluation of students' work can be grounded in how well each product meets the client's stated purpose. For example, in Appendix B of chapter 6, this volume, the quality assessment guide that is given provides guidelines for assessing the usefulness of both preliminary and final products—or for assessing the relative quality of alternative results. These guidelines can be used by anyone—including students—for real life, problem solving situations where it is clear what, when, why, and for whom work is being done.

In projects that focus on performance assessment, a quality assessment guide of the type just mentioned sometimes is referred to as a "scoring rubric" because, from a client's perspective and in the client's voice, five levels of quality are identified that can be used to sort products from "noteworthy" to "needs redirection." But, for most of the purposes emphasized in research, instruction, and assessment, labeling a product along a simplistic good–bad continuum is only one trivial purpose for such a guide. Far more important purposes involve helping students (as well as teachers or parents) to identify strengths and weaknesses in the work that is produced so that improvements can be made and additional learning can occur.

As the example problems in the previous section (and Appendix B to this chapter) suggest, traditional mathematics textbooks and tests include many superficially precise questions that fail to give any clues about the matters that answers to such questions would be intended to inform in real life situations. Consequently, the scoring of answers to such questions usually must involve factors that are quite different from those that would influence the quality of responses in real situations. For example, even in many performance assessment materials that are intended to be authentic (in the sense of being similar to those that occur in real life situations), scoring rubrics often focus on criteria that were not stated in the original problem and that would not be likely to apply to the real life situations that the problems are intended to simulate. They often favor "one rule solutions" using standard algorithms or equations over nonstandard procedures or informal methods that might be more reasonable in a practical sense. They may favor lengthy prose communication over elegant graphical representations. But, if quality scores are based on something besides how well the solution meets the stated goals of the problem, then the real "problem" that students need to address is not the problem that was stated; instead, it also involves addressing unstated school expectations that often are applied inequitably across students. For example, two groups may produce equally useful solutions to a given problem, but one group may be penalized because it did not use a favored strategy involving graphs or particular types of equations; on another problem, the same two groups again may produce equally useful solutions to the problem, but the same group may be penalized again because of some new unstated criteria that are imposed after the fact. Such experiences give the appearance of changing the rules for some students but not for others, and following such experiences, many students quickly learn to turn off their real life knowledge and experiences. Getting the "right" answers to school problems often means focusing more attention on interpreting and complying with nonmathematical norms imposed by teachers, textbooks, or tests—and less on interpreting significant, powerful, interesting, and useful mathematical constructs.

## The Construct Documentation Principle

For the purposes discussed in this chapter, the problem solving situations that are needed must be more than merely thought eliciting; they also must be thought revealing. Therefore, the construct documentation principle poses the question: Will responding to the question require students to reveal explicitly how they are thinking about the situation by revealing the givens, goals, and possible solution paths that they took into account? In particular, will it provide an "audit trail" that can be examined to determine what kinds of systems (objects, relations, operations, patterns, and regularities) the students were thinking with and about?

One reason the construct-documentation principle is important is because both researchers and teachers often are interested in activities that do more than stimulate and facilitate the development of important mathematical constructs. Sometimes, students also need to be able to document the constructs that they develop. Therefore, the construct-documentation principle is aimed at activities that are intended to contribute simultaneously to both learning and the documentation of learning, while at the same time they facilitate self-assessment and thinking about thinking.

The construct-documentation principle is essential not only for the purposes of the researcher (or teacher), but also for the student. In fact, fostering self-reflection is perhaps the most significant reason the construct-documentation principle is important. This is because, in general, it is not easy for students (or teachers, or researchers) to go beyond thinking to also think about thinking. Therefore, to facilitate reflection, effective thought revealing activities should encourage students to externalize their thought processes as much as possible. One way to make it natural for students to externalize their ways of thinking is to have them work in groups where such processes as planning, monitoring, and assessing must be carried out explicitly. However, an even more effective method is to focus on activities in which the products that students create require them to disclose automatically what kinds of mathematical objects, relations, operations, and patterns they are thinking about. For example, when an activity satisfies the construct documentation principle, students' solutions should reveal, as explicitly as possible, how they are thinking about the givens, goals, and solution processes. That is, the descriptions and explanations that they produce also should reveal answers to the following kinds of questions:

- What kinds of mathematical "objects" did the students employ? (Some possible answers are ratios, trends, and coordinates.)
- What kinds of relationships or comparisons among objects did they consider? (Some possible answers are equivalence relationships, order relationships, and invariance under transformations.)
- What kinds of operations or interactions among objects did they consider? (Some possible answers are additive combinations and multiplicative interactions.)
- What principles governed the preceding comparisons and interactions? (Some possible answers are transitivity and commutativity.)
- What representational systems did they use? (Some possible answers are graphs, diagrams, written symbols, and concrete metaphors.)

For model-eliciting activities, the explanations and justifications and descriptions that are given should be integral parts of the answers themselves. Therefore, the processes of reasoning that students use to generate "answers" should be embedded in their final product. In this way, assessing the quality of the final result automatically involves assessing the quality of the mathematical reasoning used to produce it. Nonetheless, even if the products that students generate require them to reveal significant aspects of their ways of thinking, this does not guarantee that the preceding information will be apparent to students, teachers, or researchers. Therefore, to help participants analyze students' ways of thinking, the authors have found it useful to work with teams of teachers (students or researchers) to develop "ways of thinking" sheets for a variety of model-eliciting activities. Simplified versions of these "ways of thinking" sheets are included in the teachers' guides that accompany the materials known as PACKETS (Katims & Lesh, 1994). But, in classrooms where the authors have worked, these "ways of thinking" sheets often look like large posters that display snippets taken from the products that students create for a given problem. Then, these snippets are organized to suggest alternative types of products that students can be expected to create. For example:

1.  *In the Case of "The Summer Jobs Problem"* (in the Appendix to chapter 23, this volume):

    - Students may focus on money earned, time worked, or ratios or rates of money per unit of time.

    - They may rank workers in different categories and then attempt to aggregate these rankings, or they may aggregate information within categories and then attempt to rank these aggregates.

    - They may aggregate information by first calculating averages for both money and time and then calculating the ratio of these averages, or they may begin by calculating ratios or rates and then calculating the average of these ratios.

    - They may weight information differently for June, July, and August (or for periods of work that are slow, steady, or fast), or they may use graphs or tables look at trends across these categories.

    - They may make decisions about workers based on a single rule or procedure, or they may use a series of telescoping rules.

2.  In the Case of "The Sears Catalogue Problem" (in Appendix A to this chapter):

- Students may focus on additive differences between prices from 10 years ago and comparable prices today, or they may focus on multiplicative differences in the form of ratios or rates.

- They may aggregate information from 10 years ago, as well as comparable information today, and then find the difference (or ratio, or rate) between these two aggregates; or, they may begin by calculating differences (or ratios, or rates), then find a way to aggregate these differences.

- They may deal with issues of sampling in a variety of ways.

## The Construct Shareability and Reusability Principle

The construct shareability and reuseability principle poses the question: Is the model that is developed useful only to the person who developed it and applicable only to the particular situation presented in the problem, or does it provide a way of thinking that is shareable, transportable, easily modifiable, and reusable?

As conceptual tools, mathematical models and the procedures derived from them vary greatly in their generalizability. Some are highly restricted to the peculiarities of particular problem situations, but others are taken out of their initial setting and applied to a wide variety of structurally similar situations. For example, among the smart tools that people develop using spreadsheets, graphs, or graphing-calculator programs, it is easy to distinguish among:

- Tools that are designed to be reusable, and those that are not.

- Tools that work when new data are substituted, and tools that satisfy only short-term needs with particular data sets.

- Tools that are made to be shared with others, and tools intended for personal use only.

Yet, in mathematics classes, students are seldom challenged to develop reusable, modifiable, shareable smart tools. In fact, textbook and test problems rarely ask students to produce any models at all. Most often, traditional problem sets provide the relevant models or tools, then direct students to apply them to produce single-number answers. Even applied problems, which are intended to involve real life situations, usually require no more than specific answers to particularistic questions. Consequently, it is generally possible to produce perfectly acceptable solutions to such problems that use very little real mathematics.

When the answer to a problem is 12 feet, one might ask, "Where is the mathematics?" Certainly, this answer reveals little about the ways of thinking that were used to produce it. Therefore, to assess the quality of students' mathematical reasoning in the context of such problems, the temptation is to focus on *processes* rather than on *products*. Consequently, if students' work is assessed based on processes, rather than the products that they thought they were being asked to produce, they inevitably conclude (correctly) that what problems ask them to do is not what they *really* are supposed to do—and that, regardless what they produce, someone (e.g., the teacher) is going to keep *changing the rules* so that their work will not be valued.

Problems that satisfy the construct shareability and reusability principle confront students with the need to go beyond developing personal tools to developing general ways of thinking. Therefore, by asking for descriptions, explanations, or prediction procedures that can be used by others beyond the immediate situation, such problems tend to emphasize much more powerful uses of mathematics than problems that fail to call for any form of generalization. Nevertheless, to say that students have produced a general model or a transportable tool is different from (and easier than) concluding that they who created this tool can transfer the relevant knowledge to other contexts and situations. Students' products can be observed and assessed directly, whereas inferences about transferability or generalizability are much more difficult to establish.

## The Effective Prototype Principle

Does the solution provide a useful prototype, or metaphor, for interpreting other situations? Long after the problem has been solved, will students think back on it when they encounter other structurally similar situations? If so, the solution usually needs to be as simple as possible, while still creating the need for a significant construct.

Effective model-eliciting activities tend to operate like case studies in professional schools in the sense that they are most effective when they provide rich and memorable contexts for learning and for discussing important mathematical ideas. During the school year, such problem solving episodes should become an important part of the culture and history of individual classrooms. For example, in classrooms where the authors have worked, it is common to hear mathematical discourse in which students and teachers refer to the problems—"Remember when we used ratios in The Summer Jobs Problem" or "That's a lot like The Million Dollar Getaway"—because the problems serve as effective vehicles for discussing many topics and for making many different mathematical connections.

Einstein is credited with saying, "A theory should be as simple as possible, but no simpler." The same is true of model-eliciting activities. Effective thought revealing activities must be structurally significant, but it often is not necessary for them to be procedurally complex. For example, if the goal is to focus attention on underlying quantitative relationships, then it may be desirable to minimize computational complexity. That is, computational complexity should be limited to that which is needed for focusing attention on the targeted underlying conceptual relationships that are essential for dealing with the intended structure of the task. If students cannot see the conceptual "forest" because of too many procedural "trees," then they are not likely to refer to, and draw strength from, the experience when confronting similar situations in the future.

## SOME COMMON MISCONCEPTIONS ABOUT MODEL-ELICITING ACTIVITIES

Thought revealing activities are needed for teaching and assessment as well as research. Furthermore, in chapter 9 of this book, Lesh & Kelly describe how thought revealing activities for *students* often provide productive contexts to use as the basis of thought revealing activities for *teachers*. Therefore, to close this chapter, it is useful to describe some common misconceptions that have occurred frequently when model-eliciting activities have been used for the purpose of instruction, rather than research.

When teachers and researchers first see examples of the kind of model-eliciting activities discussed in this chapter, they often describe them using such terms as *cute, open-ended,* and *difficult*. But, in an important sense, effective, model-eliciting activities should be none of these; and certainly, they are not intended for the enrichment of gifted students only. In fact, the six principles in this chapter are meant to help teachers select (or create) activities that are especially appropriate for meeting the needs of students who have been labeled *average* or *below average*.

## Why "Fun" isn't a Primary Characteristic of Model-Eliciting Activities?

One commonly recognized reason why many people try to use real life problems is for motivational purposes; and, one of the first things that people often like about model-eliciting activities is that they seem "fun" or "cute". But, in general, the authors have not found motivational factors to be among those that are the most important — if the goal is to develop problems where the primary goals are to elicit important information about the nature of students' mathematical knowledge and to recognize and reward a broader range of mathematical understandings and abilities than those emphasized in traditional textbooks and tests. This is not to say that motivation is not important; but, if we try to make problems "fun" for students, there tends to be a point of diminishing returns. This is because the very problems that stimulate the interest of some students often prove to be of no interest to others. Sports, rock and roll, dinosaurs, pizza and other topics that engage some students are equally uninteresting to other students. Today's "hot" topics are out of style tomorrow. Furthermore, if attempts are made to emphasize the usefulness of problems in terms of their payoff for getting future jobs, the problems that work least well often are those that students perceive to be relevant only in low-level or low-paying jobs for adults.

Although it is wise to start with problem settings that are likely to appeal to a wide range of students, experience suggests that good teachers often are masters at stimulating students to become interested in topics that expand their interests, rather than merely catering to them. Fortunately, model-eliciting activities do not require universally appealing topics. The topics that work best are those that fit current local interests. Consequently, the most useful problem solving situations are those that teachers can modify easily to fit the interests and experiences of specific students. a goal is to provide every student with as many "low-pressure, high-interest" opportunities as possible to demonstrate their abilities and achievements within contexts that are familiar and comfortable.

We've found that, what teachers need most is not cute problems, but problems whose solutions involve the construction of conceptual tools that empower students to achieve goals that they themselves consider important. The best way to create such model-eliciting activities is not to search for what is "fun", but to ensure that the solutions that students construct can be based on extensions of their real life knowledge and experiences. Conversely, if students' legitimate ideas are not taken seriously, or if they are dismissed even though their points would be valid in real situations, then the students can be expected to   become unresponsive, even if the topic interested them initially.

## Why is "Difficult" an Inaccurate Characteristic of Model-Eliciting Activities?

The term *open-ended* often conjures up the notion of never knowing when you have finished, or of being value-free in the sense that nearly any answer is acceptable (frequently because the quality or usefulness of alternative responses cannot be compared). But, effective model-eliciting activities exhibit neither of these characteristics. They are open in the sense that "right" answers have not been predetermined, and students must select the mathematical ideas that they will use to build their solutions, but the activities are highly structured in order to encourage students to build important mathematical models and to know when they have finished their task.

Model-eliciting activities should not be unstructured. In fact, extensive research and trial testing usually make them some of the most highly structured activities that most students have encountered in their mathematics instruction. However, the structure tends to be implicit, rather than explicit; and, it unfolds naturally as students work, rather than needing to be imposed by teachers at the beginning or during the problem solving process.

## Why Is "Difficult" an Inccurate Characterization of Model-Eliciting Activities?

Teachers who have had little experience with model-eliciting activities often think that such problems are too difficult for their children. This may be because such teachers are accustomed to these rules of thumb:

- "If an activity is hard for me, it will be even harder for my students."
- "If my best students have difficulty, then my other students will be completely blown away."
- Solutions that require an hour to construct are impossible for most of their students to complete without help.

Experience with model-eliciting activities has shown that students who have excelled at "one-rule, quick-answer" word problems do not excel necessarily at activities where "one-rule, quick-answer" responses are not appropriate. Furthermore, nearly all students are successful at some level because there are no tricks and because the most straightforward approach is usually a productive one. On the other hand, many teachers or other adults often perform no better than average middle school students on model-eliciting activities, especially if they often waste too much time trying to remember and implement formal one-rule solutions instead of using common sense and a few basic principles.

# SUMMARY: THREE COMMON QUESTIONS ABOUT MODEL-ELICITING ACTIVITIES

This final section addresses the following questions that are often raised by researchers and teachers who are not familiar with model-eliciting activities.

- What role(s) should teachers play when students are working on project-size, model-eliciting activities?
- When so much content needs to be covered, how can teachers afford to spend several class periods on single, problem solving situations?
- When it took professional mathematicians so many centuries to invent the ideas in modern textbooks, how can students be expected to construct these ideas during a small number of open-ended, unstructured, problem solving activities?

## What Role(s) Should Teachers Play When Students Are Working on Project-Size, Model-Eliciting Activities?

Answers to this question depend on what purposes teachers have in mind when they choose to use model-eliciting activities. For simplicity, we focus on the case of using these activities at the beginning of units of instruction when their main purpose is to identify students' conceptual strengths and weaknesses.

In ideal instructional settings with one-to-one teacher-to-student ratios, teachers could begin each session with interviews designed to follow each student's thinking, identifying conceptual strengths and weaknesses, and strengthening relevant concrete/intuitive/informal conceptual foundations before attempting to formalize these ideas using abstract, symbolic, and formal definitions, rules, and procedures. Although individualized interviews might be time consuming, time might be saved in the long run because instructional activities could build on conceptual strengths, address (or avoid) conceptual weaknesses, and avoid rehashing issues that are understood clearly already. Also, new ideas might be remembered better because they could be embedded within familiar and meaningful contexts.

In most classroom settings, teachers do not have time to engage in activities such as conducting one-to-one interviews with each student. Nonetheless, they often realize that, if they knew more about the strengths and weaknesses on their students, their teaching could be much more effective. Therefore, model-eliciting activities were designed explicitly to help provide details about students' ways of thinking; and, to do this in topic areas that are most important, model-eliciting activities should focus explicitly on the most important "big ideas" in any given course or grade level. The goal is to enable teachers to observe their students' thinking and to identify their conceptual strengths and weaknesses, while at the same time helping students to strengthen their relevant concrete, intuitive, and informal conceptual foundations. In other words, during model-eliciting activities, some of the teacher's main role consist of being observers, facilitators, mentors, and learners.

## How Can Teachers Spend So Much Time on Project-Size Activities?

Model-eliciting activities focus in depth on a small number of major ideas rather than try to cover superficially a large number of idea fragments or isolated skills. But, this teaching strategy pays off only if:

1.  Attention is focused on 8 to 12 major ideas that: (a) lie at the heart of any given mathematics course; (b) provide conceptual frameworks in which isolated facts and skills can be embedded meaningfully; (c) are related to the most common deep misconceptions that hinder students' progress; and (d) are the most powerful and useful in a wide range of important, problem solving situations.

2.  The solutions involve more than only generating specific answers to isolated questions. They are like the case study projects in professional schools. That is, they involve constructing conceptual systems, or structural metaphors, that can be used to describe (or explain, create, manipulate, or predict) the behaviors of other systems existing in real or possible worlds. Therefore, as students proceed through a course, they can refer to these metaphors in order to make sense of new ideas or to use old ideas in new kinds of problem solving situations.

3.  The time that students devote to mathematical thinking increases. This increase will happen when students establish meaningful connections between their "school math" and the concrete, intuitive, informal, context-specific, "real math" that they use in their everyday lives and when they use their "school math" outside class, and the results of their capabilities are valued by their peers and adults.

4.  When teachers observe students during model-eliciting activities, they: (a) learn about their students' strengths and weaknesses and avoid reteaching ideas that their students know already; (b) focus on the key issues that students do not understand; and (c) use existing understandings and capabilities as foundations for new knowledge and abilities.

## How Can Average-Ability Students Be Expected to Invent Significant Mathematical Ideas?

The answer to this question stems from the following observations: (a) students do not begin from a state of having no knowledge about the relevant processes and understandings; and (b) model-eliciting activities are fashioned to facilitate certain types of inquiry and development without telling students what to do and how to think.

In the middle school curriculum, most of the ideas that are taught have been "covered" during earlier grades, and most of them will be "covered" again in following courses. Few ideas are introduced completely fresh for the first time, and few are introduced for the last time. Furthermore, before students begin to work on a given topic, they usually work on topics that are considered to be prerequisites. So, the next ideas that they are expected to learn are seldom more than extensions or refinements of ideas that have been introduced already. In particular, they usually possess the elements of a language and powerful graphic and symbolic notation systems that were designed especially to express the "new" ideas that they are expected to learn.

One way that mathematical knowledge and abilities grow is by a mechanistic process in which small ideas, facts, and skills are assembled gradually, like tinker toys, into larger and more complex ideas, facts, and skills. But, mathematical ideas and abilities also develop along a number of other dimensions such as: concrete-abstract, intuitive-symbolic, global/undifferentiated-refined, informal-formal, or specific-general. So, one of the most effective strategies for maximizing students' progress is to begin instruction with activities in which students reveal and test their concrete/intuitive/informal understandings (and mis-understandings) while extending, refining, or integrating these ideas to develop new levels of more abstract, or formal understandings. Students seldom begin to work on topics with no understanding.   Most students already have developed some concrete, intuitive, informal foundations on which the intended formalizations can be based.

In the history of science, once the need for an idea has become clear, once the right questions have been asked in the right ways, and once adequate conceptual and technical tools are available, even some breathtaking achievements often have been accomplished in short order—and nearly simultaneously by several people who were not collaborators. So, if teachers have the power to place students in contexts that make the need for targeted ideas clear, if they pose appropriate tasks or questions, and if they provide appropriate tools and incentives, then they should not be astonished if average-ability youngsters often become able to "put it all together" to create some surprisingly sophisticated constructs

At conferences these days, it is not uncommon to hear researchers presenting data showing high-achieving students at selective colleges who produce nonsense when responding to seemingly straightforward questions about proportions (Clement, 1982a), averages (Konold, 1991), or other basic ideas from mathematics or science. Yet, by engaging children in the kind of model-eliciting activities that have been described in this chapter, the authors have been more impressed that low-achieving middle school children often invent—or significantly refine, or modify, or extend—more powerful mathematical and scientific constructs than those referred to in the research on high-achieving college students, and also more powerful than those that had characterized their failure experiences in situations involving traditional textbooks, teaching, and tests. What explains this anomaly of low-achieving middle school youngsters apparently outperforming college students? The answer involves all six of the principles in this chapter. That is, students should not be expected to invent powerful constructs unless:

- They try to make sense of the situation based on extensions of their personal knowledge and experiences (the reality principle).
- They recognize the need to develop the targeted construct (the model construction principle).

- They feel the need to go beyond their first way of thinking about the problem situation (the self-assessment principle). This means that the criteria for judging the quality of alternative results must be apparent and the need to go through multiple modeling cycles obvious.

- They externalize their ways of thinking so that they can examine them and refine them (the construct documentation principle).

- They recognize the need for a general solution to a collection of specific situations (rather than only a specific solution to an isolated situation; the construct shareability and reusability principle).

- The situation can serve as a useful prototype for thinking about other structurally similar situations  (the effective prototype principle). In other words, the situation should focus as directly as possible on the important idea and should avoid needless complexity. The problems need not be computationally complex even though they are structurally rich.

# APPENDIX A

The Sears Catalogue Problem

On the day before the class began to work on The Sears Catalogue Problem, each student was given:

- A 10-year-old newspaper article describing the typical allowance that students in a given community received when the newspaper was printed.

- Two minicatalogues from two newspapers, one published 10 years ago and the other one published recently; specific dollar values were given for each item named, were adjusted appropriately for the local community, and were consistent with the local newspapers used.

- Preparatory questions that also encouraged students to read these materials with awareness of their mathematical content.

The goals of the problem are for students to determine the buying power of their allowance 10 years ago and today and write a new newspaper article describing what a comparable allowance should be now. The new article should be persuasive to parent who might not believe that children's allowances, like adults' salaries, should be increase to reflect increasing prices.

Companion web pages, sample screens of which are shown in FIGs. A1 through A4, contain similar information about the cost of items that teenagers might have wanted to purchase with their allowances 10 years ago and today.

This model-eliciting problem involves data analysis and the mathematics of change. A web page (FIG. A1) gives the context for the problem, the familiar subject of teenagers, and their allowances.

FIG. A1. The context for the problem.

A second web page (FIG. A2) presents the model-eliciting problem.

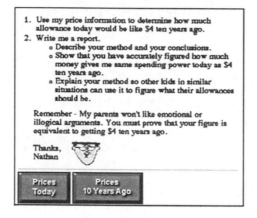

FIG. A2. The problem statement.

Other web pages provide price information for things that teenagers might buy with their allowance money. This information is organized into two collections of advertisements: one collection of items and prices from 10 years ago and the other showing current prices. Problem solvers may browse the collections to select data to use in their solutions. They also may gather additional data on their own.

Example web pages from the price collections are shown in FIGs. A3a, A3b, A4a, and A4b.

FIG. A3a. One page in the collection of advertisements from 10 years ago.

FIG. A3b. Corresponding data about prices of similar items today.

FIG. A4a. 10-year-old advertisement for athletic wear.

FIG. A4b. Advertisement for similar clothes today.

# APPENDIX B

## Using the Reality Principle to Improve Performance Assessment Activities

The critiques that follow Tables B1 and B2 were generated in a series of semester-long multitiered teaching experiments (see chap. 9 by Lesh & Kelly, this volume) in which groups of expert teachers worked together to develop the principles that are described in this chapter for creating effective, construct-eliciting activities. As the following analyses make clear, a "real" problem is not merely one that refers to a real situation. The question that is asked also should make sense in terms of students' real life knowledge and experiences.

### TABLE B1

### The Softball Problem

| The table gives the record for Joan Dyer's last 100 times at bat during the softball season. She is now coming up to bat. Use the data to answer the following questions: (a) What is the probability that Joan will get a home run? (b) What is the probability that she will get a hit? (c) How many times can she be expected to get a walk in her next 14 times at bat? | |
|---|---|
| Home Runs | 9 |
| Triples | 2 |
| Doubles | 16 |
| Singles | 24 |
| Walks | 11 |
| Outs | 38 |
| Total | **100** |

# AN ATTEMPT TO IMPROVE "THE SOFTBALL PROBLEM"

## A Teacher's Analysis

*Critique.* On the surface, this problem appears to be embedded in a real-world situation: Joan is coming up to bat, and the problem description gives some data about her prior performances. But, in a real situation, it would not be sensible for someone (other than a mathematics teacher) to want to know the answer to the questions as they are stated (concerning the probabilities of a home run or a hit). In fact, computing this "probability" using the intended rule depends on ignoring common sense and/or practical experience. In reality, the probability depends on who is pitching (Is he or she left-handed or right-handed?), on field conditions or the weather, and on a lot of other factors that people who play softball are aware of (Who is in a slump or on a streak? Who is good under pressure? And so on.). Furthermore, because we do not know who is asking the question, or why, we cannot know what to take into account, how accurate the answer needs to be, or what the risks or benefits might be. Therefore, the criteria for judging the quality of the answers are not implicit to the situation, and the solutions must be judged according to whether they conform to the calculation that was expected, rather than according to whether they succeed in any practical or meaningful sense of the word. Overall, I do not think that such a problem is realistic or that it promotes authentic performance. Real softball players would have to turn off their real life knowledge and experience.

*Analysis.* In this problem, it is not particularly necessary to have Joan coming up to bat right now. In fact, for the third question, we might wonder what coming up to bat, at this particular time, has to do with expectations about her walks for the next 14 times at bat, which may not happen in the same game. Is there some reason, now that Joan is coming up to bat, to want to know her expected number of walks for the next 14 times at bat? Why not the next 15 times at bat? Is it possible that having Joan at bat in the first place was only the awkward result of a well-intentioned effort to create a lifelike context (for a problem with essentially one appropriate solution path that leads to a single "right" answer)? Or was it a superficial gesture to suggest that even girls play sports? If not for either of these reasons, why is it there?

*Possible Improvements.* Here is a suggestion for improving this problem. Notice that the "math answer" is not an end in itself. It is a means to an end (or a tool for informing actions, decisions, and judgments). If Joan really is coming up to bat now, the mathematics should address a plausible question that might occur in that situation. I think that the revised item asks a more authentic question in the sense that it asks for a decision that might be required in the context.

## A Suggested Improvement

You are the manager of a softball team. It is the bottom of the ninth inning, two outs gone, and no one is on base. Your team is one run behind. You plan to send in a pinch hitter in the hopes of scoring the tying run. Your possibilities are Joan, Mary, and Bob. Their batting records are given in the following table. Who would you choose to bat? Explain your reasoning.

|          | Joan | Mary | Bob |
|----------|------|------|-----|
| Home Runs | 9  | 15   | 6   |
| Triples   | 2  | 5    | 3   |
| Doubles   | 16 | 11   | 8   |
| Singles   | 24 | 34   | 18  |
| Walks     | 11 | 20   | 12  |
| Outs      | 38 | 85   | 36  |

As a third iteration of how to improve this problem, one group suggested the following. The suggestion was based on the observation that, in the second version, when students were asked to explain their reasoning, it was unclear who was supposed to be given the explanation or for what purpose. So, it became virtually impossible to judge whether one explanation was better than another. By contrast, notice that, in the third iteration-refinement of the softball problem, the explanation is not only about the process that was used to arrive at a decision; it also is the product itself.

## A Third Iteration of "The Softball Problem"

You have a friend who is the manager of a softball team. It is the bottom of the ninth inning, two outs gone, and no one is on base. Your team is one run behind. The manager (your friend) has decided to send in a pinch hitter in the hopes of scoring the tying run. The possibilities are Joan, Mary, and Bob. Their batting records are given in the table below. The manager decided to send in Mary, but Mary struck out and the team lost.

In the local newspaper the next day, there were a number of nasty letters to the sports editor demanding that your friend be fired.

Write a letter to the editor describing why your friend made a wise choice, although the results did not turn out as everybody had hoped.

|          | Joan | Mary | Bob |
|----------|------|------|-----|
| Home Runs | 9  | 15   | 6   |
| Triples   | 2  | 5    | 3   |
| Doubles   | 16 | 11   | 8   |
| Singles   | 24 | 34   | 18  |
| Walks     | 11 | 20   | 12  |
| Outs      | 38 | 85   | 36  |

TABLE B2

Exploring the Size of a Million Dollars

Materials: One thousand or more fake dollar bills (play money or rectangular sheets of paper the approximate size of a dollar bill). Calculators should be available to facilitate and expedite the computation for analysis.

Begin by telling the following story: Just as you decide to go to bed one night, the phone rings and a friend offers you a chance to be a millionaire. He tells you he won $2,000,000 in a contest. The money was sent to him in two suitcases, each containing $1,000,000 in $1 bills. He will give you one suitcase of money if your mom or dad will drive him to the airport to pick it up. Could your friend be telling you the truth? Can he make you a millionaire?

Involve students in formulating and exploring questions to investigate the truth of this claim. For example: (a) Can $1,000,000 in $1 bills fit in a standard-size suitcase? If not, what is the smallest denomination of bills that could fit the money in a suitcase? (b) Could you lift the suitcase if it contained $1,000,000 in $1 bills? Estimate its weight.

*Note*: The dimensions of a $1 bill are approximately 6 inches by 2 1/2 inches.

## AN ATTEMPT TO IMPROVE "THE MILLION DOLLAR PROBLEM"

### One Teacher's Critique of "Exploring the Size of a Million Dollars"

It is easy to think of The Million Dollar Problem as a real life problem in the sense that students use mathematics to deal with a situation outside the classroom. Although the story is unlikely to happen in students' lives, the question deals with familiar things that *are* parts of their lives: a friend, a phone call, parents, dollar bills, suitcases, a request for help. At first glance, this seems like an opportunity for students to use their own knowledge and experiences to make sense of a situation. But, the more I think about it, the more things I see working against this. Who is asking this question and why? Is the phone friend wondering if the contest company made a mistake? Are the parents worried about driving to

(continued)

the airport on a fool's errand? Even in hypothetical problems, students need some sense of who is asking for a solution and for what purpose, in order to make decisions about what kinds of answers are useful. The problem lacks internal criteria for successful completion, which would help students to assess their answers as they work. The teacher is the sole audience for students' responses and, thus, the primary source of authority for evaluating their answers. In planning and monitoring their solution processes, students will ask themselves, "What does my math teacher want?" instead of "What makes the most sense?" That is what I call the "school math" mentality.

Who but a mathematics teacher with a solution in mind already would give students a thousand or more fake dollar bills? The teacher's directions list the dimensions as 6 inches by 2 1/2 inches, as if the third dimension of thickness is somehow less important than the other two, or does not matter. Fake bills may vary significantly in thickness from real bills, depending on the paper. By giving the dimensions, the authors seem to want the students to do something with these numbers, rather than to think about the relative sizes of real dollars, real pieces of paper, real stacks of paper, and so on. Teachers who would not use play money that was 3 inches long or 1 1/4 inches wide may be giving students fake bills that are half as thick, yet the effect on the volume or weight of all of these distortions is identical. Besides being extra work for teachers, providing bills for students tells them how the teacher thinks about the situation: which aspects are important and which to ignore. The teacher's way is not always the best way, as in the case of misleading students about the importance of different dimensions. Yet, this is a strongly teacher-directed activity in which students are led through a process of transforming the stated real life questions (Could your friend be telling you the truth? Can he make you a millionaire?) into estimation problems about the size and the weight of a million $1 bills. The obstacle to meaningful problem solving here is not the hypothetical nature of the situation. "What ifs" can be powerful, construct-eliciting experiences. Instead it is the obvious fact that, if such a phone call ever happens, no sensible person would respond as the teacher wants children to. In the real world, if a friend claims a million dollars are waiting at the airport, normal people do not rely on number sense to figure out what is going on. "You can't be telling the truth because my calculations prove that the prize money will not fit in an ordinary suitcase" is not the best response to such a phone call. The situation presents much more salient issues—such as where the money came from and what kind of a friend this is—than the questions that the teacher poses.

What happens when students respond seriously that—whether it be $1,000 or $1,000,000—this scenario sounds like a drug deal, or money laundering, or a practical joke? The amount of money is not what leads normal people to conclude that the caller is untruthful. The stated questions (Could your friend be telling you the truth? Can he make you a millionaire?) do not create the need for the mathematics that the teacher intends to elicit. Students are being set up not by a phone friend, but by their own teacher, who leads them along a predetermined path toward a foregone conclusion, and the whole point of all of the leading questions seemed to be to try to guarantee that all students would interpret the situation as the teacher intended. In other words, what the teacher had in mind was for students to carry out a particular computation; it was not for students to develop a sensible interpretation of the situation that would allow a sensible decision to be made.

Smart children would know that they were being set up.

A similar problem, called "The Million Dollar Getaway," (see Table B3) was published in a program called *The PACKETS Program* (Katims et al., 1994) that developed out of the kind of multitiered teaching experiments that are described in chapter 9 by Lesh & Kelly, this volume. Like the NCTM problem, "The Million Dollar Getaway" also presents a hypothetical situation. However, this problem addresses issues raised in the preceding critique, and the result is that the chances improved significantly that students would engage in sense-making that is an extension of their real life knowledge and experiences.

TABLE B3

The Million Dollar Getaway.

---

Main Bank was robbed this morning. A lone robber carried the loot away in a big leather bag. The manager of the bank said that most of the stolen bills were 1s, 5s, and 10s. Early reports said the robber took approximately $1,000,000 in small bills. The Channel 1 News team thinks this sounds like more money than one person could carry. What do you think?

Channel 1 News needs help determining how hard it would be for one person to carry $1,000,000 in small bills. Investigate this question to determine if it is possible. Prepare a report for Channel 1 News describing and explaining your findings. Your report should help investigative reporters at Channel 1 understand the situation and plan better for tonight's broadcast.

---

At first glance, the PACKETS activity appears less structured than the NCTM problem. It does not specify the denominations of the stolen currency, and it does not tell students to explore specific mathematical topics, such as weight and volume. In spite of this, the activity is not less structured; it is less teacher directed.

When students are told the specific concern—"this sounds like more money than one person could carry"—they need not resort to guessing what the task is or to straying into nonmathematical explorations or explanations; instead, they can move directly to modeling the situation with mathematics. When students know who is asking the question and why, they can sense what kinds of issues to explore and what kinds of answers might be appropriate. For example, one way in which students assess their work in progress is to play the role of Channel 1 reporters covering the story and to ask themselves, "How helpful would this result be in preparing me for the evening news broadcast?"

Because students do not know the exact denominations of the stolen bills, they must go beyond the worst-case scenario of all $1 bills to construct alternative collections of bills that are equivalent to $1,000,000 in singles. For example, some students typically consider various linear combinations of $1, $5, $10, $20, and $100 bills amounting to $1,000,000; others invent the idea of best-case and worst-case scenarios, in order to establish boundaries for the different possibilities.

# 22 Videorecording as Theory

**Rogers Hall**

*University of California–Berkeley*

Carl: They're not tattoos, they're skin ILLUSTRATIONS! Don't you ever call them tattoos. Let me tell you. Don't you look at those illustrations too long, because they'll come alive and they'll tell stories.

Rod Steiger as Carl, in a film adaptation of Ray Bradbury's *The Illustrated Man* (1951, directed by Jack Smight, 1969)

We can learn a great deal about the detailed structure of learning and teaching by watching videotape of people in action. But, we still don't know much about our own activities of collecting, watching, or interpreting video as a stable source of data for research and presentation purposes. That one can get into trouble or, worse still, get others into trouble, by showing films of study participants is apparent in the kinds of "war stories" that researchers swap outside conference meeting rooms. Relatively little has been written about this. In this chapter, I use difficulties encountered in my own research on teaching and learning mathematics to illustrate what I take to be a set of core problems with appropriate uses of video as data. These problems include:

- Processes of collecting video data and making selections from it are usually (and too easily) deleted from research accounts.
- Production values that are preserved in technical arrangements for collecting video become a permanent part of the data one is recording.

- Video databases may be public resources by virtue of accepted arrangements for scholarly review and research sponsorship, yet, we cannot fully anticipate the public use of database materials.

These problems persist because there is no single community of practice surrounding appropriate use of video records as data in research with human (and technical or organizational) participants. I present several local suggestions for overcoming some of these problems, but I expect that no single set of standard practices is possible. Instead, a heterogeneous set of agreements and conventional practices will need to emerge over time. The chapters collected in this volume are a step in that direction.


## DATA ARE TECHNOLOGY (AS WELL AS THEORY) LADEN

In this section, I focus on how video and audio records are used to capture stretches of doing, learning, and teaching. My point is only to show that inclusions/exclusions of what is "primary" about the resulting data follow directly from technical and theoretical expectations about what a record of these activities should look like. These expectations create data that are both technology and theory laden. In a later section, I consider what happens when these records "travel" outside the contexts of use in which they are collected.

### Technology and Research Practices

There is a widespread though controversial belief in the human sciences that new technologies shape the specific cultural practices we call human thinking (Eisenstein, 1979; Goody, 1977, 1987; Latour, 1986; Olson, 1994; Street, 1984; Tulviste, 1991). Given this family of conjectures, we might learn something by applying the same logic of development to the specific cultural practices we call cognitive and educational research.

To what extent do technologies for getting access to phenomena of human action matter when doing research? For example, without the widespread availability of audiotape recording and playback machines, two of the most radical innovations in close studies of human action would be completely unworkable: studies of thinking as symbolic information processing using verbal protocol analysis (Ericsson & H. A. Simon, 1984) and studies of the social order using analyses of talk-in-interaction (Garfinkel, 1967; Sacks, 1992; Schegloff, 1984). Both are scientific movements that have reorganized how we think about thinking and human action. But, starting with a common (and apparently neutral) technology to capture people talking, they have created accounts of human action that may turn out to be incommensurable (Costall & Still, 1987; Coulter, 1991; Suchman, 1987; Vera & H. A. Simon, 1993).

By considering how new combinations of text, sound, image, and interactivity can be used to report research findings about learning and teaching, we raise an interesting methodological question. How should we expect new technical media for recording human action, along with a growing suite of tools for their analysis, to shape the specific cultural practices of cognitive and educational researchers?

The first five figures (and following sections) in this chapter examine different sorts of trouble that can arise when we treat videorecordings as objective or theory neutral data. Each shows a type of activity that is important in research on learning or teaching. These activities include: making inferences, solving problems, teaching, telling, and explaining that (with one exception) are drawn from my own work. The figures show scenes from these studies, collected in ways that make aspects of the phenomena of learning or teaching more or less visible. In each case, the technical arrangements for recording data reflect and help to reproduce specific cultural practices of analysis, inference, and publication in educational research.

Scenes on the left in each figure show a narrow framing of each activity (deleted), whereas scenes on the right show a wider framing (restored).[1] In each contrasting pair of scenes, my aim is to show that any activity of interest (e.g., solving problems) must be rendered in ways that selectively delete or foreground aspects of the original setting. This is not usually an oversight on the part of researchers (Star, 1983), but rather, is driven by technical arrangements for capturing human activity and by theoretical expectations about the boundaries of that activity. How one approaches the "primary data" in each case matters a great deal to what is later available for analysis.

---

[1] The contrasting terms, *deleted* and *restored*, reflect my own interests and assumptions as a researcher. Rather than masking these interests, I use material from my own research to show how different approaches to recording can give access to different kinds of phenomena.

Deleted                              Restored

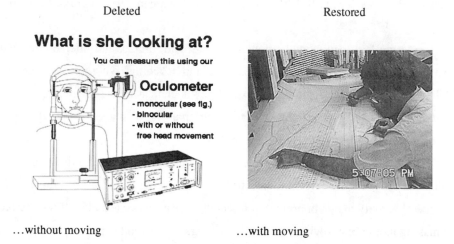

...without moving                    ...with moving

FIG. 22.1. Making inferences with and without moving.

## Thinking With and Without Moving

To the left in FIG. 22.1, a subject sits in an experimental device that records eye movements as she does things like make inferences during a reading comprehension task. In order for us to tell "What is she looking at?",[2] the subject in this situation needs to keep her body relatively still and attend to what she is shown. To the right in FIG. 22.1, two civil engineers lean into a table layered with what they call "paper space" views of a design project (Hall, 1994). Without getting their bodies into this position, they would have nothing coherent to look at or read, and so would have difficulty making inferences about their ongoing design problem. The activity that researchers hope to study across scenes in FIG. 22.1 might be the same (e.g., making inferences about complex informational displays), but in one approach the body and task are immobilized to get at inference, whereas in the other, inferences and tasks appear only when people and materials move around in coordinated ways.

---

[2] This image comes from an advertisement in the *Proceedings of the Fourth European Conference on Eye Movements* (Luer & Lass, 1987, p. 398). It is the only graphical rendering of an intact person I could find in the entire conference proceedings. The few graphical images used to report research results showed an eyeball in plan view, oriented toward a fixed, planar display for a researcher-presented task.

This is an extreme contrast, but it is a good place to start thinking about how technologies for recording primary data can influence the phenomena being studied. Though studies that use eye movements to make inferences about attention and the contents of working memory can tell us very subtle things about how people use text and graphics while working on experimental tasks (e.g., Hegarty, 1992, reported that subjects "animate" connected parts of mechanical displays while trying to explain how they work), these technical arrangements for recording data strip away many of the resources that people have in situations where they find and solve complex problems. These resources include other people, changes in perspective made possible by reorienting one's body and/or the representational forms in use, and use of one's own and others' hands to assemble and index parts of the forms displayed.

In the studies I have been doing of "math at work" (Hall & R. Stevens, 1995, 1996; R. Stevens & Hall, in press), these resources appear to be necessary for people to get their work done, to teach, and to learn. Briefly, our approach (see also C. Goodwin, 1993; Hutchins, 1995) has been to gain access to ongoing work activities, to film a "wide" view of activity with a stationary camera that can be operated by remote control, to use hand-held cameras with a steady cam feature to "follow" detailed work with representational forms, and to locate wireless audio microphones on people and in places where we have found that talk routinely occurs. By starting with multiple video and audio perspectives on activities that occur naturally in the workplace, we can do work at a theoretical level that stretches cognition (e.g., inference, calculation, teaching, learning) over people, things, and space in new and interesting ways (Lave, 1988). Again, the point here is simply that our technical arrangements for collecting primary data greatly influence the kinds of inferences we will be able to make later.

Deleted                                                        Restored

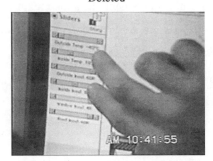

...without heads or bodies (primal screen          ...with moving (people in action)
scene)

FIG. 22.2. Solving problems with and without heads or bodies.

## Solving Problems With/Without Whole People

FIG. 22.2 shows two scenes from studies of design "problem solving" in elementary and middle school mathematics (Berg, Chiu, & Hall, 1994; Goldman, 1994; Goldman, Moschkovich, & The Middle School Mathematics Through Applications Project, 1995; Hall, 1995). In the first scene, hands are busy at the computer screen of a prototype software environment. With the computer in full frame, we can recover relatively little about whose hands are in play, how this activity at the interface got organized, or where it is going. The second scene shows a combined perspective on these same people and their activities. At the lower right, a picture-in-picture image shows a group of students and their teacher clustered around a computer. Using a digital mixing board, this wide perspective on their activity can be inserted and moved around inside a simultaneously recorded image that follows the details of work at the interface. Using the combined images, for example, we might find that a student has been systematically "carpentered" (R. P. McDermott, Gospodinoff, & Aron, 1978) out of access to a design-in-progress at the computer screen. Both scenes are records of problem-solving activity, but each gives a different sense of who is solving what problems. From the first to the second scene, what gets restored is the people who are manipulating objects on the screen (or not) and the way in which they are organizing their attempt to find a solution.

I have come to think of the leftmost video record as a "primal screen scene," because it closely reflects the interests of an interface designer (myself, along with others, at the time) in how interface objects are being used by children who are (we hope) learning and solving problems as they design things. A stationary camera sits above and behind a group working at the computer, and a single wireless microphone is taped to the side of the computer display. As a recording of action at an interface, this technical arrangement has a nice feature: We can see which objects people are pointing at as they speak, so we have a chance to recover the meaning of indexical talk[3] like, "No! Move *that* over *there*!" This would not be true of a

---

[3] Indexicality refers to the way utterances depend on their context for meaning and the fact that the meaning of words can shift as the context changes (Duranti & C. Goodwin, 1992; Hanks, 1996). It is important to realize that this is a *commonplace* feature of language use in multiparty interaction,

(continued)

record of the screen recorded by taking the video signal directly from the back of the computer display (a number of companies sell devices for doing this) or by replaying a "dribble file" that records a chronologically ordered sequence of interface events. Ironically, taking only a wide view of this interaction would show us that people are pointing at or animating objects on the screen, but we could not tell which objects were in play or what their important features were. So *both* wide and follow perspectives are necessary for understanding what people are doing in this case.

Deleted                                    Restored

...from a head with no bodies  (teacher as     ...between heads and bodies  (teaching
exhibit)                                       dioramas)

FIG. 22.3. Teaching with and without acting or listening.

## Teaching With and Without Acting or Listening

FIG. 22.3 shows two different approaches to capturing "teaching" in a middle school mathematics classroom. In the first scene, the camera frames a conventional view of teaching as talking to students, so we get a talking head without bodies and utterances without hearers. In the second scene, collected in the same classroom after thinking a little harder about the routine structure of teaching interventions, we get a frame that includes more aspects of teaching as an activity done in interaction with learners. The teacher stops in at a local group,

---

including situations where people have shared access to physical or computational artifacts (e.g., a graphical user interface). Goodwin and Goodwin (1996) described this particular kind of indexical talk as "articulating the surface" of complex representational displays.

and (most of) the participants lean in to have a conversation about the day's activity. From the first to the second scene, what gets restored is the teacher's activity and in progress relations with the students she teaches. If we thought of these two scenes as the construction of museum exhibits (i.e., images that we and our readers would later take to be representative of something), the first treats the teacher herself as the exhibit whereas the second frames the teacher's interactions with local groups as a collection of dioramas[4] that unfold over time.

Thus far we have another, relatively simple story about trying to include more of what people are doing in the records that we collect to study them. It is important to point out two things, however. First, one does not get a usable "teaching diorama" by recording a fixed, wide-angle view of an entire classroom with an open audio source. Instead, the scene shown to the right in FIG. 22.3 was recorded with a stationary camera that was operated (i.e., panning and zooming) by a person whose sole job it was to follow teaching events. The teacher wore a wireless lapel microphone, clipped at the middle of her blouse so that it would pick up local student voices without being drowned out by her own talk. As the record was made, the camera operator wore headphones that shut out ambient noise in the rest of the classroom, allowing him (me, in this case) to follow the teacher's local conversations with students quite closely. Second, by combining a record of these teaching dioramas with focused records of group work like those described in the preceding section, it is possible to treat classroom videography as a sampling scheme that weaves together the multiple, local perspectives of teachers and students as they work together across settings. This is a labor- and equipment-intensive approach,[5] of course, but it has the nice feature that subsequent

---

[4]In *Scenes from Deep Time: Early Pictorial Representations of the Prehistoric World,* Martin Rudwick (1992) analyzed the history of different technical approaches to constructing museum exhibits that were intended to "show" Cretaceous life in paleontology. His point, and the point of comparing "teachers as exhibits" with "teaching dioramas," is that the ways in which we frame actors (whether dinosaurs, students, or teachers) has a great deal to do with how we then come to see and understand their activity.

[5]In this case, three cameras and two or more microphones would be required: (a) one camera and one microphone to follow the teacher and (b) two cameras and one or more microphones to follow the local work of a group. For a less equipment-intensive alternative, see Stigler's (1995) approach to capturing the perspective of an "ideal" student as part of the Third International Mathematics and Science Study.

(continued)

analyses can question relations between students' perspectives on instruction and those of the teacher, between the curriculum as taught and the curriculum as enacted by students, etc. In addition, if the teacher visits most of the groups in a classroom, a record of teaching dioramas will also be a record, at some level of granularity, of what these groups are doing.

Deleted                                                    Restored

...without asking  (semi-structured          ...with asking, showing, and negotiated
interview)                                                  understanding  (participatory design)

FIG. 22.4. Telling with and without asking.

## Telling With and Without Asking or Interacting

In FIG. 22.4, two interview records taken with teachers are shown (Hall, Knudsen, & Greeno, 1996). In the first, we see only the "respondent" (a teacher) telling about her work without any evident access to an interviewer. That is, the teacher (it could be anyone in a typical, semistructured interview) is technically framed as a respondent: She tells us things when asked, she asks relatively few questions of her own, and we can see nothing of the interactional work of the interviewer in the resulting record. In the second scene, the same teacher (and a coworker) sit at a table with a group of researchers. Everyone is talking, not

---

Using a single camera and (I presume) an audio source attached to the teacher, camera operators were trained to "point the camera toward that which should be the focus of the ideal student at any given time" and to "be certain to capture everything that the teacher is doing to instruct the class" (p. 15). It is probably the case that stronger theoretical commitments allow one to record less, rather than more. In any case, you get what you invest in (i.e., investing in operator time, in equipment, and in later indexing and analysis of the resulting records).

only to each other, but also about records of interaction drawn from these teachers' classrooms. From the first to the second scene, what is restored is the relation between research participants (teachers), people doing the research (us), inspectable records of the phenomena up for discussion (e.g., students working on a design problem), and the negotiated character of arriving at an analysis of those records.

This comparison shifts our attention from collecting video records of people doing things (e.g., using a computer to solve a problem or teaching) to collecting records of people telling us about what they do. Interviewing people raises all the usual problems of distinguishing what they say from what they actually do (H. S. Becker & Geer, 1969; B. Jordan & Henderson, 1995), but my point here is that technical and organizational arrangements for "telling" make a difference in sorting these things out. First, as is shown in the scene to the right in FIG. 22.4, we can ask people questions in the context of prior records of what they and others have actually been doing together. How selected aspects of a prior video record can be used in an interview is a complex issue. In the scene to the right, for example, video excerpts of local student work were selected both by teachers and academic researchers, and the contrasts between what we selected turned out to be interesting for our attempts at a joint analysis of how assessment systems operate in elementary school mathematics classrooms. With these records in view, however, telling about what happened is held accountable to aspects of what did happen, at least as these happenings were captured in the video record and to the extent that discussions systematically revisit this record of interaction.[6] Second, and as implied already by this example, one can invite the people usually treated as respondents to participate in the analysis. In this case, we were working over the summer with a fifth- and sixth-grade teacher, using video records we had recorded in their classrooms during the preceding school year. We framed the collaboration as an instance of the "participatory

---

[6] This is a crowning feature of video-based interaction analysis (B. Jordan & Henderson, 1995), where the video record up for discussion is played until someone asks to "stop" (technically, to "pause") and discuss something they have seen. The discipline of returning to the tape, ironically, is supported by a feature of consumer video playback mechanisms: They resume play after they have been placed on "pause" for more than several minutes, so analysts' tendencies to pontificate are faithfully interrupted by automatic resumption of the video record.

design" (Schuler & Namioka, 1993; Suchman & Trigg, 1991a) of assessment systems, with the intention of designing and field testing new forms of assessment in their classrooms the following year.

Deleted

Restored

 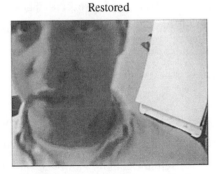

...without seeing  (observer perspective)     ...with seeing  (participant perspective)

FIG. 22.5. Explaining with and without seeing.

## Explaining With and Without Seeing

In FIG. 22.5, we see two different perspectives on a single explanation for why rates can be added together in a difficult algebra problem (Hall, 1996). In the first scene (an observer perspective), two teachers meet in a simulated act of collision, while one of them narrates a simple explanation for why combining rates would mean that two drivers are "goin' faster." In the second scene (a participant perspective), recorded later with the original explainer (wearing a plaid shirt in the first scene), we see a re-creation of the simulated collision that was filmed to examine the recipient's experience during this explanation. To do this, I carried a camera and acted like the recipient (i.e., followed instructions, marched toward the explainer, and eventually collided with him), while the original explainer read from a transcript of his earlier directives and explanatory comments. What gets restored from the first to the second scene is the fact that both of these teachers (i.e., participants in this situation) had an experience that we (i.e., observers of the situation) did not have and might easily have overlooked.

This kind of constructed video record helps raise some important questions about what we count as primary data in research on teaching and learning. First, it helps us to see that every type of video record described in this chapter encodes a particular perspective on ongoing human activity. What is more, in almost every one of these cases, the perspective that goes "on the record" is one that no participant in the recorded activity could have had. If nothing else, this should encourage us to think carefully about claims that videotape provides "objective" or "realistic" records of human action.[7]

Second, this case should help us to see that video records of human activity are weak in some ways and privileged in others. They are weak in that they systematically miss the experience of participants in the events being recorded, putting us as observers into the seemingly inescapable situation of always being perpendicular to the action. But video records are also privileged because they give us, as observers to the action, access to things that participants either miss or cannot do. That is, video records are plastic in ways that real-time experience is not: we can slow down a videotape, we can watch multiparty interactions repeatedly, we can make video and audio recordings that contain more or different things than any single participant could see or hear, and we can hold our judgments about the actions of participants in the record accountable to other observers.

## Summary and a Note About Production Values

Across these brief comparisons, I have argued that technical arrangements for collecting video records can:

- Reorganize the tasks and experiences of research participants.
- Serve different research interests by selectively attending to different aspects of human activity.
- Reinforce or break open traditional boundaries between researchers and their study participants.
- Provide both limited and privileged access to aspects of human interaction.

Across different types of activity in learning and teaching, the way technology is used to capture primary data and our expectations about what these data need to show create records of phenomena that are both technology and theory laden. Primary data are technology laden in the sense that video and audio devices are deployed to record human activity in ways that

---

[7]C. Goodwin (1994) gave an extended discussion of how the same videotape can be used to "see" entirely different things, contrasting expert legal testimony given in the trial of Los Angeles police officers accused of beating an African American motorist (Rodney King).

make selections from ongoing interaction. Primary data are also theory laden in the sense that theoretical interests focus researchers on which parts of ongoing interaction are relevant, reliable, or usable given existing methods of analysis. Technical and theoretical constraints drive toward creating data records that show just those parts of interaction we already find interesting and little more. Although they can always be questioned, the boundaries of phenomena in research on learning and teaching are largely fixed at the time primary data are constructed.

Before closing this section, it is important to consider what production values we expect of video recordings, given that most of us have grown up with television and commercial film. By production values, I mean the way we judge the quality of a filmed record of human activity (e.g., Is it well lit? Can we hear it? Is there too much or too little activity? Are we close enough or too close to the action? Can we follow what people are saying?) and the way that these judgments have a tendency to creep into both what we choose to record and how we watch it. These values are implicit but pervasive. For example, up until the last several years, almost no one seen on television was ever shown watching television (Ehrenreich, 1988). It was, ironically, as if the fictional worlds we most wanted to watch were places where everyone had something better to do than waste their time watching television. As another example (also something that has started to change recently), we rarely see any embedded evidence that television or movie images have been constructed (e.g., images of recording equipment, rapid panning or zooming, etc.), as if the viewer had unmediated access to the events unfolding on film. We should be careful about how our expectations of film records of activity, shaped in these other genre, come into play when we construct and analyze records of learning and teaching.

## A TERRAIN FOR (THINKING ABOUT) USING VIDEOTAPE

Most of the research projects that I work on are supported with public funds, so the data we collect in those projects could be considered a public resource. This is true both in the traditional sense of academics making their data available to one another for peer review and purposes of replication, but also in the sense that resources produced with public funds should be available to the public that underwrites them. This second sense of research as a public good is particularly important when the development of curricula, assessments, or software is part of the funded activity. What parts of a research project should be a public resource, and for what purposes, are deeply contested questions.

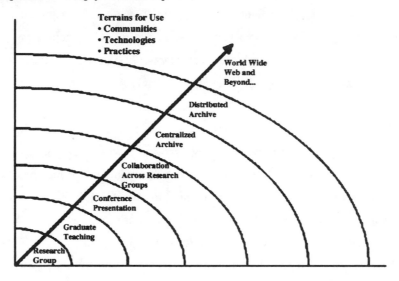

FIG. 22.6. A terrain showing contexts of use that are increasingly distant (and unpredictable) from a research project that produces video records.

FIG. 22.6 shows one way to think about records of primary data as public resources by following them as they travel inside and outside the research projects where they are collected and used.[8] The terrain for use is organized in concentric circles to show that, as one moves outward, the types of use (and users) expand, whereas the amount of information available about the actual activities of participants in a project usually contracts. Places in this terrain consist of user communities, their practices for manipulating and interpreting video records, and the technologies that (in some cases) support these practices. The cast is plural at each level out from the center, so the terrain is complicated. A small move across a boundary can bring about a very large change in the hypothetical (or actual) scenario of use.

---

[8] This view was constructed jointly by a subgroup discussing ethical uses of field data at a 1995 National Design Experiments Consortium meeting. The group included Maryl Gearhart, Janet Schofeld, Raul Zaritsky, Tammy Berman, and Eric Baumgarten. They should not, of course, be held responsible for what I have to say here.

In the previous section, I argued that collections of primary data about learning and teaching necessarily reflect deletions (or selections) brought on by technical arrangements and theoretical interests. Here, the question is: What happens when these constructed records move out from the communities that have collected them? We should immediately recognize this as a volatile mix—more people looking, with varied and unpredictable purposes, with less surrounding material to inform what they might find. The mix is particularly volatile when we talk about something as value laden as the reorganization of public schooling.

I visit three places across this terrain briefly:

- Use of primary data records within a research project.
- Using these records in a conference setting.
- Using these records to illustrate research issues and analytic categories in a public forum like the World Wide Web.

At each stop, I focus on what "informed consent" given by study participants might mean, and how new technical arrangements for recording and reporting the phenomena of learning and teaching create possible problems.

## Trouble/Heterogeneity at Home

At the center of the terrain are research or development projects that collect, analyze, and preserve the kinds of primary data contrasted in the preceding section. Even within research projects, interests and commitments are heterogeneous. This is particularly true of research projects that seek the active participation of teachers and learners in developing, documenting, or analyzing instructional interventions. As these projects mature, the people who show up in the records treated as data are still present and sometimes are actively involved in the analysis of those data, in resulting design decisions, and in report writing. In this context for use, informed consent obtained at the outset of a project can be challenged by these (traditionally absent) participants. One response is to hold the ongoing analysis accountable to the concerns of study participants who live in both worlds (observed and observer), treating their views of the data and its interpretation as privileged accounts. Another response is to give study participants the right to selectively withdraw their consent as research subjects when their informed views of use change (e.g., to remove records that include them from a corpus under study), yet still to continue collaborating in other ways with the research project.

## Trouble/Heterogeneity in the Research Community

As records of primary data travel into the research community, we need to make decisions about:

- What records to choose.
- How to provide surrounding context for these records so that they can be used in the ways we expect.
- How to limit or respond to unanticipated uses effectively.

Particularly with video records of teaching, the range of responses one gets at a public meeting seems to be enormous.[9] What one person sees as an artful interaction between a teacher and a student, another person takes as the basis for confirming generalizations about all of their worst experiences in public school. Under these circumstances, informed consent, taken at the outset of a study or renegotiated as that study unfolds, is probably inadequate to deal with challenges to reasonable use that arise outside a research project. One response is to obtain signed, restrictive agreements with viewers or users of video records in addition to releases from study participants.

## Trouble/Heterogeneity Online

Perhaps all bets are off when records of primary data are allowed to circulate freely around the Internet, as are the text and still images in this chapter.[10] In the worst-case scenario, we should expect these records to be repurposed in ways that undermine the entire research undertaking, regardless of the kind of surrounding details we attach to the records. In the average case, particularly if "reality close" media (e.g., image and sound) are included as data to illustrate research settings or analytic categories, it is likely that only people who are already interested in these issues will seek out and use these illustrations. But informed consent and the ethical treatment of research participants isn't decided on the average. Copyright protections are often suggested as a solution to this problem. But in this context of use, if we consider the expense of pursuing cases of infringement, legal protections like

---

[9] Wendy Mackay (1994) described a variety of similarly challenging situations that appear regularly among researchers in human computer interaction.

[10] A draft of this chapter (along with others in this volume) was available through a password-protected Web site for a graduate course on research methods, organized by Dick Lesh at Purdue University.

copyright are probably more about protecting the rights and limiting the liabilities of research institutions and authors than they are about protecting research participants.

## DISCUSSION

In this chapter, I have examined and then combined two issues. The first is how we should think about records of primary data we collect in research on learning and teaching. Most of us would agree that what we take as data are strongly theory laden, although the ways in which recording technologies implement these theories may be less obvious. New media for recording, analyzing, and reporting primary data necessarily delete or reorganize aspects of the original phenomena, even as they add new dimensions to what we can learn about human activity. I say this as a caution against taking these new media as being relatively complete, direct, or veridical.

The second issue carries this caution into the wider question raised by research that seeks to reform or reorganize public schooling: How can new technical arrangements for collecting, analyzing, and reporting research on teaching and learning be managed in ways that:

- Support collaboration across research projects.
- Convey vivid illustrations of complex instructional interventions to widely different audiences.
- Protect the rights and privacy of a heterogeneous group of study participants.

I have argued that our conventional understanding of informed consent breaks down as primary data move across wider contexts of use. One reason for this breakdown is that we cannot yet anticipate how different communities, technologies, and practices will take up and use these records. We need new practices as much as we need new media for doing and talking about research on learning and teaching.

## ACKNOWLEDGMENTS

An early version of this chapter was given at a symposium on "A Discussion of the 'Multimedia Journal Article' Format as a Technology for Reporting Research and Evaluation Projects" at the annual meeting of the American Educational Research Association (San Francisco, 1995). I would like to thank members of that panel, particularly Lawrence Erlbaum and Jan Hawkins, for helpful conversations about these ideas. I also would like to thank Michael Sipusic and Jeremy Roschelle for more general discussions about using videotape in educational research. The title and focus of this chapter borrows from Elinor Ochs' account of transcription as theory (Ochs, 1979). Support for this work came from a National Academy of Education/Spencer Foundation Postdoctoral Fellowship and a National Science Foundation grant (ESI-94552771) to the Math@Work Project conducted at the University of California, Berkeley.

# 23 Iterative Refinement Cycles for Videotape Analyses of Conceptual Change

**Richard Lesh**
*Purdue University*

**Richard Lehrer**
*University of Wisconsin–Madison*

Note: Before reading this chapter on iterative videotape analyses, readers may find it useful to read the transcript that is given in the Appendix to the chapter. The transcript is one of those that is referred to in the chapter; and, many of the chapter's main points make reference to it.   In this regard, the following comments are especially relevant:

- The students' goal for this problem solving session was to produce a description of the information that was given; and, the purpose of this description was to enable the students to rank workers whose summer jobs involved selling things in a park.

- The students' initial way of thinking about the information was quite barren and distorted; that is, they neglected to notice a great deal of relevant information, and, at the same time, they made assumptions that were not valid.

- To gradually arrive at a final way of thinking about the situation, the students went through a series of modeling cycles in which they interpreted givens and the goals in systematically different ways that focused on different facts, quantities, relationships, and patterns.

- The researchers' goals were to produce a description of how the students' ways of thinking evolved during the problem solving session. Consequently, the researchers also arrived at a final interpretation of the session by going through a series of modeling cycles in which their early ways of thinking were remarkably barren and distorted compared with those that evolved later.

The following issues are useful to think about when reading the transcript. What do you think was the researcher's perceived purpose for the description that he was generating? Is it likely that another purpose or another perspective might have emphasized different principles for selecting and organizing information, or for interpreting their significance? In what ways did the researchers test the usefulness of alternative interpretations? What methods did they use to determine whether a given interpretation needed to be refined, modified, or extended? If the researchers undertook the job of producing a movie to convey to audiences what was going on in the problem solving session, do you think that the best kind of movie would consist of nothing more than the videotape of the session?

This chapter about iterative videotape analyses is a companion to two others in this book. The first is about model-eliciting activities (Lesh, Hoover, Hole, Kelly, & Post, chap. 21, this volume); and, the second is about multitiered teaching experiments (Lesh & Kelly, chap. 9, this volume). In general, all three chapters focus on research whose central purpose is to investigate the nature of the constructs that students (or teachers or groups) develop to make sense of a targeted class of problem solving or decision-making situations. Also, all three chapters emphasize research designs that are potentially *shareable*; that is, it is possible to coordinate the work of several researchers who are working at multiple sites using diverse practical or theoretical perspectives.

Whereas the chapter on model-eliciting activities (chap. 21, this volume) describes principles for *designing problem solving situations* in which observations are to be made, the chapter on multitiered teaching experiments (chap. 9, this volume) focuses on principles for designing the *data collection* stages of research, and this chapter on iterative videotape analyses focuses on the stages of research that involve *data analysis*. Also, the chapter on multitiered teaching experiments concentrates on studies in which conclusions based on today's sessions influence tomorrow's data collection activities; whereas, this chapter on iterative videotape analyses focuses on research settings in which the most significant stages of data collection must be completed before the most significant stages of data interpretation begin. Therefore, in this latter case, there exist no severe constraints on the turnaround times for data interpretation.

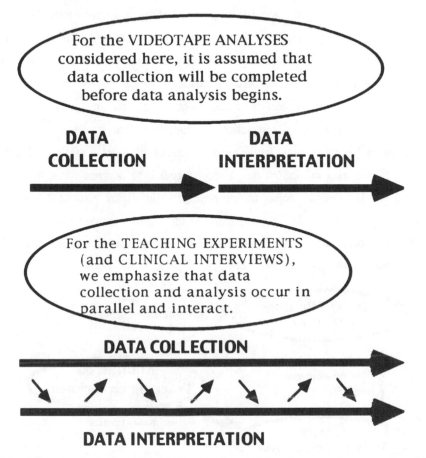

FIG. 23.1. Differences in timing of the data collection and data interpretation states for videotape analysis and teaching experiments.

FIG. 23.1 focuses on the procedures that are used to test, refine, and extend their interpretations of their data. It suggests one important way that videotape analyses sometimes need to be quite different depending on the types of context in which they occur. For example, an essential characteristic of many teaching experiments is that it is for each successive videotaped session to be designed partly to test the validity of researchers' interpretations of students' responses during similar sessions that occurred earlier. Therefore, an iterative series of hypothesis-testing or decision-making cycles may enable researchers to validate (test, refine, and extend) their own constructs gradually.[1]

In contrast to the preceding kinds of situations, an essential characteristic of many studies involving videotape analyses is that significant portions of the data interpretation stages of the project cannot begin until after many of the most significant data-gathering stages have been completed. Therefore, tentative interpretations of one videotaped session cannot influence the problems that students confront in succeeding videotaped sessions, and there may exist no effective ways for researchers to test their interpretations by making predictions from one episode to the next. Consequently, researchers' interpretations must be tested and refined in other ways. One goal of this chapter is to examine some of the most important of these other possible forms of construct validation; and, a second goal is to describe some ways that it is possible for a single research project to integrate procedures that associated with teaching experiments, clinical interviews, ethnographic observations, or videotape analyses. For example, FIG. 23.2 describes one way that iterative videotape analyses may be integrated with approaches to research that are emphasized in other chapters of this book.

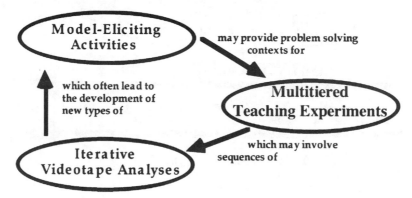

FIG. 23.2. Activity in one area of study often stimulates action in another area, and all of them can occur in the same study.

---

[1]Similarly, an essential characteristic of many clinical interviews is that researchers' interpretations of students' responses to one question often influence the next question that is

(continued)

Because the research design issues that we want to emphasize in this chapter are easier to describe in the context of specific studies, we'll refer to the problem solving session that's transcribed in the appendix to this chapter. It involves three-person teams of students who are working together on 60-minute "thought-revealing activities" of the type described in chapter 21 in this book. Nonetheless, the research design principles that are discussed are not restricted to this context; they are relevant to videotape analyses of a broad range of teaching and learning situations.[2]

## THE ROLE OF VIDEOTAPES DEPENDS ON OTHER APPROACHES USED WITH THEM

Sometimes, it is said that a researcher who is viewing videotapes may not see the forest because of the trees. Alternatively, if the researcher is too narrowly predisposed to view situations through one particular theoretical window, then other types of details or perspectives may be ignored systematically. For some of these kinds of prejudices, negative

---

asked. Again, a series of such questions provides a series of rapid hypothesis-testing and decision-making cycles in which researchers test, refine, and extend their own constructs gradually.

[2]Studies involving model-eliciting activities are of interest mainly because, in such problems, the objective for students is not merely to produce answers to questions in which the givens and goals are stated in a form that is intended to require little interpretation. Instead, when teams of students work on model-eliciting activities, a large part of their objective is to construct an explicit mathematical interpretation (description, explanation, and justification) that typically must go through several refinement cycles in which trial constructs are tested, revised, and improved repeatedly for a given purpose. Therefore, because constructs and thought processes are externalized and made explicit, students tend to reveal the nature of their mathematical constructs in a straightforward manner. Videotapes of such sessions often provide direct evidence about the nature of the constructs that students use as well as the mechanisms that contribute to the development of those constructs.

effects can be minimized if videotape analyses occur in research designs that also include ethnographic observations, clinical interviews, teaching experiments, and other methods of data collection and/or data analysis. Furthermore, the roles that videotaping is expected to play depends partly on the strengths and weaknesses of the other approaches that are employed. By seeking agreement among the interpretations that are generated from these alternative approaches, it sometimes is possible to avoid biases that would result if only a single method were used. For example:

- *Videotaping may be part of a strategy to focus on perspectives or details whose significance can be anticipated.* Suppose that videotape analyses are used in conjunction with ethnographic observations of complex situations in which the range of possible responses cannot be anticipated. In such situations, it often is wise for the attention of an on-the-scene observer to be free to adjust to circumstances, to focus attention here or there as needs arise, and to zoom in and out in ways that are judged appropriate. But, in such circumstances, even though the collection and coding of data cannot be reduced to an algorithm, it is nonetheless important for the holistic judgments of experts to be governed by ground rules that enable later judgments to be made about why one type of information was emphasized and another type was ignored. Also, in such circumstances, videotapes may be useful to provide stable and unchanging perspectives that focus on aspects of the situation that can be predicted to be important (such as particular details or particular points of view). For instance, in group problem solving activities, one preplanned videorecording may focus on a close-up view of individual students' desktop work, whereas another may focus on body language and other factors for the group as a whole. In this manner, alternative "windows on reality" may enable several diverse perspectives to be juxtaposed for easy comparison during after-the-fact analyses.

- *Videotaping may be part of a strategy to broaden perspectives or details beyond those whose significance can be anticipated.* For instance, suppose that videotape analyses are used in conjunction with clinical interviews  in which carefully preplanned and highly structured sequences of standardized questions are used. In such circumstances, videotapes may enable a variety of unforeseen factors to be recorded and considered that might not have been recognized otherwise. For example, videotapes of children's faces frequently provide clear evidence about the importance of certain aspects of their responses, even in cases where these factors were not anticipated in preplanned questioning and recording schemes.

From the point of view of research design, one danger with either of the preceding focusing or broadening strategies is that it is easy for researchers to imagine that videotapes represent complete and unbiased recordings of everything that occurred during given sessions. The truth is otherwise. Every time a videocamera focuses on one thing, it tends to de-emphasize or ignore something else, and, in general, videotapes are poorly suited to record certain types of information. For example, when three-person teams of students are engaged in 60-minute group problem solving sessions, experience shows that an on-the-scene human observer almost always notices some things (such as an uncomfortable temperature in the room or tension among members of the group) that may not be apparent in the videotapes of the session. Conversely, even when on-the-scene experts are available during videotaped sessions, they nearly always fail to notice some things that are recognized later to be very significant in the videotapes of the same sessions (perhaps because the significance of an event is not clear until its consequences are apparent). The problem of judging importance becomes even more complex for long-term studies of conceptual change. This is partly due to the difficulty of judging the significance of an event until its consequences become clear, as they unfold and emerge over time. Therefore, as information emerges about the history that is relevant to a given classroom activity, video backtracking may play an important role in establishing an adequate framework for interpretation.

Sometimes, a picture is worth a thousand words; and a moving picture sometimes has the power to reveal patterns that would not be apparent in the snapshots that they contain. For instance, videotapes often make it possible to observe changes across time (by enabling researchers to go back and forth among related segments, even in cases where the relatedness could not have been apparent to on-the-scene observers). Also, videotapes sometimes offer the possibility of viewing segments multiple times from multiple perspectives, as well as the possibility of juxtaposing segments that occur at different times (so that patterns, regularities, or trends may become apparent that would tend to be overlooked if only isolated sessions were viewed). However, even though videotapes sometimes approach the ideal of preserving raw data so that it can be analyzed multiple times from multiple perspectives, it also is true that some data interpretation always occurs each time that information is filtered, selected, simplified, or organized. Consequently, when information is filtered out and noncontiguous segments are juxtaposed, the rationales that are used to make selections, deletions, or comparisons should be explained. There is a need to make explicit the interpretation framework that is used to fill in gaps or to focus on potential relationships in the filtered data. Otherwise, concealed biases are inevitable.

To accomplish the preceding goals in a given investigation, one important step is to specify which purposes and functions videotape analyses are intended to fill. Then, steps should be taken to address these functions. For example, simply because multiple viewing is possible does not ensure that it will take place; and, simply because videotape analyses make it possible for subsequent examinations to reveal diverse and unforeseen factors in students' complex performances sometimes, this does not eliminate the need for careful preplanning.

To identify several types of preplanning that are needed in the case of videotape analyses, consider the kind of videotaping that is used habitually in assessments of preservice teachers' undergraduate, student-teaching assignments. In such settings, the following issues arise commonly:

- Which episodes should be recorded? For example, the characterization that emerges of a given teacher's abilities often depends on whether the videotaped episodes emphasize only (i) teacher-centered lectures (in which the goal may be for students to try to follow the teacher's thinking) or (ii) student-centered discussions (in which the goal may be for the teachers to follow the students' thinking).

- What perspective(s) or viewpoints should be emphasized? For example, a bird's-eye view of a classroom situation often provides very different information than a teacher's-eye view (or a given student's-eye view) of the same situation.

- Which details should be emphasized in any given perspective? For example, a video segment in which the teacher is not visible may provide information about teaching ability that is more revealing than a video segment in which the teacher is the center of attention.

- What "grain size" or unit of analysis is most useful for seeing patterns and regularities that underlie discrete pieces of information? For example, when a video segment "zooms in" on one student who is being "turned on" during a given student–teacher interaction, it may neglect to notice that 29 other students are being "turned off" by the same interaction.

By considering the preceding kinds of issues, it is clear that, to formulate the design component of a research proposal, it is not enough merely to state that an investigation will involve videotape analyses (or clinical interviews or ethnographic observations) of a particular type of situation. Furthermore, issues of validity, reliability, and generalizability do not disappear because qualitative analysis procedures are used. For example, the meaning of a given videotaped session often depends on other sessions that surround it. In this context, the following questions need to be answered:

- How typical is a session that is chosen for special attention?
- How is one session influenced by experiences in earlier sessions?
- What aspects of an isolated session only become significant in the light of sessions that followed?

Unless answers are available to these kinds of questions, analyses of isolated sessions often are misleading. Furthermore, this may be true regardless of how thoroughly and conscientiously isolated videotapes are analyzed as independent entities.

## SOME ISSUES TO CONSIDER TO IMPROVE THE QUALITY OF VIDEOTAPE ANALYSES

At their worst, proposals to conduct videotape analyses sometimes are accused of being "trust me" studies, with little effort made to assure reliability and validity. The claim that video vignettes "speak for themselves" is often given as a justification for such approaches. But, the apparent ability of video vignettes to speak for themselves tends to be an illusion; video draws its power from the interpretive framework established by researchers. In particular, researchers may find it useful to consider the following questions.

- What steps were taken to ensure that videotaped segments that are given special attention constitute a representative or unbiased sample?

- Did the researchers' interpretations go through any testing and revision cycles? If so, what types of tests were used?

- What refinement cycles were used to filter, select, weigh, organize, and code the data that were collected?

- What cross-checking or triangulation techniques were used to ensure that information from alternative viewpoints fit together to produce stable and consistent interpretations of results?

To capitalize on the potential strengths of videotape analyses, as well as to avoid their potential weaknesses, researchers should plan acceptable procedures to document and cross-check their responses to decision-making issues that arise during data collection and data interpretation. Yet, because the transcription and analysis of videotapes are expensive and time consuming, many projects end up collecting far too many videotapes and spending far too little time interpreting the data they yield. The result is that the ratio of videotaping hours to video-analysis hours becomes many-to-one rather than one-to-many, and the lure of capturing the ultimate video clip sometimes seems to become a fever for researchers that is similar to the lure of gold in the Klondike. Therefore, the next section of this chapter describes some specific techniques to avoid such occurrences.

## PROCEDURES FOR TESTING, REFINING, AND EXTENDING INTERPRETATIONS OF VIDEOTAPES

To describe appropriate procedures for testing, refining, and extending interpretations of videotaped research sessions, it is useful to focus on a particular example, and it is useful for this example to be a typical project that involves most of the types of procedures that we want to discuss. However, whenever a particular case is given special attention, it is important to emphasize that this does not imply that the underlying issues and procedures could not have been handled in other ways. On the contrary, nearly always a variety of options is available.

The study described next lasted for an entire semester (10 to 16 weeks); the participants included an entire classroom of 24 to 30 students; and, the videotaped sessions involved 60-minute problem solving sessions in which the students worked in three-person groups that had access to the appropriate tools and resources. This study is typical in the sense that it involves many of the kinds of issues that arise frequently in mathematics and science education research. But, it is not typical in the sense that support from the National Science Foundation made it possible to involve a larger number of levels and types of interacting research staff members than are available in most published studies of mathematics and science education (Lesh, 1979). Table 23.1. illustrates a typical scheme for collecting data within such studies.

TABLE 23.1

A Typical Sixteen-Week Study Involving Eight, Three-Person Groups of Students and Eight Pairs of Problem Solving Situations ($A_1$-$A_2$, $B_1$-$B_2$, ..., $H_1$-$H_2$)

| | Wk 1 | Wk 2 | Wk 3 | Wk 4 | Wk 5 | Wk 6 | Wk 7 | Wk 8 | Wk 9 | Wk 10 | Wk 11 | Wk 12 | Wk 13 | Wk 14 | Wk 15 | Wk 16 |
|---|---|---|---|---|---|---|---|---|---|---|---|---|---|---|---|---|
| Group I | Prob $A_1$ | Prob $B_1$ | Prob $C_1$ | Prob $D_1$ | Prob $E_1$ | Prob $F_1$ | Prob $G_1$ | Prob $H_1$ | Prob $A_2$ | Prob $B_2$ | Prob $C_1$ | Prob $D_2$ | Prob $E_1$ | Prob $F_1$ | Prob $G_2$ | Prob $H_2$ |
| Group II | Prob $A_1$ | Prob $B_1$ | Prob $C_1$ | Prob $D_1$ | Prob $E_1$ | Prob $F_1$ | Prob $G_1$ | Prob $H_1$ | Prob $A_2$ | Prob $B_2$ | Prob $C_1$ | Prob $D_2$ | Prob $E_1$ | Prob $F_1$ | Prob $G_2$ | Prob $H_2$ |
| Group III | Prob $A_1$ | Prob $B_1$ | Prob $C_1$ | Prob $D_1$ | Prob $E_1$ | Prob $F_1$ | Prob $G_1$ | Prob $H_1$ | Prob $A_2$ | Prob $B_2$ | Prob $C_1$ | Prob $D_2$ | Prob $E_1$ | Prob $F_1$ | Prob $G_2$ | Prob $H_2$ |
| Group IV | Prob $A_1$ | Prob $B_1$ | Prob $C_1$ | Prob $D_1$ | Prob $E_1$ | Prob $F_1$ | Prob $G_1$ | Prob $H_1$ | Prob $A_2$ | Prob $B_2$ | Prob $C_1$ | Prob $D_2$ | Prob $E_1$ | Prob $F_1$ | Prob $G_2$ | Prob $H_2$ |
| Group V | Prob $A_2$ | Prob $B_2$ | Prob $C_2$ | Prob $D_2$ | Prob $E_2$ | Prob $F_2$ | Prob $G_2$ | Prob $H_2$ | Prob $A_1$ | Prob $B_1$ | Prob $C_1$ | Prob $D_1$ | Prob $E_1$ | Prob $F_1$ | Prob $G_1$ | Prob $H_1$ |
| Group VI | Prob $A_2$ | Prob $B_2$ | Prob $C_2$ | Prob $D_2$ | Prob $E_2$ | Prob $F_2$ | Prob $G_2$ | Prob $H_2$ | Prob $A_1$ | Prob $B_1$ | Prob $C_1$ | Prob $D_1$ | Prob $E_1$ | Prob $F_1$ | Prob $G_1$ | Prob $H_1$ |
| Group VII | Prob $A_2$ | Prob $B_2$ | Prob $C_2$ | Prob $D_2$ | Prob $E_2$ | Prob $F_2$ | Prob $G_2$ | Prob $H_2$ | Prob $A_1$ | Prob $B_1$ | Prob $C_1$ | Prob $D_1$ | Prob $E_1$ | Prob $F_1$ | Prob $G_1$ | Prob $H_1$ |
| Group VIII | Prob $A_2$ | Prob $B_2$ | Prob $C_2$ | Prob $D_2$ | Prob $E_2$ | Prob $F_2$ | Prob $G_2$ | Prob $H_2$ | Prob $A_1$ | Prob $B_1$ | Prob $C_1$ | Prob $D_1$ | Prob $E_1$ | Prob $F_1$ | Prob $G_1$ | Prob $H_1$ |
| Substitute Groups | Prob $A_1$ | Prob $B_1$ | Prob $C_1$ | Prob $D_1$ | Prob $E_1$ | Prob $F_1$ | Prob $G_1$ | Prob $H_1$ | Prob $A_2$ | Prob $B_2$ | Prob $C_1$ | Prob $D_2$ | Prob $E_1$ | Prob $F_1$ | Prob $G_2$ | Prob $H_2$ |
| Substitute Groups | Prob $A_2$ | Prob $B_2$ | Prob $C_2$ | Prob $D_2$ | Prob $E_2$ | Prob $F_2$ | Prob $G_2$ | Prob $H_2$ | Prob $A_1$ | Prob $B_1$ | Prob $C_1$ | Prob $D_1$ | Prob $E_1$ | Prob $F_1$ | Prob $G_1$ | Prob $H_1$ |

In the study depicted in Table 23.1, it was possible to compare the behaviors of multiple groups students working on each of the problems: $A_1$, $B_1$, . . . , $H_1$; $A_2$, $B_2$, . . . , $H_2$). Furthermore, because several different teams of students worked on each problem, it also was possible to compare the behaviors of students who worked on a given problem at different times during the sixteen-week study; and, because the 16 problems consisted of 8 pairs of structurally similar problems,[3] and because the teams of students remained invariant over the entire 16-week study[4], it was possible to observe the development of groups across time.

Of course, in similar research investigations, more or fewer groups might have been involved; the study might have been conducted over a period of more or fewer weeks; the number of students in each group might have been more or fewer; and, other factors (such as the nature and length of the sessions that were videotaped) might have varied. But, for the purposes of this chapter, the basic structure of the study would remain essentially unchanged regardless of whether the episodes being videotaped consisted of clinical interviews involving individual students, problem solving sessions involving small groups of students, or teacher-led activities involving entire classrooms of students.

When planning a similar investigations, researchers must make choices about the following kinds of issues.

- *Practical* considerations involve the following kinds of issues. What is the purpose of the observations that are being made? For example, an on-the-scene observer might concentrate on collecting small scraps of paper, or on other physical or anecdotal evidence, that would be unlikely to be captured by other recording devices. An analysis of a typed transcript (which is based on a videotape) might focus on trends and patterns that are difficult to observe when videotapes are viewed sequentially. A meta-analysis might look for generalizations that occur in the behavior of a given group of students across a number of related videotaped sessions, or it might look for similarities and differences

---

[3] During a given session, half of the teams worked on one problem from the pair, and half of the teams worked on the other problem from the pair. Then, later in the project, each group worked on the problem that they had not addressed earlier.

[4] Students in the substitute groups were used to fill in for other students who might miss class because of illness or other reasons. Therefore, for the research design that is illustrated in Table 23.1, the 30 students were divided into 24 regular participants and 6 substitutes.

among the behaviors of several different groups across similar situations.

- *Physical* considerations involve the following kinds of issues. How many video cameras will be used? What will each camera focus on? For example, if small-group problem solving sessions are being videotaped, one camera might focus on students' desktop work and another on faces or gestures for the group as a whole. Still another perspective might be embodied in the notes of on-the-scene observers.

- *Theoretical* considerations involve the following kinds of issues. What kinds of entities or events and what kinds of relationships and patterns will be given special attention? For example, in a given physical perspective, a psychological perspective might concentrate on the changing roles of individuals within groups, a teaching perspective might converge on facts and skills that promote or inhibit progress, and a problem solving perspective might highlight the representational issues or the modeling cycles that students go though during the solution of given problems.

- *Temporal* considerations involve the following kinds of issues. What counts as an episode? A lesson? What is the period of time that is of interest? If the point of the analysis is to understand the evolution of students' epistemology or significant changes in ontological structure, then often a long time span is indicated. If, however, the interest is in characterizing local conceptual development, especially changes in strategies or slight revisions in models, then the sampling of episodes important for understanding change may be from minute to minute or problem to problem (e.g., Siegler & Jenkins, 1989).

As FIG. 23.3 suggests, it is productive to analyze videotapes from multiple standpoints such as: theoretical, physical, and practical. Usually, each perspective yields somewhat different information. Therefore, a primary way to test and refine interpretations is to go through a series of triangulation and consensus-building cycles so that descriptions based on multiple viewpoints can be compared to identify points of agreement and disagreement, and efforts can be made to reach a stable consensus.

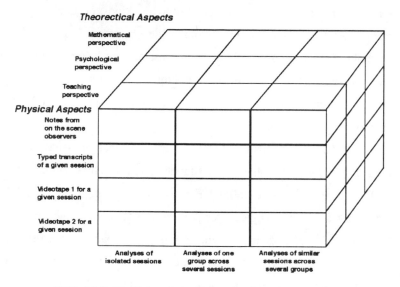

FIG. 23.3. Multiple windows for viewing given sessions.

To implement a scheme similar to the one described in Figure 23.3, it often is useful to use a series of telescoping analyses that begin by giving equal attention to all of the sessions (using procedures that are necessarily more superficial and less time consuming) and that end by focusing on deeper and more time consuming analyses of a relatively small number of specially selected sessions (whose criteria for selection and weighting are specified clearly and whose representativeness is described in an organizational scheme that is identified clearly also). Or, in general:

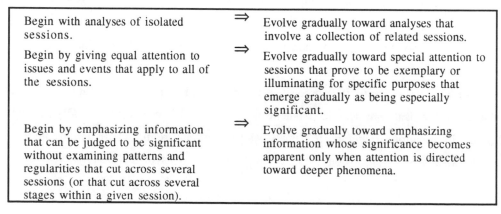

To conduct the preceding type of telescoping analyses within a 16-week study similar to the one described at the beginning of this section, the following interpretation cycles can be expected to occur.

*Interpretation Cycle 1: Begin With Debriefing Forms From the On-the-Scene Observers.* During each videotaped session, it is useful for an on-the-scene observer to be available to:

- Take notes.
- Keep the session from getting derailed by irrelevant factors (such as squabbles over who uses the calculator or other resources) or going off on unrelated tangents (such as those that occur when students make unintended assumptions about the problem solving situation).
- Ensure that the videotape equipment is working properly.
- Collect information that might get lost.

The on-the-scene observer may be a researcher, a teacher, or a graduate student in mathematics education, psychology, or another relevant field. Experience shows that on-the-scene observers often notice a great many things that go unremarked if only videotaped records are preserved. Therefore, as soon as possible after each session, it is wise for each on-the-scene observer to prepare a brief report summarizing his or her observations and appending any relevant documentation that might be lost or neglected. To get the most out of records from on-the-scene observers, careful preplanning is needed in order to anticipate the kinds of information that it may be most important to emphasize (e.g., there is no need for on-the-scene observers to focus on factors that will be recorded adequately using videotapes or results that students will produce). As mentioned already, it is important for debriefing sessions to occur as rapidly as possible following the event; otherwise, the kind of information that is distinctive to this perspective often gets misplaced or forgotten.

Of course, there are risks associated with giving too much emphasis to rapidly produced conclusions that are based on factors that are most salient to the on-the-scene observers, but the same could be said of any perspective that is produced at any time. No perspective has exclusive access to "the truth" about a given session. Yet, even if a perspective proves to be highly inaccurate in the light of later analyses, it still may contribute in positive ways to how the session is interpreted later. For example, in research on model-eliciting activities (Lesh & Akerstrom, 1982), it was discovered that the sessions that the on-the-scene observers considered to be most or least interesting at first seldom turned out to be the ones that proved to be most interesting based on deeper and more thoughtful analyses. Nonetheless, fresh firsthand assessments tended to provide powerful counterpoints to impressions that evolved from other later analyses, and they often provided important ways to cross-check the validity of interpretations generated by more remote observers. It is not necessary for later interpretations to agree with the rapidly produced impressions of the on-the-scene observers; however, in general, it does tend to be important for later interpretations to account for these observations and to offer alternative explanations.

*Interpretation Cycle 2: On-the-Scene Observers also Produce Observations of a Videotape for a Second Session.* While the results of a given session are still fresh in the minds of the on-the-scene observers, it is useful for each of them to generate a second debriefing form of at least one other session in addition to the one for which he or she was the on-the-scene observer. Furthermore, it also is useful for each session to be interpreted independently by at least two observers (one interpretation based on the comments produced by an on-the-scene observer and one based on comments produced by an observer of the videotape). When on-the-scene observers produce debriefing forms for at least two separate sessions, they tend to notice similarities and differences that stimulate observations that lead to productive refinements in both reports. Furthermore, when each session is interpreted independently by at least two separate observers, each observer often receives valuable feedback showing that how he or she interpreted students' actions is seldom the only explanation that could be given. Therefore, this feedback may provide valuable input that can be used as cross-checks for later rounds of transcript interpretation.

*Interpretation Cycle 3: Produce Written Transcripts and an Executive Summary for a Given Session.* In lengthy, complex, videotaped episodes, it may be hard to discern some patterns and trends unless the sweep of an entire session can be skimmed rapidly so that related segments can be compared in ways that tend to be difficult even when it is possible to fast-forward through a videotape. For example, consider the annotated transcript that is given in the Appendix to this chapter. This transcript is based on a 60-minute problem solving session that involved three, average-ability, middle school students. By reading this transcript and the comments that are interspersed, it should be clear how it becomes possible to see certain trends and comparisons that would have been difficult to notice otherwise. For example, note the successive interpretations of the students' conceptions in the Appendix, beginning with an initial interpretation of their activity as uncoordinated and relatively disjointed, followed by a focus on a single quantity (the total number of hours worked), and so on. In addition, note that the transcript not only is interpreted with respect to the activity of a single group but also is contextualized by comparison to other groups.

In some transcripts of this nature, the first column often ends up looking similar to the kind of script that tells actors what to do and say in a theatrical performance; the second column often includes relevant snippets of students' work and other relevant information (e.g., pictures, diagrams, tables, and notes). Then, in the later stages of transcript analysis, more columns can be added that give comments and interpretations from researchers representing a variety of perspectives and that focus on such themes as descriptions of:

- The mathematical modeling cycles that the students went through as they generated a response to the given problem.
- The metacognitive roles that various students played involving such activities as planning, monitoring, and assessment.
- Individual differences, such as those associated with tendencies for impulsiveness or excessive avoidance of risk taking.
- Problem solving strategies that the students used, such as those that are emphasized frequently in classroom instruction.

Because annotated transcripts can facilitate researchers to make comparisons involving the preceding kinds of themes, such transcripts often stimulate a level of analysis that would remain obscured to viewers of uninterpreted videotapes otherwise. Unfortunately, typed and annotated transcripts are very time consuming and expensive to produce. Therefore, it is important to take advantage of the fact that it is seldom necessary to use expensive, high-level, staff members to produce transcripts that are useful. Furthermore, it may not be necessary to produce polished and annotated transcripts for all of the sessions in a project. For example, one purpose of using telescoping methods of data analysis is that screening and weighting procedures can be used to enable researchers to focus their attention progressively on sessions that emerge as being the most interesting.

Once typed transcripts of a session have been made and debriefing forms have been produced by an on-the-scene observer and by a videotape observer, it is necessary for a member of the project's staff to view the relevant videotape and to ensure that times and quotations have been recorded accurately in the transcript, events that seem to be especially significant have been highlighted and described briefly, and relevant pictures, diagrams, and notes have been appended appropriately. This person can be one of the observers who were involved during Cycles 1 or 2 of the analysis. It is useful for this person to write a two-page, executive summary of the session, attaching the debriefing forms from both the on-the-scene observer and the videotape observer and including a brief description of the significant characteristics of the session, together with a tentative assessment of the extent to which the session appears to be worth further detailed analysis.[5]

*Interpretation Cycle 4: Produce a Summary for One Problem Across Multiple Groups.* Once executive summaries and typed transcripts have been prepared for all of the sessions that involve a given problem, it is useful for one researcher to be assigned to write a brief, two- to five-page report summarizing the results based on all of the sessions. This report should describe the similarities and the differences among all of the groups who worked on the given problem, describe and illustrate any generalizations that seem appropriate across all of the groups, and select at least one of the transcripts for indepth analysis from a specifically assigned, theoretical perspective. For example, if the researcher who is doing this analysis is a mathematician, then the transcript that is selected could be analyzed from the point of view of the kind of mathematical modeling perspective that is represented in the appendix. A mathematician might concentrate on successive cycles of modeling (e.g., focus on a single quantity to consider derived variables, like trends), whereas a social psychologist might study the events surrounding transitions in roles among the students in the group analyzing, for example, the implications of the sentence in the transcript in the appendix that reads: "Because Carla was calculating sums, she was no longer recording everybody else's results, as she had

---

[5] At this early stage of transcript analysis, it is premature to eliminate a given transcript from further examination. Furthermore, premature screening is especially hazardous if the person doing the screening represents a narrow theoretical or practical perspective. For example, a session that may appear to be uninteresting to a teacher may be very interesting to a psychologist; a session that may appear to be uninteresting to a psychologist may appear to be very interesting to a mathematician. So, in general, it is sensible to follow the "triangle rule"; that is, do not screen out transcripts until at least three distinct perspectives have been represented in the analysis.

done earlier. Therefore, the results of the calculations were not written down. . . . Consequently, at this point, Barb started writing down the results? . . ."

It is beneficial for the report to be presented at a research seminar in which the participants represent a broad range of theoretical and practical perspectives. The discussions of the report should be aimed at trying to reach a tentative consensus about how the session is described and explained. The discussions also should clarify alternative interpretations that could be given of the highlighted session, critique the summary of the entire collection of sessions, and identify issues that should be investigated during additional interpretation cycles. In particular, the discussions should assess the criteria that are emerging for selecting and eliminating sessions for further detailed analysis, identify a group of students whose performance should be investigated across multiple sessions and, it should choose a theoretical perspective that should be emphasized in the next analysis.

*Interpretation Cycle 5: Produce a Summary for One Group of Students Across Multiple Problem Solving Sessions.* Once the results are available from discussion groups focusing on a series of problems, for another researcher should write a brief, two- to five-page report summarizing the performance of a particular group of students across a series of problem solving sessions. Again, this report should describe the trends across multiple sessions and select at least one of the transcripts for indepth analysis from a new, specifically assigned, theoretical perspective. For example, if the transcript has been analyzed already from the perspective of mathematical modeling, the new analysis might concentrate on a psychological perspective and metacognitive roles and activities. The result should be a transcript with at least three columns: one dealing with what the students did and said, one interpreting the transcript from one theoretical perspective, and one interpreting the transcript from a second theoretical perspective. Again, it is helpful for the report to be presented at a research seminar in which the participants represent a broad range of theoretical and practical viewpoints and for the discussions to emphasize issues similar to those featured during Interpretation Cycle 4.

*Interpretation Cycle 6: Produce Additional Analyses of the Sessions, Groups, and Problems That Emerge as Being the Most Interesting and Promising for Further Study.* By the time Interpretation Cycle 5 occurs, a small number of sessions, groups, and problems are likely to emerge as being those most worthy of further investigation; also, complex dossiers will have been produced that include interpretations of these sessions from multiple practical and theoretical perspectives. Consequently, because alternative theoretical perspectives tend to result in mismatches and in new issues that need to be explained, one of the main goals of analysis cycles is to clarify which issues and perspectives should be highlighted in follow-up analyses. Furthermore, because highly specialized analyses may be required, it may be necessary to include researchers who were not involved in earlier analyses. Because detailed summaries are available for a small number of sessions, it often is possible for these new researchers to use advanced technologies and participate from remote sites.

# SUMMARY

The use of videotape is not a royal road to unfettered evidence about conceptual change. Like any other methodological tool, researchers must establish an interpretive framework within which the video serves as one form of evidence. The validity of any such framework is likely to be enhanced if the researchers make decisions during the design of the study (before collecting any videotape!) about:

- The primary function of the videotape, especially when a researcher can anticipate focusing on a particular issue or on obtaining additional contributions from it to fill in or broaden the potential field of inquiry.

- Likely targets of the video, such as small groups, individuals, or teacher-led discussions.

- Methods used for triangulation, including the roles and functions of additional observers, and other sources of evidence, such as students' artifacts, that could be used to buttress claims about students made in the light of the restricted lens of the camera.

- The methods used to organize and train a research team to ensure that videotape analysis is conducted in cycles of interpretation, with sufficient opportunities for different (but relevant) perspectives, cross-checking of particular episodes as well as collections of related sessions, and perhaps most important opportunities for changing and revising the interpretive framework so established painstakingly.

# APPENDIX

## The Summer Jobs Problem

Last summer Maya started a concession business at Wild Days Amusement Park. Her vendors carry popcorn and drinks around the park, selling wherever they can find customers. Maya needs your help deciding which workers to rehire next summer. Last year Maya had nine vendors. This summer, she can have only six – three full-time and three half-time. She wants to rehire the vendors who will make the most money for her. But she doesn't know how to compare them because they worked different numbers of hours. Also, when they worked makes a big difference. After all, it is easier to sell more on a crowded Friday night than on a rainy afternoon.

Maya reviewed her records from last year. For each vendor, she totaled the number of hours worked and the money collected – when business in the park was busy (high attendance), steady, and slow (low attendance). (See the table.) Please evaluate how well the different vendors did last year for the business and decide which three she should rehire full-time and which three she should rehire half-time.

Write a letter to Maya giving your results. In your letter describe how you evaluated the vendors. Give details so Maya can check your work, and give a clear explanation so she can decide whether your method is a good one for her to use.

### TABLE A1
### Hours Worked Last Summer

|  | JUNE | | | JULY | | | AUGUST | | |
|---|---|---|---|---|---|---|---|---|---|
|  | Busy | Steady | Slow | Busy | Steady | Slow | Busy | Steady | Slow |
| MARIA | 12.5 | 15 | 9 | 10 | 14 | 17.5 | 12.5 | 33.5 | 35.0 |
| KIM | 5.5 | 22 | 15.5 | 53.5 | 40 | 15.5 | 50 | 14 | 23.5 |
| TERRY | 12 | 17 | 14.5 | 20 | 25 | 21.5 | 19.5 | 20.5 | 24.5 |
| JOSE | 19.5 | 30.5 | 34 | 20 | 31 | 14 | 22 | 19.5 | 36.0 |
| CHAD | 19.5 | 26 | 0 | 36 | 15.5 | 27 | 30 | 24 | 4.5 |
| CHERI | 13 | 4.5 | 12 | 33.5 | 37.5 | 6.5 | 16 | 24 | 16.5 |
| ROBIN | 26.5 | 43.5 | 27 | 67 | 26 | 3 | 41.5 | 58 | 5.5 |
| TONY | 7.5 | 16 | 25 | 16 | 45.5 | 51 | 7.5 | 42 | 84 |
| WILLY | 0 | 3 | 4.5 | 38 | 17.5 | 39 | 37 | 22 | 12 |

(continued)

TABLE A2

Money Collected Last Summer (In Dollars)

| | JUNE | | | JULY | | | AUGUST | | |
|---|---|---|---|---|---|---|---|---|---|
| | Busy | Steady | Slow | Busy | Steady | Slow | Busy | Steady | Slow |
| MARIA | 690 | 780 | 452 | 699 | 758 | 835 | 788 | 1732 | 1462 |
| KIM | 474 | 874 | 406 | 4612 | 2032 | 477 | 4500 | 834 | 712 |
| TERRY | 1047 | 667 | 284 | 1389 | 804 | 450 | 1062 | 806 | 491 |
| JOSE | 1263 | 1188 | 765 | 1584 | 1668 | 449 | 1822 | 1276 | 1358 |
| CHAD | 1264 | 1172 | 0 | 2477 | 681 | 548 | 1923 | 1130 | 89 |
| CHERI | 1115 | 278 | 574 | 2972 | 2399 | 231 | 1322 | 1594 | 577 |
| ROBIN | 2253 | 1702 | 610 | 4470 | 993 | 75 | 2754 | 2327 | 87 |
| TONY | 550 | 903 | 928 | 1296 | 2360 | 2610 | 615 | 2184 | 2518 |
| WILLY | 0 | 125 | 64 | 3073 | 767 | 768 | 3005 | 1253 | 253 |

Note. Figures are given for times when park attendance was high (busy), medium (steady), and low (slow).

The students in Ms. Barnes' seventh-grade class worked in three-person teams, with the members of the teams being assigned by Ms. Barnes. All the members of the team whose work is described herein were all considered to be average-ability mathematics students in an average-ability inner-city classroom. However, because of Ms. Barnes' emphasis on portfolio-based assessment, the students had had considerable prior experience working on at least 10 projects similar in size to the summer jobs problem. The summer jobs problem was based on a context that was described in a "math-rich" newspaper article that was discussed by the class as a whole on the day before the summer jobs problem was presented.

The students worked at small tables where a tool kit was available that included three TI-92 calculators and other standard classroom tools. The work station included a Macintosh computer with a 12-inch color monitor and software for word processing, spreadsheets, drawing, and making geometric constructions.

After Ms. Barnes had passed out the summer jobs problem and after each group had read the problem carefully, the class as a whole answered the following questions:

- Who is the client? (Answer: Maya)
- What does Maya need you to produce? (Answer: A letter describing a procedure for deciding whom to rehire.)

- Why does she need this product from you? (Answer: So that she will know whom to rehire.)
- When does she need this letter? (Answer: At the end of tomorrow's class.)

The solution process that follows includes significant segments from a transcript for a group of students whose names are Alan, Barb, and Carla. Most of the graphs shown were produced originally using TI-83 calculators. However, when the teams presented their work in class, they used posters that contained redrawn versions of their favorite graphs. Generally, these graphs were constructed using a computer-based, graphing spreadsheet and a color printer. One of these posters is shown in Interpretation 14 at the end of this Appendix. The graph that is appended to the transcript was taken from one the posters. Only in those cases where it is so indicated were the graphs produced by Alan, Barb, and Carla.

> Approximately 5 minutes passed as the students read the problem and discussed it.

> Alan: Oh, God. We've gotta add up all this stuff? . . . You got a calculator?

> Barb: They're in here [the toolbox]? . . . Here. [She finds two TI-83 calculators in the toolbox.]

> Approximately 5 more minutes passed while Alan, Barb, and Carla added the numbers in various rows or columns of Table A1. Because the three students had made no attempt to coordinate their efforts, everybody went off in a slightly different direction. For example, Barb and Carla both added the numbers in the first row of Table A1 (which shows the number of hours that Maria worked), whereas Alan added the numbers in the first column (which shows the number of hours that all of the students worked during the busy periods in June).

> Carla: [Looking at Barb] What'd you get?...I got 159.

> Barb: Yep? . . . Um. . . . That's what I got.

> Alan: I got, let's see, . . . 116.

> Barb: You punched them in wrong. . . . Here, you read them [the numbers] and I'll punch 'em in.

> Alan: [Pointing to the numbers in the table.] 12.5, 5.5, 12, 19.9, 19.5. . . .

> Carla: Huh! . . . Not those, you dummy!

Alan: Why?

Barb: Here, . . . read these [pointing to the first row of Table A1].

---

*Interpretation #1: A Hodgepodge of Several Unstated and Uncoordinated Ways of Thinking Is Used Inconsistently.* This team's first interpretation of the summer jobs problem was similar to those generated by most of the other groups. That is, when the students first began to work on the problem:

- They tended to worry most about "What should I do?" rather than "What does this information mean?" Therefore, their first interpretations focused on computation, and the information that was given was treated as if no data interpretation or mathematization were necessary. Also, when computation was done, it nearly always involved only two-item combinations; it did not involve computations of whole rows or whole columns of numbers.

  They tended to focus on a small subset of the information only, and they tended to concentrate on isolated pieces of it rather than on searching for underlying patterns and regularities. For example, Alan, Barb, and Carla seized on the first information that they noticed, or on the information that impressed them most. In other words, they focused on only the rows or columns in the table that showed the number of hours that each vendor worked. This emphasis was not based on the thoughtful selection of which items were most important. They merely converged on the first details that came to their attention.

- Their early interpretations seldom consisted of a single coherent way of thinking about givens, goals, and possible solution procedures; instead, they usually involved a hodgepodge of several unarticulated and undifferentiated points of view. That is, different students think in different ways; even the same individual may switch sometimes (without noticing) from one

(continued)

> way of looking at the problem to another way. For example, in the transcript that is given here, when Alan finished adding the first column of numbers in Table A1, he began to add the first column of numbers in Table A2; there was no evidence that he noticed that Table A1 dealt with hours worked and that Table A2 dealt with money collected. In fact, later in the session, Alan tried to subtract data in Table A1 from data in Table A2; that is, he tried to subtract hours from dollars (e.g., 690 dollars − 12.5 hours = ?).
>
> - They tended to focus on numbers only, and ignored quantity types. For example, the quantity "12.5 hours" usually was read as "twelve point five," emphasizing "how much" but ignoring "of what."

Barb: Here, read these [again pointing to the first row of Table A1].

Alan: OK. . . . . 12.5, 15, 9, 10, 14, 17.5 12.5, 33.5, and 35. . . . [pause]. . . .

   What is it?

[pause]

Barb: It's 159.

> As Alan was reading the numbers, Carla was checking them off in her table. When Barb gave the result, Carla recorded it in a new column on the right side of her table of data.
>
> One noteworthy fact about this session with Alan, Barb, and Carla is that they began to work as a team much earlier than many of their peers. For example, the preceding differentiation of their roles (as readers, calculators, and recorders) is an indication that the students were beginning to work together as a team, rather than working as independent individuals.
>
> Next, Alan, Barb, and Carla spent approximately 5 minutes calculating the total amount of time that the other vendors worked. Carla recorded the results in the last column of her table. The table of sums that they produced corresponds to the graph shown in FIG. A1.

Interpretation #2: Focusing on Total Number of Hours For Each Worker. The graph in FIG. A1 and Table A3 focused on only the total number of hours that each worker worked. In presentations of their results, the notions of "seniority" or "willingness to work" were common justifications that students used for emphasizing "hours worked." Unlike many other groups that produced the graph in FIG. A1 as part of their final presentations, Alan, Barb, and Carla *did not* bother to produce the graph. They only produced the table of sums (see Table A3) that would have led to this graph. This seemed to be true for several reasons. First, the table of sums that Alan, Barb, and Carla produced was, in itself, enough to enable them to go on to a new and improved way of thinking about the information that was given. Second, at this point in the session, Alan, Barb, and

| TABLE A3 Total Number of Hours for Each Worker | |
|---|---|
| MARIA | 159 |
| KIM | 239.5 |
| TERRY | 174.5 |
| JOSE | 226.5 |
| CHAD | 182.5 |
| CHERI | 163.5 |
| ROBIN | 298 |
| TONY | 294.5 |
| WILLY | 173 |

Carla were only using their calculators to operate on *pairs* of numbers; they were not operating on whole *lists* of numbers. Therefore, they were not entering data into their calculators (or their computer) in a form that made it easy for them to produce automatic graphs.

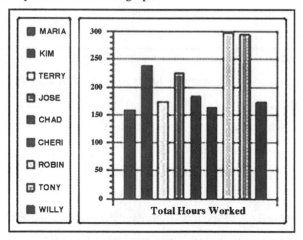

FIG. A1. Total hours each vendor worked.

Alan: OK, so who should we hire? [Alan was looking at Carla's table of sums.]

Barb: Robin looks good. . . . [pause]  So does Tony.

Alan: Maybe Kim.

[pause]

Carla: Hey! We ought to look at money, not hours. . . . Money is down here [pointing to Table A2, which shows the amount of money each student earned].

Alan: Yep, money.

[Approximately 1 minute passed while the students thought and looked at the table.]

Barb: OK, let's add these  [pointing to the rows in the second half of the table].

Barb: Here, you do Maria [gesturing to Alan]. You do Kim [gesturing to Carla]. And, I'll do Terry.

> Again, it is noteworthy that Alan, Barb, and Carla worked as a team much better than many of their peers. For example, here, they divided the task into several different pieces, with different students working on different pieces. Therefore, more planning, monitoring, cross-checking, and rethinking were likely to occur.
>
> Alan seemed to be insecure about using a calculator, so he added only one row of numbers; then, he began watching the other two students as they worked. After that, he began to act as a facilitator and a monitor for the group, rather than as a person was doing calculations.

Alan: Here, I'll read the numbers for you [looking at Carla].

> Next, approximately 3 minutes passed as the students calculated sums in the second half of the table.

Alan: So, let's see what we've got. . . . Who made the most?

> Because Carla was calculating sums, she was no longer recording everybody else's results, as she had done earlier. Therefore, the results of the calculations were not written down in an orderly fashion; they were written on scraps of paper. Consequently, at this point, Barb started writing down the results of her own calculations in a new column at the right of her table.

Barb: Where's the answer for Tony? Where did I put it? Darn, I'm going to have to do it again. . . . . Oh, here is it. . . . . No. . . . Oh, I'm not sure. . . . I'd better do it again.

Carla: My numbers are: "fourteen nine twenty-one" for Kim, "fifteen two seventy-one" for Robin, "nine three oh eight" for Willy, and "thirteen nine sixty-four" for Tony.

[pause]

Carla: Hey, I did Tony. It's "thirteen nine sixty-four." You don't need to do it.

Barb has become the temporary recorder for the group. Here, she takes several minutes to collect the results from the group and to record them in a column (like the one that Carla had constructed in the group's earlier work).

Interpretation #3: Focusing on the Total Number of Dollars That Each Worker Earned: Some teams essentially quit working on the problem at this point. For these groups, their presentations often included a graph like the one shown in FIG. A2. Again, probably for the same kinds of reasons as for Interpretation #2, Alan, Barb, and Carla used only a *table* of sums; they did *not* bother to construct the graph shown in FIG. A2.

| TABLE A4 Total Dollars Each Worker Earned | |
|---|---|
| MARIA | $8,196 |
| KIM | $14,921 |
| TERRY | $7,000 |
| JOSE | $11,373 |
| CHAD | $9,284 |
| CHERI | $11,062 |
| ROBIN | $15,271 |
| TONY | $13,964 |
| WILLY | $9,308 |

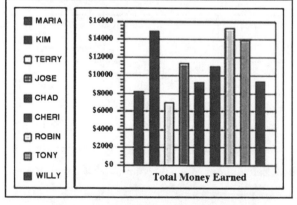

FIG. A2. Total dollars each vendor earned.

Alan: So, who's the best? . . . [pause]. . . . Robin's best. She got "fifteen two seventy-one." And, Kim got "fourteen nine twenty-one." Who's next?

Carla: Tony . . . He got "thirteen nine sixty-four."

Barb: This isn't fair. Some guys got to work a lot more than others. . . . Look at Robin and Tony. They worked more than everybody else. That's why they made more money. . . . If Maria worked that much, she'd have made that much money too. [Mumbling.]

> At this point in the session, nobody picks up on Barb's suggestion to investigate the relationship between "dollars earned" and "hours worked." Nonetheless, later in the session, Barb comes back to this same suggestion; and, at that time, her suggestion leads to the idea of investigating "dollars-per-hour" for each worker. Now, however, the idea of "dollars-per-hour" is not pursued. Instead, Barb's suggestion led the students to investigate *changes* in the dollars earned across time.

Barb: Look, Willy didn't work at all in June [pointing to the zeros by Willy's name in Table A2.]  But, he was doing great in August [pointing to the $3,005 by Willy's name in the August column of Table A2]. . . . Let's just see how much everybody got, totally, in August.

| Interpretation #4a: Using a Table to Focus on the Total Number of Dollars Each Month: Next, the group spent approximately 10 minutes making a table showing the total number of dollars each worker earned each month. At first, the group only made a list of the totals for August; but, when they were finished with August, they made a table showing | | | |
|---|---|---|---|

| TABLE A5 Dollars Earned Each Month | | | |
|---|---|---|---|
| | June | July | August |
| MARIA | $1922 | $2292 | $3982 |
| KIM | $1754 | $7121 | $6046 |
| TERRY | $1998 | $2643 | $2359 |
| JOSE | $3216 | $3701 | $4456 |
| CHAD | $2436 | $3706 | $3142 |
| CHERI | $1967 | $5602 | $3493 |
| ROBIN | $4565 | $5538 | $5168 |
| TONY | $2381 | $6266 | $5317 |
| WILLY | $189 | $4608 | $4511 |

3 months. Also, after the values were calculated using calculators, Carla entered the results into the computer spreadsheet. (Note: Alan, Barb, and Carla never used the spreadsheet to calculate values; they only used it to *record* information and to *graph* results.)

> It is significant that Table A5 was put together in a top-down fashion. Earlier tables were simple lists, and even these lists were created by doing the individual calculations first, then putting the results into a well-organized form. The organizational system was *not* generated first and used to guide the computations that were performed. That is, each of the earlier lists was constructed in a bottom-up fashion.

Alan: Look at old Willy. He's really catching on [at the end of the Summer]. . . . Look, back here [in June] he only made a hundred and eighty-nine bucks, but, out here [in August] he was really humming.

Barb: I think August should count most. Then July. . . . I don't think June should count much. They were just learning.

Alan: How we going to do that?

Barb: I don't know. Just look at them [the numbers in the table], I guess.

[pause]

Barb: Let's see, out here [in August], Kim was best. . . . Then Robin, no Tony....Then Robin....I think they're the top three. Kim, Robin, and Tony. . . . How'd they do in July?

Barb: Wow! Look at Kim. She's still the best. . . . But, uh oh, look at Cheri. She was real good in July.

Alan: Let's line 'em up in July. Who's first?

Barb: Kim. . . . [pause]  Then Tony, and Cheri, and Robin. . . .  [long pause]. . . Then Willy, Chad, and Jose. . . . [long pause]. . . . And, these guys weren't very good [referring to Maria, and Terry].

> Though Barb was doing most of the talking and overt work, Alan was watching and listening closely. But, Carla was off on her own, playing with the computer's spreadsheet program and entering lists of numbers. . . . At this point, Carla reentered the conversation.

Carla: Look you guys, I can make a graph of this stuff.

*Interpretation #4b: Using a Graph to Focus on the Total Number of Dollars Earned Each Month:* For the next 4 minutes, Carla used the computer to flip back and forth, showing the graphs in FIG. A3 that she had made, explaining how she made the graphs, and pointing out who was the top money earner each month.

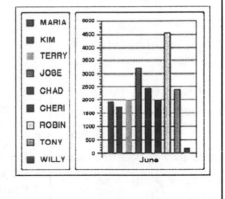

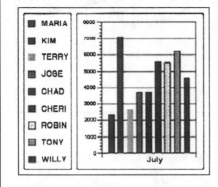

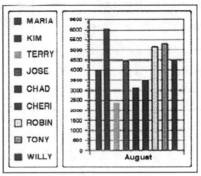

FIG. A3. Total dollars earned each month.

Barb: OK, let's, like, line 'em up for each month.

Alan: You started doing that.

Barb: OK, you [Alan] read 'em off and I'll write 'em down.

Alan: OK, here's August. . . . We got Kim, Tony, Robin, . . . Cheri, . . . Willy, Chad, and Jose; then, Maria and Terry.

| *Interpretation #5: Focusing on Trends in Rank Across Time:* For approximately 5 minutes, Alan, Barb, and Carla worked together to get a list of "top money makers" each month. Then, they noticed that the rankings were somewhat different each month; so, the "trends" shown here were used as an early attempt to reduce this information to a single list. | TABLE A6<br>Changes in Collections Across Time By Vendor<br>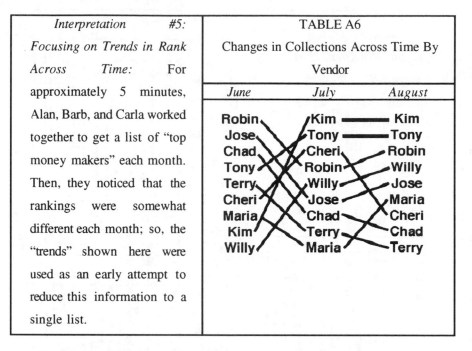 |
| --- | --- |

Alan: Look, Kim was top in July and August, and so was Tony. . . . Robin was next in August, but she wasn't as good in July. . . . [pause] . . .

But, she [Robin] was really good in June. . . . [pause]. . . . I think June is most important because some of them were just learning. . . . August is how they'll probably do next summer.

Approximately 5 more minutes passed while each of the three students nominated workers that they believed should be hired, based on the rankings and trends in the Table A6. In most cases, when the students spoke in favor of a given worker, they made up some sort of cover story to account for the "ups" and "downs" in the worker's performance. These cover stories involved the following kinds of possibilities: Some workers learned and improved, whereas others got bored; some were not able to work as much as others; and some were good during busy periods, but not during slow periods. In these discussions, the students started to pay attention to the fact that the months might not be equally important (e.g., July is the busiest month; August might be the best indicator of current abilities) and that busy, steady, and slow periods might not be equally important (e.g. the half-time workers would not be hired during slow periods). In addition, the students began to express concerns about the fact that they would have liked to have had some additional information that was not available such as: Who really needed a job badly? Who was willing to work when they were called? Finally, as Carla was looking at Table A6 (see Interpretation #5), she got the idea to make a similar graph using the computer; this idea led to Interpretation #6.

Carla: I can make a graph like that [pointing to Table A6] with the computer. Wanna see?

Alan: Sure, um, what's it look like?

Barb: . . . Let me see.

Carla: Wait a minute. . . . [long pause]...Wait a minute. . . . [long pause]. . . . Here's one. No. . . . [long pause]...Ah, here. No. . . . [long pause]. . . . OK, look at this.

*Interpretation #6: Focusing on Trends in Money Earned For June, July, and August:* Carla's graph was a line graph showing the total number of dollars that each worker earned for June, July, and August (see FIG. A4).

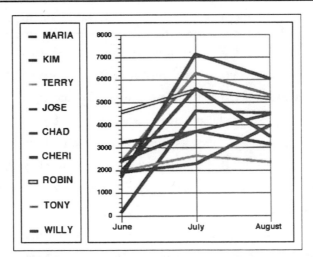

FIG. A4. Trends in money earned for June, July, and August.

Alan: Wow! Neat! How'd you do that?

Carla explained again how she had made the graphs using the computer.

Alan: Now who do we pick. . . . Who's this?

Carla: Um, let's see, it's Kim. . . . And this is . . . um . . . Tony.

Alan: Who's this?

Barb: Let me see.

Carla: Oh, it's Robin.

Barb: So, we've got Kim, . . . Tony, and Robin. Who's next?

[pause]

Carla: What about this guy? . . . Who is he? . . . Um, it's Cheri. . . . Look, she was really good here, but, then, she screwed up.

Barb: How we gonna decide which of these guys to hire? They were all good some and bad some. . . . [long pause]. . . . How many were we supposed to hire anyway? . . . [pause]. . . . Look at the problem [speaking to Alan]. What does it say?

[long pause]

Alan: We're supposed to hire three full-time and three part-time.

[long pause]

Alan: I think we should hire Willy. He was good here [pointing to July and August] . . . and he didn't get to work much here [pointing to June].

---

*Interpretation #7: Using Telescoping Decision Rules:* Up until this point in the session, the students implicitly seemed to assume that the best way to choose workers should be to use a single rule for ranking the workers. Then, if this list was successful in ranking workers from "best" to "worst," the top three workers could be hired for full time, and the next three workers could be hired for part time. But, unfortunately, life was not this simple. No single rule seemed to work to form a single list. For example, both Barb and Carla suggested the idea of using some sort of average. But, this idea was not considered in detail, because the type of averages that were mentioned didn't seem to involve equally important quantities. Therefore, the students began to consider more sophisticated decision-making rules. For example, one rule involved the following kind of two-step process: First-round decisions about who to hire could be based on the ranking in August alone; then, second-round decisions could be based on the ranking in July alone (or based on busy periods alone). _

Barb: Look, you guys. Some of these people got to work a lot more than others. . . . That's not fair. Look, Willy didn't get to work at all back here [in June].

Carla: So, what're we gonna do? [Mumbling.]

> More than 1 minute passed.

Alan: Here. I'm trying something. . . . I'm subtracting how much each guy worked. That'll kind of even things out. . . . I worked for a guy who did that once. We were cleaning up trash and he wanted us to work fast.

---

*Interpretation #8: Subtracting Time Scores From Money Scores:* The most important characteristic of this new idea is that, for the first time, it took into account a relationship between the amount of money that was earned and the amount of time that was spent working. But, because the numbers in the tables didn't include any unit labels, nobody noticed that it might not make sense to subtract hours from dollars. Nonetheless, neither Barb nor Carla were convinced that the idea made sense. What *did* make sense to Barb and Carla was to apply lessons they had learned from their own prior real-life experiences to help them make decisions in the case of the summer jobs problem. Therefore, the team didn't pursue Alan's suggestion. Instead, Alan's suggestion was used as a (transitional) way of thinking that led to a better idea that Barb suggested, which would take into account *both* time and money.

---

Barb: Hey, that's a good idea! We could figure out dollars per hour. . . . I did that for my jobs last summer.

---

*Interpretation #9: Focusing on Dollars-Per-Hour:* Barb wasn't really paying close attention to Alan's idea. The new ideas that she heard was to think about the situation in the same way that she thought about her own past jobs. That is, both Alan and Barb were using past real-life experience to make sense of the current problem. Therefore, Barb thought in terms of dollars-per-hour.

---

For the remaining minutes of the class, Alan, Barb, and Carla went back to the original data tables of hours worked and dollars collected by each vendor last summer and started calculating dollars per hour. As class ended, they decided that, to prepare for the next day's class, each student should bring a graph showing the dollars per hour collected by each vendor. Then, they planned to use these graphs to make final decisions about who to rehire. The graphs in Figs. A5 and A6 show what each student brought to class the next day.

*Interpretation #10a: Alan's Dollars-Per-Hour Graph Based on Sums For the Whole Summer:* First, Alan calculated the total amount of money that each worker earned for the whole summer. Then, he calculated how much time they worked altogether. Finally, for each worker, he divided total dollars by total time.

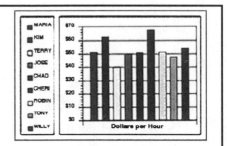

FIG. A5. Dollars-per-hour based on sums for the whole summer.

*Interpretation #10b: Barb's Dollars-Per-Hour Graph Based on Sums For Each Month*: First, Barb calculated the total amount of money that each worker earned for each month. Then, she calculated how much time they worked each month. Finally, for each month, she divided dollars earned by time worked.

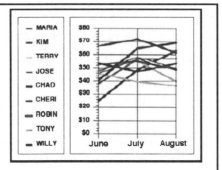

FIG. A6. Dollars-per-hour based on sums for each month.

*Interpretation #10c:* Carla got some help from her brother, who apparently suggested the idea of an average. First, Carla calculated the dollar-per-hour for each cell in the matrix shown in Table A7. Then, for each month, she calculated the average of the rates for the busy, steady, and slow periods. This procedure assumes (incorrectly) that the students intended to treat busy, steady, and slow periods as being equally important!

### TABLE A7
Average Dollars-per-Hour Rate Each Month (Where the Average Is Taken Across Busy, Steady, and Slow Periods)

|  | June | | | July | | | August | | |
|---|---|---|---|---|---|---|---|---|---|
|  | Busy | Steady | Slow | Busy | Steady | Slow | Busy | Steady | Slow |
| Maria | $55.20 | $52.00 | $50.22 | $69.90 | $54.14 | $47.71 | $63.04 | $51.70 | $41.77 |
| Kim | $86.18 | $39.73 | $26.19 | $86.21 | $50.80 | $30.77 | $90.00 | $59.57 | $30.30 |
| Terry | $87.25 | $39.24 | $19.59 | $69.45 | $32.16 | $20.93 | $54.46 | $39.32 | $20.04 |
| Jose | $64.77 | $38.95 | $22.50 | $79.20 | $53.81 | $32.07 | $82.82 | $65.44 | $37.72 |
| Chad | $64.82 | $45.08 |  | $68.81 | $43.94 | $20.30 | $64.10 | $47.08 | $19.78 |
| Cheri | $85.77 | $61.78 | $47.83 | $88.72 | $63.97 | $35.54 | $82.63 | $66.42 | $34.97 |
| Robin | $85.02 | $39.13 | $22.59 | $66.72 | $38.19 | $25.00 | $66.36 | $40.12 | $15.82 |
| Tony | $73.33 | $56.44 | $37.12 | $81.00 | $51.87 | $51.18 | $82.00 | $52.00 | $29.98 |
| Willy | $ 0.00 | $41.67 | $14.22 | $80.87 | $43.83 | $19.69 | $81.22 | $56.95 | $21.08 |

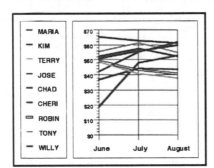

FIG. A7. Average dollars-per-hour each month (across busy, steady, and slow periods).

For approximately the first 20 minutes of the second class, Alan, Barb, and Carla showed one another their rate-per-hour graphs and explained how they were made. Then, for each graph, the team worked together to try to decide which workers should fall into these categories: full-time, part-time, and don't hire.

For Alan's list, the ranking was easy to read directly from the graph that he had drawn (see FIG. A5), but, for Barb's and Carla's graphs (see Figs. A6 and A7, respectively), it was not so obvious to determine which workers ranked first, second, third, and so on. Therefore, for both of these graphs, the team used telescoping methods of decision-making. That is, first-round (tentative) decisions were based on performances in August alone; then, to make decisions about difficult cases, information was used from July (or June). The results are shown in Table A8.

*Interpretation #11:* Three different lists were generated that ranked workers from lowest to highest based on the three, dollar-per-hour graphs that the students had produced.

### TABLE A8
Ranking of Workers Based on Students' Dollar-Per-Hour Graphs

|  | *Alan's List* | *Barb's List* | *Carla's List* |
|---|---|---|---|
|  | Cheri | Kim | Cheri |
| FULL-TIME | Kim | Cheri | Jose |
|  | Willy | Willy | Kim |
|  | Maria | Jose | Tony |
| PART-TIME | Robin | Chad | Maria |
|  | Chad | Robin | Willy |
|  | Jose | Maria | Chad |
| DO NOT HIRE | Tony | Tony | Robin |
|  | Terry | Terry | Terry |

Because the three lists were somewhat different, Alan, Barb, and Carla tried to make a new list (which they called their "agreement list"), showing points of agreement among the three lists.

Alan: Look, Cheri's in the top for all three lists. . . . Kim, too. We should
hire them for sure. Cheri and Kim. . . . What about Willy?...Nope,
he's way down on Carla's list. Damn! Now, what're we gonna go?

Barb: We can throw out Terry. He's at the bottom of every list.

Alan: Tony's pretty bad too.

Carla: I don't think he's so bad. . . . Here look at my graph.

Barb: OK, you're right. He did OK.

Carla: OK.

.... [pause] ....

Alan: Who else should we hire full-time? Willy maybe. Or Jose. . . . No, Jose's way down here on my list.

[pause]

Carla: Look, on my list, Cheri, Jose, and Kim all got A's. . . . Tony, Robin, and Willy got B's. And Chad, Robin, and Terry got C's. . . . What did they get on your lists?

Alan: What do you mean?

Carla: Give me your list, I'll show you. . . . [pause] . . . . See. Cheri got an A, and so did Kim and Willy.

Barb: What are you guys doing?

Carla: Here, watch.

---

For approximately the next 5 minutes, Carla asked the other two students to give her information to fill in the grading scale shown in Table A9.

---

*Interpretation #12:* For each list, a "grading scheme" is imposed that is similar to those used for tests in class. Then, the scores are combined (treating each of the rankings as if they were independent ratings).

(continued)

| | Alan's List | Barb's List | Carla's List | | Combined |
|---|---|---|---|---|---|
| | | | | | TABLE A9 |
| | | | | | The Grading Scheme |
| Cheri | A | A | A | | A |
| Kim | A | A | A | | A |
| Willy | A | A | B | | A- |
| Jose | C | B | A | | B |
| Robin | B | B | C | | B- |
| Chad | B | B | C | | B- |
| Maria | B | C | B | | B- |
| Tony | C | C | B | | C+ |
| Terry | C | C | C | | C |

Alan: So, it looks like the full-time people should be Cheri, and Kim, and Willy. . . . And part-time should be Jose, and...uh oh! Who should we pick next? Maria, Robin, or Chad.

Barb: Yeah. Tony and Terry are out.

Alan: These other guys are pretty close. . . . It's not fair to just pick one.

Carla: Maybe one of these guys really needs a job. I'd think we should hire guys who really need a job. . . . Maybe Willy doesn't really need a job. Maybe Jose really needs one.

Alan: Some of these guys probably didn't get to work at the good times.

[pause]

Barb: Let's make more graphs like these [pointing to FIG. A7 in Interpretation #10c] for the slow times, and the steady times, and the fast times.

More than 12 minutes passed while Alan, Barb, and Carla worked together to make the following graphs.

*Interpretation #13*: A telescoping series of rules. First round decisions are based on Interpretation #12. Then, second-round decisions are made by comparing dollars-per-hour for busy, steady, and slow periods.

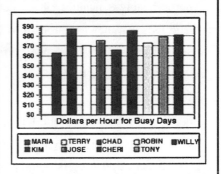

FIG. A8. Dollars-per-hour for busy periods.

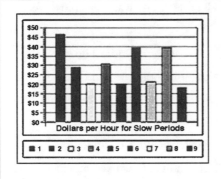

FIG. A9. Dollars-per-hour for slow periods.

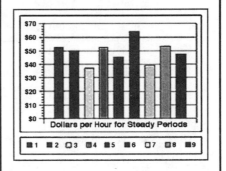

FIG. A10. Dollars-per-hour for steady periods.

Barb: [Looking at Figs. A8, A9, and A10.] I don't think this helps much.

Carla: [Looking at Figs. A8, A9, and A10.] So, which one should we hire? Maria, Robin, or Chad?

Alan: Look, Maria's only best during slow times, but we don't really care about slow times. We're only going to hire part-time people when things are happening . . . fast times. . . . [pause]

Barb: Wait a minute. Maria's not so bad. Look, um, she's better than Robin during steady times. . . and Chad too.

Approximately 8 minutes passed during which Alan, Barb, and Carla looked back over the graphs that they had brought to class and the work that they had done earlier in the period. In these discussions, they offered "stories" that might explain patterns in the dollars-per-hour collected by the various workers. In the end, they reached an agreement on the following points:

- Slow periods should not be treated as being very important because most of the money would be made during busy or steady periods and part-time workers would not be hired during slow periods.

- Performance in August (and, to a lesser extent, July) should be treated as being most important because it took into account learning and improvement and because it was the most recent indicator of capabilities.

Carla: We've got to write up our report. . . . What should we do?

Barb: I think we should make another graph like the one I made before [i.e., Interpretation #10b, FIG. A6], . . . only this time leave out slow times.

Carla: OK, you do that. . . . I'll get the poster board and stuff.

For the remainder of the class, Alan, Barb, and Carla worked together to produce a large poster like the one shown in FIG. A11.

*Interpretation 14: A Telescoping Series of Rules Based on Dollars-per-Hour Trends for Busy and Steady Periods Only.*

Dear Maya,

We think you should hire Kim and Cheri and Jose for full time, and we think you should hire Willy and Chad, and Tony for part time. Look at this graph to see why these people are best.

The graph is only about busy times and steady times. You don't make much money during slow times, and you won't hire people for slow times.

Some workers got better at the end of the summer. But, some didn't get better. So, August is most important, and July is also important. July is when you make the most money.

Alan, Barb, and Carla

(continued)

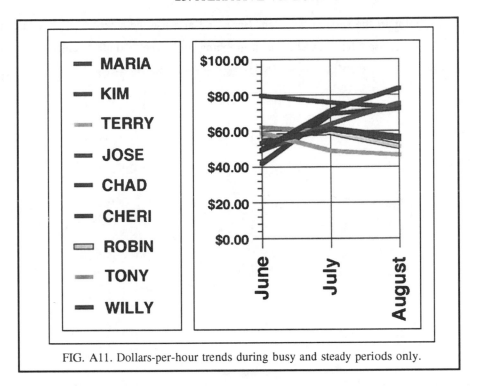

FIG. A11. Dollars-per-hour trends during busy and steady periods only.

At a similar point, another group of students produced the graph shown FIG. A12.

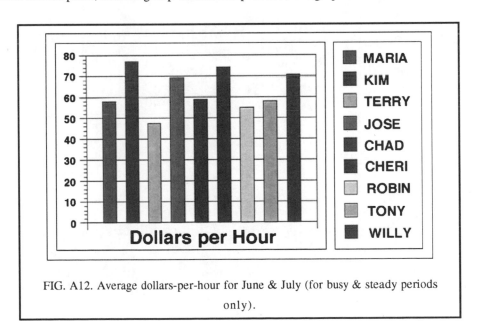

FIG. A12. Average dollars-per-hour for June & July (for busy & steady periods only).

At no point in the session did Alan, Barb, or Carla use the spreadsheet as a calculating device. They only used the spreadsheet as a graphing tool. They did all calculations on TI-83 calculators.

# 24 Choosing and Using Video Equipment for Data Collection

**Jeremy Roschelle**

*SRI International*

Video is becoming the medium of choice for collecting data for educational and social science research projects. There are many reasons for choosing video: Videotape can preserve more aspects of interaction including talking, gesture, eye gaze, manipulatives, and computer displays. Moreover, video allows repeated observation of the same event and supports microanalysis and multidisciplinary analysis. Video also enables researchers to leave controlled laboratory settings and enter naturalistic fieldwork. Finally, video provides analytical benefits: It can support grounded theory, whereby the emergence of new categories from source materials is rigorously controlled. Video can avoid the "what I say" versus "what I do" problem that can occur in self-reports. Video supports a critical incident methodology but also allows examination of the antecedents and consequences of the critical event.

Despite these strong benefits, using video as a research medium carries heavy costs. The equipment is technical and expensive. Data reduction can become an oppressive problem, because videos are very time consuming to watch. Transcription can take 10 times the duration of the source tape. Further, relying on transcription too early can eliminate the advantages of video because a transcript has but a fraction of the richness of the original source tape.

In addition, video raises some unique methodological challenges. First and most important, the experimenter must understand that video is a constructed artifact, not an "objective capture" or a "holographic memory" of the original happenings. As later chapters point out, there are major obstacles in analyzing videos and interpreting them. Finally, ethical dilemmas arise whenever recognizable images of experimental participants are presented.

This chapter aims to provide practical information for the wise choice and use of video equipment. The first section discusses the equipment needed to make research-quality videos. The second section covers basic videography techniques. Although these initial sections might seem overly pragmatic, the dictum from early computer science applies to the analysis of video data: garbage in, garbage out. Choosing equipment carefully and learning good videography techniques are essential prerequisites to obtaining data that are worthy of sophisticated research methods. Once quality data are available, the basics of valid interpretation can be discussed. The third section addresses the biases that are introduced into a video by the videographer and experimenter, with some suggestions of how one can control, or at least be aware of, these biases. The fourth and concluding section summarizes some of the methodological challenges of video through the various phases of a typical research project, from design to presentation.

## CHOOSING VIDEO EQUIPMENT

The video marketplace provides equipment with diverse features, trade-offs, and capabilities. To the beginning research videographer, these choices can seem overwhelming. This section covers each major area of choice, suggesting the most important factors that should be considered in selecting equipment. In most cases, specific models are not recommended because they change frequently.

A general issue in buying video equipment is whether to use a mail-order house or a local supplier. Mail-order houses can be satisfactory, but make sure that a full U.S. warranty is obtained and that the supplier has a long and stable track record. A reputable local shop can provide more rapid help when problems emerge, which can outweigh the slightly higher cost.

Consumer magazines such as *Camcorder, VideoMaker,* and *Consumer Reports* offer good reviews of equipment and tables comparing features. At the time of this writing, a reasonable budget for video equipment can range from $2,000 for a simple, one-camera setup to $8,000 or more for a sophisticated, two-camera setup.

## Tape Format

Digital video is becoming available. It offers superb quality and the preservation of that quality across multiple copies. Digital video also will be much easier to work with using a computer. At the moment, prices are high, but are dropping into a range that makes it worth considering. Be aware, however, that, at present, computer equipment for working with digital video is optimized for working with 1 or 2 hours of footage to produce a few minutes of commercial television. Typical research projects, which work with hundreds of hours of footage, may encounter technical limitations in this medium.

Until digital video becomes ubiquitous, the two most common formats of videotape will be VHS and 8 mm. Table 24.1 displays the variations in these formats.

TABLE 24.1

Videotape Formats

|  | *Standard Size* | *Compact* |
|---|---|---|
| **Normal Resolution** | VHS | 8-mm |
| **High Resolution** | SVHS | Hi8 |
| **Broadcast Resolution** | Beta | |

VHS is compatible with most home videocassette recorders (VCRs), whereas 8-mm tape is more compact. The high-resolution formats, SVHS and Hi8, have much higher quality images and provide much better results when copying a tape, especially when making copies of copies ("multiple generations"). In general, the author recommends Hi8 because it is compact, offers superior-quality stills, and is only slightly more expensive than 8-mm. Because SVHS is not compatible with most home VCRs, there is no reason to choose SVHS over Hi8. VHS should be selected only when the research project must have the ability to play its master tapes in a home VCR (but note that VHS copies of Hi8 master tapes can be made). One should never use the VHS-C format because the maximum duration of the tape is limited severely. Beta and other professional formats are much more expensive and should be used only when producing broadcast-quality, documentary videos.

Tape brands vary in quality, although in most research uses the variations will not be noticed. If concerned about tape quality, check the periodic reviews in consumer magazines like *Consumer Reports, VideoMaker,* and *Camcorder.* Choose a tape brand with few dropouts (frames in which the picture is missing).

A common practice among serious video researchers is to preserve original "master" tapes in a special safe place and use copies or "dubs" for analysis. Videotapes degrade in quality with use, especially with frequent starting and stopping. Furthermore, master tapes are stored off-site; data will not be lost in the case of a fire (which happened to the author).

## Camcorders

The camcorder market is highly competitive and changes quickly. Manufacturers offer many complex features on their products. Only a few are important to the researcher.

These features are essential:

- The camcorder must be able to superimpose a date and time stamp on the tape, with hours, minutes, and seconds.
- The "lux" rating should be low, which means that the camcorder will function with little ambient light.
- Insist on microphone inputs and headphone outputs.
- A high-resolution (Hi8 or SVHS) camcorder is recommended strongly by the author, even if low-resolution tapes will be made. (At the time of purchase, it costs only a little more to get a high-resolution camcorder, and there is no way to upgrade once you've committed to a low-resolution camcorder.)
- There should be a choice between fully manual operation (aperture and focus) and fully automatic operation.

Camcorders have other features that are desirable. They include stereo sound, an easy-to-use manual focus, and an adjustable viewfinder. An infrared remote control with on-off and zoom controls is handy. Medium-sized camcorders are easier to hold steady than palm-sized models.

The researcher typically does not need many of the features offered on advanced models. Superimpose, fade, and other effects are not necessary. Macro and long-zoom lens are unimportant. High shutter speeds are hardly ever used. Color viewfinders often show less detail than black-and-white ones. "Fuzzy" logic and digital jitter removal are not important.

Camcorders have the worst mean time to failure of any consumer product. Repairs typically cost 25% of the cost of the product. The purchase of a service contract for both camcorders and VCRs should be considered. Extended warranty plans should be compared because they differ widely in terms and cost. Better yet, a more robust, professional model could be contemplated.

## Microphones

The built-in microphone on a camcorder should not be used. Without good sound, tapes are useless as research data. Camcorder microphones pick up noise from all directions, and the ideal location for getting a clear picture is seldom the ideal location for getting clear sound. External microphones are required.

Three kinds of microphones are useful:

- A pressure-zone microphone (PZM) is good for small-group discussions as well as full-class lessons. They cost less than $100 and are available at Radio Shack and through mail-order stores. They work well if they can be placed close to the sound source or along a flat surface perpendicular to the sound source.

- A supercardioid directional (shotgun) microphone costs more (around $300) but can gather sound with a very tight focus. This microphone is useful for hearing one group of speakers selectively in a noisy setting, especially when proximity to the speaker is impossible.

- A wireless lapel microphone is useful for following a roving teacher or student. Beware of the transient, static-noise problems that occur with cheaper models! Some models drain batteries very quickly. If ordering multiple wireless microphones from the same manufacturer, different channels for each receiving unit should be specified. On better models, a unidirectional, rather than an omnidirectional, lapel microphone can be selected.

## Mixers

When using multiple microphones, an audio mixer is essential. A very simple audio mixer will work in most cases. It can be battery powered, and it should be possible to adjust the volumes and to mix the microphone into either the left or right stereo channel.

If using multiple videocameras, a video mixer will be needed. The Panasonic WJAVE-5 and WJAVE-7 offer excellent performance at affordable prices. Both of them permit the combination of two video signals in a variety of split-screen and picture-in-picture formats. They also contain a simple audio mixer.

## Accessories

The most important accessory is a tripod. Videography tripods must have a "fluid head" for smooth rotation, a quick release for attaching and removing the camera, good height, and stability. Padded headphones are necessary for performing sound checks during a shoot. Sometimes, a wide-angle lens can provide a good contextual overview, but severe "fish eye" distortion can be experienced on the widest models.

A padded carrying case will protect the equipment and keep miscellaneous accessories together. Among the miscellaneous accessories needed are adapters, cables, extension cords, power strips, a Swiss army knife, duct tape, and microphone stands or fasteners. If all of this equipment will be moved around, a sturdy foldable cart will be required.

Lights are generally too intrusive in research settings and, thus, are not necessary.

## Playback VCRs

Playback VCRs need only a few critical features to be useful to the researcher. First and most important, the VCR must have a hours-minutes-seconds counter. It should read "00:00:00" and not "0000." A jog-shuttle knob is helpful for spinning the tape backward and forward. A high-quality still is essential (this is hard to find on VHS equipment). On VHS gear, "HiFi" sound delivers high-quality audio, but all 8-mm equipment delivers either HiFi or digital audio.

More sophisticated researchers may want to use timecode on their tapes. A timecode means that each frame on the tape has a machine-readable number attached to it. By reading these numbers, a VCR can find the exact frame specified. A timecode is essential when trying to synchronize multiple tapes of the same event. Otherwise, it is not necessary. SMPTE is the name of the professional timecode standard. Equipment with a SMPTE timecode is very expensive and often unnecessary for a researcher. Sony's proprietary RC timecode (on 8-mm equipment) is cheaper and can be acceptable for research use.

Computer control capability can be very important too, but, unfortunately, most consumer equipment does not provide a computer remote port. Equipment designed specifically for this purpose may have to be purchased. When choosing a computer-controllable VCR, the most important requirement is that it follow a protocol that is supported by the software.

There are many protocols available that connect computers and VCRs. Sony's Control-L or LANC is the cheapest and simplest system. It is nearly ubiquitous on consumer Hi8 gear. (Note that Control-S or S-Video is not suitable for computer control.) Panasonic's Control-M or 5-pin remote is similar to Control-L, but available on Panasonic gear only. Sanyo and GoVideo also supply proprietary protocols, but they are not supported widely yet. Professional quality-VCRs use RS-422 protocols, which are compatible with studio editing suites, but not with most desktop computer software.

## Monitors

The author does not advise looking at video on a computer screen. Usually, the quality is worse than on a separate monitor, video digitizing cards are expensive, and computer screen display space is limited. Generally, any 13- or 20-inch television set or consumer-quality video monitor is satisfactory for research use. Desirable features include front-panel input jacks, a headphone output, easy-to-reach volume control, and a balance control for stereo sound. If high-resolution tape is used, a S-Video input for viewing high-resolution tape may be desirable.

## Software Support for Video Analysis

Software can make logging and analyzing tapes much easier. A full review of the software available would require more space than is possible here, so three useful packages are listed:

- The author has created an easy-to-use analysis tool called CVideo. CVideo supports making transcripts, content logs, and loose notes about videotapes. Once a tape has been logged, CVideo can locate quickly and play any scene in a tape. Contact the author at jeremy@unix.SRI.com for more information.

- MacShapa is a more sophisticated and complex video analysis tool. It has a spreadsheet (tabular) analysis format and can work with codes and predicates. It also has powerful searching and reporting capabilities. Contact Penny Sanderson (psanders@ux1.cso.uiuc.edu) for more information.

- Researchers who want to build their own video analysis tools or need to edit tapes should contact Videonics (http://www.videonics.com) and inquire about Video Toolkit.

## USING VIDEO EQUIPMENT

Making research-quality videos is difficult. Master videographers work with their:

- Hands on: confidence with operating equipment.
- Eyes on: visual aesthetics, given situational constraints.
- Minds on: managing complexity through clarity of purpose and discipline.

### Audio First!

Without top-quality audio, research videos usually will be useless. Good-quality microphones and an audio mixer are excellent investments. In audiorecording, as in real estate, the three most important rules are "location, location, and location." The microphones should be placed as close to the participants as possible. Once the microphones have been positioned, sound checks (wearing padded headphones) should be made. If the microphones have batteries, make sure that they are fresh (there are few things more frustrating than having your microphones die halfway through a session).

When using an audio mixer, the volumes should be adjusted so that the needles break into the red zone only periodically. It is best to turn up the individual microphone volumes (gain) instead of turning up the overall, master volume control. Ambient noise can be controlled by turning down the microphones that are not near currently active participants.

Before beginning to tape, the ambient noise should be decreased as much as possible. Windows and doors should be closed, and noisy equipment like air conditioners should be turned off, if possible. Computers have noisy fans; often, the main box can be moved underneath a table, and only the monitor and keyboard left on the desk. Sometimes, the reverberations in a room can be reduced with carpets and closed curtains.

## Camera Placement

Usually, the preferred shot for research use is wide (not zoomed close), stationary, and angled down slightly on the participants. Ideally, the shot should be wide enough to capture all of the participants in a joint activity and narrow enough to see the important details of what they are doing. There are several reasons to favor a stationary camera:

- A picture that moves quickly or frequently is hard to watch.

- A moving picture relies much more heavily on the quick judgment of the camera operator. This is acceptable for highly patterned activities (like a football game), but introduces a high degree of arbitrary choice otherwise.

- In quickly changing situations, camera operators tend to lag behind the action and, therefore, move the camera ineffectively. A slowly changing, wide shot is better than a quickly moving, narrow shot.

When placing cameras, glare and backlighting are to be avoided. Glare occurs when light reflects into the camera, and backlight occurs when a light source is behind the subject. Sharp changes in light intensity can happen in front of overhead projectors, computer screens, and other light sources. They should be kept out of the camera frame, if practical. Sometimes lights can be moved and curtains closed before participants arrive in order to remove glare, backlight, and sharp contrasts.

Recording should start before the participants arrive but should not stop until after they have left. This is important because participants often make revealing remarks before and after the "official" activity.

## Videography Trade-Offs

Every research recording session is subject to three dilemmas:

- Detail versus context: A videographer can never capture all of the detail nor all of the context. It is best to seek a middle ground that preserves for analysis the relevant aspects of the activity. This middle ground is discovered by paying close attention to aspects of the situation that the participants refer to directly in their work together. To augment the context, field notes and interviews can be used to supplement the video. To enlarge the detail, copies of materials (handouts, worksheets, and slides) can be collected.

- Naturalistic versus quality video: Ideally, research videography would not modify the situation being filmed. Unfortunately, researchers often need to make minor rearrangements of space and people in order to get good sound and pictures. For example, as mentioned earlier, noisy equipment and light sources should be moved. If a whiteboard is too wide to fit into the camera, part of the board can be marked off-limits by writing "please save" across it. When filming a small group, it may be necessary to rearrange the chairs around the table so that a good camera angle can be obtained. Such changes should be made before the participants arrive.

  In many cases, these small changes will not affect behavior. The easiest way to confirm this is to observe the participants a few days before and after videotaping to see if their interactions are qualitatively different.

- Storyline versus overview: In a busy setting, a videographer needs to choose between following a particular person or group and providing a good overview of the overall activity in the setting. This choice must be made before beginning to film, according to the purposes of the research.

## Minimizing Camera Effects

Introducing a video camera into a naturalistic context almost always changes how the participants behave to some degree. Although the author is not aware of any systematic studies on this topic, most researchers seem to believe that the effect of "the presence of the camera changing the event being observed" can be minimized. It never goes away completely, however. In some "high stakes" assessment contexts, the temptation to "play to the camera" may be inevitable.

The videographer can take some practical steps to reduce camera effects. They include:

- Explaining and discussing the purpose of the taping.
- Practicing "dry runs"; use the equipment in class for several days in preparation.
- Using "icebreakers"; make small jokes to relieve tension.
- Modeling natural behavior.
- Leaving the recording equipment alone during taping.

There are also a few common errors to avoid. The fact that a participant is being recorded should never be emphasized. Moving the microphones or pointing the camera in a participant's face is bad. The videographer should avoid moving but move as silently as possible if movements are necessary. Plenty of time should be allotted to set up the equipment before the event, so that it is not delayed or disrupted by equipment problems.

## About Multiple Cameras

The use of two or more cameras can provide a broader view than one camera alone. However, multiple cameras introduce numerous technical challenges.

In most cases, images from multiple cameras will be combined onto one tape. There are three basic options for combining images:

- A picture-in-picture (PIP) mix takes all of one image at quarter size and insets it in one corner of the other full-size image. The quarter-size PIP images are grainy and often have insufficient resolution for details. When using a PIP, the shot should be arranged so that nothing important is happening in the obscured corner of the full-size image.

- A split-screen image places half of each image side by side, split either horizontally or vertically. When filming, nothing important should be in the half of each image that will be discarded.
- A-B cuts show you all of either image, in alternation over time. This is typical for a sporting event. Generally, complex, video-editing equipment is required to do them well. In a live situation, the editor will tend to lag behind the action.

Another difficult decision is whether to mix images at recording time or later. Usually, it is much easier to mix images when they are recorded. This avoids synchronization problems and saves time. Because the videographer can get immediate feedback on the final product, composing good shots is easier.

If the images are to be combined in a studio, the tapes need to be synchronized. Generally, a professional will do this using a SMPTE timecode, which is very expensive. If SMPTE is not available, the most difficult problem is synchronizing the audio because time lags in audio are very annoying. It is best to use the audio from one source tape only. The audio should be mixed onto this source tape in the field, and the audio on the other source tape should be ignored. To avoid losing quality, high-resolution tape should be used, because the mix will be a new level of master tape.

A third option is to view the tapes on multiple monitors. Unfortunately, anything less than professional SMPTE video gear does not support this option well. The author is not aware of any video analysis software that can control multiple decks in synchrony. However, if identical VCRs are available, sometimes the remote control can be set so that it controls both decks at once. Then, the play and pause controls of both VCRs can be used synchronously. The VCRs will stay roughly synchronized as long as only the play and pause controls are used.

## Tape Management

A labeling system for tapes should be developed and adhered to. The labels should include the date, place, and tape number. Tapes should be labeled immediately after they have been used and the record-protect tab should be set to prevent accidental erasure.

It is also helpful to keep a small notebook log of your recording sessions. Alternatively, you can use the back of the tape label to jot down major activities and overall impressions.

As a rule, airport X-ray machines will not harm tapes. However, if the same tape will go through many X-ray machines, it is advisable to have it inspected manually.

# UNDERSTANDING BIASES IN RESEARCH VIDEOS

Video offers the researcher large gains in data-gathering capabilities compared to audiorecording or direct observation. The gains can cause researchers to overlook the limitations of the medium, leading to dangerous misconceptions. Four misconceptions are discussed next, along with suggestions of how the researcher can control the biases of the medium.

## Misconception: Video Captures What an Observer Would See

Compared to the human eye, a video camera has many limitations. For example, because video has low resolution, it is usually impossible to see writing on a document or blackboard without zooming in. But such zooming will exclude the broader activity. The human eye can see both at once easily.

Video has a low contrast ratio. This means that it can tolerate only a limited range of brightness. Whereas a human observer can see both an image cast by an overhead projector and the participants in a darkened room, a video camera will overexpose the image or underexpose the participants.

Video has less depth of field than the human eye. This means that it takes constant work to keep the different elements of a situation in focus in a video camera. In general, we are unaware of focusing problems as direct observers. Video also has a narrower field of vision, especially because direct observers can turn their heads rapidly to track action as it occurs. An observer can watch easily the faces of two participants who are having a dialogue across a classroom. A single video camera that tries to move from participant to participant will make the viewer seasick.

Audio microphones have less selectivity than human hearing. For the most part, it is much easier to pay attention to one conversation out of many when observing a situation directly. In a recording, any extraneous noise becomes annoying and distracting.

## Misconception: Video Has No Point of View

In part because of the aforementioned limitations, the process of recording introduces a distinctive point of view on the proceedings. This point of view can distort the underlying event and impede inquiry severely.

For example, in recording the audio portion of the event, it is good practice to put the microphones as close to the participants as possible. However, a unidirectional lapel microphone on the teacher can do an exceptional job of selecting the teacher's voice and reducing classroom noise. This can make the classroom seem unnaturally "dead." Conversely, poor microphone choice and placement can pick up every cough and chair squeak, making it hard to hear the teacher. This amplified background noise can make a classroom seem chaotic, unruly, or inattentive.

Likewise, one might put microphones near a particular group of students. These microphones can pick up whispered comments that would be inaudible to an observer otherwise. If the students are making disparaging remarks, the classroom's climate might appear very different than it seems to an observer. If only good students have microphones, the class will seem better than if only a few bad students have them.

Video images are highly composed. Distortions can occur by focusing on one participant to the exclusion of others. Using video directly from a computer screen will capture a flicker-free image of the screen, but miss the participants' gestures in front of the screen. Focusing on the materials that the students are using can lead to neglect of their facial expressions.

Generally, a neutral point of view cannot be achieved. The reason for making the videorecording will have to be clarified and used to guide the construction of a video point of view.

## Misconception: Video Captures Context

Because video captures so many more features of human interactions than other media do, it is common to say that video captures context. To say whether a context has been captured, one needs some definition of what it is. As a working definition, let's assume that context refers to those aspects of the shared situation that are available to the participants and relevant to the meaning of their actions.

Assuming this definition, it is clear that video can capture many aspects of local, short-term context, such as the materials students are manipulating. But video is a poor medium for preserving nonlocal, long-term context. For example, while working together, the students know what they did yesterday and the day before. Capturing a long-term sequence on video is difficult, and it is time consuming to watch. A journal or diary is much better at compressing chronological contextual information. Likewise, a teacher knows a lot about the personal history of each student. A transcribed interview is a much better technique for gaining access to this context. In some situations, like a school playground, participants move rapidly among many activities and settings. Giving an appropriate overview of this activity on a video would be very challenging. Field notes from a participant's observations might give a more coherent view of the playground context.

## Misconception: A Research Video Is Like a Research Paper

Unfortunately, the author has witnessed the following scene too many times: A researcher attends a prestigious conference armed with a project video to show. After brief introductory remarks, the researcher says, "I am going to let the data speak for themselves." But contrary to his or her expectation, the audience sees events in the video that did not appear in the researcher's analysis. Soon, the session is spinning out of control, with the researcher unable to inject his or her point of view into what is becoming a charged and confrontational atmosphere.

One of the unique powers of video is its ability to support a wide range of types of analysis and possibly conflicting interpretations. One of its disadvantages is that it is difficult to compress the meaning of a large corpus of video data. Video is not structured like a fractal; a small snippet is unlikely to preserve much of the structure of a very large data set. Thus, "letting the data speak" is a dangerous proposition.

A contributing factor in this problem is the lack of established genres for presenting research videos, especially compared to traditional genres for presenting other forms of data. A genre introduces constraints that enable an audience to make appropriate inferences from a presentation. Where no genre is available, the audience may generate inappropriate and conflicting interpretations. A research video is not like a research paper because a research video lacks a commonly understood genre.

Even worse, all of us have watched hours of video on television prior to watching any research footage; thus, the genre of broadcast television forms our expectations. We expect video to be action packed. Footage from a real classroom will look boring and slow compared to a situation comedy on television. We also expect video performers to be polished and perfect. Again, data from real life will look bumbling and messy.

Until a distinctive research video genre emerges and is well established, presenting research videos will require extra care, whether in a conference presentation or one of the emerging multimedia journals. Directing the viewers' attention to key features of the video and supplying appropriate contextual support can help to provide the constraints that a viewer needs in order to make a valid interpretation. Legal and ethical guidelines for publishing research videos also need to be established.

## METHODOLOGICAL CHALLENGES OF VIDEO DATA

It should be clear from the preceding sections that merely using video does not eliminate any of the standard issues involved in designing the research. Aside from the problems of purchasing equipment and developing videography skills, the research team must establish an appropriate logic and a set of procedures to guide the inquiry through the maze of potential pitfalls described previously.

Many issues surrounding video are no different from any other data medium. Questions of designing a data-gathering protocol, sampling the data, drawing valid inferences, and presenting conclusions share much in common with traditional media. However, there are some special considerations that arise when using video. The following section summarizes them, following the chronological order of a typical research project from design through data collection, data analysis, and presentation.

### Designing the Logic of a Research Project

Video can be used in many experimental logics ranging from top-down, planned comparisons to bottom-up participant observation. Both qualitative and quantitative logics can be employed, without one excluding the other. Conditions can be either controlled or naturalistic. Video does not require or best support any single type of experimental design.

However, video does create opportunities for serious mistakes to be made in the design of the logic for a particular inquiry. A researcher operating in a traditional, planned, comparison paradigm might reduce all video data quickly to a set of predetermined codes for analysis. Although this is efficient, it neglects the strongest benefit of using video data—the potential of allowing insights from rich data to restructure preconceived categories and thus account for observations better. At the other extreme, a researcher operating in a bottom-up, data-driven mode can be overwhelmed by the sheer volume of the data available. Information overload can paralyze an inquiry. Inevitably a higher order structure must be imposed on the data, based on the goals and interests of the research team.

In either case, the critical problem in the design phase of the project is coping with the related issues of open-endedness and information overload. Remaining open to insights requires planning in order to allow observations that fall outside the predetermined structures, whereas information overload requires imposing structure on an otherwise open inquiry.

This double-edged sword of structure can be controlled best by a form of iterative progressive refinement of the categories, questions, and procedures that organize the research. A plan for progressive refinement might include a set of small-scale pilot projects before the major data collection. For example, it could be appropriate to start with broad contextual footage. Later, the videographer might sample the same setting more selectively, to capture details needed for more focused research questions. Progressive refinement also might include opportunities for open-ended brainstorming about the videos collected. These brainstorming sessions might result in reshaping the categories to be used in the analysis. Certainly coding schemes and data analysis procedures should be subjected to refinement too.

A second set of potential mistakes results from overreliance on video data. As detailed earlier, video is a constructed artifact with serious limitations. Every filming session samples aspects of the situation while suppressing others. Therefore, most research designs will benefit from a form of triangulation. Interviews, journals, and observations of participants can provide some of the long-term context that video leaves out. Direct field observations offer an alternative way of capturing a secondary record of the stream of events. Though a human observer may catch less overall information, human eyes and ears have better receptors than any video camera and may be able to apprehend aspects of the overall situation that a camera or videographer might miss. Through direct observation, many small groups of students can be viewed and, thus, the representativeness of the single group in the video can be gauged. Likewise, field notes can contribute a good concise overview of the events that occurred on a particular day and can point out topics worth investigating.

Finally, collecting artifacts such as samples of a participant's work can fill in some of the details missing on video. Copies of a participant's worksheets, overhead slides, computer software, or textbooks are invaluable when trying to make sense of a video. Additionally, it is a good idea to make a floor plan if the participants were in a complicated space (like a classroom). Photographs of fixed features of the room, such as posters and workspaces, can be helpful as well.

## Ethics and Informed Consent

Generally, it is legal to tape public behavior in a public space (e.g., a speaker at an outdoor rally in which anyone can participate). A classroom is a private space and, therefore, requires consent. Taping a private conversation in a public space is not legal either. All private taping requires the written consent of those involved, and the Human Subjects Review Board and the school or school district administration should be consulted beforehand. In usual circumstances, there are three issues in informed consent:

- Is the subject free to refuse to participate in the taping?
- Does the subject understand the use of the tapes?
- Can the subject request the destruction of a tape?

As a practical matter, subjects seldom request the destruction of tapes. But, sometimes, highly damaging material can be acquired accidentally. For example, the author once had a remote lapel microphone on a teacher who had a whispered, 5-minute conversation with a student about a psychiatric problem. This tape was destroyed.

In general, it is a good idea to get progressive levels of consent only as they are needed. Three common levels are for:

- Small research group use only.
- Scientific conferences and meetings.
- General broadcast via TV, CD-ROM, or computer networks.

## Data Collection

Explicit, careful planning of the guidelines for the videographer is essential to obtaining useful research footage and should be a part of the research design. There is no simple recipe for overcoming the biases of the video medium. The researchers must be aware that videos are a constructed record and investigate them as such. This means that the researchers must be clear about the purpose of their research before taping begins and must develop a systematic videorecording strategy that is true to those purposes. As a part of any data collection, the researchers should document what camera angles and microphone placements were chosen, and why.

Because so many factors are involved in recording research-quality videos, it is essential to pilot the videograpic techniques before taping the core corpus. During pilot studies, the videographer may want to experiment with alternative priorities for capturing images and sound. If the camera will be moved or zoomed during filming, these procedures should be practiced and the resulting footage examined carefully. It is especially important to practice techniques for combining images from two cameras or using mixing equipment in the field. Throughout the pilot phase, the team should notice the different perspectives and biases that each variation introduces. Through practice, the researchers can create a systematic approach to getting the desired data.

A pilot phase is also a good time to examine the potential role of camera effects. The easiest way to examine camera effects is through direct field observation before, during, and after the days when the videographer is present. Almost always, some trivial effects will be noticed: Participants may giggle a bit, be more reluctant to begin speaking, or be more anxious. The key question is not whether any effects occur, but whether the participants' behavior changes in ways that are relevant to the research questions being asked. In most cases, a little giggling will not disturb core behavioral patterns that have been established over a long time. If camera effects are a problem, it is possible that they may die down over a more extended period of practice videography.

## Data Analysis

In addition to the usual issues of any data analysis process, video introduces some unique potentials:

- Video offers repeated viewing of the same event. Watching a rich complex scene many times often can lead to insights that cannot be gleaned from a textual transcript of the same scene.
- Video can support interpretations from many frames of analysis. Thus, it is possible to use video as a common medium for a rich multidisciplinary analysis from many points of view.

- Video can be shared with the participants in it, thus creating the opportunity for getting a participant's own point of view about his or her behaviors.

If a research project is going to the effort of capturing video data, it is worth structuring the analysis process so that advantage can be taken of some of these potentials.

Data reduction is always an especially pressing problem with video data, and some forms of sampling and the progressive reduction of detail are always required. Planning a systematic approach to move from hundreds of hours of video to presentable results is the central challenge in the productive use of video data. Computer-based analysis tools can be extremely helpful in this regard by retaining the connection between an analysis and the actual scenes. This can make it possible to go back from the more reduced form to the richer data in order to check an interpretation. Computer-based tools also can make it possible to begin the analysis with a rough coding, such as a content log, and proceed to more fine-grained analysis, such as a transcript, on only those segments that contain interesting events.

## Presentation

Video can be an extremely compelling medium for presentations because it allows a researcher to make more direct connections between observable behaviors and interpretations. However, video can be used inappropriately as well. It is tempting to select the best case for presentation, rather than a more typical performance. Indeed, researchers often present video clips without describing the criteria for their selection. Furthermore, a short clip, taken out of context, can be highly misleading. The research community should begin to establish guidelines for presenting video clips in order to ward off such problems.

Guidelines might be developed for more than one genre. For example, a documentary movie might present intentionally a point of view or a set of points of view and be organized around a narrative. Documentaries often have extended segments in which the participants can tell their own story. In contrast, video that is intended to exemplify data analysis procedures might use shorter segments that juxtapose the data and its coding. Finally, it can be appropriate to produce a deliberately promotional video. In fact, such videos can be helpful in disseminating results.

# CONCLUSION

Video data can be an exceptional tool for educational research. Yet, like all tools, video has strengths and limitations. Realizing the strengths requires care in selecting equipment, practicing videography, and designing a logic of inquiry. Counteracting the limitations requires attention to the potential weaknesses and biases of the medium and devising appropriate complementary techniques. Although the process of producing rigorous results from video data can be lengthy and difficult, the beginning researcher should not be dissuaded from becoming involved in it. Even the fairly casual use of video data can produce compelling personal insights. It may be hard to get started with video, but, once embarked, it is unlikely that a researcher will want to revert to the former tools and techniques.

# ACKNOWLEDGMENTS

I would like to thank Michael Sipusic for his contributions to my thinking about videography. I am also grateful for Raul Zaritsky's insight about the future of digital video.

# APPENDIX

## Checklists

Things to do before the day of the shoot:

- Inform students and parents.
- Plan the shoot, considering class plan, activities, and materials.
- Do a dry run. Practice!
- Make sure that all necessary cables, adapters, extension cords, duct tape, and so on, are assembled.
- Set the time of day on the camera correctly.
- Choose a tape length at least 15 minutes longer than the anticipated need.
- Check the batteries in the microphones with a voltmeter and/or replace the batteries.

Things to do before recording:

- Select a primary focus (e.g., group work or full-class discussion).
- Get good sight lines to the primary focus.
- Place the microphones as close as possible to the primary participants.
- Try to capture faces and hands.
- Set the camera to manual focus and focus on an object in the focal plane.
- Check the sound.
- Check glare and backlights.

More things to do before recording:

- Consider secondary focuses.
- Keep wires away from heavy foot traffic.
- Tape down wires.
- Label tapes.
- Record with a time stamp visible.
- Consider the biases of the picture and the sound.

- Experiment with alternative angles.
- Use an electrical outlet, not batteries.

Things to do while recording:

- Start recording before the class begins; stop when the classroom is empty.
- Use a tripod as often as possible.
- The teacher should use "icebreakers" (small jokes) to relieve tension.
- Try to capture faces and hands.
- Use close-up shots only to capture materials temporarily.
- Capture the linkage between talk and materials.
- Be invisible (avoid sudden movement, noise, and intrusion).
- Do not focus on the teacher to the exclusion of the students.
- Do not move the microphones or overtly make participants aware suddenly that they are being taped.
- Do not move the camera rapidly.
- Avoid MTV-type production values (frames spilling over with action and rapid disconnected shots, similar to the techniques used on MTV).

# VI Curriculum Design As Research

Part VI focuses on productive relationships that should exist between projects aimed at the development of knowledge and information and those that emphasize the development of programs, software, or other curriculum materials for instruction and assessment. In fact, authors in this section describe how, even within a given project, interactions often should occur that involve knowledge development, curriculum development, and program development—or among the development of students, teachers, curriculum materials, and assessment instruments. These interactions are important because, during the past several decades, if any progress has been made in the development of programs and curriculum materials, it is because more is known. Yet, in mathematics and science education, more money has gone into the development of materials and programs than into the development of basic understandings about teaching, learning, and problem solving. In fact, curriculum developers and program developers are seldom given adequate support to go beyond addressing simple-minded questions such as: *Does it work?* —Of course it works. Virtually all programs and materials work in some ways, for some students, under some circumstances. Therefore, more significant questions might focus on when, where, why, how, for whom, and in what ways does it work.

In Part VI, each of the first three chapters deals with the following types of basic questions: How can we deal with curriculum design as a scientific enterprise? How can this enterprise be made more cumulative, so that new efforts build on past efforts in systematic ways? What can be done to optimize the probability that, when curriculum development projects end, more is known? Do certain resources, tools, or enabling capabilities need to be developed so that greater progress could be made by all? If curriculum development projects focus on making incremental improvements in existing practices, then what can be done to avoid neglecting opportunities that cannot be addressed in incremental ways?

In the first two closely related chapters in Part VI, Battista and Clements look first at curriculum development in general, and then at software development in particular, as activities that need to be subjected to the same level of testing and evaluation that is applied to more basic types of research on teaching and learning. Next, Roschelle and Jackiw explore similar themes while presenting a view of how the development of technology-oriented curriculum materials can adopt a more encompassing outlook than the simple one-software-solution-to-one-educational-need approach. Finally, in Part VI, Dennis shows how the curricula that many take for granted in mathematics and science education are the results of choices and opportunities that were made in the past, and that may not have been well informed by either educational needs or solid perspectives about teaching and learning. Dennis' chapter also sensitizes researchers to the fact that, for progress to be made in curriculum development, it often is productive to approach problems from a variety of perspectives: for example, (a) *a psychological perspective* about how fundamental constructs develop in the minds of children in typical learning environments; (b) *a mathematical perspective* about how fundamental constructs develop according to logical constructions; (c) *a pedagogical perspective* about a variety of ways that fundamental constructs can be approached in a variety of curriculum materials that are available; and (d) *a historical perspective* about how basic constructs developed in the history of science.

Before reading the chapters in Part VI, readers may find it useful to formulate responses to the following questions for a research that they themselves might want to conduct:

1. In mathematics and science education, many innovative curriculum developers are well known for the attention they have given to investigations about the historical development of relevant constructs. One reason for this fact is that historical investigations often yield insights about what conditions were required to create the need for targeted ways of thinking. Therefore, innovative instructional materials often aim at putting students in situations in which they confront similar needs. Describe some ways that historical investigations might be relevant to your research.  What limitations do you see in the historical approach?

2. The research designs emphasized in this book are those that have helped mathematics and science education researchers focus on projects that make a difference in both theory and practice; and, the primary practitioners whose views are emphasized have been teachers. But, it is also important not to neglect other relevant practitioners. They include: curriculum developers, software developers, assessment developers, program developers, parents, and policymakers. Which practitioners do you want to emphasize in your own research? In what ways might a choice to emphasize different practitioners have different influences on the questions you ask, the data you collect, and the perspectives you adopt?

3. When researchers attempt to address the needs of teachers, administrators, and policymakers, it sometimes is important to go beyond answering questions that people *do* ask, to help them formulate new ways of thinking about questions that they *should* ask. For issues that might be related to your own research, what unfortunate outcomes could result if you simply accept naive formulations of issues that decision makers may raise?

4. Under what circumstances do you consider project evaluations to be research? Under what circumstances do you consider other types of assessment to be research?

# 25 Mathematics Curriculum Development as a Scientific Endeavor

**Michael T. Battista**
*Kent State University*

**Douglas H. Clements**
*The State University of New York–Buffalo*

> If I have seen farther than others, it is because I have stood on the shoulders of giants.
>
> —Isaac Newton (as quoted by Steen, 1990b, p. 7)

Because of the chaotic way that mathematics curricula are developed in the United States, it is unlikely that we will soon hear Newton's words repeated by a curriculum developer in mathematics education. In this chapter, we argue that curriculum development in mathematics education makes little progress because it fails to adhere to scientific methodology. We discuss weaknesses in the current development process, how such development can become scientific, how curriculum development should be related to research on learning and teaching, and some possible criticisms of taking a scientific approach.

# A FLAWED PROCESS

A curriculum[1] is a detailed instructional blueprint for guiding students' acquisition of certain culturally valued concepts, procedures, intellectual dispositions, and ways of reasoning. Mathematics curricula link the practice of teaching to curriculum developers' knowledge and beliefs about mathematics, learning, teaching, schools, and culture. Ideally, mathematics curricula should form concrete ties that link research on learning and teaching to classroom instruction in a synergistic system.

But, belying its critical importance, the development of mathematics curricula in the United States is chaotic and suffers from major methodological flaws. First, almost anyone can engage in it. University professors and graduate students in mathematics and mathematics education, teachers, school administrators, parents, school districts, publishing companies, state departments of education, professional organizations, and funding agencies are all involved in the development of mathematics curricula. Curriculum development activities are taking place in National Science Foundation projects whose major goals are research, curriculum development, teacher enhancement, and systemic change. The difficulty with this plethora of players is that there are no established standards for development, peer review, communication, or professional training.

Second, too often the development of mathematics curricula is totally disconnected from research on students' mathematics learning. Frequently it is planned in "brainstorming" sessions in which the most prevalent justifications for curricular decisions are based on traditional "prerequisite analysis" ("We have to teach this because it is needed next year in..."), personal experience ("An activity that I used when I taught was . . ."), vague intuitions ("This doesn't feel right."), and duplication of previously published treatments ("Did you see the activity written by so and so?"). Such sessions rarely explicitly incorporate research findings and theoretical perspectives into instructional design. Some curriculum developers even state

---

[1]Throughout this chapter, we use the term *curriculum* to refer to what many would call the "intended curriculum," as opposed to the "implemented curriculum."

privately that research on learning does not seem very helpful in designing curricula; so they make no attempt to carefully consider it during the design process. Additionally, curriculum materials relying on technology often are based more on what is possible with the technology rather than on what research suggests is possible or desirable for students (Battista, 1988).

Third, there is little reflection on or documentation of the *process* of developing mathematics curricula. Because this process has not been subjected to the critical scrutiny of scientific analysis and review, curriculum developers continually "reinvent the wheel," frequently evidencing little progress over previous efforts. In fact, K. J. Wilson and Daviss (1994) likened the current state of curriculum development in the United States to that of aeronautics before the time of the Wright brothers at Kitty Hawk:

> A century ago, people making airplanes were usually solitary, self-taught visionaries or eccentrics following their own theories or hunches. They lacked a good deal of information about aerodynamics. . . . They continued to work separately, often unknowingly crossing and recrossing each other's tracks, unable to take advantage of or build on each other's successes. (p. 98)

## AN EXAMPLE: GENERAL GOALS, NEBULOUS OUTCOMES

The following draft of an instructional activity for second-grade students was created by a team of educators (including the authors) involved in an elementary mathematics curriculum development project funded by the National Science Foundation. The curriculum was intended to be consistent with the National Council of Teachers of Mathematics' *Curriculum and Evaluation Standards* (1989). Its general goals were: (a) to offer students meaningful mathematical problems; (b) to emphasize depth in mathematical thinking rather than exposure to a series of fragmented topics; and (c) to have students invent their own strategies and approaches rather than rely on memorized procedures.

In the following sections, we provide the lesson plan given to a teacher familiar with the goals of the curriculum. We then analyze the class discussion in which the teacher attempted to help students integrate the ideas they had worked on for several days.

## The Lesson Plan

*Goals.* This lesson provides another context in which students can see several skip-counting sequences. It also will be good experience for students who in later grades are going to explore the enumeration of cubes in three-dimensional rectangular buildings.

*Description.* Students use interlocking cubes to construct buildings, pretending that each cube is a room in a building. The teacher shows three cubes attached together in a row (see FIG. 25.1) and says:

FIG. 25.1.

> This is a one-story building. How many rooms does it have? How many rooms will there be in the building if you make it two stories or floors high? There must be the same number of rooms on each floor. Try it and see. How many rooms would there be if the building were three stories high? Four stories? Can you predict, without building it, how many rooms would be in the building if it were 10 stories high?

The rectangles lettered A, B, C, D, and E show the outline of the bottom story of five different buildings (see FIG. 25.2). Students record in a table the number of rooms in each building if the building were one story high, two stories high, and so on.

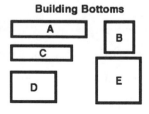

**Building Bottoms**

| Building | 1 Story | 2 Stories | 3 Stories | 4 Stories | 5 Stories | 10 Stories |
|----------|---------|-----------|-----------|-----------|-----------|------------|
| A B C    |         |           |           |           |           |            |
| D E      |         |           |           |           |           |            |

FIG. 25.2.

*Suggestions for Class Discussion.* Ask students to share their findings for Building A. As they state their results, record the numbers on the board: 5, 10, 15, 20, 25, 50. *Look at these numbers. Where have we seen this pattern before?* Students may point out that they are counting by fives or skip-counting. Ask them if they can explain why they are counting by fives.

Ask students to share results for Buildings B and C. *Why do the numbers come out the same?* Ask students to build three-story buildings for B and C and compare them. *What is the same about the buildings? What is different?*

## Observation of the Final Class Discussion

- Teacher: Look at your numbers on the *Build a Building* sheet. Tell me what you have written about building A.

- Marti: 5, 10, 15, 20, 25, 50.

- Teacher: Look at those numbers. What's going on?

- John: That's the same as counting by fives. When I got 25, I doubled it to get 50.

- Teacher: How come you got started counting by fives?

- Bob: Because A is five cubes.

- Nate: How come they don't build any buildings like that?

- Teacher: I don't know.

- Monica: I know the numbers in some of the others.

- Teacher: I want to hear more about A.

- Sherry: You can find 25 + 25. 20 + 20 is 40, and not forgetting the two 5s, that's 10. Add 10 + 40 = 50.

- Teacher: You wanted to share how to add 25 and 25. Now let's hear about B. Look at the numbers for Building B.

- Mikal: I discovered something about the fives. The second number goes 5, 0, 5, 0.

- Teacher: Mikal noticed a pattern.

- Marti: On the 10 stories, all of them have zeros at the end.

- Walter: Building B counts by four; 4, 8, 12, 16, 20, and then you double it to get 40.

- Teacher: How is that counting by fours? Can you explain that? [Walter looks up, thinks, and shakes his head to indicate a negative response.] Is that something that's so clear in your head, that you can't figure out how to explain it?

- Walter: Yeah.

- Monica: How I got the numbers. I didn't know exactly how to count by fours, so I built it and then I counted.

- Teacher: Counting by fours doesn't come as quickly as counting by fives, so you found a good way to get the answer.

- Alan: I noticed something. B and C are the same [in the table].

- Teacher: Read us the numbers.

- Alan: 4, 8, 12, 16, 20.

- Marti: B and C have the same amount of cubes, but they're a different shape.

- Tina: So if C was really long and wide, it wouldn't fit. Or if B was small and really tiny, it wouldn't fit.

The teacher asks Tina if what she is saying is that they can be different shapes on the bottom but have the same number of cubes. Tina shakes her head to indicate a negative response. The teacher asks students to make Buildings B and C each three layers high (see FIG. 25.3).

Teacher: How are these [the buildings] the same and different?

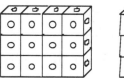

FIG. 25.3.

- Tina: One building goes up in a different way.

- Megan: One building has two on each one and the other has four on each one.

- Bob: One is fatter.

- Monica: I noticed that one building has three holes on one side and six holes on the other.

The teacher asks if she can call the holes windows, and the students agree. The teacher counts 12 windows on one face of Building C and 6 on one face of Building B.

- Nate: That would be a cube if you take off one floor. [The teacher agrees.]

- Mikal: If you build A up to ten, the front would be a building, but what would be the back?

- Teacher: Are you noticing that in one building they just have one room?

- Mikal: Yes.

- Teacher: How many windows would you have in each building?

- Mikal counts 24 in one and 30 in another.

- Teacher: If windows were very expensive, which kind of building would you build?

- Students: A.

- Teacher: Maybe that's why they don't build many buildings that way.

## A Rudderless Ship

This episode is an example of a rather diffuse type of "inquiry teaching." The teacher, her aide, and an observer from the curriculum development staff all expressed praise for what happened in class on the day of the discussion. They saw enthusiastic students actively engaged in mathematical exploration, thinking, and communication. We agree. However, we also see substantial difficulties. The discussion resembled a "show-and-tell" sharing session and lacked a clear conceptual focus. It is true that the comments of several students indicate that some nice thinking had occurred. But, that thinking rarely became the focus of discussion. How did the students know that doubling the number of rooms for 5 stories gave the number of rooms for 10 stories? When a student commented that taking a layer off one of the buildings would make a cubical building, there was no follow-up. The teacher pursued the "windows" idea, but the resulting discussion did not seem to lead to anything worthwhile, and it was unrelated to the goals of the lesson. In fact, there was only one attempt by the teacher to get the students to think about one of the major objectives of the lesson from the curriculum designer's point of view—the meaningful application of skip-counting. But this attempt failed to promote the desired discussion.

Furthermore, we wonder how meaningful the students' enumeration of cubes was. Were students determining the number of cubes in each building by spatially organizing the cubes then enumerating them, or did they merely detect a number pattern that they connected superficially to the structure of the buildings? Subsequently we asked three second-graders who had correctly completed Buildings A through D (only one student had time to complete Building E) to enumerate cubes in a building that measured three by three by four cubes.[2] Two of the three gave incorrect answers. The first counted the cubes one-by-one by columns but omitted the middle four by three layer of cubes; she got 24. When asked to check her answer, she said that there were three layers, but she still enumerated by columns of four. The second student gave an answer of 40, saying, "That's how many it looks like." The third student correctly skip-counted cubes by columns, not by layers. Thus, the students' work on the *Build the Buildings* activity did not seem to have caused any of them to abstract a layer structuring for enumerating cubes in spite of the fact that the activity directed students to determine the number of cubes layer by layer. Instead, it seems that the students used number patterns that were not well connected to spatial quantities. In fact, research shows that older elementary, and even middle school, students have great difficulty meaningfully enumerating cubes in three-dimensional rectangular arrays (Battista & D. H. Clements, 1996).

In conclusion, the original, intuitively derived claim that students' work with the *Build the Buildings* activity would be "good experience" for dealing with cube buildings in later grades is a conjecture that should not have been taken for granted but should have been investigated explicitly. The practical goal of giving students experience with skip-counting in the context of cube buildings seemed to have caused the curriculum developers to ignore relevant research on students' understanding of three-dimensional arrays of cubes.

This episode, then, illustrates what happens when instruction is designed with only general goals in mind and with little or no connection to relevant research on students' cognitive constructions. The educators in the classroom judged the unit successful because it supported a spirit of inquiry in which students were employing skip-counting and making

---

[2] These students were tested at a site different from that in which the class discussion took place.

discoveries.[3]    However, because the curriculum designers did not adequately attend to the nature of students' mental constructions, as our interviews suggest, it is quite likely that the students' solutions to the instructional problems were the result of superficial application of number patterns. Furthermore, as the classroom observation illustrates, the focus of the lesson was so diffuse that it is unlikely that the activities promoted meaningful learning of a planned set of concepts. Thus, although the unit may have possessed many characteristics of effective mathematics instruction, its lack of conceptual coherence caused it to be much less effective than it could have been.

## CURRICULUM DEVELOPMENT AS SCIENTIFIC ACTIVITY

In the mainstream of our culture, scientific knowledge is particularly valued because of the reliability it provides us in dealing with our experiences while in pursuit of our goals. "Our faith [in science] rests entirely on the certainty of producing or seeing again a certain phenomenon by means of certain well defined acts" (Valery, 1957, as quoted by von Glasersfeld, 1995, p. 117). In fact, scientific knowledge is deemed more reliable than commonsense knowledge because it employs the "scientific method" to ensure that it is built up in a way that is explicit and repeatable (von Glasersfeld, 1995). Such knowledge is constructed according to standards that are upheld by scientific communities of scholars committed to particular sets of questions, lines of reasoning, methods for verifying predictions, and shared ways of "seeing" the world    (Romberg, 1992a). Members of these

---

[3] We do not mean to ignore the benefits of such an inquiry environment on students' beliefs about the nature of mathematics and the way that proper beliefs can affect students' practice of mathematics. But we believe that such inquiry can and should take place while carefully promoting the construction of the specific concepts that students need to acquire to be mathematically literate.

communities review, critique, and build on each other's work to produce knowledge that they take as established and reliable.[4]

To provide explicit and repeatable treatments of phenomena in need of explanation, the scientific method generally includes four steps, all of which must be documented in the dissemination of results (von Glasersfeld, 1995):

1.  The conditions under which a phenomenon is observed are made explicit so that the observation can be repeated.

2.  A theory is proposed to explain how the observed phenomenon arises.

3.  The theory is used to deduce a prediction about an event that has not yet been observed.

4.  An attempt is made to produce the predicted event by generating the conditions under which the theory predicted it would happen. The conditions actually generated and the resulting observations are made explicit.

In implementing the scientific method, the social sciences generally place less emphasis on establishing "predictability," focusing instead on finding "plausible interpretations" (Bruner, 1990). Nevertheless, there is still an assumption that the interpretations and conclusions drawn from observations in one context will be generalizable or applicable to similar contexts not yet studied (Martin & Sugarman, 1993). Moreover, social scientists adhere to the fundamental scientific principles of documentation, explicitness, theory building, peer review, and commitment to the systematic cooperative construction of knowledge in their respective disciplines.

---

[4] However, the extent to which individual members of scientific communities believe in this knowledge depends on the degree to which they have found that the knowledge personally viable (i.e., it has "worked" for them in the past), and that their understanding of the knowledge is shared by others (von Glasersfeld, 1995).

In mathematics education, research about the learning and teaching of mathematics is one example of scientific activity. It is disciplined inquiry involving the use of procedures accepted by a community of researchers to systematically investigate and explain phenomena in teaching and learning mathematics (Kilpatrick, 1992; Romberg, 1992a). We contend that for curriculum development in mathematics education to progress beyond its current state of chaos and inefficiency, it too must become scientific. To move beyond the "intellectually soft, intuitive, informal and cookbooky" nature historically attributed to "design sciences," such disciplines must develop and adhere to "a body of intellectually tough, analytic, partly formalizable, partly empirical, teachable doctrine about the design process" (H. A. Simon, 1970, as quoted in Wittmann, 1995, p. 362). In fact, it has been argued that only by becoming scientific can such enterprises make "progress" (Kuhn, 1962/1970).

In the following two sections, we provide a framework for making curriculum development more scientific. This framework not only can guide curriculum development efforts, it can serve as a backdrop, or set of standards, against which the process of curriculum development can be studied and evaluated.

## ELEMENTS OF A SCIENTIFIC APPROACH TO CURRICULUM DEVELOPMENT

> The whole of science is nothing more than a refinement of everyday thinking.—Albert Einstein (quoted by Donadio, J. Smith, Mesner, & Davison, 1992, p. 370)

To take the first step toward becoming scientific, curriculum developers need to explicate their theoretical standpoints, judgments, purposes, and procedures so that the development process is recorded, shared, and opened to critical reflection and discussion. Such explication includes the six activities described as follows (cf. Gravemeijer, 1994; Romberg, 1992a). Partial implementations of these activities within actual curriculum development projects are illustrated in Battista and D. H. Clements (1988, in press), D. H. Clements, Battista, and Sarama (in press), and Gravemeijer (1994).[5]

## Describe the Problem That the Curriculum Development Effort Seeks to Solve

The "problem" is the creation of a certain type of curriculum. What is the nature of the curriculum? What are the general philosophy and goals for the curriculum; why are they desirable; are they compatible; why should we believe they are attainable? Why is the new curriculum needed? What is novel about the curriculum and what purpose does the novelty serve? Of course, the goals might be quite eclectic, including notions such as teaching mathematics in a way that is consistent with the National Council of Teachers of Mathematics' *Standards* (1989), teaching mathematics through inquiry or problem solving, teaching mathematics in a way that is consistent with the radical constructivist view of learning, offering students meaningful mathematical problems; emphasizing depth rather than exposure to topics, expanding the pool of mathematically literate students, and increasing the success rate for at-risk students. The goals for the curriculum may also extend to factors related to the institutional, economic, political, and cultural contexts in which schools are situated (Apple, 1992).

## Provide a Theoretical Explanation of How the Curriculum Development Effort Should Solve the Problem

Based on their beliefs about what mathematics is, how it is learned, and how it should be taught, curriculum developers should have a theory about how their curriculum ensures that students will learn what is intended (Gravemeijer, 1994). The developers' sense making in this regard must be explicit. They must clearly elaborate not only how the development process will lead to a curriculum that will meet the goals they have articulated, but exactly how this curriculum will enable students to learn particular concepts, procedures, and ways of

---

[5] We do not think that any curriculum developers, including us, perform all of these activities. But that is not a reason for claiming that such activities should not or cannot be done.

reasoning. They must identify the mental operations that underlie the mathematical capabilities their curriculum seeks to develop and describe how their instructional tasks will engender these capabilities.

To be scientific, a curriculum development effort must describe how it is related to the relevant work of others (Romberg, 1992a). This includes comparing development work with existing curricula, and, more important, explicitly connecting the design of instructional activities to theories of learning and teaching and related research. The developers should describe how extant theories and research are applied or connected to the derivation of specific instructional activities. Predictions about what will happen and why should be made. What cognitive changes are expected in students? How will the proposed instructional activities cause these changes? How will cognitive changes alter students' mathematical behaviors? Several elements of research on students' learning of mathematics that are essential in this regard are described in the next section.

Finally, curriculum developers must explicate their decisions about the inclusion of topics in a curriculum. Too often, such decisions are arbitrary or based solely on tradition. Why should a particular topic be included in the curriculum? What evidence is there that students who study this topic will be able to make it meaningful? How will students make sense of it and why will it be significant for them (as opposed to the curriculum developers)? Often, research on students' learning provides insights into the sense that students make of particular mathematical topics. Other times, curriculum developers must rely on personal theories that they will need to confirm or disconfirm.

As an example, once it had been decided that a curriculum we were developing would deal with volume in fifth grade, we set out to determine what aspects of this topic fifth-graders could make sense of. In examining the research relevant to this area, we found suggestions that older students confused volume and surface area. So we decided to have students make boxes out of square grid paper and determine their surface area and volume, hoping that this would help students discriminate the two concepts. However, when we gave our original instructional tasks to students and carefully examined how they thought about them, we found that merely determining how many cubes were needed to fill a box was far more difficult for students than we had imagined. But it was not because they were confusing surface area and volume. The students intended to enumerate cubes, but because of inadequate spatial structuring of the three-dimenional array, they were unable to do so correctly (Battista & D. H. Clements, 1996). Furthermore, because of the complexity of the situation, some students apparently failed to maintain the distinction between what they were looking at as they counted (squares) and what they intended to count (cubes); (Battista & D. H. Clements, 1996). Asking such students to determine surface area would have required them to use these squares for another purpose, something that we judged would add to their confusion. Thus, our careful work with students suggested that we abandon our original instructional strategy.

## Describe the Testing and Data Collection Procedures

Curriculum developers should explain the specific procedures that will be used for:

- Testing and revising materials.
- Collecting data during the formative period of testing and revising materials.
- Collecting data during the summative evaluation of the curriculum.

Developers must describe the general testing and revising cycle that will be used in designing specific instructional activities. For example, after examining both the research and instructional literature relevant to a particular topic, potential instructional activities will be created for testing. How will those activities be tested? With members of the development team working first with individual students, then, after appropriate revisions, with teachers using materials in their classrooms? What kinds of data will be collected during this formative period? What criteria will be used to decide if the activities are good enough to include in the finished curriculum?

Both for formative and summative evaluation, the curriculum development team must determine what types of data need to be collected to investigate how instructional activities are affecting learning. Qualitative methods seem especially well suited for such investigations (Gravemeijer, 1994; Wittmann, 1995). What combination of teaching experiments, classroom observations, interviews, case studies, and paper-and-pencil tests are needed to make sense of what is going on in the classroom against the background of the theoretical analysis that formed the basis for development? For example, once key cognitive processes, instructional tasks, and categories of students' reasoning have been established using teaching experiments and interviews, it is important to conduct long-term case studies of students' classroom learning and compare the results to those predicted by the underlying theoretical framework.

## Document the Development of Instructional Activities and the Collection of Data

Curriculum developers should describe how the process of development proceeds for each major topic in the curriculum. What substantial revisions of materials are made and why? How are these revisions related to data collected about students' learning? All data that are collected on students' learning with newly produced instructional materials should be reported. In fact, by describing things that did and did not work and why, curriculum developers can add to the knowledge base on learning and instructional design instead of attempting to convince others that their curriculum works. Taking this approach necessitates that all testing of instructional tasks be recorded on video- or audiotapes so that the evolution of students' learning with successively better tasks is recorded and can be analyzed. It represents a departure from the standard practice of working on activities until they "seem right," then moving on to an evaluation phase in which students' learning is evaluated formally. If the curriculum development has been connected properly to theory and research on learning, the data collected during this period can form a significant component of an associated research program.

## Analyze the Data and Records of Development

The development team should conduct an analysis to determine what has been learned about the effectiveness of the curriculum in promoting students' learning, the curriculum development process, and the theoretical and research base on which the curriculum development was based.

## Disseminate the Data and Analysis

Members of the development team should transmit their written analyses to others by publishing them in professional journals and by giving presentations at professional meetings.

# THE INTERPLAY BETWEEN CURRICULUM DEVELOPMENT AND RESEARCH

We emphasize that we are not calling for curriculum development to become "research." The scientific development of curricula differs from what we classically think of as research in that curriculum development focuses on the production of instructional activities, with most of the knowledge gained remaining implicit (Gravemeijer, 1994). In research, knowledge gain is the main concern; the focus is on building theories and descriptions that can be put before the research community.

Making curriculum development scientific will cause the knowledge generated therein to become explicit so that future development efforts can build on it. It will enable mathematics educators to integrate curriculum development and research on learning into a synergistic system, improving not only curriculum development and research but also teaching. To make curriculum development scientific and integrated with research, however, requires that curriculum developers explicitly connect design efforts with research findings, perspectives, and methodologies.

## Connecting Curriculum Development to Research Findings

Scientifically sound curriculum development cannot be based solely on *general* theories or philosophies. For example, as we saw in the illustrative example earlier, broad goals by themselves, even if worthwhile, are insufficient to effectively guide the design of instructional activities. A scientific approach to curriculum development requires that *all* relevant research on learning and teaching be considered. There are several findings in that research that mathematics curriculum developers cannot ignore.

First, it is well accepted among researchers that learners construct their own personal knowledge of mathematics rather than receive it ready-made from a teacher or textbook (Hiebert & T. P. Carpenter, 1992; Lester, 1994; Romberg, 1992a; Steffe & Kieren, 1994). For instructional activities to provide opportunities for students to produce such personally meaningful mathematical knowledge, the activities must be "grounded in detailed analyses of children's mathematical experiences and the processes by which they construct mathematical knowledge" (Cobb et al., 1990, p. 130). Curricula that focus on students' behaviors rather than on their cognitions and the nature of their experiences are inconsistent with this premise.

Second, all current research paradigms in mathematics education take it as axiomatic that instructional decisions must be based on knowledge about how students learn particular content, not merely on general theories of learning (Baroody & Ginsburg, 1990; Battista & Larson, 1994; Hiebert & Wearne, 1991; Koehler & Grouws, 1992). In fact, contemporary researchers in mathematics education have gone beyond Piaget's original psychological and epistemological theories to develop specific models of students' ways of operating as they construct increasingly sophisticated mathematical knowledge *in particular mathematical situations* (Steffe & Kieren, 1994). It is this elaboration and particularization of Piaget's general theory that "makes it possible to consider children's construction of mathematical knowledge in a way relevant to instructional issues" (Cobb et al., 1990, p. 126). Of utmost importance in this view of learning is the identification and description of key cognitive processes that underlie students' competence in various mathematical domains (Hiebert & Wearne, 1991). Thus, to formulate possible learning paths along which students' conceptual development in a particular mathematical domain might progress, curriculum developers must possess a model of how students' cognitive processes and structures in that domain can be gradually transformed into increasingly sophisticated conceptualizations (von Glasersfeld, 1987). Ideas for instructional activities must constantly be evaluated in terms of this model. That is, curriculum developers must frame the goals and success of instructional activities in terms of the cognitive processes these activities are meant to engender.

Third and finally, as reflective practitioners, teachers' knowledge, theories, and belief systems about teaching and learning mathematics influence their instructional plans, decisions, and actions as well as their utilization of curricula (T. P. Carpenter & Fennema, 1991). So if developers expect their curricula to be used as intended, in addition to instructional activities, they must provide materials that help teachers clearly understand not only their approach to learning and teaching, but the various learning paths that teachers are likely to see in their students.

## Connecting Curriculum Development to Research Perspectives

There is general agreement among researchers that students' learning of mathematics needs to be viewed from several different complementary perspectives, the most important of which are the psychological and sociocultural (Cobb, 1990; Cobb & Yackel, 1995). From the psychological perspective, we attempt to describe and interpret students' mathematical experiences; we try to understand the nature of students' personal mathematical creations. How do students view situations that we consider as requiring mathematical thinking? What strategies do they use to solve problems and why? What mental operations give rise to the mathematical concepts, strategies, and experiences that students are inferred to have? These include general operations such as abstraction, assimilation, and accommodation (von

Glasersfeld, 1995), and those utilized in specific situations such as the unitizing and partitioning operations described by Steffe and Cobb (1988), or the structuring, coordinating, and integrating operations described by Battista and D. H. Clements (1996).

From the sociocultural perspective, we attempt to describe the social and cultural factors that affect students' construction of mathematical meanings. We try to describe the development and functioning of mathematical classroom cultures. How are classroom norms and practices in mathematics formed? How are students' beliefs about their own and the teacher's roles in the classroom, as well as their beliefs about the mathematical enterprise, affected by their participation in classroom cultures? How does socially supported thought—say, the spirit of inquiry—become a mathematics classroom norm, and how does it become "internalized" by students? Though we generally focus our analysis on the culture of the classroom, sometimes we must extend it to the culture of the surrounding school and community (Cobb & Yackel, 1995).

Significantly, the relative weights that developers give to these two perspectives might greatly affect the procedures used in developing a curriculum. For instance, as developers design instructional tasks, how do they envision the resulting materials being used? If they intend to have students construct and sufficiently refine ideas without interacting with others, they will incorporate opportunities for perturbation and self-checking of students' theories into the tasks. They will develop and test materials first by conducting teaching experiments with individual students. Psychological factors will be at the forefront of their theoretical perspective. It is only during the second phase of development, when they have teachers test the materials with whole classes of students, that they will attend to sociocultural factors.

Alternatively, developers might envision instructional tasks as tools for guiding the evolution of mathematical practices and discourse in the classroom culture. A critical component in the design of these tasks is the expectation that students' learning will result from their adoption of socially negotiated classroom practices developed in response to the tasks. Initially, these developers might envision and test activities with whole classes of students; their perspective is primarily sociocultural. In our view, placing initial emphasis on sociocultural factors can be valid. But it must be accompanied by the psychological perspective—the developers must also carefully examine individual students' learning.

We conclude, therefore, that both the psychological and the sociocultural perspectives are critical in a scientific approach to developing mathematics curricula. Taking a psychological perspective is essential because the goal of instructional tasks is to change the ways that students think; we want to induce students' development of increasingly more sophisticated cognitive operations for dealing with particular domains of mathematics. But because students will be using these tasks within a classroom culture consisting of many students and a teacher, we also need to take a sociocultural perspective to understand how students' individual construction of meanings is related to their participation in the classroom community. Though it might be useful for one perspective to take precedence in the initial design of an instructional activity, it is imperative to consider both in the overall conceptualization and development of the activity.

A good example of how these two perspectives can be utilized in curriculum analysis is offered by the *Build the Buildings* activity described earlier. The educators in the classroom seemed to take primarily an implicit sociocultural perspective, judging that members of the classroom culture were productively engaged in mathematical inquiry.[6] But it was the psychological perspective that revealed the shortcomings in the instructional unit. The unit did not seem to effectively encourage individual students' construction of a set of targeted concepts. We could return to a sociocultural analysis to relate individual learning to the operation of the classroom culture. In a productive culture of inquiry, discussions involve more than show and tell; students listen to and critique each others' comments so that knowledge is acquired collaboratively.

## Connecting Curriculum Development to Research Methodologies

Methodologies utilized in research on mathematics learning frequently can be adapted to provide scientific rigor in curriculum development. As an example, we illustrate how teaching experiment-based methodologies advocated by constructivists (Steffe, 1996; von Glasersfeld, 1987b) can be used in the scientific development of mathematics curricula.

---

[6] It is likely that much of what the students did in this regard was due to the mathematical culture the teacher had engendered over many months.

*Preliminary Work.* Curriculum developers should determine the categories of mathematical minds, or ways of operating, that students have with respect to particular mathematical topics that are to be taught. In addition to reviewing relevant research, this should be accomplished by interviewing students or engaging them in exploratory teaching. In this step, curriculum developers generate tentative theoretically grounded models of students' present conceptions of and ways of reasoning about target topics. They also develop hypotheses about how students' current ways of operating can be guided toward adult competence.

*Teaching, Model Building, and Hypothesis Testing for Individual Students.* During teaching experiments conducted with individual (or perhaps pairs of) students, curriculum developers should formulate and test detailed working models of how students construct specific areas of mathematical knowledge. At this time, the goals should be to gain understanding of students' mathematical sense making and ways of operating, and to experiment with methods of modifying student's understandings and ways of operating. The psychological perspective will be dominant. By observing students' work on appropriately selected tasks, curriculum developers formulate hypotheses concerning what students' in each category of mathematical mind might learn. To test these hypotheses, developers present tasks to students and allow them to establish their own history of constructions.

*Retrospective Analysis for Individual Students.* After collecting data on individual students, curriculum developers should use videotape records of teaching episodes to perform a retrospective analysis of students' actions and interactions during the experiment. As part of this analysis, developers should constantly attempt to determine exactly what mathematical ideas students were personally constructing as they worked on instructional tasks, no matter how much these ideas differ from standard mathematical concepts.

*Teaching, Model Building, and Hypothesis Testing with Classes of Students.* Once curriculum developers have sufficient knowledge to effectively teach the desired topics interactively to individuals, they should use this knowledge to design instructional sequences that a teacher might use for an entire class. These sequences must accommodate the different mathematical minds that will exist in a class of students. Developers should test these instructional sequences and the models underlying them by conducting classroom teaching experiments in which whole classes are taught by students' regular classroom teachers. At this time, the goals should be to ascertain how students construct knowledge of the target concepts within a classroom setting, and to determine ways of modifying instructional sequences to maximize students' learning as they interact with the materials, the teacher, and other students. Although the sociocultural perspective will dominate, the psychological viewpoint cannot be forgotten. One way to accomplish the synthesis in perspectives required in this step is to conduct case studies of individual or pairs of students within the context of the study of the whole class.

*Retrospective Analysis for Classes of Students.* Curriculum developers should construct a retrospective analysis of classroom teaching experiments. In this analysis, they should seek to understand how students with different mathematical minds learned within classroom situations, and how aspects of classroom cultures affected individual student learning.

*Final Curriculum Revision and Scientific Model Building.* Curriculum developers should make final revisions to the curriculum, which includes instructional tasks, rationale for tasks, descriptions of how to implement tasks, and conceptual analyses of how students are likely to progress on them. They should also conduct a research-based analysis of learning and instruction within the completed curriculum. In this analysis, the activity of model building that was present throughout the development of instructional activities is revisited with the intention of building a final model that can be presented to the research community. Explanations in this model should be based on concepts in the core of the research program like assimilation, accommodation, mental model, scheme, reflection, and forms of social interaction, as well as concepts particular to the topic at hand, such as unitizing, structuring, coordination, and integration. Together, the retrospective analysis and scientific model building should provide a complete account of the development of students' mathematical knowledge and the effects of instruction on student learning within the completed curriculum. This account should include a description of how particular instructional tasks, learning environments, and sociocultural factors affected students' learning.

## Benefits

In addition to adding rigor to the curriculum development process, employing appropriately adapted research methodology can make the acquisition of knowledge during curriculum development methodologically sound and properly framed theoretically. Consequently, the resulting knowledge about learning and teaching, which traditionally has remained implicit, can meet the standards required to be published in research journals, adding vital information about learning and teaching to our knowledge base. Moreover, such "curriculum development research" can help practitioners better appreciate mathematics education research as applicable to classroom use.

Another benefit of applying research methodology to curriculum development is that it can focus attention on traditionally neglected aspects of the development process. For instance, both Guba and Lincoln (1989) and Cobb (1996) suggested that researchers include the perspectives of major stakeholders in research studies. Implementing this suggestion would require curriculum developers to systematically collect and represent the views of teachers and students who are using the newly developed instructional materials. Instead of researchers conducting studies about teachers' use or misuse of innovative curricula, or curriculum developers merely taking informal note of teachers' views—both of which are valuable activities—developers should systematically acquire teachers' comments about using the materials. They should then honestly represent the teachers' views in scholarly reports on the curriculum. Similarly, developers could gather and present the views of students.

## POSSIBLE CRITICISMS OF SCIENTIFIC CURRICULUM DEVELOPMENT

There are several potential criticisms that could be directed toward a scientific approach to curriculum development. In each case, however, we find that examining the criticism reveals strengths of this approach. First, not every mathematical topic that one wishes to include in a curriculum has been researched sufficiently to provide clear guidance for the design of instructional tasks. Consequently, curriculum designers often will have to conduct their own developmental research on these topics. The advantage of approaching curriculum development scientifically is that work done in this regard enters the professional literature in mathematics education, thus increasing the store of knowledge for curriculum development and research alike.

Another possible criticism of a scientific approach to developing curricula is that it will slow down the pace of development. Actually, we view this as an advantage. Rarely have funding agencies given curriculum development projects enough time to accomplish their goals. Quality curriculum development cannot be rushed. Much work in this field is like most current mathematics instruction—forever doing the same things, but doing them badly, so they have to be repeated. In fact, construing curriculum development as a scientific undertaking should cause the mathematics education community to drastically rethink the time frames and resources required for this essential activity.

It also might be argued that a scientific approach will stifle the creativity of developers. Though having standards for curriculum development might feel constraining to some initially, developers will learn to channel their creativity within these constraints, as have practitioners in other scientific disciplines. In fact, they will be members of the community that cooperatively establishes these constraints.[7]

An additional potential criticism to making curriculum development scientific is that it will make some curriculum development efforts legitimate and others illegitimate. Although some may view this practice as exclusionary, it is a necessary price for making curriculum development scientific. Indeed, the practice of any science is restricted to those who are willing to learn its core knowledge and become fluent in its established ways of operating. Besides, in today's haphazard world of curriculum development, there are many efforts that should be excluded (Wittmann, 1995). For instance, many current commercial projects are doing more harm than good. Too often, these projects tout traditional curricula with surface-level changes

---

[7]Thinking of scientific activity as problem solving can help researchers and scientifically minded curriculum developers avoid putting themselves into methodological straitjackets that impede, not accelerate, progress. When we are perplexed by a difficult problem, we often cycle through different phases in our attempts at finding a solution. In one phase, we try to generate good ideas, potentially fruitful paths to a solution. During this phase, it is unproductive to attend to all the details, to verify each step in possible solution paths. Doing so can waste time, and ultimately prove futile. In the second phase, after we have chosen a solution path, careful analysis is mandatory; we must painstakingly check our proposed solution. Because the science of curriculum development, and some would say research in mathematics education, is still in its infancy, we should be careful not to prematurely overspecify rigid methodologies for its practice.

as "reform curricula," giving school personnel who adopt them the impression that needed changes have occurred. Because the lack of genuine change is obscured, the mathematical miseducation of students continues.

Finally, it might be argued that making curriculum development scientific will devalue the wisdom of practice of experienced designers and teachers. It is true that intuition and experience can be valuable in guiding the development of curricula. But this "craft knowledge" can also be wrong (Leinhardt, 1990). To separate the wheat from the chaff, to refine this knowledge and preserve it so that others can build on it instead of duplicating it, requires a scientific approach. Indeed, taking a scientific approach is probably the only way to deal with the difficult problem of recording and learning from the "wisdom of practice" of experienced curriculum developers (cf. Leinhardt, 1990).

## CONCLUSION

Curriculum development, teaching, and learning are the core activities in the educational enterprise—educators develop curricula and teach so that students learn. Through research in mathematics education, the processes of teaching and learning mathematics have been brought under the scrutiny of scientific analysis, resulting in clear knowledge gains about both. But, so far, the process of curriculum development has eluded the organization, analysis, and progress that can come from adopting appropriate scientific standards. Until we make curriculum development more scientific, firmly establishing this critical link between research and practice, mathematics teaching will continue to flounder.

## ACKNOWLEDGMENT

Partial support for this work was provided by Grant RED 8954664 from the National Science Foundation. The opinions expressed, however, are those of the authors and do not necessarily reflect the views of the foundation.

# 26 Designing Effective Software

**Douglas H. Clements**
*The State University of New York-Buffalo*

**Michael T. Battista**
*Kent State University*

There is little doubt that technology will have a major impact on the teaching and learning of mathematics and science. However, we contend that results from the enterprise of designing effective software have fallen short of their potential. We take "effective" to mean simultaneously pedagogically efficacious and fecund in the development of theoretical and empirical research. In this chapter, we describe a model for integrated research and software and curricula development that we believe will help to fulfill the potential of software development and correlated research.

What of present practice limits software from fulfilling its promise? In the majority of cases, testing the software with target users is rare (which may account for the generally low quality of the software). Often, there is only minimal formative research, such as a polling of easily accessible peers, rather than any systematic testing with an appropriate target audience. "Beta" testing is done sometimes, but late enough in the process that changes are minimal, given the time and resources dedicated to the project already and the limited budget and pressing deadlines that remain (Char, 1989). Such testing is more summative than formative (Schauble, 1990).

Even when conducted, most summative evaluations are limited in scope. The majority of studies have used traditional quantitative designs in which the "computer" was the "treatment." The general conclusion drawn was that such treatments lead to moderate but statistically significant learning gains, especially in mathematics (H. J. Becker, 1992; D. H. Clements & Nastasi, 1992; Kelman, 1990; Roblyer, Castine, & King, 1988). However, this conclusion must be tempered with the realization that most of the software used presented drill and practice exercises. Therefore, the potential of software based on different approaches to learning (as well as the appropriateness of the methodology for evaluating such different types of software) has not been addressed adequately.

What of software based on other approaches to, philosophies of, and goals for learning? Many pieces of software are created from a vision that computers can provide experiences far beyond such drill and practice work. This recalls Duckworth's analysis of how Piagetian thought circa 1970 did and did not inspire good curricula. Simply put, details of children's learning and development obtained from Piagetian research failed to guide curricula development in direct useful ways (Duckworth, 1979). However, Piaget's constructivist vision did suggest, in general, the validity of encouraging children to "have wonderful ideas" (Duckworth, 1973). Similarly, some software is developed based on a vision of encouraging children to have and explore wonderful ideas with technology. Many developers proceed from intuition and unbridled creativity; often, their products are fascinating and may be worthwhile educationally, but typically they are unconnected to theory and research. Other developers are familiar with mathematics education research and theory and have extensive experience doing informal research with students and computers. Their products, then, are connected to theory and research, albeit indirectly, and can be of high quality (W. D. Crown, personal communication, December 4, 1995).

In contrast to either of these approaches, we argue that the time is ripe for research and software design to be more intimately connected, mutually supporting processes. Compared to Duckworth's era, the state of the art is such that we have models with sufficient explanatory power to permit design to grow concurrently with the refinement of these models (Biddlecomb, 1994; D. H. Clements & Sarama, 1995; Hennessy, 1995). Thus, software design can and should have an explicit theoretical and empirical foundation, beyond its genesis in someone's intuitive grasp of children's learning, and it should interact with the ongoing development of theory and research—reaching toward the ideal of testing a theory by testing the software. To maximize its contributions to both mathematics and science curricula and to theory and research, software development must take a large number of issues into consideration and proceed through a variety of phases.

# A MODEL FOR INTEGRATED RESEARCH AND CURRICULA AND SOFTWARE DEVELOPMENT

Capitalizing fully on both research and curriculum development opportunities requires the maintenance of explicit connections between these two domains and formative research with users throughout the development process (cf. Laurillard & J. Taylor, 1994). The complexity of computer-enhanced teaching and learning, including the need to examine both the processes and the products of learning and the variety of relevant social transactions, necessitates the use of multiple methodologies (see, e.g., D. H. Clements & Sarama, 1995; P. W. Thompson, 1992).

The research design model described herein moves through phases in a sequence that is as much recursive as linear. The phases begin with a draft of initial values and educational goals, proceed through a series of investigations with small numbers of children (e.g., clinical interviews and teaching experiments), and end (for the time being) in more summative, classroom implementations. Each phase is described and illustrated with examples from projects that used the model or aspects of it.

## Phase 1: Draft the Initial Goals

*Mathematical Learning Goals.* The first phase begins with the identification of a problematic domain of mathematics. This domain should be significant in two ways: The learning of the domain would make a substantive contribution to students' mathematical development, and learning about students' mathematical activity in the domain would make a substantive contribution to research and theory. For example, one team designed rational numbers microworlds (RNMs) (Biddlecomb, 1994; Olive, 1996; Steffe & Wiegel, 1994). We designed Logo environments for the learning of elementary geometry and the use of geometric models in other areas of mathematics (Battista & D. H. Clements, 1991; D. H. Clements & Battista, 1991).

In establishing mathematical learning goals, intense study of reform recommendations (National Council of Teachers of Mathematics, 1989, 1991b; National Research Council, 1989), the history of the curriculum domain (see Dennis, chap. 28, this volume), and equity issues is recommended. Equity issues (see Confrey, chap. 5, this volume) imply that considerable thought be given to the students who are envisioned as users and who participate in field tests; a convenience sample may be inappropriate. Systemic sociocultural issues, and, finally, technical issues should be considered as well.

*The Advantages and Disadvantages of Technocentrism.* Technocentrism refers to the tendency to place a technical object, such as a computer, in a central position (Papert, 1987). This leads to questions such as, "What is the effect of the computer on mathematics development?" There are palpable disadvantages to this perspective when considered in such a simplistic manner. It belies the complexity of the educational situation, omits considerations of types of software and types of mathematics (Skemp, 1976), and ignores the classroom culture. It also implies that the computer is an entity separate from other curricular considerations. In contrast, most designers of educational software who follow procedures consistent with the model described herein consider themselves creators of activities or curricula, not merely of software (Char, 1990; D. H. Clements & Sarama, 1995). They view software as one, albeit critical, piece of a situation involving planning to use the computer, using the computer, making sense of their experiences, and reasoning about them both at and away from the computer (P. W. Thompson, personal communication, November 29, 1995). Their goal is that students learn concepts and processes that are worthwhile with and without their experiences with the computer. They do not invent a tool first without asking, early in the process, for what it will be used (R. Lehrer, personal communication, November 30, 1995).

Can a focus on technology be advantageous? Reflecting on the actions and activities that are enabled by a new technology can catalyze a reconceptualization of the nature and the content of the mathematics that could and should be learned. Also, the developer can focus designs by thinking about how software might provide tools (that enhance students' actions and imagination or that suggest an encapsulation of a process) or constraints (obstacles they meet by design that force them to grapple with an important idea or issue); (Kaput, 1994). Finally, the flexibility of computer technologies allows the creation of a vision less hampered by the limitations of traditional materials and pedagogical approaches (cf. Confrey, in press). For example, computer-based communication can extend the model for science and mathematical learning beyond the classroom, and computers can allow representations and actions not possible with other media. Such thinking anticipates Phase 3 and illustrates the nonlinear nature of the design model.

The product of this first phase is a description of a problematic aspect of mathematics. This description should be quite detailed, especially if the purpose is developing innovative software and if the mathematics differs from that in common use.

## Phase 2: Build an Explicit Model of Students' Knowledge and Learning in the Goal Domain

The next step is to build a model of students' learning that is sufficiently explicit to describe the processes involved in the construction of the goal mathematics. Frequently, extant models are available, although they vary in degree of specificity; some highly specific models can be used directly (e.g., Steffe & Cobb, 1988), whereas others are general and, therefore, mostly suggestive (e.g., D. H. Clements & Battista, 1991; van Hiele, 1986). Especially in the latter case, the developer uses clinical interviews and observations to examine students' knowledge of the content domain, including conceptions, strategies, and intuitive ideas used to solve problems. Students may use paper and physical materials (although these can be configured to anticipate the software experiences that will be designed). In these experiments, the teacher tries to set up a situation or task that will elicit pertinent concepts and processes. The interviewer asks follow-up questions to ascertain in as much detail as possible what and how the students are thinking about the situation. Pairs of children may be observed working on problems, because they can be more relaxed and expressive about their thinking and problem-solving activity with a peer. Once a (static) model has been partially developed, it is tested and extended with exploratory teaching (see Steffe & Thompson, chap. 11, this volume). This approach contrasts with that of the "wonderful ideas" perspective, with its initial focus on what the computer can do and succeeding attempts to use these technological capabilities to teach mathematics.

If specific activities are planned as a component of the software, similar techniques are used to assess the relative appropriateness of proposed problems. That is, there must be teaching that is exploratory and intuitive, followed by analyses. The researchers' mental models of students' thinking in the domain guide their design of the activities. As is true at each phase of development, the researchers' further experiences with new students provide feedback that leads to modification of that mental model. Other approaches are possible. For example, Char (1989) analyzed major textbook activities, examining such dimensions as curriculum goals, types of problem levels, nature of presentation, and nature of user response.

The end result of this phase is an explicit model of students' learning of mathematics in the target domain. Ideally, such models specify knowledge structures, the development of these structures, and mechanisms or processes of development. To repeat a caveat: Activities and results of this phase are connected, even overlapping, with those in the following phases, with the model of students' learning developing constantly.

## Phase 3: Create an Initial Design for Software and Activities

*Plan the Design.* Our descriptions and illustrations of this phase become more specific. We continue our focus on the design of theoretically based and research-based microworlds. However, there are many other possibilities, such as producing:

- A cognitive tool (specifically, a computer enactment of lower level operations, obviating the need for novices to achieve automatization of these skills prior to carrying out higher order thinking; Lajoie, 1990).
- A simulation (Hennessy, 1995).
- A programming language (e.g., Logo).
- Specialized programming language (e.g., StarLogo).
- Scriptable, modular components that may represent any of these types.

The software might be embedded in a student-centered design. Though details of the design model would need to be modified for such diverse types of software, most of the components of our model apply.

Based on the model of students' learning generated in Phase 2, developers create a basic design to describe the objects that will constitute the software environment and the actions that may be performed on these objects. These actions-on-objects should mirror the hypothesized mathematical activity of students as closely as possible. The design also describes how the actions are to be instantiated (including the questions of what choices and options are available to the learners, and what should be decided by the developers). The rationale for these and all of the other design decisions is critical to the development and research process (Kaput, 1994).

For example, the RNM team (Biddlecomb, 1994; Steffe & Wiegel, 1994) included actions for creating objects ("Toys" in one program, line segments or "Sticks" in another), copying objects, uniting and disembedding objects, and hiding objects. In the Sticks microworld, for instance, students can segment sticks into parts or combine them into higher order units. Methods of production also illustrate these developers' theory-design connections. Objects can be produced by clicking (producing single objects) or (in Sticks) by dragging (producing an entire cluster that is constituted as a unit). "Covers" that hide some objects were included to encourage students' internalization of perceptual counting schemes. Finally, the authors wanted students to create and reason with composite units, so, they incorporated such objects as "strings," "chains," and "stacks" of toys.

Such actions on objects—in this case, creating, copying, uniting, disembedding, and hiding both individual units and composite units—are in line with the mental actions that the developers wanted students to construct (D. H. Clements & McMillen, 1996). Further, the provision of objects and actions on these objects is consistent with the Vygotskian theory that mediation by tools and signs is critical in the development of human cognition (Steffe & Tzur, 1994).

The "Turtle Math" (D. H. Clements & Meredith, 1994) software was designed to include the traditional "turtle" object and actions on that object (e.g., entering commands on the computer such as "fd 30" or "rt 120") because children's initial representations of space are based on action, rather than on the passive "copying" of sensory data (Piaget & Inhelder, 1967). That is, we hypothesized that the use of Logo commands that correspond to the motions necessary for constructing geometric figures (e.g., moving forward and turning) increases the salience of the critical components of the figure. We also went beyond this by including objects that resulted from that activity (e.g., line segments or polygons) and actions on those objects (e.g., motions, scaling, and other transformations). Our early research indicated that such transformations are consistent with elementary students' mental motions (e.g., in "proving" congruency) and can extend these motions to more general and abstract levels (Johnson-Gentile, D. H. Clements, & Battista, 1994). Finally, we designed dynamic and consistent relationships between different representations of the same object (D. H. Clements & Battista, 1992). In other words, there is a dynamic link between the commands in the command center and the geometry of the drawn figure. Any change in the commands in "Turtle Math" leads to a corresponding change in the figure, so that the commands in the command center reflect the geometry in the figure precisely. In this way, command center code constitutes what we call a proleptic procedure. Thus, the Logo code in the command center stands halfway between traditional, immediate-mode records and procedures created in an editor, helping to link the symbolic and visual representations. The second basic issue is the directionality of the visual-symbol connection. One of Logo's main strengths has been its support of linkages between visual and symbolic representations. One of its limitations has been the lack of bidirectionality between these modes (Noss & Hoyles, 1992). That is, one creates or modifies symbolic code to produce visual effects, but not the reverse. "Turtle Math" provides a "draw commands" tool that allows the student to use the mouse to turn and move the turtle, with corresponding Logo commands created automatically. The student creates continuously first a turn ("rt" or "lt") command, then a movement ("fd" or "bk") command until he or she clicks outside the window. "Turtle Math" also provides a "change shape" tool that allows the student to use the mouse to alter the geometric figure directly, with corresponding changes made automatically to the Logo commands. Thus, Logo students benefit from the direct manipulation of geometric figures (cf. de Villiers, 1995). Such direct manipulation is consistent with students' mental operations (see, e.g., D. H. Clements & Battista, 1991, 1992; Johnson-Gentile et al., 1994) and, through dynamic connections, aids children in the abstraction and generalization of these operations.

Designs based on objects and actions force the developer to focus on explicit actions or processes and what they will mean to the students. This characteristic mirrors the benefit attributed to cognitive science models of human thinking; they did not allow "black boxes" to hide weaknesses in the theory. It must be emphasized that designs are not determined fully by this line of reasoning: Intuition and the art of teaching play critical roles in the design of software (cf. Confrey, in press). That is, this phase often involves the developers, as individuals and groups, decentering and imaging the projected activities and interactions.

*Consider Unique Characteristics of Computers.* Expanding on a theme introduced previously, developers should consider the potential unique contributions of the computer in planning objects and actions. For example, the dynamic aspect of Toys and Sticks (Biddlecomb, 1994; Steffe & Wiegel, 1994) captured students' interest, according to the developers. Students used their schemes in ways not possible when working in a mathematics textbook or with structured learning material such as Cuisenaire rods. From the students' perspective, acting in the microworlds created experiential situations that metamorphosed with every accommodation. That is, as the children added structure to the situations through their actions, the situations changed correspondingly and new possibilities for action emerged. The microworlds opened pathways for mathematical activity (Steffe & Wiegel, 1994). Additional conceivable characteristics of computer manipulatives include (D. H. Clements & McMillen, 1996, includes a discussion):

- Offering flexibility.
- Changing arrangement or representation.
- Storing and later retrieving configurations.
- Recording and replaying students' actions.
- Linking the concrete and the symbolic with feedback.
- Dynamically linking multiple representations.
- Focusing attention and increasing motivation.

- Changing the nature of the manipulative.

In addition to the aforementioned characteristics, the following have been identified as unique contributions of Logo and "Turtle Math" in particular (i.e., more so than previous versions of Logo):

- Promoting the connection of formal representations with dynamic visual representations, supporting the construction of mathematical strategies and ideas out of initial intuitions and visual approaches.
- Encouraging the manipulation of specific shapes in ways that help students to view them as mathematical representatives of a class of shapes.
- Encouraging wondering about and posing problems by providing an environment in which to test ideas and receive feedback about them
- Facilitating students' reflection on and modification of their Logo code (more than traditional versions of Logo).
- Providing sufficient flexibility so the range of opportunities to explore mathematics is enlarged for both students and teachers (D. H. Clements & Sarama, 1995; Sarama, 1995).

*Outline the Activities.* A sketch of the anticipated instructional tasks that use the software should be created. Preliminary activities for using the software should be based on:

- The model of students' learning.
- A review of the professional literature, from reform recommendations (National Council of Teachers of Mathematics, 1989, 1991; National Research Council, 1989) to activities from the literature.
- One's own past experiences.

Given the importance yet paucity of student-designed projects in mathematics education and the support that the computer can offer to such projects (D. H. Clements, 1997), provision for such self-motivated, self-maintained work should be considered. Specific teaching strategies should be included as part of the plan (see Hoyles & Noss, 1992). Again, the developers create a vision of the projected activities and interactions that may occur.

## Phase 4: Investigate the Components

During this phase, components of the software are tested using clinical interviews and observations of a small number of students. Critical questions include: Are children able to control the software with the input device(s)? How do children interpret and understand the screen design, objects, and actions? Because we wish to understand the meaning that students give to the objects and actions that we have created for their mathematical learning, there is a mix of model (or hypothesis) testing and model generation (e.g., a microethnographic approach; see Spradley, 1979).

This phase may use paper or physical material mock-ups of the software or early prototype versions. Some developers may use software that can create prototypes quickly, before programming in a faster, lower level language. Clements and Sarama (D. H. Clements & Meredith, 1994) used a generic version of Logo to create microworlds and activities that approximated the implementation desired. The researchers learned, for example, that two simultaneous representations of the geometric figure under construction were of maximum use to the children. With fewer, they lost connections between representations; with more than two, they became frustrated and confused (e.g., about which one could be edited). The RNM team (Biddlecomb, 1994; Steffe & Wiegel, 1994) also used Logo as their authoring language. This programming environment allowed them to make rapid changes in design features in response to children's use of the microworlds and their perceived needs.

In this and the following phase, communication between the designer and the developer (if they are different people) is essential. In our work, design, programming, and research were conducted by the same people. We believe that this approach has advantages for this type of software development and research. However, if programming is carried out separately, full communication about all of the aspects (e.g., goals, actions, objects, aesthetics, etc.) should be ensured.

## Phase 5: Assess Prototypes and Curriculum

This phase continues the evaluation of the prototype, rendered now in a more complete form. A major goal is to test hypotheses concerning features of the computer environment that are designed to correspond to students' thinking. Do their actions on the objects substantiate the actions of the researcher's mental model of children's mathematical activity? If not, what needs alteration: the mental model or the way in which this model is instantiated in the software?

In a similar vein, pedagogical features of the software are evaluated. That is, the software may go beyond the provision of objects and actions mirroring students' (hypothesized) cognitive structures. Creating dissonance may be a goal also. For example, we believe that one benefit of Logo is that students have to specify steps to a noninterpretive agent, with thorough specification and detail. The results of these commands can be observed, reflected on, and corrected; the computer serves as an explicative agent. In noncomputer (manipulative or paper) environments, one can make intuitive actions and corrections without such explicit awareness. Therefore, in evaluating early Logo microworlds (D. H. Clements & Battista, 1991) and prototypes of "Turtle Math" (D. H. Clements & Sarama, 1995), we were especially sensitive to students' interpretations and reactions to computer feedback. We found that the dynamic connection between the symbolic Logo commands and the graphic was critical, so we developed those connections further in succeeding versions.

*The Role of Teaching Experiments.* To this end, teaching experiments (see Steffe & Thompson, chap. 11, this volume) are conducted with a small number of students (as few as 2 on occasion, but often as many as 12). Although this phase mainly takes a model-testing approach, there remains significant adaptation to students' input. Often, a free exploration phase precedes the introduction of activities. In addition, the contributions of children are interpreted by the developer, and new tasks or questions are posed. Students' responses may indicate a need—or, more positively stated, an opportunity—to change the cognitive model, software, and activities.

For example, in their initial teaching experiments, the developers of "Toys" found some students could iterate composite units; therefore, they modified the computer environments to incorporate the iteration of units more explicitly (Biddlecomb, 1994). By way of illustration, one task presented students with two piles of toys (numbering 30 and 15) and asked how many strings of three could be made. A student who could not anticipate the results of iterating might add 30 and 15, then segment 45 by counting in threes. The student who anticipates may segment the 15 into 5 threes and the 30 into 10 threes and sum for a total of 15 threes. For such students, the result of iterating a unit could be either a unit of the same spatial dimensionality (e.g., a longer string of toys) or a composite unit of higher spatial dimensionality, such as a string iterated into a chain. Both of these actions were built into the software.

In addition, responses and advice of teachers playing the role of students may be sought in this phase. Based on these investigations, the prototypes are revised. This is the most iterative research-design phase; sometimes evaluation and redesign may cycle in quick succession, often as much as every 24 hours (Char, 1990; D. H. Clements & Sarama, 1995; see also S. Hennessy, personal communication, December 4, 1995). In this way, the computer environment (and the original model) is modified in ways not anticipated originally to fine tune, correct problems, check speed, and add functions whose need was not foreseen.

The teaching experiments, especially the latter ones during this phase, are rich with research possibilities. Using the model of mathematics learning as a guide, and the software and activities as a catalyst, the developer creates more refined models of particular students. Also collected is more detailed information about the worth of various features of the software and the teaching and learning interventions, some of which will be knowledge emerging from, and mutually constituted by, the developer-teacher and the student in the software context. Valuable empirical data may be garnered from the interactions of the students with the software, the activities (writ large), their peers, the teacher-developer, and combinations of them.

With so many possibilities, extensive documentation is vital. Videotapes (for later microgenetic analysis), audiotapes, and field notes can be collected.[1] Using the computer as a data collection assessment tool should not be overlooked either, a function to which we turn.

*Computer-based Assessment.* Computer-based assessment can take many forms (Lesh, 1990). As an example of a direct assessment approach, specially designed, computer-based, assessment items might use intelligent-answer checking, help functions, hints, feedback, follow-up questions, and information that is available, but only on request. Such items approximate human forms of dynamic assessment (e.g., as in Feuerstein, Rand, & Hoffman, 1979) and may be useful for research and educational practice (Gerber, Semmel, & Semmel, 1994). Lesh illustrated how such unique features of the computer can allow students to examine the mental models that they use to solve mathematical and scientific problems and to reconsider the validity of their solutions. He also suggested considering the use of computer-based story problems, graph- or table-based problems, and simulations.

Computers also can store data documenting students' ongoing activity. Solution-path recording is a particularly useful technique (Gerber et al., 1994; Lesh, 1990). Solution paths can be reexecuted and examined by the teacher, student, or researcher (and analyzed in many ways); they can be modified, as well. Issues such as the efficiency, simplicity, and elegance of particular solutions—even those that result in the same answer—can be assessed (Lesh, 1990).

---

[1]These sources, along with others, should be used also to reflect on those aspects of the design that were based on intuition, aesthetics, and subconscious beliefs; a detailed discussion of this is beyond the scope of this chapter (see Confrey, in press).

As another example, "dribble" files can record a complete, dynamic, visual recording of every step that a student takes in programming the Logo turtle. Then, each student's interaction with Logo can be analyzed, for example, to determine progression through SOLO learning cycles (Olive, 1991). Techniques such as videorecording a mix of two inputs, traditional camera video, and computer screen output serve similar purposes.

## Phase 6: Conduct Pilot Tests in a Classroom

There are two research thrusts during this phase. First, teaching experiments continue, but in a different form. We conducted such classroom-based teaching experiments (including what we call interpretive case studies) with one or two children. The goal was making sense of the curricular activities as they were experienced by individual students (Gravemeijer, 1994). Such interpretive case studies serve similar research purposes as teaching experiments (see Steffe & Thompson, chap. 11, this volume) but are conducted in a naturalistic classroom setting. Videotapes and extensive field notes are required so that students' performance can be examined repeatedly for evidence of their interpretations and learning.

Second and simultaneously, the entire class is observed for information about the usability and effectiveness of the software and the curriculum. Ethnographic participant observation is used heavily because we wish to research the teacher and the students as they construct new types of classroom cultures and interactions together (Spradley, 1980). Thus, the focus is on how the materials are used and how the teacher guides students through the activities. Attention is given to how software experiences reinforce, complement, and extend learning experiences with manipulatives or print (Char, 1989). Print materials, especially, are revised in this phase.

We reserve this pilot test phase for teachers familiar with the software and the curriculum. The class is taught either by one of the developers, standing in for the classroom teacher, or by a teacher intimately familiar with and intensively involved in curricula development.

## Phase 7: Conduct Field Tests in Multiple Classrooms

These field tests are conducted with several teachers who were not initially connected intimately with development. Again, the entire class is observed for information about the effectiveness and usability of the software and the curriculum, but more emphasis is placed on the usability by such teachers. We wish to know whether the software and its supporting materials are flexible enough to support multiple situations (e.g., variation in the number of computers available), various modes of instruction (e.g., demonstration to a class, class discussion, small-group work), and different modes and styles of management (e.g., how the teachers track students' progress through the materials, monitor students' problem solving with the materials, and assess students' learning). Again, ethnographic research (Spradley, 1979, 1980) is important, for two reasons. First, although the teachers may agree with the curriculum's goals and approach, their implementation of them may not be veridical to the developers' vision (Sarama, Clements, & Henry, in press). Second, in this phase, we need to determine the meaning that the various curricular materials have for both teachers and the students. In addition, of course, the final field tests may include summative evaluations.

There are other distinguishing features of this phase. Time is often more extensive; for example, we must give students long periods to use (and, ideally, to internalize, or to construct mental processes that mirror) the software tools. Assessment of students' competence and learning potential must include extended interaction and work on the activities and may require repeated engagements with the software. If projects were an aspect of the curriculum, extended time is especially important. Further, interactions become complex; researchers need to consider the activity, personal goals, where and when students become perplexed, how (or whether) they can recover, and so on.

In summary, Phases 4 to 7 provide a comprehensive approach to obtain advice from users and significant research data. Not every project can or should employ each phase; however, the reasons for omitting any phase and the coherence of the phases that are to be included should be considered carefully.

## Phase 8: Recurse

Interative and recursive actions within and between phases have been described already. However, often substantive progress is often made when a complete project (in our case, Battista & D. H. Clements, 1991; D. H. Clements & Battista, 1991) is revisited, refined, reconceptualized, and reborn (D. H. Clements & Meredith, 1994; D. H. Clements & Sarama, 1995).

## Phase 9: Publish

This phase appears obvious. The software and curricula may be disseminated through a variety of channels, from commercial publishers to the Internet. What is emphasized here, however, is the equal importance of publishing the research—both summative and formative. Many interesting pieces of software have been created. Frequently, though, the expertise developed during the production of that software is not disseminated. Whether because resources are exhausted (finances, time, and emotional energy) or because there is no interest, nonpublication has a strong deleterious effect on the field of curricula development and research.

# CONCLUSIONS

This chapter presented one model of "principled design," a way of linking development closely with scientific research. Those using such a model assume a responsibility to describe the details of their theoretical and empirical foundations and their design and to conduct the research deemed necessary not only to see if the design is successful, but also to trace whether that success can be attributed to the posited, theory–design connections.

Theoretical assumptions are involved always, of course, in the design of any educational materials. In this model, however, they have to be articulated clearly because they are to be reflections of the developer's model of children's mathematical concepts and processes. This explicitness guides and aids research as well, leading to questions and hypotheses that cannot be glossed over in summative evaluations.

Realizing the full potential of both the research and the curricula development opportunities requires consistent, coherent, formative research using multiple methodologies. Some have been discussed, among them clinical interviews, protocol analyses of students' problem solving, classroom observations, and interviews with teachers, students, and administrators. Others, such as systems thinking instruments, paired teachers' observations, students' immediate retrospective reports of their strategies, performance assessment, portfolio development, and content analyses of students' work, may be more suitable in certain situations. In any case, repeated intensive investigations are required.

Several caveats should be considered:

- It is a rare project that can afford to follow each phase of this model. Developers should plan either to treat each of these issues and phases comprehensively or to address a coherent subsection of them.
- Technology and its use in our culture are changing rapidly. Our designs, research questions, and methodologies should remain sensitive to new possibilities.
- No theory, research, or design can answer the question "What is best?" for numerous reasons, from practical limitations on branching at each

stage to recognition that such questions are inherently grounded in goals and values.

- The model and examples described here emphasize one class of effective software (one that is rooted in certain constructivist assumptions). The developmental model would need to be modified for other classes, such as intelligent tutorials with microadaptation assessment. However, the basic goals and procedures would be quite similar.

- Although this model offers comprehensive, rich data collection, the diversity of the methodologies employed could lead to incoherence and confusion between theoretical assumptions. Constant reflection and checks are ever more important in models such as this one.

- Our theoretical models and the software—to an extent, instantiations of these models—may funnel our perceptions and conceptions. Testing or refining our theories by testing or refining our software has significant advantages: We make our theories more explicit and we extend our visions of what students can do mathematically. Given the emotional investment in such a complex process, however, we must take precautions that our work does not contain self-gratifying, self-fulfilling circularities.

- The internal coherence and comprehensiveness of the proposed approach should not be mistaken for comprehensiveness at a global level of theory and research. There are many other issues and questions that must be addressed, from the myriad styles of instructional interaction to the social organization of the learning–teaching environment, to the social-cultural-political interactions at the school and community levels that affect implementation.

There is much to consider. There is also much to gain. The separation of curricula development, classroom teaching, and research in mathematics education has vitiated each of these efforts. Flexible application of the model proposed here can help to achieve the ideal of testing theory by testing software and activities.

# 27 Technology Design as Educational Research: Interweaving Imagination, Inquiry, and Impact

**Jeremy Roschelle**

*SRI International*

**Nicholas Jackiw**

*Key Curriculum Press Technologies*

> The reason why we are on a higher imaginative level is not because we have a finer imagination, but because we have better instruments. . . . The gain is more than mere additions; it is a transformation.
>
> —Alfred North Whitehead (1963, p. 107)

Designing educational experiences is an imaginative art. As designers, we anticipate and fabricate activities, resources, and conversations that will bring learners' inquiry to fulfillment, enabling their growth toward desirable skills, intuitions, and understandings. As Whitehead suggested, success in this art requires highly developed tools, and the computer, in its protean flexibility, is the most evolved tool of educational imagination.

The tools for our imagination have grown extremely quickly in the past decades. Logo, which was developed in the mid-1970s, inspired Seymour Papert and his followers to imagine "gears of the mind," powerful tools that allowed learners to make sense of complex phenomena (Papert, 1980). Multimedia enabled Howard Gardner's readers to imagine tools that leverage the "multiple intelligences" for learning, and reduced the influence of formal symbol systems in excluding learners (Gardner, 1993). Powerful visualization, simulation, and animation capabilities led scientists to imagine a new "third path" for learning that is neither empirical nor theoretical, but merges these two through the art of modeling (Horwitz & Barowy, 1994; Snir, Smith, & Grosslight, 1993). Miniaturization allowed Alan Kay, Adele Goldberg, and other educational pioneers to imagine "Dynabooks," which packaged powerful learning technologies in portable, hand-held devices (Goldberg, 1979; Kay & Goldberg, 1977).

Following close behind these inspired imaginations, a second wave of research has examined the consequences of technology for learning. New methods of teaching and learning have emerged, along with sound evidence of technology's potential to deepen understanding and improve access to difficult ideas. For example, new methods of teaching physics using microcomputer-based sensors have been developed (Mokris & Tinker, 1987; Thornton, 1987). Large-scale experiments have shown that desktop simulations can enable 6th-graders to understand physics concepts better than their 12th-grade counterparts (White, 1993). Geometry has been reinvigorated through the use of dynamic graphical construction (Jackiw, 1988-1997). Intelligent tutors have produced a reliable standard deviation gain in students' learning (Anderson, Corbett, Koedinger, & Pelletier, 1995). Most important, we have learned that successful deployment requires simultaneous innovation in software, curricula, pedagogy, teacher training, and assessment (Fisher et al., 1996).

Today, the strands of imagination and inquiry are continuing forward into exciting new technological platforms. Networking, an old technology with new currency, has many researchers exploring communities of learners unrestricted by geographical boundaries, physical abilities, and other barriers to collaboration (e.g., Riel & Levin, 1990; Ruopp, Gal, Drayton, & Pfister, 1993). Group-oriented software ("groupware") exploiting this connectivity affords electronically mediated conversations that both facilitate and guide well-structured scientific discourse (Pea, 1993a). Another important strand of current research examines the potential of hand-held personal devices to complement computers (Tinker, 1996b). At the far extreme of technical accomplishment, cognitive scientists have implemented intelligent tutors that can control the branching path of a learning experience to match an expert model (Wenger, 1987).

In part due to the imagination and inquiries of the researchers cited previously and many more unnamed colleagues, educational technology now has widespread legitimacy. In the United States, one finds computers—in labs and classrooms—in almost every school. The organizations that proctor standardized tests permit calculators in ever-growing number. The call for a greater and closer integration of technology and teaching is heard not only from manifestos written on the research fringe, but also from curriculum committees, textbook authors, and teachers' organizations.

Despite this sense of flourishing accomplishment, optimism about educational technology is clouded by awareness of the difficulties that lie ahead. Too many of the aforementioned victories have produced glowing research reports but left no trace in classroom practice. Learning technology has a dark history of marginalization in mainstream institutions; technology is dismissed from the classroom as quickly as it arrives. Each wave of "revolutionary" new technology—television, film, and audio workstations—has disappeared quietly into relatively circumscribed niches. In these niches, older technologies surely serve a useful role, although this role is negligible in the overall scale of the institutions involved. By and large, newer technologies and conceptions of the educational mission have not displaced the roles of "chalk and talk" as the predominant tools and practices of teaching. Whether it supports this old pedagogy or seeks radically novel approaches, computer technology is by no means immune from this marginalization. Indeed, very few high-quality tools have crossed the gap from research prototype into mainstream curricula.

In this chapter, we suggest that technology design as educational research can focus no longer on just imagination and inquiry. Research on technology is like a three-legged stool, and an explicit quest for impact is the third leg required to stabilize research programs. Without this third leg, research totters between boutique studies, which produce much excitement and knowledge about circumstances that defy replication, and large demographic studies, which provide knowledge about the success and failure of today's educational technology but little direction for tomorrow's.

We maintain that research has an important role in the future of educational technology because the problems of designing for learning are distinct from the problems of designing for corporate productivity that dominate the mainstream industry (Soloway & Guzdial, 1996). But to be successful, the mission for research must expand to include equal emphasis on imagination, inquiry, and impact. New models of the research projects that include technology design are needed that draw on the idealistic potential of technology, but engage with the practical problems of educational reform in a rapidly changing society.

We begin by reviewing briefly some of the characteristics that have made past research projects successful. Next we consider why successes in designing learning technology have been mostly localized, with few innovations crossing the threshold to broadscale acceptance. Then we suggest three emerging models for high-impact research: open project architecture, principled design experiment consortia, and reusable software kits. We conclude by listing some criteria that span the three models and may provide guidance for future research projects.

## CHARACTERISTICS OF SUCCESSFUL PROJECTS

A wide variety of research methodologies can be applied successfully to design of educational technology. Indeed, most of the chapters in this book apply equally well to the technology component of educational research. It is doubtful that the universe of successful projects could result from a monolithic methodological program. Thus, we restrict ourselves to describing broad characteristics that obtain in many successful projects.

### Integrated Attention to Learning, Curriculum, and Technology

Many successful projects draw on deep wells of understanding of learning. Although it is doubtful that any one theory gives the best account of how technology facilitates learning, it appears to be important that design of technology grows from grounding in a theory. Learning theories of Piaget, Vygotsky, Dewey, and cognitive science have been particularly provocative.

A key element of Piaget's theory was the progression from concrete to abstract thinking (Corsini, 1994). Many designers in the Piagetian tradition have turned this into a design principle by making concrete, manipulable, constructible manifestations of abstract intangible concepts, thus enabling the powerful, sense-making capabilities that learners can apply to concrete objects to guide their development of difficult concepts (Harel & Papert, 1991). For example, Papert developed the "turtle" (originally a hardware device!) in order to provide a concrete manifestation of mathematical procedures that students could build (Papert, 1980).

Vygotskian theory describes a mediational role for artifacts in establishing a context for development (Vygotsky, 1986). Thus, Vygotskian-inspired designers emphasize enhancing a collaborative context for discourse by creating tools that mediate conversation. For example, Pea (1994) described how distributed multimedia environments create opportunities for transformative conversations. Likewise, the Cognition and Technology Group at Vanderbilt created (1992) a set of "macrocontexts" that ground student problem solving in motivating, resource-rich settings.

Dewey's theory of learning technology stresses the creation of conditions that will support a community of inquiry (Dewey, 1938; Hickman, 1990). Dewey has stimulated designers to extend students' ability to engage with situations that they find problematic through an experimental practice (Roschelle, 1996). For example, simulations can allow students to experiment with controlling a steam engine that would be too dangerous to play with in real life (Hollan, Hutchins, McCandless, Rosenstein, & Weitzman, 1986).

Cognitive science is developing the capability to represent aspects of learning as the transformation of symbolic structures (Newell & Simon, 1972). Designers of intelligent tutoring systems use this capability to draw implications from the differences between a student's behavior and the idealized expert behavior (Wenger, 1987). For example, geometry tutors (Anderson, Boyle, & Reiser, 1985) follow a student's progress in completing a proof and remediate when the student falters.

Although grounding in a learning theory appears to be a central element in many successful projects, attention to the deep structure of subject matter is equally important. Indeed, productive projects often have principal investigators whose primary training is in a subject matter field. In a review article entitled *Technology and Mathematics Education*, Kaput (1992) identified aspects of successful technology specific to mathematics. In mathematics, the concept of a "notation system" brings together cognitive, subject matter, and technological perspectives, and Kaput argued that the unique potential of technology in mathematics lies in the prospect of being able to create radically innovative notation systems. For example, computer-based notation systems can create new opportunities for learning because computer-based notation can be dynamic, include interactive constraints, support multiple linked representations, and capture procedures as objects for reflection. Similarly in science education, researchers have understood the subject matter implications of technology in terms of a unifying "modeling" perspective (e.g., Hestenes, 1987; Niedderer, Schecker, & Bethge, 1991). The modeling perspective draws out the specific capabilities of technology to bring together simulation and visualization with strong empirical tools in ways that open up new pedagogical possibilities.

Finally, successful projects cultivate a deep understanding of the affordances of technology. Rather than merely applying technology to a design conceived in terms of learning theory and subject matter, researchers develop a sense of the unique capabilities of technology for education. This sense interpenetrates the conception of subject matter and the understanding of the learning process.

For example, some researchers have drawn on the capability of computers to propagate constraints automatically. This has led to dynamic geometry environments such as Cabri Géomètre (Laborde, Baulac, & Bellemain, 1988–1997) and The Geometer's Sketchpad (Jackiw, 1988–1997). In the dynamic geometry paradigm, the identity of a geometric diagram is determined by its logical description—the compass and straightedge construction steps used to assemble it—rather than by its physical characteristics (location, orientation, and scale). This constraint-based representation enables students to alter the geometric appearance of a construction interactively, by dragging component objects with a mouse while other objects stretch and transform to maintain the logical structure of the total diagram. Students working in such environments find that dragging illuminates the mathematical structure of a construction, revealing the general case (of which any static illustration is merely a single example) as the emergent totality of the endless stream of continuously related example illustrations generated in response to their mouse motion. In addition to this open-ended mode of inquiry and intuition building, dragging addresses more focused questions or learner issues raised by a particular construction, in that one can manipulate a construction into a single, precise configuration easily—as, for instance, when dragging a general triangle into a configuration in which it becomes a right triangle (or an equilateral triangle or an isosceles triangle). In practice, the dragging paradigm allows students to move fluidly between open-ended and goal-directed modes of inquiry, as special cases, local extrema, and other interesting mathematical phenomena emerge from a continuous deformation of a geometric construction, drawing attention naturally to the configurations in which the construction reveals them.

## Technology Design as Iterative and Transformative

In the broad human-computer interaction community, views of software design driven by means–ends analysis are giving way to a more iterative and transformative view. The idea of developing high-quality software by a process that runs sequentially from requirements through delivery (e.g., the waterfall model; Budgen, 1994) is largely discredited now. Psychological theory is less powerful in informing design than grounded empiricism (Landauer, 1991). Rapid prototyping and iterative refinement have taken hold (Schrage, 1996), and the results can be found in popular products like Quicken. Similarly, the view of technology design as automating existing practice has given way to a more encompassing view that "technology changes the task" (Norman, 1991). Leading designers now argue for a more contextualized view of their role, with more attention to the transformative potential of new software designs (e.g., Winograd, Bennet, & De Young, 1996).

Fortunately, most educational researchers have not adopted linear software engineering models in the first place. Given that successful research involves simultaneous innovation in curricula, pedagogy, and technology (as we argued earlier), automating existing practices does not make sense. Indeed, many projects begin with the stated objective of transforming practice. Some of the transformations that are usually sought include:

- From rote procedures to active construction.
- From character string representations to graphic visualizations.
- From concept definitions to mental models.

Progressing through iterative phases requires cultivating attention to how students learn from prototypes. Video analysis (see other chapters in this book) has proved to be one useful technique for gathering information for iterative design (Suchman & Trigg, 1991). Some successful projects go farther by engaging with teachers and students in participatory design

(Greenberg, 1991b). For example, the Mathematics Through Applications project (Greeno et al., in press) developed a mathematics curriculum and software through a process of long-term engagement between researchers, teachers, and designers.

Iteration, by itself, is insufficient for coping with the thousands of detailed decisions required in any real technology design. Design guidelines would seem to be helpful but have a rather checkered history. Some, like the Macintosh Human Interface Guidelines (Apple Computer, 1993), have influenced thousands of software products. But, although many research projects have suggested design guidelines for educational software, it is unclear whether any of them are influential. Instead, the best approach appears to be to cultivate good taste, harvest folklore, and adopt conventions. Good taste requires appreciating elegant solutions to common design problems; fortunately, available products offer abundant examples of clean, functional designs and complicated, confusing ones (e.g., Norman, 1991). Folklore, often discovered at conferences and informal discussions with other designers, provides a wealth of design guidance not found in a book. For example, a designer of children's multimedia once explained that young children sometimes cannot perform drag operations (holding the mouse button down while moving it), so they redesigned their product to use only single clicks. Finally, conventions and standards can clarify many design decisions, while lowering the learning curve for newcomers. With standards, there is always an interesting trade-off between convention and innovation. Adopting a coherent design language (Rheinfrank & Evenson, 1996) for a product can shortcut many rounds of iteration.

## THE DILEMMA OF IMPACT

Using technology to advance education will require attention to the interplay between local and systemic factors in design. In a sense, all learning is local: Students construct knowledge in response to the problem and resources at hand. Most research projects address local conditions, processes, and resources that enhance learning. Nevertheless, if technology design addresses only these local factors, the result is often systemic failure: software that is fragmentary, poorly supported, and easily marginalized. Every research project could observe these characteristics, and yet the overall impact could be marginal. For broad educational improvement, we must begin to address factors that will enable local successes to plug into larger agendas, scale up to widespread audiences, and evolve to meet new challenges.

Far-reaching impact is elusive for a couple of reasons. First, achieving even local success is hard. The characteristics discussed previously, such as the interpenetration of theory, curriculum, and technology, are difficult to achieve. Second, the educational community is distributed and diversified. The participants in the educational reform enterprise include professionals with different agendas and vocabularies: teachers, curriculum developers, assessment providers, professional development centers, textbook and software publishers, along with technology designers. In addition, political considerations enter all serious attempts to reform education.

From an enterprise standpoint, the assumption that each technology research project can produce a corresponding impact directly is sharply flawed. Large-scale changes, at a minimum, require coordination of reforms across multiple processes, materials, and situations. Moreover, for changes to spread beyond a single site, this coordination must extend to the organizations that hold the power to propagate changes: curriculum groups such as the National Council of Teachers of Mathematics, teacher education and professional development programs, and assessment providers such as the Educational Testing Service. The mutual relationships among these organizations are weak, the sense of collaborative endeavor is thin, and exchanges of value are minimal. Achieving impact at the enterprise level from a single research project requires heroic effort.

Despite the difficulties involved, we reject the notion that educational researchers who are designing technology should abandon striving for direct impact and focus on scholarly publication. Education is a practical enterprise, with enormous societal consequences. Due in part to the low profits in educational technology, the marketplace has been slow to provide the scope and scale of quality software that schools require (Office of Technology Assessment, 1988). Important to note, the problems of designing for learning will not be solved by the techniques of designing for usability that are at the heart of most business productivity tools (Guzdial & Soloway, 1996; Norman & Spohrer, 1996). The enterprise needs researchers who focus jointly on learning and technology in order to provide revolutionary inspiration and disciplined inquiries. The question, then, is how to continue to foster creative imagination and thoughtful inquiry while facilitating stronger impact.

In the sections that follow, we outline three emerging forms of research organization that provide potential answers to this question. Before proceeding, we consider one fairly obvious but fatally flawed answer.

The image of a dysfunctional distributed enterprise with many power centers but no coordination suggests a move toward centralizing control. Indeed some projects have succeeded by instituting centralized control over technology, curriculum, pedagogy, and assessment, under the direction of a single research team. Although this approach can work at the scale of a single project, several factors argue against expanding it. First, technology is changing too rapidly and becoming inherently more distributed. It is doubtful that centralized committees could make as wise decisions as a free marketplace of ideas and innovations. Second, a strong tradition of unsolicited research and academic freedom prevails in the educational community. Destroying traditions that have been successful historically in a quest for more impact seems shortsighted. Third, education genuinely needs more radical innovation and reform, not less. Centralized procurement and the propagation of research are unlikely to encourage the requisite risk taking.

Hence the sections that follow present models of research organization that maintain the tradition of decentralized, unsolicited research and encourage adventuresome innovation. The first model, open project architecture, integrates the efforts of diverse participants in a long-term commitment to accumulate research in a specific community. The second model, principled design experiment consortia, seeks deep exploration of a set of design options by articulating a common experimental methodology. The third model, reusable software kits, stresses the accumulation of independent results in a technical platform that provides for interoperability, integration, and incremental evolution.

# OPEN PROJECT ARCHITECTURE

As we argued earlier, dramatic success in applying technology in education requires simultaneous innovations in software, curriculum, pedagogy, and assessment. Here we add further that it is critical for nonprofit research projects to engage in realistic contexts. This means technological innovations cannot be tested only in special schools, with elite students. Unfortunately, the necessity of creating a realistic context taps much of the effort of a research team. It is prohibitively expensive to create and manage an entire reform movement solely to study a particular idea. This suggests that research about educational technology must begin to let go of the idea of "controlled conditions" and, instead, embed its innovations directly in reform projects. Shared contexts, managed by a consortium, may provide a more powerful setting for individual investigators taking a special interest in one aspect of the innovation under way. "Technology" research in such a consortium becomes a special focus on the role of designed artifacts in an integrated teaching and learning effort.

On the other hand, consortia have a dangerous side: They can consolidate power in the hands of very few researchers, leading to a research cartel. To differentiate the more benevolent form of consortia, we suggest the idea of "open project architecture." In an open project architecture, a reform context is created by organizing a set of researchers, reformers, and schools around a core, long-term mission. Once a strong context has been established, outside researchers can be invited to participate by performing studies that will advance the mission and the needs of the participants. In order to avoid overtaxing classrooms, outside researchers may need to submit competitive proposals for the studies that they wish to perform. The core group works closely with outside researchers to make sure that integrated results emerge, organized by the research and reform mission.

The Apple Classrooms of Tomorrow (ACOT) project offers a leading example of the power of open project architecture. The ACOT project (Fisher et al., 1996) began with a simple question, "What happens when teachers and students have access to technology whenever they need it?" To answer the question, Apple created classrooms where every teacher and student had a computer, both at school and at home. But ACOT did more than give away technology; it created and managed a context for exploring how technology could change schools. Furthermore, the ACOT team did not mandate a core ideology or program but, rather, allowed teachers to construct their own future (Walker, 1996). In addition, ACOT classrooms were open to a large collection of researchers, who could establish joint projects with teachers involving technology and curricula. Researchers were available as experts who could help teachers, and to summarize the vast amounts of data that were generated from observations, weekly e-mail reports, and journals. This open project architecture allowed an amazing diversity of technologies, pedagogies, and experiments to thrive in ACOT.

In an edited volume (Fisher et al., 1996), ACOT participants reflected on the first decade of this shared context. These reflections exhibit a class of findings that goes well beyond the typical, stand-alone research project. For example, the researchers were able to rise above the parochial nature of experiments with particular innovations and summarize the large-scale, most important factors in successful school reform.

Among these factors, the strongest theme is the need for radical changes in teaching practice in order for technology to make a difference. Indeed, it is telling that the reflections in the beginning of the volume begin with the promise of technology, but as the book closes, the authors focus increasingly on the nature of changes in teaching practice. Important to note, ACOT was able to perform longitudinal studies of changes to teaching practice, resulting in a five-phase model: *entry, adoption, adaptation, appropriation*, and *invention* (Dwyer, Ringstaff, & Sandholtz, 1990). ACOT also produced longitudinal studies of students, showing that as they gradually appropriated computer technology their reports became more dynamic and visual, and their thought processes became more creative and collaborative, and criscrossed more perspectives (Tierney, 1996). Many of the chapters in the volume provide personal histories of researchers. It is clear from these accounts that not only students and teachers changed, but also the researchers involved with ACOT underwent personal transformations, resulting in deeper understanding of the issues and more intense engagement with classroom-based teaching and learning.

ACOT's open project architecture allowed the project leaders to speak powerfully to national and international audiences about the prospects for and problems of technology and education. The sites that ACOT created became an infrastructure for integrating the work of many innovators and researchers. From the rich, long-term, well-documented experiences at the sites, ACOT was able to address issues that matter to the public and policymakers. For example, ACOT was able to show that ubiquitous computing enables students to be more social, not less (Dwyer, 1996). Additionally, ACOT was able to provide a model of private–public partnerships that engage with the teachers in schools on a long-term basis, and accomplish meaningful change (David, 1996).

An open project architecture is a powerful structure for an educational project because it leverages the costs of setting up a complex reform context. In this context, teachers, students, and researchers can have the time they need to appropriate technology fully and enter the inventive phase. Moreover, longitudinal, integrative, interdisciplinary research can be performed. This research can accumulate in actual practice, rather than in neglected journals on dusty shelves. By maintaining a long-term commitment to supporting change at particular sites, an open project architecture also supports an interweaving of imagination, rigorous inquiry, and lasting impact.

## PRINCIPLED DESIGN EXPERIMENT CONSORTIA

In the early days of educational computing, there were few developers and, therefore, little need to define the appropriate role for research projects as distinct from commercial endeavors. Today, that situation is changed dramatically; the marketplace for educational software is valued at hundreds of millions of dollars a year and is growing rapidly. Research funding is a fraction of that amount, and is not likely to grow much. At this time, it is increasingly necessary to leverage these few research dollars for the greatest possible impact.

The marketplace in educational technology is quite dynamic and innovating quickly. Particularly in the area of human interface, rapid evolution has occurred independently of the role of university-based research. Now, as the number of educational products available grows, we can anticipate that commercial publishers will have high incentives to make incremental improvements to current applications. Thus, it makes little sense to spend research funds on creating products that exist already. It is particularly important that research projects not automate existing teaching and learning practices; the commercial marketplace is more than adequate to exploit such potential fully.

Indeed, if optimal learning technologies could evolve in an incremental way from products already in the marketplace, there would be little reason to invest in research at all. Therefore, research-based technological innovations often explore novel possibilities that have much higher risks than incremental evolution allows, but also the potential of proportionately higher rewards. DiSessa and Abelson's work on Boxer is one example of a principled design experiment with a higher risk and a higher potential reward than related commercial efforts, in this case, commercial versions of Logo (diSessa & Abelson, 1986). At leaving the laboratory in the early 1970s, various commercial developers have published Logo, along with a string of incremental enhancements. However, diSessa (1985) did not seek merely an incremental improvement to Logo, but rather a reconceptualization according to a set of principles (spatial metaphor, naive realism, and incremental learnability). The implementation of these principles in Boxer moves from the Logo experiment (a child's programming language) to a much richer design space, "reconstructible computational media," in which the technology moves from tool to expressive medium (diSessa & Abelson, 1986). Thus, Boxer explores a design space that is at least a generation removed from incremental variations to Logo; this exploration is riskier than most commercial endeavors could tolerate, but it has potentially greater rewards.

A problem with individual principled design experiments is that each is highly idiosyncratic. This obstructs the synthesis of results across experiments. A methodology is needed to guide the exploration of the space of high-risk/high-reward design options in a more systematic pattern, so that comparisons across experiments can be performed, and so that strong recommendations for future directions can emerge (Collins, 1990).

A promising direction for such a methodology is the formation of a principled design experiment consortium (PDEC). A PDEC is a group of projects that develops:

- A common map of the overall design space, which can organize the different explorations of individual experiments.
- A common methodology, to support the comparison and aggregation of results from individual experiments.

- A common commitment to achieving impact through the synthesis of the most effective ideas across the individual experiments.

Whereas an open project architecture situates individual research projects in a shared infrastructure (e.g., a set of schools and base technologies), a PDEC situates individual research projects in a shared conceptual superstructure. The primary example to date is the National Design Experiments Consortium (NDEC), (Hawkins, 1997). This project created a national conversation among researchers from a range of highly innovative, individual design experiments. Specific goals included working toward a common methodology for design experiments, creating a shared collection of reusable resources, and seeking synthesis of results.

From the work of NDEC members to date, it is obvious that there is no easy methodological solution that will allow grand syntheses across innovative technology projects. The methodologies required in technology design experiments are complex and messy. Collins (1990) suggested teachers as coinvestigators, flexible design revisions, and multiple measures of success or failure. A. Brown (1992) recognized the need for a combination of classroom-based and laboratory-based research as well as a mix of qualitative and quantitative methods, and a mix of classical controlled experiments and more transformative explorations. Herman (1993) noted the difficulty of imposing methodological conditions on design experiments, such as the need to design new assessments to match new curricula, the need to investigate process as well as outcome, and the need to understand not only local effects but also how to replicate them in different conditions. Herman suggested more focus on communicating the outcome and process goals of design experiments, more emphasis on triangulation and meta-analysis, and increased recognition that cost-effectiveness questions must be conceived broadly. Given these methodological complexities, NDEC did not immediately make progress toward a grand synthesis (Hawkins, 1997), but instead focused on articulating ways of documenting the advances made by design experiments, collecting and sharing resources, and shifting the nature of publications from archival journals to more useful intermediate products.

Although progress in a PDEC may appear slow, policymakers in government, schools, and industry need structured syntheses of design options that go beyond incremental improvements. Merely aggregating idiosyncratic projects, each with its own innovations, methodologies, and dissemination plans, is unlikely to achieve a concentrated impact on policy. Through a consortium, a researcher can seek a conceptual superstructure that allows individual design experiments to be conceived as parts of a systematic exploration of a wide range of options. Thus a consortium provides a structure in which individual principled design experiments can be organized to maximize impact.

## REUSABLE SOFTWARE KITS

Advancement in both research and technology depends on the accumulation and dissemination of knowledge. In technology, growth occurs because prior efforts produce components that encapsulate the complexity of one level of detail and enable the next generation to tackle a higher level of detail. Transistors allow the design of gate circuitry, which allows the design of logic units, which allows the design of microprocessors, and so forth, all the way up to programming languages. Rarely has educational research on technology evolved along such a vertical trajectory; instead of accumulating knowledge and innovation, each project starts from the same level (a programming language) and builds a stand-alone, monolithic, closed product (an application, a CD-ROM, or a Web site).

The classroom impact of a new technology is dependent on an entire complex of dissemination issues that surround and embed the technology itself (as is clear from the ACOT research cited earlier). Some of these issues derive directly from sweeping questions that must be faced and answered by the researcher, such as: What is the curricular function of the technology? What assessment metric is suitable for evaluating its effect? Other components of the dissemination complex, however, resist centralized or "top-down" solutions. For example, how does the technology interact with the basal text used by particular school district X? What form of training materials will help teachers familiar with previous technology Y? What is the best deployment technique in schools that are experimenting with class scheduling strategy Z? Frequently, answers to these local questions arise only within the communities in which the questions are relevant. Thus, in addition to the opportunity for encoding a vertical accumulation of knowledge in an emerging technology, there is also a horizontally vast dissemination context to which each new technology must adapt.

The reusable software kit is a research strategy that attempts to maximize the penetration of a technology's key ideas into the vertical strata of future educational thinking and technology development and to pluralize the dissemination context as broadly as possible. Software kits pursue these twin goals by offering "open" architectures, thereby making it easy or attractive to integrate, extend, and customize the technology. These open architectures may manifest themselves as code-level building blocks for rearrangement and combination by future technology researchers, or as authoring environments and authoring functionality for use by curricula designers, professional development mentors, classroom teachers, and even students.

Though examples of code-level reuse are rare in today's educational technology milieu, we believe that the emerging component software architectures represented by Java and ActiveX afford unique opportunities to create software building blocks (see Roschelle & Kaput, 1996a). Each of these industry-standard infrastructures allows developers to create modules that can be integrated into larger scale activities, curricula, and assessments. (In contrast, tools built to older, "stand-alone application" architectures resist any attempt at integration.) The newer component architecture facilitates vertical integration because useful modules (such as a graph, a table, or an equation editor) can be combined into containers (such as a Web browser, a notebook, or an assessment portfolio) to form higher order products. Furthermore, because component architectures enable such embedding recursively, this pattern of vertical integration can continue again at a higher scale.

Component architectures also make horizontal diversity possible because local schools, teachers, or students can replace standard components with other components that suit their specific needs. Indeed, software kit research designs often include authoring tools that allow core innovations to be expressed in educational contexts that are designed by users (beyond or in addition to those contexts generated explicitly by the developers). From a functional perspective, authoring features range from simple provisions that permit users to record their comments, thoughts, and ideas while interacting with the technology, to the ability to develop complete supplemental curricular activities in the form of interactive notebooks (e.g.,

Mathematica, MathCad), multimedia presentations (e.g., Sketchpad; Jackiw, 1988–1997) or custom-configured simulation environments (e.g., MathWorlds; Roschelle, Kaput, & DeLaura, 1996). From the standpoint of impact, these tools encourage users to rework raw technology concepts into the forms that are most appropriate for their particular uses and to distribute and expand the network of interest groups who incorporate technology into the classroom.

Several products in the history of educational technology suggest the powerful benefits of supporting authoring and composition through open standards and reusable modular components (see Roschelle, Kaput, Stroup, & Kahn, 1998, for full discussion). Most impressively, the World Wide Web has energized an enormous audience of potential educational authors by providing open standards for delivering, displaying, and linking multimedia documents. At its best, component architecture can engage both grassroots authors and major publishers to accomplish the horizontal and vertical dimensions of integration. Component architectures (such as Java, ActiveX, and OpenDoc) are overcoming the limitations of the World Wide Web to static text and images and allowing fully interactive environments to be embedded in curricular documents. This trend should encourage a broad move toward reusable software kits among educational developers, authors, and publishers.

Reusable software kits can be a powerful strategy because they extend the progressive, cumulative, and communitarian properties of scientific practice to the development of technology. Science improves knowledge rapidly because it permits distributed inquiry in which results accumulate and are subject to the standards of a self-critical community. Component software architectures replace the monolithic, stand-alone, closed systems of past designs for educational technologies with the potential for modular, interoperable, open systems. Eventually, these systems could allow a more progressive, cumulative, self-critical community of practitioners in educational technology.

A community of practice based around reusable software kits could have three desirable characteristics. First, the community could engage in rapid prototyping and experimental comparison. Researchers, activity designers, teachers, and students would be able to design new, technology-rich settings and curricula by combining preexisting modules. Because modules can be exchanged easily, experimental comparisons become feasible. Second, the community could aim for scalable integration of the best innovations. The products of multiple research projects could be integrated into a suite of tools that scale to support the full needs of a classroom, a school, or a school district. Finally, reusable software kits could enable incremental evolution. An innovator could focus on improving one particular tool in a reusable kit, without needing to rewrite all of the auxiliary and complementary components in the suite. Focused innovation could lead to faster progress. Moreover, component strategy would allow an improvement in a single tool to be substituted into an overall activity, a curriculum, or an assessment without affecting the other pieces. Thus, instead of needing to rewrite all the software to accommodate each innovation, a suite of powerful tools could assimilate improved components incrementally.

## CONCLUSION

We have argued that the design of technology as educational research is maturing in phases. A first phase focused on radical imagination and the transformative opportunities that new technology brings. A second phase stressed rigorous inquiry and the need to understand how, what, and why children learn with technological resources. Increasing maturation and large-scale investment are leading to a third phase where the quest for impact will take its place alongside imagination and inquiry. Research will continue to be a strong element in the design and use of educational technology as long as researchers manage to maintain a balance among these three phases—imagination, inquiry, and impact—which now might be understood better as three aspects of the overall problem.

The history of learning technologies will support no easy generalizations about necessary or sufficient methodological principles for successful research-based innovation. At the level of general guidelines, however, it appears that research projects seek a deep interpenetration of learning theory, subject matter, and technological affordances. Learning theories may draw on Dewey, Piaget, Vygotsky, cognitive science, or alternative frameworks. The consideration of subject matter often leads to a large organizing idea, like "notation systems" or "modeling," which creates a disciplinary viewpoint on the potential power of new media. Finally, careful attention to the affordances of technology, such as the possibility of creating manipulable constraint systems, frequently catalyzes new insights into subject matter and the nature of learning.

In terms of design practices, we noted that the normative mode of design in educational technology is iterative and transformative. Yet, the vast number of design decisions in any realistic technology project cannot be made through iterative experimentation alone. Hence, designers cultivate good taste, harvest folklore, and utilize appropriate conventions. Again, no single design methodology integrates the balance of factors that a successful team must bring to bear in creating a worthy new technology. Technology design as educational research remains a skilled art that aspires to greater rigor and replicability.

We argued further that the quest for impact requires aggregating, integrating, and synthesizing design experiments above the level of the individual project. At this point, there is little possibility for an individual project to have a simple correlation to a large-scale change in educational practice. We suggested three strategies for achieving larger scale impacts. The open project architecture strategy manages a common school-based infrastructure that can serve as a site for integrating many research studies. A natural complement to this strategy is the PDEC, which creates a common conceptual superstructure. This superstructure enables individual experiments to be seen as exploring interesting points in an overall design space, and the push toward a common methodology allows extrapolation across points in the design space. The reusable software kit strategy seeks to create a chance for vertical integration and horizontal diversification of the ideas of software developers, authors, teacher-educators, teachers, and students.

All three strategies contain some common elements. Taken together, these common elements might indicate the overall direction in which a methodology for educational technology is evolving. First, each of the three strategies deliberately creates a mechanism for accumulating contributions, integrating partial solutions, and supporting widespread dissemination. In the open project architecture strategy, the mechanism is a common school-based infrastructure; in the principled design experiment consortia strategy, the mechanism is a common conceptual superstructure; and in the reusable software kit strategy, the mechanism is a common technological architecture. Research methodologies probably will emerge that draw on all three of these possible means for accumulating work, and that achieve both vertical and horizontal integration. Second, each of the three strategies involves closer partnerships (and indeed leads to communities) that cross the traditional barriers between researchers, commercial publishers, and teachers. This list of participants might easily grow to include parents, students, and policymakers. We can expect that research methodologies for technological innovations will continue to respect the value that each participant brings and to seek opportunities for mutually valuable contributions. Third and finally, we note that each strategy presumes a growing legion of sophisticated participants who can balance the creativity and rigor needed to succeed. At present, there are too few places where a student can learn the wide variety of research and innovation skills that any of the strategies requires. We close by urging educational technologists to focus some of their energies an expanding their own community of practice and increasing the opportunities for diverse participants to enter the practice and thrive.

## ACKNOWLEDGMENTS

The work reported in this chapter was supported by the National Science Foundation (Awards: RED-9353507 & REC-9705650). Thanks also go to Dick Lesh, for comments and encouragement, and to Jim Kaput, for his readiness to come to our aid, or at least, to have lunch.

# 28 The Role of Historical Studies in Mathematics and Science Educational Research

**David Dennis**

*University of Texas–El Paso*

Some of the most profound educational research in mathematics and science has employed historical studies of the origins of mathematical and scientific concepts. These studies have proven to be fruitful in the design of curricula, in the creation of environments for teaching experiments, and in the formation of theories of cognition. Piaget and Vygotsky both espoused forms of "genetic epistemology," which compel educators to examine the historical, social, and cultural genesis of all knowledge (Confrey, 1994b). Differences in theoretical framework and methodology direct educational researchers to study and use historical materials differently, and this chapter addresses such questions as: What kinds of historical investigations are desirable? Where and how should they be presented and discussed? What sort of reforms of curricula can history inspire? What kind of history, if any, should be presented directly to secondary students? or to teacher candidates? What part should history play in educational philosophy and epistemology?

Responses to these questions are framed in three different approaches to the use of the history of mathematics and science in educational research. These three approaches to historical and educational research require increasing levels of scholarly engagement with historical materials and offer correspondingly increased levels of insight. Each of these approaches is discussed in the three subsequent sections of this chapter. Summarized briefly, they are:

- Historical background as an addendum to traditional curricula, used mainly to inspire students and to lend to mathematics and science a humanistic face and to give an idea of their place in culture.

- The use of original, historical, source material to gain insights into the problems, situations, and intellectual environments that led to the genesis of scientific concepts, focusing on alternative and diverse views that no longer exist in standard modern curricula but could be revised and revived in light of new educational situations.

- Study of the broader social history in which the original sources of mathematics and science are embedded in order to see how certain views came to be valued over others and subsequently enshrined in traditional curricula, that is, the history of the values implied by our choice of curricula.

These three directions for historical and educational research can be summarized as: context, content, and critique. In other words, the first approach provides students with a cultural context for existing curricula. The second approach provides researchers with new ideas for curricula and for the design of learning environments. The third provides researchers with the tools to engage in a broad critique of existing curricular concepts in order to redirect education in the service of the larger society and its newly emerging goals.

Educational research is inherently interdisciplinary and, therefore, can place exorbitant intellectual demands on researchers. The researcher must combine an expertise on student voice and perspective with a detailed knowledge of mathematical and scientific concepts. This already requires a researcher to wear two hats. In addition, I am proposing that such researchers could benefit greatly from knowledge about the historical origins of science itself, as evidenced in the documents that reveal the voice and perspective of its genesis. I am aware that this seems to place unrealistic demands on any one researcher (three hats? four hats?), but a successful educational research program is nearly always a cooperative endeavor, and it seems quite realistic that such programs could include a historian on the team or at least the possibility to consult with one occasionally, although, in order to be useful, such a historian would have to be acutely aware of the direction of the research and be able to locate and interpret appropriate historical material.

History and its uses have little pretense to objectivity; someone tells a story and such stories are rooted deeply in particular perspectives. History as an educational research methodology must begin with the establishment of an appropriate stance from which to conduct historical research. Hence, before laying out a methodological theory that integrates education, history, mathematics, and science, I begin with a brief description of how I came to be engaged in such activity. My initial training was in mathematics, but as I began to attempt a doctoral thesis I became intensely curious about the history of mathematics, so much so that I abandoned my first thesis and began reading original source material. The original works of Gauss, Galois, Lagrange, Euler, Leibniz, Newton, Pascal, Descartes, or Apollonius were not at all what I would have expected from my modern studies based on modern textbooks. I also found that even the best modern mathematical training left me sadly lacking in a variety of backgrounds that were fundamental to understanding historical development, for example, geometry, physics, engineering, and technology, to name a few. I also found that there existed scant opportunity to write a doctoral dissertation on the history of mathematics, so I pursued my interests privately for over a decade while teaching at small colleges as a mathematics instructor.

My introduction to educational research began when I gave up teaching for a few years and went to work as a research assistant for Jere Confrey's Mathematics Education Research Project, which was funded by the National Science Foundation at Cornell University. I studied various theories of intellectual development and research methodologies, focusing first on radical constructivism and videotaped clinical teaching interviews. I wore three hats: those of mathematician, historian, and educational researcher. In Dennis (1995) I integrated all three of these areas of research, and I continue to see huge opportunities in this direction (these would correspond roughly to the second approach listed earlier). I have begun to gain enough background in social history only recently to effectively pursue the third. Therefore, my fourth hat as a social historian is being woven still; the demands are great but the possible benefits are tremendous. For these reasons, in the following sections the illustrative sketches are all taken from the history of mathematics, physics, engineering, and technology.

Each of the three approaches listed previously stems from quite different theoretical imperatives. The first approach is fairly consistent with a progressive absolutist view of science. It can be used to enhance traditional curricula without making broad changes; however, when done carefully, some direct content and pedagogical changes are inevitable. The second approach emerges from the works of Piaget and the radical constructivists in that it calls for the design of innovative curricula and learning environments that are informed by genetic epistemology (Piaget & Garcia, 1989). However, within this approach, historical genesis is taken as mostly the history of ideas and concepts in and of themselves largely divorced from a broader social context. The third approach is tied more to a Vygotskian framework where the genesis of knowledge must be seen as a socially mediated construction

(Wertsch, 1985). All of these approaches have certain benefits and they are not mutually exclusive in terms of classroom practice, even though it might be difficult or impossible to reconcile the differences in theoretical framework (Confrey, 1994b).

Each of the following three sections includes brief examples of some historical material and their possible implications for the reform of curricula. In order to illuminate the three different historical approaches, the examples focus mostly on the same subject: analytic geometry. Although this subject no longer exists as a full course in high school or college, analytic geometry nevertheless remains one of the fundamental topics in secondary school mathematics and, as a part of calculus, constitutes a stumbling block that impedes the progress of students in all of the sciences. A great many curricular changes are occurring in the reform of analytic geometry and calculus without enough direct discussion. Some of these changes are related to changing technology, such as graphing calculators and computers. As we see later, the study of history can be a great aid in rethinking these curricula especially when it is combined with other educational research methods.

## HISTORICAL BACKGROUND AS AN ADDENDUM TO TRADITIONAL CURRICULA

Jahnke (1994) argued for the importance of seeing mathematics in a cultural setting. In order to accomplish this, he suggested that secondary school students be exposed to historical material and possibly some original historical sources that complement and diversify conceptually the traditional curricula. Mathematics entirely stripped of its origins and cultural setting was called by Jahnke "fast food mathematics," and, he argued, it cannot be appreciated fully nor comprehended entirely. He advocated exposing students to the questions and problems that led to the genesis of mathematics, and he saw this exposure as an important, but separate, part of curricula that does not fundamentally change content or pedagogy. Jahnke reminded us that "history of mathematics is difficult!" (p. 141), and he felt that teachers with limited classroom time cannot fail to discuss the usual content material.

A mathematician and historian like Jahnke is suggesting the use of carefully selected and profound historical material that will illuminate and situate important concepts culturally, but a word of caution is necessary. Recently, many mathematics and science textbooks have begun to include brief historical pieces, usually biographical, even though many of these tidbits are oversimplified, misleading, or incorrect. For example, several textbooks have a picture and brief biography of René Descartes (1596–1650) at the beginning of a unit on graphing linear and quadratic equations. Descartes never used equations to plot points and create curves, and a scholar like Jahnke would never make such a blunder. Such attempts at history serve only to perpetuate the mythological status of a few selected scientists, often to the detriment of students for whom the subject is mystified further.

So what would an appropriate historical addendum for our example, analytic geometry, look like? It would have to begin with a discussion of François Viète (1540–1603) and the evolution of "syncopated algebra," that is, the symbolic algebra that the students are learning, and then go on to discuss the movement towards using such language as a possible model for geometry. During the early 17th century, within this movement, Descartes and Pierre de Fermat (1601–1665) approached this problem independently and simultaneously. Descartes started with mechanical devices that drew curves, then studied the motion of such devices, and found ways to represent and classify them with coordinates and equations. In the opposite direction, Fermat studied equations and how they could be represented geometrically by the curves traced by the ends of line segments with appropriately variable lengths (i.e., graphs). Descartes demonstrated, for example, that no matter how you draw a conic section, and no matter what coordinate system you choose, the resulting equation always will have degree two. On the other hand, Fermat demonstrated that given any equation of degree two, no matter how you represent it with line segments, the resulting locus always will be a conic section. Descartes and Fermat both made free use of coordinate systems with arbitrary angles between the axes. Descartes went on in his work to try to represent mechanics and physics mathematically, whereas Fermat became more concerned with patterns in tables of numbers, maximum–minimum problems, and number theory.

This brief synopsis is oversimplified, but an important historical point could be made to students. This is that there are two distinct approaches to analytic geometry: one that begins with mechanically or geometrically constructed curves and then attempts to represent them in the language of algebraic equations, and the other that begins with data or equations and then plots a graph as a representation in order to gain insight into the nature of numerical phenomena (e.g., maximum values). If there is to be no fundamental change in the curricula, it should be pointed out to students that they will be dealing almost entirely with the latter activity, namely the approach of Fermat.

At this point, Jahnke probably would advocate showing students at least a brief example of a problem taken directly from Descartes' *Geometry* (1638/1952) and one from Fermat

(Mahoney, 1973). Then a relevant question would be where might an educational researcher get hold of appropriate historical material at this level. Although the sources cited earlier generally are found in university libraries, they can be difficult for a nonmathematically trained historian to read. Lately, however, such mathematical history has become much more widely accessible in more reliable secondary sources such as V. J. Katz (1993), or in annotated source books such as Callinger (1995) or Struik (1969), which make selected original material much more readable. Similar publications have come out in all of the sciences (e.g., Densmore & Donahue, 1995; Hagen, Allchin, & Singer, 1996) and such publications make conceptually accurate, historical material far more available to educational researchers.

## NEW CURRICULA INSPIRED BY ORIGINAL HISTORICAL SOURCE MATERIAL

Piaget's theory of genetic epistemology compels educational researchers to examine the historical process of development within which scientific concepts were constructed. As interpreted by von Glasersfeld (1982, 1984) and Confrey (1994b), this theory rejects the notion that science is progressing linearly toward an increasingly accurate picture of "the way things really are." Scientific knowledge is viewed as actions and reflections on those actions. The theory calls for educational researchers to seek broad and diverse environments that "create the need" for an idea (Confrey, 1994b). It is here that historical studies can play a vital role, but the type of historical investigation that is required necessitates going beyond most readily obtainable secondary sources.

In order to gain useful historical insights that will direct researchers toward profound curricular innovations, one must examine carefully original historical documents that provide a full range of the ideas, tools, and environments that led to the formation of scientific concepts. Often, the most helpful ideas are those that have been pruned from both modern curricula and the usual histories of science (e.g., Allchin, 1997). In order to use history as a source for the creation of innovative curricula, one need not re-create exactly for students the historical problems and situations, nor does this process necessarily entail the inclusion of historical background.

Let us return to our example of analytic geometry to see how this process can work. Once one becomes aware of the fundamental difference between the analytic geometry of Descartes and that of Fermat, a question arises as to what kind of a curriculum might result from adopting some of the tools, actions, and concepts of the Cartesian approach. What happens if the mechanical or geometrical construction of curves is taken as a primary action, with coordinates and algebraic equations acting as secondary analytical facilitators? This view forces a reversal in the conceptual foreground and background. Students traditionally think of the coordinate system as the background, and then, by plotting pairs of numbers as points (usually from an equation), a curve is produced. Any geometrical analysis of the curve (such as a tangent line) occurs in the last foreground layer. Many students think that the only way to create a curve is to start with an equation, and, indeed, this view is reinforced strongly through the use of a graphing calculator.

Descartes' conceptual space reverses this entire process. A researcher might think first about what experiences of curve drawing remain in the curriculum. Generally, they are limited to a compass and perhaps a loop of string over two tacks used to draw ellipses. An indepth reading of Descartes' *Geometry* (1638/1952) is then required, along with some modern intellectual history of the work's intentions (e.g., Lenoir, 1979). A reconceptualization occurs as one realizes that all algebraic curves can be drawn with linkages (i.e., simple mechanical devices consisting only of hinged rigid rods). Techniques for finding equations directly from the actions that produced a curve are scarcely known among modern mathematicians, although the most important technique is iterated similarity relations, which was studied by Confrey (1994a) as a fundamental cognitive issue in children's development of ratio concepts. History yields new curricular possibilities that link early cognition of ratio directly with more advanced scientific modeling concepts.

Further historical research into the history of curve-drawing mechanisms and their role in the development of the notions of functions and calculus proves to be a rich topic. Such devices played very important roles in the work of Pascal, Newton, Leibniz, and others (Dennis, 1995, 1997; Dennis & Confrey, 1995; 1997). Hence, following a Piagetian constructivist model entails that the educational researcher then reflect on the curricular possibilities of curve-drawing actions as a crucial developmental phase in the evolution of analytic geometry, mechanics, and calculus, although this does not mean that students must relive the exact historical chain of events.

The next questions involve how this historical environment with its tools, actions, and inquiries can be made fruitful for modern students. What are the appropriate modern environments? Clearly, the usual curriculum with its new attendant tool, the graphing calculator, will not work. Some of these devices can be built easily from cardboard, wood, or strings, whereas the more complicated ones can be simulated readily using a computer with dynamic geometry software. This combination of physical reconstructions along with computer simulations allows students to engage and experiment actively with some of the most profound conceptions of 17th century mechanics (Dennis, 1995, 1997; Dennis & Confrey, 1998).

Certainly, it must be asked what is to be gained intellectually from such a curricular innovation. Perhaps curve drawing was merely an awkward phase in mathematical history and contemporary students would do well to ignore it. A careful reading of historical sources along with a consideration of the modern possibilities leads to the opposite conclusion (Dennis, 1995). This reversed approach to analytic geometry involves students in direct modeling situations where the language of algebra is only as good as its ability to articulate what they can see happening in their own experiments (physically or on a computer). Students' investigations in historically inspired, educational environments lead in directions that complement much of the latest educational theory (Dennis & Confrey, 1998). Curve-drawing experiments conceivably could be done with young students well before the advent of algebra, and, in this environment, young students could begin discussing tangents, areas, and arc lengths not only before calculus but also well before algebra. This history suggests manipulatives that could provide effective background experiences so that the symbolic languages of algebra and calculus have strong physical referents.

An important methodological question is: What level of historical research is required to obtain insights that can lead to profound curricular innovations. In the example described earlier, I began by reading a side-by-side French/English version of Descartes' *Geometry* (1638/1952), followed by other works such as *The Mathematical Papers of Isaac Newton* (1967). Eventually I found that some of the best material is available only in original Latin texts from the 17th century, which can be found solely in rare books collections (e.g., Schooten, 1657).

Others who have pursued educational and historical research have had similar experiences. For example, Reinhard Laubenbacher and David Pengelley at New Mexico State University recently have created college mathematics courses that are taught entirely from original historical sources. Their researches, for example, led them to some surprising conclusions that came from reading the original letters of Sophie Germain (1776–1831). They are now preparing a book entitled *Recovering Motivation in Mathematics: Teaching From Original Sources*, which will make these sources accessible. In physics, Falk Riess, at Carl von

Ossietzky University in Oldenburg, Germany, has created a year of physics experiments done on replicas of original equipment for university students preparing to become secondary teachers. In order to re-create the environments that led to new concepts, Riess' research led him to many original historical archives and some unanticipated conclusions that would never have been found in secondary historical sources (Heering, 1992; Reiss, 1995). Such research is difficult, but, once done, vast rewards can be shared broadly.

Are historically grounded curricula valuable? According to Falk Riess, having students verify Ohm's Law in electronics using a modern Ohm meter is circular and absurd. Ohm's law is built into the device; it is assumed in the construction of the tool. He prefers his students to see the process by which Ohm came to formulate his famous law of electrical resistance. Most educational theorists agree that an understanding of the methods and conceptual frameworks of mathematics and science have increasingly become our educational goals. If we are to continue in this direction, then the development of historically informed curricula will be crucial so that our students avoid such circularity.

The examples thus far described have all implied large curriculum changes involving many weeks of student activities, but historically informed curricula need not always imply such global conceptual innovations. Recently I worked on a project-based approach to an introductory course on discrete mathematics aimed mainly at students majoring in computer science. It was required that the students understand modular arithmetic notation and how it functions algebraically (i.e., $a = b \mod n$, which means that $a$ and $b$ both have the same remainder upon division by $n$). The professor teaching the course, Art Duval, wrote several introductory problems that he hoped would create the need for this notation, but, in every case he found direct ways to solve them without ever using modular notation. So what situation would create the need for modular arithmetic? Thinking about the question historically, the notation was created by C. F. Gauss in his work of 1801, the *Disquisitiones Arithmeticae,* in which he developed his famous quadratic reciprocity theorems (Gauss, 1801/1965). Because quadratic reciprocity and related theorems are considered beyond the scope of the course in question, a radical constructivist perspective would suggest that modular notation is being forced on students prematurely. As a compromise, we created the following project:

> Given an arbitrary arithmetic sequence of integers with any starting point and any common difference, develop a method for determining whether such a sequence ever contains a perfect square. How far must you search in such a sequence to be sure that no perfect square will ever occur?

In the context of the course, this project is tied to a variety of other situations, but, even standing alone, it has the feel of computer science, and we both felt convinced that it was indeed the simplest investigation that might create the need for modular notation. Although no formal theorems on quadratic reciprocity are discussed herein, the project gets at the heart of quadratic reciprocity in that if students start checking examples randomly, roughly half of the sequences will contain squares. History was a great guide here in the search for a good, one-week project. This and related projects are now being tested at the University of Texas at El Paso as part of a National Science Foundation project.

## SOCIAL HISTORY OF CURRICULA AND IMPLIED VALUES

Mathematics and science curricula for kindergarten through Grade 12 are controlled by a variety of state institutions from almost uniform, statewide mandates as in New York, Texas, or California to almost complete control at local school district levels in other states. University curricula rarely fall under such direct bureaucratic control; however, they often display remarkable uniformity nationally and even internationally (e.g., college calculus sequences). In this section, I examine how historical studies could inform educational research by showing how certain curricula came to be what they are, whose interests are being served by the use of these curricula, and what viable alternatives might exist. This approach to social history is situated in a largely Vygotskian perspective where science and mathematics are considered to be linguistic tools, and tools are seen as socially mediated agents that transform human endeavors in which society and the state have an interest (Confrey, 1994b).

Historical studies in this context can present researchers with an array of possible directions, and the most fruitful investigations may not always be in the same chronological frame of reference. For example, when thinking about the reform of school mathematics it is certainly necessary to look back at the last major attempt at reform: the new math movement of the early 1960s. What parts of this movement were successful? Why did other parts fail? Who created this curriculum and whose interests did it intend to serve? Why was the "new math" movement almost universally rejected by 1980? How did its rejection contribute to the curricular backlash of the 1980s known as the "back-to-basics" movement? Why did the back-to-basics movement fail even more spectacularly than the "new math" movement? It is crucial to consider these recent historical questions in the light of both culture and technology before proceeding to launch any kind of new research aimed at the reform of mathematics curricula, especially if such initiatives are to have large-scale government funding.

An understanding of such recent curricular history alone, however, is not enough to see clearly how certain concepts came to be standard curricula and what other alternatives are socially and culturally possible. When considering the example of mandatory mathematics curricula from a historical perspective, the most immediately striking feature is that the majority of the curricula comes directly from 17th century Europe. From the beginning of algebra in middle school to the end of differential equations in college, the curricula focus on mathematics that began with Descartes and Fermat about 1620 and concluded with Leonard Euler (1707–1783) about 1740. This includes all secondary and college mathematics for even the most capable students except for a tiny number who are majoring in mathematics and physics. The only important standard topics that fall outside this historical period are some Euclidean geometry from the third century B.C. and some statistics from the 19th century A.D.

Studies of these curricula must address larger historical issues than merely the past few decades of attempted reform. What are our social and cultural intentions? Why, for example, are mandatory mathematics curricula so firmly rooted in a narrow historical period? Most educational researchers are keenly aware that sociocultural pedagogical reforms can never be made independently of curricula and so a larger historical perspective has to address both issues simultaneously. In order to illustrate the role of history here, I return once again to the example that has been discussed in the previous two sections (analytic geometry) but, this time, the subject must be seen as part of a larger social history. What follows here is a very brief sketch of the kind of historical analysis that could provide profound insights for educational researchers. This analysis is provided as an example only of how one might begin to think through such issues, and it is not fully detailed or referenced.

There are some important social-historical reasons why most of our mandatory mathematics curricula originates in 17th century Europe, although these issues are not discussed in educational research usually. Most important, perhaps, is the fact that the formation of the modern state originates from that period. The two most important institutions that mark the origin of the modern state are a professional bureaucracy and a professional military. Government-supported scientific research programs and broadly based educational institutions appear only after the establishment of a modern state with these two institutions. Briefly put, the shift in power relations caused by the social transition to a modern state produced the "scientific revolution" (Foucault, 1977). During the early 17th century, these social changes took place very rapidly in France (Beik, 1985), and it is here that one finds the earliest development of algebra and analytic geometry, which remain parts of our modern curricula.

One must investigate how social and political environments influenced the development of mathematical conceptions. Consider again the work of Fermat and Descartes. Place the genesis of their ideas in a cultural setting and look at the differences between their approaches to mathematics in the light of their respective social positions.

Pierre Fermat was born into a moderately wealthy family in Languedoc. His father was a prosperous leather merchant and a "bourgeois second consul" in the region, a man whose fortunes were rising and who wanted to translate his finances into political power. The family chose a legal career for their son Pierre, as this was one common path for upward social mobility at that time. Pierre studied law at a new university, and, in anticipation of his graduation, his parents had purchased the offices of *Conseiller au Parlement de Toulouse* and *Commissaire aux Requêtes du Palais*. Pierre Fermat became Pierre *de* Fermat. He became a member of the new lesser nobility, the *noblesse de robe* (nobles of the robe). Throughout his life he would remain a member of the newly organized, centralized bureaucracy of the emerging absolutist monarchy of France. Fermat's mathematical investigations began in earnest once he took up his office (Mahoney, 1973).

Descartes, by contrast, was born into a family of the old nobility, the *noblesse de épeé* (nobles of the sword). He studied military geometry and law at the Jesuit school at La Fléche. As he was not the oldest son, he took up a military career and participated in several campaigns with the Dutch, Bavarian, and French armies. Having obtained enough of a fortune as a mercenary to live in modest comfort, Descartes spent the remainder of his life constructing a grand scheme for the creation of a new philosophical and scientific system in which mathematical abstraction played a key role (V. J. Katz, 1993; Lenoir, 1979).

Many aspects of their different approaches to analytic geometry can be explained by looking at the social backgrounds and intentions of these two men. Descartes' view always remains grounded in mechanics and engineering. He also was concerned with the relationship of his mathematics to the ancient geometrical and philosophical traditions, but the problems that he chose and the metaphors that he selected to describe them inevitably reveal his background in military engineering. For example, he described the phenomenon of refraction by describing a cannonball breaking through a tightly streched cloth. Fermat, by contrast, was a government bureaucrat. He began his career by making a series of arguments concerning tax collection and monetary policy. His legal arguments were mathematical and largely ignored because few people understood them. He wanted a way to display complicated numerical relationships. His mathematical treatises created the concept of graphs as a visual display of numerical phenomena, and it is not surprising in this context that he developed the first effective algorithms for solving maximum–minimum problems. Fermat's description of refraction thinks of light as information seeking the most efficient path.

It is revealing that in modern public schools we say that we are teaching analytic geometry in the Cartesian plane, but what actually is taught is almost entirely the method of Fermat. The coordinate system is always laid down first, and then used to make a picture of a numerical relationship (i.e., points are plotted on a grid from a preexisting equation). Students are rarely taught to construct curves geometrically and then choose an appropriate coordinate system to create an algebraic model of a geometrical action. It would seem that our educational intentions are aimed far more toward bureaucratic interests than engineering ones. One could go on to trace the social history of how these Cartesian mechanical curve-drawing devices slowly disappeared from standard curricula only after many experiments convinced mathematicians that algebraic language, including calculus, was an adequate model of mechanics.

So now, given the new social and technological environments, an educational researcher can ask how do we want to transform the study of analytic geometry. Dynamic geometry computer environments allow for the rapid geometric construction of curves (Dennis & Confrey, 1997). Descartes' approach can be made readily available now for students to explore (Dennis, 1995), but then researchers face the social question of whether society wants to institute a curriculum that has strong ties to mechanical engineering. Such a curricular shift would be greatly beneficial not only in engineering, but also in physics, astronomy, geology, and chemistry, where students' lack of experience with the physical models that underlie mathematical language is a constant drawback. On the other hand, perhaps the overriding interests of society lie more with data-oriented bureaucratic mathematics. The analytic geometry of Fermat is more appropriate in a computer spreadsheet environment and perhaps that is a dominant concern, but, if so, then a historical study of that conceptual framework would lead from Fermat to John Wallis (1616–1703), mathematician and code breaker for Oliver Cromwell (Dennis & Confrey, 1996). Any balance of values that is to be achieved in curricula surely must benefit from a larger informed, social-historical view that addresses the question of how mathematics and science serve us. Everything old is new again, but socially different.

# CONCLUSIONS

These three approaches to the use of history in mathematics and science education have different research implications, but are not mutually exclusive with respect to development of curricula. For example, one might combine the first two methods by creating a set of historically based environments for students' investigations and then following up such investigations by having students look at various events that happened in history. Afterwards students could write essays that compare and contrast different historical investigations with each other and with what happened in their own class, thus achieving a richer constructivist curriculum along with a broader cultural interpretation.

Social historical investigations can shed important light on how to choose intellectual historical material that directs and informs the choices of curricula in accord with the social and philosophical intentions of a given educational research agenda. The process of original, scientific, historical research generally entails going back and forth between social and intellectual history; for example, it is impossible to separate Descartes' geometry from his larger philosophical goals, and, in order to understand his mathematics, it is essential to see his philosophy in relation to his society (Lenoir, 1979). In educational research, the historical and social setting of a concept must be compared constantly to current social settings in order to make appropriate choices of tools and environments.

Confrey's constructivist philosophy calls on all teachers to be good listeners and to have the intellectual flexibility to respond to the voices of students with rich and stimulating activities. This entails that teachers must become, to some extent, impromptu curriculum developers in their classrooms. This can happen only if such teachers have access to a wealth of sound conceptual material, which should include good historical material that is tied to descriptions of possible learning environments that are conceptually rich. It is here that the fruits of educational research based on genetic epistemology ultimately must find their audience.

A narrow oversimplified history of science will not serve, but neither will impenetrable original sources. New works are appearing in this area that make these educational research goals increasingly obtainable. For example, Densmore and Donahue (1995) published a translation of the central ideas from Newton's *Principia* along with commentaries that render this work understandable and yet preserve the essential geometry that makes it quite strange to a modern reader. Such resources make historically based educational research much easier, although the design of activities and environments remains a difficult task.

An initial step that would help to foster the kinds of discussions that need to take place would be to have educational researchers participate in seminars with historians of mathematics and science. Participating historians would need to be made aware of the needs and concerns of educational research. Although this might be difficult, such discussions often energize historical researchers when they see the profound impact that educational studies can have for students. I hope that such discussions will become a widespread part of both educational research and teacher education programs. For those who face the difficult task of creating and implementing rich and stimulating curricula in our schools, creative, well-directed, historical research can provide an abundant flow of diverse ideas.

## ACKNOWLEDGMENTS

This research was supported by the National Science Foundation under the Partnership for Excellence in Teacher Eduction at the University of Texas at El Paso. I wish to thank Jere Confrey, Anil Nerode, and David Sabean for introducing me, respectively, to educational research, mathematical history, and social history.

# VII Toward Assessment Design

Throughout most of the parts of this book, authors have emphasized that, especially in emerging new research designs being pioneered in mathematics and science education, important stages of data interpretation and data analysis begin much earlier than many novice researchers were led to believe in training focused on traditional research methodologies. For example, data analysis begins as soon as decisions begin to be made about which information to include and which to ignore, how to sort and organize and name the information that is collected, how much emphasis to give to various categories of information, and so on. During each of these activities, researchers introduce prejudices that go beyond anything that is a necessary part of the given situation.

Part VII reconsiders a number of issues that were raised in Part II on instruments and methods. But, Part VII focuses on research activities in which it is even more clear than in earlier sections that interpretations and analyses must go beyond the information given. That is, Part VII focuses on activities in which information is quantified (e.g., through assessment), or in which computations are carried out to simplify (or interpolate/extrapolate beyond) the information given. A major point is that, even when computations involve procedures as simple as averaging, implicit assumptions may be introduced that are antithetical to those the researcher intended to adopt. Therefore, if assessment instruments or statistics are applied thoughtlessly, then risks increase that misleading or counterproductive results will occur.

Liebovitch and his colleagues point out that concepts as apparently simple as the mean involve assumptions about phenomena and distribution characteristics that may not be warranted. Next, Cooper returns attention to many of the issues about assessment that were introduced by Lesh and Clarke or by Cline and Mandinach in Part II of this book. But, for Cooper, these issues arise in the context of multifaceted and technology-rich interventions in physics education. Returning to many of the issues that were introduced by Mestre and others in earlier parts of this book, Cooper concludes that, when instruction and assessment are not aligned, serious negative consequences frequently arise. By exploring similar themes, Stroup and Wilensky take on the difficult challenge of laying the foundation for using statistics that takes constructivist thinking into consideration. Finally, Tatsuoka and Boodoo illustrate how newly developed statistical techniques can help researchers examine their own underlying assumptions while at the same time deriving information that is more rich than that typically mined from standardized tests.

The chapter by Tatsuoka and Boodoo describes substantial advances in the subfield of psychometric research focused on large-sample cognitive analyses. For example, Tatsuoka has developed a statistical classification technique called "rule-space analysis" that attempts to classify test takers according to their profiles on what she calls the "attributes" or underlying factors measured by tests. These factors could include general test-taking skill, the ability to solve multistep problems, or the mastery of specific basic principles in mathematics or the sciences. In particular, Tatsuoka and Boodoo illustrate the power of one rule-space analysis as it is applied to the Educational Testing Service's Graduate Record Examination Quantitative Test. To demonstrate some straightforward uses of such techniques, they point out that, although the study described in this chapter involves a very large sample (10,000), individual profiles of strengths and weaknesses can be computed. The reference section of the chapter points the reader to other uses of rule-space analyses on smaller samples and simpler tests. Furthermore, they also describe how the task of completing a rule-space analysis can help researchers examine their own assumptions concerning the assessment instruments they have used, as well as having salubrious effects on subsequent test design because the rule-space analysis cannot "salvage" poorly designed tests.

Liebovitch and his colleagues use games and data on heart rhythms to demonstrate that, in some cases, the concept of the mean is not defined. Consequently, when simple statistics such as means are calculated, if characteristics of the phenomenon are ignored, and if the statistic is used blindly, then, in cases such as the ones these authors consider, results may lead to errors that threaten life-and-death situations. Although the stakes in educational research are not as high as those described here, the theme struck by Liebovitch and his colleagues mirrors that propounded by Stroup and Wilensky, who fear similar mismeasurements of learning and teaching by the unreflective use of statistical methods.

Cooper goes beyond discussing errors associated with inappropriate uses of statistics to focus on fundamental conceptual errors that may be committed when researchers isolate and reify technology or other similar "treatments" as though they were disembodied factors that can be added or subtracted as an educational intervention. Her work points out that an instructional experience for students typically involves many pedagogical strategies that may or may not support learning in a technology-rich learning environment. The methodological lessons that Cooper draws from her work are that, in general, studies focusing on the adoption, use, and transfer of technology in classrooms must be long term and multidimensional, and that they must entail field-based involvement by the researchers.

Cooper also makes the observation (shared by others in earlier sections of this book) that the process of collecting data in such a manner often provides additional instructional experiences that, although clearly desirable for the students, may confound efforts to conduct "pure" research.

Stroup and Wilensky share many of the misgivings expressed by others about standardized tests used poorly. Yet, they go further to identify what they believe are even more fundamental problems associated with the tendency of psychometric measurement to rely exclusively on numeric characterizations of relevant factors. Number, they argue, is degenerate in the sense that much information is lost in its computation. Further, harking back to points emphasized in earlier chapters in the section, number representations invite additional manipulations (such as averaging) that often are not legitimate. In general, Stroup and Wilensky argue that the model of learning implied by standard statistical models is seriously at variance with what constructivist models say about teaching, learning, and problem solving. Following their portrayal of standard statistics as a "handmaiden of behaviorism," Stroup and Wilensky describe a class of "nonuniversal constructivist statistics" that they believe may be more consistent with assumptions underlying most modern research in mathematics and science education.

Before reading the chapters in Part VI, readers may find it useful to formulate responses to the following questions for a research that you yourself might want to conduct:

1. If the study you plan to conduct involves statistical analyses of data, what assumptions do these techniques presuppose about the nature of the relevant information?

2. If the study you plan to conduct involves several interacting processes, characteristics, or factors, are you assuming that these interactions are additive, multiplicative, or based on some other simple arithmetic relationships (such as differences, quotients, vector sums)? Or, more generally, are you assuming that that the relevant relationships, patterns, or trends fit some other simple type of closed form algebraic equation?

3.  If interactions among variables are involved in your study, are you assuming that relevant factors can be isolated from one another without significantly altering their character? Is it possible that results of first-order interactions may be significantly altered by second-order effects, or effects based on other types of recursive or higher order interactions?

# 29

## Subgroup Differences on the GRE Quantitative Test Based on the Underlying Cognitive Processes and Knowledge

**Kikumi K. Tatsuoka**
**Gwyneth M. Boodoo**
*Educational Testing Service*

The cognitive processing and knowledge requirements of individuals taking the Graduate Record Examination Quantitative Test (GRE–Q) were investigated by K. K. Tatsuoka and Gallagher (in press). The study described in this chapter adopted their findings, especially the cognitive processing and knowledge requirements called "attributes," for investigating subgroup differences such as major field of study, gender, and racial-ethnic backgrounds of students taking the GRE–Q. The study also investigated the effects of content, contexts, and processing variables on students' performance on a GRE–Q. The taxonomy that divides the performance variables on mathematics tests into three categories—content, contexts, and processing variables—is based on Webb's (1984) suggestions. The content variables consist of the domains of arithmetic, elementary and intermediate algebra, and geometry, and the context variables are problem types, answer types, and the presentation of the tasks. The processing requirements are adapted from K. K. Tatsuoka and Gallagher in which several protocols were studied.

Tatsuoka's rule-space method (K. K. Tatsuoka 1983, 1985, 1995a) is employed for validating the cognitive processing model used in this study and for classifying the subjects on the GRE–Q into the students' latent states of knowledge. Several studies have demonstrated the usefulness of the rule-space model for such purposes (e.g., Birenbaum, Kelly, & K. K. Tatsuoka, 1993; K. K. Tatsuoka, 1990; K. K. Tatsuoka, Birenbaum, & Arnold, 1989; Tatsuoka, Linn, Tatsuoka, & Yamamoto, 1988; K. K. Tatsuoka, & M. M. Tatsuoka, 1992; M. M. Tatsuoka, & K. K. Tatsuoka, 1989).

This study provides information about the nature of the GRE–Q, namely, what the test measures, the underlying causes of group differences, and how test items can be improved to measure appropriate constructs for targeted subgroups. Several other researchers have investigated group differences too, but they used total scores and/or item scores (Bridgeman & Lewis, 1994; Wainer & Steinberg, 1992); no one has investigated the differences at the levels of the underlying cognitive processes and knowledge needed for a large-scale assessment. The results of the study provide information that will be helpful for developing new items appropriate for male or female GRE test-takers as well as Asian, Black, Hispanic, and White test takers, while measuring effectively the abilities required for graduate-level education in different disciplines. In addition, the results will enable test developers to design appropriate new items by helping them to decide which knowledge and cognitive skills ought to be included in new items or what types of items are better for measuring underlying cognitive skills.

Research on the association between scores on Scholastic Aptitude Test (SAT), the American College Test (ACT), or the GRE general tests and the quality of schooling or socioeconomic status of students indicate that curricular choices made during high school and undergraduate school correlate highly with the scores (Angoff & E. G. Johnson, 1988; Pennock-Roman, 1994). This study confirms these findings.

The chapter begins with a short account of the rule-space model used for the determination of the attribute probabilities for the examinees for Section I of the GRE–Q. After that the attributes identified for solving GRE–Q items are described, then the rule-space methodology is illustrated using the classification results of 10,000 examinees. The analyses of group differences by using the rule-space classification results are discussed next. These classification results consist of the weighted probabilities (the probabilities of using each attribute successfully) of the 14 attributes for an examinee who is classified into one of the predetermined latent knowledge states. The chapter ends with the conclusions drawn from the study and a discussion of their implications.

## A BRIEF SUMMARY OF THE RULE-SPACE MODEL

The rule-space model is a probabilistic model for cognitive diagnosis that offers a general and cost-effective method. The mechanism of diagnosis used in the rule-space methodology is not domain-specific like other diagnostic systems (such as computer programs) using expert systems approaches: Thus, it is applicable to a wide range of content domains. Traditional paper-and-pencil tests as well as computerized tests can be analyzed by this approach at relatively low cost.

Diagnosing the cognitive errors of examinees taking the GRE–Q can be considered as a pattern classification problem that is designed to classify a sequential input of stimuli into one of several predetermined groups (Fukunaga, 1990; K. K. Tatsuoka, 1995a, 1997). For this study, the sequential inputs are the responses to the 30 items in Section I of the GRE–Q, and the predetermined groups are the various cognitive states of knowledge and capabilities resulting from the different degrees of knowledge or misconception in a quantitative domain. The rule-space model was developed to solve this classification problem. In the model, two main steps are essential for diagnosing cognitive errors: the formulation of a classification space and classification procedures, and the determination of classification groups. The classification groups are defined as students' knowledge states or cognitive states. Each knowledge state is expressed by an attribute pattern consisting of mastered and nonmastered attributes.

The formulation of a classification space is done by utilizing item-response theory (IRT) in order to preserve continuity with current psychometric theories (K. K. Tatsuoka, 1983, 1985, 1990; K. K. Tatsuoka & M. M. Tatsuoka, 1987). IRT probability functions are used as tools to formulate a Cartesian product space of IRT ability $\theta$ and the variables, $\zeta$s, which are sensitive to the unusualness of item-response patterns (Tatsuoka, 1984; K. K. Tatsuoka & Linn, 1983). Bayes' decision rules for minimum errors are used to classify a student into one of the predetermined knowledge states.

The classification groups (knowledge states) must be determined before the classification procedure is applied. The number of knowledge states can be several hundreds, or several thousands (K. K. Tatsuoka, 1991). Several studies as, for example, an analysis of SAT mathematics (Buck, VanEssen, Tatsuoka, & Kostin, 1997; K. K. Tatsuoka & C. M. Tatsuoka, 1998a), have shown that even though 6,000 or 7,000 knowledge states exist, only 70 to 80 of them each contained at least 5% of the examinees, several hundred had only one or two students classified in them, and the remaining knowledge states were empty.

However, until we can design an experimental study in which unobservable cognitive tasks become measurable, it is impossible to observe knowledge and capability states directly. In practical testing situations, designing experimental studies for such data collection is not only unrealistic but also undoable. Because the rule-space model assumes that item scores are the only source of the scores obtainable, the model has to have the capability of making inferences about students' performances on unobservable cognitive tasks from observable item scores. The difficulty imposed on the rule-space model (namely, that only item scores are observable and that the underlying cognitive tasks are not observable) was solved by introducing a Boolean description function (BDF); (K. K. Tatsuoka, 1991; Varadi & Tatsuoka, 1989). The BDF makes the model applicable to many domains of interest. Unobservable cognitive states are determined systematically by applying various theories in Boolean algebra to item data. The BDF maps these cognitive states into observable item score patterns (called ideal item-response patterns).

The basic idea that initiated an application of Boolean algebra to the determination of knowledge states originated from a matrix representation of the relationships between attributes and items. The relationship between the cognitive tasks (attributes) identified and the items is expressed by an incidence matrix Q, whose order is $K \times n$, where $K$ is the number of cognitive tasks and $n$ is the number of items. If item $j$ involves cognitive task $k$, then $q_{kj} = 1$, otherwise $q_{kj} = 0$. Thus, each item can be characterized by a set of cognitive tasks required for solving it. The set of subsets of row vectors (corresponding to attributes) forms a Boolean algebra. Therefore, all possible item-response patterns that are associated with attribute-mastery patterns can be derived from this incidence matrix Q. An example of an incidence matrix, which is described later, is given in Table 29.1.

# OBTAINING ATTRIBUTE PROBABILITIES USING THE RULE-SPACE MODEL

## The Data Set

The data used in this study are the item responses of 10,000 examinees who took the GRE–Q in 1991. The first 30 items in the Quantitative Test (Section I) were used for our analysis. Examinees used in the analyses were majoring in 33 areas of study from six categories: humanities and art, natural sciences, physical sciences, engineering and nonengineering, social sciences, business, and social work and education (see Appendix A for the fields studied). Differences in the use of the attributes demonstrated by students in the 33 major fields of studies, as well as differences in their use by gender and race-ethnicity are investigated in terms of the 14 attributes described in the article by K. K. Tatsuoka and Gallagher (in press) and given in Appendix B.

## Phase 1: Obtaining an Incidence Matrix for Use in Rule-Space Analysis

An attribute for a task on the GRE Quantitative Test is a description of the content, processes, and contexts that an examinee must know in order to complete the task successfully.

### Identifying the Attributes

As noted earlier, the attributes (the cognitive processing and the knowledge) required to complete the tasks specified in Section I of the GRE–Q were investigated by K. K. Tatsuoka and Gallagher (in press) and are listed in Appendix B. These researchers identified the four content, two context, and eight processing variables (attributes) needed to complete the tasks measured by the GRE–Q successfully. Readers are referred to the K. K. Tatsuoka and Gallagher article for a full description of the procedure followed in identifying the 14 attributes.

### Developing the Incidence Matrix

The 30 items from Section I of the GRE–Q were coded by the 14 attributes in a Q matrix, summarized in Table 29.1, in which $q_{kj} = 1$ if attribute $k$ is involved in item $j$, $q_{kj} = 0$ if not (K. K. Tatsuoka, 1990).

## Validating the Incidence Matrix

Regression analysis was used to regress the item difficulties on the attribute vectors. As mentioned in K. K. Tatsuoka and Gallagher (in press), the 14 attributes explained 78% of the variance in the 30 item difficulties. The process attributes, especially $A_{10}$, $A_{11}$, $A_{13}$, and $A_{14}$ are strong predictors of item difficulty. Difficult items usually involve quite a few such process variables, and easy items do not. The same result was obtained for SAT mathematics (K. K. Tatsuoka, Birenbaum, Lewis, & Sheehan, 1993).

TABLE 29.1

Incidence Matrix for the 14 Attributes Required to Answer Correctly 30 Items on the GRE Quantitative Test

| Items | Difficulty of Item | Attributes Involved in Items |
|:---:|:---:|:---:|
| 1 | -.995 | 1, 6, 7 |
| 2 | -1.362 | 4, 6, 9, 12 |
| 3 | -.808 | 2, 6, 8 |
| 4 | -1.023 | 2, 5, 6, 7 |
| 5 | .077 | 4, 6, 9, 11, 14 |
| 6 | -.634 | 1, 6, 7, 9 |
| 7 | .097 | 4, 6, 7, 8, 10 |
| 8 | .584 | 2, 3, 6, 7, 8, 10, 13 |
| 9 | .398 | 4, 6, 10, 11, 13 |
| 10 | 1.207 | 3, 6, 7, 8, 11, 12, 14 |
| 11 | 1.362 | 1, 2, 6, 7, 10, 11, 12, 14 |
| 12 | -.086 | 5, 6, 7 |
| 13 | .069 | 3, 6, 7, 8 |
| 14 | .785 | 1, 6, 7, 10, 11 |
| 15 | 1.351 | 1, 4, 6, 9, 10, 12, 13, 14 |
| 16 | -1.389 | 1, 5, 6 |
| 17 | -.609 | 3, 8, 9 |
| 18 | -.949 | 2, 8 |

(continued)

| 19 | .039 | 1, 7, 9, 11, 12 |
| 20 | .354 | 4, 8, 9, 10, 11, 13 |
| 21 | -2.475 | 1, 12 |
| 22 | -.719 | 1, 12, 14 |
| 23 | -.897 | 1, 7, 12 |
| 24 | .401 | 1, 5, 7, 12 |
| 25 | .819 | 1, 5, 7, 10, 12 |
| 26 | .312 | 4, 7, 8, 12, 14 |
| 27 | 1.247 | 1, 2, 5, 7, 8, 12, 14 |
| 28 | 1.168 | 3, 8, 9, 13 |
| 29 | 1.294 | 4, 5, 7, 8, 10, 12 |
| 30 | 2.580 | 1, 3, 7, 10, 11, 14 |

TABLE 29.2

Summary of the Weights Associated With the 14 Attributes in the Regression Analysis and the Attributes Required to Answer Items Correctly

| Attribute | Coefficient in Regression Probability[1] | | Items Involving Attribute |
|---|---|---|---|
| 1 | 0.12 | 0.78 | 1, 6, 11, 14, 15, 16, 19, 21–25, 27, 30 |
| 2 | -0.27 | 0.49 | 3, 4, 8, 11, 18, 27 |
| 3 | 0.19 | 0.71 | 8, 10, 13, 17, 28, 30 |
| 4 | -0.33 | 0.61 | 2, 5, 7, 9, 15, 20, 26, 29 |
| 5 | 0.67 | 0.29 | 4, 12, 16, 24, 25, 27, 29 |
| 6 | -0.23 | 0.25 | 1–16 |
| 7 | 0.71 | 0.01 | 1, 4, 6–8, 10–14, 19, 23–27, 29, 30 |
| 8 | 0.59 | 0.13 | 3, 7, 8, 10, 13, 17, 18, 20, 26–29 |
| 9 | 0.49 | 0.09 | 2, 5, 6, 15, 17, 19, 20, 28 |
| 10 | 0.81 | 0.03 | 7–9, 11, 14, 15, 20, 25, 29, 30 |
| 11 | 0.78 | 0.02 | 5, 9–11, 14, 19, 20, 30 |
| 12 | -0.28 | 0.30 | 2, 10, 11, 15, 19, 21–27, 29 |
| 13 | 0.93 | 0.03 | 8, 9, 15, 20, 28 |
| 14 | 1.06 | 0.00 | 5, 10, 11, 15, 22, 26, 27, 30 |

---

[1]$R^2 = .89$, adjusted $R^2 = .78$

Table 29.2 gives the β -weights associated with each of the 14 attributes in the regression analysis and the items that require the successful use of the attribute for completion. Difficult items, such as Items 30 and 11, require the use of Process Attributes 10, 11, and 14 to obtain the correct answer, whereas easy items, such as Item 21, do not require the use of any of the process variables.

## Phase 2: Rule-Space Analysis

### Determining Ideal Item-Response Patterns, Latent Knowledge States, Latent Classes

When we have obtained an acceptable incidence matrix, we are ready for Phase 2. Before the classification procedure can start, we have to determine and prepare the classification groups (the latent knowledge states or latent classes).

For a set of items, the ideal item-response patterns correspond to examinees' possible knowledge states identified by the attributes required to complete the items successfully. For example, for the 30 GRE items, there are $2^{30}$ possible item-response patterns ranging from incorrect responses to all of the items, resulting in the following pattern (0 = incorrect response, 1 = correct response):

Item   1 2  3 4   5 6 7 8  9   10 11  12 13  14 15  16 17  18 19  20 21  22 23   24 25  26  27 28 29 30

00 00  00 00 0  0  0  0  0  0  0  0  0  0  0  0  0  0  0  0  0  0

to correct responses on some of the items as, for example:

1 1  1 1  0 1  0 0 0  0  0  1  0  0  0  1  1  1  0  0  1  1  1  0  0  0  0  0  0  0

to a pattern of all correct responses:

1 1  1 1  1 1 1 1  1  1  1  1  1  1  1  1  1  1  1  1  1  1  1  1  1  1  1  1  1  1

Not all of these $2^{30}$ response patterns are ideal item-response patterns because they do not all correspond exactly to possible combinations of the 14 attributes representing examinees' knowledge states.

*An Illustration.* Let us suppose that each item measures a task that requires only one attribute for its correct solution, as follows:

Item   1 2  3 4   5 6 7 8  9   10 11  12 13  14 15  16 17  18 19  20 21  22 23   24 25  26  27 28 29 30

Att.   1 2  3 4   5 6 7 8  9   10 11  12 13  14  1   2   3   4   5   6   7   8   9   10 11  12  13 14  1   2

There are many different knowledge states based on these 14 attributes. In fact, there could be up to $2^{14}$ different knowledge states corresponding to all possible combinations of the attributes. For example, for examinees who can do $A_1$ but not $A_2$ through $A_{14}$, the ideal item-response pattern corresponding to this knowledge state is

1 0  0 0  0 0 0 0  0  0  0  0  0  0  1  0  0  0  0  0  0  0  0  0  0  0  0  0  1  0

In other words, these examinees should answer items 1, 15, and 29 correctly. For those who can do $A_1$ and $A_2$ but not $A_3$ through $A_{14}$, the ideal item-response pattern is:

1 1  0 0  0 0 0 0  0  0  0  0  0  0  1  1  0  0  0  0  0  0  0  0  0  0  0  0  1  1

Similarly, we could derive the $2^{14}$ ideal item-response patterns corresponding to each of the $2^{14}$ attribute patterns.

*The GRE Case.* In fact, because each of the 30 GRE–Q items requires more than one attribute for a correct response (see Table 29.1), the combinatorial problem is more complicated than the one described previously, leading to a reduction in the number of knowledge states needed to explain test takers' performance on the GRE–Q. The BDF serves to reduce the number of knowledge states and hence the number of possible ideal item-response patterns. A computer program called BUGSHELL2, written by C. M. Tatsuoka, Varadi, and K. K. Tatsuoka (1992), derived 1,664 ideal response patterns based on the 14 attributes for classifying students across the 33 majors. The number of latent knowledge states in which at least one student was classified was 450. Sixty-six percent of the examinees were classified into one of the 1,664 predetermined latent knowledge states. The number of predetermined states, 1,664, was an enormously large number, and if there are too many classification groups in a space, the separation of such groups is very poor. Various techniques for reducing irrelevant states were used in BUGSHELL2, and hence the number of latent knowledge states was decreased to less than 1,000. Details of the classification procedures and technical issues were described in another report by K. K. Tatsuoka (in press), so readers who are interested in statistics should read that report. This chapter emphasizes the analyses of group differences.

## Classification

Because all of the students do not respond to the 30 items in such a way that their responses are the same as the ideal item-response patterns corresponding to the predetermined latent knowledge states, a classification criterion is used for making a decision about how close each student's response pattern is to one of the centroids corresponding to the predetermined latent knowledge states in the rule-space methodology.

The classification criterion used was that the squared Mahalanobis distance (four dimensional rule-space was used for computing Mahalanobis distance) be less than 6, ($D^2 <$ 6); that is, if the squared Mahalanobis distance between student X and the centroid of a distribution representing a latent knowledge state is less than 6 ($1 - p < .80$, $df = 4$), then X is judged to be classified. The probability of misclassification (error probability) and the posterior probability of X coming from the group in which his or her latent knowledge state is classified are computed. The classification rate is calculated by taking the ratio of the classified examinees to the total number of examinees in a sample group (; C. M. Tatsuoka & K. K. Tatsuoka, in press; K. K. Tatsuoka & M. M. Tatsuoka, 1987). Table 29.3 summarizes the number of students in each major, the classification rates, and the average probabilities of misclassification in each major.

TABLE 29.3
Summary of the Number of Students in Each Major, Classification Rates, and the
Average Probabilities of Misclassification in Each Major

| Major | Number of Students[2] | Classification Rate | Average Probability of Misclassification |
|---|---|---|---|
| Agriculture | 172 | .62 | .26 |
| Anthropology | 109 | .59 | .25 |
| Architecture | 102 | .73 | .25 |
| Art History | 99 | .67 | .28 |
| Biology | 796 | .62 | .22 |

(continued)

---

[2]Total $N < 10,000$ because some major groups were small and were omitted from the analysis.

| | | | |
|---|---|---|---|
| Business Administration | 168 | .68 | .30 |
| Chemical Engineering | 52 | .71 | .11 |
| Chemistry | 177 | .65 | .17 |
| Child Education | 64 | .78 | .53 |
| Civil Engineering | 102 | .75 | .15 |
| Communication | 406 | .67 | .34 |
| Computer Science | 182 | .62 | .14 |
| Earth Atmospheric, and Marine Sciences | 94 | .68 | .22 |
| Economics | 164 | .68 | .15 |
| Electrical Engineering | 277 | .75 | .16 |
| Elementary Education | 347 | .67 | .40 |
| English | 738 | .64 | .30 |
| Foreign Languages | 188 | .62 | .23 |
| History | 433 | .63 | .27 |
| Home Economics | 63 | .78 | .48 |
| Industrial Engineering | 43 | .74 | .17 |
| Mathematics | 222 | .68 | .11 |
| Mechanical Engineering | 185 | .69 | .12 |
| Medicine | 708 | .65 | .34 |
| Performing Arts | 240 | .63 | .32 |
| Philosophy | 102 | .65 | .20 |
| Physics | 138 | .74 | .12 |
| Political Science | 477 | .65 | .27 |
| Psychology | 1,381 | .64 | .25 |
| Secondary Education | 166 | .71 | .36 |
| Social Work | 76 | .71 | .49 |
| Sociology | 225 | .64 | .50 |
| Special Education | 99 | .74 | .46 |
| Total | 8,795 | .66 | .28 |

For agriculture majors, 107 students (see Table 29.3) were classified successfully, with a classification rate of 62% and an average error probability of .26. For electrical engineering majors, 208 students were classified, with a classification rate of 75% and an average misclassification probability of .16. The average misclassification probability for all students across the 33 majors is about .28.

If a less strict classification criterion had been used, say $D^2 < 10$, then more than 66% of the students would have been classified. However, because the purpose of this study was to investigate the differences between and among groups, it was important to preserve group characteristics by setting a strict classification criterion.

### Validity of the 14 Attributes: Variance of the IRT Ability Measure Accounted for by the 14 Attributes

Three multiple regression analyses, regressing IRT $\theta$[3] values onto the attribute-mastery patterns[4] (denoted by AMP), attribute-probability vectors[5] (APV), and item-response patterns (IRP) of all of the students classified were computed, and $R$-squares of .70 for AMP, .80 for APV, and .90 for IRP were obtained. Further, multiple $R$-squares and their adjusted $R$-squares for the 33 majors, female and male groups, Asian, Black, Hispanic, and White examinees were computed also; they are summarized in Table 29.4 and Table 29.5.

TABLE 29.4

The Use of Multiple $R$-Squares to Predict ability Levels By Major From Attribute-Mastery Patterns, Attribute-Probability Vectors, and Item-Response Patterns for the GRE–Q

| | Humanities and Art | | | | | | |
|---|---|---|---|---|---|---|---|
| | Architecture | Art History | English | Foreign Languages | History | Performing Arts | Philosophy |
| N | 74 | 66 | 470 | 116 | 271 | 151 | 66 |
| AMP | .79(.74)[a6] | .85(.81) | .81(.81) | .74(.70) | .67(.66) | .76(.74) | .77(.72) |
| APV | .82(.78) | .89(.86) | .86(.85) | .78(.75) | .78(.76) | .81(.79) | .80(.74) |
| IRP | .91(.84) | .99(.98) | .97(.97) | .93(.91) | .91(.90) | .93(.92) | .91(.83) |

(continued)

---

[3] The values are estimated from a two-parameter logistic model using item-response patterns.

[4] An attribute-mastery pattern (AMP) is a pattern of mastered and nonmastered attributes defining a knowledge state. A knowledge state can be defined by an ideal item-response pattern or an ideal attribute-mastery pattern.

[5] An attribute probability vector (APV) is a vector of the estimated probabilities of the successful use of each attribute by an individual.

[6] Adjusted $R$-square.

### Natural Sciences

|       | Agriculture | Biology | Home Economics | Medicine |
|-------|-------------|---------|----------------|----------|
| N     | 106         | 490     | 49             | 459      |
| AMP   | .79(.76)    | .71(.70)| .86(.80)       | .84(.83) |
| APV   | .83(.80)    | .74(.73)| .93(.89)       | 89(.89)  |
| IRP   | .92(.88)    | .88(.88)| .99(.99)       | .99(.99) |

### Social Sciences and Business

|       | Anthropology | Business Admin. | Communication | Economics | Political Science | Psych. | Sociology |
|-------|--------------|-----------------|---------------|-----------|-------------------|--------|-----------|
| N     | 64           | 114             | 271           | 112       | 309               | 883    | 144       |
| AMP   | .88(.85)     | .83(.81)        | .84(.83)      | .78(.76)  | .66(.64)          | .72(.71)| .75(.73) |
| APV   | .91(.88)     | .88(.86)        | .90(.90)      | .79(.77)  | .76(.75)          | .80(.80)| .80(.78) |
| IRP   | .99(.98)     | .98(.97)        | .99(.99)      | .88(.83)  | .91(.90)          | .93(.92)| .92(.90) |

### Social Work and Education

|       | Child Education | Elementary Education | Secondary Education | Special Education | Social Work |
|-------|-----------------|----------------------|---------------------|-------------------|-------------|
| N     | 50              | 232                  | 118                 | 73                | 54          |
| AMP   | .84(.77)        | .82(.81)             | .89(.88)            | .83(.79)          | .90(.87)    |
| APV   | .90(.86)        | .88(.88)             | .93(.92)            | .91(.89)          | .96(.94)    |
| IRP   | .99(.99)        | .99(.99)             | .99(.99)            | .99(.99)          | .99(.99)    |

### Physical Sciences (Nonengineering)

|       | Chemistry | Computer Science | Earth, Atmospheric, Marine Sciences | Mathematics | Physics |
|-------|-----------|------------------|-------------------------------------|-------------|---------|
| N     | 115       | 112              | 64                                  | 150         | 102     |
| AMP   | .71(.67)  | .69(.65)         | .84(.81)                            | .67(.65)    | .68(.65)|
| APV   | .77(.74)  | .72(.68)         | .89(.86)                            | .70(.68)    | .75(.72)|
| IRP   | .85(.79)  | .83(.77)         | .98(.97)                            | .78(.74)    | .78(.69)|

### Physical Sciences (Engineering)

|       | Chemical Engineering | Civil Engineering | Electrical Engineering | Industrial Engineering | Mechanical Engineering |
|-------|----------------------|-------------------|------------------------|------------------------|------------------------|
| N     | 37                   | 76                | 209                    | 32                     | 127                    |
| AMP   | .71(.67)             | .83(.81)          | .66(.64)               | .71(.63)               | .62(.59)               |
| APV   | .74(.69)             | .86(.84)          | .71(.69)               | .77(.69)               | .74(.72)               |
| IRP   | .87(.57)             | .94(.90)          | .81(.78)               | .96(.81)               | .81(.75)               |

Note: $N$ = sample size; AMP = attribute-mastery patterns; APV = attribute-probability vectors; IRP = item-response pattern; GRE = Graduate Record Examination.

TABLE 29.5

The Use of Multiple *R*-Squares to Predict Ability Levels by Gender and Racial-Ethnic Group from Attribute-Mastery Patterns, Attribute-Probability Vectors, and Item-Response Patterns for the GRE–Q

*Gender*

|  | Male | Female |
|---|---|---|
| *N* | 2,647 | 3,916 |
| AMP | .68(.68)[7] | .76(.76) |
| APV | .75(.75) | .82(.82) |
| IRP | .88(.87) | .94(.94) |

*Racial-Ethnic Group*

|  | *Asian* | *Black* | *Hispanic* | *White* |
|---|---|---|---|---|
| *N* | 236 | 369 | 219 | 2,819 |
| AMP | .62(.60) | .83(.82) | .79(.77) | .72(.72) |
| APV | .74(.72) | .90(.90) | .90(.90) | .78(.78) |
| IRP | .84(.82) | .99(.99) | .99(.99) | .91(.91) |

Note: Analyses were carried out to classify the 10,000 examines separately by majors, and gender and race-ethnic groups. This accounts for the difference in the total numbers classified by gender and race in this table and by majors in Table 29.4. *N* = sample size; AMP = attribute–mastery patterns; APV = attribute–probability vectors; IRP = item-response pattern; GRE = Graduate Record Examination.

The item-response patterns predict IRT $\theta$ very well for all of the groups because the $\theta$s are estimated from these item-response patterns. Across the 33 majors, the adjusted R-squared values vary from .99 for the majors in communication, education, home economics, and medicine (nurses are included) to .57 in chemical engineering. The average value for R-square

---

[7] Adjusted *R*-square.

for the 33 majors is .89. The attribute probability vectors, APV, account for about 80% percent of the variance of IRT $\theta$. This implies that the 14 attributes do almost as well as the 30 items in predicting IRT $\theta$. The APVs are better than the AMPs for predicting $\theta$. Similar trends were observed (IRP > APV > AMP) for the two gender and the four racial-ethnic groups.

*Cross Validation.* The total sample of classified examinees was divided randomly into two subsamples, one of which was used as a training sample whereas the other functioned as a validation sample. A multiple regression equation using 14 APVs was estimated from the training sample, and the same regression equation was used to predict $\theta$ values for the examinees in the validation sample. The correlation between the original and the predicted $\theta$s for the validation sample was .85.

# ANALYSIS OF THE RULE-SPACE CLASSIFICATION RESULTS

## Means and Standard Deviations of the 14 Attributes for the 33 Majors and 6 Gender and Racial-Ethnic Groups

*Differences Among Majors.* The means and standard deviations (*SDs*) of $\theta$ and the 14 attributes across 33 majors, males, females, Asians, Blacks, Hispanics, and Whites are computed. The histograms of 14 attributes across various $\theta$ levels for the 33 majors, genders, and racial ethnic groups are plotted in Figs. 29.1 through 29.5.

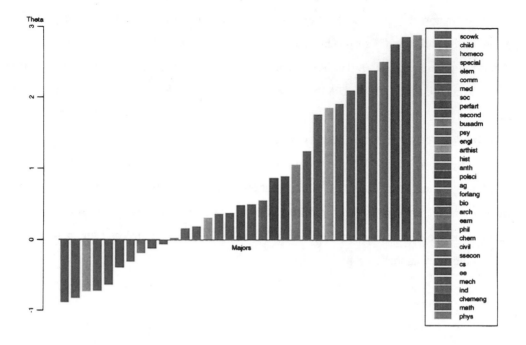

FIG. 29.1. Mean theta values for 33 majors.

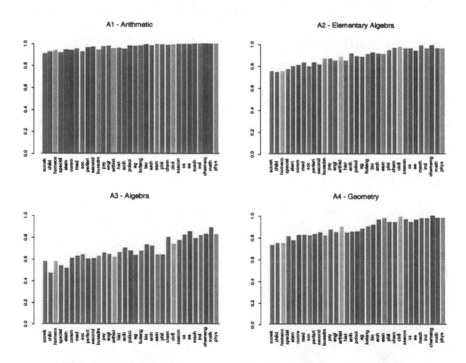

FIG. 29.2. Mean values of 33 majors for attributes 1 through 4.

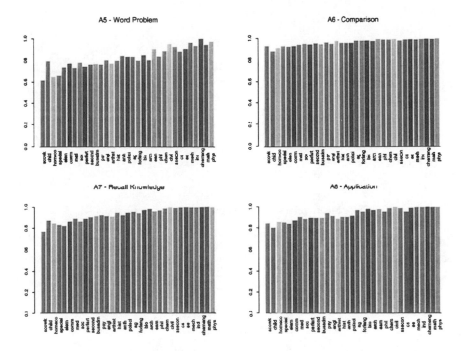

FIG. 29.3. Mean values of 33 majors for attributes 5 through 8.

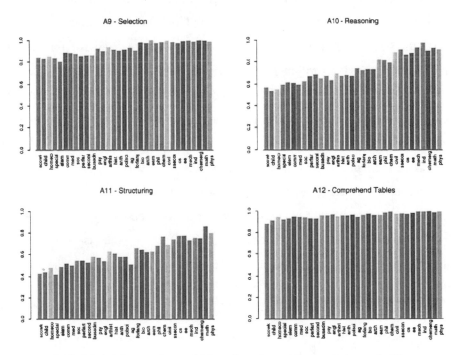

FIG. 29.4. Mean values of 33 majors for attributes 9 through 12.

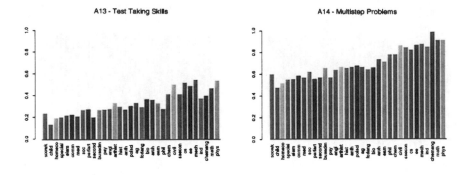

FIG. 29.5. Mean values of 33 majors for attributes 13 and 14.

FIG. 29.1 shows the bar graph of the mean IRT θ values for the 33 majors. Social work majors have the lowest mean value for θ, followed by child education and home economics majors. Physics and mathematics majors have the highest mean scores for θ, followed by a group of engineering majors.

The average probability values and their standard deviations of all of the 33 majors for the 14 attributes are .97(.14) for Attribute 1 (arithmetic), .87(.26) for Attribute 2 (elementary algebra), .68(.37) for Attribute 3 (intermediate algebra), .87(.25) for Attribute 4 (geometry), .81(.35) for Attribute 5 (translation of word problems), .97(.14) for Attribute 6 (comparison item type), .93 (.21) for Attribute 7 (application of knowledge), .93(.20) for Attribute 8 (application of rules and algorithms), .92(.20) for Attribute 9 (selection of rules and theorems), .71(.38) for Attribute 10 (reasoning and logical thinking), .59(.41) for Attribute 11 (analytical thinking and structuring the problem), .96(.15) for Attribute 12 (comprehend graphs, tables and figures), .31(.35) for Attribute 13 (test-taking skills), and .66(.40) for Attribute 14 (sorting multiple goals and solving them step by step).

The means of the 14 attribute-probability values of the examinees for the 33 majors are plotted in Figs. 29.2 through 29.5. In each figure, the x-axis represents the 33 majors ordered by their mean θ-values. The common characteristic of the 14 plots is that the attribute probability values increase generally as the IRT θ value increases although the slopes vary across the plots.

For the attributes that are the content variables, the slopes are gradual, not steep. The high means across all of the majors in Attribute 1 indicate that basic knowledge and skills in arithmetic are easy and it is mastered or nearly mastery by almost all of the groups. Attribute 3, basic knowledge and skills in intermediate algebra, is much harder than Attribute 2, which is basic knowledge and skills in elementary algebra. Only physics, mathematics, chemistry, computer science, and the engineering (chemical engineering, industrial engineering, electrical engineering) majors achieved the probability of .8 in Attribute 3. Basic knowledge and skills in geometry (Attribute 4) are not difficult for most of the majors, except for those majoring in social work, child education, home economics, and elementary education. $A_{12}$, a context variable that includes following verbal instructions and comprehending terminologies, tables, and figures, seems easy for most majors.

As for the process variables, application attributes $A_7$, $A_8$, and $A_9$ have almost identical profiles across the majors. But the thinking-translation attributes are obviously more difficult, and their slopes are steeper than the application attributes. Attribute 13, test-taking skills, is the most difficult; indeed, it is more difficult than the reasoning skills, $A_{10}$, analytical thinking skills, $A_{11}$, dealing with multistep problems, $A_{14}$ and translating verbal problems to algebraic, arithmetic expressions, $A_5$.

*Gender and Racial-Ethnic Differences.* With regards to gender differences, men achieve better than women in all of the attributes in the content and process areas and $\theta$. However, this result is expected because more men are majoring in science, engineering, and economics, whereas more women are studying education, home economics, and psychology. It confirms the known fact that the GRE–Q is much easier for mathematics, science, and engineering students. FIGS. 29.6 through 29.8 show the box plots of mean values for the gender groups.

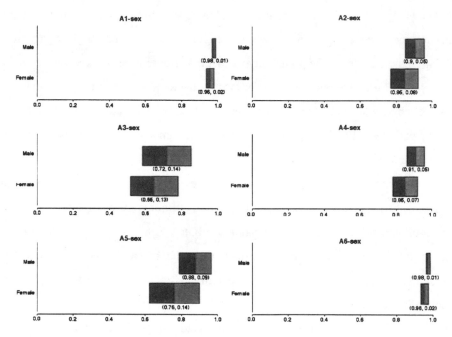

FIG. 29.6. Box plot of mean values for the two gender groups: Attributes 1 through 6.

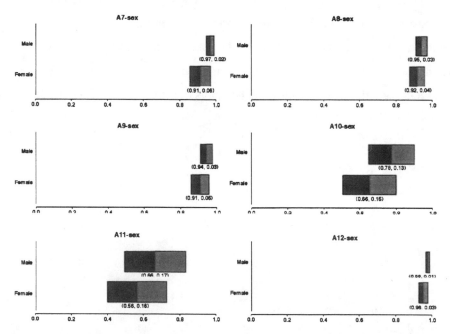

FIG. 29.7. Box plot of mean values for the two gender groups: Attributes 7 through 12.

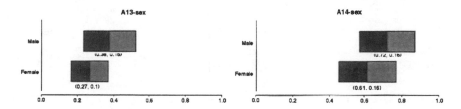

FIG. 29.8. Box plot of mean values for the two gender groups: Attributes 13 and 14.

The four racial-ethnic ethnic groups are also compared with respect to their attribute-probability scores (see Figs. 29.9, 29.10, and 29.11). Because the majority of Asians are majoring in mathematics, science, and engineering, this group outperformed the other three groups on the GRE–Q. Whites performed much better on the attributes in the content and context variables than Hispanics and Blacks, but the differences were much smaller in terms of their standard errors on the attributes in the process variables. The most difficult attribute, $A_{13}$, has the same mean value for Whites and Blacks; Hispanics' mean value is the smallest. However, Whites performed better than Hispanics, and Hispanics performed better than Blacks on the other attributes. In general, the differences in the attribute scores across the racial-ethnic groups are much smaller than the differences in $\theta$ values.

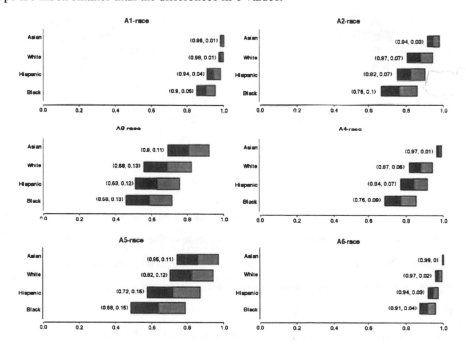

FIG. 29.9. Box plot of mean values for the four racial-ethnic groups: Attributes 1 through 6.

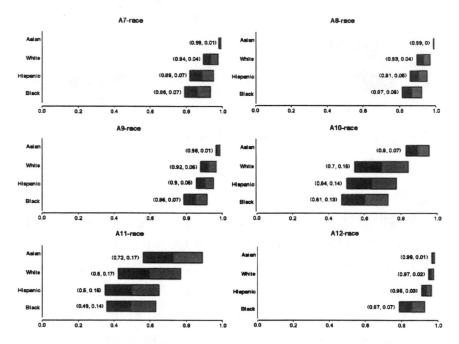

FIG. 29.10. Box plot of mean values for the four racial-ethnic groups: Attributes 7 through 12.

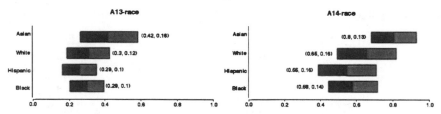

FIG. 29.11. Box plot of mean values for the four racial-ethnic groups: Attributes 13 and 14.

## Cluster Analysis

Cluster analysis is used for finding which majors, genders, and racial-ethnic groups formulate homogeneous categories with respect to the 14 attributes. The attribute scores are weighted probabilities whose values are between 0 and 1, so similarity measures are computed by Ward's (1963) minimum-variance method in which the distance is the analysis of variance sum of squares between two clusters added up for all 14 variables. The within-cluster sum of the squares is minimized over all of the partitions that can be obtained by merging two clusters at each step of cluster generation. The criterion for joining clusters at each level is to maximize the likelihood by assuming a multivariate normal mixture, equal spherical covariance matrices, and equal sampling probabilities.

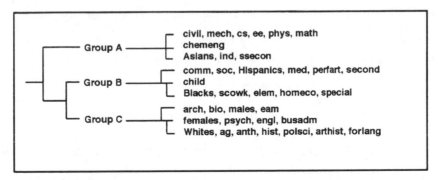

FIG. 29.12. Tree representation of clustered groups A, B, and C.

Using Ward's (1963) method, three major clusters were obtained and are depicted in FIG. 29.12. The groups included 31 out of 33 majors; chemistry and philosophy majors are omitted because they did not cluster with any of the three groups.

- Group A consists of industrial engineering, economics, chemical engineering, civil engineering, mechanical engineering, physics, computer science, electrical engineering, and mathematics majors.

- Group B is composed of social work, elementary education, home economics, special education, child education, communication, sociology, medicine, performing arts, and secondary education majors.

- Group C comprises agriculture, anthropology, history, political science, art history, foreign languages, business administration, English, psychology, architecture, biology, and earth atmospheric, marine majors.

The majors in science, mathematics, and engineering clustered in Group A. Asian students are in this group. The education majors clustered with social workers, medical students (mostly nurses), and sociologists in the second group. Hispanic and Black students are clustered in this group. The third group consists of most of the humanity majors, behavioral scientists, biology, and agriculture majors. White students are also in this group. Women and men also clustered in this group.

Each group has its unique characteristics. Group A consists of engineers and scientists, Group B is oriented toward services and education, and Group C consists of the humanities and psychology. Asian students were classified in Group A, Black and Hispanic students in Group B, and White students in group C. In Group C, women cluster with psychology and English majors whereas men cluster with architecture and biology majors. Because the gender and racial-ethnic groups are not statistically independent of the majors, the discriminant analyses for the majors, gender groups, and racial-ethnic groups are carried out separately for the investigation of the subgroups' characteristics.

## Discriminant Analysis for the Majors

In order to enhance the characterization of the three Groups A, B, and C, a canonical discriminant analysis was performed with the 14 attribute scores as independent variables and the three groups as categorical dependent variables. The gender and racial-ethnic groups are analyzed independently. Group-level information, frequencies, and distances between the groups are listed in Table 29.6.

TABLE 29.6

Squared Mahalanobis Distances Between Groups A, B, and C, and Their Frequencies

| Groups | Frequency[8] | Group A | Group B |
|---------|---------|---------|---------|
| Group A | 957 | | |
| Group B | 1601 | 0.49 | |
| Group C | 3027 | 1.49 | 3.36 |

Two canonical discriminant functions are obtained; the means of the three groups are given in Table 29.7 and plotted in FIG. 29.13.

---

[8] The three groups consist of 31 majors ($N = 5,585$). They do not include the chemistry and philosophy majors ($N=181$); these two majors did not cluster with any of the Groups A, B, and C.

TABLE 29.7.

Standardized Canonical Coefficients and Group Means for Groups A, B, and C

| Attributes | Canonical Coefficient 1 | Canonical Coefficient 2 |
|---|---|---|
| $A_1$ (Arithmetic) | 0.077 | 0.166 |
| $A_2$ (Elementary algebra) | 0.088 | 0.074 |
| $A_3$ (Intermediate algebra) | 0.243 | -0.204 |
| $A_4$ (Geometry) | 0.019 | 0.062 |
| $A_5$ (Word problem) | 0.277 | -0.031 |
| $A_6$ (Comparison format) | 0.107 | 0.236 |
| $A_7$ (Application of knowledge) | 0.338 | 0.446 |
| $A_8$ (Application of rules and algorithms) | 0.100 | 0.413 |
| $A_9$ (Selection of rules and theorems) | 0.126 | 0.271 |
| $A_{10}$ (Reasoning and logical thinking) | 0.351 | -0.477 |
| $A_{11}$ (Analytical thinking) | 0.272 | -0.165 |
| $A_{12}$ (Working with figures and tables ) | 0.067 | 0.184 |
| $A_{13}$ (Test-taking skills) | 0.267 | -0.390 |
| $A_{14}$ (Sorting subgoals) | 0.472 | -0.397 |
| Group A | 1.170 | -0.140 |
| Group B | -0.662 | -0.155 |
| Group C | -0.020 | 0.126 |

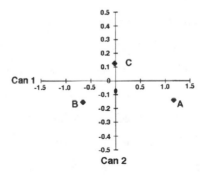

FIG. 29.13. Means plot of groups A, B, and C.

The larger the value of the coefficient, the more powerful the corresponding attribute is as a discriminator of the groups. The first canonical discriminant function indicates that the members of Group A can do well in "sorting and setting goals in multistep problems" ($A_{14}$), are "knowledgeable in general mathematics at the high school levels" ($A_7$), have strong "mathematical reasoning skills" ($A_{10}$), can "translate word problems into algebraic or arithmetic relationships" ($A_5$) well, can "separate a problem into components (implicit) and restructure them into a solvable form" ($A_{11}$), and can solve problems in unusual but clever ways ($A_{13}$). As for the content areas, they know intermediate algebra ($A_3$) well.

The second canonical discriminant function characterizes the students as being "knowledgeable in general mathematics at the high school level" ($A_7$), able to "apply rules and algorithms for solving equations" ($A_8$), and able to "select appropriate rules and theorems" ($A_9$), but not so good in using "mathematical reasoning skills" ($A_{10}$), "sorting and setting goals in multistep problems" ($A_{14}$), and weak in using "test-taking skills" ($A_{13}$).

In short, the students in Group A tend to be excellent in using process-oriented attributes, and they know more mathematics than the students in the other two groups. The members of Group C tend to be good in application-oriented attributes, but not process-oriented attributes. They have better language skills than the members of the other two groups, and they may be good in arithmetic, but they are not good in either algebra or geometry. Group B is the opposite of Group A in terms of canonical discriminant function 1, but very similar to Group A in terms of canonical discriminant function 2.

## Discriminant Analysis for Racial-Ethnic Groups

Discriminant analysis was carried out for the four racial-ethnic groups: Asians, Blacks, Hispanics, and Whites. Table 29.8 gives group-level information on the frequencies in the four groups and the Mahalanobis distances between the groups. The distance between the Asian and the Black groups is the largest, followed by the distance between the Asian and the Hispanic groups; but the distances between the White and Hispanic, and the Black and Hispanic groups are smaller. Discriminant analysis optimizes these group differences with respect to the attribute- probability scores. Table 29.8 summarizes the discriminant analysis.

TABLE 29.8.

Squared Mahalanobis Distances Between Four Racial-Ethnic Groups and Their Frequencies

| Group | Frequency | Asian | Black | Hispanic |
|---|---|---|---|---|
| Asian | 236 | | | |
| Black | 369 | 2.92 | | |
| Hispanic | 219 | 1.66 | 0.57 | |
| White | 2,819 | 0.64 | 1.33 | 0.35 |

## TABLE 29.9.

Standardized Canonical Coefficients and Group Means for the Four Racial-Ethnic Groups

| Attributes | Canonical Coefficient 1 | Canonical Coefficient 2 | Canonical Coefficient 3 |
|---|---|---|---|
| $A_1$ (Arithmetic) | 0.246 | -0.273 | 0.356 |
| $A_2$ (Elementary algebra) | 0.088 | 0.062 | -0.197 |
| $A_3$ (Intermediate algebra) | 0.163 | 0.215 | -0.162 |
| $A_4$ (Geometry) | 0.173 | -0.116 | -0.288 |
| $A_5$ (Word problem) | 0.320 | -0.230 | 0.341 |
| $A_6$ (Comparison format) | 0.240 | -0.121 | 0.176 |
| $A_7$ (Application of knowledge) | 0.219 | 0.140 | 0.266 |
| $A_8$ (Application of rules and algorithms) | 0.147 | -0.070 | 0.017 |
| $A_9$ (Selection of rules and theorems) | 0.013 | 0.066 | -0.343 |
| $A_{10}$ (Reasoning and logical thinking) | 0.204 | 0.464 | -0.405 |
| $A_{11}$ (Analytical thinking) | 0.107 | 0.298 | 0.284 |
| $A_{12}$ (Working with figures and tables) | 0.440 | -0.402 | -0.365 |
| $A_{13}$ (Test-taking skills) | -0.083 | 0.303 | 0.268 |
| $A_{14}$ (Sorting subgoals) | 0.223 | 0.393 | 0.357 |
| Asian | 0.665 | 0.512 | -0.070 |
| Black | -1.014 | 0.202 | 0.041 |
| Hispanic | -0.420 | -0.166 | -0.227 |
| White | 0.110 | -0.057 | 0.018 |

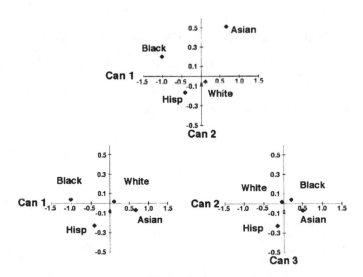

FIG. 29.14. Class means for the four racial-ethnic groups.

The racial-ethnic groups are fairly well separated, and they are different with respect to their attributes. Group differences can be seen clearly in FIG. 29.14, which gives plots of the four centroids with respect to the canonical discriminant functions described in Table 29.9. In Table 29.9, the first canonical discriminant function has large coefficients for Attributes 12 (following verbal instructions, comprehending tables, figures, and terminologies), 5 (word problems), and 1 (basic knowledge and skills in arithmetic). The dimension defined by the first canonical discriminant function denotes examinees having a better foundation in mathematics and being able to do the problems associated with verbal competency.

The second canonical discriminant function has large coefficients for Attributes 10 (mathematical reasoning skills), 14 (sorting the goals in multistep problems), 13 (test-taking skills), and 11 (analytical thinking skills) in the positive direction, and for Attributes 12 and 1 in the negative direction. The second dimension measures competency in mathematical thinking skills, including test-taking skills. The third canonical discriminant function is characterized by Attributes 1, 5, 14, 11, and 7 in the positive direction, and Attributes 4, 9, 10, and 12 in the negative direction.

The summary of the group descriptions shows that Asian and White students are at the positive end of the first dimension, but Black and Hispanic students are not. However, Black students are doing as well as White students in the second dimension, whereas Asian students obtain the highest positive mean. It should be noted that the mean of $A_{13}$ for Black students is as high as that for White students, and the differences of the means for $A_{10}$, $A_{11}$, and $A_{14}$ among White, Black, and Hispanic students are very close, less than 1 SD. Hispanic students have a tendency to have negative values for the third canonical discriminant function. Unfortunately, it is difficult to interpret this third function.

## Discriminant Analysis for the Gender Differences

The female and male groups are investigated by discriminant analysis too. Table 29.10 summarizes their group-level information, frequencies, and Mahalanobis distances between the groups. The total-sample standardized canonical coefficients for the gender groups are given in Table 29.11. FIG. 29.15 shows the plot of the canonical means for these groups.

TABLE 29.10.

Squared Mahalanobis Distances Between the Two Gender Groups and Their Frequencies

| Gender | Frequency | Female |
|--------|-----------|--------|
| Female | 3,916 | |
| Male | 2,647 | 0.45 |

TABLE 29.11

Total-Sample, Standardized Canonical Coefficients and Group Means for the Two Gender Groups

| Attributes | Canonical Coefficient 1 |
|---|---|
| $A_1$ (Arithmetic) | 0.038 |
| $A_2$ (Elementary algebra) | 0.071 |
| $A_3$ (Intermediate algebra) | 0.128 |
| $A_4$ (Geometry) | 0.039 |
| $A_5$ (Word problems) | 0.398 |
| $A_6$ (Comparison format) | 0.034 |
| $A_7$ (Application of knowledge) | 0.361 |
| $A_8$ (Application of rules and algorithms) | -0.054 |
| $A_9$ (Selection of rules and theorems) | -0.001 |
| $A_{10}$ (Reasoning and logical thinking) | 0.331 |
| $A_{11}$ (Analytical thinking) | 0.217 |
| $A_{12}$ (Working with figures and tables ) | 0.158 |
| $A_{13}$ (Test-taking skills) | 0.289 |
| $A_{14}$ (Sorting subgoals) | 0.355 |
| Female | -0.270 |
| Male | 0.400 |

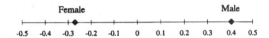

FIG. 29.15. Class means for the two gender groups.

With regard to the gender differences (FIG. 29.15), men perform better than women on Attributes 5, 7, 10, 13, and 14. Men tend to be more knowledgeable, stronger in translating word problems, and to have better mathematical reasoning skills and have better test-taking skills than women. However, the differences at the attribute levels are much smaller in relation to their standard errors than the total score levels or IRT $\theta$ levels, and the mean differences for the attribute scores are not statistically significant.

## CONCLUSIONS

This study showed that an analysis of the attributes required to answer correctly items in Section I of the GRE–Q utilizing the rule-space methodology is useful in answering several educational and psychometric questions:

- Predicting the difficulty of items from a Q-matrix—a matrix representing item-and-attribute involvement relationships—is useful in tapping the underlying cognitive processes and knowledge that are required to solve the problems, especially when the number of items is substantially larger than the number of attributes. The matrix indicates clearly that difficult items involve more mathematical thinking attributes than easy items do. The content attributes are often statistically weak in predicting the difficulty of items.

- Attribute-probability scores are a better predictor of IRT $\theta$ values than attribute-mastery patterns. Because, in this study, the number of attributes is 14 and the number of items is 30, a multiple $R^2$ of around .80 with 14 variables is very good when $R^2 = .89$ with 30 variables.

- For gender and racial-ethnic groups, the differences in attribute means are much smaller in relation to their standard errors than the differences in the means of $\theta$s or in the total scores. The differences in the attribute means are smaller than a standard deviation, whereas the differences in the means of $\theta$s or the means of scale scores are larger than a standard deviation. It is obvious that we have an "amplified effect;" that is, the accumulation of small differences in each of the 14 attribute scores becomes a large difference.

- For racial-ethnic groups, the content attributes and the attributes involving verbal comprehension have much larger mean differences in relation to their standard errors than thinking attributes and application attributes have. Some thinking attributes (such as Attribute 13) that may not require cumulative training have the same mean value for Black and White students.

- Cluster analyses of the 33 majors, 4 racial-ethnic groups, and 2 gender groups were performed, and three main groups were identified. The first group (Group A) consists of Asian students, and those majoring in civil engineering, computer science, economics, chemical engineering, industrial engineering, mechanical engineering, physics, electrical engineering, and mathematics. The second group (Group B) is characterized by Black and Hispanic students and those majoring in social work, elementary education, home economics, special education, child education, communications, sociology, medicine, performing art, and secondary education. The third group (Group C) is characterized by White students, men and women, and students majoring in agriculture, anthropology, history, political science, art history, foreign languages, business administration, English, psychology, architecture, biology, and earth-atmospheric-marine science.

- A discriminant analysis characterized three clustered groups: Group A is associated with an excellent use of processing skills and knows more mathematics than the other two groups. Group B is associated with better application skills, but not better processing skills. Group B is the opposite of Group A with respect to the first canonical coordinates, but they are about same with respect to the second canonical coordinates. Group C is identified by large second canonical coordinates; that is, members of Group C are better in arithmetic, have a better knowledge of middle-school-level mathematics in general, and are excellent in application skills. They are more likely to lack knowledge and basic skills in higher level algebra and mathematics and are naive in using mathematical thinking skills.

- For racial-ethnic groups, discriminant analysis revealed Hispanics and Blacks tend to be considerably weaker in basic knowledge and skills in arithmetic, elementary algebra, and geometry than Asians and Whites. However, they are less weak in terms of process attributes.

- Concerning gender differences, men tend to be more knowledgeable, to be stronger in solving word problems, and to have better mathematical reasoning skills and better test-taking skills than women do. However, the differences in relation to their standard errors at the attribute level are much smaller than at the total score level or at the IRT $\theta$ level. The mean differences for the attribute scores are not statistically significant. In Group C, women cluster with English, psychology, and business administration majors, whereas men cluster with architecture, biology, and earth-atomospheric-marine-majors.

# DISCUSSION

An incidence matrix Q of attributes and items, whose elements indicate the involvement or noninvolvement of each attribute in the items, prompts new item-analysis techniques associated closely with attribute statistics. Rule-space methodology enables us to calculate attribute difficulties and discriminating powers. By knowing the difficulties and the values of point-biserials for the attributes and total scores for the attributes and IRT $\theta$, and by knowing which attributes are involved in an item, one should be able to estimate the item difficulties and item-discriminating powers from the difficulties and the discriminating powers of attributes. There should be a mathematical relationship between the reliability of the total score by items and the total scores by attributes.

Test developers can select a set of attributes that they would like to test by looking into the values of attribute difficulties and discrimination powers. By selecting the appropriate attributes, the difficulty of items can be manipulated. If this relationship were developed fully, then the current practice of item development can be improved, and the costs incurred in developing tests can be substantially reduced. Most of all, the costs of administering pretests will be much reduced. However, new psychometric theories will need to be developed.

This chapter shows that there are subgroup differences in terms of performances on the attributes. Hence it becomes easier to tailor item difficulties to a particular population by selecting an appropriate set of attributes, such as the use of analytical thinking skills. The developers of quantitative tests for science and engineering majors can ignore easy attributes such as $A_1$, $A_2$, $A_4$, and $A_{12}$ when constructing tests. What science and engineering students have to know are more difficult mathematical thinking skills interacting with knowledge of higher level mathematics than those tested in the current GRE–Q tests.

The development of a fair test for all of the subgroups is very important. To achieve this goal, we must know the sources of the differences between the groups. Studying protocols has been one of the most useful techniques for investigating the cognitive aspect of items. If taking protocols and/or interviewing were done in conjunction with using these statistical techniques, then the shortcomings associated with either of the two approaches would be compensated for by the other. Statistical analysis is objective, but it lacks substantive information. Protocol analyses can give us qualitative and descriptive information, which may not be objective enough. In other words, the rule-space methodology can be used together with protocol analyses.

The methodology used in this study has opened up various possibilities for the future such as the development of new test theories that can be useful for generating new items associated with attributes, the diagnosis of students' latent knowledge states and the use of that information for improving learning and teaching (K. K. Tatsuoka & C. M. Tatsuoka, 1998), and the development of conditional probability curves for attributes and the use of the curves for proficiency scaling (K. K. Tatsuoka, et al., 1994).

Chipman and Nichols (1995) suggested that the rule-space methodology should be helpful in creating cognitive models. Researchers have already used it for guiding the development of their cognitive models in such complex domains as architecture (I. R. Katz, Martinez, Sheehan, & Tatsuoka, 1994), algebra (Birenbaum, et al., 1993) and the GRE–Q (K. K. Tatsuoka & Gallagher, in press).

## ACKNOWLEDGMENTS

The authors gratefully acknowledge and thank Maurice Tatsuoka who gave much editorial help and statistical consultation, Curtis Tatsuoka who engaged in many useful discussions with the authors, Phil Leung for data analyses and graphic design, and Liz Brophy for preparing the manuscript.

# APPENDIX A

## Major Fields of Study

*Humanities and Art*

- Architecture
- Art history
- English
- Foreign languages
- History
- Performing arts
- Philosophy

*Natural Sciences*

- Agriculture
- Biology
- Home economics
- Medicine

*Physical Sciences: Nonengineering*

- Chemistry
- Computer science
- Earth, atmospheric, and marine sciences
- Mathematics
- Physics

*Physical Sciences: Engineering*

- Chemical engineering
- Civil engineering
- Electrical engineering

- Industrial engineering
- Mechanical engineering

*Social Sciences and Business*

- Anthropology
- Business administration
- Communication
- Economics
- Political science
- Psychology
- Sociology

*Social Work and Education*

- Social work
- Child education
- Elementary education
- Secondary education
- Special education

# APPENDIX B

Attributes Required by Examinees to Answer Correctly Items on the GRE Quantitative Test

*Content Variables*

$A_1$ *(Arithmetic—Numbers and Operations).* Can work with odd and even integers, prime numbers, factors, rational numbers, ordering, ratios, percentages, square of positive numbers, square root of small positive numbers such as 4, 9, 16, average of positive numbers.

$A_2$ *(Elementary Algebra).* Can work with variables (addition and subtraction only), linear equations, linear algebraic expressions, signed numbers, absolute values, irrational numbers (such as the square root of 3).

*$A_3$ (Intermediate Algebra)*. Can work with factorable quadratic equations, complicated algebraic expressions, functions, sets, simple probability, simple combinations, exponents with variables, simple statistics such as modes and medians.

*$A_4$ (Geometry and Analytic Geometry)*. Can work with perimeter, area, and volume of triangles, circles, rectangles, and other geometric figures. In analytic geometry, can work with points, lines, and their expressions in terms of a coordinate system.

*Process Variables*

*$A_5$ (Translating Word Problems)*. Can translate a word problem into an arithmetic expression(s), algebraic expression(s), equation(s). Can identify implicit variables and relationships.

*$A_7$ (Application of Knowledge)*. Can recall and interpret knowledge about basic concepts and properties in arithmetic, elementary algebra, intermediate algebra, geometry, and analytic geometry. Can perform computations in arithmetic (ratio, powers), geometry, signed numbers, absolute values, median, and mode.

*$A_8$ (Application of Rules and Algorithms)*. Can solve equations, solve simultaneous linear equations, derive algebraic expressions, compute algebraic expressions, factor algebraic equations, factor algebraic expressions, substitute numbers and/or variables in algebraic expressions and algebraic equations.

*$A_9$ (Selection of Rules and Theorems)*. Can select and apply to the task the relevant concept, theorem, rule, and/or strategy from a large knowledge base.

*$A_{10}$ (Reasoning and Logical Thinking)*. Can reason from cause to effect, identify and understand necessary and sufficient conditions and apply them appropriately to solve problems, check that solutions hold true in the general case as opposed to a specific case.

*$A_{11}$ (Analytical Thinking and Problem Structuring)*. Can analyze the problem into component parts or constituent elements, which are implicit, and structure the component parts so that a problem becomes solvable.

*$A_{13}$ (Test-Taking Skills)*. Can take advantage of the form of the test items and other test-taking methods without solving the problem in the manner intended by the item writer. Can solve a task by working back from the multiple-choice options, producing one or two examples and, from them, inferring the correct option, substituting numbers for selecting the

correct option, eliminating one or more of the options, and guessing from among the remaining options.

$A_{14}$ *(Degree of Complexity)*. Can deal with problems that involve several steps. These steps may be explicit or implicit. Can establish the subgoals of the problem, organize them in relation to each other, rate them in order of priority, and execute them in the proper sequence in a step-by-step fashion.

*Context Variables*

$A_6$ *(Comparison Format)*. The item is written in a comparison format.

$A_{12}$ *(Working With Figures, Tables and Graphs)*. Can comprehend tables, figures, and graphs. Can follow verbally described mathematical problems. In the statement of the problem, the student can relate the geometric terms with figures, graphs, and charts. Can generate figures for using external representations to facilitate problem-solving activities.

# 30 Cautions and Considerations: Thoughts on the Implementation and Evaluation of Innovation in Science Education

**S. Marie A. Cooper**

*Immaculata College*

Educational researchers direct their attention increasingly to the use of new technologies in the classroom. Various demonstration technologies at every educational level, from kindergarten through university, draw considerable scrutiny, and the number of pilot programs grows rapidly. This is particularly true in the area of science education where technology-based programs hold promise for increased cognitive gains for students, efficiency of delivery for instructors, and positive affect for both. Though evaluative studies are still relatively few and limited in scope, a review of the emerging literature suggests important lessons, both for the optimum implementation of such programs and for research methodologies to assess their effectiveness.

Two areas of concern demand special consideration. The researcher who wishes to study the genuine, long term impact of technology-based educational programs must maintain an acute awareness that the instructional effectiveness of an innovation can depend in large part on the continuing presence and involvement of its designer. Reflection on early programs indicates that the gains in cognitive achievement, and even in affect, that occur when the designer of a program is involved intimately in the instructional process do not transfer necessarily when the innovation is passed to other instructors for their use.

The evaluation process itself is another vital area of concern. Current technology-based instructional programs are diverse, and any single program may employ a broad range of cognitive strategies. The complexity of the innovations and the subtlety of cognitive change demand long term and multifaceted approaches to the evaluation of the new curricula if any clear picture of their value is to emerge. In this chapter, I consider representative instructional innovations that use technological delivery vehicles and discuss outcome limitations and methodological lessons from my own research.

## TECHNOLOGY-BASED PROGRAMS IN SCIENCE CURRICULA

Science instructors at all levels strive toward two goals in their instructional plans. They want their students to achieve a strong conceptual competence, with principles rooted firmly in the students' own cognitive frameworks and easily retrievable, and a utilization competence that promotes fluidity in the application of these principles to new situations (Gelman & Greeno, 1989). Both conceptual and utilization competence build on basic skills and simple facts as well as higher order thinking and problem solving skills, and more advanced knowledge (N. Cole, 1990), and both require the replacement of naive preconceptions about the physical world with understandings in accord with sound scientific principles (Heller, Keith, & S. Anderson, 1992). The challenge of guiding students through the development of these competencies lies in delivering an extensive prescription of basic skills and facts while attending carefully to a growth in higher order thinking skills and an understanding of the overarching nature of science. The manner in which students learn science teaches them much about the nature of science, the work of scientists, and the scientific process (Bruffee, 1993). Yet, although what the world knows about science is developed, synthesized, and refined in ongoing conversations among scientists, traditionally, the explanation, revision, and interpretation that mark the scientific enterprise have been absent from the science classroom. These, with the approximation methods that are essential to new understandings, have been replaced too often by transmission–reception modes of instruction. Such instructional modes leave students with little chance at long term learning and the erroneous picture of science as a closed body of immutable facts and precise final answers.

This is true at all levels, but nowhere more so than in introductory university classes with their large lectures. In physics education, for example, studies (e.g., Hestenes, et al., 1992; Mazur, 1996; Thornton, 1989; Thornton & Sokoloff, 1990) show consistently that the traditional curricula and methods are inadequate, especially for those students who are not majoring in science, but who will be the citizenry of an increasingly technological society. One such study (Van Heuvelen, 1991) indicates that only 5% of the students taking introductory science courses manage to make the transformation from a pre-Newtonian to a Newtonian understanding of motion, even after a full year of instruction in calculus-based physics. Most students fail to build any coherent scientific model of the subject matter they have studied (Redish, J. M. Wilson, & McDaniel, 1992). Many continue to view physics as merely a collection of facts and unrelated equations, gaining little understanding of effective reasoning or the nature of a good explanation (L. C. McDermott, 1996; Redish, 1996).

Members of the science education community have searched for the reasons and remedies for these deficiencies for more than 40 years. Researchers suggest a number of possible reasons for students' failure to acquire a firm understanding of the subject matter or the true nature of science. In two studies (Tobias, 1990; Tobias & Hake, 1988), nonscience graduate students and faculty members auditing introductory physics courses found that the professors made little overt connection among the concepts covered in class or between these concepts and the students' experience. Students were intimidated by large, lecture-format classes, and found, even in smaller classes, little opportunity for discussion or for questions. Courses focused strongly on problem solving, with little emphasis on the concepts underlying the problems. The reward for successful solution tended to be a more difficult problem. Students never felt secure. The volume of material covered in a short period led a number of the participants to invest more energy in preparing for their physics classes than they did for more advanced classes in their own fields, with less encouraging outcomes. Frustration resulted. The inclusion of laboratory work afforded procedural experience but fell far short of giving students a view of the activity of professional scientists (Redish, et al., 1992) or the opportunity for reflection and discussion that can restructure thinking (Johsua & Dupin, 1987).

Any change in students' learning outcomes for an introductory physics course, or indeed for any science course, demands a shift in focus from the content of the course to how students learn that content. Edward Redish (1996), echoing Robert Glaser (as referenced in Gelman & Greeno, 1989), reminds the physics educational community that, in building an effective instructional program, it is essential to examine the goals for learning and the initial state of the students' knowledge, then consider ways to facilitate the transition from initial to goal state. Studies conducted in a diverse setting by representatives from physics, cognitive science. and social science draw similar conclusions and make similar recommendations for the restructuring of teaching and learning that have potential for facilitating the transition. Robust learning requires the interplay of declarative and procedural knowledge (J. R. Anderson, 1983). This needed blend of declarative knowledge and procedural skills, built into an integrated and coherent cognitive structure, is facilitated by the immediate application of new learning in a variety of tasks (Reif & Allen, 1992). Such experiences should be grounded firmly in the relevant domain (Doolittle, 1995; C. H. Walker, 1987), with common elements evident among the various tasks. Indeed, the strength of the learning may depend on associations between the new knowledge and culturally grounded activities in which that learning is applied, along with the immediacy and frequency of that application (Koschmann, Myers, Feltovich, & Barrows, 1994).

The integration of the microcomputer into curricular development has afforded the opportunity to implement these conclusions of cognitive research in a way that is efficient in its use of financial, temporal, and human resources. Because computers are a common tool used by professional scientists, any instructional program seeking to introduce students to the culture of scientists would be expected to make some use of the computer. Recently, however. beyond its use as a tool, the computer has become a vital part of the total learning environment as an instructional instrument. Over the last 30 years and at all levels of schooling, computer-integrated learning systems (ILS) have been developed and implemented with a broad range of outcomes. Early educational applications used computers for drill and practice, but research suggests that they have a stronger impact on new learning, particularly for more able students (Hativa, 1994). At the very least, students in an ILS environment tend to spend more time engaged diligently in learning tasks (Worthen, VanDusen, & Sailor. 1994). Although there has been mixed evidence of the effect of such systems on academic outcomes, they have been shown to have strong affective outcomes for both students and teachers, to encourage persistence, and to increase motivation and self-esteem (D. D. Adams & Shrum, 1990; VanDusen & Worthen, 1994). Originally considered a vehicle for individualizing learning, the computer has been shown most effective in a collaborative setting (Cox, 1992), and the combination of an ILS environment with a collaborative structure and Socratic dialogue provides not only cognitive, but also metacognitive, support (Hake, 1995; Hativa, 1994; Mevarech, 1994). There is evidence that this collaborative, computer-integrated setting gives students the opportunity to build their own theories of science; thus, they have a clearer understanding of the true nature of science (Cox, 1992). Palincsar and colleagues (Palincsar, C. Anderson, & David, 1993) demonstrated the power of collaborative problem solving in general in helping students to develop a clearer idea of the nature of scientific work. There is evidence that integrating this collaborative interaction into a computer-based format enhances its effects (Cox, 1992). Any potential positive effects depend on the deliberate development of programs grounded in cognitive theory (Winn, 1990) and designed to achieve the closest possible match to true scientific understanding, the nature of scientific learning, and the effectiveness of scientific activity (Hawkins & Pea, 1987).

In its use as an educational medium in a carefully structured learning environment based on the principles of cognitive research, the computer may serve as a strong mechanism for reorganizing mental processes, aiding students in developing the hierarchical structure for their new knowledge (Pea, 1986, 1993b). Such guidance in organization is not easy to accomplish in the progress of a traditional educational program, but the collaborative use of computer tools under the guidance of a mentoring instructor may provide students with greater opportunity to work in their zones of proximal development, Lev Vygotsky's (1978) term for functioning just beyond their current level of competence. Interaction with peers in a learning task provides the occasion to refine one's own ideas and to broaden and extend them through exposure to the thoughts of others.

Aspects of the intelligence of the collaborators, of their mentors, and of those who produced the materials for classroom use are distributed across symbolic and physical tools available in the learning environment, so that the intelligence available to the individual in an enriched environment is far greater than his or her own (Pea, 1993b). The distribution of intelligence across the social environment meshes with the ideas of Vygotsky (1962) as well and is validated in the research. Patricia Heller and her colleagues (1992) presented long term experimental evidence that solutions to problems negotiated within structured groups are consistently better than the best individual solutions of the best problem solver within the group, and that this skill transfers to individual work. The process of cognition is inextricably linked to its physical and social context (L. B. Resnick, Salmon, Zeitz, Wathen, & Holowchak, 1993). A feedback loop persists between the student's activity and cognition, with adjustments occurring on both sides as the student interacts with the environment, and with the reciprocal relationships among learner, task, environment, social structure, and activity, as noted by Salomon (1993) in his elaboration of distributed cognition. It would seem, then, that an ideal setting for enhancing students' understandings of the process and content of science is one in which new material is presented linked to prior learning and future goals, learning is reinforced by a variety of activities in which students collaboratively work with the same concept in a variety of contexts, thinking is reorganized through reflection and discussion, and all is accomplished within a technologically appropriate environment.

The last 15 years, especially, have seen significant progress in the drive for innovation based on cognitive studies. Several innovative programs have arisen during these years, each incorporating selected suggestions from cognitive research, most employing computer-based environments, and all boasting varying degrees of success and exportability. At the University of Washington, Lillian McDermott and her colleagues have developed tutorials, based on Socratic dialogue and structured group-learning activities, as a supplement to the introductory physics program (L. C. McDermott, 1996). These activities are designed to help learners confront their long-standing preconceptions and develop a framework for scientific thinking. The use of Socratic dialogue employs distributed intelligence (Pea, 1993b) and responds to the call for articulation of understandings (Redish, 1996), affording the occasion to engage and correct naive understandings (Gorsky & Finegold, 1994).

Ron Thornton and his colleagues at Tufts University have developed Tools for Scientific Thinking and their accompanying microcomputer-based laboratory materials to answer the need for laboratory investigations that are efficient and profitable to the student, devoid of computational drudgery, but not of active participation or meaningful content (Thornton & Sokoloff, 1990). The use of computer-interfaced measurement tools direct transfer of data to the computer, where it can be recorded in a spreadsheet. In tune with Arons' (1993) prescriptions for effective learning, the program gives students the responsibility to choose what measures to make and the format in which to display them. Mathematical tools, including integration and differentiation, are built into the system, and data lists and graphs may be displayed immediately, making a firm connection between the external phenomenon, the data that summarize it, and its graphical representation. The availability of multiple graphing windows on a single screen helps to reinforce the connection between related characteristics, such as force and acceleration, or position, velocity, and acceleration. The visual comparison of graphs gives credence to comparison of the more theoretical equations. Because the process is quick, students have the chance to try "what if?" scenarios, make predictions, compare those predictions to outcomes, and explain their revisions. In addition, the use of the computer applications helps demonstrate the use of numerical approximations and dispel the myth of the exactness of outcomes (Thornton, 1989; Thornton & Sokoloff, 1990).

Priscilla Laws and her colleagues at Dickinson College contributed Workshop Physics, a "hands-on, minds-on," activity-based introductory course (Laws, 1991, 1996). In this course, conducted in small classes, all conceptual instruction is anchored in, and is the outcome of, experimental observations.

Eric Mazur, at Harvard University, converted a standard lecture format to a conceptual, collaborative format, coupled with the use of short ConcepTests and an electronic response system for immediate response-feedback to his presentations (Mazur, 1996). This allows for greater interaction even when large classes are unavoidable.

Jack Wilson, at Rensselaer Polytechnic Institute, has introduced the highly integrated, strongly structured, multimedia, computer-based CUPLE Studio Physics Course, an outgrowth of the Comprehensive Unified Physics Learning Environment (CUPLE). This program combines elements of the others into a new entity. Powerful computer tools, small-group and whole-group discussions, Socratic dialogue, collaborative problem solving, mentoring instructors, and realistic and contemporary instances of physical principles combine to give students every chance to confront and amend naive or incomplete understandings, to strengthen concepts and skills, and to build confidence and poise through collaboration and presentation (Redish, et al., 1992; J. M. Wilson, 1994, 1996; J. M. Wilson & Redish, 1992).

Across the country and around the world, innovations multiply at an amazing rate. Testing of the programs has found all of the fully implemented, designer-guided ones to have achieved some measure of cognitive success. Drawbacks, where they exist, are related to the expense of implementation, size constraints, or lack of faculty support.

# EVALUATING TECHNOLOGY-BASED PROGRAMS

If recent technology-amplified innovations in science education are to provide a catalyst for effective, robust learning, educators must examine them carefully and honestly for their outcomes, their comparative benefits, their possible difficulties, and their ease of adoption or adaptation by nondesigners. Programs like the CUPLE Studio are strong efforts to respond to the recommendations of cognitive science by using sound educational principles in technological applications anchored in contemporary reality. Can the Studio program, or others like it, help the learner effectively to build a stronger, more cohesive knowledge base? Can such a program model expert problem solving and explanation techniques and guide students into more expert modes of thinking and acting? Can it be used with equal effectiveness by any instructor?

## Difficulties in Implementing Innovation

Iterative testing and revision will preserve the best of the innovations while allowing for the redesign of ineffective components (Winn, 1990). Matching finished product to educational goals demands the ongoing comparison of processes and strategies to predetermined criteria. It is obvious that the midprocess alteration of criteria is likely to result in a product that is different from the original innovation in its very essence. What may not be so obvious is that losing sight of those criteria, or failing to express them adequately to persons implementing the innovation, may have the same effect. In such circumstances, the most careful researcher may find himself or herself studying a program that shows rapidly vanishing similarities to the original design.

This phenomenon was evident in the first widespread use of Thornton's and Sokoloff's Tools for Scientific Thinking (Thornton, 1989; Thornton & Sokoloff, 1990), one of the earliest of the current crop of computer-aided innovations. Pilot testing of the program at Tufts University showed encouraging results. High percentages of students made strong transitions from naive to accurate Newtonian thinking. When the program was made available, on a limited basis, for use in high schools and other colleges, some results for these secondary implementations were just as encouraging, whereas others were markedly less so. Investigation revealed a seemingly minor change only in the less successful uses of the program: the elimination of whole-group discussions. The designers intended a whole-group discussion to follow each laboratory experience, promoting exchange of students' understandings of the investigation and reflection on, and integration of, those understandings. Early response to the laboratory exercises by both teachers and students was strongly positive. A number of teachers, observing students' complete involvement in the tasks, their discussions in small groups, their interpretations within the exercise, their apparent understanding of the principles underlying them, and their obvious enjoyment of the activities, discarded the discussions as unnecessary when time was needed for other activities. Vygotsky (1962) told of the primacy of social interaction during the development of knowledge, and ongoing research has confirmed that importance. Without discussion, there may be no challenge to incorrect or inadequate beliefs. Without exception, classes that neglected the follow-up discussions demonstrated markedly lower results on the corresponding parts of the *Motion and Force Conceptual Evaluation* than the groups that retained them, despite the appearance of understanding during the progress of the activities. The follow-up, whole-group discussions proved to be a mediating factor in altering students' naive understandings. This is not to say that positive results vanished. All of the students using the program showed improvement in understanding and positive affect, but those working under the altered program gained less. The same finding has been repeated in a series of innovative programs since the 1950s: The continued presence and involvement of the designer help determine success (DiStefano, 1996).

One of the most striking components of the evaluation of the early implementation of the CUPLE Studio Physics Course at Rensselaer Polytechnic Institute (Cooper, 1995, Cooper & O'Donnell, 1996) was the marked contrast between results in the presence of a designer and in the designer's absence. The original vision of this program called for a highly structured curriculum set in a laboratory classroom designed for communication among students in collaborative learning experiences and between students and instructors in Socratic interaction. Weekly class meetings are confined to two 2-hour sessions, the 4 hours matching the credit hours for the course. This is in contrast to the total of 6 hours for the former and more traditional physics class at Rensselaer and common elsewhere. The 2-hour sessions are subdivided into activity sessions of approximately 1 half-hour each. Concepts encountered previously are reviewed at the outset of the class in conjunction with students' presentations, explanations, and refinement of homework problems. This is followed by a short laboratory experience in small groups geared to the concept under focus. In response to research, every laboratory segment is summarized in a whole-group discussion, giving students a forum to share understandings, questions, and insights, and to make the connection overtly between the practical activity and its theoretical underpinnings. A second group project of 1 half-hour duration may be a second laboratory exercise, collaborative problem solving activity, or an interactive computer exercise related to the topic under study. Again, in summary, whole-group discussion completes the activity. Finally, a mini-lecture of 1 half-hour summarizes new ideas, offers illustrative demonstrations, presents mathematical representations, and sets the stage for the next class.

The course was piloted during the spring semester of 1994 for a class of 29 students under the guidance of the designer and a co-instructor. Implementation was true to the vision and the original design. At the end of this semester, students achieved comparable or higher scores with traditional students on a common final examination written by the instructors of the traditional physics course. As noted earlier, students in the more traditional class had met for a total of 6 hours each week whereas those in the Studio class had worked together for 4 hours weekly. Evaluations at the end of the course were strongly positive, with 91% of the students responding that they would recommend the school on the basis of the Studio Course alone.

As a continuation of the experiment, a Studio Physics II Course was held in the fall of 1994, again for 29 students. At the start of this semester, some of the original studio students had transferred to the traditional class and some traditional students had entered the studio class. Studio II was conducted by the coinstructor of the original pilot. Though not a designer, this professor had become convinced of the value of the program and preserved the original design. In interviews held at the end of the fall semester, both with students from the Studio class and with students in the more traditional class who participated in Studio I, responses were highly positive. All of the students interviewed stated without hesitation that they would recommend the course to others. Some believed it to be especially helpful to students with weak backgrounds in physics, whereas others believed it to be ideal for physics majors. Students appreciated the direct interaction between students and instructors and among students. They valued the opportunity to ask questions as they arose and to implement activities in search of answers. Several stated that questions led frequently to whole-group discussions that guided them to deeper learning and confidence in their own work. In this setting, students must be involved and responsible for their own work constantly. A number of them said explicitly that the constant interaction, involvement, and discussion gave them a clearer picture of the way in which physicists work and helped them to think and work more like professional physicists.

After the highly encouraging results from the pilot implementation of the CUPLE Studio Course, the physics department made the decision to implement the program for a full introductory class during fall 1994, concurrent with Studio II. Outcomes, although positive, were less so than in the original study (Cooper, 1995; Cooper & O'Donnell, 1996). In this implementation, pairs of coinstructors led five studio classes. This time, the designer served as a consultant but was not involved directly in instruction, which was undertaken by professors with outstanding reputations as teachers of traditional classes. These professors believed in the value of the Studio endeavor and conferred regularly with the designer on its implementation, but they had not taught in the studio format before.

During the course of the semester, the progress of a daily class changed character. Two aspects of the studio course that did not emerge in practice were the students' presentations of materials, and the whole-group discussion. A professor or teaching assistant presented homework solutions, from the beginning and in both. This contrasts with the intended use of the studio in which students were expected to present their solutions and to contribute to those of other students. Though teachers elicited responses from students, the students themselves never presented, and, generally, discussion was limited to responses by students and summaries or corrections by instructors. This represented a lost occasion for students to refine and clarify ideas and to develop self-regulatory skills. Two of the instructors always asked for justifications of responses and the reasoning that provided the structure for solutions. "What if" questions were not unusual with these instructors, and students were reminded to check for the reasonableness of their answers. This pattern was not universal, however; other instructors accepted a simple statement of final answer as sufficient. All made connections among the homework, previous concepts, and upcoming material. In all cases, the instructor was increasingly the center of the activity, and most students worked at correcting their own work from his presentations. The introduction of new material and the review of major concepts also approached the traditional mode increasingly more closely after the opening weeks. As students encountered more difficulty with the material, professors employed more familiar teaching patterns.

As the homework review gradually increased in length through the semester, so, too, did the principal activity, whether it was a laboratory investigation or a collaborative problem solving session. With this extension of these parts of the class, follow-up discussion decreased accordingly and existed only as a summary of results or, most frequently, did not occur at all. Discussions of procedures, outcomes, and interpretations maintained their place in the interactions between instructors and smaller groups, but the benefits of these discussions were seldom available to the full class, nor were the insights of other members of the class available to individuals. Students working in dyads tended to move into groups of four when more input was needed, but, again, the absence of the whole-group discussions limited the availability of the insights gained to these individual small groups. Students' involvement and sense of ownership were less pronounced than with the original group. Extension of the time devoted to the laboratory work precluded, in many instances, the possibility of a second task.

Affective responses to the Studio Course remained largely positive, with 60% of the students stating that they would choose a Studio Course and recommend it to others. Students appreciated the variety of modes of interaction, the ability to ask questions as they arose, and the direct contact with instructors in small-group activities. They found it especially helpful to apply concepts immediately in a laboratory investigation.

The use of the Force Concept Inventory (Hestenes, et al., 1992) gave a means for the objective comparison of these students' achievements with those in traditional classes in the absence of a local control group. In recent years, Richard Hake (1994) has kept an extensive national database of students' scores on this instrument, sorted according to level of instruction, school, and type of program. Students in the 4-hour Studio Course scored comparably to students in more traditional 6-hour courses, but not in the range that Hake considered truly interactive. Students demonstrated little change in their ability to analyze and solve problems or in their interpretation of graphical representations, despite the use of computer-assisted graphing tools.

Innovations change gradually when they pass from the hands of their designers into those of others. Indeed, in Hake's first summary publication of test outcomes for secondary and postsecondary introductory physics courses, only one of the programs listed as highly successful, or FINE (Fulfilling Interactive Engagement [Hake, 1994]), was taught by a person other than its original designer.

Although instructors at the secondary stage of implementation may be at least as expert in their profession as the designers of innovations, the vision that drives the designers cannot be transmitted completely with the innovation. Commitment to all of the aspects of the design is not likely to be as strong in secondary implementers because they have not been a part of the research that established the design. As individual pieces of a curriculum are altered and results change accordingly, the likelihood of further change increases.

Technological innovations and, indeed, educational reforms in general, have not fared well over the years. Hailed at introduction, their long term use has been universally less widespread than anticipated (Cuban, 1986). Larry Cuban (1995), who has chronicled the history of technology in the American classroom, suggests that the success or demise of the innovation rests ultimately with the individual instructor. Whatever organizational constraints exist, teachers face their classrooms and their students alone. In classrooms, laboratories, and lecture halls, instructors exercise their profession within personal and unique frameworks of belief, practice, and practical pedagogy. Every experienced teacher has acquired, honed, and polished a repertoire of tested techniques for conveying extensive bodies of procedural and conceptual knowledge while maintaining the focus and control of the class (Cuban, 1984). When aspects of an innovation do not meet the perceived instructional needs of a teacher, alteration is the likely outcome. The support and commitment of the faculty are essential to the success of any planned innovation  (Tobias, 1990), and these are determined by the comfort level of the instructors with the technology and the attitude of the instructors toward the program (Wedman, 1986). Innovators must maintain an awareness of the teachers' classroom realities, their need for sufficient preparation, and the benefits of ongoing communication (Kao, Wedman, & Placier, 1994). The inclusion of faculty members in the planning of an implementation, consultation with them about its underlying cognitive structure, brainstorming with them over procedures, and troubleshooting with them about the possible and actual difficulties may provide the teaching staff with a more informed picture and a greater stake in the process.

## Evaluation Protocols

The matter of any science course is quite complex, and any plan for its implementation must be well defined by its cognitive aims and well structured for the attainment of these aims. The growing response to this demand is resulting in classrooms and laboratories designed and conducted within the cognitive apprenticeship model of constructivist theory. Such learning environments are guided by educators who view themselves as mentors, designing and directing the students' tasks to optimize their cognitive impact. New designs employ the ancient tools of Socratic dialogue, framing them within a contemporary computer environment. Laboratory experiences range from those that students can manipulate and measure easily to those that become part of the classroom by way of videos and network links. The collaborative construction of learning with peers helps students to confront and restructure naive beliefs, and explanation and discussion enhance the rehearsal and refinement of new knowledge. All of these elements are linked in a highly structured learning environment.

If the construction of an effective instructional design is a difficult and complex process, measuring its effects can be even more so  (Hawkins & Pea, 1987). Any attempt to evaluate the impact of such manifold programs will fall far short of its goal unless it is well-matched to the subtlety and complexity of the cognitive change that the program seeks to engender. If they are not to be short-sightedly limited, evaluation protocols for multifaceted, integrated, technology-based innovations must bear two vital characteristics: They must be longitudinal, and they must be wide-ranging. The studies must be longitudinal because it takes time for students to make the cognitive transitions and to develop the insights that the programs seek to encourage. Though studies extended through time may run the risk of being weakened by confounding factors, the risk may be necessary if growth in expertise, depth of background, and confidence are to be seen clearly. Tracking students from an introductory course through their college careers and into their first year in the workplace may provide more information about the long term effects of instruction on their understanding and their view of science than any single test instrument can.

In the short term, the measurement of progress must be multifaceted. Certainly, the success of a curriculum in science instruction will evidence itself in students' mastery of essential concepts. Growth in this mastery can be measured, at least to some extent, by some of the well-designed standardized instruments like the Force Concept Inventory (Hestenes, et al., 1992) and the Mechanics Baseline test (Hestenes & M. Wells, 1992). These tests are good first indicators when used as pre- and posttests. Their benefits are extended by the existence of a national database of test results maintained by Richard Hake of Indiana University (Hake, 1994, 1995). Hake's database lists results on these tests according to the level of the program (secondary, postsecondary), the type of school (university, college, 2-year community college, high school), the nature of the program, and the number of students involved. This gives opportunities for comparison beyond limited local control groups. However, the tests are endpoint measures, and cognitive change is not solely an endpoint phenomenon.

An evaluator who wishes to understand the full effects of an innovation must find a way to measure cognitive change at stages along the process. This is especially true in programs that emphasize prediction, explanation, and discussion (Hein, 1987). One effective technique is to measure students' ability to solve problems associated with the concepts they have met and to apply them in unfamiliar situations (Shavelson & Baxter, 1992). Textbook-style problems yield insufficient information here. Although they may be challenging, textbook problems generally provide all the information needed with little extraneous information included. A more realistic test of problem solving expertise lies in the information-rich problems proposed and designed by Patricia Heller and her colleagues (Heller, et al., 1992). These problems are story based and anchored in real experience, do not provide information that students can find or estimate easily, and include extraneous information as distracters. Such problems give students experience in transferring concepts to real applications and offer evaluators insights into students' thinking. A number of researchers make suggestions concerning expert skills that will serve as benchmarks of progress. Effectiveness of diagram, representation of information, logical flow, match of equations to situation, appropriateness of mathematical operations, and consistency of units are representative of expert skills (Chi, et al., 1981; Chi, R. Glaser, & Rees, 1983; Heller, et al., 1992).

The explanation of problem solutions is an indicator that can give an excellent picture of students' growth in mental organization, interpretation of understandings, and integration and application of concepts. Although most students consider description of procedure to be an adequate substitute for real explanation, true explanation involves the use of underlying concepts as rationale for problem solutions. The transition from one to the other represents a genuine transition to more expert modes of reasoning. The SOLO (Structure of Observed Learning Outcomes) taxonomy (Biggs & Collis, 1982) may serve as a guide in gathering criteria for evaluating students' explanations. Because students' explanation skills typically lag their solution skills (Vygotsky, 1962), the combination of problem solutions and explanations should give a more complete view of reasoning and application skills than either criterion alone.

The use of problem solving interviews with "think-aloud" protocols can fine-tune the researcher's understanding of students' thought processes even further. Students advancing in expert patterns of reasoning will relate new topics to those already known, recognize match between situations and concepts, tend to solve their problems in a forward process from known information rather than looking backward from a sought answer, and use self-regulating skills, analyzing and adjusting their performance throughout the process (N. Cole, 1990). In the course of an interview, the investigator sees the difference between students' effective and noneffective strategies and gives a view of their metacognitive processes, their strategies for coping with failure, and even their realization or nonrealization of their own failure to understand a situation.

Two difficulties arise in problem solving and explanation as data. Such information may represent a further intrusion on the progress of the class, unless the exercises can serve as data for the instructor as well as for the investigator. If the choice is made to use problem solutions and explanations as pure data and the students understand that they do not contribute to their class grade, then a self-selection process limits their effectiveness. Even in the face of this, they may contribute valuable information. A second source of difficulty resides in the interview. An investigator may be meticulous in giving no indication of the correctness of a student's work, may ask no leading questions, and still may introduce a confounding factor into the research. Having students solve problems aloud and explain their solutions to the interviewer can serve as an instructional technique in itself. The student who expects to carry out such an exercise every week or two gradually begins to reflect more deeply on how he or she does it. The reflection itself may add to the level of expertise. Given the possibility of these difficulties, both evaluation elements still provide valuable information, especially about the extent and pace of cognitive change. Their combination may give a view of those cognitive behaviors that are not amenable to direct observation (Winn, 1990).

Interviews also help the researcher gain information about those elements of the program that students find to be very helpful, less helpful, or even obstructive. In one study (Cooper, 1995), students listed helpful and difficult aspects of the course with their weekly problem solutions. Tabulations of these statements gave answers to the questions asked directly and insight into gradual changes of view as the semester progressed. Interviews with students who were enrolled in a second semester of the course yielded additional information, as did interviews with instructors and teaching assistants.

One final evaluation element must be recommended strongly. The investigator who seeks to understand the process and outcomes of an innovation must take the time to observe the progress of the classes on a regular basis. This observation is essential if one is to understand the course as it truly is and the gradual changes in students' cognitive and procedural competences. It is impossible to have a clear understanding of the dynamics of any educational program without observing it directly. Structures are altered and refined in delivery and the balance of activities shifts. Documenting that shift may be essential to the explanation of some results. Moreover, there are inevitably observations that could not be foreseen as important, but that lend understanding to conclusions after the fact.

Researchers should take note of interactions within and between groups. When are questions asked? What kinds of questions are asked? Who asks them? Are they answered? In what manner? By whom? Do questions lead to discussion or do they meet with definitive closed answers?

Observation opens a window on students' progress, evidenced in small-group laboratory investigations and collaborative problem solving sessions, and in whole-group discussions. Besides the elements of expertise listed earlier, students demonstrate advances in cognitive functioning in their persistence, their confidence, their use of "what if" questions in the progress of an experiment, and their questioning attitude in general. Artifacts of the laboratory experience or collaborative problem solving session may lend themselves to later, deeper analysis as well. Do students' products evidence reflection? Does the level of reflection change over time? Do they connect new learning to previously mastered concepts? Do they show an aptitude for investigation? Do they ask effective questions in their groups?

# CONCLUSION

The well-planned and carefully structured use of interactive computers in authentic, collaborative learning environments may serve as a mediating factor for learning activity, especially in the sciences, creating opportunities for students, engaged in active social construction of learning, to operate within their zones of proximal development (Pea, 1993b). This may encourage progress not only in the concepts of science, but also in the understanding of the nature of science and scientific enterprise, equipping the students for informed decision-making in an increasingly technological society.

Innovative and promising programs that employ the findings of cognitive research while adhering carefully to rigorous scientific study exist already, and their number grows rapidly. If such programs are to fulfill their promise, those who implement them must have access to the vision and rationale of their designers. Moreover, the programs must be subject to intense formative evaluation to guard against erosion of the original design, and encourage the continued refinement and development of strategies. An evaluation program that is longitudinal and broad-based, and employs quantitative and qualitative protocols may give the truest possible picture of the effects of innovation. With care and study, the promise of new technology-based instructional programs will be fulfilled in the more effective education of future researchers and a more informed, scientifically literate citizenry.

# 31

## Assessing Learning as Emergent Phenomena: Moving Constructivist Statistics Beyond the Bell Curve

**Walter M. Stroup**
*University of Texas-Austin*

**Uriel Wilensky**
*Northwestern University*

## TAKING THE MEASURE OF MEASURING

### Reconsidering the Beginnings and Ends of Assessment

Assessment, in the context of learning, serves two purposes. First, assessment renders or typifies the nature of understanding for an individual or a group. Second, assessment addresses expectations about learners' possible future performance. As a practical matter it is reasonable for educators and researchers to ask: Has an intervention succeeded? Can one intervention inform another? Are there expectations we might reasonably have about what learners can now do in other settings?

More formally, assessment is an attempt to establish equivalence classes that can typify and form the basis for reasoning about groups of learners and individuals within those groups.[1] This chapter takes up the issue of formal assessment and the rendering of knowing on a scale larger than one (or even a few) learner(s). It is addressed principally to our colleagues within the constructivist research community, but it may be of interest to other researchers or educators who see learning as the emergence or the development of cognitive structures[2] in a rich web of intellectual and social connections.

In this chapter, our principal goal is to critique the standard statistical model of assessment used by educational researchers both to depict the state of knowledge of a group of learners and to track the evolution over time of the group's knowledge in order to evaluate the success of an educational intervention (activity). We show that the standard assessment models based on the use of standard parametric statistics are *both* fundamentally flawed and essentially incompatible with constructivist theory. A subsidiary goal, which will serve as an introduction to our critique of standard statistical models of *group* assessment, is to critique the "technology" and methodologies of assessment of *individual* students over time, arguing that the methods of assessment employed are impoverished and that, in an attempt to summarize performances quickly, they throw out qualities of performance that are essential to getting adequate accounts of an individual's understandings. We continue by outlining the qualities that must be characteristic of an adequate assessment methodology and sketch a nonstandard assessment methodology that addresses many of the flaws of traditional methods. Some limitations of the new methods are addressed. We conclude by suggesting ways in which new computational technologies can be employed to create richer assessment methodologies that both correspond more closely with constructivist theory and provide a much more detailed and illuminating account of learners' development.

---

[1] An example of an equivalence class is all students receiving a five on a given Advanced Placement examination. The expectation about the future performance of this class of students is that they could perform adequately in subsequent courses in the same domain.

[2] Although there seems to be a good deal of confusion about what is meant by structure in the research community, our intended use is close to that articulated in Piaget's Structuralism (1970b) and/or what Seymour Papert called "powerful ideas" (1980, 1991).

## What's in a Number? How Does Standard Numerical Assessment Depict Learning?

The principal goal of critiquing the methodology of group assessment (and the assessment of educational interventions) exists against the backdrop of problematic, school-based, assessment practice. For most school districts, the end of a school year is marked by each student receiving a collection of numerical (or letter) grades, usually arrived at by averaging performances over the year. Averages are also computed for various groupings of learners: sections of a given course, schools in a system, and even districts as a whole. All of this is so standard as to be beyond the reach of criticism—as unavoidable as the changing of the seasons. The need to summarize students' performance is seen as natural as the expectation that averages (and standard parametric procedures) would be the methods used to create these summaries. What we hope to do is separate the need to summarize or typify learning from the particular methodologies employed currently. We seek to distinguish the *assessment of learning* from the simple *averaging* of numerical quantities. In this section, we point out that such numerical averaging methods exist as a point or a small region within a vast space of possible assessment methodologies. Moreover, standard averaging methods are particularly impoverished ways of typifying learning and knowing, ways that give educators and researchers very little of the insights they need in order to practice their crafts better. Additionally, the computing of these averages carries with it a deeply suspect model of learning and knowing that may undermine efforts at meaningful reform.

Among the observations we make is that a computed average—for example, B+ or 85—is, by nature, degenerate. We use *degenerate* in the mathematical sense—that it represents a huge reduction in the dimension and richness of learner performance. A final course grade reduces hundreds of hours of performances, activities, beliefs, thoughts, emotions, and peer interactions to a single value. This richness is lost irretrievably to the larger educational enterprise. Consequently, there is a profound reduction in what can be said about learner understanding. This, in turn, provides inadequate feedback for educators to use in developing classroom activities and little information for researchers to use in reconstructing learner thought. Both classroom activity and research into understanding are compromised by the degeneracy of the averaging methodology.

A subtle and widely held "misconception" about averaging is that it is the most objective and theoretically neutral technology for reporting summaries of multiple performances. Because objectivity and neutrality are seen as desirable in assessment, averaging is seen as desirable. In principle, there are an infinite number of ways of combining values, all comparably objective, none theoretically neutral. Thus, averaging is not a privileged methodology. A basic example illustrates the point that even a report of something as simple as a calculated average requires a selection of methods and a theory or model to suggest what the number signifies and how it could come to represent such a thing.

In what sense can we speak of an average square? Suppose we have two squares, square A with side 2 and square B with side 10. What is the average of these two squares? In computing this average, a question is provoked immediately over whether we are referring to the sides of the squares or the areas. In the former case, we average the length of the sides and find that the average square is of side $(2 + 10) / 2 = 6$ units of length. In the other case, we average the areas of the squares, which yields an average area of $(100 + 4) / 2 = 52$ square units. So, on the one hand, the average of the two squares is a square of side 6. On the other hand, the average square is of area 52. Even if we corrected for the dimensionality by taking the square root, we end up with an average square with side of length greater than 7. Which is the real average square: the 6 or the 7? When averaging, one needs to be explicit about what one is paying attention to.

A more significant observation about this example is that *neither average* says anything at all about squareness as such (if, indeed, there is any such thing as squareness as such). So average *squareness* is underdefined or missed altogether, *even if agreement is reached* about which numbers are used to compute the average (sides or areas). All sorts of averages can be created and defined operationally as measuring a given property (like the average square). Our argument is that even when careful attention *is* paid to such operational definitions, it still may be the case that the model implied by averaging of this sort does not fit with, or in any way render, the intended object of attention. In the example given previously, squareness itself is missed. Instead, one ends up with various averagings of selected features of certain geometric figures and not an account of the presence of squareness that is presumed to be at the center of the investigation.

The situation is similar, we argue, with assessing learner understandings. Various averages can be computed. Often, ambiguity of the sort alluded to in the square example is present: Are we talking about analogs to areas or to sides (or a mixture of these and still other properties)? More fundamental, however, is the question of whether a statistic based on averaging is a statistic that can say anything meaningful about understandings as such. When using computed averages in assessing understandings, we want to ask: Are we merely measuring somewhat arbitrary features of human activity and missing the mark altogether in our attempt to give an account of understanding as a developing, structured, and structuring whole? We believe that cognitive statistics—as a rendering of equivalence classes among learners—are indeed possible. But, in order for the intended objects of our attention—understandings—to be rendered, it is not expected that these statistics will be based on a notion of average understanding or that they will be well served by the use of various kinds of related parametric procedures.

In educational assessment, we believe that a part of the reason that averages have been selected from among the vast range of possible renderings is because they are comparatively easy to compute. That is, given the technologies of pencil and paper, adding machines, and so forth, the average is among the simplest of computations. "Averagers" customarily ignore the role of computing technologies in forming and biasing the selection of the standard average. This lack of awareness of dependency on the ease of computation has numerous consequences. Among them is that even with the advent of new, computer-based technologies, we have failed to address the new possibilities inherent in the more powerful medium and, instead, have carried over the old methodology to the new medium. In our concluding section, we suggest assessment renderings that make better use of powerful new technologies.

Given that any reporting of outcomes results from theory and norm-based selection of procedure, we note that, under current practice, the possibility of having this valuation and consequent analyses informed by, and reflective of, local norms and emphases is not considered. This means that local educators are tacitly deferring to a centralized testing authority to decide important issues of valuation. This deference may relate to the presumption of greater objectivity associated with averaging, discussed previously. New computing tools would allow the analyses to be powerfully contextualized and tailored to better address local needs and norms.

In the next section, we take up the major argument of this chapter—the critique of standard statistical methodology for group assessment. In doing so, we are aware that we are taking a strong stance regarding the interaction of methods and models of learning. Although positivism, as a philosophy proper and as a theory of scientific method in particular, has been widely rejected, some positivistic assumptions about methodology still linger in the education research community. Most notable is the assumption that methods can be cleanly separated from models or that given methods can be "theory neutral" (see, e.g., Kuhn, 1957, 1962/1970). The argument that follows assumes that methods and models are inextricably linked and mutually informing.

# CRITIQUE OF STANDARD GROUP ASSESSMENT METHODOLOGY: REJECTING THE EFFICACY OF METHODS WITHOUT MODELS

Now we come to our principal argument—that standard statistical methodology implies a model of learning that is largely incompatible with fundamental elements of constructivist theories of learning centered on the development of cognitive structure. If, in fact, the emergence of whole cognitive structures does typify the developmental sequence, then we would expect individuals' progress to show a more discrete quality to it and not be well modeled through a continuous distribution with an incremental time-evolution. The *understandings* of groups of learners would emerge as vectors in an evolving, structural, *n*-space. The time-evolution of the locations of populations associated with these vectors would not be monotonically incremental but, rather, would have a significant stochastic aspect. The image is less like a planet processing and more like the discrete restructurings associated with various quantum phenomena. In this section, we expand on and develop these ideas further. Subsequently, we present the outlines of a nonstandard statistical methodology more compatible with fundamental elements of constructivist learning theory.

The reasonable rejection (avoidance) by some constructivists of the standard model and its associated methodology has resulted in the creation of what we see as a problematic response—a methodology that we call "radical individualism." In the work associated with this methodology, it is sometimes unclear in what sense the reported work is about more than one (or a few) person(s). Such work risks being too individual in a way that Piaget rejected explicitly as a characterization of his constructivism (Bringuier, 1980). In this chapter, we outline an alternative to either standard parametric methodologies or the methodologies of radical individualism.

Admittedly, the topic of formal assessment is an awkward one among constructivists and one that most are hesitant to engage. For many, there is the danger of becoming too consumed by methodological issues that will take them far afield from the kinds of learner-centered research activities that interest them most. Piaget expressed something like this idea[3] and Duckworth (1987) expressed similar sentiment.[4]     Papert (personal communication, April 1993) justified his lack of interest in statistical assessment methodology by saying that if you need statistics to show an educational improvement then the improvement was not significant enough to warrant our attention. Problems, however, are created by this inattention. On the one hand, this *seeming* incoherence in the methodologies of various cognitive researchers can hamper efforts to have one set of results inform another and, on the other hand, it can give critics a too facile reason for not engaging the substance of the research findings. Most significant to us, however, is the possibility that some researchers' allowance that standard parametric methods are acceptable could, in the end, advance indirectly a model of learning largely incompatible with constructivism's attention to the emergence and development of learners' cognitive structures.

Skepticism has been expressed about the utility of statistical assessment in the educational reform community. This skepticism has had a significant impact on discussions of practice and attempts to create new educational standards. Many reform documents and articles call for nonstatistical assessment techniques including portfolio assessment (Cai, Lane, & Jakabcsin 1996; Cai, Magone, Wang, & Lane, 1996; Lambdin, Kehle, & Preston, 1996; Mathematical Sciences Education Board, 1993a, 1993b; National Council of Teachers of

---

[3] "Once the work of clearing away, of groundbreaking, has been done, which consists of discovering new things, and finding things that hadn't been anticipated, you can begin to standardize —at least if you like that sort of thing—and to produce accurate statistics" (Bringuier, 1980, p. 25).

[4] "The virtues involved in not knowing are the ones that really count in the long run. . . . Standardized tests can never, even at their best, tell us anything other than whether a given fact, notion, or ability is already within a child's repertoire" (Duckworth, 1987).

Mathematics, 1989, 1992a, 1992b, 1995; Vermont Department of Education, 1991). Whereas constructivist educators have made some significant inroads on assessing individual learners, constructivist researchers have had much less to say on large-scale assessments (classrooms, schools, districts, states, countries). Moreover, as a practical concern, the aggregate of portfolios overwhelms the capacity of the classroom educator to process the input in a way that would inform ongoing practice. Additionally, a number of critiques of statistical assessment methodology in relation to educational research have emerged. Some have noted that "classical" educational research, with its use of standard statistical methodologies, emphasizes product over process (Schoenfeld, 1987b). Others have noted that standard statistical methodologies can do little to inform the interventions needed for children with special needs (Meltzer, 1994). There have been calls for a temporary suspension of statistical assessment until methods integrated more closely with analyses of thinking processes are found (Kilpatrick, 1978). Our sense is that significant work needs to be done related to analyzing the theoretical aspects of the relationship between standard statistical methodologies and constructivism and to providing constructivist alternatives for large-scale assessment.

Ours, then, is a very pragmatic concern. We see the edifice of school-based, behaviorist practice that resists putting the ideas of learners at the center of education discourse as standing on a foundation of standard parametric methods. Therefore, we believe it is worth considering how an embrace of the latter may do much to reinforce the former. One purpose of this chapter is to encourage developmentalists and constructivists of the various hues to take up again the issue of how we render learning formally on a scale larger than one (or even a few in a teaching experiment). We intend this chapter to begin this process of reconsideration even as it seeks to give specific guidance to researchers and educators "in the field" looking for ways of analyzing the activities of learners.

## Heuristic Realism and the Gaussian Distribution

*The Fit Between the Use of Standard Parametric Methods and Behaviorist Learning Theory.* Although, in discussing learning research, many cognitivists—including constructivists (e.g., Piaget, as quoted by Bringuier, 1980) and Gestaltists (e.g., Köhler, 1959)—have allowed that standard statistical methods could be used after the more important work of discovery has been done, it is argued here that the use of standard norm-based statistics (classical parametric methods, as discussed by Siegel [1956] and S. S. Stevens [1946, 1951]) implies a model of learning that fits better with the central features of behaviorism than with structure-based cognitivism. Deeper reasons why Piaget, in particular, may have continued to allow for the use of parametric methods may have more to do with his philosophical stances regarding the foundations of chance-based reasoning and the relations between science and religion than as an assertion about the adequacy or appropriateness of these methods in the realm of learning research (Stroup, 1994, 1996). These reasons are not the focus of this chapter because they take us quite far away from an analysis of standard parametric methods as vehicles of learning research and assessment.

Later herein, we give an example of where Piaget, despite his seeming allowance for the use of standard statistics, did advance nonetheless a kind of nonstandard statistic in reporting the results of some work with learners. We believe that this nonstandard statistic may hint at the possibility of advancing a more thoroughgoing effort to develop nonstandard statistics that fit better with the central tenets of structure-emergent, learning theory. Thus, although the ambivalence regarding standard statistics is long-standing within cognitivism, the possibility of resolving the internal tension in a way that allows for the creation of formal equivalence classes (necessary for the creation of any kind of statistic) while remaining true to cognitive theory is highlighted. To move toward this resolution, it is important to make clear the ways in which standard statistics seem to fit better with behaviorism as a theory of learning. The behaviorism considered is the classical stance represented in the writings of B. F. Skinner, the chief architect of this now traditional model of learning.

The precursors to parametric statistics certainly predate their application to what Skinner called a "science of behavior." The first efforts to develop a formal manner for discussing fluctuations or errors in scientific measurement came in the field of astronomy in the latter half of the 18th century. Early astronomers needed a system for talking about the variations occurring in their measurements of specific celestial objects (Heidelberger, 1987). A notion of what eventually became "standard deviation" was developed. If the standard deviation (SD) for a particular set of measurements was relatively large, then other scientists would know that a good deal of fluctuation had occurred in the measured results. A relatively low standard deviation meant that the results were relatively consistent.

In the 19th century, Karl Friedrich Gauss helped to formalize the discussion of standard deviation (Swijtink, 1987) and give it the numerical interpretation that it has today (i.e., allowing that the results are consistent with the central limit theorem, within 1 SD of the mean, one can expect to find nearly 68% of the trials in a normal distribution). In the realm of celestial observations, the assumption that there is some one thing being examined (assuming a certain level of competence) and that this same one thing continues to exist while observations are made seems entirely reasonable.[5]

Social theory based on the use of statistics inverts this argument. Rather than moving from a real object being observed to the use of a certain kind of statistics, the argument in social science (including traditional forms of behaviorist analysis) moves from the use of a certain kind of statistics to the assumption that there is something *there* that is being measured. A kind of operationally defined or heuristic realism takes hold:

> When a concept is defined in terms of the operations, manipulations, and measurements that are made in referring to it we have an *operational* definition. Intelligence might be defined as the score obtained on a particular test, a character trait like generosity might be defined as the proportion of one's income that one gives away. (Cowles, 1989, p. 41, emphasis in the original)

As noted in the quotation, intelligence is defined operationally as that which the score on an intelligence quotient (IQ) test measures—what the statistics *point to*. Even characteristics like "generosity" can be *made real* by the similar use of an operational definition.

The positivist commitments of operationalism require that "meaning is equated with verifiability" and that constructs that are not accessible instrumentally to observation "are meaningless" (Cowles, 1989, p. 41). Of course, this approach is "closely akin to the doctrine of behaviorism" (Cowles, 1989, p. 41). The language of *thought*, *meaning*, or *intent* (to say nothing of aesthetics) is eschewed in scientific discourse and is replaced by the objective measurement of behavior.

Although positivism, as such, is decidedly antirealist, a kind of implicit notion of deterministic mechanism still informs behaviorist discourse:

> It is a working assumption which must be adopted at the very start. We cannot apply the methods of science to a subject matter which is assumed to

---

[5]Even in this seemingly uncontroversial case, there have been cases of false attributions.

move about capriciously. Science not only describes, it predicts. It deals not only with the past but with the future. . . . If we are to use the methods of science in the field of human affairs, *we must assume that behavior is lawful and determined.* (Skinner quoted in Cowles, 1989, p. 22, emphasis added)

The "field of human affairs," including education, "must" be "lawful and determined" in much the same way that the motions of planets are objectively determined. The "methods of science" require that this be so. Thus, in using these methods, it is "assumed" that the behavior under consideration is as lawful and determined as it is seen to be (at least under classical models) in other realms of science. The flow of the argument is not from the object (e.g., a planet) to a method. Instead, the move is from the application of certain "methods of science" to the assumption that there must be something "lawful and determined" there to be measured. In this particular way, behaviorism labors under the assumption of a kind of operational or heuristic realism.

Extending the sense in which behaviors are analogues of physical objects, such as planets, a new class of object is introduced—a behavioral object. Some objects of behavior are immovable (like the "fixed" stars). Still others can be advanced (like planets traveling in their orbits). Intelligence as a behavioral object, *usually* is seen to be fixed. It is the *first mover* of knowing-type behaviors. A properly calibrated test simply measures where this unmoved mover is located. In this way, intelligence is understood to be largely above interventions of any kind (except, of course, certain types of physical trauma).[6]

---

[6]Recently, there has been significant literature that questions the assumption of fixed intelligence (see, e.g., Dweck & Leggett, 1988; S. J. Gould, 1993).

Examples of intellectual objects that can be seen to move include performance or achievement in some field of knowledge.[7] Achievement in doing sums or in doing physics can be measured using a testing instrument. Usually by some form of intervention (the behavioral equivalent of a physical push or shove), the level of achievement can be improved. This improvement can be measured in individuals and in groups. By using properly calibrated instruments, the motion or movement of the behavioral object can be assessed experimentally.

For a group of learners working on a standardized examination in physics (e.g., like those produced by the Educational Testing Service), an improvement in scores represents a "real" improvement in achievement.

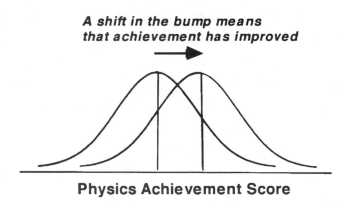

FIG. 31.1. The significance of a change in achievement scores.

If the bump of collective performance moves to the right, as illustrated in FIG. 31.1, then the intervention (e.g., increased class time, use of a particular text, or animated lectures) is labeled effective. Performance, understanding, or ability in almost any area can be defined

---

[7] This distinction in the nature of the behavioral object being measured is commonplace in standardized testing. Scholastic Aptitude Tests, for instance, are represented as measuring relatively immovable aptitudes, whereas achievement tests measure relatively moveable achievement.

operationally in such a manner, and the effectiveness of an intervention can be established objectively. School curricula and pedagogy rise and fall according to their ability to shift the bump of (what is assumed to be) a normalized distribution.

*Some Characteristics of Traditional Statistical Models.* In light of the radical epistemic shifts that have taken place in physics and astronomy since they became modern (including specifically the use of nonstandard statistical distributions), it might seem reasonable to ask whether methods borrowed from the natural sciences during their mechanistic (classical) period might need to be updated. Certainly, there has to be some irony in the fact that one of the few major realms of formal academic discourse where a kind of mechanistic realism persists is in the quantitative methods divisions of the various social science departments (including education). These observations notwithstanding, it remains beyond the scope of this chapter to review fully, much less engage in detail, the extensive literature concerning the validity of using traditional statistical methods.[8] For the purposes of analysis, a few features of the traditional model need to be highlighted:

- The distribution of intelligence, achievement, or understanding in a group looks like a bump (a Gaussian distribution) in the traditional schema (see FIG. 31.2).

---

[8] For a historical overview, see Statistics in Psychology: An Historical Perspective, by Michael Cowles (1989).

## **Gaussian Distribution (Normal Bump)**

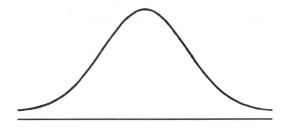

FIG. 31.2. The Guassian distribution.

- At least in principle, the distribution of learnable performance for a group of individuals (the bump shown in FIG. 31.2) can move quasi-continuously (there may be small jumps due to the discrete nature of the assessment items; nonetheless, the mathematics, in a sense, requires that the distribution approach—as a limit—a continuous curve and be able to move up or down relatively smoothly). Complex behavior is analyzed into "small steps" and behavior is shaped "through a program of progressive approximation" (Skinner, 1978, p. 135). Based on the results gleaned from the "laboratory," learning "material is so designed that correct responses are highly probable" (Skinner, 1978, p. 135). Ability is advanced incrementally as correct responses to individual contingencies become more probable (Skinner, 1978). Illustrating Skinner's (1968) strong commitment to incrementalism is his own "conservative estimate" of "the total number of contingencies which may be arranged during ... the first four years" of schooling (Skinner, 1968, p. 17). His estimate for these years alone is "perhaps 50,000"

(Skinner, 1968, p. 17). For a scale with such fine-grained increments, global advancement would appear near-continuous.[9]

- The bump is assumed to stand for, or represent, a single thing (e.g., general intelligence for fixed bumps, or understanding of mathematics for movable bumps) or a single cluster of abilities (e.g., scholastic aptitude). For movable achievement, this identity is preserved even as the bump moves up or down the range of possible values. The sense is that there is some one thing, like a planet, being moved and, when the bump moves, the something—for example, achievement—is now located in a new place.

- There is no need to engage, or even to acknowledge, the existence of learners' ideas, models, or modes of reasoning. Not only are investigations of such structures a distraction from empirical investigations of behavior, but also they are doomed in principle to be misleading. Skinner (1978) argued specifically that "introspective knowledge is limited by anatomy" (p. 73). For a person, self-observation and the ability to investigate "why he behaves as he does" are seen to have "arose very late in the evolution of the species" (Skinner, 1978, p. 73). When "why" questions are asked about ourselves (or, even more difficult, when "why" questions are asked about others), "the only nervous systems available" are those that have "evolved for entirely different reasons" (Skinner, 1978, p. 73). That is, the nervous systems that had "proved useful in the internal economy of

---

[9] Note that structuralist accounts do not need to take a stance regarding the fine structure of learning and knowing in a domain. It is sufficient that an account of such learning and knowing can be given meaningfully through engagement with macrolevel structures. Some cognitivists would trace the emergence of macrostructures to combinations of similar fine-grained structures (see, e.g., Dennett, 1991; Minsky, 1987).

the organism, in the coordination of movement, and in operating upon the environment" are being pushed well beyond their specific capacities in being asked about ideas or internal models (Skinner, 1978, p. 73). According to Skinner, there is "no reason why they [the nervous systems] should be suitable in supplying information about those very extensive systems that mediate behavior" (Skinner, 1978, p. 73). The nervous systems simply are not designed to do this. Fundamentally introspection is suspect: "Introspection cannot be very relevant or comprehensive because the human organism does not have nerves going to the right places" (Skinner, 1978, pp. 73–74).

In the end, Skinner's very personal theory or model of the evolution, purposes, and design of the nervous systems (briefly outlined in the preceding discussion) preemptively precludes the possibility of engaging the thoughts or reasoning of learners.[10] The whole of semiotic activity as such is suspect as the stuff of formal ("scientific") investigation. All there is to teaching within his behaviorist framework is the programatic manipulation of the contingencies of reinforcement. Learners' ideas, symbolizations, or structures of thought are absolutely irrelevant to Skinner's notion of a science of behavior.

Taken together, these assumptions are seen to underlie or reinforce the use of statistics in ways closely identified with the larger behaviorist program. Having outlined the bases for the external identification of standard statistics with behaviorist learning theory, we now take up some issues related to the internal inconsistency of standard statistical methods as they are applied to learning.

*Internal Deficiencies of Standard Parametric Methods.* Setting aside, for a moment, the *external* identification of standard parametric methods with largely discredited, behaviorist learning theory, significant *internal* fault lines can be found in the systematic application of standard paramentric methods to assessing learning. In education, standard parametric methods

---

[10] There are aspects of Skinner's personal theory that many cognitivists would embrace. In particular, it is noncontroversial that some aspects of our internal processing are inaccessible to our introspection.

have shown themselves to be well suited to sorting and ranking learners within a consistent interpretive scheme. Beyond simply sorting learners, however, the methods fail to say much that is meaningful or useful about learning itself. The processes, beliefs, content, and activities of learning are not illuminated. By examining closely some of the internal theoretical and practical deficiencies of the application of standard parametric methods, we hope to raise serious questions about the integrity of seeking to apply these methods in education contexts.

Classical statistical theory as applied to social science, has a number of fundamental assumptions. Among the five that Siegel (1956) listed is "the observations must be drawn from normally distributed populations" (p. 19). In actual practice, however, the appearance of normal distributions, even in large-scale achievement and psychometric measures, is extraordinarily rare. An article by Micceri (1989) with the provocative title "The Unicorn, the Normal Curve, and Other Improbable Creatures" made this point convincingly. Micceri undertook a review of 440 large-sample achievement and psychometric measures. The striking result of this review was that *less than 7%* of these data sets exhibited the symmetry and tail weights of the normal (Gaussian) distribution. In addition to mixed-normal distributions (distinct peaks), other important kinds of distributions occurred regularly. A more recent survey (Sawilowsky, 1990) of these issues highlights a similar sense in which typical distributions associated with learning research and assessment *almost never satisfy the fundamental assumptions required for the use of parametric tests* such as the $t$ and $F$ tests for analyzing sets of experimental data.

In part as a way around these very significant failures of the standard parametric model to work as a statistic in the learning sciences, a rather defensive response has emerged from parametric researchers. The goal seems to be to preserve the calculating machinery of various analysis of variance (ANOVA) techniques even when the fundamental assumptions that structure the use of the techniques fail. Strategically, an effort is being made to avoid linking specific forms of calculation with either theories of behavior or classical theories of parametric method (e.g., Siegel, 1956; S. S. Stevens, 1946). The break with the fundamental assumptions of classical parametric method is startling. Even when fundamental assumptions (like normality, etc.) that structured the use of these algorithms are violated, these researchers still want to continue to use the calculating machinery.

The argument of these researchers is that the calculating techniques themselves become a model and are no longer to be considered methods associated with other models. In justification, it is no longer a question of whether the "normal theory ANOVA assumptions" (as discussed by Siegel [1956, p. 19], for example) are "met," but "whether the plausible violations of the assumptions have serious consequences on the validity of probability statements based on the standard assumptions" (Glass, Peckham, & Sanders, 1972). For these researchers, the probabilities associated with ANOVA tests being run on various nonnormal distributions (see Siegel, 1956) were close to the probabilistic results from Monte Carlo simulations. Because the numbers worked out to be very similar, there was little danger in continuing to use ANOVA statistics *even when the conditions that structured the use of these statistics are absent.* Glass summarized the situation somewhat cavalierly this way: "The assumptions of most mathematical models are always false to a greater or lesser extent." The statistical bottom line was (and is) this: ANOVA tests work and there is no need to become engaged in trying to justify their continued use in any other way. Formally, the *ANOVA tests themselves* are to be considered a kind of "model." Researchers can act *as if* this model is true just so long as reasonable probabilities are produced.

Although the point needs to be developed further in future work, those familiar with the history of science may recognize some striking parallels with other important moments of paradigm shift. By the time of the Copernican revolution, the mathematical machinery used to calculate the position of various planets and the stars *assuming a geocentric model* was quite advanced. There was little (if anything) in the formalism that could have compelled the major revision that was the Copernican revolution. The mathematical model was quite powerful.[11] What became increasingly untenable was the effort to see in the world the structures that would allow the formalism to make sense.

---

[11]Thomas Kuhn (1962/1970) made this point:

> The Ptolemaic system . . . was admirably successful in predicting the changing positions of both stars and planets. No other ancient system had performed so well; for the stars, Ptolemaic astronomy is still widely used today as an engineering approximation; for the planets, Ptolemy's predictions were as good as Copernicus'. (p. 68)

Similarly, the criticism of traditional statistical models advanced in this chapter is not particularly informed by failures of the mathematics to "save the phenomena." Instead, it is informed by the failure of the mathematics of the parametric model to make sense of itself *and* to make sense of learning. At this point in our intellectual history, it seems as if the methods of various tests have been divorced from the assumptions that grounded the use of these tests. Moreover, the whole of the effort to do research in statistical methods has attempted to divorce itself from discourse about the nature and processes of cognitive activity. Once again, there is an attempt to separate neatly the methods from the content and meaning of the work done with those methods.

One of our aims in this section is to remind ourselves that, historically, there *were* links between models of learning and methods. Additionally, we hope to advance the idea that coherent alternatives to the current pastiche of methods, mathematics, and theories of education might are possible. This sense of alternatives emerges, we believe, in underdeveloped strands from the constructivist literature. We begin with an example from Piaget.

## An Early Example of a Constructivist Statistic

Piaget's book, *The Child's Conception of Movement and Speed* (1946/1970a), reports his investigations of children's ideas about changes in position and speed. Methodologically, the findings are largely the product of clinical interviews. At one point, however, Piaget summarized his results in a way that is distinctly quantitative. He used a simple quantification scheme—quoted later—to draw together important strands in his work. This quantification conveys insights about children's ideas of motion, aspects of his larger developmental project (with its specific references to age), and an overview of the collective performance of "some sixty subjects of 5 to 10 years of age" (Piaget, 1946/1970a, p. 227). This rendering allows Piaget to speak "both" to "their agreement with previous results" and to "the individual light thrown on the problem of speed" (p. 227). Both general (i.e., developmental) and quite narrow (motion-specific) concerns are thereby addressed. Though a weakness of his account might be that it does not seem to allow for the full bidirectional interaction of collective results and individual reports that the nonstandard statistical methodology developed in this chapter does allow, it is still the case that what Piaget did report instantiates an effort on his part to articulate collective results in ways consistent with his larger developmental claims.

Piaget (1946/1970a) advanced a nonstandard "model" centered on learning issues related to the development of motion and rate structures. This brief quantitative report we view as significant because it suggests new methodological and theoretical possibilities for the development of nonstandard statistics centered on the emergence of cognitive structure. It is precisely to this possibility that we want to draw attention and we would like to see it extended by other cognitive researchers.

Piaget (1946/1970a) summarized some of his motion-related results from "some sixty" learners in the following way:

> From the point of view of time, first of all, confirmation is found of what has already been seen in other work: simultaneousness of finishing points (or even starting points) is acquired at the age of 5 years by only 25% of the subjects; at 6 years by 50% and at 7 years by 75%. As for the equality of synchronous durations, this is on average slightly delayed: 33% at 5 years, 25% at 6 years, 70% at 7 years, and 75% only at 8 years. (p. 227)

The report is nonstandard in that no (even implicit) reference to a normal distribution is advanced nor are related reports of uncertainty (plus or minus) made. Instead, specific assertions about shifts in understanding are reported as a function of age. In the context of the quotation, *simultaneousness* refers to learners identifying that objects moving together for the same amount of time but for different displacements finish together (as opposed to a single object that went farther for more time). *Synchronous duration* concerns learners seeing the objects as having moved for the same amount of time (duration, as opposed to stopping *at* the same instant, as with simultaneousness).

If Piaget's findings are plotted on three-dimensional axes, the respective graphs for the development (time-evolution) of simultaneousness and synchronous duration that result are shown on FIG. 31.3 and 31.4.

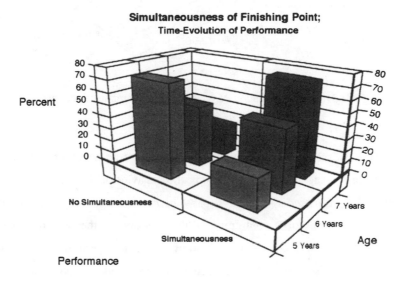

FIG. 31.3. Time evolution of performance for simultaneousness.

As Piaget reported, synchronous duration is "slightly delayed," so the shift in performance comes later ("75% . . . at 8 years").

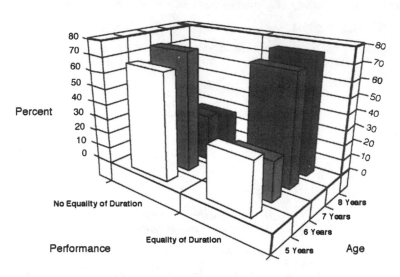

FIG. 31.4. Time-evolution of equality of synchronous durations.

"Performance" is seen as the exhibition ("acquisition") or nonexhibition of a way of thinking about a task. Piaget's way of analyzing the behavior of the learners is organized in terms of *shifts in understanding or ways of thinking*—simultaneousness or equality of duration—and *not* in terms of a continuity in the identity of the specific collections of students either exhibiting or not exhibiting a kind of behavior or performance (this identity is required under the heuristic realism associated with the standard statistical model). It is expected that the individual students associated with particular kinds of performance would change over time.

Students restructure their thinking and their performances change. Although the results that Piaget reported are not from a longitudinal study, it is clear that he *did* expect that his finding would typify the development of any particular group if it were followed over time. This means the narrative is not merely a description of 14 separate groups of students (represented by each bar of the graphs in FIG. 31.3 and 31.4). Rather, an overarching account of development is being advanced.

Attention to shifts in learners' *understanding* is the salient feature of this framework. This contrasts with the standard model based on the incremental acquisition of *ability*, judged in relation to changes in a particular collection or sample. What are conserved in Piaget's model are the modes of thinking, not the populations associated with these modes. The traditional notion of sample is largely abandoned. Piaget even went so far as to allow that the reports at various ages can be of *completely distinct groups of learners*. He was *that* confident in his account, which is centered on shifts in understanding.

Not only is the organization of the analysis of performance distinctive, but so, too, is his treatment of children not exhibiting simultaneousness or equality of duration. The ways in which learners do not exhibit simultaneousness or equality of duration *are as important* to Piaget's investigations as the characterization of the thinking of the students who have operationalized these conceptions. Nonsimultaneity and inequality of durations are still seen as ways of thinking and acting. Indeed, at least as much time is spent analyzing and making sense of the properties of the students not exhibiting simultaneousness or equality of duration as is spent articulating what it means for students to have acquired these structures of thought.

This attention to earlier thought and to changes in thought reflects general theoretical commitments that Piaget advanced throughout the whole of his life's work. These commitments are a starting place for the possible nonstandard quantification system suggested in this chapter. Themes in Piaget's universalistic developmental project can be drawn on to begin examining of the nonstandard quantification scheme presented herein. However, the particular commitments of the methods that we outline do not require the structures to be universal in the way that Piaget pushed for. Instead of focusing only on universally emergent structures that may characterize the development of intelligence itself, the methods we propose would allow for attention to nonuniversal structures that can characterize understanding within particular realms of human accomplishment and creativity (Stroup, 1994, 1996). The methods we propose take seriously the role the forms of embodiment and types of symbolization we use have in actually shaping emergence of nonuniversal structures (Wilensky, 1993, 1997). The representations we use shape what it is that we know. The development of these non-universal structures are recognized by at least some neo-Piagetians as what "most of the energy of most of the people in most of the world" is spent trying to "achieve" (D. Feldman, 1980, p. xiii–xiv; see also H. Gardner, 1989, p. 114).

The nonstandard quantification scheme, introduced later, is presented as an alternative to standard analyses based on the use of normalized distributions. In presenting this nonstandard quantification scheme, an explicit connection is made between particular theories of learning and certain methods of quantification. The positivistic presumption that there is a clean line separating method from message is rejected. The idea advanced is that although Piaget did allow for the use of standard statistics at some points, on the whole, a nonstandard statistic (of roughly the sort that he invoked earlier) needs to be developed to analyze the changes in thinking of learners. This nonstandard quantification system should fit better with the morphology of the cognitivist theories of learning that are centered largely on the emergence of structure.

# TOWARD A NONUNIVERSAL CONSTRUCTIVIST STATISTIC

## Outlines of an Emergent Framework

The characteristics of a nonuniversal constructivist framework for the analysis of collective performance are outlined next. This nonstandard quantitative framework will fit with and extend the cognitivist model hinted at in Piaget's example. The idea is to cross the positivistic divide of meaning and method. The quantitative features of the constructivist statistics discussed in the following have sufficient experimental content so that they are applicable to the interpretation of the data sets that our fellow researchers may encounter. This framework is emergent because, unlike the behaviorist stance outlined previously where the emphasis is on uncovering and measuring already existent objects of performance, it seeks to inform us about understandings that come into being in relation to activity. These understandings are constructed in ways that can not be reduced to the individual "responses" or "contingencies" of performance, or to the linear summation (accumulation) of these "responses" or "contingencies" (see the earlier discussion of Skinner). Here, then, are the characteristics of the framework:

1. The distribution of performance on a complex task will not belong properly under one bump. In general, the frequency distributions will be bi- or even multimodal (see FIG. 31.5).

Although, conceivably, various parametric tests might show that there are indeed two (or more) distinct modes present, no presumption of normal distribution in any of the modes is advanced. Among other significant shortcomings, the time-evolution discussed later in Item 6 would be difficult to account for if one expects the identity of the populations associated with each mode to be preserved. The assertion made in this work is merely that distinct modes will appear in the data.

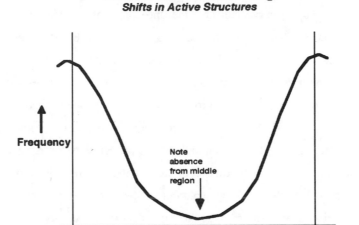

**Multimodel Understanding:**
*Shifts in Active Structures*

Frequency

Note absence from middle region

Performance/Outcome on Complex Task

Nonexpert or Noncompetent Understanding Mode(s)

Expert or Compentent Understanding Mode(s)

FIG. 31.5. Shifts between modes of understanding.

In this framework, *expert* is viewed as a convenient shorthand for a well-connected (see Wilensky, 1991, 1993, 1997) form of understanding as it exists among other forms of understanding. It does not refer to a fixed or final intellectual resting spot. Moreover, what constitutes expert or what is *seen* to constitute expert in this framework has significant sociocultural dimensions in ways that might not be compatible with the ways in which expert is used traditionally in "expert systems" or novice–expert study parlance. Under this framework, *competent* performance is associated with a less well connected form of understanding that has some properties of expert understanding. The labels *nonexpert* and *noncompetent* simply denote other ways of understanding not currently identified as "expert" or "competent."

In 1982, S. Strauss and Stavy also outlined a theory of U-shaped development that might appear morphologically similar to this theory. In substance, however, these theories are distinct.  For Strauss and Stavy, "Such a [U-shaped] curve indicates the appearance of a behavior, a later dropping out of that behavior, and what appears to be its subsequent reappearance" (p. 1)  This work, in contrast, does not argue that a certain kind of behavior disappears and then reemerges. Instead, it argues that the initial behavior of members of a group is structured by one (or more) set(s) of relational ideas and that later behavior becomes structured by other ways of understanding a task.  Additionally, U-shaped growth for Strauss and Stavy is a description of the time-evolution of performance for *individuals*. What is articulated herein is a quantitative theory of the distribution and time-evolution (see Item 6 as follows) of performance for *groups* of individuals.

2.  The movement of groups of individuals along the range of values (scores on a scale of performance) will not be smooth. Instead, the movement will be characterized by more or less discontinuous jumps between the modes associated with the activity of certain structures or ways of understanding. Boundaries between the modes can be well defined. Instances of mixed or unstable performance may occur in a data set sometimes.  However, these in-between scores are seen to result from an alternation between ways of understanding within a performance and do not suggest a separate form of understanding or anything like an average understanding.

3.   The bumps will not stand for the same thing. Because understanding is relational and because different relations (structures) draw together qualitatively different kinds of performance, the bumps along an axis of performance will not stand for one kind of thing called understanding (or ability, etc.). Understandings are plural and depend on which kinds of structures or ways of relating elements of a whole are active.

4.   What some researchers and educators could see as expert or competent responses to a complex problem (including the responses of competent learners who have jumped) will form an *organized whole* and will be located as a group at one extreme in a performance evaluation. This placement at an extreme means that there is a good deal of coherence to the expert and competent responses. This coherence can be described quantitatively.

5.   Other kinds of responses also will be clustered and potentially well removed from expert or competent performance. Unlike traditional frameworks for discussing "wrong" answers, an analysis of the novice responses reveals a coherence that can be accounted for (ideally) in terms of a relatively small set of active structures (ways of reasoning). The responses can be viewed as the projection of nonexpert ways of understanding onto an axis of expert performance. The image is similar to that of a mountain range viewed in silhouette. The fact that the mountain peaks appear together does not mean they are linked physically. A silhouette is just a way of looking at what is a multidimensional reality. Despite the fact that they appear on the same performance axis (in the same intellectual silhouette), the modes of a distribution—like the silhouetted peaks of a mountain range—may be quite far removed from one another in reality. Within this framework, the most important silhouettes or the most important ways of analyzing understanding are those that best articulate the distinctive peaks in the

full range of learners' thinking. The best assessments are those that help to produce meaningful peaks or that help to articulate of ways of thinking present in a group of learners.

6.  The time-evolution will be such that the locations of the modes will remain the same even as the size of the populations identified with the modes decreases or increases. As novice understanding shifts to expert or competent understanding, portions of the population associated with the novice mode will move (jump) to the expert mode (see FIG. 31.6). The relative absence of scores in between the modes will be preserved.

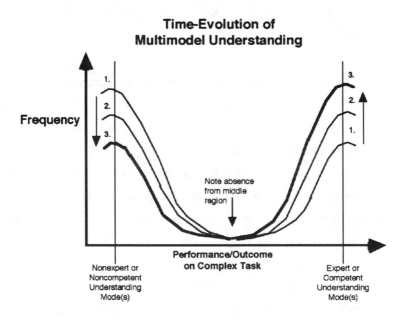

FIG. 31.6. Shifts in population associated with changing modes of understanding.

In sharp contrast with a normally distributed, multimodal theory (which might presume that each mode is distributed normally and that the identity of the populations associated with the modes is preserved during a near-continuous sliding along the performance axis), the discontinuous time-evolution described here does not allow for the preservation of the identity of the population associated with any one mode. In a normally distributed, multimodal theory, the identity of the populations would be preserved and the location of the modes would change. For the alternative theory (and for a given learning domain), *the location of the modes is preserved but not the identity of the population associated with each respective mode.*

7. A consequence of applying the nonstandard model is that the notion of sample is redefined. Traditionally, the notion of sample means that the researcher is drawing instances from a stable, larger (e.g., that of the population as a whole), sample space. For standard parametric sampling, the distribution is presumed to be normal; for nonparametric sampling, the distribution is nonnormal but stable. Formally, this stability means that the integral of the probability density function over an interval of the domain is presumed to be constant (if unknown). This stability can be preserved under translation (see the sliding of the bump discussed later).

For the nonstandard model outlined earlier (which, in this respect, is like those found in some areas of quantum physics), this stability cannot be presumed. The shape of the overall distribution is not constant and is determined largely by the circumstances or context of the experiment or learning tasks. What one is left with are statements about the time-evolution of the chances of finding individual events in certain regions of the sample space. Unlike quantum physics, however, there is no analytic model that determines the shape of the density function. We have only the macrophenomena of the relocating population *and* models of what structures are present that characterize the thinking of learners associated with certain modes.

## Limitations of the Nonstandard Methodology

Although we have devoted considerable space to the description of a particular nonstandard methodology for assessing group learning, we have not addressed adequately the rendering and assessment of individual learning up to now. There is an implicit relationship between the methodology advanced for groups and an analogous methodology for individuals. In this model, the individual's location in the intellectual n-space could be characterized and tracked as relatively discrete movement between modes of thought. In this section, we discuss individual learning and, in so doing, provoke an analysis of some of the limitations of the nonstandard methodology.

Under the proposed nonstandard framework, the space of possible performance is organized in terms of the forms of thinking that the students manifest. It is the organization of this analytic space in terms of the learners' thoughts, ideas, and structures that we consider to be a significant improvement over standard statistical methodologies giving preference to a particular form of averaging (and attendant expectations about distribution). Within the new framework, individuals can relocate from one form of thinking to others. As a form of assessment, features of performance and understanding typifying populations associated with a particular statistical mode can be seen to typify the understanding of an individual associated with the given mode. Expectations about future performance that are associated with a particular mode of thought can be expected to apply to any individual located in that mode (for as long as her or his thought is structured in a certain way).

These aspects of the nonstandard model make it clear that the model addresses the purposes of assessment: to render equivalence classes and address expectations about future performance. We view it as a significant improvement over the current state of the art in that the methodology centers on the thinking of learners. A vector in an intellectual *n*-space does reveal much more about what that person understands than a dimensionless average can. Moreover, this methodology is practicable, it could make good use of sophisticated computational capability, and it is capable of informing the activity of the larger educational enterprise.

Despite these very real advances, the methodology outlined earlier does have important limitations. Among the individuals associated with a mode, we fully expect that there would be local diversity not well rendered under the model. Second, the model assumes implicitly that the structures are self-contained, do not depend on the path taken to them, and do not retain traces of that path. Not only does this cause problems for the claims of equivalence that we have made for these structures, but also we would fully expect that these path dependencies and local diversities would manifest themselves in nonequivalent future performance. Third, novelty may appear undervalued and even ignored because the expectation might be that learners would move between well-established modes in the n-space. We see the last limitation as especially problematic because we do not see novelty as a rarity. Instead, we see novelty manifesting itself regularly at multiple levels of constructive activity: At the level of the learner, all constructions are novel and will be experienced as such; at the level of the *n*-space, new locations will be created continually; and to the extent that path dependency is taken seriously as an attribute of constructive processes, there will be uniqueness with the potential for novel expression in every learner's cognitive development. Finally, the model also may be problematic in the impression that it gives of the nature and operation of domains; an expectation could be set up that structure would manifest itself in a cross-context way that would ignore the intradomain, cognitive, and social contextuality of the lived experience of structure.

In the next section, we suggest ways in which new computational technologies can be employed to create richer assessment methodologies that both correspond more closely with constructivist theory and provide a much more detailed and illuminating account of learners' development.

## THE COEVOLUTION OF TECHNOLOGY, METHOD, AND EPISTEMOLOGY

As researchers, we believe that technology, method (or technique), and epistemology coevolve. Constructivism specifically allows that epistemology (including epistemologies that are constructivist) will evolve and that this evolution can be expected to happen in relation with the tools and the media of symbolization and activity that we create. For assessment, we believe this means that the epistemological and methodological shifts pointed to earlier need to happen together with the advances in the technologies that we use to think with and to render our experience. In particular, we hope that with cognitivism free of the need to reduce results to an average, the richness of possibility for rendering associated with increasingly powerful computing environments will allow us to look with new eyes and minds at the ways in which we depict what we know of learning. Moreover, with improved communication and networking, assessment can happen now in a way that is close to the fabric of the day-to-day learning activity and not as separate tests.

We close this chapter with a couple of examples of how increasingly sophisticated forms of representation enabled by the technology of the computer might advance this revision in our thinking.

The first example is relatively modest in its computing requirements and is most transparent in its links to the theoretical outline given in the previous section. Like the earlier work of Piaget (1946/1970a), it depicts results related to the development of learners' understanding of motion. These results are from an investigation of learners' ideas of *how much* (amount) and *how fast* (rate) as they are expressed graphically (Stroup, 1996). A taxonomy was used to encode the learners' graphical responses to a series of assessments given at three different times. Then, these responses were compared to the expert responses and the results plotted on an axis of expert performance (see earlier Item 5 and FIG. 31.7).

## Matching for Position versus Time

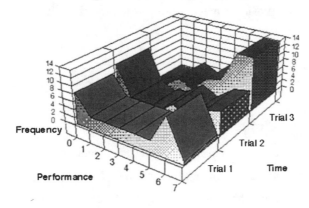

FIG. 31.7. The time-evolution of performance on a matching task.

FIG. 31.7 depicts shifts in understanding of the sort expected under the constructivist model outlined earlier. This general fit is important but so, too, is the fact that the ways of thinking associated with the nonexpert modes of thinking can be identified readily and investigated carefully (see Stroup, 1994, 1996). These other forms of understanding are as important to the work of cognitive researchers and educators as are the forms of understanding typically identified as expert or competent. Increasingly sophisticated and nuanced forms of rendering results can be drawn for the purposes of analysis that move well beyond the rather limiting capabilities associated with various parametric statistics.

Although the example given previously is intended to be illustrative, it does not exhaust the possibilities for the development of cognitivist statistics. A goal for this chapter is to open the door to possibilities and begin a conversation, rather than to pretend that where this process will end up is already well formed. Indeed, it is expected that the research community will need to construct and explore the power of new forms of rendering and symbolization of learning. To get a glimpse of where the richness of possibilities could lead, our suggestions include looking to areas of human investigation that deal with making sense of highly complex emergent phenomena. As an example, we are struck by the ways in which weather[12] statistics are generated and how the results are depicted using color and dimension in increasingly novel fashion. Weather maps are rich stores of information that capture the current state of the system and enable predictions about future system states (see FIG. 31.8). A map is built up from meaningful attributes of weather systems (temperature, pressure, precipitation, etc.) which, in turn, can be read out of the map and interpreted by a range of users including individual citizens, event planners, city officials, meteorologists, and climatologists. Though certain features of the map are arrived at by various forms of averaging, the meaningful attributes (e.g., an isobar or an isotherm) are not aggregated. Pressure is not averaged with temperature.

---

[12] We are indebted to Richard Lesh (1996) for suggesting the example of weather.

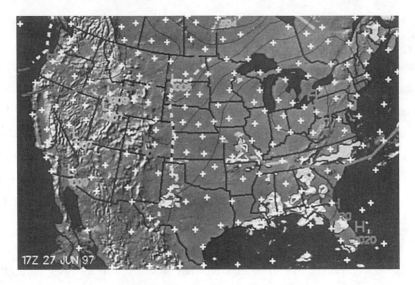

FIG. 31.8. Weather maps integrate complex, disparate, information in ways that can be interpreted readily for different purposes.

Moreover, the same map can be interpreted in contextually relevant ways. What the map tells and what activities the residents might undertake in different parts of the country are expected to be quite different. Local consumers can make informed decisions about what matters to them. The creation and display of such maps make extensive use of sophisticated technological tools. There are rapid advances in the techniques of rendering weather maps with increasingly sophisticated dynamic capabilities with which the changing weather can be visualized. In turn, these capabilities allow for the exploration and invention of new analytic approaches. The analogue of all of these features, we believe, can be constructed for educational assessment. Assessment should reveal the significant meaningful structures of students' understanding in ways that could inform future expectations and learning activities. It should not aggregate cognitively meaningful and distinct features of the processes of students' reasoning. It should serve a range of potential users from classroom educator to district superintendent and beyond. The assessments should be interpretable in different ways across different contexts. We would expect that what a map tells us about them in one context would be quite different from what it tells us about learners in another context. Such maps would enable local educators to make decisions about evaluation without having to default to the norms of a central testing authority. The rendering of assessment should be dynamic and interactive in ways that we have come to associate with advanced computational technologies. Maps could display processes spread out over time, highlight specific features, and allow for various degrees of zooming in and zooming out, enabling educators to see the finely grained detail of students' understanding as well as the large-scale summary of the educational system.

The point of including these examples is to highlight the need to push our current sense of possible statistical renderings and symbolizations well past the present state of the art in education. These renderings should center on the ideas of learners in a richly situated way. Accordingly, we hope that there is room for a full range of possibilities to be explored before the urge to collapse to standards holds sway. The development of nonstandard statistics or ways of rendering equivalence classes needs to be a jointly constructed effort. As such, the process cannot be seen as one where the outcome is determined in advance.

# 32

## When Using the Mean Is Meaningless: Examples From Probability Theory and Cardiology

**Larry S. Liebovitch**
**Angelo T. Todorov**
*Florida Atlantic University*

**Mark A. Wood**
**Kenneth A. Ellenbogen**
*Medical College of Virginia*

Abraham Maslow (1966), writing on the psychology of science, noted that, "If the only tool you have is a hammer, you tend to treat everything as if it were a nail." The corollary of this proposition is that sometimes we drive nails, and sometimes we smash windows. The statistical tools that we use to analyze data each carry with them certain assumptions about the characteristics of the data. We use these methods so often that we can easily forget these assumptions. Frequently, we have concentrated so much on teaching how to use these methods that we may not have made clear the assumptions on which these methods are based, or we may not even know those assumptions. When the data satisfy these assumptions, then the analysis that we perform can provide faithful models of the phenomena that we wish to describe. Otherwise, the analysis may be worthless, or dangerous, and worse yet, we may not even question our methods. Like a chess player, we must look not only at the piece our opponent just moved, but also remain aware of the move's strategic implications. We can easily forget that a method as simple, as commonplace, as seemingly innocuous, as taking the arithmetic mean of a set of numbers depends on certain assumptions. In this chapter, we see

913

how important it is to stay open to the possibility that our analytic technique fails to satisfy those assumptions.

## ASSUMPTIONS ON WHICH THE MEAN IS BASED

We measure something in nature. We repeat the measurements a number of different times. By combining these separate measurements, we hope that the errors in each measurement will cancel and the result will be more accurate. A way to do this is to compute the arithmetic mean. We have computed so many means in our life, and seen the means computed by so many other people, that this seems the natural, and perhaps even the only, way to handle the data. It seems almost absurd to question the value of the mean. Yet, the usefulness of the mean depends on the data satisfying certain assumptions. Surprisingly, many experimental data do not meet these assumptions! The means computed from such data can lead to a false picture of what the data represent.

The assumption that underlies the use of the mean is that a set of numbers have about the same value, with some a bit smaller and others a bit larger, as shown in FIG. 32.1a. In this case, the mean provides a good estimate of the best guess of a typical value. The probability density function (PDF) characterizes the number of times each value is found in the data. More technically, the probability that we find a value $x$, in the range $(x, x + dx)$ is given by PDF$(x)$. Usually, we assume that the PDF is Gaussian, or asymptotically Gaussian. That is, it has the form commonly called a bell curve or a normal distribution. The mean of such a Gaussian PDF is well defined and easy to compute. The best guess (maximum likelihood estimator) of the mean of the PDF is the arithmetic mean of the data.

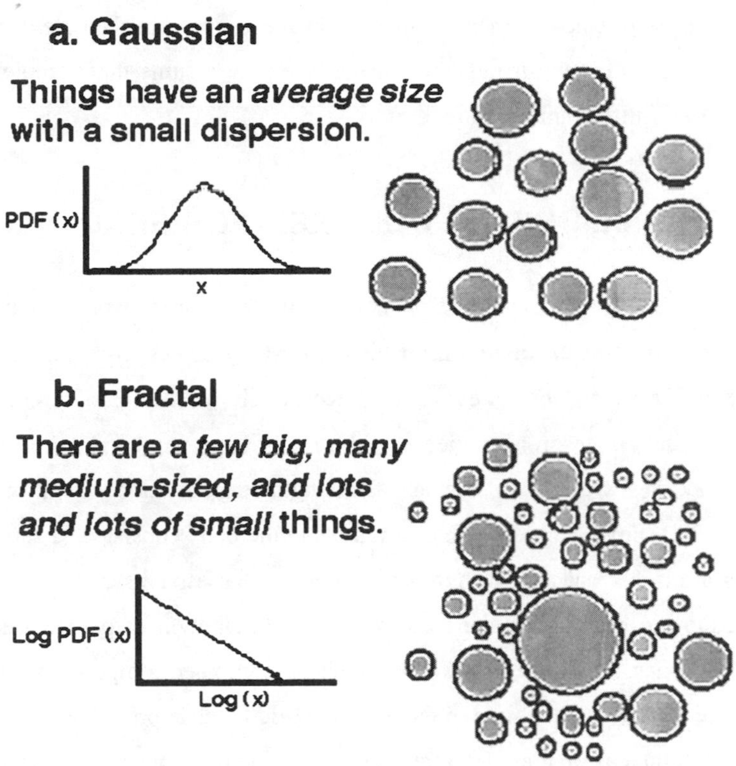

## a. Gaussian

**Things have an *average size* with a small dispersion.**

PDF (x)

x

## b. Fractal

**There are a *few big, many medium-sized, and lots and lots of small* things.**

Log PDF (x)

Log (x)

FIG. 32.1. (a) We are used to thinking that a set of similar objects, such as these circles, have approximately the same diameter, with some a bit smaller and others a bit larger. The mean of the diameters of these circles is a good way to characterize the size of these objects. The probability that a circle has a diameter in the range $x$, $x + dt$ is given by the probability density function, PDF($x$). The PDF is a Gaussian distribution, which is characterized by its mean and variance. (b) Many things in the natural world are fractal. They consist of an ever larger number of ever smaller objects. The mean is not defined and is not a good way to characterize the size of these objects. The PDF is a power law and thus a straight line on a log-log plot.

The mean value of data sampled from the population is called the sample mean. As we include ever more data, the fluctuations in the values around the typical value cancel out, and the sample means approach a finite limiting value. We consider this limiting value the "true" value of the population, which we define as the population mean. Technically, the central limit theorem guarantees that as we collect more data, the values of the sample means approach that of the population mean. Our faith in the central limit theorem may lead us to believe that it applies equally to all phenomena. We may assume that sample means of all data converge to a finite limiting value.

## THE MEAN IS NOT DEFINED FOR FRACTALS

Data drawn from many processes and phenomena in the natural world do not satisfy the assumptions underpinning the central limit theorem. Many objects in nature can be described as consisting of a larger number of ever finer pieces, as shown in FIG. 32.1b. Typically, there are a few big pieces, many smaller pieces, and a really large number of tiny pieces. Objects with these properties are called "fractals" (Bassingthwaighte, Liebovitch, & West, 1994; Mandelbrot, 1983). For example, the blood vessels in the body consist of a few large arteries, many smaller arterioles, and a huge number of tiny capillaries. This characteristic description can be applied to the branching patterns of trees, the distribution of particles in the soil, the clustering of galaxies, the timing between failures in computer components, and many other objects in space or processes in time in the natural world (Mandelbrot, 1983).

For these fractals, as we include more data or examine more pieces at finer resolution, the sample means do not approach a finite limiting value. For example, for some fractals, as we include more data, the increasing number of smaller pieces dominates the mean, and consequently the mean approaches zero. For other fractals, as we include more data, the small number of very large pieces dominates the mean, and consequently the mean increases without bound; that is, it approaches infinity. Because the sample means do not approach a finite limiting value, the population mean is not defined!

What happens if we do not realize this, and we try to use the mean of a set of measurements to characterize a fractal? The value of the mean depends on the amount of data analyzed. If we measure the same fractal object twice, but use different amounts of data, we will find two different values of the mean. If we measure two similar fractal objects, but use different amounts of data, we will find two different values of the mean.  Thus, there are important consequences to our failure to realize that the usual interpretation of the mean depends on certain assumptions that are not satisfied by the data from fractals. These consequences can affect life-and-death decisions, as we see later in the analysis of the time intervals between episodes of abnormal heart rhythms. These intervals have fractal properties and as a result, cannot be characterized by a mean value. Therefore the state of one patient, or a group of patients, and the consequences of their medical therapies cannot be assessed by the changes in the mean value of these time intervals.

# HISTORICAL BACKGROUND

Sometimes, pure mathematics is motivated by the need to solve worldly problems. About 400 years ago, mathematicians began to study games in order to determine the odds that gambling houses should offer their customers. This was the beginning of probability theory and, subsequently, statistics. About 250 years ago, Niklaus Bernoulli, in Russia, created a game with a PDF with fractal properties, which was published by his cousin Daniel Bernoulli and became known as the St. Petersburg Paradox (Dutka, 1988).

In the 1920s, the French mathematician Paul Lévy analyzed these distributions, which became known as stable or Lévy stable distributions (Mandelbrot, 1983). In these PDFs, the parameters of the sum of independently distributed random variables are linear combinations of the parameters of the individual distributions (Feller, 1971). The standard Gaussian distribution is a subset of these stable PDFs. However, these stable PDFs also include more general distributions.

One way to characterize any PDF is by its moments. The moments are the values of variables, raised to a power, and weighted by their frequency of occurrence in the PDF. For example, the first moment is the mean, the average of all of the values in the data set. The second moment is the variance, which characterizes the spread in the values around that average value. The mean and the variance are the most common methods used to analyze and characterize a set of any measurements. The mean and the variance are well defined for the standard bell curve, that is, the Gaussian PDF. However, the moments, such as mean and variance, do not necessarily exist for stable PDFs. The properties of these stable PDFs are different from those predicted by the central limit theorem, which assumes that the second moment exists and is finite.

Mandelbrot developed the properties of fractals further and introduced them to the wider scientific community (Mandelbrot, 1983). Although the properties of the stable PDFs of fractals were well known to a small group of mathematicians, these properties were not known to most people in the natural sciences. That is why these properties appear so strange at first sight. We have been too used to dealing only with Gaussian, or asymptotically Gaussian, distributions. With the realization that many objects and processes in nature have fractal properties, understanding the properties of stable PDFs and how they are different from Gaussian distributions is essential in order to analyze and understand data from the many fractals that are found in nature. We now illustrate these ideas with two examples of fractals: one from probability theory and another from the world of medicine.

## AN EXAMPLE WHERE THE MEAN EXISTS: A GAUSSIAN COIN GAME

Consider the game that consists of one toss of a coin. If the coin lands heads up, we win $1; if the coin lands tails up, we win $0. The expected winnings is the probability of each outcome multiplied by the winnings of that outcome. The probability that the coin lands heads up is 1/2 and the probability that the coin lands tails up is 1/2. Thus, the expected winnings of one game is equal to $(1/2)(\$1) + (1/2)(\$0) = \$0.50$. In a fair gambling house, the house should charge the player $0.50 to play each game, and the player would accept this as a fair charge.

If we play the game many times, in the long run, the winnings, averaged over all of the games, should be the same as the expected winnings of one game, which is $0.50. The more games that are played, the closer the mean winnings of all of the games will be to $0.50. That is, as more games are played, the sample means computed from all of those games approach $0.50. This game can be simulated with a computer. FIG. 32.2a shows the average winnings after playing $N$ games as a function of $N$. The average winnings after $N$ games is the sample mean for $N$ games. As expected, as more games are played, the average winnings after $N$ games approaches $0.50 rapidly.

### a. Gaussian Coin Game

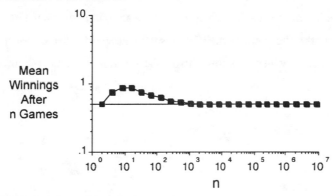

### b. St. Petersburg Game

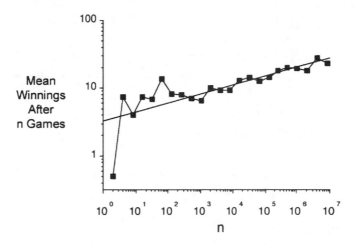

FIG. 32.2. (a) In the Gaussian coin game, as the number of games $N$ played increases, the mean winnings after n games approaches a finite limit ($.50) that we identify as the population mean. (b) In the fractal St. Petersburg coin game, as the number of games $N$ played increases, the mean winnings after $N$ games increases without bound. Therefore, the population mean is not defined.

We can compute the PDF of the winnings for this game. Let us say that we play a set of 100 games. The PDF($x$) is the probability that $x$, the mean winnings, that is, the winnings of all of those games divided by the number of games, is between $x$ and $x + dx$. The most probable value of the mean winnings $x$ is $0.50. It is less probable that the mean winnings will be a little lower or a little higher than $0.50. It is very less probable that the mean winnings will be much lower or much higher than \$0.50. Thus, the PDF has a peak at the mean winnings of \$0.50 and decreases as the mean winnings increases or decreases from \$0.50. Consequently, the curve of the PDF has the characteristic shape of a bell. Therefore, it is called a bell curve, which is known also as a normal, or a Gaussian, distribution. FIG. 32.3a shows the PDF, this Gaussian curve, computed for a set of 100 such games.

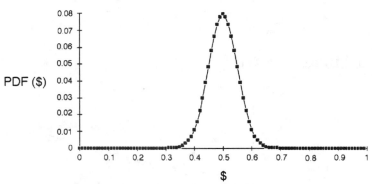

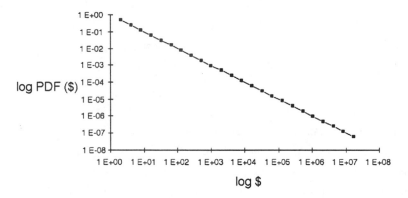

FIG. 32.3. (a) The PDF of the Gaussian coin game is a Gaussian distribution. Shown here is the distribution computed for 100 games. (b) The PDF of the fractal St. Petersburg game is a power law distribution and thus a straight line on a log-log plot. (Note computer printout notation $1\ E + a = 1.0 \times 10^{+a}$.)

# AN EXAMPLE WHERE THE MEAN IS NOT DEFINED: THE ST. PETERSBUG PARADOX, A FRACTAL COIN GAME

Now let us play the game formulated by the Bernoullis. In this game, we toss a coin as many times as needed until we get a head. If the coin lands heads up on the first toss, we win $2. If the first toss is a tail, and then on the second toss we get a head, we win $4. If the first and second tosses are tails, and then on the third toss we get a head, we win $8. If the first, second, and third tosses are tails, and then we get a head on the fourth toss, we win $16, and so on. That is, if we get a head on the $m$-th toss, we win $2^m$. The probability of getting a head on the first toss is 1/2. The probability of getting a tail on the first toss and then a head on the second toss is 1/4. The probability of getting a tail on the first two tosses and then a head on the third toss is 1/8. The probability of getting a tail on the first three tosses and then a head on the fourth toss is 1/16, and so on. That is, the probability of getting a head on the $m$-th toss is $2^{-m}$. The expected winnings of one game are $(1/2)(\$2) + (1/4)(\$4) + (1/8)(\$8) + (1/16)(\$16) + . . . = $ infinity!  This game became known as the St. Petersburg Paradox because the house wants to charge the player more than all the money in the world to play even one game, whereas the player feels he or she should be charged only $2 to play because he or she has a 50-50 chance of winning that amount on one play of the game.

We can simulate this game on a computer. FIG. 32.2b shows the average winnings after playing $N$ games as a function of $N$. The average winnings after $N$ games is the sample mean for $N$ games. The more games are played, the larger the mean winnings!  The mean does not approach a finite limiting value. There is no limiting value that we can identify as the population mean. The value that we find for a sample mean will depend on the number of games played.

We will find different values for the mean winnings evaluated after different numbers of games. Our experience with Gaussian statistics suggests that when the moments of a data set are constant in time, then the rules that generated the data must also be constant in time; when the moments vary in time, then the rules that generated the data must also vary in time. For example, the most commonly used moment is the mean. If the mean is constant in time, we think that the process that generated the data must be constant in time. When the mean varies in time, we think that the process that generated the data must be changing in time. With only our Gaussian thinking cap on, we would think that these changing means imply that the rules of the game are changing over time. But the rules of the St. Petersburg game are <u>not</u> changing over time. Our experience with Gaussian statistics does <u>not</u> give us the right intuition for dealing with stable PDFs.

The probability PDF($2^m$) of winning $\$2^m$ is equal to $2^{-m}$. The PDF as a function of the amount won is a straight line when log[PDF($2^m$)] is plotted versus log($2^m$). This is shown in FIG. 32.3b. This power law form is characteristic of the stable PDFs of fractals. It means that as this game is played again and again, very often the winnings are small, sometimes the winnings are larger, and very rarely the winnings are huge. This pattern of geometric repetition of an ever smaller number of ever larger winnings is characteristic of a fractal.

The infinite value of the mean in this game (the expected winnings) troubled those who were developing probability theory (Dutka, 1988). Yet, this game is as reasonable and as logical as the first coin toss game described earlier with a finite mean. Somehow, though, the infinite value of the mean of this game and its paradox did not seem like a "fair" game. Probability problems with these characteristics were still studied by some mathematicians over the next 250 years, but PDFs with these characteristics were not considered in the main thread of probability theory that became popular in the natural sciences. That is why the properties of this game seem so odd. But, they are not odd at all. The many fractal objects in nature have these fractal properties. We must be able to recognize and interpret these properties properly when we find them in nature, if we are to understand the natural world, as shown in the following example.

## AN EXAMPLE FROM HEART DATA

Sudden cardiac death is the single, most common cause of death in the United States. It almost always arises from abnormalities in the rhythm of the beating of the heart. The heart normally contracts in an organized wave that pushes blood out of the ventricles, the main pumping chambers of the heart. When each small segment of the heart beats separately, the wall of the heart twitches like a bag of worms and the blood is not pumped. This condition is called ventricular fibrillation and it leads to death within minutes. Work is underway to determine what other abnormal rhythms of the heart presage the onset of ventricular fibrillation. This work may make it possible to predict the onset of fibrillation and perhaps prevent it by the timely use of drugs or electrical stimulation. One dangerous rhythm that can lead to ventricular fibrillation is called ventricular tachycardia, or "v-tach" in the medical jargon. In v-tach, the ventricles beat over three times their normal rate. It is now possible to implant small computers in the chest, called cardioverter defibrillators, that monitor the heart rate. When an episode of v-tach is detected, these devices send a strong shock throughout the heart that resets it to a normal rhythm. These computers can record when each episode occurs. These times can be read back later by radio communication with a device that triggers the computer to replay the information that it has stored.

If one did not know anything about fractals or stable PDFs, one might think that a good way, perhaps the only way, to characterize how a heart patient is doing is to determine the mean time between episodes of v-tach. One might also think that measuring how the mean time changed when different drugs were taken would be a good way to determine the effects of the drugs. This is exactly what the medical community had thought.

We measured the PDF of the times between events of v-tach in 30 patients, recorded by their implanted cardioverter defibrillators (Liebovitch et al., 1999). For 28 patients, these events were infrequent enough that we had to combine the data from different patients in order to have enough event times to determine the PDF. For two patients, there were enough events of v-tach to determine the PDF from each patient separately.

As shown in FIG. 32.4, the PDFs from all of these heart patients have the same form. That is, the plot of the log(number of events in the range $t$ to $t + dt$) versus $\log(t)$ is a straight line. This power law form is characteristic of the stable PDF of a fractal. The computation of the PDF and its presentation on a log-log plot have revealed a new and striking form that would not have been revealed by the computation of the sample mean, or even by a linear plot of the PDF.

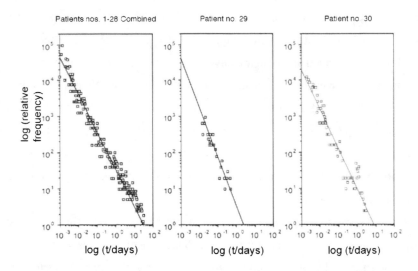

FIG. 32.4. The relative frequency, which is proportional to the PDF, of the times t between episodes of abnormally rapid heart rhythms (ventricular tachycardia). These PDFs have the power law form of the stable PDFs of fractals, like that 32.3b. The mean time between episodes is not defined. The time between episodes is often very brief, sometimes longer, and rarely very long. The mean fails to properly characterize these data. However, the true nature of these data is revealed clearly by the straight lines on these log-log plots of the PDFs.

The simple, clean form of the power law of the PDF in the data combined from 28 different patients is most likely due to the fact that each patient also has a PDF of the same power law form. If the PDF from each patient were different, then combining the data from different patients would produce an unrecognizable form of the PDF. This conjecture is supported by the fact that the two additional patients (Nos. 29 and 30) each have the same power law PDF as that of the combined data.

This power law PDF extended over an impressive range of five orders of magnitude in times between v-tach events from seconds to days. This range of five magnitudes is one of the largest ever reported for a power law PDF in biomedical data. This observation is remarkable considering that these patients have different types of heart disease and different medical treatments. These data may be revealing a completely unanticipated property of the how the heart works.

The central lesson is that the mean is not an appropriate method to characterize these data. There is no mean value that can characterize the time between episodes of v-tach. These times can be very long, more often they are short, and most often they are very brief. The form of the PDF, revealed as a straight line on a log-log plot, reveals, for the first time, the true nature of the timing of these life-threatening events.

This striking finding would not have been revealed if we had determined only the mean time between events of v-tach. In fact, because there are different amounts of data from each patient, the mean is different for each patient. This also shows that determining the mean time between events of v-tach, before and after a drug is given, will not be a meaningful way to test the effectiveness of drugs. Here then is a concrete example where the mean fails because the data have fractal, rather than Gaussian, characteristics. Not understanding the properties of these data could lead us to a meaningless, and maybe even a life-threatening, conclusion.

Another irregularity of the heart beat occurs when the larger ventricles beat before the smaller atria. These beats are called premature ventricular contractions, or PVCs in the jargon. It is not known when PVCs become dangerous. Many people without severe heart disease were given drugs to eliminate their PVCs. Unfortunately, these drugs may have caused more harm than good (Moore, 1995). A decade ago, it was found that the variation in the frequency of these PVCs increased as the larger amount of data over a longer time period was analyzed (G. Schmidt et al., 1988). This behavior surprised the researchers who discovered it. Illuminated by the light of our knowledge of stable PDFs, this suggests that the second moment, the variance, is increasing without bound as it is measured over longer time intervals. This indicates that even healthy people can be expected to have PVCs when observed over long time periods. Perhaps here, too, log-log plots of the PDF may make it possible to characterize the normal rates of occurrence of PVCs and thus determine when they are harmless and should be left alone, and when they are dangerous and should be treated.

## SUMMARY

Patterns in our data may be clarified or obscured by the mathematical tools we choose. Each mathematical method makes certain assumptions about the data. We must remain aware of those assumptions and whether our data satisfy them. Even commonplace tools, such as the arithmetic mean, make assumptions about the data. When the data do not satisfy those assumptions, our analysis may not be meaningful. The worst case is when we do not know that the results are meaningless.

In this chapter, we have described how the mean of fractal processes, such as the winnings in the St. Petersburg game or the timing between episodes of dangerously rapid heartbeats, does not exist and is not a meaningful measure of such data.

When the mean is not meaningful, how then should we analyze such data? For the many fractals found in nature, the meaningful measure is how the mean depends on the amount of data analyzed or the resolution used to analyze it. Technically, there is a scaling relationship where the logarithm of the mean is a linear function of the logarithm of the resolution used to measure it. This shows up dramatically as a straight line on a log-log plot of the PDF. The slope of this line is related to a parameter called the fractal dimension. We are exploring whether the fractal dimension can be used to characterize the degree of risk of life-threatening heart rhythm problems and assess the ability of different medical therapies to lower that risk.

So, mathematics from hundreds of years ago has brought new insight into a current problem, enabling us to see things in a different way, which may lead to saving lives.

## ACKNOWLEDGMENT

This work was supported in part by Grant EY6234 from the National Institutes of Health.

# References

Abreu, G. de (1995). Understanding how children experience the relationship between home and school mathematics. *Mind, Culture and Activity, 2,* 119–142.

Ackermann, E. (1995). Construction and transference of meaning through form. In L. P. Steffe & J. Gale (Eds.), *Constructivism in education* (pp. 341–354). Hillsdale, NJ: Lawrence Erlbaum Associates.

Ackoff, R. L. (1972). *The second industrial revolution.* Philadelphia, PA: Wharton School of Finance and Commerce.

Adams, D. D., & Shrum, J. (1990). The effects of microcomputer–based laboratory exercises on the acquisition of line graph construction and interpretation skills. *Journal of Research in Science Teaching, 27*(8), 777–787.

Alderson, J. C. (1990). Testing reading comprehension skills: Part 2. Getting students to talk about taking a reading test (pilot study). *Reading in a Foreign Language, 7*(1), 465–503.

Allchin, D. (1997). Rekindling phlogiston: From classroom case study to interdisciplinary relationships. *Science and Education, 6*(5), 473-509.

Altrichter, H., Posch, P., & Somekh, B. (1993). *Teachers investigate their work: An introduction to the methods of action research.* New York: Routledge.

American Association for the Advancement of Science. (1993). *Benchmarks for science literacy.* Washington, DC: American Association for the Advancement of Science.

Anderman, E. M., & Maehr, M. L. (1994). Motivation and schooling in the middle grades. In F. B. Murray & J. Raths (Eds.), *Review of educational research* (pp. 287–309). Washington, DC: American Educational Research Association.

Anderson, J. R. (1983). *The architecture of cognition.* Hillsdale, NJ: Lawrence Erlbaum Associates

Anderson, J., Boyle, F., & Reiser, B. (1985). Intelligent tutoring systems. *Science, 223,* 456–462.

Anderson, J. R., Corbett, A. T., Koedinger, K., & Pelletier, R. (1995). Cognitive tutors: Lessons learned. *Journal of Learning Sciences, 4,* 167–207.

Angoff, W. H., & Johnson, E. G. (1988). *A study of the differential impact of curriculum on aptitude test scores* (ETS Research Report No. RR-88-46). Princeton, NJ: Educational Testing Service.

Apple Computer, Inc. (1993). *Macintosh human interface guidelines.* Reading, MA: Addison–Wesley.

Apple, M. W. (1992). Do the *Standards* go far enough? Power, policy, and practice in mathematics education. *Journal for Research in Mathematics Education, 23*(5), 412–431.

Arons, A. (1993). Guiding insights and inquiry in the introductory physics laboratory. *The Physics Teacher, 31,* 278–282.

Atkinson, P., Delamont, S., & Hammersley, M. (1988). Qualitative research traditions: A British response to Jacob. *Review of Educational Research, 58,* 231–250.

Au, K. H., & Mason, J. M. (1981). Social organizational factors in learning to read: The balance of rights hypothesis. *Reading Research Quarterly, 17,* 115–152.

Aveni, A. (1989). *Empires of Time.* New York: Basic Books.

Ayer, A. J. (1946). *Language, truth, and logic.* London: Gollancz.

Azmitia, M., & Perlmutter, M. (1989). Social influences on children's cognition: State of the art and future directions. *Advances in Child Development and Behavior, 22,* 89–143.

Balacheff, N. (1987). Processus de preuve et situations de validation. *Educational Studies in Mathematics, 18,* 147–176.

Balacheff, N., Howson, G., Sfard, A., Steinbring, H., Kilpatrick, J., & Sierpinska, A. (1993). What is research in mathematics education, and what are its results? *ICMI Bulletin, 33,* 17–23.

Ball, D. (1988). *Knowledge and reasoning in mathematical pedagogy: Examining what prospective teachers bring to teacher education.* Unpublished doctoral dissertation, Michigan State University, East Lansing.

Ball, D. L. (1990). Breaking with experience in learning to teach mathematics: The role of a preservice methods course. *For the Learning of Mathematics, 10*(2), 10–16.

Ball, D. L. (1991). Research on teaching mathematics: Making subject matter knowledge part of the equation. In J. E. Brophy (Ed.), *Advances in research on teaching: Teachers' subject matter knowledge and classroom instruction* (Vol. 2, pp. 1–48). Greenwich, CT: JAI.

Ball, D. L. (1993a). Halves, pieces, and twoths: Constructing representational contexts in teaching fractions. In T. Carpenter, E. Fennema, & T. Romberg (Eds.), *Rational numbers: An integration of research.* Hillsdale, NJ: Lawrence Erlbaum Associates.

Ball, D. L. (1993b). With an eye on the mathematical horizon: Dilemmas of teaching elementary school mathematics. *Elementary School Journal, 93*(4), 373–397.

Ball, D. L. (1995). Transforming pedagogy: Classrooms as mathematical communities. A response to Timothy Lensmire and John Pryor. *Harvard Educational Review, 65,* 670–677.

Ball, D. L. (in press). Fundamental questions, impossible conclusions: What are students learning? In I. Goodson, B. Biddle, & T. Good (Eds.), *International handbook on teachers and teaching.* Dordrecht, Netherlands: Kluwer.

Barlow, C. (Ed.). (1991). *From gaia to selfish genes: Selected writings in the life sciences.* Cambridge, MA: MIT Press.

Barlow, C. (Ed.). (1994). *Evolution extended: Biology debates on the meaning of life.* Cambridge, MA: MIT Press.

Baroody, A. J., & Ginsburg, H. P. (1990). Children's learning: A cognitive view. In R. B. Davis, C. A. Maher, & N. Noddings (Eds.), *Constructivist views on the teaching and learning of mathematics* (*Journal for Research in Mathematics Education,* Monograph No. 4, pp. 51–64). Reston, VA: National Council of Teachers of Mathematics.

Bassingthwaighte, J. B., Liebovitch, L. S., & West, B. J. (1994). *Fractal physiology.* New York: Oxford University Press.

Battista, M. T. (1988, June). Mathematics and technology: A call for caution. *Educational Technology,* pp. 31–33.

Battista, M. T., & Clements, D. H. (1988). A case for a Logo–based elementary school geometry curriculum. *Arithmetic Teacher, 36,* 11–17.

Battista, M. T., & Clements, D. H. (1991). *Logo geometry.* Morristown, NJ: Silver Burdett & Ginn.

Battista, M. T., & Clements, D. H. (1996). Students' understanding of three–dimensional rectangular arrays of cubes. *Journal for Research in Mathematics Education, 27*(3), 258–292.

Battista, M. T., & Clements, D. H. (in press). Students' understanding of 3D cube arrays: Findings from a research and curriculum development project. In R. Lehrer & D. Chazan (Eds.), *Designing learning environments for developing understanding of geometry and space.* Mahwah, NJ: Lawrence Erlbaum Associates.

Battista, M. T., & Larson, C. L. (1994). The role of *JRME* in advancing the learning and teaching of elementary school mathematics. *Teaching Children Mathematics, 1,* 178–182.

Bauersfeld, H. (1988). Interaction, construction, and knowledge: Alternative perspectives for mathematics education. In T. J. Cooney & D. Grouws (Eds.), *Effective mathematics teaching* (pp. 27–46). Reston, VA: National Council of Teachers of Mathematics.

Bauersfeld, H., Krummheuer, G., & Voigt, J. (1988). Interactional theory of learning and teaching mathematics and related microethnographical studies. In H. G. Steiner & A. Vermandel (Eds.),

*Foundations and methodology of the discipline of mathematics education* (pp. 174–188). Antwerp, Belgium: Proceedings of the Theory of Mathematics Education Conference.

Becker, H. J. (1992). Computer–based integrated learning systems in the elementary and middle grades: A critical review and synthesis of evaluation reports. *Journal of Educational Computing Research, 8,* 1–41.

Becker, H. S., & Geer, B. (1969). Participant observation and interviewing: A comparison [and commentaries]. In G. J. McCall & J. L. Simmons (Eds.), *Issues in participant observation: A text and reader* (pp. 322–341). Reading, MA: Addison–Wesley.

Bednarz, N., Dufour–Janvier, B., Poirier, L., & Bacon, L. (1993). Socioconstructivist viewpoint on the use of symbolism in mathematics education. *Alberta Journal of Educational Research, 39,* 41–58.

Behar, R. (1996). *The vulnerable observer: Anthropology that breaks your heart.* Boston: Beacon Press.

Behr, M., Harel, G., Lesh, R., & Post, T. (1991). Rational number, ratio, and proportion. In D. Grouws (Ed.), *Handbook of research on mathematics teaching and learning* (pp. 296–333). New York: Macmillan.

Behr, M., Wachsmuth, I., Post, T., & Lesh, R. (1984). Order and equivalence of rational number concepts: A clinical teaching experiment. *Journal for Research in Mathematics Education, 15*(5), 323-341.

Beik, W. (1985). *Absolutism and society in seventeeth–century France.* Cambridge, England: Cambridge University Press.

Bell, A. (1979). The learning process aspects of mathematics. *Educational Studies in Mathematics, 10,* 361–387.

Berg, R., Chiu, M., & Hall, R. (1994, April). *Interactive construction of familiar, fantastic, and formal models in middle school mathematics.* Paper presented at the annual meeting of the American Educational Research Association, New Orleans, LA.

Biddlecomb, B. D. (1994). Theory–based development of computer microworlds. *Journal of Research in Childhood Education, 8*(2), 87–98.

Biggs, J. B., & Collis, K. F. (1982). *Evaluating the quality of learning: The SOLO taxonomy (structure of observed learning outcome).* New York: Academic Press.

Biklen, S. (1991). Public schools can benefit from qualitative research. *Homework, 3*(1–2), 9.

Biklen, S., Patterson, J., Tinto, P., Yamini, A., Mitchell, J., Zarach, N., & Thomas, H. (Eds.). (1992). *Mathematics task force report.* Syracuse, NY: Nottingham High School, Syracuse City School District.

Birenbaum, M., Kelly, A. E., & Tatsuoka, K. K. (1993). Diagnosing knowledge states in algebra using the rule–space model. *Journal for Research in Mathematics Education, 24*(5), 442–459.

Bishop, A. (1985). The social construction of meaning—A significant development for mathematics education? *For the Learning of Mathematics, 5*(1), 24–28.

Bishop, A. J. (1991). *Mathematical enculturation.* Dordrecht, Netherlands: Kluwer.

Bishop, A. J. (1992). International perspectives on research in mathematics education. In D. Grouws (Ed.), *Handbook of research on mathematics teaching and learning* (pp. 710–723). New York: Macmillan.

Bodner, B. L., & Goldin, G. A. (1991a). *Cognitive obstacles of developmental–level college students in drawing diagrams.* Paper presented at the Thirteenth Annual Meeting of the North American Chapter of the International Group for the Psychology of Mathematics Education, Blacksburg, VA.

Bodner, B. L., & Goldin, G. A. (1991b). *Drawing a diagram: Observing a partially developed heuristic process in college students.* Paper presented at the Fifteenth International Conference for the Psychology of Mathematics Education, Genoa, Italy.

Borg, W., Gall, J., & Gall, M. (1993). *Applying eductional research, a practical guide* (3rd ed.). New York: Longman.

Borko, H., Brown, C., Eisenhart, M., & Underhill, R. (1992). Learning to teach hard mathematics: Do novice teachers and their instructors give up too easily? *Journal for Research in Mathematics Education, 23*(3), 194–222.

Bowers, J. (1995). *Designing computer learning activities based on the theory of realistic mathematics education.* Paper presented at the Nineteenth International Conference for the Psychology of Mathematics Education, Recife, Brazil.

Bradbury, R. (1951). *The illustrated man.* Garden City, NY: Doubleday.

Brenner, M. E. (1985). *Arithmetic and classroom interaction as cultural practice among the Vai of Liberia.* Unpublished doctoral dissertation, University of California, Irvine.

Brenner, M. E. (1989, March). *Everyday problem solving: Dollar wise, penny foolish.* Paper presented at the annual meeting of the National Association for Research on Science Teaching, San Francisco.

Brenner, M. E. (1998a). Adding cognitive to the formula for culturally relevant instruction in mathematics. *Anthropology and Education Quarterly, 29,* 214–244.

Brenner, M. E. (1998b). Meaning and money. *Educational Studies in Mathematics, 36,* 123–155.

Bridgeman, B., & Lewis, C. (1994). *Gender differences in college mathematics grades and SAT–M scores: A reanalysis of Wainer and Steinberg.* Unpublished manuscript.

Bringuier, J. C. (1980). *Conversations with Jean Piaget.* Chicago: University of Chicago Press.

Briscoe, C. (1993). Using cognitive referents in making sense of teaching: A chemistry teacher's struggle to change assessment practices. *Journal of Research in Science Teaching, 30,* 971–987.

Bronfenbrenner, U. (1977). Toward an experimental ecology of human development. *American Psychologist, 32,* 513–531.

Brophy, J. (1986). Where are the data? A reply to Confrey. *Journal for Research in Mathematics Education, 17*(5), 361–368.

Brousseau, G. (1981). Problemes de didactique des decimaux [Problems in teaching decimals]. *Recherches en Didactiques des Mathematiques, 2.1,* 37–125.

Brousseau, G. (1984). The crucial role of the didactical contract in the analysis and construction of situations in teaching and learning mathematics. In H. G. Steiner (Ed.), *Theory of mathematics education* (pp. 110–119). Bielefeld, Germany: Institut fur Didaktik der Mathematik.

Brousseau, G. (1986). Fondements et methodes de la didactique des mathematiques. *Recherches en Didactique des Mathematiques, 7*(2), 33–115.

Brown, A. (1992). Design experiments: Theoretical and methodological challenges in creating complex interventions in classroom settings. *The Journal of the Learning Sciences, 2*(2), 141–178.

Brown, C. A., & Cooney, T. J. (1982). Research on teacher education: A philosophical orientation. *Journal of Research and Development in Education, 15*(4), 13–18.

Brown, J. S., & Burton, R. B. (1978). Diagnostic models for procedural bugs in basic mathematical skills. *Cognitive Science, 2,* 155–192.

Brown, J. S., & VanLehn, K. (1980). Repair theory: A generative theory of bugs in procedural skills. *Cognitive Science, 4,* 379–426.

Brownell, W. A. (1928). *The development of children's number ideas in the primary grades.* Chicago: University of Chicago Press.

Bruer, J. (1993). *Schools for thought: A science for learning in the classroom.* Cambridge, MA: MIT Press.

Bruffee, K. A. (1993). *Collaborative learning: Higher education, interdependence, and the authority of knowledge.* Baltimore: Johns Hopkins University Press.

Bruner, J. (1973). In J. Anglin (Ed.), *Beyond the information given.* New York: Norton.

Bruner, J. (1990). *Acts of meaning.* Cambridge, MA: Harvard University Press.

Bruner, J. (1996). *The culture of education.* Cambridge, MA: Harvard University Press.

Bruner, J., Goodnow, J. J., & Austin, G. A.  (1956).  *A study of thinking.*  New York: Wiley.

Budgen, D.  (1994).  *Software design.*  Reading, MA: Addison–Wesley.

Burnaford, G., Fischer, J., & Hobson, D. (Eds.).  (1996).  *Teachers doing research: Practical possibilities.*  Mahwah, NJ: Lawrence Erlbaum Associates.

Burton, R. B.  (1982).  DEBUGGY: Diagnosis of errors in basic mathematical skills.  In D. Sleeman & J. S. Brown (Eds.), *Intelligent tutoring systems.*  New York: Academic Press.

Bybee, R. W., & McInerney, J. (Eds.).  (1995).  *Redesigning the science curriculum.*  Colorado Springs: Biological Sciences Curriculum Study.

Cai, J., Lane, S., & Jakabcsin, M. S.  (1996).  The role of open–ended tasks and holistic scoring rubrics: Assessing students' mathematical reasoning and communication.  In P. C. Elliott (Ed.), *Communication in mathematics, K–12 and beyond* (pp. 137–145).  Reston, VA: National Council of Teachers of Mathematics.

Cai, J., Magone, M. E., Wang, N., & Lane, S.  (1996).  Describing student performance qualitatively.  *Mathematics Teaching in the Middle School, 1,* 835–928.

Calhoun, E.  (1993).  Action research: Three approaches.  *Educational Leadership, 51,* 62–65.

Calhoun, E.  (1994).  *How to use action research in the self–renewing school.*  Alexandria, VA: Association for Supervision and Curriculum Development.

Calinger, R.  (1995).  *Classics of mathematics.*  Engelwood Cliffs, NJ: Prentice-Hall.

Camp, C., Clement, J., Brown, D., Gonzalez, K., Kudukey, J., Minstrell, J., Schultz, K., Steinberg, M., Veneman, V., & Zietsman, A.  (1994).  *Preconceptions in mechanics: Lessons designed to deal with student's conceptual difficulties.*  Dubuque, IA: Kendall/Hunt.

Campbell, D.  (1979).  Degrees of freedom and the case study.  In T. Cook & C. Reichardt (Eds.), *Qualitative and quantitative methods in evaluation research.*  Beverly Hills, CA: Sage.

Campbell, D. T., & Stanley, J. C.  (1963).  Experimental and quasi–experimental designs for research on teaching.  In N. L. Gage (Ed.), *Handbook on research on teaching* (pp. 171–246).  Chicago: Rand McNally.

Campbell, N.  (1957).  *Physics: The elements.*  Cambridge, England: Cambridge University Press.  (Original work published 1920)

Carpenter, P. A., & Just, M. A.  (1975).  Sentence comprehension: A psycholinguistic processing model of verification.  *Psychological Review, 82,* 45–73.

Carpenter, T. P., & Fennema, E.  (1991).  Research and cognitively guided instruction.  In E. Fennema, T. P. Carpenter, & S. J. Lamon (Eds.), *Integrating research on teaching and learning mathematics,* (pp. 1–16).  Albany, NY: State University of New York Press.

Carpenter, T. P., & Fennema, E.  (1992).  Cognitively guided instruction: Building on the knowledge of students and teachers.  In W. Secada (Ed.), *Curriculum reform: The case of mathematics in the United States* (Special issue of *International Journal of Educational Research* pp. 457–470).  Elmsford, NY: Pergamon.

Carpenter, T., Fennema, E., & Lamon, S. J. (Eds).  (1988).  *Integrating research on teaching and learning mathematics.*  Madison: Wisconsin Center for Education Research.

Carpenter, T., Fennema, E., & Romberg, T.  (1993).  *Rational numbers: An integration of research.*  Hillsdale, NJ: Lawrence Erlbaum Associates.

Carr, W., & Kemmis, S.  (1986).  *Becoming critical: Education, knowledge and action research.*  London: Falmer Press.

Carraher, T. N., & Schliemann, A. D.  (1985).  Computation routines prescribed by schools: Help or hindrance?  *Journal for Research in Mathematics Education, 16,* 37–44.

Carter, K.  (1990).  Teacher's knowledge and learning to teach.  In R. Houston (Ed.), *Handbook of research on teacher education* (pp. 291–310).  New York: Macmillan.

Carter, K.  (1993).  The place of story in the study of teaching and teacher education.  *Educational Researcher, 22*(1), 5–18.

Char, C. A.  (1989).  *Formative research in the development of mathematics software for young children.*  San Francisco: American Educational Research Association.

Char, C. A. (1990). *Click on the clock: Formative research in the development of mathematics software for young children* (90–1). Newton, MA: Educational Development Center.

Chazan, D. (1992). Knowing school mathematics: A personal reflection on the NCTM's teaching standards. *Mathematics Teacher, 85,* 371–375.

Chazan, D. (1996). Algebra for all students? *Journal of Mathematical Behavior, 15*(4), 455–477.

Chi, M. (1995). Analyzing verbal data to represent knowledge: A practical guide. *Journal of the Learning Sciences.*

Chi, M. T. H., Feltovich, P. J., & Glaser, R. (1981). Categorization and representation of physics problems by experts and novices. *Cognitive Science, 5,* 121–152.

Chi, M. T. H., Glaser, R., & Rees, E. (1983). Expertise in problem solving. *Advances in the psychology of human intelligence* (Vol. II, pp. 7–75). Hillsdale, NJ: Lawrence Erlbaum Associates

Chipman, S. F., & Nichols, P. D. (1995). Introduction. In P. D. Nichols, S. F. Chipman, & R. L. Brennan (Eds.), *Cognitively diagnostic assessment.* Hillsdale, NJ: Lawrence Erlbaum Associates.

Chubin, D. E. (in press). Systemic evaluation and evidence of education reform. In D. M. Bartels & J. O. Sandler (Eds.), *Implementing science education reform: Are we making an impact?* Washington, DC: American Association for the Advancement of Science.

Clarke, D. J. (1996). Assessment. In A. Bishop et al. (Eds.), *International handbook of mathematics education: Part 1* (pp. 327–330). Dordrecht, Netherlands: Kluwer.

Clarke, D. J., & Stephens, M. (1996). The ripple effect: The instructional impact of the systemic introduction of performance in mathematics. In M. Birenhaum & F. J. R. C. Dochy (Eds.), *Alternatives in assessment of achievements, learning processes and prior knowledge* (pp. 63–92). Boston, MA: Kluwer.

Clement, J. (1979). Mapping a student's casual conceptions from a problem solving protocol. In J. Lochhead & J. Clement (Eds.), *Cognitive process instruction* (pp. 133–146). Hillsdale, NJ: Lawrence Erlbaum Associates.

Clement, J. (1982a). Algebra word problem solutions: Thought processes underlying a common misconception. *Journal for Research in Mathematics Education, 13*(1), 16–30.

Clement, J. (1982b). *The University of Massachusetts Mechanics Diagnostic.*

Clement, J. (1988). Observed methods for generating analogies in scientific problem solving. *Cognitive Science, 12,* 563–586.

Clement, J. (1989a). The concept of variation and misconceptions in Cartesian graphing. *Focus on Learning Problems in Mathematics, 11*(2), 77–87.

Clement, J. (1989b). Learning via model construction and criticism: Protocol evidence on sources of creativity in science. In J. Glover, R. Ronning, & C. Reynolds (Eds.), *Handbook of creativity: Assessment, theory and research* (pp. 341–381). New York: Plenum.

Clement, J., & Brown, D. E. (1989). Overcoming misconceptions via analogical reasoning: Abstract transfer versus explanatory model construction. *Instructional Science, 18,* 327–361.

Clements, D. H. (1997). *From exercises and tasks to problems and projects: Unique contributions of computers to innovative mathematics education.* Manuscript submitted for publication.

Clements, D. H., & Battista, M. T. (1991). *The development of a Logo–based elementary school geometry curriculum* (Final Report: NSF Grant MDR-8651668). Buffalo: State University of New York.

Clements, D. H., & Battista, M. T. (1992). Geometry and spatial reasoning. In D. A. Grouws (Ed.), *Handbook of research on mathematics teaching and learning* (pp. 420–464). New York: Macmillan.

Clements, D. H., Battista, M. T., & Sarama, J. (in press). Students' development of geometric and measurement ideas: Results from a research and curriculum development project. In R. Lehrer

& D. Chazan (Eds.), *Designing learning environments for developing understanding of geometry and space.* Mahwah, NJ: Lawrence Erlbaum Associates.

Clements, D. H., & McMillen, S. (1996). Rethinking "concrete" manipulatives. *Teaching Children Mathematics, 2*(5), 270–279.

Clements, D. H., & Meredith, J. S. (1994). *Turtle math* [Computer software]. Montreal, Quebec: Logo Computer Systems, Inc.

Clements, D. H., & Nastasi, B. K. (1992). Computers and early childhood education. In M. Gettinger, S. N. Elliot, & T. R. Kratochwill (Eds.), *Advances in school psychology: Preschool and early childhood treatment directions* (pp. 187–246). Hillsdale, NJ: Lawrence Erlbaum Associates.

Clements, D. H., & Sarama, J. (1995). Design of a Logo environment for elementary geometry. *Journal of Mathematical Behavior, 14,* 381–398.

Clements, M. A., & Ellerton, N. F. (1996). *Mathematics education research: Past, present, and future.* Bangkok, Thailand: United Nations Educational, Scientific, and Cultural Organization.

Cobb, P. (1986, September). *Clinical interviewing in the context of research programs.* Paper presented at the Eighth Annual Meeting of the North American Chapter of the International Group for the Psychology of Mathematics Education: Plenary Speeches and Symposium, East Lansing, MI.

Cobb, P. (1990). Multiple perspectives. In L. Steffe, P. Wood, & T. Wood (Eds.), *Transforming children's mathematics education* (pp. 200–215). Hillsdale, NJ: Lawrence Erlbaum Associates.

Cobb, P. (1995). Continuing the conversation: A response to Smith. *Educational Researcher, 24*(5), 25–27.

Cobb, P. (1996, April). *Some criteria to consider when judging classroom teaching experiments.* Paper presented at the Annual Meeting of the American Educational Research Association, New York.

Cobb, P., & Bauersfeld, H. (Eds.). (1995). *Emergence of mathematical meaning: Interaction in classroom cultures.* Hillsdale, NJ: Lawrence Erlbaum Associates.

Cobb, P., Gravemeijer, K., Yackel, E., McClain, K., & Whitenack, J. (in press). Mathematizing and symbolizing: The emergence of chains of signification in one first–grade classroom. In D. Kirshner & J. A. Whitson (Eds.), *Situated cognition theory: Social, semiotic, and neurological perspectives.* Mahwah, NJ: Lawrence Erlbaum Associates.

Cobb, P., & Steffe, L. P. (1983). The constructivist researcher as teacher and model builder. *Journal for Research in Mathematics Education, 14*(2), 83–94.

Cobb, P., & Whitenack, J. W. (1996). A method for conducting longitudinal analyses of classroom videorecordings and transcripts. *Educational Studies in Mathematics, 30,* 213–228.

Cobb, P., Wood, T., & Yackel, E. (1990). Classrooms as learning environments for teachers and researchers. In R. B. Davis, C. A. Maher, & N. Noddings (Eds.), *Constructivist views of the teaching and learning of mathematics* (*Journal for Research in Mathematics Education* Monograph No. 4, pp. 125–146). Reston, VA: National Council of Teachers of Mathematics.

Cobb, P., Wood, T., & Yackel, E. (1993). Discourse, mathematical thinking, and classroom practice. In E. Forman, N. Minick, & A. Stone (Eds.), *Contexts for learning: Sociocultural dynamics in children's development* (pp. 91–119). New York: Oxford University Press.

Cobb, P., Wood, T., Yackel, E., & McNeal, B. (1992). Characteristics of classroom mathematics traditions: An interactional analysis. *American Educational Research Journal, 29*(3), 573–604.

Cobb, P., & Yackel, E. (1995, October). *Constructivist, emergent, and sociocultural perspectives in the context of developmental research.* Paper presented at the Seventeenth Annual Meeting of the North American Chapter of the International Group for the Psychology of Mathematics Education, Columbus, OH.

Cobb, P., Yackel, E., & Wood, T. (1989). Young children's emotional acts while doing mathematical problem solving. In D. B. McLeod & V. M. Adams (Eds.), *Affect and mathematical problem solving: A new perspective* (pp. 117–148). New York: Springer–Verlag.

Cobb, P., Yackel, E., & Wood, T. (1993). Learning mathematics: Multiple perspectives, theoretical orientation. In T. Wood, P. Cobb, E. Yackel, & D. Dillon (Eds.), *Rethinking elementary school mathematics: Insights and issues* (*Journal for Research in Mathematics Education* Monograph Series, Vol. 6, pp. 21–32). Reston, VA: National Council of Teachers of Mathematics.

Cochran–Smith, M., & Lytle, S. (1990). Research on teaching and teacher research: The issues that divide. *Educational Researcher, 19*(2), 2–11.

Cochran–Smith, M., & Lytle, S. (1993). *Inside/outside: Teacher research and knowledge.* New York: Teachers College Press.

Cognition and Technology Group at Vanderbilt. (1992). The Jasper experiment: An exploration of issues in learning and instructional design. *Educational Technology Research and Development, 40*(1), 65–80.

Cohen, J., & Cohen, P. (1983). *Applied multiple regression: Correlational analysis for the behavioral sciences.* Hillsdale, NJ: Lawrence Erlbaum Associates.

Cole, M., Hood, L., & McDermott, R. P. (1978). *Ecological niche picking: Ecological invalidity as an axiom of experimental cognitive psychology.* Unpublished manuscript, University of California, San Diego.

Cole, N. (1990). Conceptions of educational achievement. *Educational Reaseacher, 19*(3), 2–7.

Collins, A. (1990). *Towards a design science of education* (Tech. Rep. No. 1). New York: Center for Children and Technology, Educational Development Center.

*Comprehensive School Mathematics Program.* (1982). St. Louis, MO: Central Midwest Regional Educational Laboratory.

Confrey, J. (1986). A critique of teacher effectiveness research in mathematics education. *Journal for Research in Mathematics Education, 17*(5), 347–360.

Confrey, J. (1988, November). *Multiplication and splitting: Their role in understanding exponential functions.* Paper presented at the Tenth Annual Meeting of the North American Chapter of the International Group for the Psychology of Mathematics Education, DeKalb, IL.

Confrey, J. (1989). *Splitting and counting: A conjecture.* Paper presented at the annual meeting of the American Educational Research Association, San Francisco.

Confrey, J. (1990). A review of the research on student conceptions in mathematics, science and programming. *Review of Research in Education, 16*, 3–56.

Confrey, J. (1991). Learning to listen: A student's understanding of powers of ten. In E. von Glasersfeld (Ed.), *Radical constructivism in mathematics education* (pp. 141–178). Dordecht, Netherlands: Kluwer.

Confrey, J. (1992, April). *First graders' understanding of similarity.* Paper presented at the annual meeting of the American Educational Research Association, San Francisco.

Confrey, J. (1993). Learning to see children's mathematics: Crucial challenges in constructivist reform. In K. Tobin (Ed.), *The practice of constructivism in science education* (pp. 299–321). Washington, DC: American Association for the Advancement of Science.

Confrey, J. (1994). A theory of intellectual development. Appearing in three consecutive issues: *For the Learning of Mathematics, 14*(3), 2–8; *15*(1), 38–48; *15*(2).

Confrey, J. (1995, July). *Student voice in examining "splitting" as an approach to ratio, proportion, and fractions.* Paper presented at the Nineteenth Annual Meeting of the International Group for the Psychology of Mathematics Education, Recife, Brazil.

Confrey, J. (1996, April). *Strengthening elementary education through a splitting approach as preparation for reform algebra*. Paper presented at the annual meeting of the American Education Research Association, New York.

Confrey, J. (in press). Designing mathematics education: The role of new technologies. In C. Fisher (Ed.), *Education & technology: Reflections on a decade of experience in classrooms*. San Francisco: Jossey–Bass & Apple Corp.

Confrey, J., & Scarano, G. H. (1995). *Splitting reexamined: Results from a three–year longitudinal study of children in grades three to five*. Paper presented at the Seventeenth Annual Meeting of the North American Chapter of the International Group for the Psychology of Mathematics Education, Columbus, OH.

Confrey, J., & Smith, E. (1989, October). *Alternative representations of ratio: The Greek concept of anthphairesis and modern decimal notation*. Paper presented at the First Annual Conference of the History and Philosophy of Science in Science Teaching, Tallahassee, FL.

Confrey, J., & Smith, E. (1995). Splitting, covariation, and their role in the development of exponential functions. *Journal for Research in Mathematics Education, 26*(1), 66–86.

Cooper, S. M. A. (1995). *An evaluation of the implementation of an integrated learning system for introductory college physics*. Unpublished doctoral dissertation, Rutgers University, New Brunswick, NJ.

Cooper, S. M. A., & O'Donnell, A. M. (1996, March). *Innovation and persistence: The evaluation of the CUPLE Studio Physics Course*. Paper presented at the annual meeting of the American Educational Research Association, New York.

Corsini, R. J. (1994). *Encyclopedia of psychology* (2nd ed.). New York: Wiley.

Costall, A., & Still, A. (1987). *Cognitive psychology in question*.

Coulter, J. (1991). Logic: Ethnomethodology and the logic of language. In G. Button (Ed.), *Ethnomethodology and the human sciences* (pp. 20–50). Cambridge, England: Cambridge University Press.

Coveney, P., & Highfield, R. (1990). *The arrow of time*. New York: Fawcett Columbine.

Cowles, M. (1989). *Statistics in psychology: An historical perspective*. Hillsdale, NJ: Lawrence Erlbaum Associates.

Cox, M. J. (1992). The computer in the science curriculum. *International Journal of Educational Research, 17*(1), 19–35.

Cuban, L. (1984). *How teachers taught: Constancy and change in American classrooms*. New York: Longman.

Cuban, L. (1986). *Teachers and machines: The classroom use of technology since 1920*. New York: Teachers College Press.

Cuban, L. (1995). The hidden variable: How organizations influence teacher responses to secondary science curriculum reform. *Theory into Practice, 34*(1), 4–11.

Darden, L. (1991). *Theory change in science: Strategies from Mendelian genetics*. New York: Oxford University Press.

Darling-Hammond, L. (1992). Educational indicators and enlightened policy. *Educational Policy, 6*, 235–265.

David, J. L. (1996). Developing and spreading accomplished teaching: Policy lessons from a unique partnership. In C. Fisher, D. C. Dwyer, & K. Yocam (Eds.), *Education and technology: Reflections on computing in classrooms* (pp. 237–250). San Francisco: Jossey–Bass.

Davies, P. (1995). *About time*. New York: Simon & Schuster.

Davis, R. B. (1984). *Learning mathematics: The cognitive science approach to mathematics education*. Norwood, NJ: Ablex.

Davis, R. B., Maher, C. A., & Noddings, N. (1990). Constructivist views on the teaching and learning of mathematics. *Journal for Research in Mathematics Education, 21*(4).

Davydov, V. V. (1988). Problems of developmental teaching (Part I). *Soviet Education, 30*(8), 6–97.

Dawkins, R. (1976). *The selfish gene.* New York: Oxford University Press.

Dawkins, R. (1986). *The blind watchmaker: Why the evidence of evolution reveals a universe without design.* New York: Norton.

Dawkins, R. (1995). *River out of Eden: A Darwinian view of life.* New York: Norton.

DeBellis, V. A. (1996). *Interactions between affect and cognition during mathematical problem solving: A two year case study of four elementary school children.* Unpublished doctoral dissertation, Rutgers University, New Brunswick, NJ.

DeBellis, V. A., & Goldin, G. A. (1991). *Interactions between cognition and affect in eight high school students' individual problem solving.* Paper presented at the Thirteenth Annual Meeting of the North American Chapter of the International Group for the Psychology of Mathematics Education, Blacksburg, VA.

DeBellis, V. A., & Goldin, G. A. (1993). *Analysis of interactions between affect and cognition in elementary school children during problem solving.* Paper presented at the Fifteenth Annual Meeting of the North American Chapter of the International Group for the Psychology of Mathematics Education, Pacific Grove, CA.

DeBellis, V. A., & Goldin, G. A. (1997). *The affective domain in mathematical problem solving.* Paper presented at the Twenty-First International Conference for the Psychology of Mathematics Education, Helsinki, Finland.

Dennett, D. (1991). *Consciousness explained.* Boston: Little, Brown.

Dennis, D. (1995). *Historical perspectives for the reform of mathematics curriculum: Geometric curve–drawing devices and their role in the transition to an algebraic description of functions.* Unpublished doctoral dissertation, Cornell University, Ithaca, NY.

Dennis, D. (1997). René Descartes' curve-drawing devices: Experiments in the relations between mechanical motion and symbolic language. *Mathematics Magazine, 70*(3), 163-174. Washington, DC: Mathematical Association of America.

Dennis, D., & Confrey, J. (1995). Functions of a curve: Leibniz's original notion of functions and its meaning for the parabola. In *The College Mathematics Journal* (Vol. 26, pp. 124–131). Washington, DC: Mathematical Association of America.

Dennis, D., & Confrey, J. (1996). The creation of continuous exponents: A study of the methods and epistemology of Alhazen, and Wallis. In J. Kaput & E. Dubinsky (Eds.), *Research in Collegiate Mathematics II* (pp. 33-60). Providence, RI: American Mathmematical Society.

Dennis, D., & Confrey, J. (in press). Drawing logarithmic and exponential curves with the computer software Geometer's Sketchpad: A method inspired by historical sources. In J. King & D. Schatschneider (Eds.), *Geometry turned on: Dynamic software in learning, teaching and research.* Washington, DC: Mathematical Association of America.

Densmore, D., & Donahue, W. (1995). *Newton's principia: The central argument.* Santa Fe, NM: Green Lion Press.

Descartes, R. (1952). *The geometry* (D. E. & Smith M. L. Latham, Trans.) LaSalle, IL: Open Court. (Original work published 1638)

de Villiers, M. D. (1995). An alternative introduction to proof in dynamic geometry. *MicroMath, 11*(12), 14–19.

Dewey, J. (1938). *Experience and education.* New York: Macmillan.

Dienes, Z. P. (1960). *Building up mathematics.* New York: Hutchinson.

Dienes, Z. P., & Jeeves, M. A. (1965). *Thinking in structures.* London: Hutchinson.

Dienes, Z. P., & Jeeves, M. A. (1970). *The effects of structural relations on transfer.* London: Hutchinson.

Dillon, D. R. (1993). The wider social context of innovation in mathematics education. In T. Wood, P. Cobb, E. Yackel, & D. Dillon (Eds.), *Rethinking elementary school mathematics: Insights and issues* (*Journal for Research in Mathematics Education,* Monograph No. 6, pp. 71–96). Reston, VA: National Council of Teachers of Mathematics.

diSessa, A. A. (1985). A principled design for an integrated computational environment. *Human–Computer Interaction, 1,* 1–47.

diSessa, A. (1988). Knowledge in pieces. In G. Forman & P. Pufall (Eds.), *Constructivism in the computer age* (pp. 49–70). Hillsdale, NJ: Lawrence Erlbaum Associates.

diSessa, A. A., & Abelson, H. (1986). Boxer: A reconstructible computational medium. *Communications of the ACM, 29*(9), 859–868.

diSessa, A., & Minstrell, J. (1998). Cultivating conceptual change with benchmark lessons. In J. G. Greeno (Ed.), *Thinking practices.* Mahwah, NJ: Lawrence Erlbaum Associates.

DiStefano, R. (1996). The IUPP evaluation: What we were trying to learn and how we were trying to learn it. *American Journal of Physics, 64*(1), 49–57.

Doerr, H. (1994). *A model building approach to constructing student understanding of force, motion, and vectors.* Unpublished doctoral dissertation, Cornell University, Ithaca, NY.

Donadio, S., Smith, J., Mesner, S., & Davison, R. (1992). *The New York public library book of twentieth–century American quotations.* New York: Warner Books.

Doolittle, P. E. (1995, June). *Understanding cooperative learning through Vygotsky's zone of proximal development.* Paper presented at the Lilly National Conference on Excellence in College Teaching, Columbia, SC.

Dorfler, W. (1989). *Protocols of actions as a cognitive tool for knowledge construction.* Paper presented at the Thirteenth Conference of the International Group for the Psychology of Mathematics Education, Paris.

Dorfler, W. (1995, September). *Means for meaning.* Paper presented at the Symposium on Symbolizing, Communication, and Mathematizing, Nashville, TN.

Dowrick, P. W. (1991). *Practical guide to using video in the behavioral sciences.* New York: Wiley.

Driver, R. (1973). *The representation of conceptual frameworks in young adolescent science students.* Unpublished doctoral dissertation, University of Illinois, Urbana-Champaign.

Driver, R., & Easley, G. (1983). Pupils and paradigms: A review of literature related to conceptual development in adolescent science studies. *Studies in Science Education, 5,* 61–84.

Duckworth, E. (1973). The having of wonderful ideas. In M. Schwebel & J. Raph (Eds.), *Piaget in the classroom* (pp. 258–277). New York: Basic Books.

Duckworth, E. (1979). Either we're too early and they can't learn it or we're too late and they know it already: The dilemma of "applying Piaget." *Harvard Educational Review, 49,* 297–312.

Duckworth, E. (1987). *"The having of wonderful ideas" and other essays on teaching and learning.* New York: Teachers College Press.

Dufresne, R. J., Gerace, W. J., Hardiman, P. T., & Mestre, J. P. (1992). Constraining novices to perform expert–like problem analyses: Effects on schema acquisition. *Journal of the Learning Sciences, 2,* 307–331.

Dunbar, K. (1994). *Scientific discovery heuristics: How current day scientist generate new hypotheses and make scientific discoveries.* Paper presented at the Sixteenth Annual Meeting of the Cognitive Science Society.

Duranti, A., & Goodwin, C. (1992). *Rethinking context: Language as an interactive phenomenon.* Cambridge, England: Cambridge University Press.

Dutka, J. (1988). On the St. Petersburg paradox. *Archive for History of Exact Sciences, 39,* 13–39.

Dweck, C. S., & Leggett, E. L. (1988). A social–cognitive approach to motivation and personality. *Psychological Review, 95*(2), 256–273.

Dwyer, D. C. (1996). The imperative to change our schools. In C. Fisher, D. C. Dwyer, & K. Yocam (Eds.), *Education & technology: Reflections on computing in classrooms* (pp. 15–33). San Francisco: Jossey-Bass.

Dwyer, D. C., Ringstaff, C., & Sandholtz, J. (1990). *The evolution of teachers' instructional beliefs and practices in high-access-to-technology classrooms.* Paper presented at the annual meeting of the American Educational Research Association, Boston.

Easley, J. A. (1974). The structural paradigm in protocol analysis. *Journal of Research in Science Teaching, 2,* 281–290.

Easley, J. A. (1978). Symbol manipulation reexamined: An approach to bridging a chasm. In B. Presseisen, D. Goldstein, & M. Appel (Eds.), *Topics in cognitive development* (Vol. 2, pp. 99–112). New York: Plenum.

Eckert, P. (1989). *Jocks and burnouts: Social categories and identity in the high school.* New York: Teachers College Press.

Ehrenreich, B. (1988). Ode to a couch potato. *Mother Jones, 13*(3), 9.

Einstein, A., & Infeld, L. (1967). *The evolution of physics.* New York: Simon & Schuster Clarion Book. (Original work published 1938)

Eisenhart, M., Borko, H., Underhill, R., Brown, C., Jones, D., & Agard, P. (1993). Conceptual knowledge falls throught the cracks: Complexities of learning to teach mathematics for understanding. *Journal for Research in Mathematics Education, 24*(1), 8–40.

Eisenhart, M. A. (1988). The ethnographic research tradition and mathematics education research. *Journal for Research in Mathematics Education, 19,* 99–114.

Eisenstein, E. (1979). *The printing press as an agent of change.* Cambridge, England: Cambridge University Press.

El'konin, D. B. (1967). The problem of instruction and development in the works of L. S. Vygotsky. *Soviet Psychology, 5*(3), 34–41.

Ellerton, N. F., & Clements, M. A. (1994). *The national curriculum debacle.* Perth, Australia: Meridian Press.

Ellerton, N. F., & Clements, M. A. (1996). Transforming the international mathematics education research agenda. In A. Sierpinska & J. Kilpatrick (Eds.), *What is mathematics education, and what are its results?* Dordrecht, Netherlands: Kluwer.

Elliott, J. (1991). *Action research for educational change.* Buckingham, England: Open University Press.

Emerson, R. M., Fretz, R. I., & Shaw, L. L. (1995). *Writing ethnographic fieldnotes.* Chicago: University of Chicago Press.

Erickson, F. (1986). Qualitative methods in research on teaching. In M. C. Wittrock (Ed.), *The handbook of research on teaching* (3rd ed., pp. 119–161). New York: Macmillan.

Erickson, F. (1998). Qualitative research methods for science education. In B. J. Fraser & K. Tobin (Eds.), *The international handbook of science education,* (pp. 1155–1173). Dordrecht, Netherlands: Kluwer.

Ericsson, K. A., & Simon, H. A. (1984). *Protocol analysis: Verbal reports as data.* Cambridge, MA: MIT Press.

Erlandson, D. A., Harris, E. L., Skipper, B. L., & Allen, S. D. (1993). *Doing naturalistic inquiry: A guide to methods.* Newbury Park, CA: Sage.

Erlwanger, S. H. (1973). Benny's conception of rules and answers in IPI mathematics. *Journal of Children's Mathematical Behavior, 1*(2), 7–25.

Ernest, P. (1991). *The philosophy of mathematics education.* Basinstoke, Hampshire, England: Falmer Press.

Erzberger, A., Fottrell, S., Hiebart, L., Merrill, T., Rappleyea, A., Weinmann, L., & Woosman, T. (1996). A framework for physics projects. *The Physics Teacher, 34*(1), 26–28.

Fals–Borda, O., & Anisur, M. (Eds.). (1991). *Action and knowledge: Breaking the monopoly with participatory action research.* New York: Apex Press.

Feldman, A. (1993). *Teachers learning from teachers: Knowledge and understanding in collaborative action research.* Ph. D., Stanford University.

Feldman, A. (1996). Enhancing the practice of physics teachers: Mechanisms for the generation and sharing of knowledge and understanding in collaborative action research. *Journal of Research in Science Teaching, 33*(5), 513–540.

Feldman, A. (1998). Implementing and assessing the power of conversation in the teaching of action research. *Teacher Education Quarterly, 25*,(2), 27–42.

Feldman, A., Alibrandi, M., Capifali, E., Floyd, D., Gabriel, J., Henriques, B., Hitchens, F., Lucey, J., & Mera, M. (1998). Looking at ourselves look at ourselves: An action research self–study of doctoral students' roles in teacher education programs. *Teacher Education Quarterly, 25*(3), 5–28.

Feldman, A., & Atkin, J. (1995). Embedding action research in professional practice. In S. E. Noffke & R. B. Stevenson (Eds.), *Educational action research: Becoming practically critical* (pp. 127–137). New York: Teachers College Press.

Feldman, A., Mason, C., & Goldberg, F. (1992). *Action research: Reports from the field, 1991–92.* San Diego: Center for Research in Mathematics and Science Education.

Feldman, A., Mason, C., & Goldberg, F. (1993). *Action research: Reports from the field, 1992–93.* San Diego: Center for Research in Mathematics and Science Education.

Feldman, D. (1980). *Beyond universals in cognitive development.* Norwood, NJ: Ablex.

Feller, W. (1971). *An introduction to probability theory and its applications* (Vol. II). New York: Wiley.

Ferrini–Mundy, J., & Clements, M. A. (1994). Recognizing and recording reforms in mathematics—New questions, many answers. *Mathematics Teacher, 88,* 380–389.

Feuerstein, R., Rand, Y. A., & Hoffman, M. B. (1979). *The dynamic assessment of retarded performers: The Learning Potential Assessment Device, theory, instruments, and techniques.* Baltimore: University Park Press.

Fine, M. (1994). Working the hyphens: Reinventing self and other in qualitative research. In N. K. Denzin & Y. S. Lincoln (Eds.), *Handbook of qualitative research* (pp. 70–82). Thousand Oaks, CA: Sage.

Firestone, W. A. (1993). Alternative arguments for generalizing from data as applied to qualitative research. *Educational Researcher, 22,* 16–23.

Fischbein, E. (1987). *Intuition in science and mathematics.* Dordrecht, Netherlands: Reidel.

Fischbien, F., Deri, M., Nello, M. S., & Marino, M. S. (1985). The role of implicit models in solving verbal problems in multiplication and division. *Journal for Research in Mathematics Education, 6*(1), 3–17.

Fisher, C., Dwyer, D. C., & Yocam, K. (Eds.). (1996). *Education and technology: Reflections on computing in classrooms.* San Francisco: Apple Press/Jossey-Bass.

Fisher, K. (1990). Semantic networking: The new kid on the block. *Journal of Research in Science Teaching, 27*(10), 1001–1018.

Flanders, N. (1970). *Analyzing teaching behavior.* Reading, MA: Addison–Wesley.

Forrester, J. (1961). *Industrial dynamics.* Cambridge, MA: MIT Press.

Forrester, J. (1968). *Principles of systems.* Cambridge, MA: MIT Press.

Forrester, J. (1969). *Urban dynamics.* Cambridge, MA: MIT Press.

Forrester, J. (1971). *World dynamics.* Cambridge, MA: Wright–Allen Press.

Foucault, M. (1977). *Discipline and punish: The birth of the prison* (A. Sheridan, Trans.). New York: Pantheon Books.

Frankenstein, M. (1995). Equity in mathematics education: Class in the world outside the class. In W. G. Secada, E. Fennema, & L. B. Adajian (Eds.), *New directions for equity in mathematics education* (pp. 165–19002). London: Cambridge University Press.

Freudenthal, H. (1991). *Revisiting mathematics education.* Dordrecht, Netherlands: Kluwer.

Fukunaga, K. (1990). *Introduction to statistical pattern recognition: Computer science and scientific computing.* New York: Academic Press.

Gadamer, H. (1992). *Truth and method* (2nd rev. ed.). New York: Crossroad.

Gal, I., & Garfield, J. (1997). *The assessment challenge in statistics education*. Netherlands: The International Statistical Institute, IOS Press.

Galtung, J. (1980). *The true worlds: A transnational perspective*. New York: The Free Press.

Gamoran, A. (in press). Goals 2000 in organizational perspective: Will it make a difference for states, districts, and schools? In K. Borman, P. Cookson, A. Sadovnik, & J. Z. Spade (Eds.), *Implementing federal legislation: Sociological perspectives on policy*. Norwood, NJ: Ablex.

Gardner, H. (1989). *To open minds*. New York: Basic Books.

Gardner, H. (1993a). *Frames of mind: The theory of multiple intelligences*. Tenth anniversary edition. New York: Basic Books.

Gardner, H. (1993b). *Multiple intelligences: The theory in practice*. New York: Basic Books.

Garfinkel, H. (1967). *Studies in ethnomethodology*. Englewood Cliffs, NJ: Prentice-Hall.

Garrison, J. (1995, April). *Using technology to prepare effective and responsible educators*. Paper presented at the annual meeting of the American Educational Research Association, San Francisco.

Gauss, C. F. (1965). *Disquisitones Arithmeticae* (A. A. Clarke, Trans.). New Haven, CT: Yale University Press. (Original work published 1801)

Geertz, C. (1988). *Works and lives: The anthropologist as author*. Stanford, CA: Stanford University Press.

Gelman, R., & Greeno, J. G. (1989). On the nature of competence: Principles for understanding in a domain. In L. B. Resnick (Ed.), *Knowing, learning, and instruction: Essays in honor of Robert Glaser* (pp. 125–186). Hillsdale, NJ: Lawrence Erlbaum Associates.

Gerber, M. M., Semmel, D. S., & Semmel, M. I. (1994). Computer–based dynamic assessment of multidigit multiplication. *Exceptional Children, 61*, 114–125.

Giere, R. (1988). *Explaining science*. Chicago: University of Chicago Press.

Ginsburg, H. (1981). The clinical interview in psychological research on mathematical thinking: Aims, rationales, techniques. *For the Learning of Mathematics, 1*(3), 4–11.

Ginsburg, H. (1983). Protocol methods in research on mathematical thinking. In H. Ginsburg (Ed.), *The development of mathematical thinking*. New York: Academic Press.

Glaser, B. G., & Strauss, A. L. (1967). *The discovery of grounded theory: Strategies for qualititative research*. New York: Aldine.

Glaser, R. (1994). Learning theory and instruction. In G. d'Ydewalle, P. Eelen, & P. Bertelson (Eds.), *International perspectives on psychological science* (pp. 342–357). Hove, England: Lawrence Erlbaum Associates.

Glaser, R., & Silver, E. (1994). Assessment, testing, and instruction: Retrospect and prospect. In L. Darling–Hammond (Ed.), *Review of research in education* (pp. 393–419). Washington, DC: American Educational Research Association.

Glass, G., Peckham, P., & Sanders, J. R. (1972). Consequences of failure to meet assumptions underlying the fixed effects analysis of variance and covariance. *Review of Educational Research, 42*, 237–288.

Glesne, C., & Peshkin, A. (1992). *Becoming qualitative researchers: An introduction*. White Plains, NY: Longman.

Goetz, J., & LeCompte, M. (1984). *Ethnograpy and qualitative design in educational research*. New York: Academic Press.

Goldberg, A. (1979). Educational uses of a dynabook. *Computers and Education, 3*, 247–266.

Goldenberg, P. (1988). Mathematics, metaphors, and human factors: Mathematical, technical, and pedagodgical challenges in the educational use of graphical representations of functions. *Journal of Mathematical Behavior, 7*, 135–173.

Goldin, G. A. (1980). Structure variables in problem solving. In G. A. Goldin & C. E. McClintock (Eds.), *Task variables in mathematical problem solving* (pp. 103–169). Philadelphia: Franklin Institute Press (subsequently acquired by Lawrence Erlbaum Associates, Hillsdale, NJ).

Goldin, G. A. (1982). The measure of problem–solving outcomes. In J. F. K. Lester & J. Garofalo (Eds.), *Mathematical problem solving: Issues in research*, (pp. 87–101). Philadelphia, PA: Franklin Institute Press, subsequently acquired by Lawrence Erlbaum Associates, Hillsdale, NJ.

Goldin, G. A. (1985). *Studying children's use of heuristic processes for mathematical problem solving through structured clinical interviews*. Paper presented at the Seventh Annual Meeting of the North American Chapter of the International Group for the Psychology of Mathematics Education, Columbus, OH.

Goldin, G. A. (1986). *Comments on structured individual interview methods for the study of problem solving*. Paper presented at the Eighth Annual Meeting of the North American Chapter of the International Group for the Psychology of Mathematics Education: Plenary Speeches and Symposium, East Lansing, MI.

Goldin, G. A. (1987). Cognitive representational systems for mathematical problem solving. In C. Janvier (Ed.), *Problems of representation in the teaching and learning of mathematics* (pp. 125–145). Hillsdale, NJ: Lawrence Erlbaum Associates.

Goldin, G. A. (1990). Epistemology, constructivism, and discovery learning in mathematics. In R. B. Davis, C. A. Maher, & N. Noddings (Eds.), *Constructivist views on the teaching and learning of mathematics* (pp. 31–47). Reston, VA: National Council of Teachers of Mathematics.

Goldin, G. A. (1992a). Meta–analysis of problem–solving studies: A critical response. *Journal for Research in Mathematics Education, 23*(3), 274–283.

Goldin, G. A. (1992b). *On developing a unified model for the psychology of mathematical learning and problem solving*. Paper presented at the Sixteenth International Conference for the Psychology of Mathematics Education, Durham, NH.

Goldin, G. A. (1992c). Toward an assessment framework for school mathematics. In R. Lesh & S. J. Lamon (Eds.), *Assessment of authentic performance in school mathematics* (pp. 63–88). Washington, DC: American Association for the Advancement of Science.

Goldin, G. A. (1993a). *Observing mathematical problem solving: Perspectives on structured, task-based interviews*. Paper presented at the Sixteenth Annual Conference of the Mathematics Educational Research Group of Australasia: Contexts in Mathematics Education (MERGA–16), Queensland University of Technology, Kelvin Grove, Australia.

Goldin, G. A. (1993b). Reply to the letter of S. B. Gray. *Journal for Research in Mathematics Education, 24*(2), 181–182.

Goldin, G. A., DeBellis, V. A., DeWindt–King, A. M., Passantino, C. B., & Zang, R. (1993). *Task-based interviews for a longitudinal study of children's mathematical development*. Paper presented at the Seventeenth International Conference for the Psychology of Mathematics Education, Tsukuba, Japan.

Goldin, G. A., & Kaput, J. J. (1996). A joint perspective on the idea of representation in learning and doing mathematics. In L. P. Steffe, P. Nesher, P. Cobb, G. A. Goldin, & B. Greer (Eds.), *Theories of mathematical learning* (pp. 397–430). Mahwah, NJ: Lawrence Erlbaum Associates.

Goldin, G. A., & Landis, J. H. (1986, July). *A study of children's mathematical problem solving heuristics*. Paper presented at the Tenth International Conference for the Psychology of Mathematics Education, London.

Goldin, G. A., & Landis, J. H. (1995, October). *A problem–solving interview with "Stan" (age 11)*. Paper presented at the Seventh Annual Meeting of the North American Chapter of the International Group for the Psychology of Mathematics Education, Columbus, OH.

Goldin, G. A., & Luger, G. F. (1975). *Problem structure and problem solving behavior*. Paper presented at the Fourth International Conference on Artificial Intelligence, Cambridge, MA.

Goldin, G. A., & Passantino, C. B. (1996, July). *A longitudinal study of children's fraction representations and problem solving behavior.* Paper presented at the Twentieth International Conference for the Psychology of Mathematics Education, Valencia, Spain.

Goldin, G. A., & Waters, W. M. (1982). *Strategy use and effectiveness in successive concept acquisition tasks.* Paper presented at the Fourth Annual Meeting of the North American Chapter of the International Group for the Psychology of Mathematics Education, Athens, GA.

Goldman, S. (1994). *Middle school mathematics through applications project (MMAP): Second year progress report to the National Science Foundation* (Tech. Rep.). Palo Alto, CA: Institute for Research on Learning.

Goldman, S., Moschkovich, J., & The Middle School Mathematics Through Applications Project. (1995). *Environments for collaborating mathematically: The middle school mathematics through applications project.* Paper presented at the CSCL 95: The First International Conference on Computer Support for Collaborative Learning, Hillsdale, NJ.

Goleman, D. (1997). *Emotional intelligence.* New York: Bantam Books.

Goodenough, W. (1956). Componential analysis and the study of meaning. *Language, 32,* 195–216.

Goodwin, C. (1992). Recording human interaction in natural settings. *Pragmatics, 3*(2), 181–209.

Goodwin, C. (1994). Professional vision. *American Anthropologist, 96*(3), 606–633.

Goody, J. (1977). *The domestication of the savage mind.* Cambridge, England: Cambridge University Press.

Goody, J. (1987). *The interface between the written and the oral.* Cambridge, England: Cambridge University Press.

Gore, J., & Zeichner, K. (1991). Action research and reflective teaching in preservice teacher education: A case study from the United States. *Teaching and Teacher Education, 7*(2), 119–136.

Gorsky, P., & Finegold, M. (1994). The role of anomaly and of cognitive dissonance in restructuring students' concepts of force. *Instructional Science, 22,* 75–90.

Goswami, D., & Stillman, P. (Eds.). (1987). *Reclaiming the classroom: Teacher research as an agency for change.* Portsmouth, NH: Boynton/Cook.

Gould, J. (1981). *Ever since Darwin.* New York: Norton.

Gould, S. J. (1988). *Time's arrow, time's cycle.* Harmondsworth, England: Penguin.

Gould, S. J. (1993). *The mismeasure of man.* New York: Norton.

Gravemeijer, K. (1994). Educational development and developmental research in mathematics education. *Journal for Research in Mathematics Education, 25*(5), 443–471.

Gravemeijer, K. P. E. (1995). *Developing realistic mathematics instruction.* Utrecht, Netherlands: Freudenthal Institute.

Greenberg, S. (Ed.). (1991). *Computer supported cooperative work and groupware.* London: Academic Press.

Greeno, J. (1991). Number sense as situated knowing in a conceptual domain. *Journal for Research in Mathematics Education, 22*(3), 170–218.

Greeno, J. G., McDermott, R., Engle, R. A., Knudsen, J., Cole, K., Lauman, B., Goldman, S., & Linde, C. (in press). *Research, reform, and aims in education: Modes of action in search of each other.*

Greer, B., & Harel, G. (1998). The role of isomorphisms in mathematical cognition. *Journal of Mathematical Behavior, 17*(1).

Grouws, D. A., & Cooney, T. J. (Eds.). (1988). *Research agenda in mathematics education: Perspectives on research on effective mathematics teaching.* Reston, VA: National Council of Teachers of Mathematics.

Gruber, H. (1974). *Darwin on man.* New York: Dutton.

Guba, E. G. (1990). The alternative paradigm dialog. In E. G. Guba (Ed.), *The paradigm dialog* (pp. 17–31). Newbury Park, CA: Sage.

Guba, E. G. (1993). Foreword. In D. A. Erlandson, E. L. Harris, & B. L. Skipper (Eds.), *Doing naturalistic inquiry: A guide to methods* (pp. ix–xv). Newbury Park, CA: Sage.

Guba, E. G., & Lincoln, Y. S. (1989). *Fourth generation evaluation.* Newbury Park, CA: Sage Publications.

Guberman, S. (1992). *Math and money: A comparative study of the arithmetical achievements and out–of–school activities of Latino and Korean American children.* Unpublished doctoral dissertation, University of California, Los Angeles.

Hagen, J. B., Allchin, D., & Singer, F. (1996). *Doing biology.* Glenview, IL: HarperCollins.

Hake, R. R. (1994, August). Survey of test data for introductory mechanics courses. Paper presented at the meeting of the American Association of Physics Teachers, Notre Dame, IN.

Hake, R. R. (1995, June). Socratic dialogue inducing laboratories: Do they work? Talk delivered at Project Kaleidoscope Workshop on "Revitalizing Introductory Physics," Miami University, Oxford, OH.

Hall, R. (1994). *Visual reasoning in instruction.* Paper presented at the Sixteenth Annual Conference of the Cognitive Science Society, Hillsdale, NJ.

Hall, R. (1995). Realism(s) for learning algebra. In C. B. LaCampagne, W. Blair, & J. Kaput (Eds.), *The Algebra Initiative Colloquium* (Vol. 2, pp. 33–51). Washington, DC: U.S. Department of Education, Office of Educational Research and Improvement.

Hall, R. (1996). Representation as shared activity: Situated cognition and Dewey's cartography of experience. *Journal of the Learning Sciences, 5*(3), 209–238.

Hall, R., Knudsen, J., & Greeno, J. G. (1996). A case study of systemic attributes of assessment technologies. *Educational Assessment, 3*(4), 315–361.

Hall, R., & Stevens, R. (1995). Making space: A comparison of mathematical work in school and professional design practices. In S. L. Star (Ed.), *The cultures of computing* (pp. 118–145). London: Basil Blackwell.

Hall, R., & Stevens, R. (1996). *Teaching/learning events in the workplace: A comparative analysis of their organizational and interactional structure.* Paper presented at the Eighteenth Annual Conference of the Cognitive Science Society, Hillsdale, NJ.

Hanks, W. F. (1996). *Language and communicative practices.* Boulder, CO: Westview Press.

Hanna, G. (1990). Some pedagogical aspects of proof. *Interchange, 21*(1), 6–13.

Hannahs, N. J. (1983). *Native Hawaiian educational assessment project.* Honolulu: Kamehameha Schools.

Hanson, N. R. (1958). *Patterns of discovery.* Cambridge, England: Cambridge University Press.

Hardiman, P. T., Dufresne, R. J., & Mestre, J. P. (1989). The relation between problem categorization and problem solving among experts and novices. *Memory & Cognition, 17,* 627–638.

Harel, I., & Papert, S. (Eds.). (1991). *Constructionism.* Norwood, NJ: Ablex.

Harre, R. (1961). *Theories and things.* London: Newman History and Philosophy of Science Series.

Harre, R. (1967). Philosophy of science: History of. In P. Edwards (Ed.), *The encyclopedia of philosophy* (pp. 289–296). New York: The Free Press.

Hart, K. (1984). *Ratio: Children's strategies and errors. A report of the strategies and srrors in secondary mathematics project.* London: The NFER-Nelson Publishing Company, Ltd.

Hart, L. (1986, September). *Small group problem solving as a data source for the individual.* Paper presented at the Eighth Annual Meeting of the North American Chapter of the International Group for the Psychology of Mathematics Education: Plenary Speeches and Symposium, East Lansing, MI.

Hatano, G. (1988). Social and motivational bases for mathematical understanding. In G. Saxe & M. Gearhart (Eds.), *Children's mathematics* (pp. 55–70). San Francisco: Jossey–Bass.

Hativa, N. (1994). What you design is not what you get: Cognitive, affective, and social implications of learning with ILS—An integration of findings from six years of qualitative and quanititative studies. *International Journal of Educational Research, 21*(1), 81–111.

Hawking, S. W. (1988). *A brief history of time.* New York: Bantam.

Hawkins, J. (1997). *The national design experiments consortium: Final report.* New York: Center for Children and Technology, Educational Development Center.

Hawkins, J., & Pea, R. D. (1987). Tools for bridging the culture of everyday and scientific thinking. *Journal of Research in Science Teaching, 24*(4), 291–307.

Hayes, J. R. (1978). *Cognitive psychology: Thinking and creating.* Homewood, IL: Dorsley.

Hayes, J. R., & Flower, L. S. (1978, March). *Protocol analysis of writing processes.* Paper presented at the annual meeting of the American Educational Research Association.

Heath, S. B. (1983). *Ways with words.* Cambridge, England: Cambridge University Press.

Heaton, R. M. (1992). Who is minding the mathematics content? A case study of a fifth-grade teacher. *Elementary School Journal, 93,* 153–162.

Heaton, R. M. (1994). *Creating and studying a practice of teaching elementary mathematics for understanding.* Unpublished doctoral dissertation, Michigan State University, East Lansing.

Heering, P. (1992). *On J. P. Joule's determination of the mechanical equivalent of heat.* Paper presented at the Second International Conference on the History and Philosophy of Science in Science Education, Kingston, Ontario.

Hegarty, M. (1992). Mental animation: Inferring motion from static displays of mechanical systems. *Journal of Experimental Psychology: Learning, Memory, and Cognition, 18*(5), 1084–1102.

Heidelberger, M. (1987). Fechner's indeterminism: From freedom to laws of chance. In L. Kruger, L. Daston, & M. Heidelberger (Eds.), *The probabilistic revolution,* (Vol. 2). Cambridge, MA: MIT Press.

Hein, G. E. (1987). The right test for hands–on learning? *Science and Children, 25*(2), 8–12.

Helfgott, D., Helfgott, M., & Hoof, B. (1994). Inspiration [Computer software]. Inspiration Software, Inc.

Heller, P., Keith, R., & Anderson, S. (1992). Teaching problem solving through cooperative grouping: Part 1. Group versus individual problem solving. *American Journal of Physics, 60*(7), 627–636.

Hennessy, S. (1995). Design of a computer–augmented curriculum for mechanics. *International Journal of Science Education, 17*(1), 75–92.

Herman, J. L. (1993). *Finding the reality behind the promise: Assessing the effects of technology in school reform.* Paper presented at the annual meeting of the American Educational Research Association, Atlanta.

Hesse, M. (1967). Models and analogies in science. In P. Edwards (Ed.), *The encyclopedia of philosophy* (pp. 354–359). New York: The Free Press.

Hestenes, D. (1987). A modeling theory of physics instruction. *American Journal of Physics, 53,* 1056–1065.

Hestenes, D. (1994). Toward a modeling theory of physics instructions. *American Journal of Physics, 60,* 440–454.

Hestenes, D., & Wells, M. (1992). A mechanics baseline test. *The Physics Teacher, 30,* 159–166.

Hestenes, D., Wells, M., & Swackhamer, G. (1992). Force concept inventory. *The Physics Teacher, 30,* 141–158.

Hickman, L. A. (1990). *John Dewey's pragmatic technology.* Indianapolis, IN: Indiana University Press.

Hicks, D. (1995). Discourse, learning, and teaching. In M. W. Apple (Ed.), *Review of research in education* (pp. 49–95). Washington, DC: American Educational Research Association.

Hiebert, J., & Behr, M. (Eds.). (1988). *Research agenda in mathematics education: Number concepts and operations in the middle grades*. Reston, VA: National Council of Teachers of Mathematics.

Hiebert, J., & Carpenter, T. P. (1992). Learning and teaching with understanding. In D. A. Grouws (Ed.), *Handbook of research on mathematics teaching*, (pp. 65–97). New York: Macmillan.

Hiebert, J., & Wearne, D. (1991). Methodologies for studying learning to inform teaching. In E. Fennema, T. P. Carpenter, & S. J. Lamon (Eds.), *Integrating research on teaching and learning mathematics* (pp. 153–176). Albany: State University of New York Press.

Hollan, Hutchins, McCandless, Rosenstein, & Weitzman. (1986). Graphical interfaces for simulation. In Rouse (Ed.), *Advances in man-machine systems* (Vol. 3). Greenwich, CT: Jai.

Hollingsworth, S. (1994). *Teacher research and urban literacy education: Lessons and conversations in feminist key*. New York: Teachers College Press.

Horwitz, P., & Barowy, W. (1994). Designing and using open–ended software to promote conceptual change. *Journal of Science Education and Technology, 3*, 161–185.

Howe, K. (1985). Two dogmas of educational research. *Educational Researcher, 14*, 10–18.

Howe, K., & Eisennhart, M. (1990). Standards for qualitative (and quantitative) research: A prolegomenon. *Educational Researcher, 19*(4), 2–9.

Hoyles, C., & Noss, R. (1992). A pedagogy for mathematical microworlds. *Educational Studies in Mathematics, 23*, 31–57.

Hubbard, R. S., & Power, B. M. (1993). *The art of classroom inquiry: A handbook for teacher-researchers*. Portsmouth, NH: Heinemann.

Hulse, R. A. (1995, September). *System dynamics and computer modeling for education: A physicist/computer modeler's perspective on what is all about and why it is important for education*. Paper presented at the System Dynamics and Computer Modeling Conference, Princeton Plasma Physics Laboratory, Princeton, NJ.

Hunt, E., & Minstrell, J. (1994). A cognitive approach to the teaching of physics. In K. McGilly (Ed.), *Classroom lessons: Integrating cognitive theory and classroom practice*. Cambridge, MA: MIT Press.

Hunting, R. (1983). Emerging methodologies for understanding internal processes governing children's mathematical behavior. *The Australian Journal of Education, 27*(1), 45–61.

Hunting, R. P. (1997). Clinical interview methods in mathematics education research and practice. *Journal of Mathematical Behavior, 16*(2), 145–165.

Hurd, P. (1995). Reinventing the science curriculum: Historical reflections and new directions. In R. W. Bybee & J. McInerney (Eds.), *Redesigning the science curriculum* (pp. 1–11). Colorado Springs: Biological Sciences Curriculum Study.

Hutchins, E. (1995). *Cognition in the wild*. Cambridge, MA: MIT Press.

Inagaki, K. (1981). Facilitation of knowledge integration through classroom discussion. *The Quarterly Newsletter of the Laboratory of Comparative Human Cognition, 3*, 26–28.

Irwin, T. (1985). *Aristotle's Nichomachean ethics*. Indianapolis, IN: Hackett.

Jackiw, N. (1988–1997). The Geometer's Sketchpad [Computer software: various versions]. Berkeley, CA: Key Curriculum Press.

Jacob, E. (1987). Qualitative research traditions: A review. *Review of Educational Research, 57*, 1–50.

Jahnke, H. N. (1994, July). *The historical dimension of mathematical understanding-objectifying the subjective*. Paper presented at the Eighteenth International Conference for the Psychology of Mathematics Education, Lisbon, Portugal.

Jeeves, M. A., & Greer, G. B. (1983). *Analysis of structural learning*. London: Academic Press.

Jick, T. D. (1979). Mixing qualitative and quantitative methods: Triangulation in action. In J. V. Maanen (Ed.), *Qualitative methodology* (pp. 135–148). Beverly Hills, CA: Sage.

Johnson, M. (1987). *The body in the mind: The bodily basis of meaning, imagination, and reason*. Chicago: University of Chicago Press.

Johnson–Gentile, K., Clements, D. H., & Battista, M. T. (1994). The effects of computer and noncomputer environment on students' conceptualizations of geometric motions. *Journal of Educational Computing Research, 11*(2), 121–140.

Johsua, S., & Dupin, J. J. (1987). Taking into account student conceptions in instructional strategy: An example in physics. *Cognition and Instruction, 4*(2), 117–135.

Jordan, B., & Henderson, A. (1995). Interaction analysis: Foundations and practice. *Journal of the Learning Sciences, 4*(1), 39–103.

Jordan, C. (1985). Translating culture: From ethnographic information to educational program. *Anthropology and Education Quarterly, 16,* 105–123.

Just, M. A., & Carpenter, P. A. (1987). *The psychology of reading and language comprehension.* Newton, MA: Allyn & Bacon.

Kao, H., Wedman, J., & Placier, P. (1994, February). *Implementation of an interactive videodisc program: An ethnographic study.* Paper presented at the Sixteenth National Convention of the Association for Educational Communications and Technology, Nashville, TN.

Kaput, J. (1985). Representation and problem solving: Methodological issues related to modeling. In E. Silver (Ed.), *Teaching and learning mathematical problem solving: Multiple research perspectives* (pp. 381–398). Hillsdale, NJ: Lawrence Erlbaum Associates.

Kaput, J. (1987). Representation systems and mathematics. In C. Janvier (Ed.), *Problems of representation in the teaching and learning of mathematics* (pp. 19–26). Hillsdale, NJ: Lawrence Erlbaum Associates.

Kaput, J. (1991). Notations and representations as mediators of constructive processes. In E. v. Glasersfeld (Ed.), *Constructivism in mathematics education* (pp. 53–74). Dordrecht, Netherlands: Kluwer.

Kaput, J. (1992). Technology and mathematics education. In D. Grouws (Ed.), *A handbook of research on mathematics teaching and learning* (pp. 515–556). New York: Macmillan.

Kaput, J. (1994). Rational numbers and rationality: What are we learning and what needs to be done? *Journal of Research in Childhood Education, 8*(2), 142–149.

Kaput, J. (in press). Overcoming physicality and the eternal present: Cybernetic manipulatives. In R. Sutherland & J. Mason (Eds.), *Visualization and technology in mathematics education.* New York: Springer-Verlag.

Kaput, J., & Nemirovsky, R. (1995). Moving to the next level: A mathematics of change theme througout the K–16 curriculum. *UME Trends, 6*(6), 21–21.

Kaput, J., & Roschelle, J. (1993). SimCalc: Simulations for calculus learning [Computer software]. North Dartmouth, MA.

Karplus, R. (1974). *SCIS teacher's handbook.* Berkeley, CA: Science Curriculum Improvement Study, University of California.

Karplus, R. & Peterson, (1970). In R. Lesh & M. Landau (Eds.), *Acquisition of mathematics concepts & processes.* New York: Academic Press.

Katims, N., & Lesh, R.., Hole, B., & Hoover, M. (Eds.). (1994a). *PACKETS: A guidebook for inservice mathematics teacher development.* Lexington, MA: Heath.

Katims, N., Lesh, R., Hole, B., & Hoover, M. (1994b). *PACKETS: A program for integrating learning and performance assessment for mathematics.* Lexington, MA: Heath.

Katz, V. J. (1993). *A history of mathematics: An introduction.* New York: HarperCollins.

Kauffman, S. (1993). *The origins of order: Self organization and selection in evolution.* New York: Oxford University Press.

Kauffman, S. (1995). *At home in the universe: The search for the laws of self-organization and complexity.* New York: Oxford University Press.

Kay, A., & Goldberg, A. (1977). Personal dynamic media. *IEEE Computer, 10*(3), 31–41.

Keeves, J. (1997). *Educational research, methodology, and measurement: An international handbook.* Oxford, England: Pergamon. (Original work published 1988)

Keitel, C. (1987). What are the goals of mathematics for all? *Journal of Curriculum Studies, 19*(5), 393–407.

Keitel, C., & Ruthven, K. (Eds.). (1993). *Learning from computers: Mathematics education and technology.* New York: Springer–Verlag.

Kelman, P. (1990, June). *Alternatives to integrated instructional systems.* Paper presented at the meeting of the National Educational Computing Conference, Nashville, TN.

Kieren, T. (1994). Play and mathematical understanding. *Journal of Research in Childhood Education, 8*(2), 132–141.

Kilpatrick, J. (1978). Research on problem solving in mathematics. *School, Science, and Mathematics, 78*(3), 189–192.

Kilpatrick, J. (1987, July). *What constructivism might mean in mathematics education.* Paper presented at the Eleventh International Conferenced on the Psychology of Mathematics Education, Montreal.

Kilpatrick, J. (1992). A history of research in mathematics education. In D. A. Grouws (Ed.), *Handbook of research on mathematics teaching and learning* (pp. 3–38). New York: Macmillan.

Kilpatrick, J., & Wirszup, I. (1975). *Methods of teaching mathematics* (Vol. VIII). Chicago: University of Chicago Press.

Knapp, N. F., & Peterson, P. L. (1995). Teachers' interpretations of "CGI" after four years: Meanings and practices. *Journal for Research in Mathematics Education, 26,* 40–65.

Koehler, M., & Grouws, D. A. (1992). Mathematics teaching practices and their effects. In D. A. Grouws (Ed.), *Handbook of research on mathematics teaching* (pp. 115–126). New York: Macmillan.

Kohl, H. (1967). *36 children.* New York: Penguin Books.

Kohl, H. (1984). *Growing minds: On becoming a teacher.* New York: Harper & Row.

Köhler, W. (1959). *Gestalt psychology: An introduction to new concepts in modern psychology.* New York: Mentor.

Konold, C. (1991). Understanding students' beliefs about probability. In E. von Glaserfeld (Ed.), *Radical constructivism in mathematics education* (pp. 139–156) Dordrecht, Netherlands: Kluwer.

Koschmann, T. D., Meyers, A. C., Feltovich, P. J., & Barrows, H. S. (1994). Using technology to assist in realizing effective learning and instruction: A principled approach to the use of computers in collaborative learning. *The Journal of the Learning Sciences, 3,* 227–264.

Kota, H., & Feldman, A. (1993). *The transformative effect of action research on educational reform* [Photocopy]. School of Education, University of Massachusetts.

Krieger, S. (1991). *Social science and the self: Personal essays on an art form.* New Brunswick, NJ: Rutgers University Press.

Kuhn, T. (1957). *The Copernican revolution.* Cambridge, MA: Harvard University Press.

Kuhn, T. (1970). *The structure of scientific revolutions.* Chicago: University of Chicago Press. (Original work published 1962)

Kuhn, T. (1977). Concepts of cause in the development of physics. In T. Kuhn (Ed.), *The essential tension: Selected studies in scientific tradition and change* (pp. 21–30). Chicago: University of Chicago Press.

Kvale, S. (1996). *InterViews.* Newbury Park, CA: Sage.

Laborde, J. M., Baulac, Y., & Bellemain, F. (1988–1997). Cabri Geométre [Software, various versions]. Grenoble, France: IMAG–CNRS, Universite Joseph Fourier.

Lachance, A. (1996). *From ratios to decimals: Introducing students to decimal notation through ratio and proportion.* Unpublished master's thesis, Cornell University, Ithaca, NY.

Lajoie, S. P. (1990, April). *Computer environments as cognitive tools for enhancing mental models.* Paper presented at the meeting of the American Educational Research Association, Boston.

Lakatos, I. (1976). *Proofs and refutations: The logic of mathematical discovery.* London: Cambridge University Press.

Lakatos, I. (1978). *The methodology of scientific research programmes* (Vol. 1). Cambridge, England: Cambridge University Press.

Lambdin, D. V., Kehle, P. E., & Preston, R. V. (Eds.). (1996). *Emphasis on assessment: Readings from NCTM's school-based journals.* Reston, VA: National Council of Teachers of Mathematics.

Lampert, M. (1985). How do teachers manage to teach? Perspectives on problems in practice. *Harvard Educational Review, 55,* 178–194.

Lampert, M. (1986). Knowing, doing, and teaching multiplication. *Cognition and Instruction, 3*(4), 305–342.

Lampert, M. (1988). The teacher's role in reinventing the meaning of mathematical knowing in the classroom. In *Proceedings of the North American Chapter of the Psychology of the Mathematics Education Group* (pp. 433-480). DeKalb: Northern Illinois University Press.

Lampert, M. (1990). When the problem is not the question and the solution is not the answer: Mathematical knowing and teaching. *American Educational Research Journal, 27*(1), 29–63.

Lampert, M. (1992). Practices and problems in teaching authentic mathematics. In F. K. Oser, A. Dick, & J. L. Patry (Eds.), *Effective and responsible teaching: The new synthesis.* San Francisco: Jossey–Bass.

Lampert, M. (1998). Studying teaching as a thinking practice. In J. Greeno & S. G. Goldman (Eds.), *Thinking practices* (pp. 53–78). Mahwah, NJ: Lawrence Erlbaum Associates.

Landauer, T. K. (1991). Let's get real: A position paper on the role of cognitive psychology in humanly useful and usable systems. In J. M. Carrol (Ed.), *Designing interaction* (pp. 60–73). Cambridge, MA: Cambridge University Press.

Larkin, J. H. (1981). Enriching formal knowledge: A model for learning to solve problems in physics. In J. R. Anderson (Ed.), *Cognitive skills and their acquisition* (pp. 311–334). Hillsdale, NJ: Lawrence Erlbaum Associates.

Larkin, J. H. (1983). The role of problem representation in physics. In D. Gentner & A. L. Stevens (Eds.), *Mental models* (pp. 75–98). Hillsdale, NJ: Lawrence Erlbaum Associates.

Larkin, J. H., McDermott, J., Simon, D. P., & Simon, H. A. (1980). Expert and novice performance in solving physics problems. *Science, 208,* 1335–1342.

Lash, A., & Kirkpatrick, S. L. (1994). Interrupted lessons: Teacher views of transfer student education. *American Educational Research Journal, 31*(4), 813–843.

Latour, B. (1986). Visualization and cognition: Thinking with eyes and hands. *Knowledge and Society: Studies in the Sociology of Culture Past and Present, 6,* 1–40.

Laurillard, D., & Taylor, J. (1994). Designing the Stepping Stones: An evaluation of interactive media in the classroom. *Journal of Educational Television, 20,* 169–184.

Lave, J. (1988). *Cognition in practice: Mind, mathematics and culture in everyday life.* Cambridge, MA: Cambridge University Press.

Lave, J. (1993). Word problems: A microcosm of theories of learning. In P. Light & G. Butterworth (Eds.), *Context and cognition: Ways of learning and knowing* (pp. 74–92). Hillsdale, NJ: Lawrence Erlbaum Associates.

Lave, J., & Kvale, S. (1995). What is anthropological research? An interview with Jean Lave by Steinar Kvale. *Qualitative Studies in Education, 8,* 219–228.

Lave, J., & Wenger, E. (1991). *Situated learning: Legitimate peripheral participation.* New York: Cambridge University Press.

Laws, P. (1991, July/August). Workshop physics: Learning introductory physics by doing it. *Change,* pp. 20–27.

Laws, P. (1996). A new order for mechanics. In J. M. Wilson (Ed.), *Conference on the introductory physics course* (pp. 125–136). New York: Wiley.

Lawson, A. (1977). Classroom test of formal operations.

LeCompte, M. D., & Preissle, J. (1993). *Ethnography and qualitative design in educational research* (2nd ed.). San Diego: Academic Press.

Lehrer, R., Horvath, J., & Schauble, L. (1994). Developing model based reasoning. *Interactive Learning Environments, 4*(3), 218–232.

Lein, L., Johnson, J., & Ragland, M. (1996). *Successful Texas schoolwide programs: Research study results.* Austin: Charles A. Dana Center, University of Texas.

Leinhardt, G. (1990). Capturing craft knowledge in teaching. *Educational Researcher, 19*(2), 18–25.

Lemke, J. L. (1995). *Textual politics: Discourse and social dynamics.* London: Taylor & Francis.

Lemke, J. L. (in press). Cognition, context, and learning: A social semiotic perspective. In D. Kirshner & J. A. Whitson (Eds.), *Situated cognition theory: Social, semiotic, and neurological perspectives.* Hillsdale, NJ: Lawrence Erlbaum Associates.

Lenoir, T. (1979). Descartes and the geometrization of thought: The methodological background of Descartes' geometry. *Historia Mathematica, 6,* 355–379.

Lensmire, T. J. (1991). *Intention, risk, and writing in a third grade writing workshop.* Unpublished doctoral dissertation, Michigan State University, East Lansing.

Lensmire, T. J. (1994). *When children write: Critical re–visions of the writing workshop.* New York: Teachers College Press.

Lesh, R. (1979). *Using mathematics in everyday problem solving situations* (NSF Grant NSF–79–1173). Arlington, VA: National Science Foundation.

Lesh, R. (1981). Applied mathematical problem–solving. *Educational Studies in Mathematics, 12*(2), 235–264.

Lesh, R. (1983). Conceptual analyses of problem–solving performance. In E. Silver (Ed.), *Teaching and learning mathematical problem solving* (pp. 309–329). Hillsdale, NJ: Lawrence Erlbaum Associates.

Lesh, R. (1985a). Conceptual analyses of problem solving performance. In E. Silver (Ed.), *Teaching and learning mathematical problem solving* (pp. 309–329). Hillsdale, NJ: Lawrence Erlbaum Associates.

Lesh, R. (1985b). Processes, skills and abilities needed to use mathematics in everyday situations. *Education and Urban Society, 17*(4), 439–446.

Lesh, R. (1990). Computer-based assessment of higher order understandings and processes in elementary mathematics. In G. Kulm (Ed.), *Assessing higher order thinking in mathematics* (pp. 81–110). Washington, DC: American Association for the Advancement of Science.

Lesh, R. (1998). The development of representational abilities in middle school mathematics: The development of student's representations during model eliciting activites. In I. Sigel (Ed.), *Representations and student learning.* Mahwah, NJ: Lawrence Erlbaum Associates.

Lesh, R., & Akerstrom, M. (1982). Applied problem solving: Priorities for mathematics education research. In F. Lester & J. Garofalo (Eds.), *Mathematical problem solving: Issues in research* (pp. 117–129). Philadelphia: Franklin Institute Press.

Lesh, R., Hoover, M., & Kelly, A. (1993). Equity, technology, and teacher development. In I. Wirszup & R. Streit (Eds.), *Developments in school mathematics education around the world* (Vol. 3). Reston, VA: National Council of Teachers of Mathematics.

Lesh, R., & Kaput, J. (1988). Interpreting modeling as local conceptual development. In J. DeLange & M. Doorman (Eds.), *Senior secondary mathematics education.* Utrecht, Netherlands: OW & OC.

Lesh, R., & Lamon, S. (Eds.). (1992). *Assessment of authentic performance in school mathematics.* Washington, DC: American Association for the Advancement of Science.

Lesh, R., & Lamon, S. (1994). *Assessments of authentic performance in school mathematics.* Hillsdale, NJ: Lawrence Erlbaum Associates.

Lesh, R., Post, T., & Behr, M. (1987). Representations and translations among representations in mathematics learning and problem solving. In C. Janvier (Ed.), *Problems of representation in teaching and learning mathematics.* Hillsdale, NJ: Lawrence Erlbaum Associates.

Lesh, R., Post, T., & Behr, M. (1989). Proportional reasoning. In J. Hiebert & M. Behr (Eds.), *Number concepts and operations in the middle grades* (pp. 93–118). Reston, VA: National Council of Teachers of Mathematics.

Lesh, R., & Zawojewski, J. (1987). Problem solving. In T. Post (Ed.), *Teaching mathematics in grades K–8: Research-based methods.* Boston: Allyn & Bacon.

Lester, F. K. (1994). Musing about mathematical problem solving research:1970–1994. *Journal for Research in Mathematics Education, 25*(6), 660–675.

Levidow, B., Hunt, E., & McKee, C. (1991). The Diagnoser: A HyperCard tool for building theoretically based tutorials. *Behavior Research Methods, Instruments, and Computers, 23*(2), 249–252.

Levin, P., Brenner, M. E., & McClellan, M. (1993). The social context of early literacy in Hawaiian homes. In R. N. Roberts (Ed.), *Coming home to preschool: The sociocultural context of early education* (pp. 195–219). Norwood, NJ: Ablex.

Liebovitch, L. S., Todorov, A. T., Wood, M. A., Herre, J. M., Bernstein, R. C., & Ellenbogen, K. A. (1999). Nonlinear properties of cardiac rhythm abnormalities. *Physical Review, E59,* 3312-3319.

Lincoln, Y. (1990). Toward a categorical imperative for qualitative reserch. In E. Eisner & A. Peshkin (Eds.), *Qualitative inquiry in education: The continuing debate* (pp. 277–295). New York: Teacher's College Press.

Lincoln, Y., & Guba, E. (1985). *Naturalistic inquiry.* Beverly Hills, CA: Sage.

Linde, C. (1993). *Life stories: The creation of coherence.* New York: Oxford University Press.

Lovell, K. (1972). Intellectual growth and understanding mathematics. *Journal for Research in Mathematics Education, 3*(3), 164–182.

Lucas, J. F., Branca, N., Goldberg, D., Kantowski, M. G., Kellogg, H., & Smith, J. P. (1980). A process–sequence coding system for behavioral analysis of mathematical problem solving. In G. A. Goldin & C. E. McClintock (Eds.), *Task variables in mathematical problem solving* (pp. 353–378). Philadelphia: Franklin Institute Press (subsequently acquired by Lawrence Erlbaum Associates, Hillsdale, NJ).

Luer, G., & Lass, U. (1987). *Proceedings of the Fourth European Conference on Eye Movements.* Volume 1. (p. 398). Toronto, Canada: C. J. Hogrefe, Inc.

Luger, G. F. (1980). State-space representation of problem solving behavior. In G. A. Goldin & C. E. McClintock (Eds.), *Task variables in mathematical problem solving* (pp. 311–325). Philadelphia: Franklin Institute Press (subsequently acquired by Lawrence Erlbaum Associates, Hillsdale, NJ).

Mackay, W. E. (1994). *Ethics, lies and videotape.* Paper presented at the Computer–Human Interaction '95: Mosaic of Creativity, Denver, CO.

Mager, R. (1962). *Preparing instructional objectives.* Palo Alto, CA: Fearon.

Mahoney, M. S. (1973). *The mathematical career of Pierre de Fermat.* Princeton, NJ: Princeton University Press.

Malinowski, B. (1922). *Argonauts of the Western Pacific.* London: Routledge.

Mandelbrot, B. B. (1983). *Fractals: Form, chance, and dimension.* San Francisco: Freeman.

Mandinach, E. B., & Cline, H. F. (1994a). *Classroom dynamics: Implementing a technology-based learning environment.* Hillsdale, NJ: Lawrence Erlbaum Associates.

Mandinach, E. B., & Cline, H. F. (1994b). Modeling and simulation in the secondary school curriculum: The impact on teachers. *Interactive Learning Environments, 4*(3), 271–289.

Mandinach, E. B., & Cline, H. F. (1996). Classroom dynamics: The impact of a technology–based curriculum innovation on teaching and learning. *Journal of Educational Computing Research, 14*(1), 83–102.

Marshall, C., & Rossman, G. (1995). *Designing qualitative research.* Newbury Park, CA: Sage.

Martin, J., & Sugarman, J. (1993). Beyond methodolatry: Two conceptions of relations between theory and research in research on teaching. *Educational Researcher, 22*(8), 17–24.

Maslow, A. H. (1966). *The psychology of science: A reconnaissance*. New York: Harper & Row.

Mason, J. (1994, May). *Researching from the inside in mathematics education*. Paper presented at the conference "What is research in mathematics education and what are its results?," College Park, MD.

Mathematical Sciences Education Board. (1989). *Everybody count: A report to the nation on the future of mathematics education*. Washington, DC: National Academy Press.

Mathematical Sciences Education Board. (1990). *Reshaping school mathematics*. Washington, DC: National Academy Press.

Mathematical Sciences Education Board, National Research Council. (1993a). *Measuring up: Prototypes for mathematics assessment*. Washington, DC: National Academy Press.

Mathematical Sciences Education Board, National Research Council. (1993b). *Measuring what counts: A conceptual guide for mathematics assessment*. Washington, DC: National Academy Press.

Maturana, H. (1978). Biology of language: The epistemology of language. In G. A. Miller & E. Lenneberg (Eds.), *Psychology and biology of language and thought: Essays in honor of Eric Lenneberg* (pp. 27–63). New York: Academic Press.

Matyas, M., & Malcom, S. (1991). *Investing in human potential: Science and engineering at the crossroads*. Washington, DC: American Association for the Advancement of Science.

Matz, M. (1982). Towards a process model for high school algebra errors. In D. Sleeman & J. S. Brown (Eds.), *Intelligent tutoring systems* (pp. 25–50). London: Academic Press.

Maxis. (1989). *SimCity* [Computer software]. Morago, CA: Maxis.

Maxis. (1990). *SimEarth* [Computer software]. Orinda, CA: Maxis.

Mazur, E. (1996). Understanding or memorization: Are we teaching the right thing? In J. M. Wilson (Ed.), *Conference on the introductory physics course* (pp. 113–123). New York: Wiley.

McDermott, L. (1984). An overview on conceptual understanding in physics. *Physics Today, 37*, 636–649.

McDermott, L. C. (1996). How research can guide us in improving the introductory course. In J. M. Wilson (Ed.), *Conference on the introductory physics course* (pp. 33–45). New York: Wiley.

McDermott, R. P., Gospodinoff, K., & Aron, J. (1978). Criteria for an ethnographically adequate description of activities and their contexts. *Semiotica, 24*, (245–275).

McLellan, J. A., & Dewey, J. (1895). *The psychology of number*. New York: Appleton.

McNeal, B., & Simon, M. (1994, November). *Development of classroom social norms and mathematical practices with preservice teachers*. Paper presented at the Sixteenth Annual Meeting of the North American Chapter of the International Group for the Psychology of Mathematics Education, Baton Rouge, LA.

McNeal, B. & Simon, M. (1999). Mathematics culture clash: Negotiating new classroom norms with pre-service teachers. *Journal of Mathematical Behavior, 18*.

McNeil, L. (1988). *Contradictions of control: School structure and school knowledge*. New York: Routledge.

McNiff, J. (1993). *Teaching as learning: An action research approach*. New York: Routledge.

McRobbie, C. J., & Tobin, K. (1995). Restraints to reform: The congruence of teacher and student actions in a chemistry classroom. *Journal of Research in Science Teaching, 32*, 373–385.

McRobbie, C. J., & Tobin, K. (1997). A social constructivist perspective on learning environments. *International Journal of Science Education, 19*, 193–208.

McTaggart, R. (1994). Participatory action research: Issues in theory and practice. *Educational action research, 2*(3), 313–337.

Meltzer, L. (1994). New directions in the assessment of students with special needs: The shift toward a constructivist perspective. *Journal of Special Education, 28*(3).

Mestre, J. P., Dufresne, R. J., Gerace, W. J., Hardiman, P. T., & Touger, J. S. (1992). Enhancing higher-order thinking skills in physics. In D. Halpern (Ed.), *Enhancing thinking skills in the sciences and mathematics* (pp. 77–94). Hillsdale, NJ: Lawrence Erlbaum Associates.

Mestre, J. P., Dufresne, R. J., Gerace, W. J., Hardiman, P. T., & Touger, J. S. (1993). Promoting skilled problem solving behavior among beginning physics students. *Journal of Research in Science Teaching, 30,* 303–317.

Mevarech, Z. R. (1994). The effectiveness of individualized versus cooperative computer–based integrated learning systems. *International Journal of Educational Research, 21*(1), 39–52.

Micceri, T. (1989). The unicorn, the normal curve, and other improbable creatures. *Psychological Bulletin, 105*(1), 156–166.

Miles, M. B., & Huberman, A. M. (1984). *Qualitative data analysis: A sourcebook of new methods.* Beverly Hills, CA: Sage.

Minsky, M. (1987). *The society of mind.* New York: Simon & Schuster Inc.

Minstrell, J. (1982a). Explaining the 'at rest' condition of an object. *The Physics Teacher, January.*

Minstrell, J. (1982b). Conceptual development research in the natural setting of the classroom. In M. B. Rowe (Ed.), *Education for the 80's: Science.* Washington, DC: National Education Association.

Minstrell, J. (1992). *Facets of students' knowledge and relevant instruction.* Paper presented at the international workshop "Research in Physics Learning: Theoretical Issues and Emprical Studies," Kiel, Germany.

Minstrell, J., & Stimpson, V. (1986). *Instruction for understanding: A cognitive process framework* (Final Report to NIE for NIE G-83-0059).

Mohr, M. M., & MacLean, M. S. (1987). *Working together: A guide for teacher-researchers.* Urbana, IL: National Council of Teachers of English.

Mokris, J. R., & Tinker, R. F. (1987). The impact of microcomputer–based labs on children's ability to interpret graphs. *Journal of Research in Science Teaching, 24*(4), 369–383.

Moore, T. J. (1995). *Deadly medicine.* New York: Simon & Schuster.

Moschkovich, J. N. (1992). *Making sense of linear equations and graphs: An analysis of students' conceptions and language use.* Unpublished doctoral dissertation, University of California, Berkeley.

Moschkovich, J. N. (1996). Moving up and getting steeper: Negotiating shared descriptions of linear graphs. *The Journal of the Learning Sciences, 5,* (3) 239–277.

Moschkovich, J. N. (1998). Resources for refining conceptions: Case studies in the domain or linear functions. *The Journal of the Learning Sciences, 7,* (2) 209–237.

Moschkovich, J. N. (1999). Students' use of the $x$-intercept: An instance of a transitional conception. *Educational Studies in Mathematics, 37,* 169-197.

Nagel, E. (1961). *The structure of science.* New York: Harcourt, Brace & World.

National Board for Professional Teaching Standards. (1994). *What teachers should know and be able to do.* Washington, DC: Author.

National Board for Professional Teaching Standards. (1997). *Standards.* Washington, DC: Author.

National Center for Improving Student Learning and Achievement in Mathematics and Science. (1998). *The project on models and modeling in mathematics and science education.* Madison, WI: University of Wisconsin. Available at *http://www.wcer.wisc.edu/ncisla/*

National Center of Education and the Economy and the University of Pittsburgh. (1997). *New standards performance standards,* Vol. 1 (Elementary), Vol. 2 (Middle School), Vol. 3 (High School). USA: Author.

National Commission on Excellence in Education. (1983). *A nation at risk: The imperative for educational reform.* Washington, DC: U.S. Government Printing Office.

National Council of Teachers of Mathematics. (1980). *An agenda for action: Recommendations for school mathematics of the 1980s.* Reston, VA: Author.

National Council of Teachers of Mathematics. (1989). *Curriculum and evaluation standards for school mathematics.* Reston, VA: Author.

National Council of Teachers of Mathematics. (1991a). Exploring the size of a million dollars. In *Developing number sense in the middle grades, addenda series, grades 5–8,* (p. 22). Reston, VA: Author.

National Council of Teachers of Mathematics. (1991b). *Professional standards for teaching mathematics.* Reston, VA: Author.

National Council of Teachers of Mathematics. (1992a). Alternative assessment [Focus issue]. *Arithmetic Teacher, 85*(8).

National Council of Teachers of Mathematics. (1992b). Alternative assessment [Theme issue]. *Mathematics Teacher, 85*(8).

National Council of Teachers of Mathematics. (1995). *Assessment standards for school mathematics.* Reston, VA: Author.

National Institute for Science Education. (1996). Principles of effective professional development for mathematics and science education: A synthesis of standards. *NISE BRIEF, 1.*

National Research Council. (1989). *Everybody counts: A report to the nation on the future of mathematics education.* Washington, DC: National Academy Press.

National Research Council. (1996). *National science education standards.* Washington, DC: National Academy Press.

National Science Board Commission on Precollege Education in Mathematics Science and Technology. (1983). *Educating Americans for the 21st century: A plan of action for improving the mathematics, science and technology education for all American elementary and secondary students so that their achievement is the best in the world by 1995.* Washington, DC: National Science Foundation.

National Science Foundation. (1996). *Instrument for annual report of progress in systemic reform.* Washington, DC: Author.

Nemirovsky, R., Tierney, C., & Wright, T. (1995, April). Body motion and graphing. Paper presented at the annual meeting of the American Educational Research Association, San Francisco.

Nersessian, N. (1984). *Faraday to Einstein: Constructing meaning in scientific explanation.* Dordrecht, Netherlands: Martinus Nijhoff.

Nersessian, N. (1992). How do scientists think? Capturing the dynamics of conceptual change in science. In R. Giere (Ed.), *Cognitive models of science.* Minneapolis: University of Minnesota Press.

Newell, A., & Simon, H. A. (1972). *Human problem solving.* Englewood Cliffs, NJ: Prentice-Hall.

Newman, D. (1990). Opportunities for research on the organizational impact of school computers. *Educational Researcher, 19*(3), 8–13.

Newman, D., Griffin, P., & Cole, M. (1989). *The construction zone: Working for cognitive change in school.* New York: Cambridge University Press.

Newmann, F. M., & Associates. (Eds.). (1996). *Authentic achievement: Restructuring schools for intellectual quality.* San Francisco: Jossey-Bass.

Newton, I. (1967). *The mathematical papers of Isaac Newton.* Cambridge, England: Cambridge University Press.

Niedderer, H., Schecker, H., & Bethge, T. (1991). The role of computer aided modeling in learning physics, *Computer Aided Learning.*

Nisbett, R., & Wilson, T. (1977). Telling more than we can know: Verbal reports on mental processes. *Psychological Review, 84,* 231–259.

Noble, T., Flerlage, D., & Confrey, J. (1993). *Experiment, simulation, and analysis: Teaching and learning in an integrated physics and mathematics class.* Atlanta: American Education Research Association.

Noddings, N. (1985). Formal modes of knowing. In E. Eisner (Ed.), *Learning and teaching the ways of knowing: Eighty-fourth yearbook of the National Society for the Study of Education, Part II*. Chicago: University of Chicago Press.

Noddings, N. (1990). Constructivism in mathematics education. In R. B. Davis, C. A. Maher, & N. Noddings (Eds.), *Constructivist views on the teaching and learning of mathematics* (pp. 7–18). Reston, VA: National Council of Teachers of Mathematics.

Noffke, S. (1994). Action research: Towards the next generation. *Educational Action Research, 2*(1), 9–21.

Noffke, S. (1996). Professional, personal, and political dimensions of action research. In M. Apple (Ed.), *Review of research in education*, (Vol. 22). Washington, DC: American Educational Research Association.

Noffke, S. E., & Stevenson, R. B. (Eds.). (1995). *Educational action research: Becoming practically critical*. New York: Teachers College Press.

Norman, D. A. (1991). *The psychology of everyday things*. New York: Basic Books.

Norman, D. A., & Spohrer, J. C. (1996). Learner–centered education. *Communications of the ACM, 39*(4), 24–27.

Noss, R., & Hoyles, C. (1992). Afterword: Looking back and looking forward. In C. Hoyles & R. Noss (Eds.), *Learning mathematics and Logo* (pp. 427–468). Cambridge, MA: MIT Press.

Nunes, T. (1992). Ethnomathematics and everyday cognition. In D. A. Grouws (Ed.), *Handbook of research on mathematical teaching and learning* (pp. 557–574). New York: Macmillan.

Nunes, T., Schliemann, A. D., & Carraher, D. W. (1993). *Street mathematics and school mathematics*. New York: Cambridge University Press.

Ochs, E. (1979). Transcription as theory. In E. Ochs & B. Schieffelin (Eds.), *Developmental pragmatics* (pp. 43–72). New York: Academic Press.

O'Day, J. A., & Smith, M. (1993). Systemic reform and educational opportunity. In S. H. Fuhrman (Ed.), *Designing coherent education policy: Improving the system* (pp. 250–312). San Francisco: Jossey-Bass.

Office of Technology Assessment. (1988). *Power on! New tools for teaching and learning*. Washington, DC: U.S. Government Printing Office.

Oja, S., & Smulyan, L. (1989). *Collaborative action research: A developmental approach*. New York: Falmer Press.

Olive, J. (1991). Logo programming and geometric understanding: An in–depth study. *Journal for Research in Mathematics Education, 22*, 90–111.

Olive, J. (1996, July). *Constructing multiplicative operations with fractions using tools for interactive mathematical activity (TIMA) microworlds*. Paper presented at the meeting of the Eighth International Congress on Mathematical Education (ICME–8), Topic Group 19, Seville, Spain.

Olson, D. (1994). *The world on paper: The conceptual and cognitive implications of writing and reading*. Cambridge, England: Cambridge University Press.

Osborne, M. D. (1993). *Teaching with and without mirrors: Examining science teaching in elementary school from the perspective of a teacher and learner*. Unpublished doctoral dissertation, Michigan State University, East Lansing.

Paley, V. G. (1979). *White teacher*. Cambridge, MA: Harvard University Press.

Paley, V. G. (1981). *Wally's stories*. Cambridge, MA: Harvard University Press.

Paley, V. G. (1995). *Kwanzaa and me: A teacher's story*. Cambridge, MA: Harvard University Press.

Palincsar, A. S., Anderson, C., & David, Y. M. (1993). Pursuing literacy in the middle grades through collaborative problem solving. *The Elementary School Journal, 93*, 643–658.

Papert, S. (1980). *Mindstorms: Children, computers, and powerful ideas*. New York: Basic Books.

Papert, S. (1987). Computer criticism vs. technocentric thinking. *Educational Researcher, 16*, 22–30.

Papert, S. (1991). Situating constructionism. In I. Harel & S. Papert (Eds.), *Constructionism*. Norwood, NJ: Ablex.

Patai, D. (1994, February 23). Sick and tired of nouveau solipsism. *The Chronicle of Higher Education*.

Patton, M. (1980). *Qualitative evaluation methods*. Beverly Hills, CA: Sage.

Patton, M. Q. (1990). *Qualitative evaluation and research methods*. Newbury Park, CA: Sage.

Pea, R. D. (1986, April). *Beyond amplification: Using computers to reorganize mental functioning*. Paper presented at the annual meeting of the American Educational Research Association, Chicago.

Pea, R. D. (1993a). Distributed multimedia learning environments: The collaborative visualization project. *Communications of the ACM, 36*(5), 60–63.

Pea, R. D. (1993b). Practices of distributed intelligence and designs for education. In G. Salomon (Ed.), *Distributed cognitions: Psychological and educational considerations* (pp. 47–87). New York: Cambridge University Press.

Pea, R. D. (1994). Seeing what we build together: Distributed multimedia learning environments for transformative communications. *Journal of the Learning Sciences, 3*(3), 283–298.

Peirce, C. S. (1958). *Collected papers* (8 Vols.) (C. Hartshorne, P. Weiss, & A. Burks, Eds.). Cambridge, MA: Harvard University Press.

Pennock–Roman, M. (1994). *Background characteristics and future plans of high–scoring GRE general test examinees* (ETS Research Rep. No. RR-94-12). Princeton, NJ: Educational Testing Service.

Phillips, D. (1987). Validity in qualitative research: Why the worry about warrants will not wane. *Education and Urban Society, 20*(1), 9–24.

Piaget, J. (1964). Development and learning. In R. E. Ripple & V. N. Rockcastle (Eds.), *Piaget rediscovered: Report of the conference on cognitive studies and curriculum development*. Ithaca, NY: Cornell University Press.

Piaget, J. (1965). *The child's conception of number*. New York: Norton.

Piaget, J. (1970a). *The child's conception of movement and speed*. New York: Basic Books. (Original work published 1946)

Piaget, J. (1970b). *Structuralism*. New York: Basic Books.

Piaget, J. (1975). *The child's conception of the world*. Totowa, NJ: Littlefield, Adams.

Piaget, J. (1980). The psychogenesis of knowledge and its epistemological significance. In M. Piattelli–Palmarini (Ed.), *Language and learning: The debate between Jean Piaget and Noam Chomsky* (pp. 23–34). Cambridge, MA: Harvard University Press.

Piaget, J., & Beth, E. (1966). *Mathematical epistemology and psychology*. Dordrecht, Netherlands: D. Reidel.

Piaget, J., & Garcia, G. (1989). *Psychogenesis and the history of science*. New York: Columbia University Press.

Piaget, J., & Inhelder, B. (1958). *The growth of logical thinking from childhood to adolescence*. London: Routledge & Kegan Paul.

Piaget, J., & Inhelder, B. (1967). *The child's conception of space*. New York: Norton.

Piaget, J., & Inhelder, B. (1974). *The child's conception of quantities*. Boston: Routledge & Kegan Paul.

Piaget, J. & Szeminska, A. (1952). *The child's conception of number*. London: Routledge & Kegan Paul.

Piliero, S. (1994). *An investigation of teacher knowledge, beliefs and practices in the implementation of a problem-based curriculum using multi-representational software in a technology-rich classroom*. Unpublished doctoral dissertation, Cornell University, Ithaca, NY.

Pimm, D. (1987). *Speaking mathematically: Communication in mathematics classrooms*. London: Routledge & Kegan Paul.

Popper, K. R. (1965). Towards a rational theory of tradition. In K. R. Popper (Ed.), *Conjectures and refutations: The growth of scientific knowledge.* New York: Harper & Row.

Porter, A. C., Archbald, D. A., & Tyree, A. K., Jr. (1991). Reforming the curriculum: Will empowerment policies replace control? In S. Fuhrman & B. Malen (Eds.), *The politics of curriculum and testing* (pp. 11–36). Bristol, PA: Falmer Press.

Post, T., Behr, M., Lesh, R., & Harel, G. (1988). Intermediate teachers' knowledge of rational number concepts. In E. Fennema, T. Carpenter, S. J. Lamon (Eds.), *Integrating research on teaching and learning mathematics.* Madison, WI: National Center for Research in the Mathematical Sciences Education.

Post, T., Lesh, R., Cramer, K., Behr, M., & Harel, G. (1993). Curriculum implications of research on the learning, teaching, and assessing of rational number concepts. In T. Carpenter, E. Fennema, & T. Romberg (Eds.), *Rational numbers: An integration of research.* Hillsdale, NJ: Lawrence Erlbaum Associates.

Powers, W. (1973). *Behavior: The control of perception.* Chicago: Aldine.

Powers, W. (1978). Quantitative analysis of purposive systems: Some spadework at the foundations of scientific psychology. *Psychological Review, 85*(5), 417–435.

Presmeg, N. C. (1992). Prototypes, metaphors, metonymies and imaginative reality in high school mathematics. *Educational Studies in Mathematics, 23,* 595–610.

Preyer, R. (1996). *Tool based investigation and the development of experiences that support mathematical understanding.* Unpublished master's thesis, Cornell University, Ithaca, NY.

Raizen, S. A., & Britton, E. D. (Eds.). (1996–1997). *Bold ventures.* (Vols. 1–3). Dordrecht, Netherlands: Kluwer.

Raymond, A., Rafferty, C., & Dutt, K. (Eds.). (1996). *Collaborative action research: Case studies of school–university initiatives.* Terre Haute: Indiana State University, School of Education, Curriculum Research and Development Center.

Reason, P. (1994). Three approaches to participative inquiry. In N. K. Denzin & Y. S. Lincoln (Eds.), *Handbook of qualitative research* (pp. 324–339). Thousand Oaks, CA: Sage.

Reddy, M. (1979). The conduit metaphor: A case of frame conflict in our language about language. In A. Ortony (Ed.), *Metaphor and thought.* New York: Cambridge University Press.

Redish, E. F. (1996). What can a physics teacher do with a computer? In J. M. Wilson (Ed.), *Conference on the introductory physics course* (pp. 47–60). New York: Wiley.

Redish, E. F., Wilson, J. M., & McDaniel, C. (1992). The CUPLE Project: A hyper- and multimedia approach to restructuring physics education. In E. Barrett (Ed.), *Sociomedia—Multimedia, hypermedia, and the social construction of knowledge* (pp. 119–155). Cambridge, MA: MIT Press.

Reif, F., & Allen, S. (1992). Cognition for interpreting scientific concepts: A study of acceleration. *Cognition and Instruction, 9*(1), 1–44.

Reiss, F. (1995). *Teaching science and the history of science by redoing historical experiments.* Paper presented at the Third International History, Philosophy and Science Teaching Confrerence, Minneapolis, MN.

Resnick, L., & Ford, W. W. (1981). *The psychology of mathematics for instruction.* Hillsdale, NJ: Lawrence Erlbaum Associates.

Resnick, L. B., Nesher, P., Leonard, F., Magone, M., Omanson, S., & Peled, I. (1989). Conceptual bases of arithmetic errors: The case of decimal fractions. *Journal for Research in Mathematics Education, 20*(1), 8–27.

Resnick, L. B., Salmon, M., Zeitz, C. M., Wathen, S. H., & Holowchak, M. (1993). Reasoning and conversation. *Cognition and Instruction, 11*(3 & 4), 347–364.

Resnick, M., & Ocko, S. (1991). LEGO/Logo: Learning through about design. In I. Harel & S. Papert (Eds.), *Constructivism* (pp. 141–150). Norwood, NJ: Ablex.

Rheinfrank, J., & Evenson, S. (1996). Design Languages. In T. Winograd (Ed.), *Bringing design to software* (pp. 63–80). New York: Addison-Wesley.

Richmond, B. (1985). *STELLA* [Computer software]. Lyme, NH: High Performance Systems.

Riel, M., & Levin, J. (1990). Building electronic communities: Successes and failures in computer networking. *Instructional Science, 19*, 145–169.

Robinson, V. (1993). *Problem-based methodology: Research for the improvement of practice.* Oxford, England: Pergamon.

Roblyer, M. D., Castine, W. H., & King, F. J. (1988). *Assessing the impact of computer-based instruction: A review of recent research.* New York: Haworth Press.

Romberg, T. A. (1992a). Perspectives on scholarship and research methods. In D. A. Grouws (Ed.), *Handbook of research on mathematics teaching and learning* (pp. 49–64). New York: Macmillan.

Romberg, T. A. (1992b). Problematic features of the school mathematics curriculum. In P. Jackson (Ed.), *Handbook on research on curriculum* (pp. 749–788). New York: Macmillan.

Romberg, T. A., & Carpenter, T. P. (1986). Research on teaching and learning mathematics: Two disciplines of inquiry. In M. C. Wottrock (Ed.), *Handbook of reasearch on teaching* (pp. 850–873). New York: Macmillan.

Romberg, T., Fennema, E., & Carpenter, T. (1993). *Integrating research on the graphical representation of functions.* Hillsdale, NJ: Lawrence Erlbaum Associates.

Romberg, T. A., Wilson, L., & Khaketla, M. (1991). *The alignment of six standardized tests with the NCTM Standards.* Madison: University of Wisconsin Press.

Roschelle, J. (1996). Designing for cognitive communication: Epistemic fidelity or mediating collaborating inquiry. In D. L. Day & D. K. Kovacs (Eds.), *Computers, communication and mental models* (pp. 13–25). London: Taylor & Francis.

Roschelle, J., & Kaput, J. (1996a). Educational software architecture and systemic impact: The promise of component software. *Journal of Educational Computing Research, 14*(3), 217–228.

Roschelle, J., & Kaput, J. (1996b). SimCalc MathWorlds for mathematics of change. *Communications, 39*(8), 97–99.

Roschelle, J., Kaput, J., Stroup, W., & Kahn, T. (1998). Scalable integration of educational software: Exploring the promise of component architectures. *Journal of Interactive Media in Education. http://www–jime.open.ac.uk/98/6.*

Rosenblueth, A., & Wiener, N. (1945). The role of models in science. *Philosophy of Science, 12,* 316–321.

Rosenthal, W. (1994, February). *Student voice in an "improbable context": Telling underground calculus tales in school.* Paper presented at the Fifteenth Annual Ethnography in Education Research Forum, University of Pennsylvania, Philadelphia.

Rudwick, M. J. S. (1992). *Scences from deep time: Early pictorial representations of the prehistoric world.* Chicago: University of Chicago Press.

Ruopp, R., Gal, S., Drayton, B., & Pfister, M. (Eds.). (1993). *LabNet: Towards a community of practice.* New York: Lawrence Erlbaum Associates.

Rutherford, F. J., & Ahlgren, A. (1990). *Science for all Americans.* New York: Oxford University Press.

Rutherford, F., Holton, G., & Watson, F. (1970). *Project physics text.* New York: Holt, Rinehart & Winston.

Sachs, R. (1987). *The physics of time reversal.* Chicago: University of Chicago Press.

Sacks, H. (1992). *Lectures on conversation.* Oxford, England: Blackwell.

Sagor, R. (1992). *How to conduct action research.* Alexandria, VA: Association for Supervision and Curriculum Development.

Salomon, G. (1993). No distribution without individuals' cognition: A dynamic interactional view. In G. Salomon (Ed.), *Distributed cognition: Psychological and educational considerations.* New York: Cambridge University Press.

Sarama, J. (1995). *Redesigning Logo: The turtle metaphor in mathematics education.* Unpublished doctoral dissertation, State University of New York, Buffalo.

Sarama, J., Clements, D., & Henry, J. J. (in press). Network of influences in an implementation of a mathematics curriculum innovation. *International Journal of Computers for Mathematical Learning.*

Sawilowsky, S. (1990). Nonparametic tests of interaction in experimental design. *Review of educational research, 60*(1), 91–126.

Saxe, G. B. (1991). *Culture and cognitive development: Studies in mathematical understanding.* Hillsdale, NJ: Lawrence Erlbaum Associates.

Saxe, G. B., & Bermudez, T. (1996). Emergent mathematical environments in children's games. In P. Nesher, L. P. Steffe, P. Cobb, G. Goldin, & B. Greer (Eds.), *Theories of mathematical learning* (pp. 51–68). Hillsdale, NJ: Lawrence Erlbaum Associates.

Scarano, G. H., & Confrey, J. (1996, April). *Results from a three–year longitudinal teaching experiment designed to investigate splitting, ratio and proportion.* Paper presented at the annual meeting of the American Education Research Association, New York.

Schauble, L. (1990). Formative evaluation in the design of educational software at the Children's Television Workshop. In B. N. Flagg (Ed.), *Formative evaluation for educational technologies* (pp. 51–66). Hillsdale, NJ: Lawrence Erlbaum Associates.

Scheffler, I. (1975). *Basic mathematical skills: Some philosophical and practical remarks.* Los Alamitos, CA: SWRL Educational Research and Development.

Schegloff, E. A. (1984). On some gestures' relation to talk. In J. Maxwell & J. Heritage (Eds.), *Structures of social action* (pp. 266–296). New York: Cambridge University Press.

Schifter, D. (Ed.). (1996a). *What's happening in math class? Envisioning new practices through teacher narratives* (Vol. 1). New York: Teachers College Press.

Schifter, D. (Ed.). (1996b). *What's happening in math class? Reconstructing professional identities* (Vol. 2). New York: Teachers College Press.

Schifter, D., & Fosnot, C. T. (1993). *Reconstructing mathematics education: Stories of teachers meeting the challenge of reform.* New York: Teachers College Press.

Schmidt, F. L. (1996). Statistical significance testing and cumulative knowledge in psychology: Implications for training of researchers. *Psychological Methods, 1*(2), 115–129.

Schmidt, G., Ulm, K., Barthel, P., Goedel–Meinen, L., Jahns, G., & Baedeker, W. (1988). Spontaneous variability of simple and complex ventricular premature contractions during long time intervals in patients with severe organic heart disease. *Circulation, 78,* 296–301.

Schoenfeld, A. H. (1983). Beyond the purely cognitive: Belief systems, social cognitions, and metacognitions as driving forces in intellectual performance. *Cognitive Science, 7,* 329–363.

Schoenfeld, A. H. (1985). Making sense of "out loud" problem solving protocols. *The Journal of Mathematical Behavior, 4,* 171–191.

Schoenfeld, A. H. (1987a). *Cognitive science and mathematics education.* Hillsdale, NJ: Lawrence Erlbaum Associates.

Schoenfeld, A. H. (1987b). Cognitive science and mathematics education: An overview. In A. H. Schoenfeld (Ed.), *Cognitive science and mathematics education.* Hillsdale, NJ: Lawrence Erlbaum Associates.

Schoenfeld, A. H. (1992). Learning to think mathematically. In D. Grouws (Ed.), *Handbook for research on mathematics teaching and learning* (pp. 334–370). New York: Macmillan.

Schoenfeld, A. H., Smith, J. P., & Arcavi, A. (1993). Learning: The microgenetic analysis of one student's evolving understanding of a complex subject matter domain. In R. Glaser (Ed.), *Advances in instructional psychology* (Vol. 4, pp. 55–175). Hillsdale, NJ: Lawrence Erlbaum Associates.

Schön, D. A. (1983). *The reflective practitioner: How professionals think in action.* New York: Basic Books.

Schön, D. A. (1987). *Educating the reflective practitioner: Toward a new design for teaching and learning in the professions.* San Francisco: Jossey-Bass.

Schön, D. A. (1991). *The reflective turn: Case studies in and on educational practice.* New York: Teachers College Press.

Schön, D. A. (1995, Nov./Dec.). Knowing-in-action: The new scholarship requires a new epistemology. *Change,* pp. 27–34.

Schooten, F. V. (1657). *Exercitationum mathematicorum, Liber IV, organica coniccarum sectionum in plano descriptione.* Leiden.

Schrage, M. (1996). The culture(s) of prototyping. *Design Management Journal, 4*(1), 55–65.

Schuler, D., & Namioka, A. (1993). *Participatory design: Principles and practices.* Hillsdale, NJ: Lawrence Erlbaum Associates.

Scribner, S. (1984). Studying working intelligence. In B. R. J. Lave (Ed.), *Everyday cognition: Its development in social context* (pp. 9–40). Cambridge, MA: Harvard University Press.

Searle, J. (1984). *Minds, brains and science.* Cambridge, MA: Harvard University Press.

Secada, W. G. (1992). Race, ethnicity, social class, language and achievement in mathematics. In D. A. Grouws (Ed.), *Handbook of research on mathematics teaching and learning* (pp. 623–660). New York: Macmillan.

Sfard, A. (1991). On the dual nature of mathematical conceptions: Reflections on processes and objects as different sides of the same coin. *Educational Studies in Mathematics, 22,* 1–36.

Sfard, A. (1994, September). *The development of the concept of concept development: From God's eye view to what can be seen with the mind's eye.* Paper presented at the symposium on Trends and Perspectives in Mathmatics Education, Klagenfurt, Austria.

Shavelson, R. J., & Baxter, G. P. (1992). What we've learned about assessing hands-on science. *Educational Leadership, 49*(8), 20–25.

Shimahara, N. (1988). Anthroethnography: A methodological considerarion. In R. R. Sherman & R. B. Webb (Eds.), *Qualitative research in education: Focus and methods* (pp. 76–89). Philadelphia: Falmer Press.

Shlain, L. (1991). *Art & physics: Parallel visions in space, time & light.* New York: Morrow.

Shulman, L. S. (1985). On teaching problem solving and solving problems of teaching. In E. Silver (Ed.), *Teaching and learning mathematical problem solving: Multiple research perspectives* (pp. 439–450). Hillsdale, NJ: Lawrence Erlbaum Associates.

Shulman, L. S. (1986). Those who understand: Knowledge growth in teaching. *Educational Researcher, 15*(2), 4–14.

Shumway, R. J. (Ed.). (1980). *Research in mathematics education.* Reston, VA: National Council of Teachers of Mathematics.

Siegel, S. (1956). *Non–parametric statistics for the behavioral sciences.* New York: McGraw–Hill.

Sierpinska, A. (1993). Criteria for scientific quality and relevance in the didactics of mathematics. In G. Nissen & M. Blomhoj (Eds.), *Criteria for scientific quality and relevance in the didactics of mathematics* (pp. 36–74). Roskilde: Danish Research Council for the Humanities.

Silva, C. M., Moses, R. P., Rivers, J., & Johnson, P. (1990). The algebra project: Making middle schools mathematics count. *Journal of Negro Education, 59*(3), 375–390.

Silver, E. A., & Cai, J. (1996). An analysis of arithmetic problem posing by middle school students. *Journal for Research in Mathematics Education, 27*(5), 521–539.

Simon, D. P., & Simon, H. A. (1978). Individual differences in solving physics problems. In R. Siegler (Ed.), *Children's thinking: What develops?* (pp. 325–348). Hillsdale, NJ: Lawrence Erlbaum Associates.

Simon, M. (1995). Reconstructing mathematics pedagogy from a constructivist perspective. *Journal for Research in Mathematics Education, 26*(2), 114–145.

Simon, M. (1989). *The impact of intensive classroom followup in a constructivist mathematics teacher education program*. Paper presented at the annual meeting of the American Educational Research Association, San Francisco.

Simon, M. (1997). Developing new models of mathematics teaching: An imperative for research on mathematics teacher development. In E. Fennema & B. Nelson (Eds.), *Mathematics teachers in transition* (pp. 55–86). Mahwah, NJ: Lawrence Erlbaum Associates.

Simon, M., & Blume, G. (1994a). Building and understanding multiplicative relationships: A study of prospective elementary teachers. *Journal for Research in Mathematics Education, 25*(5), 472–494.

Simon, M., & Blume, G. (1994b). Mathematical modeling as a component of understanding ratio–as–measure: A study of prospective elementary teachers. *Journal of Mathematical Behavior, 13*, 183–197.

Simon, M., & Blume, G. (1996). Justification in the mathematics classroom: A study of prospective elementary teachers. *Journal of Mathematical Behavior, 15*, 3–31.

Simon, M., & Schifter, D. (1991). Towards a constructivist perspective: An intervention study of mathematics teacher development. *Educational Studies in Mathematics, 22*, 309–331.

Simon, M., & Tzur, R. (1999). Explicating the teacher's perspective from the researchers' perspectives: Generating accounts of mathematics teachers' practice. *JRME, 30*, 252-264.

Sinclair, H. (1987, July). *Constructivism and the psychology of mathematics*. Paper presented at the Eleventh International Confrence on the Psychology of Mathematics Education, Montreal.

Skemp, R. (1976, December). Relational understanding and instrumental understanding. *Mathematics Teaching, 77*, 20–26.

Skinner, B. F. (1953). *Science and human behavior*. New York: The Free Press.

Skinner, B. F. (1968). *The technology of teaching*. Englewood Cliffs, NJ: Prentice–Hall.

Skinner, B. F. (1974). *About behaviorism*. New York: Knopf.

Skinner, B. F. (1978). *Reflections on behaviorism and society*. Englewood Cliffs, NJ: Prentice-Hall.

Skovsmose, O. (1994). Towards a critical mathematics education. *Educational Studies in Mathematics Education, 27*(1), 35–57.

Smight, J. D. (1969). *The illustrated man* [Film]. (Available from Warner Home Video).

Smith, E. E., Shoben, E. J., & Rips, L. J. (1974). Structure and process in semantic memory: A featural model for semantic decisions. *Psychological Review, 81*, 214–241.

Smith, J. K. (1989). *The nature of social and educational inquiry: Empiricism versus interpretation*. Norwood, NJ: Ablex.

Smith, M. L. (1987). Publishing qualitative research. *American Educational Research Journal, 24*(2), 173–183.

Snir, J., Smith, C., & Grosslight, L. (1993). Conceptual–enhanced simulations: A computer tool for science teaching. *Journal of Science Education and Technology, 2*(2), 373–388.

Sockett, H. (1993). *The moral base for teacher professionalism*. New York: Teachers College Press.

Soloway, E., & Guzdial, M. (1996). Designing for learners. In M. Guzdial & F. W. Weingarten (Eds.), *Setting a computer science research agenda for educational technology* (pp. 10–22). Washington, DC: Computing Research Association.

Sowder, J. T. (Ed.). (1989). *Research agenda in mathematics education: Setting a research agenda*. Reston, VA: National Council of Teachers of Mathematics.

Spindler, G., & Spindler, L. (1987). Ethnography: An anthropological view. In G. Spindler (Ed.), *Education and cultural process* (pp. 151–156). Prospect Heights, IL: Waveland Press.

Spradley, J. P. (1979). *The ethnographic interview*. New York: Holt, Rhinehart & Winston.

Spradley, J. P. (1980). *Participant observation*. New York: Holt, Rhinehart & Winston.

Stake, R. (1978). The case study method in social inquiry. *Educational Researcher, 7*(2), 5–8.

Stake, R. E. (1988). Case study methods in educational research: Seeking sweet water. In R. M. Jaeger (Ed.), *Complementary methods for research in education* (pp. 253–265). Washington, DC: American Educational Research Association.

Star, S. L. (1983). Simplification in scientific work: An example from neuroscience research. *Social Studies of Science, 13*, 206–228.

Steen, L. A. (1990). Pattern. In L. A. Steen (Ed.), *On the shoulders of giants: New approaches to numeracy* (pp. 1–10). Washington, D.C.: National Academy Press.

Steffe, L. P. (1991). The constructivist teaching experiment: Illustrations and implications. In E. v. Glasersfeld (Ed.), *Radical constructivism in mathematics education*, (pp. 177–194). The Netherlands: Kluwer.

Steffe, L. P. (1983). *The teaching experiment methodology in a constructivist research program.* Paper presented at the Fourth International Congress on Mathematical Education, Boston.

Steffe, L. P. (1988). Children's construction of number sequences and multiplying schemes. In J. Hiebert & M. Behr (Eds.), *Number concepts and operations in the middle grades* (pp. 119–140). Hillsdale, NJ: Lawrence Erlbaum Associates.

Steffe, L. P. (1995). Alternative epistemologies: An educator's perspective. In L. P. Steffe & J. Gale (Eds.), *Constructivism in education* (pp. 489–523). Hillsdale, NJ: Lawrence Erlbaum Associates.

Steffe, L. P. (1996, April). *Teaching experiment methodology: Underlying principles and essential elements.* Paper presented at the NCTM Research Presession, San Diego.

Steffe, L. P., & Cobb, P. (1988). *Construction of arithmetical meanings and strategies.* New York: Springer-Verlag.

Steffe, L. P., Cobb, P., & von Glaserfeld, E. (1988). *Constructions of arithmetical meanings and strategies.* New York: Springer-Verlag.

Steffe, L. P., & D'Ambrosio, B. S. (1995). Toward a working model of constructivist teaching: A reaction to Simon. *Journal for Research in Mathematics Education, 26*(2), 146–159.

Steffe, L. P., & Gale, J. (Eds.). (1995). *Constructivism in education.* Hillsdale, NJ: Lawrence Erlbaum Associates.

Steffe, L. P., Hirstein, J., & Spikes, W. C. (1976). *Quantitative comparisons and class inclusion as readiness variables for learning first grade arithmetical content* (PMDC Report No. 9). Athens: University of Georgia, Department of Mathematics Education.

Steffe, L. P., & Kieran, T. (1994). Radical constructivism and mathematics education. *Journal for Research in Mathematics Education, 25*(6), 711–733.

Steffe, L. P., Nesher, P., Cobb, P., Goldin, G. A., & Greer, B. (Eds.). (1996). *Theories of mathematical learning.* Mahwah, NJ: Lawrence Erlbaum Associates.

Steffe, L. P., & Tzur, R. (1994). Interaction and children's mathematics. *Journal of Research in Childhood Education, 8*(2), 99–116.

Steffe, L. P., & Wiegel, H. (1992). On reforming practice in mathematics education. *Educational Studies in Mathematics, 23*, 445–465.

Steffe, L. P., & Wiegel, H. (1994). Cognitive play and mathematical learning in computer microworlds. In P. Cobb (Ed.), *Learning mathematics: Constructivist and interactionist theories of mathematical development*, (pp. 7–30). Dordrecht, Netherlands: Kluwer.

Steier, F. (1995). From universing to conversing: A ecological constructionist approach to leaning and multiple description. In L. P. Steffe & J. Gale (Eds.), *Constructivism in education* (pp. 647–684). Hillsdale, NJ: Lawrence Erlbaum Associates.

Stenhouse, L. (1975). *An introduction to curriculum research and development.* London: Heinemann.

Stevens, R., & Hall, R. (in press). Disciplined perception: Learning to see in technoscience. In M. Lampert & M. Blunk (Eds.), *Mathematical talk and school learning: What, when, why.* New York: Cambridge University Press.

Stevens, S. S. (1946). On the theory of scales of measurement. *Science, 103*, 677–680.

Stevens, S. S. (1951). *Handbook of experimental psychology.* New York: Wiley.

Stigler, J. W. (1995). *Large–scale video surveys for the study of classroom processes.* Washington, DC: U.S. Department of Education.

Stolzenberg, G. (1984). Can an inquiry into the foundations of mathematics tell us anything interesting about mind? In P. Watzlawick (Ed.), *The invented reality: How do we know what we believe we know?* (pp. 257–308). New York: Norton.

Strauss, A., & Corbin, J. (1990). *Basics of qualitative research: Grounded theory procedures and techniques.* Newbury Park, CA: Sage.

Strauss, S., & Stavy, R. (1982). *U-shaped behavioral growth.* New York: Academic Press.

Streeck, J. (1979). Sandwich. Good for you. In J. Dittman (Ed.), *Arbeiten zur knoversations alyse* (pp. 235–257). Tubingen, Germany: Niemeyer.

Streefland, L. (1991). *Fractions in realistic mathematics education.* Dordrecht, Netherlands: Kluwer.

Street, B. (1984). *Literacy in theory and practice.* Cambridge, England: Cambridge University Press.

Strike, K., & Posner, G. (1982). Conceptual change and science teaching. *European Journal of Science Education, 4*(3), 231–240.

Stroup, W. (1994). *What the development of non–universal understanding look like: An investigation of results from a series of qualitative calculus assessments* (Tech. Rep. No. TR94-1). Cambridge, MA: Harvard University, Educational Technology Center.

Stroup, W. (1996). *Embodying a nominalist constructivism: Making graphical sense of learning the calculus of how much and how fast.* Unpublished doctoral dissertation, Harvard University, Cambridge, MA.

Struik, D. J. (1969). *A source book in mathematics, 1200–1800.* Cambridge, MA: Harvard University Press.

Suchman, L. A. (1987). *Plans and situated actions: The problem of human–machine communication.* Cambridge, England: Cambridge University Press.

Suchman, L. A., & Trigg, R. H. (1991). Understanding practice: Video as a medium for reflection and design. In J. Greenbaum & M. Kyng (Eds.), *Design at work: Cooperative design of computer systems* (pp. 65–90). Hillsdale, NJ: Lawrence Erlbaum Associates.

Sund, R., & Picard, A. (1972). *Behavioral objectives and evaluational measures: Science and mathematics.* Columbus, OH: Merrill.

Suppe, F. (1977). *The structure of scientific theories.* (2nd Ed.). Chicago: University of Illinois Press.

Suter, L. E. (1996). *The learning curve: What we are discovering about U.S. science and mathematics education* (NSF-96-53). Washington, DC: National Science Foundation, Division of Research, Evaluation and Communication, Directorate for Education and Human Resources.

Suzuka, K. (1996, April). *The impossible role of the teacher educator.* Paper presented at the annual meeting of the American Educational Research Association, Chicago.

Sweller, J. (1992). Cognitive theories and their implications for mathematics instruction. In G. Leder (Ed.), *Assessment and learning of mathematics.* Hawthorn: Australian Council for Educational Research.

Swijtink, D. (1987). The objectification of observation: Measurement and statistical methods in the nineteenth century. In L. Kruger, L. Daston, & M. Heidelberger (Eds.), *The probabilistic revolution* (Vol. 2). Cambridge, MA: MIT Press.

Tall, D. (1989). Concept images, generic organizers, computers, and curriculum change. *For the Learning of Mathematics, 9*(3), 37–42.

Tate, W. F. (1995a). Economics, equity, and the national mathematics assessment: Are we creating a national toll road? In W. G. Secada, E. Fennema, & L. B. Adajian (Eds.), *New directions for equity in mathematics education* (pp. 191–204). New York: Cambridge University Press.

Tate, W. F. (1995b). School mathematics and African American students: Thinking seriously about opportunity-to-learn standards. *Educational Administration Quarterly, 31,* 424–448.

Tatsuoka, C. M., Varadi, F., & Tatsuoka, K. K. (1992). *BUGSHELL2* [Computer software]. Trenton, NJ: Tanar Software.

Tatsuoka, K. K. (1983). Rule space: An approach for dealing with misconcepts based on item response theory. *Journal of Educational Measurement, 20*(4), 345–354.

Tatsuoka, K. K. (1985). A probabilistic model for diagnosing misconception by the pattern classification approach. *Journal of Educational Statistics, 10*(1), 55–73.

Tatsuoka, K. K. (1990). Toward an integration of item-response theory and cognitive error diagnoses. In N. Frederiksen, R. L. Glaser, A. M. Lesgold, & M. G. Shafto (Eds.), *Diagnostic monitoring of skill and knowledge acquisition* (pp. 453–488). Hillsdale, NJ: Lawrence Erlbaum Associates.

Tatsuoka, K. K. (1991). *Boolean algebra applied to determination of the universal set of misconception states* (ONR-Tech. Rep. No. RR-91-44). Princeton, NJ: Educational Testing Service.

Tatsuoka, K. K. (1995). Architecture of knowledge structures and cognitive diagnosis: A statistical pattern recognition and classification approach. In P. D. Nichols, S. F. Chipman, & R. L. Brennan (Eds.), *Cognitively diagnostic assessment* (pp. 327–359). Hillsdale, NJ: Lawrence Erlbaum Associates.

Tatsuoka, K. K. (in press). *Cognitive assessment: A link between statistical pattern recogniton and classification and psychometrics.* Mahwah, NJ: Lawrence Erlbaum Associates

Tatsuoka, K. K., Birenbaum, M., & Arnold, J. (1989). On the stability of students' rules of operation for solving aritmetic problems. *Journal of Educational Measurement, 26*(4), 351–361.

Tatsuoka, K. K., Birenbaum, M., Lewis, C., & Sheehan, K. K. (1993). *Proficiency scaling based on conditional probability functions for attributes* (Research Report 93–50). Princeton, NJ: Educational Testing Service.

Tatsuoka, K. K., & Gallagher, A. (in press). *Variables that are involved in the underlying cognitive processes and knowledge of GRE Quantitative* (Technical Report). Princeton, NJ: Educational Testing Service.

Tatsuoka, K. K., & Linn, R. L. (1983). Indices for detecting unusual patterns: Links between two general approaches and potential applications. *Applied Psychological Measurement, 7*(1), 81–96.

Tatsuoka, K. K., Linn, R. L., Tatsuoka, M. M., & Yamamoto, K. (1988). Differential item functioning resulting from the use of different solution strategies. *Journal of Educational Measurement, 25*(4), 301–319.

Tatsuoka, K. K., & Tatsuoka, M. M. (1987). Bug distribution and statistical pattern classification. *Psychometrika, 52*(2), 193–206.

Tatsuoka, M. M., & Tatsuoka, K. K. (1989). Rule space. In Kotz & Johnson (Eds.), *Encyclopedia of statistical sciences.* New York: Wiley.

Tatsuoka, K. K., & Tatsuoka, M. M. (1992). *A psychometrically sound cognitive diagnostic model: Effect of remediation as empirical validity* (ETS Research Rep. No. RR-92-38-ONR). Princeton, NJ: Educational Testion Service.

Taylor, S. J., & Bogdan, R. (1984). *Introduction to qualitative research methods: The search for meanings* (2nd ed.). New York: Wiley.

Thagard, P. (1992). *Conceptual revolutions.* Princeton, NJ: Princeton University Press.

Thompson, A. (1984). The relationship of teachers' conceptions of mathematics and mathematics teaching to instructional practice. *Educational Studies in Mathematics, 15,* 105–127.

Thompson, A. (1989). Learning to teach mathematical problem solving. In R. I. Charles & E. A. Silver (Eds.), *Research agenda for mathematics education: The teaching and assessing of mathematical problem solving* (pp. 232–243). Reston, VA: National Council of Teachers of Mathematics.

Thompson, A. (1992). Teachers' beliefs and conceptions: A synthesis of research. In D. A. Grouws (Ed.), *Handbook of research on mathematics teaching and learning* (pp. 127–146). New York: MacMillan.

Thompson, P. W. (1979, April). *The teaching experiment in mathematics education research.* Paper presented at the NCTM Research Presession, Boston.

Thompson, P. W. (1982). Were lions to speak, we wouldn't understand. *Journal of Mathematical Behavior, 3*(2), 147–165.

Thompson, P. W. (1991, October). *Getting ahead, with theories: I have a theory about this.* Paper presented at the Annual Meeting of the North American Chapter, International Group for the Psychology of Mathematics Education, Blacksburg, VA.

Thompson, P. W. (1992). Notations, principles, and constraints: Contributions to the effective use of concrete manipulatives in elementary mathematics. *Journal for Research in Mathematics Education, 23,* 123–147.

Thompson, P. W. (1994a). The development of the concept of speed and its relationship to concepts of rate. In G. Harel & J. Confrey (Eds.), *The development of multiplicative reasoning in the learning of mathematics* (pp. 181–236). Albany, NY: State University of New York Press.

Thompson, P. W. (1994b). Images of rote and operational understanding of the Fundamental Theorem of Calculus. *Educational Studies in Mathematics, 26,* 229–274.

Thorne, K. S. (1994). *Black holes and time warps.* New York: Macmillan.

Thornton, R. K. (1989, September). *Using the microcomputer-based laboratory to improve student conceptual understanding in physics.* Paper presented at The International Conference on the Microcomputer in Physics Education, Adana, Turkey.

Thornton, R. K. (1987). Tools for scientific thinking: Microcomputer-based laboratory for physics teaching. *Physics Education, 22,* 230–238.

Thornton, R. K., & Sokoloff, D. R. (1990). Learning motion concepts using real-time microcomputer-based laboratory tools. *American Journal of Physics, 58*(9), 858–867.

Tierney, R. J. (1996). Redefining computer appropriation: A five-year study of ACOT students. In C. Fisher, D. C. Dwyer, & K. Yocam (Eds.), *Education and technology: Reflections on computing in classrooms* (pp. 169–183). San Francisco: Jossey-Bass.

Tinker, R. (1996a). *Information technologies in science and mathematics education.* The Concord Consortium Inc.

Tinker, R. (1996b). *The whole world in their hands* [on–line]. Washingon, DC: U.S. Department of Education. Available: http://www.ed.gov/Technology/Futures/tinker.html).

Tinto, P. (1993). Teacher as researcher: Creating a classroom environment which supports both student and teacher learning. *Homework, 4*(2).

Tinto, P. (1996a, April). *Breading the routine! Improving instruction through teacher research.* Paper presented at the National Council of Teachers of Mathematics 74th Annual Meeting, San Diego.

Tinto, P. (1996b, April). *A teachers's portfolio for change: A multimedia demonstration.* CD presented at the American Educational Research Association annual meeting, New York.

Tinto, P., & Shelly, B. (1996, Nov.). *Leaving a legacy: Outcomes of an action research project.* Paper presented at the 3rd Annual New York State Graduate Mathematics Education Research Conference, Syracuse.

Tinto, P., Shelly, B., & Zarach, N. (1993, March). *Teachers as researchers: The classroom as learning environment for teachers.* Paper presented at the National Council of Supervisors of Mathematics 25th Annual Conference, Seattle, WA.

Tinto, P. P., Shelly, B., & Zarach, N. (1994a). Classroom research and classroom practice: Blurring the boundaries. *The Mathematics Teacher, 87*(8), 644–648.

Tinto, P., Shelly, B., & Zarach, N. (1994b). Shared meanings: Cooperative learning in high school mathematics classrooms. *Cooperative Learning Magazine, 14*(1), 31–33.

Tinto, P., Shelly, B., Zarach, N., & Graver, J. (1995, April). *Changing practice: Lessons from the classroom.* Paper presented at the National Educational Computing Conference, Boston.

Tinto, P., Zarach, N., & Shelly, B. (1993, June). *Cooperative groups: Conjecturing and technology in the geometry classroom.* Paper presented at the National Educational Computing Conference, Orlando, FL.

Tobias, S. (1990). *They're not dumb, they're different: Stalking the second tier.* Tucson, AZ: Research Corporation.

Tobias, S., & Hake, R. R. (1988). Professors as physics students: What can they teach us? *American Journal of Physics, 56*(9), 786–794.

Tobin, K. (Ed.). (1993). *The practice of constructivism in science education.* Washington, DC: AAAS Press.

Tobin, K., & Espinet, M. (1989). Impediments to change: An application of peer coaching in high school science. *Journal of Research in Science Teaching, 26,* 105–120.

Tobin, K., Espinet, M., Byrd, S. E., & Adams, D. (1988). Alternative perspectives of effective science teaching. *Science Education, 72,* 433–451.

Tobin, K., & Gallagher, J. J. (1987). What happens in high school science classrooms? *Journal of Curriculum Studies, 19,* 549–560.

Tobin, K., Kahle, J. B., & Fraser, B. J. (Eds.). (1990). *Windows into science classrooms: Problems associated with higher-level learning.* London: Falmer Press.

Tobin, K., & LaMaster, S. (1995). Relationships between metaphors, beliefs and actions in a context of science curriculum change. *Journal of Research in Science Teaching, 32,* 225–242.

Tobin, K., McRobbie, C. J., & Anderson, D. (1997). Dialectical constraints to the discursive practices of a high school physics community. *Journal of Research in Science Teaching, 34,* 491–507.

Tobin, K., & Tippins, D. (1996). Metaphors as seeds for learning and the improvement of science teaching. *Science Education, 80,* 711–730.

Treffers, A. (1987). *Three dimensions: A model of goal and theory description in mathematics instruction—The Wiskobas Project.* Dordrecht, Netherlands: Reidel.

Tripp, D. (1990). Socially critical action research. *Theory into Practice, 29*(3), 158–166.

Tulviste, P. (1991). *The cultural-historical development of verbal thinking.* Commack, NY: Nova Science Publishers.

Tweney, R. (1985). Faraday's discovery of induction: A cognitive approach. In D. Gooding & F. James (Eds.), *Faraday rediscovered: Essays on the life and work of Michael Faraday, 1791–1867* (pp. 189–209). New York: Stockton Press.

Tzur, R. (1995). *Interaction and children's fraction learning.* Unpublished doctoral dissertation, University of Georgia, Athens.

Ulichny, P., & Schoener, W. (1996). Teacher–researcher collaboration from two perspectives. *Harvard Educational Review, 66*(3), 496–524.

U. S. Congressional Senate Committee on Indian Affairs. (1994). *Reauthorization of theNative Hawaiian Education Act: Hearing before the Committee on Indian Affairs.* Washington, DC: U.S. Government Printing Office.

U.S. Department of Education. (1991a). *America 2000: An education strategy.* Washington, DC: Author.

U.S. Department of Education. (1991b). *National education goals.* Washington, DC: Author.

U.S. Department of Education. (1996b). *National Commission on Teaching an American Future.* Washington, DC: Author.

U. S. National Research Center for the Third International Mathematics and Science Study. (1996). *A splintered vision: The status quo of U.S. science and mathematics education.* East Lansing, MI: Author.

van Dormolen, J. (1977). Learning to understand what giving a proof really means. *Educational Studies in Mathematics, 8,* 27–34.

VanDusen, L., & Worthen, B. R. (1994). The impact of integrated learning system implementation for student outcomes: Implications for research and evaluation. *Journal of Educational Research, 21*(1), 13–24.

Van Heuvelen, A. (1991). Learning to think like a physicist: A review of research–based instructional strategies. *American Journal of Physics, 59,* 891–897.

van Hiele, P. M. (1986). *Structure and insight.* Orlando, FL: Academic Press.

van Manen, M. (1991). *The tact of teaching: The meaning of pedagogical thoughfulness.* Albany: State University of New York Press.

van Oers, B. (1995, September). *The appropriation of mathematical symbols: A psychosemiotic approach to mathematics learning.* Paper presented at the Symposium on Symbolizing, Communication, and Mathematizing, Nashville, TN.

van Oers, B. (1996). Learning mathematics as meaningful activity. In P. Nesher, L. Steffe, P. Cobb, G. Goldin, & B. Greer (Eds.), *Theories of mathematical learning* (pp. 91–114). Mahwah, NJ: Lawrence Erlbaum Associates.

Vera, A. H., & Simon, H. A. (1993). Situated action: A symbolic interpretation. *Cognitive Science, 17,* 7–48.

Vergnaud, G. (1982). A classification of cognitive tasks and operations of thought involved in addition and subtraction problems. In T. P. Carpenter, J. M. Moser, & T. A. Romberg (Eds.), *Addition and subtraction: A cognitive perspective* (pp. 39–59). Hillsdale, NJ: Lawrence Erlbaum Associates.

Vergnaud, G. (1987, July). *About constructivism.* Paper presented at the Eleventh International Conference on the Psychology of Mathematics Education, Montreal.

Vermont Department of Education. (1991). *Looking beyond "the answer:" The report of Vermont's mathematics portfolio assessment program.* Montpelier, VT: Author.

Voigt, J. (1994). Negotiation of mathematical meaning of learning mathematics. *Educational Studies in Mathematics, 26*(2–3), 273–298.

Voigt, J. (1995). Thematic patterns of interaction and sociomathematical norms. In P. Cobb & H. Bauersfeld (Eds.), *Emergence of Mathematical Meaning: Interaction in classroom cultures* (pp. 163–201). Hillsdale, NJ: Lawrence Erlbaum Associates.

von Foerster, H. (1982). To know and to let know an applied theory of knowledge. *Canadian Library Journal, 39*(5), 47–55.

von Foerster, H. (1984). On constructing a reality. In P. Watzlawick (Ed.), *The invented reality: How do we know what we believe we know* (pp. 41–61). New York: W. W. Norton.

von Glasersfeld, E. (1982). An interpretation of Piaget's constructivism. *Review Internationale de Philosophy, 142*(3), 612–635.

von Glasersfeld, E. (1984). An introduction to radical constructivism. In P. Watzlawick (Ed.), *The invented reality* (pp. 17–40). New York: Norton.

von Glasersfeld, E. (1987a). *The construction of knowledge.* Seaside, CA: Intersystems Publications.

von Glasersfeld, E. (1987b). Learning as a constructive activity. In C. Janvier (Ed.), *Problems of representation in the teaching and learning of mathematics* (pp. 3–17). Hillsdale, NJ: Lawrence Erlbaum Associates.

von Glasersfeld, E. (1989). Cognition, construction of knowledge, and teaching. *Synthese, 80,* 121–140.

von Glasersfeld, E. (1990). Environment and communication. In L. P. Steffe & T. Wood (Eds.), *Transforming children's mathematics education* (pp. 30–38). Hillsdale, NJ: Lawrence Erlbaum Associates.

von Glasersfeld, E. (1991). Abstraction, re-presentation, and reflection: An interpretation of experience and Piaget's approach. In L. P. Steffe (Ed.), *Epistemological foundations of mathematical experience* (pp. 45–67). New York: Springer-Verlag.

von Glasersfeld, E. (1995). *Radical constructivism: A way of knowing and learning.* Washington, DC: Falmer Press.

von Glasersfeld, E. (1996). Aspects of radical constructivism and its educational recommendations. In L. P. Steffe, P. Nesher, P. Cobb, G. A. Goldin, & B. Greer (Eds.), *Theories of mathematical learning* (pp. 307–314). Mahwah, NJ: Lawrence Erlbaum Associates.

Vygotsky, L. S. (1962). *Thought and language.* Cambridge, MA: MIT Press.

Vygotsky, L. S. (1978). *Mind in society.* Cambridge, MA: Harvard University Press.

Vygotsky, L. S. (1986). *Thought and language.* Cambridge, MA: MIT Press.

Wagner, S., & Kieran, C. (Eds.). (1989). *Research agenda in mathematics education: The teaching and assessing of mathematical problem solving.* Reston, VA: National Council of Teachers of Mathematics.

Wainer, H., & Steinberg, L. (1992). Sex differences in performance on mathematics section of the Scholastic Aptitude Test: A bidirectional validity study. *Harvard Educational Review, 62,* 323–336.

Walker, C. H. (1987). Relative importance of domain knowledge and overall aptitude on acquisition of domain-related information. *Cognition and Instruction, 4*(1), 25–42.

Walkerdine, V. (1988). *The mastery of reason: Cognitive development and the production of rationality.* London: Routledge.

Warren, B., Rosenberg, A., & Conant, F. (1994). Discourse and social practice: Learning science in bilingual classrooms. In D. Spener (Ed.), *Biliteracy: Theory and practice.* Englewood Cliffs, NJ: Prentice-Hall.

Waters, W. M. (1980). Concept acquisition tasks. In G. A. Goldin & C. E. McClintock (Eds.), *Task variables in mathematical problem solving* (pp. 277–296). Philadelphia: Franklin Institute Press (subsequently acquired by Lawrence Erlbaum Associates, Hillsdale, NJ).

Webb, N. (1984). Content and context variables in problem tasks. In G. Goldin & C. E. McClintock (Eds.), *Task variables in mathematical problem solving.* Philadelphia: Franklin Institute Press.

Webb, N., & Romberg, T. (1992). Implications of the NCTM standards for mathematics assessment. In T. A. Romberg (Ed.), *Mathematics assessment and evaluation* (pp. 37–60). Albany: State University of New York Press.

Wedman, J. F. (1986, January). *Educational computing in-service design: Implications from teachers' concern research.* Paper presented at the annual conventio of the Association for Educational Communications and Technology, Las Vegas, NV.

Wells, G. (Ed.). (1994). *Changing schools from within: Creating communities of inquiry.* Toronto: OISE Press.

Wenger, E. (1987). *Artificial intelligence and tutoring systems.* Los Altos, CA: Morgan Kaufmann.

Werner, O., & Shoepfle, G. M. (1987). *Systematic fieldwork.* Newbury Park, CA: Sage.

Wertsch, J. V. (1985). *Vygotsky and the social formation of mind.* Cambridge, MA: Harvard University Press.

Wheeler, D. (1987). *The world of mathematics: Dream, myth, or reality.* Paper presented at the Eleventh International Conference on the Psychology of Mathematics Education, Montreal.

White, B. Y. (1993). ThinkerTools: Causal models, conceptual change, and science education. *Cognition and Instruction, 10*(1), 1–100.

Whitehead, A. N. (1963). *Science and the modern world.* New York: New American Library.

Whitson, J. A. (in press). Cognition as a semiotic process: Grounding, mediation, and critical reflective transcendence. In D. Kirshner & J. A. Whitson (Eds.), *Situated cognition theory: Social semiotic, and neurological perspectives.* Mahwah, NJ: Lawrence Erlbaum Associates.

Wickelgren, W. (1974). *How to solve problems.* San Francisco: Freeman.

Wilensky, U. (1991). Abstract meditations on the concrete and concrete implications for mathematics education. In I. Harel & S. Papert (Eds.), *Constructionism* (pp. 193–203). Norwood, NJ: Ablex.

Wilensky, U. (1993). *Connected mathematics: Building concrete relationships with mathematical knowledge.* Unpublished doctoral dissertation, Massachusetts Institute of Technology, Cambridge, MA.

Wilensky, U. (1995). Paradox, programming and learning probability: A case study in a connected mathematics framework. *Journal of Mathematical Behavior, 14*(2), 231–280.

Wilensky, U. (1997). What is normal anyway? Therapy for Epistemological Anxiety. In R. Noss (Ed.), *Educational Studies in Mathematics, 33*(2), 171–202.

Wilson, J. M. (1994). The CUPLE physics studio. *The Physics Teacher, 32,* 518–523.

Wilson, J. M. (1996). Some possible futures for the introductory physics course. In J. M. Wilson (Ed.), *Conference on the introductory physics course* (pp. 21–31). New York: Wiley.

Wilson, J. M., & Redish, E. F. (1992). The comprehensive unified physics learning environment: Part I. Background and system operation. *Computers in Physics, 6*(2), 202–209.

Wilson, J. T. (1994). *Situational motivation: Structuring classrooms to enhance intrinsic motivation to learn.* Unpublished doctoral dissertation, University of California, Santa Barbara.

Wilson, K. G., & Davis, B. (1994). *Redesigning education.* New York: Holt.

Wilson, S. M. (1990). The secret garden of teacher education. *Phi Delta Kappan, 72*(3), 204–209.

Wilson, S. M. (in press). Mastodons, maps, and Michigan: Exploring uncharted territory while teaching elementary school social studies. *Elementary School Journal.*

Wilson, S. M., & Gudmundsdottir, S. (1987). What is this case of? Exploring some conceptual issues in case study research. *Education and Urban Society, 20*(1), 42–54.

Winn, W. (1990). Some implications of cognitive theory for instructional design. *Instructional Science, 19,* 53–69.

Winograd, T., Bennet, J., & De Young, L. (Eds.). (1996). *Bringing design to software.* Reading, MA: Addison-Wesley.

Wirszup, I., & Kilpatrick, J. (Eds.). (1975–1978). *Soviet studies in the psychology of mathematics education* (Vols. 1–14). Palo Alto, CA: School Mathematics Study Group.

Wittmann, E. (1995). Mathematics education as "design science." *Educational Studies in Mathematics, 29*(4), 355–374.

Wong, E. D. (1995). Challenges confronting the researcher/teacher: Conflicts of purpose and conduct. *Educational Researcher, 24*(3), 22–28.

Wood, T., Cobb, P., & Yackel, E. (1991). Change in teaching mathematics: A case study. *American Educational Research Journal, 28*(3), 587–616.

Worthen, B. R., VanDusen, L., & Sailor, P. J. (1994). A comparative study of the impact of integrated learning systems on students' time–on–task. *International Journal of Educational Research, 21*(1), 25–37.

Yackel, E. (1995). *The classroom teaching experiment.* Unpublished manuscript, Department of Mathematical Sciences, Purdue University, Calumet, IN.

Yackel, E., & Cobb, P. (1996). Sociomath norms, argumentation, and autonomy in mathematics. *Journal for Research in Mathematics Education, 27*(4), 458–477.

Zack, V., Mousley, J., & Breen, C. (Eds.). (1997). *Developing practice: Teachers' inquiry and educational change.* Melbourne, Australia: Deakin University Press.

Zang, R. A. (1994). *Inferring internal strategic problem representation and its development: A two-year case study with four elementary school children.* Unpublished doctoral dissertation, Rutgers University, East Rutherford, NJ.

Zang, R. A. (1995, October). *Inferring internal strategic problem representation and its development: A two–year case study with Marcia.* Paper presented at the Seventeenth Annual Meeting of the North American Chapter of the International Group for the Psychology of Mathematics Education, Columbus, OH.

Zweng, M., Green, T., Kilpatrick, J., Pollack, H., & Suydam, M. (Eds.). (1983). *Proceedings of the Fourth International Congress on Mathematical Education.* Boston: Birkhauser.

# Author Index

## A

Abelson, H., 796
Abreu, G. de, 457, 472
Ackermann, E., 269, 277, 278, 282, 292, 295
Ackoff, R. L., 75
Adams, D. D., 487, 495, 869
Agard, P., 374
Ahlgren, A., 74
Akerstrom, M., 617, 680
Alibrandi, M., 434
Allchin, D., 810
Allen, S., 457, 458, 459, 478, 479, 868
Altrichter, H., 413, 437, 450
Anderman, E. M., 96
Anderson, C., 869
Anderson, D., 487
Anderson, J., 787
Anderson, J. R., 784, 868
Anderson, S., 866, 880
Angoff, W. H., 828
Apple, M. W., 750
Arcavi, A., 468
Archbald, D. A., 91
Arnold, J., 828
Aron, J., 652
Arons, A., 871
Atkin, J., 406, 435, 452
Atkinson, P., 328
Au, K. H., 470
Austin, G. A., 520
Aveni, A., 121
Ayer, A. J., 535
Azmitia, M., 469

## B

Bacon, L., 310
Baedeker, W., 931
Balacheff, N., 27, 347
Ball, D., 56, 95, 312, 319, 330, 365, 366, 372, 383
Baroody, A. J., 755
Barowy, W., 784
Barrows, H. S., 868
Barthel, P., 931

Bassingthwaighte, J. B., 922
Battista, M. T., 741, 746, 750, 752, 755, 756, 767, 769, 771, 772, 775, 779
Bauersfeld, H., 56, 307, 310, 328, 337, 457
Baulac, Y., 788
Baxter, G. P., 120, 880
Becker, H. J., 766
Becker, H. S., 655
Bednarz, N., 310
Behar, R., 399, 400, 401
Behr, M., 56, 124, 204, 238, 339, 604
Beik, W., 816
Bell, A., 347
Bellemain, F., 788
Berg, R., 652
Bermudez, T., 318
Bernstein, R. C., 929
Beth, E., 124, 212
Bethge, T., 788
Biddlecomb, B. D., 766, 767, 771, 773, 775, 776
Biggs, J. B., 880
Biklen, S., 422, 425
Birenbaum, M., 828, 832, 860
Bishop, A., 27, 323, 457
Blume, G., 346, 347
Bodner, B. L., 518
Bogdan, R., 329
Borg, W., 431
Borko, H., 374
Bowers, J., 320
Boyle, F., 787
Branca, N., 518
Brenner, M. E., 457, 467, 470, 474, 480, 481, 483, 484, 485
Bridgeman, B., 828
Bringuier, J. C., 891, 892
Briscoe, C., 487
Bronfenbrenner, U., 466
Brophy, J., 273
Brousseau, G., 27, 324, 383
Brown, A., 352, 387, 395, 463, 797
Brown, C., 374
Brown, C. A., 374
Brown, D., 441
Brown, D. E., 319
Brown, J. S., 460

971

# Subject Index

**S**